Fundamentals of Corporate Finance

Fundamentals of Corporate Finance

Fourth Edition

ROBERT PARRINO
Department Chair and Lamar Savings
Centennial Professor of Finance
University of Texas at Austin

THOMAS W. BATES
Department Chair and
Associate Professor of Finance
Arizona State University

STUART L. GILLAN
Associate Professor of Finance
University of Georgia

DAVID S. KIDWELL
Professor of Finance and Dean Emeritus
University of Minnesota

WILEY

DIRECTOR	Michael McDonald
CONTENT MANAGER	Dorothy Sinclair
ACQUISITIONS EDITOR	Emily Marcoux
SENIOR PRODUCTION EDITOR	Valerie A. Vargas
EDITORIAL ASSISTANT	Alden Farrar
ASSOCIATE DEVELOPMENT EDITOR	Courtney Jordan
PROJECT MANAGER	Jennifer Welter
PRODUCT MARKETING MANAGER	John LaVacca III
PRODUCT MARKETING ASSISTANT	Ashley Migliaro
SENIOR MEDIA SPECIALIST	Elena Santa Maria
SENIOR DESIGNER	Maureen Eide
COVER PHOTO	©Aeriform/Getty Images

This book was set in Minion Pro by Aptara, Inc. and printed and bound by Quad/Graphics. The cover was printed by Quad/Graphics.

This book is printed on acid free paper. ∞

ISBN: 978-1-119-37140-3

Printed in the United States of America

V10003067_080418

Dedication

ROBERT PARRINO

To my parents, whose life-long support and commitment to education inspired me to become an educator, and to my wife, Emily, for her unending support.

THOMAS BATES

To my wife, Emi, and our daughters, Abigail and Lillian. Your support, patience, fun, and friendship make me a better educator, scholar, and person.

STUART GILLAN

To the memory of my father, and to my family for their never-ending support and encouragement.

DAVID KIDWELL

To my parents, Dr. William and Margaret Kidwell, for their endless support of my endeavors; to my son, David Jr., of whom I am very proud; and to my wife, Jillinda, who is the joy of my life.

About the Authors

ROBERT PARRINO

Department Chair and Lamar Savings Centennial Professor of Finance
Director, Hicks, Muse, Tate & Furst Center for Private Equity Finance
McCombs School of Business, University of Texas at Austin

A member of the faculty at University of Texas since 1992, Dr. Parrino teaches courses in regular degree and executive education programs at the University of Texas, as well as in customized executive education courses for industrial, financial, and professional firms. He has also taught at the University of Chicago, University of Rochester, and IMADEC University in Vienna. Dr. Parrino has received numerous awards for teaching excellence at the University of Texas from students, faculty, and the Texas Exes (alumni association).

Dr. Parrino has been involved in advancing financial education outside of the classroom in a variety of ways. As a Chartered Financial Analyst (CFA) charterholder, he has been very active with the CFA Institute, having been a member of the candidate curriculum committee, served as a regular speaker at the annual Financial Analysts Seminar, spoken at over 20 Financial Analyst Society meetings, and served as a member of the planning committee for the CFA Institute's Annual Meeting. In addition, Dr. Parrino is the founding director of the Hicks, Muse, Tate & Furst Center for Private Equity Finance at the University of Texas. The center sponsors conferences and other educational activities in areas related to private equity finance. Dr. Parrino was Vice President for Financial Education of the Financial Management Association (FMA) from 2008 to 2010 and an academic director of the FMA from 2011 to 2013. In 2017 he was elected to be VP-Program for the 2019 FMA annual meeting.

Dr. Parrino also co-founded the Financial Research Association and is Associate Editor of the *Journal of Corporate Finance*. Dr. Parrino's research focus includes corporate governance, financial policies, restructuring, mergers and acquisitions, and private equity markets. He has published his research in a number of journals, including the *Journal of Finance*, *Journal of Financial Economics*, *Journal of Financial and Quantitative Analysis*, *Journal of Law and Economics*, *Journal of Portfolio Management*, and *Financial Management*. Dr. Parrino has won a number of awards for his research, including the 2013–2014 Career Award for Outstanding Research Contributions at the McCombs School of Business.

Dr. Parrino has experience in the application of corporate finance concepts in a variety of business situations. Since entering the academic profession, he has been retained as an advisor on valuation issues concerning businesses with enterprise values ranging to more than $1 billion and has consulted in areas such as corporate financing, compensation, and corporate governance. Dr. Parrino was previously President of Sprigg Lane Financial, Inc., a financial consulting firm with offices in Charlottesville, Virginia, and New York City. While at Sprigg Lane, he was on the executive, banking, and portfolio committees of the holding company that owns Sprigg Lane. Before joining Sprigg Lane, Dr. Parrino was on the Corporate Business Planning and Development staff at Marriott Corporation. At Marriott, he conducted fundamental business analyses and preliminary financial valuations of new business development opportunities and potential acquisitions. Dr. Parrino holds a B.S. in chemical engineering from Lehigh University, an MBA degree from The College of William and Mary, and M.S. and Ph.D. degrees in applied economics and finance, respectively, from the University of Rochester.

THOMAS W. BATES

Department Chair and Associate Professor of Finance W. P. Carey School of Business, Arizona State University

Dr. Bates is the Chair of the Department of Finance and Dean's Council of 100 Distinguished Scholar at the W. P. Carey School of Business, Arizona State University. He has also taught courses in finance at the University of Delaware, the Ivey School of Business at the University of Western Ontario, and the University of Arizona where he received the Scrivner teaching award. During his career as an educator, Professor Bates has taught corporate finance to students in undergraduate, MBA, executive MBA, and Ph.D. programs, as well as in custom corporate educational courses.

Professor Bates is a regular contributor to the academic finance literature in such journals as the *Journal of Finance*, *Journal of Financial Economics*, *Journal of Financial and Quantitative Analysis*, and *Financial Management*. His research addresses a variety of issues in corporate finance including the contracting environment in mergers and acquisitions, corporate liquidity decisions and cash holdings, and the governance of corporations. In practice, Dr. Bates has worked with companies and legal firms as an advisor on issues related to the valuation of companies and corporate governance. Dr. Bates received a B.A. in Economics from Guilford College and his doctorate in finance from the University of Pittsburgh.

STUART L. GILLAN

Associate Professor of Finance, Terry College of Business, University of Georgia

Dr. Gillan is Associate Professor of Finance in the Terry College of Business at the University of Georgia. His industry experience includes time as Associate Chief Economist at the United States Securities and Exchange Commission (SEC) and Senior Research Fellow with TIAA, a New York-based financial services company.

Before joining the University of Georgia, he held academic positions at Arizona State University, the University of Delaware, the University of Hong Kong, the University of Otago, and Texas Tech University. He has also been a visiting scholar at the Chinese University of Hong Kong, University of Canterbury, the Hong Kong Polytechnic University, and a William Evans Fellow at the University of Otago. In addition to teaching corporate finance classes to undergraduate, masters, MBA and Executive MBA students, Dr. Gillan has taught in several customized executive education and corporate programs. In recognition of his teaching, he also received a Terry College of Business Hugh O. Nourse Outstanding MBA Teacher Award.

Additionally, Dr. Gillan has served as Co-Editor of the *Journal of Corporate Finance*, Associate Editor at the *Review of Financial Studies*, Associate Editor at *Accounting and Finance*, and on the editorial advisory board of the *Journal of Applied Corporate Finance*. He has written and published extensively on corporate finance and corporate governance including topics such as corporate restructuring, executive compensation, shareholder activism, shareholder voting, and the structure and activity of corporate boards. His research has been published in the *Journal of Finance, Journal of Financial Economics, Review of Financial Studies, Journal of Corporate Finance, Journal of Risk and Insurance, Financial Management,* and the *Journal of Applied Corporate Finance*, amongst others. His has also received best paper awards from academic finance groups including the Financial Management Association International, the Indian School of Business Center for Analytical Finance, and the Western Finance Association.

Dr. Gillan received his Ph.D. from the Graduate School of Business at the University of Texas, Austin. His Bachelor of Commerce (Honors) and Masters of Commerce degrees are from the University of Otago, New Zealand.

DAVID S. KIDWELL

Professor of Finance and Dean Emeritus, Curtis L. Carlson School of Management, University of Minnesota

Dr. Kidwell has over 30 years experience in financial education, as a teacher, researcher, and administrator. He has served as Dean of the Carlson School at the University of Minnesota and of the School of Business Administration at the University of Connecticut. Prior to joining the University of Connecticut, Dr. Kidwell held endowed chairs in banking and finance at Tulane University, the University of Tennessee, and Texas Tech University. He was also on the faculty at the Krannert Graduate School of Management, Purdue University where he was twice voted the outstanding undergraduate teacher of the year.

An expert on the U.S. financial system, Dr. Kidwell is the author of more than 80 articles dealing with the U.S. financial system and capital markets. He has published his research in the leading journals, including *Journal of Finance, Journal of Financial Economics, Journal of Financial and Quantitative Analysis, Financial Management,* and *Journal of Money, Credit, and Banking*. Dr. Kidwell has also participated in a number of research grants funded by the National Science Foundation to study the efficiency of U.S. capital markets, and to study the impact of government regulations upon the delivery of consumer financial services.

Dr. Kidwell has been a management consultant for Coopers & Lybrand and a sales engineer for Bethlehem Steel Corporation. He served on the Board of Directors for the Schwan Food Company and was the Chairman of the Audit and Risk Committee. Dr. Kidwell is the past Secretary-Treasurer of the Board of Directors of AACSB, the International Association for Management Education and is a past member of the Boards of the Minnesota Council for Quality, the Stonier Graduate School of Banking, and Minnesota Center for Corporate Responsibility. Dr. Kidwell has also served as an Examiner for the 1995 Malcolm Baldrige National Quality Award, on the Board of Directors of the Juran Center for Leadership in Quality, and on the Board of the Minnesota Life Insurance Company.

Dr. Kidwell holds an undergraduate degree in mechanical engineering from California State University at San Diego, an MBA with a concentration in finance from California State University at San Francisco, and a Ph.D. in finance from the University of Oregon.

Preface

We have written *Fundamentals of Corporate Finance* for use in an introductory course in corporate finance at the undergraduate level. It is also suitable for advanced undergraduate, executive development, and traditional or executive MBA courses when supplemented with cases and outside readings. The main chapters in the book assume that students are well-versed in algebra and that they have taken courses in principles of economics and financial accounting. Optional chapters covering important economic and financial accounting concepts are included for students and instructors seeking such coverage.

Balance Between Conceptual Understanding and Computational Skills

We wrote this corporate finance text for one very important reason. We want to provide students and instructors with a book that strikes the best possible balance between helping students develop an intuitive understanding of key financial concepts and providing them with problem-solving and decision-making skills. In our experience, teaching students at all levels and across a range of business schools, we have found that students who understand the intuition underlying the basic concepts of finance are better able to develop the critical judgment necessary to apply financial tools to a broad range of real-world situations. An introductory corporate finance course should provide students with a strong understanding of both the concepts and tools that will help them in their subsequent business studies and their personal and professional lives.

Market research supports our view. Many faculty members who teach the introductory corporate finance course to undergraduates want a book that bridges the gap between conceptually-focused and computationally-focused books. This text is designed to bridge this gap. Specifically, it develops the fundamental concepts underlying corporate finance in an intuitive manner while maintaining a strong emphasis on developing computational skills. This text also takes the students one step further by emphasizing the use of intuition and analytical skills in decision making.

Our ultimate goal has been to write a book and develop associated learning tools that help our colleagues succeed in the classroom—materials that are genuinely helpful in the learning process. Our book offers a level of rigor that is appropriate for finance majors and yet presents the content in a manner that both finance and non-finance students find accessible and want to read. Writing a book that is both *rigorous* and *accessible* has been one of our key objectives, and both faculty and student reviews of the previous editions suggest that we have achieved this objective.

We have also tried to provide solutions to many of the challenges facing finance faculty in the current environment, who are asked to teach ever-increasing numbers of students with limited resources. Faculty members need a book and associated learning tools that help them effectively leverage their time. The organization of this book and the supplemental materials, along with the innovative *WileyPLUS* Web-based interface, which offers extensive problem solving opportunities and other resources for students, provides such leverage.

A Focus on Value Creation

This book is more than a collection of ideas, equations, and chapters. It has an important integrating theme—that of value creation. This theme, which is carried throughout the book, provides a framework that helps students understand the relations between the various concepts covered in the book and makes it easier for them to learn these concepts.

The concept of value creation is the most fundamental notion in corporate finance. It is in stockholders' best interests for value maximization to be at the heart of the financial decisions made within the firm. Thus, it is critical that students be able to analyze and make business decisions with a focus on value creation. The concept of value creation is introduced in the first chapter of the book and is further developed and applied throughout the remaining chapters.

The theme of value creation is operationalized through the net present value (NPV) concept. Once students grasp the fundamental idea that financial decision makers should only choose courses of action whose benefits exceed their costs, analysis and decision making using the NPV concept becomes second nature. By helping students better understand the economic rationale for a decision from the outset, rather than initially focusing on computational skills, our text keeps students focused on the true purpose of the calculations and the decision at hand.

Integrated Approach: Intuition, Analysis, and Decision Making

To support the focus on value creation, we have emphasized three things: (1) providing an intuitive framework for understanding fundamental finance concepts, (2) teaching students how to analyze and solve finance problems, and (3) helping students develop the ability to use the results from their analyses to make good financial decisions.

1. **An Intuitive Approach:** We believe that explaining finance concepts in an intuitive context helps students develop a richer understanding of those concepts and gain better insights into how finance problems can be approached. It is our experience that students who have a strong conceptual understanding of financial theory better

understand how things really work and are better problem solvers and decision makers than students who focus primarily on computational skills.

2. **Analysis and Problem Solving:** With a strong understanding of the basic principles of finance, students are equipped to tackle a wide range of financial problems. In addition to the many numerical examples that are solved in the text of each chapter, this book has 1,200 end-of-chapter homework and review problems that have been written with Bloom's Taxonomy in mind. Solutions for these problems are provided in the Instructor's Manual. We strive to help students acquire the ability to analyze and solve finance problems.
3. **Decision Making:** In the end, we want to prepare students to make sound financial decisions. To help students develop these skills, throughout the text we illustrate how the results from financial analyses are used in decision making.

Organization and Coverage

In order to help students develop the skills necessary to tackle investment and financing decisions, we have arranged the book's 21 chapters into five major building blocks, that collectively comprise the seven parts of the book, as illustrated in the accompanying exhibit and described below.

Introduction

Part 1, which consists of Chapter 1, provides an introduction to corporate finance. It describes the role of the financial manager, the types of fundamental decisions that financial mangers make, alternative forms of business organization, the goal of the firm, agency conflicts and how they arise, and the importance of ethics in financial decision-making. These discussions set the stage and provide a framework that students can use to think about key concepts as the course progresses.

Foundations

Part 2 of the text consists of Chapters 2 through 4. These chapters present the basic institutional, economic, and accounting knowledge and tools that students should understand before they begin the study of financial concepts. Most of the material in these chapters is typically taught in other courses. Since students come to the corporate finance course with varying academic backgrounds, and because the time that has elapsed since students have taken particular prerequisite courses also varies, the chapters in Part 2 can help the instructor ensure that all students have the same base level of knowledge early in the course. Depending on the educational background of the students, the instructor might not find it necessary to cover all or any of the material in these chapters. Some or all of these chapters might, instead, be assigned as supplemental readings.

Chapter 2 describes the services financial institutions provide to businesses, how domestic and international financial markets work, the concept of market efficiency, how firms use financial markets, and how interest rates are determined in the economy. Chapter 3 describes the key financial statements and how they are related, as well as how these statements are related to cash flows to investors. Chapter 4 discusses ratio analysis and other tools used to evaluate financial statements. Throughout Part 2, we emphasize the importance of cash flows to get students thinking about cash flows as a critical component of all valuation calculations and financial decisions.

Basic Concepts and Tools

Part 3 presents basic financial concepts and tools and illustrates their application. This part of the text, which consists of Chapters 5 through 9, introduces time value of money and risk and return concepts and then applies these concepts to bond and stock valuation. These chapters provide students with basic financial intuitions and computational tools that will serve as the building blocks for analyzing investment and financing decisions in subsequent chapters.

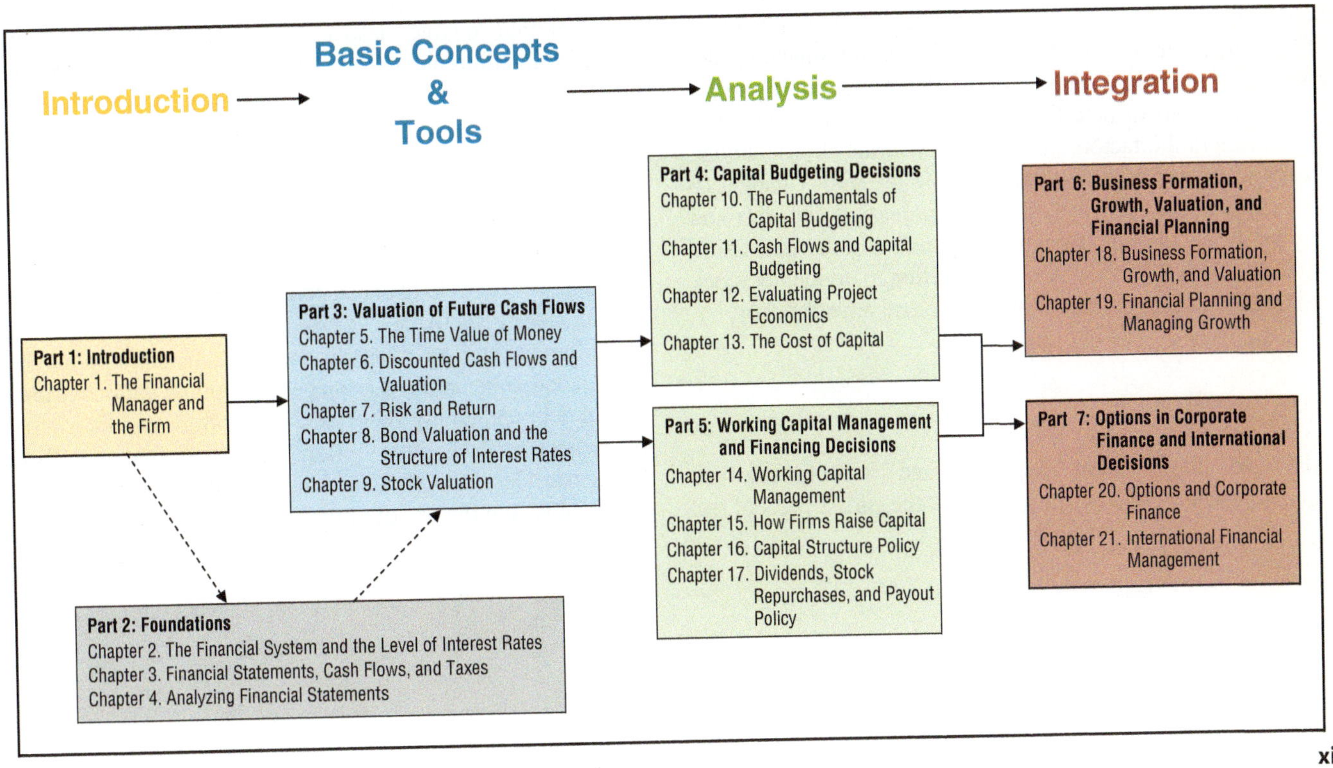

Analysis

Parts 4 and 5 of the text focus on investment and financing decisions. Part 4 covers capital budgeting. Chapter 10 introduces the concept of net present value and illustrates its application as the principle tool for evaluating capital projects. It also discusses alternative capital budgeting decision rules, such as internal rate of return, payback period, and accounting rate of return, and compares them with the net present value criterion. Finally, Chapter 10 also discusses investment decisions with capital rationing. The discussions in Chapter 10 provide a framework that will help students in the rest of Part 4 as they learn the nuances of capital budgeting analysis in realistic settings.

Chapters 11 and 12 follow with in-depth discussions of how cash flows are calculated and forecast. The cash flow calculations are presented in Chapter 11 using a valuation framework that helps students think about valuation concepts in an intuitive way and that prepares them for the extension of these concepts to business valuation in Chapter 18. Chapter 12 covers analytical tools—such as breakeven, sensitivity, scenario, and simulation analysis—that give students a better appreciation for how they can deal with the uncertainties associated with cash flow forecasts.

Chapter 13 explains how the discount rates used in capital budgeting are estimated. This chapter uses an innovative concept—that of the finance balance sheet—to help students develop an intuitive understanding of the relations between the costs of the individual components of capital and the firm's overall weighted average cost of capital. It also provides a detailed discussion of methods used to estimate the costs of the individual components of capital that are used to finance a firm's investments and how these estimates are used in capital budgeting.

Part 5 covers working capital management and financing decisions. It begins, in Chapter 14, with an introduction to how firms manage their working capital and the implications of working capital management decisions for financing decisions and firm value. This is followed, in Chapters 15 and 16, with discussions of how firms raise capital to fund their real activities and the factors that affect how firms choose among the various sources of capital available to them. Chapter 16 also includes an extensive appendix on leasing concepts and buy vs. lease analysis. Chapter 17 rounds out the discussion of financing decisions with an introduction to dividends, stock repurchases, stock dividends and splits, and payout policy.

Integration

Part 6, which consists of Chapters 18 and 19, brings together many of the key concepts introduced in the earlier parts of the text. Chapter 18 covers financial aspects of business formation and growth and introduces students to business valuation concepts for both private and public firms. The discussions in this chapter integrate the investment and financing concepts discussed in Parts 4 and 5 to provide students with a more complete picture of how all the financial concepts fit together. Chapter 19 covers concepts related to financial planning, forecasting, and managing growth.

Part 7 introduces students to some important issues that managers must deal with in applying the concepts covered in the text to real-world problems. Chapter 20 introduces call and put options and discusses how they relate to investment and financing decisions. It describes options that are embedded in the securities that firms issue. It also explains, at an accessible level, the idea behind real options and why traditional NPV analysis does not take such options into account. In addition, the chapter discusses agency costs of debt and equity and the implications of these costs for investment and financing decisions. Finally, Chapter 20 illustrates the use of options in risk management. Instructors can cover the topics in Chapter 20 near the end of the course or insert them at the appropriate points in Parts 4 and 5. Chapter 21 examines how international considerations affect the application of concepts covered in the book.

Unique Chapters

Chapter on Business Formation, Growth, and Valuation

We wrote Chapter 18 in response to students' heightened interest in new business formation (entrepreneurship) and in order to draw together, in a comprehensive way, the key concepts from capital budgeting, working capital management, and financial policy. This capstone chapter provides an overview of practical finance issues associated with forecasting cash flows and capital requirements for a new business, preparing a business plan, and business valuation. The discussion of business valuation extends far beyond that found in other introductory corporate finance textbooks.

Chapter on Options and Corporate Finance

Many other corporate finance textbooks have a chapter that introduces students to financial options and how they are valued. This chapter goes further. It provides a focused discussion of the different types of financial and non-financial options that are of concern to financial managers, including options embedded in debt and equity securities, real options and their effect on project analysis, how option-like payoff functions faced by stockholders, bond holders, and managers affect agency relationships, and the use of options in risk management.

Proven Pedagogical Framework

We have developed several distinctive features throughout the book to aid student learning. The pedagogical features included in our text are as follows:

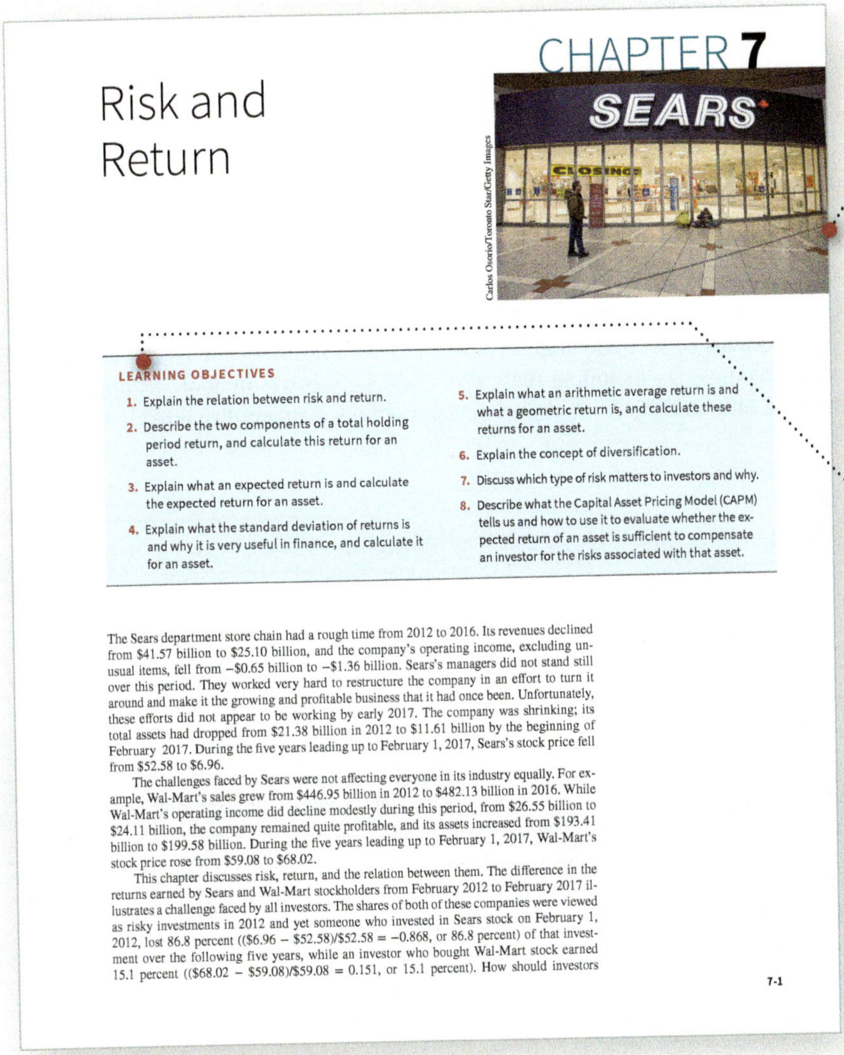

CHAPTER 7

Risk and Return

Carlos Osorio/Toronto Star/Getty Images

LEARNING OBJECTIVES

1. Explain the relation between risk and return.
2. Describe the two components of a total holding period return, and calculate this return for an asset.
3. Explain what an expected return is and calculate the expected return for an asset.
4. Explain what the standard deviation of returns is and why it is very useful in finance, and calculate it for an asset.
5. Explain what an arithmetic average return is and what a geometric return is, and calculate these returns for an asset.
6. Explain the concept of diversification.
7. Discuss which type of risk matters to investors and why.
8. Describe what the Capital Asset Pricing Model (CAPM) tells us and how to use it to evaluate whether the expected return of an asset is sufficient to compensate an investor for the risks associated with that asset.

The Sears department store chain had a rough time from 2012 to 2016. Its revenues declined from \$41.57 billion to \$25.10 billion, and the company's operating income, excluding unusual items, fell from −\$0.65 billion to −\$1.36 billion. Sears's managers did not stand still over this period. They worked very hard to restructure the company in an effort to turn it around and make it the growing and profitable business that it had once been. Unfortunately, these efforts did not appear to be working by early 2017. The company was shrinking; its total assets had dropped from \$21.38 billion in 2012 to \$11.61 billion by the beginning of February 2017. During the five years leading up to February 1, 2017, Sears's stock price fell from \$52.58 to \$6.96.

The challenges faced by Sears were not affecting everyone in its industry equally. For example, Wal-Mart's sales grew from \$446.95 billion in 2012 to \$482.13 billion in 2016. While Wal-Mart's operating income did decline modestly during this period, from \$26.55 billion to \$24.11 billion, the company remained quite profitable, and its assets increased from \$193.41 billion to \$199.58 billion. During the five years leading up to February 1, 2017, Wal-Mart's stock price rose from \$59.08 to \$68.02.

This chapter discusses risk, return, and the relation between them. The difference in the returns earned by Sears and Wal-Mart stockholders from February 2012 to February 2017 illustrates a challenge faced by all investors. The shares of both of these companies were viewed as risky investments in 2012 and yet someone who invested in Sears stock on February 1, 2012, lost 86.8 percent ((\$6.96 − \$52.58)/\$52.58 = −0.868, or 86.8 percent) of that investment over the following five years, while an investor who bought Wal-Mart stock earned 15.1 percent ((\$68.02 − \$59.08)/\$59.08 = 0.151, or 15.1 percent). How should investors

7-1

Chapter Opener Vignettes

Each chapter begins with a vignette that describes a real company or personal application. The vignettes illustrate concepts that will be presented in the chapter and are meant to heighten student interest, motivate learning, and demonstrate the real-life relevance of the material in the chapter.

Learning Objectives

The opening vignette is accompanied by learning objectives that identify the most important material for students to understand while reading the chapter. At the end of the chapter, the Summary of Learning Objectives summarizes the chapter content in the context of the learning objectives.

LEARNING BY DOING

WileyPLUS

Need more help? Visit your WileyPLUS course.

APPLICATION 7.1 | Calculating the Return on an Investment

Problem You purchased a beat-up 1974 Datsun 240Z sports car a year ago for $1,500. Datsun is what Nissan, the Japanese car company, was called in the 1970s. The 240Z was the first in a series of cars that led to the Nissan 370Z that is being sold today. Recognizing that a mint-condition 240Z is a much sought-after car, you invested $7,000 and a lot of your time fixing up the car. Last week, you sold it to a collector for $18,000. Not counting the value of the time you spent restoring the car, what is the total return you earned on this investment over the one-year holding period?

Approach Use Equation 7.1 to calculate the total holding period return. To calculate R_T using Equation 7.1, you must know P_0, P_1, and CF_1. In this problem, you can assume that the $7,000 was spent at the time you bought the car to purchase parts and materials. Therefore, your initial investment, P_0, was $1,500 + $7,000 = $8,500. Since there were no other cash inflows or outflows between the time that you bought the car and the time that you sold it, CF_1 equals $0.

Solution The total holding period return is:

$$R_T = R_{CA} + R_I = \frac{P_1 - P_0 + CF_1}{P_0} = \frac{\$18{,}000 - \$8{,}500 + \$0}{\$8{,}500} = 1.118, \text{ or } 111.8\%$$

Learning by Doing Applications

Along with a generous number of in-text examples, most chapters include several Learning by Doing Applications. These applications contain quantitative problems with step-by-step solutions to help students better understand how to apply their intuition and analytical skills to solve important problems. By including these exercises, we provide students with additional practice in the application of the concepts, tools, and methods that are discussed in the text.

Building Intuition

Students must have an intuitive understanding of a number of important principles and concepts to successfully master the finance curriculum. Throughout the book, we emphasize these important concepts by presenting them in Building Intuition boxes. These boxes provide a statement of an important finance concept, such as the relation between risk and expected return, along with an intuitive example or explanation to help the student "get" the concept. These boxes help the students develop finance intuition. Collectively the Building Intuition boxes cover the most important concepts in corporate finance.

Building Intuition

More Risk Means a Higher Expected Return

The greater the risk associated with an investment, the greater the return investors expect from it. A corollary to this idea is that investors want the highest return for a given level of risk or the lowest risk for a given level of return. When choosing between two investments that have the same level of risk, investors prefer the investment with the higher return. Alternatively, if two investments have the same expected return, investors prefer the less risky alternative.

EXAMPLE 7.2 | Choosing between Two Investments

DECISION MAKING

Situation You are trying to decide whether to invest in one or both of two different stocks. Stock 1 has a beta of 0.8 and an expected return of 7.0 percent. Stock 2 has a beta of 1.2 and an expected return of 9.5 percent. You remember learning about the CAPM in school and believe that it does a good job of telling you what the appropriate expected return should be for a given level of risk. Since the risk-free rate is 4 percent and the market risk premium is 6 percent, the CAPM tells you that the appropriate expected rate of return for an asset with a beta of 0.8 is 8.8 percent. The corresponding return for an asset with a beta of 1.2 is 11.2 percent. Should you invest in either or both of these stocks?

Decision You should not invest in either stock. The expected returns for both of them are below the values predicted by the CAPM for investments with the same level of risk. In other words, both would plot below the line in Exhibit 7.11. This implies that they are both overpriced.

Decision-Making Examples

Throughout the book, we emphasize the role of the financial manager as a decision maker. To that end, twenty chapters include Decision-Making Examples. These examples, which emphasize the decision-making process rather than computation, provide students with experience in financial decision making. Each Decision-Making Example outlines a scenario and asks the student to make a decision based on the information presented.

End of Chapter Pedagogy

Summary of Learning Objectives and Key Equations

At the end of the chapter, you will find a summary of the key chapter content related to each of the learning objectives listed at the beginning of the chapter, as well as an exhibit listing the key equations in the chapter.

Summary of Learning Objectives

1 Explain the relation between risk and return.

Investors require higher returns for taking greater risk. They prefer the investment with the highest possible return for a given level of risk or the investment with the lowest risk for a given level of return.

2 Describe the two components of a total holding period return, and calculate this return for an asset.

The total holding period return on an investment consists of a capital appreciation component and an income component. This return is calculated using Equation 7.1. It is important to recognize that investors do not care whether they receive a dollar of return through capital appreciation or as a cash dividend. Investors value both sources of return equally.

3 Explain what an expected return is and calculate the expected return for an asset.

persion of returns. In other words, it tells us about the probability that a return will fall within a particular distance from the expected value or within a particular range. To calculate the standard deviation, the variance is first calculated using Equation 7.3. The standard deviation of returns is then calculated by taking the square root of the variance.

5 Explain what an arithmetic average return is and what a geometric return is, and calculate these returns for an asset.

The arithmetic average return is the return earned in an average period while the geometric average return is the average compounded return earned by an investor. Equations 7.4 and 7.5 are used to calculate these returns.

6 Explain the concept of diversification.

Diversification entails reducing risk by investing in two or more assets whose values do not always move in the same direction at the same time. Investing in a portfolio containing assets whose prices do

Summary of Key Equations

Equation	Description	Formula
7.1	Total holding period return	$R_T = R_{CA} + R_I = \frac{P_1 - P_0}{P_0} + \frac{CF_1}{P_0} = \frac{\Delta P + CF_1}{P_0}$
7.2	Expected return on an asset	$E(R_{Asset}) = \sum_{i=1}^{n} (p_i \times R_i)$
7.3	Variance of return on an asset	$Var(R) = \sigma_R^2 = \sum_{i=1}^{n} \{p_i \times [R_i - E(R)^2]\}$

Self-Study Problems with Solutions

Five problems similar to the in-text Learning by Doing Applications follow the summary and provide additional examples with step-by-step solutions to help students further develop their problem-solving and computational skills.

Self-Study Problems

7.1 Kaaran made a friendly wager with a colleague that involves the result from flipping a coin. If heads comes up, Kaaran must pay her colleague \$15; otherwise, her colleague will pay Kaaran \$15. What is Kaaran's expected cash flow, and what is the variance of that cash flow if the coin has an equal probability of coming up heads or tails? Suppose Kaaran's colleague is willing to handicap the bet by paying her \$20 if

Solutions to Self-Study Problems

7.1 Part 1: $E(\text{cash flow}) = (0.5 \times -\$15) + (0.5 \times \$15) = 0$

$$\sigma^2_{\text{Cash flow}} = [0.5 \times (-\$15 - \$0)^2] + [0.5 \times (\$15 - \$0)^2] = 225$$

Part 2: $E(\text{cash flow}) = (0.5 \times -\$15) + (0.5 \times \$20) = \$2.50$

$$\sigma^2_{\text{Cash flow}} = [0.5 \times (-\$15 - \$2.50)^2] + [0.5 \times (\$20 - \$2.50)^2] = 306.25$$

7.2 The expected return for CFI based on today's stock price is (\$12 − \$11)/\$11 = 9.09 percent, which is lower than 20 percent. Since the stock price one year from today is fixed, the only way that you will generate a 20 percent return is if the price of the stock drops today. Consequently, the price of the stock today must drop to \$10. It is found by solving the following: $0.2 = (\$12 - x)/x$, or $x = \$10$.

7.3 Since you know that 1.645 standard deviations around the expected return captures 90 percent of the distribution, you can set up either of the following equations:

$$\$40 = \$50 - 1.645\sigma \quad \text{or} \quad \$60 = \$50 + 1.645\sigma$$

and solve for σ. Doing this with either equation yields:

$$\sigma = \$6.079 \text{ and } \sigma^2 = 36.954$$

7.4 The value in 2015 is:

$$V_{2015} = \$1 \times (1 + -0.0326) \times (1 + 0.1823) \times (1 + 0.4507) \times (1 + 0.0292) \times (1 + -0.0360) = \$1.646$$

Substituting into Equation 7.4 and solving for the geometric average yields:

$$R_{\text{Geometric average}} = [(1 + R_1) \times (1 + R_2) \times \cdots \times (1 + R_n)]^{1/n} - 1 = [\$1.646]^{1/5} - 1 = 0.1048, \text{ or } 10.48 \text{ per year}$$

Discussion Questions

At least ten qualitative questions, called Discussion Questions, require students to think through their understanding of key concepts and apply those concepts to a problem.

Discussion Questions

7.1 Suppose that you know the risk and the expected return for two stocks. Discuss the process you might utilize to determine which of the two stocks is a better buy. You may assume that the two stocks will be the only assets held in your portfolio.

7.2 What is the difference between the expected rate of return and the required rate of return? What does it mean if they are different for a particular asset at a particular point in time?

7.3 Suppose that the standard deviation of the returns on the shares of stock at two different companies is exactly the same. Does this mean that the required rate of return will be the same for these two stocks? How might the required rate of return on the stock of a third company be greater than the required rates of return on the stocks of the first two companies even if the standard deviation of the returns of the third company's stock is lower?

7.4 The correlation between Stocks A and B is 0.50, while the correlation between Stocks A and C is −0.5. You already own Stock A

7.6 Which investment category included in Exhibit 7.3 has shown the greatest degree of risk in the United States since 1926? Explain why that makes sense in a world where the value of an asset in this investment category is likely to be more sensitive to changes in market conditions than is the price of a corporate bond.

7.7 You are concerned about one of the investments in your fully diversified portfolio. You just have an uneasy feeling about the CFO, Iam Shifty, of that particular firm. You do believe, however, that the firm makes a good product and that it is appropriately priced by the market. Should you be concerned about the effect on your portfolio if Shifty embezzles a portion of the firm's cash?

7.8 The CAPM is used to price the risk (estimate the expected return) for any asset. Our examples have focused on stocks, but we could also use CAPM to estimate the expected rate of return for bonds. Explain why.

7.9 In recent years, investors have agreed that the market portfolio consists of more than just a group of U.S. stocks and bonds. If you are

Questions and Problems

The Questions and Problems, numbering 26 to 48 per chapter, are primarily quantitative and are classified as Basic, Intermediate, or Advanced.

Questions and Problems

Excel — *Excel templates and resources available in* **WileyPLUS**

Basic

7.1 **Returns:** Describe the difference between a total holding period return and an expected return.

7.2 **Expected returns:** John is watching an old game show rerun on television called *Let's Make a Deal* in which the contestant chooses a prize behind one of two curtains. Behind one of the curtains is a gag prize worth $150, and behind the other is a round-the-world trip

7.5 **Single-asset portfolios:** Stocks A, B, and C have expected returns of 15 percent, 15 percent, and 12 percent, respectively, while their standard deviations are 45 percent, 30 percent, and 30 percent, respectively. If you were considering the purchase of each of these stocks as the only holding in your portfolio and the risk-free rate is 0 percent, which stock should you choose?

Excel Problems

Nearly all problems can be solved using Excel templates within *WileyPLUS*.

Intermediate

7.15 **Expected returns:** José is thinking about purchasing a soft drink machine and placing it in a business office. He knows that there is a 5 percent probability that someone who walks by the machine will make a purchase from the machine, and he knows that the profit on each soft drink sold is $0.10. If José expects a thousand

7.20 **Single-asset portfolios:** Using the information from Problems 7.17, 7.18, and 7.19, calculate the coefficient of variation for each of the investments in those problems.

7.21 **Portfolios with more than one asset:** Emmy is analyzing a two-

Advanced

7.29 David is going to purchase two stocks to form the initial holdings in his portfolio. Iron stock has an expected return of 15 percent, while Copper stock has an expected return of 20 percent. If David plans to invest 30 percent of his funds in Iron and the remainder in Copper, what will be the expected return from his

you think that this will have a large or a small impact on the beta of the asset? Explain your opinion.

7.35 Draw the Security Market Line (SML) for the case where the market risk premium is 5 percent and the risk-free rate is 7 percent. Now suppose an asset has a beta of −1.0 and an expected return of

CFA Problems

4.38 Common-size analysis is used in financial analysis to:

a. evaluate changes in a company's operating cycle over time.

b. predict changes in a company's capital structure using regression analysis.

c. compare companies of different sizes or compare a company with itself over time.

d. restate each element in a company's financial statement as a

4.40 DuPont analysis involves breaking return-on-assets ratios into their:

a. profit components.

b. marginal and average components.

c. operating and financing components.

d. profit margin and turnover components.

4.41 If a company's net profit margin is −5 percent, its total asset

CFA Problems

Problems from CFA readings are included in the Question and Problem section in appropriate chapters.

Sample Test Problems

Finally, five or more Sample Test Problems call for straightforward applications of the chapter concepts. These problems are intended to be representative of the kind of problems that may be used in a test, and instructors can encourage students to solve them as if they were taking a quiz. Solutions are provided in the Instructor's Manual.

Sample Test Problems

7.1 Given the following information from Capstone Corporation, what price would the CAPM predict that the company's stock will trade for one year from today?

Risk free rate: 3%
Market risk premium: 8%
Beta: 0.65
Current stock price: $64.61
Annual dividend: $1.92

7.2 You are considering investing in a mutual fund. The fund is expected to earn a return of 15 percent in the next year. If its annual return is normally distributed with a standard deviation of 6.5 percent, what return can you expect the fund to beat 95 percent of the time?

7.3 You have just invested in a portfolio of three stocks. The amount of money that you invested in each stock and its beta are summarized below. Calculate the beta of the portfolio and use the Capital Asset Pricing Model (CAPM) to compute the expected rate of return for the portfolio. Assume that the expected rate of return on the market is 15 percent and that the risk-free rate is 7 percent.

Stock	Investment	Beta
A	$200,000	1.50
B	300,000	0.65
C	500,000	1.25

7.4 What would you recommend to an investor who is considering making an investment in a stock that plots *below* the Security Market Line (SML)? Explain.

7.5 Why does an investor want a diversified portfolio? Can an investor eliminate all risk?

Ethics Case

America's Ailing Drug Prices

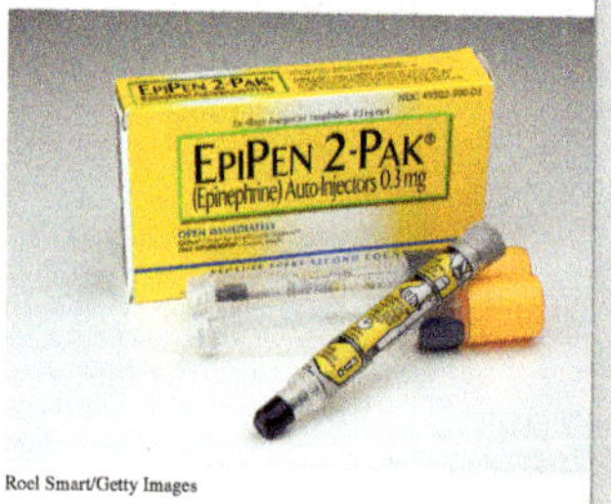

Roel Smart/Getty Images

In September 2016, Mylan CEO Heather Bresch appeared before the U.S. House Oversight Committee to address the controversial issue of rising prescription drug prices. Mylan was in the spotlight because of a dramatic 600 percent increase in the price of the EpiPen, a steroidal injector that treats severe and sometimes deadly allergic reactions. The rise in the cost of EpiPens was stunning. Priced at $100 for a two-pack in 2009, the same medication sold for over $600 by the fall

prices for a large proporti

Ethics Cases

Ethics is an important topic in Finance. Key concepts are discussed in Chapter 1 and eight cases are included throughout this book to help students better understand how to analyze ethicals dilemmas. Real company examples are presented, including timeless cases about Arthur Anderson and Martha Stewart's scandal involving ImClone, and more timely topics such as the controversy surrounding drug price increases at firms like Mylan (EpiPen) and the cross-selling scandal at Wells Fargo. Each case includes questions for follow-up discussion in class or as an assignment.

In revising Fundamentals of Corporate Finance we have improved the presentation and organization of key topics, added important new content, updated the text to reflect changes in market and business conditions since the third edition was written, improved key in-chapter pedagogical features, and added to the number and quality of the end-of-chapter problem sets.

Improved Content, Presentation, and Organization

In preparing this edition of *Fundamentals of Corporate Finance*, we extensively edited discussions throughout the text and added new content to improve the depth and effectiveness of the presentation. We also substantially modified the layout of the text to enhance the accessibility of the content in on line applications, such as WileyPLUS. The changes that we made to the content and writing are too numerous to discuss in detail here. However, examples include the addition of more in-text calculations related to cash flows associated with working capital and long term investments in Chapter 3, the addition of a new section on arithmetic versus geometric returns in Chapter 7, and streamlining of some of bond calculation discussions in Chapter 8. Throughout the text we added callouts for the Learning by Doing Applications and Decision Making Examples to improve the flow of the presentation. We also added two new ethics cases, one on pricing in the pharmaceutical industry and a second on the controversy at Wells Fargo regarding the establishment of new accounts without customer permission. These new cases, along with updated versions of six of the ethics cases from the previous edition, provide the instructor with a broad range ethical issues from which to choose.

Current Financial Market and Business Information

Throughout the text, all financial market and business information for which more current data are available have been updated. Not only have the exhibits been updated, but financial values such as interest rates, risk premia, and foreign currency exchange rates have been updated throughout the discussions in text, in-text examples, and end-of-chapter problems. In addition, all of the chapter opener vignettes have either been replaced or updated. Six of these examples are from 2016 and 15 are from 2017. All of the chapter openers provide timely examples of how the material covered in the chapter is relevant to financial decision-making.

In-Chapter Features

The **Learning Objectives** at the beginning of each chapter have been revised to more fully reflect the important content in the associated sections of the chapters.

New **Building Intuition Boxes** have been added where appropriate and existing Building Intuition Boxes have been edited to ensure clarity.

All **Learning by Doing Applications** have been reviewed and, where appropriate, updated or replaced.

All **Decision-Making Examples** have been reviewed and updated where necessary.

The **Summary of Learning Objectives** and **Key Equations** at the end of each chapter have been updated to reflect changes in the chapter text and to improve the pedagogical value of these features.

Refined and Extended Problem Sets

We have carefully edited the end-of-chapter questions and problems throughout the book to ensure that the examples are current and clearly presented. New Self-Study Problems, Discussion Questions, and Questions and Problems have been added to ensure appropriate coverage of key concepts at all levels of difficulty. The total number of end-of-chapter questions and problems, including self-study problems and self-test questions, for the entire text has increased to 1,200.

Engaging Digitally

Fundamentals of Corporate Finance, Fourth Edition, is completely integrated with WileyPLUS, featuring a suite of teaching and learning resources developed under the close review of the authors. Driven by the same basic beliefs as the textbook, WileyPLUS allows students to create a personalized study plan, assess their progress along the way, and access the content and resources needed to master the material. WileyPLUS provides immediate insight to student strengths and problem areas with visual reports that highlight what's most important for both the instructor and student.

Many dynamic resources are integrated into the course to help students build their knowledge and understanding, stay motivated, and prepare for decision making in a real-world context. WileyPLUS also includes **Orion**, an integrated adaptive practice that helps students build proficiency and use their study time most effectively. Additional features of the WileyPLUS course include:

Chapter 0 Math and Skills Review offering students adaptive review and practice for essential math topics necessary to master Corporate Finance. Built to serve as a refresher of remedial content, this chapter includes reading content, algorithmic practice, and **Figuring Finance Interactive Tutorials** built to improve student retention and help connect difficult math and finance concepts.

Learning by Doing Interactive Tutorials containing quantitative problems with step-by-step solutions to help students better understand how to apply their intuition and analytical skills to solve problems.

Solution Walkthrough Lightboard Videos featuring the authors working through a 1–3 of end of chapter problems per chapter, offering 24/7 just-in-time homework assistance and problem solving techniques.

Excel Templates and Excel Function Videos providing students with step-by-step examples of how to use specific Excel functions as it applies to Corporate Finance. Excel templates will be available for all applicable end of chapter question while videos feature select end-of-chapter problems to support Excel function examples.

Acknowledgments

The nearly 400 colleagues listed below provided valuable feedback during the development process and added greatly to the content and pedagogy of the program. Their commitment to teaching and willingness to become involved in such a project was a source of inspiration to the authors. We would like to acknowledge the contribution made by the following professors whose thoughtful comments contributed to the quality, relevancy, and accuracy of the Parrino Corporate Finance program.

Reviewers

Saul Adelman, Miami University
Kenneth Ahern, University of Southern California
Evrim Akdogu, Koç University
Kofi Amoateng, North Carolina Central University
Esther Ancel, University of Wisconsin—Milwaukee
Kavous Ardalan, Marist College
Ronald Anderson, Temple University
Michael Anderson, University of Mass-Dartmouth
Michael Andrews, Roosevelt University
Gene Andrusco, California State University San Bernardino
Bala Arshanapalli, Indiana University Northwest
Saul Auslander, Bridgewater State College
Sung C. Bae, Bowling Green State University
Alan Bailey, University of Texas San Antonio
Robert Balik, Western Michigan University
John Banko, University of Florida
Babu Baradwaj, Towson University
Nina Baranchuk, University of Texas at Dallas
Karen Barnhart, Missouri State University
Janet Bartholow, Kent State University
John Becker-Blease, Washington State University
Basma Bekdache, Wayne State University
Omar Benkato, Ball State University
Vashishta Bhaskar, Duquesne University
Wilfred Jerome Bibbins, Troy University
Hamdi Bilici, California State University Long Beach
Ken Bishop, Florida Atlantic University
David Blackwell, University of Kentucky
Charles Blaylock, Murray State University
Vigdis Boasson, Central Michigan University
David Bourff, Boise State University
Carol Boyer, Long Island University
Joe Brocato, Tarleton State University
Jeffrey Brookman, Idaho State University
Jeff Bruns, Bacone College
James Buck, East Carolina University
Juan Cabrera, Ramapo College
Michael Carter, University of North Texas—Dallas
[illegible]heodore Chadwick, Boston University
[illegible]helikani, Quinnipiac University
[illegible], University of Southern Indiana
[illegible]rsity of Colorado Denver
[illegible]rsity of North Carolina at Charlotte
[illegible] San Francisco State University
Paul Chiou, Shippensburg University
William Chittenden, Texas State University
Tarun Chordia, Emory University
Ting-Heng Chu, East Tennessee State University
Cetin Ciner, University of North Carolina at Wilmington
Jonathan Clarke, Georgia Tech
Brandon Cline, Mississippi State University
Thomas Coe, Quinnipiac University
Hugh Colaco, Aston University
Colene Coldwell, Baylor University
Boyd D. Collier, Tarleton State University
Roger Collier, Northeastern State University
Georges Courtadon, Cuny Queens College
Lary B. Cowart, The University of Alabama at Birmingham
Susan J. Crain, Missouri State University
Tony Crawford, University of Montana
Sandeep Dahiva, Georgetown University
Julie Dahlquist, University of Texas at San Antonio
Brent Dalrymple, University of Central Florida
Amadeu DaSilva, California State University, Fullerton
Sergio Davalos, University of Washington
Zane Dennick-Ream, Robert Morris University
Hendrik Devos, University of Texas-El Paso
John Dexter, Northwood University
Robert Dildine, Metropolitan State University
Michael Drake, Brigham Young University-Provo
Robert Dubil, University of Utah
Heidi Dybevik, University of Iowa
Michael Dyer, University of Illinois at Urbana-Champaign
David Eckmann, University of Miami
Susan Edwards, Grand Valley State University
Ahmed El-Shahat, Bradley University
Marco Elia, Drexel University
Susan Elkinawy, Loyola Marymount University
Frank Elston, University of South Queensland
Maryellen Epplin, University of Central Oklahoma
Omar Esqueda, Tarleton State University
Stephen Ferris, University of Missouri Columbia
Ron Filante, Pace University
J. Howard Finch, Samford University
Dov Fobar, Brooklyn College/CUNY
Kathy Fogel, Suffolk University
Marianne Fortuna, University of Georgia
Joann Fredrickson, Bemidji State University
Sally Fulkert, University of South Carolina
Sharon Garrison, University of Arizona
Louis Gasper, University of Dallas
John Gawryk, Central Michigan University
Ashley Geisewite, Southwest Tennessee Community College
John Goodell, University of Akron
Edward Graham, University of North Carolina at Wilmington
Richard P. Gregory, East Tennessee State University
Nicolas Gressis, Wright State University
Anthony Gu, SUNY Geneseo
Diane Del Guercio, University of Oregon
Roxane Gunser, University of Wisconsin Platteville
Manak Gupta, Temple University

Sally Guyton, Texas A&M University
Matthew Haertzen, Northern Arizona University
Karen Hallows, University of Maryland
Karen Hamilton, Georgia Southern University
Mahfuzul Haque, Indiana State University
John Hatem, Georgia Southern University
George Haushalter, Pennsylvania State University
Andrew Head, Western Kentucky University
Matthew Hood, University of Southern Mississippi
James Howard, University of Maryland University College
Emily Huang, California State University, Chico
Jian Huang, Towson University
Christy Huebner Caridi, Marist College
Stephen Huffman, University of Wisconsin Oshkosh
Rob Hull, Washburn University
Kenneth Hunsader, University of South Alabama
Jae-Kwang Hwang, Virginia State University
Zahid Iqbal, Texas Southern University
Jide Iwawere, Howard University
Subramanian Iyer, University of New Mexico
Victoria Javine, University of Alabama
Xiaoquan Jiang, Florida International University
Benjamas Jirasakuldech, Slippery Rock University
Steve Johnson, Sam Houston State University
Surendranath Jory, University of Sussex
Jarl Kallberg, Thunderbird School of Global Management
Ahmet Karagozoglu, Hofstra University
Burhan Kawosa, Wright State University
Gary Kayakachoian, University of Rhode Island
Ayla Kayhan, Louisianna State University Baton Rouge
James Kehr, Miami University of Ohio
Peppi Kenny, Western Illinois University
Andrew Kern, University of Missouri
James Keys, Florida International University
Robert Kieschnick, University of Texas Dallas
Jaemin Kim, San Diego State University
Kee Kim, Missouri State University
Kenneth Kim, SUNY Buffalo
Brett King, University of North Alabama
Halil Kiymaz, Rollins College
Roger Klee, Cleveland State University
John Knight, University of the Pacific
C.R. Krishna-Swamy, Western Michigan University
Robert Krell, University of Phoenix
Thomas J. Krissek, Northeastern Illinois University
Raman Kumar, Virginia Tech University
George Kutner, Marquette University
Frances Kwansa, University of Delaware
Julia Kwok, Northeastern State University
Pamela LaBorde, Western Washington University
Stephen Lacewell, Murray State University
Gene Lai, Washington State University
Mark Laplante, University of Wisconsin-Madison
Duong Le, University of Arkansas at Little Rock
Jerry Leabman, Bentley College
Gregory La Blanc, University of California Berkeley
Rick Le Compte, Wichita State University
Alice Lee, San Francisco State University
Cheng Few Lee, Rutgers University
Jeong Lee, University of North Dakota
Richard Lee, Barton College
Canlin Li, The Federal Reserve System
Mingsheng Li, Bowling Green State University
Bing Liang, University of Massachusetts Amherst
Wendell Licon, Arizona State University Tempe
Steven Lifland, High Point University
Ralph Lim, Sacred Heart University
Bingxuan Lin, University of Rhode Island
Hong-Jen Lin, Brooklyn College
Jason Lin, Truman State University
David Lins, University of Illinois
Kenneth Lobo, Herbert H. Lehman College
Peter Locke, Texas Christian University
Robert Lutz, University of Utah
Yulong Ma, California State University Long Beach
Y. Lal Mahajan, Monmouth University
Dana Manner, University of Miami
Carol Mannino, Milwaukee School of Engineering
Timothy Manuel, University of Montana
Barry Marchman, Georgia Tech
Richard Mark, Dowling College
Brian Maris, Northern Arizona University
Rand Martin, Bloomsburg University of Pennsylvania
John Masserwick, Farmingdale State College
Richmond Matthews, University of Maryland
Leslie Mathis, University of Memphis
Stefano Mazzotta, Kennesaw State University
Joseph McCarthy, Bryant University
Lee McClain, Western Washington University
Michael McNamara, Washington State University
Kathleen McNichol, La Salle University
Seyed Mehdian, University of Michigan at Flint
Robert Meiselas, St. John's University
Timothy Michael, Univeristy of Houston Clear Lake
Jill Misuraca, University of Tampa
Sunil Mohanty, Brooklyn CUNY
Sunil Mohanty, University of St. Thomas
Cathileen Montesarchio, Broward College Central
Dianne Morrison, University of Wisconsin, La Crosse
Shane Moser, University of Mississippi
Tammie Mosley, California State University, East Bay
Michael Muoghalu, Pittsburg State University
Suzan Murphy, University of Tennessee
Dina Naples-Layish, SUNY Binghamton
Vivian Nazar, Ferris State University
Steven Nenninger, Sam Houstin State University
Chee Ng, Fairleigh Dickinson University
Brian Nichols, Missouri Southern State University
Terry D. Nixon, Miami University
Mark Norrell, Indiana University-Bloomington
Deniz Ozenbas, Montclair State University
Vivek Pandey, University of Texas Tyler
James Pandjiris, University of Missouri at St. Louis
Nick Panepinto, Flagler College
Coleen Pantalone, Northeastern University
Robert Pavlik, Elon University
Ivelina Pavlova, University of Houston, Clear Lake,
Anil Pawar, San Diego State University
Janet Payne, Texas State University
Chien-Chih Peng, Morehead State University
G. Michael Phillips, California State University Northridge
James Philpot, Missouri State University
Greg Pierce, Pennsylvania State University
Steve Pilloff, George Mason University
Wendy Pirie, CFA Institute
Tony Plath, University of North Carolina, Charlotte

Vassilis Polimenis, Aristotle University of Thessaloniki
Richard Ponarul, California State University, Chico
Percy Poon, University of Nevada Las Vegas
Terry Pope, Abilene Christian University
Gary Powell, Queens University of Charlotte
Richard Powell, Villanova University
Dev Prasad, University of Massachusetts Lowell
Rose Prasad, Central Michigan University
Shoba Prekumar, Iowa State University
Robert Puelz, Southern Methodist University
Russell B. Raimer, Cleveland State University
S. Rao, University of Louisiana at Lafayette
Vadhindran K. Rao, Metropolitan State University
Thomas Rearick, Indiana University
Jong Rhim, University of Southern Indiana
Greg Richey, California State University, San Bernadino
Hong Rim, Shippensburg University
Luis Rivera, Arcadia University
Kenneth Roskelley, Mississippi State University
Bruce Rubin, Old Dominion University
David Rystrom, Western Washington University
Helen Saar, Dixie State University
Murray Sabrin, Ramapo College
Sundarrajan Sankar, Tarleton State University
Muku Santhanakrishnan, Southern Methodist University
Mukunthan Santhanakrishnan, Idaho State University
Salil Sarkar, University of Texas Arlington
Atul Saxena, Georgia Gwinnett College
Steven Scheff, Florida Gulf Coast University
Adam Schwartz, Washington and Lee University
George Seldat, Southwest Minnesota State University
Vivek Sharma, University of Michigan Dearborn
Val Sibilkov, University of Wisconsin, Milwaukee
Ana Silva, Merrimack College
Betty Simkins, Oklahoma State University Stillwater
Sudhir Singh, Frostburg State University
Kim Small, Illinois State University
Joe Smolira, Belmont University
Andrew Spieler, Hofstra University
Cliff Stephens, Louisiana State University
Mark Hoven Stohs, California State University, Fullerton
Gene Stout, Central Michigan University
Jan Strockis, Santa Clara University
David Suk, Rider University
Charlene Sullivan, Purdue University
Michael Sullivan, University of Nevada at Las Vegas
Alice Sun, California State Polytechnic University Pomona
Srinivasan Sundaram, Ball State University
Janikan Supanvanij, St. Cloud State University
Robert Sweeney, Wright State University
Philip Swensen, Summit Capital Investment Group
Chu-Sheng Tai, Texas Southern University
Thomas Tallerico, Stony Brook University
Richard Taylor, Arkansas State University
Bill Templeton, Butler University
Diana Tempski, University of Wisconsin, La Crosse
-nda Tenkku, University of Missouri at St. Louis
-wari, The College at Brockport, State University of

California State University Long Beach
Minnesota State University
versity of Nevada at Las Vegas
Nancy Titus-Piersma, Oklahoma State at Stillwater
Damir Tokic, ESC Rennes School of Business
Roger Torneden, Webster University
K.C. Tseng, California State University Fresno
Sergey Tsyplakov, University of South Carolina
David Tufte, Southern Utah University
Cathyann Tully, Kean University
Marian Turac, College of Charleston
Harry Turtle, Washington State University
Pieter Vandenberg, San Diego State University
Bonnie Van Ness, University of Mississippi
Kristen Van Rensselaer, University of North Alabama
Zoë L. Van Schyndel, Evergreen State College
Sanjay Varshney, California State University Sacramento
Rahul Verma, University of Houston Downtown
Jill Lynn Vihtelic, Saint Mary's College
Anna Vygodina, California State University Sacramento
Jonathan Wagoner, Fairmont State University
Joe Walker, University of Alabama at Birmingham
Peggy Ward, Wichita State University
Jim Washam, Arkansas State University
Ethan Watson, University of N Carolina-Wilmington
Gwendolyn Webb, Baruch College
Mark Weinstein, University of Southern California
Paul Weinstock, Ohio State University
Susan White, University of Maryland
Alayna Williamson, University of Utah
Michael Willoughby, University of California San Diego
Rachel Wilson, Wittenberg University
Alexander Wilson, University of Arizona
K. Matthew Wong, St. John's University
Yangru Wu, Rutgers Business School
Wenjuan Xie, University of New Hampshire
Feixue Xie, University of Texas at El Paso
Yan (Alice) Xie, University of Michigan Dearborn
Devrim Yaman, Western Michigan University
Hua Yang, Old Dominion University
David Yamoah, Kean University
Keven Yost, Auburn University
Lei Yu, University of Notre Dame
Jasmine Yur-Austin, California State University, Long Beach
David Zhang, Arizona State University West
Ge Zhang, William Patterson University
Zhong-guo Zhou, California State University Northridge
Kermit C. Zieg, Florida Institute of Technology

Advisory Board

Francisca M. Beer, California State University, San Bernardino
Susan J. Crain, Missouri State University
Praveen Kumar Das, University of Louisiana
Amadeu DaSilva, California State University, Fullerton
Beverly Hadaway, The University of Texas at Austin
James D. Keys, Florida International University
G. Michael Phillips, California State University, Northridge
Helen Saar, Dixie State University
Mark Stohs, California State University, Fullerton
Devrim Yaman, Western Michigan University
Jasmine Yur-Austin, California State University, Long Beach
Kermit C. Zieg, Florida Institute of Technology

Class Testers

Saul W. Adelman, Miami University
Babu Baradwaj, Towson University
Jeffrey Brookman, Idaho State University
Juan Cabrera, Ramapo College
Michael Carter, University of North Texas
Jun Chen, University of North Carolina at Charlotte
Jonathan Clarke, Georgia Tech
Thomas Coe, Quinnipiac College
Hugh Colaco, Aston University
Boyd Collier, Tarleton State University
Roger Collier, Northeastern State University
James Cordiero, The College at Brockport, State University of New York
Irving DeGraw, St. Petersburg Junior College
Zane Dennick-Ream, Robert Morris College
Michael Dyer, University of Illinois, Urbana-Champaign
Ronald Filante, Pace University
Louis Gasper, University of Dallas
J. Edward Graham, University of North Carolina, Wilmington
Richard Gregory, East Tennessee State University
Nicolas Gressis, Wright State University
Matthew Haertzen, Northern Arizona University
Karen L. Hamilton, Georgia Southern University
Gary Kayakachoian, University of Rhode Island
Peppi Kenny, Western Illinois University
Julia Kwok, Northeastern State University
Pamela LaBorde, Western Washington University
Duong Le, University of Arkansas at Little Rock
Mingsheng Li, Bowling Green State University
Wendell Licon, Arizona State University
Steven Lifland, High Point University
Jason Lin, Truman State University
Hong-Jen Lin, Brooklyn College
Robert Lutz, University of Utah
Brian A. Maris, Northern Arizona University
Suzan Murphy, University of Tennessee
S. P. UMA Rao, University of Louisiana at Lafayette
Luis Rivera, Arcadia University
David Rystrom, Western Washington University
Murray Sabrin, Ramapo College
Michael Sullivan, University of Nevada at Las Vegas
Chu-Sheng Tai, Texas Southern University
Thomas Tallerico, Stony Brook University
Diana Tempski, University of Wisconsin, La Crosse
Jonathan Wagoner, Fairmont State College

Accuracy Checkers

Tom Arnold, University of Richmond
Robert J. Balik, Western Michigan University
Babu Baradwaj, Towson University
Deb Bauer, University of Oregon
Dalton Bigbee, Northeastern State University
Deanne Butchey, Florida International University
Julie Dahlquist, Texas Christian University
Jim P. DeMello, Western Michigan University
Sharon Garrison, University of Arizona
James Hilliard, Northern Arizona University
Samira Hussein, Johnson County Community College
Sanjay Jain, Salem State University
Benjamas Jirasakuldech, Slipper Rock University
Inayat U. Mangla, Western Michigan University
Dianne Morrison, University of Wisconsin
Jill Misuraca, University of Tampa
Napoleon Overton, University of Memphis
Craig A. Peterson, Western Michigan University
James Philpot, Missouri State University
Andrew Prevost, University of Vermont
Mary Lou Poloskey, The University of Texas at Austin
Judith Swisher, Western Michigan University
Alex Tan, University of Tampa
Rhonda Tenkku, University of Missouri

The following people developed and revised valuable student and instructor resources and made tremendous contributions to WileyPLUS with Orion:

Babu Baradwaj, Towson University
Charles Beauchamp, Middle Tennessee State University
Kristine Beck, California State University, Northridge
Michael Carter, University of North Texas, Dallas
James DeMello, Western Michigan University
James Dow, California State University, Northridge
James Hilliard, Northern Arizona University
James Keys, Florida International University
Patrick Lach, Eastern Illinois University
Pamela LaBorde, Western Washington University
Wendell Licon, Arizona State University
Steven Lifland, High Point University
Bridget Lyons, Sacred Heart University
Dianne Morrison, University of Wisconsin, La Crosse
G. Michael Phillips, California State University, Northridge
Mary Lou Poloskey, The University of Texas at Austin
Andrew Prevost, University of Vermont
Timothy Sargent, California State University, Northridge
Mary Jane Sterling, Bradley University
Philip Thames, California State University, Long Beach
Susan White, University of Maryland
Devrim Yaman, Western Michigan University

Contributor Team

We owe a special thanks to members of the contributor team for their hard work, exceptional creativity, consummate communications skills, and advice: Dr. Babu Baradwaj of Towson State University and Dr. Wendell Licon of Arizona State University who contributed significantly to the Instructor's Manual, and major sections of the end-of-chapter materials for the First Edition. Dr. Norm Bowie of the University of Minnesota wrote number of the ethics cases.

Publishing Team

We also thank the Wiley publishing team for always being calm, supportive, and gracious under fire as we suffered the travails of college textbook writing and revising, where deadlines are always yesterda Those showing extraordinary patience and support include Mic McDonald, Director of Accounting and Finance; and Emily Mar Acquisitions Editor for Accounting and Finance. Those war special praise are Courtney Jordan, Associate Development Editor; and Jenny Welter, Project Manager and the Wiley sales force for their creativity and success in selling our book.

Colleagues

Robert Parrino would also like to thank some of his colleagues for their inspiration and helpful discussions. Among those who have significantly influenced this book are Robert Bruner of University of Virginia, Jay Hartzell of University of Texas at Austin, and Mark Huson of University of Alberta. Special thanks are owed to Clifford Smith, of University of Rochester, whose classes helped Dr. Parrino make sense of finance. In addition, recognition should go to Michael J. Barclay, who inspired generations of students through his selfless support and example and who was both a great researcher and teacher.

Thomas Bates would like to thank the professors, co-authors, and colleagues who have made him a better scholar and educator, including Robert Williams, who first introduced him to the analytical elegance of economics, and Kenneth Lehn who inspired him to pursue excellence in research and teaching in the field of finance.

Stuart Gillan would like to thank his professors and classmates at the University of Texas at Austin (for sharing the journey through the PhD program) and to the many friends, colleagues, mentors, and students who have helped him become a better researcher and teacher. A special thanks to his dissertation chair, Laura T. Starks.

David Kidwell would like to thank some of his former professors and colleagues for their inspiration and willingness to share their intellectual capital. George Kaufman and Michael Hopewell who contributed to Dr. Kidwell's knowledge of economics and finance and were critical professors during his doctoral program at the University of Oregon. Richard West, former dean and professor at the University of Oregon, who unlocked the secrets of research and inspired Dr. Kidwell's love of teaching and scholarship. Robert Johnson of Purdue University whose dignity and academic bearing served as an academic role model and whose love of teaching and research inspired Dr. Kidwell to follow in his footsteps and to write this book. David Blackwell of Texas A&M University who helped conceptualize the idea for the book and contributed numerous insights to various chapters during the book's writing. Finally, to John Harbell and Jonas Mittelman, of San Francisco State University who started Dr. Kidwell on his academic journey.

Brief Contents

Contents

CHAPTER 1

The Financial Manager and the Firm

Kerem Yucel/Getty Images

LEARNING OBJECTIVES

1. Identify the key financial decisions facing the financial manager of any business.
2. Identify common forms of business organization in the United States and their respective strengths and weaknesses.
3. Describe the typical organization of the financial function in a large corporation.
4. Explain why maximizing the value of the firm's stock is the appropriate goal for management.
5. Discuss how agency conflicts affect the goal of maximizing stockholder value.
6. Explain why ethics is an appropriate topic in the study of corporate finance.

On July 25, 2016, Verizon Communications announced an agreement to buy Yahoo's core internet business for $4.8 billion. Why did Verizon's management decide to purchase Yahoo's internet business, and how did the Yahoo and Verizon management teams agree on the $4.8 billion price tag?

In a press release about the deal, Tim Armstrong, the chief executive officer of Verizon-owned AOL, suggested that "this transaction is about unleashing Yahoo's full potential, building upon our collective synergies, and strengthening and accelerating that growth. Combining Verizon, AOL, and Yahoo will create a new powerful competitive rival in mobile media." In the same press release, Marissa Mayer, Yahoo's chief executive officer, said that the deal was an important step in her company's plan to "unlock shareholder value for Yahoo."[1]

However, in mid-December 2016, Yahoo reported that more than 1 billion user accounts were hacked in one of the largest data breaches in history. Following the news release, Yahoo's stock price dropped 2.5 percent. Over the next few months, many questioned whether the deal would be completed. In the end, Verizon did acquire Yahoo, but paid $350 million less than the original price of $4.8 billion.

Surely Verizon and its investors were not expecting the bad news about the data breach. Nor did they make an investment in Yahoo with the expectation of losing money on the deal. Rather, by taking advantage of the operational experience of Verizon's and AOL's management teams and the potential overlap with Yahoo's business, Verizon's management was expecting to earn solid returns for its investors.

The managers of companies like Verizon and Yahoo use many of the concepts covered in this chapter and elsewhere in this book to create the most value possible. Managers can create value by buying companies only when the expected benefits exceed the cost, managing the assets of those companies as efficiently as possible, and financing those companies with the least expensive combination of debt and equity. This chapter introduces you to the key financial aspects of these activities, and the remainder of the book fills in many of the details.

[1]http://www.verizon.com/about/news/verizon-acquire-yahoos-operating-business

Chapter Preview

This book provides an introduction to corporate finance. In it we focus on the responsibilities of the financial manager, who oversees the accounting and treasury functions and sets the overall financial strategy for the firm. We pay special attention to the financial manager's role as a decision maker. To that end, we emphasize the mastery of fundamental financial concepts and tools that are used to make sound financial decisions that create value for stockholders. These financial concepts and tools apply not only to business organizations but also to other venues, such as government entities, not-for-profit organizations, and sometimes even our own personal finances.

We begin this chapter by discussing the three major types of decisions that a financial manager makes. We then describe common forms of business organization. After next discussing the major responsibilities of the financial manager, we explain why maximizing the value of the firm's stock is an appropriate goal for a financial manager. We go on to describe the conflicts of interest that can arise between stockholders and managers and the mechanisms that help align the interests of these two groups. Finally, we discuss the importance of ethical conduct in business.

1.1 The Role of the Financial Manager

LEARNING OBJECTIVE

1. Identify the key financial decisions facing the financial manager of any business.

The financial manager is responsible for making decisions that are in the best interests of the firm's owners, whether the firm is a start-up business with a single owner or a billion-dollar corporation owned by thousands of stockholders. The decisions made by the financial manager or owner should be one and the same. In most situations this means that the financial manager should make decisions that maximize the value of the owners' stock. This helps maximize the owners' **wealth**, which is the economic value of the assets the owner possesses. Our underlying assumption in this book is that most people who invest in businesses do so because they want to increase their wealth. In the following discussion, we describe the responsibilities of the financial manager in a new business in order to illustrate the types of decisions that such a manager makes.

wealth the economic value of the assets someone possesses

Stakeholders

Before we discuss the new business, you may want to look at **Exhibit 1.1**, which shows the cash flows between a firm and its owners (in a corporation, the stockholders) and various stakeholders. A **stakeholder** is someone other than an owner who has a claim on the cash flows of the firm: *managers,* who want to be paid salaries and performance bonuses; *other employees*, who want to be paid wages; *suppliers*, who want to be paid for goods or services they provide; *creditors*, who want to be paid interest and principal; and the *government*, which wants the firm to pay taxes. Stakeholders may have interests that differ from those of the owners. When this is the case, they may exert pressure on management to make decisions that benefit them. We will return to these types of conflicts of interest later in the book. For now, though, we are primarily concerned with the overall flow of cash between the firm and its stockholders and stakeholders.

stakeholder anyone other than an owner (stockholder) with a claim on the cash flows of a firm, including employees, suppliers, creditors, and the government

It's All About Cash Flows

To produce its products or services, a new firm needs to acquire a variety of assets. Most will be long-term assets, which are also known as **productive assets**. Productive assets can be tangible assets, such as equipment, machinery, or a manufacturing facility, or intangible assets, such as patents, trademarks, technical expertise, or other types of intellectual capital. Regardless of the type of asset, the firm tries to select assets that will generate the greatest cash flows for the firm's owners. The decision-making process through which the firm purchases productive assets is called *capital budgeting,* and it is one of the most important decision processes in a firm.

productive assets the long-term tangible and intangible assets a firm uses to generate cash flows

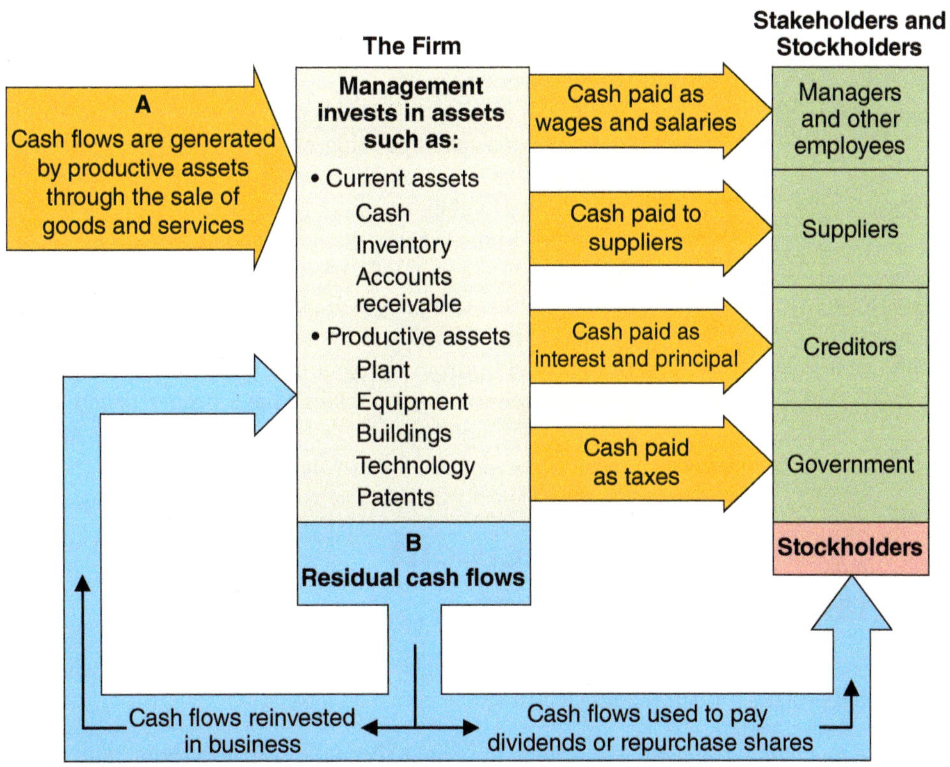

EXHIBIT 1.1 Cash Flows Between the Firm and Its Stakeholders and Owners (Stockholders)

A. Making business decisions is all about cash flows, because only cash can be used to pay bills and buy new assets. Cash initially flows into the firm as a result of the sale of goods or services. These cash inflows are used in a number of ways: to pay wages and salaries, to buy supplies, to repay creditors, and to pay taxes.

B. Any cash that is left over (residual cash flows) can be reinvested in the business or paid as dividends to stockholders.

Once the managers of a firm have selected the firm's productive assets, they must raise money to pay for them. *Financing decisions* determine the ways in which firms obtain and manage long-term financing to acquire and support their productive assets. There are two basic sources of funds: debt and equity. Every firm has some equity because equity represents ownership in the firm. It consists of capital contributions by the owners plus cash flows that have been reinvested in the firm. In addition, most firms borrow from a bank or issue some type of long-term debt to finance productive assets.

After the productive assets have been purchased and the business is operating, the managers of the firm will try to produce products at the lowest possible cost while maintaining quality. This means buying raw materials at the lowest possible cost, holding production and labor costs down, keeping management and administrative costs to a minimum, and seeing that shipping and delivery costs are competitive. In addition, day-to-day finances must be managed so that the firm will have sufficient cash on hand to pay salaries, purchase supplies, maintain inventories, pay taxes, and cover the myriad of other expenses necessary to run a business. The management of current assets, such as money owed by customers who purchase on credit, inventory, and current liabilities, such as money owed to suppliers, is called *working capital management.*[2]

A firm generates cash flows by selling the goods and services it produces. A firm is successful when these cash inflows exceed the cash outflows needed to pay operating expenses, creditors, and taxes. After meeting these obligations, managers of the firm can distribute the remaining cash, called **residual cash flows**, to the owners as a cash dividend or by repurchasing some shares, or reinvest the cash in the business. The reinvestment of residual cash flows in the business to buy more productive assets is a very important concept. If these funds are invested wisely, they provide the foundation for the firm to grow and provide larger residual cash flows in the future for the owners. The reinvestment of cash flows (earnings) is the most fundamental

residual cash flows the cash remaining after a firm has paid operating expenses and what it owes creditors and in taxes; can be distributed to the owners as a cash dividend or by repurchasing some shares, or reinvested in the business

[2] From accounting, *current assets* are assets that will be converted into cash within one year, and *current liabilities* are liabilities that must be paid within one year.

Building Intuition

Cash Flows Matter Most to Investors

Cash is what investors ultimately care about when making an investment. The value of any asset—a share of stock, a bond, or a business—is determined by the cash flows it is expected to generate in the future. To understand this concept, just consider how much you would pay for an asset from which you could never expect to obtain any cash flows. Buying such an asset would be like giving your money away. It would have a value of exactly zero. Conversely, as the expected cash flows from an investment increase, you would be willing to pay more and more for it.

way that businesses grow in size. Exhibit 1.1 illustrates how the revenue generated by productive assets ultimately becomes residual cash flows.

A firm is unprofitable when it fails to generate sufficient cash inflows to pay operating expenses, creditors, and taxes. Firms that are unprofitable over time will be forced into **bankruptcy** by their creditors if the owners do not shut them down first. In bankruptcy the company will be reorganized or the company's assets will be liquidated, whichever is more valuable. If the company is liquidated, creditors are paid in a priority order according to the structure of the firm's financial contracts and prevailing bankruptcy law. If anything is left after all creditor and tax claims have been satisfied, which usually does not happen, the remaining cash, or residual value, is distributed to the owners.

bankruptcy legally declared inability of an individual or a company to pay its creditors

Three Fundamental Decisions in Financial Management

Based on our discussion so far, we can see that financial managers are concerned with three fundamental decisions when running a business:

1. *Capital budgeting decisions:* Identifying the productive assets the firm should buy.
2. *Financing decisions:* Determining how the firm should finance or pay for assets.
3. *Working capital management decisions:* Determining how day-to-day financial matters should be managed so that the firm can pay its bills, and how surplus cash should be invested.

Exhibit 1.2 shows the impact of each decision on the firm's balance sheet. We briefly introduce each decision here and discuss them in greater detail in later chapters.

Capital Budgeting Decisions

A firm's capital budget is simply a list of the productive (capital) assets that management wants to purchase over a budget cycle, typically one year. The capital budgeting decision process addresses which productive assets the firm should purchase and how much money the firm can afford to spend. As shown in Exhibit 1.2, capital budgeting decisions affect the asset side of the balance sheet and are concerned with a firm's long-term investments. Capital budgeting decisions, as we mentioned earlier, are among management's most important decisions. Over the long run, they have a large impact on the firm's success or failure. The reason is twofold. First, capital (productive) assets generate most of the cash flows for the firm. Second, capital assets are long term in nature. Once they are purchased, the firm owns them for a long time, and they may be hard to sell without taking a financial loss.

The fundamental question in capital budgeting is this: Which productive assets should the firm purchase? A capital budgeting decision may be as simple as a movie theater's decision to buy a popcorn machine or as complicated as Boeing's decision to invest more than $6 billion to design and build the 787 *Dreamliner* passenger jet. Capital investments may also involve the purchase of an entire business, such as Microsoft's June 2016 purchase of the professional networking software company LinkedIn for $26 billion.

Regardless of the project, a good investment is one in which the benefits are worth more to the firm than the cost of the asset. For example, in January 2015 AT&T bid more than $18 billion in a Federal Communications Commission auction for Advanced Wireless Services (the right to use radio frequencies over which voice and data signals are sent). Presumably, AT&T expects that the investment will produce a stream of cash flows worth more than $18 billion. Suppose AT&T estimates that in terms of the current market value, the future cash flows from the wireless spectrum purchase are worth $21 billion. Is the purchase a good deal for AT&T? The answer is yes because the value of the expected cash flow benefits from the purchase exceeds

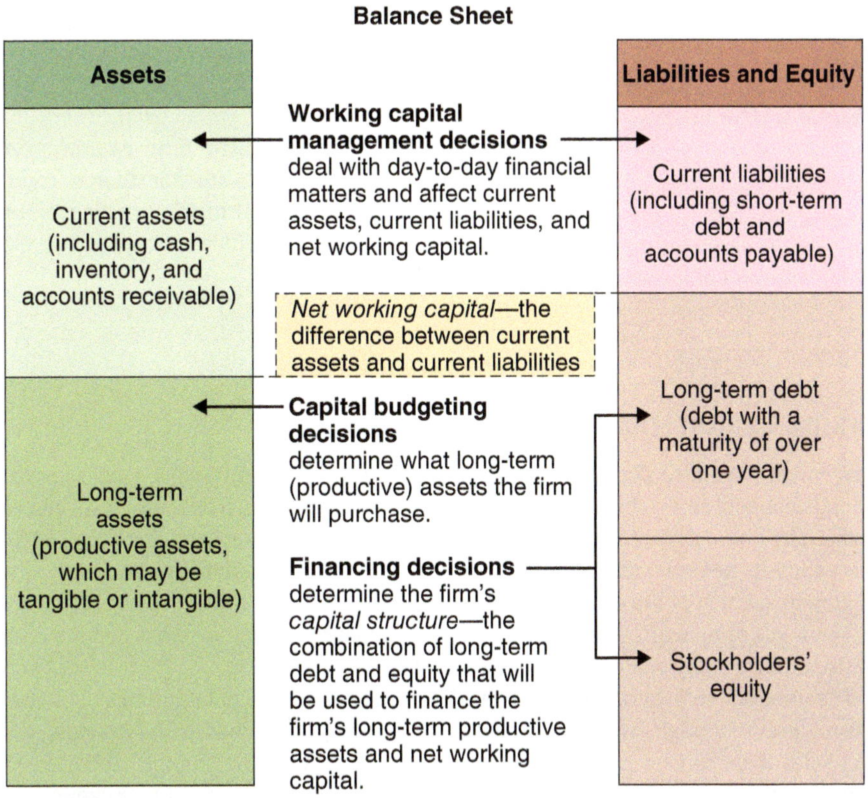

EXHIBIT 1.2 **How the Financial Manager's Decisions Affect the Balance Sheet**

Financial managers are concerned with three fundamental types of decisions: capital budgeting decisions, financing decisions, and working capital management decisions. Each type of decision has a direct and important effect on the firm's balance sheet and, ultimately, the success or failure of the firm.

the cost by \$3 billion (\$21 billion − \$18 billion = \$3 billion). If the purchase of the wireless spectrum works out as planned, the value of AT&T will be increased by \$3 billion!

Not all investment decisions are successful. Just open the business section of any newspaper on any day, and you will find stories of bad decisions. For example, Universal Pictures' 2014 action movie *47 Ronin* reportedly cost over \$225 million in production and advertising expenses, but made only \$152 million in worldwide box office receipts. Even with U.S. DVD sales of approximately \$16.5 million, the overall cash flows from sales of the movie did not come close to covering its up-front costs.

> **Building Intuition**
>
> **Sound Investments Are Those Where the Value of the Benefits Exceeds Their Cost**
>
> Financial managers should invest in a capital project only if the value of its future cash flows exceeds the cost of the project (benefits > cost). Such investments increase the value of the firm and thus increase stockholders' (owners') wealth. This rule holds whether you're making the decision to purchase new machinery, build a new plant, or buy an entire business.

Financing Decisions

Financing decisions determine how firms raise cash to pay for their investments, as shown in Exhibit 1.2. Productive assets, which are long term in nature, are financed by long-term borrowing, equity investment, or both. Financing decisions involve trade-offs between the advantages and disadvantages of these financing alternatives for the firm.

A major advantage of debt financing is that debt payments are tax deductible for many corporations. However, debt financing increases a firm's risk because it creates a contractual obligation to make periodic interest payments and, at maturity, to repay the amount that is borrowed. Contractual obligations must be paid regardless of the firm's operating cash flow, even if the firm suffers a financial loss. If the firm fails to make payments as promised, it defaults on its debt obligation and could be forced into bankruptcy.

In contrast, equity has no maturity, and there are no guaranteed payments to equity investors. In a corporation, the board of directors has the right to decide whether dividends should be paid to stockholders. This means that if a dividend payment is reduced or omitted

Building Intuition

Financing Decisions Affect the Value of the Firm

How a firm is financed with debt and equity affects the value of the firm. The reason is that the mix between debt and equity affects the taxes the firm pays and the probability that the firm will go bankrupt. The financial manager's goal is to determine the combination of debt and equity that minimizes the cost of financing the firm.

altogether, the firm will not be in default. Unlike interest payments, however, dividend payments to stockholders are not tax deductible.

The mix of debt and equity on the balance sheet is known as a firm's **capital structure**. The term *capital structure* is used because long-term funds are considered capital, and these funds are raised in **capital markets**—financial markets where equity and debt instruments with maturities greater than one year are traded.

capital structure the mix of debt and equity that is used to finance a firm

capital markets financial markets where equity and debt instruments with maturities greater than one year are traded

net working capital the dollar difference between total current assets and total current liabilities

Working Capital Management Decisions

Management must also decide how to manage the firm's current assets, such as cash, inventory, and accounts receivable, as well as its current liabilities, such as trade credit and accounts payable. The dollar difference between a firm's total current assets and its total current liabilities is called its **net working capital**, as shown in Exhibit 1.2. As mentioned earlier, working capital management is the day-to-day management of the firm's short-term assets and liabilities. The goals of managing working capital are to ensure that the firm has enough cash to pay its bills and invest any spare cash to earn interest.

The mismanagement of working capital can cause a firm to default on its debt and go into bankruptcy, even though, over the long term, the firm may be profitable. For example, a firm that makes sales to customers on credit but is not diligent about collecting the accounts receivable can quickly find itself without enough cash to pay its bills. If this condition becomes chronic, creditors can force the firm into bankruptcy if the firm is not able to obtain alternative financing.

A firm's profitability can also be affected by its inventory level. If the firm has more inventory than it needs to meet customer demands, it has too much capital tied up in assets that are not earning cash. Conversely, if the firm holds too little inventory, it can lose sales because it does not have products to sell when customers want them. Management must therefore determine the optimal inventory level.

Before You Go On

1. What are the three basic types of financial decisions managers must make?
2. Explain why you would make an investment if the value of the expected cash flows exceeds the cost of the project.
3. Why are capital budgeting decisions among the most important decisions in the life of a firm?

1.2 Forms of Business Organization

LEARNING OBJECTIVE

2. Identify common forms of business organization in the United States and their respective strengths and weaknesses.

Firms are organized in a number of different ways in the United States. In this section we discuss some of the more common forms of organization and the factors that business owners consider when they choose which to use. **Exhibit 1.3** summarizes key characteristics of common forms of business organization.

EXHIBIT 1.3 **Characteristics of Different Forms of Business Organization**

Choosing the appropriate form of business organization is an important step in starting a business. This exhibit compares key characteristics of the most popular forms of business organization in the United States.

	Sole Proprietorship	Partnership		Corporation		Limited Liability Partnership (LLP) or Company (LLC)
		General	Limited	S-Corp.	C-Corp.	
Cost to establish	Inexpensive	More costly	More costly	More costly	More costly	More costly
Life of entity	Limited	Flexible	Flexible	Indefinite	Indefinite	Flexible
Control by founder over business decisions	Complete	Shared	Shared	Depends on ownership	Depends on ownership	Shared
Access to capital	Very limited	Limited	Less limited	Less limited	Excellent	Less limited
Cost to transfer ownership	High	High	High	High	Can be low	High
Separation of management and investment	No	No	Yes	Yes	Yes	Yes
Potential owner/manager conflicts	No	No	Some	Potentially high	Potentially high	Some
Ability to provide incentives to attract and retain high-quality employees	Limited	Good	Good	Good	Good	Good
Liability of owners	Unlimited	Unlimited	Unlimited for general partner	Limited	Limited	Limited
Tax treatment of income	Flow-through	Flow-through	Flow-through	Flow-through	Double tax	As elected
Tax deductibility of owner benefits	Limited	Limited	Limited	Limited	Less limited	Limited

Sole Proprietorships

A **sole proprietorship** is a business that is owned by a single person. Its life is limited to the period that the owner (proprietor) is associated with the business because there is no ownership interest that can be transferred to someone else—there is no stock or other such interest that can be sold. A sole proprietorship ceases to exist when the proprietor stops being involved with the business. Many small businesses in the United States are organized this way.

sole proprietorship a business owned by a single person

A sole proprietorship is the simplest and least expensive form of business to set up and is the least regulated. To start a sole proprietorship, all you have to do is obtain the business licenses required by your local and state governments.

The ownership structure of a sole proprietorship has both advantages and disadvantages. Among the advantages is the fact that the proprietor does not have to share decision-making authority with anyone and can run the business as he or she chooses.

There are several disadvantages related to the fact that there is no stock or other ownership interest to sell. First, the amount of equity capital that can be raised to finance the business is limited to the owner's personal wealth. This can restrict growth for the business unless the proprietor is very wealthy. Second, it can be more costly to transfer ownership. The proprietor must sell the assets of the business directly, rather than indirectly through the sale of an ownership interest in an operating business. The business must essentially be re-established every time it is sold. Third, because the proprietor provides all of the equity capital and manages the business, there is no separation of the management and investment roles. This limits the ability of good managers to form a business if they do not also have capital to invest. Fourth, it is not possible to provide employees with compensation in the form of ownership interests, such as stock or stock options, which can help motivate them to work harder.

Another disadvantage of a sole proprietorship is that proprietor faces *unlimited liability*. If someone is harmed by the business, the proprietor's liability extends beyond the money invested in the business. The proprietor can lose some or all of his or her personal wealth, too.

Finally, profits from a sole proprietorship *flow through* to the sole proprietor's personal tax return, meaning that the business does not pay taxes before profits are distributed to the owner. Because the business is not subject to income taxes, profits are not subject to double taxation as is a C-corporation (described later). There are limitations on tax deductions for personal expenses, such as those associated with health insurance, but the costs of these limitations are often outweighed by the benefits from the flow-through of profits in a sole proprietorship.

Partnerships

partnership two or more owners who have joined together legally to manage a business and share its profits

A **partnership** consists of two or more owners who have joined together legally to manage a business. To form a partnership, the owners (partners) enter into an agreement that details how much capital each partner will invest in the partnership, what their management roles will be, how key management decisions will be made, how the profits will be divided, and how ownership will be transferred in case of specified events, such as the retirement or death of a partner. A *general partnership* is a partnership in which all of the partners are owners of (investors in) the business and active in managing it. In contrast, a *limited partnership* has both *general partners*, who are owners and managers, and *limited partners*, who are owners but not managers.

Partnerships are more costly to form than sole proprietorships because the partners must hire an attorney to draw up and maintain the *partnership agreement*, which specifies the nature of the relationships between or among the partners. On the other hand, partnership agreements can be amended to allow for the business to continue when a partner leaves. The ability to make the life of a business independent of that of the partners increases the liquidity of the ownership interests, making it easier to raise capital and less costly for the partners to sell their interests at an attractive price.

Many of the other advantages and disadvantages of a general partnership are similar to those of a sole proprietorship. A key disadvantage of a *general partnership* is that, like the proprietor in a sole proprietorship, all partners have unlimited liability. This liability can be even worse than in a sole proprietorship because a general partner can be held liable for all of the partnership's debts and other obligations, regardless of what proportion of the business he or she owns or how the debt or other obligations were incurred.

The problem of unlimited liability is avoided for some partners in a *limited partnership* because limited partners can generally only lose the amount of money that they have invested in the business. In a limited partnership one or more general partners have unlimited liability and actively manage the business, while each limited partner is liable for business obligations only up to the amount of capital he or she invested in the partnership. In other words, the limited partners have **limited liability**. To qualify for limited partner status, a partner cannot be actively engaged in managing the business.

limited liability the legal liability of an investor is limited to the amount of capital invested in the business

Corporations

corporation a legal entity formed and authorized under a state charter; in a legal sense, a corporation is a "person" distinct from its owners

Most large businesses are organized as corporations. A **corporation** is a legal entity authorized under a state charter. In a legal sense, it is a "person" distinct from its owners. For example, corporations can sue and be sued, enter into contracts, borrow money, and own assets. They can also be general or limited partners in partnerships, and they can own stock in certain types of other corporations. Because a corporation is an entity that is distinct from its owners, it can have an indefinite life. Corporations hold the majority of all business assets and generate the majority of business revenues and profits in the United States. The owners of a corporation are its stockholders.

Starting a corporation is more costly than starting a sole proprietorship. For example, it requires writing articles of incorporation and by-laws that conform to the laws of the state of incorporation. These documents spell out the name of the corporation, its business purpose, its intended life span (unless explicitly stated otherwise, the life is indefinite), the amount of stock to be issued, and the number of directors and their responsibilities. Over the life of a successful business, these costs are not very important. However, to a cash-strapped entrepreneur, they can seem substantial.

On the other hand, the corporate form of organization has several advantages. For example, shares in a corporation can be sold to raise capital from investors who are not involved in the business. This can greatly increase the amount of capital that can be raised to fund the business.

Another major advantage of a corporation is that stockholders have limited liability for debts and other obligations. Owners of corporations have limited liability because corporations are *legal persons* that take actions in their own names, not in the names of individual owners.

An *S-corporation* is a form of corporation that can be used by private businesses that meet certain requirements. An S-corporation can have only one class of stock and cannot have more than one hundred stockholders or any stockholders that are corporations or nonresident alien investors. In contrast, a *C-corporation*, which is the form used by public corporations, does not face such limits.

While there are more restrictions on S-corporations, there are also advantages. Specifically, all profits earned by an S-corporation pass directly to the stockholders, just as they pass to a sole proprietor or the partners in a partnership. This means that no taxes are paid at the corporate level.

Weblink

Visit the Web sites of the NYSE and NASDAQ at http://www.nyse.com and http://www.nasdaq.com to get more information about market activity.

In contrast, a major disadvantage of a C-corporation is that it must pay taxes on the income it earns. If the corporation pays a cash dividend, the stockholders must also pay taxes on the dividends they receive. Thus, the owners of C-corporations are subject to double taxation—first at the corporate level and then at the personal level when they receive dividends.

Corporations can be classified as public or private. Most large companies prefer to operate as public corporations because large amounts of capital can be raised in public markets at a relatively low cost. **Public markets**, such as the New York Stock Exchange (NYSE) and NASDAQ, are regulated by the Securities and Exchange Commission (SEC).[3]

public markets markets regulated by the Securities and Exchange Commission in which securities such as stocks and bonds are publicly traded

In contrast, **privately held,** or **closely held, corporations** are owned by a small number of investors, and their shares are not traded publicly. When a corporation is first formed, the common stock is often held by a few investors, typically the founder, a small number of key managers, and financial backers. Over time, as the company grows in size and needs larger amounts of capital, management may decide that the company should "go public" in order to gain access to the public markets. Not all privately held corporations go public, however.

privately held, or **closely held, corporations** corporations whose stock is not traded in the public markets

Limited Liability Partnerships and Companies

Historically, law firms, accounting firms, investment banks, and other professional groups were organized as sole proprietorships or partnerships. For partners in these firms, all income was taxed as personal income, and general partners had unlimited liability for all debts and other obligations of the firm. It was widely believed that in professional partnerships, such as those of attorneys, accountants, or physicians, the partners should be liable individually and collectively for the professional conduct of each partner. This structure gave the partners an incentive to monitor each other's professional conduct and discipline poorly performing partners, resulting in a higher quality of service and greater professional integrity. Financially, however, misconduct by one partner could result in disaster for the entire firm. For example, a physician found guilty of malpractice exposes every partner in the medical practice to financial liability, even if the others never treated the patient in question.

In the 1980s, because of sharp increases in the number of professional malpractice cases and large damages awards in the courts, professional groups began lobbying state legislators to create hybrid forms of business organization. One such hybrid is known as a **limited liability partnership (LLP)**. An LLP combines some of the limited liability characteristics of a corporation with the tax advantage of a partnership. While liability varies from state to state, LLP partners in general have more limited liability than general partners in regular partnerships.

limited liability partnership (LLP) and limited liability company (LLC) hybrid business organizations that combine some of the advantages of corporations and partnerships; in general, income to the partners is taxed only as personal income, but the partners have limited liability

[3]We examine the public and private markets in more detail in Chapters 2 and 15.

Typically, they are not personally liable for any other partner's malpractice or professional misconduct. Like regular partnerships, income to the partners of an LLP is taxed as personal income.

A **limited liability company (LLC)** is another hybrid form of organization that is becoming increasingly common. Like LLPs, LLCs have benefited founders of many businesses that would otherwise have been organized as limited partnerships. They also provide limited liability to the people who make the business decisions in the firm while enabling all investors to retain the flow-through tax advantages of a limited partnership.

You will notice that Exhibit 1.3 indicates that the lives of partnerships, LLPs, and LLCs are flexible. This is because, while partnership, LLP, and LLC agreements can be written so that their lives are indefinite, they can also be written with a fixed life in mind. For example, private equity and venture capital limited partnerships and LLCs are typically structured so that they last only 10 years.

Before You Go On

1. Why are many businesses operated as sole proprietorships or partnerships?
2. What are some advantages and disadvantages of operating as a public corporation?
3. Explain why professional partnerships such as physicians' groups organize as limited liability partnerships.

1.3 Managing the Financial Function

LEARNING OBJECTIVE

3. Describe the typical organization of the financial function in a large corporation.

chief financial officer or CFO the most senior financial manager in a company

As we discussed earlier, financial managers are concerned with a firm's investment, financing, and working capital management decisions. The senior financial manager holds one of the top executive positions in the firm. In a large corporation, the senior financial manager usually has the rank of vice president or senior vice president and goes by the title of **chief financial officer** or **CFO**. In smaller firms, the job tends to focus more on the accounting function, and the top financial officer may be called the controller or chief accountant. In this section we focus on the financial function in a large corporation.

Organizational Structure

Exhibit 1.4 shows a typical organizational structure for a large corporation, with special attention to the financial function. As shown, the top management position in the firm is the chief executive officer (CEO), who has the final decision-making authority among all the firm's executives. The CEO's most important responsibilities are to set the strategic direction of the firm and see that the management team executes the strategic plan. The CEO reports directly to the board of directors, which is accountable to the company's stockholders. The board's responsibility is to see that the top management makes decisions that are in the best interest of the stockholders.

The CFO reports directly to the CEO and focuses on managing all aspects of the firm's finances, as well as working closely with the CEO on strategic issues. A number of positions report directly to the CFO. In addition, the CFO often interacts with people in other functional areas on a regular basis because all senior executives are involved in financial decisions that affect the firm and their areas of responsibility.

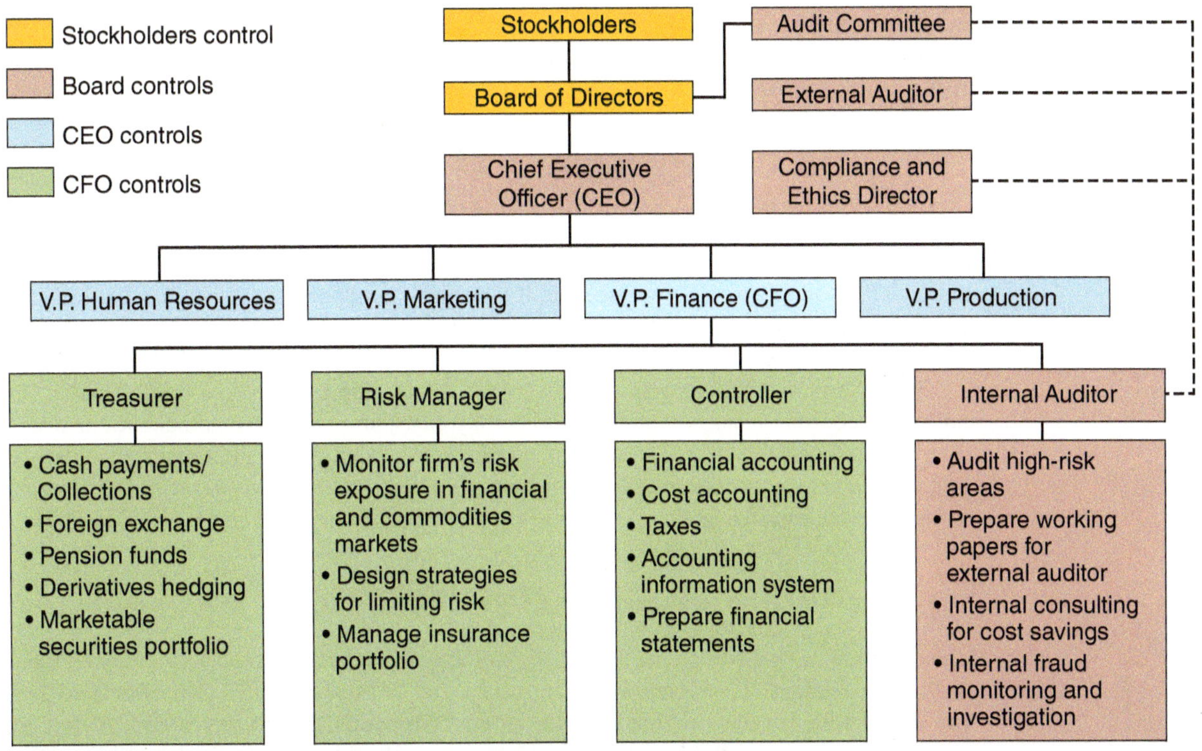

EXHIBIT 1.4 **Simplified Corporate Organization Chart**

The firm's top finance and accounting executive is the CFO, who reports directly to the CEO. Positions that report directly to the CFO include the treasurer, risk manager, and controller. The internal auditor reports both to the CFO and to the audit committee of the board of directors. The external auditor and the compliance and ethics director also are ultimately responsible to the audit committee.

Positions Reporting to the CFO

Exhibit 1.4 also shows the positions that typically report to the CFO in a large corporation and the activities managed in each area.

- The *treasurer* looks after the collection and disbursement of cash, investing excess cash so that it earns interest, raising new capital, handling foreign exchange transactions, and overseeing the firm's pension fund managers. The treasurer also assists the CFO in handling important Wall Street relationships, such as those with investment bankers and credit rating agencies.
- The *risk mana*ger monitors and manages the firm's risk exposure in financial and commodity markets and the firm's relationships with insurance providers.
- The *controller* is really the firm's chief accounting officer. The controller's staff prepares the financial statements, maintains the firm's financial and cost accounting systems, prepares the taxes, and works closely with the firm's external auditors.
- The *internal auditor* is responsible for identifying and assessing major risks facing the firm and performing audits in areas where the firm might incur substantial losses. The internal auditor reports to the board of directors as well as the CFO.

External Auditor

Virtually every large corporation hires a licensed certified public accounting (CPA) firm to provide an independent annual audit of the firm's financial statements. Through this audit the CPA comes to a conclusion as to whether the firm's financial statements present fairly, in all material respects, the financial position of the firm and results of its activities, or in other words, whether the financial numbers are reasonably accurate, accounting principles have been consistently applied year to year and do not significantly distort the firm's performance,

Weblink

Go to the Web site of CFO magazine at http://www.cfo.com to get a better idea of the responsibilities of a CFO.

and the accounting principles used conform to those generally accepted by the accounting profession. Creditors and investors require independent audits, and the SEC requires publicly traded firms to supply audited financial statements.

The Audit Committee

The audit committee, a powerful subcommittee of the board of directors, has the responsibility of overseeing the accounting function and the preparation of the firm's financial statements. In addition, the audit committee oversees or, if necessary, conducts investigations of significant fraud, theft, or malfeasance in the firm, especially if it is suspected that senior managers in the firm may be involved.

The external auditor reports directly to the audit committee to help ensure his or her independence from management. On a day-to-day basis, however, the external auditor works closely with the CFO's staff. The internal auditor also reports to the audit committee to help ensure his or her independence from management. On a day-to-day basis, however, the internal auditor, like the external auditor, works closely with the CFO staff.

The Compliance and Ethics Director

Many publicly traded companies have a compliance and ethics director who oversees three mandated programs: (1) a compliance program that ensures that the firm complies with federal and state laws and regulations, (2) an ethics program that promotes ethical conduct among executives and other employees, and (3) a compliance hotline, which must include a whistleblower program. Like the internal auditor, the compliance director reports to the audit committee to ensure independence from management, though on a day-to-day basis the director typically reports to the firm's legal counsel.

Before You Go On

1. What are the major responsibilities of the CFO?
2. Identify three financial officers who typically report to the CFO and describe their duties.
3. Why does the internal auditor report to both the CFO and the board of directors?

1.4 The Goal of the Firm

LEARNING OBJECTIVE

4. Explain why maximizing the value of the firm's stock is the appropriate goal for management.

For business owners, it is important to determine the appropriate goal for management decisions. Should the goal be to try to keep costs as low as possible? Or to maximize sales or market share? Or to achieve steady growth and earnings? Let's look at this fundamental question more closely.

What Should Management Maximize?

Suppose you own and manage a pizza parlor. Depending on your preferences and tolerance for risk, you can set any goal for the business that you want. For example, you might have a fear of bankruptcy and losing money. To avoid the risk of bankruptcy, you could focus on keeping your costs as low as possible, paying low wages, avoiding borrowing, advertising minimally, and remaining reluctant to expand the business. In short, you will avoid any action that increases your firm's risk. You will sleep well at night, but you may eat poorly because of meager profits.

Conversely, you could focus on maximizing market share and becoming the largest pizza business in town. Your strategy might include cutting prices to increase sales, borrowing heavily to open new pizza parlors, spending lavishly on advertising, and developing exotic menu items such as *pizza de foie gras.* In the short run, your high-risk, high-growth strategy will have you both eating poorly and sleeping poorly as you push the firm to the edge. In the long run, you will either become very rich or go bankrupt! There must be a better operational goal than either of these extremes.

Why Not Maximize Profits?

One goal for decision making that seems reasonable is *profit maximization.* After all, don't stockholders and business owners want their companies to be profitable? Although profit maximization seems a logical goal for a business, it has some serious drawbacks.

A problem with profit maximization is that it is hard to pin down what is meant by "profit." To the average businessperson, profits are just revenues minus expenses. To an accountant, however, a decision that increases profits under one set of accounting rules can reduce it under another. A second problem is that accounting profits are not necessarily the same as cash flows. For example, many firms recognize revenues at the time a sale is made, which is typically before the cash payment for the sale is received. Ultimately, the owners of a business want cash because only cash can be used to make investments or to buy goods and services.

Yet another problem with profit maximization as a goal is that it does not distinguish between getting a dollar today and getting a dollar some time in the future. In finance, the timing of cash flows is extremely important. For example, the longer you go without paying your credit card balance, the more interest you must pay the bank for the use of the money. The interest accrues because of the *time value of money*; the longer you have access to money, the more you have to pay for it. The time value of money is one of the most important concepts in finance and is the focus of Chapters 5 and 6.

Finally, profit maximization ignores the uncertainty, or risk, associated with cash flows. A basic principle of finance is that there is a trade-off between expected return and risk. When given a choice between two investments that have the same expected returns but different risk, most people choose the less risky one. This makes sense because most people do not like bearing risk and, as a result, must be compensated for taking it. The profit maximization goal ignores differences in value caused by differences in risk. We return to the important topics of risk, its measurement, and the trade-off between risk and return in Chapter 7. What is important at this time is that you understand that investors do not like risk and must be compensated for bearing it.

In sum, it appears that profit maximization is not an appropriate goal for a firm because the concept is difficult to define and does not directly account for the firm's cash flows. What we need is a goal that looks at a firm's cash flows and considers both their timing and their riskiness. Fortunately, we have just such a measure: the market value of the firm's stock.

Building Intuition

The Timing of Cash Flows Affects Their Value

A dollar today is worth more than a dollar in the future because if you have a dollar today, you can invest it and earn interest. For businesses, cash flows can involve large sums of money, and receiving money one day late can cost a great deal. For example, if a bank has $100 billion of consumer loans outstanding and the average annual interest payment is 5 percent, it would cost the bank $13.7 million if every consumer decided to make an interest payment one day later.

Building Intuition

The Riskiness of Cash Flows Affects Their Value

A risky dollar is worth less than a safe dollar. The reason is that investors do not like risk and must be compensated for bearing it. For example, if two investments have the same return—say, 5 percent—most people will prefer the investment with the lower risk. Thus, the more risky an investment's cash flows, the less it is worth.

Maximize the Value of the Firm's Stock

The underlying value of any asset is determined by the cash flows it is expected to generate in the future. This principle holds whether we are buying a bank certificate of deposit, a corporate bond, or an office building. Furthermore, as we will discuss in Chapter 9, when security analysts and investors on Wall Street determine the value of a firm's stock, they consider (1) the size of the expected cash flows, (2) the timing of the cash flows, and (3) the riskiness of the cash flows. Notice that the mechanism for determining stock values overcomes all the cash flow objections we raised with regard to profit maximization as a goal.

Thus, an appropriate goal for management is to maximize the current value of the firm's stock. Maximizing the value of the firm's stock is an unambiguous objective that is easy to measure for a firm whose stock is traded in a public market. We simply look at the market value of the stock in the newspaper or online on a given day to determine the value of the stockholders' shares and whether it went up or down. Publicly traded securities are ideally suited for this task because public markets are wholesale markets with large numbers of buyers and sellers where securities trade near their true value.

What about firms whose stock is not publicly traded, such as private corporations and partnerships? The total value of the stockholder or partner interests in such a business is equal to the value of the owner's equity. *Thus, our goal can be restated for these firms as this: Maximize the current value of owner's equity.* The only other restriction is that the entities must be for-profit businesses.

It is important to recognize that maximizing the value of stock, or owner's equity, is not necessarily inconsistent with maximizing the value of claims to the firm's other stakeholders. For example, suppose the managers of a firm decide to delay paying suppliers in an effort to increase the cash flows to the firm's owners. An action such as this is likely to be met by resistance from suppliers who might increase the prices they charge the firm in order to offset the cost of this policy to them. In the extreme, the suppliers might stop selling their products to the firm, and then both the firm's owners and the suppliers can end up worse off. For example, IBM's annual report to shareholders highlights that company's business model is built to support two principal goals: (1) helping the firm's enterprise clients to become more innovative, efficient, and competitive, and (2) providing long-term value to shareholders. Consequently, in maximizing the value of the owner's equity, managers make decisions that account for the interests all stakeholders. Quite often, what is best for the firm's owners also benefits other stakeholders.

Building Intuition

The Financial Manager's Goal Is to Maximize the Value of the Firm's Stock

The goal for financial managers is to make decisions that maximize the firm's stock price. By maximizing stock price, management will help maximize stockholders' wealth. To do this, managers must make investment and financing decisions so that the total value of cash inflows exceeds the total value of cash outflows by the greatest possible amount (benefits > costs). Notice that the focus is on maximizing the value of cash flows, not profits.

Can Management Decisions Affect Stock Prices?

An important question is whether management decisions actually affect the firm's stock price. Fortunately, the answer is yes. As noted earlier, a basic principle in finance is that the value of an asset is determined by the future cash flows it is expected to generate. As shown in **Exhibit 1.5**, a firm's management makes numerous decisions that affect its cash flows. For example, management decides what type of products or services to produce and what productive assets to purchase. Managers also make decisions concerning the mix of debt and equity financing the firm uses, debt collection policies, and policies for paying suppliers, to mention a few examples. In addition, cash flows are affected by how efficient management is in making products, the quality of the products, management's sales and marketing skills, and the firm's investment in research and development for new products. Some of these decisions affect cash flows over the long term, such as the decision to build a new plant, and other decisions have a short-term impact on cash flows, such as launching an advertising campaign. For example, on January 10, 2017, Merck & Co. reported that the Food and Drug Administration (FDA) had accepted its appplication to combine one of its drugs with chemotherapy as a lung cancer treatment. Merck & Co.'s stock price increased almost 4 percent the day after the announcement, suggesting that this therapy would was expected to have a positive impact on the firm's long run cash flows.

The firm's managers also must deal with a number of external factors over which they have little or no control, such as economic conditions (recession or expansion), war or peace, and new government regulations. External factors are constantly changing, and management must weigh the impact of these changes and adjust its strategy and decisions accordingly.

The important point here is that, over time, management makes a series of decisions when executing the firm's strategy that affects the firm's cash flows and, hence, the price of the firm's stock. Firms that have a better business strategy, are more nimble, make better business

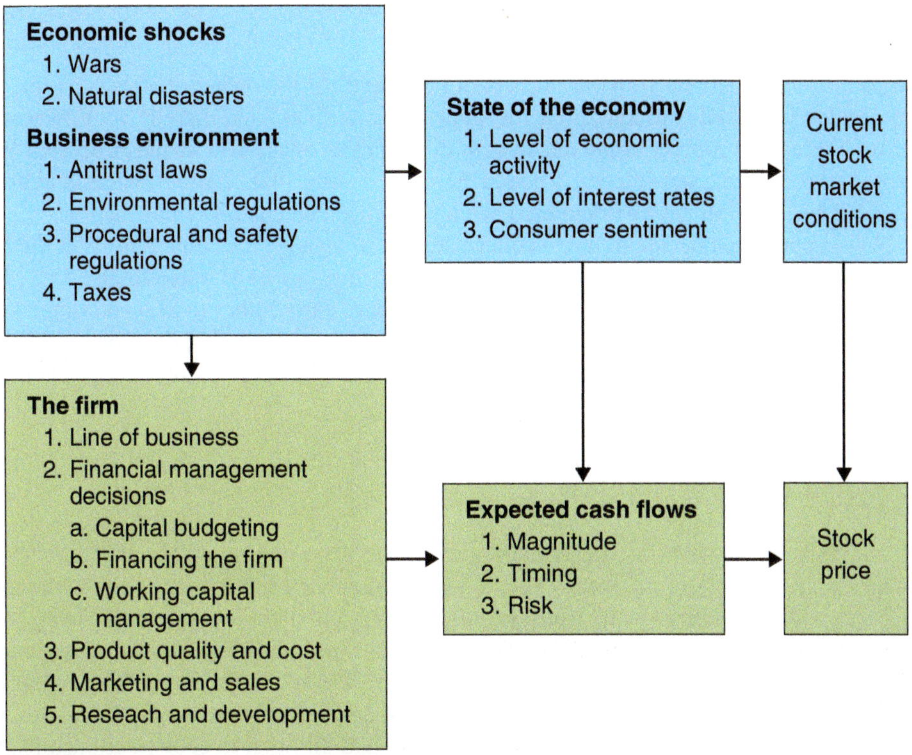

EXHIBIT 1.5 Major Factors Affecting Stock Prices

The firm's stock price is affected by a number of factors, and management can control only some of them. Managers exercise little control over external conditions (blue boxes), such as the state of the general economy, although they can closely observe these conditions and make appropriate changes in strategy. Also managers make many other decisions that directly affect the firm's expected cash flows (green boxes)—and hence the price of the firm's stock.

decisions, and can execute their plans well will have a higher stock price than similar firms that just can't get it right.

Before You Go On

1. Why is profit maximization an unsatisfactory goal for managing a firm?
2. Explain why maximizing the current market price of a firm's stock is an appropriate goal for the firm's management.
3. What is the fundamental determinant of an asset's value?

1.5 Agency Conflicts: Separation of Ownership and Control

LEARNING OBJECTIVE

5. Discuss how agency conflicts affect the goal of maximizing stockholder value.

We turn next to an important issue facing stockholders of large corporations: the separation of ownership and control of the firm. In a large corporation, ownership is often spread over a large number of small stockholders who may have little control over management. Managers may therefore make decisions that benefit their own interests rather than those of the stockholders. In contrast, in smaller firms owners and managers are usually one and the same, and there is no conflict of interest between them. As you will see, this self-interested behavior may affect the value of the firm.

Ownership and Control

To illustrate, let's continue with our pizza parlor example. As the owner of a pizza parlor, you have decided your goal is to maximize the value of the business and thereby your ownership interest. There is no conflict of interest in your dual roles as owner and manager because your personal and economic self-interest is tied to the success of the pizza parlor. The restaurant has succeeded because you have worked hard and have focused on customer satisfaction.

Now suppose you decide to hire a college student to manage the restaurant. Will the new manager always act in your interest? Or could the new manager be tempted to give free pizza to friends now and then or, after an exhausting day, leave early rather than spend time cleaning and preparing for the next day? From this example, you can see that once ownership and management are separated, managers may be tempted to pursue goals that are in their own self-interest rather than the interests of the owners.

Agency Relationships

The relationship we have just described between the pizza parlor owner and the student manager is an example of an agency relationship. An agency relationship arises whenever one party, called the *principal*, hires another party, called the *agent*, to perform some service on behalf of the principal. The relationship between stockholders and management is an agency relationship. Legally, managers (who are the agents) have a fiduciary duty to the stockholders (the principals), which means managers are obligated to put the interests of the stockholders above their own. However, in these and all other agency relationships, the potential exists for a conflict of interest between the principal and the agent. These conflicts are called **agency conflicts**.

agency conflicts conflicts of interest between a principal and an agent

Do Managers Really Want to Maximize Stock Price?

It is not difficult to see how conflicts of interest between managers and stockholders can arise in the corporate setting. In most large corporations, especially those that are publicly traded, there is a significant degree of separation between ownership and management. The largest corporations can have more than one million stockholders. As a practical matter, it is not possible for all of the stockholders to be active in the management of the firm or to individually bear the high cost of monitoring management. The bottom line is that stockholders own the corporation, but managers control the money and have the opportunity to use it for their own benefit.

How might management be tempted to indulge itself and pursue its self-interest? We need not look far for an answer to this question. Corporate excesses are common. High on the list are palatial office buildings, corporate hunting and fishing lodges in exotic places, expensive corporate jets, extravagant expense-account dinners kicked off with bottles of Dom Perignon and washed down with 1953 Margaux—and, of course, a king's compensation package.[4] Besides economic nest feathering, corporate managers may focus on maximizing market share, their industry prestige, and their job security.

Needless to say, these types of activities and spending conflict with the goal of maximizing a firm's stock price. The costs of these activities are called **agency costs**. Agency costs are the costs incurred because of conflicts of interest between a principal and an agent. Examples are the cost of the lavish dinner mentioned earlier and the cost of a corporate jet for executives. However, not all agency costs are frivolous. The cost of hiring an external auditor to certify financial statements is also an agency cost because it is a cost that is incurred to limit actions by managers that result in agency costs.

agency costs the costs arising from conflicts of interest between a principal and an agent—for example, between a firm's owners and its managers

[4]A favorite premeal "quaffing" champagne of young investment bankers on Wall Street is Dom Perignon, known as the "Domer," which, depending on the vintage, can cost as much as $500 a bottle. Senior partners who are more genteel are reported to favor a 1953 Margaux, a French Bordeaux wine from Château Margaux; 1953 is considered a stellar vintage year, and Margaux 1953 is an excellent but very pricey (about $1,800 per bottle in 2017) choice.

Aligning the Interests of Managers and Stockholders

If the linkage between stockholder and manager goals is weak, a number of mechanisms can help to better align the behavior of managers with the goals of stockholders. These include (1) board of directors, (2) management compensation, (3) managerial labor market, (4) other managers, (5) large stockholders, (6) the takeover market, and (7) the legal and regulatory environment.

Board of Directors

A corporation's board of directors has a legal responsibility to represent stockholders' interests. The board's duties include hiring and firing the CEO, setting his or her compensation, and monitoring his or her performance. The board also approves major decisions concerning the firm, such as the firm's annual capital budget or the acquisition of another business. These responsibilities make the board a key mechanism for ensuring that managers' decisions are aligned with the interests of stockholders.

How well boards actually perform in this role has been questioned in recent years. As an example, critics point out that some boards are unwilling to make hard decisions such as firing the CEO when a firm performs poorly. Other people believe that a lack of independence from management is a reason that boards are not as effective as they might be. For example, the CEO often chairs the board of directors. This dual position can give the CEO undue influence over the board, as the chairperson sets the agenda for and chairs board meetings, appoints committees, and controls the flow of information to the board.

Management Compensation

The most effective means of aligning the interests of managers with those of stockholders is a well-designed compensation (pay) package that rewards managers when they do what stockholders want them to do and penalizes them when they do not. This type of plan is effective because a manager will quickly internalize the benefits and costs of making good and bad decisions and, thus, will be more likely to make the decisions that stockholders want. Therefore, there is no need for some outside monitor, such as the board of directors, to try to figure out whether the managers are making the right decisions. The information that outside monitors have is not as good as the managers' information, so these outside monitors are always at a disadvantage in trying to determine whether a manager is acting in the interest of stockholders.

Most corporations have management compensation plans that tie compensation to the performance of the firm. The idea behind these plans is that if compensation is sensitive to the performance of the firm, managers will have greater incentives to make decisions that increase the stockholders' wealth. Although these incentive plans vary widely, they usually include (1) a base salary, (2) a bonus based on accounting performance, and (3) some compensation that is tied to the firm's stock price.[5] The base salary ensures the executive of receiving some minimum compensation as long as he or she remains with the firm, and the bonus and stock price–based compensation are designed to align the manager's incentives with those of the stockholders. The trick in designing such a program is to choose the right mix of these three components so that the manager has the right incentives and the overall package is sufficiently appealing to attract and retain high-quality managers at the lowest possible cost.

Managerial Labor Market

The managerial labor market also provides managers with incentives to act in the interests of stockholders. Firms that have a history of poor performance or a reputation for "shady operations" or unethical behavior have difficulty hiring top managerial talent. Individuals who are top performers have better alternatives than to work for such firms. Therefore, to the extent that managers want to attract high-quality people, the labor market provides incentives to run a good company.

[5]This component, which may include stock options, will increase and decrease with the stock price.

Furthermore, studies show that executives who "manage" firms into bankruptcy or are convicted of white-collar crimes can rarely secure equivalent positions after being fired for poor performance or convicted for criminal behavior. Thus, the penalty for extremely poor performance or a criminal conviction is a significant reduction in the manager's lifetime earnings potential. Managers know this, and the fear of such consequences helps keep them working hard and honestly.[6]

Other Managers

Competition among managers within firms also helps provide incentives for each manager to act in the interests of stockholders. Managers compete to attain the CEO position and in doing so try to attract the board of directors' attention by acting in the stockholders' interests. Furthermore, even when a manager becomes CEO, he or she is always looking over his or her shoulder because other managers covet that job.

Large Stockholders

All stockholders have an interest in providing managers with incentives to maximize stockholder value. However, as we noted earlier, most stockholders in large corporations own too few shares to make it worthwhile for them to actively monitor managers. Only large stockholders, those with a significant investment in the firm, have enough money at stake and enough power to make it worthwhile for them to actively monitor managers and to try to influence their decisions. For firms that are publicly traded, many of the large stockholders are institutional investors, such as mutual funds, large commercial banks, or hedge funds.

The Takeover Market

The market for takeovers provides incentives for managers to act in the interests of stockholders. When a firm performs poorly because its current managers are doing a poor job, an opportunity arises for astute investors, so-called corporate raiders, to make money by buying the company at a price that reflects its poor performance and replacing the current managers with a top-flight management team. If the investors have evaluated the situation correctly, the firm will soon be transformed into a strong performer, its stock price will increase, and investors can sell their stock for a significant profit. The possibility that a firm might be discovered by corporate raiders provides incentives for managers to perform well.

The Legal and Regulatory Environment

Finally, the laws and regulations that firms must adhere to limit the ability of managers to make decisions that harm the interests of stockholders. An example is federal and state statutes that make it illegal for managers to steal corporate assets. Similarly, regulatory reforms such as the Sarbanes-Oxley Act, discussed next, limit the ability of managers to mislead stockholders.

Sarbanes-Oxley and Other Regulatory Reforms

Weblink

To find out more about the Sarbanes-Oxley Act, visit http://www.soxlaw.com.

Managers of public firms in the United States have long been required to make audited financial statements available to investors that show how their firms have been performing, what their assets are, and how those assets have been financed. Prior to 1933, these disclosure requirements were specified by the individual states in which firms were incorporated. Since the passage of the Securities Act of 1933, also known as the *Truth in Securities Act*,

[6]Nonquantifiable costs of convictions for crimes are the perpetrators' personal embarrassment and the embarrassment of their families and the effect it may have on their lives. On average, the overall cost of such convictions is higher than even that suggested by the labor market argument.

these requirements have been standardized throughout the country. They have evolved to the point at which financial reports must adhere to the Generally Accepted Accounting Principles (GAAP), which are discussed in Chapter 3.

With the longstanding disclosure requirements for public firms, many investors during the latter part of the 1900s were comfortable with the quality of corporate financial statements. However, a series of accounting scandals and ethical lapses by corporate officers shocked the nation in the early years of the twenty-first century. A case in point was WorldCom's bankruptcy filing in 2002 and the admission that its officers had "cooked the books" by misstating $7.2 billion of expenses, which allowed WorldCom to report profits when the firm had actually lost money. The accounting fraud at WorldCom followed similar scandals at Enron, Global Crossing, Tyco, and elsewhere. These scandals—and the resulting losses to stockholders—led to a set of far-reaching regulatory reforms passed by Congress in 2002.[7] The most significant reform measure to date is the Sarbanes-Oxley Act, which focuses on (1) reducing agency costs in corporations, (2) restoring ethical conduct within the business sector, and (3) improving the integrity of the accounting reporting system within firms.

Overall, the new regulations require all public corporations to implement five overarching strategies. (Private corporations and partnerships are not required to implement these measures.)

1. **Ensure greater board independence.** Firms must restructure their boards so that the majority of the members are outside directors. Furthermore, it is recommended that the positions of chair and CEO be separated. Finally, Sarbanes-Oxley makes it clear that board members have a fiduciary responsibility to represent and act in the interest of stockholders, and board members who fail to meet their fiduciary duty can be fined and receive jail sentences.
2. **Establish internal accounting controls.** Firms must establish internal accounting control systems to protect the integrity of the accounting systems and safeguard the firms' assets. The internal controls are intended to improve the reliability of accounting data and the quality of financial reports and to reduce the likelihood that individuals within the firm engage in accounting fraud.
3. **Establish compliance programs.** Firms must establish corporate compliance programs that ensure that they comply with important federal and state regulations. For example, a compliance program would document whether a firm's truck drivers complied with all federal and state truck and driver safety regulations, such as the number of hours one can drive during the day and the gross highway weight of the truck.
4. **Establish an ethics program.** Firms must establish ethics programs that monitor the conduct of employees and executives. Among other features, these programs must include a whistleblower protection provision. The intent is to create an ethical work environment so that employees will know what is expected of them in their relationships with customers, suppliers, and other stakeholders.
5. **Expand the audit committee's oversight powers.** The external auditor, the internal auditor, and the compliance and ethics director owe their ultimate legal responsibilities to the audit committee, not to the firm. In addition, the audit committee has the unconditional power to probe and question any person in the firm, including the CEO, regarding any matter that might materially impact the firm or its financial statements.

Exhibit 1.6 summarizes some of the regulatory requirements that are designed to reduce agency costs.

A noticeable shift has occurred in the behavior of board members and management since the Sarbanes-Oxley Act was passed. Boards appear much more serious about monitoring firms' performance and ratifying important decisions by management. Audit committees,

[7]The major laws passed by Congress in this area in 2002 were the Public Accounting Reform and Investor Protection Act and the Sarbanes-Oxley Act.

EXHIBIT 1.6 Corporate Governance Regulations Designed to Reduce Agency Costs

These are regulatory requirements that are designed to reduce agency costs. The most important requirements resulted from the Sarbanes-Oxley Act, passed by Congress in 2002. The act was aimed at reducing agency costs, promoting ethical conduct, and improving the integrity of accounting reporting systems.

Board of Directors

- Board has a fiduciary responsibility to represent the best interest of the firm's owners.
- Majority of the board must be outside independent directors.
- Firm is required to have a code of ethics, which has to be approved by the board.
- Firm must establish an ethics program that has a complaint hotline and a whistleblower protection provision that is approved by the board.
- Separation of chairperson and CEO positions is recommended.
- Board members can be fined or receive jail sentences if they fail to fulfill their fiduciary responsibilities.

Audit Committee

- External auditor, internal auditor, and compliance and ethics director's fiduciary (legal) responsibilities are to the audit committee.
- Audit committee approves the hiring, firing, and fees paid to external auditors.
- CEO and CFO must certify financial statements.
- All audit committee members must be outside independent directors.
- One member must be a financial expert.

External Auditor

- Lead partner must change every five years.
- There are limits on consulting (nonaudit) services that external auditors can provide.

Sources: Sarbanes-Oxley Act, Public Accounting Reform and Investor Protection Act, and NYSE and NASDAQ new listing requirements.

with their new independence and investigative powers, are providing greater oversight over the preparation of financial statements. Stronger internal accounting control systems, compliance programs, and ethics programs are improving the integrity of accounting systems and reducing the likelihood of fraud and other illegal activities. Thus, the Sarbanes-Oxley Act does appear to be having an effect. The major complaint from business has been the cost of compliance.

More recently, the Dodd-Frank Wall Street Reform and Consumer Protection Act of 2010 introduced a number of other requirements for public companies. Two that have received a great deal of attention relate to executive compensation. The first requires that companies allow stockholders a nonbinding advisory vote on executive compensation policies—the so-called "say-on-pay" rule. The aim of say-on-pay is to provide shareholders with a way to send a message to the company if there are concerns about the firm's compensation practices. The second requirement is that all companies adopt "clawback" policies to recover compensation from executives if compensation is paid based on financial statements that later have to be "materially restated." The goal of clawbacks is to discourage executives from misreporting the firm's accounting numbers in order to increase their pay, as any compensation they earn as a result would ultimately be "clawed back" from them.

Before You Go On

1. What are agency conflicts?
2. What are corporate raiders?
3. List the three main objectives of the Sarbanes-Oxley Act.

1.6 The Importance of Ethics in Business

LEARNING OBJECTIVE

6. Explain why ethics is an appropriate topic in the study of corporate finance.

We have just seen that Congress included ethics program requirements in the Sarbanes-Oxley Act. Why are ethics important to business?

Business Ethics

The term *ethics* describes a society's ideas about what actions are right and wrong. Ethical values are not moral absolutes, and they can and do vary across societies. Regardless of cultural differences, however, if we think about it, all of us would probably prefer to live in a world where people behave ethically—where people try to do what is right.

In our society, ethical rules include considering the impact of our actions on others, being willing to sometimes put the interests of others ahead of our own interests, and realizing that we must follow the same rules we expect others to follow. The golden rule—"Do unto others as you would have done unto you"—is an example of a widely accepted ethical norm.[8]

Are Business Ethics Different from Everyday Ethics?

Perhaps business is a dog-eat-dog world where ethics do not matter. People who take this point of view link business ethics to the ethics of the poker game and not to the ethics of everyday morality. Poker players, they suggest, must practice cunning deception and must conceal their strengths and their intentions. After all, they are playing the game to win. How far does one go to win?

In 2002, investors learned the hard way about a number of firms that had been behaving according to the ethics of the poker game: Cunning deception and concealment of information were the order of the day at WorldCom, Enron, Global Crossing, Tyco, and a host of other firms. The market's reaction to the behavior of these firms was to wipe out $2.3 trillion of stockholder value. More recently, in 2016, it was revealed that Wells Fargo employees had opened millions of unauthorized checking and credit card accounts for the bank's customers. Wells Fargo dismissed more than 5,300 low-level employees and was fined $185 million; the value of the firm's equity dropped $28 billion as this scandal developed.

We believe that those who argue that ethics do not matter in business are mistaken. Indeed, most academic studies on the topic suggest that traditions of morality are very relevant to business and to financial markets in particular. The reasons are practical as well as ethical. Corruption in business creates inefficiencies in an economy, inhibits the growth of capital markets, and slows a country's rate of economic growth.

For example, as Russia made the transition to a market economy, it had a difficult time establishing a stock market and attracting foreign investment. The reason was a simple one. Corruption was rampant in local government and in business. Contractual agreements were not enforceable, and there was no reliable financial information about Russian companies. Not until the mid-1990s did some Russian companies begin to display enough financial transparency to attract investment capital.[9]

[8]The golden rule can be stated in a number of ways. One version, in the Gospel of Matthew, states, "In everything do to others as you would have them do to you." A less noble version you occasionally hear in business is "he who has the gold makes the rules."

[9]In economics, *transparency* refers to openness and access to information.

Types of Ethical Conflicts in Business

We turn next to a consideration of the ethical problems that arise in business dealings. Most problems involve three related areas: agency costs, conflicts of interest, and informational asymmetry.

Agency Costs

As we discussed earlier in this chapter, many relationships in business are agency relationships. Agents can be bound both legally and ethically to act in the interest of the principal. Financial managers have agency obligations to act honestly and to see that subordinates act honestly with respect to financial transactions. A product recall or environmental offense may cause a decline in a firm's stock price. However, revelations of dishonesty, deception, and fraud in financial matters can have a larger and longer-lasting impact on the stock price. If the dishonesty is flagrant, the firm may go bankrupt, as we saw with the bankruptcies of Enron and WorldCom.

Conflicts of Interest

Conflicts of interest often arise in agency relationships. A conflict of interest in such a situation can arise when the agent's interests are different from those of the principal. For example, suppose you're interested in buying a house and a local real estate agent is helping you find the home of your dreams. As it turns out, the dream house is one for which your agent is also the listing agent. Your agent has a conflict of interest because her professional obligation to help you find the right house at a fair price conflicts with her professional obligation to get the highest price possible for the client whose house she has listed.

Organizations can be either principals or agents and, hence, can be parties to conflicts of interest. In the past, for example, many large accounting firms provided both consulting services and audits for corporations. This dual function may compromise the independence and objectivity of the audit opinion, even though the work is done by different parts of the firm. For example, if consulting fees from an audit client become a large source of income, the auditing firm may be less likely to render an adverse audit opinion and thereby risk losing the consulting business.

Conflicts of interest are typically resolved in one of two ways. Sometimes complete disclosure is sufficient. Thus, in real estate transactions, it is not unusual for the same lawyer or realtor to represent both the buyer and the seller. This practice is not considered unethical as long as both sides are aware of the fact and give their consent. Alternatively, the conflicted party can withdraw from serving the interests of one of the parties. Sometimes the law mandates this solution. For example, public accounting firms are not permitted to provide certain types of consulting services to their audit clients.

Information Asymmetry

information asymmetry the situation in which one party in a business transaction has information that is unavailable to the other parties in the transaction

Information asymmetry exists when one party in a business transaction has information that is unavailable to the other parties in the transaction. The existence of information asymmetry in business relationships is commonplace. For example, suppose you decide to sell your 10-year-old car. You know much more about the real condition of the car than does the prospective buyer. The ethical issue is this: How much should you tell the prospective buyer? In other words, to what extent is the party with the information advantage obligated to reduce the amount of information asymmetry?

Society imposes both market-based and legal solutions for transactional information asymmetries. Consider the prospective car buyer in the previous example. You can be reasonably sure that the buyer understands that he or she has less information about the car's condition than the seller and, as a result, will pay a lower price for the vehicle. Conversely, sellers who certify or provide a warranty with respect to the condition of the vehicle reduce the concerns that buyers have about information asymmetries and therefore tend to receive higher prices.

Legal solutions often require sellers to disclose material facts to buyers or prohibit trading on information that is not widely available. For example, when you sell a car, you are required to disclose to the seller whether it has been in an accident and whether the odometer has been altered. Similarly, in many states home sellers must disclose if they are aware of any major defects in their home. In the investment world, the trading of stocks based on material inside information (e.g., which is not available to the public) has been made illegal in an effort to create a "level playing field" for all investors.

The Importance of an Ethical Business Culture

Some economists have noted that the legal system and market forces impose substantial costs on individuals and institutions that engage in unethical behavior. As a result, these forces provide important incentives that foster ethical behavior in the business community. The incentives include financial losses, legal fines, jail time, and bankruptcy. Ethicists argue, however, that laws and market forces are not enough. For example, the financial sector is one of the most heavily regulated areas of the U.S. economy. Yet despite heavy regulation, the sector has a long and rich history of financial scandals.

In addition to laws and market forces, many people argue that it is important to create an ethical culture in the firm. Why is this important? An ethical business culture means that people have a set of principles—a moral compass, so to speak—that helps them identify moral issues and make ethical judgments without being told what to do. The culture has a powerful influence on the way people behave and the way they make decisions.

The people at the top of a company determine whether or not the culture of that company is ethical. At Enron, for example, top officers promoted a culture of aggressive risk taking and willingness, at times, to cross over ethical and even legal lines. The motto "do no evil" was adopted by Google's founders before they took the firm public in 2004.

More than likely, you will be confronted with ethical issues during your professional career. Knowing how to identify and deal with ethical issues is an important part of your professional skill set. Exhibit 1.7 presents a framework for making ethical judgments.

Serious Consequences

In recent years the rules have changed, and the cost of ethical mistakes can be extremely high. In the past, the business community and legal authorities often dismissed corporate scandals as a "few rotten apples" in an otherwise sound barrel. This is no longer true today. In 2005, for instance, Bernard J. Ebbers, the 63-year-old CEO of WorldCom, was found guilty of fraud and theft and was sentenced to 25 years in prison. Judge Barbara S. Jones, acknowledging that Ebbers would probably serve the rest of his days in jail, said, "I find a sentence of anything less would not reflect the seriousness of the crime." In the past, sentences for white-collar crimes

EXHIBIT 1.7 A Framework for the Analysis of Ethical Conflicts

Dealing with ethical conflicts is an inescapable part of professional life for most people. An analytical framework can be helpful in understanding and resolving such conflicts.

The first step toward ethical behavior is to recognize that you face a moral issue. In general, if your actions or decisions will cause harm to others, you are facing a moral issue. When you find yourself in this position, you might ask yourself the following questions:

1. What does the law require? When in doubt, consult the legal department.
2. What do your role-related obligations require? What is your station, and what are its duties? If you are a member of a profession, what does the code of conduct of your profession say you should do in these circumstances?
3. Are you an agent employed on behalf of another in these circumstances? If so, what are the interests and desires of the employing party?
4. Are the interests of the stockholders materially affected? Your obligation is to represent the best interests of the firm's owners.
5. Do you have a conflict of interest? Will full diclosure of the conflict be sufficient? If not, you must determine what interest has priority.
6. Are you abusing an information asymmetry? Is your use of the information asymmetry fair? It probably is fair if you would make the same decision if the roles of the parties were reversed or if you would publicly advocate the principle behind your decision.
7. Would you be willing to have your action and all the reasons that motivated it reported in the *Wall Street Journal*?

were minimal; even for serious crimes, there often was no jail time at all. Clearly, business ethics is a topic of high interest and increasing importance in the business community and one that will be discussed throughout this book.

Before You Go On

1. What is a conflict of interest in a business setting?
2. How would you define an ethical business culture?

Summary of Learning Objectives

1 Identify the key financial decisions facing the financial manager of any business.

The financial manager faces three basic decisions: (1) which productive assets the firm should buy (capital budgeting decisions), (2) how the firm should finance the productive assets purchased (financing decisions), and (3) how the firm should manage its day-to-day financial activities (working capital decisions). The financial manager should make these decisions in a way that maximizes the current value of the firm's stock.

2 Identify common forms of business organization in the United States and their respective strengths and weaknesses.

Businesses in the United States are commonly organized as a sole proprietorship, a general or limited partnership, a corporation, or a limited liability partnership or company. Most large firms elect to organize as C-corporations because of the ease of raising money; the major disadvantage is double taxation. Smaller companies tend to organize as sole proprietorships or partnerships. The advantages of these forms of organization include ease of formation and taxation at the personal income tax rate. The major disadvantage is the owners' unlimited personal liability. Limited liability partnerships and companies and S-corporations provide owners of small businesses who make the business decisions with limited personal liability.

3 Describe the typical organization of the financial function in a large corporation.

In a large corporation, the financial manager generally has the rank of vice president and goes by the title of chief financial officer. The CFO reports directly to the firm's CEO. Positions reporting directly to the CFO generally include the treasurer, the risk manager, the controller, and the internal auditor. The audit committee of the board of directors is also important in the financial function. The committee hires the external auditor for the firm, and the internal auditor, external auditor, and compliance and ethics director all report to the audit committee.

4 Explain why maximizing the value of the firm's stock is the appropriate goal for management.

Maximizing the firm's stock value is an appropriate goal because it forces management to focus on decisions that will generate the greatest amount of wealth for stockholders. Since the value of a share of stock (or any asset) is determined by its cash flows, management's decisions must consider the size of the cash flow (larger is better), the timing of the cash flow (sooner is better), and the riskiness of the cash flow (given equal returns, lower risk is better).

5 Discuss how agency conflicts affect the goal of maximizing stockholder value.

In most large corporations, there is a significant degree of separation between management and ownership. As a result, stockholders have little control over corporate managers, and management may thus be tempted to pursue its own self-interest rather than maximizing the value of the owners' stock. The resulting conflicts give rise to agency costs. Ways of reducing agency costs include developing compensation agreements that link employee compensation to the firm's performance and having independent boards of directors monitor management.

6 Explain why ethics is an appropriate topic in the study of corporate finance.

If we lived in a world without ethical norms, we would soon discover that it would be difficult to do business. As a practical matter, the law and market forces provide important incentives that foster ethical behavior in the business community, but they are not enough to ensure ethical behavior. An ethical culture is also needed. In an ethical culture, people have a set of moral principles—a moral compass—that helps them identify ethical issues and make ethical judgments without being told what to do.

Self-Study Problems

1.1 Give an example of a capital budgeting decision and a financing decision.

1.2 What is the appropriate decision criterion for financial managers to use when selecting a capital project?

1.3 What are some of the things that managers do to manage a firm's working capital?

1.4 Which one of the following characteristics does not pertain to corporations?

- **a.** Can enter into contracts.
- **b.** Can borrow money.
- **c.** Are the easiest type of business to form.
- **d.** Can be sued.
- **e.** Can own stock in other companies.

1.5 What are typically the main components of an executive compensation package?

Solutions to Self-Study Problems

1.1 Capital budgeting involves deciding which productive assets the firm invests in, such as buying a new plant or investing in the renovation of an existing facility. Financing decisions determine how a firm will raise capital. Examples of financing decisions include the decision to borrow from a bank or issue debt in the public capital markets.

1.2 Financial managers should select a capital project only if the value of the project's expected future cash flows exceeds the cost of the project. In other words, managers should only make investments that will increase firm value and thus increase the stockholders' wealth.

1.3 Working capital management is the day-to-day management of a firm's short-term assets and liabilities. Working capital can be managed by maintaining the optimal level of inventory, managing receivables and payables, deciding to whom the firm should extend credit, and making appropriate investments with excess cash.

1.4 The answer that does *not* pertain to corporations is: **c.** Are the easiest type of business to form.

1.5 The three main components of a typical executive compensation package are base salary, bonus based on accounting performance, and compensation tied to the firm's stock price.

WileyPLUS

Questions and Problems, Solution Walkthrough Videos, Learning by Doing Tutorials, and additional study tools and resources are available in WileyPLUS.

Discussion Questions

1.1 Describe the cash flows between a firm and its stakeholders.

1.2 What are the three fundamental decisions the financial manager is concerned with, and how do they affect the firm's balance sheet?

1.3 What is the difference between stockholders and stakeholders?

1.4 Suppose that a group of accountants wants to start an accounting business. What organizational form would they most likely choose, and why?

1.5 Why would the owners of a business choose to form a corporation even though they will face double taxation?

1.6 Explain why profit maximization is not the best goal for a company. What is a better goal?

1.7 What are some of the major external and internal factors that affect a firm's stock price? What is the difference between the two general types of factors?

1.8 Identify the sources of agency costs. What are some ways these costs can be controlled in a company?

1.9 What is the Sarbanes-Oxley Act, and what is its focus? Why does it focus in these areas?

1.10 Give an example of a conflict of interest in a business setting, other than the one involving the real estate agent discussed in the chapter text.

Questions and Problems

Excel *Excel templates and resources available in* **WileyPLUS**

Basic

1.1 Capital: What are the two basic sources of funds for all businesses?

1.2 Management role: What is net working capital?

1.3 Cash flows: Explain the difference between profitable and unprofitable firms.

1.4 Management role: What three major decisions are of most concern to financial managers?

1.5 Cash flows: What is the appropriate decision rule for a firm considering undertaking a capital project? Give a real-life example.

1.6 Management role: What is a firm's capital structure, and why is it important?

1.7 Management role: What are some of the working capital decisions that a financial manager faces?

1.8 Organizational form: What are the common forms of business organization discussed in this chapter?

1.9 Organizational form: What are the advantages and disadvantages of a sole proprietorship?

1.10 Organizational form: What is a partnership, and what is the biggest disadvantage of this form of business organization? How can this disadvantage be avoided?

1.11 Organizational form: Who are the owners of a corporation, and how is their ownership represented?

1.12 Organizational form: Explain what is meant by stockholders' limited liability.

1.13 Organizational form: What is double taxation?

1.14 Organizational form: What is the form of business organization taken by most large companies and why?

1.15 Finance function: What is the primary responsibility of the board of directors in a corporation?

1.16 Finance function: All public companies must hire a certified public accounting firm to perform an independent audit of their financial statements. What exactly does the term *audit* mean?

1.17 Firm's goal: What are some of the drawbacks to setting profit maximization as the main goal of a company?

1.18 Firm's goal: What is the appropriate goal of financial managers? How do managers' decisions affect how successful the firm is in achieving this goal?

1.19 Firm's goal: What are the major factors that affect a firm's stock price?

1.20 Agency conflicts: What is an agency relationship, and what is an agency conflict? How can agency conflicts be reduced in a corporation?

1.21 Firm's goal: What can happen if a firm is poorly managed and its stock price falls substantially below its maximum potential price?

1.22 Agency conflicts: What are some of the regulations that pertain to boards of directors that were put in place to reduce agency conflicts?

1.23 Business ethics: How can a lack of business ethics negatively affect the performance of an economy? Give an example.

1.24 Agency conflicts: What are some ways to resolve a conflict of interest?

1.25 Information asymmetry: Describe what an information asymmetry is in a business transaction. Explain how the inequity associated with an information asymmetry might be, at least partially, solved through the market for goods or services.

1.26 Business ethics: What ethical conflict does insider trading present?

Sample Test Problems

1.1 Identify three fundamental types of decisions that financial managers make and identify which part of the balance sheet each of these decisions affects.

1.2 Which of the following is/are advantages of the corporate form of organization?

- **a.** Reduced start-up costs.
- **b.** Greater access to capital markets.
- **c.** Unlimited liability.
- **d.** Single taxation.

1.3 Why is stock value maximization superior to profit maximization as a goal for management?

1.4 What are agency costs? Explain.

1.5 Identify seven mechanisms that can help better align the goals of managers with those of stockholders.

Ethics Case

Incentives And Ethics: Cross-Selling at Wells Fargo

Spencer Platt/Getty Images

In September 2016 news broke of Wells Fargo's $185 million settlement with the Consumer Financial Protection Bureau, the Los Angeles City Attorney, and the Office of the Comptroller of the Currency. The penalties were assessed after investigations revealed that, over the course of five years, Wells Fargo employees had opened more than two million bank or credit card accounts without customers' knowledge or permission. As a result, Wells Fargo fired more than 5,300 employees. In addition, the firm's Board Chairman and Chief Executive Officer (CEO), John Stumpf, was required to give up more than $69 million of compensation and retired shortly after the settlement was announced.

How did such a massive fraud happen for such a long period without being discovered? At its heart, it appeared that the bank was on a strong trajectory of solid growth, which was built on the notion of cross-selling its various financial products. However, as we will see, this turned out to be problematic.

Cross-selling: Eight is Great!

Wells Fargo bank employees were encouraged to "cross-sell" products to customers. That is, if someone had a checking account, they could also be offered overdraft protection, a savings account, a credit card, a home equity loan, wealth management services, or other financial products that would generate additional fees for the bank. The idea behind cross-selling is that it is less costly to sell a new product to an existing customer than to a new customer. Thus, cross-selling to current customers increases fee income for the bank while keeping costs down resulting in higher profits.

In the 2010 Wells Fargo Annual Report, John Stumpf was quoted as saying "I'm often asked why we set a cross-sell goal of eight. The answer is, it rhymed with 'great.' Perhaps our new cheer should be: 'Let's go again, for ten!'" By 2015 the retail banking cross-sell was 6.11 products per household, but the message to employees was clear - "Eight is great," and selling more products to current customers was a key focus in the firm's Community Banking division.

Is Eight *that* Great?

As a business strategy, cross-selling is a perfectly reasonable practice. And while it certainly added to Wells Fargo's growth and the bottom line, signs of potential problems came to light in an LA Times story that ran in late 2013.[1] The article outlined a laser focus on increased sales with employees being assigned daily targets for signing up customers for additional products. Not only was employee compensation tied to the number of new accounts opened, but at least some employees were told that if they did not meet their daily targets, they would have to stay and work evenings and weekends to do so. Some employees even said that they were threatened with being fired if they failed to make their sales goals. The LA Times article suggested that the bank had a "...pressure cooker sales culture..." and reported that branch managers were asked not just to meet, but to exceed daily quotas handed down from the regional head office. When commenting on the regional managers' daily conference calls to review sales progress, one former branch manager said "If you do not make your goal, you are severely chastised and embarrassed in front of 60-plus managers in your area by the Community Banking president."

News of potential problems in the LA area first came to light after about 30 Wells Fargo employees had been fired for opening accounts that had never been used, and for manipulating customer approval surveys. The newspaper also quoted a senior spokesman for the region saying that "We found a breakdown in a small number of our team members."[2] As it turned out, the problems were considerably larger than this quote would suggest. In fact, because of the newspaper reporting, the Los Angeles City Attorney initiated an investigation that ultimately led them to sue Wells Fargo over the opening of unauthorized accounts.[3] Other authorities including the Consumer Financial Protection Bureau and the Office of the Comptroller of the Currency also started to scrutinize the bank's activities.

The subsequent investigations discovered that employees opened additional accounts without customer permission, transferred funds to those accounts without the customer's knowledge or consent, ordered new credit cards without customer approval, issued and activated debit cards without authorization, created fake email addresses to enroll customers in online banking, and in some cases allegedly forged customer signatures in order to open new accounts. Many customers were charged for insufficient funds or overdraft fees because the money was not in their original accounts, and credit card customers were charged annual fees, finance or interest charges, and other fees. But perhaps just as important, their trust in the company they had asked to look after their finances had been betrayed.

The Fallout

While the $185 million fine was small relative to their 2016 revenues of $94 billion and profits of $23 billion, in the weeks following the announcement of the settlement Wells Fargo's stock price declined

[1] http://www.latimes.com/business/la-fi-wells-fargo-sale-pressure-20131222-story.html

[2] http://articles.latimes.com/2013/oct/03/business/la-fi-1004-wells-fargo-firings-20131004

[3] http://www.lacityattorney.org/single-post/2016/09/08/Los-Angeles-City-Attorney-Mike-Feuer-Achieves-Historic-Result-in-Consumer-Action-Against-Wells-Fargo-Bank-to-Make-Restitution-to-Customers-Pay-50-million-in-Penalties-Unprecedented-Coordination-with-Federal-Regulators-to-Benefit-Consumers-Nationwide

from $49.90 (on September 8) to $44.28 by month-end - a drop of about 11%. And since that time, the firm has repeatedly been the focus of negative headlines in the business press. Other investigations have ensued. Board Chairman and CEO John Stumpf was called to testify before the Senate Banking Committee where he was grilled over the bank's practices. Senator Elizabeth Warren told Stumpf "You should resign ... and you should be criminally investigated." In the Committee hearings Stumpf was also asked if the firm's board of directors would try to "claw back" any compensation paid to senior executives who were associated with the fraud. This was, perhaps, in part because Carrie Tolstedt (the head of the Community Banking division where the problems occurred) would leave the firm with an exit package worth an estimated $125 million. Stumpf's response was "I am not part of that process. I want to make sure nothing I say will prejudice their process."[4] Of course, the implication was that he too should be financially penalized.

When it comes to recovering payments from executives in cases of fraud or financial irregularities, the Securities and Exchange Commission (SEC) has the regulatory authority to "claw back" payments for senior executives, but only if there is a "material misstatement" of a firm's financials. The problems at Wells Fargo, however, did not rise to this level. At the same time, Wells Fargo had their own clawback policy that allowed the board to recover compensation from executives if their actions caused "reputational harm" to the company. But only after external pressure mounted to a crescendo did the board act to claw back compensation. Intially the company announced that Tolstedt would not receive a bonus or severance, and would forfeit $19 million worth of unvested stock awards. She also agreed not to exercise around $34 million in stock options. Similarly, John Stumpf would forgo most of his 2016 salary, receive no bonus for 2016, and would give up some $41 million in stock awards. The firm later announced it would claw back an additional $47 million from Tolstedt and another $28 million from Stumpf. Stumpf decided to retire around this time. This was a dramatic fall from grace for someone who had been named as CEO of the year by Morningstar the prior year.

The fallout at Wells Fargo continues, with ongoing investigations by the company and regulators, several senior bank executives including the regional heads of Los Angeles and Arizona being dismissed, and lawsuits being filed by customers, former employees, and shareholders. At the same time, as part of the settlement agreement the company has agreed to overhaul its sales practices, removing product sales goals, untying employee compensation from the number of new accounts opened, and basing pay more on branch-level as opposed to individual performance. Will these changes fix the problems? Only time will tell. What we do know is that Wells Fargo has experienced double-digit declines in new checking accounts and credit card applications every month since the settlement.

Discussion Questions

1. Should employee pay be linked to sales targets?
2. Should the practice of cross-selling be eliminated?
3. What other steps could Wells Fargo have taken ahead of time to avoid the problems that it faced?
4. Should senior executives Carrie Tolstedt and John Stumpf have been financially penalized by the company?
5. How important is it to have regulators like the Securities and Exchange Commission or congress involved in the oversight of situations such as that at Wells Fargo?

Source: https://www.washingtonpost.com/business/capitalbusiness/with-2519b-in-deposits-wells-fargo-remains-the-areas-largest-bank/2014/10/03/daef0fdc-4811-11e4-a046-120a8a855cca_story.html?utm_term=.a521c7505a0a

[4]https://www.nytimes.com/2016/09/21/business/dealbook/wells-fargo-ceo-john-stumpf-senate-testimony.html?_r=0

CHAPTER 2

The Financial System and the Level of Interest Rates

LEARNING OBJECTIVES

1. Describe the role of the financial system in the economy and the two basic ways in which money flows through the system.
2. Discuss direct financing and the important role that investment banks play in this process.
3. Describe the primary, secondary, and money markets, explaining the special importance of secondary and money markets to business organizations.
4. Explain what an efficient market is and why market efficiency is important to financial managers.
5. Explain how financial institutions serve the needs of consumers and small businesses.
6. Compute the nominal and the real rates of interest, differentiating between them.

One of the most important institutional players in the financial system is the Federal Reserve System (called the Fed). In fact, it is sometimes said that the chairperson of the Federal Reserve System Board of Governors is the second most powerful person in the United States—second only to the president. Where does all of this power come from?

It comes from the Fed's role as the nation's central bank—the institution that controls the money supply. The Fed manages a key component of the nation's economy by conducting monetary policy, which affects how much money is available in the economy. One way it does this is by setting a target short-term interest rate at which large money center banks lend to each other (called the federal funds rate) and by buying and selling Treasury and federal agency securities to achieve this rate. Increases in the money supply put downward pressure on short-term interest rates. Over time, this can lead to increases in the level of economic activity, along with higher inflation. Conversely, decreases in the money supply put upward pressure on short-term interest rates. This can lead to a lower level of economic activity and lower inflation.

Small wonder that when the Fed speaks, everyone stops and listens. Ben Bernanke, the chairperson of the Fed Board of Governors from 2006 to 2014, described the effects of Fed announcements on the stock market as follows:

> *Normally, the Federal Open Market Committee, or FOMC, the monetary policymaking arm of the Federal Reserve, announces its interest rate decisions at around 2:15* P.M. *following each of its eight regularly scheduled meetings each year. An air of expectation reigns in financial markets in the few minutes before the announcement. If you happen to have access to a monitor that tracks key market indexes, at 2:15* P.M. *on an announcement day you can watch those indexes quiver as if trying to digest the information in the rate decision and the FOMC's accompanying statement of explanation. Then the black line representing each market index moves quickly up or down, and the markets have priced the FOMC action into the aggregate values of U.S. equities, bonds, and other assets.*[1]

[1]Ben S. Bernanke, "Remarks at the Fall 2003 Banking and Finance Lecture," Widener University, Chester, Pennsylvania, October 2, 2003.

As you can see, the Fed's policy actions are transmitted quickly through the financial system and ultimately affect the economic well-being of nearly all consumers and businesses. This chapter provides a basic explanation of how the financial system works and discusses interest rates and their movements.

Chapter Preview

Chapter 1 identified three kinds of decisions that financial managers make: *capital budgeting decisions*, which concern the purchase of productive assets; *financing decisions*, which concern how assets will be financed or paid for; and *working capital management decisions*, which concern day-to-day financial matters. In making capital budgeting decisions, financial managers should select projects whose cash flows increase the value of the firm's stock. The financial models used to evaluate these projects require an understanding of the concepts covered in this chapter. In making financing decisions, financial managers want to obtain capital at the lowest possible cost, which means that they need to understand how financial markets work and what financing alternatives are available. Finally, working capital management is concerned with whether a firm has enough money to pay its bills and how it invests its spare cash to earn interest. Making decisions in these areas requires knowledge of the financial system and what determines the level of *interest* rates.

This chapter provides an overview of key concepts, many of which we will revisit in later chapters. We begin the chapter by looking at how the financial system facilitates the transfer of money from those who have it to those who need it. Then we describe direct financing, through which businesses finance themselves by issuing debt and equity, and the important role that investment banks play in the process. Next we describe different types of financial markets that are in the financial system and discuss the concept of market efficiency. We then examine indirect financing and the services that financial institutions provide to large and small businesses. Finally, we discuss the factors that determine the general level of interest rates in the economy and explain how interest rates vary over the business cycle.

2.1 The Financial System

LEARNING OBJECTIVE

1. Describe the role of the financial system in the economy and the two basic ways in which money flows through the system.

The financial system consists of financial markets and financial institutions. *Financial market* is a general term that includes a number of different types of markets for the creation and exchange of financial assets, such as stocks and bonds. *Financial institutions* are firms such as commercial banks, credit unions, insurance companies, pension funds, and finance companies that provide financial services to the economy. The distinguishing feature of financial institutions is that they invest their funds in **financial assets**, such as business loans, stocks, and bonds, rather than **real assets**, such as plant and equipment.

financial assets assets that are claims on the cash flows from other assets; business loans, stocks, and bonds are financial assets

real assets nonfinancial assets such as plant and equipment; productive assets are real assets; many financial assets are claims on cash flows from real assets

The critical role of the financial system in the economy is to gather money from households (individuals), businesses, and governments with surplus funds to invest and channel that money to those who need it. Businesses need money to invest in new productive assets to expand their operations and increase the firm's cash flow, which should increase the value of the firm. Consumers, too, need money, which they use to purchase things such as homes, cars, and boats—or to pay college tuition bills. Some of the players in the financial system are well-known names such as the New York Stock Exchange, Bank of America, Goldman Sachs, and State Farm Insurance. Others are lesser-known but important firms, such as the multinational giant AIG.

A well-developed financial system is critical for the operation of a complex industrial economy such as that of the United States. Highly industrialized countries cannot function without a competitive and sound financial system that efficiently gathers money and channels it into the best investment opportunities. Let's look at a simple example to illustrate how the financial system channels money to businesses.

The Financial System at Work

Suppose that, at the beginning of the school year, you receive a $10,000 student loan to help pay your expenses for the year, but you need only $5,000 for the first semester. You wisely decide to invest the remaining $5,000 to earn some interest income. After shopping at several banks near campus, you decide that the best deal is a $5,000 consumer certificate of deposit (CD) that matures in three months and pays 2 percent interest. (CDs are debt instruments issued by a bank that pay interest and are insured by the federal government.)

The bank pools your money with funds from checking and savings accounts and other CDs and uses this money to make business and consumer loans. In this case, the bank makes a loan to the pizza parlor near campus: $30,000 for five years at a 7 percent interest rate. The bank decides to make the loan because of the pizza parlor's sound credit rating and because it expects the pizza parlor to generate enough cash flows to repay the loan with interest. The pizza parlor owner wants the money to invest in additional real (productive) assets to earn greater profits (cash flows) and thereby increase the value of her business. During the same week, the bank makes loans to other businesses and also rejects a number of loan requests because the borrowers have poor credit ratings or the proposed projects have low rates of return.

From this example, we can draw some important inferences about financial systems:

- If the financial system is *competitive,* the interest rate the bank pays on CDs will be at or near the highest rate that you can earn on a CD of similar maturity and risk at another bank. At the same time, the pizza parlor and other businesses will have borrowed at or near the lowest possible interest cost, given their risk class. Competition among banks will drive CD rates up and loan rates down.
- The bank gathers money from you and other consumers in small dollar amounts, aggregates it, and then makes loans in much larger dollar amounts. Saving by consumers in small dollar amounts is the origin of much of the money that funds business loans.
- An important function of the financial system is to direct money to the best investment opportunities in the economy. If the financial system works properly, only business projects with high rates of return and good credit will be financed. Those with low rates of return or poor credit will be rejected. Thus, financial systems contribute to higher production and efficiency in the overall economy.
- Finally, note that the bank has earned a tidy profit from the deal. The bank has borrowed your money at 2 percent by selling you a CD and has lent the money to the pizza parlor at 7 percent. Thus, the bank's gross profit is 5 percent (7 percent − 2 percent = 5 percent), which is the difference between the bank's lending and borrowing rates. Banks earn much of their profits from this *spread* between the lending and borrowing rates.

How Funds Flow through the Financial System

We have seen that the financial system plays a critical role in the economy. The system moves money from *lender-savers* (whose income exceeds their spending) to *borrower-spenders* (whose spending exceeds their income), as shown schematically in **Exhibit 2.1**. The most important group of lender-savers in the economy are households, but some businesses and many state and local governments at times have excess funds to lend to those who need money. As a group, businesses are the borrower-spenders that borrow the most in the economy, followed by the federal government.

The arrows in Exhibit 2.1 show that there are two basic mechanisms by which funds flow through the financial system: (1) Funds can flow *directly* through financial markets (the route at the top of the diagram) and (2) funds can flow *indirectly* through financial institutions (the

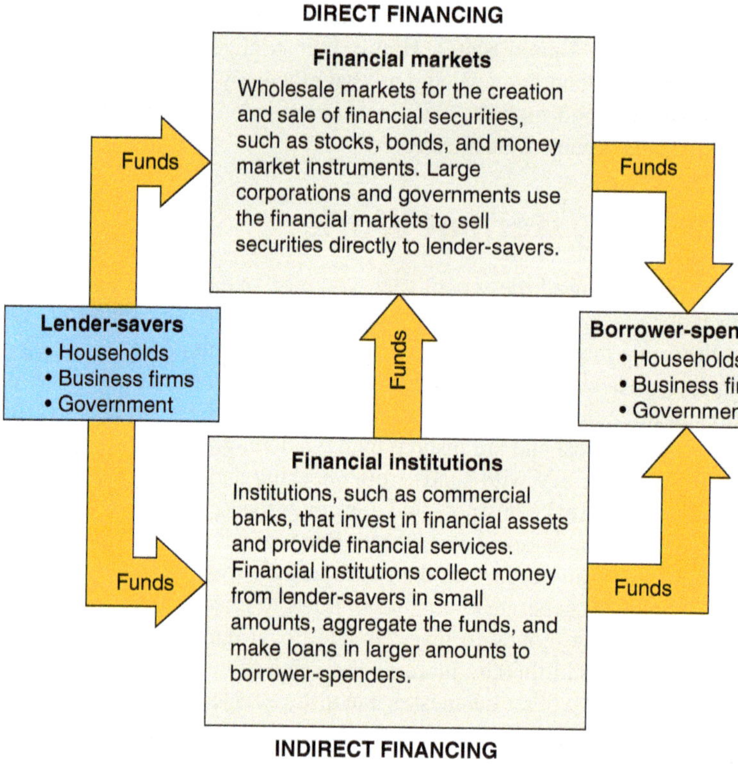

EXHIBIT 2.1 The Flow of Funds through the Financial System

The role of the financial system is to gather money from households, businesses, or governments with surplus funds and channel it to those who need it. Money flows through the financial system in two basic ways: *directly,* through wholesale financial markets, as shown in the top route of the diagram, and *indirectly,* through financial institutions, as shown in the bottom route.

route at the bottom of the diagram). In the following three sections, we look more closely at the direct flow of funds and at the financial markets. After that, we discuss financial institutions and the indirect flow of funds.

Before You Go On

1. What critical economic role does the financial system play in the economy?
2. What are the two basic ways in which funds flow through the financial system from lender-savers to borrower-spenders?

2.2 Direct Financing

LEARNING OBJECTIVE

2. Discuss direct financing and the important role that investment banks play in this process.

In this section we turn our attention to direct financing, in which funds flow directly through the financial system. In direct transactions, the lender-savers and the borrower-spenders deal directly with one another; borrower-spenders sell securities, such as stocks and bonds, to lender-savers in exchange for money. These securities represent claims on the borrowers' future income or assets. A number of different interchangeable terms are used to refer to securities, including *financial securities*, *financial instruments,* and *financial claims.*

The financial markets in which direct transactions take place are wholesale markets with a typical minimum transaction size of $1 million. For most business firms, these markets provide funds at the lowest possible cost. The major buyers and sellers of securities in the direct financial markets are commercial banks; other financial institutions, such as insurance companies and business finance companies; large corporations; federal, state, and local governments; hedge funds; and some wealthy individuals. It is important to note that financial institutions are major buyers of securities in the direct financial markets. For example, life and casualty insurance companies buy large quantities of corporate bonds and stocks for their investment portfolios. In Exhibit 2.1 the arrow leading from financial institutions to financial markets depicts this flow.

Although few individuals participate in direct financial markets, individuals can gain access to many of the financial products produced in these markets through retail channels at investment or commercial banks or independent brokerage firms (the lower route in Exhibit 2.1). For example, individuals can buy or sell stocks and bonds in small dollar amounts at Merrill Lynch, a Bank of America retail brokerage business, or the discount brokerage firm TD Ameritrade. We discuss indirect financing through financial institutions later in this chapter.

A Direct Market Transaction

Let's look at a typical direct market transaction. When managers decide to engage in a direct market transaction, they often have in mind a specific capital project that needs financing, such as building a new manufacturing facility. Suppose that Apple Inc. needs $200 million to build a new facility and decides to fund it by selling long-term bonds with a 15-year maturity (Apple is planning on borrowing the money). While searching for the financing, Apple contacts a group of insurance companies, which expresses an interest in buying Apple's bonds. The insurance companies will buy Apple's bonds only after determining that they are priced fairly for their level of risk. Apple will sell its bonds to the insurance companies only after shopping the market to be sure these investors are offering a competitive price.

If Apple and the insurance companies strike a deal, the flow of funds between them will be as shown below:

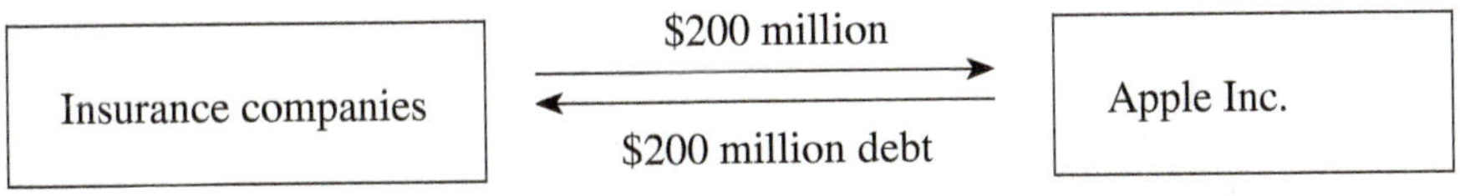

Apple sells its bonds to the insurance group for $200 million and gets the use of the money for 15 years. For Apple, the bonds are a liability, and it pays the insurance companies (bondholders) interest for use of the money. For the insurance companies, the bonds are an asset that earns interest.

Investment Banks and Direct Financing

Two important participants in the direct financial markets are investment banks and money center banks. **Investment banks** specialize in helping companies sell new debt or equity, although they can also provide other services, such as the broker and dealer services discussed later in this chapter and traditional banking services. **Money center banks** are large commercial banks that provide both traditional and investment banking services throughout the world.

investment banks firms that specialize in helping companies sell new security issues

money center banks large commercial banks that provide both traditional and investment banking services throughout the world

Historically, there was a clear distinction between the activities of investment and money center banks. After the Great Depression (1929–1933), commercial banks were prohibited from engaging in investment banking activities because it was believed that these activities encouraged them to take too many risks. However, this prohibition ended in 1999 with passage of the Financial Services Modernization Act, after which the major money center banks, such as Bank of America, JPMorgan Chase, and Citigroup, started providing investment banking services. After the financial meltdown in 2008, the remaining major independent investment banks, specifically Goldman Sachs and Morgan Stanley, converted themselves into traditional bank holding companies to qualify for government assistance. While there are still small investment banks that focus only on investment banking activities, the large investment and commercial banks are now quite similar.

Weblink

To get a better idea of all the lines of business in which large investment banking firms engage, go to Goldman Sachs's home page at http://www.goldmansachs.com.

Origination

Origination is the process of preparing a security issue for sale. During the origination phase, the investment banker may help the client company determine the feasibility of the project being funded and the amount and type of capital that needs to be raised. Once this is done, the investment banker helps secure a credit rating, if needed, determines the sale date, obtains legal clearances to sell the securities, and gets the securities printed. If securities are to be sold in the public markets, the issuer must also file a registration statement with the Securities and Exchange Commission (SEC). Issuers that sell securities in the private markets are not required to file a registration statement with the SEC.

Underwriting

Underwriting is the process by which the investment banker helps the company sell its new security issue. In the most common type of underwriting arrangement, called *firm-commitment underwriting*, the investment banker buys the new securities from the issuing company and resells them to investors. Because the investment banker buys the entire security issue from the company at a fixed price, the issuing company is guaranteed that price. On the other hand, the investment banker takes the risk that the actual price at which the securities are sold is less than the price that is paid to the company. Since issuing companies typically need a certain amount of money to pay for a particular project or to fund operations, and getting anything less than this amount can pose a serious problem, financial managers almost always prefer to have their new security issues underwritten on a firm-commitment basis.[2]

Once the investment bankers buy the securities from the issuer, they immediately offer to resell individual securities to institutional investors and the public at a specified offering price. The underwriters hope to be able to sell the offering at the market-clearing price, which is the price that will allow the entire security issue to be sold during the first day of sale. Underwriting involves considerable risk because it is difficult to estimate the price that will clear the market. If the investment bank has to sell the securities at a price below the price that it paid to the issuing company, the investment bank suffers a financial loss.

LEARNING BY DOING

WileyPLUS

Need more help? Visit your WileyPLUS course.

APPLICATION 2.1 | Underwriter's Compensation

Problem Dairy Queen needs to raise $5 million to build three new restaurants and its financial manager decides to issue long-term bonds. The financial manager hires an investment banking firm to help design the bond issue and underwrite it. The issue consists of 5,000 bonds, and the investment banker agrees to purchase the entire issue for $4.8 million. The investment banker then resells the bonds to investors at the offering price. The sale totals $5.0 million. What is the underwriter's compensation?

Approach The underwriter's compensation is the underwriting spread, which is the difference between the price at which the bonds were resold to investors and the price the underwriter paid for the issue. The underwriting spread per bond is then calculated by dividing the total spread by the number of bonds that are issued.

Solution

$$\text{Underwriting spread: } \$5{,}000{,}000 - \$4{,}800{,}000 = \$200{,}000$$

$$\text{Underwriting spread per bond: } \$200{,}000/5{,}000 \text{ bonds} = \$40$$

Since the bonds are sold for $1,000 each ($5,000,000/5,000 bonds = $1,000 per bond), the underwriting spread is 4 percent of the bond price. Notice that because of the guarantee Dairy Queen gets a check from the underwriter for $4.8 million regardless of the price at which the bonds are resold.

[2]If the risk of underwriting a new security issue is high, investment bankers may refuse to underwrite the securities for a guaranteed price. Instead, they will underwrite the new issue on a *best-efforts basis,* which means that they will sell the securities for the highest price that investors are willing to pay. These issues are discussed in more detail in Chapter 15.

The investment banker's compensation is called the *underwriting spread*. It is the difference between the offering price and the price the investment banker pays for the security issue. The underwriting spread is one of the costs to the firm of selling new securities.

Learning by Doing Application 2.1 illustrates how the underwriting spread is calculated.

Distribution

Distribution is the process of marketing and reselling the securities to investors. Because security prices can take large, unexpected swings, a quick resale of all the securities is important. To that end, the underwriters often form sales syndicates, consisting of a number of different investment banking firms, to sell the securities. If the securities are not sold within a few days, the syndicate is disbanded, and the individual syndicate members sell the unsold securities at whatever price they can get.

Before You Go On

1. Why is it difficult for individuals to participate in direct financial markets?
2. Why might a firm prefer to have a security issue underwritten by an investment banking firm?

2.3 Types of Financial Markets

LEARNING OBJECTIVE

3. Describe the primary, secondary, and money markets, explaining the special importance of secondary and money markets to business organizations.

We have seen that direct flows of funds occur in financial markets. However, as already mentioned, *financial market* is a very general term. A complex industrial economy such as ours includes many different types of financial markets, and not all of them are involved in direct financing. Next, we examine some of the more important ways to classify financial markets. Note that these classifications overlap to a large extent. Thus, for example, the New York Stock Exchange fits into several different categories.

Primary and Secondary Markets

A **primary market** is any market where companies sell new security issues (debt or equity). For example, suppose Hewlett-Packard (HP) needs to raise $100 million for business expansion and decides to raise the money through the sale of common stock. The company will sell the new equity issue in the primary market for corporate stock—probably with the help of an underwriter, as discussed in Section 2.2. The primary markets are not well known to the general public because they are wholesale markets and the sales take place outside of the public view. A key characteristic of a primary market is that the transaction results in new money going into the firm.

primary market a financial market in which new security issues are sold by companies directly to investors

A **secondary market** is any market where owners of outstanding securities can sell them to other investors. Secondary markets are like used-car markets in that they allow investors to buy or sell previously owned securities for cash. These markets are important because they enable investors to buy and sell securities as frequently as they want. As you might expect, investors are willing to pay higher prices for securities that have active secondary markets. Secondary markets are important to corporations as well because investors are willing to pay higher prices for securities in primary markets if the securities have active secondary

secondary market a financial market in which the owners of outstanding securities can sell them to other investors markets. Thus, companies whose securities have active secondary markets enjoy lower funding costs than similar firms whose securities do not have active secondary markets. In contrast to primary markets, no new money goes into the firm when a secondary market transaction takes place.

Marketability versus Liquidity

marketability the ease with which a security can be sold and converted into cash

An important characteristic of a security to investors is its marketability. **Marketability** is the ease with which a security can be sold and converted into cash. A security's marketability depends in part on the costs of trading and searching for information, so-called *transaction costs*. The lower the transaction costs, the greater a security's marketability. Because secondary markets make it easier to trade securities, their presence increases a security's marketability.

liquidity the ability to convert an asset into cash quickly without loss of value

A term closely related to marketability is **liquidity**. Liquidity is the ability to convert an asset into cash quickly without loss of value. In common use, the terms *marketability* and *liquidity* are often used interchangeably, but they are different. Liquidity implies that when the security is sold, its value will be preserved; marketability does not carry this implication.

Brokers versus Dealers

brokers market specialists who bring buyers and sellers together, usually for a commission

Two types of market specialists facilitate transactions in secondary markets. **Brokers** are market specialists who bring buyers and sellers together when a sale takes place. They execute the transaction for their client and are compensated for their services with a commission fee. They bear no risk of ownership of the securities during the transaction; their only service is that of matchmaker.

dealers market specialists who make markets for securities by buying and selling from their own inventories

Dealers, in contrast, make markets for securities and do bear risk. They make a market for a security by buying and selling from an inventory of securities they own. Dealers make their profit, just as retail merchants do, by selling securities at prices above what they paid for them. The risk that dealers bear is *price risk*, which is the risk that they will sell a security for less than they paid for it.

Exchanges and Over-the-Counter Markets

Financial markets can be classified as either organized markets (more commonly called exchanges) or over-the-counter markets. Traditional exchanges, such as the New York Stock Exchange (NYSE), provide a physical meeting place and communication facilities for members to buy and sell securities or other assets (such as commodities like oil or wheat) under a specific set of rules and regulations. Members are individuals who represent securities firms as well as people who trade for their own accounts. Only members can use the exchange.

Securities not listed on an exchange are bought and sold in the over-the-counter (OTC) market. The OTC market differs from organized exchanges in that the OTC market has no central trading location. Instead, investors can execute OTC transactions by visiting or telephoning an OTC dealer or by using a computer-based electronic trading system linked to the OTC dealer. Historically, stocks traded over the counter were those of small and relatively unknown firms, most of which would not qualify to be listed on a major exchange. However, electronic trading has become much more important as computer-based trading technologies have advanced. Many large well-known firms, such as Alphabet (Google's parent company), Facebook, and Microsoft, now trade on electronic exchanges such as NASDAQ. In fact, even in organized markets like the NYSE, most trades are now completed electronically.

Money and Capital Markets

money markets markets where short-term debt instruments are traded

Money markets are global markets where short-term debt instruments, which have maturities of less than one year, are traded. Money markets are wholesale markets in which the minimum transaction is \$1 million and transactions of \$10 million or \$100 million are not uncommon. Money market instruments are lower in risk than other securities because of their high liquidity and low default risk. In fact, the term *money market* is used because these instruments are close substitutes for cash. The most important and largest money markets are in New York City, London, and Tokyo. **Exhibit 2.2** lists the most common money market instruments and the dollar amounts outstanding as of December 2016.

Large companies use money markets to adjust their liquidity positions. Liquidity, as mentioned, is the ability to convert an asset into cash quickly without loss of value. Liquidity problems arise because companies' cash receipts and expenditures are rarely perfectly synchronized. To manage liquidity, a firm can invest idle cash in money market instruments; then, if the firm has a temporary cash shortfall, it can raise cash overnight by selling money market instruments.

Recall from Chapter 1 that capital markets are markets where equity and debt instruments with maturities of greater than one year are traded. In these markets, large firms finance capital assets such as plants and equipment. The NYSE, as well as the London and Tokyo stock exchanges, are capital markets. Exhibit 2.2 also lists the major U.S. capital market instruments and the dollar amounts outstanding. Compared with money market instruments, capital market instruments are less marketable, have higher default risk, and have longer maturities.

Public and Private Markets

Public markets are organized financial markets where the general public buys and sells securities through their stockbrokers. The NYSE, for example, is a public market. The SEC regulates public securities markets in the United States. This agency is responsible for overseeing the securities industry and regulating all primary and secondary markets in which securities are traded. Many corporations want access to the public markets because they are wholesale markets where issuers can sell their securities at the lowest possible funding cost. The downside for corporations selling in the public markets is the cost of complying with the various SEC regulations.

In contrast to public markets, *private markets* involve direct transactions between two parties. Transactions in private markets are often called **private placements**. In private markets, a company contacts investors directly and negotiates a deal to sell them all or part of a security

private placement the sale of an unregistered security directly to an investor, such as an insurance company or a wealthy individual

EXHIBIT 2.2 **Selected Money Market and Capital Market Instruments, December 2016 ($ billions)**

The exhibit shows the size of the U.S. market for each of the most important money market and capital market instruments. Notice that the largest security market is the market for corporate stock, followed by those for mortgage debt, corporate bonds, and Treasury notes. Compared with money market instruments, capital market instruments are less marketable, have higher default risk, and have longer maturities.

Money Market Instruments		
Treasury bills		$ 1,818
Commercial paper		911
	Total	$ 2,729
Capital Market Instruments		
Treasury notes		$ 8,659
Treasury bonds*		3,444
State and local government bonds		3,051
Corporate bonds		9,741
Corporate stock (at market value)		30,077
Mortgage debt		14,188
	Total	$69,160

*Includes Treasury inflation-protected securities, floating rate notes, and Federal Financing Bank securities.

Sources: Board of Governors, Federal Reserve System, Flow of Funds, Balance Sheets, and Integrated Macroeconomic Accounts (December 8, 2016) and Bureau of Public Debt, Monthly Statement of the Public Debt of the United States (December 31, 2016).

issue. Larger firms may be equipped to handle these transactions themselves. Smaller firms are more likely to use the services of an investment bank, which will help locate investors, help negotiate the deal, and handle the legal aspects of the transaction. The major advantages of a private placement are the speed at which funds can be raised and low transaction costs. The downsides are that privately placed securities cannot legally be sold in the public markets because they lack SEC registration and the dollar amounts that can be raised tend to be smaller.

Futures and Options Markets

Markets also exist for trading in futures and options. Perhaps the best-known futures markets are the New York Board of Trade and the Chicago Board of Trade. The Chicago Board Options Exchange is a major options market.

Futures and options are often called *derivative securities* because they derive their value from some underlying asset. Futures contracts are contracts for the future delivery of assets such as securities, foreign currencies, interest cash flows, or commodities. Corporations use these contracts to reduce (hedge) risk exposure caused by fluctuation in things such as foreign exchange rates or commodity prices. We illustrate the use of futures contracts further in Chapter 21.

Options contracts call for one party (the option writer) to perform a specific act if called upon to do so by the option buyer or owner. Options contracts, like futures contracts, can be used to hedge risk in situations where the firm faces risk from price fluctuations. Chapter 20 discusses options in detail.

Before You Go On

1. What is the difference between primary and secondary markets?
2. How and why do large business firms use money markets?
3. What are capital markets, and why are they important to corporations?

2.4 Market Efficiency

LEARNING OBJECTIVE

4. Explain what an efficient market is and why market efficiency is important to financial managers.

Financial markets, such as the bond and stock markets, help bring together buyers and sellers of securities. They reduce the cost of buying and selling securities by providing a physical location or computer trading system where investors can trade securities. The supply and demand for securities are better reflected in organized markets because much of the total supply and demand for securities flows through these centralized locations or trading systems. Any price that balances the overall supply and demand for a security is a market equilibrium price.

true (intrinsic) value for a security, the present value of the cash flows an investor who owns that security can expect to receive in the future

Ideally, economists would like financial markets to price securities at their **true (intrinsic) value**. A security's true value is the present value (the value in today's dollars) of the cash flows an investor who owns that security can expect to receive in the future. This present value, in turn, reflects all available information about the size, timing, and riskiness of the cash flows at the time the price was set.[3] As new information becomes available, investors adjust their cash flow estimates and, through buying and selling, the price of a security adjusts to reflect this information.

[3]We discuss how to calculate the present value of future cash flows in Chapters 5 and 6.

Markets such as those just described are called efficient markets. More formally, in an **efficient market**, security prices fully reflect the knowledge and expectations of all investors at a particular point in time. If markets are efficient, investors and financial managers have no reason to believe the securities are not priced at or near their true value. The more efficient a market is, the more likely securities are to be priced at or near their true value.

efficient market market where prices reflect the knowledge and expectations of all investors

The overall efficiency of a market depends on its *operational efficiency* and its *informational efficiency*. **Market operational efficiency** concerns the cost of bringing together buyers and sellers. The costs of bringing together buyers and sellers are called *transaction costs* and include such things as broker commissions and other fees and expenses. The lower these costs, the more operationally efficient markets are. Why is operational efficiency important? If transaction costs are high, market prices will be more volatile, fewer financial transactions will take place, and prices will not reflect the knowledge and expectations of investors as accurately.

market operational efficiency the degree to which the transaction costs of bringing buyers and sellers together are minimized

Market informational efficiency is exhibited if market prices reflect all relevant information about securities at a particular point in time. As suggested above, informational efficiency is influenced by operational efficiency, but it also depends on the availability of information and the ability of investors to buy and sell securities based on that information. In an informationally efficient market, market prices adjust quickly to new information as it becomes available. Prices adjust quickly because many security analysts and investors are gathering and trading on information about securities to make a profit. Note that competition among investors is an important driver of informational efficiency.

market informational efficiency the degree to which current market prices reflect relevant information and, therefore, the true value of the security

Weblink

The concept of market efficiency originated with the Ph.D. dissertation that Eugene Fama wrote at the University of Chicago. In 2013, Dr. Fama received the Nobel Prize in Economics for his research on market efficiency. You can see a video of an interview with Dr. Fama about market efficiency at http://www.youtube.com/watch?v=bM9bYOBuKF4.

Efficient Market Hypotheses

Public financial markets are efficient in part because regulators such as the SEC require issuers of publicly traded securities to disclose a great deal of information about those securities to investors. Investors are constantly evaluating the prospects for these securities and acting on the conclusions from their analyses by trading them. If the price of a security is out of line with what investors think it should be, then investors will buy or sell that security, causing its price to adjust to reflect their assessment of its value. The ability of investors to easily observe transaction prices and trade volumes and to inexpensively trade securities in public markets contributes to the efficiency of this process. This buying and selling by investors is the mechanism through which prices adjust to reflect the market's consensus. The theory about how well this mechanism works is known as the **efficient market hypothesis**. We next discuss the three forms of the efficient market hypothesis, which describe different degrees of market efficiency.

efficient market hypothesis a theory concerning the extent to which information is reflected in security prices and how information gets incorporated into security prices

Strong-Form Efficiency The market for a security is perfectly informationally efficient if the security's price always reflects all information. The idea that all information about a security is reflected in its price is known as the **strong-form of the efficient market hypothesis**. Few people really believe that market prices of public securities reflect all available information, however. It is widely accepted that insiders have information that is not reflected in the security prices. Thus, the concept of strong-form market efficiency represents the ideal case rather than the real world.

strong-form of the efficient market hypothesis the theory that security prices reflect all information

If a security market were strong-form efficient, then it would not be possible to earn abnormally high returns (returns greater than those justified by the risks) by trading on **private information**—information unavailable to other investors—because there would be no such information. In addition, since all information would already be reflected in security prices, the price of a share of a particular security would change only when new information about its prospects became available.

private information information that is not available to all investors

Semistrong-Form Efficiency A weaker form of the efficient market hypothesis, known as the **semistrong-form of the efficient market hypothesis**, holds only that all **public information**—information that is available to all investors—is reflected in security prices. Investors who have private information are able to profit by trading on this information before it becomes public. For example, suppose that conversations with the customers of a firm indicate to an investor that the firm's sales, and thereby its cash flows, are increasing more rapidly than other investors expect. To profit from this information, the investor buys the firm's stock. By buying the stock, the investor helps drive up the price to the point where it accurately reflects the higher level of cash flows.

semistrong-form of the efficient market hypothesis the theory that security prices reflect all public information but not all private information

public information information that is available to all investors

The concept of semistrong-form efficiency is a reasonable representation of the public stock markets in developed countries such as the United States. In a market characterized by this sort of efficiency, as soon as information becomes public, it is quickly reflected in stock prices through trading activity. Studies of the speed at which new information is reflected in stock prices indicate that by the time you read a hot tip in the *Wall Street Journal* or a business magazine, it is too late to benefit by trading on it.

weak-form of the efficient market hypothesis the theory that security prices reflect all information in past prices but do not reflect all private or all public information

Weak-Form Efficiency The weakest form of the efficient market hypothesis is known, aptly enough, as the **weak-form of the efficient market hypothesis**. This hypothesis holds that all information contained in past prices of a security is reflected in current prices but that there is both public and private information that is not. In a weak-form efficient market, it would not be possible to earn abnormally high returns by looking for patterns in security prices, but it would be possible to do so by trading on public or private information.

An important conclusion of the efficient market hypothesis is that at any point in time, all securities with the same risk should be priced to offer the same expected return. The more efficient the market, the more likely this is to happen. Since both the bond and stock markets are relatively efficient, this means that securities of similar risk will offer the same expected return. This conclusion is important because it provides the basis for identifying the proper discount rate to use in applying the bond and stock valuation models developed in Chapters 8 and 9.

Weblink

For an in-depth discussion of market efficiency, visit http://www.investorhome.com/emh.htm.

Before You Go On

1. How does information about a firm's prospects get reflected in its share price?
2. What is strong-form market efficiency? semistrong-form market efficiency? weak-form market efficiency?

2.5 Financial Institutions and Indirect Financing

LEARNING OBJECTIVE

5. Explain how financial institutions serve the needs of consumers and small businesses.

As we mentioned earlier, many business firms are too small to sell their debt or equity directly to investors. They have neither the expert knowledge nor the financing requirements to make transacting in wholesale markets cost-effective. When these companies need funds for capital investments or for liquidity adjustments, their only feasible choice is to borrow in the *indirect* market from a financial institution. These financial institutions act as intermediaries, converting financial securities with one set of characteristics into securities with another set of characteristics. This process is called **financial intermediation**. The hallmark of indirect financing is that a financial institution—an intermediary—stands between the lender-saver and the borrower-spender. This route is shown at the bottom of Exhibit 2.1.

financial intermediation conversion of securities with one set of characteristics into securities with another set of characteristics

Indirect Market Transactions

We worked through an example of indirect financing at the beginning of the chapter. In that situation, a college student had $5,000 to invest for three months. A bank sold the student a three-month consumer CD for $5,000, pooled this $5,000 with the proceeds from checking and savings accounts and other CDs, and used the money to make small-business loans, one of which was a $30,000 loan to a pizza parlor owner. Following is a schematic diagram of that transaction:

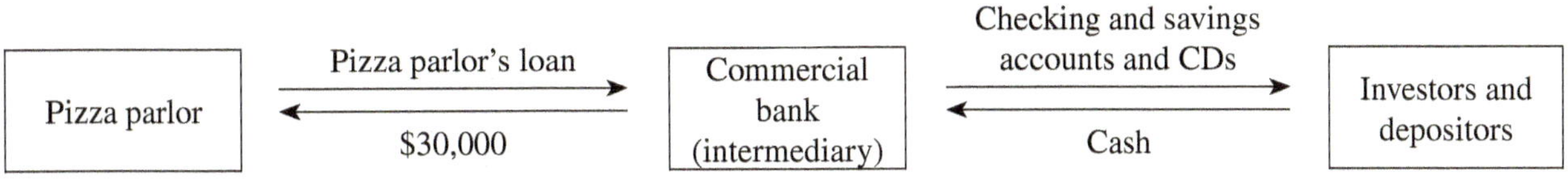

The bank raises money from deposits to checking and savings accounts and by selling CDs and then uses the money to make loans to businesses or consumers.

On a larger scale, insurance companies provide much of the long-term financing in the economy through the indirect credit market. These companies invest heavily in corporate bonds and equity securities using funds they receive when they sell insurance policies to individuals and businesses. The schematic diagram for intermediation by an insurance company is as follows:

Notice an important difference between indirect and direct financial markets. In the direct market, as securities flow between lender-savers and borrower-spenders, the form of the securities remains unchanged. In indirect markets, however, as securities flow between lender-savers and borrower-spenders, they are repackaged, and their form is changed. In the example above, money from the sale of insurance policies becomes investments in corporate debt or equity. By repackaging securities, financial intermediaries tailor-make a wide range of financial products and services that meet the needs of consumers, small businesses, and large corporations. Their products and services are particularly important for smaller businesses that do not have access to direct financial markets.

Somewhat surprisingly, indirect markets are a much larger and more important source of financing to businesses than the more newsworthy direct financial markets. This is true not only in the United States, but in all industrial countries as well.

Financial Institutions and Their Services

We have briefly discussed the role of financial institutions as intermediaries in the indirect financial market. Next, we look at various types of financial institutions and the services they provide to small businesses as well as large corporations. We discuss only financial institutions that provide a significant amount of services to businesses.

Commercial Banks

Commercial banks are the most prominent and largest financial intermediaries in the economy and offer the widest range of financial services to businesses. Nearly every business, small or large, has a significant relationship with a commercial bank—usually a checking or transaction account and some type of credit or loan arrangement. For businesses, the most common type of bank loan is a line of credit (often called revolving credit), which works much like a credit card. A line of credit is a commitment by the bank to lend a firm an amount up to a predetermined limit, which can be used as needed. Banks also make term loans, which are fixed-rate loans with a maturity of one year to 10 years. In addition, banks do a significant amount of equipment lease financing. A lease is a contract that gives a business the right to use an asset, such as office space, a truck, or a computer mainframe, for a period of time in exchange for periodic payments. Leases are discussed in the Appendix to Chapter 16.

Weblink

For an example of the range of services provided by commercial banks to businesses, visit the small business section of http://www.pncbank.com.

Life and Casualty Insurance Companies

Two types of insurance companies are important in the financial markets: (1) life insurance companies and (2) casualty insurance companies, which sell protection against loss of property from fire, theft, accidents, and other causes. The cash flows for both types of companies are fairly predictable. As a result, they are able to provide funding to corporations through the purchase of stocks and bonds in the direct credit markets as well as funding for both public and private corporations through private placement financing. Businesses of all sizes purchase life insurance programs as part of their employee benefit packages and purchase casualty insurance policies to protect physical assets such as automobiles, truck fleets, equipment, and entire plants.

Pension Funds

Pension funds invest retirement funds on behalf of businesses or government agencies that provide retirement programs for their employees. Pension funds obtain money from employee and employer contributions during the employee's working years, and they provide monthly cash payments upon retirement. Because of the predictability of these cash flows, pension fund managers invest in corporate bonds and equity securities purchased in the direct financial markets and participate in the private placement market.

Investment Funds

Investment funds, such as mutual funds, sell shares to investors and use the funds to purchase securities. As a result, they are an important source of business funding. For example, mutual funds may focus on purchasing (1) equity or debt securities; (2) securities of small or medium-size corporations; (3) securities of companies in a particular industry, such as energy, computer, or information technology, or (4) foreign investments.

Business Finance Companies

Business finance companies obtain the majority of their funds by selling short-term debt, called commercial paper, to investors in direct credit markets. These funds are used to make a variety of short- and intermediate-term loans and leases to small and large businesses. The loans are often secured by accounts receivable or inventory. Business finance companies are typically more willing than commercial banks to make loans and leases to firms with higher levels of default risk.

Corporations and the Financial System

We began this chapter by saying that financial managers need to understand the financial system in order to make sound decisions. We now follow up on that statement by briefly describing how corporations operate within the financial system. The interaction between the financial system and a large public corporation is shown in **Exhibit 2.3**. The arrows show the major cash flows for a firm over a typical operating cycle. These cash flows relate to some of the key decisions that the financial manager must make. As you know, those decisions involve three major areas: capital budgeting, financing, and working capital management.

Let's work through an example using Exhibit 2.3 to illustrate how corporate businesses use the financial system. Suppose you are the CFO of a new high-tech firm that is being formed in a joint venture with 3M Corporation. The new firm has a well-thought-out business plan, owns some valuable technology, and will operate one manufacturing facility. The company will be large enough to have access to public markets. The company plans to use its core technology to develop and sell a number of new products that the marketing department believes will generate a strong market demand.

To start the new company, management's first task is to sell equity and debt to finance the firm. The senior management team and 3M will provide 40 percent of the equity, and the balance will come from an **initial public offering (IPO)** of common stock. An IPO is a corporation's first offering of its stock to the public. In this example, management hires Morgan Stanley as its investment bank to underwrite the new securities. After the deal is underwritten,

initial public offering (IPO) the first offering of a corporation's stock to the public

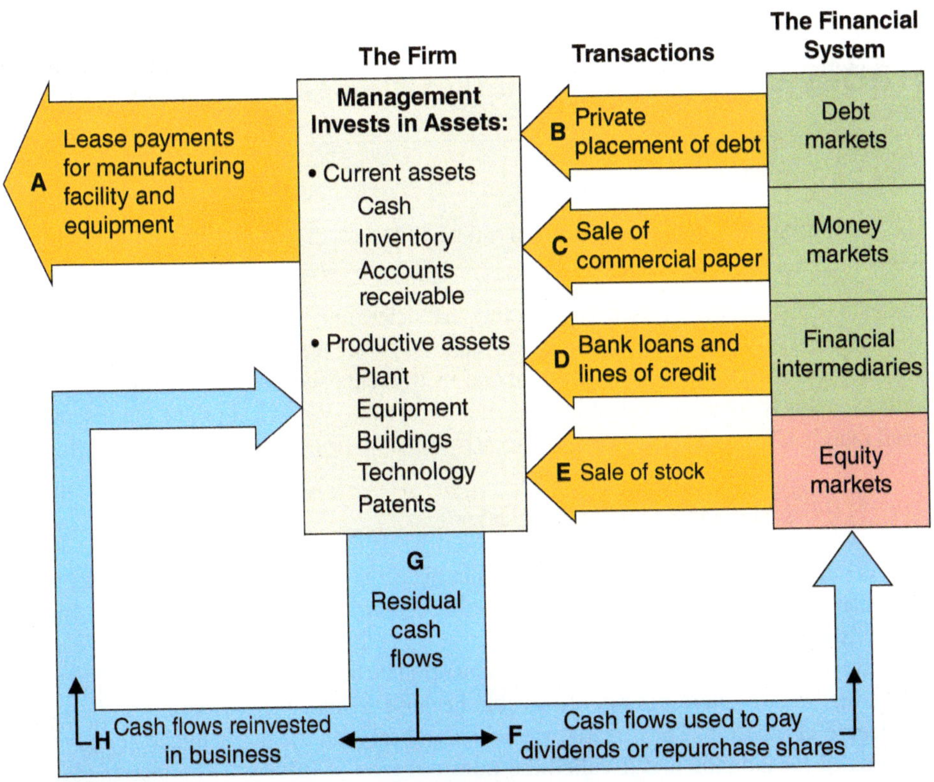

EXHIBIT 2.3 **Cash Flows between the Firm and the Financial System**

This exhibit shows how the financial system helps businesses finance their activities. The arrows in the exhibit indicate the major cash flows into and out of a firm over a typical operating cycle. Money obtained from the financial system, combined with reinvested cash flows from operations, enables a firm to make necessary investments and fund any other requirements.

the new venture receives the proceeds from the stock sale, less Morgan Stanley's underwriting fees (see arrow E in the exhibit).[4]

In addition to the equity financing, 30 percent of the firm's total funding will come from the sale of long-term debt through a private placement deal with a large insurance company (see arrow B). Management decided to use a private placement because the lender is willing to commit to lend the firm additional money in the future if the firm meets certain performance goals. Since management has ambitious growth plans, locking in a future source of funds is important.

Once the funds from the debt and equity sales are in hand, they are deposited in the firm's checking account at a commercial bank. Management then decides to lease an existing manufacturing facility and the equipment necessary to manufacture the new high-technology products; the cash outflows are represented by arrow A.

To begin manufacturing, the firm needs to raise working capital and does this by (1) selling commercial paper in the money markets (arrow C) and (2) obtaining a line of credit from a bank (arrow D). As the firm becomes operational, it generates cash inflows from its productive assets (arrow G). Some of these cash inflows are reinvested in the business (arrow H), and the remainder is used to pay cash dividends to stockholders or repurchase shares (arrow F).

Before You Go On

1. What is financial intermediation, and why is it important?
2. What are some services that commercial banks provide to businesses?
3. What is an IPO, and what role does an investment banker play in the process?

[4]Chapter 15 contains a detailed discussion of the IPO process.

2.6 The Determinants of Interest Rate Levels

LEARNING OBJECTIVE

6. Compute the nominal and the real rates of interest, differentiating between them.

We conclude this chapter by examining factors that determine the general level of interest rates in the economy and describing how interest rates vary over the business cycle. Understanding interest rates is important because the financial instruments and most of the financial services discussed in this chapter are priced in terms of interest rates. We will continue our discussion of interest rates in Chapter 8, where we consider why different firms have different borrowing costs.

The Real Rate of Interest

real rate of interest the interest rate that would exist in the absence of inflation

nominal rate of interest the rate of interest that is unadjusted for inflation

One of the most important economic variables in the economy is the **real rate of interest**—an interest rate determined in the absence of inflation. *Inflation* is the amount by which aggregate price levels rise over time. The real rate of interest is (1) the inflation-adjusted return earned by lender-savers and (2) the inflation-adjusted cost incurred by borrower-spenders when they borrow.

The real rate of interest is not observable because all industrial economies operate with some degree of inflation. The rate that we actually observe in the marketplace at a given time is unadjusted for inflation and is called the **nominal rate of interest**. The factors that determine the real rate of interest, however, are the underlying determinants of all interest rates we observe in the marketplace. For this reason, an understanding of the real rate is important.

Determinants of the Real Rate of Interest

The fundamental determinants of interest rates are the returns earned on investments in productive assets (capital investments) and individuals' time preference for consumption. Let's examine how these two factors interact to determine the real rate of interest.

Returns on Investments Recall from Chapter 1 that businesses invest in capital projects that are expected to generate positive cash flows by producing additional real output, such as cars, machinery, computers, and video games. The output generated by a capital project constitutes its return on investment, which is usually measured as a percentage. For example, if a capital project costs $1,000 and produces $180 in cash flows each year, the project's return on investment is 18 percent ($180/$1,000 = 0.18, or 18 percent).

For a capital project to be attractive, its return on investment must exceed the cost of the funds (debt and equity) used to finance it. Intuitively, this makes sense because if an investment earns a return greater than the cost of funding, it should be profitable and thus should increase the value of the firm. For example, if the cost of funding—often called the *cost of capital*—is 15 percent, the capital project mentioned above would be attractive (18 percent > 15 percent) and would therefore be undertaken. If the capital project was expected to earn only 13 percent, though, the project would be rejected (13 percent < 15 percent). The cost of capital is the minimum acceptable rate of return on a capital project.

Decision Making Example 2.1 illustrates an application of the idea that an attractive project is one for which the return on investment exceeds the cost of funds.

Time Preference for Consumption All other things being equal, most people prefer to consume goods today rather than tomorrow. This is called a positive time preference for consumption. For example, most people who want to buy a new car prefer to have it now rather than wait until they have earned enough cash to make the purchase. When people consume today, however, they realize that their future consumption may be less because they have forgone the opportunity to save and earn interest on their savings.

Given people's positive time preference for consumption, the interest rate offered on financial instruments determines how much people will save. At low rates of interest, it hardly makes sense to save, so most people will continue to spend money rather than put money aside in savings. To coax people to postpone current spending, interest rates must be raised. At higher

EXAMPLE 2.1 | Capital Budgeting Preview

DECISION MAKING

Situation Sonic Manufacturing Company's capital budget includes six projects that management has identified as having merit. The CFO's staff computed the return on investment for each project. The average cost of funding each project is 10 percent. The projects are as follows:

Project	Return on Investment
A	13.0%
B	12.0
C	10.9
D	10.5
E	9.8
F	8.9

Which capital projects should the firm undertake?

Decision The firm should accept all projects with a return on investment greater than the average cost of funding, which is 10 percent in all cases. These projects are A, B, C, and D. As noted in the text, this decision-making principle makes intuitive sense because all projects with a return on investment greater than the cost of funds will increase the value of the firm. In Chapters 10 through 13, we will delve much more deeply into capital budgeting, and you will find out a great deal more about how these decisions are made.

Equilibrium Condition. Higher interest rates reduce business investment (or spending) because fewer capital projects can earn a high enough return on investment to cover the added interest cost. They also reduce demand for borrowing by consumers. At the same time, lender-savers spend less and want to lend more money when interest rates are high. The real rate of interest depends on the interaction between these two opposing factors. Using a supply-and-demand framework, **Exhibit 2.4** shows that the equilibrium market rate of interest (*r*) is the point where the desired level of borrowing (B) by borrower-spenders equals the desired level of lending (L) by lender-savers.[5]

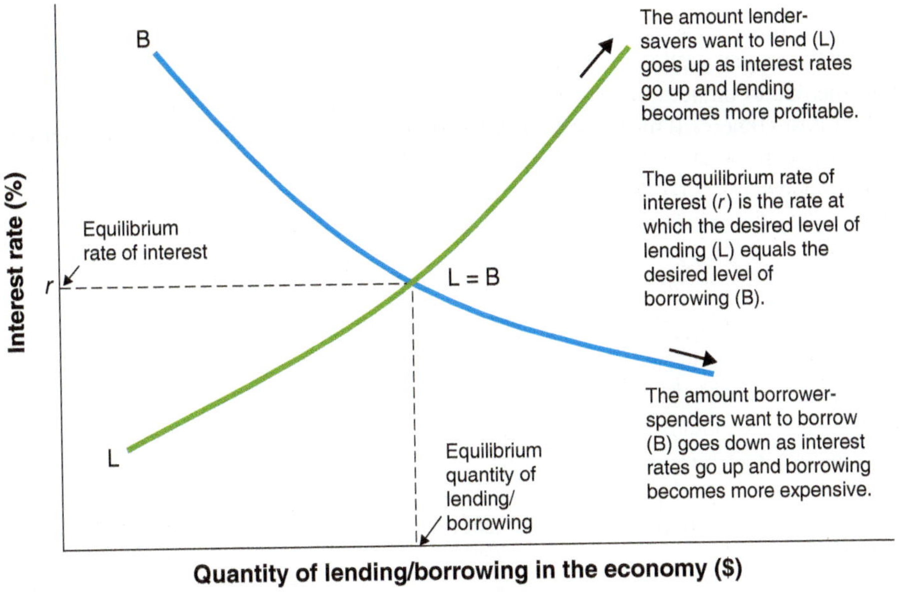

EXHIBIT 2.4 **The Determinants of the Equilibrium Rate of Interest**

The equilibrium rate of interest is a function of supply and demand. Lender-savers are willing to supply more funds as interest rates go up, but borrower-spenders demand fewer funds at higher interest rates. The interest rate at which the supply of funds equals the demand for those funds is the equilibrium rate.

[5]The model presented here is based on the loanable funds theory of market equilibrium. Saving (or giving up current consumption) is the source of loanable funds, and personal and business spending (or investment) is the use of funds.

Fluctuations in the Real Rate

In the supply-and-demand framework discussed previously, any economic factor that causes a shift in desired lending or desired borrowing will cause a change in the equilibrium rate of interest. For example, a major breakthrough in technology should cause a shift to the right in the desired level of borrowing schedule, thus increasing the real rate of interest. This makes intuitive sense because the new technology should spawn an increase in investment opportunities, increasing the desired level of borrowing. Similarly, a reduction in the corporate tax rate should provide businesses with more money to spend on investments, which should increase the desired level of borrowing schedule, causing the real rate of interest to increase.

One factor that would shift the desired level of lending to the right, and hence lead to a decrease in the real rate of interest, would be a decrease in the tax rates for individuals. Lower individual tax rates would leave lender-savers with more money to lend. Also, with lower individual tax rates, lender-savers could receive a lower interest rate and earn the same after-tax return. Another factor would be monetary policy action by the Federal Reserve System Board of Governors to increase the money supply. A larger money supply would increase the amount of money available for lending.

Other forces that could affect the real rate of interest include growth in population, demographic variables such as the age of the population, and cultural differences. In sum, the real rate of interest reflects a complex set of forces that control the desired level of lending and borrowing in the economy. The real rate of interest has historically been around 3 percent for the U.S. economy but has typically varied between 2 and 4 percent because of changes in economic conditions.

Loan Contracts and Inflation

The real rate of interest does not account for inflation, but price-level changes in the real world are a fact of life, and these changes affect the value of a loan contract or, for that matter, any financial contract. For example, if prices rise due to inflation during the life of a loan contract, the purchasing power of the dollar decreases because the borrower repays the lender with inflated dollars—dollars with less buying power.[6]

To see the impact of inflation on a loan, let's look at an example. Suppose that you lend a friend $1,000 for one year at a 4 percent interest rate. Furthermore, you plan to buy a new surfboard for $1,040 in one year when you graduate from college. With the $40 of interest you earn ($1,000 × 0.04 = $40), you will have just enough money to buy the surfboard. At the end of the year, you graduate, and your friend pays off the loan, giving you $1,040. Unfortunately, the rate of inflation during the year was an unexpected 10 percent, and your surfboard now will cost 10 percent more, or $1,144 ($1,040 × 1.10 = $1,144). You have experienced a 10 percent decrease in your purchasing power due to the unanticipated inflation. The loss of purchasing power is $104 ($1,144 – $1,040 = $104).

The Fisher Equation and Inflation

How do we write a loan contract that provides protection against loss of purchasing power due to inflation? We have no crystal ball to tell us what the actual rate of inflation will be when the loan contract is written. However, market participants collectively (often called "the market") have expectations about how prices will change during the contract period.

To incorporate these inflation expectations into a loan contract, we need to adjust the real rate of interest by the amount of inflation that is expected during the contract period. The mathematical formula used to adjust the real rate of interest for the expected rate of inflation is as follows:

$$\begin{aligned} 1 + i &= (1 + r) \times (1 + \Delta P_e) \qquad (2.1) \\ 1 + i &= 1 + r + \Delta P_e + r\Delta P_e \\ i &= r + \Delta P_e + r\Delta P_e \end{aligned}$$

[6]Recall from economics two important relations: (1) The value of money is its purchasing power—what you can buy with it, and (2) there is a negative relation between changes in price level and the value of money. As the price level increases (inflation), the value of money decreases, and as the price level decreases (deflation), the value of money increases. This makes sense because when we have rising prices (inflation), our dollars will buy less.

where:

i = nominal (or market) rate of interest
r = real rate of interest
ΔP_e = expected annualized price-level change
$r\Delta P_e$ = adjustment of the interest rate for expected price-level change

Equation 2.1 is called the Fisher equation. It is named after Irving Fisher, who first developed the concept and is considered by many to be one of America's greatest economists.

Applying Equation 2.1 to our surfboard example, we can find out what the nominal rate of interest should be if the expected inflation rate is 10 percent and the real rate of interest is 4 percent:

$$\begin{aligned} i &= r + \Delta P_e + r\Delta P_e \\ &= 0.04 + 0.10 + (0.04 \times 0.10) \\ &= 0.1440, \text{ or } 14.40\% \end{aligned}$$

Looking at Equation 2.1, notice that ΔP_e is the *expected* price-level change and not the *realized* (actual) rate of inflation (ΔP_a). Thus, to properly determine the nominal rate of interest, it is necessary to predict prices over the life of the loan contract. Also, recall that the nominal rate of interest is the market rate of interest—the rate actually observed in financial markets. The real and nominal rates of interest are equal only when the expected rate of inflation over the contract period is zero ($\Delta P_e = 0$).[7]

When either r or ΔP_e is a small number, or when both are small, then $r\Delta P_e$ is very small and is approximately equal to zero. In these situations, it is common practice to write the Fisher equation as a simple additive function, where the nominal rate of interest is divided into two parts: (1) the real rate of interest and (2) the anticipated percent change in the price level. The simplified (or approximate) Fisher equation can be written as follows:

$$i = r + \Delta P_e \tag{2.2}$$

Thus, for our one-year loan example:

$$i = 0.04 + 0.10 = 0.1400, \text{ or } 14.00\%$$

The difference in the contract loan rates between the two variations of the Fisher equation is 0.40 percent (14.40 percent − 14.00 percent = 0.40 percent), a difference of less than 3 percent (0.40/14.40 = 0.0278, or 2.78 percent). Thus, dropping $r\Delta P_e$ from the equation makes the equation easier to understand without creating a significant computational error.

Learning by Doing Application 2.2 and **2.3** illustrate applications of the Fisher equation.

APPLICATION 2.2 | Calculating a New Inflation Premium

LEARNING BY DOING

Problem The current one-year Treasury bill rate is 2.0 percent. On the evening news, several economists at leading investment and commercial banks predict that the annual inflation rate is going to be 0.25 percent higher than originally expected. The higher inflation forecasts reflect unexpectedly strong employment figures released by the government that afternoon. What is the current inflation premium if the real rate of interest is 0.5 percent? When the market opens tomorrow, what should happen to the one-year Treasury bill rate?

Approach You must first estimate the current inflation premium using Equation 2.2. You should then adjust this premium to reflect the economists' revised beliefs. Finally, this revised inflation premium can be used in the simplified Fisher equation to estimate what the Treasury rate will be tomorrow morning.

[7] In economics the terms *nominal* and *real* are frequently used as modifiers, as in *nominal GNP* and *real GNP*. *Nominal* means that the data are from the marketplace; thus, the values may contain price-level changes due to inflation. *Real* means the data are corrected for changes in purchasing power.

Solution Current inflation premium:

$$i = r + \Delta P_e$$
$$\Delta P_e = i - r$$
$$= 2.0\% - 0.5\%$$
$$= 1.5\%$$

New inflation premium:

$$\Delta P_e = 1.5\% + 0.25\% = 1.75\%$$

The opening Treasury rate in the morning:

$$i = r + \Delta P_e = 0.5\% + 1.75\% = 2.25\%$$

LEARNING BY DOING

APPLICATION 2.3 | International Loan Rate

Problem You are a financial manager at a manufacturing company that is going to make a one-year loan to a key supplier in another country. The loan will be made in the supplier's local currency. The supplier's government controls the banking system, and there are no reliable market data available. For this reason, you have spoken with five economists who have some knowledge about the economy. Their predictions for inflation next year are 30, 40, 45, 50, and 60 percent.

What rate should your firm charge for the one-year business loan if you are not concerned about the possibility that your supplier will default? You recall from your corporate finance course that the real rate of interest is, on average, 3 percent over the long run.

Approach Although the sample of economists is small, an average of the economists' estimates should provide a reasonable estimate of the expected rate of inflation (ΔP_e). This value can be used in Equation 2.2 to calculate the nominal rate of interest.

Solution

$$\Delta P_e = (30\% + 40\% + 45\% + 50\% + 60\%)/5$$
$$= 225\%/5$$
$$= 45\%$$

Nominal rate of interest:

$$i = r + \Delta P_e$$
$$= 3\% + 45\%$$
$$= 48\%$$

This number is a reasonable estimate, given that you have no market data.

Cyclical and Long-Term Trends in Interest Rates

Now let's look at some market data to see how interest rates have actually fluctuated over the past five decades in the United States. **Exhibit 2.5** plots the interest rate yield on 10-year government bonds since 1960 to represent interest rate movements. In addition, the exhibit plots the annual rate of inflation, represented by the annual percent change in the consumer price index (CPI). The CPI is a price index that measures the change in prices of a market basket of goods and services that a typical consumer purchases. Finally, the shaded areas on the chart indicate periods of recession. Recession occurs when real output from the economy is decreasing and unemployment is increasing. Each shaded area begins

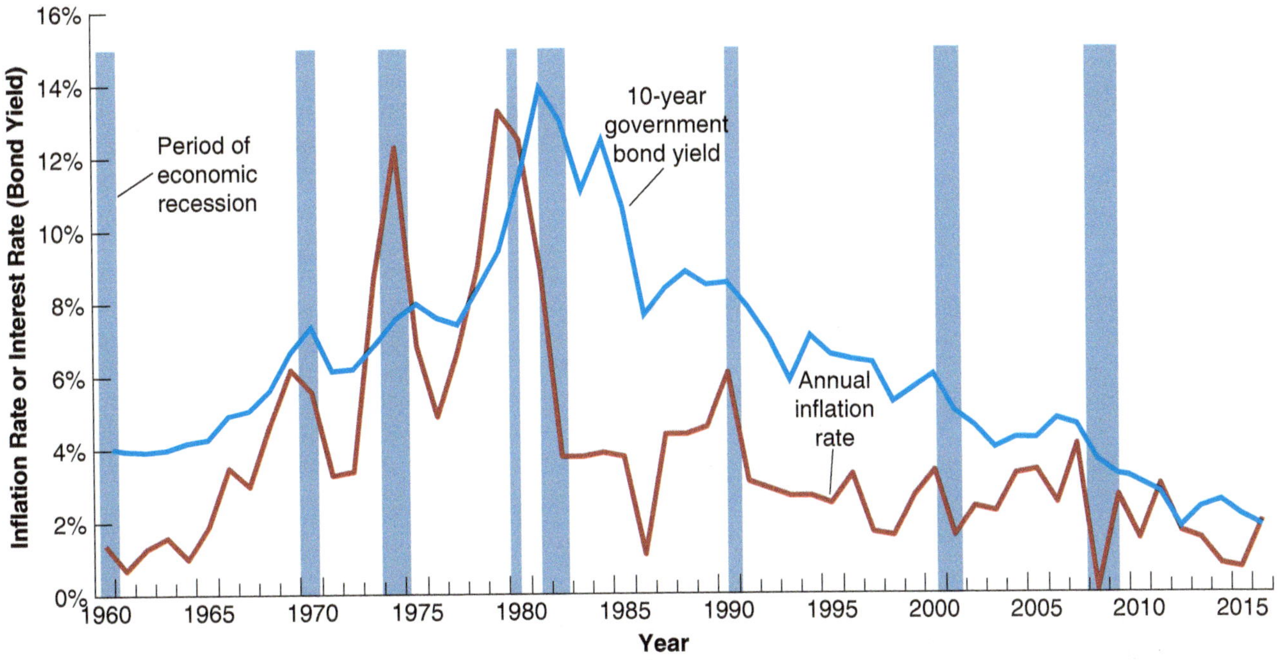

EXHIBIT 2.5 Relation between Annual Inflation Rate and Long-Term Interest Rate (1960–2016)

Based on the graph shown in the exhibit, we can draw two important conclusions about interest rate movements. First, the level of interest rates tends to rise and fall with the actual rate of inflation—a conclusion also supported by the Fisher equation, which suggests that interest rates rise and fall with the *expected* rate of inflation. Second, the level of interest rates tends to rise during periods of economic expansion and decline during periods of economic contraction.

Sources: Bureau of Labor Statistics, U.S. Department of Labor (http://www.bls.gov/cpi), U.S. Department of the Treasury (http://www.treasury.gov), and Wikipedia (http://en.wikipedia.org).

at the peak of the business cycle and ends at the bottom (or trough) of the recession. From our discussion of interest rates and an examination of Exhibit 2.5, we can draw two general conclusions:

1. *The level of interest rates tends to rise and fall with changes in the actual rate of inflation.* The positive relation between the rate of inflation and the level of interest rates is what we should expect given Equation 2.1. Thus, we feel comfortable concluding that inflationary expectations have a major impact on interest rates.

   Our findings also explain in part why interest rates can vary substantially between countries. For example, in 2016 the long-term expected rate of inflation in the United States was 2.0 percent; during the same period, the rate of inflation in Russia was 5.8 percent. If the real rate of interest is 3.0 percent, the long-term interest rate in the United States in 2016 should have been around 5.0 percent (3.0 percent + 2.0 percent = 5.0 percent) and the Russian interest rate should have been around 8.8 percent (3.0 percent + 5.8 percent = 8.8 percent). In fact, at the end of December 2016 the U.S. 10-year interest rate was about 2.45 percent and the Russian rate was 10.00 percent. Though hardly scientific, this analysis illustrates the point that countries with higher rates of inflation or expected rates of inflation will have higher interest rates than countries with lower inflation rates.

2. *The level of interest rates tends to rise during periods of economic expansion and decline during periods of economic contraction.* It makes sense that interest rates should increase during years of economic expansion. The reasoning is that as the economy expands, businesses begin to borrow money to build up inventories and to invest in more production capacity in anticipation of increased sales. As unemployment begins to decrease, the economic future looks bright, and consumers begin to buy more homes, cars, and other durable items on credit. As a result, the demand for funds by both businesses and consumers increases, driving interest rates up. Also, near the end of expansion, the rate of inflation begins to accelerate, which puts upward pressure on interest rates. At some point, the Fed

becomes concerned over the increasing inflation in the economy and begins to tighten credit, which further raises interest rates, slowing down the economy. The higher interest rates in the economy choke off spending by both businesses and consumers.

During a recession, the opposite takes place; businesses and consumers rein in their spending and their use of credit, putting downward pressure on interest rates. To stimulate demand for goods and services, the Fed will typically begin to make more credit available to lower interest rates in the economy and encourage business and consumer spending.

Also notice in Exhibit 2.5 that periods of business expansion tend to be much longer than periods of contraction (recessions). Since the end of the Great Depression, the average period of economic expansion has lasted three to four years and the average period of contraction about nine months. Keep in mind that the numbers given are averages and that actual periods of economic expansion and contraction can vary widely from averages. For example, the business expansion from October 2001 to December 2007 lasted 6 years and two months and the recession that followed it lasted 18 months, from December 2007 to June 2009.

Before You Go On

1. Explain how the real rate of interest is determined.
2. How are inflationary expectations accounted for in the nominal rate of interest?
3. Explain why interest rates follow the business cycle.

Summary of Learning Objectives

1 Describe the role of the financial system in the economy and the two basic ways in which money flows through the system.

The role of the financial system is to gather money from households, businesses, and governments with surplus funds to invest (lender-savers) and channel that money to households, businesses, and governments who need money (borrower-spenders). If the financial system works properly, only investment projects with high rates of return and good credit are financed and all other projects are rejected. Money flows through the financial system in two basic ways: (1) directly, through financial markets, or (2) indirectly, through financial institutions.

2 Discuss direct financing and the important role that investment banks play in this process.

Direct markets are wholesale markets where lender-savers and borrower-spenders deal directly with one another. For example, corporations sell securities, such as stocks and bonds, directly to investors in exchange for money, which they use to invest in their businesses. Investment banks are important in the direct markets because they help borrower-spenders sell their new security issues. The services provided by investment bankers include origination, underwriting, and distribution.

3 Describe the primary, secondary, and money markets, explaining the special importance of secondary and money markets to business organizations.

Primary markets are markets in which new securities are sold for the first time. Secondary markets are markets for securities that were previously issued. Not all securities have active secondary markets. Active secondary markets are important because they enable investors to convert securities easily to cash. Business firms whose securities are traded in secondary markets are able to issue new securities at a lower cost than they otherwise could because investors are willing to pay a higher price for securities that have active secondary markets.

Large corporations use money markets to adjust their liquidity because cash inflows and outflows are rarely perfectly synchronized. Thus, on the one hand, if cash expenditures exceed cash receipts, a firm can borrow short-term in the money markets. If that firm holds a portfolio of money market instruments, it can sell some of these securities for cash. On the other hand, if cash receipts exceed expenditures, the firm can temporarily invest the funds in short-term money market instruments. Businesses are willing to invest large amounts of idle cash in money market instruments because of their high liquidity and their low default risk.

4 Explain what an efficient market is and why market efficiency is important to financial managers.

An efficient market is a market where security prices reflect the knowledge and expectations of all investors. Public markets, for example, are more efficient than private markets because issuers of public securities are required to disclose a great deal of information about these securities to investors and investors are constantly evaluating the prospects for these securities and acting on the conclusions from their analyses by trading them. Market efficiency is important to investors because it assures them that the securities they buy are priced close to their true value.

5 Explain how financial institutions serve the needs of consumers and small businesses.

One problem with direct financing is that it takes place in a wholesale market. Most consumers and small businesses do not have the skills, financing requirements, or money to transact in this market. In contrast, a large portion of the indirect market focuses on providing financial services to consumers and small businesses. For example, commercial banks collect money from consumers in small dollar amounts through checking accounts, savings accounts, and consumer CDs. They then aggregate the funds and make loans in larger amounts to consumers and businesses. The financial services provided by financial institutions are tailor-made to fit the needs of the markets they serve. Exhibit 2.3 illustrates how businesses use the financial system.

6 Compute the nominal and the real rates of interest, differentiating between them.

Equations 2.1 and 2.2 are used to compute the nominal (real) rate of interest when you have the real (nominal) rate and the inflation rate. The real rate of interest is the interest rate that would exist in the absence of inflation. It is determined by the interaction of (1) the rate of return that businesses can expect to earn on capital projects and (2) individuals' time preference for consumption. The interest rate we observe in the marketplace is called the nominal rate of interest. The nominal rate of interest is composed of two parts: (1) the real rate of interest and (2) the expected rate of inflation.

Summary of Key Equations

Equation	Description	Formula
2.1	Fisher equation	$1 + i = (1 + r) \times (1 + \Delta P_e)$ $i = r + \Delta P_e + r\Delta P_e$
2.2	Simplified or approximate Fisher equation	$i = r + \Delta P_e$

Self-Study Problems

2.1 Economic units that need to borrow money are said to be:

a. Lender-savers.

b. Borrower-spenders.

c. Balanced budget keepers.

d. None of the above.

2.2 Explain what the marketability of a security is and how it is determined.

2.3 What are over-the-counter markets (OTCs), and how do they differ from organized exchanges?

2.4 What effect does an increase in demand for business goods and services have on the real interest rate? What other factors can affect the real interest rate?

2.5 How does the business cycle affect the nominal interest rate and inflation rate?

2.6 You lent $100 to a friend for one year at a nominal rate of interest of 3 percent. Inflation during that year was 2 percent. Did you experience an increase or decrease in the purchasing power of your money? How much did it increase or decrease?

Solutions to Self-Study Problems

2.1 Such units are said to be: b. Borrower-spenders.

2.2 Marketability refers to the ease with which a security can be sold and converted into cash. The level of marketability depends on the cost of trading the security and the cost of searching for information. The lower these costs are, the greater the security's marketability.

2.3 Securities that are not listed on an organized exchange are sold OTC. An OTC market differs from an organized exchange in that there is no central trading location. OTC security transactions are made via phone or computer as opposed to on the floor of an exchange.

2.4 An increase in the demand for business goods and services will cause the borrowing schedule in Exhibit 2.4 to shift to the right, thus increasing the real rate of interest. Other factors that can affect the real interest rate include increases in productivity, changes in technology, or changes in the corporate tax rate. Demographic factors, such as growth or age of the population, and cultural differences can also affect the real rate of interest.

2.5 Both the nominal interest and inflation rates tend to follow the business cycle; that is, they rise with economic expansion and fall during a recession.

2.6 Since the interest rate that you received (3 percent) exceeded the rate of inflation, the amount that you received from your friend when the loan was repaid had greater purchasing power than $100. The amount by which the purchasing power increased can be calculated using Equation 2.1:

$$1 + i = (1 + r) \times (1 + \Delta P_e)$$

Solving for r yields:

$$r = (1 + i)/(1 + \Delta P_e) - 1$$

$$r = (1 + 0.03)/(1 + 0.02) - 1$$

$$r = 0.0098, \text{ or } 0.98\%$$

Therefore, the purchasing power increased by slightly less than 1 percent.

WileyPLUS

Questions and Problems, Solution Walkthrough Videos, Learning by Doing Tutorials, and additional study tools and resources are available in WileyPLUS.

Discussion Questions

2.1 Explain why total financial assets in the economy must equal total financial liabilities.

2.2 Why don't small businesses make greater use of the direct credit markets since these markets enable firms to finance their activities at a very low cost?

2.3 Explain the economic role of brokers and dealers. How does each make a profit?

2.4 Why were commercial banks prohibited from engaging in investment banking activities until 1999?

2.5 What are two basic services that investment banks provide in the economy?

2.6 How do large corporations adjust their liquidity in the money markets?

2.7 The CFO of a certain company always wears his green suit on a day that the firm is about to release positive information about his company. You believe that you can profit from this information by buying the firm's shares at the beginning of every day that the CFO shows up wearing this green suit. Describe which form of market efficiency is consistent with your belief.

2.8 Shouldn't the nominal rate of interest (Equation 2.1) be determined by the actual rate of inflation (ΔP_a), which can be easily measured, rather than by the expected rate of inflation (ΔP_e)?

2.9 How does Exhibit 2.5 help explain why interest rates were so high during the early 1980s as compared to the relatively low interest rates in the early 1960s?

2.10 When determining the real interest rate, what happens to businesses that find themselves with unfunded capital projects whose rate of return exceeds the cost of capital?

Questions and Problems

Excel *Excel templates and resources available in* **WileyPLUS**

Basic

2.1 **Financial system:** What is the role of the financial system, and what are the two major components of the financial system?

2.2 **Financial system:** What does a competitive financial system imply about interest rates?

2.3 **Financial system:** What is the difference between saver-lenders and borrower-spenders, and who are the major representatives of each group?

2.4 **Financial markets:** List the two ways in which a transfer of funds takes place in an economy. What is the main difference between these two?

2.5 **Financial markets:** Suppose you own a security that you know can be easily sold in the secondary market, but the security will sell at a lower price than you paid for it. What does this imply for the security's marketability and liquidity?

2.6 Financial markets: Why are direct financial markets also called wholesale markets?

2.7 Financial markets: Trader Inc. is a $300 million company, as measured by asset value, and Horst Corp. is a $35 million company. Both are privately held corporations. Explain which firm is more likely to go public and register with the SEC, and why.

2.8 Primary markets: What is a primary market? What does IPO stand for?

2.9 Primary market: Identify whether the following transactions are primary market or secondary market transactions.

a. Jim Hendry bought 300 shares of IBM through his brokerage account.

b. Peggy Jones bought $5,000 of General Motors bonds from another investor.

c. Hathaway Insurance Company bought 500,000 shares of Trigen Corp. when the company issued stock.

2.10 Investment banking: What does it mean to "underwrite" a new security issue? What compensation does an investment banker get from underwriting a security issue?

2.11 Investment banking: Cranjet Inc. is issuing 10,000 bonds, and its investment banker has guaranteed a price of $985 per bond. If the investment banker sells the entire issue to investors for $10,150,000:

a. What is the underwriting spread for this issue?

b. What is the percentage underwriting cost?

c. How much will Cranjet raise?

2.12 Financial institutions: What are some of the ways in which a financial institution or intermediary can raise money?

2.13 Financial institutions: How do financial institutions act as intermediaries to provide services to small businesses?

2.14 Financial institutions: Which financial institution is usually the most important to businesses?

2.15 Financial markets: What is the main difference between money markets and capital markets?

2.16 Money markets: What is the primary role of money markets? Explain how the money markets work.

2.17 Money markets: What are the main types of securities in the money markets?

2.18 Capital markets: How do capital market instruments differ from money market instruments?

2.19 Market efficiency: Describe the informational differences that distinguish the three forms of market efficiency.

2.20 Market efficiency: Zippy Computers announced strong fourth quarter results. Sales and earnings were both above analysts' expectations. You notice in the newspaper that Zippy's stock price went up sharply on the day of the announcement. If no other information about Zippy became public on the day of the announcement and the overall market was down, is this evidence of market efficiency?

2.21 Market efficiency: In Problem 2.20, if the market is efficient, would it have been possible for Zippy's stock price to go down in the day that the firm announced the strong fourth quarter results?

2.22 Market efficiency: If the market is strong-form efficient, then trading on tips you hear from Jim Cramer (the host of *Mad Money* on CNBC) will generate no excess returns (i.e., returns in excess of fair compensation for the risk you are bearing). True or false?

2.23 Financial markets: What are the major differences between public and private markets?

2.24 Financial instruments: What are the two risk-hedging instruments discussed in this chapter?

2.25 Interest rates: What is the real rate of interest, and how is it determined?

2.26 Interest rates: How does the nominal rate of interest vary over time?

2.27 Interest rates: What is the Fisher equation, and how is it used?

2.28 Interest rates: Imagine you borrow $500 from your roommate, agreeing to pay her back $500 plus 7 percent nominal interest in one year. Assume inflation over the life of the contract is expected to be 4.25 percent. What is the total dollar amount you will have to pay her back in a year? What percentage of the interest payment is the result of the real rate of interest?

2.29 Interest rates: Your parents gave you $1,000 a year before your graduation date so that you can take a trip when you graduate. You wisely decide to invest the money in a bank CD that pays 6.75 percent interest. You know that the trip costs $1,025 right now and that inflation for the year is predicted to be 4 percent. Will you have enough money in a year to purchase the trip?

2.30 Interest rates: When are the nominal and real interest rates equal?

Sample Test Problems

2.1 What are the two basic mechanisms through which funds flow through the financial system, and how do they differ?

2.2 You just purchased a share of IBM stock on the New York Stock Exchange. What kind of transaction was this?

a. Primary market transaction.

b. Secondary market transaction.

c. Futures market transaction.

d. Private placement.

2.3 How are brokers different from dealers?

2.4 List the three forms of the efficient market hypothesis, and describe what information is assumed to be reflected in security prices under each of these hypotheses.

2.5 If the nominal rate of interest is 4.25 percent and the expected rate of inflation is 1.75 percent, what is the real rate of interest?

2.6 What is the relation between business cycles and the general level of interest rates?

CHAPTER **3**

Financial Statements, Cash Flows, and Taxes

ROBYN BECK/AFP/Getty Images

LEARNING OBJECTIVES

1. Discuss generally accepted accounting principles (GAAP) and their importance to the economy.
2. Explain the balance sheet identity and why a balance sheet must balance.
3. Describe how market-value balance sheets differ from book-value balance sheets.
4. Identify the basic equation for the income statement and the information it provides.
5. Understand the calculation of cash flows from operating, investing, and financing activities required in the statement of cash flows.
6. Explain how the four major financial statements discussed in this chapter are related.
7. Identify the cash flow to a firm's investors using its financial statements.
8. Discuss the difference between average and marginal tax rates.

On October 16, 2016, after the close of U.S. financial markets, Tesla Motors Inc. announced that its corporate earnings for the third quarter of the year were $21.9 million or 14 cents per share. The news shocked both investors and Wall Street analysts who had forecast that the firm would lose money during the quarter. The performance was particularly surprising given that the maker of electric vehicles, including the popular Model S, had failed to earn a profit over the preceding 12 quarters. In a press release, Tesla attributed its financial results to unexpected revenue from California clean-car credits and record production and sales of its automobiles. Tesla's share price surged with the news, gaining nearly 5 percent in the hours following the earnings announcement.

This example illustrates the close relation between the information contained in a firm's accounting statements and its stock performance. Public corporations in the United States communicate their financial performance to their investors through their financial statements, leading to Wall Street's virtual obsession with accounting earnings. Analysts estimate what a firm's revenue should be and how much the firm should earn in a particular reporting period, and if the firm fails to meet these estimates it can be punished by a drop in its stock price. If a firm consistently fails to meet these estimates, its CEO can be out of a job. Pressure to meet analyst expectations has occasionally led managers to misstate accounting results in an attempt to mislead analysts and investors. In the wake of several large-scale accounting frauds, involving firms such as Enron and WorldCom, Congress and federal regulators tightened accounting standards and oversight of the accounting profession in the early 2000s. Passage of the Sarbanes-Oxley Act, discussed in Chapter 1, is an example of these steps.

Clearly, the correct preparation of financial statements is crucial for investors. In this chapter and the next, we focus on the preparation, interpretation, and limitations of financial statements. The concepts that we discuss in these chapters provide an important foundation for the material discussed in the rest of this book.

Chapter Preview

In Chapter 1 we noted that all businesses have owners and stakeholders—managers, creditors, suppliers, and the government, among others—who have claims on the firms' cash flows. The owners and stakeholders in a firm need to monitor the firm's progress and evaluate its performance. Financial statements enable them to do this. The accounting system is the framework that gathers information about the firm's business activities and translates the information into objective numerical financial reports.

Most firms prepare financial statements on a regular basis and have independent auditors certify that the financial statements have been prepared in accordance with generally accepted accounting principles and contain no material misstatements. The audit increases the confidence of the owners and stakeholders that the financial statements prepared by management present a "fair and accurate" picture of the firm's financial condition at a particular point in time. In fact, it is difficult to get any type of legitimate business loan without audited financial statements.

This chapter reviews the basic structure of a firm's financial statements and explains how the various statements fit together. It also explains the relation between accounting income and cash flow to investors. We begin by examining the preparation of the balance sheet, the income statement, the statement of retained earnings, and the statement of cash flows. As you read through this part of the chapter, pay particular attention to the differences between (1) book value and market value and (2) accounting income and cash flow to investors. Understanding the differences between these concepts is necessary to avoid serious analytical and decision-making errors. The last part of the chapter discusses essential features of the federal tax code for corporations. In finance we make most decisions on an after-tax basis, so understanding the tax code is very important.

3.1 Financial Statements and Accounting Principles

LEARNING OBJECTIVE

1. Discuss generally accepted accounting principles (GAAP) and their importance to the economy.

Before we can meaningfully interpret and analyze financial statements, we need to understand some accounting principles that guide their preparation. Thus, we begin the chapter with a discussion of generally accepted accounting principles, which guide firms in the preparation of financial statements. First, however, we briefly describe the annual report.

The Annual Report

The *annual report* is the most important report that firms issue to their stockholders and make available to the general public. Historically, annual reports were dull, black-and-white publications that presented audited financial statements for firms. Today some annual reports, especially those of large public companies, are slick, picture-laden, full-color documents with orchestrated media messages.

Weblink

To find annual reports and other corporate filings for U.S. corporations, visit the EDGAR search page maintained by the U.S. Securities and Exchange Commission (SEC) at http://www.sec.gov/edgar.shtml.

Annual reports typically are divided into three distinct sections. First are the financial tables, which contain financial information about the firm and its operations for the year, and an accompanying summary explaining the firm's performance over the past year. For example, the summary might explain that sales and profits were down because of declining consumer demand. Often, there is a letter from the chairperson or CEO that provides some insights into the reasons for the firm's performance, a discussion of new developments, and a high-level view of the firm's strategy and future direction. It is important to note that the financial tables are historical records reflecting past performance of the firm and do not necessarily indicate what the firm will do in the future.

The second part of the report is often a corporate public relations piece discussing the firm's product lines, its services to its customers, and its contributions to the communities in which it operates.

The third part of the annual report presents the audited financial statements: the balance sheet, the income statement, the statement of retained earnings, and the statement of cash flows. Overall, the annual report provides a good overview of the firm's operating and financial performance and states why, in management's judgment, things turned out the way they did.

Generally Accepted Accounting Principles

In the United States, accounting statements are prepared in accordance with **generally accepted accounting principles (GAAP)**, a set of widely agreed-upon rules and procedures that defines how companies are to maintain financial records and prepare financial reports. These principles are important because without them, financial statements would be less standardized. Accounting standards such as GAAP make it easier for analysts and management to make meaningful comparisons of a company's performance against that of other companies.

generally accepted accounting principles (GAAP) a set of rules that defines how companies are to prepare financial statements

Accounting principles and reporting practices for U.S. firms are promulgated by the Financial Accounting Standards Board (FASB), a not-for-profit body that operates in the public interest. FASB derives its authority from the Securities and Exchange Commission (SEC). GAAP and reporting practices are published in the form of FASB standards, and certified public accountants are required to follow these standards in their auditing and accounting practices.

Weblink

You can find more information about FASB at http://www.fasb.org.

Fundamental Accounting Principles

To better understand financial statements, it is helpful to look at some fundamental accounting principles embodied in GAAP. These principles determine the manner of recording, measuring, and reporting company transactions. As you will see, the practical application of these principles requires professional judgment, which can result in considerable differences in financial statements.

The Assumption of Arm's-Length Transactions

Accounting is based on the recording of economic transactions that can be quantified in dollar amounts. It assumes that the parties to a transaction are economically rational and are free to act *independently* of each other. In other words, all transactions are assumed to be "arm's-length transactions." The price you pay for something or the price for which you sell something is what gets recorded on the financial statements. To illustrate, let's assume that you are preparing a personal balance sheet for a bank loan on which you must list all your assets. You are including your BMW 325 as an asset. You bought the car a few months ago from your father for $3,000 when the market value of the car was $15,000. You got a good deal. However, the price you paid, which would be the number recorded on your balance sheet, was not the market value. Since you did not purchase the BMW in an arm's-length transaction, your balance sheet would not reflect the true value of the asset.

The Cost Principle

Generally, the value of an asset that is recorded on a company's "books" reflects its historical cost. The historical cost is assumed to represent the fair market value of the item at the time it was acquired and is recorded as the **book value**. Over time, it is unlikely that an asset's book value will be equal to its market value because market values tend to change over time. The major exception to this principle is marketable securities, such as the stock of another company, which are recorded at their current market value.

book value the net value of an asset or liability recorded on the financial statements—normally reflects historical cost

It is important to note that accounting statements are records of past performance; they are based on historical costs, not on current market prices or values. Accounting statements translate the business's past performance into dollars and cents, which helps management and investors better understand how the business has performed in the past.

The Realization Principle

Under the realization principle, revenue is recognized only when the sale is virtually completed and the exchange value for the goods or services can be reliably determined. As a practical matter, this means that most revenues are recognized at the time of sale whether or not cash is actually received. At this time, if a firm sells to its customers on credit, an account receivable is recorded. The firm receives the cash only when the customer actually makes the payment. Although the realization principle seems straightforward, there can be considerable ambiguity in its interpretation. For example, should revenues be recognized when goods are ordered, when they are shipped, or when payment is received from the customer?

The Matching Principle

Accountants try to match revenue on the income statement with the expenses incurred to generate the revenue. In practice, this matching principle means that revenue is first recognized (according to the realization principle) and then is matched with the costs associated with producing the revenue. For example, if we manufacture a product and sell it on credit (accounts receivable), the revenue is recognized at the time of sale. The expenses associated with manufacturing the product—expenditures for raw materials, labor, equipment, and facilities—are recognized at the same time. Notice that the actual cash outflows for expenses may not occur at the same time the expenses are recognized. The figures on the income statement more than likely will not correspond to the actual cash inflows and outflows during the period.

The Going Concern Assumption

The going concern assumption is the assumption that a business will remain in operation for the foreseeable future. This assumption underlies much of what is done in accounting. For example, suppose that Sears has $4.6 billion of inventory on its balance sheet, representing what the firm actually paid for the inventory in arm's-length transactions. If we assume that Sears is a going concern, the balance sheet figure is a reasonable number because in the normal course of business we expect Sears to be able to sell the goods for their cost plus some reasonable markup.

However, suppose Sears declares bankruptcy and is forced by its creditors to liquidate its assets. If this happens, Sears is no longer a going concern. What will the inventory be worth then? We cannot be certain, but 50 cents on the dollar might be a high figure. The going concern assumption allows the accountant to record assets at cost rather than their value in a liquidation sale, which is usually much less.

You can see that the fundamental accounting principles just discussed leave considerable professional discretion to accountants in the preparation of financial statements. As a result, financial statements can and do differ because of honest differences in professional judgments. Of course, there are limits on honest professional differences, and at some point an accountant's choices can cross a line and result in "cooking the books."

International GAAP

Accounting is often called the language of business. Just as there are different dialects within languages, there are different international "dialects" in accounting. For example, the set of generally accepted accounting principles in the United Kingdom is called U.K. GAAP. Given the variation in accounting standards, accountants must adjust financial statements so that meaningful comparisons can be made between firms that utilize different accounting principles. The cost of making these adjustments represents an economic inefficiency that adds to the overall cost of international business transactions.

By the end of the 1990s, the two predominant international reporting standards were the U.S. GAAP and the International Financial Reporting Standards, also known as IFRS. Both FASB and the International Accounting Standards Board (IASB) have been working toward a convergence of these rules in an effort to provide a truly global accounting standard. Today most international jurisdictions utilize IFRS or some close variant of those standards. Consistent with these practices, the U.S. SEC has been reviewing proposals for U.S. corporations to adopt IFRS for financial reporting, but to date there has been no move to change the accounting standard from U.S. GAAP.

Weblink

You can read more about IFRS at http://www.ifrs.com.

Illustrative Company: Diaz Manufacturing

In the next part of this chapter, we turn to a discussion of four fundamental financial statements: the balance sheet, the income statement, the statement of retained earnings, and the statement of cash flows. To more clearly illustrate these financial statements, we use data from Diaz Manufacturing Company, a fictional Houston-based provider of petroleum and industrial equipment and services worldwide.[1] Diaz Manufacturing was formed in 2013 as a spin-off of several divisions of a large multinational corporation. The firm specializes in the design and manufacturing of systems used in petroleum production and has two divisions: (1) Diaz Energy Services, which sells oil and gas compression equipment, and (2) Diaz Manufacturing, which makes valves and related parts for energy production.

In 2017 Diaz Manufacturing's sales were $1.56 billion, an increase of 12.8 percent from the previous year. A letter to stockholders in the 2017 annual report stated that management did not expect earnings in 2018 to exceed the 2017 earnings. The reason for caution was that Diaz's earnings are very susceptible to changes in the political and economic environment in the world's energy-producing regions, and in 2017 the environment in the Middle East was highly unstable. Management reassured investors, however, that Diaz had the financial strength and the management team needed to weather any economic adversity.

Before You Go On

1. What types of information does a firm's annual report contain?
2. What is the realization principle, and why may it lead to a difference in the timing of when revenues are recognized on the books and cash is collected?

3.2 The Balance Sheet

LEARNING OBJECTIVE

2. Explain the balance sheet identity and why a balance sheet must balance.

The **balance sheet** reports the firm's financial position at a particular point in time. **Exhibit 3.1** shows the balance sheets for Diaz Manufacturing on December 31, 2016, and December 31, 2017. The left-hand side of the balance sheet identifies the firm's assets, which are listed at book value. These assets are owned by the firm and are used to generate income. The right-hand side of the balance sheet includes liabilities and stockholders' equity, which tell us how the firm has financed its assets. Liabilities are obligations of the firm that represent claims against its assets. These claims arise from

balance sheet a financial statement that shows a firm's financial position (assets, liabilities, and equity) at a point in time

[1]Although Diaz Manufacturing Company is not a real firm, the financial statements and situations presented are based on a composite of actual firms.

EXHIBIT 3.1 Diaz Manufacturing Balance Sheets as of December 31 ($ millions)

The left-hand side of the balance sheet lists the assets that the firm has at a particular point in time, while the right-hand side shows how the firm has financed those assets.

Assets	2017	2016	Liabilities and Stockholders' Equity	2017	2016
Cash[a]	$ 288.5	$ 16.6	Accounts payable and accruals	$ 349.3	$ 325.0
Accounts receivable	306.2	268.8	Notes payable	10.5	4.2
Inventories	423.8	372.7	Accured taxes	18.0	16.8
Other current assets	21.3	29.9	Total current liabilities	$ 377.8	$ 346.0
Total current assets	$1,039.8	$ 688.0	Long-term debt	574.0	305.6
			Total liabilities	$ 951.8	$ 651.6
Plant and equipment	911.6	823.3	Preferred stock[b]	—	—
Less: Accumulated depreciation	512.2	429.1	Common stock (54,566,054 shares)[c]	50.0	50.0
Net plant and equipment	$ 399.4	$ 394.2	Additional paid-in capital	842.9	842.9
			Retained earning	67.8	(50.7)
Goodwill and other assets	450.0	411.6	Treasury stock (571,320 shares)	(23.3)	—
			Total stockholders equity	$ 937.4	$ 842.2
Total assets	$1,889.2	$1,493.8	Total liabilities and equity	$1,889.2	$1,493.8

[a]Cash includes investments in marketable securities.
[b]10,000,000 preferred stock shares authorized.
[c]150,000,000 common stock shares authorized.

debts and other obligations to pay creditors, employees, or the government. In contrast, stockholders' equity represents the residual claim of the owners on the remaining assets of the firm after all liabilities have been paid.[2] The basic balance sheet identity can thus be stated as follows:[3]

$$\text{Total assets} = \text{Total liabilities} + \text{Total stockholders' equity} \tag{3.1}$$

Weblink

You can go to Yahoo! Finance to obtain financial statements and other information about public companies at http://finance.yahoo.com.

Since stockholders' equity is the residual claim, stockholders would receive any remaining value if the firm decided to sell off all of its assets and use the money to pay its creditors. That is why the balance sheet always balances. Simply put, if you total what the firm owns and what it owes, then the difference between the two is the total stockholders' equity:

$$\text{Total stockholders' equity} = \text{Total assets} - \text{Total liabilities}$$

Notice that total stockholders' equity can be positive, negative, or equal to zero.

It is important to note that balance sheet items are listed in a specific order. Assets are listed in order of their liquidity, with the most liquid assets, cash and marketable securities, at the top. The liquidity of an asset is defined by how quickly it can be converted into cash without loss of value. Thus, an asset's liquidity has two dimensions: (1) the speed and ease with which the asset can be sold and (2) whether the asset can be sold without loss of value. Of course, any asset can be sold easily and quickly if the price is low enough. Liabilities on the balance sheet are listed based on their maturity, with the liabilities having the shortest maturities listed at the top. Maturity refers to the length of time remaining before the obligation must be paid.

Next, we examine some important balance sheet accounts of Diaz Manufacturing as of December 31, 2017 (see Exhibit 3.1). As a matter of convention, accountants classify assets and liabilities as short-term (or current) or long-term. We will start by looking at current assets and liabilities.

[2]The terms *owners' equity, stockholders' equity, shareholders' equity, net worth, and equity* are used interchangeably to refer to the ownership of a corporation's stock.
[3]An *identity* is an equation that is true by definition; thus, a balance sheet must balance.

Current Assets and Liabilities

Current assets are assets that can reasonably be expected to be converted into cash within one year. Besides cash, which includes investments in marketable securities such as money market instruments, other current assets are accounts receivable, which are typically due within 30 to 45 days, and inventory, which is money invested in raw materials, work-in-process inventory, and finished goods. Diaz's current assets at the end of 2017 totaled \$1,039.8 million.

Current liabilities are obligations payable within one year. Typical current liabilities are accounts payable, which arise in the purchases of goods and services from vendors and are normally paid within 30 to 45 days; notes payable, which are formal borrowing agreements with a bank or some other lender that have a stated maturity; and accrued taxes from federal, state, and local governments, which are taxes Diaz owes but has not yet paid. Diaz's total current liabilities were \$377.8 million at the end of 2017.

Net Working Capital

Recall from Chapter 1 that the dollar difference between total current assets and total current liabilities is the firm's net working capital:

$$\text{Net working capital} = \text{Total current assets} - \text{Total current liabilities} \tag{3.2}$$

Net working capital is a measure of a firm's ability to meet its short-term obligations as they come due. One way that firms maintain their liquidity is by holding more current assets than current liabilities.

For Diaz Manufacturing, total current assets at the end of 2017 were \$1,039.8 million, and total current liabilities were \$377.8 million. The firm's net working capital was thus:

$$\begin{aligned}\text{Net working capital} &= \text{Total current assets} - \text{Total current liabilities}\\ &= \$1{,}039.8 \text{ million} - \$377.8 \text{ million}\\ &= \$662.0 \text{ million}\end{aligned}$$

To interpret this number, if Diaz Manufacturing took its current stock of cash and liquidated its marketable securities, accounts receivables, and inventory at book value, it would have \$1,039.8 million with which to pay off its short-term liabilities of \$377.8 million, leaving \$662.0 million of "cushion." As a short-term creditor, such as a bank, you would have a positive view of the net working capital position of Diaz because current assets exceed current liabilities by almost three times (\$1,039.8/\$377.8 = 2.75).

Accounting for Inventory

Inventory, as noted earlier, is a current asset on the balance sheet, but it is usually the least liquid of the current assets. The reason is that it can take a long time for a firm to convert inventory into cash. For a manufacturing firm, the inventory cycle begins with raw materials, continues with goods in process, proceeds with finished goods, and finally concludes with selling the asset for cash or an account receivable. For a firm such as The Boeing Company, for example, the inventory cycle in manufacturing an aircraft can be nearly a year.

An important decision for management is the selection of an inventory valuation method. The most common methods are FIFO (first in, first out) and LIFO (last in, first out). During periods of changing price levels, how a firm values its inventory affects both its balance sheet and its income statement. For example, suppose that prices have been rising (inflation). If a company values its inventory using the FIFO method, when the firm makes a sale, it assumes the sale is from the oldest, lowest-cost inventory—first in, first out. Thus, during rising prices, firms using FIFO will have the lowest cost of goods sold, the highest net income, and the highest inventory value. In contrast, a company using the LIFO method assumes the sale is from the newest, highest-cost inventory—last in, first out. During a period of inflation, firms using LIFO will have the highest cost of goods sold, the lowest net income, and the lowest inventory value.

Because inventory valuation methods can have a significant impact on both the income statement and the balance sheet, when financial analysts compare different companies, they make adjustments for differences in inventory valuation methods. Although firms can switch from one inventory valuation method to another, this type of change is an extraordinary event and cannot be done frequently.

Diaz Manufacturing reports inventory values in the United States using the LIFO method. The remaining inventories, which are located outside the United States and Canada, are calculated using the FIFO method. Diaz's total inventory is $423.8 million at the end of 2017.

Long-Term Assets and Liabilities

The remaining assets on the balance sheet are classified as long-term assets. Typically, these assets are financed by long-term liabilities and stockholders' equity.

Long-Term Assets

Long-term (productive) assets are the assets that the firm uses to generate most of its income. Long-term assets may be tangible or intangible. Tangible assets are balance sheet items such as land, mineral resources, buildings, equipment, machinery, and vehicles that are used over an extended period of time. In addition, tangible assets can include other businesses that a firm wholly or partially owns, such as foreign subsidiaries. Intangible assets are items such as patents, copyrights, licensing agreements, technology, and other intellectual capital the firm owns.

Goodwill is an intangible asset that arises only when a firm purchases another firm. Conceptually, goodwill is a measure of how much the price paid for the acquired firm exceeds the sum of the values of the acquired firm's individual assets. There are a variety of reasons why the purchase price of an asset might exceed its value to the seller. Goodwill may arise from improvements in efficiency, the reputation or brands associated with products or trademarks, or even a valuable client base for a particular service. For example, if Diaz Manufacturing paid $2.0 million for a company that had individual assets with a total fair market value of $1.9 million, the goodwill paid would be $100,000 ($2.0 million − $1.9 million = $0.1 million).

Diaz Manufacturing's long-term assets at the end of 2017 included net plant and equipment of $399.4 million and intangible and other assets of $450.0 million, as shown in Exhibit 3.1. The term *net plant and equipment* indicates that accumulated depreciation has been subtracted to arrive at the net value. That is, net plant and equipment equals total plant and equipment less accumulated depreciation; accumulated depreciation is the total amount of depreciation expense taken on plant and equipment up to the balance sheet date. For Diaz Manufacturing, net plant and equipment for 2017 is calculated as follows:

$$\begin{aligned}\text{Net plant and equipment} &= \text{Total plant and equipment} - \text{Accumulated depreciation}\\ &= \$911.6 \text{ million} - \$512.2 \text{ million}\\ &= \$399.4 \text{ million}\end{aligned}$$

Accumulated Depreciation

depreciation the allocation of the cost of an asset over its estimated useful life to reflect the wear and tear on the asset as it is used to produce the firm's goods and services

When a firm acquires a tangible asset that deteriorates with use and wears out, accountants try to allocate the asset's cost over its estimated useful life. The matching principle requires that the cost be expensed during the period in which the firm benefited from use of the asset. Thus, **depreciation** allocates the cost of a limited-life asset to the periods in which the firm is assumed to benefit from the asset. Tangible assets with an unlimited life, such as land, are not depreciated. Depreciation affects the balance sheet through the accumulated depreciation account; we discuss its effect on the income statement in Section 3.4.

Management of a company can elect whether to depreciate its assets using straight-line depreciation or one of the approved accelerated depreciation methods. All of these methods allow the same amount of total depreciation over an asset's life. However, accelerated depreciation methods allow for more depreciation expense in the early years of an asset's life than straight-line depreciation.

Diaz Manufacturing uses the straight-line method of depreciation. Had Diaz elected to use accelerated depreciation, the value of its depreciable assets would have been written off to the income statement more quickly as a higher depreciation expense, which results in a lower net plant and equipment account on its balance sheet and a lower net income for the period.

Long-Term Liabilities

Long-term liabilities include debt instruments due and payable beyond one year as well as other long-term obligations of the firm. They include bonds, bank term loans, mortgages, and other types of liabilities, such as pension obligations and deferred compensation. Typically, firms finance long-term assets with long-term liabilities. Diaz Manufacturing has a single long-term liability of $574.0 million at the end of 2017, which is a long-term debt.

Equity

We have summarized the types of assets and liabilities that appear on the balance sheet. Now we look at the equity accounts. Diaz Manufacturing's total stockholders' equity at the end of 2017 is $937.4 million and is made up of four accounts—common stock, additional paid-in capital, retained earnings, and treasury stock—which we discuss next. We conclude with a discussion of preferred stock. Although a line item for preferred stock appears on Diaz Manufacturing's balance sheets, the company has no shares of preferred stock outstanding.

The Common Stock Accounts

The most important equity accounts are those related to common stock, which represent the true ownership of the firm. Certain basic rights of ownership typically come with common stock; those rights are as follows:

1. The right to vote on corporate matters, such as the election of the board of directors or important actions such as the purchase of another company.
2. The preemptive right, which allows stockholders to purchase any additional shares of stock issued by the corporation in proportion to the number of shares they currently own. This allows common stockholders to retain the same percentage of ownership in the firm, if they choose to do so.
3. The right to receive cash dividends if they are paid.
4. If the firm is liquidated, the right to all remaining corporate assets after all creditors and preferred stockholders have been paid.

A common source of confusion is the number of different common stock accounts on the balance sheet, each of which identifies a source of the firm's equity. The *common stock account* identifies the funding from equity investors that was used to start and maintain the business and is priced at a par value. The par value is an arbitrary number set by management, usually a nominal amount such as $1.

Clearly, par value has little to do with the market value of the stock when it is sold to investors. The *additional paid-in capital* is the amount of capital received from the sale of common stock in excess of par value. Thus, for example, if a new business is started with $40,000 from the sale of 1,000 shares of common stock with a par value of $1, the owners' equity account looks as follows:

Common stock (1,000 shares @ $1 par value)	$ 1,000
Additional paid-in capital	39,000
Total paid-in capital	$40,000

Note the money put up by the initial investors: $1,000 in total par value (1,000 shares of common stock with a par value of $1) and $39,000 additional paid-in capital, for a total of $40,000.

As you can see in Exhibit 3.1, Diaz manufacturing has 54,566,054 shares of common stock with a par value of 91.63 cents, for a total value of $50.0 million (54,566,054 shares ×

91.63 cents = $50 million). The additional paid-in capital is $842.9 million. Thus, Diaz's total paid-in capital is $892.9 million ($50.0 million + $842.9 million = $892.9 million).

Retained Earnings

The retained earnings account represents earnings that have been retained and reinvested in the business over time rather than being paid out as cash dividends. The change in retained earnings from one period to the next can be computed as the difference between net income and dividends paid. Diaz Manufacturing's retained earnings account is $67.8 million in 2017. Reading the annual report, we learn that in the recent past the company "wrote down" the value of a substantial amount of assets. This transaction, which will be discussed later in this chapter, reduced the size of the retained earnings account by reducing net income.

Note that retained earnings are not the same as cash. In fact, as we discuss in Section 3.7 of this chapter, a company can have a very large retained earnings account and no cash. Conversely, it can have a lot of cash and a very small retained earnings account. Because retained earnings appear on the liability side of the balance sheet, they do not represent an asset, as do cash and marketable securities.

Treasury Stock

treasury stock stock that the firm has repurchased from investors

The **treasury stock** account represents stock that the firm has repurchased from investors. Publicly traded companies can simply buy shares of stock from stockholders on the market at the prevailing price. Typically, repurchased stock is held as "treasury stock," and the firm can reissue it in the future if it desires. Diaz Manufacturing has spent a total of $23.3 million during 2017 to repurchase the 571,320 shares of common stock it currently holds as treasury stock. The company has had a policy of repurchasing common stock, which has been subsequently reissued to senior executives under the firm's stock-option plan.

You may wonder why a firm's management would repurchase its own stock. This is a classic finance question, and it has no simple answer. One reason is that when a company has excess cash and management believes its stock price is undervalued, it makes sense to purchase stock with the cash. We discuss this in more detail in Chapter 17.

Preferred Stock

Preferred stock is a cross between common stock and long-term debt. Preferred stock pays dividends at a specified fixed rate, which means that the firm cannot increase or decrease the dividend rate, regardless of whether the firm's earnings increase or decrease. However, like common stock dividends, preferred stock dividends are declared by the board of directors, and in the event of financial distress, the board can elect not to pay a preferred stock dividend. If preferred stock dividends are not paid, the firm is typically required to pay dividends that have been skipped in the past before they can pay dividends to common stockholders. In the event of bankruptcy, preferred stockholders are paid before common stockholders but after bondholders and other creditors. As shown in Exhibit 3.1, Diaz Manufacturing has no preferred stock outstanding, but the company is authorized to issue up to 10 million shares of preferred stock.

Before You Go On

1. What is net working capital? Why might a low value for this number be considered undesirable?
2. Explain the accounting concept behind depreciation.
3. What is treasury stock?

3.3 Market Value versus Book Value

LEARNING OBJECTIVE

3. Describe how market-value balance sheets differ from book-value balance sheets.

Although accounting statements are helpful to analysts and managers, they have a number of limitations. One of these limitations, mentioned earlier, is that accounting statements are historical—they are based on data such as the cost of a building that was built years ago. Thus, the value of assets on the balance sheet is generally what the firm paid for them and not their current **market value**—the amount they are worth today.

market value the price at which an item can be sold

Investors and management, however, care about how the company will do in the future. The best information concerning how much a company's assets can earn in the future, as well as how much of a burden its liabilities are, comes from the current market value of those assets and liabilities. Accounting statements would therefore be more valuable if they measured current value. The process of recording assets at their current market value is often called *marking to market.*

In theory, everyone agrees that it is better to base financial statements on current information. Marking to market provides decision makers with financial statements that more closely reflect a company's true financial condition; thus, they have a better chance of making the correct economic decision, given the information available. For example, providing current market values means that managers can no longer conceal a failing business or hide unrealized gains on assets.

Weblink

For some perspective on mark-to-market accounting, go to http://www.investopedia.com/articles/fundamental-analysis/09/mark-to-market-accounting.asp.

On the downside, it can be difficult to identify the market value of an asset, particularly if there are few transactions involving comparable assets. Critics also point out that estimating market value can require complex financial modeling, and the resulting numbers can be open to manipulation and abuse. Finally, mark-to-market accounting can become inaccurate if market prices deviate from the "fundamental" values of assets and liabilities. This might occur because buyers and sellers have either incorrect information or overally optimistic or overally pessimistic expectations about the future.

A More Informative Balance Sheet

To illustrate why market value provides better economic information than book value, let's revisit the balance sheet components discussed earlier. Our discussion will also help you understand why there can be such large differences between some book-value and market-value balance sheet accounts.

Assets

For current assets, market value and book value may be reasonably close. The reason is that current assets have a short life cycle and typically are converted into cash quickly. Then, as new current assets are added to the balance sheet, they are entered at their current market price.

In contrast, long-term assets, which are also referred to as fixed assets, have a long life cycle and their market value and book value are not likely to be equal. In addition, if an asset is depreciable, the amount of depreciation shown on the balance sheet does not necessarily reflect the actual loss of economic value. As a general rule, the longer the time that has passed since an asset was acquired, the more likely it is that the current market value will differ from the book value.

For example, suppose a firm purchased land for a trucking depot in Atlanta, Georgia, 30 years ago for $100,000. Today the land is nestled in an expensive suburban area and is worth $5.5 million. The difference between the book value of $100,000 and the market value is $5.4 million.

Liabilities

The market value of liabilities can also differ from their book value, though typically by smaller amounts than is the case with assets. For liabilities, the balance sheet shows the amount of money that the company has promised to pay. This figure is generally close to the actual market value for short-term liabilities because of their relatively short maturities.

For long-term debt, however, book value and market value can differ substantially. The market value of debt with fixed interest payments is affected by the level of interest rates in the economy. More specifically, after long-term debt is issued, if the market rate of interest increases, the market value of the debt will decline. Conversely, if interest rates decline, the value of the debt will increase. For example, assume that a firm has $1 million of 20-year bonds outstanding. If the market rate of interest increases from 5 to 8 percent, the price of the bonds will decline to around $700,000.[4] Thus, changes in interest rates can have an important effect on the market values of long-term liabilities, such as corporate bonds. Even if interest rates do not change, the market value of long-term liabilities can change if the performance of the firm declines and the probability of default increases.

Stockholders' Equity

The book value of the firm's equity is one of the least informative items on the balance sheet. The book value of equity, as suggested earlier, is simply a historical record. As a result, it says very little about the current market value of the stockholders' stake in the firm.

In contrast, on a balance sheet where both assets and liabilities are marked-to-market, the firm's equity is more informative to management and investors. *The difference between the market values of the assets and liabilities provides a better estimate of the market value of stockholders' equity than the difference in the book values.* Intuitively, this makes sense because if you know the true market values of the firm's assets and liabilities, the difference must equal the market value of the stockholders' equity.

You should be aware, however, that the difference between the sum of the market values of the individual assets and total liabilities will not give us an exact estimate of the market value of stockholders' equity. The reason is that the total value of a firm's assets depends on how these assets are utilized. By utilizing the assets efficiently, management can make the total value greater than the simple sum of the individual asset values. We will discuss this idea in more detail in Chapter 18.

Finally, if you know the market value of the stockholders' equity and the number of shares of stock outstanding, it is easy to compute the stock price. Specifically, the price of a share of stock is the market value of the firm's stockholders' equity divided by the number of shares outstanding.

A Market-Value Balance Sheet

Let's look at an example of how a market-value balance sheet can differ from a book-value balance sheet. Marvel Airline is a small regional carrier that has been serving the Northeast for five years. The airline has a fleet of short-haul jet aircraft, most of which were purchased over the past two years. The fleet has a book value of $600 million. Recently, the airline industry has suffered substantial losses in revenue due to price competition, and most carriers are projecting operating losses for the foreseeable future. As a result, the market value of Marvel's aircraft fleet is only $400 million. The book value of Marvel's long-term debt is $300 million, which is near its current market value. The firm has 100 million shares outstanding. Using these data, we can construct two balance sheets, one based on historical book values and the other based on market values:

Marvel Airlines
Book-Value versus Market-Value Balance Sheets ($ millions)

Assets			Liabilities and Stockholders' Equity		
	Book	**Market**		**Book**	**Market**
Aircraft	$600	$400	Long-term debt	$300	$300
			Stockholders' equity	300	100
Total	$600	$400		$600	$400

[4]We will discuss how changes in interest rates affect the market price of debt in Chapter 8, so for now don't worry about the numerical calculation.

Based on the book-value balance sheet, the firm's financial condition looks fine; the book value of Marvel's aircraft at $600 million reflects what the firm paid, and the stockholders' equity account is $300 million. But when we look at the market-value balance sheet, a different story emerges. We immediately see that the value of the aircraft has declined by $200 million and the stockholders' equity has declined by $200 million!

Why the decline in stockholders' equity? Recall that in Chapter 1 we argued that the value of any asset—stocks, bonds, or a firm—is determined by the future cash flows the asset will generate. At the time the aircraft were purchased, it was expected that they would generate a certain amount of cash flow over time. Now that hard times plague the industry, the cash flow expectations have been lowered, leading to a decline in the value of stockholders' equity.

Learning by Doing Application 3.1 presents another example of a market-value balance sheet and what it tells us.

APPLICATION 3.1 | The Market-Value Balance Sheet

LEARNING BY DOING

WileyPLUS

Need more help? Visit your WileyPLUS course.

Problem Grady Means and his four partners in Menlo Park Consulting (MPC) have developed a revolutionary new continuous audit program that can monitor high-risk areas within a firm and identify abnormalities so that corrective actions can be taken. The partners have spent about $300,000 developing the program. The firm's bookkeeper records the audit program on the firm's balance sheet as an asset valued at cost, which is $300,000. To launch the product, the four partners recently invested an additional $1 million, and the money is currently in the firm's bank account. At a recent trade show, a number of accounting and financial consulting firms tried to buy the new continuous product—the highest offer being $15 million. Assuming these are MPC's only assets and liabilities, prepare the firm's book-value and market-value balance sheets and explain the difference between the two.

Approach The main differences between the two balance sheets will be the treatment of the $300,000 already spent to develop the program and the $15 million offer. The book-value balance sheet is a historical document, which means all assets are valued at what it cost to put them in service, while the market-value balance sheet reflects the value of the assets if they were sold under current market conditions. The differences between the two approaches can be considerable.

Solution The two balance sheets are as follows:

Menlo Park Consulting
Book-Value versus Market-Value Balance Sheets ($ thousands)

Assets			Liabilities and Stockholders' Equity		
	Book	Market		Book	Market
Cash in bank	$1,000	$ 1,000	Long-term debt	$ —	$ —
Intangible assets	300	15,000	Stockholders' equity	1,300	16,000
Total	$1,300	$16,000		$1,300	$16,000

The book-value balance sheet provides little useful information. The book value of the firm's total assets is $1.3 million, which consists of cash in the bank and the cost of developing the audit program. Since the firm has no debt, total assets must equal the book value of stockholders' equity. The market value tells a dramatically different story. The market value of the audit program is estimated to be $15.0 million; thus, the market value of stockholders' equity is $16.0 million and not $1.3 million as reported in the book-value balance sheet.

Before You Go On

1. What is the difference between book value and market value?
2. What are some objections to the preparation of marked-to-market balance sheets?

3.4 The Income Statement and the Statement of Retained Earnings

LEARNING OBJECTIVE

4. Identify the basic equation for the income statement and the information it provides.

In the previous sections, we examined a firm's balance sheet, which is like a financial snapshot of the firm at a point in time. In contrast, the income statement illustrates the flow of operating activity and tells us how profitable a firm was between two points in time.

The Income Statement

income statement a financial statement that reports a firm's revenues, expenses, and profits or losses over a period of time

The **income statement** summarizes the revenues, expenses, and profitability (or losses) of the firm over some period of time, usually a month, a quarter, or a year. The basic equation for the income statement can be expressed as follows:

$$\text{Net income} = \text{Revenues} - \text{Expenses} \tag{3.3}$$

Let's look more closely at each element in this equation.

Revenues

A firm's revenues (sales) arise from the products and services it creates through its business operations. For manufacturing and merchandising companies, revenues come from the sale of merchandise. Service companies, such as consulting firms, generate fees for the services they perform. Other kinds of businesses earn revenues by charging interest or collecting rent. Regardless of how they earn revenues, most firms either receive cash or create an account receivable for each transaction.

Expenses

Expenses are the various costs that the firm incurs to generate revenues. Broadly speaking, expenses are (1) the value of long-term assets consumed through business operations, such as depreciation expense, and (2) the costs incurred in conducting business, such as labor, utilities, materials, and taxes.

Net Income

earnings per share (EPS) net income divided by the number of common shares outstanding

The firm's net income reflects its accomplishments (revenues) relative to its efforts (expenses) during a time period. If revenues exceed expenses, the firm generates net income for the period. If expenses exceed revenues, the firm has a net loss. Net income is often referred to as profits, as income, or simply as the "bottom line," since it is the last item on the income statement. Net income is often reported on a per-share basis and is then called **earnings per share (EPS)**, where EPS equals net income divided by the number of common shares outstanding. A firm's earnings per share tell a stockholder how much the firm has earned (or lost) for each share of stock outstanding.

Income statements for Diaz Manufacturing for 2016 and 2017 are shown in **Exhibit 3.2**. You can see that in 2017 total revenues from all sources (net sales) were $1,563.7 million. Total expenses for producing and selling those goods were $1,445.2 million—the total of the amounts for cost of goods sold, selling and administrative expenses, depreciation, interest expense, and taxes.[5]

[5]Looking at Exhibit 3.2, we find that the total expenses (in millions) are as follows: $1,081.1 + $231.1 + $83.1 + $5.6 + $44.3 = $1,445.2.

EXHIBIT 3.2 **Diaz Manufacturing Income Statements for the Fiscal Year Ending December 31 ($ millions)**

The income statement shows the sales, expenses, and profit earned by the firm over a specific period of time.

	2017	2016
Net sales[a]	$1,563.7	$1,386.7
Cost of goods sold	1,081.1	974.8
Selling and administrative expenses	231.1	197.4
Earnings before interest, taxes, depreciation, and amortization (EBITDA)	$ 251.5	$ 214.5
Depreciation and amortization	83.1	75.3
Earnings before interest and taxes (EBIT)	$ 168.4	$ 139.2
Interest expense	5.6	18.0
Earnings before taxes (EBT)	$ 162.8	$ 121.2
Taxes	44.3	16.1
Net income	$ 118.5	$ 105.1
Common stock dividend	—	—
Addition to retained earnings	$ 118.5	$ 105.1
Per-share data:		
Common stock price		
Earnings per share (EPS)	$ 2.17	$ 1.93
Dividends per share (DPS)	—	—
Book value per share (BVPS)	—	—
Cash flow per share (CFPS)	$ 3.69	$ 3.31

[a]Net sales is defined as total sales less all sales discounts and sales returns and allowances.

Using Equation 3.3, we can use these numbers to calculate Diaz Manufacturing's net income for the year:

$$\begin{aligned}\text{Net income} &= \text{Revenues} - \text{Expenses}\\ &= \$1{,}563.7\text{ million} - \$1{,}445.2\text{ million}\\ &= \$118.5\text{ million}\end{aligned}$$

Since Diaz Manufacturing had 54,566,054 common shares outstanding at year's end, its EPS was $2.17 per share ($118.5 million/54,566,054 shares = $2.17 per share).

A Closer Look at Some Expense Categories

Next, we take a closer look at some of the expense items on the income statement. We discussed depreciation earlier in relation to the balance sheet, and we now look at the role of depreciation expense in the income statement.

Depreciation Expense. An interesting feature of financial reporting is that companies are allowed to prepare two sets of financial statements: one for tax purposes and one for financial reporting to the SEC and investors. For tax purposes, most firms elect to accelerate depreciation as quickly as is permitted under the tax code. The reason is that accelerated depreciation results in a higher depreciation expense to the income statement, which in turn results in a lower earnings before taxes (EBT) and a lower tax liability in the first few years after the asset is acquired. The good news about accelerating depreciation for tax purposes is that the firm pays lower taxes but the depreciation expense does not represent a cash flow. The depreciation method does not affect the cost of the asset. In contrast, straight-line depreciation results in lower depreciation expenses to the income statement, which results in higher EBT and higher tax payments. Firms generally use straight-line depreciation in the financial statements they report to the SEC and investors because it makes their earnings look better. The higher a firm's EBT, the higher its net income.

It is important to understand that, as we noted earlier, the company does not take more total depreciation under accelerated depreciation methods than under the straight-line method;

the total amount of depreciation expensed to the income statement over the life of an asset is the same. Total depreciation cannot exceed the price paid for the asset. Accelerating depreciation only alters the timing of when the depreciation is expensed.

Amortization Expense. Amortization is the process of writing off expenses for intangible assets—such as patents, licenses, copyrights, and trademarks—over their useful life. Since depreciation and amortization are very similar, they are often lumped together on the income statement. Both are noncash expenses, which means that an expense is recorded on the income statement, but the associated cash does not necessarily leave the firm in that period. For Diaz Manufacturing, the depreciation and amortization expense for 2017 was $83.1 million.

At one time, goodwill was one of the intangible assets subject to amortization. Beginning in June 2001, however, goodwill could no longer be amortized. The value of the goodwill on a firm's balance sheet is now subject to an annual *impairment test.* This test requires that the company annually value the businesses that were acquired in the past to see if the value of the goodwill associated with those businesses has declined below the value at which it is being carried on the balance sheet. If the value of the goodwill has declined (been impaired), management must expense the amount of the impairment. This expense reduces the firm's reported net income.

Extraordinary Items. Other items reported separately in the income statement are extra-ordinary items, which are reserved for nonoperating gains or losses. Extraordinary items are unusual and infrequent occurrences, such as gains or losses from floods, fires, earthquakes, or accidents. For example, in February 2011 BP plc, the large oil company, reported a loss of $4.9 billion for 2010. This was the company's first loss since 1992 and was a direct result of a $40.9 billion extraordinary expense associated with the large 2010 oil spill in the Gulf of Mexico. Diaz Manufacturing has no extraordinary expense item during 2017.

Step by Step to the Bottom Line

You probably noticed in Exhibit 3.2 that Diaz Manufacturing's income statement showed income at several intermediate steps before reaching net income, the so-called bottom line. These intermediate income figures, which are typically included on a firm's income statement, provide important information about the firm's performance and help identify what factors are driving the firm's income or losses.

EBITDA. The first intermediate income figure is EBITDA, or earnings before interest, taxes, depreciation, and amortization. The importance of EBITDA is that it shows what is earned purely from operations and reflects how efficiently the firm can manufacture and sell its products without taking into account the cost of the productive asset base (plant and equipment and intangible assets). For Diaz Manufacturing, EBITDA was $251.5 million in 2017.

EBIT. Subtracting depreciation and amortization from EBITDA yields the next intermediate figure, EBIT, or earnings before interest and taxes. EBIT for Diaz Manufacturing was $168.4 million.

EBT. When interest expense is subtracted from EBIT, the result is EBT, or earnings before taxes. Diaz Manufacturing had EBT of $162.8 million in 2017.

Net Income. Finally, taxes are subtracted from EBT to arrive at net income. For Diaz Manufacturing, as we have already seen, net income in 2017 was $118.5 million.

In Chapter 4 you will see how to use these intermediate income figures to evaluate the firm's financial condition. Next, we look at the statement of retained earnings, which provides detailed information about how management allocated the $118.5 million of net income earned during the period.

The Statement of Retained Earnings

Corporations often prepare a statement of retained earnings, which identifies the changes in the retained earnings account from one accounting period to the next. During any accounting period, two events can affect the retained earnings account balance:

1. When the firm reports net income or loss.
2. When the board of directors declares and pays a cash dividend.

EXHIBIT 3.3 **Diaz Manufacturing Statement of Retained Earnings for the Fiscal Year Ending December 31, 2017 ($ millions)**

The statement of retained earnings accompanies the balance sheet and shows the beginning balance of retained earnings, the adjustments made to retained earnings during the year, and the ending balance.

Balance of retained earnings, December 31, 2016	$ (50.7)
Add: Net income, 2017	118.5
Less: Dividends to common stockholders, 2017	—
Balance of retained earnings, December 31, 2017	$ 67.8

Exhibit 3.3 shows the activity in the retained earnings account for 2017 for Diaz Manufacturing. The beginning balance is a negative $50.7 million. The firm's annual report explains that the retained earnings deficit resulted from a $441 million write-down of assets that occurred when Diaz Manufacturing became a stand-alone business in June 2013. As reported in the 2017 income statement (Exhibit 3.2), the firm earned $118.5 million that year, and the board of directors elected not to declare any dividends. Retained earnings consequently went from a negative $50.7 million to a positive balance of $67.8 million, an increase of $118.5 million.

Before You Go On

1. How is net income computed?
2. What is EBITDA, and what does it measure?
3. What accounting events trigger changes to the retained earnings account?

3.5 The Statement of Cash Flows

LEARNING OBJECTIVE

5. Understand the calculation of cash flows from operating, investing, and financing activities required in the statement of cash flows.

There are times when the financial manager wants to know the details of all the cash inflows and outflows that have taken place during the year and to reconcile the beginning-of-year and end-of-year cash balances. The reason for the focus on cash flows is very practical. Managers must have a complete understanding of the uses of cash and the sources of cash in the firm. Firms must have the cash to pay wages, suppliers, and other creditors, and they often elect to defer cash receipts from sales by providing credit to customers. Managers may also decide to issue new securities to raise cash or may retire existing liabilities or repurchase equity to use cash. Finally, the purchase and sale of long-term productive assets can have a measurable impact on a firm's cash position. In sum, managers are responsible for a wide variety of transactions that involve sources and uses of cash over an accounting period. The statement of cash flows provides them with what amounts to an inventory of these transactions, and helps them understand why the cash balance changed as it did from the beginning to the end of the period.

Sources and Uses of Cash

The **statement of cash flows** shows the company's cash inflows (receipts) and cash outflows (payments and investments) for a period of time. We derive these cash flows by looking at the firm's net income during the period and at changes in balance sheet accounts from the

statement of cash flows a financial statement that shows a firm's cash receipts, cash payments, and investments for a period of time beginning of the period (end of the previous period) to the end of the period. In analyzing the statement of cash flows, it is important to understand that changes in the balance sheet accounts reflect cash flows. More specifically, increases in assets or decreases in liabilities and equity are uses of cash, while decreases in assets or increases in liabilities and equity are sources of cash. These changes in balance sheet items can be summarized by the following:

- *Working capital.* An increase in current assets (such as accounts receivable and inventory) is a use of cash. For example, if a firm increases its inventory, it must use cash to purchase the additional inventory. Conversely, the sale of inventory increases a firm's cash position. An increase in current liabilities (such as accounts or notes payable) is a source of cash. For example, if during the year a firm increases its accounts payable, it has effectively borrowed money from suppliers and increased its cash position.
- *Fixed assets.* An increase in long-term fixed assets is a use of cash. If a company purchases fixed assets during the year, it decreases cash because it must use cash to pay for the purchase. If the firm sells a fixed asset during the year, the firm's cash position will increase.
- *Long-term liabilities and equity.* An increase in long-term debt (bonds and private placement debt) or equity (common and preferred stock) is a source of cash. The retirement of debt or the purchase of treasury stock requires the firm to pay out cash, reducing its cash balance.
- *Dividends.* Any cash dividend payment decreases a firm's cash balance.

Organization of the Statement of Cash Flows

The statement of cash flows is organized around three business activities—operating activities, long-term investing activities, and financing activities—and the reconciliation of the cash account. We discuss each element next and illustrate them with reference to the statement of cash flows for Diaz Manufacturing, which is shown in **Exhibit 3.4**.

Operating Activities. Cash flows from operating activities in the statement of cash flows are the net cash flows that are related to a firm's principal business activities. The most important items are the firm's net income, depreciation and amortization expense, and working capital accounts (other than cash and short-term debt obligations, which are classified elsewhere).

In Exhibit 3.4, the first section of the statement of cash flows for Diaz Manufacturing shows the cash flow from operations. The section starts with the firm's net income of $118.5 million for the year ending December 31, 2017. Depreciation expense ($83.1 million) is added because it is a noncash expense on the income statement.

Next come changes in the firm's working capital accounts that affect operating activities. Note that working capital accounts that involve financing (bank loans and notes payable) and cash reconciliation (cash and marketable securities) will be classified separately. For Diaz, the working capital accounts that are *sources* of cash are (1) increase in accounts payable of $24.3 million ($349.3 – $325.0 = $24.3), (2) decrease in other current assets of $8.6 million ($29.9 – $21.3 = $8.6), and (3) increase in accrued income taxes of $1.2 million ($18.0 – $16.8 = $1.2). Changes in working capital items that are *uses* of cash are (1) increase in accounts receivable of $37.4 million ($306.2 – $268.8 = $37.4) and (2) increase in inventory of $51.1 million ($423.8 – $372.7 = $51.1). The total cash provided to the firm from operations is $147.2 million.

To clarify why changes in working capital accounts affect the statement of cash flows, let's look at some of the changes. Diaz had a $37.4 million increase in accounts receivable, which is subtracted from net income as a use of cash because the number represents sales that were included in the income statement but for which no cash has been collected. Diaz provided financing for these sales to its customers. Similarly, the $24.3 million increase in accounts payable represents a source of cash because goods and services the company purchased have been received but no cash has been paid out.

Long-Term Investing Activities. Cash flows from long-term investing activities relate to the buying and selling of long-term assets. In Exhibit 3.4, the second section shows the cash

EXHIBIT 3.4 **Diaz Manufacturing Statement of Cash Flows for the Fiscal Year Ending December 31, 2017 ($ millions)**

The statement of cash flows shows the sources of the cash that has come into the firm during a period of time and the ways in which this cash has been used.

Operating Activities	
Net income	$ 118.5
Additions (sources of cash)	
Depreciation and amortization	83.1
Increase in accounts payable	24.3
Decrease in other current assets	8.6
Increase in accrued income taxes	1.2
Subtractions (uses of cash)	
Increase in accounts receivable	(37.4)
Increase in inventories	(51.1)
Net cash provided by operating activities	$ 147.2
Long-Term Investing Activities	
Property, equipment, and other assets	$ (88.3)
Increase in goodwill and other assets	(38.4)
Net cash used in investing activities	$(126.7)
Financing Activities	
Increase in long-term debt	$ 268.4
Purchase of treasury stock	(23.3)
Increase in notes payable	6.3
Net cash provided by financing activities	$ 251.4
Cash Reconciliation[a]	
Net increase in cash and marketable securities	$ 271.9
Cash and securities at beginning of year	16.6
Cash and securities at end of year	$ 288.5

[a]Cash includes investments in marketable securities.

flows from long-term investing activities. Diaz Manufacturing made long-term investments in two areas, which resulted in a cash outflow of $126.7 million. They were as follows: (1) the purchase of plant and equipment, totaling $88.3 million ($911.6 – $823.3 = $88.3) and (2) an increase in goodwill and other assets of $38.4 million ($450.0 – $411.6 = $38.4). Diaz's investments in property, equipment, and other assets resulted in a cash outflow of $126.7 million.

Financing Activities. Cash flows from financing occur when cash is obtained from or repaid to creditors or owners (stockholders). Typical financing activities involve cash received from the issuance of common or preferred stock, as well as cash from bank loans, notes payable, and long-term debt. Cash payments of dividends to stockholders and cash purchases of treasury stock reduce a company's cash position.

Diaz Manufacturing's financing activities include the sale of bonds for $268.4 million ($574.0 – $305.6 = $268.4), which is a source of cash, and the purchase of treasury stock for $23.3 million, which is a use of cash. The firm's notes payable position also increased by $6.3 million ($10.5 – $4.2 = $6.3). Overall, Diaz had a net cash inflow from financing activities of $251.4 million.

Cash Reconciliation. The final part of the statement of cash flows is a reconciliation of the firm's beginning and ending cash positions. For Diaz Manufacturing, these cash positions are shown on the 2016 and 2017 balance sheets. The first step in reconciling the company's beginning and ending cash positions is to add together the amounts from the first three sections of the statement of cash flows: (1) the net cash inflows from operations of $147.2 million, (2) the net cash outflow from long-term investment activities of –$126.7 million,

(3) and the net cash inflow from financing activities of $251.4 million. Together, these three items represent a total net increase in cash to the firm of $271.9 million ($147.2 − $126.7 + $251.4 = $271.9). Finally, we add this amount ($271.9 million) to the beginning cash balance of $16.6 million to obtain the ending cash balance for 2017 of $288.5 million ($271.9 + $16.6 = $288.5).

Before You Go On

1. How do increases in fixed assets from one period to the next affect cash holdings for the firm?
2. Name two working capital accounts that represent sources of cash for the firm.
3. Explain the difference between cash flows from financing and investment activities.

3.6 Tying Together the Financial Statements

LEARNING OBJECTIVE

6. Explain how the four major financial statements discussed in this chapter are related.

Up to this point, we have treated a firm's financial statements as if they were independent of one another. As you might suspect, though, the four financial statements presented in this chapter are related. Let's see how.

Recall that the balance sheet summarizes what assets the firm has at a particular point in time and how the firm has financed those assets with debt and equity. From one year to the next, the firm's balance sheet will change because the firm will buy or sell assets and the dollar value of the debt and equity financing will change. These changes are exactly the ones presented in the statement of cash flows. In other words, the statement of cash flows is a summary of the changes in a firm's balance sheet from the beginning of a period to the end of that period.

This concept is illustrated in **Exhibit 3.5**, which presents summaries of the four financial statements for Diaz Manufacturing for the year 2017. The exhibit also presents the balance sheet for the beginning of that year, which is dated December 31, 2016. If you compare the changes in the balance sheet numbers from the beginning of the year to the end of the year, you can see that these changes are in fact summarized in the statement of cash flows. For example, the change in the cash balance of $271.9 million ($288.5 − $16.6 = $271.9) appears at the bottom of the statement of cash flows. Similarly, excluding cash and notes payable, the change in net working capital from the beginning to the end of 2017 is $54.4 million, which is calculated as follows: [($751.3 − $367.3) − ($671.4 − $341.8)] = ($384.0 − $329.6) = $54.4.[6] This number is equal to the net working capital investment reflected in the statement of cash flows. Note, too, that the net working capital investment in Diaz's statement of cash flows is just the total change in the firm's investment in the following working capital accounts: accounts payable, other current assets, accrued income taxes, accounts receivable, and inventories. You can also see in Exhibit 3.5 that the change in fixed assets, which includes net property, plant, and equipment, goodwill, and other long-term assets, is $43.6 million ($849.4 − $805.8 = $43.6). This number is equal to the sum of the cash flows from investing activities and depreciation and amortization, −$126.7 + $83.1 = −$43.6, in the statement of cash flows. We add depreciation to investing activities in the latter calculation because the fixed asset accounts in the balance sheet are net of depreciation.

[6]From the 2017 balance sheet ($ millions): (1) Current assets − Cash = $1,039.8 − $288.5 = $751.3, and (2) Current liabilities − Notes payable = $377.8 − $10.5 = $367.3. The calculations are similar for the 2016 balance sheet.

Income Statement, 12/31/17	
Revenues	$1,563.7
Expenses	(1,312.2)
Net income	118.5

Balance Sheet, 12/31/16	
Cash	$ 16.6
Current assets (less cash)	671.4
Fixed assets	805.8
Current liabilities (less notes)	341.8
Long-term debt and notes	309.8
Capital stock	892.9
Retained earnings	(50.7)

Statement of Cash Flows, 12/31/17	
Net income	$118.5
Depreciation and amortization	83.1
Net working capital investment (excluding cash and notes payable)	(54.4)
Operating activities	$147.2
Investing activities	(126.7)
Financing activities	251.4
Net increase in cash	$271.9

Balance Sheet, 12/31/17	
Cash	$288.5
Current assets (less cash)	751.3
Fixed assets	849.4
Current liabilities (less notes)	367.3
Long-term debt and notes	584.5
Capital stock	869.6
Retained earnings	67.8

Statement of Retained Earnings 12/31/17	
Retained earnings, 12/31/16	$(50.7)
Net income	118.5
Dividends	
Retained earnings, 12/31/17	$67.8

EXHIBIT 3.5 The Interrelations among the Financial Statements: Illustrated Using Diaz Manufacturing Financial Results ($ millions)

The statement of cash flows ties together the income statement with the balance sheets from the beginning and the end of the period. The statement of retained earnings shows how the retained earnings account has changed from the beginning to the end of the period.

Turning to the liability and equity side of the balance sheet, notice the change in the amount of debt plus equity that the firm has sold in 2017, which is represented by the sum of the long-term liabilities and notes and capital stock in the balance sheet. This sum equals the value of the financing activities in the statement of cash flows. The change in the balance sheet values is calculated as follows: [($584.5 + $869.6) – ($309.8 + $892.9)] = ($1,454.1 – $1,202.7) = $251.4 million.[7] Finally, since Diaz did not pay a dividend in 2017, the change in retained earnings of $118.5 million [$67.8 – (–$50.7) = $118.5] exactly equals the company's net income, which appears on the top line of the statement of cash flows.

Again, the important point here is that the statement of cash flows summarizes the changes in the balance sheet. How do the other financial statements fit into the picture? Well, the income statement calculates the firm's net income, which is used to calculate the retained earnings at the end of the year and is included as the first line in the statement of cash flows. The income statement provides an input that is used in the balance sheet and the statement of cash flows. The statement of retained earnings just summarizes the changes to the retained earnings account a little differently than the statement of cash flows. This different format makes it simpler for managers and investors to see why retained earnings changed as it did.

Before You Go On

1. Explain how the four financial statements are related.

[7]From the 2017 balance sheet, note the following ($ millions): Debt = $574.0 (long-term debt) + $10.5 (notes payable) = $584.5 and equity = $50.0 (common stock) + $842.9 (additional paid-in capital) – $23.3 (treasury stock) = $869.6. The calculations for 2016 are made in a similar manner.

3.7 Cash Flow to Investors

LEARNING OBJECTIVE

7. Identify the cash flow to a firm's investors using its financial statements.

As we discussed in Chapter 1, the concept of cash flow is very important in corporate finance. Financial managers are concerned with maximizing the value of stockholders' shares, which means making decisions that maximize the value of the cash flows that stockholders can expect to receive. Similarly, the firm has interest and principal obligations to its debt holders that must be met. It is important to recognize that the revenues, expenses, and net income reported in a firm's income statement provide an incomplete picture of the cash flows available to its investors.

Net Income versus the Cash Flow to Investors

cash flow to investors the cash flow that a firm generates for its investors in a given period, excluding cash inflows from the sale of securities to investors

Managers and investors are primarily interested in a firm's ability to generate cash flows to meet the firm's obligations to its debt holders and that can be distributed to stockholders; the **cash flow to investors**. These cash obligations and distributions include interest payments and the repayment of principal to the firm's debt holders, as well as distributions of cash to its stockholders in the form of dividends or stock repurchases. Cash flow to investors is the cash flow that a firm generates for its investors in a given period (cash receipts less cash payments and investments), excluding cash inflows from investors themselves, such as from the sale of new equity or long-term interest-bearing debt.

So how is cash flow to investors different from net income? One significant difference arises because accountants do not necessarily count the cash coming into the firm and the cash going out when they prepare financial statements. Under GAAP, accountants recognize revenue at the time a sale is substantially completed, not when the customer actually pays the firm. In addition, because of the matching principle, accountants match revenues with the costs of producing those revenues regardless of whether these are cash costs to the firm during that period.[8] Finally, cash flows for capital expenditures occur at the time that an asset is purchased, not when it is expensed through depreciation and amortization. As a result of these accounting rules, there can be a substantial difference between the time when revenues and expenses are recorded and when cash is actually collected (in the case of revenue) or paid (in the case of expenses).

Cash flow to investors is one of the most important concepts in finance as it identifies the cash flow in a given period that is available to meet the firm's obligations to its debt holders and that can be distributed to its stockholders. This, in turn, defines the value of their investments in the firm. The cash flow to investors is calculated as the cash flow to investors from operating activity, minus the cash flow invested in net working capital, minus the cash flow invested in long-term assets.

Cash Flow to Investors from Operating Activity

Accounting profits can be converted into cash flow to investors from operating activity by subtracting the taxes that the firm paid during the period from earnings before interest and taxes (EBIT) and adding back all of the firm's noncash expenses. This calculation results in a number that is different from the net cash provided by operating activities that is reported in the statement of cash flows because it does not include cash flows associated with working capital accounts. Unlike the statement of cash flows, when we calculate cash flow to investors, we compute cash flows associated with net working capital separately. We also start from EBIT since interest paid to debt holders has been deducted in the net income calculation and

[8]The accounting practice of recognizing revenues and expenses as they are earned and incurred, and not when cash is received or paid, is called accrual accounting.

we want to include it in cash flow to investors. Cash flow to investors from operating activity (CFOA) can be formally written as:

$$\text{CFOA} = \text{EBIT} - \text{Current taxes} + \text{Noncash expenses} \tag{3.4}$$

For most businesses, the largest noncash expenses are depreciation and amortization of long-term assets. These are noncash expenses because they are deducted from revenues on the income statement during the years after a long-term asset was purchased, even though no cash is actually being paid out. The cash outflow took place when the asset was purchased. Other noncash items include the following:

- Depletion charges, which are like depreciation but apply to extractive natural resources, such as crude oil, natural gas, timber, and mineral deposits (noncash expense).
- Deferred taxes, which are the portion of a firm's income tax expense that is postponed because of differences in the accounting policies adopted for financial reporting and for tax reporting (noncash expense).
- Expenses that were paid in cash in a previous period (prepaid expenses), such as for rent and insurance (noncash expense).
- Revenues previously received as cash but not yet earned (deferred revenues). An example of deferred revenue would be prepaid magazine subscriptions to a publishing company that are recorded as revenue in a period after the cash has been paid (noncash revenue).

We can use the data from Diaz Manufacturing's 2017 income statement in Exhibit 3.2 to illustrate the calculation of CFOA. If the company had no deferred taxes and the taxes reported in the income statement equal the taxes actually paid by the firm, Diaz's CFOA in 2017 was:

$$\text{CFOA}_{2017} = \$168.4 \text{ million} - \$44.3 \text{ million} + \$83.1 \text{ million} = \$207.2 \text{ million}$$

Decision Making Example 3.1 presents another illustration of the CFOA concepts.

EXAMPLE 3.1 | Cash Flow to Investors from Operating Activity

DECISION MAKING

Situation You are a financial manager at Bonivo Corporation and are preparing a report for senior management. You have asked two analysts who work for you to compute cash flow to investors from operating activity during the year that just ended. A short while later they come to your office and report that they cannot agree on how to do the calculation.

The first analyst thinks it should be computed as:

Net income
+ Depreciation and amortization
+ Increase in accounts payable
+ Increase in accrued income taxes
− Increase in accounts receivables
− Increase in inventories
− Increase in other current assets
= Cash flow to investors from operating activity

The second analyst proposes that the calculation is:

EBIT
− Current taxes
+ Depreciation and amortization
= Cash flow to investors from operating activity

Which calculation should you use for your report to senior management?

Decision You should use the calculation proposed by the second analyst. This is the correct calculation. The calculation proposed by the first analyst is incorrect. The first analyst has computed the net cash from operating activities as it is calculated in a statement of cash flows. This calculation does account for the firm's noncash depreciation and amortization expenses, but unlike the calculation of cash flow to investors from operating activity, it incorporates changes in the firm's working capital accounts other than cash and marketable securities. The first analyst also started from net income rather than EBIT. It is important to start from EBIT rather than net income when calculating cash flows for investors because the interest payments to debt holders are not deducted when EBIT is calculated.

Cash Flow Invested in Net Working Capital

As we discussed in Section 3.5, changes in current assets and liabilities from one period to the next represent sources and uses of cash. When we calculate the cash flow to investors we account for these sources and uses by computing the change in net working capital during the period. This change takes into account all the money that has been invested in current assets, including cash and marketable securities, accounts receivable and inventories, and all of the financing that has been received from current liabilities, such as accounts payable and notes payable, during the period. These sources and uses all directly affect the cash flow that is available to investors during the period.

Recall from Equation 3.2 that a firm's investment in net working capital (NWC) at any point in time can be computed as the difference between its total current assets and total current liabilities:

$$\text{Net working capital (NWC)} = \text{Total current assets} - \text{Total current liabilities}$$

We saw earlier that Diaz Manufacturing's investment in NWC at the end of 2017 was:

$$\text{NWC}_{2017} = \$1{,}039.8 \text{ million} - \$377.8 \text{ million} = \$662.0 \text{ million}$$

The corresponding value at the end of 2016 was:

$$\text{NWC}_{2016} = \$688.0 \text{ million} - \$346.0 \text{ million} = \$342.0 \text{ million}$$

As is the case with all balance sheet items, the investment in NWC is a snapshot at a point in time. To determine the flow of cash into, or out of, working capital we compute the cash flow invested in net working capital (CFNWC). This equals the difference between NWC at the end of the current period and NWC at the end of the previous period:

$$\text{CFNWC} = \text{NWC}_{\text{current period}} - \text{NWC}_{\text{previous period}} \qquad (3.5)$$

For Diaz Manufacturing, CFNWC is:

$$\text{CFNWC}_{2017} = \text{NWC}_{2017} - \text{NWC}_{2016} = \$662.0 \text{ million} - \$342.0 \text{ million} = \$320.0 \text{ million}$$

The positive difference between Diaz Manufacturing's net working capital in 2017 and 2016 indicates that current assets increased by $320.0 million more than current liabilities during 2017. This net investment in NWC reduced the amount of cash that might otherwise have been available for distribution to the Diaz investors in 2017. Of course, investments in NWC are likely to yield positive cash flows in the future. For example, accounts receivable can be collected, and inventories will eventually be sold. Also, selling items on credit or having a greater stock of finished inventories can help the company attract new customers. For Diaz Manufacturing, the single largest investment in working capital is the addition of $271.9 million to cash and marketable securities. We will discuss reasons why firms make investments in cash in Chapter 14.

Cash Flow Invested in Long-Term Assets

Long-term assets, such as land, buildings, and plant and equipment, represent a large portion of the total assets of many firms. Because the purchases and sales of such assets can have a substantial impact on the cash flow to investors, it is very important that we account for them in our cash flow calculations. If a firm is a net investor (buys more than it sells) in long-term assets during a given year, its cash flow to investors will be reduced by the amount of the net purchases. If the firm is a net seller of long-term assets, its cash flow to investors will increase by the value of the net sales.

As we discussed earlier, Diaz Manufacturing had $911.6 million invested in plant and equipment and $450.0 million invested in goodwill and other assets at the end of 2017 (Exhibit 3.1). The company's total investment in long-term assets at the end of 2017 was therefore $911.6 million + $450.0 million = $1,361.6 million. The corresponding value at the end of 2016 was $823.3 million + $411.6 million = $1,234.9 million. As with investments in net working capital, we use the change in the value of the long-term assets to compute the amount that a firm invested in long-term investments during a period. Specifically, the cash flow invested in long-term assets (CFLTA) is computed as:

$$\text{CFLTA} = \text{Long-term assets}_{\text{current period}} - \text{Long-term assets}_{\text{previous period}} \tag{3.6}$$

It is very important to remember that, since depreciation is a noncash charge, we ignore accumulated depreciation when we compute the effects of investment in long-term assets on cash flow to investors. For Diaz Manufacturing, CFLTA in 2017 was:

$$\text{CFLTA}_{2017} = \$1{,}361.6 \text{ million} - \$1{,}234.9 \text{ million} = \$126.7 \text{ million}$$

where the $1,361.6 million and $1,234.9 million values represent the long-term asset values before accumulated depreciation. This calculation indicates that Diaz Manufacturing invested a total of $126.7 million in long-term assets during 2017. Of this total, $88.3 million ($911.6 – $823.3 = $88.3) was invested in plant and equipment and $38.4 million ($450 – $411.6 = $38.4) was invested in goodwill and other assets. As with investment in net working capital, investments in long-term assets are likely to generate positive cash flows in the future but reduce the cash flow to investors in the current period.

Learning by Doing Application 3.2 illustrates another CFNWC and CFLTA calculation.

APPLICATION 3.2 | LEARNING BY DOING

Problem Alexi Ghosh and Paul Heaton are the founding partners of BitByte Inc., a leading developer of application delivery management software and solutions. Since opening for business in 2014, BitByte's revenue has nearly tripled. The partners would like to know more about how much cash flow the firm is investing in net working capital and long-term assets to facilitate this growth. While the firm has no inventory for software development, it has increasingly relied on accounts receivable as a term of sale. In addition, growth has required additional investment in long-term assets such as computing hardware, networking equipment, and facilities. Using the information in the following financial statements, calculate the cash flow invested in net working capital and the cash flow invested in long-term assets during fiscal year 2017 for BitByte Inc.

BitByte Inc. Balance Sheets as of December 31, 2017, and December 31, 2016

Assets	2017	2016
Cash and marketable securities		
Accounts receivable	$ 15,844	$ 26,103
Inventory	573,228	421,670
Other current assets	3,554	10,007
Total current assets	$592,626	$457,780
Plant and equipment	309,675	205,480
Less: Accumulated depreciation	(91,410)	(48,295)
Net plant and equipment	$218,265	$157,185
Goodwill and other assets	12,689	12,689
Total assets	$823,580	$627,654

Liabilities and Equity	2017	2016
Accounts payable and accurals	$ 157,090	$ 94,137
Notes payable	101,159	59,815
Other current liabilities	—	—
Total current liabilities	$ 258,249	$ 153,952
Long-term debt	—	—
Total liabilities	$ 258,249	$ 153,952
Preferred stock	—	—
Common stock (8,000 shares)	8,000	8,000
Additional paid-in capital	493,231	493,231
Retained earnings	64,100	(27,529)
Less: Treasury stock	—	—
Total common eqiuity	$565,331.00	$473,702.00
Total liabilities and equity	$823,580.00	$627,654.00

Approach The cash flow invested in net working capital during fiscal year 2017 can be computed as the difference between the net working capital observed at the end of fiscal year 2017 and the net working capital observed at the end of fiscal year 2016. Net working capital for a given year can be computed as the difference between total current assets and total current liabilities. The cash flow invested in long-term assets is calculated as the change in long-term assets from the end of fiscal year 2016 to the end of fiscal year 2017. Long-term assets for BitByte include plant and equipment as well as goodwill and other assets. Since depreciation on plant and equipment is a noncash charge, we ignore accumulated depreciation in the calculation.

Solution Net working capital (NWC) for 2016 and 2017 can be computed as follows:

$$NWC_{2016} = \$457,780 - \$153,952 = \$303,828$$
$$NWC_{2017} = \$592,626 - \$258,249 = \$334,377$$

The cash flow invested in net working capital (CFNWC) for 2017 can be computed as:

$$CFNWC_{2017} = \$334,377 - \$303,828 = \$30,549$$

The cash flow invested in long-term assets (CFLTA) for 2017 is the difference in the long-term asset accounts for 2017 and 2016 ignoring accumulated depreciation.

$$CFLTA_{2017} = \$322,364 - \$218,169 = \$104,195$$

BitByte did not make any new investments in goodwill and other assets during the fiscal year; thus, the cash flow invested in long-term assets reflected only $104,195 of new investment in plant and equipment.

Cash Flow to Investors: Putting It All Together

Having calculated the cash flow from operating activity, cash flow invested in net working capital, and cash flow invested in long-term assets, we are now ready to compute cash flow to investors (CFI). We use Equation 3.7 to do this:

$$CFI = CFOA - CFNWC - CFLTA \tag{3.7}$$

Note that in this calculation, CFNWC and CFLTA are subtracted from CFOA because investments in both net working capital and long-term assets reduce the cash flow available to investors. Of course, it is possible for either or both of these figures to be negative in a given period. For example, CFLTA will be negative if proceeds for the sale of long-term assets exceed total investments in these assets.

Putting this all together for Diaz Manufacturing, we can see that the company's CFI in 2017 was:

$$CFI_{2017} = \$207.2 \text{ million} - \$320.0 \text{ million} - \$126.7 \text{ million} = -\$239.5 \text{ million}$$

The negative value indicates that Diaz invested more cash than was produced by its operating activity during 2017. This is not uncommon for a rapidly growing company like Diaz, which experienced a net sales increase of almost 13 percent from 2016 to 2017. Fast-growing firms often must invest more cash than they generate. The difference is financed by selling stock to investors or by borrowing money. In such situations, both the old and new investors are counting on the firm to produce cash flows in the future that will compensate them for the investment that they are making now. A brief look at the liability side of the Diaz balance sheet suggests that the negative cash flow to investors was funded largely by issuing new long-term debt.

Before You Go On

1. How does the calculation of net income differ from the calculation of cash flow to investors from operating activity?
2. All else being equal, if a firm increases its accounts payable, what effect will this have on cash flow to investors?
3. What does it mean when a firm's cash flow to investors is negative?

3.8 Federal Income Tax

LEARNING OBJECTIVE

8. Discuss the difference between average and marginal tax rates.

We conclude this chapter with a discussion of corporate income taxes. Taxes take a big bite out of the income of most businesses and represent one of their largest cash outflows. For example, as shown in the income statement for Diaz Manufacturing (Exhibit 3.2), the firm's earnings before interest and taxes (EBIT) in 2017 amounted to $168.4 million, and its tax bill was $44.3 million, or 26.3 percent of EBIT ($44.3/$168.4 = 0.263, or 26.3 percent)—not a trivial amount by any standard. Because of their magnitude, taxes play a critical role in most business financial decisions.

As you might suspect, corporations spend a considerable amount of effort and money employing tax specialists to find legal ways to minimize their tax burdens. The tax laws are complicated, continually changing, and at times seemingly bizarre—in part because the tax code is not an economically rational document; rather, it reflects the changing and sometimes conflicting political and social values of Congress and the president over time.

If you work in the finance or accounting area, a tax specialist will advise you on the tax implications of most decisions in which you will be involved as a businessperson. Consequently, we will not try here to make you a tax expert, but we will present a high-level view of the major portions of the federal tax code that have a significant impact on business decision making.

Corporate Income Tax Rates

Exhibit 3.6 shows the 2016 U.S. federal income tax schedule for corporations. As you can see, the marginal tax rate varies from 15 percent to 39 percent (column 3). In general, companies with lower taxable incomes have lower tax rates than larger companies with higher taxable incomes. Historically, the federal income tax code has given preferential treatment to small businesses and start-up companies as a means of stimulating new business formation. In addition, the federal system is a progressive income tax system; that is, as the level of income rises, the tax rate rises. Under the current tax code, which has its origins in the Tax Reform Act of 1986, marginal tax rates do not increase continuously through the income brackets, however. As you can see in Exhibit 3.6, marginal tax rates rise from 15 percent to 39 percent for incomes up to $335,000; they decrease to 34 percent, then increase to 38 percent for incomes up to $18.3 million; and they ultimately rest at 35 percent for all taxable income above $18.3 million.

Weblink

The U.S. Department of the Treasury provides a comprehensive tax information site at http://www.irs.gov.

Exhibit 3.6 **U.S. Federal Corporate Income Tax Rates for 2016**

The federal corporate marginal tax rate varies from 15 to 39 percent. Generally speaking, smaller companies with lower taxable income have lower tax rates than larger companies with higher taxable incomes. Smaller businesses are given preferential treatment to encourage new business formation.

(1)	(2)	(3)	(4)
Corporations' Taxable Income	Pay This Amount on the Base of the Bracket	Marginal Tax Rate: Tax Rate on the Excess Over the Base	Average Tax Rate at Top of Bracket
\$0–\$50,000	\$ 0	15%	15.0%
50,001–75,000	7,500	25	18.3
75,001–100,000	13,750	34	22.3
100,001–335,000	22,250	39	34.0
335,001–10,000,000	113,900	34	34.0
10,000,001–15,000,000	3,400,000	35	34.3
15,000,001–18,333,333	5,150,000	38	35.0
More than 18,333,333	6,416,667	35	35.0

Average versus Marginal Tax Rates

average tax rate total taxes paid divided by taxable income

marginal tax rate the tax rate paid on the last dollar of income earned

The difference between the average tax rate and the marginal tax rate is an important consideration in financial decision making. The **average tax rate** is simply the total taxes paid divided by taxable income. In contrast, the **marginal tax rate** is the tax rate that is paid on the last dollar of income earned. Exhibit 3.6 shows both the marginal tax rates and average tax rates for corporations.

A simple example will clarify the difference between the average and marginal tax rates. Suppose a corporation has a taxable income of \$150,000. Using the data in Exhibit 3.6, we can determine the firm's federal income tax bill, its marginal tax rate, and its average tax rate. The firm's total tax bill is computed as follows:

$$\begin{aligned}
0.15 \times \$50{,}000 \quad &= \$\ 7{,}500\\
0.25 \times (\$75{,}000 - \$50{,}000) &= \quad 6{,}250\\
0.34 \times (\$100{,}000 - \$75{,}000) &= \quad 8{,}500\\
0.39 \times (\$150{,}000 - \$100{,}000) &= \underline{\quad 19{,}500}\\
&\quad\ \$41{,}750
\end{aligned}$$

The firm's average tax rate is equal to the total taxes divided by the firm's total taxable income; thus, the average tax rate is \$41,750/\$150,000 = 0.278, or 27.8 percent. The firm's marginal tax rate is the rate paid on the last dollar earned, which is 39 percent.

When you are making investment decisions for a firm, the relevant tax rate to use is usually the marginal tax rate. The reason is that new investments (projects) are expected to generate new cash flows, which will be taxed at the firm's marginal tax rate.

To simplify calculations throughout the book, we will generally specify a single tax rate for a corporation, such as 40 percent. The rate may include some payment for state and local taxes, which will make the total tax rate the firm pays greater than the federal rate.

Learning by Doing Application 3.3 presents another example of the tax calculations for a firm.

Unequal Treatment of Dividends and Interest Payments

An interesting anomaly in the U.S. tax code is the unequal treatment of interest and dividend payments. For C-corporations (discussed in Chapter 1), interest paid on debt obligations is a

APPLICATION 3.3 | The Difference between Average and Marginal Tax Rates

LEARNING BY DOING

Problem Taxland Corporation has taxable income of $90,000. What is the firm's federal corporate income tax liability? What are the firm's average and marginal tax rates?

Approach Use Exhibit 3.6 to calculate the firm's tax bill. To calculate the average tax rate, divide the total amount of taxes paid by the $90,000 of taxable income. The marginal tax rate is the tax rate paid on the last dollar of taxable income.

Solution

$$\begin{aligned}\text{Tax bill} &= (0.15 \times \$50{,}000) + [0.25 \times (\$75{,}000 - \$50{,}000)] \\ &\quad + [0.34 \times (\$90{,}000 - \$75{,}000)] \\ &= \$7{,}500 + \$6{,}250 + \$5{,}100 \\ &= \$18{,}850 \\ \text{Average tax rate} &= \$18{,}850/\$90{,}000 = 0.209, \text{ or } 20.9\% \\ \text{Marginal tax rate} &= 34\end{aligned}$$

tax-deductible business expense. Dividends paid to common or preferred stockholders are not deductible, however.

The unequal treatment of interest and dividend payments is not without consequences. In effect, it lowers the cost of debt financing compared with the cost of an equal amount of common or preferred stock financing. Thus, there is a tax-induced bias toward the use of debt financing, which we discuss more thoroughly in later chapters.

Before You Go On

1. Why is it important to consider the consequences of taxes when financing a new project?
2. Which type of tax rate, marginal or average, should be used in analyzing the expansion of a product line, and why?
3. What are the tax implications of a decision to finance a project using debt rather than new equity?

Summary of Learning Objectives

1 Discuss generally accepted accounting principles (GAAP) and their importance to the economy.

GAAP are a set of authoritative guidelines that define accounting practices at a particular point in time. The principles determine the rules for how a company maintains its accounting system and how it prepares financial statements. Accounting standards are important because without them each firm could develop its own unique accounting practices. This would make it difficult for anyone to monitor the firm's true performance or compare the performance of different firms. The result would be a loss of confidence in the accounting system and the financial reports it produces. Fundamental accounting principles include arm's-length transactions, the cost principle, the realization principle, the matching principle, and the going concern assumption.

2 Explain the balance sheet identity and why a balance sheet must balance.

A balance sheet provides a summary of a firm's financial position at a particular point in time. It identifies the current assets that a firm has and the productive assets that it uses to generate income, as well as the sources of funding from creditors (liabilities) and owners (stockholders' equity) that were used to buy the assets. The balance sheet identity is Total assets = Total liabilities + Total stockholders' equity. Stockholders' equity represents ownership in the firm and is the residual claim of the owners after all other obligations to creditors, employees, and vendors have been paid. The balance sheet must always balance because the owners get what is left over after all creditors have been paid—that is, Total stockholders' equity = Total assets − Total liabilities.

3 Describe how market-value balance sheets differ from book-value balance sheets.

Book value is the amount a firm paid for its assets at the time of purchase. The current market value of an asset is the amount that a firm would receive for the asset if it were sold on the open market (not in a forced liquidation). Most managers and investors are more concerned about what a firm's assets can earn in the future than about what the assets cost in the past. Thus, marked-to-market balance sheets are more helpful in showing a company's true financial condition than balance sheets based on historical costs. The reason that marked-to-market balance sheets are not commonly used is that it is difficult to estimate market values for some assets and liabilities.

4 Identify the basic equation for the income statement and the information it provides.

An income statement presents a firm's profit or loss for a period of time, usually a month, quarter, or year. The income statement identifies the major sources of revenues generated by the firm and the corresponding expenses needed to generate those revenues. The equation for the income statement is Net income = Revenues − Expenses. If revenues exceed expenses, the firm generates a net profit for the period. If expenses exceed revenues, the firm generates a net loss. Net profit or net income is the most comprehensive accounting measure of a firm's performance.

5 Understand the calculation of cash flows from operating, investing, and financing activities required in the statement of cash flows.

Cash flows from operating activities in the statement of cash flows are the net cash flows that are related to a firm's principal business activities. The most important items are the firm's net income, depreciation and amortization expense, and working capital accounts (other than cash and short-term debt obligations, which are classified elsewhere). Cash flows from long-term investing activities relate to the buying and selling of long-term assets. Cash flows from financing occur when cash is obtained from or repaid to creditors or owners (stockholders). Typical financing activities involve cash received from the issuance of common or preferred stock, as well as cash from bank loans, other notes payable, and long-term debt. Cash payments of dividends to stockholders and cash purchases of treasury stock reduce a company's cash position.

6 Explain how the four major financial statements discussed in this chapter are related.

The four financial statements discussed in the chapter are the balance sheet, the income statement, the statement of retained earnings, and the statement of cash flows. The key financial statement that ties together the other three statements is the statement of cash flows, which summarizes changes in the balance sheet from the beginning of the year to the end. These changes reflect the information in the income statement and in the statement of retained earnings.

7 Identify the cash flow to a firm's investors using its financial statements.

Cash flow to investors is the cash flow that a firm generates in a given period (cash receipts less cash payments and investments), excluding cash inflows from new equity sales or long-term debt issues. Cash flow to investors is the cash flow that is used to meet the firm's obligations to its debt holders and that is distributed to its stockholders, which in turn defines the value of their investments in the firm over time. The cash flow to investors is calculated as the cash flow to investors from operating activity, minus the cash flow invested in net working capital, minus the cash flow invested in long-term assets.

8 Discuss the difference between average and marginal tax rates.

The average tax rate is computed by dividing the total taxes paid by taxable income. It takes into account the taxes paid at all levels of income and will normally be lower than the marginal tax rate, which is the rate that is paid on the last dollar of income earned. When companies are making financial investment decisions, they use the marginal tax rate because new projects are expected to generate additional cash flows, which will be taxed at the firm's marginal tax rate.

Summary of Key Equations

Equation	Description	Formula
3.1	Balance sheet identity	Total assets = Total liabilities + Total stockholders' equity
3.2	Net working capital	Net working capital = Total current assets − Total current liabilities
3.3	Income statement equation	Net income = Revenues − Expenses
3.4	Cash flow from operating activity	CFOA = EBIT − Current taxes + Noncash expenses
3.5	Cash flow invested in net working capital	$\text{CFNWC} = \text{NWC}_{\text{current period}} - \text{NWC}_{\text{previous period}}$
3.6	Cash flow invested in long-term assets	$\text{CFLTA} = \text{Long-term assets}_{\text{current period}} - \text{Long-term assets}_{\text{previous period}}$
3.7	Cash flow to investors	CFI = CFOA − CFNWC − CFLTA

Self-Study Problems

3.1 The *going concern assumption* of GAAP implies that the firm:

a. Is going under and needs to be liquidated at historical cost.

b. Will continue to operate and its assets should be recorded at historical cost.

c. Will continue to operate and that all assets should be recorded at their cost rather than at their liquidation value.

d. Is going under and needs to be liquidated at liquidation value.

3.2 The Ellicott City Ice Cream Company management has just completed an assessment of the company's assets and liabilities and has obtained the following information. The firm has total current assets worth $625,000 at book value and $519,000 at market value. In addition, its long-term assets include plant and equipment valued at market for $695,000, while their book value is $940,000. The company's total current liabilities are valued at market for $543,000, while their book value is $495,000. Both the book value and the market value of long-term debt are $350,000. If the company's total assets are equal to a market value of $1,214,000 (book value of $1,565,000), what are the book value and market value of its stockholders' equity?

3.3 Depreciation and amortization expenses are:

a. Part of current assets on the balance sheet.

b. After-tax expenses that reduce a firm's cash flows.

c. Long-term liabilities that reduce a firm's net worth.

d. Noncash expenses that cause a firm's after-tax cash flows to exceed its net income.

3.4 You are given the following information about Clarkesville Plumbing Company. Revenues in 2017 totaled $896, depreciation expenses $75, costs of goods sold $365, and interest expenses $54. At the end of the year, current assets were $121 and current liabilities were $107. The company has an average tax rate of 34 percent. Calculate its net income by setting up an income statement.

3.5 The Huntington Rain Gear Company had $633,125 in taxable income in the year ending September 30, 2017. Calculate the company's tax using the tax schedule in Exhibit 3.6.

Solutions to Self-Study Problems

3.1 One of the key assumptions under GAAP is the *going concern assumption,* which states that the firm: **c.** Will continue to operate and that all assets should be recorded at their cost rather than at their liquidation value.

3.2 The book value and market value of stockholders' equity are shown below (in $ thousands):

Assets	**Book**	**Market**	**Liabilities and Equity**	**Book**	**Market**
Total current assets	$ 625	$ 519	Total current liabilities	$ 495	$ 543
Fixed assets	940	695	Long-term debt	350	350
			Stockholders' equity	720	321
Total assets	$1,565	$1,214	Total liabilities and equity	$1,565	$1,214

3.3 Depreciation and amortization expenses are: **d.** Noncash expenses that cause a firm's after-tax cash flows to exceed its net income.

3.4 Clarkesville's income statement and net income are as follows:

Clarkesville Plumbing Company
Income Statement for the Fiscal Year Ending
December 31, 2017

	Amount
Revenues	$896.00
Costs	365.00
EBITDA	$531.00
Depreciation	75.00
EBIT	$456.00
Interest	54.00
EBT	$402.00
Taxes (34%)	136.68
Net income	$265.32

3.5 Huntington's tax bill is calculated as follows:

Tax Rate	Income Taxed at Indicated Rate	Tax
15%	$50,000	$ 7,500
25	75,000 – 50,000	6,250
34	100,000 – 75,000	8,500
39	335,000 – 100,000	91,650
34	633,125 – 335,000	101,363
Total taxes payable		$215,263

WileyPLUS

Questions and Problems, Solution Walkthrough Videos, Learning by Doing Tutorials, and additional study tools and resources are available in WileyPLUS.

Discussion Questions

3.1 What is a major reason for the accounting scandals in the early 2000s? How do firms sometimes attempt to meet Wall Street analysts' earnings projections?

3.2 Why are taxes and the tax code important for managerial decision making?

3.3 Identify the five fundamental principles of GAAP, and explain briefly their importance.

3.4 Explain why firms prefer to use accelerated depreciation methods over the straight-line method for tax purposes.

3.5 What is treasury stock? Why do firms have treasury stock?

3.6 Define book-value accounting and market-value accounting.

3.7 Compare and contrast depreciation expense and amortization expense.

3.8 Why are retained earnings not considered an asset of the firm?

3.9 What is the statement of cash flows, and what is its role?

3.10 How does a firm's cash flow to investors from operating activity differ from net income, and why?

Questions and Problems

Excel *Excel templates and resources available in* **WileyPLUS**

Basic

3.1 **Balance sheet:** Given the following information about Elkridge Sporting Goods, Inc., construct a balance sheet for June 30, 2017. On that date the firm had cash and marketable securities of $25,135, accounts receivable of $43,758, inventory of $167,112, net fixed assets of $325,422, and other assets of $13,125. It had accounts payables of $67,855, notes payables of $36,454, long-term debt of $223,125, and common stock of $150,000. How much retained earnings did the firm have?

3.2 **Inventory accounting:** What is the difference between FIFO and LIFO accounting.

3.3 **Inventory accounting:** Explain how the choice of FIFO versus LIFO can affect a firm's balance sheet and income statement.

3.4 **Market-value accounting:** How does the use of market-value accounting help managers?

3.5 **Working capital:** Laurel Electronics reported the following information at its annual meeting: The company had cash and marketable securities worth $1,235,455, accounts payables worth $4,159,357, inventory of $7,121,599, accounts receivables of $3,488,121, short-term notes payable worth $1,151,663, and other current assets of $121,455. What is the company's net working capital?

3.6 **Working capital:** The financial information for Laurel Electronics referred to in Problem 3.5 is all at book value. Suppose marking to market reveals that the market value of the firm's inventory is 20 percent below its book value, its receivables are 25 percent below their book value, and the market value of its current liabilities is identical to the book value. What is the firm's net working capital using market values? What is the percentage difference in net working capital using market versus book values?

3.7 **Income statement:** The Oakland Mills Company has disclosed the following financial information in its annual reports for the period ending March 31, 2017: sales of $1.45 million, cost of goods sold of $812,500, depreciation expenses of $175,000, and interest expenses of $89,575. Assume that the firm has an average tax rate of 35 percent. What is the company's net income? Set up an income statement to answer the question.

3.8 **Cash flows:** Describe the organization of the statement of cash flows.

3.9 **Cash flows:** During 2017, Towson Recording Company increased its investment in marketable securities by $36,845, funded fixed-assets acquisitions of $109,455, and had marketable securities of $14,215 mature. What is the net cash used in investing activities?

3.10 **Cash flows:** Caustic Chemicals management identified the following cash flows as significant in its year-end meeting with analysts: During the year, Caustic repaid existing debt of $312,080 and raised additional debt capital of $650,000. It also repurchased stock in the open market for a total of $45,250. What is the net cash provided by financing activities?

3.11 **Cash flows:** Identify and describe the noncash expenses that a firm may incur.

3.12 **Cash flows:** Given the data for Oakland Mills Company in Problem 3.7, compute the cash flows to investors from operating activity.

3.13 **Cash flows:** Hillman Corporation reported current assets of $3,495,055 on December 31, 2017, and current assets of $3,103,839 on December 31, 2016. Current liabilities for the firm were $2,867,225 and $2,760,124 at the end of 2017 and 2016, respectively. Compute the cash flow invested in net working capital at Hillman Corporation during 2017.

3.14 **Cash flows:** Del Bridge Construction had long-term assets before depreciation of $990,560 on December 31, 2016, and $1,211,105 on December 31, 2017. How much cash flow was invested in long-term assets by Del Bridge during 2017?

3.15 **Tax:** Define average tax rate and marginal tax rate.

3.16 **Tax:** What is the relevant tax rate to use when making financial decisions? Explain why.

3.17 **Tax:** Manz Property Management Company announced that in the year ended June 30, 2017, its earnings before taxes amounted to $1,478,936. Calculate its taxes using Exhibit 3.6.

Intermediate

3.18 **Balance sheet:** Tim Dye, the CFO of Blackwell Automotive, Inc., is putting together this year's financial statements. He has gathered the following balance sheet information: The firm had a cash balance of $23,015, accounts payable of $163,257, common stock of $313,299, retained earnings of $512,159, inventory of $212,444, goodwill and other assets equal to $78,656, net plant and equipment of $711,256, and short-term notes payable of $21,115. It also had accounts receivable of $141,258 and other current assets of $11,223. How much long-term debt does Blackwell Automotive have?

3.19 **Working capital:** Mukhopadhya Network Associates has a current ratio of 1.60, where the current ratio is defined as follows: Current ratio = Current assets/Current liabilities. The firm's current assets are equal to $1,233,265, its accounts payables are $419,357, and its notes payables are $351,663. Its inventory is currently at $721,599. The company plans to raise funds in the short-term debt market and invest the entire amount in additional inventory. How much can notes payable increase without the current ratio falling below 1.50?

3.20 **Market value:** Reservoir Bottling Company reported the following information at the end of the year. Total current assets are worth $237,513 at book value and $219,344 at market value. In addition, plant and equipment have a market value of $343,222 and a book value of $362,145. The company's total current liabilities are valued at market for $134,889 and have a book value of $129,175. Both the book value and the market value of long-term debt are $144,000. If the company's total assets have a market value of $562,566 and a book value of $599,658, what is the difference between the book value and market value of its stockholders' equity?

3.21 **Income statement:** Nimitz Rental Company provided the following information to its auditors. For the year ended March 31, 2017, the company had revenues of $878,412, general and administrative expenses of $352,666, depreciation expenses of $131,455, leasing expenses of $108,195, and interest expenses equal to $78,122. If the company's average tax rate is 34 percent, what is its net income after taxes?

3.22 **Income statement:** Sosa Corporation recently reported an EBITDA of $31.3 million and net income of $9.7 million. The company had $6.8 million in interest expense, and it's average corporate tax rate was 35 percent. What was its depreciation and amortization expense?

3.23 **Income statement:** Fraser Corporation has announced that its net income for the year ended June 30, 2017, was $1,353,412. The company had EBITDA of $4,967,855, and its depreciation and amortization expense was equal to $1,112,685. The company's average tax rate is 34 percent. What was its interest expense?

3.24 Income Statement: For its most recent fiscal year, Carmichael Hobby Shop recorded EBITDA of $512,725.20, EBIT of $362,450.20, zero interest expense, and cash flow to investors from operating activity of $348,461.25. Assuming there are no noncash revenues recorded on the income statement, what is the firm's net income after taxes?

3.25 Retained earnings: Columbia Construction Company earned $451,888 during the year ended June 30, 2017. After paying out $225,794 in dividends, the balance went into retained earnings. If the firm's total retained earnings were $846,972 at the end of fiscal year 2017, what were the retained earnings on its balance sheet on July 1, 2016?

3.26 Cash flows: Refer to the information given in Problem 3.21. What is the cash flow from operating activity for Nimitz Rental?

3.27 Tax: Mount Hebron Electrical Company's financial statements indicated that the company had earnings before interest and taxes of $718,323. The interest rate on its $850,000 debt was 8.95 percent. Calculate the taxes the company is likely to owe. What are the marginal and average tax rates for this company?

Advanced

3.28 The Centennial Chemical Corporation announced that, for the period ending March 31, 2017, it had earned income after taxes of $2,768,028.25 on revenues of $13,144,680. The company's costs (excluding depreciation and amortization) amounted to 61 percent of sales, and it had interest expenses of $392,168. What is the firm's depreciation and amortization expense if its average tax rate is 34 percent?

3.29 Eau Claire Paper Mill, Inc., had, at the beginning of the current fiscal year, April 1, 2016, retained earnings of $323,325. During the year ended March 31, 2017, the company produced net income after taxes of $713,445 and paid out 45 percent of its net income as dividends. Construct a statement of retained earnings and compute the year-end balance of retained earnings.

3.30 Menomonie Casino Company earned $23,458,933 before interest and taxes for the fiscal year ending March 31, 2017. If the casino had interest expenses of $1,645,123, calculate its tax obligation using Exhibit 3.6. What are the marginal and the average tax rates for this company?

3.31 Vanderheiden Hog Products Corp. provided the following financial information for the quarter ending June 30, 2017:

Net income: $189,425
Depreciation and amortization: $63,114
Increase in receivables: $62,154
Increase in inventory: $57,338
Increase in accounts payable: $37,655
Decrease in other current assets: $27,450

What is this firm's cash flow from operating activities during this quarter?

3.32 Cash flows: Analysts following the Tomkovick Golf Company were given the following balance sheet information for the years ended June 30, 2017, and June 30, 2016:

Assets	2017	2016
Cash and marketable securities	$ 33,411	$ 16,566
Accounts receivable	260,205	318,768
Inventory	423,819	352,740
Other current assets	41,251	29,912
Total current assets	$ 758,686	$ 717,986
Plant and equipment	1,931,719	1,609,898
Less: Accumulated depreciation	(419,044)	(206,678)
Net plant and equipment	$1,512,675	$1,403,220
Goodwill and other assets	382,145	412,565
Total assets	$2,653,506	$2,533,771

Liabilities and Equity	2017	2016
Accounts payable and accruals	$ 378,236	$ 332,004
Notes payable	14,487	7,862
Accrued income taxes	21,125	16,815
Total current liabilities	$ 413,848	$ 356,681
Long-term debt	679,981	793,515
Total liabilities	$1,093,829	$1,150,196
Preferred stock	—	—
Common stock (10,000 shares)	10,000	10,000
Additional paid-in capital	975,465	975,465
Retained earnings	587,546	398,110
Less: Treasury stock	(13,334)	—
Total common equity	$1,559,677	$1,383,575
Total liabilities and equity	$2,653,506	$2,533,771

In addition, it was reported that the company had a net income of $3,155,848 and that depreciation expenses were equal to $212,366 during 2017. Assume amortization expense was $0 in 2017.

a. Construct a 2017 cash flow statement for this firm.

b. Calculate the net cash provided by operating activities for the statement of cash flows.

c. What is the net cash used in investing activities?

d. Compute the net cash provided by financing activities.

3.33 **Cash flows:** Based on the financial statements for Tomkovick Golf Company in Problem 3.32, compute the cash flow invested in net working capital and the cash flow invested in long-term assets that you would use in a calculation of the cash flow to investors for 2017.

Sample Test Problems

3.1 What is the matching principle, and how can it cause accounting expenses to differ from actual cash outflows?

3.2 Wolf Pack Enterprises has total current assets of $346,002 and fixed assets of $476,306. The company also has long-term debt of $276,400, $100,000 in its common stock account, and retained earnings of $187,567. What is the value of its total current liabilities?

3.3 What is the difference between a book-value balance sheet and a market-value balance sheet? Which provides better information to investors and management?

3.4 ACME Corporation had revenues of $867,030. It also had expenses (excluding depreciation) of $356,240, depreciation of $103,456, and interest expense of $52,423. What was the company's net income after taxes if its average tax rate was 40 percent?

3.5 True Blue Company increased its investments in marketable securities by $323,370 and paid $1,220,231 for new fixed assets during 2017. The company also repaid $779,200 of existing long-term debt while raising $913,455 of new debt capital. In addition, True Blue had a net cash inflow of $345,002 from the sale of fixed assets, and repurchased stock in the open markets for a total of $56,001. What is the net cash used in long-term investing activities by True Blue? What is the net cash provided by the company's financing activities?

3.6 Sun Devil Corporation reported EBITDA of $7,300,125 and net income of $3,328,950 for the fiscal year ended December 31, 2017. During the same period, the company had $1,155,378 in interest expense, $1,023,285 in depreciation and amortization expense, and an average corporate tax rate of 35 percent. What was the cash flow to investors from operating activity during 2017?

CHAPTER 4

Analyzing Financial Statements

Christopher Polk/Getty Images for Mindless Behavior

LEARNING OBJECTIVES

1. Explain the three perspectives from which financial statements can be viewed.
2. Describe common-size financial statements, explain why they are used, and be able to prepare and use them to analyze the historical performance of a firm.
3. Discuss how financial ratios facilitate financial analysis and be able to compute and use them to analyze a firm's performance.
4. Describe the DuPont system of analysis and be able to use it to evaluate a firm's performance and identify corrective actions that may be necessary.
5. Explain what benchmarks are, describe how they are prepared, and discuss why they are important in financial statement analysis.
6. Identify the major limitations in using financial statement analysis.

The last three decades witnessed a major shift in the U.S. retailing marketplace. By taking advantage of logistic and purchasing advantages, large-scale discount chains have been able to reduce their costs and lower prices for consumers, fueling the explosive expansion of retailers such as the Target and Wal-Mart Stores. Competition for customers between these two firms is intense, with Target pursuing a strategy reliant on consumer discretionary purchases, and Wal-Mart focused on very low prices for consumer basics.

Just how do analysts compare the performance of companies like Target and Wal-Mart? One approach is to compare accounting data from the financial statements that companies file with the SEC. Below are data for total sales and net income for Target and Wal-Mart for their fiscal years ending January 2016:

	Target ($ millions)	Wal-Mart ($ millions)
Total sales	$73,785	$482,130
Net income	$ 3,363	$ 14,694

The accounting numbers by themselves are not very revealing. Wal-Mart is a much larger firm than Target, with greater sales and net income. This difference in size makes it difficult to assess the actual performance differences between the two firms. However, if we compute the net profit margin, one of the profitability ratios discussed in this chapter, we can identify more clearly the performance difference between the two retailers. The net profit margins (net income/total sales) for Target and Wal-Mart are 4.56 percent and 3.05 percent, respectively. This means that for every $100 in revenues, Target is able to generate $4.56 in profit, whereas Wal-Mart generates only $3.05. As this example illustrates, one advantage of using ratios is that they make direct comparisons of companies possible by adjusting for size differences.

This chapter discusses financial ratio analysis (or financial statement analysis), which involves the calculation and comparison of ratios derived from financial statements. These ratios can be used to draw useful conclusions about a company's financial condition, its operating efficiency, and the attractiveness of its securities as investments.

Chapter Preview

In Chapter 3 we reviewed the basic structure of financial statements. This chapter explains how financial statements are used to evaluate a company's overall performance and assess its strengths and shortcomings. The basic tool used to do this is financial ratio analysis. Financial ratios are computed by dividing one number from a firm's financial statements by another such number in order to allow for meaningful comparisons between firms or areas within a firm.

Management can use the information from this type of analysis to help maximize the firm's value by identifying areas where performance improvements are needed. For example, the analysis of data from financial statements can help determine why a firm's cash flows are increasing or decreasing, why a firm's profitability is changing, and whether a firm will be able to pay its bills next month.

We begin the chapter by discussing some general guidelines for financial statement analysis, along with three different perspectives on financial analysis: those of the stockholder, manager, and creditor. Next, we describe how to prepare common-size financial statements, which allow us to compare firms that differ in size and to analyze a firm's financial performance over time. We then explain how to calculate and interpret key financial ratios and discuss the DuPont system, a diagnostic tool that uses financial ratios. After a discussion of benchmarks, we conclude with a description of the limitations of financial statement analysis.

4.1 Background for Financial Statement Analysis

LEARNING OBJECTIVE

1. Explain the three perspectives from which financial statements can be viewed.

financial statement analysis the use of financial statements to analyze a company's performance and assess its strengths and weaknesses

This chapter will guide you through a typical **financial statement analysis**, which involves the use of financial statements to analyze a company's performance and assess its strengths and weaknesses. First, we look at the different perspectives we can take when analyzing financial statements; then we present some helpful guidelines for financial statement analysis.

Perspectives on Financial Statement Analysis

Stockholders and stakeholders may differ in the information they want to gain when analyzing financial statements. In this section, we discuss three perspectives from which we can view financial statement analysis: those of (1) stockholders, (2) managers, and (3) creditors.

Stockholders' Perspective

Stockholders are primarily concerned with the value of their stock and with how much cash they can expect to receive from dividends and capital appreciation over time. Therefore, stockholders want financial statements to tell them how profitable the firm is, what the return on their investment is, and how much cash is available for stockholders, both in total and on a per-share basis. Ultimately, stockholders are interested in how much a share of stock is worth. We address pricing issues in detail in Chapter 9, but financial analysis is a key step in valuing a company's stock.

Managers' Perspective

Broadly speaking, management's perspective of financial statement analysis is similar to that of stockholders. The reason is that stockholders own the firm and managers have a fiduciary responsibility to make decisions that are in the owners' best interests. Thus, managers are interested in the same performance measures as stockholders: profitability, how much cash is available for stockholders, capital appreciation, return on investment, and the like.

Managers, however, are also responsible for running the business on a daily basis and must make decisions that will maximize the value of the stockholders' shares in the long run. Maximizing the value of the stockholders' shares does not involve a single big decision, but rather a series of smaller day-to-day decisions. Thus, managers need feedback on the short-term impact these day-to-day decisions have on the firm's financial statements and its current stock price. For example, managers can track trends in sales and can determine how well they are controlling expenses and how much of each sales dollar goes to the bottom line. In addition, managers can see the impact of their capital budgeting, financing, and working capital decisions reflected in the financial statements. Keep in mind that managers, as insiders, have access to much more detailed financial information than those outside the firm. Generally, outsiders only have access to published financial statements for publicly traded firms.

Creditors' Perspective

The primary concern of creditors is whether and when they will receive the interest payments they are entitled to and when they will be repaid the money they loaned to the firm. Thus, a firm's creditors, including long-term bondholders, closely monitor how much debt the firm is currently using, whether the firm is generating enough cash to pay its day-to-day bills, and whether the firm will have sufficient cash in the future to make interest and principal payments on long-term debt *after* satisfying obligations that have a higher legal priority, such as paying employees' wages. Of course, the firm's ability to pay interest and principal ultimately depends on cash flows and profitability; hence, creditors—like stockholders and managers—are interested in those aspects of the firm's financial performance.

Guidelines for Financial Statement Analysis

We turn now to some general guidelines that will help you when analyzing a firm's financial statements. First, make sure you understand which perspective you are adopting to conduct your analysis: stockholder, manager, or creditor. The perspective will dictate the type of information you need for the analysis and may affect the actions you take based on the results.

Second, always use audited financial statements if they are available. As we discussed in Chapter 1, an audit means that an independent accountant has attested that the financial statements present fairly, in all material respects, the firm's financial condition at a point in time. If the statements are unaudited, your analysis will require extra effort. For example, if you are a creditor considering making a loan, you will need to undertake an especially diligent examination of the company's books before closing the deal. It would also be a good idea to make sure you know the company's management team and accountant very well. This will provide additional insight into the creditworthiness of the firm.

Third, use financial statements that cover three to five years, or more, to conduct your analysis. This enables you to perform a **trend analysis**, which involves looking at historical financial statements to see how various ratios are increasing, decreasing, or staying constant over time.

trend analysis analysis of trends in financial data over time

Fourth, when possible, it is always best to compare a firm's financial statements with those of competitors that are roughly the same size and that offer similar products and services. If you compare firms of disparate size, the results may be meaningless because the two firms may have very different infrastructures, sources of financing, production capabilities, product mixes, and distribution channels. For example, comparing The Boeing Company's financial statements with those of Piper Aircraft, a firm that manufactures small aircraft, makes no sense whatsoever, although both firms manufacture aircraft. You will have to use your judgment as to whether relevant comparisons can be made between firms with large size differences.

benchmark a standard against which performance is measured

In business it is common to **benchmark** a firm's performance, as discussed in the previous paragraph. The most common type of benchmarking involves comparing a firm's performance with the performance of similar firms that are relevant competitors. For example, Ford Motor Company management may want to benchmark the firm's performance against General Motors and Toyota, a broader group of Ford's competitors in the world market, or the industry as a whole. Firms can also be benchmarked against themselves. For example, they can compare this year's performance with last year's performance or with a specific goal, such as a 10 percent growth in sales. We discuss benchmarking in more detail later in this chapter.

Before You Go On

1. Why is it important to look at a firm's historical financial statements?
2. What is the primary concern of a firm's creditors?

4.2 Common-Size Financial Statements

LEARNING OBJECTIVE

2. Describe common-size financial statements, explain why they are used, and be able to prepare and use them to analyze the historical performance of a firm.

common-size financial statement a financial statement in which each number is expressed as a percentage of a base number, such as total assets or net revenues (net sales)

A **common-size financial statement** is one in which each number is expressed as a percentage of some base number, such as total assets or net revenues (net sales). For example, each number on a balance sheet may be divided by total assets. Dividing numbers by a common base to form a ratio is called *scaling*. Scaling is an important concept, and you will read more about it later in this chapter in the discussion of financial ratios. Financial statements scaled in this manner are also called *standardized financial statements*.

Common-size financial statements make it easier to evaluate changes in a firm's performance and financial condition over time. They also allow you to make more meaningful comparisons between the financial statements of two firms that are different in size. For example, in the oil and gas field equipment market, Schlumberger Limited is the major competitor of Diaz Manufacturing, the illustrative firm introduced in Chapter 3. However, Schlumberger has over $55 billion in total assets while Diaz Manufacturing's assets total only $1.9 billion. Without common-size financial statements, comparisons of these two firms would be difficult to interpret. Common-size financial statements are also useful for analyzing trends within a single firm over time, as you will see.

Common-Size Balance Sheets

To create a *common-size balance sheet,* we divide each of the asset accounts by total assets. We also divide each of the liability and equity accounts by total assets since Total assets = Total liabilities + Total equity. You can see the common-size balance sheet for Diaz Manufacturing in **Exhibit 4.1**. Assets are shown in the top portion of the exhibit, and liabilities and stockholders' equity in the lower portion. The calculations are simple. For example, on the asset side in 2017, cash and marketable securities were 15.3 percent of total assets ($288.5/$1,889.2 = 0.153, or 15.3 percent), and inventory was 22.4 percent of total assets ($423.8/$1,889.2 = 0.224, or 22.4 percent). Notice that the percentages of total assets add up to 100 percent. On the liability side, accounts payable and accruals are 18.5 percent of total assets ($349.3/$1,889.2 = 0.185, or 18.5 percent), and long-term debt is 30.4 percent ($574.0/$1,889.2 = 0.304, or 30.4 percent). To test yourself, see if you can re-create the

EXHIBIT 4.1 **Common-Size Balance Sheets for Diaz Manufacturing on December 31 ($ millions)**

In common-size balance sheets, such as those in this exhibit, each asset account and each liability and equity account are expressed as a percentage of total assets. Common-size statements allow financial analysts to compare firms that are different in size and to identify trends within a single firm over time.

	2017		2016		2015	
		% of Assets		% of Assets		% of Assets
Assets						
Cash and marketable securities	$ 288.5	15.3	$ 16.6	1.1	$ 8.2	0.6
Accounts receivable	306.2	16.2	268.8	18.0	271.5	19.4
Inventories	423.8	22.4	372.7	24.9	400.0	28.6
Other current assets	21.3	1.1	29.9	2.0	24.8	1.8
Total current assets	$1,039.8	55.0	$ 688.0	46.1	$ 704.5	50.4
Plant and equipment (net)	399.4	21.1	394.2	26.4	419.6	30.0
Goodwill and other assets	450.0	23.8	411.6	27.6	273.9	19.6
Total assets	$1,889.2	100.0	$1,493.8	100.0	$1,398.0	100.0
Liabilities and Stockholders' Equity:						
Accounts payable and accruals	$ 349.3	18.5	$ 325.0	21.8	$ 395.0	28.3
Notes payable	10.5	0.6	4.2	0.3	14.5	1.0
Accrued income taxes	18.0	1.0	16.8	1.1	12.4	0.9
Total current liabilities	$ 377.8	20.0	$ 346.0	23.2	$ 421.9	30.2
Long-term debt	574.0	30.4	305.6	20.5	295.6	21.1
Total liabilities	$ 951.8	50.4	$ 651.6	43.6	$ 717.5	51.3
Common stock (54,566,054 shares)	0.5	0.0	0.5	0.0	0.5	0.0
Additional paid-in capital	892.4	47.2	892.4	59.7	892.4	63.8
Retained earnings	67.8	3.6	(50.7)	(3.4)	(155.8)	(11.1)
Less: Treasury stock	(23.3)	(1.2)	—	—	(56.6)	(4.0)
Total stockholders' equity	$ 937.4	49.6	$ 842.2	56.4	$ 680.5	48.7
Total liabilities and equity	$1,889.2	100.0	$1,493.8	100.0	$1,398.0	100.0

percentages in Exhibit 4.1 using your calculator. Make sure the percentages add up to 100, but realize that you may obtain slight variations from 100 because of rounding.

What kind of information can Exhibit 4.1 tell us about Diaz Manufacturing's operations? Here are some examples. Notice that in 2017, inventories accounted for 22.4 percent of total assets, down from 24.9 percent in 2016 and 28.6 percent in 2015. In other words, Diaz Manufacturing has been steadily reducing the proportion of its money tied up in inventory. This is probably good news because it is usually a sign of more efficient inventory management.

Weblink

A good source for financial statements is http://finance.yahoo.com.

Now look at liabilities and equity, and notice that in 2017 total liabilities represent 50.4 percent of Diaz Manufacturing's total liabilities and equity. This means that common stockholders have provided 49.6 percent of the firm's total financing and that creditors have provided 50.4 percent of the financing. In addition, you can see that from 2015 to 2017, Diaz Manufacturing substantially increased the proportion of financing from long-term debt holders. Long-term debt provided 21.1 percent ($295.6/$1.398.0 = 0.211, or 21.1 percent) of the financing in 2015 and 30.4 percent ($574.0/$1,889.2 = 0.304, or 30.4 percent) in 2017.

Overall, we can identify the following trends in Diaz Manufacturing's common-size balance sheet. First, Diaz Manufacturing is a growing company. Its assets increased from $1,398.0 million in 2015 to $1,889.2 million in 2017. Second, the percentage of total assets held in current assets grew from 2015 to 2017, a sign of increasing liquidity. Recall from Chapter 2 that assets are liquid if they can be sold easily and quickly for cash without a loss of value. Third, the percentage of total assets in plant and equipment declined from 2015 to 2017, a sign that Diaz Manufacturing is becoming more efficient because it is using fewer long-term assets in producing sales (below you will see that net sales have increased over the same period). Finally, as mentioned, Diaz Manufacturing has significantly increased the percentage of its financing from long-term debt. Generally, these are considered signs of a solidly performing company, but we have a long way to go before we can confidently reach that conclusion. We will now turn to Diaz Manufacturing's common-size income statement.

Common-Size Income Statements

The most useful way to prepare a *common-size income statement* is to express each account as a percentage of net sales, as shown for Diaz Manufacturing in **Exhibit 4.2**. *Net sales* are defined as total sales less all sales discounts and sales returns and allowances. You should note that when looking at accounting information and sales numbers as reported, they almost always mean net sales, unless otherwise stated. We will follow this convention in the book. Again, the percent calculations are simple. For example, in 2017 selling and administrative expenses are 14.8 percent of sales ($231.1/$1,563.7 = 0.148, or 14.8 percent), and net income is 7.6 percent of sales ($118.5/$1,563.7 = 0.076, or 7.6 percent). Before proceeding, make sure that you can verify each percentage in Exhibit 4.2 with your calculator.

Interpreting the common-size income statement is also straightforward. As you move down the income statement, you will find out exactly what happens to each dollar of sales that the firm generates. For example, in 2017 it cost Diaz Manufacturing 69.1 cents in cost of goods sold to generate one dollar of sales. Similarly, it cost 14.8 cents in selling and administrative expenses to generate a dollar of sales. The government takes 2.8 percent of sales in the form of taxes.

Weblink

This MSN Web site offers lots of financial information, including ratios for firms of your choice: http://money.msn.com/investing/.

The common-size income statement can tell us a lot about a firm's efficiency and profitability. For example, in 2015, Diaz Manufacturing's cost of goods sold and selling and administrative expenses totaled 86.9 percent of sales (73.0 percent + 13.9 percent = 86.9 percent). By 2017, these expenses declined to 83.9 percent of sales (69.1 percent + 14.8 percent = 83.9 percent). This might mean that Diaz Manufacturing is negotiating lower prices from its suppliers or is more efficient in its use of materials and labor. It could also mean that the company is getting higher prices for its products, perhaps by offering fewer discounts or rebates. The important point, however, is that more of each dollar of sales is contributing to net income.

EXHIBIT 4.2 **Common-Size Income Statements for Diaz Manufacturing for Fiscal Years Ending December 31 ($ millions)**

Common-size income statements express each account as a percentage of net sales. These statements allow financial analysts to better compare firms of different sizes and to analyze trends in a single firm's income statement accounts over time.

	2017		2016		2015	
		% of Net Sales		% of Net Sales		% of Net Sales
Net sales	$1,563.7	100.0	$1,386.7	100.0	$1,475.1	100.0
Cost of goods sold	1,081.1	69.1	974.8	70.3	1,076.3	73.0
Selling and administrative expenses	231.1	14.8	197.4	14.2	205.7	13.9
Earnings before interest, taxes, depreciation, and amortization (EBITDA)	$ 251.5	16.1	$ 214.5	15.5	$ 193.1	13.1
Depreciation	83.1	5.3	75.3	5.4	71.2	4.8
Earnings before interest and taxes (EBIT)	$ 168.4	10.8	$ 139.2	10.0	$ 121.9	8.3
Interest expense	5.6	0.4	18.0	1.3	27.8	1.9
Earnings before taxes (EBT)	$ 162.8	10.4	$ 121.2	8.7	$ 94.1	6.4
Taxes	44.3	2.8	16.1	1.2	27.9	1.9
Net income	$ 118.5	7.6	$ 105.1	7.6	$ 66.2	4.5
Dividends	—		—		—	
Addition to retained earnings	$ 118.5		$ 105.1		$ 66.2	

The trends in the income statement and balance sheet suggest that Diaz Manufacturing is improving along a number of dimensions. The real question, however, is whether Diaz Manufacturing is performing as well as other firms in the same industry. For example, the fact that 7.6 cents of every dollar of sales reaches the bottom line may not be a good sign if we find out that Diaz Manufacturing's competitors average 10 cents of net income for every dollar of sales.

Before You Go On

1. Why does it make sense to standardize financial statements?
2. What are common-size, or standardized, financial statements, and how are they prepared?

4.3 Financial Ratios and Firm Performance

LEARNING OBJECTIVE

3. Discuss how financial ratios facilitate financial analysis and be able to compute and use them to analyze a firm's performance.

In addition to the common-size ratios we have just discussed, other specialized financial ratios help analysts interpret the myriad of numbers in financial statements. In this section we examine financial ratios that measure a firm's liquidity, efficiency, leverage, profitability, and market value, using Diaz Manufacturing as an example. Keep in mind that for ratio analysis to be most useful, it should also include trend and benchmark analyses, which we discuss in more detail later in this chapter.

Why Ratios are Better Measures

A **financial ratio** is simply one number from a financial statement that has been divided by another financial number. Like the percentages in common-size financial statements, ratios eliminate problems arising from differences in size because the denominator of the ratio adjusts, or scales, the numerator to a common base.

financial ratio a number from a financial statement that has been scaled by dividing by another financial number

Here's an example. Suppose you want to assess the profitability of two firms. Firm A's net income is $5, and firm B's is $50. Which firm had the best performance? You really cannot tell because you have no idea what asset base was used to generate the income. In this case, a relevant measure of financial performance for a stockholder might be net income scaled by the firm's stockholders' equity—that is, the return on equity (ROE):

$$\text{ROE} = \frac{\text{Net income}}{\text{Stockholders' equity}}$$

If firm A's total stockholders' equity is $25 and firm B's stockholders' equity is $5,000, the ROE for each firm is as follows:

Firm	ROE Calculation	ROE
A	$5/$25	0.20, or 20%
B	$50/$5,000	0.01, or 1%

As you can see, the ROE for firm A is 20 percent—much larger than the ROE for firm B at 1 percent. Even though firm B had the higher net income in absolute terms ($50 versus $5), its stockholders had invested more money in the firm ($5,000 versus $25), and it generated less income per dollar of invested equity than firm A. Clearly, firm A's performance is better than firm B's, given its smaller equity investment. The bottom line is that accounting numbers are more easily compared and interpreted when they are scaled.

Choice of Scale Is Important

An important decision is your choice of the "size factor" for scaling. The size factor you select must be relevant and make economic sense. For example, suppose you want a measure that will enable you to compare the productivity of employees at a particular plant with the productivity of employees at other plants that make similar products. Your assistant makes a suggestion: divide net income by the number of parking spaces available at the plant. Will this ratio tell you how productive labor is at a plant? Clearly, the answer is no.

Your assistant comes up with another idea: divide net income by the number of employees. This ratio makes sense as a measure of employee productivity. A higher ratio indicates that employees are more productive because, on average, each employee is generating more income. In business, the type of variable most commonly used for scaling is a measure of size, such as total assets or total net sales. Other scaling variables are used in specific industries where they are especially informative. For example, in the airline industry, a key measure of performance is revenue per available seat mile; in the steel industry, it is sales or cost per ton; and in the automobile industry, it is cost per car.

Other Comments on Ratios

The ratios we present in this chapter are widely accepted and are almost always included in any financial workup. However, you will find that different analysts will compute many of these standard ratios slightly differently. Modest variation in how ratios are computed is not a problem as long as the analyst carefully documents the work done and discloses the ratio formula. These differences are particularly important when you are comparing data from different sources.

Short-Term Liquidity Ratios

Liquid assets have active secondary markets and can be sold quickly for cash without a loss of value. Some assets are more liquid than others. For example, short-term marketable securities are very liquid because they can be easily sold in the secondary market at or near the original purchase price. In contrast, plant and equipment can take months or years to sell and often must be sold substantially below the cost of building or acquiring them.

When we examine a company's *liquidity position*, we want to know whether the firm can pay its bills when cash flow from operations is insufficient to pay short-term obligations, such as payroll, invoices from vendors, and maturing bank loans. As the name implies, *short-term liquidity ratios* focus on whether the firm has the ability to convert current assets into cash quickly without loss of value. As we have noted before, even a profitable business can fail if it cannot pay its current bills on time. The inability to pay debts when they are due is known as **insolvency**. Thus, liquidity ratios are also known as *short-term solvency ratios*. The two most important liquidity ratios are the current ratio and the quick ratio.

insolvency the inability to pay debts when they are due

The Current Ratio

To calculate the current ratio, we divide current assets by current liabilities.[1] The formula is presented below, along with a calculation of the current ratio for Diaz Manufacturing for 2017 based on balance sheet account data from Exhibit 4.1:

$$\begin{aligned}\text{Current ratio} &= \frac{\text{Current assets}}{\text{Current liabilities}} \qquad (4.1)\\ &= \frac{\$1{,}039.8}{\$377.8}\\ &= 2.75\end{aligned}$$

[1]This calculation involves dividing total current assets by total current liabilities. We drop the word *total* in the interest of brevity.

Diaz Manufacturing's current ratio is 2.75, which should be read as "2.75 times." What does this number mean? If Diaz Manufacturing were to take its current supply of cash and add to it the proceeds of liquidating its other current assets—such as marketable securities, accounts receivable, and inventory—it would have $1,039.8 million. This $1,039.8 million would cover the firm's short-term obligations of $377.8 million approximately 2.75 times, leaving a cushion of $662.0 million ($1,039.8 million − $377.8 million = $662.0 million).

Now turn to **Exhibit 4.3**, which shows the ratios discussed in this chapter for Diaz Manufacturing for the three-year period 2015 to 2017. The exhibit will allow us to identify important trends in the company's financial statements. Note that Diaz Manufacturing's current ratio has been steadily increasing over time. What does this trend mean? From the perspective of a potential creditor, it is a positive sign. To a potential creditor, more liquidity is better because it means that the firm has a greater ability, at least in the short term, to make payments. From a stockholder's perspective, however, too much liquidity is not necessarily a good thing. If we were to discover that Diaz Manufacturing has a much higher current ratio than its competitors, it could mean that management is being too conservative by keeping too much money tied up

EXHIBIT 4.3 **Ratios for Time-Trend Analysis for Diaz Manufacturing for Fiscal Years Ending December 31**

Comparing how financial ratios, such as these ratios for Diaz Manufacturing, change over time enables financial analysts to identify trends in company performance.

Financial Ratio	2017	2016	2015
Liquidity Ratios:			
Current ratio	2.75	1.99	1.67
Quick ratio	1.63	0.91	0.72
Efficiency Ratios:			
Inventory turnover	2.55	2.62	2.69
Days' sales in inventory	143.14	139.31	135.69
Accounts receivable turnover	5.11	5.16	5.43
Days' sales outstanding	71.43	70.74	67.22
Total asset turnover	0.83	0.93	1.06
Fixed asset turnover	3.92	3.52	3.52
Leverage Ratios:			
Total debt ratio	0.50	0.44	0.51
Debt-to-equity ratio	1.02	0.77	1.05
Equity multiplier	2.02	1.77	2.05
Times interest earned	30.07	7.73	4.38
Cash coverage	44.91	11.92	6.95
Profitability Ratios:			
Gross profit margin	30.86%	29.70%	27.04%
Operating profit margin	10.77%	10.04%	8.26%
Net profit margin	7.58%	7.58%	4.49%
EBIT return on assets	8.91%	9.32%	8.72%
Return on assets	6.27%	7.04%	4.74%
Return on equity	12.64%	12.48%	9.73%
Market-Value Indicators:			
Price-earnings ratio	22.40	18.43	14.29
Earnings per share	$ 2.17	$ 1.93	$ 1.21
Market-to-book ratio	2.83	1.63	1.39

Note: Numbers may not add up because of rounding.

in current assets, leaving less cash flow for investors. Generally, more liquidity is better and is a sign of a healthy firm. Only a benchmark analysis can tell us the complete story, however.

The Quick Ratio

The quick ratio is similar to the current ratio except that *inventory* is subtracted from current assets in the numerator. The quick ratio accounts for the fact that inventory is often much less liquid than other current assets. Inventory is the most difficult current asset to convert to cash without loss of value. Of course, the liquidity of inventory varies with the industry. For example, inventory of a raw material commodity, such as gold or crude oil, is more likely to be sold with little loss in value than inventory consisting of perishables, such as fruit, or fashion items, such as basketball shoes. Another reason for excluding inventory in the quick ratio calculation is that the book value of inventory may be significantly more than its market value because it may be obsolete, partially completed, spoiled, out of fashion, or out of season.

To calculate the quick ratio—or *acid-test ratio,* as it is sometimes called—we divide current assets, less inventory, by current liabilities. The calculation for Diaz Manufacturing for 2017 is as follows, based on balance sheet data from Exhibit 4.1:

$$\text{Quick ratio} = \frac{\text{Current assets} - \text{Inventory}}{\text{Current liabilities}} \tag{4.2}$$

$$= \frac{\$1{,}039.8 - \$423.8}{\$377.8}$$

$$= 1.63$$

The quick ratio of 1.63 times means that if we exclude inventory, Diaz Manufacturing had \$1.63 of current assets for each dollar of current liabilities. You can see from Exhibit 4.3 that Diaz Manufacturing's liquidity position, as measured by its quick ratio, has been increasing over time.

Note that the quick ratio is usually less than the current ratio, as it was for Diaz Manufacturing in 2017.[2] The quick ratio is a very conservative measure of liquidity because the calculation assumes that the inventory is valued at zero, which in most cases is not a realistic assumption. Even in a bankruptcy "fire sale," the inventory can be sold for some small percentage of its book value, generating at least some cash.

Decision Making Example 4.1 illustrates how short-term liquidity ratios vary across different types of businesses.

DECISION MAKING

EXAMPLE 4.1 | The Liquidity Paradox

Situation You are asked by your boss whether Wal-Mart or H&R Block is more liquid. You have the following information:

	Wal-Mart	H&R Block
Current ratio	0.93	1.18
Quick ratio	0.24	1.18

You also know that Wal-Mart carries a large inventory and that H&R Block is a service firm that specializes in income-tax preparation. Which firm is more liquid? Your boss asks you to explain the reasons for your answers and also to explain why H&R Block's current and quick ratios are the same.

Decision Wal-Mart is much less liquid than H&R Block. The difference between the quick ratios—0.24 versus 1.18—pretty much tells the story. Inventory is the least liquid of all the current assets. Because H&R Block does not manufacture or sell goods, it has no inventory; hence, the current and quick ratios are equal. Wal-Mart has a lot of inventory relative to the rest of its current assets, and that explains the large numerical difference between the current and quick ratios.

[2]The quick ratio will always be less than the current ratio for any firm that has inventory.

Efficiency Ratios

We now turn to a group of ratios called *efficiency ratios* or *asset turnover ratios*, which measure how efficiently a firm uses it assets. These ratios are quite useful for managers and financial analysts in identifying the inefficient use of current and long-term assets. They are also valuable for a firm's investors who use the ratios to find out how quickly a firm is selling its inventory and converting receivables into cash flow for investors.

Inventory Turnover and Days' Sales in Inventory

We measure inventory turnover by dividing the cost of goods sold from the income statement by inventory from the balance sheet (see Exhibits 4.1 and 4.2). The cost of goods sold is used because it reflects the book value of the inventory that is sold by a firm. The formula for inventory turnover and its value for Diaz Manufacturing in 2017 are:

$$\text{Inventory turnover} = \frac{\text{Cost of goods sold}}{\text{Inventory}} \tag{4.3}$$
$$= \frac{\$1{,}081.1}{\$423.8}$$
$$= 2.55$$

The firm "turned over" its inventory 2.55 times during the year. Looking back at Exhibit 4.3, you can see that this ratio remained about the same over the period covered.

What exactly does "turning over" inventory mean? Consider a simple example. Assume that a firm starts the year with inventory worth $100 and replaces the inventory when it is all sold; that is, when the inventory goes to zero. If, over the course of the year, the firm sells the inventory and replaces it three times, the firm is said to have an inventory turnover of three times.

As a general rule, turning over inventory faster is a good thing because it means that the firm is doing a good job of minimizing its investment in inventory. Nevertheless, like all ratios, inventory turnover can be either too high or too low. Too high of an inventory turnover ratio may signal that the firm has too little inventory for its customers and could be losing sales as a result. If the firm's inventory turnover level is too low, it could mean that management is not managing the firm's inventory efficiently or that an unusually large portion of the inventory is obsolete or out of date. In sum, inventory turnover that is significantly lower or significantly higher than that of competitors calls for further investigation.

Based on the inventory turnover figure, and using a 365-day year, we can also calculate the *days' sales in inventory,* which tells us how long it takes a firm to turn over its inventory on average. The formula for days' sales in inventory, along with the 2017 calculation for Diaz Manufacturing, is as follows:

$$\text{Days' sales in inventory} = \frac{365 \text{ days}}{\text{Inventory turnover}} \tag{4.4}$$
$$= \frac{365 \text{ days}}{2.55}$$
$$= 143.14 \text{ days}$$

Note that inventory turnover in the formula is computed using Equation 4.3. On average, Diaz Manufacturing takes about 143 days to turn over its inventory. Generally speaking, the smaller the number, the more efficient the firm is at moving its inventory.

Alternative Calculation for Inventory Turnover

Normally, we determine inventory turnover by dividing cost of goods sold by the inventory level at the end of the period. However, if a firm's inventory fluctuates widely or is growing (or decreasing) over time, some analysts prefer to compute inventory turnover using the average inventory value for the time period. In this case, the inventory turnover is calculated in two steps:

1. We first calculate average inventory by adding beginning and ending inventory and dividing by 2:

$$\text{Average inventory} = \frac{\text{Beginning inventory} + \text{Ending inventory}}{2}$$

2. We then divide the cost of goods sold by average inventory to find inventory turnover:

$$\text{Average inventory} = \frac{\text{Cost of goods sold}}{\text{Average inventory}}$$

Note that all six efficiency ratios presented in the chapter (Equations 4.3 through 4.8) can be computed using an average asset value. For simplicity, we will generally use the end of the period asset value in our calculations.

Learning by Doing Application 4.1 illustrates the alternative calculation for efficiency ratios using financial data for Diaz Manufacturing.

Accounts Receivable Turnover and Days' Sales Outstanding

Many firms make sales to their customers on credit, which creates an account receivable on the balance sheet. It does not do the firm much good to ship products or provide the services on credit if it cannot ultimately collect the cash from its customers. A firm that collects its receivables faster is generating cash faster. We can measure the speed at which a firm converts its receivables into cash with a ratio called accounts receivable turnover; the formula and calculated values for Diaz Manufacturing in 2017 are as follows:

$$\text{Accounts receivable turnover} = \frac{\text{Net sales}}{\text{Accounts receivable}} \quad (4.5)$$

$$= \frac{\$1{,}563.7}{\$306.2}$$

$$= 5.11$$

The data to compute this ratio is from Diaz's balance sheet and income statement (Exhibits 4.1 and 4.2). Roughly, this ratio means that Diaz Manufacturing loans out and collects an amount equal to its outstanding accounts receivable 5.11 times over the course of a year.

In most circumstances, higher accounts receivable turnover is a good thing—it means that the firm is making fewer sales on credit and collecting cash payments from its credit customers faster. Such credit is a customer incentive that is used to promote sales, but it can be

LEARNING BY DOING

APPLICATION 4.1 | Alternative Calculations for Efficiency Ratios

Problem For Diaz Manufacturing, compute inventory turnover during 2017 using the average inventory. Then compare that value with 2.55, the turnover ratio computed using Equation 4.3. Why do the two values differ?

Approach Use the alternative calculation described above. In comparing the two values, you should consider fluctuations in inventory over time.

Solution

1. $$\text{Average inventory} = \frac{\text{Beginning inventory} + \text{Ending inventory}}{2}$$

$$= \frac{\$372.7 + \$423.8}{2}$$

$$= \$398.3$$

2. $$\text{Inventory turnover} = \frac{\text{Cost of goods sold}}{\text{Average inventory}}$$

$$= \frac{\$1{,}081.1}{\$398.3}$$

$$= 2.71$$

The 2017 inventory turnover computed with average inventory, 2.71 times, is slightly higher than 2.55 because the inventory increased during the year.

expensive. As shown in Exhibit 4.3, Diaz's collection speed slowed down slightly from 2015 to 2017. This may be a cause for management concern for at least three reasons. First, Diaz's system for collecting accounts receivable may be inefficient. Second, the firm's customers may not be paying on time because their businesses are slowing down due to industry or general economic conditions. Finally, Diaz may be extending credit to customers that are poor credit risks. Making a determination of the cause would require us to compare Diaz's accounts receivable turnover with corresponding figures from its competitors.

You may find it easier to evaluate a firm's credit and collection policies by using days' sales outstanding, often referred to as DSO, which is calculated as follows:

$$\begin{aligned}\text{Days' sales outstanding} &= \frac{365 \text{ days}}{\text{Accounts receivable turnover}} \\ &= \frac{365 \text{ days}}{5.11} \\ &= 71.43 \text{ days}\end{aligned} \tag{4.6}$$

Note that accounts receivable turnover is computed using Equation 4.5. The DSO for Diaz Manufacturing means that, on average, the company converts its credit sales into cash in 71.43 days. DSO is commonly called the *average collection period.*

Generally, faster collection is better. Whether 71.43 days is fast enough really depends on industry norms and on the credit terms Diaz Manufacturing extends to its customers. For example, if the industry average DSO is 77 days and Diaz Manufacturing gives customers 90 days to pay, then a DSO of 71.43 days is an indication of good management. If, in contrast, Diaz gives customers 60 days to pay, the company has a problem, and management needs to determine why customers are not paying on time.

Asset Turnover Ratios

We turn next to a discussion of some broader efficiency ratios. In this section we discuss two ratios that measure how efficiently management is using the firm's assets to generate sales.

Total asset turnover measures the dollar amount of sales generated with each dollar of total assets. Generally, the higher the total asset turnover, the more efficiently management is using total assets. Thus, if a firm increases its asset turnover, management is squeezing more sales out of a constant asset base. When a firm's asset turnover ratio is high for its industry, the firm may be approaching full capacity. In such a situation, if management wants to increase sales, it will need to make an investment in additional fixed assets. Total asset turnover should be interpreted with care when examining trends for a given firm or when benchmarking against competitors. Younger firms and firms with more recent purchases of fixed assets will have a higher book value of assets and therefore lower total asset turnover for a given level of net sales.

The formula for total asset turnover and the calculation for Diaz Manufacturing's turnover value in 2017 (based on data from Exhibits 4.1 and 4.2) are as follows:

$$\begin{aligned}\text{Total assets turnover} &= \frac{\text{Net sales}}{\text{Total assets}} \\ &= \frac{\$1{,}563.7}{\$1{,}889.2} \\ &= 0.83\end{aligned} \tag{4.7}$$

Total asset turnover for Diaz Manufacturing is 0.83 times. In other words, in 2017, Diaz Manufacturing generated $0.83 in sales for every dollar in assets. In Exhibit 4.3 you can see that Diaz Manufacturing's total asset turnover has declined since 2015. This does not necessarily mean that the company's management team is performing poorly. The decline could be part of a typical industry sales cycle, or it could be due to a slowdown in the business of Diaz Manufacturing's customers. As always, getting a better fix on potential problems requires comparing Diaz Manufacturing's total asset turnover with comparable figures for its close competitors.

The turnover of total assets is a "big picture" measure. In addition, management may want to see how particular types of assets are being put to use. A common asset turnover ratio measures sales per dollar invested in fixed assets (plant and equipment). The fixed asset turnover formula and the 2017 calculation for Diaz are:

$$\text{Fixed assets turnover} = \frac{\text{Net sales}}{\text{Net fixed assets}} \tag{4.8}$$

$$= \frac{\$1{,}563.7}{\$3994}$$

$$= 3.92$$

Diaz Manufacturing generated \$3.92 of sales for each dollar of net fixed assets in 2017, which is an increase over the 2016 value of \$3.52. This means that the firm is generating more sales for every dollar in fixed assets. In a manufacturing firm that relies heavily on plant and equipment to generate output, the fixed asset turnover number is an important ratio. In contrast, in a service-industry firm with little plant and equipment, *total* asset turnover is more relevant.

Decision Making Example 4.2 illustrates how fixed asset turnover ratios vary across firms from different industries.

Leverage Ratios

Leverage ratios measure the extent to which a firm uses debt rather than equity financing and indicate the firm's ability to meet its long-term financial obligations, such as interest payments on debt and lease payments. The ratios are also called *long-term solvency ratios.* They are of interest to the firm's creditors, stockholders, and managers. Many different leverage ratios are used in industry; in this chapter we present some of the most widely used.

Financial Leverage

financial leverage the use of debt in a firm's capital structure; the more debt, the higher the financial leverage

The term **financial leverage** refers to the use of debt in a firm's capital structure. When a firm uses debt financing, rather than only equity financing, the returns to stockholders may be magnified. This so-called leveraging effect occurs because the interest payments associated with much long-term debt and some short-term debt are fixed, regardless of the level of the firm's operating profits. On the one hand, if the firm's operating profits increase from one year to the next, fixed debt holders continue to receive only their fixed-interest payments, and all of the increase goes to the stockholders. On the other hand, if the firm falls on hard times and suffers an operating loss, these debt holders receive the same fixed-interest payment (assuming that the firm does not become insolvent and default on its obligations to debt holders), and the loss is charged against the stockholders' equity. Thus, debt increases the returns to stockholders during good times and reduces the returns during bad times. In Chapter 16 we discuss financial leverage in greater depth and present a detailed example of how debt financing creates the leveraging effect.

DECISION MAKING

EXAMPLE 4.2 | Ranking Firms by Fixed Asset Turnover

Situation Different industries use different amounts of fixed assets to generate their revenues. For example, the airline industry is capital intensive, with large investments in airplanes, whereas firms in service industries use more human capital (people) and have very little invested in fixed assets. As a financial analyst, you are given the following fixed asset turnover ratios: 1.77, 4.13, and 10.35. You must decide which ratios match up with three firms: Delta Air Lines, H&R Block, and Wal-Mart. Make this decision, and explain your reasoning.

Decision At the extremes, Delta is a capital-intensive firm, and H&R Block is a service firm. We would expect firms with large investments in fixed assets (Delta) to have lower asset turnover than service-industry firms, which have few fixed assets. Wal-Mart is the middle-ground firm, with fixed asset holdings primarily in stores and land. Thus, the firms and their respective fixed asset turnover ratios are Delta = 1.77, Wal-Mart = 4.13, and H&R Block = 10.35.

The use of debt in a company's capital structure increases the firm's **default (insolvency) risk**—the risk that it will not be able to pay its debt as it comes due. The explanation is, of course, that debt payments are a fixed obligation and debt holders must be paid the interest and principal payments they are owed, regardless of whether the company earns a profit or suffers a loss. If a company fails to make an interest payment on the prescribed date, the company defaults on its debt and could be forced into bankruptcy by creditors.

default (insolvency) risk the risk that a firm will not be able to pay its debt obligations as they come due

Debt Ratios

We next look at three leverage ratios that focus on how much debt, rather than equity, the firm employs in its capital structure. The more debt a firm uses, the higher its financial leverage, the more volatile its earnings, and the greater its risk of default.

Total Debt Ratio. The total debt ratio measures the extent to which the firm finances its assets from sources other than the stockholders. The higher the total debt ratio, the more debt the firm has in its capital structure. The total debt ratio and a calculation for Diaz Manufacturing for 2017 based on data from Exhibit 4.1 appear as follows:

$$\text{Total debt ratio} = \frac{\text{Total debt}}{\text{Total assets}} \tag{4.9}$$

$$= \frac{\$951.8}{\$1{,}889.2}$$

$$= 0.50$$

How do we determine the figure to use for total debt? Many variations are used, but perhaps the easiest is to subtract total equity from total assets. In other words, total debt is equal to total liabilities. A common alternative measure of debt is the sum of all the firm's interest-bearing liabilities, such as notes payable and long-term debt. Using data from Exhibit 4.1, we can calculate total debt for Diaz Manufacturing in 2017 as follows:

$$\text{Total debt} = \text{Total assets} - \text{Total equity} = \$1{,}889.2 - \$937.4 = \$951.8$$

As you can see from Equation 4.9, the total debt ratio for Diaz Manufacturing is 0.50, which means that 50 percent of the company's assets are financed with debt. Looking back at Exhibit 4.3, we find that Diaz Manufacturing increased its use of debt from 2016 to 2017. The 2017 total debt ratio of 50 percent appears high, raising questions about the company's financing strategy. Whether a high or low value for the total debt ratio is good or bad, however, depends on how the firm's capital structure affects the value of the firm. We explore this topic in greater detail in Chapter 16.

We turn next to two common variations of the total debt ratio: the debt-to-equity ratio and the equity multiplier.

Debt-to-Equity Ratio. The *total debt ratio* tells us the amount of debt for each dollar of total assets. The *debt-to-equity ratio* tells us the amount of debt for each dollar of equity. Based on data from Exhibit 4.1, Diaz Manufacturing's debt-to-equity ratio for 2017 is 1.02:

$$\text{Debt-to-equity ratio} = \frac{\text{Total debt}}{\text{Total equity}} \tag{4.10}$$

$$= \frac{\$951.8}{\$937.4}$$

$$= 1.02$$

The total debt ratio and the debt-to-equity ratio are directly related by the following formula, shown with a calculation for Diaz Manufacturing:

$$\text{Total debt ratio} = \frac{\text{Debt-to-equity ratio}}{1 + \text{Debt-to-equity ratio}}$$

$$= \frac{1.02}{1 + 1.02}$$

$$= 0.50$$

As you can see, once you know one of these ratios, you can compute the other. Which of the two ratios you use is really a matter of personal preference.

Learning by Doing Application 4.2 and **Learning by Doing Application 4.3** illustrate additional debt ratio calculations.

LEARNING BY DOING

APPLICATION 4.2 | Finding a Total Debt Ratio

Problem A firm's debt-to-equity ratio is 0.5. What is the firm's total debt ratio?

Approach Use the equation that relates the total debt ratio to the debt-to-equity ratio.

Solution

$$\begin{aligned}\text{Total debt ratio} &= \frac{\text{Debt-to-equity ratio}}{1 + \text{Debt-to-equity ratio}}\\ &= \frac{0.5}{1 + 0.5}\\ &= 0.33\end{aligned}$$

LEARNING BY DOING

APPLICATION 4.3 | Solving for an Unknown Using the Debt-to-Equity Ratio

Problem You are given the following information about Delta Air Lines' year-end balance sheet for 2015. The firm's debt-to-equity ratio is 3.90, and its total equity is $10.85 billion. Determine the book (accounting) values for Delta Air Lines' total debt and total assets.

Approach We know that the debt-to-equity ratio is 3.90 and that total equity is $10.85 billion. We also know that the debt-to-equity ratio (Equation 4.10) is equal to total debt divided by total equity, and we can use this information to solve for total debt. Once we have a figure for total debt, we can use the balance sheet identity to solve for total assets.

Solution

$$\begin{aligned}\text{Total debt} &= \text{Debt-to-equity ratio} \times \text{Total equity}\\ &= 3.90 \times \$10.85 \text{ billion}\\ &= \$42.32 \text{ billion}\\ \text{Total assets} &= \text{Total debt} + \text{Total equity}\\ &= \$42.32 \text{ billion} + \$10.85 \text{ billion}\\ &= \$53.17 \text{ billion}\end{aligned}$$

Equity Multiplier. The equity multiplier tells us the amount of assets that the firm has for every dollar of equity. Diaz Manufacturing's equity multiplier ratio in 2017 was 2.02, as shown here:

$$\begin{aligned}\text{Equity multiplier} &= \frac{\text{Total assets}}{\text{Total equity}} \qquad (4.11)\\ &= \frac{\$1{,}889.2}{\$937.4}\\ &= 2.02\end{aligned}$$

Notice that the equity multiplier is directly related to the debt-to-equity ratio:

$$\text{Equity multiplier} = 1 + \text{Debt-to-equity ratio}$$

This is no accident. Recall the balance sheet identity: Total assets = Total liabilities (debt) + Total stockholders' equity. This identity can be substituted into the numerator of the equity multiplier formula (Equation 4.11):

$$\begin{aligned}\text{Equity multiplier} &= \frac{\text{Total assets}}{\text{Total equity}}\\ &= \frac{\text{Total equity} + \text{Total debt}}{\text{Total equity}}\end{aligned}$$

$$
\begin{aligned}
&= \frac{\text{Total equity}}{\text{Total equity}} + \frac{\text{Total debt}}{\text{Total equity}} \\
&= 1 + \frac{\text{Total debt}}{\text{Total equity}} \\
&= 1 + \frac{\$951.8}{937.4} \\
&= 1 + 1.02 \\
&= 2.02
\end{aligned}
$$

Therefore, all three of these leverage ratios (Equations 4.9–4.11) are related by the balance sheet identity, and once you know one of the three ratios, you can compute the other two ratios.

Coverage Ratios

A second type of leverage ratio measures the firm's ability to service its debt, or how easily the firm can "cover" its debt payments out of earnings or cash flow. We assess this using coverage ratios. For example, if your monthly take-home pay from your part-time job is \$400 and the rent on your apartment is \$450, your monthly coverage ratio with respect to rent is \$400/\$450 = 0.89 times. Because this ratio is less than 1 you will be in some financial distress. Your income does not cover your \$450 fixed obligation to pay the rent. If, on the other hand, your take-home pay is \$900, your monthly coverage ratio with respect to rent is \$900/\$450 = 2 times. This means that for every dollar of rent you must pay, you earn two dollars of revenue. The higher your coverage ratio, the less likely you are to default on your rent payments.

Times Interest Earned. Our first coverage ratio is times interest earned, which measures the extent to which operating profits (earnings before interest and taxes, or EBIT) cover the firm's interest expenses. Creditors prefer to lend to firms whose EBIT is far in excess of their interest payments. The equation for the times-interest-earned ratio and a calculation for Diaz Manufacturing from its income statement (Exhibit 4.2) for 2017 are:

$$
\begin{aligned}
\text{Times interest earned} &= \frac{\text{EBIT}}{\text{interest expense}} \qquad (4.12) \\
&= \frac{\$168.4}{\$5.6} \\
&= 30.07
\end{aligned}
$$

Diaz Manufacturing can cover its interest charges about 30 times with its operating income. This figure appears to point to a good margin of safety for creditors. In general, the larger the times interest earned, the more likely the firm is to make its interest payments.

Cash Coverage. As we have discussed before, depreciation is a noncash expense, and as a result, no cash goes out the door when depreciation is deducted on the income statement. Thus, rather than asking whether operating profits (EBIT) are sufficient to cover interest payments, we might ask how much cash is available to cover interest payments. The cash a firm has available from operations to meet interest payments is better measured by EBIT plus depreciation and amortization (EBITDA).[3] Thus, the cash coverage ratio for Diaz Manufacturing in 2017 is:

$$
\begin{aligned}
\text{Cash coverage} &= \frac{\text{EBITDA}}{\text{interest expense}} \qquad (4.13) \\
&= \frac{\$251.5}{\$5.6} \\
&= 44.91
\end{aligned}
$$

[3]EBITDA can differ from actual cash flows because of the accounting accruals and the investment in net working capital and fixed assets that we discussed in Chapter 3.

For a firm with depreciation or amortization expenses, which includes virtually all firms, EBITDA coverage will be larger than times interest earned coverage.

Profitability Ratios

Profitability ratios measure management's ability to efficiently use the firm's assets to generate sales and manage the firm's operations. These measurements are of interest to stockholders, creditors, and managers because they focus on the firm's earnings. The profitability ratios presented in this chapter are among a handful of such ratios commonly used by stockholders, managers, and creditors when analyzing a firm's performance. In general, the higher the profitability ratios, the better the firm is performing.

Gross Profit Margin

The gross profit margin measures the percentage of net sales remaining after the cost of goods sold is paid. It captures the firm's ability to manage the expenses directly associated with producing the firm's products or services. Using data from Exhibit 4.2, the gross profit margin formula, along with a calculation for Diaz Manufacturing in 2017, is:

$$\text{Gross profit margin} = \frac{\text{Net sales} - \text{Cost of goods sold}}{\text{Net sales}} \tag{4.14}$$
$$= \frac{\$1{,}563.7 - \$1{,}081.1}{\$1{,}563.7}$$
$$= 0.3086\text{, or } 30.86\%$$

Thus, after paying the cost of goods sold, Diaz Manufacturing has 30.86 percent of the sales amount remaining to pay other expenses. From Exhibit 4.3, you can see that Diaz Manufacturing's gross profit margin has been increasing over the past several years, which is good news.

Operating Profit Margin and EBITDA Margin

Moving farther down the income statement, you can measure the percentage of sales that remains after payment of cost of goods sold and all other expenses, except for interest and taxes. Operating profit is typically measured as EBIT. The operating profit margin, therefore, gives an indication of the profitability of the firm's operations, independent of its financing policies or tax management strategies. The operating profit margin formula, along with Diaz Manufacturing's 2017 operating profit margin calculated using data from Exhibit 4.2, is as follows:

$$\text{Operating profit margin} = \frac{\text{EBIT}}{\text{Net sales}} \tag{4.15}$$
$$= \frac{\$168.4}{\$1{,}563.7}$$
$$= 0.1077\text{, or } 10.77\%$$

Many analysts and investors are concerned with cash flows generated by operations rather than operating earnings and will use EBITDA in the numerator instead of EBIT. Calculated in this way, the operating profit margin is known as the EBITDA margin.

Net Profit Margin

The net profit margin is the percentage of sales remaining after all of the firm's expenses, including interest and taxes, have been paid. The net profit margin formula is shown here, along with the calculated value for Diaz Manufacturing in 2017, using data from the firm's income statement (Exhibit 4.2):

$$\text{Net profit margin} = \frac{\text{Net income}}{\text{Net sales}} \tag{4.16}$$
$$= \frac{\$118.5}{\$1{,}563.7}$$
$$= 0.0758\text{, or } 7.58\%$$

As you can see from Exhibit 4.3, Diaz Manufacturing's net profit margin improved dramatically from 2015 to 2017. This is good news. The question remains, however, whether 7.58 percent is a good profit margin. Answering this question requires that we compare Diaz Manufacturing's performance to the performance of its competitors, which we will do later in this chapter. What qualifies as a good profit margin varies significantly across industries. Generally speaking, the higher a company's profit margin, the better the company's performance.

Return on Assets

So far, we have examined profitability as a percentage of sales. It is also important that we analyze profitability as a percentage of investment, either in assets or in equity. First, let's look at return on assets. In practice, return on assets is calculated in two different ways.

One approach provides a measure of operating profit (EBIT) per dollar of assets. This is a powerful measure of return because it tells us how efficiently management utilized the assets under their command, independent of financing decisions and taxes. It can be thought of as a measure of the pre-tax return on the total net investment in the firm from operations. The formula for this version of return on assets, which we call EBIT return on assets (EROA), is shown next, together with the calculated value for Diaz Manufacturing in 2017, using data from Exhibits 4.1 and 4.2:

$$\begin{aligned}\text{EBIT return on assets(EROA)} &= \frac{\text{EBIT}}{\text{Total assets}} \\ &= \frac{\$168.4}{\$1{,}889.2} \\ &= 0.0891, \text{ or } 8.91\%\end{aligned} \tag{4.17}$$

Exhibit 4.3 shows us that, unlike the other profitability ratios, Diaz Manufacturing's EROA did not really improve from 2015 to 2017. The very similar EROA values for 2015 and 2017 indicate that assets increased at approximately the same rate as operating profits.

Some analysts calculate return on assets (ROA) as:

$$\begin{aligned}\text{Return on assets(ROA)} &= \frac{\text{Net income}}{\text{Total assets}} \\ &= \frac{\$118.5}{\$1{,}889.2} \\ &= 0.0627, \text{ or } 6.27\%\end{aligned} \tag{4.18}$$

Although it is a common calculation, we advise against using the calculation in Equation 4.18 unless you are using the DuPont system, which we discuss shortly. The ROA calculation divides a measure of earnings available to stockholders (net income) by total assets (debt plus equity), which is a measure of the investment in the firm by both stockholders and creditors. Constructing a ratio of those two numbers is like mixing apples and oranges. The information that this ratio provides about the efficiency of asset utilization is obscured by the financing decisions the firm has made and the taxes it pays. You can see this in Exhibit 4.3, which shows that, in contrast to the very small change in EROA, ROA increases substantially from 2015 to 2017. This increase in ROA is not due to improved efficiency, but rather to a large decrease in interest expense (see Exhibit 4.2).

The key point is that EROA surpasses ROA as a measure of how efficiently assets are utilized in operations. Dividing a measure of earnings to both debt holders and stockholders by a measure of how much both debt holders and stockholders have invested gives us a clearer view of what we are trying to measure.

In general, when you calculate a financial ratio, if you have a measure of income to stockholders in the numerator, you want to make sure that you have only investments by stockholders in the denominator. Similarly, if you have a measure of total profits from operations in the numerator, you want to divide it by a measure of total investments by both debt holders and stockholders.

Return on Equity

Return on equity (ROE) measures net income as a percentage of the stockholders' investment in the firm. The return on equity formula and the calculation for Diaz Manufacturing in 2017 based on data from Exhibits 4.1 and 4.2 are as follows:

$$\text{Return on equity (ROE)} = \frac{\text{Net income}}{\text{Total equity}} \tag{4.19}$$

$$= \frac{\$118.5}{\$937.4}$$

$$= 0.1264, \text{ or } 12.64\%$$

Alternative Calculation of ROA and ROE

As with efficiency ratios, the calculation of ROA and ROE involves dividing an income statement value, which relates to a period of time, by a balance sheet value from the end of the time period. Some analysts prefer to calculate ROA and ROE using the average asset value or equity value, where the average value is determined as follows:

$$\text{Average asset or equity value} = \frac{\text{Begining value} + \text{Ending value}}{2}$$

Using the average asset or equity value makes sense because the earnings over a period are generated with the average value of assets or equity.

Learning by Doing Application 4.4 illustrates the alternative calculations for EROA and ROE using financial data for Diaz Manufacturing.

LEARNING BY DOING

WileyPLUS

Need more help? Visit your WileyPLUS course.

APPLICATION 4.4 | Alternative Calculations for EROA and ROE Ratios

Problem Calculate the EROA and ROE for Diaz Manufacturing in 2017 using average balance sheet values and compare the results with the calculations based on Equations 4.17 and 4.19.

Approach First find average values for the asset and equity accounts using data from Exhibit 4.1. Then use these values to calculate the EROA and ROE. In explaining why some analysts might prefer the alternative calculation, consider possible fluctuations of assets or equity over time.

Solution

$$\text{Average asset or equity value} = \frac{\text{Beginnning value} + \text{Ending value}}{2}$$

$$\text{Average asset value} = \frac{\$1{,}493.8 + \$1{,}889.2}{2}$$

$$= \$1{,}691.5$$

$$\text{Average equity value} = \frac{\$842.2 + \$937.4}{2}$$

$$= \$889.8$$

$$\text{EROA} = \frac{\text{EBIT}}{\text{Total assets}} = \frac{\$168.4}{\$1{,}691.5}$$

$$= 0.0996, \text{ or } 9.96\%$$

$$\text{ROE} = \frac{\text{Net income}}{\text{Total equity}} = \frac{\$118.5}{\$889.8}$$

$$= 0.1332, \text{ or } 13.32\%$$

Both EROA (9.96 percent versus 8.91 percent) and ROE (13.32 percent versus 12.64 percent) are higher when the average values are used. The reason is that Diaz's total assets grew from \$1,493.8 million in 2016 to \$1,889.2 million in 2017 and its equity grew from \$842.2 million to \$937.4 million during the same period.

Market-Value Indicators

The ratios we have discussed so far rely solely on the firm's financial statements, and we know that much of the data in those statements are historical and do not represent current market values. Also, as we discussed in Chapter 1, the appropriate objective for the firm's management is to maximize stockholder value, and the market value of the stockholders' claims is the value of the *cash flows* that they are entitled to receive, which is not necessarily the same as accounting income. To find out how the stock market evaluates a firm's liquidity, efficiency, leverage, and profitability, we need ratios based on market values.

Over the years, financial analysts have developed a number of ratios, called *market-value ratios*, which combine market-value data with data from a firm's financial statements. Here we examine the most commonly used market-value ratios: earnings per share, the price-earnings ratio, and the market-to-book ratio.

Earnings per Share

Dividing a firm's net income by the number of shares outstanding yields earnings per share (EPS). At the end of 2017, Diaz Manufacturing had 54,566,054 shares outstanding (see Exhibit 3.1 in Chapter 3) and net income of $118.5 million (Exhibit 4.2). Its EPS at that point is calculated as follows:

$$\text{Earning per share} = \frac{\text{Net income}}{\text{Shares outstanding}} \tag{4.20}$$

$$= \frac{\$118{,}500{,}000}{54{,}566{,}054} = \$2.17 \text{ per share}$$

Price-Earnings Ratio

The price-earnings (P/E) ratio relates earnings per share to price per share. The formula, with a calculation for Diaz Manufacturing for the end of 2017, is as follows:

$$\text{Price-earnings ratio} = \frac{\text{Price per share}}{\text{Earnings per share}} \tag{4.21}$$

$$= \frac{\$48.61}{\$2.17} = 22.4$$

Price per share on a given date can be obtained from listings in the *Wall Street Journal* or from an online source, such as Yahoo! Finance.

What does it mean for a firm to have a price-earnings ratio of 22.4? It means that the stock market places a value of $22.40 on every $1 of net income. Why are investors willing to pay $22.40 for a claim on $1 of earnings? The answer is that the stock price does not only reflect the earnings this year. It reflects all future cash flows from earnings. An especially high P/E ratio can indicate that investors expect the firm's earnings to grow rapidly in the future. Alternatively, a high P/E ratio might be due to unusually low earnings in a particular year and investors might expect earnings to recover to a normal level soon. We will discuss how expected growth affects P/E ratios in detail in later chapters. As with other measures, to understand whether the P/E ratio is too high or too low, we must compare the firm's P/E ratio with those of competitors and also look at movements in the firm's P/E ratio relative to market trends.

Market-to-Book Ratio

The market-to-book ratio compares the market value of the firm's investments to its book value. The formula, with a calculation for Diaz at the end of 2017, is:

$$\text{Market-to-book ratio} = \frac{\text{Market value or equity per share}}{\text{Book value of equity per share}} \tag{4.22}$$

$$= \frac{\$48.61}{\$937.4/54.566}$$

$$= \frac{\$48.61}{\$17.18} = 2.83$$

Book value per share is an accounting number that reflects the cumulative historical investment into the firm's equity account on a per share basis. Market value of equity per share is simply the price per share. A higher market-to-book ratio suggests that the firm has been more effective at investing in projects that add value for its stockholders. A value of less than one could mean that the firm has not created any value for its stockholders.

Concluding Comments on Ratios

We could have covered many more ratios. However, the group of ratios presented in this chapter is a fair representation of the ratios needed to analyze the performance of a business. When using ratios, it is important that you ask yourself, "What does this ratio mean, and what is it measuring?" rather than trying to memorize a definition. Good ratios should make good economic sense when you look at them.

Before You Go On

1. What are the efficiency ratios, and what do they measure? Why, for some firms, is the total asset turnover more important than the fixed asset turnover?
2. List the leverage ratios discussed in this section, and explain how they are related.
3. List the profitability ratios discussed in this section, and explain how they differ from each other.

4.4 The Dupont System: A Diagnostic Tool

LEARNING OBJECTIVE

4. Describe the DuPont system of analysis and be able to use it to evaluate a firm's performance and identify corrective actions that may be necessary.

By now, your mind may be swimming with ratios. Fortunately, some enterprising financial managers at the DuPont Company developed a system that ties together some of the most important financial ratios and provides a systematic approach to financial ratio analysis.

An Overview of the DuPont System

The DuPont system of analysis is a diagnostic tool that uses financial ratios to evaluate a company's financial health. The process has three steps. First, management assesses the company's financial health using the DuPont ratios. Second, if any problems are identified, management corrects them. Finally, management monitors the firm's financial performance over time, looking for differences from ratios established as benchmarks by management.

Under the DuPont system, management is charged with making decisions that maximize the firm's return on equity as opposed to maximizing the value of the stockholders' shares. The system is primarily designed to be used by management as a diagnostic and corrective tool, though investors and other stakeholders have found its diagnostic powers of interest.

The DuPont system is derived from two equations that link the firm's return on assets (ROA) and return on equity (ROE). The system identifies three areas where management should focus its efforts in order to maximize the firm's ROE: (1) how much profit management can earn on sales, (2) how efficient management is in using the firm's assets, and (3) how much financial leverage management is using. Each of these areas is monitored by a single ratio, and together the ratios comprise the *DuPont equation.*

The ROA Equation

The ROA equation links the firm's return on assets with its total asset turnover and net profit margin. We derive this relation from the ROA equation as follows:

$$\begin{aligned} \text{ROA} &= \frac{\text{Net income}}{\text{Total assets}} \\ &= \frac{\text{Net income}}{\text{Total assets}} \times \frac{\text{Net sales}}{\text{Net sales}} \\ &= \frac{\text{Net income}}{\text{Net sales}} \times \frac{\text{Net sales}}{\text{Total assets}} \\ &= \text{Net profit margin} \times \text{Total asset turnover} \end{aligned}$$

As you can see, we start with the ROA formula presented earlier as Equation 4.18. Then we multiply ROA by net sales divided by net sales. In the third line, we rearrange the terms, coming up with the expression ROA = (Net income/Net sales) × (Net sales/Total assets). You may recognize the first ratio in the third line as the firm's net profit margin (Equation 4.16) and the second ratio as the firm's total asset turnover (Equation 4.7). Thus, we end up with the final equation for ROA, which is restated as Equation 4.23:

$$\text{ROA} = \text{Net profit margin} \times \text{Total asset turnover} \tag{4.23}$$

Equation 4.23 says that a firm's ROA is determined by two factors: (1) the firm's net profit margin and (2) the firm's total asset turnover. Let's look at the managerial implications of each of these terms.

Net Profit Margin. The net profit margin ratio can be written as follows:

$$\text{Net profit margin} = \frac{\text{Net income}}{\text{Net sales}} = \frac{\text{EBIT}}{\text{Net sales}} \times \frac{\text{EBT}}{\text{EBIT}} \times \frac{\text{Net income}}{\text{EBT}}$$

As you can see, the net profit margin can be viewed as the product of three ratios: (1) the operating profit margin (EBIT/Net sales), which is Equation 4.15, (2) a ratio that measures the impact of interest expenses on profits (EBT/EBIT), and (3) a ratio that measures the impact of taxes on profits (Net income/EBT). Thus, the net profit margin focuses on management's ability to generate profits from sales by efficiently managing the firm's (1) operating expenses, (2) interest expenses, and (3) tax expenses.

Total Asset Turnover. Total asset turnover, which is defined as Net sales/Total assets, measures how efficiently management uses the assets under its command—that is, how much output management can generate with a given asset base.

Net Profit Margin versus Total Asset Turnover

The ROA equation provides some very interesting managerial insights. It says that if management wants to increase the firm's ROA, it can increase the net profit margin, total asset turnover, or both. Of course, every firm would like to make both terms as large as possible so as to earn the highest possible ROA. Though every industry is different, competition, marketing considerations, technology, and manufacturing capabilities, to name a few, place upper limits on asset turnover and net profit margins and, thus, ROA. Equation 4.23 suggests that management can follow two distinct strategies to maximize ROA. Deciding between the strategies involves a trade-off between total asset turnover and net profit margin.

The first management strategy emphasizes high profit margin and low asset turnover. Examples of companies that use this strategy are luxury stores, such as jewelry stores, high-end

EXHIBIT 4.4 Two Basic Strategies to Earn a Higher ROA[a]

To maximize a firm's ROA, management can focus more on achieving high profit margins or on achieving high asset turnover. High-end retailers like Tiffany & Co. and Burberry Group plc focus more on achieving high profit margins. In contrast, grocery and discount stores like Whole Foods Market and Wal-Mart tend to focus more on achieving high asset turnover because competition limits their ability to achieve very high profit margins.

Company	Asset Turnover	×	Profit Margin (%)	=	ROA (%)
High Profit Margin:					
Tiffany & Co.	0.80		11.30		9.04
Burberry Group plc	1.09		12.33		13.44
High Turnover:					
Whole Foods Market	2.48		3.22		7.99
Wal-Mart Stores	2.42		3.05		7.38

[a]Ratios are calculated using financial results for the fiscal year ending closest to December 2015.

department stores, and upscale specialty boutiques. Such stores carry expensive merchandise that has a high profit margin but tends to sell slowly. The second management strategy depends on low profit margins and high turnover. Examples of firms that use this strategy are discount stores and grocery stores, which have very low profit margins but make up for it by turning over their inventory very quickly. A typical chain grocery store, for example, turns over its inventory more than 12 times per year.

Exhibit 4.4 illustrates both strategies. The exhibit shows asset turnover, profit margin, and ROA for four retailing firms for the fiscal year ending closest to December 2015. Tiffany & Co. is a nationwide retailer of high-end jewelry, and Burberry is a British seller of upscale clothing for men and women. At the other end of the spectrum are Whole Foods Market, a grocery chain based in Austin, Texas, and Wal-Mart, which is famous for its low-price, high-volume strategy.

Notice that the two luxury-item retailers (Tiffany & Co. and Burberry) have lower asset turnover and higher profit margins, while the grocery and discount stores have lower profit margins and much higher asset turnover. Whole Foods and Wal-Mart are strong financial performers in their industry sectors. Their relatively low ROAs of 7.99 and 7.38 percent, respectively, reflect the high degree of competition in the grocery and discount store businesses.

The ROE Equation

To derive the ROE equation, we start with the formula from Equation 4.19:

$$\begin{aligned}\text{ROE} &= \frac{\text{Net income}}{\text{Total equity}}\\ &= \frac{\text{Net income}}{\text{Total equity}} \times \frac{\text{Total assets}}{\text{Total assets}}\\ &= \frac{\text{Net income}}{\text{Total assets}} \times \frac{\text{Total assets}}{\text{Total equity}}\\ &= \text{ROA} \times \text{Equity multiplier}\end{aligned}$$

Next, we multiply by total assets divided by total assets, and then we rearrange the terms so that ROE = (Net income/Total assets) × (Total assets/Total equity), as shown in the third line. By this definition, ROE is the product of two ratios already familiar to us: ROA

(Equation 4.18) and the equity multiplier (Equation 4.11). The equation for ROE is shown as Equation 4.24:

$$\text{ROE} = \text{ROA} \times \text{Equity multiplier} \tag{4.24}$$

Interesting here is the fact that ROE is determined by the firm's ROA and its use of leverage. The greater the use of debt in the firm's capital structure, the greater the ROE. Thus, increasing the use of leverage is one way management can increase the firm's ROE—but at a price. That is, the greater the use of financial leverage, the more risky the firm. How aggressively a company uses this strategy depends on management's preference for risk and the willingness of creditors to lend money and bear the risk.

The DuPont Equation

Now we can combine our two equations into a single equation. From Equation 4.24, we know that ROE = ROA × Equity multiplier; and from Equation 4.23, we know that ROA = Net profit margin × Total asset turnover. Substituting Equation 4.23 into Equation 4.24 yields an expression formally called the DuPont equation, as follows:

$$\text{ROE} = \text{Net profit margin} \times \text{Total asset turnover} \times \text{Equity multiplier} \tag{4.25}$$

We can also express the DuPont equation in ratio form:

$$\text{ROE} = \frac{\text{Net income}}{\text{Net sales}} \times \frac{\text{Net sales}}{\text{Total asets}} \times \frac{\text{Total assets}}{\text{Total equity}} \tag{4.26}$$

To check the DuPont relation, we will use some values from Exhibit 4.3, which lists financial ratios for Diaz Manufacturing. For 2017, Diaz's net profit margin is 7.58 percent, total asset turnover is 0.83, and the equity multiplier is 2.02. Substituting these values into Equation 4.25 yields:

$$\begin{aligned}\text{ROE} &= \text{Net profit margin} \times \text{Total asset turnover} \times \text{Equity multiplier}\\ &= 7.58 \times 0.83 \times 2.02\\ &= 12.71\%\end{aligned}$$

With rounding error, this agrees with the value computed for ROE using Equation 4.19.

Applying the DuPont System

In summary, the DuPont equation tells us that a firm's ROE is determined by three factors: (1) net profit margin, which measures the firm's operating efficiency and how it manages its interest expense and taxes; (2) total asset turnover, which measures the efficiency with which the firm's assets are utilized; and (3) the equity multiplier, which measures the firm's use of financial leverage. The schematic diagram in **Exhibit 4.5** shows how the three key DuPont ratios are linked together and how they relate to the balance sheet and income statement for Diaz Manufacturing.

The DuPont system of analysis is a useful tool to help identify problem areas within a firm. For example, suppose that North Sails Group, a sailboat manufacturer located in San Diego, California, is having financial difficulty. Management hires you to find out why the ship is financially sinking. You calculate the DuPont ratio values for the firm and obtain some industry averages to use as benchmarks, as shown.

DuPont Ratios	Firm	Industry
ROE	8%	16%
ROA	4%	8%
Equity multiplier	2	2
Net profit margin	8%	16%
Asset turnover	0.5	0.5

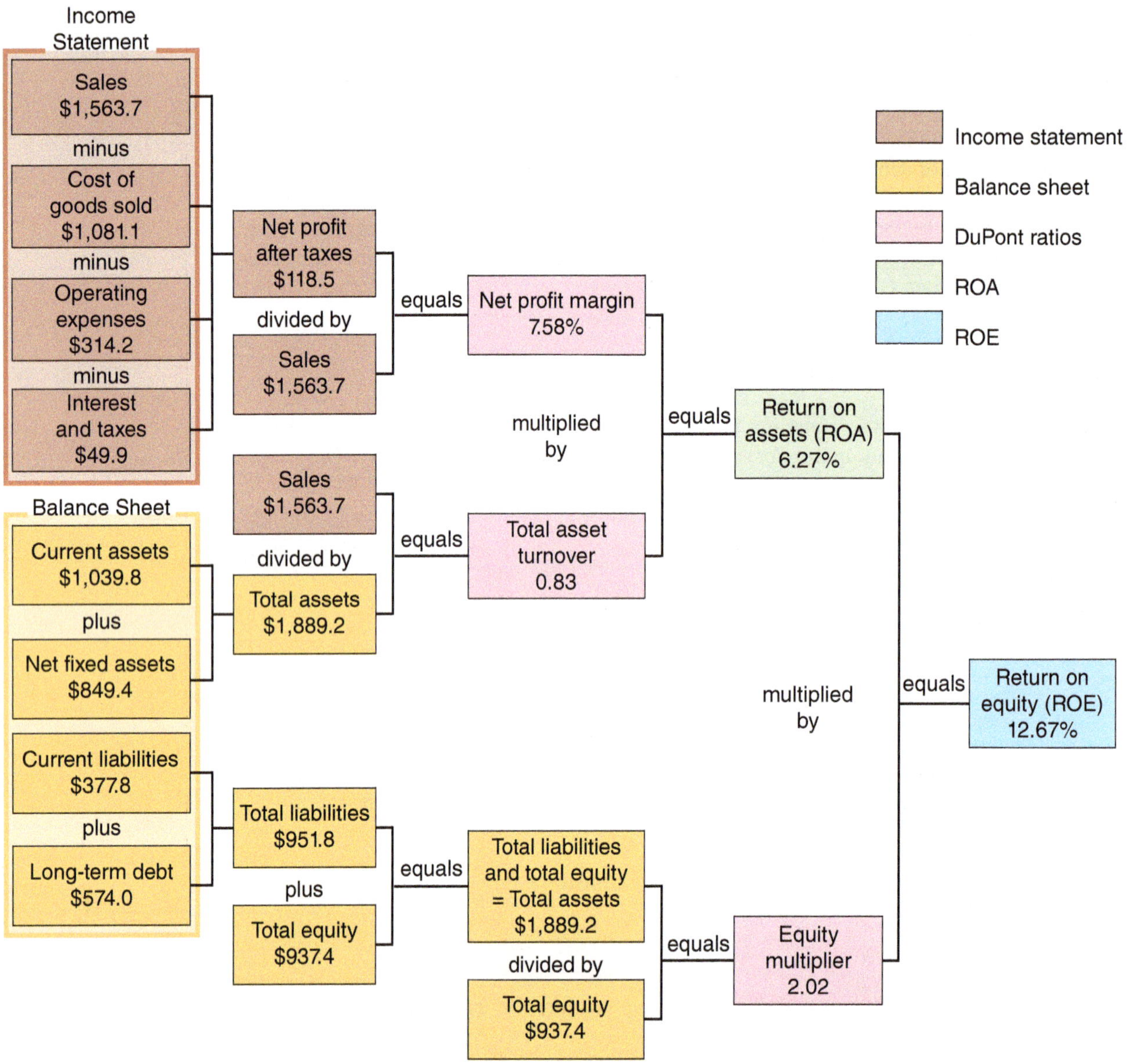

EXHIBIT 4.5 **Relations in the DuPont System of Analysis for Diaz Manufacturing in 2017 ($ millions)**

The diagram shows how the three key DuPont ratios are linked together and to the firm's balance sheet and income statement. Numbers in the exhibit are in millions of dollars and represent 2017 data from Diaz Manufacturing. The ROE of 12.67 percent differs from the 12.64 percent in Exhibit 4.3 due to rounding.

Clearly, the firm's ROE is quite low compared to its industry (8 percent versus 16 percent), so without question the firm has problems. Next, you examine the values for the firm's ROA and equity multiplier. The firm's use of financial leverage is equal to the industry standard of 2 times, but its ROA is half that of the industry (4 percent versus 8 percent). Because ROA is the product of net profit margin and total asset turnover, you next examine these two ratios. Asset turnover does not appear to be a problem because the firm's ratio is equal to the industry standard of 0.5 times. However, the firm's net profit margin is substantially below the benchmark standard (8 percent versus 16 percent). Thus, the firm's performance problem stems from a low profit margin.

Identifying the low profit margin as an area of concern is only a first step. Further investigation is necessary to determine the underlying problem and its causes. The point to remember is that financial analysis identifies areas of concern within the firm, but rarely does it tell us all we need to know.

Is Maximizing ROE an Appropriate Goal?

Throughout this book we have stressed the notion that management should make decisions that maximize the current value of the company stock. An important question is whether maximizing the value of ROE, as suggested by the DuPont system, is equivalent to maximizing share price. The short answer is that the two goals are not equivalent, but some discussion is warranted.

A major shortcoming of ROE is that it does not directly consider cash flow. ROE considers earnings, but earnings are not the same as future cash flows. Second, ROE does not consider risk. As discussed in Chapter 1, management and stockholders are very concerned about the degree of risk they face. Third, ROE does not consider the size of the initial investment or the size of future cash payments. As we stressed in Chapter 1, the essence of any business or investment decision is this: What is the size of the cash flows to be received, when do you expect to receive the cash flows, and how likely are you to receive them?

In spite of these shortcomings, ROE analysis is widely used in business as a measure of operating performance. Proponents of ROE analysis argue that it provides a systematic way for management to work through the income statement and balance sheet and to identify problem areas within the firm. Furthermore, they note that ROE and stockholder value are often highly correlated.

Before You Go On

1. What is the purpose of the DuPont system of analysis?
2. What is the equation for ROA in the DuPont system, and how do the factors in that equation influence the ratio?
3. What are the three major shortcomings of ROE?

4.5 Selecting a Benchmark

LEARNING OBJECTIVE

5. Explain what benchmarks are, describe how they are prepared, and discuss why they are important in financial statement analysis.

How do you judge whether a ratio value is too high or too low? Is the value good or bad? We touched on these questions several times earlier in this chapter. As we suggested, the starting point for making these judgments is selecting an appropriate benchmark—a standard that will be the basis for meaningful comparisons. Financial managers can gather appropriate benchmark data in three ways: through trend, industry, and peer group analysis.

Weblink

Visit the Web site of the Risk Management Association for a variety of ratio definitions and sample financial ratio benchmarks across different industries: http://www.rmahq.org/tools-publications/publications/annual-statement-studies.

Trend Analysis

Trend analysis uses history as its standard by evaluating a single firm's performance over time. This sort of analysis allows management to determine whether a given ratio value has increased or decreased over time and whether there has been an abrupt shift in a ratio value. An increase or decrease in a ratio value is in itself neither good nor bad. However, a ratio value that is changing typically prompts the financial manager to sort out the issues surrounding the change and to take any action that is warranted. Exhibit 4.3 shows the trends in Diaz Manufacturing's ratios. For example, the increase in Diaz's current ratio indicates that the company's liquidity has improved.

Industry Analysis

A second way to establish a benchmark is to conduct an industry group analysis. To do that, we identify a group of firms that have the same product line, compete in the same market, and are about the same size. The average ratio values for these firms will be our benchmarks. Since no two firms are identical, deciding which firms to include in the analysis is always a judgment call. If we can construct a sample of reasonable size, however, the average values provide defensible benchmarks.

Financial ratios and other financial data for industry groups are published by a number of sources—the U.S. Department of Commerce, Dun & Bradstreet, the Risk Management Association, and Standard & Poor's (S&P), to name a few. One widely used system for identifying industry groups is the **Standard Industrial Classification (SIC) System**. The SIC codes are four-digit numbers established by the federal government for statistical reporting purposes. The first two digits describe the type of business in a broad sense (for example, firms engaged in building construction, mining of metals, manufacturing of machinery, food stores, or banking). Diaz's two-digit code is 35: "Industrial and commercial machinery and computer equipment manufacturing."

Standard Industrial Classification (SIC) System a numerical system developed by the U.S. government to classify businesses according to the type of activity they perform

More than 400 companies fall into the "Industrial and commercial machinery and computer equipment manufacturing" code category. To narrow the group, we use more digits. Diaz Manufacturing's four-digit code is 3533 ("oil and gas field machinery and equipment manufacturing"), and there are only 35 firms in this category. Among firms within an SIC code, financial ratio data can be further categorized by asset size or by sales, which allows for more meaningful comparisons.

In 1977, the **North American Industry Classification System (NAICS)** was introduced as a new classification system. It was intended to refine and replace the older SIC codes, but it has been slow to catch on. Industry databases still allow you to sort data by either SIC or NAICS classifications.

North American Industry Classification System (NAICS) a classification system for businesses introduced to refine and replace the older SIC system

Weblink

You can find information about the SIC and NAICS systems at http://www.census.gov/eos/www/naics/.

Although industry databases are readily available and easy to use, they are far from perfect. When trying to find a sample of firms that are similar to your company, you may find the classifications too broad. For example, Wal-Mart and Nordstrom have the same four-digit SIC code (5311), but they are very different retailing firms. Another problem is that different databases may compute ratios differently. Thus, when making benchmark comparisons, you must be careful that your calculations match those in the database, or there could be some distortions in your findings.

Peer Group Analysis

The third way to establish benchmark information is to identify a group of firms that compete with the company we are analyzing. Ideally, the firms are in similar lines of business, are about the same size, and are direct competitors of the target firm. These firms form a *peer group*. Once a peer group has been identified, management can obtain the associated financial information and compute average ratio values against which the firm can compare its performance.

How do we determine which firms should be in the peer group? The senior management team within a company will know its competitors. If you're working outside the firm, you can look at the firm's annual report and at financial analysts' reports. Both of these sources usually identify key competitors. Exhibit 4.6 shows ratios for a five-firm peer group constructed for Diaz Manufacturing for 2015 through 2017.

EXHIBIT 4.6 Peer Group Ratios for Diaz Manufacturing

Peer group analysis is one way to establish benchmarks for a firm. Ideally, a firm's peer group is made up of firms that are direct competitors and are about the same size. The exhibit shows the average financial ratios for public companies that make up the peer group for Diaz Manufacturing for 2015, 2016, and 2017.

	2017	2016	2015
Liquidity Ratios:			
Current ratio	2.10	2.20	2.10
Quick ratio	1.50	1.60	1.50
Efficiency Ratios:			
Inventory turnover	5.40	5.30	5.20
Days' sales in inventory	67.59	68.87	70.19
Accounts receivable turnover	4.90	4.20	4.10
Days' sales outstanding	76.70	89.80	90.00
Total asset turnover	0.87	0.90	0.80
Fixed asset turnover	3.50	3.30	2.40
Leverage Ratios:			
Total debt ratio	0.18	0.11	0.21
Debt-to-equity ratio	0.40	0.20	0.50
Equity multiplier	2.02	1.77	2.05
Times interest earned	7.00	5.60	1.60
Cash coverage	7.50	8.20	1.30
Profitability Ratios:			
Gross profit margin	26.80%	24.10%	19.20%
Operating profit margin	12.00%	6.90%	2.70%
Net profit margin	10.74%	3.30%	0.10%
Return on assets	9.34%	3.30%	0.80%
Return on equity	13.07%	7.00%	1.00%
Market-Value Indicators:			
Price-earnings ratio	18.10	38.40	44.60
Earnings per share	$1.65	$3.85	$3.78
Market-to-book ratio	2.84	1.82	1.64

We consider the peer group methodology the best way to establish a benchmark if financial data for peer firms are publicly available. We should note, however, that comparison against a single firm is acceptable when there is a clear market leader and we want to compare a firm's performance and other characteristics against those of a firm considered the best. For example, Ford Motor Company may want to compare itself directly against the automobile manufacturer that is the most productive. It is worthwhile to compare a firm with the market leader to identify areas of relative strength and weakness.

Before You Go On

1. In what three ways can a financial manager choose a benchmark?
2. Explain what the SIC codes are, and discuss the pros and cons of using them in financial analysis.

4.6 Using Financial Ratios

LEARNING OBJECTIVE

6. Identify the major limitations in using financial statement analysis.

So far, our focus has been on the calculation of financial ratios. As you may already have concluded, however, the most important tasks are to *correctly interpret* the ratio values and to *make appropriate decisions* based on this interpretation. In this section we discuss using financial ratios in performance analysis.

Performance Analysis of Diaz Manufacturing

Let's examine Diaz Manufacturing's performance during 2017 using the DuPont system of analysis as our diagnostic tool and the peer group sample in Exhibit 4.6 as our benchmark. For ease of discussion, Diaz's financial ratios and the peer group data are assembled in **Exhibit 4.7**.

We start our analysis by looking at the big picture—the three key DuPont ratios for the firm and a peer group of firms (see Exhibit 4.7). We see that Diaz Manufacturing's ROE of 12.64 percent is below the benchmark value of 13.07 percent, a difference of 0.43 percent, which is not good news. More dramatically, Diaz's ROA is 3.07 percent below the peer group benchmark, which is a serious difference. Clearly, Diaz Manufacturing has some performance problems that need to be investigated.

To determine the problems, we examine the firm's equity multiplier and ROA results in more detail. The equity multiplier value of 2.02, versus the benchmark value of 1.40, suggests that Diaz Manufacturing is using more leverage than the average firm in the benchmark sample. Management is comfortable with the higher-than-average leverage.

EXHIBIT 4.7 Peer Group Analysis for Diaz Manufacturing in 2017

Examining the differences between the ratios of a firm and its peer group is a good way to spot areas that require further analysis.

	(1) Diaz Ratio	(2) Peer Group Ratio	(3) Difference (Column 1 – Column 2)
DuPont Ratios:			
Return on equity (%)	12.64	13.07	(0.43)
Return on assets (%)	6.27	9.34	(3.07)
Equity multiplier (%)	2.02	1.40	0.62
Net profit margin (%)	7.58	10.74	(3.16)
Total asset turnover	0.83	0.87	(0.04)
Asset Ratios:			
Current ratio	2.75	2.10	0.65
Fixed asset turnover	3.92	3.50	0.42
Inventory turnover	2.55	5.40	(2.85)
Accounts receivable turnover	5.11	4.90	0.21
Profit Margins:			
Gross profit margin (%)	30.86	26.80	4.06
Operating margin (%)	10.77	12.00	(1.23)
Net profit margin (%)	7.58	10.74	(3.16)

Conversations with the firm's investment banker, however, indicate that the company's debt could become a problem if the economy deteriorated and went into a recession.

Without the higher equity multiplier and management's willingness to bear additional risk, Diaz Manufacturing's ROE would be much lower. To illustrate this point, suppose management reduced the company's leverage to the peer group average equity multiplier of 1.40 (see Exhibit 4.7). With an equity multiplier of 1.40, the firm's ROE would be only 8.78 percent (0.0627 × 1.40 = 0.0878, or 8.78 percent); this is 3.86 percent below the firm's current ROE of 12.64 percent and 4.29 percent below the peer group benchmark. Thus, the use of higher leverage has, to some extent, masked the severity of the firm's problem with ROA.

Recall that ROA equals the product of the net profit margin and total asset turnover. Diaz's net profit margin is 3.16 percentage points lower than the benchmark value (7.58 percent − 10.74 percent = −3.16 percent), and its total asset turnover ratio is slightly below the benchmark value (0.83 versus 0.87). Thus, both ratios that comprise ROA are below the peer group benchmark standard, but the net profit margin appears to be the larger problem.

Turning to the asset turnover ratios shown in Exhibit 4.7, we find that the ratios for Diaz are generally similar to the corresponding peer group ratios. An exception is the inventory turnover ratio, which is substantially below the benchmark: 2.55 for Diaz versus 5.40 for the benchmark. Diaz's management needs to investigate why the inventory turnover ratio is off the mark.

Because Diaz Manufacturing's net profit margin is low, we next look at the various profit margins shown in Exhibit 4.7 to gain insight into this situation. Diaz Manufacturing's gross profit margin is 4.06 percentage points above the benchmark value (30.86 percent − 26.80 percent = 4.06 percent), which is good news. Since gross profit margin is a factor of sales and the cost of goods sold, we can conclude that there is no problem with the price the firm is charging for its products or with its cost of goods sold.

Diaz's problems begin with its operating margin of 10.77 percent, which is 1.23 percentage points below the peer group benchmark of 12.00 percent (10.77 percent − 12.00 percent = −1.23 percent). The major controllable expense here is selling and administrative costs, and management needs to investigate why these expenses appear to be out of line.

In sum, the DuPont analysis of Diaz Manufacturing has identified two areas that warrant detailed investigation by management: (1) the larger-than-average inventory (slow inventory turnover) and (2) the above-average selling and administrative expenses. Management must now investigate each of these areas and come up with a course of action. Management may also want to give careful consideration to the firm's high degree of financial leverage and whether it represents a prudent degree of risk.

Financial ratio analysis is an excellent diagnostic tool. It helps management identify the problem areas in the firm—the symptoms. However, it does not tell management what the causes of the problems are or what course of action should be taken. Management must drill down into the accounting data, talk with managers in the field, and if appropriate, talk with people outside the firm, such as suppliers, to understand what is causing the problems and how best to fix them.

Learning by Doing Application 4.5 and **Decision Making Example 4.3** illustrate more calculations from a DuPont analysis and their interpretation.

LEARNING BY DOING

APPLICATION 4.5 | Ron's Jewelry Store and the Missing Data

Problem Ron Roberts has owned and managed a profitable jewelry business in San Diego County for the past five years. He believes his jewelry store is one of the best managed in the county, and he is considering opening several new stores.

When Ron started the store, he supplied all the equity financing himself and financed the rest with personal loans from friends and family members. To open more stores, Ron needs a bank loan. The bank will want to examine his financial statements and know something about the competition he faces.

Ron has asked his brother-in-law, Dennis O'Neil, a CPA, to analyze the financials. Ron has also gathered some financial information about a company he considers the chief competition in the San Diego County market. The competitor has been in business for 25 years, has a number of stores, and is widely admired for its owners' management skills. Dennis organizes the available information in the following table:

Financial Ratio/Data	Ron's Store	Competitor
Net sales ($ thousands)	$240	$300
Net income ($ thousands)	$ 6	—
ROE	13.13%	—
Net profit margin	—	5.84%
Asset turnover	1.5	1.5
Equity multiplier	—	1.5
Debt-to-equity ratio	2.5	—

Calculate the missing values for the financial data above.

Approach Use the ratio equations discussed in the text to calculate the missing financial ratios for both Ron's store and the competitor.

Solution

Ron's jewelry store:

1. $\text{Net profit margin} = \dfrac{\text{Net income}}{\text{Net sales}} = \dfrac{\$6}{\$240} = 0.025, \text{ or } 2.5\%$

2. Equity multipier = 1 + Debt-to-equity ratio = 1 + 2.5 = 3.5

Competitor:

1. Net income = Net profit margin × Net sales = 0.0584 × $300 = $17.52

2. ROE = Net profit margin × Total asset turnover × Equity multiplier
   = 0.0584 × 1.5 × 1.5 = 0.1314, or 13.14%

3. $\text{Debt-to-equity ratio} = \dfrac{\text{Total debt}}{\text{Total equity}} = \dfrac{\$66.82}{\$133.1} = 0.50$

   (a) $\text{Total equity} = \dfrac{\text{Net income}}{\text{Net income/Total equity}} = \dfrac{\$17.5}{0.1314} = \$133.18$

   (b) $\text{Total assets} = \dfrac{\text{Net sales}}{\text{Total asset turnover}} = \dfrac{\$300}{1.5} = \$200.00$

   (c) Total debt = Total assets − Total equity = $200.00 − $133.18 = $66.82

DECISION MAKING

EXAMPLE 4.3 | Ron's Jewelry Store and the DuPont Analysis

Situation Let's continue with our analysis of Ron's jewelry store, introduced in Learning by Doing Application 4.5. Brother-in-law Dennis has been asked to analyze the company's financials. He decides to use the DuPont system of analysis as a framework. He arranges the critical information as follows:

Financial Ratios	Ron's Store	Competitor
ROE	13.13%	13.14%
ROA	3.75%	8.76%
Net profit margin	2.50%	5.84%
Asset turnover	1.5	1.5
Equity multiplier	3.5	1.5
Debt-to-equity ratio	2.5	0.5
Net sales ($ thousands)	$240	$300
Net income ($ thousands)	$ 6.0	$ 17.5

Given the above financial ratios, what recommendations should Dennis make regarding Ron's jewelry store and its management?

Decision The good news is that Ron is able to earn about the same ROE as his major competitor. Unfortunately for Ron, it's pretty much downhill from there. Turning to the first two DuPont system ratios, we can see that Ron's ROA of 3.75 percent is much lower than his major competitor's ROA of 8.76 percent. Ron's business is also very highly leveraged, with an equity multiplier of 3.5 times, compared with 1.5 times for the competitor. In fact, the only reason Ron's ROE is comparable to the competitor's is the high leverage. Ron's debt-to-equity ratio is 2.5 whereas the competitor's is only 0.5.

Breaking the ROA into its components, we find that Ron's asset turnover ratio is the same as the competitor's, 1.5. However, the profitability of Ron's store is extremely poor as measured by the firm's net profit margin of 2.50 percent, compared with the competitor's margin of 5.84 percent. One possible explanation is that to stimulate sales and maintain asset turnover, Ron has been selling his merchandise at too low a price.

In summary, Ron's jewelry store is not well managed. Ron needs to either increase his net profit margin or increase his inventory turnover to bring his ROA into line with that of his major competitor. Ron may also need to reduce his dependence on financial leverage, but it makes sense to review interest coverage ratios before deciding whether he should do so.

Limitations of Financial Statement Analysis

Financial statement and ratio analysis as discussed in this chapter presents two major problems. First, it depends on accounting data based on historical costs. As we discussed in Chapter 3, knowledgeable financial managers would prefer to use financial statements in which all of the firm's assets and liabilities are valued at market. Financial statements based on current market values more closely reflect a firm's true economic condition than do statements based on historical cost.

Second, there is little theory to guide us in making judgments based on financial statement and ratio analysis. That is why it is difficult to say a current ratio of 2.0 is good or bad or to say whether ROE or ROA is a more important ratio. The lack of theory explains, in part, why rules of thumb are often used as decision rules in financial statement analysis. The problem with decision rules based on experience rather than theory is that they may work fine in a stable economic environment, but may fail when a significant shift takes place. For example, if you developed a set of decision rules to help manage your business in an economic environment with low inflation, those decision rules might fail if the economy became inflationary.

Despite the limitations, we know that financial managers and analysts routinely use financial statements and ratio analysis to evaluate a firm's performance and to make a variety of decisions about the firm. These financial statements and the resulting analysis are the primary means by which financial information is communicated both inside and outside of firms. The availability of market-value data is limited for public corporations and such data are not available for privately held firms and other entities such as government units.

Thus, practically speaking, historical accounting information often represents the best available information. However, times are changing. As the accounting profession becomes more comfortable with the use of market-value data and as technology increases its availability and reliability and lowers its cost, we expect to see an increase in the use of market-based financial statements.

Before You Go On

1. Explain how the DuPont system allows us to evaluate a firm's performance.
2. What are the limitations on traditional financial statement analysis?
3. List some of the problems that financial analysts confront when analyzing financial statements.

Summary of Learning Objectives

1 Explain the three perspectives from which financial statements can be viewed.

Financial statements can be viewed from the owners', managers', or creditors' perspective. All three groups are ultimately interested in a firm's profitability, but each group takes a different view. Stockholders want to know how much cash they can expect to receive, what their return on investment will be, and how much their stock is worth in the market. Managers are concerned with maximizing the firm's long-term value through a series of day-to-day management decisions; thus, they need to see the impact of their decisions on the financial statements to confirm that things are going as planned. Creditors are concerned with how much debt the firm is using and whether the firm will have enough cash to meet its debt obligations.

2 Describe common-size financial statements, explain why they are used, and be able to prepare and use them to analyze the historical performance of a firm.

Common-size financial statements are financial statements in which each number has been scaled by a common measure of firm size: Balance sheets are expressed as a percentage of total assets, and income statements are expressed as a percentage of net sales. Common-size financial statements make it easier to evaluate changes in a firm's performance and financial condition over time. They are also useful when comparing firms that are significantly different in size. The preparation of common-size financial statements and their use are illustrated for Diaz Manufacturing in Section 4.2.

3 Discuss how financial ratios facilitate financial analysis and be able to compute and use them to analyze a firm's performance.

Financial ratios are used in financial analysis because they eliminate problems caused by comparing two or more companies of different size, or when looking at the same company over time as the size changes. Financial ratios can be divided into five categories: (1) Liquidity ratios measure the ability of a company to cover its current bills. (2) Efficiency ratios tell how efficiently the firm uses its assets. (3) Leverage ratios tell how much debt a firm has in its capital structure and whether the firm can meet its long-term financial obligations. (4) Profitability ratios focus on the firm's earnings. (5) Market value indicators look at a company based on market data as opposed to historical data used in financial statements. The computation and analysis of major financial ratios are presented in Section 4.3 (also see the Summary of Key Equations that follows).

4 Describe the DuPont system of analysis and be able to use it to evaluate a firm's performance and identify corrective actions that may be necessary.

The DuPont system of analysis is a diagnostic tool that uses financial ratios to assess a firm's financial condition. Once the financial ratios are calculated and the assessment is complete, management can focus on correcting the problems within the context of maximizing the firm's ROE. For analysis, the DuPont system breaks ROE into three components: net profit margin, which measures operating efficiency; total asset turnover, which measures how efficiently the firm's assets are being used; and the equity multiplier, which measures financial leverage. A diagnostic analysis of a firm's performance using the DuPont system is illustrated in Section 4.4.

5 Explain what benchmarks are, describe how they are prepared, and discuss why they are important in financial statement analysis.

Benchmarks are used to provide a standard for evaluating the financial performance of a firm. In financial statement analysis, a number of benchmarks are used. Most often, benchmark comparisons involve competitors that are roughly the same size and that offer a similar range of products. Another form of benchmarking is time-trend analysis, which compares a firm's current financial ratios against the same ratios from past years. Time-trend analysis tells us whether a ratio has increased, decreased, or remained the same over time. The preparation and use of peer group benchmark data are illustrated in Section 4.6.

6 Identify the major limitations in using financial statement analysis.

The major limitations to financial statement and ratio analysis are the use of historical accounting data and the lack of theory to guide the decision maker. The lack of theory explains, in part, why there are so many rules of thumb. Rules of thumb are useful in that they may work under certain conditions. However, they may also lead to poor decisions if circumstances change.

Summary of Key Equations

Equation	Description	Formula
4.1	Liquidity Ratio	$\text{Current ratio} = \dfrac{\text{Current assets}}{\text{Current liabilities}}$
4.2	Liquidity Ratio	$\text{Quick ratio} = \dfrac{\text{Current assets} - \text{Inventory}}{\text{Current liabilities}}$
4.3	Efficiency Ratio	$\text{Inventory turnover} = \dfrac{\text{Cost of goods sold}}{\text{Inventory}}$
4.4	Efficiency Ratio	$\text{Day's sales in inventory} = \dfrac{\text{365 days}}{\text{Inventory turnover}}$

continued

continued

Equation	Description	Formula
4.5	Efficiency Ratio	$\text{Accounts receivable turnover} = \dfrac{\text{Net sales}}{\text{Accounts receivable}}$
4.6	Efficiency Ratio	$\text{Day's sales outstanding} = \dfrac{\text{365 days}}{\text{Accounts receivable turnover}}$
4.7	Efficiency Ratio	$\text{Total asset turnover} = \dfrac{\text{Net sales}}{\text{Total assets}}$
4.8	Efficiency Ratio	$\text{Fixed asset turnover} = \dfrac{\text{Net sales}}{\text{Net fixed assets}}$
4.9	Leverage Ratio	$\text{Total debt ratio} = \dfrac{\text{Total debt}}{\text{Total assets}}$
4.10	Leverage Ratio	$\text{Debt-to-equity ratio} = \dfrac{\text{Total debt}}{\text{Total equity}}$
4.11	Leverage Ratio	$\text{Equity multiplier} = \dfrac{\text{Total assets}}{\text{Total equity}}$
4.12	Leverage Ratio	$\text{Times interest earned} = \dfrac{\text{EBIT}}{\text{Interest expense}}$
4.13	Leverage Ratio	$\text{Cash coverage} = \dfrac{\text{EBITDA}}{\text{Interest expense}}$
4.14	Profitability Ratio	$\text{Gross profit margin} = \dfrac{\text{Net sales} - \text{Cost of goods sold}}{\text{Net sales}}$
4.15	Profitability Ratio	$\text{Operating profit margin} = \dfrac{\text{EBIT}}{\text{Net sales}}$
4.16	Profitability Ratio	$\text{Net profit margin} = \dfrac{\text{Net income}}{\text{Net sales}}$
4.17	Profitability Ratio	$\text{EBIT return on assets (EROA)} = \dfrac{\text{EBIT}}{\text{Total assets}}$
4.18	Profitability Ratio	$\text{Return on assets (ROA)} = \dfrac{\text{Net income}}{\text{Total assets}}$
4.19	Profitability Ratio	$\text{Return on equity (ROE)} = \dfrac{\text{Net income}}{\text{Total equity}}$
4.20	Market-Value-Indicator	$\text{Earning per share} = \dfrac{\text{Net income}}{\text{Shares outstanding}}$
4.21	Market-Value Indicator	$\text{Price-earnings ratio} = \dfrac{\text{Price per share}}{\text{Earnings per share}}$
4.22	Market-Value Indicator	$\text{Market-to-book ratio} = \dfrac{\text{Market value of equity per share}}{\text{Book value of equity per share}}$
4.23	ROA Breakdown	$\text{ROA} = \text{Net profit margin} \times \text{Total asset turnover}$
4.24	ROE Breakdown	$\text{ROE} = \text{ROA} \times \text{Equity multiplier}$
4.25	DuPont Equation	$\text{ROE} = \text{Net profit margin} \times \text{Total asset turnover} \times \text{Equity multiplier}$
4.26	DuPont Equation	$\text{ROE} = \dfrac{\text{Net income}}{\text{Net sales}} \times \dfrac{\text{Net sales}}{\text{Total assets}} \times \dfrac{\text{Total assets}}{\text{Total equity}}$

Self-Study Problems

4.1 The Abercrombie Supply Company reported the following information for 2017. Prepare a common-size income statement for the year ended June 30, 2017.

Abercrombie Supply Company Income Statement for the Fiscal Year Ended June 30, 2017 ($ thousands)	
Net sales	$2,110,965
Cost of goods sold	1,459,455
Selling and administrative expenses	312,044
Nonrecurring expenses	27,215
Earnings before interest, taxes, depreciation, and amortization (EBITDA)	$ 312,251
Depreciation	112,178
Earnings before interest and taxes (EBIT)	$ 200,073
Interest expense	117,587
Earnings before taxes (EBT)	$ 82,486
Taxes (35%)	28,870
Net income	$ 53,616

4.2 Prepare a common-size balance sheet from the following information for Abercrombie Supply Company.

Abercrombie Supply Company Balance Sheet as of June 30, 2017 ($ thousands)			
Assets:		Liabilities and Equity:	
Cash and marketable securities	$ 396,494	Accounts payable	$ 817,845
Accounts receivable	708,275	Notes payable	101,229
Inventory	1,152,398	Accrued income taxes	41,322
Other current assets	42,115	Total current liabilities	$ 960,396
Total current assets	$2,299,282	Long-term debt	1,149,520
Net plant and equipment	1,978,455	Total liabilities	$2,109,916
		Common stock	1,312,137
		Retained earnings	855,684
		Total common equity	$2,167,821
Total assets	$4,277,737	Total liabilities and equity	$4,277,737

4.3 Using the 2017 data for the Abercrombie Supply Company, calculate the following liquidity ratios:

a. Current ratio.

b. Quick ratio.

4.4 Refer to the balance sheet and income statement for Abercrombie Supply Company for the year ended June 30, 2017. Calculate the following ratios:

a. Inventory turnover.

b. Days' sales outstanding.

c. Total asset turnover.

d. Fixed asset turnover.

e. Total debt ratio.

f. Debt-to-equity ratio.

g. Times-interest-earned.

h. Cash coverage.

4.5 Last year ABC companies had accounts receivable turnover of 15, total asset turnover of 4.5, and total assets of $1,000,000. What was the value of ABC's accounts receivable? What was the value of its net sales?

4.6 The equity multiplier for Spiffy Corporation is 1.75, its EBIT return on assets (EROA) is 0.07, and the value of its equity is $850,000. What is the value of Spiffy's total assets? What is the value of its EBIT?

4.7 Refer again to the balance sheet and income statement for Abercrombie Supply Company for the fiscal year ended June 30, 2017. Use the DuPont equation to calculate the return on equity (ROE). In the process, calculate the following ratios: profit margin, EBIT return on assets, return on assets, equity multiplier, and total asset turnover.

Solutions to Self-Study Problems

4.1 The common-size income statement for Abercrombie Supply Company should look like the following one:

Abercrombie Supply Company
Common-Size Income Statement for the Fiscal Year Ended June 30, 2017 ($ thousands)

		% of Net Sales
Net sales	$2,110,965	100.0
Cost of goods sold	1,459,455	69.1
Selling and administrative expenses	312,044	14.8
Nonrecurring expenses	27,215	1.3
Earnings before interest, taxes, depreciation, and amortization (EBITDA)	$ 312,251	14.8
Depreciation	112,178	5.3
Earnings before interest and taxes (EBIT)	$ 200,073	9.5
Interest expense	117,587	5.6
Earnings before taxes (EBT)	$ 82,486	3.9
Taxes (35%)	28,870	1.4
Net income	$ 53,616	2.5

4.2 Abercrombie Supply's common-size balance sheet is as follows:

Abercrombie Supply Company
Common-Size Balance Sheet as of June 30, 2017 ($ thousands)

Assets:		% of Assets	Liabilities and Equity:		% of Assets
Cash and marketable securities	$ 396,494	9.3	Accounts payable and accruals	$ 817,845	19.1
Accounts receivable	708,275	16.5	Notes payable	101,229	2.4
Inventory	1,152,398	26.9	Accrued income taxes	41,322	1.0
Other current assets	42,115	1.0	Total current liabilities	$ 960,396	22.5
Total current assets	$2,299,282	53.7	Long-term debt	1,149,520	26.9
Net plant and equipment	1,978,455	46.3	Total liabilities	$2,109,916	49.3
			Common stock	1,312,137	30.7
			Retained earnings	855,684	20.0
			Total common equity	$2,167,821	50.7
Total asssets	$4,277,737	100.0	Total liabilities and equity	$4,277,737	100.0

4.3 Abercrombie Supply's current ratio and quick ratio are calculated as follows:

a. $\text{Current ratio} = \dfrac{\$2,299,282}{\$960,396} = 2.39$

b. $\text{Quick ratio} = \dfrac{\$2,299,282 - \$1,152,398}{\$960,396} = 1.19$

4.4 The ratios are calculated as shown in the following table:

Ratio	Calculation	Value
Inventory turnover	$1,459,455 / 1,152,398	1.27
Days' sales outstanding	$708,275 / ($2,110,965/365)	122.5 days
Total asset turnover	$2,110,965 / $4,277,737	0.49
Fixed asset turnover	$2,110,965 / $1,978,455	1.07
Total debt ratio	$2,109,916 / $4,277,737	0.493
Debt-to-equity ratio	$2,109,916 / $2,167,821	0.974
Times-interest-earned	$200,073 / $117,587	1.7
Cash coverage	$312,251 / $117,587	2.66

4.5 In this problem we can use the accounts receivable turnover equation (Equation 4.5) and total asset turnover equation (Equation 4.7) to solve for the values of accounts receivable and net sales.

$$\text{Accounts receivable turnover} = \frac{\text{Net sales}}{\text{Accounts receivable}}$$

$$\text{Total asset turnover} = \frac{\text{Net sales}}{\text{Total assets}}$$

Dividing accounts receivable turnover by total asset turnover yields:

$$\frac{\text{Net sales}}{\text{Accounts receivable}} / \frac{\text{Net sales}}{\text{Total assets}} = \frac{\text{Total assets}}{\text{Accounts receivable}}$$

$$= \frac{15}{4.5}$$

$$= 3.333$$

With total assets of \$1,000,000, accounts must receivable equal:

$$\text{Accounts receivable} = \frac{\text{Total assets}}{3.3333}$$

$$= \frac{\$1{,}000{,}00}{3.3333}$$

$$= \$300{,}000$$

From the total asset turnover equation, net sales equal:

$$\text{Total asset turnover} = \frac{\text{Net sales}}{\text{Total assets}}$$

$$4.5 = \frac{\text{Net sales}}{\$1{,}000{,}000}$$

$$\text{Net sales} = (4.5)(\$1{,}000{,}000) = \$4{,}500{,}000$$

4.6 In this problem we can use the equity multiplier equation (Equation 4.11) and the EROA equation (Equation 4.17) to solve for the values of total assets and EBIT.

$$\text{Equity multiplier} = \frac{\text{Total assets}}{\text{Total equity}}$$

$$\text{EROA} = \frac{\text{EBIT}}{\text{Total assets}}$$

First, use the equity multiplier equation to solve for total assets:

$$\text{Equity multiplier} = \frac{\text{Total assets}}{\text{Total equity}}$$

$$1.75 = \frac{\text{Total assets}}{\$850{,}000}$$

$$\text{Total assets} = 1.75 \times \$850{,}000$$

$$= \$1{,}487{,}500$$

Next, use the EROA equation to solve for EBIT:

$$\text{EROA} = \frac{\text{EBIT}}{\text{Total assets}}$$

$$0.07 = \frac{\text{EBIT}}{\$1{,}487{,}500}$$

$$\text{EBIT} = 0.07 \times \$1{,}487{,}500$$

$$= \$104{,}125$$

4.7 Following are the calculations for the ROE and associated ratios:

$$\text{Net profit margin} = \frac{\text{Net income}}{\text{Net sales}} = \frac{\$53{,}616}{\$2{,}110{,}965} = 0.0254, \text{ or } 2.54\%$$

$$\text{EBIT ROA} = \frac{\text{EBIT}}{\text{Total assets}} = \frac{\$200{,}073}{\$4{,}277{,}737} = 0.0468, \text{ or } 4.68\%$$

$$\text{Return on assets} = \frac{\text{Net income}}{\text{Total assets}} = \frac{\$53{,}616}{\$4{,}277{,}737} = 0.0125, \text{ or } 1.25\%$$

$$\text{Equity multiplier} = \frac{\text{Total assets}}{\text{Total equity}} = \frac{\$4{,}277{,}737}{\$2{,}167{,}821} = 1.97$$

$$\text{Total asset turnover} = \frac{\text{Net sales}}{\text{Total assets}} = \frac{\$2{,}110{,}965}{\$4{,}277{,}737} = 0.49$$

DuPont identity:

$$\begin{aligned}\text{ROE} &= \text{ROA} \times \text{Equity multiplier}\\ &= \text{Net profit margin} \times \text{Total asset turnover ratio} \times \text{Equity multiplier}\\ &= \frac{\text{Net income}}{\text{Net sales}} \times \frac{\text{Net sales}}{\text{Total assets}} \times \frac{\text{Total assets}}{\text{Total equity}}\\ &= 0.0254 \times 0.49 \times 1.97\\ &= 0.0245, \text{ or } 2.45\%\end{aligned}$$

WileyPLUS

Questions and Problems, Solution Walkthrough Videos, Learning by Doing Tutorials, and additional study tools and resources are available in WileyPLUS.

Discussion Questions

4.1 What does it mean when a company's return on assets (ROA) is equal to its return on equity (ROE)?

4.2 Why is too much liquidity not a good thing?

4.3 Inventory is excluded when the quick ratio or acid-test ratio is calculated because inventory is the most difficult current asset to convert to cash without loss of value. What types of inventory are likely to be most easily converted to cash without loss of value?

4.4 What does a very high inventory turnover ratio signify?

4.5 How would one explain a low receivables turnover ratio?

4.6 What additional information does the fixed asset turnover ratio provide over the total asset turnover ratio? For which industries does it carry greater significance?

4.7 How does financial leverage help stockholders?

4.8 Why is ROE generally much higher than ROA for banks relative to other industries?

4.9 Why is the ROE a more appropriate proxy for stockholder value maximization for some firms than for other firms?

4.10 Why is it not enough for an analyst to look at just the short-term and long-term debt on a firm's balance sheet when assessing the firm's fixed obligations?

Questions and Problems

Excel *Excel templates and resources available in* **WileyPLUS**

Basic

4.1 **Liquidity ratios:** Explain why the quick ratio or acid-test ratio is a better measure of a firm's liquidity than the current ratio.

4.2 **Liquidity ratios:** Flying Penguins Corp. has total current assets of \$11,845,175, current liabilities of \$5,311,020, and a quick ratio of 0.89. How much inventory does it have?

4.3 Efficiency ratio: If Newton Manufacturers has an accounts receivable turnover of 4.8 times and net sales of $7,812,379, what would its receivables be?

4.4 Efficiency ratio: Bummel and Strand Corp. has a gross profit margin of 33.7 percent, sales of $47,112,365, and inventory of $14,595,435. What is its inventory turnover ratio?

4.5 Efficiency ratio: Sorenson Inc. has sales of $3,112,489, a gross profit margin of 23.1 percent, and inventory of $833,145. What are the company's inventory turnover ratio and days' sales in inventory?

4.6 Leverage ratios: Breckenridge Ski Company has total assets of $422,235,811 and a debt ratio of 29.5 percent. Calculate the company's debt-to-equity ratio and equity multiplier.

4.7 Leverage ratios: Norton Company has a debt-to-equity ratio of 1.65, ROA of 11.3 percent, and total equity of $1,322,796. What are the company's equity multiplier, debt ratio, and ROE?

4.8 DuPont equation: The Rangoon Timber Company has the following ratios:

Net sales/Total assets = 2.23   ROA = 9.69%   ROE = 16.4%

What are Rangoon's profit margin and debt ratios?

4.9 DuPont equation: Lemmon Enterprises has a total asset turnover of 2.1 and a net profit margin of 7.5%. If its equity multiplier is 1.90, what is the ROE for Lemmon Enterprises?

4.10 Benchmark analysis: List the ways a company's financial manager can benchmark the company's own performance.

4.11 Benchmark analysis: Trademark Corp.'s financial manager collected the following information to compare its performance against that of its peers.

Ratios	Trademark	Peer Group
DSO	33.5 days	27.9 days
Total asset turnover	2.3	3.7
Inventory turnover	1.8	2.8
Quick ratio	0.6	1.3

a. Explain how Trademark is performing relative to its peers.

b. How do the industry ratios help Trademark's management?

4.12 Market-value ratios: Rockwell Jewelers management announced that the company had net earnings of $6,481,778 for this year. The company has 2,543,800 shares outstanding, and the year-end stock price is $54.21. What are Rockwell's earnings per share and P/E ratio?

4.13 Market-value ratios: Chisel Corporation has 3 million shares outstanding at a price per share of $3.25. If the debt-to-equity ratio is 1.7 and total book value of debt equals $12,400,000, what is the market-to-book ratio for Chisel Corporation?

Intermediate

4.14 Liquidity ratios: Laurel Electronics has a quick ratio of 1.15, current liabilities of $5,311,020, and inventories of $7,121,599. What is the firm's current ratio?

4.15 Efficiency ratio: Lambda Corporation has current liabilities of $450,000, a quick ratio of 1.8, inventory turnover of 5.0, and a current ratio of 3.5. What is the cost of goods sold for Lambda Corporation?

4.16 Efficiency ratio: Norwood Corp. currently has accounts receivable of $1,223,675 on net sales of $6,216,900. What are its accounts receivable turnover and days' sales outstanding (DSO)?

4.17 Efficiency ratio: If Norwood Corp.'s management wants to reduce the DSO from that calculated in Problem 4.16 to an industry average of 56.3 days and its net sales are expected to decline by about 12 percent, what would the new level of receivables be?

4.18 Coverage ratios: Nimitz Rental Company had depreciation expenses of $108,905, interest expenses of $78,112, and an EBIT of $1,254,338 for the year ended June 30, 2017. What are the times-interest-earned and cash coverage ratios for this company?

4.19 Leverage ratios: Conseco, Inc., has a debt ratio of 0.56. What are the company's debt-to-equity ratio and equity multiplier?

4.20 Profitability ratios: Cisco Systems has total assets of $35.594 billion, total debt of $9.678 billion, and net sales of $22.045 billion. Its net profit margin for the year is 20 percent, while the operating profit margin is 30 percent. What are Cisco's net income, EROA, ROA, and ROE?

4.21 Profitability ratios: Procter & Gamble reported the following information for its fiscal year end: On net sales of $51.407 billion, the company earned net income after taxes of $6.481 billion. It had cost of goods sold of $25.076 billion and EBIT of $9.827 billion. What are the company's gross profit margin, operating profit margin, and net profit margin?

4.22 Profitability ratios: Wal-Mart, Inc., has net income of $9,054,000 on net sales of $256,329,812. The company has total assets of $104,912,112 and stockholders' equity of $43,623,445. Use the extended DuPont identity to find the return on assets and return on equity for the firm.

4.23 Profitability ratios: Xtreme Sports Innovations has disclosed the following information:

EBIT = $25,664,300	Net income = $13,054,000
Net sales = $83,125,336	Total debt = $20,885,753
Total assets = $71,244,863	

Compute the following ratios for this firm using the DuPont identity: debt-to-equity ratio, EROA, ROA, and ROE.

4.24 Market-value ratios: Cisco Systems had net income of $4.401 billion and, at year end, 6.735 billion shares outstanding. Calculate the earnings per share for the company.

4.25 Market-value ratios: Use the information for Cisco Systems in Problem 4.24. In addition, the company's EBITDA was $6.834 billion and its share price was $22.36. Compute the firm's price-earnings ratio.

4.26 DuPont equation: Carter, Inc., a manufacturer of electrical supplies, has an ROE of 23.1 percent, a profit margin of 4.9 percent, and a total asset turnover ratio of 2.6 times. Its peer group also has an ROE of 23.1 percent, but has outperformed Carter with a net profit margin of 5.3 percent and a total asset turnover ratio of 3.0 times. Explain how Carter managed to achieve the same level of profitability as reflected by the ROE.

4.27 DuPont equation: Grossman Enterprises has an equity multiplier of 2.6 times, total assets of $2,312,000, an ROE of 14.8 percent, and a total asset turnover ratio of 2.8 times. Calculate the firm's sales and ROA.

Advanced

4.28 Complete the balance sheet of Flying Roos Corporation.

Flying Roos Corporation Balance Sheet as of December 31, 2017			
Assets:		Liabilities and Equity:	
Cash and marketable securities		Accounts payable and accruals	
Accounts receivable		Notes payable	$ 300,000
Inventory		Total current liabilities	
Total current assets			
		Long-term debt	$2,000,000
Net plant and equipment		Common stock	
		Retained earnings	$1,250,000
Total assets	$8,000,000	Total liabilities and equity	

You have the following information:

Debt ratio = 40%	DSO = 39 days
Current ratio = 1.5	Inventory turnover ratio = 3.375
Net sales = $2.25 million	Cost of goods sold = $1.6875 million

4.29 For the year ended June 30, 2017, Northern Clothing Company has total assets of $87,631,181, ROA of 11.67 percent, ROE of 21.19 percent, and a net profit margin of 11.59 percent. What are the company's net income and net sales? Calculate the firm's debt-to-equity ratio.

4.30 Blackwell Automotive's balance sheet at the end of its most recent fiscal year shows the following information:

Blackwell Automotive Balance Sheet as of March 31, 2017			
Assets:		Liabilities and Equity:	
Cash and marketable securities	$ 23,015	Accounts payable and accruals	$ 163,257
Accounts receivable	141,258	Notes payable	21,115
Inventory	212,444	Total current liabilities	$ 184,372
Total current assets	$ 376,717	Long-term debt	168,022
Net plant and equipment	711,256	Total liabilities	$ 352,394
Goodwill and other assets	89,879	Common stock	313,299
		Retained earnings	512,159
Total assets	$1,177,852	Total liabilities and equity	$1,177,852

In addition, it was reported that the firm had a net income of $156,042 on net sales of $4,063,589.

a. What are the firm's current ratio and quick ratio?

b. Calculate the firm's days' sales outstanding, total asset turnover ratio, and fixed asset turnover ratio.

4.31 The following are the financial statements for Nederland Consumer Products Company for the fiscal year ended September 30, 2017.

Nederland Consumer Products Company Income Statement for the Fiscal Year Ended September 30, 2017	
Net sales	$51,407
Cost of products sold	25,076
Gross profit	$26,331
Marketing, research, administrative expense	15,746
Depreciation	758
Operating income (loss)	$ 9,827
Interest expense	477
Earnings (loss) before income taxes	$ 9,350
Income taxes	2,869
Net earnings (loss)	$ 6,481

Nederland Consumer Products Company Balance Sheet as of September 30, 2017			
Assets:		Liabilities and Equity:	
Cash and marketable securities	$ 5,469	Accounts payable	$ 3,617
Investment securities	423	Accrued and other liabilities	7,689
Accounts receivable	4,062	Taxes payable	2,554
Inventory	4,400	Debt due within one year	8,287
Deferred income taxes	958	Total current liabilities	$22,147
Prepaid expenses and other receivables	1,803	Long-term debt	12,554
		Deferred income taxes	2,261
Total current assets	$17,115	Other noncurrent liabilities	2,808
Property, plant, and equipment, at cost	25,304	Total liabilities	$39,770
		Convertible class A preferred stock	1,526
Less: Accumulated depreciation	11,196		
Net property, plant, and equipment	$14,108	Common stock	2,141
Net goodwill and other intangible assets	23,900	Retained earnings	13,611
		Total stockholders' equity	$17,278
Other noncurrent assets	1,925		
Total assets	$57,048	Total liabilities and equity	$57,048

Calculate all the ratios, for which industry figures are available below, for Nederland and compare the firm's ratios with the industry ratios.

Ratio	Industry Average
Current ratio	2.05
Quick ratio	0.78
Gross margin	23.9%
Net profit margin	12.3%
Debt ratio	0.23
Long-term debt to equity	0.98
Interest coverage	5.62
ROA	5.3%
ROE	18.8%

4.32 Refer to the preceding information for Nederland Consumer Products Company. Compute the firm's ratios for the following categories and briefly evaluate the company's performance using these numbers.

a. Efficiency ratios. **b.** Asset turnover ratios.

c. Leverage ratios. **d.** Coverage ratios.

4.33 Refer to the earlier information for Nederland Consumer Products Company. Using the DuPont identity, calculate the return on equity for Nederland, after calculating the ratios that make up the DuPont identity.

4.34 Nugent, Inc., has a gross profit margin of 31.7 percent on net sales of $9,865,214 and total assets of $7,125,852. The company has a current ratio of 2.7 times, accounts receivable of $1,715,363, cash and marketable securities of $315,488, and current liabilities of $870,938.

a. What is Nugent's total current assets?

b. How much inventory does the firm have? What is the inventory turnover ratio?

c. What is Nugent's days' sales outstanding?

d. If management sets a target DSO of 30 days, what should Nugent's accounts receivable be?

4.35 Recreational Supplies Co. has net sales of $11,655,000, an ROE of 17.64 percent, and a total asset turnover of 2.89 times. If the firm has a debt-to-equity ratio of 1.43, what is the company's net income?

4.36 Nutmeg Houseware Inc. has an operating profit margin of 10.3 percent on revenues of $24,547,125 and total assets of $8,652,352.

a. Calculate the company's total asset turnover ratio and its operating profit (EBIT).

b. The company's management has set a target for the total asset turnover ratio of 3.25 for next year. If there is no change in the total assets of the company, what will the new net sales level have to be next year? Calculate the dollar change in sales necessary and the percentage change in sales necessary.

c. If the operating profit margin declines to 10 percent, what will be the EBIT at the new level of net sales?

4.37 Modern Appliances Corporation has reported its financial results for the year ended December 31, 2017.

Modern Appliances Corporation Income Statement for the Fiscal Year Ended December 31, 2017	
Net sales	$5,398,412,000
Cost of goods sold	3,432,925,255
Gross profit	$1,965,486,745
Selling, general, and administrative expenses	1,036,311,231
Depreciation	299,928,155
Operating income	$ 629,247,359
Interest expense	35,826,000
EBT	$ 593,421,359
Income taxes	163,104,554
Net earnings	$ 430,316,805

Modern Appliances Corporation Balance Sheet as of December 31, 2017			
Assets:		Liabilities and Equity:	
Cash and cash equivalents	$ 514,412,159	Short-term borrowings	$ 117,109,865
Accounts receivable	1,046,612,233	Trade accounts payable	466,937,985
Inventory	981,870,990	Other current liabilities	994,289,383
Other current assets	313,621,610	Total current liabilities	$1,578,337,233
Total current assets	$2,856,516,992	Long-term debt	1,200,691,565
Net fixed assets	754,660,275	Common stock	397,407,352
Goodwill	118,407,710	Retained earnings	1,218,207,588
Other assets	665,058,761		
Total assets	$4,394,643,738	Total liabilities and equity	$4,394,643,738

Using the information from the financial statements, complete a comprehensive ratio analysis for Modern Appliances Corporation.

a. Calculate these liquidity ratios: current and quick ratios.
b. Calculate these efficiency ratios: inventory turnover, accounts receivable turnover, DSO.
c. Calculate these asset turnover ratios: total asset turnover, fixed asset turnover.
d. Calculate these leverage ratios: total debt ratio, debt-to-equity ratio, equity multiplier.
e. Calculate these coverage ratios: times interest earned, cash coverage.
f. Calculate these profitability ratios: gross profit margin, net profit margin, ROA, ROE.
g. Use the DuPont identity, after calculating the component ratios, to compute ROE.

CFA Problems

4.38 Common-size analysis is used in financial analysis to:

a. evaluate changes in a company's operating cycle over time.
b. predict changes in a company's capital structure using regression analysis.
c. compare companies of different sizes or compare a company with itself over time.
d. restate each element in a company's financial statement as a proportion of the similar account for another company in the same industry.

4.39 The TBI Company has a number of days of inventory of 50. Therefore, the TBI Company's inventory turnover is closest to:

a. 4.8 times.
b. 7.3 times.
c. 8.4 times.
d. 9.6 times.

4.40 DuPont analysis involves breaking return-on-assets ratios into their:

a. profit components.
b. marginal and average components.
c. operating and financing components.
d. profit margin and turnover components.

4.41 If a company's net profit margin is −5 percent, its total asset turnover is 1.5 times, and its financial leverage ratio is 1.2 times, its return on equity is closest to:

a. −9.0 percent.
b. −7.5 percent.
c. −3.2 percent.
d. 1.8 percent.

Sample Test Problems

Greenfern Corporation recently filed the following financial statements with the SEC.

Greenfern Corporation Income Statement for the Fiscal Year Ended July 31, 2017	
Net sales	$ 73,236
Cost of products sold	52,092
Gross profit	$ 21,144
Selling, general, and administrative expenses	9,333
Depreciation	1,060
Operating income (loss)	$ 10,751
Interest expense	649
Earning (loss) before income taxes	10,102
Income taxes	3,536
Net earnings (loss)	$ 6,566

Greenfern Corporation Balance Sheet as of July 31, 2017			
Assets:		**Liabilities and Equity:**	
Cash and marketable securities	$ 9,118	Accounts payable	$ 6,379
Accounts receivable	7,844	Accrued and other liabilities	5,663
Inventory	8,900	Taxes payable	4,821
Deferred income taxes	878	Debt due within one year	10,778
Prepaid expenses and other	2,803	Total current liabilities	$27,641
Total current assets	$29,543		
Property, plant, and equipment, at cost	62,467	Long-term debt	24,280
		Deferred income taxes	6,903
Less: Accumulated depreciation	22,196	Other non current liabilities	5,608
Net property, plant, and equipment	$40,271	Total liabilities	$64,432
		Common stock	3,667
Net goodwill and other intangible assets	16,270	Retained earnings	17,985
		Total stockholders' equity	$21,652
Total assets	$86,084	Total liabilities and stockholders' equity	$86,084

4.1 Refer to the preceding balance sheet and income statement for Greenfern Corporation for the fiscal year ended July 31, 2017. What are the company's current ratio and quick ratio? What do these ratios tell us about Greenfern?

4.2 Refer to the preceding balance sheet and income statement for Greenfern Corporation for the fiscal year ended July 31, 2017. Calculate the following ratios:

a. Inventory turnover

b. Days' sales outstanding.

c. Total asset turnover.

d. Fixed asset turnover.

e. Total debt ratio.

f. Debt-to-equity ratio.

g. Times interest earned ratio.

h. Cash coverage ratio.

4.3 Refer to the preceding balance sheet and income statement for Greenfern Corporation for the fiscal year ended July 31, 2017. Use the DuPont identity to calculate the return on equity (ROE). In the process, calculate the following ratios: net profit margin, total asset turnover, equity multiplier, EBIT return on assets (EROA), and return on assets.

4.4 Last year Pontiff Enterprises reported net sales of $13,144,680, a gross profit $4,127,429, EBIT of $2,586,150, and net income of $867,555. Compute Pontiff's cost of goods sold, gross profit margin, operating profit margin, and net profit margin.

4.5 National City Bank has 646,749,650 shares of common stock outstanding that are currently selling for $37.55 per share on the New York Stock Exchange. If National City's net income was $2,780,955,000 in the year that just ended, what was its earnings per share and what is its current price-earnings ratio? If the typical price-earnings ratio for a bank is currently 15, what does the price-earnings ratio for National City tell you about its prospects?

Ethics Case

A Sad Tale: The Demise of Arthur Andersen

In January 2002, there were five major public accounting firms: Arthur Andersen, Deloitte Touche, KPMG, Pricewaterhouse-Coopers, and Ernst & Young. By late fall of that year, the number had been reduced to four. Arthur Andersen became the first major public accounting firm to be found guilty of a felony (a conviction later overturned), and as a result it virtually ceased to exist.

Ken Cedeno/Bloomberg/Getty Images

That such a fate could befall Andersen is especially sad given its early history. When Andersen and Company was established in 1918, it was led by Arthur Andersen, an acknowledged man of principle, and the company had a credo that became firmly embedded in the culture: "Think Straight and Talk Straight." Andersen became an industry leader partly on the basis of high ethical principles and integrity.

How did a one-time industry leader find itself in a position where it received a corporate death penalty over ethical issues? First, the market changed. During the 1980s, a boom in mergers and acquisitions and the emergence of information technology fueled the growth of an extremely profitable consulting practice at Andersen. The profits from consulting contracts soon exceeded the profits from auditing, Andersen's core business. Many of the consulting clients were also audit clients, and the firm found that the audit relationship was an ideal bridge for selling consulting services. Soon the audit fees became "loss leaders" to win audits, which allowed the consultants to sell more lucrative consulting contracts.

Tension between Audit and Consulting

At Andersen, tension between audit and consulting partners broke into open and sometimes public warfare. At the heart of the problem was how to divide the earnings from the consulting practice between the two groups. The resulting conflict ended in divorce, with the consultants leaving to form their own firm. The firm, Accenture, continues to thrive today.

Once the firm split in two, Andersen began to rebuild a consulting practice as part of the accounting practice. Consulting continued to be a highly profitable business, and audit partners were now asked to sell consulting services to other clients, a role that many auditors found uncomfortable.

Although the accountants were firmly in charge, the role of partners as salespersons compounded an already existing ethical issue—that of conflict of interest. It is legally well established that the fiduciary responsibility of a certified public accounting (CPA) firm is to the investors and creditors of the firm being audited. CPA firms are supposed to render an opinion as to whether a firm's financial statements are reasonably accurate and whether the firm has applied generally accepted accounting principles in a consistent manner over time so as not to distort the financial statements. To meet their fiduciary responsibilities, auditors must maintain independence from the firms they audit.

What might interfere with the objective judgment of the public accounting firms? One problem arises because it is the audited companies themselves that pay the auditors' fees. Auditors might not be completely objective when auditing a firm because they fear losing consulting business. This is an issue that regulators and auditors have not yet solved. But another problem arises in situations where accounting firms provide consulting services to the companies they audit. Although all of the major accounting firms were involved in this practice to some extent, Andersen had developed an aggressive culture for engaging partners to sell consulting services to audit clients.

Andersen's Problems Mount

The unraveling of Andersen began in the 1990s with a series of accounting scandals at Sunbeam, Waste Management, and Colonial Realty—all firms that Andersen had audited. But scandals involving the energy giant Enron proved to be the firm's undoing. The account was huge. In 2000 alone, Andersen received $52 million in fees from Enron, approximately 50 percent for auditing and 50 percent for other consulting services, especially tax services. The partner in charge of the account and his entire 100-person team worked out of Enron's Houston office. Approximately 300 of Enron's senior and middle managers had been Andersen employees.

Enron went bankrupt in December 2001 after large-scale accounting irregularities came to light, prompting an investigation by the Securities and Exchange Commission (SEC). It soon became clear that Enron's financial statements for some time had been largely the products of accounting fraud, showing the company to be in far better financial condition than was actually the case. The inevitable question was asked: Why hadn't the auditors called attention to Enron's questionable accounting practices? The answer was a simple one. Andersen had major conflicts of interest. Indeed, when one member of Andersen's Professional Standards Group objected to some of Enron's accounting practices, Andersen removed him from auditing responsibilities at Enron—in response to a request from Enron management.

Playing Hardball and Losing

The SEC was determined to make an example of Andersen. The U.S. Justice Department began a criminal investigation, but investigators were willing to explore some "settlement options" in return for Andersen's cooperation. However, Andersen's senior management appeared arrogant and failed to grasp the political mood in Congress and in the country after a series of business scandals that had brought more than one large company to bankruptcy.

After several months of sparring with the Andersen senior management team, the Justice Department charged Andersen with a felony offense—obstruction of justice. Andersen was found guilty in 2002 of illegally instructing its employees to destroy documents relating to Enron, even as the government was conducting inquiries into Enron's finances. During the trial, government lawyers argued that by instructing its staff to "undertake an unprecedented campaign of document destruction," Andersen had obstructed the government's investigation.

Since a firm convicted of a felony cannot audit a publicly held company, the conviction spelled the end for Andersen. But even before the guilty verdict, there had been a massive defection of Andersen clients to other accounting firms. The evidence presented at trial showed a breakdown in Andersen's internal controls, a lack of leadership, and an environment in Andersen's Houston office that fostered recklessness and unethical behavior by some partners.

In 2005, the United States Supreme Court unanimously overturned the Andersen conviction on the grounds that the jury was given overly broad instructions by the federal judge who presided over the case. But by then it was too late. Most of the Andersen partners had either retired or gone to work for former competitors, and the company had all but ceased to exist.

Discussion Questions

1. To what extent do market pressures encourage unethical behavior? Can the demise of Andersen be blamed on the fact that the market began rewarding consulting services of the kind Andersen could provide?
2. How serious are the kinds of conflicts of interest discussed in this case? Did Sarbanes-Oxley eliminate the most serious conflicts?
3. Was it fair for the government to destroy an entire company because of the misdeeds of some of its members, or had Andersen become such a serious offender that such an action on the part of the government was justified?

CHAPTER 5

The Time Value of Money

Lethbridge Herald-Al Beeber/The Canadian Press

LEARNING OBJECTIVES

1. Explain the concept of time value of money and why it is so important in the field of finance.
2. Explain the concept of future value, including the meaning of the terms *principal, simple interest,* and *compound interest*, and use the future value formula to make business decisions.
3. Explain the concept of present value and how it relates to future value, and use the present value formula to make business decisions.
4. Discuss why the concept of compounding is not restricted to money, and use the future value formula to calculate growth rates.

When you buy a piece of equipment for a business, the decision of whether to pay cash or to use debt financing can affect the price that you pay. For example, equipment manufacturers often offer customers a choice between a cash rebate and low-cost financing. Both of these alternatives affect the cost of the equipment, but one alternative can be worth more than the other to the buyer.

For example, consider the following. In January 2017, the Ford Motor Company offered special financing terms on its 2017 Super Duty F-350 XL pickup truck. These trucks are commonly used in a wide range of businesses, such as those involved with construction, landscaping, and home repair, among others.

In an effort to increase sales of its F-350 XL truck, Ford offered buyers a choice between (1) receiving $1,000 off a base (suggested retail) price of $33,705 if they paid cash and (2) receiving 4.9 percent financing on a five-year loan if they paid the base price. For a business that had enough cash to buy the truck outright and did not need the cash for other uses, the decision of whether to pay cash or finance the purchase of an F-350 XL truck depended on the rate of return that could be earned by investing the cash. On the one hand, if it was only possible to earn a 5 percent interest rate, the buyer was better off paying cash and taking the discount. On the other hand, if it was possible to earn a 7 percent interest rate, the buyer was better off taking the financing and investing the money. With a 6.15 percent interest rate, the buyer would have been indifferent about choosing between the two alternatives (You can see how this 6.15 percent value is calculated in WileyPLUS.)

As with most business transactions, a crucial element in the analysis of the alternatives offered by Ford is the value of the expected cash flows. Because the cash flows for the two alternatives take place in different time periods, they must be adjusted to account for the time value of money before they can be compared. The buyer of the F-350 XL truck wants to select the alternative with the cash flows that have the lowest value (price). This chapter and the next provide the knowledge and tools you need to make the correct decision (as well as to calculate the rate of return at which the buyer would be indifferent). You will learn that at the bank, in the boardroom, or at the truck dealer, money has a time value—dollars today are worth more than dollars in the future—and you must account for this reality when making financial decisions.

Chapter Preview

Businesses routinely make decisions to invest in productive assets to earn income. Some assets, such as plant and equipment, are tangible, and other assets, such as patents and trademarks, are intangible. Regardless of the type of investment, a firm pays out money now in the hope that the value of the future benefits (cash inflows) will exceed the cost of the asset. This process is what *value creation* is all about—buying productive assets that are worth more than they cost.

The valuation models presented in this book will require you to compute the present and future values of cash flows. This chapter and the next one provide the fundamental tools for making these calculations. Chapter 5 explains how to value a single cash flow in different time periods, and Chapter 6 covers valuation of multiple cash flows. These two chapters are critical for your understanding of corporate finance.

We begin this chapter with a discussion of the time value of money. We then look at future value, which tells us how funds will grow if they are invested at a particular interest rate. Next, we discuss present value, which answers the question "What is the value today of cash payments that are to be received in the future?" We conclude the chapter with a discussion of several additional topics related to time value of money calculations.

5.1 The Time Value of Money

Weblink

Take an online lesson on the time value of money from TeachMeFinance.com at http://teachmefinance.com/timevalueofmoney.html.

LEARNING OBJECTIVE

1. Explain the concept of time value of money and why it is so important in the field of finance.

In financial decision making, one basic problem managers face is determining the value of (or price to pay for) cash flows expected in the future. Why is this a problem? Consider as an example the popular Mega Millions lottery game.[1] In Mega Millions, the jackpot continues to build up until some lucky person buys a winning ticket—the payouts for a number of jackpot winning tickets have exceeded $100 million.

If you won $100 million, headlines would read "Lucky Student Wins $100 Million Jackpot!" Does this mean that your ticket is worth $100 million on the day you win? The answer is no. A Mega Millions jackpot is paid either as a series of 30 payments over 29 years or as a cash lump sum. If you win "$100 million" and choose to receive the series of payments, the 30 payments will total $100 million. If you choose the lump sum option, Mega Millions will pay you less than the stated value of $100 million. This amount was about $59 million in January 2017. Thus, the value, or market price, of a "$100 million" winning Mega Millions ticket is really about $59 million because of the time value of money and the timing of the 30 cash payments. An appropriate question to ask now is "What is the time value of money?" (See WileyPLUS for an illustration of how to answer this question for the Mega Millions example.)

Consuming Today or Tomorrow

time value of money the difference in value between a dollar in hand today and a dollar promised in the future; a dollar today is worth more than a dollar in the future

The **time value of money** is based on the idea that people prefer to consume goods today rather than wait to consume similar goods in the future. Most people would prefer to have a large-screen TV today than to have one a year from now, for example. Money has a time

[1] Mega Millions is operated by a consortium of the state lottery commissions in 44 states plus the District of Columbia and the U.S. Virgin Islands. To play the game, a player pays one dollar and picks five numbers from 1 to 75 and one additional number from 1 to 15 (the Mega Ball number). Twice a week a machine mixes numbered balls and randomly selects six balls (five white balls and one Mega Ball), which determines the winning combination for that drawing. There are various winning combinations, but a ticket that matches all six numbers, including the Mega Ball number, is the jackpot winner.

value because a dollar in hand today is worth more than a dollar to be received in the future. This makes sense because if you had the dollar today, you could buy something with it—or, instead, you could invest it and earn interest. For example, if you had $100,000 and you could buy a one-year bank certificate of deposit paying 5 percent interest, you could earn $5,000 interest for the year. At the end of the year, you would have $105,000 ($100,000 + $5,000 = $105,000). The $100,000 today is worth $105,000 a year from today. If the interest rate was higher, you would have even more money at the end of the year.

Based on this example, we can make several generalizations. First, the value of a dollar invested at a positive interest rate grows over time. Thus, the further in the future you receive a dollar, the less it is worth today. Second, the trade-off between money today and money at some future date depends in part on the rate of interest you can earn by investing. The higher the rate of interest, the more likely you will elect to invest your funds and forgo current consumption. Why? At the higher interest rate, your investment will earn more money.

In the next two sections, we look at two views of time value—future value and present value. First, however, we describe time lines, which are pictorial aids to help solve future and present value problems.

Building Intuition

The Value of Money Changes with Time

The term *time value of money* reflects the notion that people prefer to consume things today rather than at some time in the future. For this reason, people require compensation for deferring consumption. The effect is to make a dollar in the future worth less than a dollar today.

Time Lines as Aids to Problem Solving

Time lines are an important tool for analyzing problems that involve cash flows over time. They provide an easy way to visualize the cash flows associated with investment decisions. A time line is a horizontal line that starts at time zero and shows cash flows as they occur over time. The term **time zero** is used to refer to the beginning of a transaction in time value of money problems. Time zero is often the current point in time (today).

time zero the beginning of a transaction; often the current point in time

Exhibit 5.1 shows the time line for a five-year investment opportunity and its cash flows. Here, as in most finance problems, cash flows are assumed to occur at the end of the period. The project involves a $10,000 initial investment (cash outflow), such as the purchase of a new machine, that is expected to generate cash inflows over a five-year period: $5,000 at the end of Year 1, $4,000 at the end of Year 2, $3,000 at the end of Year 3, $2,000 at the end of Year 4, and $1,000 at the end of Year 5. Because of the time value of money, it is critical that you identify not only the size of the cash flows but also their timing.

If it is appropriate, the time line will also show the relevant interest rate for the problem. In Exhibit 5.1 this is shown as 5 percent. Also, note in Exhibit 5.1 that the initial cash flow of $10,000 is represented by a negative number. It is conventional that cash outflows from the firm, such as for the purchase of a new machine, are treated as negative values on a time line and that cash inflows to the firm, such as revenues earned, are treated as positive values. The −$10,000 therefore means that there is a cash outflow of $10,000 at time zero. As you will see, it makes no difference how you label cash inflows and outflows as long as you are consistent. That is, if *all* cash outflows are given a negative value, then *all* cash inflows must have a positive value. If the signs get mixed up—if some cash inflows are negative and some positive—you will get the wrong answer to any problem you are trying to solve.

Financial Calculator

We recommend that students purchase a financial calculator for this course. A financial calculator will provide the computational tools to solve most problems in the book. A financial calculator is just an ordinary calculator that has preprogrammed future value and present value algorithms. To solve problems, all you have to do is press the proper keys. The instructions in this book are generally meant for Texas Instruments calculators, such as the TI BA II Plus. If you are using an HP, Sharp, or other calculator, consult the user's manual for instructions.

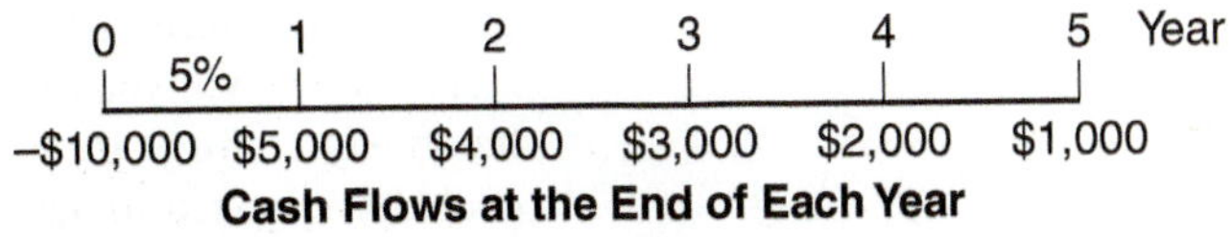

EXHIBIT 5.1 Five-Year Time Line for a $10,000 Investment

Time lines help us to correctly identify the size and timing of cash flows—critical tasks in solving time value problems. This time line shows the cash flows generated over five years by a $10,000 investment where the relevant interest rate is 5 percent.

It may sound as if the financial calculator will solve problems for you. It won't. To get the correct answer you must first analyze the problem correctly and then identify the cash flows (size and timing), placing them correctly on a time line. Only then will you enter the correct inputs into the financial calculator.

A calculator can help you eliminate computation errors and save you a great deal of time. However, it is important that you understand the calculations that the calculator is performing. For this reason we recommend when you first start using a financial calculator that you solve problems without using the calculator's financial functions and then use the financial functions to check your answers.

To help you master your financial calculator, throughout this chapter we provide hints on how to best use the calculator. We also recognize that some professors or students may want to solve problems using one of the popular computer spreadsheet programs. In this chapter and a number of other chapters, we provide solutions to several problems that lend themselves to spreadsheet analysis. In solving these problems, we used Microsoft Excel. The analysis and basic commands are similar for other spreadsheet programs. We also provide spreadsheet solutions for additional problems on WileyPlus, the Web site for this book. Since spreadsheet programs are commonly used in industry, you should make sure to learn how to use one of these programs early in your studies and become proficient with it before you graduate.

Before You Go On

1. Why is a dollar today worth more than a dollar one year from now?
2. What is a time line, and why is it important in financial analysis?

5.2 Future Value and Compounding

LEARNING OBJECTIVE

2. Explain the concept of future value, including the meaning of the terms *principal*, *simple interest*, and *compound interest*, and use the future value formula to make business decisions.

future value (FV) the value of an investment after it earns interest for one or more periods

The **future value (FV)** of an investment is what the investment will be worth after earning interest for one or more time periods. The process of converting the initial amount into a future value is called *compounding*. We will define this term more precisely later. First, though, we illustrate the concepts of future value and compounding with an example.

Single-Period Investment

Suppose you place \$100 in a bank savings account that pays interest at 10 percent a year. How much money will you have in one year? Go ahead and make the calculation. Most people can intuitively arrive at the correct answer, \$110, without the aid of a formula. Your calculation could have looked something like this:

$$\begin{aligned}\text{Future value at the end of Year 1} &= \text{Principal} + \text{Interest earned}\\ &= \$100 + (\$100 \times 0.10)\\ &= \$100 \times (1 + 0.10)\\ &= \$100 \times (1.10)\\ &= \$110\end{aligned}$$

This approach computes the amount of interest earned ($100 × 0.10) and then adds it to the initial, or *principal*, amount ($100). Notice that when we solve the equation, we factor out the $100. Recall from algebra that if you have the equation $y = c + (c \times x)$, you can factor out the common term c and get $y = c \times (1 + x)$. By doing this in our future value calculation, we arrived at the term (1 + 0.10). This term can be stated more generally as $(1 + i)$, where i is the interest rate. As you will see, this is a pivotal term in all time value of money calculations.

Let's use our intuitive calculation to generate a more general formula. First, we need to define the variables used to calculate the answer. In our example, $100 is the principal amount (P_0), which is the amount of money deposited (invested) at the beginning of the transaction (time zero); the 10 percent is the simple interest rate (i); and the $110 is the future value (FV_1) of the investment after one year. We can write the formula for a single-period investment as follows:

$$\begin{aligned} FV_1 &= P_0 + (P_0 \times i) \\ &= P_0 \times (1 + i) \end{aligned}$$

Looking at the formula, we more easily see mathematically what is happening in our intuitive calculation. P_0 is the principal amount invested at time zero. If you invest for one period at an interest rate of i, your investment, or principal, will grow by $(1 + i)$ per dollar invested. The term $(1 + i)$ is the *future value interest factor*—often called simply the *future value factor*—for a single period, such as one year. To test the equation, we plug in our values:

$$\begin{aligned} FV_1 &= \$100 \times (1 + 0.10) \\ &= \$100 \times 1.10 \\ &= \$110 \end{aligned}$$

Good, it works!

Two-Period Investment

We have determined that at the end of one year (one period), your $100 investment has grown to $110. Now let's say you decide to leave this new principal amount (FV_1) of $110 in the bank for another year earning 10 percent interest. How much money would you have at the end of the second year (FV_2)? To arrive at the value for FV_2, we multiply the new principal amount by the future value factor $(1 + i)$. That is, $FV_2 = FV_1 \times (1 + i)$. Since $FV_1 = P_0 \times (1 + i)$, we can write this as:

$$\begin{aligned} FV_2 &= FV_1 \times (1 + i) \\ &= [P_0 \times (1 + i)] \times (1 + i) \\ &= P_0 \times (1 + i)^2 \end{aligned}$$

The future value of your $110 at the end of the second year (FV_2) is as follows:

$$\begin{aligned} FV_2 &= P_0 \times (1 + i)^2 \\ &= \$100 \times (1 + 0.10)^2 \\ &= \$100 \times (1.10)^2 \\ &= \$100 \times 1.21 \\ &= \$121 \end{aligned}$$

Another way of thinking of a two-period investment is that it is two single-period investments back to back.

Turning to **Exhibit 5.2**, we can see what is happening to your $100 investment over the two years we have already discussed and beyond. The future value of $121 at Year 2 consists of three parts. First is the initial *principal* of $100 (first row of column 2). Second is the $20 ($10 + $10 = $20) of *simple interest* earned at 10 percent for the first and second years (first and second rows of column 3). Third is the $1 interest earned during the second year (second row of column 4) on the $10 of interest from the first year ($10 × 0.10 = $1.00). This is called *interest on interest.* The total amount of interest earned is $21 ($10 + $11 = $21), which is shown in column 5 and is called *compound interest.*

EXHIBIT 5.2 Future Value of $100 at 10 Percent

With compounding, interest earned on an investment is reinvested so that, in future periods, interest is earned on interest as well as on the principal amount. Here, interest on interest begins accruing in Year 2.

		Interest Earned					
Year (1)	Value at Beginning of Year (2)	Simple Interest (3)		Interest on Interest (4)		Total (Compound) Interest (5)	Value at End of Year (6)
1	$100.00	$10.00	+	$ 0.00	=	$10.00	$110.00
2	110.00	10.00	+	1.00	=	11.00	121.00
3	121.00	10.00	+	2.10	=	12.10	133.10
4	133.10	10.00	+	3.31	=	13.31	146.41
5	146.41	10.00	+	4.64	=	14.64	161.05
Five-year total	$100.00	$50.00	+	$11.05	=	$61.05	$161.05

principal the amount of money on which interest is paid

simple interest interest earned on the original principal amount only

interest on interest interest earned on interest that was earned in previous periods

compounding the process by which interest earned on an investment is reinvested, so in future periods interest is earned on the interest as well as the original principal

compound interest interest earned both on the original principal amount and on interest previously earned

We are now in a position to formally define some important terms already mentioned in our discussion. The **principal** is the amount of money on which interest is paid. In our example, the principal amount is $100. **Simple interest** is the amount of interest paid on the original principal amount. With simple interest, the interest earned each period is paid only on the original principal. In our example, the simple interest is $10 per year or $20 for the two years. **Interest on interest** is the interest earned on the reinvestment of previous interest payments. In our example, the interest on interest is $1. **Compounding** is the process by which interest earned on an investment is reinvested so that in future periods, interest is earned on the interest previously earned as well as the original principal. In other words, with compounding you are able to earn **compound interest**, which consists of both simple interest and interest on interest.

The Future Value Equation

Let's continue our bank example. Suppose you decide to leave your money in the bank for three years. Looking back at equations for a single-period and a two-period investment, you can probably guess that the equation for the future value of money invested for three years would be:

$$FV_3 = P_0 \times (1 + i)^3$$

With this pattern clearly established, we can see that the general equation to find the future value after any number of periods is as follows:

$$FV_n = P_0 \times (1 + i)^n$$

which is often written as:

$$FV_n = PV \times (1 + i)^n \qquad (5.1)$$

where:

FV_n = future value of investment at the end of period n
PV = original principal (P_0); this is often called the present value, or PV
i = the rate of interest per period
n = the number of periods; a period can be a year, a quarter, a month, a day, or some other unit of time
$(1 + i)^n$ = the future value factor

Let's test our general equation. Suppose you leave your \$100 invested in the bank savings account at 10 percent interest for five years. How much would you have in the bank at the end of five years? Applying Equation 5.1 yields the following:

$$\begin{aligned} FV_5 &= \$100 \times (1 + 0.10)^5 \\ &= \$100 \times (1.10)^5 \\ &= \$100 \times 1.6105 \\ &= \$161.05 \end{aligned}$$

Exhibit 5.2 shows how the interest is earned on a year-by-year basis. Notice that the total compound interest earned over the five-year period is \$61.05 (column 5) and that it is made up of two parts: (1) \$50.00 of simple interest (column 3) and (2) \$11.05 of interest on interest (column 4). Thus, the total compound interest can be expressed as follows:

$$\begin{aligned} \text{Total compound interest} &= \text{Total simple interest} + \text{Total interest on interest} \\ &= \$50.00 + \$11.05 \\ &= \$61.05 \end{aligned}$$

The simple interest earned is $\$100 \times 0.10 = \$10.00$ per year, and thus the total simple interest for the five-year period is \$50.00 (5 years × \$10.00 = \$50.00). The remaining balance of \$11.05 (\$61.05 − \$50.00 = \$11.05) comes from earning interest on interest.

A helpful equation for calculating simple interest can be derived by using the future value equation for a single-period investment and solving for the term $FV_1 - P_0$:

$$\begin{aligned} FV_1 &= P_0 + (P_0 \times i) \\ FV_1 - P_0 &= P_0 \times i \\ SI &= P_0 \times i \end{aligned}$$

where SI is the simple interest earned. Thus, the calculation for simple interest is:[2]

$$SI = P_0 \times i = \$100 \times 0.10 = \$10.00$$

Weblink

CNNMoney's Web site has a savings calculator at http://cgi.money.cnn.com/tools/savingscalc/savingscalc.html.

Exhibit 5.3 shows graphically how the compound interest in Exhibit 5.2 grows. Notice that the simple interest earned each year remains constant at \$10 per year but that the amount of interest on interest increases every year. The reason, of course, is that interest on interest increases with the cumulative interest that has been earned. As more and more interest is earned, the compounding of interest accelerates the growth of the interest on interest and therefore the total interest earned.

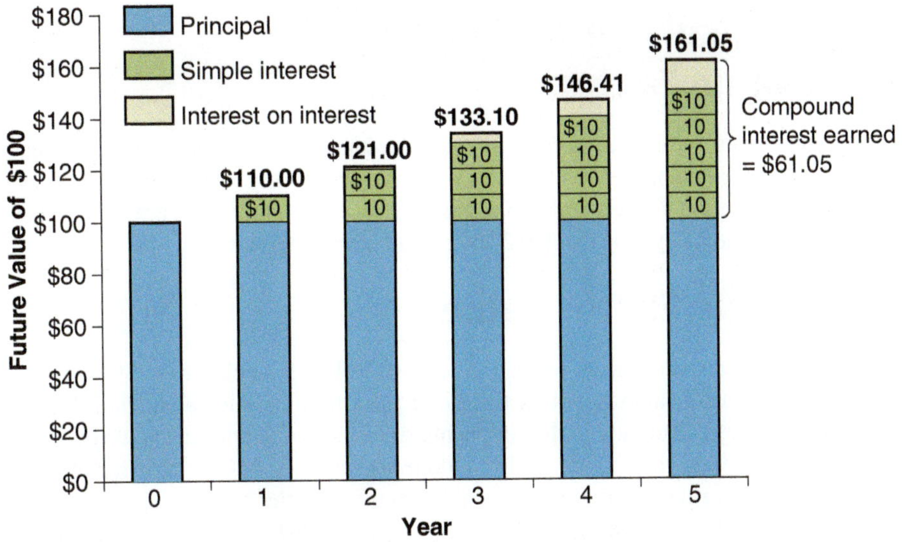

EXHIBIT 5.3 **How Compound Interest Grows on \$100 at 10 Percent**

The amount of simple interest earned on \$100 invested at 10 percent remains constant at \$10 per year, but the amount of interest earned on interest increases each year. As more and more interest builds, the effect of compounding accelerates the growth of the total interest earned.

[2] Another helpful equation is the one that computes the total simple interest (TSI) over several periods: $TSI = \text{Number of periods} \times SI = \text{Number of periods} \times (P_0 \times i)$.

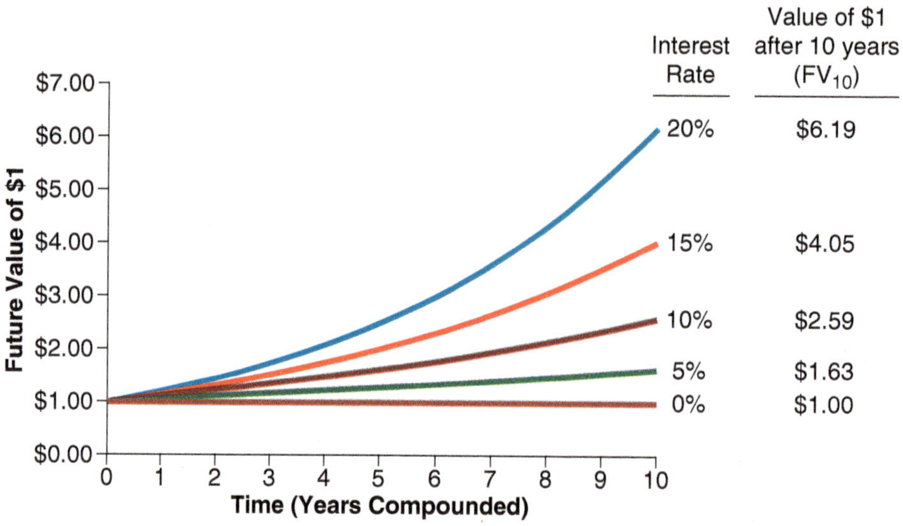

EXHIBIT 5.4 **Future Value of $1 for Different Periods and Interest Rates**

The higher the interest rate, the faster the value of an investment will grow, and the larger the amount of money that will accumulate over time. Because of compounding, the growth over time is not linear but exponential—the dollar increase in the future value is greater in each subsequent period.

An interesting observation about Equation 5.1 is that the higher the interest rate, the faster the investment will grow. This fact can be seen in Exhibit 5.4, which shows the growth in the future value of $1.00 at different interest rates and for different time periods into the future. First, notice that the growth in the future value over time is exponential, not linear. The dollar value of the invested funds does not increase by the same dollar amount from year to year. It increases by a greater amount each year. In other words, the growth of the invested funds is accelerated by the compounding of interest. Second, the higher the interest rate is, the more the monies accumulated for any time period. Looking at the right side of the exhibit, you can see the difference in total dollars accumulated if you invest a dollar for 10 years: At 5 percent, you will have $1.63; at 10 percent, you will have $2.59; at 15 percent, you will have $4.05; and at 20 percent, you will have $6.19. Finally, as you should expect, if you invest a dollar at 0 percent for 10 years, you will only have a dollar at the end of the 10 years.

Using a Calculator to Compute the Future Value Factor

To solve a future value problem, we need to know the future value factor, $(1 + i)^n$. Fortunately, almost any calculator suitable for college-level work has a power key (the y^x key) that we can use to make this computation. For example, to compute $(1.08)^{10}$, we enter 1.08, press the y^x key and enter 10, and press the = key. The number 2.159 should emerge. Give it a try with your calculator.

Future Value Factor Tables

Before calculators and spreadsheets became widely available, a financial analyst would typically use a future value factor table to obtain the factor for a future value calculation. Doing this reduced the necessary calculation to the simple multiplication of the present value by the future value factor—something that could easily be done by hand. A future value factor table, an example of which is provided in Table A-1 in Appendix A at the back of this book, provides future value factors for a range of interest rates and years. While such tables are no longer commonly used, you might find the one at the back of this book useful in checking some of the calculations that you do throughout this course.

Applying the Future Value Formula

Next, we will review a number of examples of future value problems to illustrate the typical types of problems you will encounter in business and in your personal life.

The Power of Compounding

Our first example illustrates the effects of compounding. Suppose you have an opportunity to make a \$5,000 investment that pays 15 percent per year. How much money will you have at the end of 10 years? The time line for the investment opportunity is:

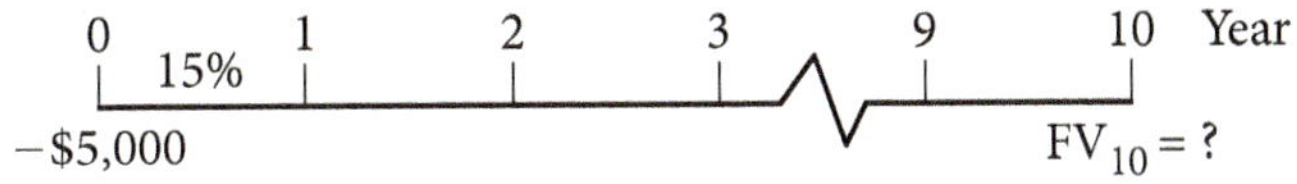

where the \$5,000 investment is a cash outflow and the future value you will receive in 10 years is a cash inflow.

We can apply Equation 5.1 to find the future value of \$5,000 invested for 10 years at 15 percent interest. We want to multiply the original principal amount (PV) times the appropriate future value factor for 10 years at 15 percent, which is $(1 + 0.15)^{10}$; thus:

$$\begin{aligned} FV_n &= PV \times (1 + i)^n \\ FV_{10} &= \$5{,}000 \times (1 + 0.15)^{10} \\ &= \$5{,}000 \times 4.045558 \\ &= \$20{,}227.79 \end{aligned}$$

Weblink

You can find a compound interest calculator at Bankrate.com: http://www.bankrate.com/calculators/savings/compound-interest-calculator-tool.aspx.

Now let's determine how much of the interest is from simple interest and how much is from interest on interest. The total compound interest earned is \$15,227.79 (\$20,227.79 − \$5,000.00 = \$15,227.79). The simple interest is the amount of interest paid on the original principal amount: $SI = P_0 \times i = \$5{,}000 \times 0.15 = \$750$ per year, which over 10 years is \$750 × 10 years = \$7,500. The interest on interest must be the difference between the total compound interest earned and the simple interest: \$15,227.79 − \$7,500 = \$7,727.79. Notice how quickly the value of an investment increases and how the reinvestment of interest earned impacts the total compound interest when the interest rate is high.

LEARNING BY DOING

APPLICATION 5.1 | The Power of Compounding

Problem Your wealthy uncle passed away, and one of the assets he left to you was a savings account that your great-grandfather had set up 100 years ago. The account had a single deposit of \$1,000 and paid 10 percent interest per year. How much money have you inherited, what is the total compound interest, and how much of the interest earned came from interest on interest?

Approach We first determine the value of the inheritance, which is the future value of \$1,000 retained in a savings account for 100 years at a 10 percent interest rate. Our time line for the problem is:

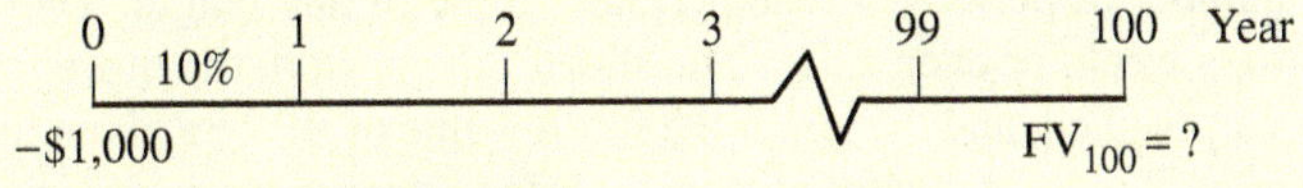

To calculate FV_{100}, we begin by computing the future value factor. We then plug this number into the future value formula (Equation 5.1) and solve for the total inheritance. Once we have computed FV_{100}, we calculate the total compound interest and the total simple interest and find the difference between these two numbers, which will give us the interest earned on interest.

Solution First, we find the future value factor:

$$(1 + i)^n = (1 + 0.10)^{100} = (1.10)^{100} = 13{,}780.612$$

Then we find the future value:

$$\begin{aligned} FV_n &= PV \times (1 + i)^n \\ FV_{100} &= \$1{,}000 \times (1.10)^{100} \\ &= \$1{,}000 \times 13{,}780.612 \\ &= \$13{,}780{,}612 \end{aligned}$$

Your total inheritance is \$13,780,612. The total compound interest earned is this amount less the original \$1,000 investment, or \$13,779,612:

$$\$13{,}780{,}612 - \$1{,}000 = \$13{,}779{,}612$$

The total simple interest earned is calculated as follows:

$$P_0 \times i = \$1{,}000 \times 0.10 = \$100 \text{ per year}$$
$$\$100 \times 100 \text{ years} = \$10{,}000$$

The interest earned on interest is the difference between the total compound interest earned and the simple interest:

$$\$13{,}779{,}612 - \$10{,}000 = \$13{,}769{,}612$$

That's quite a difference!

Building Intuition

Compounding Drives Much of the Earnings on Long-Term Investments

The earnings from compounding drive much of the return earned on a long-term investment. The reason is that the longer the investment period, the greater the proportion of total earnings from interest earned on interest. Interest earned on interest grows exponentially as the investment period increases.

As **Learning by Doing Application 5.1** indicates, the relative importance of interest earned on interest is especially great for long-term investments. For many people, retirement savings include the longest investments they will make. As you might expect, interest earned on interest has a great impact on how much money people ultimately have for their retirement. For example, consider someone who inherits and invests $10,000 on her 25th birthday and earns 8 percent per year for the next 40 years. This investment will grow to:

$$\$10{,}000 \times (1 + 0.08)^{40} = \$217{,}245.22$$

by the investor's 65th birthday. In contrast, if the same individual waited until her 35th birthday to invest the $10,000, she would have only:

$$\$10{,}000 \times (1 + 0.08)^{30} = \$100{,}626.57$$

when she turned 65.

Of the $116,618.65 difference in these amounts, the difference in simple interest accounts for only $8,000 (10 years × $10,000 × 0.08 = $8,000). The remaining $108,618.65 is attributable to the difference in interest earned on interest. This example illustrates both the importance of compounding for investment returns and the importance of getting started early when saving for retirement. The sooner you start saving, the better off you will be when you retire.

Compounding More Frequently Than Once a Year

Interest can be compounded more frequently than once a year. In Equation 5.1, the term n represents the number of periods. These periods can be of any length. They can be a year, a quarter, a month, a week, or even a day. The shorter the period, the more frequently interest payments are compounded, and the larger the future value of $1 for a given time period. Equation 5.1 can be rewritten to explicitly recognize different compounding periods:

$$FV_n = PV \times (1 + i/m)^{m \times n} \tag{5.2}$$

where m is the number of times per year that interest is compounded and n is the number of periods specified in years.

Weblink

Moneychimp.com also provides a compound interest calculator at http://www.moneychimp.com/calculator/compound_interest_calculator.htm.

Let's say you invest $100 in a bank account that pays a 5 percent interest rate semiannually (2.5 percent twice a year) for two years. In other words, the annual rate quoted by the bank is 5 percent, but the bank calculates the interest it pays you based on a six-month rate of 2.5 percent. In this example there are four six-month periods, and the amount of principal and interest you would have at the end of the four periods would be:

$$\begin{aligned} FV_2 &= \$100 \times (1 + 0.05/2)^{2\times 2} \\ &= \$100 \times (1 + 0.025)^4 \\ &= \$100 \times 1.1038 \\ &= \$110.38 \end{aligned}$$

It is not necessary to memorize Equation 5.2; using Equation 5.1 will do fine. All you have to do is determine the interest paid per compounding period (i/m) and calculate the total number of compounding periods ($m \times n$) as the exponent for the future value factor. For example, if the bank compounds interest quarterly, then both the interest rate and number of compounding periods must be expressed in quarterly terms: ($i/4$) and ($4 \times n$).

If the bank in the preceding example paid interest annually instead of semiannually, you would have:

$$FV_2 = \$100 \times (1 + 0.05)^2 = \$110.25$$

at the end of the two-year period. The difference between this amount and the $110.38 is due to the additional interest earned on interest when the compounding period is shorter and the interest payments are compounded more frequently.

During the late 1960s, the effects of compounding periods became an issue in banking. At that time, the interest rates that banks and thrift institutions could pay on consumer savings accounts were limited by regulation. However, financial institutions discovered they could keep their rates within the legal limit and pay their customers additional interest by increasing the compounding frequency. Prior to this, banks and thrifts had paid interest on savings accounts quarterly. You can see the difference between quarterly and daily compounding in **Learning by Doing Application 5.2**.

APPLICATION 5.2 | Changing the Compounding Period

LEARNING BY DOING

WileyPLUS

Need more help? Visit your WileyPLUS course.

Problem Your grandmother has $10,000 she wants to put into a bank savings account for five years. The bank she is considering is within walking distance, pays 5 percent annual interest compounded quarterly (5 percent per year/4 quarters per year = 1.25 percent per quarter), and provides free coffee and doughnuts in the morning. Another bank in town pays 5 percent interest compounded daily. Getting to this bank requires a bus trip, but your grandmother can ride free as a senior citizen. More important, though, this bank does not serve coffee and doughnuts. Which bank should your grandmother select?

Approach We need to calculate the difference between the two banks' interest payments. Bank A, which compounds quarterly, will pay one-fourth of the annual interest per quarter, 0.05/4 = 0.0125, and there will be 20 compounding periods over the five-year investment horizon (5 years × 4 quarters per year = 20 quarters). The time line for quarterly compounding is as follows:

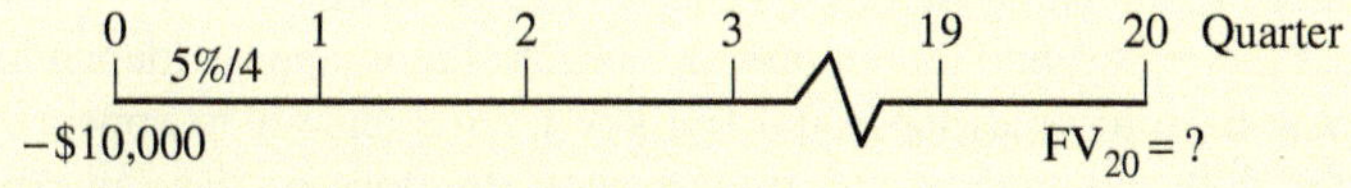

Bank B, which compounds daily, has 365 compounding periods per year. Thus, the daily interest rate is 0.000137 (0.05/365 = 0.000137), and there are 1,825 (5 years × 365 days per year = 1,825 days) compounding periods. The time line for daily compounding is:

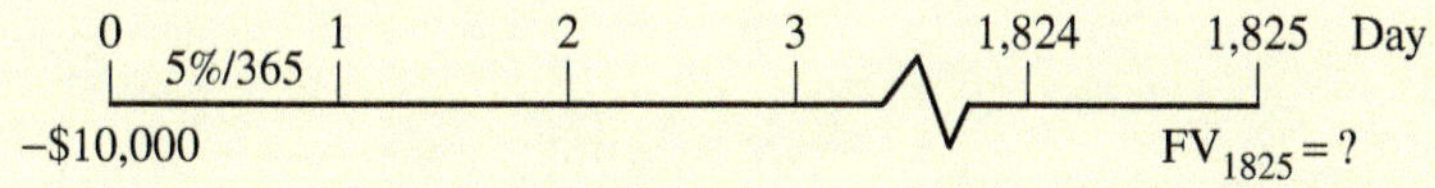

We use Equation 5.2 to solve for the future values the investment would generate at each bank. We then compare the two.

Solution

Bank A:

$$\begin{aligned} FV_n &= PV \times (1 + i/m)^{m \times n} \\ FV_{qtrly} &= \$10{,}000 \times (1 + 0.05/4)^{4 \times 5} \\ &= \$10{,}000 \times (1 + 0.0125)^{20} \\ &= \$12{,}820.37 \end{aligned}$$

Bank B:

$$\begin{aligned} FV_n &= PV \times (1 + i/m)^{m \times n} \\ FV_{daily} &= \$10{,}000 \times (1 + 0.05/365)^{365 \times 5} \\ &= \$10{,}000 \times (1 + 0.000137)^{1{,}825} \\ &= \$12{,}840.03 \end{aligned}$$

With daily compounding, the additional interest earned by your grandmother is $19.66:

$$\$12{,}840.03 - \$12{,}820.37 = \$19.66$$

Given that the interest gained by daily compounding is less than $20, your grandmother should probably select her local bank and enjoy the daily coffee and doughnuts. (If she is on a diet, of course, she should take the higher interest payment and walk to the other bank.)

It is worth noting that the longer the investment period, the greater the additional interest earned from daily compounding versus quarterly compounding. For example, if $10,000 was invested for 40 years instead of five years, the additional interest would increase to $899.91. You should confirm this by doing the calculation.

Continuous Compounding

We can continue to divide the compounding interval into smaller and smaller time periods, such as minutes and seconds, until, at the extreme, we would compound continuously. In this case, *m* in Equation 5.2 would approach infinity (∞). The formula to compute the future value for continuous compounding (FV_∞) is:

$$FV_\infty = PV \times e^{i \times n} \quad (5.3)$$

where *e* is the exponential function, which has a known mathematical value of about 2.71828, *n* is the number of periods specified in years, and *i* is the annual interest rate. Although the formula may look a little intimidating, it is really quite easy to apply. Look for a key on your calculator labeled e^x. If you don't have the key, you still can work the problem.

Let's go back to the example in Learning by Doing Application 5.2, in which your grandmother wants to put $10,000 in a savings account at a bank. How much money would she have at the end of five years if the bank paid 5 percent annual interest compounded continuously? To find out, we enter these values into Equation 5.3:

$$\begin{aligned} FV_\infty &= PV \times e^{i \times n} \\ &= \$10{,}000 \times e^{0.05 \times 5} \\ &= \$10{,}000 \times e^{0.25} \\ &= \$10{,}000 \times 2.71828^{0.25} \\ &= \$10{,}000 \times 1.284025 \\ &= \$12{,}840.25 \end{aligned}$$

If your calculator has an exponent key, all you have to do to calculate $e^{0.25}$ is enter the number 0.25, then press the e^x key, and the number 1.284025 should appear (depending on your calculator, you may have to press the equal [=] key for the answer to appear). Then multiply 1.284025 by $10,000, and you're done! If your calculator does not have an exponent key, then you can calculate $e^{0.25}$ by inputting the value of *e* (2.71828) and raising it to the 0.25 power using the y^x key, as described earlier in this chapter.

Let's look at your grandmother's $10,000 bank balance at the end of five years with several different compounding periods: yearly, quarterly, daily, and continuous:[3]

(1) Compounding Period	(2) Total Earnings	(3) Compound Interest	(4) Additional Interest
Yearly	$12,762.82	$2,762.82	—
Quarterly	$12,820.37	$2,820.37	$57.55 more than yearly compounding
Daily	$12,840.03	$2,840.03	$19.66 more than quarterly compounding
Continuous	$12,840.25	$2,840.25	$0.22 more than daily compounding

Notice that your grandmother's total earnings get larger as the frequency of compounding increases, as shown in column 2, but the earnings increase at a decreasing rate, as shown in column 4. The biggest gain comes when the compounding period goes from an annual interest

[3]The future value calculation for annual compounding is $FV_5 = \$10{,}000 \times (1.05)^5 = \$12{,}762.82$.

DECISION MAKING

EXAMPLE 5.1 | Which Bank Offers Depositors the Best Deal?

Situation You have just received a bonus of $10,000 and are looking to deposit the money in a bank account for five years. You investigate the annual deposit rates of several banks and collect the following information:

Bank	Compounding Frequency	Annual Rate
A	Annually	5.00%
B	Quarterly	5.00%
C	Monthly	4.80%
D	Daily	4.85%

You understand that the more frequently interest is compounded in each year, the more you will have at the end of your five-year investment horizon. To determine in which bank you should deposit your money, you calculate how much money you will have at the end of five years at each bank. You apply Equation 5.2 and obtain the following results. Which bank should you choose?

Bank	Investment Amount	Compounding Frequency	Rate	Value after 5 Years
A	$10,000	Annually	5.00%	$12,762.82
B	$10,000	Quarterly	5.00%	$12,820.37
C	$10,000	Monthly	4.80%	$12,706.41
D	$10,000	Daily	4.85%	$12,744.11

Decision Without making any calculations, we can exclude Bank A from consideration because we know that Bank B's CD will have a higher value at the end of five years. The reason is that the CDs from Banks A and B have the same investment amount ($10,000), maturity (five years), and annual interest rate (5 percent); they differ only in their compounding frequency. Bank B's quarterly compounding will result in a higher value than Bank A's annual compounding. Since the CDs from Banks B, C, and D differ in both their annual rates and compounding frequencies, there is no way to determine the most attractive among them without doing future value calculations. These calculations reveal that the CD from Bank B will provide the highest value at the end of five years. You should choose Bank B.

payment to quarterly interest payments. The gain from daily compounding to continuous compounding is small on a modest savings balance such as your grandmother's. Twenty-two cents over five years will not buy your grandmother a cup of coffee, let alone a doughnut. However, for businesses and governments with very large dollar balances at financial institutions, the difference in compounding periods can be substantial.

Decision Making Example 5.1 provides another illustration of how compounding period can affect investment choice.

Calculator Tips for Future Value Problems

As we have mentioned, all types of future value calculations can be done easily on a financial calculator. Here we discuss how to solve these problems, and we identify some potential problem areas to avoid.

A financial calculator includes the following five basic keys for solving future value and present value problems:

N i PV PMT FV

The keys represent the following inputs:

- **N** is the number of periods. The periods can be years, quarters, months, days, or some other unit of time.
- **i** is the interest rate per period, expressed as a percentage.
- **PV** is the present value or the original principal (P_0).
- **PMT** is the amount of any recurring payment.[4]
- **FV** is the future value.

[4]The PMT key is used for annuity calculations, which we will discuss in Chapter 6.

Given any four of these inputs, the financial calculator will solve for the fifth. Note that the interest rate key i differs with different calculator brands: Texas Instruments uses the I/Y key; Hewlett-Packard an i, %i, or I/Y key; and Sharp the i key.

For future value problems, we use only four of the five keys: N for the number of periods, i for the interest rate (or growth rate), PV for the present value (at time zero), and FV for the future value in *n* periods. The PMT key is not used, but, when working on a problem, you should always enter a zero for PMT to clear the register.

To solve a future value problem, enter the known data into your calculator. For example, if you know that the number of periods is five, key in 5 and press the N key. Repeat the process for the remaining known values. Once you have entered all of the values you know, then press the key for the unknown quantity, and you have your answer. Note that with some calculators, including the TI BA II Plus, you get the answer by first pressing the key labeled CPT (compute).

Let's try a problem to see how this works. Suppose we invest $5,000 at 15 percent for 10 years. How much money will we have in 10 years? To solve the problem, we enter data on the keys as displayed in the following calculation and solve for FV. Note that the initial investment of $5,000 is a negative number because it represents a cash outflow. Use the +/– key to make a number negative.

Enter	**10**	**15**	**–5,000**	**0**	
	N	i	PV	PMT	FV
Answer					**20,227.79**

If you did not get the correct answer of $20,227.79, you may need to consult the instruction manual that came with your financial calculator. However, before you do that, you may want to look through **Exhibit 5.5**, which lists the most common problems with using financial calculators. Also, note again that PMT is entered as zero to clear the register.

One advantage of using a financial calculator is that if you have values for any three of the four variables in Equation 5.1, you can solve for the remaining variable at the press of a button. Suppose that you have an opportunity to invest $5,000 in a bank and that the bank will pay you $20,227.79 at the end of 10 years. What interest rate does the bank pay? The time line for our situation is as follows:

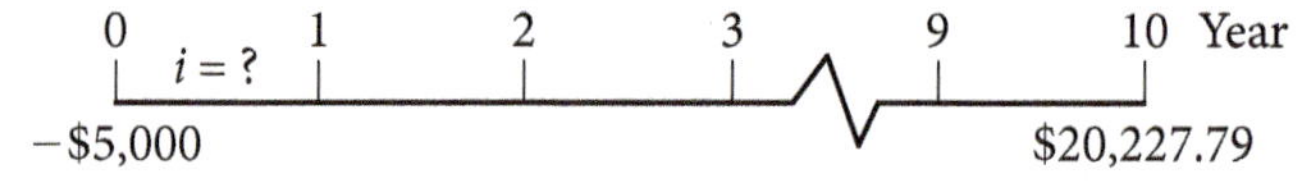

EXHIBIT 5.5 Tips for Using Financial Calculators

Following these tips will help you avoid problems that sometimes arise in solving time value of money problems with a financial calculator.

Use the Correct Compounding Period. Make sure that your calculator is set to compound one payment per period or per year. Because financial calculators are often used to compute monthly payments, some will default to monthly payments unless you indicate otherwise. You will need to consult your calculator's instruction manual because procedures for changing settings vary by manufacturer. Most of the problems you will work in other chapters of this book will compound annually.

Clear the Financial Register of the Calculator Before Starting. Be sure you clear the data from the financial register before starting to work a problem because most calculators retain information between calculations. Since the information may be retained even when the calculator is turned off, turning the calculator off and on will not solve this problem. Check your instruction manual for the correct procedure for clearing the financial register of your calculator.

Ensure the Signs on Cash Outflows and Inflows Are Consistent. For certain types of calculations, you must input a negative (positive)sign for all cash outflows and a positive (negative) sign for all cash inflows. Otherwise, the calculator cannot make the computation, and the answer screen will display an error message, or the answer will be incorrect.

Putting a Negative Sign on a Number. To create a number with a negative sign, enter the number first and then press the "change of sign key." These keys are typically labeled "CHS" or "+/–".

Entering an Interest Rate as a Percentage. Most financial calculators require that interest rate data be entered in percentage form, not in decimal form. For example, enter 7.125 percent as 7.125 and not 0.07125. Unlike nonfinancial calculators, financial calculators assume that rates are stated as percentages.

Rounding Off Numbers. Never round off any numbers until all your calculations are complete. If you round off numbers along the way, you can generate significant rounding errors.

Adjusting the Decimal Setting. Most calculators are set to display two decimal places. You will find it convenient at times to display four or more decimal places when making financial calculations, especially when working with interest rates or present value factors. Again, consult your instruction manual.

Having the mode correctly set to BEG or END. In finance, most problems that you solve will involve cash payments that occur at the end of each time period. Most calculators normally operate in this mode, which is usually designated as "END" mode. However, in some problems the cash payments occur at the beginning of each period. This setting is designated as the "BEG" mode. When your financial calculator was purchased, it was set in the END mode. Financial calculators allow you to switch between the END and BEG modes.

We know the values for N (10 years), PV ($5,000), and FV ($20,227.79), so we can enter these values into our financial calculator:

Enter	**10**		**−5,000**	**0**	**20,227.79**
	N	i	PV	PMT	FV
Answer		**15.00**			

Press the interest rate (i) key, and 15.00 percent appears as the answer. Notice that the cash outflow ($5,000) was entered as a negative value and the cash inflow ($20,227.79) as a positive value. If both values were entered with the same sign, your financial calculator algorithm could not compute the equation, yielding an error message. Go ahead and try it.

The following **Using Excel Example** illustrates the use of a computer spreadsheet program to compute future values with different compunding rates.

Using Excel

Time Value of Money

Spreadsheet programs are a popular method for setting up and solving finance and accounting problems. Throughout this book, we will show you how to structure and calculate some problems using the Microsoft Excel spreadsheet program. Spreadsheet programs are like your financial calculator but are especially efficient at doing repetitive calculations. For example, once the spreadsheet program is set up, it will allow you to make computations using preprogrammed formulas. Thus, you can simply change any of the input cells, and the preset formula will automatically recalculate the answer based on the new input values. For this reason, we recommend that you use formulas whenever possible.

We begin our spreadsheet applications with time value of money calculations. As with the financial calculator approach, there are five variables used in these calculations, and knowing any four of them will let you calculate the fifth one. Excel includes preset formulas for you to use. These are as follows:

Solving for	**Formula**
Present Value	= PV(RATE, NPER, PMT, FV)
Future Value	= FV(RATE, NPER, PMT, PV)
Discount Rate	= RATE(NPER, PMT, PV, FV)
Payment	= PMT(RATE, NPER, PV, FV)
Number of Periods	= NPER(RATE, PMT, PV, FV)

To enter a formula, all you have to do is type in the equal sign, the abbreviated name of the variable you want to compute, and an open parenthesis, and Excel will automatically prompt you to enter the rest of the variables. Here is an example of what you would type to compute the future value:

	A	B	C	D	E	F
1						
2	**Time Value of Money Calculations**					
3						
4	Your grandmother wants to put $10,000 into a bank savings account for five years. Bank A pays 5 percent					
5	interest compounded quarterly, while Bank B offers 5 percent compounded daily. Which bank should your					
6	grandmother choose?					
7						
8	To answer the question, we need to solve for the future value.					
9						
10	**Problem setup and solution:**					
11						
12		**Bank A**	**Bank B**		**Comment**	
13	Present value	($10,000)	($10,000)		Value given	
14	Interest rate	0.01250	0.00014		Interest rate/# compounding periods per year	
15	Number of periods	20	1825		# years × # compounding periods per year	
16	**Future value**	**$12,820.37**	**$12,840.03**		See note below	
17						
18–22	The formula entered to calculate the future value for Bank A in cell B16 is =FV(B14, B15, 0, B13). Similarly, the formula to calculate the future value for Bank B in cell C16 is =FV(C14, C15, 0, C13). Since there are no payments, we enter PMT as zero. Also, notice that to be consistent with what we have said about cash inflows and outflows so far, the present value is entered as a negative number.					
23						

1. =
2. FV
3. (

Here are a few important things to note when entering the formulas: (1) be consistent with signs for cash inflows and outflows; (2) enter the rate of return as a decimal number, not a percentage; and (3) enter the amount of an unknown payment as zero.

To see how a problem is set up and how the calculations are made using a spreadsheet, let's return to Learning by Doing Application 5.2.

Before You Go On

1. What is compounding, and how does it affect the future value of an investment?
2. What is the difference between simple interest and compound interest?
3. How does changing the compounding period affect the amount of interest earned on an investment?

5.3 Present Value and Discounting

LEARNING OBJECTIVE

3. Explain the concept of present value and how it relates to future value, and use the present value formula to make business decisions.

In our discussion of future value, we asked the question "If you put \$100 in a bank savings account that pays 10 percent annual interest, how much money would accumulate in one year?" Another type of question that arises frequently in finance concerns present value. This question asks, "What is the value today of a cash flow promised in the future?" We'll illustrate the present value concept with a simple example.

Single-Period Investment

Suppose that a rich uncle gives you a bank certificate of deposit (CD) that matures in one year and pays \$110. The CD pays 10 percent interest annually and cannot be redeemed until maturity. Being a student, you need the money now and would like to sell the CD. What would be a fair price if you sold the CD today?

From our earlier discussion, we know that if we invest \$100 in a bank at 10 percent for one year, it will grow to a future value of $\$100 \times (1 + 0.10) = \$110$. It seems reasonable to conclude that if a CD has an interest rate of 10 percent and will have a value of \$110 a year from now, it is worth \$100 today.

More formally, to find the present value of a future cash flow, or its value today, we reverse the compounding process and divide the future value (\$110) by the future value factor $(1 + 0.10)$. The result is $\$110/(1 + 0.10) = \$100$, which is the same answer we derived from our intuitive calculation. If we write the calculations above as a formula, we have a one-period model for calculating the present value of a future cash flow:

$$PV = \frac{FV_1}{1 + i}$$

The numerical calculation for the present value (PV) from our one-period model follows:

$$\begin{aligned} PV &= \frac{FV_1}{1 + i} \\ &= \frac{\$110}{1 + 0.10} \\ &= \frac{\$110}{1.10} \\ &= \$100 \end{aligned}$$

We have noted that while future value calculations involve *compounding* an amount forward into the future, *present value* calculations involve the reverse. That is, present value calculations involve determining the current value (or present value) of a future cash flow. The process of calculating the present value is called **discounting**, and the interest rate i is known as the **discount rate**. Accordingly, the **present value (PV)** can be thought of as the *discounted value of a future amount.* The present value is simply the current value of a future cash flow that has been discounted at the appropriate discount rate.

discounting the process by which the present value of future cash flows is obtained

discount rate the interest rate used in the discounting process to find the present value of future cash flows

present value (PV) the current value of a future cash flow discounted at the appropriate discount rate

Just as we have a future value factor, $(1 + i)$, we also have a *present value factor,* which is more commonly called the *discount factor.* The discount factor, which is $1/(1 + i)$, is the reciprocal of the future value factor. This expression may not be obvious in the equation above, but note that we can write that equation in two ways:

1. $PV = \dfrac{FV_1}{1 + i}$

2. $PV = FV_1 \times \dfrac{1}{1 + i}$

These equations represent the same calculation, but the discount factor is explicit in the second one.

Multiple-Period Investment

Now suppose your uncle gives you another 10 percent CD, but this CD matures in two years and pays \$121 at maturity. Like the other CD, it cannot be redeemed until maturity. From the previous section, we know that if we invest \$100 in a bank at 10 percent for two years, it will grow to a future value of $\$100 \times (1 + 0.10)^2 = \$121$. To calculate the present value, or today's price, we divide the future value by the future value factor. If we write this as an equation, the result is a two-period model for computing the present value of a future cash flow:

$$PV = \frac{FV_2}{(1 + i)^2}$$

Plugging the data from our example into the equation yields:

$$\begin{aligned} PV &= \frac{FV_2}{(1 + i)^2} \\ &= \frac{\$121}{(1 + 0.10)^2} \\ &= \frac{\$121}{1.21} \\ &= \$100 \end{aligned}$$

By now, you know the drill. We can extend the equation to a third year as:

$$PV = \frac{FV_3}{(1 + i)^3}$$

and so on for the fourth year and beyond.

The Present Value Equation

Given the pattern shown above, we can see that the general formula for the present value equation is:

$$PV = \frac{FV_n}{(1 + i)^n} \tag{5.4}$$

where:

PV = the value today (time zero) of a cash flow
FV_n = the future value at the end of period n
i = the discount rate, which is the interest rate per period
n = the number of periods, which can be years, quarters, months, days, or some other unit of time

Note that Equation 5.4 can be written in slightly different ways, which we will sometimes do in this book. The first form, introduced earlier, separates out the discount factor, $1/(1 + i)$:[5]

$$PV = FV_n \times \frac{1}{(1 + i)^n}$$

In the second form, DF_n is the discount factor for the nth period: $DF_n = 1/(1 + i)^n$:

$$PV = FV_n \times DF_n$$

Future and Present Value Equations Are the Same

Equation 5.4 is just a restatement of the future value equation, Equation 5.1. That is, to get the future value (FV_n) of funds invested for n years, we multiply the original investment by $(1 + i)^n$. To find the present value of a future payment (PV), we divide FV_n by $(1 + i)^n$. Stated another way, we can start with the future value equation (Equation 5.1), $FV_n = PV \times (1 + i)^n$, and then solve it for PV; the resulting equation is the present value equation (Equation 5.4), $PV = FV_n/(1 + i)^n$.

[5]Equation 5.4 can also be written as $PV = FV_n \times (1 + i)^{-n}$.

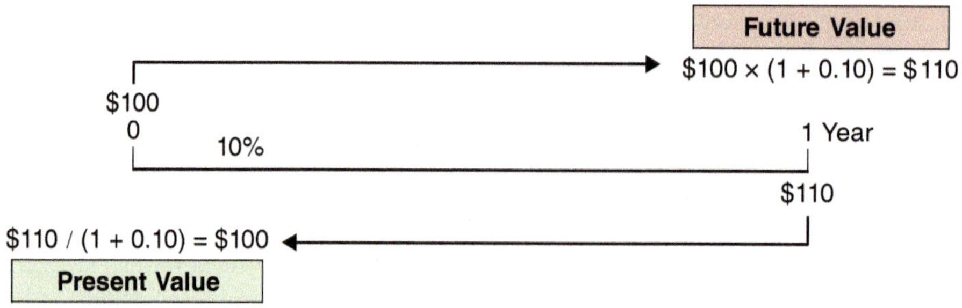

EXHIBIT 5.6 Comparing Future Value and Present Value Calculations

The future value and present value formulas are one and the same; the present value factor, $1/(1 + i)^n$, is just the reciprocal of the future value factor, $(1 + i)^n$.

Exhibit 5.6 illustrates the relation between the future value and present value calculations for $100 invested at 10 percent interest. You can see from the exhibit that present value and future value are just two sides of the same coin. The formula used to calculate the present value is really the same as the formula for future value, just rearranged.

Applying the Present Value Formula

Let's work through some examples to see how the present value equation is used. Suppose you are interested in buying a new sports coupe a year from now. You estimate that the car will cost $40,000. If your local bank pays 5 percent interest on savings deposits, how much money will you need to save in order to buy the car as planned? The time line for the car purchase problem is as follows:

Solving this problem involves a direct application of Equation 5.4. What we want to know is how much money you have to put in the bank today to have $40,000 a year from now to buy your car. To find out, we compute the present value of $40,000 using a 5 percent discount rate:

$$\begin{aligned} PV &= \frac{FV_1}{1 + i} \\ &= \frac{\$40{,}000}{1 + 0.05} \\ &= \frac{\$40{,}000}{1.05} \\ &= \$38{,}095.24 \end{aligned}$$

Weblink

Marketwatch.com's personal finance Web site provides a lot of useful information for day-to-day finance dealings at http://www.marketwatch.com/personal-finance?showsmscrim=true.

If you put $38,095.24 in a bank savings account at 5 percent today, you will have the $40,000 to buy the car in one year.

Since that's a lot of money to come up with, your mother suggests that you leave the money in the bank for two years instead of one year. If you follow her advice, how much money do you need to invest? The time line is as follows:

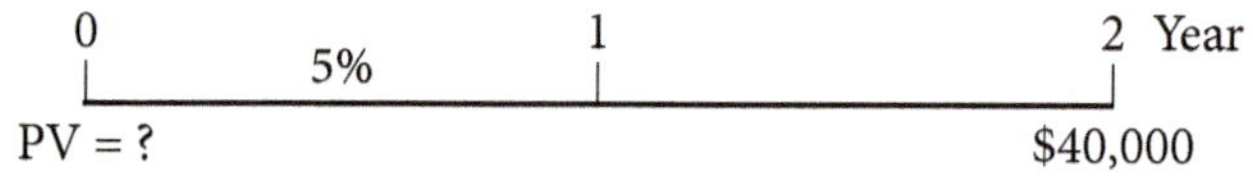

For a two-year waiting period, assuming the car price will stay the same, the calculation is:

$$\begin{aligned} PV &= \frac{FV_2}{(1 + i)^2} \\ &= \frac{\$40{,}000}{(1 + 0.05)^2} \\ &= \frac{\$40{,}000}{1.1025} \\ &= \$36{,}281.18 \end{aligned}$$

Given the time value of money, the result is exactly what we would expect. The present value of \$40,000 two years out is lower than the present value of \$40,000 one year out—\$36,281.18 compared with \$38,095.24. Thus, if you are willing to leave your money in the bank for two years instead of one, you can make a smaller initial investment to reach your goal.

Now suppose your rich neighbor says that if you invest your money with him for one year, he will pay you 15 percent interest. The time line is:

0	15%	1 Year
PV = ?		\$40,000

The calculation for the initial investment at this new rate is as follows:

$$\begin{aligned} PV &= \frac{FV_1}{1+i} \\ &= \frac{\$40{,}000}{1+0.15} \\ &= \frac{\$40{,}000}{1.15} \\ &= \$34{,}782.61 \end{aligned}$$

Thus, when the interest rate, or discount rate, is 15 percent, the present value of \$40,000 to be received in a year's time is \$34,782.61, compared with \$38,095.24 at a rate of 5 percent and a time of one year. Holding maturity constant, an increase in the discount rate decreases the present value of the future cash flow. This makes sense because when interest rates are higher, it is more valuable to have dollars in hand today to invest; thus, dollars in the future are worth less.

Learning By Doing Application 5.3 shows another present valuation calculation.

APPLICATION 5.3 | European Graduation Fling

LEARNING BY DOING

Problem Suppose you plan to take a vacation to Europe when you graduate from college in two years. If your savings account at the bank pays 6 percent, how much money do you need to set aside today to have \$8,000 when you leave for Europe?

Approach The money you need today is the present value of the amount you will need for your trip in two years. The value of FV_2 is \$8,000 and the interest rate is 6 percent. Using these values and the present value equation, we can calculate how much money you must put in the bank at 6 percent to generate \$8,000. The time line is:

0	6%	1	2 Year
PV = ?			\$8,000

Solution

$$\begin{aligned} PV &= FV_n \times \frac{1}{(1+i)^n} \\ &= FV_2 \times \frac{1}{(1+i)^2} \\ &= \$8{,}000 \times \frac{1}{(1.06)^2} \\ &= \$8{,}000 \times 0.889996 \\ &= \$7{,}119.97 \end{aligned}$$

Thus, if you invest \$7,119.97 in your savings account today, at the end of two years you will have exactly \$8,000.

WileyPLUS

Need more help? Visit your WileyPLUS course.

The Relations Among Time, the Discount Rate, and Present Value

From our discussion so far, we can see that (1) the farther in the future a dollar will be received, the less it is worth today, and (2) the higher the discount rate, the lower the present value of a dollar to be received in the future. Let's look a bit more closely at these relations.

Recall from Exhibit 5.4 that the future value of a dollar increases with time because of compounding. In contrast, the present value of a dollar becomes smaller the farther into the future that dollar is to be received. The reason is that the present value factor $1/(1 + i)^n$ is the reciprocal of the future value factor $(1 + i)^n$. Thus, the present value of $1 must become smaller the farther into the future that dollar is to be received.

Exhibit 5.7 shows the present values of $1 for different time periods and discount rates. For example, the present value of $1 discounted at 5 percent for 10 years is 61 cents, at 10 percent it is 39 cents, and at 20 percent, 16 cents. Thus, the higher the discount rate, the lower the present value of $1 for a given time period. Exhibit 5.7 also shows that, just as with future value, the relation between the present value of $1 and time is not linear, but exponential. Finally, it is worth noting that if interest rates are zero, the present value of $1 is $1; that is, there is no time value of money. In this situation, $1,000 today has the same value as $1,000 a year from now or, for that matter, 10 years from now.

Calculator Tips for Present Value Problems

Calculating the discount factor (present value factor) on a calculator is similar to calculating the future value factor but requires an additional keystroke on most calculators because the discount factor, $1/(1 + i)^n$, is the reciprocal of the future value factor, $(1 + i)^n$. The additional keystroke involves the use of the reciprocal key ($1/x$) to find the discount factor. For example, to compute $1/(1.08)^{10}$, first enter 1.08, press the y^x key and enter 10, then press the equal (=) key. The number on the screen should be 2.159. This is the future value factor. It is a

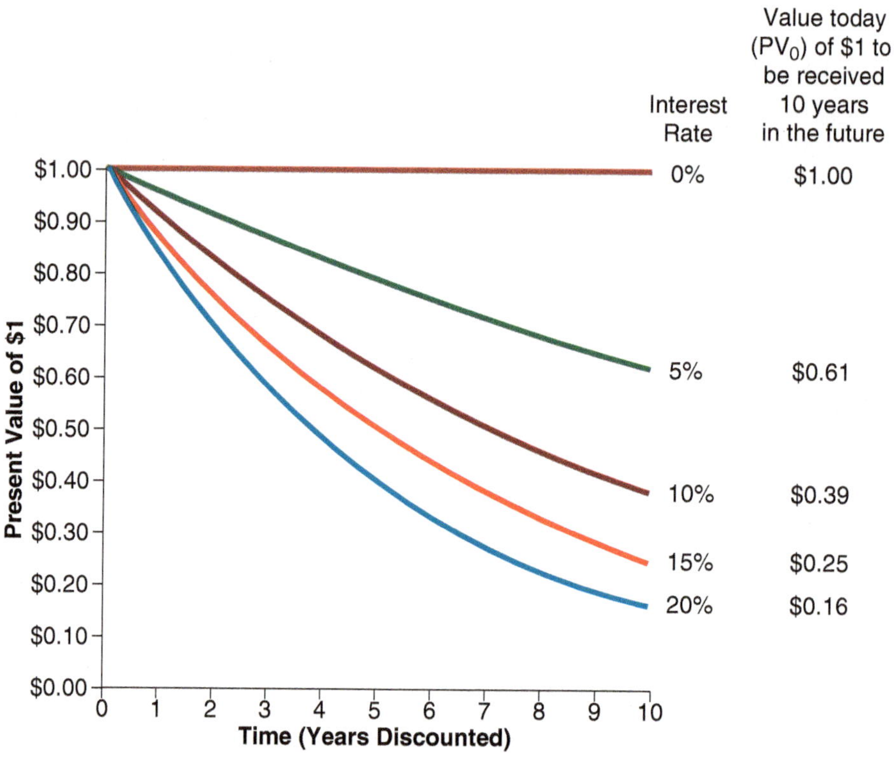

EXHIBIT 5.7 **Present Value of $1 for Different Time Periods and Discount Rates**

The higher the discount rate, the lower the present value of $1 for a given time period. Just as with future value, the relation between the present value and time is not linear, but exponential.

calculation you have made before. Now press the $1/x$ key, then the equal key, and you have the present value factor, 0.463!

Calculating the present value (PV) on a financial calculator is the same as calculating the future value (FV_n) except that you solve for PV rather than FV_n. For example, what is the present value of $1,000 received 10 years from now at a 9 percent discount rate? To find the answer on your financial calculator, enter the following keystrokes:

Enter	**10**	**9**		**0**	**1,000**
	N	i	PV	PMT	FV
Answer			**−422.41**		

then solve for the present value (PV), which is −$422.41. Notice that the answer has a negative sign. As we discussed previously, the $1,000 represents an inflow, and the $442.41 represents an outflow.

Decision Making Example 5.2 illustrates another application of the present value concept.

Note that, just as financial analysts used future value factor tables to help with calculations before calculators and computer spreadsheets became widely available, they also used present value (discount) factor tables. Table A-2 in Appendix A at the back of this book is an example of such a table.

Future Value Versus Present Value

We can analyze financial decisions using either future value or present value techniques. Although the two techniques approach the decision differently, both yield the same result. Both techniques focus on the valuation of cash flows received over time. In corporate finance, future value problems typically measure the value of cash flows at the end of a project, whereas present value problems measure the value of cash flows at the start of a project (time zero).

EXAMPLE 5.2 | Picking the Best Lottery Payoff Option

DECISION MAKING

Situation Congratulations! You have won the $1 million lottery grand prize. You have been presented with several payout alternatives, and you have to decide which one to accept. The alternatives are as follows:

- $1 million today
- $1.2 million lump sum in two years
- $1.5 million lump sum in five years
- $2 million lump sum in eight years

You are intrigued by the choice of collecting the prize money today or receiving double the amount of money in the future. Which payout option should you choose?

Your cousin, a stockbroker, advises you that over the long term you should be able to earn 10 percent on an investment portfolio. Based on that rate of return, you make the following calculations:

Alternative	Future Value	Present Value
Today	$1 million	$1 million
2 years	$1.2 million	$991,736
5 years	$1.5 million	$931,382
8 years	$2 million	$933,015

Decision As appealing as the higher amounts may sound, waiting for the big payout is not worthwhile in this case. Applying the present value formula has enabled you to convert future dollars into present, or current, dollars. Now the decision is simple—you can directly compare the present values. Given the choices here, you should take the $1 million today.

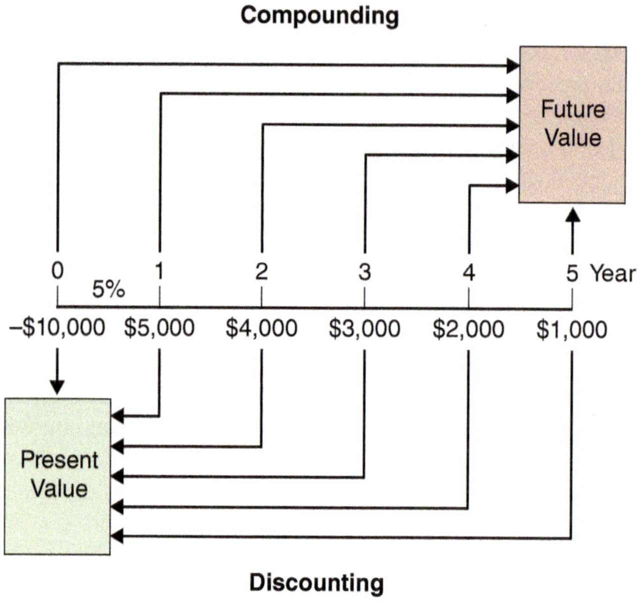

EXHIBIT 5.8 Future Value and Present Value Compared

Compounding converts a present value into its future value, taking into account the time value of money. Discounting is just the reverse—it converts future cash flows into their present value.

Exhibit 5.8 compares the $10,000 investment decision shown in Exhibit 5.1 in terms of future value and present value. When managers are making a decision about whether to accept a project, they must look at all of the cash flows associated with that project with reference to the same point in time. As Exhibit 5.8 shows, for most business decisions, that point is either the start (time zero) or the end of the project (in this example, Year 5). In Chapter 6 we will discuss calculation of the future value or the present value of a series of cash flows like that illustrated in Exhibit 5.8.

Before You Go On

1. What is the present value, and when is it used?
2. What is the discount rate? How does the discount rate differ from the interest rate in the future value equation?
3. What is the relation between the present value factor and the future value factor?
4. Explain why you would expect the discount factor to be smaller when the time to payment is longer.

5.4 Additional Concepts and Applications

LEARNING OBJECTIVE

4. Discuss why the concept of compounding is not restricted to money, and use the future value formula to calculate growth rates.

In this final section, we discuss several additional issues concerning present and future value, including how to find an unknown discount rate, the time required for an investment to grow by a certain amount, a rule of thumb for estimating the length of time it will take to "double your money," and how to find the growth rates of various kinds of investments.

Finding the Interest Rate

In finance, some situations require you to determine the interest rate (or discount rate) for a given future cash flow. These situations typically arise when you want to determine the return on an investment. Consider a *zero coupon bond,* which is essentially a loan that pays no periodic interest. The issuer (the firm that borrows the money) makes a single payment when the bond matures (the loan is due) that includes repayment of the amount borrowed plus all of the interest. Needless to say, the issuer must prepare in advance to have the cash to pay the bondholders.

Suppose a firm is planning to issue $10 million worth of zero coupon bonds with 20 years to maturity. The bonds are issued in denominations of $1,000 and are sold for $90 each. In other words, the investor buys a bond today for $90, and 20 years from now the firm pays the investor $1,000. If you bought one of these bonds, what would be your return on investment?

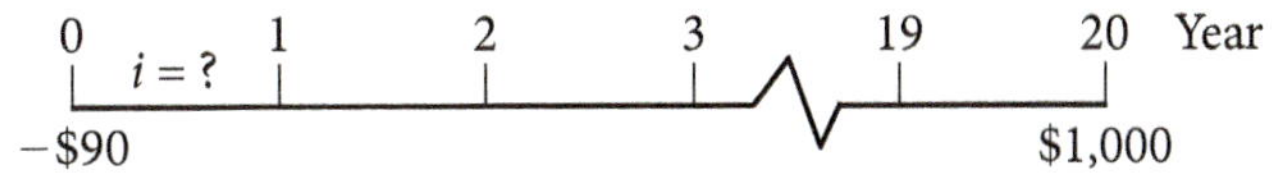

To find the return, we need to solve Equation 5.1, the future value equation, for i, the interest, or discount, rate. The $90 you pay today is the PV (present value), the $1,000 you get in 20 years is the FV (future value), and n (number of periods) is 20 years. The calculation is as follows:

$$\begin{aligned} FV_n &= PV \times (1+i)^n \\ \$1{,}000 &= \$90 \times (1+i)^{20} \\ (1+i)^{20} &= \frac{\$1{,}000}{\$90} \\ 1+i &= \left(\frac{\$1{,}000}{\$90}\right)^{1/20} \\ i &= (11.1111)^{1/20} - 1 \\ &= 1.1279 - 1 \\ &= 0.1279, \text{ or } 12.79\% \end{aligned}$$

The rate of return on your investment, compounded annually, is 12.79 percent. Using a financial calculator, we arrive at the following solution:

	N	i	PV	PMT	FV
Enter	**20**		**−90**	**0**	**1,000**
Answer		**12.79**			

Learning by Doing Application 5.4 illustrates another interest rate calculation.

APPLICATION 5.4 | Interest Rate on a Loan

LEARNING BY DOING

Problem Greg and Joan Hubbard are getting ready to buy their first house. To help make the down payment, Greg's aunt offers to loan them $15,000, which can be repaid in 10 years. If Greg and Joan borrow the money, they will have to repay Greg's aunt the amount of $23,750. What rate of interest would Greg and Joan be paying on the 10-year loan?

Approach In this case, the present value is the value of the loan ($15,000), and the future value is the amount due at the end of 10 years ($23,750). To solve for the rate of interest on the loan, we can use the future value equation, Equation 5.1. Alternatively, we can use a financial calculator to compute the interest rate. The time line for the loan, where the $15,000 is a cash inflow to Greg and Joan and the $23,750 is a cash outflow, is as follows:

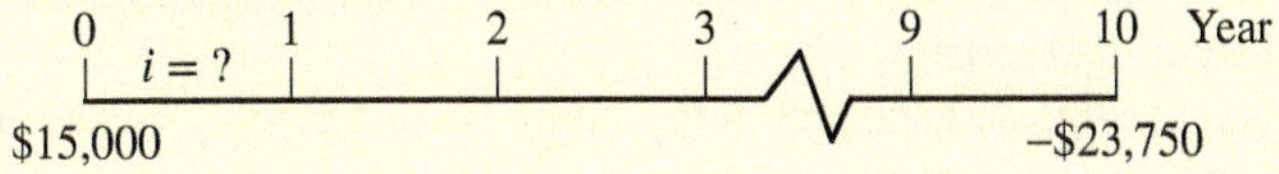

WileyPLUS

Need more help? Visit your WileyPLUS course.

Solution Using Equation 5.1:

$$\begin{aligned} FV_n &= PV \times (1+i)^n \\ \$23{,}750 &= \$15{,}000 \times (1+i)^{10} \\ (1+i)^{10} &= \frac{\$23{,}750}{\$15{,}000} \\ 1+i &= \left(\frac{\$23{,}750}{\$15{,}000}\right)^{1/10} \\ i &= (1.58333)^{1/10} - 1 \\ &= 1.04703 - 1 \\ &= 0.04703, \text{ or } 4.703\% \end{aligned}$$

Using a financial calculator:

Enter	10		15,000	0	223,750
	N	i	PV	PMT	FV
Answer		**4.703**			

Finding How Many Periods It Takes an Investment to Grow a Certain Amount

Up to this point we have used variations of Equation 5.1:

$$FV_n = PV \times (1+i)^n$$

to calculate the future value of an investment (FV_n), the present value of an investment (PV), and the interest rate necessary for an initial investment (the present value) to grow to a specific value (the future value) over a certain number of periods (i). Note that Equation 5.1 has a total of four variables. You may have noticed that in all of the previous calculations, we took advantage of the mathematical principle that if we know the values of three of these variables we can calculate the value of the fourth.

The same principle allows us to calculate the number of periods (n) that it takes an investment to grow a certain amount. This is a more complicated calculation than the calculations of the values of the other three variables, but it is an important one for you to know and understand.

Suppose that you would like to purchase a new motorcycle to ride on dirt trails near campus. The motorcycle dealer will finance the bike that you are interested in if you make a down payment of \$1,175. Right now you only have \$1,000. If you can earn 5 percent by investing your money, how long will it take for your \$1,000 to grow to \$1,175?

To find this length of time, we must solve Equation 5.1, the future value equation, for n.

$$\begin{aligned} FV_n &= PV \times (1+i)^n \\ \$1{,}175 &= \$1{,}000 \times (1+0.05)^n \\ \frac{\$1{,}175}{\$1{,}000} &= (1+0.05)^n \\ \ln\left(\frac{\$1{,}175}{\$1{,}000}\right) &= n \times \ln(1+0.05) \\ n &= \frac{\ln\left(\frac{\$1{,}175}{\$1{,}000}\right)}{\ln(1+0.05)} \\ n &= \frac{0.16127}{0.04879} \\ n &= 3.31 \text{ years} \end{aligned}$$

It will take 3.31 years for your investment to grow to \$1,175. If you don't want to wait this long to get your motorcycle, you cannot rely on your investment earnings alone. You will have to put aside some additional money.

Note that because n is an exponent in the future value formula, we have to take the natural logarithm, $\ln(x)$, of both sides of the equation in the fourth line of the preceding calculations to compute the value of n directly. Your financial calculator should have a key that allows you to calculate natural logarithms. Just enter the value in the parentheses and then press the LN key.

Using a financial calculator, we obtain the same solution.

Enter		5	−1,000	0	1,175
	N	i	PV	PMT	FV
Answer	**3.31**				

The Rule of 72

People are fascinated by the possibility of doubling their money. Infomercials on television tout speculative land investments, often claiming that some investors have doubled their money in a short period of time, such as four years. Before there were financial calculators, people used rules of thumb to approximate difficult present value calculations. One such rule is the Rule of 72, which was used to determine the approximate amount of time it takes to double the value of an investment. The **Rule of 72** says that the time to double your money (TDM) approximately equals $72/i$, where i is the rate of return expressed as a percentage. Thus,

Rule of 72 a rule proposing that the time required to double an amount of money (TDM) approximately equals $72/i$, where i is the rate of return expressed as a percentage

$$\text{TDM} = \frac{72}{i} \tag{5.5}$$

Applying the Rule of 72 to the preceding investment example suggests that if you double your money in four years, your annual rate of return will be 18 percent ($i = 72/4$ years $= 18$ percent).

Let's check the rule's accuracy by applying the future value formula to the land example. We are assuming that we will double our money in four years, so $n = 4$ years. We did not specify a present value or future value amount; however, doubling our money means that we will get back $2 (FV) for every $1 invested (PV). Using Equation 5.1 and solving for the interest rate (i), we find that $i = 0.1892$, or 18.92 percent.[6]

That's not bad for a simple rule of thumb: 18.92 percent versus 18 percent. Within limits, the Rule of 72 provides a quick method for determining approximately how long it will take to double an investment for a particular rate of return. The Rule of 72 is a linear approximation of a nonlinear function, and as such, the rule is fairly accurate for interest rates between 5 and 20 percent. Outside these limits, the rule is not very accurate.

Compound Growth Rates

The concept of compounding is not restricted to money. Any number that changes over time, such as the population of a city, changes at some compound growth rate. Compound growth occurs when the initial value of a number increases or decreases each period by the factor (1 + growth rate). As we go through the book, we will discuss many different types of interest rates, such as the discount rate on capital budgeting projects, the yield on a bond, and the internal rate of return on an investment. All of these interest rates can be thought of as growth rates (g) that relate future values to present values.

When we refer to the compounding effect, we are really talking about what happens when the value of a number increases or decreases by $(1 + \text{growth rate})^n$. That is, the future value of a number after n periods will equal the initial value times $(1 + \text{growth rate})^n$. Does this sound familiar? We can also rewrite Equation 5.1 in a more general form as a compound growth rate formula, substituting g, the growth rate, for i, the interest rate:

$$FV_n = PV \times (1 + g)^n \tag{5.6}$$

where:

FV_n = future value of the economic factor, such as sales or population, at the end of period n
PV = original amount or present value of the economic factor
g = growth rate per period
n = number of periods, which can be years, quarters, months, weeks, days, minutes, or some other unit of time

Suppose, for example, that because of an advertising campaign, a firm's sales increased from 20 million units in 2011 to more than 35 million units in 2014. What has been the average annual

[6] Solve $FV_n = PV \times (1 + i)^n$ for i with $FV_n = \$2$, $PV = \$1$, and $n = 4$ years.

growth rate in unit sales? Here, the future value is 35 million, the present value is 20 million, and n is 3 since we are interested in the average annual growth rate over three years. The time line is:

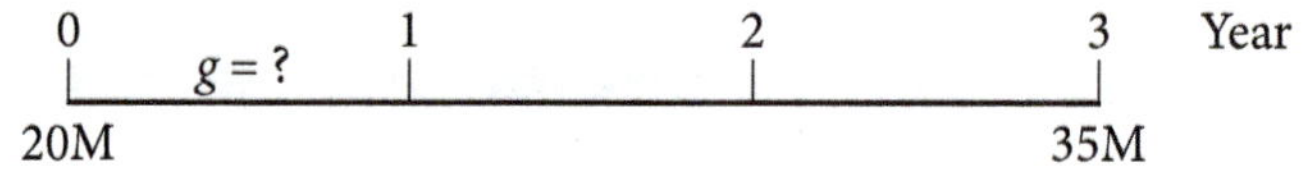

Applying Equation 5.6 and solving for the growth factor (g) yields:

$$\begin{aligned} FV_3 &= PV \times (1 + g)^3 \\ 35 &= 20 \times (1 + g)^3 \\ 1.75 &= (1 + g)^3 \\ g &= (1.75)^{1/3} - 1 \\ &= 1.2051 - 1 \\ &= 0.2051, \text{ or } 20.51\% \end{aligned}$$

compound annual growth rate (CAGR) the average annual growth rate over a specified period of time

Thus, unit sales grew nearly 21 percent per year. More precisely, we could say that unit sales grew at a average annual growth rate, or **compound annual growth rate (CAGR)**, of nearly 21 percent. If we use our financial calculator, we find the same answer:

	N	i	PV	PMT	FV
Enter	3		−20	0	35
Answer		**20.51**			

Note that we enter 20 million as a negative number even though it is not a cash outflow. This is because one value must be negative when using a financial calculator. It makes no difference which number is negative and which is positive.

Learning by Doing Application 5.5 and **Learning by Doing Application 5.6** illustrate other growth rate calculations.

LEARNING BY DOING

WileyPLUS

Need more help? Visit your WileyPLUS course.

APPLICATION 5.5 | The Growth Rate of the World's Population

Problem Hannah, an industrial relations major, is writing a term paper and needs an estimate of how fast the world population is growing. In her almanac, she finds that the world's population was an estimated 7.4 billion people as of August 2016. The United Nations estimates that the population will reach 11.2 billion people in August 2100. Calculate the annual population growth rate implied by these numbers. At that growth rate, what will be the world's population in August 2030?

Approach We first find the annual rate of growth through August 2100 by applying Equation 5.6 for the 84-year period 2016–2100. For the purpose of this calculation, we can use the estimated population of 7.4 billion people in 2016 as the present value, the estimated future population of 11.2 billion people as the future value, and 84 years as the number of compounding periods (n). We want to solve for g, which is the annual compound growth rate over the 84-year period. We can then plug the 84-year population growth rate in Equation 5.6 and solve for the world's population in August 2030 (FV_{14}). Alternatively, we can get the answer by using a financial calculator.

Solution Using Equation 5.6, we find the growth rate as follows:

$$\begin{aligned} FV_n &= PV \times (1 + g)^n \\ 11.2 &= 7.4 \times (1 + g)^{84} \\ 1.51 &= (1 + g)^{84} \\ (1.51)^{1/84} &= 1 + g \\ g &= (1.51)^{1/84} - 1 \\ &= 1.005 - 1 \\ &= 0.005, \text{ or } 0.5\% \end{aligned}$$

The world's population at the end of 2030 is therefore estimated to be:

$$\begin{aligned} FV_{14} &= 7.4 \times (1 + 0.005)^{14} \\ &= 7.4 \times 1.072 \\ &= 7.94 \text{ billion people} \end{aligned}$$

Using a financial calculator:

	N	i	PV	PMT	FV
Enter	14	0.5	−7.4	0	
Answer					**7.94**

LEARNING BY DOING

APPLICATION 5.6 | Calculating Projected Earnings

Problem IBM's net income in 2015 was $13.36 billion. Wall Street analysts expect IBM's earnings to increase by 6 percent per year over the next three years. Using your financial calculator, determine what IBM's earnings should be in three years.

Approach This problem involves the growth rate (g) of IBM's earnings. We already know the value of g, which is 6 percent, and we need to find the future value. Since the general compound growth rate formula, Equation 5.6, is the same as Equation 5.1, the future value formula, we can use the same calculator procedure we used earlier to find the future value. We enter the data on the calculator keys as shown below, using the growth rate value for the interest rate. Then we solve for the future value:

Solution

Enter	3	6	−13.36	0	
	N	i	PV	PMT	FV
Answer					**15.91**

Concluding Comments

This chapter has introduced the basic principles of present value and future value. The table at the end of the chapter summarizes the key equations developed in the chapter. The equations for future value (Equation 5.1) and present value (Equation 5.4) are two of the most fundamental relations in finance and will be applied throughout the rest of this textbook.

Before You Go On

1. What is the difference between the interest rate (i) and the growth rate (g) in the future value equation?

Summary of Learning Objectives

1 Explain the concept of time value of money and why it is so important in the field of finance.

The idea that money has a time value is one of the most fundamental concepts in the field of finance. The concept is based on the idea that most people prefer to consume goods today rather than wait to have similar goods in the future. Since money buys goods, they would rather have money today than in the future. Thus, *a dollar today is worth more than a dollar received in the future.* Another way of viewing the time value of money is that your money is worth more today than at some point in the future because, if you had the money now, you could invest it and earn interest. Thus, the time value of money is the opportunity cost of forgoing consumption today.

Applications of the time value of money focus on the trade-off between current dollars and dollars received at some future date. This is an important element in financial decisions because most investment decisions require the comparison of cash invested today with the value of expected future cash inflows. Time value of money calculations facilitate such comparisons by accounting for both the magnitude and timing of cash flows. Investment opportunities are undertaken only when the value of future cash inflows exceeds the cost of the investment (the initial cash outflow).

2 Explain the concept of future value, including the meaning of the terms *principal*, *simple interest*, and *compound interest*, and use the future value formula to make business decisions.

The future value is what the investment will be worth after earning interest for one or more periods. The *principal* is the amount of the investment. *Simple interest* is the interest paid on the original investment; the amount of *simple interest* remains constant from period to period. *Compound interest* includes not only *simple interest* but also interest earned on the reinvestment of previously earned interest, the so-called *interest earned on interest*. For future value calculations, the higher the interest rate, the faster the investment will grow. The application of the future value formula in business decisions is presented in Section 5.2.

3 Explain the concept of present value and how it relates to future value, and use the present value formula to make business decisions.

The present value is the value today of a future cash flow. Computing the present value involves discounting future cash flows back to the present at an appropriate discount rate. The process of discounting cash flows adjusts the cash flows for the time value of money. Computationally, the present value factor is the reciprocal of the future value factor, or $1/(1 + i)$. The calculation and application of the present value formula in business decisions is presented in Section 5.3.

4 Discuss why the concept of compounding is not restricted to money, and use the future value formula to calculate growth rates.

Any number of changes that are observed over time in the physical and social sciences follow a compound growth rate pattern. The future value formula can be used in calculating these growth rates, as illustrated in Section 5.4.

Summary of Key Equations

Equation	Description	Formula
5.1	Future value of an n-period investment	$FV_n = PV \times (1 + i)^n$
5.2	Future value with more frequent than annual compounding	$FV_n = PV \times (1 + i/m)^{m \times n}$
5.3	Future value with continuous compounding	$FV_\infty = PV \times e^{i \times n}$
5.4	Present value of an n-period investment	$PV = \frac{FV_n}{(1 + i)^n}$
5.5	Rule of 72	$TDM = \frac{72}{i}$
5.6	Future value with general growth rate	$FV_n = PV \times (1 + g)^n$

Self-Study Problems

5.1 Amit Patel is planning to invest $10,000 in a bank certificate of deposit (CD) for five years. The CD will pay interest of 9 percent. What is the future value of Amit's investment?

5.2 Megan Gaumer expects to need $50,000 for a down payment on a house in six years. How much would she have to invest today in an account paying 7.25 percent in order to have $50,000 in six years?

5.3 Kelly Martin has $10,000 that she can deposit into a savings account for five years. Bank A compounds interest annually, Bank B twice a year, and Bank C quarterly. Each bank has a stated interest rate of 4 percent. What account balance would Kelly have at the end of the fifth year if she left all the interest paid on the deposit in each bank?

5.4 You have an opportunity to invest $2,500 today and receive $3,000 in three years. What would be the return on your investment if you accepted this opportunity?

5.5 Emily Smith deposits $1,200 in her bank today.

a. If the bank pays 4 percent interest per year without compounding, how much simple interest will she have earned and how much money will she have at the end of five years?

b. How much money will she have in five years if the bank pays compound interest with annual compounding?

c. How much of the earnings in part b, will be interest on interest?

Solutions to Self-Study Problems

5.1 Present value of Amit's investment = PV = $10,000
Interest rate = i = 9%
Number of years = n = 5

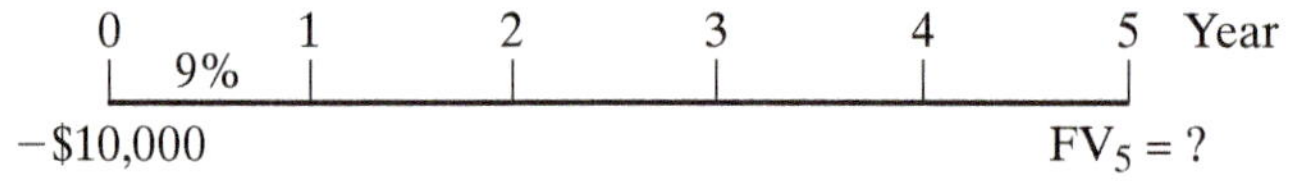

$$FV_n = PV \times (1 + i)^n$$
$$FV_5 = \$10{,}000 \times (1 + 0.09)^5$$
$$= \$15{,}386.24$$

5.2 Amount Megan will need in six years = FV_6 = \$50,000
Number of years = $n = 6$
Interest rate = $i = 7.25\%$
Amount that has to be invested now = PV = ?

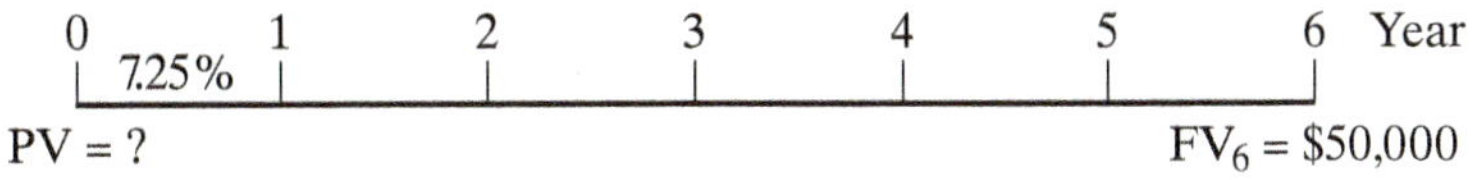

$$PV = \frac{FV_n}{(1 + i)^n}$$
$$= \frac{\$50{,}000}{(1 + 0.0725)^6}$$
$$= \$32{,}853.84$$

5.3 Present value of Kelly's deposit = PV = \$10,000
Number of years = $n = 5$
Interest rate = $i = 4\%$
Compound period (m):

A = 1

B = 2

C = 4

Amount at the end of five years = FV_5 = ?

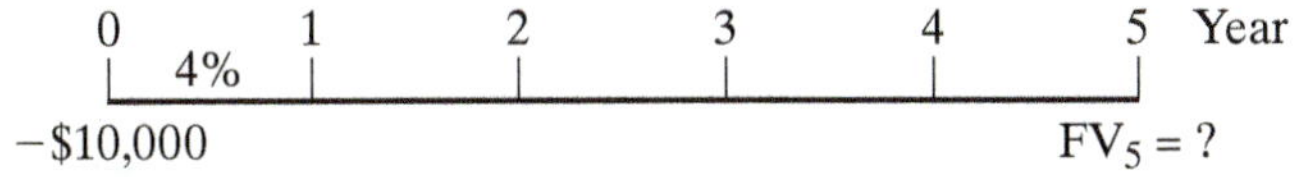

Bank A: $FV_n = PV \times (1 + i/m)^{m \times n}$
$$FV_5 = \$10{,}000 \times (1 + 0.04/1)^{1\times5}$$
$$= \$12{,}166.53$$

Bank B: $FV_5 = \$10{,}000 \times (1 + 0.04/2)^{2\times5}$
$$= \$12{,}189.94$$

Bank C: $FV_5 = \$10{,}000 \times (1 + 0.04/4)^{4\times5}$
$$= \$12{,}201.90$$

5.4 Your investment today = PV = \$2,500
Amount to be received = FV_3 = \$3,000
Time of investment = $n = 3$
Return on the investment = i = ?

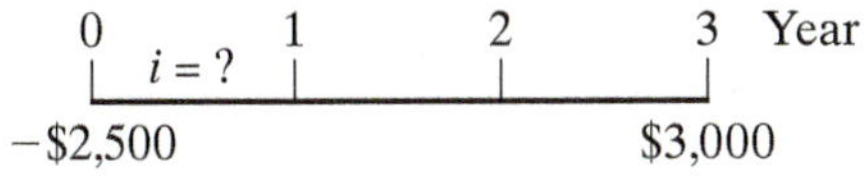

$$FV_n = PV \times (1 + i)^n$$
$$\$3{,}000 = \$2{,}500 \times (1 + i)^3$$
$$\frac{\$3{,}000}{\$2{,}500} = (1 + i)^3$$
$$i = \left(\frac{\$3{,}000}{\$2{,}500}\right)^{1/3} - 1$$
$$i = 0.0627, \text{ or } 6.27\%$$

5.5 Emily's deposit today = PV = \$1,200

a. Interest rate = $i = 4\%$
Number of years = $n = 5$
Amount to be received = FV_5 = ?

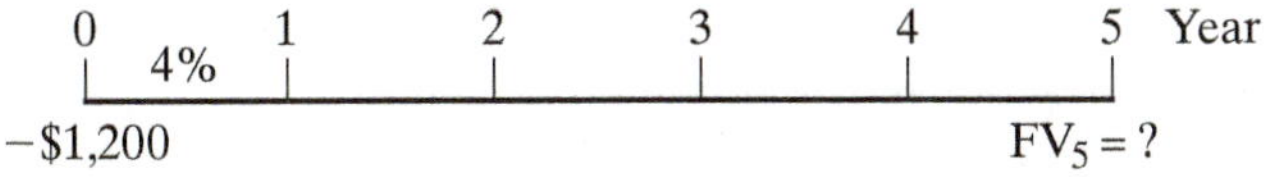

Future value with only simple interest
Simple interest per year = $\$1{,}200 \times 0.04 = \$48$
Simple interest for 5 years = $\$48 \times 5$ years = $\$240$
$FV_5 = \$1{,}200 + \$240 = \$1{,}440$

b. Future value with compound interest and annual compounding
$FV_5 = \$1{,}200 \times (1 + 0.04)^5$
$= \$1{,}459.98$

c. Simple interest = $240
Interest on interest = $\$1{,}459.98 - \$1{,}200 - \$240 = \$19.98$

WileyPLUS

Questions and Problems, Solution Walkthrough Videos, Learning by Doing Tutorials, and additional study tools and resources are available in WileyPLUS.

Discussion Questions

5.1 Explain the phrase "a dollar today is worth more than a dollar tomorrow."

5.2 Explain the importance of a time line.

5.3 What are the two factors to be considered in time value of money?

5.4 Explain the difference between future value and present value.

5.5 Explain the difference between compounding and discounting.

5.6 Explain how compound interest differs from simple interest.

5.7 If you were given a choice between investing in a savings account that paid quarterly interest and one that paid monthly interest, which one should you choose if they both offered the same stated interest rate and why?

5.8 Compound growth is exponential over time. Explain.

5.9 What is the Rule of 72?

5.10 You are planning to take a spring break trip to Cancun your senior year. The trip is exactly two years away, but you want to be prepared and have enough money when the time comes. Explain how you would determine the amount of money you will have to save in order to pay for the trip.

Questions and Problems

Excel *Excel templates and resources available in* **WileyPLUS**

Basic

5.1 **Future value:** Chuck Tomkovick is planning to invest $25,000 today in a mutual fund that will provide a return of 8 percent each year. What will be the value of the investment in 10 years?

5.2 **Future value:** Ted Rogers is investing $7,500 in a bank CD that pays a 6 percent annual interest. How much will the CD be worth at the end of five years?

5.3 **Future value:** Your aunt is planning to invest in a bank CD that will pay 7.5 percent interest semiannually. If she has $5,000 to invest, how much will she have at the end of four years?

5.4 **Future value:** Kate Eden received a graduation present of $2,000 that she is planning on investing in a mutual fund that earns 8.5 percent each year. How much money will she have in three years?

5.5 **Future value:** Your bank pays 5 percent annual interest compounded semiannually on your savings account. You don't expect to add to the current balance of $2,700 over the next four years. How much money can you expect to have at the end of this period?

5.6 **Future value:** Your birthday is next week and instead of other presents, your parents promised to give you $1,000 in cash. Since you have a part-time job and, thus, don't need the cash immediately, you decide to invest the money in a bank CD that pays 5.2 percent, compounded quarterly, for the next two years. How much money can you expect to earn in this period of time?

5.7 **Multiple compounding periods:** Find the future value of a five-year $100,000 investment that pays 8.75 percent and that has the following compounding periods:

a. Quarterly.
b. Monthly.
c. Daily.
d. Continuous.

5.8 **Growth rates:** Joe Mauer, a catcher for the Minnesota Twins, is expected to hit 15 home runs in 2018. If his home-run-hitting ability is expected to grow by 12 percent every year for the following five years, how many home runs is he expected to hit in 2023?

5.9 Present value: Roy Gross is considering an investment that pays 7.6 percent, compounded annually. How much will he have to invest today so that the investment will be worth $25,000 in six years?

5.10 Present value: Maria Addai has been offered a future payment of $750 two years from now. If she can earn an annual rate of 6.5 percent, compounded daily, on her investment, what should she pay for this investment today?

5.11 Present value: Your brother has asked you for a loan and has promised to pay you $7,750 at the end of three years. If you normally invest to earn 6 percent per year, how much will you be willing to lend to your brother if you view this purely as a financial transaction (i.e., you don't give your brother a special deal)?

5.12 Present value: Tracy Chapman is saving to buy a house in five years. She plans to put 20 percent down at that time, and she believes that she will need $35,000 for the down payment. If Tracy can invest in a fund that pays 9.25 percent annual interest, compounded quarterly, how much will she have to invest today to have enough money for the down payment?

5.13 Present value: You want to buy some bonds that will have a value of $1,000 at the end of seven years. The bonds pay 4.5 percent interest annually. How much should you pay for them today?

5.14 Present value: Elizabeth Sweeney wants to accumulate $12,000 by the end of 12 years. If the annual interest rate is 7 percent and interest compounds semiannually, how much will she have to invest today to achieve her goal?

5.15 Interest rate: You are in desperate need of cash and turn to your uncle, who has offered to lend you some money. You decide to borrow $1,300 and agree to pay back $1,500 in two years. Alternatively, you could borrow from your bank that is charging 6.5 percent interest annually. Should you borrow from your uncle or the bank?

5.16 Number of periods: You invest $150 in a mutual fund today that pays 9 percent interest annually. How long will it take to double your money?

Intermediate

5.17 Future value: Your finance textbook sold 53,250 copies in its first year. The publishing company expects the sales to grow at a rate of 20 percent each year for the next three years and by 10 percent in the fourth year. Calculate the total number of copies that the publisher expects to sell in Years 3 and 4. Draw a time line to show the sales level for each of the next four years.

5.18 Future value: CelebNav, Inc., had sales last year of $700,000, and the analysts are predicting strong future performance for the start-up, with sales growing 20 percent a year for the next three years. After that, the sales should grow 11 percent per year for two years, at which time the owners are planning to sell the company. What are the projected sales for the last year before the sale?

5.19 Future value: You decide to take advantage of the current online dating craze and start your own Web site. You know that you have 450 people who will sign up immediately and, through a careful marketing research and analysis, determine that membership can grow by 27 percent in the first two years, 22 percent in Year 3, and 18 percent in Year 4. How many members do you expect to have at the end of four years?

5.20 Multiple compounding periods: Find the future value of an investment of $2,500 made today for the following rates and periods:

a. 6.25 percent compounded semiannually for 12 years.

b. 7.63 percent compounded quarterly for 6 years.

c. 8.9 percent compounded monthly for 10 years.

d. 10 percent compounded daily for 3 years.

e. 8 percent compounded continuously for 2 years.

5.21 Multiple compounding periods: Find the present value of $3,500 under each of the following rates and periods:

a. 8.9 percent compounded monthly for five years.

b. 6.6 percent compounded quarterly for eight years.

c. 4.3 percent compounded daily for four years.

d. 5.7 percent compounded continuously for three years.

5.22 Multiple compounding periods: Samantha plans to invest some money so that she has $5,500 at the end of three years. Determine how much should she invest today given the following choices:

a. 4.2 percent compounded daily.

b. 4.9 percent compounded monthly.

c. 5.2 percent compounded quarterly.

d. 5.4 percent compounded annually.

5.23 Time to grow: Zephyr Sales Company has sales of $1.125 million. If the company's management expects sales to grow 6.5 percent annually, how long will it be before sales double? Use a financial calculator to solve this problem.

5.24 Time to grow: You are going to deposit $850 in a bank CD today, and you will withdraw the money only once the balance is $1,000. If the bank pays 5 percent interest, how long will it take for the balance to reach $1,000?

5.25 Time to grow: Neon Lights Company is a private company with sales of $1.3 million a year. Management wants to take the company public but has to wait until the sales reach $2 million. If sales are expected to grow 12 percent annually, when is the earliest that Neon Lights will go public?

5.26 Time to grow: You have just inherited $550,000. You plan to save this money and continue to live off the money that you are earning in your current job. If you can invest the money in a bond that pays 4.6 percent interest annually, how long will it be before your inheritance is worth $1 million?

5.27 Growth rates: Xenix Corp had sales of $353,866 in 2017. If management expects its sales to be $476,450 in three years, what is the rate at which the company's sales are expected to grow?

5.28 Growth rate: Infosys Technologies, Inc., an Indian technology company, reported net income of $419 million this year. Analysts expect the company's earnings to be $1.468 billion in five years. What is the expected growth rate in the company's earnings?

5.29 Present value: Caroline Weslin needs to decide whether to accept a bonus of $1,820 today or wait two years and receive $2,100 then. She can invest at 6 percent. What should she do?

5.30 Present value: Congress and the President have decided to increase the federal tax rate in an effort to reduce the budget deficit. Suppose that Caroline Weslin, from problem 5.29, will pay 35 percent of her bonus to the federal government for taxes if she accepts the bonus today and 40 percent if she receives her bonus in two years. Will the increase in tax rates affect her decision?

Advanced

5.31 You have $2,500 that you want to invest in your classmate's start-up business. You believe the business idea to be great and expect to get $3,700 back at the end of three years. If all goes according to plan, what will be the return on your investment?

5.32 Patrick Seeley has $2,400 to invest. His brother approached him with an investment opportunity that could double his money in four years. What interest rate would the investment have to yield in order for Patrick's brother to deliver on his promise?

5.33 You have $12,000 in cash. You can deposit it today in a mutual fund earning 8.2 percent semiannually, or you can wait, enjoy some of it, and invest $11,000 in your brother's business in two years. Your brother is promising you a return of at least 10 percent on your investment. Whichever alternative you choose, you will need to cash in at the end of 10 years. Assume your brother is trustworthy and both investments carry the same risk. Which one would yield the larger amount in 10 years?

5.34 When you were born, your parents set up a bank account in your name with an initial investment of $5,000. You are turning 21 in a few days and will have access to all your funds. The account was earning 7.3 percent for the first seven years, but then the rates went down to 5.5 percent for six years. Your account then earned 8.2 percent three years in a row. Unfortunately, the next two years you earned only 4.6 percent. Finally, as the economy recovered, the return jumped to 7.6 percent for the last three years.

a. How much money was in your account before the rates went down drastically at the end of Year 16?

b. How much money is in your account now, at the end of Year 21?

c. What would be the balance now if your parents made another deposit of $1,200 at the end of Year 7?

5.35 Jared Goff, the number 1 draft pick of the NFL Los Angeles Rams in 2016, and his agent are evaluating three contract options. Each option offers a signing bonus and a series of payments over the life of the contract. Goff uses a 10.25 percent rate of return to evaluate the contracts. Given the cash flows for each option, which one should he choose?

Year	Cash Flow Type	Option A	Option B	Option C
0	Signing Bonus	$3,100,000	$4,000,000	$4,250,000
1	Annual Salary	$ 650,000	$ 825,000	$ 550,000
2	Annual Salary	$ 715,000	$ 850,000	$ 625,000
3	Annual Salary	$ 822,250	$ 925,000	$ 800,000
4	Annual Salary	$ 975,000	$1,250,000	$ 900,000
5	Annual Salary	$1,100,000		$1,000,000
6	Annual Salary	$1,250,000		

5.36 Surmec, Inc., reported sales of $2.1 million last year. The company's primary business is the manufacture of nuts and bolts. Since this is a mature industry, analysts are confident that sales will grow at a steady rate of 7 percent per year. The company's net income equals 23 percent of sales. Management would like to buy a new fleet of trucks but can only do so once the net income reaches $620,000 a year. At the end of what year will Surmec be able to buy the trucks? What will sales and net income be in that year?

5.37 You will be graduating in two years and are thinking about your future. You know that you will want to buy a house five years after you graduate and that you will want to put down $60,000. As of right now, you have $8,000 in your savings account. You are also fairly certain that once you graduate, you can work in the family business and earn $32,000 a year, with a 5 percent raise every year. You plan to live with your parents for the first two years after graduation, which will enable you to minimize your expenses and put away $10,000 each year. The next three years, you will have to live on your own as your younger sister will be graduating from college and has already announced her plan to move back into the family house. Thus, you will be able to save only 13 percent of your annual salary. Assume that you will be able to earn 7.2 percent on the savings from your salary. At what interest rate will you need to invest the current savings account balance in order to achieve your goal? *Hint:* Draw a time line that shows all the cash flows for years 0 through 7. Remember, you want to buy a house seven years from now and your first salary will be in Year 3.

Sample Test Problems

5.1 Holding all else constant, what will happen to the present value of a future amount if you increase the discount rate? What if you increase the number of years?

5.2 Juliette Bronson anticipates needing $500,000 to start a business. If she can earn 4.5 percent compounded annually on her investments, how much money would Juliette have to invest today to have $500,000 in three years?

5.3 Christopher Thompkins must decide how to invest $10,000 that he just inherited. What would be the future value of his investment after five years under each of the following three investment opportunities?

a. 6.28 percent compounded quarterly.

b. 6.20 percent compounded monthly.

c. 6.12 percent compounded continuously.

5.4 Tina DeLeon deposited $2,500 today in an account paying 6 percent interest annually. What would be the simple interest earned on this investment in five years? With annual compounding, how much interest on interest would Tina earn in five years?

5.5 The state of Texas had 42,725 active patient care physicians in 2013 and by 2017 this number had grown to 47,663. What was the compound annual growth rate (CAGR) in the number of active care physicians during this period?

CHAPTER 6

Discounted Cash Flows and Valuation

ODD ANDERSEN/AFP/Getty Images

Elon Musk: Tesla CEO

LEARNING OBJECTIVES

1. Explain why cash flows occurring at different times must be adjusted to reflect their value as of a common date before they can be compared, and compute the present value and the future value for multiple cash flows.
2. Explain the difference between an ordinary annuity and an annuity due, and calculate the present value and the future value of an ordinary annuity and an annuity due.
3. Explain what a perpetuity is and where we see them in business, and calculate the value of a perpetuity.
4. Discuss growing annuities and perpetuities, as well as their application in business, and calculate their values.
5. Discuss why the effective annual interest rate (EAR) is the appropriate way to annualize interest rates, and calculate the EAR.

On November 17, 2016, the stockholders of Tesla voted to acquire SolarCity Corporation, a producer of solar power systems, for $2.6 billion. Four days later the acquisition was complete. The SolarCity acquisition was part of a plan by Elon Musk, Tesla's founder and CEO, to make Tesla into an integrated energy generation and storage company, in addition to a manufacturer of ground transportation vehicles such as its iconic electric cars.

The SolarCity acquisition did not happen without controversy. The June 2016 announcement that Tesla was considering purchasing SolarCity was met with suspicion. Mr. Musk was a major SolarCity stockholder and chairman of its board of directors. Furthermore, the CEO of SolarCity was Mr. Musk's first cousin and SolarCity had never earned a profit from its solar power systems business. A prominent firm that advises stockholders on how to vote on proposals like this characterized the acquisition as a "thinly veiled bailout" of SolarCity. Tesla's closing stock price declined from $219.61 to $193.15 in the three days following the announcement, a 12 percent drop.

On the other side, supporters of the deal described it as a key step in transforming Tesla into the energy and transportation company that Mr. Musk envisioned. Tesla management maintained that the acquisition price made sense because they would be able to achieve annual cost savings of $150 million in the first full year after the acquisition. Also, because Tesla would purchase SolarCity's shares with its own stock (0.11 share of Tesla stock would be exchanged for each share of SolarCity stock) rather than cash, the transaction would add $500 million in cash to Tesla's balance sheet over the following three years. This last point was especially important because Tesla was a rapidly growing company that needed cash to fund its growth.

In the excitement of an acquisition proposal such as this, it is important not to lose sight of the central question: What are the shares of the target firm really worth? Investors invest in an asset—whether it is a financial asset like a company's shares or a real asset like a capital project—because they expect the asset to be worth more than it costs. That's how investors create value for themselves. The value of a financial or real asset is the sum of the discounted cash flows that it is expected to produce in the future. Thus, the crucial task for both Tesla and SolarCity's stockholders was to estimate how the acquisition would change the value of the cash flows that they might expect to receive from ownership of their respective shares. This chapter, which discusses the discounting of future cash flows, presents fundamental tools that you must understand in order to answer questions such as what the SolarCity shares were worth and whether the SolarCity acquisition was a good deal for Tesla stockholders, SolarCity stockholders, or both

Chapter Preview

In Chapter 5 we introduced the concept of the time value of money: Dollars today are more valuable than dollars to be received in the future. Starting with that concept, we developed the basics of simple interest, compound interest, and future value calculations. We then went on to discuss present value calculations and discounted cash flow analysis. This was all done in the context of a single cash flow.

In this chapter, we consider the value of multiple cash flows. Most business decisions, after all, involve a series of cash flows over time. For example, if Hatteras Hammocks, a North Carolina–based firm that manufactures hammocks, swings, and rockers, wants to consider building a new factory, the decision will require an analysis of the project's expected cash flows over a number of periods. Initially, there will be large cash outlays to build and get the new factory operational. Thereafter, the project should produce cash inflows for many years. Because the cash flows occur over time, the analysis must consider the time value of money, discounting each of the cash flows by using the present value formula we discussed in Chapter 5.

We begin the chapter by describing calculations of future and present values for multiple cash flows. We then examine some situations in which future cash flows are level over time: These involve annuities, in which the cash flow stream goes on for a finite period, and perpetuities, in which the stream goes on forever. Next, we examine annuities and perpetuities in which the cash flows grow at a constant rate over time. These cash flows resemble common cash flow patterns encountered in business. Finally, we describe the effective annual interest rate and compare it with the annual percentage rate (APR), which is a rate that is used to describe the interest rate in consumer loans.

6.1 Multiple Cash Flows

LEARNING OBJECTIVE

1. Explain why cash flows occurring at different times must be adjusted to reflect their value as of a common date before they can be compared, and compute the present value and the future value for multiple cash flows.

We begin our discussion of the value of multiple cash flows by calculating the future value and then the present value of multiple cash flows. These calculations, as you will see, are nothing more than applications of the techniques you learned in Chapter 5.

Future Value of Multiple Cash Flows

In Chapter 5, we worked through several examples that involved the future value of a lump sum of money invested in a savings account that paid 10 percent interest per year. But suppose

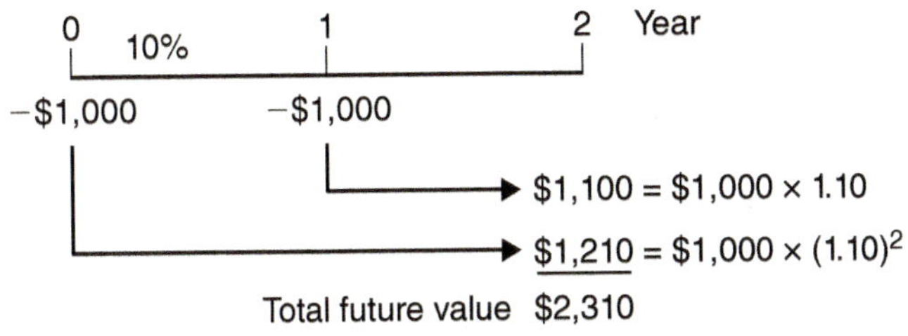

EXHIBIT 6.1 **Future Value of Two Cash Flows**

This exhibit shows a time line for two cash flows invested in a savings account that pays 10 percent interest annually. The total amount in the savings account after two years is $2,310, which is the sum of the future values of the two cash flows.

you are investing more than one lump sum. Let's say you put $1,000 in your bank savings account today and another $1,000 a year from now. If the bank continues to pay 10 percent interest per year, how much money will you have at the end of two years?

To solve this future value problem, we can use Equation 5.1: $FV_n = PV \times (1 + i)^n$. First, however, we construct a time line so that we can see the magnitude and timing of the cash flows. As **Exhibit 6.1** shows, there are two cash flows into the savings account. The first cash flow is invested for two years and compounds to a future value as follows:

$$\begin{aligned} FV_2 &= PV \times (1 + i)^2 \\ &= \$1{,}000 \times (1 + 0.10)^2 \\ &= \$1{,}000 \times (1.10)^2 \\ &= \$1{,}000 \times 1.21 \\ &= \$1{,}210 \end{aligned}$$

The second cash flow earns simple interest for a single period only and grows to:

$$\begin{aligned} FV_1 &= PV \times (1 + i) \\ &= \$1{,}000 \times (1 + 0.10) \\ &= \$1{,}000 \times 1.10 \\ &= \$1{,}100 \end{aligned}$$

As Exhibit 6.1 shows, the total amount of money in the savings account after two years is the sum of these two amounts, which is $2,310 ($1,100 + $1,210 = $2,310).

Now suppose that you expand your investment horizon to three years and invest $1,000 today, $1,000 a year from now, and $1,000 at the end of two years. How much money will you have at the end of three years? First, we draw a time line to be sure that we have correctly identified the magnitude and timing of each cash flow. This is shown in **Exhibit 6.2**. Then

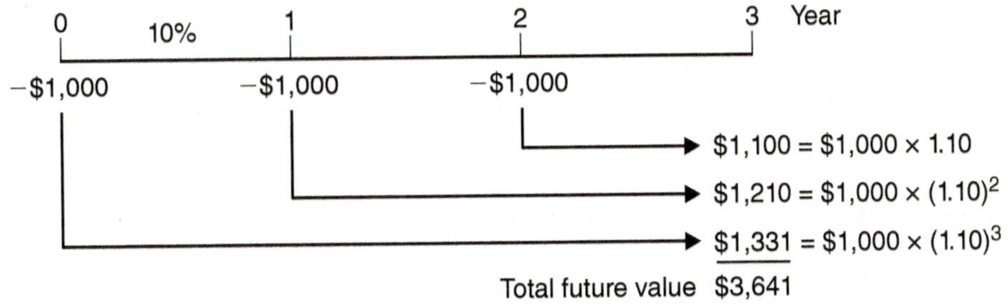

EXHIBIT 6.2 **Future Value of Three Cash Flows**

The exhibit shows a time line for an investment program with a three-year horizon. The value of the investment at the end of three years is $3,641, the sum of the future values of the three separate cash flows.

we compute the future value of each of the individual cash flows using Equation 5.1. Finally, we add up the future values. The total future value is \$3,641. The calculations are as follows:

$$FV_1 = PV \times (1 + i) = \$1{,}000 \times (1 + 0.10) = \$1{,}000 \times 1.100 = \$1{,}100$$
$$FV_2 = PV \times (1 + i)^2 = \$1{,}000 \times (1 + 0.10)^2 = \$1{,}000 \times 1.210 = \$1{,}210$$
$$FV_3 = PV \times (1 + i)^3 = \$1{,}000 \times (1 + 0.10)^3 = \$1{,}000 \times 1.331 = \underline{\$1{,}331}$$
$$\text{Total future value} \quad \$3{,}641$$

To summarize, solving future value problems with multiple cash flows involves a simple process. First, draw a time line to make sure that each cash flow is placed in the correct time period. Second, calculate the future value of each cash flow for its time period. Third, add up the future values.

Let's use this process to solve a practical problem. Suppose you want to buy a condominium in three years and estimate that you will need \$20,000 for a down payment. If the interest rate you can earn at the bank is 8 percent and you can save \$3,000 now, \$4,000 at the end of the first year, and \$5,000 at the end of the second year, how much money will you have to obtain from other sources at the end of the third year to have a \$20,000 down payment?

The time line for the future value calculation in this problem looks like this:

To solve the problem, we need to calculate the future value for each of the cash flows, add up these values, and then calculate the difference between this amount and the \$20,000 needed for the down payment. Using Equation 5.1, we find that the future values of the cash flows at the end of the third year are:

$$FV_1 = PV \times (1 + i) = \$5{,}000 \times 1.08 = \$5{,}000 \times 1.0800 = \$\ 5{,}400.00$$
$$FV_2 = PV \times (1 + i)^2 = \$4{,}000 \times (1.08)^2 = \$4{,}000 \times 1.1664 = \$\ 4{,}665.60$$
$$FV_3 = PV \times (1 + i)^3 = \$3{,}000 \times (1.08)^3 = \$3{,}000 \times 1.2597 = \underline{\$\ 3{,}779.14}$$
$$\text{Total future value} \quad \$13{,}844.74$$

At the end of the third year, you will have \$13,844.74, so you will need an additional \$6,155.26 (\$20,000 − \$13,844.74 = \$6,155.26) at that time to make the down payment.

Learning by Doing Application 6.1 illustrates another future value calculation with multiple cash flows.

LEARNING BY DOING

WileyPLUS

Need more help? Visit your WileyPLUS course.

APPLICATION 6.1 | Bidding on a Contract to Rebuild a Bridge

Problem The firm you work for is considering bidding on a contract to rebuild an old bridge that has reached the end of its useful life. The two-year contract will pay the firm \$1,100,000 at the end of the second year. The firm's estimator believes that the project will require an initial expenditure of \$700,000 for equipment. The expenses for Years 1 and 2 are estimated at \$150,000 per year. Because the cash inflow of \$1,100,000 at the end of the contract exceeds the total cash outflows of \$1,000,000 (\$700,000 + \$150,000 + \$150,000 = \$1,000,000), the estimator believes that the firm should accept the job. Drawing on your knowledge of finance from college, you point out that the estimator's decision process ignores the time value of money. Not fully understanding what you mean, the estimator asks you how the time value of money should be incorporated into the decision process. Assume that the appropriate interest rate is 8 percent.

Approach First, construct the time line for the costs in this problem, as shown here:

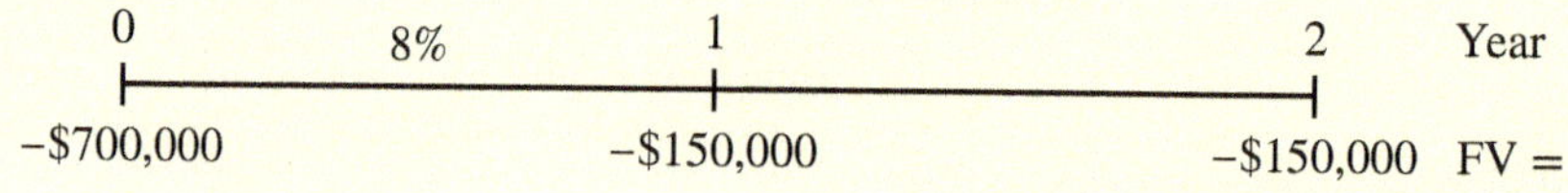

Second, use Equation 5.1 to convert each of the cash outflows into Year 2 dollars. This will make all the cash flows comparable. Finally, compare the sum of the cash outflows, stated in Year 2 dollars, to the \$1,100,000 that you would receive under the contract in Year 2.

Solution

$$FV_2 = PV \times (1+i)^2 = -\$700{,}000 \times (1.08)^2 = -\$700{,}000 \times 1.1664 = -\$\ \ 816{,}480$$
$$FV_1 = PV \times (1+i) = -\$150{,}000 \times 1.08 = -\$150{,}000 \times 1.0800 = -\$\ \ 162{,}000$$
$$FV_0 = PV \times (1+i)^0 = -\$150{,}000 \times (1.08)^0 = -\$150{,}000 \times 1.0000 = \underline{-\$\ \ 150{,}000}$$
$$\text{Total net future value} \quad -\$1{,}128{,}480$$

Once the future value calculations have been made, the decision is self-evident. With all the dollars stated as Year 2 dollars, the cash inflow (benefits) is $1,100,000 and the cash outflow (costs) is $1,128,480. Thus, the costs exceed the benefits, and the firm's management should reject the contract. If management accepts the contract, the value of the firm will decline by $28,480 ($1,100,000 – $1,128,480 = –$28,480).

Calculator Tip: Calculating the Future Value of Multiple Cash Flows

To calculate the future value of multiple cash flows with a financial calculator, we can use exactly the same process we used in Chapter 5. We simply calculate the future value of each of the individual cash flows, write down each computed future value, and add them up.

Alternatively, we can generally use a shortcut. More than likely, your financial calculator has a memory where you can store numbers; refer to your calculator's instruction manual for the keys to use. For the preceding example, you would use your financial calculator's memory (M) as follows: Calculate the future value of the first number, then store the value in the memory (M1); compute the second value, and store it in the memory (M2); compute the third value, and store it in the memory (M3). Finally, retrieve the three numbers from the memory and add them up (M1 + M2 + M3). The advantage of using the calculator's memory is that you eliminate two potential sources of error: (1) writing down a number incorrectly and (2) making a mistake when adding up the numbers.

Present Value of Multiple Cash Flows

In business situations, we often need to compute the present value of a series of future cash flows. We do this, for example, to determine the market price of a bond, to decide whether to purchase a new machine, or to determine the value of a business. Solving present value problems involving multiple cash flows is similar to solving future value problems involving multiple cash flows. First, we prepare a time line so that we can see the magnitude and timing of the cash flows. Second, we calculate the present value of each individual cash flow using Equation 5.4: $PV = FV_n/(1+i)^n$. Finally, we add up the present values. The sum of the present values of a stream of future cash flows is their current market price, or value. There is nothing new here!

Weblink

You can find plenty of future value and present value problems to work on at StudyFinance.com. Go to: http://www.studyfinance.com/lectures/timevalue/.

Using the Present Value Equation

Let's work through some examples to see how we can use Equation 5.4 to find the present value of multiple cash flows. Suppose that your best friend needs cash and offers to pay you $1,000 at the end of each of the next three years if you will give him $3,000 cash today. You realize, of course, that because of the time value of money, the cash flows he has promised to pay are worth less than $3,000. If the interest rate on similar loans is 7 percent, how much should you pay for the cash flows your friend is offering?

To solve the problem, we first construct a time line, as shown in Exhibit 6.3. Then, using Equation 5.4, we calculate the present value for each of the three cash flows, as follows:

$$PV = FV_1 \times 1/(1+i) = FV_1 \times 1/1.07 = \$1{,}000 \times 0.9346 = \$\ \ 934.58$$
$$PV = FV_2 \times 1/(1+i)^2 = FV_2 \times 1/(1.07)^2 = \$1{,}000 \times 0.8734 = \$\ \ 873.44$$
$$PV = FV_3 \times 1/(1+i)^3 = FV_3 \times 1/(1.07)^3 = \$1{,}000 \times 0.8163 = \underline{\$\ \ 816.30}$$
$$\text{Total present value} \quad \$2{,}624.32$$

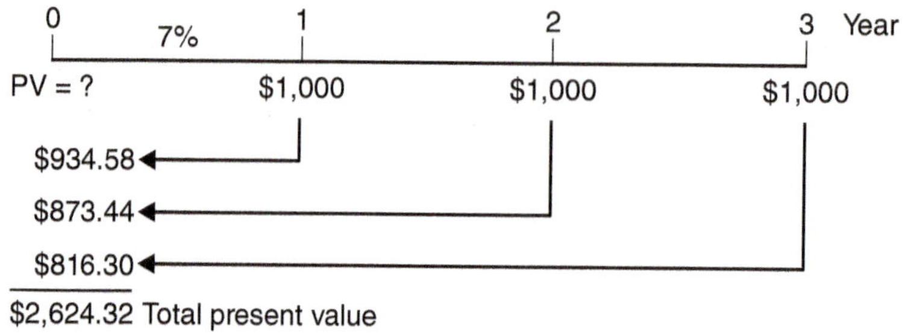

EXHIBIT 6.3 Present Value of Three Cash Flows

This exhibit shows the time line for a three-year loan with a payment of \$1,000 at the end of each year and an annual interest rate of 7 percent. To calculate the value of the loan today, we compute the present value of each of the three cash flows and then add them up. The present value of the loan is \$2,624.32.

If you view this transaction from a purely business perspective, you should not give your friend more than \$2,624.32, which is the sum of the individual discounted cash flows.

Now let's consider another example. Suppose you have the opportunity to buy a small business while you are in school. The business involves selling sandwiches, soft drinks, and snack foods to students from a truck that you drive around campus. The annual cash flows from the business have been predictable. You believe you can expand the business, and you estimate that cash flows will be as follows: \$2,000 in the first year, \$3,000 in the second and third years, and \$4,000 in the fourth year. At the end of the fourth year, the business will be closed down because the truck and other equipment will need to be replaced. The total of the estimated cash flows is \$12,000. You did some research and found that a 10 percent discount rate would be appropriate. How much should you pay for the business?

To value the business, we compute the present value of the expected cash flows, discounted at 10 percent. The time line for the investment is:

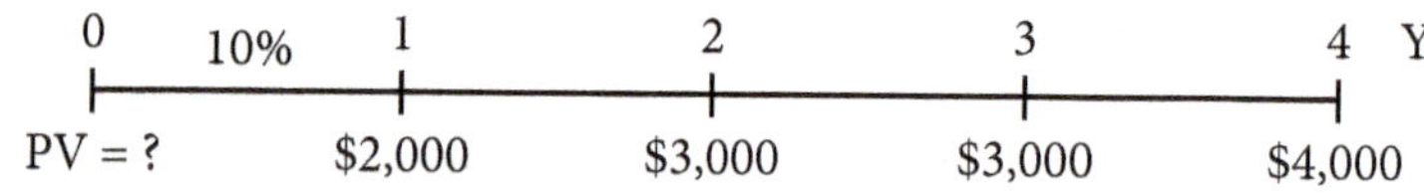

We compute the present value of each cash flow and then add them up:

$$
\begin{aligned}
PV &= FV_1 \times 1/(1+i) = \$2{,}000 \times 1/1.10 = \$2{,}000 \times 0.9091 = \$1{,}818.18 \\
PV &= FV_2 \times 1/(1+i)^2 = \$3{,}000 \times 1/(1.10)^2 = \$3{,}000 \times 0.8264 = \$2{,}479.34 \\
PV &= FV_3 \times 1/(1+i)^3 = \$3{,}000 \times 1/(1.10)^3 = \$3{,}000 \times 0.7513 = \$2{,}253.94 \\
PV &= FV_4 \times 1/(1+i)^4 = \$4{,}000 \times 1/(1.10)^4 = \$4{,}000 \times 0.6830 = \underline{\$2{,}732.05} \\
& \text{Total present value} \quad \$9{,}283.51
\end{aligned}
$$

This tells us that the present value of the expected cash flows is \$9,283.51. If you pay \$9,283.51 for the business, you will earn a return of exactly 10 percent. Of course, you should buy the business for the lowest price possible, but you should never pay more than the \$9,283.51 value today of the expected cash flows. If you do, you will be paying more than the investment is worth.

Learning by Doing Application 6.2, **Learning by Doing Application 6.3**, and **Decision Making Example 6.1** illustrate additional present value calculations and their application in decision-making.

Calculator Tip: Calculating the Present Value of Multiple Cash Flows

To calculate the present value of future cash flows with a financial calculator, we use exactly the same process we used in finding the future value, except that we solve for the present value instead of the future value. We can compute the present values of the individual cash flows, save them in the calculator's memory, and then add them up to obtain the total present value.

You should note that from this point forward we will use a different notation. Up to this point, we have used the notation FV_n to represent a cash flow in period n. We have done this to stress that, for $n > 0$, we were referring to a future value. From this point on, we will use the notation CF_n, instead of FV_n, because the CF_n notation is more commonly used by financial analysts. When you work through Learning by Doing Application 6.2, you will see the new notation.

APPLICATION 6.2 | The Value of a Gift to the University

LEARNING BY DOING

WileyPLUS

Need more help? Visit your WileyPLUS course.

Problem Suppose that in your senior year, as part of the senior class gift campaign, you pledge to donate to your university $1,000 per year for four years and $3,000 for the fifth year, for a total of $7,000. Immediately after making the third payment, you decide to make a payment with a value equal to the present value of the final two payments of your pledge because your financial situation has improved. How much should you pay to the university if the interest rate is 6 percent?

Approach The key to understanding this problem is recognizing the need for a present value calculation. Because your pledge to the university is for future cash payments, the value of the amount you will pay for the remaining two years is worth less than the $4,000 ($1,000 + $3,000 = $4,000) you promised. If the appropriate discount rate is 6 percent, the time line for the cash payments for the remaining two years of the pledge is as follows:

0	6%	1	2 Year
PV = ?		−$1,000	−$3,000

We now need only calculate the present value of the last two payments.

Solution The present value calculation for the last two payments is:

$$PV = CF_1 \times 1/(1+i) = -\$1{,}000 \times 1/1.06 = -\$\ 943.40$$
$$PV = CF_2 \times 1/(1+i)^2 = -\$3{,}000 \times 1/(1.06)^2 = -\$2{,}669.99$$
$$\text{Total present value} \quad -\$3{,}613.39$$

A payment of $3,613.39 to the university today (the end of Year 3) is a fair payment because at a 6 percent interest rate, it has precisely the same value as paying the university $1,000 at the end of Year 4 and $3,000 at the end of Year 5. In other words, if you pay the university $3,613.39 and the university invests that amount at 6 percent in a bank, it will be able to withdraw $1,000 in one year and $3,000 in two years.

APPLICATION 6.3 | Buying a Used Car—Help!

LEARNING BY DOING

Problem For a student—or anyone else—buying a used car can be a harrowing experience. Once you find the car you want, the next difficult decision is choosing how to pay for it—cash or a loan. Suppose the cash price you have negotiated for the car is $5,600, but that amount will stretch your budget for the year. The dealer says, "No problem. The car is yours for $4,000 down and payments of $1,000 per year for the next two years. Or you can put $2,000 down and pay $2,000 per year for two years. The choice is yours." Which offer is the best deal if the interest rate you can earn on your money is 8 percent?

Approach In this problem, there are three alternative streams of cash flows. We need to convert all of the cash flows (CF_n) into today's dollars (present value) and select the alternative with the lowest present value (price). The time line for the three alternatives, along with the cash flows for each, is as follows:

0	8%	1	2 Year
Cash price or down payment		CF_1	CF_2

The cash flows at time zero represent the cash price of the car in the case of Alternative A and the down payment in the cases of Alternatives B and C.

	Cash Price or Down Payment	CF_1	CF_2	Total
Alternative A	−$5,600	—	—	−$5,600
Alternative B	−$4,000	−$1,000	−$1,000	−$6,000
Alternative C	−$2,000	−$2,000	−$2,000	−$6,000

Now we can use Equation 5.4 to find the present value of each alternative.

Solution

Alternative A:

$$-\$5{,}600 \times 1/(1.08)^0 = -\$5{,}600.00$$

Alternative B:

$$-\$4{,}000 \times 1/(1.08)^0 = -\$4{,}000.00$$
$$-\$1{,}000 \times 1/1.08 = -\$\ 925.93$$
$$-\$1{,}000 \times 1/(1.08)^2 = -\$\ 857.34$$
$$\text{Total} \quad -\$5{,}783.27$$

Alternative C:

$$-\$2{,}000 \times 1/(1.08)^0 = -\$2{,}000.00$$
$$-\$2{,}000 \times 1/1.08 = -\$1{,}851.85$$
$$-\$2{,}000 \times 1/(1.08)^2 = -\$1{,}714.68$$
$$\text{Total} \quad -\$5{,}566.53$$

Once we have converted the three cash flow streams to present values, the answer is clear. Alternative C has the lowest cost, in present value terms, and is the alternative you should choose.

DECISION MAKING

EXAMPLE 6.1 | The Investment Decision

Situation You are thinking of buying a business, and your investment adviser presents you with two possibilities. Both businesses are priced at $60,000, and you have only $60,000 to invest. She has provided you with the following annual and total cash flows for each business, along with the present value of the cash flows discounted at 10 percent:

	Cash flow ($ thousands)				
Business	**1**	**2**	**3**	**Total**	**PV at 10%**
A	$50	$30	$ 20	$100	$85.27
B	$ 5	$ 5	$100	$110	$83.81

Which business should you acquire?

Decision At first glance, Business B may look to be the best choice because its undiscounted cash flows for the three years total $110,000, versus $100,000 for A. However, to make the decision on the basis of the undiscounted cash flows ignores the time value of money. By discounting the cash flows, we convert them to current dollars, or their present values. The present value of Business A is $85,270 and that of B is $83,810. While both of these investment opportunities are attractive, you should acquire Business A if you only have $60,000 to invest. Business A is expected to produce more valuable cash flows for your investment.

Before You Go On

1. Explain how to calculate the future value of a stream of cash flows.
2. Explain how to calculate the present value of a stream of cash flows.
3. Why is it important to adjust all cash flows to a common date?

6.2 Level Cash Flows: Annuities and Perpetuities

LEARNING OBJECTIVE

2. Explain the difference between an ordinary annuity and an annuity due, and calculate the present value and the future value of an ordinary annuity and an annuity due.

In finance we commonly encounter contracts that call for the payment of equal amounts of cash over several time periods. For example, most business term loans and insurance policies require the holder to make a series of equal payments, usually monthly. Similarly, nearly all consumer loans, such as auto, personal, and home mortgage loans, call for equal monthly payments. Any financial contract that calls for equally spaced and level cash flows over a finite number of periods is called an **annuity**. If the cash flow payments continue forever, the contract is called a **perpetuity**. Most annuities are structured so that cash payments are received at the end of each period. Because this is the most common structure, these annuities are often called **ordinary annuities**.

> **annuity** a series of equally spaced and level cash flows extending over a finite number of periods
>
> **perpetuity** a series of equally spaced and level cash flows that continues forever
>
> **ordinary annuity** an annuity in which payments are made at the end of each period
>
> **present value of an annuity (PVA)** the present value of the cash flows from an annuity, discounted at the appropriate discount rate

Present Value of an Annuity

We frequently need to find the **present value of an annuity (PVA)**. Suppose, for example, that a financial contract pays $2,000 at the end of each year for three years and the appropriate discount rate is 8 percent. The time line for the contract is:

0	8%	1	2	3 Year
PV = ?		$2,000	$2,000	$2,000

What is the most we should pay for this annuity? We have worked problems like this one before. All we need to do is calculate the present value of each individual cash flow (CF_n) and add them up. Using Equation 5.4, we find that the present value of the three-year annuity (PVA_3) at 8 percent interest is:

$$\begin{aligned}
PVA_3 &= \left[CF_1 \times \frac{1}{1+i}\right] + \left[CF_2 \times \frac{1}{(1+i)^2}\right] + \left[CF_3 \times \frac{1}{(1+i)^3}\right] \\
&= \left[\$2{,}000 \times \frac{1}{1.08}\right] + \left[\$2{,}000 \times \frac{1}{(1.08)^2}\right] + \left[\$2{,}000 \times \frac{1}{(1.08)^3}\right] \\
&= \$1{,}851.85 + \$1{,}714.68 + \$1{,}587.66 \\
&= \$5{,}154.19
\end{aligned}$$

This approach to computing the present value of an annuity works as long as the number of cash flows is relatively small. In many situations that involve annuities, however, the number of cash flows is large, and doing the calculations by hand would be tedious. For example, a typical 30-year home mortgage has 360 monthly payments (12 months per year × 30 years = 360 months).

Fortunately, our problem can be simplified because the cash flows (CF) for an annuity are all the same ($CF_1 = CF_2 = \cdots = CF_n = CF$). Thus, the present value of an annuity (PVA_n) with n equal cash flows (CF) at interest rate i is the sum of the individual present value calculations:

$$PVA_n = \left[CF \times \frac{1}{1+i}\right] + \left[CF \times \frac{1}{(1+i)^2}\right] + \cdots + \left[CF \times \frac{1}{(1+i)^n}\right]$$

With some mathematical manipulations that are beyond the scope of this discussion, we can simplify this equation to yield a useful formula for the present value of an annuity:

$$\text{PVA}_n = \frac{\text{CF}}{i} \times \left[1 - \frac{1}{(1+i)^n}\right] \quad (6.1)$$

$$= \text{CF} \times \left[\frac{1 - 1/(1+i)^n}{i}\right]$$

where:
PVA_n = present value of an n period annuity
CF = equally spaced and level cash flow
i = discount rate, or interest rate
n = number of periods (often called the annuity's maturity)

Notice in Equation 6.1 that $1/(1+i)^n$ is a term you have already encountered: It is the present value factor. Thus, we can also write Equation 6.1 as follows:

$$\text{PVA}_n = \text{CF} \times \frac{1 - \text{Present value factor}}{i}$$

where the term on the right is what we call the PV annuity factor:

$$\text{PV annuity factor} = \frac{1 - \text{Present value factor}}{i}$$

It follows that yet another way to state Equation 6.1 is:

$$\text{PVA}_n = \text{CF} \times \text{PV annuity factor}$$

Weblink

Visit New York Life Insurance Company's Web site to learn more about investment products that pay out annuities: http://www.newyorklife.com.

Let's apply Equation 6.1 to the example involving a three-year annuity with a $2,000 annual cash flow. To solve for PVA_n, we first compute the PV annuity factor for three years at 8 percent. The calculation is made in two steps:

1. Calculate the present value factor for three years at 8 percent:

$$\text{Present value factor} = \frac{1}{(1+i)^n} = \frac{1}{(1+0.08)^3} = \frac{1}{(1.08)^3} = \frac{1}{1.2597} = 0.7938$$

2. Use the present value factor to calculate the PV annuity factor:

$$\text{PV annuity factor} = \frac{1 - \text{Present value factor}}{i} = \frac{1 - 0.7938}{0.08} = 2.577$$

We now can calculate PVA_3 by plugging our values into the equation:

$$\text{PVA}_3 = \text{CF} \times \text{PV annuity factor} = \$2{,}000 \times 2.577 = \$5{,}154.00$$

Weblink

Investopedia is a great Web site for learning about a variety of finance topics. For example, you can find a discussion of annuities at http://www.investopedia.com/articles/03/101503.asp.

This is almost the same as the $5,154.19 we calculated by hand earlier. The difference is due to rounding.

Learning by Doing Application 6.4 illustrates another calculation of a PV anuity factor.

Calculator Tip: Finding the Present Value of an Annuity

There are four variables in a present value of an annuity equation (PVA_n, CF, n, and i), and if you know three of them, you can solve for the fourth in a few seconds with a financial calculator. The calculator key that you have not used so far is the PMT (payment) key, which is the key for level cash flows over the life of an annuity.

To illustrate problem solving with a financial calculator, we will revisit the financial contract that paid $2,000 per year for three years, discounted at 8 percent. To find the present value of the contract, we enter 8 percent for the interest rate (i), $2,000 for the payment (PMT), and 3 for the number of periods (N). The key for FV is not relevant for this calculation, so we enter zero into this register to clear it. The key entries and the answer are as follows:

Enter	**3**	**8**		**2,000**	**0**
	N	i	PV	PMT	FV
Answer			**−5,154.19**		

The price of the contract is $5,154.19, which agrees with our other calculations. As discussed in Chapter 5, the negative sign on the financial calculator box indicates that $5,154.19 is a cash outflow.

PV Annuity Factor Tables

Just as financial analysts once used future value and present value factor tables to help with future value and present value calculations, they also used PV annuity factor tables, which contain PV annuity factors for a range of interest rates and annuity lengths. Table A-4 in Appendix A is an example of a PV annuity factor table.

APPLICATION 6.4 | Computing a PV Annuity Factor

LEARNING BY DOING

Problem Compute the PV annuity factor for 30 years at a 10 percent interest rate.

Approach First, we calculate the present value factor at 10 percent for 30 years. Then, using this value, we calculate the PV annuity factor.

Solution

$$\text{Present value factor} = \frac{1}{(1+i)^n}$$
$$= \frac{1}{(1.10)^{30}}$$
$$= \frac{1}{17.4494}$$
$$= 0.0573$$

Using this value, we calculate the PV annuity factor to be:

$$\text{PV annuity factor} = \frac{1 - \text{Present value factor}}{i}$$
$$= \frac{1 - 0.0573}{0.10}$$
$$= 9.427$$

We worked through the tedious calculations to show where the numbers come from and how the calculations are made. Financial analysts typically use financial calculators or spreadsheet programs for these calculations. You might check the answer to this problem using your calculator.

Finding Monthly or Yearly Payments

A very common problem in finance is determining the payment schedule for a loan on a consumer asset, such as a car or a home. Nearly all consumer loans call for equal monthly payments. Suppose, for example, that you have just purchased a $450,000 condominium in Miami's South Beach district. You were able to put $50,000 down and obtain a 30-year, fixed-rate mortgage at 6.125 percent for the balance. What are your monthly payments?

In this problem we know the present value of the annuity. It is $400,000, the price of the condominium less the down payment ($450,000 − $50,000 = $400,000). We also know the number of payments; since the payments will be made monthly for 30 years, you will make 360 payments (12 months per year × 30 years = 360 months). Because the payments are monthly, both the interest rate and maturity must be expressed in monthly terms. For consumer loans, to get the monthly interest rate, we divide the annual interest rate by 12. Thus, the monthly interest rate equals 0.51042 percent (6.125 percent per year/12 months per year = 0.51042 percent per month). What we need to calculate is the monthly cash payment (CF) over the loan period. The time line looks like the following:

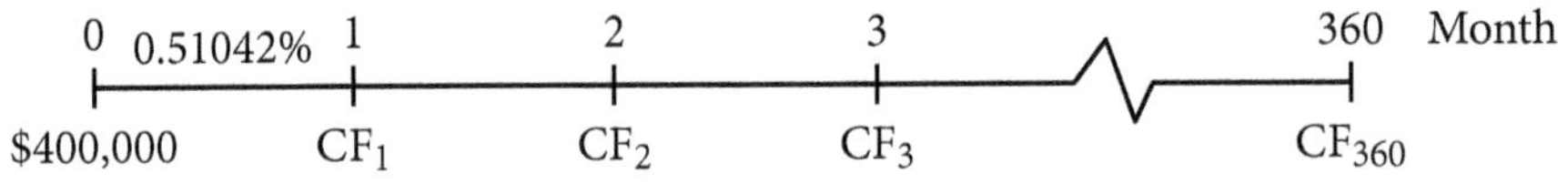

To find CF (remember that $CF_1 = CF_2 = \cdots = CF_{360} = CF$), we use Equation 6.1. We need to make two preliminary calculations:

1. First, we calculate the present value factor for 360 months at 0.51042 percent per month (or, in decimal form, 0.0051042):

$$\begin{aligned}\text{Present value factor} &= \frac{1}{(1+i)^n}\\ &= \frac{1}{(1.0051042)^{360}}\\ &= \frac{1}{6.25160595}\\ &= 0.1599589\end{aligned}$$

2. Next, we solve for the PV annuity factor:

$$\begin{aligned}\text{PV annuity factor} &= \frac{1 - \text{Present value factor}}{i}\\ &= \frac{1 - 0.1599589}{0.0051042}\\ &= \frac{0.8400411}{0.0051042}\\ &= 164.578406\end{aligned}$$

We can now plug all the data into Equation 6.1 and solve it for CF:

$$\begin{aligned}\text{PVA}_n &= \text{CF} \times \text{PV annuity factor}\\ \$400{,}000 &= \text{CF} \times 164.578406\\ \text{CF} &= \frac{\$400{,}000}{164.578406}\\ \text{CF} &= \$2{,}430.45\end{aligned}$$

Your mortgage payments will be $2,430.45 per month.

Solving the problem on a financial calculator takes only a few seconds once the time line is prepared. The most common error students make when using financial calculators is failing to convert all contract variables to be consistent with the compounding period. If the contract calls for monthly payments, the interest rate and contract duration must be stated in monthly terms.

Having converted our data to monthly terms, we enter the following into the calculator: N = 360 months (30 years × 12 months per year = 360 months), i = 0.51042 (6.125 percent per year/12 months per year = 0.51042 percent per month), PV = $400,000, and FV = 0 (to clear the register). Then, pressing the payment button (PMT), we find the answer, which is −$2,430.44. The keystrokes are:

	N	i	PV	PMT	FV
Enter	**360**	**0.51042**	**400,000**		**0**
Answer				**−2,430.44**	

Note that the financial calculator provides the most precise answer, but that the hand and financial calculator answers differ by only 1 cent ($2,430.45 − $2,430.44 = $0.01) in this example. The answers are so close because when doing the hand calculation, we carried six to eight decimal places through the entire set of calculations. Had we rounded off each number as the calculations were made, the difference between the answers from the two calculation methods would have been greater. The more numbers that are rounded during the calculations, the greater the possible rounding error.

Learning by Doing Application 6.5 presents another example in which a calculator is used to compute a periodic payment.

APPLICATION 6.5 | What Are Your Monthly Car Payments?

LEARNING BY DOING

Problem You have decided to buy a new car, and the dealer's best price is $16,000. The dealer agrees to provide financing with a five-year auto loan at 3 percent interest. Using a financial calculator, calculate your monthly payments.

Approach All the problem data must be converted to monthly terms. The number of periods is 60 months (5 years × 12 months per year = 60 months), and the monthly interest charge is 0.25 percent (3 percent per year/12 months per year = 0.25 percent per month). The time line for the car purchase is as follows:

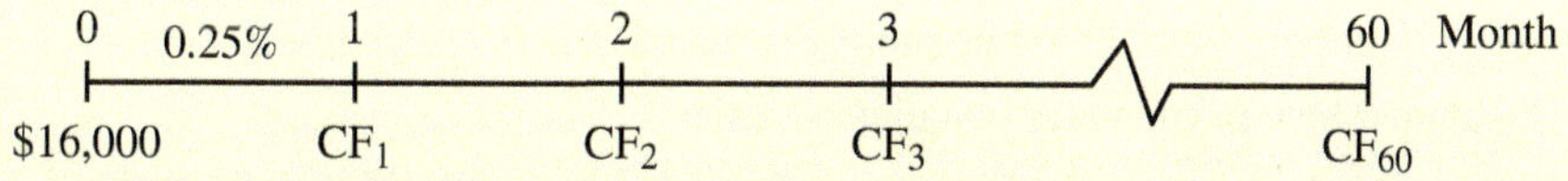

Having converted our data to monthly terms, we enter the following values into the calculator: N = 60 months, i = 0.25, PV = $16,000, and FV = 0 (to clear the register). Pressing the payment key (PMT) will give us the answer.

Solution

	N	i	PV	PMT	FV
Enter	**60**	**0.25**	**16,000**		**0**
Answer				**−287.50**	

Note that since we entered $16,000 as a positive number (because it is a cash inflow to you), the monthly payment of $287.50 is a negative number.

WileyPLUS

Need more help? Visit your WileyPLUS course.

Preparing a Loan Amortization Schedule

Once you understand how to calculate a monthly or yearly loan payment, you have all of the tools that you need to prepare a loan amortization schedule. The term *amortization* describes the way in which the principal (the amount borrowed) is repaid over the life of a loan. With an amortizing loan, some portion of each loan payment goes to paying down the principal. When the final loan payment is made, the unpaid principal is reduced to zero and the loan is paid off. The other portion of each loan payment is interest, which is payment for the use of outstanding principal (the amount of money still owed). Thus, with an **amortizing loan**, each

amortizing loan a loan for which each loan payment contains repayment of some principal and a payment of interest that is based on the remaining principal to be repaid loan payment contains some repayment of principal and an interest payment. Nearly all loans to consumers are amortizing loans.

amortization schedule a table that shows the loan balance at the beginning and end of each period, the payment made during that period, and how much of that payment represents interest and how much represents repayment of principal

A loan **amortization schedule** is a table that shows the loan balance at the beginning and end of each period, the payment made during that period, and how much of that payment represents interest and how much represents repayment of principal. To see how an amortization schedule is prepared, consider an example. Suppose that to purchase a car you have just borrowed $10,000 at a 5 percent interest rate from a bank. Typically, you would make monthly payments on such a loan. For simplicity, however, we will assume that the bank allows you to make annual payments and that the loan will be repaid over five years. **Exhibit 6.4** shows the amortization schedule for this loan.

To prepare a loan amortization schedule, we must first compute the loan payment. Since, for consumer loans, the amount of the loan payment is fixed, all the payments are identical in amount. Applying Equation 6.1 we calculate the payment as follows:

$$\text{PVA}_n = \text{CF} \times \left[\frac{1 - 1/(1+i)^n}{i}\right]$$

$$\$10{,}000 = \text{CF} \times \left[\frac{1 - 1/(1+0.05)^5}{0.05}\right]$$

$$\$10{,}000 = \text{CF} \times 4.329$$

$$\text{CF} = \frac{\$10{,}000}{4.329}$$

$$\text{CF} = \$2{,}310.00 \text{ per year}$$

Alternatively, we enter in a financial calculator the values N = 5 years, i = 5 percent, and PV = $10,000 and then press the PMT key to solve for the loan payment amount. The answer is −$2,309.75 per year. The difference between the two answers results from rounding. For the amortization table calculation, we will use the more precise answer from the financial calculator.

Turning to Exhibit 6.4, we can work through the amortization schedule to see how the table is prepared. For the first year, the values are determined as follows:

1. The amount borrowed, or the beginning principal balance (P_0), is $10,000.
2. The annual loan payment, as calculated earlier, is $2,309.75.
3. The interest payment for the first year is $500 and is calculated as follows:

$$\begin{aligned}\text{Interest payment} &= i \times P_0\\ &= 0.05 \times \$10{,}000\\ &= \$500\end{aligned}$$

Year	Beginning Principal Balance (1)	Total Annual Payment[a] (2)	Interest Paid[b] (3)	Principal Paid (2)–(3) (4)	Ending Principal Balance (1)–(4) (5)
1	$10,000.00	$2,309.75	$500.00	$1,809.75	$8,190.25
2	8,190.25	2,309.75	409.51	1,900.24	6,290.02
3	6,290.02	2,309.75	314.50	1,995.25	4,294.77
4	4,294.77	2,309.75	214.74	2,095.01	2,199.76
5	2,199.76	2,309.75	109.99	2,199.76	0.00

[a]The total annual payment is calculated using the formula for the present value of an annuity, Equation 6.1. The total annual payment is CF in PVA_n = CF × PV annuity factor.

[b]Interest paid equals the beginning balance times the interest rate.

EXHIBIT 6.4 Amortization Table for a Five-Year, $10,000 Loan with an Interest Rate of 5 Percent

A loan amortization table shows how regular payments of principal and interest are applied to repay a loan. The exhibit is an amortization table for a five-year, $10,000 loan with an interest rate of 5 percent and annual payments of $2,309.75. Notice that the interest paid declines with each payment, while the principal paid increases.

4. The principal paid for the year is $1,809.75, calculated as follows:

$$\begin{aligned}\text{Principal paid} &= \text{Loan payment} - \text{Interest payment}\\ &= \$2{,}309.75 - \$500\\ &= \$1{,}809.75\end{aligned}$$

5. The ending principal balance is $8,190.25, computed as follows:

$$\begin{aligned}\text{Ending principal balance} &= \text{Begining principal balance} - \text{Principal paid}\\ &= \$10{,}000 - \$1{,}809.75\\ &= \$8{,}190.25\end{aligned}$$

Note that the ending principal balance for the first year ($8,190.25) becomes the beginning principal balance for the second year ($8,190.25), which in turn is used in calculating the interest payment for the second year:

$$\begin{aligned}\text{Interest payment} &= i \times P_1\\ &= 0.05 \times \$8{,}190.25\\ &= \$409.51\end{aligned}$$

This calculation makes sense because each loan payment includes some principal repayment. This is why the interest paid in column 3 declines each year. We repeat the calculations until the loan is fully amortized, at which point the principal balance goes to zero and the loan is paid off.

The **Using Excel Example** below shows the amortization table calculations in spreadsheet form.

Note, in Exhibit 6.4, the amounts of interest and principal that are paid each year change over time. Interest payments are greatest in the early years of an amortizing loan because much of the principal has not yet been repaid (see columns 1 and 3). However, as the principal

Using Excel

Loan Amortization Table

Loan amortization tables are most easily constructed using a spreadsheet program. Here, we have reconstructed the loan amortization table shown in Exhibit 6.4 using Excel.

Notice that all the values in the amortization table are obtained by using formulas. Once you have built an amortization table like this one, you can change any of the input variables, such as the loan amount or the interest rate, and all of the other numbers will automatically be updated.

	A	B	C	D	E	F	G	H	I	J	K	L	M
1													
2						Loan Amortization Table							
3													
4		Loan amount		$10,000									
5		Interest rate		0.05									
6		Loan period		5									
7		**PMT**		**$2,309.75**									
8													
9		**Year**		**Beginning Balance**		**Total Annual Payment**		**Simple Interest Paid**		**Principal Paid**		**Ending Balance**	
10		1		$10,000.00		$2,309.75		$500.00		$1,809.75		$8,190.25	
11		2		8,190.25		2,309.75		409.51		1,900.24		6,290.02	
12		3		6,290.02		2,309.75		314.50		1,995.25		4,294.77	
13		4		4,294.77		2,309.75		214.74		2,095.01		2,199.76	
14		5		2,199.76		2,309.75		109.99		2,199.76		0.00	
15													
16	**Corresponding formulas:**												
17													
18		**PMT**		=PMT(D5, D6, -D4)									
19													
20		**Year**		**Beginning Balance**		**Total Annual Payment**		**Simple Interest Paid**		**Principal Paid**		**Ending Balance**	
21		1		=D4		=$D$7		=D10*$D$5		=F10-H10		=D10-J10	
22		2		=L10		=$D$7		=D11*$D$5		=F11-H11		=D11-J11	
23		3		=L11		=$D$7		=D12*$D$5		=F12-H12		=D12-J12	
24		4		=L12		=$D$7		=D13*$D$5		=F13-H13		=D13-J13	
25		5		=L13		=$D$7		=D14*$D$5		=F14-H14		=D14-J14	
26													

balance is reduced over time, the interest payments decline and more of each payment goes toward paying down the principal (see columns 3 and 4).

If we were preparing an amortization table for monthly payments, all of the principal balances, loan payments, and interest rates would have to be adjusted to a monthly basis. For example, to calculate monthly payments for our auto loan, we would make the following adjustments: $n = 60$ payments (12 months per year × 5 years = 60 months), $i = 0.4167$ percent (5 percent per year/12 months per year = 0.4167 percent per month), and monthly payment = $188.71.

Finding the Interest Rate

Another important calculation in finance is determining the interest, or discount, rate for an annuity. The interest rate tells us the rate of return on an annuity contract. For example, suppose your parents are getting ready to retire and decide to convert some of their retirement portfolio, which is invested in the stock market, into an annuity that guarantees them a fixed annual income. Their insurance agent asks for $350,000 for an annuity that guarantees to pay them $50,000 a year for 10 years. What is the rate of return on the annuity?

We can insert these values into Equation 6.1:

$$\text{PVA}_n = \text{CF} \times \left[\frac{1 - 1/(1+i)^n}{i}\right]$$

$$\$350{,}000 = \$50{,}000 \times \left[\frac{1 - 1/(1+i)^{10}}{i}\right]$$

To determine the rate of return for the annuity, we need to solve the equation for the unknown value i. Unfortunately, it is not possible to solve the resulting equation for i algebraically. The only way to solve the problem is by trial and error. We normally solve this kind of problem using a financial calculator or spreadsheet program that finds the solution for us. However, it is important to understand how the solution is arrived at by trial and error, so let's work this problem by hand.

To start the process, we must select an initial value for i, plug it into the right side of the equation, and solve the equation to see if the present value of the annuity cash flows equals $350,000, which is the left side of the equation. If the present value of the annuity is too large (PVA > $350,000), we need to select a higher value for i. If the present value of the annuity cash flows is too small (PVA < $350,000), we need to select a smaller value. We continue the trial-and-error process until we find the value of i for which PVA = $350,000.

The key to getting started is to make the best guess we can as to the possible value of the interest rate given the information and data available to us. We will assume that the current bank savings rate is 4 percent and that the annuity rate of return must exceed the bank rate to entice your parents to purchase the annuity rather than place their money in a bank. We will start our calculations with a 5 percent discount rate. The present value of the annuity is:

$$\begin{aligned}\text{PVA} &= \$50{,}000 \times \frac{1 - 1/(1+0.05)^{10}}{0.05}\\ &= \$50{,}000 \times 7.722\\ &= \$386{,}100\end{aligned}$$

That's a pretty good first guess, but our present value is greater than $350,000, so we need to try a higher discount rate.[1] Let's try 7 percent:

$$\begin{aligned}\text{PVA} &= \$50{,}000 \times \frac{1 - 1/(1+0.07)^{10}}{0.07}\\ &= \$50{,}000 \times 7.024\\ &= \$351{,}200\end{aligned}$$

[1]Notice that we have rounded the PV annuity factor to three decimal places (7.722). If we use a financial calculator and do not round, we get a more precise answer of $386,086.75.

The present value of the annuity is still slightly higher than $350,000, so we still need a larger value of *i*. How about 7.10 percent:

$$\begin{aligned} \text{PVA} &= \$50{,}000 \times \frac{1 - 1(1 + 0.071)^{10}}{0.071} \\ &= \$50{,}000 \times 6.991 \\ &= \$349{,}550 \end{aligned}$$

The value is too small, but we now know that *i* is between 7.00 and 7.10 percent. On the next try, we need to use a slightly smaller value of *i*—say, 7.07 percent:

$$\begin{aligned} \text{PVA} &= \$50{,}000 \times \frac{1 - 1/(1 + 0.0707)^{10}}{0.0707} \\ &= \$50{,}000 \times 7.001 \\ &= \$350{,}050 \end{aligned}$$

Since this value is slightly too high, we should try a number for *i* that is only slightly greater than 7.07 percent. We'll try 7.073 percent:

$$\begin{aligned} \text{PVA} &= \$50{,}000 \times \frac{1 - 1/(1 + 0.07073)^{10}}{0.07073} \\ &= \$50{,}000 \times 7.000 \\ &= \$350{,}000 \end{aligned}$$

The cost of the annuity, $350,000, is now exactly the same as the present value of the annuity ($350,000); thus, 7.073 percent is the rate of return earned by the annuity.

It often takes more guesses to solve for the interest rate than it did in this example. Clearly, solving for *i* by trial and error can be a long and tedious process. Fortunately, as mentioned, these types of problems are easily solved with a financial calculator or spreadsheet program. Next, we describe how to compute the interest rate or rate of return on an annuity on a financial calculator.

Calculator Tip: Finding the Interest Rate

To illustrate how to find the interest rate for an annuity on a financial calculator, we will enter the information from the previous example. We know the number of periods (N = 10), the payment amount (PMT = $50,000), and the present value (PV = −$350,000), and we want to solve for the interest rate (i):

Enter	**10**		**−350,000**	**50,000**	**0**
	N	i	PV	PMT	FV
Answer		**7.073**			

As with our calculations above, the interest rate is 7.073 percent. The **Using Excel Example** below illustrates how a spreadsheet is used to perform this calculation.

Using Excel

Calculating the Interest Rate For an Annuity

You can also solve for the interest rate using the =RATE function in Excel as illustrated below.

	A	B	C	D	E	F
1						
2		N		10		
3		PMT		$50,000		
4		PV		−$350,000		
5		FV		$0		
6						
7		Interest Rate		7.073%		
8		Formula		= RATE(D2,D3,D4,D5)		
9						

Learning by Doing Application 6.6 and **Decision Making Example 6.2** illustrate another interest rate calculation and application of the concepts discussed in this section to investment decision-making.

LEARNING BY DOING

APPLICATION 6.6 | Return on Investments: Good Deal or Bad?

Problem With some business opportunities you know the price of a financial contract and the promised cash flows, and you want to calculate the interest rate or rate of return on the investment. For example, suppose you have a chance to invest in a small business. The owner wants to borrow $200,000 from you for five years and will make yearly payments of $60,000 at the end of each year. Similar types of investment opportunities will pay 5 percent. Is this a good investment opportunity?

Approach First, we draw a time line for this loan:

0 ($i = ?$)	1	2	3	4	5 Year
−$200,000	$60,000	$60,000	$60,000	$60,000	$60,000

To compute the rate of return on the investment, we need to compute the interest rate that equates the initial investment of $200,000 to the present value of the promised cash flows of $60,000 per year. We can use the trial-and-error approach with Equation 6.1, a financial calculator, or a spreadsheet program (for example, using the RATE function in Excel) to solve this problem. Here we will use a financial calculator.

Solution The financial calculator steps are:

	N	i	PV	PMT	FV
Enter	**5**		**−200,000**	**60,000**	**0**
Answer		**15.24**			

The return on this investment is 15.24 percent, well above the market interest rate of 5 percent. It is a good investment opportunity.

DECISION MAKING

EXAMPLE 6.2 | The Pizza Dough Machine

Situation As the owner of a pizza parlor, you are considering whether to buy a fully automated pizza dough preparation machine. Your staff is wildly supportive of the purchase because it would eliminate a tedious part of their work. Your accountant provides you with the following information:

- The cost, including shipping, for the pizza dough machine is $25,000.
- Cash savings, including labor, raw materials, and tax savings due to depreciation, are $3,500 per year for 10 years.
- The present value of the cash savings is $21,506 at a 10 percent discount rate.[2]

Given the above data, what should you do?

Decision As you arrive at the pizza parlor in the morning, the staff is in a festive mood because word has leaked out that the new machine will save the shop $35,000 and only cost $25,000.

With a heavy heart, you explain that the analysis done at the water cooler by some of the staff is incorrect. To make economic decisions involving cash flows, even for a small business such as your pizza parlor, you cannot compare cash values from different time periods unless they are adjusted for the time value of money. The present value formula takes into account the time value of money and converts the future cash flows into current dollars. The cost of the machine is already in current dollars.

The correct analysis is as follows: the machine costs $25,000, and the present value of the cost savings is $21,506. Thus, the cost of the machine exceeds the benefits; the correct decision is not to buy the new dough preparation machine.

Future Value of an Annuity

future value of an annuity (FVA) the value of an annuity at some point in the future

Generally, when we are working with annuities, we are interested in computing their present value. On occasion, though, we need to compute the **future value of an annuity (FVA)**. Such

[2]The annuity present value factor for 10 years at 10 percent is 6.1446. Thus, PVA_{10} = CF × Annuity factor = $3,500 × 6.1446 = $21,506.10. Using a financial calculator, PVA_{10} = $21,505.98. The difference is due to rounding errors.

computations typically involve some type of saving activity, such as a monthly savings plan. Another application is computing future values for retirement or pension plans with constant contributions.

We will start with a simple example. Suppose that you plan to save \$1,000 at the end of every year for four years with the goal of buying a racing bicycle. The bike you want is a Colnago C60, a top-of-the-line Italian racing bike that costs around \$4,500. If your bank pays 8 percent interest a year, will you have enough money to buy the bike at the end of four years?

To solve this problem, we can first lay out the cash flows on a time line, as we discussed earlier in this chapter. We can then calculate the future value for each cash flow using Equation 5.1, which is $FV_n = PV \times (1 + i)^n$. Finally, we can add up all the cash flows. The time line and calculations are shown in **Exhibit 6.5**. Given that the total future value of the four deposits is \$4,506.11, as shown in the exhibit, you should have enough money to buy the bike.

Future Value of Annuity Equations

Of course, most business applications involve longer periods of time than the Colnago bike example. One way to solve more complex problems involving the future value of an annuity is first to calculate the present value of the annuity, PVA, using Equation 6.1, and then to use Equation 5.1 to calculate the future value of the PVA. In practice, many analyses condense this calculation into a single step by using the future value of annuity (FVA) formula, which we obtain by substituting PVA for PV in Equation 5.1.

$$
\begin{aligned}
FVA_n &= PVA_n \times (1 + i)^n \\
&= \frac{CF}{i} \times \left[1 - \frac{1}{(1 + i)^n}\right] \times (1 + i)^n \\
&= \frac{CF}{i} \times [(1 + i)^n - 1] \\
&= CF \times \left[\frac{(1 + i)^n - 1}{i}\right]
\end{aligned} \tag{6.2}
$$

where:

FVA_n = future value of an annuity at the end of n periods
PVA_n = present value of an n period annuity
CF = equally spaced and level cash flow
i = discount rate, or interest rate
n = number of periods

We can rearrange Equation 6.2 to write it in terms of the future value factor and the FV annuity factor:

$$
\begin{aligned}
FVA_n &= CF \times \left[\frac{(1 + i)^n - 1}{i}\right] \\
&= CF \times \frac{\text{Future value factor} - 1}{i} \\
&= CF \times \text{FV annuity factor}
\end{aligned}
$$

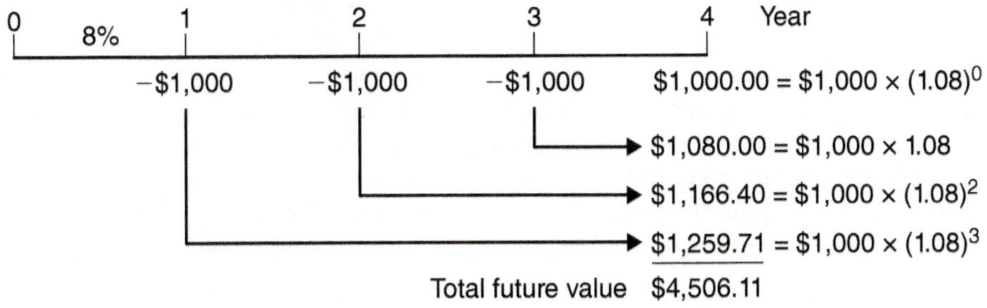

EXHIBIT 6.5 Future Value of a Four-Year Annuity: Colnago C60 Bicycle

The exhibit shows a time line for a savings plan to buy a Colnago C60 bicycle. Under this savings plan, \$1,000 is invested at the end of each year for four years at an annual interest rate of 8 percent. We find the value at the end of the four-year period by adding the future values of the separate cash flows, just as in Exhibits 6.1 and 6.2.

As with PV annuity factors, there are tables listing FV annuity factors. Table A-3 in Appendix A, at the back of this book, includes a table that shows the FV annuity factors for various interest rates and annuity lengths (years).

Using Equation 6.2 to compute FVA for the Colnago bike problem is straightforward. The calculation and process are similar to those we developed for PVA problems. That is, we first calculate the FV annuity factor for four years at 8 percent:

$$\text{Future value factor} = (1 + i)^n = (1.08)^4 = 1.36049$$

$$\text{FV annuity factor} = \frac{\text{Future value factor} - 1}{i} = \frac{1.36049 - 1}{0.08} = 4.5061$$

We then compute the future value of the annuity by multiplying the constant cash flow (CF) by the FV annuity factor. We plug our computed values into the equation:

$$\text{FVA}_n = \text{CF} \times \text{FV annuity factor} = \$1{,}000 \times 4.5061 = \$4{,}506.10$$

This value differs slightly from the one we calculated in Exhibit 6.5 because of rounding.

Calculator Tip: Finding the Future Value of an Annuity

The procedure for calculating the future value of an annuity on a financial calculator is precisely the same as the procedure for calculating the present value of an annuity discussed earlier. The only difference is that we use the FV (future value) key instead of the PV (present value) key. The PV key is entered as a zero to clear the register.

Let's work the Colnago bicycle problem on a calculator. Recall that we decided to put \$1,000 in the bank at the end of each year for four years. The bank pays 8 percent interest. Clear the financial register and make the following entries:

Enter	**4**	**8**	**0**	**−1000**	
	N	i	PV	PMT	FV
Answer					**4,506.11**

The calculated value of \$4,506.11 is the same as in Exhibit 6.5.

Perpetuities

LEARNING OBJECTIVE

3. Explain what a perpetuity is and where we see them in business, and calculate the value of a perpetuity.

A perpetuity is a series of equally spaced and level cash flows that goes on forever. Perpetuities in the form of bonds were used by the British Treasury Department to pay off the debt incurred by the government to finance the Napoleonic wars. These perpetual bonds, called *consols,* have no maturity date and are still traded in the international bond markets today. They will only be retired when the British Treasury repurchases them all in the open market.

The most important perpetuities in the securities markets today are preferred stock issues. The issuer of preferred stock promises to pay investors a fixed dividend forever unless a retirement date for the preferred stock has been set. Since, as we discussed in Chapter 1, a corporation can have an indefinite life, the expected cash flows from a corporation might also go on forever. When these expected cash flows are constant, they can be viewed as a perpetuity.

From Equation 6.1, we can calculate the present value of a perpetuity by setting n, which is the number of periods, equal to infinity (∞).[3] When that is done, the value of the term

[3]Conversely, we can derive the formula for the present value of an ordinary annuity, Equation 6.1, from the formula for a perpetuity, as explained in the appendix at the end of this chapter.

$1/(1 + i)^{\infty}$ approaches 0, and thus the present value of a perpetuity that begins next period (PVP) equals:

$$\begin{aligned} \text{PVP} &= \frac{\text{CF}}{i} \times \left[1 - \frac{1}{(1+i)^{\infty}}\right] \\ &= \frac{\text{CF}}{i} \times [1 - 0] \\ &= \frac{\text{CF}}{i} \end{aligned} \tag{6.3}$$

As you can see, the present value of a perpetuity is the promised constant cash payment (CF) divided by the interest rate (i). A nice feature of the final equation (PVP = CF/i) is that it is algebraically very simple to work with, since it allows us to solve for i directly rather than by trial and error, as is required with Equations 6.1 and 6.2.

To see how we use the perpetuity formula, suppose you had a great experience during your studies at the school of business and decided to endow a scholarship fund for finance students. The goal of the fund is to provide the university with $100,000 of financial support each year forever. If the rate of interest is 8 percent, how much money will you have to give the university to provide the desired level of support? Using Equation 6.3, we find that the present value of the perpetuity is:

$$\text{PVP} = \frac{\text{CF}}{i} = \frac{\$100{,}000}{0.08} = \$1{,}250{,}000$$

Thus, a gift of $1.25 million will provide constant annual funding of $100,000 to the university forever.

Before we finish our discussion of perpetuities, we should point out that the present value of a perpetuity is typically not very different from the present value of a very long annuity. For example, suppose that instead of funding the scholarship forever, you only plan to fund it for 100 years. If you compute the present value of a 100-year annuity of $100,000 using an interest rate of 8 percent, you will find that it equals $1,249,431.76, which is only slightly less than the $1,250,000 value of the perpetuity. Making your gift a perpetuity would only cost you an additional $568.24. This is because the present value of the cash flows to be received after 100 years is extremely small. The key point here is that cash flows that are to be received far in the future can have very small present values.

Learning by Doing Application 6.7 illustrates another application of the present value of a perpetuity formula, Equation 6.3.

Annuities Due

So far we have discussed annuities whose cash flow payments occur at the end of the period, so-called *ordinary annuities*. Another type of annuity that is fairly common in business is known as an **annuity due**. Here, cash payments start immediately, at the beginning of the first period. For example, when you rent an apartment, the first rent payment is typically due immediately. The second rent payment is due the first of the second month, and so on. In this kind of payment pattern, you are effectively prepaying for the service.

annuity due an annuity in which payments are made at the beginning of each period

APPLICATION 6.7 | Preferred Stock Dividends

LEARNING BY DOING

Problem Suppose that you are the CEO of a public company and your investment banker recommends that you issue some preferred stock at $50 per share. Similar preferred stock issues are yielding 6 percent. What annual cash dividend does the firm need to offer to be competitive in the marketplace? In other words, what cash dividend paid annually forever would be worth $50 with a 6 percent discount rate?

Approach As we have already mentioned, preferred stock is a type of perpetuity; thus, we can solve this problem by applying Equation 6.3. As usual, we begin by laying out the time line for the cash flows:

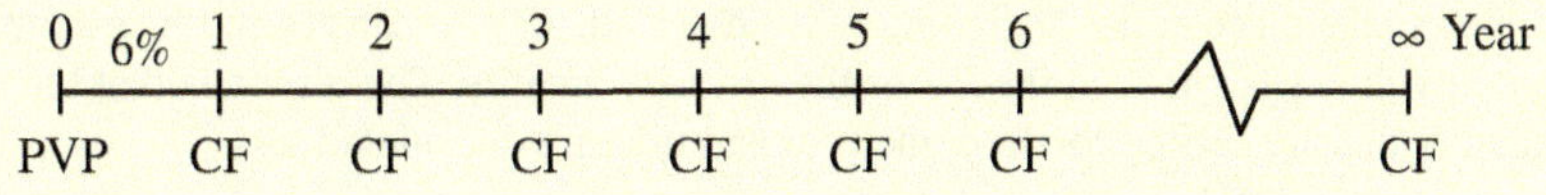

For preferred stock, PVP is the value of a share of stock, which is $50 per share. The discount rate is 6 percent. CF is the fixed-rate cash dividend, which is the unknown value. Using this information, we can use Equation 6.3 and solve for CF.

Solution

$$\text{PVP} = \frac{\text{CF}}{i}$$

$$\begin{aligned}\text{CF} &= \text{PVP} \times i \\ &= \$50 \times 0.06 \\ &= \$3\end{aligned}$$

The annual dividend on the preferred stock would be $3 per share.

Exhibit 6.6 compares the cash flows for a four-year ordinary annuity and a four-year annuity due. Note that both annuities are made up of four $1,000 cash flows and carry an 8 percent interest rate. Exhibit 6.6 A shows an ordinary annuity, in which the cash flows take place at the end of the period, and Exhibit 6.6 B shows an annuity due, in which the cash flows take place at the beginning of the period. There are several ways to calculate the present and future values of an annuity due, and we discuss them next.

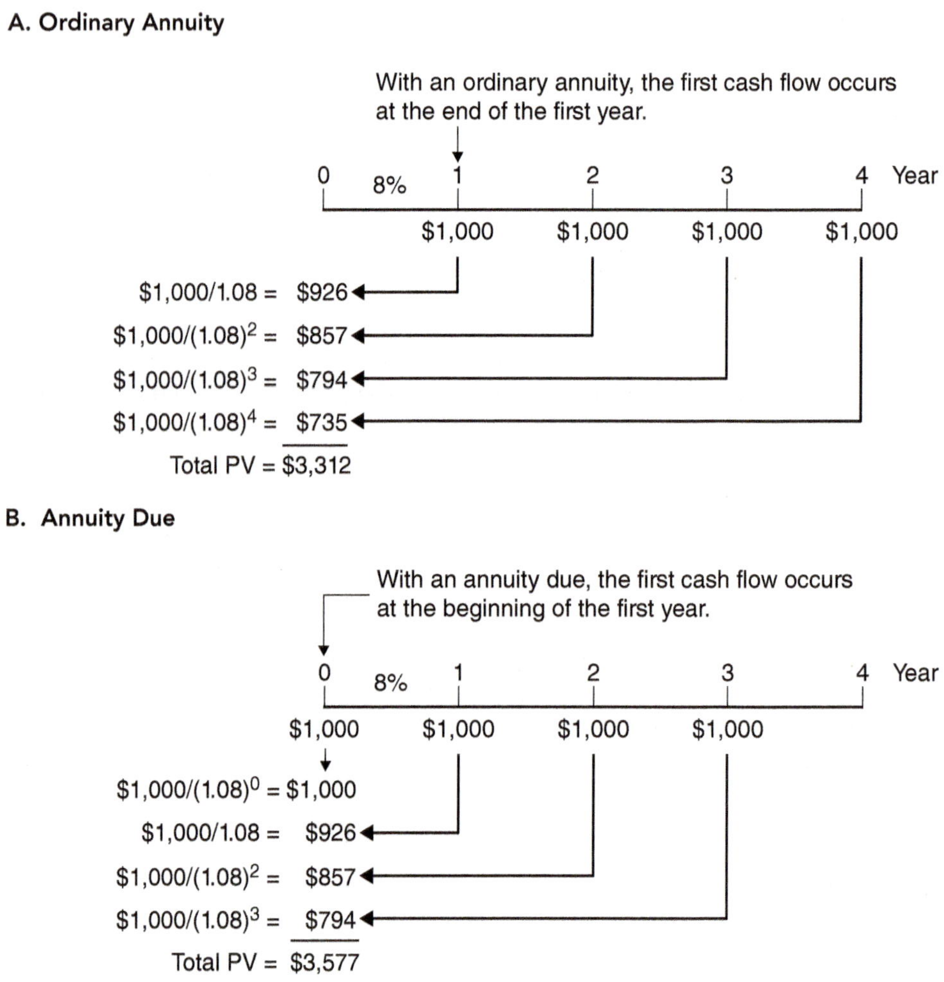

EXHIBIT 6.6 Ordinary Annuity versus Annuity Due

The difference between an ordinary annuity (part A) and an annuity due (part B) is that with an ordinary annuity, the cash flows take place at the end of each period, while with an annuity due, the cash flows take place at the beginning of each period. As you can see in this example, the PV of the annuity due is larger than the PV of the ordinary annuity. The reason is that the cash flows of the annuity due are shifted forward one year and thus are discounted less.

Present Value Method

One way to compute the present value of an annuity due is to discount each individual cash flow to the present, as shown in Exhibit 6.6 B. Note that since the first $1,000 cash flow takes place now, that cash flow is already in present value terms. The present value of the cash flows for the annuity due is $3,577.

Compare this present value with the present value of the cash flows for the ordinary annuity, $3,312, as calculated in Exhibit 6.6 A. It should be no surprise that the present value of the annuity due is larger than the present value of the ordinary annuity ($3,577 > $3,312), even though both annuities have four $1,000 cash flows. The reason is that the cash flows of the annuity due are shifted forward one year and, thus, are discounted less.

Annuity Transformation Method

An easier way to work annuity due problems is to transform the formula for the present value of an annuity (Equation 6.1) so that it will work for annuity due problems. To do this, we pretend that each cash flow occurs at the end of the period (although it actually occurs at the beginning of the period) and use Equation 6.1. Since Equation 6.1 discounts each cash flow by one period too many, we then correct for the extra discounting by multiplying our answer by $(1 + i)$, where i is the discount rate or interest rate.

The relation between an ordinary annuity and an annuity due can be formally expressed as:

$$\text{Annuity due value} = \text{Ordinary annuity value} \times (1 + i) \tag{6.4}$$

This relation is especially helpful because it works for both present value and future value calculations. Calculating the value of an annuity due using Equation 6.4 involves three steps:

1. Adjust the problem time line as if the cash flows were an ordinary annuity.
2. Calculate the present or future value as though the cash flows were an ordinary annuity.
3. Multiply the answer by $(1 + i)$.

Let's calculate the value of the annuity due shown in Exhibit 6.6 B using Equation 6.4, the transformation technique. First, we restate the time line as if the problem were an ordinary annuity; the revised time line looks like the one in Exhibit 6.6 A. Second, we calculate the present value of the annuity as if the problem involved an ordinary annuity. The value of the ordinary annuity is $3,312, as shown in Exhibit 6.6 A. Finally, we use Equation 6.4 to make the adjustment to an annuity due:

$$\begin{aligned}\text{Annuity due value} &= \text{Ordinary annuity value} \times (1 + i)\\ &= \$3{,}312 \times 1.08\\ &= \$3{,}577\end{aligned}$$

As they should, the answers for the two methods of calculation are identical.

Another easy way to calculate the present value or future value of an annuity due is by using the BEG/END switch in your financial calculator. All financial calculators have a key that switches the cash flow from the end of each period to the beginning of each period. The keys are typically labeled "BEG" for cash flows at the beginning of the period and "END" for the cash flows at the end of the period. To calculate the PV of an annuity due: (1) switch the calculator to the BEG mode, (2) enter the data, and (3) press the PV key for the answer. As an example, work the problem from Exhibit 6.6 B using your financial calculator.

Before You Go On

1. What are the differences between an ordinary annuity, an annuity due, and a perpetuity?
2. Give two examples of perpetuities.
3. What is the annuity transformation method?

6.3 Cash Flows That Grow at a Constant Rate

LEARNING OBJECTIVE

4. Discuss growing annuities and perpetuities, as well as their application in business, and calculate their values.

So far, we have been examining level cash flow streams. Often, though, management needs to value a cash flow stream that increases at a constant rate over time. These cash flow streams are called growing annuities or growing perpetuities.

Growing Annuity

growing annuity an annuity in which the cash flows increase at a constant rate

Financial managers often need to compute the value of multiyear product or service contracts with cash flows that increase each year at a constant rate. These are called **growing annuities**. For example, you may want to value the cost of a 25-year lease that adjusts annually for the expected rate of inflation over the life of the contract. Equation 6.5 can be used to compute the present value of an annuity growing at a constant rate for a finite time period:[4]

$$\text{PVA}_n = \frac{\text{CF}_1}{i - g} \times \left[1 - \left(\frac{1 + g}{1 + i}\right)^n\right] \tag{6.5}$$

where:

PVA_n = present value of a growing annuity with n periods
CF_1 = cash flow one period in the future ($t = 1$)
i = interest rate, or discount rate
g = constant growth rate per period

You should be aware of several important points when applying Equation 6.5. First, the cash flow (CF_1) used is not the cash flow for the current period (CF_0); rather, it is the cash flow to be received in the next period ($t = 1$). The relation between these two cash flows is $\text{CF}_1 = \text{CF}_0 \times (1 + g)$. Second, a necessary condition for using Equation 6.5 is that $i > g$. If this condition is not met ($i \leqslant g$), the calculations from the equation will be meaningless, as you will get a negative or infinite value for finite positive cash flows. A negative value essentially says that someone would have to pay you money to get you to accept a positive cash flow.

As an example of how Equation 6.5 is applied, suppose you work for a company that owns a number of coffee shops in the New York City area. One coffee shop is located in the Empire State Building, and your boss wants to know how much it is worth.[5] The coffee shop has a 50-year lease, so we will assume that it will be in business for 50 years. It produced cash flows of \$300,000 after all expenses this year, and the discount rate used by similar businesses is 15 percent. You estimate that, over the long term, cash flows will grow at 2.5 percent per year because of inflation. Thus, you calculate that the coffee shop's cash flow next year (CF_1) will be \$307,500, or \$300,000 × (1 + 0.025).

Plugging the values from the coffee shop example into Equation 6.5 yields the following result:

$$\begin{aligned}\text{PVA}_n &= \frac{\$307{,}500}{0.15 - 0.025} \times \left[1 - \left(\frac{1.025}{1.15}\right)^{50}\right] \\ &= \$2{,}460{,}000 \times 0.9968 \\ &= \$2{,}452{,}128\end{aligned}$$

The estimated value of the coffee shop is \$2,452,128.

[4]In Equation 6.5 we represent the present value of a growing annuity of n periods using the same notation (PVA_n) that we use for a regular annuity in Equation 6.1. We do this because the regular annuity is just a special case of the growing annuity, where $g = 0$. Equation 6.5 is the more general form of the annuity formula.

[5]For those interested, the Empire State Building has three coffee shops.

Growing Perpetuity

Sometimes cash flows are expected to grow at a constant rate indefinitely. In this case the cash flow stream is called a **growing perpetuity**. The formula to compute the present value for a growing perpetuity that begins next period (PVP) is as follows:

growing perpetuity a cash flow stream that grows at a constant rate forever

$$\text{PVP} = \frac{\text{CF}_1}{i - g} \tag{6.6}$$

As before, CF_1 is the cash flow occurring at the end of the first period, i is the discount or interest rate, and g is the constant rate of growth of the cash flow (CF). Equation 6.6 is an easy equation to work with, and it is used widely in the valuation of common stock for firms that have a policy and history of paying dividends that grow at a constant rate. It is also widely used in the valuation of entire companies, as we will discuss in Chapter 18.

Notice that we can derive Equation 6.6 from Equation 6.5 by setting n equal to ∞. If i is greater than g, as we said it must be, the term $[(1 + g)/(1 + i)]^{\infty}$ is equal to 0, leading to the following result:

$$\begin{aligned}\text{PVP} &= \frac{\text{CF}_1}{i - g} \times \left[1 - \left(\frac{1 + g}{1 + i}\right)^{\infty}\right] \\ &= \frac{\text{CF}_1}{i - g} \times [1 - 0] \\ &= \frac{\text{CF}_1}{i - g}\end{aligned}$$

This makes sense, of course, since Equation 6.5 describes a growing annuity and Equation 6.6 describes a growing cash flow stream that goes on forever. Notice that both Equations 6.5 and 6.6 are exactly the same as Equations 6.1 and 6.3 when g equals zero.

To illustrate a growing perpetuity, we will consider an example. Suppose that, after graduating from college, you started a health and athletic club. Your concept included not only providing workout facilities, such as weights, treadmills, and elliptical trainers, but also promoting a healthy lifestyle through a focus on cooking and nutrition. The concept has proved popular, and after only five years, you have seven clubs in operation. Your accountant reports that the firm's cash flow last year was \$450,000, and the appropriate discount rate for the club is 18 percent. You expect the firm's cash flows to increase by 5 percent per year, which includes 2 percent for expected inflation. Since the business is a corporation, you can assume it will continue operating indefinitely into the future. What is the value of the firm?

We can use Equation 6.6 to solve this problem. Although the equation is very easy to use, a common mistake is using the current period's cash flow (CF_0) and not the *next* period's cash flow (CF_1). Since the cash flow is growing at a constant growth rate, g, we simply multiply CF_0 by $(1 + g)$ to get the value of CF_1. Thus,

$$\text{CF}_1 = \text{CF}_0 \times (1 + g)$$

We can then substitute the result into Equation 6.6, which yields a helpful variant of this equation:

$$\text{PVP} = \frac{\text{CF}_1}{i - g} = \frac{\text{CF}_0 \times (1 + g)}{i - g}$$

Now we can insert the values for the health club into the equation and solve for PVP:

$$\begin{aligned}\text{PVP} &= \frac{\text{CF}_0 \times (1 + g)}{i - g} \\ &= \frac{\$450{,}000 \times (1 + 0.05)}{0.18 - 0.05} \\ &= \$3{,}634{,}615\end{aligned}$$

The business is worth \$3,634,615.

The growing annuity and perpetuity formulas are useful, and we will apply them later on in this book. Unfortunately, even though advanced financial calculators have special programs for annuities and perpetuities with constant cash flows, typical financial calculators do not include programs for growing annuities and perpetuities.

Before You Go On

1. What is the difference between a growing annuity and a growing perpetuity?

6.4 The Effective Annual Interest Rate

LEARNING OBJECTIVE

5. Discuss why the effective annual interest rate (EAR) is the appropriate way to annualize interest rates, and calculate the EAR.

So far in this chapter and the preceding one, there has been little question about which interest rate to use in a particular computation. In most cases, a single interest rate has been supplied. When working with real market data, however, the situation is not so clear-cut. We often encounter interest rates that can be computed in different ways. In this final section, we try to untangle some of the issues that can cause problems.

Why the Confusion?

To better understand why interest rates can be so confusing, consider the following situation. Suppose you borrow $100 on your bank credit card and plan to keep the balance outstanding for one year. The credit card's stated interest rate is 1 percent per month. The federal Truth-in-Lending Act requires the bank and other financial institutions to disclose to consumers the **annual percentage rate (APR)** charged on a loan. The APR is the annualized interest rate using *simple interest.* It ignores the interest earned on interest associated with compounding periods of less than one year. Thus, the APR is defined as the simple interest charged per period multiplied by the number of periods per year. For the bank credit card loan, the APR is 12 percent (1 percent per month × 12 months = 12 percent).

annual percentage rate (APR) the simple interest rate charged per period multiplied by the number of periods per year

At the end of the year, you go to pay off the credit card balance as planned. It seems reasonable to assume that with an APR of 12 percent your credit card balance at the end of one year would be $112 (1.12 × $100 = $112). Wrong! The bank's *actual* interest rate is 1 percent per month, meaning that the bank will compound your credit card balance monthly, 12 times over the year. The bank's calculation for the balance due is $112.68 [$\$100 \times (1.01)^{12} = \$112.68$].[6] The bank is actually charging you 12.68 percent per year, and the total interest paid for the one-year loan is $12.68 rather than $12.00. This example raises a question: What is the correct way to annualize an interest rate?

Weblink

Many useful financial calculators, including an APR calculator, can be found at eFunda.com. Go to http://www.efunda.com/formulae/finance/apr_calculator.cfm.

Calculating the Effective Annual Interest Rate

effective annual interest rate (EAR) the annual interest rate that reflects compounding within a year

In making financial decisions, the correct way to annualize an interest rate is to compute the effective annual interest rate. The **effective annual interest rate (EAR)** is defined as the

[6]If you have any doubt about the total credit card debt at the end of one year, make the calculation 12 times on your calculator: the first month is $100 × 1.01 = 101.00; the second month is $101.00 × 1.01 = $102.01; the third month is $102.01 × 1.01 = $103.03; and so on for 12 months.

annual interest rate that takes compounding into account. Mathematically, the EAR can be stated as follows:

$$\text{EAR} = \left[1 + \frac{\text{Quoted interest rate}}{m}\right]^m - 1 \tag{6.7}$$

where m is the number of compounding periods during a year. The **quoted interest rate** is by definition a *simple* annual interest rate, like the APR. That means that the quoted interest rate has been annualized by multiplying the rate per period by the number of periods per year. The EAR conversion formula accounts for the number of compounding periods and, thus, effectively adjusts the annualized quoted interest rate for the time value of money. Because the EAR is the true cost of borrowing and lending, it is the rate that should be used for making all finance decisions.

quoted interest rate a simple annual interest rate, such as the APR

We will use our bank credit card example to illustrate the use of Equation 6.7. Recall that the credit card has an APR of 12 percent (1 percent per month). The APR is the quoted interest rate and the number of compounding periods (m) is 12. Applying Equation 6.7, we find that the effective annual interest rate is:

$$\begin{aligned}
\text{EAR} &= \left(1 + \frac{\text{Quoted interest rate}}{m}\right)^m - 1 \\
&= \left(1 + \frac{0.12}{12}\right)^{12} - 1 \\
&= (1.01)^{12} - 1 \\
&= 1.1268 - 1 \\
&= 0.1268, \text{ or } 12.68\%
\end{aligned}$$

The EAR value of 12.68 percent is the true cost of borrowing the \$100 on the bank credit card for one year. The EAR calculation adjusts for the effects of compounding and, hence, the time value of money.

Finally, notice that interest rates are quoted in the marketplace in three ways:

1. *The quoted interest rate.* This is an interest rate that has been annualized by multiplying the rate per period by the number of compounding periods. The APR is an example. All consumer borrowing and lending rates are annualized in this manner.
2. *The interest rate per period.* The bank credit card rate of 1 percent per month is an example of this kind of rate. You can find the interest rate per period by dividing the quoted interest rate by the number of compounding periods.
3. *The effective annual interest rate (EAR).* This is the interest rate actually paid (or earned) after accounting for compounding. Sometimes it is difficult to distinguish a quoted rate from an EAR. Generally, however, an annualized consumer rate is an APR rather than an EAR.

Comparing Interest Rates

When borrowing or lending money, it is sometimes necessary to compare and select among interest rate alternatives. Quoted interest rates are comparable when they cover the same overall time period, such as one year, and have the same number of compounding periods. If quoted interest rates are *not* comparable, we must adjust them to a common time period. The easiest way, and the correct way, to make interest rates comparable for making finance decisions is to convert them to effective annual interest rates. Consider an example.

Suppose you are the chief financial officer of a manufacturing company. The company is planning a \$1 billion plant expansion and will finance it by borrowing money for five years. Three financial institutions have submitted interest rate quotes; all are APRs:

Lender A: 10.40 percent compound monthly

Lender B: 10.90 percent compounded annually

Lender C: 10.50 percent compounded quarterly

Although all the loans have the same maturity, they are not comparable because the APRs have different compounding periods. To make the adjustments for the different time periods, we apply Equation 6.7 to convert each of the APR quotes into an EAR:

$$\begin{aligned}
\text{Lender A: EAR} &= \left(1 + \frac{0.1040}{12}\right)^{12} - 1 \\
&= (1.0087)^{12} - 1 \\
&= 1.1091 - 1 \\
&= 0.1091, \text{ or } 10.91\% \\
\text{Lender B: EAR} &= \left(1 + \frac{0.1090}{1}\right)^{1} - 1 \\
&= 1.1090 - 1 \\
&= 0.1090, \text{ or } 10.90\% \\
\text{Lender C: EAR} &= \left(1 + \frac{0.1050}{4}\right)^{4} - 1 \\
&= (1.0263)^{4} - 1 \\
&= 1.1092 - 1 \\
&= 0.1092, \text{ or } 10.92\%
\end{aligned}$$

As shown, Lender B offers the lowest interest cost at 10.90 percent.

Notice the shift in rankings that takes place as a result of the EAR calculations. When we initially looked at the APR quotes, it appeared that Lender A offered the lowest rate and Lender B had the highest. After computing the EAR, we find that when we account for the effect of compounding, Lender B actually offers the lowest interest rate.

Another important point is that if all the interest rates are quoted as APRs with the same annualizing period, such as monthly, the interest rates are comparable and you can select the correct rate by simply comparing the quotes. That is, the lowest APR corresponds with the lowest cost of funds. Thus, it is correct for borrowers or lenders to make economic decisions with APR data as long as interest rates have the same maturity and the same compounding period. To find the true cost of the loan, however, it is still necessary to compute the EAR.

Learning by Doing Application 6.8 illustrates another effective annual interest rate calculation.

LEARNING BY DOING

WileyPLUS

Need more help? Visit your WileyPLUS course.

APPLICATION 6.8 | What Is the True Cost of a Loan?

Problem During a period of economic expansion, Frank Smith became financially overextended and was forced to consolidate his debt with a loan from a consumer finance company. The consolidated debt provided Frank with a single loan and lower monthly payments than he had previously been making. The loan agreement quotes an APR of 20 percent, and Frank must make monthly payments. What is the true cost of the loan?

Approach The true cost of the loan is the EAR, not the APR. Thus, we must convert the quoted rate into the EAR, using Equation 6.7, to get the true cost of the loan.

Solution

$$\begin{aligned}
\text{EAR} &= \left(1 + \frac{\text{Quoted interest rate}}{m}\right)^{m} - 1 \\
&= \left(1 + \frac{0.20}{12}\right)^{12} - 1 \\
&= (1 + 0.0167)^{12} - 1 \\
&= (1.0167)^{12} - 1 \\
&= 1.2194 - 1 \\
&= 0.2194, \text{ or } 21.94\%
\end{aligned}$$

The true cost of the loan is 21.94 percent, not the 20 percent APR.

Consumer Protection Acts and Interest Rate Disclosure

In 1968 Congress passed the **Truth-in-Lending Act** to ensure that all borrowers receive meaningful information about the cost of credit so that they can make intelligent economic decisions.[7] The act applies to all lenders that extend credit to consumers, and it covers credit card loans, auto loans, home mortgage loans, home equity loans, home improvement loans, and some small-business loans. Similar legislation, the so-called **Truth-in-Savings Act**, applies to consumer savings vehicles such as certificates of deposit (CDs). These two pieces of legislation require by law that the APR be disclosed on all consumer loans and savings plans and that it be prominently displayed on advertising and contractual documents.

Truth-in-Lending Act a federal law requiring lenders to fully inform borrowers of important information related to loans, including the annual percentage rate charged

Truth-in-Savings Act a federal law requiring institutions offering consumer savings vehicles, such as certificates of deposit (CDs), to fully inform consumers of important information about the savings vehicles, including the annual percentage rate paid

We know that the EAR, not the APR, represents the true economic interest rate. So why did the Truth-in-Lending and Truth-in-Savings Acts specify that the APR must be the disclosed rate? The APR was selected because it's easy to calculate and easy to understand. When the legislation was passed, personal computers and handheld calculators did not exist. Down at the auto showroom, salespeople needed an easy way to explain and annualize the monthly interest charge, and the APR provided just such a method. And most important, if all the auto lenders quoted monthly APR, consumers could use this rate to select the loan with the lowest economic interest cost.

Today, although lenders and borrowers are legally required to quote the APR, they run their businesses using interest rate calculations based on the present value and future value formulas. Consumers are bombarded with both APR and EAR rates, and confusion reigns. At the car dealership, for example, you may find that your auto loan's APR is 5 percent but the actual borrowing rate is 5.12 percent. And at the bank where your grandmother gets free coffee and doughnuts, she may be told that the bank's one-year CD has an APR of 3 percent, but it really pays 3.04 percent. Because of confusion arising from conflicting interest rates in the marketplace, some observers believe that the APR calculation has outlived its usefulness and should be replaced by the EAR.

Weblink

You can read more about credit protection laws, including the latest laws, at the Debt.org Website http://www.debt.org/credit/your-consumer-rights/protection-act/.

In addition to requiring that lenders report the APR on all consumer loans, the Truth-in-Lending Act provides other important protections for consumers. For example, it also limits the liability of credit card holders to $50 if a credit card is stolen or used without the cardholder's approval. Since this act was passed in 1968, a number of subsequent acts have added to the protections of the Truth-in-Lending Act. The most recent of these, which you may be familiar with, is the Credit Card Act of 2009. This act was passed in response to criticisms of actions by credit card companies leading up to the financial crisis of 2008. Among other things, it places new limits on the ability of credit card companies to raise interest rates, limits the fees that they can charge, requires better disclosure of rate increases and how long it will take a cardholder to pay off the outstanding balance with minimum monthly payments, and makes it more difficult for credit card companies to issue new cards to people under age 21.

The Appropriate Interest Rate Factor

Here is a final question to consider: What is the appropriate interest rate to use when making future or present value calculations? The answer is simple: use the EAR. Under no circumstance should the APR or any other quoted rate be used as the interest rate in present or future value calculations. Consider an example of using the EAR in such a calculation.

Petra, a student at University of Texas, has purchased from a small consumer finance company a $100 savings note with a two-year maturity. The contract states that the note has a 20 percent APR and pays interest quarterly. The quarterly interest rate is thus 5 percent (20 percent/4 quarters = 5 percent per quarter). Petra has several questions about the note: (1) What is the note's effective annual interest rate (EAR)? (2) How much money will she have at the end of two years? (3) When making the future value calculation, should she use the quarterly interest rate or the EAR?

[7]The Truth-in-Lending Act is Title I of the Consumer Credit Protection Act.

To answer Petra's questions, we first compute the EAR, which is the actual interest earned on the note:

$$\begin{aligned} \text{EAR} &= \left(1 + \frac{\text{APR}}{m}\right)^m - 1 \\ &= \left(1 + \frac{0.20}{4}\right)^4 - 1 \\ &= (1 + 0.05)^4 - 1 \\ &= 1.21551 - 1 \\ &= 0.21551\text{, or } 21.551\% \end{aligned}$$

Next, we calculate the future value of the note using the EAR. Because the EAR is an annual rate, for this problem we use a total of two compounding periods. The calculation is as follows:

$$\begin{aligned} \text{FV}_2 &= \text{PV} \times (1 + i)^n \\ &= \$100 \times (1 + 0.21551)^2 \\ &= \$100 \times 1.4775 \\ &= \$147.75 \end{aligned}$$

We can also calculate the future value using the quarterly rate of interest of 5 percent with a total of eight compounding periods. In this case, the calculation is as follows:

$$\begin{aligned} \text{FV}_2 &= \$100 \times (1 + 0.050)^8 \\ &= \$100 \times 1.4775 \\ &= \$147.75 \end{aligned}$$

The two calculation methods yield the same answer: $147.75.

In summary, any time you do a future value or present value calculation, you must use either the interest rate per period (quoted rate/m) or the EAR as the interest rate factor. It does not matter which of these you use. Both will properly account for the impact of compounding on the value of cash flows. Interest rate proxies such as the APR should never be used as interest rate factors for calculating future or present values, because they do not properly account for the number of compounding periods.

Before You Go On

1. What is the APR, and why are lending institutions required to disclose this rate?
2. What is the correct way to annualize an interest rate in financial decision making?
3. Distinguish between quoted interest rate, interest rate per period, and effective annual interest rate.

Summary of Learning Objectives

1 Explain why cash flows occurring at different times must be adjusted to reflect their value as of a common date before they can be compared, and compute the present value and the future value for multiple cash flows.

When making decisions involving cash flows over time, we should first identify the magnitude and timing of the cash flows and then adjust each individual cash flow to reflect its value as of a common date. For example, the process of discounting (compounding) cash flows adjusts them for the time value of money because today's dollars are not equal in value to dollars in the future. Once all of the cash flows are in present (future) value terms, they can be compared to make decisions. Section 6.1 discusses the computation of present values and future values of multiple cash flows.

2 Explain the difference between an ordinary annuity and an annuity due, and calculate the present value and the future value of an ordinary annuity and an annuity due.

An ordinary annuity is a finite series of equally spaced, level cash flows over time. The cash flows for an ordinary annuity are assumed to take place at the end of each period. To find the present value of an ordinary annuity, we multiply the present value of an annuity factor, which is equal to (1 − present value factor)/i, by the amount of the constant cash flow. We multiply the present value of an ordinary annuity by $(1 + i)^n$ to calculate its future value in n periods.

An annuity due is an annuity in which the cash flows occur at the beginning of each period. A lease is an example of an annuity due. In this case, we are effectively prepaying for the service. To calculate the value of an annuity due, we calculate the present value (or future value) as though the cash flows are from an ordinary annuity. We then multiply the ordinary annuity value times $(1 + i)$. Section 6.2 discusses the calculation of the present value and future value of an ordinary annuity and an annuity due.

3 Explain what a perpetuity is and where we see them in business, and calculate the value of a perpetuity.

A perpetuity is like an annuity except that the cash flows are perpetual—they never end. British Treasury Department bonds, called consols, were the first widely used securities of this kind. The most common example of a perpetuity today is preferred stock. The issuer of preferred stock promises to pay fixed-rate dividends forever. The cash flows from corporations can also look like perpetuities. To calculate the present value of a perpetuity, we simply divide the constant cash flow (CF) by the interest rate (i).

4 Discuss growing annuities and perpetuities, as well as their application in business, and calculate their values.

Financial managers often need to value cash flow streams that increase at a constant rate over time. These cash flow streams are called growing annuities or growing perpetuities. An example of a growing annuity is a 10-year lease with an annual adjustment for the expected rate of inflation over the life of the contract. If the cash flows continue to grow at a constant rate indefinitely, this cash flow stream is called a growing perpetuity. Since a C-corporation has an indefinite life, when the cash flows from such a corporation are growing at a constant rate, they can be thought of as a growing perpetuity. The calculation of the value of a cash flow stream that grows at a constant rate is discussed in Section 6.3.

5 Discuss why the effective annual interest rate (EAR) is the appropriate way to annualize interest rates, and calculate the EAR.

The EAR is the annual interest rate that takes compounding into account. Thus, the EAR is the true cost of borrowing or lending money. When we need to compare interest rates, we must make sure that the rates to be compared have the same time and compounding periods. If interest rates are not comparable, they must be converted into common terms. The easiest way to convert rates to common terms is to calculate the EAR for each interest rate. The use and calculation of EAR are discussed in Section 6.4.

Summary of Key Equations

Equation	Description	Formula
6.1	Present value of an ordinary annuity	$\text{PVA}_n = \frac{\text{CF}}{i} \times \left[1 - \frac{1}{(1+i)^n}\right]$ $= \text{CF} \times \left[\frac{1 - 1/(1+i)^n}{i}\right]$ $= \text{CF} \times \frac{1 - \text{Present value factor}}{i}$ $= \text{CF} \times \text{PV annuity factor}$
6.2	Future value of an ordinary annuity	$\text{FVA}_n = \frac{\text{CF}}{i} \times [(1+i)^n - 1]$ $= \text{CF} \times \left[\frac{(1+i)^n - 1}{i}\right]$ $= \text{CF} \times \frac{\text{Future value factor} - 1}{i}$ $= \text{CF} \times \text{FV annuity factor}$
6.3	Present value of a perpetuity	$\text{PVP} = \frac{\text{CF}}{i}$
6.4	Value of an annuity due	Annuity due value = Ordinary annuity value $\times (1 + i)$

continued

continued

Equation	Description	Formula
6.5	Present value of a growing annuity	$\text{PVA}_n = \dfrac{\text{CF}_1}{i - g} \times \left[1 - \left(\dfrac{1+g}{1+i}\right)^n\right]$
6.6	Present value of a growing perpetuity	$\text{PVP} = \dfrac{\text{CF}_1}{i - g}$
6.7	Effective annual interest rate	$\text{EAR} = \left(1 + \dfrac{\text{Quoted interest rate}}{m}\right)^m - 1$

Self-Study Problems

6.1 Kronka, Inc., is expecting cash inflows of \$13,000, \$11,500, \$12,750, and \$9,635 over the next four years. What is the present value of these cash flows if the appropriate discount rate is 8 percent?

6.2 Your grandfather has agreed to deposit a certain amount of money each year into an account paying 7.25 percent annually to help you go to graduate school. Starting next year, and for the following four years, he plans to deposit \$2,250, \$8,150, \$7,675, \$6,125, and \$12,345 into the account. How much will you have at the end of the five years?

6.3 Mike White is planning to save up for a trip to Europe in three years. He will need \$7,500 when he is ready to make the trip. He plans to invest the same amount at the end of each of the next three years in an account paying 6 percent. What is the amount that he will have to save every year to reach his goal of \$7,500 in three years?

6.4 Becky Scholes has \$150,000 to invest. She wants to be able to withdraw \$12,500 every year forever without using up any of her principal. What interest rate would her investment have to earn in order for her to be able to do so?

6.5 Dynamo Corp. is expecting annual payments of \$34,225 for the next seven years from a customer. What is the present value of this annuity if the discount rate is 8.5 percent?

Solutions to Self-Study Problems

6.1 The time line for Kronka's cash flows and their present value is as follows:

Year	0	1	2	3	4
Rate	8%				
Cash flow		\$13,000	\$11,500	\$12,750	\$9,635

$$\text{PV}_4 = \frac{\$13{,}000}{1.08} + \frac{\$11{,}500}{(1.08)^2} + \frac{\$12{,}750}{(1.08)^3} + \frac{\$9{,}635}{(1.08)^4}$$
$$= \$12{,}037.03 + \$9{,}859.40 + \$10{,}121.36 + \$7{,}082.01$$
$$= \$39{,}099.80$$

6.2 The time line for your cash flows and their future value is as follows:

Year	0	1	2	3	4	5
Rate	7.25%					
Cash flow		−\$2,250	−\$8,150	−\$7,675	−\$6,125	−\$12,345

$$\text{FV}_5 = [\$2{,}250 \times (1.0725)^4] + [\$8{,}150 \times (1.0725)^3] + [\$7{,}675 \times (1.0725)^2] + [\$6{,}125 \times 1.0725] + \$12{,}345$$
$$= \$2{,}976.95 + \$10{,}054.25 + \$8{,}828.22 + \$6{,}569.06 + \$12{,}345.00$$
$$= \$40{,}773.48$$

6.3 Amount Mike White will need in three years = FVA_3 = \$7,500

Number of years = $n = 3$

Interest rate on investment = $i = 6.0\%$

Amount that Mike needs to invest every year = PMT = ?

Year	0	1	2	3
Rate	6%			
Cash flow	CF = ?	CF = ?	CF = ?	FVA_3 = \$7,500

$$\text{FVA}_n = \text{CF} \times \frac{(1+i)^n - 1}{i}$$

$$\$7{,}500 = \text{CF} \times \frac{(1+0.06)^3 - 1}{0.06}$$

$$= \text{CF} \times 3.1836$$

$$\text{CF} = \frac{\$7{,}500}{3.1836}$$

$$= \$2{,}355.82$$

Mike will have to save $2,355.82 every year for the next three years.

6.4 Present value of Becky Scholes's investment = $150,000
Amount needed annually = $12,500
This is a perpetuity.

$$\text{PVP} = \frac{\text{CF}}{i}$$

$$i = \frac{\text{CF}}{\text{PVP}} = \frac{\$12{,}500}{\$150{,}000}$$

$$i = 8.33\%$$

6.5 The time line for Dynamo's cash flows and their present value is as follows:

0 (8.5%)	1	2	3	4	5	6	7	Year
PVA = ?	$34,225	$34,225	$34,225	$34,225	$34,225	$34,225	$34,225	

$$\text{PVA}_7 = \text{CF} \times \frac{1 - 1/(1+i)^n}{i}$$

$$= \$34{,}225 \times \frac{1 - 1/(1+0.085)^7}{0.085}$$

$$= \$34{,}225 \times 5.118514$$

$$= \$175{,}181.14$$

WileyPLUS

Questions and Problems, Solution Walkthrough Videos, Learning by Doing Tutorials, and additional study tools and resources are available in WileyPLUS.

Discussion Questions

6.1 Identify the steps involved in computing the future value when you have multiple cash flows.

6.2 What is the key economic principle involved in calculating the present value or future value of multiple cash flows?

6.3 What is the difference between a perpetuity and an annuity?

6.4 Define *annuity due.* Would an investment be worth more if it were an ordinary annuity or an annuity due? Explain.

6.5 Raymond Bartz is trying to choose between two equally risky annuities, each paying $5,000 per year for five years. One is an ordinary annuity, and the other is an annuity due. Which of the following statements is most correct?

a. The present value of the ordinary annuity must exceed the present value of the annuity due, but the future value of an ordinary annuity may be less than the future value of the annuity due.

b. The present value of the annuity due exceeds the present value of the ordinary annuity, while the future value of the annuity due is less than the future value of the ordinary annuity.

c. The present value of the annuity due exceeds the present value of the ordinary annuity, and the future value of the annuity due also exceeds the future value of the ordinary annuity.

d. If interest rates increase, the difference between the present value of the ordinary annuity and the present value of the annuity due remains the same.

6.6 Which of the following investments will have the highest future value at the end of three years? Assume that the effective annual rate for all investments is the same.

a. You earn $3,000 at the end of three years (a total of one payment).

b. You earn $1,000 at the end of every year for the next three years (a total of three payments).

c. You earn $1,000 at the beginning of every year for the next three years (a total of three payments).

6.7 Explain whether or not each of the following statements is correct.

a. A 15-year mortgage will have larger monthly payments than a 30-year mortgage of the same amount and same interest rate.

b. If an investment pays 10 percent interest compounded annually, its effective annual rate will also be 10 percent.

6.8 When will the annual percentage rate (APR) be the same as the effective annual rate (EAR)?

6.9 Why is the effective annual rate (EAR) superior to the annual percentage rate (APR) in measuring the true economic cost or return?

6.10 Suppose three investments have equal lives and multiple cash flows. A high discount rate tends to favor:

a. The investment with large cash flows early.

b. The investment with large cash flows late.

c. The investment with even cash flows.

d. None of the investments since they have equal lives.

Questions and Problems

Excel *Excel templates and resources available in* **WileyPLUS**

Basic

6.1 **Future value with multiple cash flows:** Konerko, Inc., management expects the company to earn cash flows of $13,227, $15,611, $18,970, and $19,114 over the next four years. If the company uses an 8 percent discount rate, what is the future value of these cash flows at the end of Year 4?

6.2 **Future value with multiple cash flows:** Ben Woolmer has an investment that will pay him the following cash flows over the next five years: $2,350, $2,725, $3,128, $3,366, and $3,695. If his investments typically earn 7.65 percent, what is the future value of the investment's cash flows at the end of five years?

6.3 **Future value with multiple cash flows:** You are a freshman in college and are planning a trip to Europe when you graduate from college at the end of four years. You plan to save the following amounts annually, starting today: $625, $700, $700, and $750. If you can earn 5.75 percent annually, how much will you have at the end of four years?

6.4 **Present value with multiple cash flows:** Saul Cervantes has just purchased some equipment for his landscaping business. For this equipment he must pay the following amounts at the end of each of the next five years: $10,450, $8,500, $9,675, $12,500, and $11,635. If the appropriate discount rate is 10.875 percent, what is the cost in today's dollars of the equipment Saul purchased today?

6.5 **Present value with multiple cash flows:** Jeremy Fenloch borrowed some money from his friend and promised to repay him $1,225, $1,350, $1,500, $1,600, and $1,600 over the next five years. If the friend normally discounts investment cash flows at 8 percent annually, how much did Jeremy borrow?

6.6 **Present value with multiple cash flows:** Biogenesis Inc. management expects the following cash flow stream over the next five years. They discount all cash flows using a 23 percent discount rate. What is the present value of this cash flow stream?

1	2	3	4	5 Year
−$1,133,676	−$978,452	$275,455	$878,326	$1,835,444

6.7 **Present value of an ordinary annuity:** An investment opportunity requires a payment of $750 for 12 years, starting a year from today. If your required rate of return is 8 percent, what is the value of the investment to you today?

6.8 **Present value of an ordinary annuity:** Dynamics Telecommunications Corp. has made an investment in another company that will guarantee it a cash flow of $22,500 each year for the next five years. If the company uses a discount rate of 15 percent on its investments, what is the present value of this investment?

6.9 **Future value of an ordinary annuity:** Robert Hobbes plans to invest $25,000 a year at the end of each year for the next seven years in an investment that will pay him a rate of return of 11.4 percent. How much money will Robert have at the end of seven years?

6.10 **Future value of an ordinary annuity:** Cecelia Thomas is a sales executive at a Baltimore firm. She is 25 years old and plans to invest $3,000 every year in an IRA account, beginning at the end of this year until she reaches age 65. If the IRA investment will earn 9.75 percent annually, how much will she have in 40 years, when she turns 65?

6.11 **Future value of an annuity due:** Refer to Problem 6.10. If Cecelia invests at the beginning of each year, how much will she have at age 65?

6.12 **Computing annuity payment:** Kevin Winthrop is saving for an Australian vacation in three years. He estimates that he will need $5,000 to cover his airfare and all other expenses for a week-long holiday in Australia. If he can invest his money in an S&P 500 equity index fund that is expected to earn an average annual return of 10.3 percent over the next three years, how much will he have to save every year if he starts saving at the end of this year?

6.13 **Computing annuity payment:** The Elkridge Bar & Grill has a seven-year loan of $23,500 with Bank of America. It plans to repay the loan in seven equal installments starting today. If the rate of interest is 8.4 percent, how much will each payment be?

6.14 **Perpetuity:** Your grandfather is retiring at the end of next year. He would like to ensure that his heirs receive payments of $10,000 a year forever, starting when he retires. If he can earn 6.5 percent annually, how much does your grandfather need to invest to produce the desired cash flow?

6.15 **Perpetuity:** Calculate the annual cash flows for each of the following investments:

a. $250,000 invested at 6 percent.

b. $50,000 invested at 12 percent.

c. $100,000 invested at 10 percent.

6.16 Effective annual interest rate: Marshall Chavez bought a Honda Civic for $17,345. He put down $6,000 and financed the rest through the dealer at an APR of 4.9 percent for four years. What is the effective annual interest rate (EAR) if the loan payments are made monthly?

6.17 Effective annual interest rate: Cyclone Rentals borrowed $15,550 from a bank for three years. If the quoted rate (APR) is 6.75 percent, and the compounding is daily, what is the effective annual interest rate (EAR)?

6.18 Growing perpetuity: You are evaluating a growing perpetuity investment from a large financial services firm. The investment promises an initial payment of $20,000 at the end of this year and subsequent payments that will grow at a rate of 3.4 percent annually. If you use a 9 percent discount rate for investments like this, what is the present value of this growing perpetuity?

Intermediate

6.19 Future value with multiple cash flows: Trigen Corp. management will invest $331,000, $616,450, $212,775, $818,400, $1,239,644, and $1,617,848 in research and development over the next six years. If the appropriate interest rate is 6.75 percent, what is the future value of these investments eight years from today?

6.20 Future value with multiple cash flows: Stephanie Watson is 20 years old and plans to make the following investments beginning next year. She will invest $3,125 in each of the next three years and will then make investments of $3,650, $3,725, $3,875, and $4,000 over the following four years. If the investments are expected to earn 11.5 percent annually, how much will Stephanie have when she turns 30?

6.21 Present value with multiple cash flows: Carol Jenkins, a lottery winner, will receive the following payments over the next seven years. She has been approached by an investor who will pay Carol a lump sum today for the rights to those future cash flows. If she can invest her cash flows in a fund that will earn 10.5 percent annually, how much should Carol require the investor to pay for the cash flows?

0	1	2	3	4	5	6	7 Year
	$200,000	$250,000	$275,000	$300,000	$350,000	$400,000	$550,000

6.22 Computing annuity payment: Gary Whitmore is a high school sophomore. He currently has $7,500 in a savings account that pays 5.65 percent annually. Gary plans to use his current savings plus what he can save over the next four years to buy a car. He estimates that the car will cost $12,000 in four years. How much money should Gary save each year if he wants to buy the car?

6.23 Growing annuity: Modern Energy Company owns several gas stations. Management is looking to open a new station in the western suburbs of Baltimore. One possibility that managers at the company are evaluating is to take over a station located at a site that has been leased from the county. The lease, originally for 99 years, currently has 73 years before expiration. The gas station generated a net cash flow of $92,500 last year, and the current owners expect an annual growth rate of 6.3 percent. If Modern Energy uses a discount rate of 14.5 percent to evaluate such businesses, what is the present value of this growing annuity?

6.24 Future value of annuity due: Jeremy Denham plans to save $5,000 every year for the next eight years, starting today. At the end of eight years, Jeremy will turn 30 years old and plans to use his savings toward the down payment on a house. If his investment in a mutual fund will earn him 10.3 percent annually, how much will he have saved in eight years when he buys his house?

6.25 Present value of an annuity due: Grant Productions borrowed some money from the California Finance Company at a rate of 17.5 percent for a seven-year period. The loan calls for a payment of $1,540,862.19 each year beginning today. How much did Grant borrow?

6.26 Present value of an annuity due: Sharon Kabana has won a state lottery and will receive a payment of $89,729.45 every year, starting today, for the next 20 years. If she invests the proceeds at a rate of 7.25 percent, what is the present value of the cash flows that she will receive? Round to the nearest dollar.

6.27 Present value of an annuity due: You wrote a piece of software that does a better job of allowing computers to network than any other program designed for this purpose. A large networking company wants to incorporate your software into its systems and is offering to pay you $500,000 today, plus $500,000 at the end of each of the following six years, for permission to do this. If the appropriate interest rate is 6 percent, what is the present value of the cash flow stream that the company is offering you?

6.28 Present value of an annuity: Suppose that the networking company in Problem 6.27 will not start paying you until the first of the new systems that uses your software is sold in two years. What is the present value of that annuity? Assume that the appropriate interest rate is still 6 percent.

6.29 Perpetuity: Calculate the present value of the following perpetuities:

a. $1,250 discounted to the present at 7 percent.

b. $7,250 discounted to the present at 6.33 percent.

c. $850 discounted to the present at 20 percent.

6.30 Effective annual interest rate: Find the effective annual interest rate (EAR) for each of the following:

a. 6 percent compounded quarterly.
b. 4.99 percent compounded monthly.
c. 7.25 percent compounded semiannually.
d. 5.6 percent compounded daily.

6.31 Effective annual interest rate: Which of the following investments has the highest effective annual interest rate (EAR)?

a. A bank CD that pays 8.25 percent compounded quarterly.
b. A bank CD that pays 8.25 percent compounded monthly.
c. A bank CD that pays 8.45 percent compounded annually.
d. A bank CD that pays 8.25 percent compounded semiannually.
e. A bank CD that pays 8 percent compounded daily (on a 365-day per year basis).

6.32 Effective annual interest rate: You are considering three alternative investments: (1) a three-year bank CD paying 7.5 percent compounded quarterly; (2) a three-year bank CD paying 7.3 percent compounded monthly; and (3) a three-year bank CD paying 7.75 percent compounded annually. Which investment has the highest effective annual interest rate (EAR)?

Advanced

6.33 You have been offered the opportunity to invest in a project that is expected to provide you with the following cash flows: $4,000 in one year, $12,000 in two years, and $8,000 in three years. If the appropriate interest rates are 6 percent for the first year, 8 percent for the second year, and 12 percent for the third year, what is the present value of these cash flows?

6.34 Tirade Owens, a professional athlete, currently has a contract that will pay him a large amount in the first year of his contract and smaller amounts thereafter. He and his agent have asked the team to restructure the contract. The team, though reluctant, obliged. Tirade and his agent came up with a counteroffer. What are the present values of each of the three alternatives below using a 14 percent discount rate? Which of the three has the highest present value?

Year	Current Contract	Team's Offer	Counteroffer
1	$8,125,000	$4,000,000	$5,250,000
2	$3,650,000	$3,825,000	$7,550,000
3	$2,715,000	$3,850,000	$3,625,000
4	$1,822,250	$3,925,000	$2,800,000

6.35 Gary Kornig is 30 years old and wants to retire when he is 65. So far he has saved (1) $6,950 in an IRA account in which his money is earning 8.3 percent annually and (2) $5,000 in a money market account in which he is earning 5.25 percent annually. Gary wants to have $1 million when he retires. Starting next year, he plans to invest the same amount of money every year until he retires in a mutual fund in which he expects to earn 9 percent annually. How much will Gary have to invest every year to achieve his savings goal?

6.36 The top prize for the state lottery is $100,000,000. You have decided it is time for you to take a chance and purchase a ticket. Before you purchase the ticket, you must decide whether to choose the cash option or the annual payment option. If you choose the annual payment option and win, you will receive $100,000,000 in 25 equal payments of $4,000,000—one payment today and one payment at the end of each of the next 24 years. If you choose the cash payment, you will receive a one-time lump sum payment of $59,194,567.18. If you can invest the proceeds and earn 6 percent, which option should you choose?

6.37 At what interest rate would you be indifferent between the cash and annual payment options in Problem 6.36?

6.38 Babu Baradwaj is saving for his son's college tuition. His son is currently 11 years old and will begin college in seven years. Babu has an index fund investment worth $7,500 that is earning 9.5 percent annually. Total expenses at the University of Maryland, where his son says he plans to go, currently total $15,000 per year but are expected to grow at roughly 6 percent each year. Babu plans to invest in a mutual fund that will earn 11 percent annually to make up the difference between the college expenses and his current savings. In total, Babu will make seven equal investments with the first starting today and the last being made a year before his son begins college.

a. What will be the present value of the four years of college expenses at the time that Babu's son starts college? Assume a discount rate of 5.5 percent.

b. What will the value of the index mutual fund be when his son just starts college?

c. What is the amount that Babu will have to have saved when his son turns 18 if Babu plans to cover all of his son's college expenses?

d. How much will Babu have to invest every year in order to have enough funds to cover all his son's expenses?

6.39 You are now 50 years old and plan to retire at age 65. You currently have a stock portfolio worth $150,000, a 401(k) retirement plan worth $250,000, and a money market account worth $50,000. Your stock portfolio is expected to provide annual returns of 12 percent, your 401(k) investment will earn 9.5 percent annually, and the money market account earns 5.25 percent, compounded monthly.

a. If you do not save another penny, what will be the total value of your investments when you retire at age 65?

b. Assume you plan to invest $12,000 every year in your 401(k) plan for the next 15 years (starting one year from now). How much will your investments be worth when you retire at age 65?

c. Assume that you expect to live 25 years after you retire (until age 90). Today, at age 50, you take all of your investments and place them in an account that pays 8 percent (use the scenario from part b in which you continue saving). If you start withdrawing funds starting at age 66, how much can you withdraw every year (e.g., an ordinary annuity) and leave nothing in your account after a 25th and final withdrawal at age 90?

d. You want your current investments, which are described in the problem statement, to support a perpetuity that starts a year from now. How much can you withdraw each year without touching your principal?

6.40 Trevor Diaz wants to purchase a Maserati Quattroporte sedan, which has an invoice price of $121,737 and a total cost of $129,482. Trevor plans to put down $20,000 and will pay the rest by taking on a 5.75 percent five-year bank loan. What is the monthly payment on this auto loan? Prepare an amortization table using Excel.

6.41 The Yan family is buying a new 3,500-square-foot house in Muncie, Indiana, and will borrow $237,000 from Bank One at a rate of 6.375 percent for 15 years. What will be their monthly loan payment? Prepare an amortization schedule using Excel.

6.42 Assume you will start working as soon as you graduate from college. You plan to start saving for your retirement on your 25th birthday and retire on your 65th birthday. After retirement, you expect to live at least until you are 85. You wish to be able to withdraw $40,000 (in today's dollars) every year from the time of your retirement until you are 85 years old (i.e., for 20 years). The average inflation rate is likely to be 5 percent.

a. Calculate the lump sum you need to have accumulated at age 65 to be able to draw the desired income. Assume that the annual return on your investments is likely to be 10 percent.

b. What is the dollar amount you need to invest every year, starting at age 26 and ending at age 65 (i.e., for 40 years), to reach the target lump sum at age 65?

c. Now answer questions **a.** and **b.** assuming the rate of return to be 8 percent per year, then again at 15 percent per year.

d. Now assume you start investing for your retirement when you turn 30 years old and analyze the situation under rate of return assumptions of (i) 8 percent, (ii) 10 percent, and (iii) 15 percent.

e. Repeat the analysis by assuming that you start investing when you are 35 years old.

Sample Test Problems

6.1 Freisinger, Inc., management is expecting a new project to start paying off, beginning at the end of next year. Cash flows are expected to be as follows:

0	7.8%	1	2	3	4	5 Year
		$433,676	$478,452	$475,455	$478,326	$535,444

If Freisinger can reinvest these cash flows to earn a return of 7.8 percent, what is the future value of this cash flow stream at the end of five years? What is its present value?

6.2 Compare an annuity due with an ordinary annuity. The payments for both are made annually and are of the same dollar amounts. The two annuities also have the same duration in years and the same discount rate. Which of the following statements is/are correct?

a. The present value of the ordinary annuity is greater.
b. The present value of the annuity due is greater.
c. The future value of the ordinary annuity is greater.
d. The future value of the annuity due is greater.

6.3 You plan to set up an endowment at your alma mater that will fund $200,000 of scholarships each year indefinitely. If the principal (the amount you donate) can be invested at 5.5 percent, compounded annually, how much do you need to donate to the university today, so that the first scholarships can be awarded beginning one year from now?

6.4 Annalise Genric wants to open a restaurant in a historic building. The property can be leased for 20 years but not purchased. She believes her restaurant can generate a net cash flow of $76,000 the first year and expects an annual growth rate of 4 percent thereafter. If a discount rate of 15 percent is used to evaluate this business, what is the present value of the cash flows that it will generate?

6.5 A credit card offers financing at an APR of 18 percent, with monthly compounding on outstanding charges. What is the effective annual rate (EAR)?

6.6 Thomas Nguyen currently has $10,000 in the bank earning interest of 6 percent per year, compounded monthly. If he needs $25,000 to purchase a car and can save an additional $100 a month stating at the end of this month, how long will it take him to accumulate the $25,000?

Appendix: Deriving the Formula for the Present Value of an Ordinary Annuity

In this chapter we showed that the formula for a perpetuity can be obtained from the formula for the present value of an ordinary annuity if n is set equal to ∞. It is also possible to go the other way. In other words, the present value of an ordinary annuity formula can be derived from the formula for a perpetuity. In fact, this is how the annuity formula was originally obtained. To see how this was done, assume that someone has offered to pay you $1 per year forever, beginning next year, but that, in return, you will have to pay that person $1 per year forever, beginning in year $n + 1$.

The cash flows you will receive and the cash flows you will pay are represented in the following time line:

	0	1	2	3		n-1	n	n+1	n+2	Year
Receive		$1	$1	$1		$1	$1	$1	$1	→ ∞
Pay		$0	$0	$0		$0	$0	$1	$1	→ ∞

The first row of dollar values shows the cash flows for the perpetuity that you will receive. This perpetuity is worth:

$$\text{PVP}_{Receive} = \frac{\$1}{i} = \frac{\text{CF}}{i}$$

The second row shows the cash flows for the perpetuity that you will pay. The present value of what you owe is the value of a $1 perpetuity that is discounted for n years.

$$\text{PVP}_{Pay} = \frac{\$1/i}{(1 + i)^n} = \frac{\text{CF}/i}{(1 + i)^n}$$

Notice that if you subtract, year by year, the cash flows you would pay from the cash flows you would receive, you get the cash flows for an n-year annuity.

	0	1	2	3		n-1	n	n+1	n+2	Year
Difference		$1	$1	$1		$1	$1	$0	$0	→ ∞

Therefore, the value of the offer equals the value of an n-year annuity. Solving for the difference between $PVP_{Receive}$ and PVP_{Pay} we see that this is the same as Equation 6.1.

$$
\begin{aligned}
PVA_n &= PVP_{Receive} - PVP_{Pay} \\
&= \frac{CF}{i} - \frac{CF/i}{(1+i)^n} \\
&= \frac{CF}{i} \times \left[1 - \frac{1}{(1+i)^n}\right]
\end{aligned}
$$

Problem

6A.1 In the chapter text, you saw that the formula for a growing perpetuity can be obtained from the formula for the present value of a growing annuity if n is set equal to ∞. It is also possible to go the other way. In other words, the present value of a growing annuity formula can be derived from the formula for a growing perpetuity. In fact, this is how Equation 6.5 was actually derived. Show how Equation 6.5 can be derived from Equation 6.6.

Ethics Case

America's Ailing Drug Prices

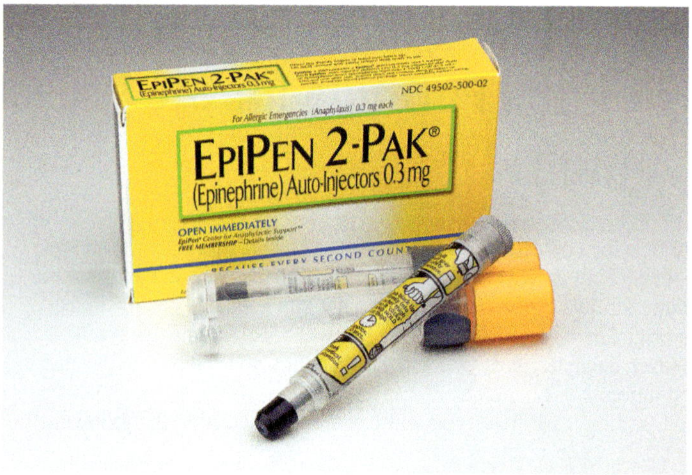

Roel Smart/Getty Images

In September 2016, Mylan CEO Heather Bresch appeared before the U.S. House Oversight Committee to address the controversial issue of rising prescription drug prices. Mylan was in the spotlight because of a dramatic 600 percent increase in the price of the EpiPen, a steroidal injector that treats severe and sometimes deadly allergic reactions. The rise in the cost of EpiPens was stunning. Priced at \$100 for a two-pack in 2009, the same medication sold for over \$600 by the fall of 2016. Members of the House of Representatives expressed their outrage over the surge in pricing for this important drug. Representative Elijah Cummings, from Maryland, accused the pharmaceutical maker of raising EpiPen prices "to get filthy rich at the expense of our constituents." Mylan CEO Bresch countered this criticism claiming that the price increases were necessary to ensure that Mylan could continue to invest in the research and development (R&D) necessary for new drug discovery, as well as improvements to existing products including the EpiPen.

The price increase for the EpiPen is hardly unusual in the U.S. drug market. Most drug makers added significant markups to the retail price of their compounds over the same time period. For example, AbbVie Inc. raised the price of the arthritis drug Humira more than 126 percent from 2011 to 2015, while Teva Pharmaceutical Industries Ltd. increased the price for its multiple sclerosis drug Copaxone by 118 percent over the same period. Data from National Health Statistics Group, summarized in the accompanying figure, illustrate that overall U.S. retail expenditures on prescription drugs grew steadily over the last 15 years. Between 2014 and 2015 prices increased 9.0 percent, to a total of \$324.6 billion.[1]

Boosting the Bottom Line at Patients' Expense?

To be sure, price increases are an important way for drug company executives to increase profits and benefit their stockholders. Like most manufacturers, pharma giant Pfizer Inc. routinely raises prices for a large proportion of its offerings, including more than 133 of its products in 2015. Similarly, Merck & Co. raised its list prices by an average of 9.6 percent in 2016. In some cases, increases for just a single prescription can give a major boost to a company's bottom line. For example, Pfizer increased the price of its popular painkiller Lyrica by 51.7 percent over a three-year period. Analyst projections suggest that Lyrica will generate close to \$5 billion in annual sales for Pfizer through 2019.[2]

While the increasing cost of medications certainly hit patient's pocketbooks, the consequences can be dire when sharp price increases impact lifesaving drugs. In one high-profile 2015 case, Turing Pharmaceuticals, headed by then CEO Martin Shkreli,

[1]Centers for Medicare & Medicaid Services, Office of the Actuary, National Health Statistics Group.

[2]https://www.bloomberg.com/news/articles/2015-10-02/pfizer-raised-prices-on-133-drugs-this-year-and-it-s-not-alone.

acquired the drug Daraprim, a 62-year-old medicine used to treat a parasitic infection that can cause brain damage and death in infants and people with AIDS. Following the acquisition, Turing raised the price of Daraprim overnight from $13.50 to $750 a pill—a 5,000 percent increase! When asked by investors about the impact of the decision on the company's profits, Shkreli cynically wrote, "I think it will be huge. . . . So 5,000 paying bottles at the new price is $375,000,000—almost all of it is profit, and I think we will get three years of that or more. Should be a very handsome investment for all of us." While not illegal, the price increase prompted public outrage and Shkreli was subpoenaed to appear before the U.S. House Oversight Committee to answer questions about the move. While Shkreli resigned as the CEO of Turing later in the year, the company continues to resist numerous calls to reduce the cost of the medication.

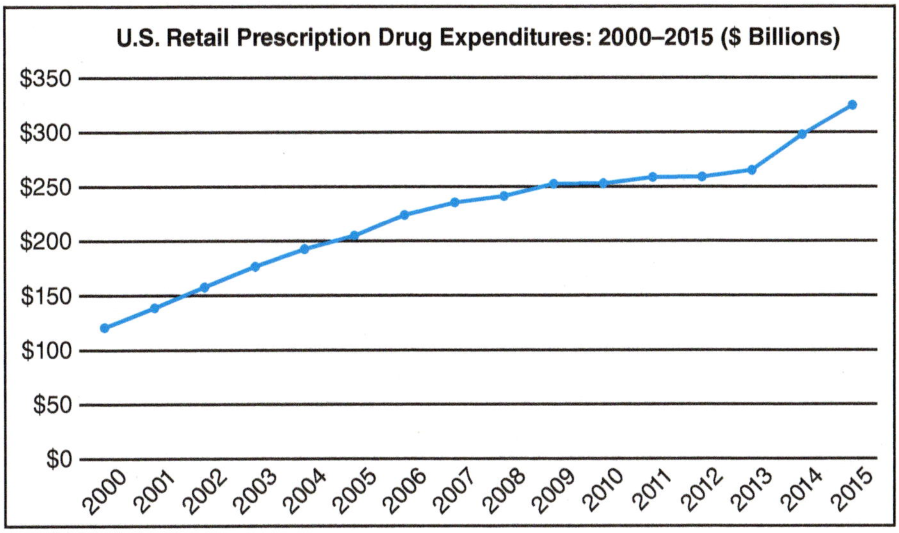

While the price increases associated with Daraprim are extreme, there is little doubt that the widespread increase in prescription drug prices is making health care increasingly unaffordable in the United States. Indeed, some health care advocates are now arguing that price increases actually translate into poorer health outcomes and dangerous medical conditions because some patients can no longer afford to take drugs at their prescribed dosage.[3]

The High Cost of Drug Development

Bringing a new drug to market typically involves many years of very costly research, development, and testing by the pharmaceutical maker. Once a new drug is discovered and developed for human use, its safety and efficacy are evaluated by the U.S. Food and Drug Administration (FDA). As part of its evaluation, the FDA assesses the outcomes of three stages of clinical trials involving clinical researchers, doctors, and thousands of patients over several years. This process of discovery and testing can be very expensive with researchers estimating that the average R&D cost of developing a new FDA-approved medication was $2.6 billion (in 2013 dollars) over the last decade.[4] Given these costs, it is little wonder that most pharmaceutical companies make enormous investments in R&D every year. Pfizer, for example, expensed over $7.5 billion in R&D in 2015 alone!

Drug development and testing are also exceedingly time consuming and risky. On average, it takes a successful experimental drug 15 years to go from lab to patient.[5] Unfortunately, the vast majority of drugs that are developed actually fail to ever receive FDA approval for use. In a recent industry study of clinical trials between 2006 and 2015, only 9.6 percent of all developmental drugs successfully made it through even the first stage of clinical trials. Of those that succeeded in the first phase, only 30.7 percent ended up making it through the second set of clinical trials.[6]

Given this very high development expense, the FDA grants a period of market exclusivity from 5 to 12 years when a new patented drug is approved for patient use. During the exclusivity period, no competing low-cost or generic version of the drug can be sold in the U.S. market. While exclusivity gives the company a veritable monopoly on the marketing and pricing of the drug, executives and regulators agree that it provides pharmaceutical companies with a critical economic incentive to develop new drugs. This incentive is important for the stockholders of drug companies because they have to finance R&D expenses and they bear the costs associated with the duration and risk of drug development.

Innovation or Gaming the System

While market exclusivity provides pharmaceutical companies with an important economic incentive to develop new drugs and improve existing medications, many of these same companies attempt to game the exclusivity rules through maneuvers commonly known as "hard switching" and "evergreening."

Hard switching happens when a manufacturer discontinues the sale of a drug immediately before the end of its exclusivity period and replaces the drug with a new, market-exclusive compound. In many cases patients are prescribed the new medication before the lower-cost generic medication hits the market. If patients are unaware and never informed of the availability of generic versions of the older drug, they will continue to use the more expensive brand-name medication.

Evergreening occurs when a pharmaceutical company makes small changes to a drug before the end of its exclusivity period in an effort to gain a new patent and a new exclusivity period. Typically these changes involve modifications to a medication's dosage or form of release. Drug makers claim that the alterations improve the efficacy of the medication and typically promote the new higher-priced product as superior to the older version. Critics of evergreening, however, argue that the majority of these changes are trivial and yield only minor benefits for patients, while allowing pharmaceutical makers to continue to charge exorbitant prices for equivalent drugs.

[3] http://www.cbsnews.com/news/whats-behind-the-sharp-rise-in-prescription-drug-prices/.

[4] Pharmaceutical Research and Manufacturers of America (PhRMA) estimates based on Tufts Center for the Study of Drug Development (CSDD) Briefing: "Cost of Developing a New Drug," November 2014. Tufts CSDD and School of Medicine. http://www.phrma.org/advocacy/research-development/clinical-trials.

[5] J.A. DiMasi, H.G. Grabowski and R.A. Hansen, "Innovation in the Pharmaceutical Industry: New Estimates of R&D Costs," *Journal of Health Economics*, 47, 2016, 20–33.

[6] Clinical Development Success Rates 2006–2015 BIO, Biomedtracker, Amplion 2016. https://www.bio.org/sites/default/files/Clinicalpercent20Development percent20Successpercent20Ratespercent202006-2015percent20-percent 20BIO,percent20Biomedtracker,percent20Amplionpercent202016.pdf

Can Consumers Fight Back Against High Drug Prices?

Like any product, drug prices are determined by supply and demand. While consumers may have a number of alternative options when they purchase a car or a gallon of milk in the grocery store, patients typically face far fewer options when they purchase medications as an individual or through one of many forms of medical insurance.

There are often many drugs to choose from when treating common conditions. For example, a "statin" lowers cholesterol in the body and is one of the most commonly prescribed medicines in the United States today. Given the high demand for the product, many pharmaceutical companies have developed their own branded statin including Pfizer (Lipitor), Astra Zeneca (Crestor), and Merck (Zocor), and there is a variety of very low-cost generic versions of these drugs available on the market today.

On the other end of the spectrum, exclusivity rules and a lack of viable alternative medications can severely limit a patient's options. In the most extreme cases, patients with rare conditions must rely on pharmaceutical companies to develop so-called "orphan" drugs. Under the 1983 Orphan Drug Act (ODA), drug companies producing orphan treatments expected to be used by 200,000 patients or less can qualify for additional exclusivity, special tax treatment, and R&D grants to incentivize research for these relatively small populations. Once a treatment is developed, however, the lack of competition can leave patients vulnerable to price increases. For example, in 2015 Valeant Pharmaceuticals raised the price of Cuprimine, a drug to treat an extremely rare malady known as Wilson's disease, by 400 percent to $26,189 for the annual treatment.

To many it seems that consumers are at a distinct disadvantage in the prescription drug market. In many other countries, however, drug prices are negotiated by government health programs that have effectively curbed the increases observed in the U.S. market. Since the government programs are the only large buyers, they can drive hard bargains with manufacturers and the savings for consumers can be huge. For example, a recent report by CNN noted that the monthly prescription price for the common acid reflex drug Nexium costs $215 in the United States but just $23 per month in the Netherlands.[7] These low prices have driven many U.S. consumers to try to fill their prescriptions outside of the United States, typically in Canada and Mexico, although U.S. law prohibits pharmacies and people with prescriptions from filling their orders over the border.

For the majority of Americans, drug prices are negotiated indirectly through their insurers that have a limited ability to constrain surging prices. The Medicare and Medicaid programs are the largest insurers of patients in the United States, covering more than 125 million people. Federal law, however, prohibits the U.S. Centers for Medicare and Medicaid from negotiating drug prices with the pharmaceutical companies.

Private insurers have some options available to reduce excessive drug pricing. One tool at their disposal is the requirement that a patient receive prior authorization from the insurer before receiving coverage for a given prescription. While prior authorization can cause some drug makers to think twice about exorbitant charges, the practice is under fire by state attorneys general who contend that the threat of nonauthorization for expensive drugs is inconsistent with an insurer's obligation to cover the medical needs of the insured.

Insurers also rely on drug formularies and tiered co-payments by patients for medications to moderate pharmaceutical costs. Drug formularies are the lists of drugs that a health insurer agrees to pay for, at least partially, for a given medical condition. In setting the formulary, health experts try to provide access to effective but low-cost drugs. In many cases this means providing access to generic rather than brand-name drugs for the same indication. Higher patient co-payments reduce drug affordability for consumers, reducing the demand for certain drugs. The effect of co-payments on demand, however, is limited by state laws that cap out-of-pocket expenses by the insured.

Discussion Questions

1. Is it ethical for pharmaceutical companies to charge high prices for certain drugs—even if the drugs are required to sustain lives?
2. What would be the potential benefits and consequences of allowing the Medicare and Medicaid programs to directly negotiate drug prices?
3. Many have called for the FDA to lower its review standard for the approval of prescription drugs and speed up the clinical trial process. How do you think these changes will affect the stock prices of pharmaceutical companies? How do you think these changes will affect patients?

[7]http://www.cnn.com/2015/09/28/health/us-pays-more-for-drugs.

CHAPTER 7

Risk and Return

Carlos Osorio/Toronto Star/Getty Images

LEARNING OBJECTIVES

1. Explain the relation between risk and return.
2. Describe the two components of a total holding period return, and calculate this return for an asset.
3. Explain what an expected return is and calculate the expected return for an asset.
4. Explain what the standard deviation of returns is and why it is very useful in finance, and calculate it for an asset.
5. Explain what an arithmetic average return is and what a geometric return is, and calculate these returns for an asset.
6. Explain the concept of diversification.
7. Discuss which type of risk matters to investors and why.
8. Describe what the Capital Asset Pricing Model (CAPM) tells us and how to use it to evaluate whether the expected return of an asset is sufficient to compensate an investor for the risks associated with that asset.

The Sears department store chain had a rough time from 2012 to 2016. Its revenues declined from \$41.57 billion to \$25.10 billion, and the company's operating income, excluding unusual items, fell from −\$0.65 billion to −\$1.36 billion. Sears's managers did not stand still over this period. They worked very hard to restructure the company in an effort to turn it around and make it the growing and profitable business that it had once been. Unfortunately, these efforts did not appear to be working by early 2017. The company was shrinking; its total assets had dropped from \$21.38 billion in 2012 to \$11.61 billion by the beginning of February 2017. During the five years leading up to February 1, 2017, Sears's stock price fell from \$52.58 to \$6.96.

The challenges faced by Sears were not affecting everyone in its industry equally. For example, Wal-Mart's sales grew from \$446.95 billion in 2012 to \$482.13 billion in 2016. While Wal-Mart's operating income did decline modestly during this period, from \$26.55 billion to \$24.11 billion, the company remained quite profitable, and its assets increased from \$193.41 billion to \$199.58 billion. During the five years leading up to February 1, 2017, Wal-Mart's stock price rose from \$59.08 to \$68.02.

This chapter discusses risk, return, and the relation between them. The difference in the returns earned by Sears and Wal-Mart stockholders from February 2012 to February 2017 illustrates a challenge faced by all investors. The shares of both of these companies were viewed as risky investments in 2012 and yet someone who invested in Sears stock on February 1, 2012, lost 86.8 percent ((\$6.96 − \$52.58)/\$52.58 = −0.868, or 86.8 percent) of that investment over the following five years, while an investor who bought Wal-Mart stock earned 15.1 percent ((\$68.02 − \$59.08)/\$59.08 = 0.151, or 15.1 percent). How should investors have viewed the risks of investing in shares of these companies in 2012? How is risk related to the returns that investors might expect to earn? How does diversification reduce the overall risk of an investor's portfolio? These questions are among the topics that we discuss in this chapter.

Chapter Preview

Up to this point, we have often mentioned the rate of return that we use to discount cash flows, but we have not explained how that rate is determined. We have now reached the point where it is time to examine key concepts underlying the discount rate. This chapter introduces a quantitative framework for measuring risk and return. This framework will help you develop an intuitive understanding of how risk and return are related and what risks matter to investors. The relation between risk and return has implications for the rate we use to discount cash flows because the time value of money concepts that we discussed in Chapters 5 and 6 are directly related to the returns that investors require. We must understand these concepts in order to determine the correct present value for a series of cash flows and to be able to make investment decisions that create value for stockholders.

We begin this chapter with a discussion of the general relation between risk and return to introduce the idea that investors require a higher rate of return from riskier assets. This is one of the most fundamental relations in finance. We next develop the statistical concepts required to quantify holding period returns, expected returns, and risk. We then apply these concepts to portfolios with a single asset and with more than one asset to illustrate the benefit of diversification. From this discussion, you will see how investing in more than one asset enables an investor to reduce the total risk associated with his or her investment portfolio, and you will learn how to quantify this benefit.

Once we have discussed the concept of diversification, we examine what it means for the relation between risk and return. We find that the total risk associated with an investment consists of two components: (1) unsystematic risk and (2) systematic risk. Diversification enables investors to eliminate the unsystematic risk associated with an individual asset. Investors do not require higher returns for the unsystematic risk that they can eliminate through diversification. Only systematic risk—risk that cannot be diversified away—affects expected returns on an investment. The distinction between unsystematic and systematic risk and the recognition that unsystematic risk can be diversified away are extremely important in finance. After reading this chapter, you will understand precisely what the term risk means in finance and how it is related to the rates of return that investors require.

7.1 Risk and Return

LEARNING OBJECTIVE

1. Explain the relation between risk and return.

The rate of return that investors require for an investment depends on the risk associated with that investment. The greater the risk, the larger the return investors require as compensation for bearing that risk. This is one of the most fundamental relations in finance. The *rate of return* is what you earn on an investment, stated in percentage terms. We will be more specific later, but for now you might think of *risk* as a measure of how certain you are that you will receive a particular return. Higher risk means you are less certain.

To get a better understanding of how risk and return are related, consider an example. You are trying to select the best investment from among the following three stocks:

Stock	Expected Return (%)	Risk Level (%)
A	12	12
B	12	16
C	16	16

Which would you choose? If you were comparing only Stocks A and B, you should choose Stock A. Both stocks have the same expected return, but Stock A has less risk. It does not make sense to invest in the riskier stock if the expected return is the same. Similarly, you can see that Stock C is clearly superior to Stock B. Stocks B and C have the same level of risk, but Stock C has a higher expected return. It would not make sense to accept a lower return for taking on the same level of risk.

But what about the choice between Stocks A and C? This choice is less obvious. Making it requires understanding the concepts that we discuss in the rest of this chapter.

Building Intuition

More Risk Means a Higher Expected Return

The greater the risk associated with an investment, the greater the return investors expect from it. A corollary to this idea is that investors want the highest return for a given level of risk or the lowest risk for a given level of return. When choosing between two investments that have the same level of risk, investors prefer the investment with the higher return. Alternatively, if two investments have the same expected return, investors prefer the less risky alternative.

7.2 Quantitative Measures of Return

LEARNING OBJECTIVE

2. Describe the two components of a total holding period return, and calculate this return for an asset.

Before we begin a detailed discussion of the relation between risk and return, we should define more precisely what these terms mean. We begin with measures of return.

Holding Period Returns

When people refer to the return from an investment, they are generally referring to the total return over some *investment period*, or *holding period*. The **total holding period return** consists of two components: (1) capital appreciation and (2) income. The capital appreciation component of a return, R_{CA}, arises from a change in the price of the asset over the investment or holding period and is calculated as follows:

total holding period return the total return on an asset over a specific period of time or holding period

$$R_{CA} = \frac{\text{Capital appreciation}}{\text{Initial price}} = \frac{P_1 - P_0}{P_0} = \frac{\Delta P}{P_0}$$

where P_0 is the price paid for the asset at time zero and P_1 is the price at a later point in time.

The income component of a return arises from income that an investor receives from the asset while he or she owns it. For example, when a firm pays a cash dividend on its stock, the income component of the return on that stock, R_I, is calculated as follows:

$$R_I = \frac{\text{Cash flow}}{\text{Initial price}} = \frac{CF_1}{P_0}$$

where CF_1 is the cash flow from the dividend.

LEARNING BY DOING

WileyPLUS

Need more help? Visit your WileyPLUS course.

APPLICATION 7.1 | Calculating the Return on an Investment

Problem You purchased a beat-up 1974 Datsun 240Z sports car a year ago for $1,500. Datsun is what Nissan, the Japanese car company, was called in the 1970s. The 240Z was the first in a series of cars that led to the Nissan 370Z that is being sold today. Recognizing that a mint-condition 240Z is a much sought-after car, you invested $7,000 and a lot of your time fixing up the car. Last week, you sold it to a collector for $18,000. Not counting the value of the time you spent restoring the car, what is the total return you earned on this investment over the one-year holding period?

Approach Use Equation 7.1 to calculate the total holding period return. To calculate R_T using Equation 7.1, you must know P_0, P_1, and CF_1. In this problem, you can assume that the $7,000 was spent at the time you bought the car to purchase parts and materials. Therefore, your initial investment, P_0, was $1,500 + $7,000 = $8,500. Since there were no other cash inflows or outflows between the time that you bought the car and the time that you sold it, CF_1 equals $0.

Solution The total holding period return is:

$$R_T = R_{CA} + R_I = \frac{P_1 - P_0 + CF_1}{P_0} = \frac{\$18{,}000 - \$8{,}500 + \$0}{\$8{,}500} = 1.118, \text{ or } 111.8\%$$

Weblink

You can download actual realized investment returns for a large number of stock market indexes at the Callan Associates Web site, http://www.callan.com/research/periodic/.

The total holding period return, R_T, is simply the sum of the capital appreciation and income components of return:

$$R_T = R_{CA} + R_I = \frac{\Delta P}{P_0} + \frac{CF_1}{P_0} = \frac{\Delta P + CF_1}{P_0} \tag{7.1}$$

Let's consider an example of calculating the total holding period return on an investment. One year ago today, you purchased a share of Twitter, Inc., stock for $16.06. Today it is worth $19.00. What total return did you earn on this stock over the past year if Twitter paid no dividend?

Since Twitter paid no dividend, and assuming you received no other income from holding the stock, the total return for the year equals the return from the capital appreciation. The total return is calculated as follows:

$$\begin{aligned} R_T = R_{CA} + R_I &= \frac{P_1 - P_0 + CF_1}{P_0} \\ &= \frac{\$19.00 - \$16.06 + \$0.00}{\$16.06} \\ &= 0.183, \text{ or } 18.3\% \end{aligned}$$

What return would you have earned if Twitter had paid a $1 dividend and today's price was $18.00? With the $1 dividend and a correspondingly lower price, the total return is the same:

$$R_T = R_{CA} + R_I = \frac{P_1 - P_0 + CF_1}{P_0} = \frac{\$18.00 - \$16.06 + \$1.00}{\$16.06} = 0.183, \text{ or } 18.3\%$$

You can see from this example that a dollar of capital appreciation is worth the same as a dollar of income.

Learning by Doing Application 7.1 illustrates another holding period return calculation.

Expected Returns

LEARNING OBJECTIVE

3. Explain what an expected return is and calculate the expected return for an asset.

Suppose that you are a senior who plays college baseball and that your team is in the College World Series. Furthermore, suppose that you have been drafted by the Washington Nationals and are coming up for what you expect to be your last at-bat as a college player. The fact that you expect this to be your last at-bat is important because you just signed a very unusual contract with the Nationals. Your signing bonus will be determined solely by whether you get a hit in your final collegiate at-bat. If you get a hit, then your signing bonus will be \$800,000. Otherwise, it will be \$400,000. This past season, you got a hit 32.5 percent of the times you were at bat (you did not get a hit 67.5 percent of the time), and you believe this percentage reflects the likelihood that you will get a hit in your last collegiate at-bat.[1]

What is the expected value of your bonus? If you have taken a statistics course, you might recall that an expected value represents the sum of the products of the possible outcomes and the probabilities that those outcomes will be realized. In our example the expected value of the bonus can be calculated using the following formula:

$$\text{E(Bonus)} = (p_{\text{H}} \times \text{B}_{\text{H}}) + (p_{\text{NH}} \times \text{B}_{\text{NH}})$$

where E(Bonus) is your expected bonus, p_{H} is the probability of a hit, p_{NH} is the probability of no hit, B_{H} is the bonus you receive if you get a hit, and B_{NH} is the bonus you receive if you get no hit. Since p_{H} equals 0.325, p_{NH} equals 0.675, B_{H} equals \$800,000, and B_{NH} equals \$400,000, the expected value of your bonus is:

$$\begin{aligned}\text{E(Bonus)} &= (p_{\text{H}} \times \text{B}_{\text{H}}) + (p_{\text{NH}} \times \text{B}_{\text{NH}}) \\ &= (0.325 \times \$800{,}000) + (0.675 \times \$400{,}000) = \$530{,}000\end{aligned}$$

Notice that the expected bonus of \$530,000 is not equal to either of the two possible payoffs. Neither is it equal to the simple average of the two possible payoffs. This is because the expected bonus takes into account the probability of each event occurring. If the probability of each event had been 50 percent, then the expected bonus would have equaled the simple average of the two payoffs:

$$\text{E(Bonus)} = (0.5 \times \$800{,}000) + (0.5 \times \$400{,}000) = \$600{,}000$$

However, since it is more likely that you will not get a hit (a 67.5 percent chance) than that you will get a hit (a 32.5 percent chance), and the payoff is lower if you do not get a hit, the expected bonus is less than the simple average.

What would your expected payoff be if you got a hit 99 percent of the time? We intuitively know that the expected bonus should be much closer to \$800,000 in this case. In fact, it is:

$$\text{E(Bonus)} = (0.99 \times \$800{,}000) + (0.01 \times \$400{,}000) = \$796{,}000$$

The key point here is that the expected value reflects the relative likelihoods of the possible outcomes.

We calculate an **expected return** in finance in the same way that we calculate any expected value. The expected return is a weighted average of the possible returns from an investment, where each of these returns is weighted by the probability that it will occur. In general terms, the expected return on an asset, $\text{E(R}_{\text{Asset}})$, is calculated as follows:

expected return an average of the possible returns from an investment, where each return is weighted by the probability that it will occur

$$\text{E(R}_{\text{Asset}}) = \sum_{i=1}^{n} (p_i \times \text{R}_i) = (p_1 \times \text{R}_1) + (p_2 \times \text{R}_2) + \cdots + (p_n \times \text{R}_n) \qquad (7.2)$$

where R_i is possible return i and p_i is the probability that you will actually earn R_i. The summation symbol in this equation

$$\sum_{i=1}^{n}$$

is mathematical shorthand indicating that n values are added together. In Equation 7.2, each of the n possible returns is multiplied by the probability that it will be realized, and these products are then added together to calculate the expected return.

It is important to make sure that the sum of the n individual probabilities, the p_i's, always equals 1, or 100 percent, when you calculate an expected value. The sum of the probabilities cannot be less than 100 percent because you must account for all possible outcomes in the calculation. On the other hand, as you may recall from statistics, the sum of the probabilities of all possible outcomes cannot exceed 100 percent. For example, notice that the sum of the p_i's equals 1 in each of the expected bonus calculations that we discussed earlier (0.325 + 0.625 = 1 in the first calculation, 0.5 + 0.5 = 1 in the second, and 0.99 + 0.01 = 1 in the third).

The expected return on an asset reflects the return that you can expect to receive from investing in that asset over the period that you plan to own it. It is your best estimate of this return, given the possible outcomes and their associated probabilities.

[1]For simplicity, let's ignore the possibility of your hitting a sacrifice fly and other such outcomes.

Note that if each of the possible outcomes is equally likely (that is, $p_1 = p_2 = p_3 = \cdots = p_n = p = 1/n$), this formula reduces to the formula for a simple (equally weighted) average of the possible returns:

$$E(R_{Asset}) = \frac{\sum_{i=1}^{n} (R_i)}{n} = \frac{R_1 + R_2 + \cdots + R_n}{n}$$

To see how we calculate the expected return on an asset, suppose you are considering purchasing Twitter, Inc. stock for \$19.00 per share. You plan to sell the stock in one year. You estimate that there is a 30 percent chance that Twitter stock will sell for \$18.50 at the end of one year, a 30 percent chance that it will sell for \$20.50, a 30 percent chance that it will sell for \$21.00, and a 10 percent chance that it will sell for \$22.00. If Twitter pays no dividends on its shares, what is the return that you expect from this stock in the next year?

With no dividends, the total return on Twitter stock equals the return from capital appreciation:

$$R_T = R_{CA} = \frac{P_1 - P_0}{P_0}$$

Therefore, we can calculate the return from owning Twitter stock under each of the four possible outcomes using the approach we used for the Twitter problem we solved earlier in the chapter. These returns are calculated as follows:

Twitter Stock Price in One Year	Total Return
\$18.50	$\frac{\$18.50 - \$19.00}{\$19.00} = -0.0263$, or -2.63%
\$20.50	$\frac{\$20.50 - \$19.00}{\$19.00} = 0.0789$, or 7.89%
\$21.00	$\frac{\$21.00 - \$19.00}{\$19.00} = 0.1053$, or 10.53%
\$22.00	$\frac{\$22.00 - \$19.00}{\$19.00} = 0.1579$, or 15.79%

Applying Equation 7.2, the expected return on Twitter stock over the next year is therefore 6.32 percent, calculated as follows:

$$\begin{aligned} E(R_{Twitter}) &= \sum_{i=1}^{4} (p_i \times R_i) = (p_1 \times R_1) + (p_2 \times R_2) + (p_3 \times R_3) + (p_4 \times R_4) \\ &= (0.3 \times -0.0263) + (0.3 \times 0.0789) + (0.3 \times 0.1053) + (0.1 \times 0.1579) \\ &= -0.00789 + 0.02367 + 0.03159 + 0.01579 = 0.0632, \text{ or } 6.32\% \end{aligned}$$

Notice that the negative return is entered into the formula just like any other. Also notice that the sum of the p_i's equals 1.

Learning by Doing Application 7.2 and **Decision Making Example 7.1** illustrate another expected return calculation and the application of expected returns in decision making.

LEARNING BY DOING

APPLICATION 7.2 | Calculating Expected Returns

Problem You have just purchased 100 railroad cars that you plan to lease (rent) to a large railroad company. Demand for shipping goods by rail has recently increased dramatically due to the rising price of oil. You expect oil prices, which are currently at \$98.81 per barrel, to reach \$115.00 per barrel in the next year. If this happens, railroad shipping prices will increase, thereby driving up the value of your railroad cars as increases in demand outpace the rate at which new cars are being produced.

Given your oil price prediction, you estimate that there is a 30 percent chance that the value of your railroad cars will increase by 15 percent, a 40 percent chance that their value will increase by 25 percent, and a 30 percent chance that their value will increase by 30 percent in the next year. In addition to appreciation in the value of your cars, you expect to earn 10 percent on your investment over the next year (after expenses) from leasing the railroad cars. What total return do you expect to earn on your railroad car investment over the next year?

Approach Use Equation 7.1 first to calculate the total return that you would earn under each of the three possible outcomes. Next use these total return values, along with the associated probabilities, in Equation 7.2 to calculate the expected total return.

Solution To calculate the total returns using Equation 7.1,

$$R_T = R_{CA} + R_I = \frac{\Delta P}{P_0} + \frac{CF_1}{P_0}$$

you must recognize that $\Delta P/P_0$ is the capital appreciation under each outcome and that CF_1/P_0 equals the 10 percent that you expect to receive from leasing the rail cars. The expected returns for the three outcomes are:

Increase in Value of Rail Cars in One Year	Return from Leases	Total Return
15%	10%	$R_T = \frac{\Delta P}{P_0} + \frac{CF_1}{P_0} = 0.15 + 0.10 = 0.25$, or 25%
25%	10%	$R_T = \frac{\Delta P}{P_0} + \frac{CF_1}{P_0} = 0.25 + 0.10 = 0.35$, or 35%
30%	10%	$R_T = \frac{\Delta P}{P_0} + \frac{CF_1}{P_0} = 0.30 + 0.10 = 0.40$, or 40%

You can then use Equation 7.2 to calculate the expected return for your rail car investment:

$$\begin{aligned} E(R_{\text{Rail cars}}) &= \sum_{i=1}^{3} (\rho_i \times R_i) = (\rho_1 \times R_1) + (\rho_2 \times R_2) + (\rho_3 \times R_3) \\ &= (0.3 \times 0.25) + (0.4 \times 0.35) + (0.3 \times 0.40) \\ &= 0.335, \text{ or } 33.5\% \end{aligned}$$

Alternatively, since there is a 100 percent probability that the return from leasing the railroad cars is 10 percent, you could have simply calculated the expected increase in value of the railroad cars:

$$\begin{aligned} E\left(\frac{\Delta P}{P_0}\right) &= (0.3 \times 0.15) + (0.4 \times 0.25) + (0.3 \times 0.30) \\ &= 0.235, \text{ or } 23.5\% \end{aligned}$$

and added the 10 percent to arrive at the answer of 33.5 percent. Of course, this simpler approach only works if the return from leasing is known with certainty.

EXAMPLE 7.1 | Using Expected Values in Decision Making

DECISION MAKING

Situation You are deciding whether you should advertise your pizza business on the radio or on billboards placed on local taxicabs. For $1,000 per month, you can either buy 20 one-minute ads on the radio or place your ad on 40 taxicabs.

There is some uncertainty regarding how many new customers will visit your restaurant after hearing one of your radio ads. You estimate that there is a 30 percent chance that 35 people will visit, a 45 percent chance that 50 people will visit, and a 25 percent chance that 60 people will visit. Therefore, you expect the following number of new customers to visit your restaurant in response to each radio ad:

$$E(\text{New customers per ad}_{\text{Radio}}) = (0.30 \times 35) + (0.45 \times 50) + (0.25 \times 60) = 48$$

This means that you expect 20 one-minute ads to bring in $20 \times 48 = 960$ new customers.

Similarly, you estimate that there is a 20 percent chance you will get 20 new customers in response to an ad placed on a taxi, a 30 percent chance you will get 30 new customers, a 30 percent chance that you will get 40 new customers, and a 20 percent chance that you will get 50 new customers. Therefore, you expect the following number of new customers in response to each ad that you place on a taxi:

$$\begin{aligned} E(\text{New customers per ad}_{\text{Taxi}}) &= (0.2 \times 20) + (0.3 \times 30) + (0.3 \times 40) + (0.2 \times 50) \\ &= 35 \end{aligned}$$

Placing ads on 40 taxicabs is therefore expected to bring in 40 × 35 = 1,400 new customers.

Which of these two advertising options is more attractive? Is it cost-effective?

Decision You should advertise on taxicabs. For a monthly cost of $1,000, you expect to attract 1,400 new customers with taxicab advertisements but only 960 new customers if you advertise on the radio.

The answer to the question of whether advertising on taxicabs is cost-effective depends on how much the gross profits (profits after variable costs) of your business are increased by those 1,400 customers. Monthly gross profits will have to increase by $1,000, or average 72 cents per new customer ($1,000/1,400 = $0.72) to cover the cost of the advertising campaign.

Before You Go On

1. What are the two components of a total holding period return?
2. How is the expected return on an investment calculated?

7.3 Variance and Standard Deviation as Measures of Risk

LEARNING OBJECTIVE

4. Explain what the standard deviation of returns is and why it is very useful in finance, and calculate it for an asset.

We turn next to a discussion of the two most basic measures of risk used in finance—variance and standard deviation. These are the same variance and standard deviation measures that you studied if you took a course in statistics.

Calculating Variance and Standard Deviation

Let's begin by returning to our College World Series example. Recall that you will receive a bonus of $800,000 if you get a hit in your final collegiate at-bat and a bonus of $400,000 if you do not. The expected value of your bonus is $530,000. Suppose you want to measure the risk, or uncertainty, associated with the bonus. How can you do this? One approach would be to compute a measure of how much, on average, the bonus payoffs deviate from the expected value. The underlying intuition here is that the greater the difference between the actual bonus and the expected value, the greater the risk. For example, you might calculate the difference between each possible bonus payment and the expected value, and sum these differences. If you do this, you will get the following result:

$$
\begin{aligned}
\text{Risk} &= (\$800{,}000 - \$530{,}000) + (\$400{,}000 - \$530{,}000)\\
&= \$270{,}000 + (-\$130{,}000)\\
&= \$140{,}000
\end{aligned}
$$

Unfortunately, using this calculation to obtain a measure of risk presents two problems. First, since one difference is positive and the other difference is negative, one difference partially cancels the other. As a result, you are not getting an accurate measure of total risk. Second, this calculation does not take into account the number of potential outcomes or the probability of each outcome.

A better approach would be to square the differences (squaring the differences makes all the numbers positive) and multiply each squared difference by its associated probability before summing them up. This calculation yields the **variance** (σ^2) of the possible outcomes. The variance does not suffer from the two problems associated with the above calculation and provides a measure of risk that has a consistent interpretation across different situations or assets. For the original bonus arrangement, the variance is:

variance (σ^2) a measure of the uncertainty associated with an outcome

$$\begin{aligned}\text{Var(Bonus)} = \sigma^2_{\text{(Bonus)}} &= \{p_{\text{H}} \times [\text{B}_{\text{H}} - \text{E(Bonus)}]^2\} \\ &\quad + \{p_{\text{NH}} \times [\text{B}_{\text{NH}} - \text{E(Bonus)}]^2\} \\ &= [0.325 \times (\$800{,}000 - \$530{,}000)^2] \\ &\quad + [0.675 \times (\$400{,}000 - \$530{,}000)^2] \\ &= 35{,}100{,}000{,}000 \text{ dollars}^2\end{aligned}$$

Note that the square of the Greek symbol sigma, σ^2, is generally used to represent the variance.

Because it is somewhat awkward to work with units of squared dollars, in a calculation such as this we would typically take the square root of the variance. The square root gives us the **standard deviation** (σ) of the possible outcomes. For our example, the standard deviation is:

standard deviation (σ) the square root of the variance

$$\sigma_{\text{(Bonus)}} = (\sigma^2_{\text{(Bonus)}})^{1/2} = (35{,}100{,}000{,}000 \text{ dollars}^2)^{1/2} = \$187{,}349.94$$

As you will see when we discuss the normal distribution, the standard deviation has a natural interpretation that is very useful for assessing investment risks.

The general formula for calculating the variance of returns can be written as follows:

$$\text{Var(R)} = \sigma^2_{\tilde{\text{R}}} = \sum_{i=1}^{n} \{p_i \times [\text{R}_i - \text{E(R)}]^2\} \qquad (7.3)$$

Equation 7.3 simply extends the calculation illustrated above to the situation where there are n possible outcomes. Like the expected return calculation (Equation 7.2), Equation 7.3 can be simplified if all of the possible outcomes are equally likely. In this case it becomes:

$$\sigma^2_{\tilde{\text{R}}} = \frac{\sum_{i=1}^{n} [\text{R}_i - \text{E(R)}]^2}{n}$$

In both the general case and the case where all possible outcomes are equally likely, the standard deviation is simply the square root of the variance $\sigma_{\text{R}} = (\sigma^2_{\tilde{\text{R}}})^{1/2}$.

Interpreting Variance and Standard Deviation

The variance and standard deviation are especially useful measures of risk for variables that are normally distributed—those that can be represented by a normal distribution. The **normal distribution** is a symmetric frequency distribution that is completely described by its mean (average) and standard deviation. **Exhibit 7.1** illustrates what this distribution looks like. Even if you have never taken a statistics course, you have already encountered the normal distribution. It is the "bell curve" on which instructors often base their grade distributions. SAT scores and IQ scores are also based on normal distributions.

normal distribution a symmetric frequency distribution that is completely described by its mean and standard deviation; also known as a bell curve due to its shape

This distribution is very useful in finance because the returns for many assets are approximately normally distributed. This makes the variance and standard deviation practical measures of the uncertainty associated with investment returns. Since the standard deviation is more easily interpreted than the variance, we will focus on the standard deviation as we discuss the normal distribution and its application in finance.

In Exhibit 7.1, you can see that the normal distribution is symmetric: the left and right sides are mirror images of each other. The mean falls directly in the center of the distribution, and the probability that an outcome is less than or greater than a particular distance from the mean is the same whether the outcome is on the left or the right side of the distribution. For example, if the mean is 0, the probability that a particular outcome is −3 or less is the same as the probability that it is +3 or more (both are 3 or more units from the mean). This enables us to use a single measure of risk for the normal distribution. That measure is the standard deviation.

The standard deviation tells us everything we need to know about the width of the normal distribution or, in other words, the variation in the individual values. This variation is what we

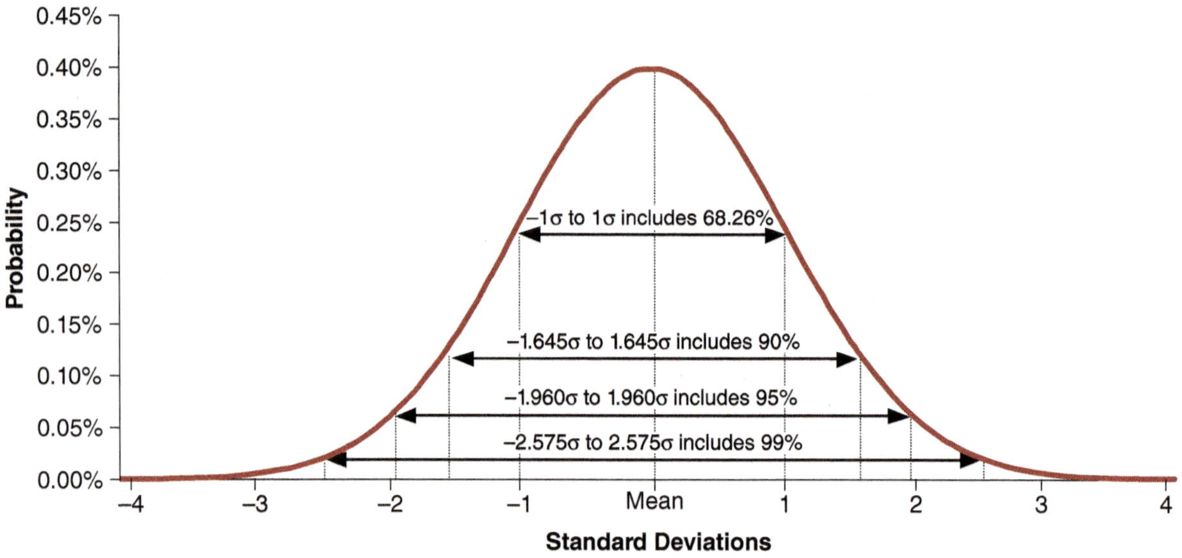

EXHIBIT 7.1 Normal Distribution

The normal distribution is a symmetric distribution that is completely described by its mean and standard deviation. The mean is the value that defines the center of the distribution, and the standard deviation, σ, describes the dispersion of the values centered around the mean.

are referring to when we talk about risk in finance. In general terms, risk is a measure of the range of potential outcomes. The standard deviation is an especially useful measure of risk because it tells us the probability that an outcome will fall a particular distance from the mean, or within a particular range. You can see this in the following table, which shows the fraction of all observations in a normal distribution that are within the indicated number of standard deviations from the mean.

Number of Standard Deviations from the Mean	Fraction of Total Observations
1.000	68.26%
1.645	90%
1.960	95%
2.575	99%

Since the returns on many assets are approximately normally distributed, the standard deviation provides a convenient way of computing the probability that the return on an asset will fall within a particular range. In these applications, the expected return on an asset equals the mean of the distribution, and the standard deviation is a measure of the uncertainty associated with the return.

For example, if the expected return for a real estate investment in Miami, Florida, is 10 percent with a standard deviation of 2 percent, there is a 90 percent chance that the actual return will be within 3.29 percent of 10 percent. How do we know this? As shown in the table above, 90 percent of all outcomes in a normal distribution have a value that is within 1.645 standard deviations of the mean value, and 1.645 × 2 percent = 3.29 percent. This tells us that there is a 90 percent chance that the realized return on the investment in Miami will be between 6.71 percent (10 percent − 3.29 percent = 6.71 percent) and 13.29 percent (10 percent + 3.29 percent = 13.29 percent), a range of 6.58 percent (13.29 percent − 6.71 percent = 6.58 percent).

You may be wondering what is *standard* about the standard deviation. The answer is that this statistic is standard in the sense that it can be used to directly compare the uncertainties (risks) associated with the returns on different investments. For instance, suppose you are comparing the real estate investment in Miami with a real estate investment in Fresno, California. Assume that the expected return on the Fresno investment is also 10 percent. If the standard deviation for the returns on the Fresno investment is 3 percent, there is a 90 percent chance that the actual return is within 4.935 percent (1.645 × 3 percent = 4.935 percent) of 10 percent. In other words, 90 percent of the time, the return will be between 5.065 percent (10 percent − 4.935 percent = 5.065 percent) and 14.935 percent (10 percent + 4.935 percent = 14.935 percent), a range of 9.87 percent (14.935 percent − 5.065 percent = 9.87 percent).

This range is exactly 9.87 percent/6.58 percent = 1.5 times as large as the range for the Miami investment opportunity. Notice that the ratio of the two standard deviations also equals 1.5 (3 percent/2 percent = 1.5). This is not a coincidence. We could have used the standard deviations to directly compute the relative uncertainty associated with the Fresno and Miami investment returns. The relation between the standard deviation of returns and the width of a normal distribution (the uncertainty) is illustrated in **Exhibit 7.2**.

Let's consider another example of how the standard deviation is interpreted. Suppose customers at your pizza restaurant have complained that there is no consistency in the number of slices of pepperoni that your cooks are putting on large pepperoni pizzas. One night you decide to work in the area where the pizzas are made so that you can count the number of pepperoni slices on the large pizzas to get a better idea of just how much variation there is. After counting the slices of pepperoni on 50 pizzas, you estimate that, on average, your pies have 18 slices of pepperoni and that the standard deviation is 3 slices.

With this information, you estimate that 95 percent of the large pepperoni pizzas sold in your restaurant have between 12.12 and 23.88 pepperoni slices. You are able to estimate this range because you know that 95 percent of the observations in a normal distribution fall within 1.96 standard deviations of the mean. With a standard deviation of three slices, this implies that the number of pepperoni slices on 95 percent of your pizzas is within 5.88 slices of the mean (3 slices × 1.96 = 5.88 slices). This, in turn, indicates a range of 12.12 (18 − 5.88 = 12.12) to 23.88 (18 + 5.88 = 23.88) slices.

Since you put only whole slices of pepperoni on your pizzas, 95 percent of the time the number of slices is somewhere between 12 and 24. No wonder your customers are up in arms! In response to this information, you decide to implement a standard policy regarding the number of pepperoni slices that go on each type of pizza.

Learning by Doing Application 7.3 illustrates application of a normal distribution to the analysis of a stock return.

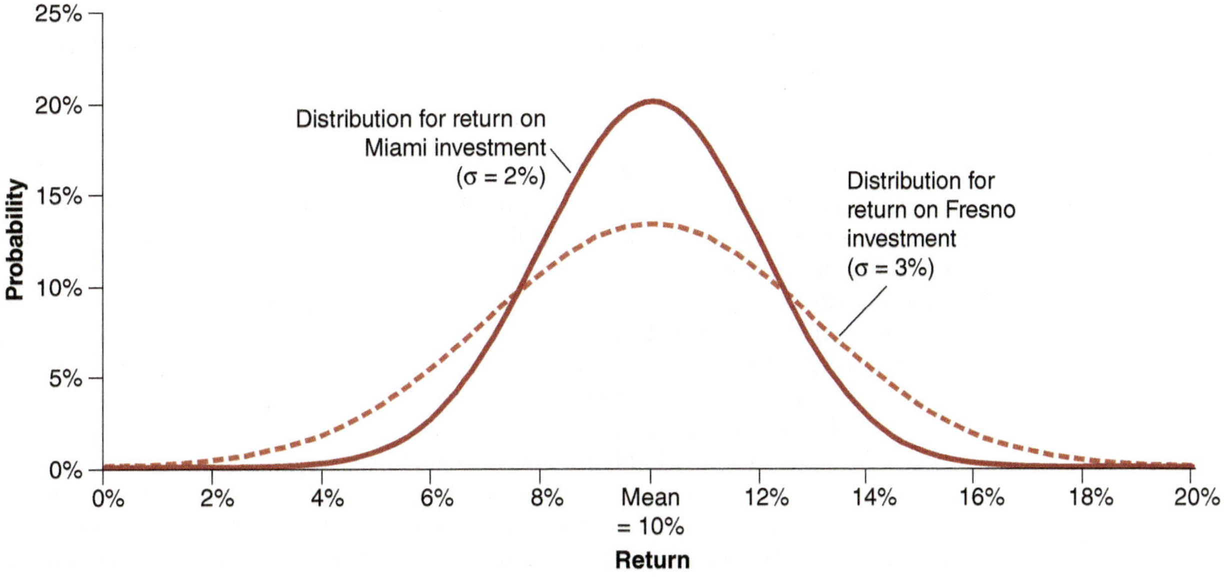

EXHIBIT 7.2 Standard Deviation and Width of the Normal Distribution

The larger standard deviation for the return on the Fresno investment means that the Fresno investment is riskier than the Miami investment. The actual return for the Fresno investment is more likely to be further from its expected return.

LEARNING BY DOING

WileyPLUS

Need more help? Visit your WileyPLUS course.

APPLICATION 7.3 | Understanding the Standard Deviation

Problem You are considering investing in a share of Google Inc. stock and want to evaluate how risky this potential investment is. You know that stock returns tend to be normally distributed, and you have calculated the expected return on Google stock to be 4.67 percent and the standard deviation of the annual return to be 23 percent. Based on these statistics, within what range would you expect the return on this stock to fall during the next year? Calculate this range for a 90 percent level of confidence (that is, 90 percent of the time, the returns will fall within the specified range).

Approach Use the values in the previous table or Exhibit 7.1 to compute the range within which Google's stock return will fall 90 percent of the time. First, find the number of standard deviations associated with a 90 percent level of confidence in the table or Exhibit 7.1 and then multiply this number by the standard deviation of the annual return for Google's stock. Then subtract the resulting value from the expected return (mean) to obtain the lower end of the range and add it to the expected return to obtain the upper end.

Solution From the table, you can see that we would expect the return over the next year to be within 1.645 standard deviations of the mean 90 percent of the time. Multiplying this value by the standard deviation of Google's stock (23 percent) yields 23 percent × 1.645 = 37.835 percent. This means that there is a 90 percent chance that the return will be between −33.165 percent (4.67 percent − 37.835 percent = −33.165 percent) and 42.505 percent (4.67 percent + 37.835 percent = 42.505 percent).

While the expected return of 4.67 percent is relatively low, the returns on Google stock vary considerably, and there is a reasonable chance that the stock return in the next year could be quite high or quite low (even negative). As you will see shortly, this wide range of possible returns is similar to the range we observe for typical shares in the U.S. stock market.

Historical Market Performance

Now that we have discussed how returns and risks can be measured, we are ready to examine the characteristics of the historical returns earned by securities such as stocks and bonds. Exhibit 7.3 illustrates the distributions of historical returns for some securities in the United States and shows the average and standard deviations of these annual returns for the period from 1926 to 2015.

Note that the statistics reported in Exhibit 7.3 are for indexes that represent total *average* returns for the indicated types of securities, not total returns on individual securities. We generally use indexes to represent the performance of the stock or bond markets. For instance, when news services report on the performance of the stock market, they often report that the Dow Jones Industrial Average (an index based on 30 large stocks), the S&P 500 Index (an index based on 500 large stocks), or the NASDAQ Composite Index (an index based on all stocks that are traded on NASDAQ) went up or down on a particular day. These and other indexes are discussed in Chapter 9.

The plots in Exhibit 7.3 are arranged in order of decreasing risk, which is indicated by the decreasing standard deviation of the annual returns. The top plot shows returns for a small-stock index that represents the 10 percent of U.S. firms that have the lowest total equity value (number of shares multiplied by price per share). The second plot shows returns for the S&P 500 Index, representing large U.S. stocks. The remaining plots show three different types of government debt: long-term government bonds that mature in 20 years, intermediate-term government bonds that mature in five years, and U.S. Treasury bills, which are short-term debts of the U.S. government, that mature in 30 days.

The key point to note in Exhibit 7.3 is that, on average, annual returns have been higher for riskier securities. Small stocks, which have the largest standard deviation of total returns, at 32.02 percent, also have the largest average annual return, 16.47 percent. On the other end of the spectrum, Treasury bills have the smallest standard deviation, 3.12 percent, and the smallest average annual return, 3.46 percent. Returns for small stocks in any particular year may have been higher or lower than returns for the other types of securities, but on average, they were higher. This is evidence that investors require higher returns for investments with greater risks.

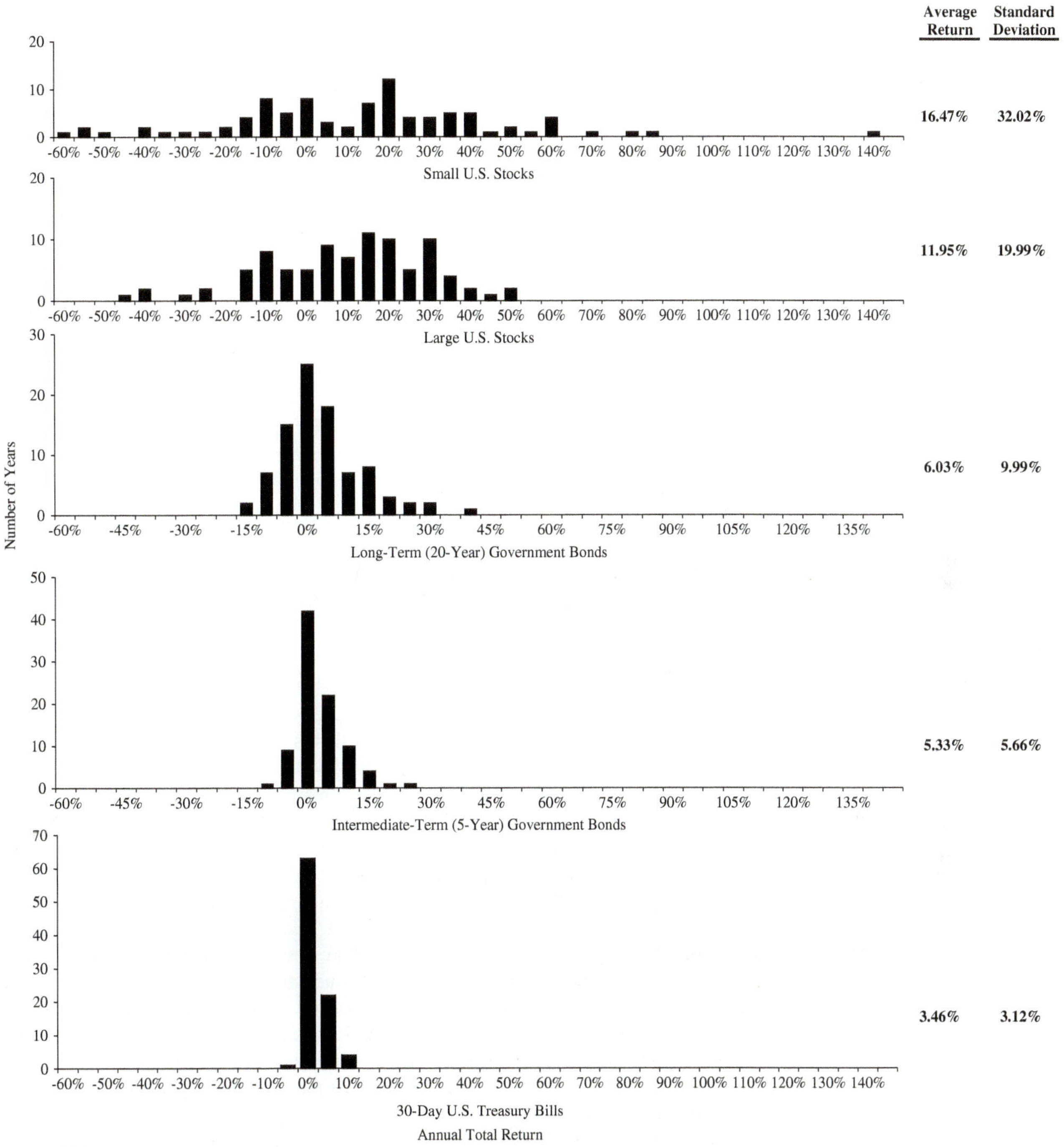

EXHIBIT 7.3 Distributions of Annual Total Returns for U.S. Stocks and Bonds from 1926 to 2015

Higher standard deviations of returns have historically been associated with higher returns. For example, between 1926 and 2015, the standard deviation of the annual returns for small stocks was higher than the standard deviations of the returns earned by other types of securities, and the average return that investors earned from small stocks was also higher. At the other end of the spectrum, the returns on Treasury bills had the smallest standard deviation, and Treasury bills earned the smallest average return.

Source: Data from Morningstar, 2016 SBBI Yearbook

The statistics in Exhibit 7.3 describe actual investment returns, as opposed to expected returns. In other words, they represent what has happened in the past. Financial analysts often use historical numbers such as these to estimate the returns that might be expected in the future. That is exactly what we did in the baseball example earlier in this chapter. We used the percentage of at-bats in which you got a hit this past season to estimate the likelihood that you would get a hit in your last collegiate at-bat. We assumed that your past performance was a reasonable indicator of your future performance.

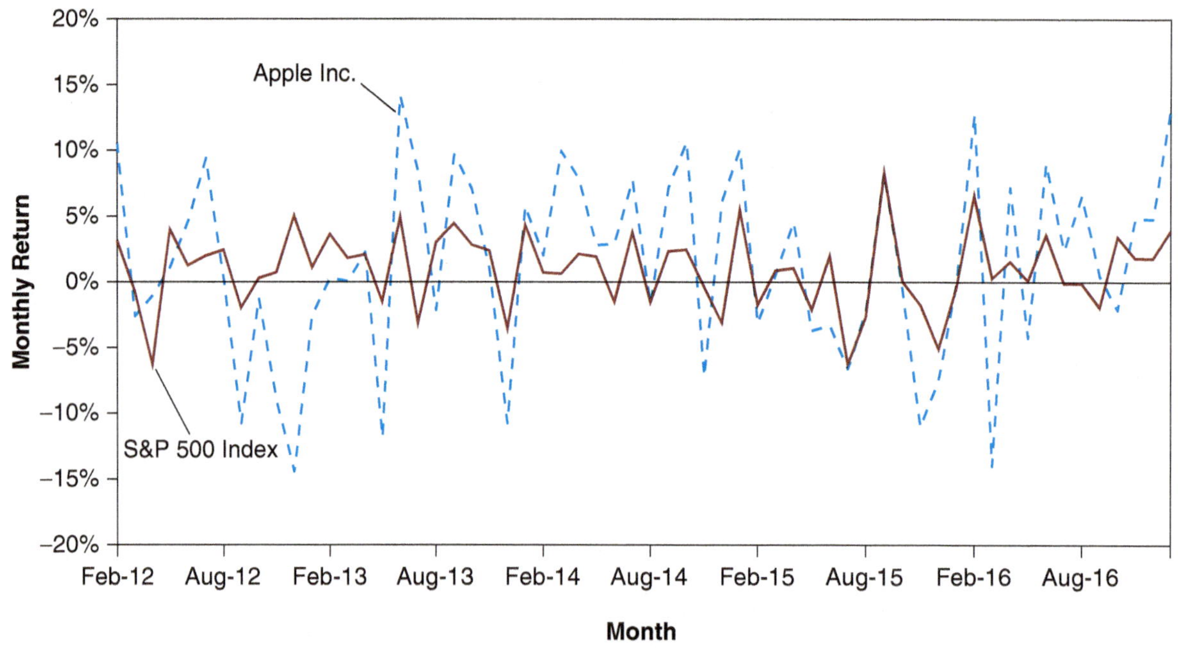

EXHIBIT 7.4 Monthly Returns for Apple Inc. stock and the S&P 500 Index from February 2012 through January 2017
The returns on shares of individual stocks tend to be much more volatile than the returns on portfolios of stocks, such as the S&P 500.

To see how historical numbers are used in finance, let's suppose that you are considering investing in a fund that mimics the S&P 500 Index (this is what we call an *index fund*) and that you want to estimate what the returns on the S&P 500 Index are likely to be in the future. If you believe that the 1926 to 2015 period provides a reasonable indication of what we can expect in the future, then the average historical return on the S&P 500 Index of 11.95 percent provides a perfectly reasonable estimate of the return you can expect from your investment in the S&P 500 Index fund. In Chapter 13 we will explore in detail how historical data can be used in this way to estimate the discount rate for evaluating projects in the capital budgeting process.

Comparing the historical returns for an individual stock with the historical returns for an index can also be instructive. **Exhibit 7.4** shows such a comparison for Apple Inc. and the S&P 500 Index using monthly returns for the period from February 2012 to January 2017. Notice in the exhibit that the returns on Apple stock are much more volatile than the average returns on the firms represented in the S&P 500 Index. In other words, the standard deviation of returns for Apple stock is higher than that for the S&P 500 Index. This is not a coincidence; we will discuss shortly why returns on individual stocks tend to be riskier than returns on indexes.

One last point is worth noting while we are examining historical returns: the value of a $1.00 investment in 1926 would have varied greatly by 2015, depending on where that dollar was invested. **Exhibit 7.5** shows that $1.00 invested in U.S. Treasury bills in 1926 would have been worth $20.57 by 2015. In contrast, that same $1.00 invested in small stocks would have been worth $26,434.04 by 2015.[2] Over a long period of time, earning higher rates of return can have a dramatic impact on the value of an investment. This huge difference reflects the impact of compounding of returns (returns earned on returns), much like the compounding of interest we discussed in Chapter 5.

[2]From a practical standpoint, it would not really have been possible to grow $1.00 to $26,434.04 by investing in small U.S. stocks because this increase assumes that an investor is able to rebalance the stock portfolio by buying and selling shares as necessary at no cost. Since buying and selling shares are costly endeavors, the final wealth would have been lower. Nevertheless, even after transaction costs, it would have been much more profitable to invest in small stocks than in U.S. Treasury bills.

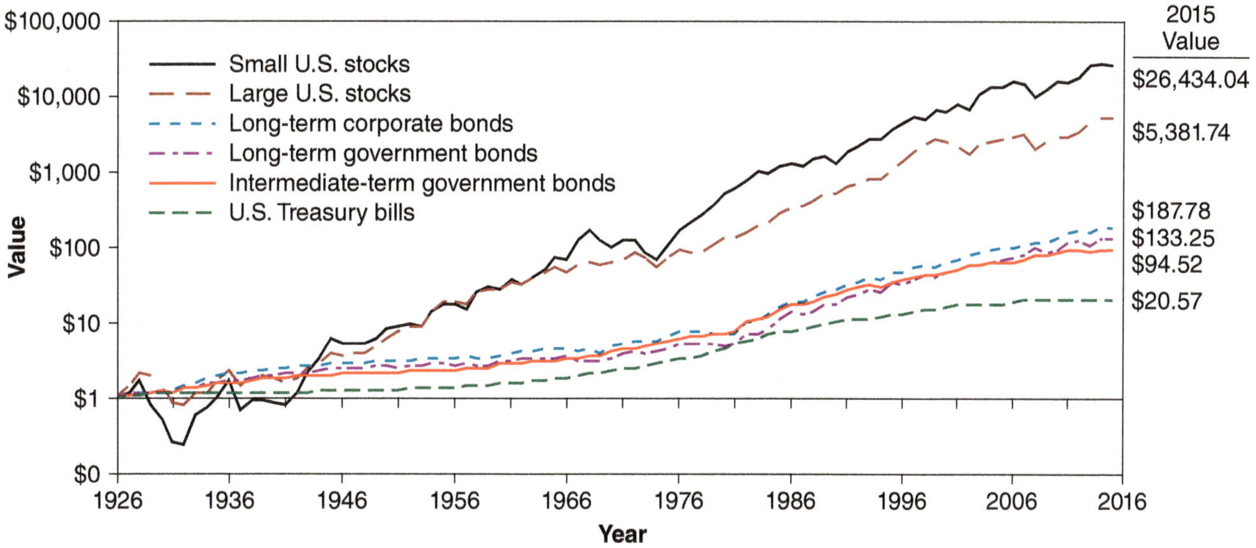

EXHIBIT 7.5 Cumulative Value of $1 Invested in 1926

The value of a $1 investment in stocks, small or large, grew much more rapidly than the value of a $1 investment in bonds or Treasury bills over the 1926 to 2015 period. This graph illustrates how earning a higher rate of return over a long period of time can affect the value of an investment portfolio. Although annual stock returns were less certain between 1926 and 2015, the returns on stock investments were much greater.

Source: Data from Morningstar, 2016 SBBI Yearbook

Arithmetic Average and Geometric (Compounded) Average Returns

LEARNING OBJECTIVE

5. Explain what an arithmetic average return is and what a geometric return is, and calculate these returns for an asset.

The average returns reported for the different types of U.S. stocks and bonds in Exhibit 7.3 are known as **arithmetic average returns**. These returns are calculated for each type of stock or bond by simply adding up the returns during each year from 1926 through 2015 and then dividing by the total number of years. This calculation tells us the return that was earned in an average year during the 90-year period from 1926 to 2015. An arithmetic average return can be calculated for an investment period of any length, such as a day, month, quarter, or year, by adding the returns across all periods and dividing by the total number of periods. Equation 7.4 shows this calculation.

arithmetic average return the return earned in an average period

$$\mathrm{R}_{\text{Arithmetic average}} = \frac{\sum_{i=1}^{n} \mathrm{R}_i}{n} \tag{7.4}$$

where:

$\mathrm{R}_{\text{Arithmetic average}}$ = arithmetic average growth rate
R_i = return in period i
n = number of periods

While the arithmetic average return is helpful in comparing the annual returns earned on investments in the different types of U.S. stocks and bonds in Exhibit 7.3, it does not tell us the average annual return an investor would have earned on an investment in a particular type of stock or bond.

For example, the 11.95 percent arithmetic average annual return on large U.S. stocks does not mean that a $1 investment in large U.S. stocks in 1926 would have grown at a compounded rate of 11.95 percent through 2015. If it had done this, that investment would have grown to $25,832.64 [$\$1 \times (1 + 0.1195)^{90} = \$25{,}832.64$], when, in fact, Exhibit 7.5 shows that it grew to only $5,381.74.

The future value formula, Equation 5.1, tells us that this $5,381.74 value implies a compounded average annual return on large U.S. stocks from 1926 to 2015 of only 10.02 percent:

$$\begin{aligned} FV_n &= PV \times (1 + i)^n \\ \$5{,}381.74 &= \$1 \times (1 + i)^{90} \\ i &= (\$5{,}381.74)^{1/90} - 1 \\ &= 0.1002, \text{ or } 10.02\% \end{aligned}$$

geometric (compounded) average return average compounded return earned by an investor

Why is there a difference between the arithmetic average return and the average return that an investor actually earned? The answer is that the compounded average annual return that an investor earns, which we call the **geometric (compounded) average return**, is sensitive to variation in returns over time. To see this, consider a two-year investment of $1 that returns 6.95 percent in Year 1 and 16.95 percent in Year 2. This investment, which has an arithmetic average return of 11.95 percent [(6.95 percent + 16.95 percent)/2 = 11.95 percent], will be worth $1.25 in Year 2 [Value in Year 2 = $(1 + 0.0695)(1 + 0.1695) = \$1.25$], which implies a geometric (compounded) average return of:

$$\begin{aligned} FV_n &= PV \times (1 + i)^n \\ \$1.25 &= \$1 \times (1 + i)^2 \\ i &= (\$1.25)^{1/2} - 1 \\ &= 0.1180, \text{ or } 11.80\% \end{aligned}$$

In contrast, if the return is 11.95 percent in both years, the arithmetic and geometric average returns both equal 11.95 percent. The fact that the return is not the same each year causes the geometric average return to differ from the arithmetic average return. The more variation there is in the year-to-year return, the greater the difference between the arithmetic and geometric returns.

Note that in the preceding example, in which the returns are 6.95 percent and 16.95 percent, we can write the equation for the geometric growth rate as:

$$\begin{aligned} i &= (\$1.25)^{1/2} - 1 \\ i &= [(1 + 0.0695)(1 + 0.1695)]^{1/2} - 1 \end{aligned}$$

If we substitute $R_{\text{Geometric average}}$ for i, the general form of this equation can be written as:

$$R_{\text{Geometric average}} = [(1 + R_1) \times (1 + R_2) \times \cdots \times (1 + R_n)]^{1/n} - 1 \qquad (7.5)$$

where:

$R_{\text{Geometric average}}$ = geometric average growth rate
R_i = return in period i
n = number of periods

The geometric average return will always be lower than the arithmetic average return when there is year-to-year variation in returns because of the difference in the way that the two calculations treat the dollar value of percentage changes. For example, suppose that you invest $1 for two years and your investment earns 15 percent in Year 1 and loses 15 percent in Year 2. The arithmetic average return would be 0 percent [(15 percent + −15 percent)/2 = 0 percent], but the geometric average would be −1.13 percent ($[(1 + 0.15)(1 + -0.15)]^{1/2} - 1 = -0.0113$). The lower geometric return reflects the fact that the positive return in Year 1 represents a $0.15 increase in value ($0.15 \times \$1 = \$0.15$) while the negative return in Year 2 represents a $0.17 decrease in value ($-0.15 \times [\$1 \times (1 + 0.15)] = -\$0.17$. The difference is that the 15 percent increase in Year 1 is based on a smaller dollar amount (the $1 starting value) than the 15 percent decrease in Year 2, which is a decrease from the Year 1 value of \$1.15. The arithmetic average return calculation treats both changes equally while the geometric average calculation accounts for the difference.

Before You Go On

1. What is the relation between the variance and the standard deviation?
2. What relation do we generally observe between risk and return when we examine historical returns?
3. What type of return tells you the average compounded return earned by an investor?

7.4 Risk and Diversification

LEARNING OBJECTIVE

6. Explain the concept of diversification.

It does not generally make sense to invest all of your money in a single asset. The reason is directly related to the fact that returns on individual stocks tend to be riskier than returns on indexes. By investing in two or more assets whose values do not always move in the same direction at the same time, an investor can reduce the risk of his or her collection of investments, or **portfolio**. This is the idea behind the concept of **diversification**.

This section develops the tools necessary to evaluate the benefits of diversification. We begin with a discussion of how to quantify risk and return for a single-asset portfolio, and then we discuss more realistic and complicated portfolios that have two or more assets. Although our discussion focuses on stock portfolios, it is important to recognize that the concepts discussed apply equally well to portfolios that include a range of assets, such as stocks, bonds, gold, art, and real estate, among others.

portfolio the collection of assets an investor owns

diversification reducing risk by investing in two or more assets whose values do not always move in the same direction at the same time

Single-Asset Portfolios

Returns for individual stocks from one day to the next have been found to be largely independent of each other and approximately normally distributed. In other words, the return for a stock on one day is largely independent of the return on that same stock the next day, two days later, three days later, and so on. Each daily return can be viewed as having been randomly drawn from a normal distribution where the probability associated with the return depends on how far it is from the expected value. If we know what the expected value and standard deviation are for the distribution of returns for a stock, it is possible to quantify the risks and expected returns that an investment in the stock might yield in the future.

To see how we might do this, assume that you are considering investing in one of two stocks for the next year: Advanced Micro Devices (AMD) or Intel. Also, to keep things simple, assume that there are only three possible economic conditions (outcomes) a year from now and that the returns on AMD and Intel under each of these outcomes are as follows:

Economic Outcome	Probability	AMD Return	Intel Return
Poor	0.2	–0.13	–0.10
Neutral	0.5	0.10	0.07
Good	0.3	0.25	0.22

With this information, we can calculate the expected returns for AMD and Intel by using Equation 7.2:

$$\begin{aligned} E(R_{AMD}) &= (p_{Poor} \times R_{Poor}) + (p_{Neutral} \times R_{Neutral}) + (p_{Good} \times R_{Good}) \\ &= (0.2 \times -0.13) + (0.5 \times 0.10) + (0.3 \times 0.25) \\ &= 0.099, \text{ or } 9.9\% \end{aligned}$$

and

$$\begin{aligned} E(R_{Intel}) &= (p_{Poor} \times R_{Poor}) + (p_{Neutral} \times R_{Neutral}) + (p_{Good} \times R_{Good}) \\ &= (0.2 \times -0.10) + (0.5 \times 0.07) + (0.3 \times 0.22) \\ &= 0.081, \text{ or } 8.1\% \end{aligned}$$

Similarly, we can calculate the standard deviations of the returns for AMD and Intel in the same way that we calculated the standard deviation for our baseball bonus example in Section 7.2:

$$\begin{aligned} \sigma^2_{R_{AMD}} &= \{p_{Poor} \times [R_{Poor} - E(R_{AMD})]^2\} + \{p_{Neutral} \times [R_{Neutral} - E(R_{AMD})]^2\} \\ &\quad + \{p_{Good} \times [R_{Good} - E(R_{AMD})]^2\} \\ &= [0.2 \times (-0.13 - 0.099)^2] + [0.5 \times (0.10 - 0.099)^2] + [0.3 \times (0.25 - 0.099)^2] \\ &= 0.01733 \\ \sigma_{R_{AMD}} &= (\sigma^2_{R_{AMD}})^{1/2} = (0.01733)^{1/2} = 0.13164, \text{ or } 13.164\% \end{aligned}$$

and

$$\begin{aligned} \sigma^2_{R_{Intel}} &= \{p_{Poor} \times [R_{Poor} - E(R_{Intel})]^2\} + \{p_{Neutral} \times [R_{Neutral} - E(R_{Intel})]^2\} \\ &\quad + \{p_{Good} \times [R_{Good} - E(R_{Intel})]^2\} \\ &= [0.2 \times (-0.10 - 0.081)^2] + [0.5 \times (0.07 - 0.081)^2] + [0.3 \times (0.22 - 0.081)^2] \\ &= 0.01241 \\ \sigma_{R_{Intel}} &= (\sigma^2_{R_{Intel}})^{1/2} = (0.01241)^{1/2} = 0.11140, \text{ or } 11.140\% \end{aligned}$$

Having calculated the expected returns and standard deviations for AMD and Intel stock, the natural question to ask is which provides the higher risk-adjusted return. Before we answer this question, let's return to the example at the beginning of Section 7.1. Recall that, in this example, we proposed choosing among three stocks: A, B, and C. We stated that investors would prefer the investment that provides the highest expected return for a given level of risk or the lowest risk for a given expected return. This made it fairly easy to choose between Stocks A and B, which had the same return but different risk, and between Stocks B and C, which had the same risk but different returns. We were stuck when trying to choose between Stocks A and C, however, because they differed in both risk and return. Now, armed with tools for quantifying expected returns and risk, we can at least take a first pass at comparing stocks such as these.

coefficient of variation (CV) a measure of the risk associated with an investment for each 1 percent of expected return

The **coefficient of variation (CV)** is a measure that can help us in making comparisons such as that between Stocks A and C. The coefficient of variation for stock *i* is calculated as:

$$CV_i = \frac{\sigma_{R_i}}{E(R_i)} \tag{7.6}$$

In this equation, CV is a measure of the risk associated with an investment for each 1 percent of expected return.

Recall that Stock A has an expected return of 12 percent and a risk level of 12 percent, while Stock C has an expected return of 16 percent and a risk level of 16 percent. If we assume that the risk level given for each stock is equal to the standard deviation of its return, we can find the coefficients of variation for the stocks as follows:

$$CV_A = \frac{0.12}{0.12} = 1.00 \quad \text{and} \quad CV_C = \frac{0.16}{0.16} = 1.00$$

Since these values are equal, the coefficient of variation measure suggests that these two investments are equally attractive on a risk-adjusted basis.

While this analysis appears to make sense, there is a conceptual problem with using the coefficient of variation to compute the amount of risk an investor can expect to realize for each

1 percent of expected return. This problem arises because investors expect to earn a positive return even when assets are completely risk free. For example, as shown in Exhibit 7.3, from 1926 to 2015 investors earned an average return of 3.46 percent each year on 30-day Treasury bills, which are considered to be risk free.[3] If investors can earn a positive risk-free rate without bearing any risk, then it really only makes sense to compare the risk of the investment, σ_{R_i}, with the return that investors expect to earn over and above the risk-free rate. As we will discuss in detail in Section 7.6, the expected return over and above the risk-free rate is a measure of the return that investors expect to earn for bearing risk.

This suggests that we should use the difference between the expected return, $E(R_i)$, and the risk-free rate, R_{rf}, instead of $E(R_i)$ alone in the coefficient of variation calculation. With this change, Equation 7.6 would be written as:

$$CV_i^* = \frac{\sigma_{R_i}}{E(R_i) - R_{rf}}$$

where CV_i^* is a modified coefficient of variation that is computed by subtracting the risk-free rate from the expected return.

Let's compute this modified coefficient of variation for the AMD and Intel example. If the risk-free rate equals 0.03, or 3 percent, the modified coefficients of variation for the two stocks are:

$$CV_{AMD}^* = \frac{\sigma_{R_{AMD}}}{E(R_{AMD}) - R_{rf}} = \frac{0.13164}{0.099 - 0.03} = 1.908$$

$$CV_{Intel}^* = \frac{\sigma_{R_{Intel}}}{E(R_{Intel}) - R_{rf}} = \frac{0.11140}{0.081 - 0.03} = 2.184$$

We can see that the modified coefficient of variation for AMD is smaller than the modified coefficient of variation for Intel. This tells us that an investment in AMD stock is expected to have less risk for each 1 percent of return. Since investors prefer less risk for a given level of return, the AMD stock is a more attractive investment.

A popular version of this modified coefficient of variation calculation is known as the Sharpe Ratio. This ratio is named after 1990 Nobel Prize Laureate William Sharpe who developed the concept and was one of the originators of the Capital Asset Pricing Model that is discussed in Section 7.7. The **Sharpe Ratio** is simply the inverse of the modified coefficient of variation:

Sharpe Ratio a measure of the return per unit of risk for an investment

$$\text{Sharpe Ratio} = S = \frac{E(R_i) - R_{rf}}{\sigma_{R_i}} \quad (7.7)$$

For the stocks of AMD and Intel, the Sharpe Ratios are:

$$S_{AMD} = \frac{1}{CV_{AMD}^*} = \frac{E(R_{AMD}) - R_{rf}}{\sigma_{R_{AMD}}} = \frac{0.099 - 0.03}{0.13164} = 0.524$$

$$S_{Intel} = \frac{1}{CV_{Intel}^*} = \frac{E(R_{Intel}) - R_{rf}}{\sigma_{R_{Intel}}} = \frac{0.081 - 0.03}{0.11140} = 0.458$$

This tells us that investors in AMD stock can expect to earn 0.524 percent for each one standard deviation of return while investors in Intel stock can expect to earn 0.458 percent for each one standard deviation of return. Many people find the Sharpe Ratio to be a more intuitive measure than the coefficient of variation because they find it easier to think about the return per unit of risk than risk per unit of return.

Learning by Doing Application 7.4 illustrates other Sharpe Ratio calculations.

Weblink

You can read more about the Sharpe Ratio and other ratios that are used to measure risk-adjusted returns for investments at the following Web site: http://en.wikipedia.org/wiki/sharpe_ratio.

Portfolios with More Than One Asset

It may seem like a good idea to evaluate investments by calculating a measure of risk for each 1 percent of expected return or the expected return per unit of risk. However, the coefficient of variation and the Sharpe Ratio have a critical shortcoming that is not quite evident when we

[3] On August 5, 2011, Standard and Poor's, the credit rating agency, lowered its rating on U.S. Treasury securities from AAA to AA+, indicating that it considered these securities to have a very small amount of default risk. The other two large credit rating agencies, Moody's and Fitch, decided not to lower their ratings of U.S. Treasury securities at that time, suggesting that if there was any default risk, it remained extremely small.

LEARNING BY DOING

APPLICATION 7.4 | Calculating and Interpreting the Sharpe Ratio

Problem You are trying to choose between two investments. The first investment, a painting by Picasso, has an expected return of 14 percent with a standard deviation of 30 percent over the next year. The second investment, a pair of blue suede shoes once worn by Elvis, has an expected return of 20 percent with a standard deviation of 40 percent. The risk-free rate of interest is 3 percent. What is the Sharpe Ratio for each of these investments, and what do these ratios tell us?

Approach Use Equation 7.7 to compute the Sharpe Ratios for the two investments.

Solution The Sharpe Ratios are:

$$S_{\text{painting}} = \frac{0.14 - 0.03}{0.3} = 0.367 \quad \text{and} \quad S_{\text{shoes}} = \frac{0.2 - 0.03}{0.4} = 0.425$$

The Sharpe Ratio for Elvis's blue suede shoes is larger than the Sharpe Ratio for the painting. This indicates that the return for each one standard deviation of risk is greater for Elvis's shoes than for the painting. The blue suede shoes are a better investment.

are considering only a single asset. In order to explain this shortcoming, we must discuss the more realistic setting in which an investor has constructed a portfolio with more than one asset.

Expected Return on a Portfolio with More Than One Asset

Suppose you own a portfolio that consists of \$500 of AMD stock and \$500 of Intel stock and that over the next year you expect to earn returns on the AMD and Intel shares of 9.9 percent and 8.1 percent, respectively. How would you calculate the expected return for the overall portfolio?

Let's try to answer this question using our intuition. If half of your funds are invested in each stock, it would seem reasonable that the expected return for this portfolio should be a 50–50 mixture of the expected returns from the two stocks, or:

$$E(R_{\text{Portfolio}}) = (0.5 \times 0.099) + (0.5 \times 0.081) = 0.09, \text{ or } 9.0\%$$

Notice that this formula is just like the expected return formula for an individual stock. However, in this case, instead of multiplying outcomes by their associated probabilities, we are multiplying expected returns for individual stocks by the fraction of the total portfolio value that each of these stocks represents. In other words, the formula for the expected return for a two-stock portfolio is:

$$E(R_{\text{Portfolio}}) = x_1 E(R_1) + x_2 E(R_2)$$

where x_i represents the fraction of the portfolio invested in asset i. The corresponding equation for a portfolio with n assets is:

$$\begin{aligned} E(R_{\text{Portfolio}}) &= \sum_{i=1}^{n} [x_i \times E(R_i)] \quad (7.8) \\ &= [x_1 \times E(R_1)] + [x_2 \times E(R_2)] + \cdots + [x_n \times E(R_n)] \end{aligned}$$

This equation is just like Equation 7.2, except that (1) the returns are expected returns for individual assets and (2) instead of multiplying by the probability of an outcome, we are multiplying by the fraction of the portfolio invested in each asset. Note that this equation can be used only if you have already calculated the expected return for each stock.

To see how Equation 7.8 is used to calculate the expected return on a portfolio with more than two assets, consider an example. Suppose that you were recently awarded a \$500,000 grant from a national foundation to pursue your interest in advancing the art of noodling—a popular pastime in some parts of the country in which people catch 40- to 50-pound catfish by putting their hands into catfish holes and wiggling their fingers like noodles to attract the fish.[4] Since your grant is intended to support your activities for five years, you kept \$100,000 to cover your expenses for the next year and invested the remaining \$400,000 in U.S. Treasury bonds and stocks. Specifically, you invested \$100,000 in Treasury bonds (TB) that yield 4.5 percent; \$150,000 in Procter & Gamble stock (P&G), which has an expected return of 7.5 percent; and \$150,000 in Exxon Mobil Corporation stock (EMC), which has an expected return of 9.0 percent. What is the expected return on this \$400,000 portfolio?

In order to use Equation 7.8, we must first calculate x_i, the fraction of the portfolio invested in asset i, for each investment. These fractions are as follows:

$$x_{TB} = \frac{\$100{,}000}{\$400{,}000} = 0.25$$

$$x_{P\&G} = x_{EMC} = \frac{\$150{,}000}{\$400{,}000} = 0.375$$

Therefore, the expected return on the portfolio is:

$$\begin{aligned} E(R_{Portfolio}) &= [x_{TB} \times E(R_{TB})] + [x_{P\&G} \times E(R_{P\&G})] + [x_{EMC} \times E(R_{EMC})] \\ &= (0.25 \times 0.045) + (0.375 \times 0.075) + (0.375 \times 0.090) \\ &= 0.0731, \text{ or } 7.31\% \end{aligned}$$

Learning by Doing Application 7.5 illustrates another expected return calculation for a portfolio.

Risk of a Portfolio with More Than One Asset

Now that we have calculated the expected return on a portfolio with more than one asset, the next question is how to quantify the risk of such a portfolio. Before we discuss the mechanics of how to do this, it is important to have some intuitive understanding of how variance in the returns for different assets interact to determine the variance of the overall portfolio.

APPLICATION 7.5 | Calculating the Expected Return for a Portfolio

LEARNING BY DOING

Problem You have become concerned that you have too much of your money invested in your pizza restaurant and have decided to diversify your personal portfolio. Right now the pizza restaurant is your only investment. To diversify, you plan to sell 45 percent of your restaurant and invest the proceeds from the sale, in equal proportions, into a stock market index fund and a bond market index fund. Over the next year, you expect to earn a return of 15 percent on your remaining investment in the pizza restaurant, 12 percent on your investment in the stock market index fund, and 8 percent on your investment in the bond market index fund. What return will you expect from your diversified portfolio over the next year?

Approach First, calculate the fraction of your portfolio that will be invested in each type of asset after you have diversified. Then use Equation 7.8 to calculate the expected return on the portfolio.

Solution After you have diversified, 55 percent (100 percent − 45 percent = 55 percent) of your portfolio will be invested in your restaurant, 22.5 percent (45 percent × 0.50 = 22.5 percent) will be invested in the stock market index fund, and 22.5 percent (45 percent × 0.50 = 22.5 percent) will be invested in the bond market index fund. Therefore, from Equation 7.8, we know that the expected return for your portfolio is:

$$\begin{aligned} E(R_{Portfolio}) &= [x_{Rest} \times E(R_{Rest})] + [x_{Stock} \times E(R_{Stock})] + [x_{Bond} \times E(R_{Bond})] \\ &= (0.550 \times 0.15) + (0.225 \times 0.12) + (0.225 \times 0.08) \\ &= 0.1275, \text{ or } 12.75\% \end{aligned}$$

At 12.75 percent, the expected return is an average of the returns on the individual assets in your portfolio, weighted by the fraction of your portfolio that is invested in each.

[4]For more information on noodling, see the April 21, 2006, *New York Times* article titled "In the Jaws of a Catfish," by Ethan Todras-Whitehill and the May 16, 2011, *Wall Street Journal* article titled "Long Arm of the Law Penalizes Texans Who Nab Catfish by Hand," by Ana Campoy.

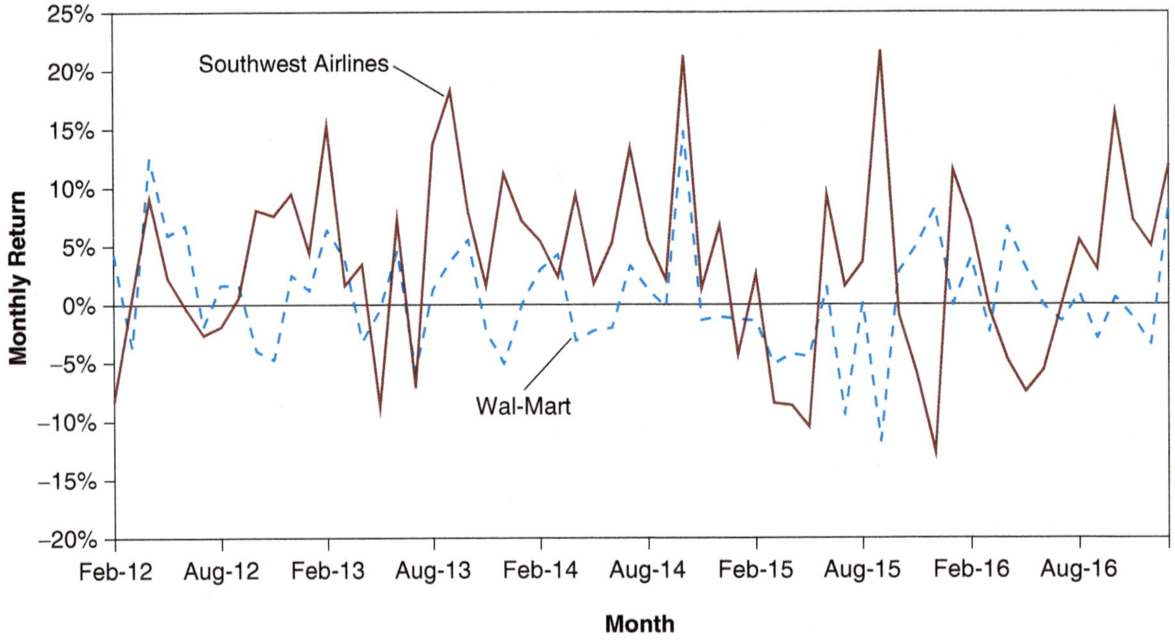

EXHIBIT 7.6 Monthly Returns for Southwest Airlines and Wal-Mart Stock from February 2012 through January 2017

The returns on two stocks are generally different. In some periods, the return on one stock is positive, while the return on the other is negative. Even when the returns on both are positive or negative, they are rarely exactly the same.

The prices of two stocks in a portfolio will rarely, if ever, change by the same amount and in the same direction at the same time. Normally, the price of one stock will change by more than the price of the other. In fact, the prices of two stocks will frequently move in different directions. These differences in price movements affect the total variance of the returns for a portfolio.

Exhibit 7.6 shows monthly returns for the stock of Southwest Airlines and Wal-Mart over the period from February 2012 through January 2017. Notice that the returns on these shares are generally different and that the prices of the shares can move in different directions in a given month (one stock has a positive return when the other has a negative return). When the stock prices move in opposite directions, the change in the price of one stock offsets at least some of the change in the price of the other stock. As a result, the level of risk for a portfolio of the two stocks is less than the average of the risks associated with the individual shares.

This means that we *cannot* calculate the variance of a portfolio containing two assets simply by calculating the weighted average of the variances of the individual stocks. We have to account for the fact that the returns on different shares in a portfolio tend to partially offset each other. For a two-asset portfolio, we calculate the variance of the returns using the following formula:

$$\sigma^2_{R_{2\ \text{Asset portfolio}}} = x_1^2\sigma^2_{R_1} + x_2^2\sigma^2_{R_2} + 2x_1x_2\sigma_{R_{1,2}} \tag{7.9}$$

where x_i represents the fraction of the portfolio invested in stock i, $\sigma^2_{R_i}$ is the variance of the return of stock i, and $\sigma_{R_{1,2}}$ is the **covariance** of the returns between stocks 1 and 2. The **covariance of returns** is a measure of how the returns on two assets covary, or move together. The third term in Equation 7.9 accounts for the fact that returns from the two assets will offset each other to some extent. The covariance of returns is calculated using the following formula:

covariance of returns a measure of how the returns on two assets covary, or move together

$$\text{Cov}(R_1, R_2) = \sigma_{R_{1,2}} = \sum_{i=1}^{n} \{p_i \times [R_{1,i} - E(R_1)] \times [R_{2,i} - E(R_2)]\} \tag{7.10}$$

where i represents outcomes rather than assets. Compare this equation with Equation 7.3, reproduced here:

$$\text{Var}(R) = \sigma^2_R = \sum_{i=1}^{n} \{p_i \times [R_i - E(R)]^2\}$$

You can see that the covariance calculation is very similar to the variance calculation. The difference is that, instead of squaring the difference between the return from each outcome and the expected return for an individual asset, we calculate the product of this difference for two different assets.

Just as it is difficult to directly interpret the variance of the returns for an asset—recall that the variance is in units of squared dollars—it is difficult to directly interpret the covariance of returns between two assets. We get around this problem by dividing the covariance of returns by the product of the standard deviations of the returns for the two assets. This gives us the correlation, ρ, between the returns on those assets:

$$\rho_{R_{1,2}} = \frac{\sigma_{R_{1,2}}}{\sigma_{R_1}\sigma_{R_2}} \tag{7.11}$$

The correlation between the returns on two assets will always have a value between −1 and +1. This makes the interpretation of this variable straightforward. A *negative correlation* means that the returns tend to have opposite signs. For example, when the return on one asset is positive, the return on the other asset tends to be negative. If the correlation is exactly −1, the returns on the two assets are perfectly negatively correlated. In other words, when the return on one asset is positive, the return on the other asset will always be negative. A *positive correlation* means that when the return on one asset is positive, the return on the other asset also tends to be positive. If the correlation is exactly equal to +1, then the returns of the two assets are said to be perfectly positively correlated. The return on one asset will always be positive when the return on the other asset is positive. Finally, a *correlation of 0* means that the returns on the assets are not correlated. In this case, the fact that the return on one asset is positive or negative tells you nothing about how likely it is that the return on the other asset will be positive or negative.

Let's work an example to see how Equation 7.9 is used to calculate the variance of the returns on a portfolio that consists of 50 percent Southwest Airlines stock and 50 percent Wal-Mart stock. Using the data plotted in Exhibit 7.6, we can calculate the variance of the annual returns for the Southwest Airlines and Wal-Mart stocks, σ_R^2, to be 0.0729 and 0.0274, respectively. The covariance between the annual returns on these two stocks is 0.0067. We do not show the calculations for the variances and the covariance because each of these numbers was calculated using 60 different monthly returns. These calculations are too cumbersome to illustrate. Rest assured, however, that they were calculated using Equations 7.3 and 7.10.[5] With these values, we can calculate the variance of a portfolio that consists of 50 percent Southwest Airlines (SW) stock and 50 percent Wal-Mart stock as:

$$\begin{aligned}\sigma^2_{R_{\text{Portfolio of SW and Wal-mart}}} &= x^2_{SW}\sigma^2_{R_{SW}} + x^2_{\text{Wal-Mart}}\sigma^2_{R_{\text{Wal-Mart}}} + 2x_{SW}x_{\text{Wal-Mart}}\sigma_{R_{\text{SW, Wal-Mart}}} \\ &= (0.5)^2(0.0729) + (0.5)^2(0.0274) + 2(0.5)(0.5)(0.0067) \\ &= 0.0284\end{aligned}$$

You can see that this portfolio variance is smaller than the average of the variances of the returns on the Southwest Airlines and Wal-Mart stocks [(0.0729 + 0.0274)/2 = 0.0501]. This is because their returns are not perfectly positively correlated.

If we calculate the standard deviations by taking the square roots of the variances, we find that the standard deviations for Southwest Airlines stock, Wal-Mart stock, and the portfolio consisting of those two stocks are 0.270 (27.0 percent), 0.166 (16.6 percent), and 0.169 (0.169 percent), respectively.

Exhibit 7.7 illustrates the monthly returns for the portfolio of Southwest Airlines and Wal-Mart stock, along with the monthly returns for the individual stocks. You can see in this exhibit that the returns on the portfolio vary quite a bit. However, as noted above, this variation is less than the average variation in the returns for the individual company shares.

Using Equation 7.11, we can calculate the correlation of the returns between Southwest Airlines and Wal-Mart stock as:

$$\rho_{R_{\text{SW, Wal-Mart}}} = \frac{\sigma_{R_{\text{SW, Wal-Mart}}}}{\sigma_{R_{SW}}\sigma_{R_{\text{Wal-Mart}}}} = \frac{0.0067}{0.270 \times 0.166} = 0.149$$

[5]The only adjustment that we had to make was to account for the fact that our calculations used monthly returns rather than annual returns. This adjustment simply required us to multiply each number we calculated by 12 because there are 12 months in a year.

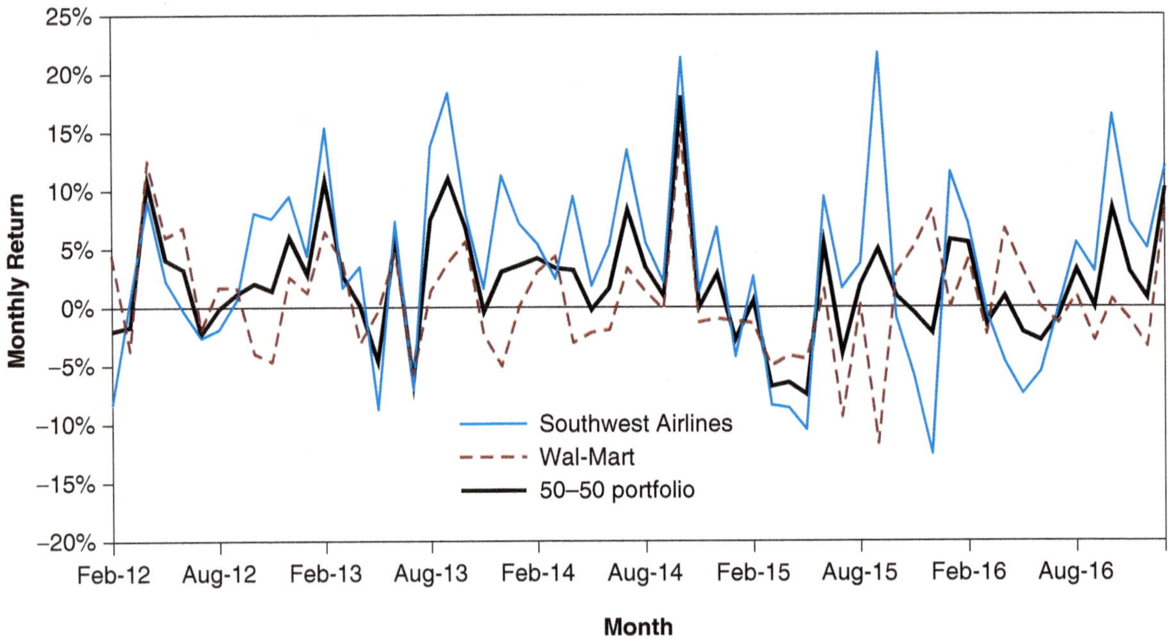

EXHIBIT 7.7 Monthly Returns for Southwest Airlines and Wal-Mart Stock and for a Portfolio with 50 Percent of the Value in Each of These Two Stocks from February 2012 through January 2017
The variation in the returns from a portfolio that consists of Southwest Airlines and Wal-Mart stock in equal proportions is less than the variation in the returns from either of those stocks alone.

The positive correlation tells us that the prices of Southwest Airlines and Wal-Mart stock tend to move in the same direction. However, the correlation of less than one tells us that they do not always do so. The fact that the prices of these two shares do not always move together is the reason that the returns on a portfolio of the two stocks have less variation than the average of the returns on the individual company shares. This example illustrates the benefit of *diversification*—how holding more than one asset with different risk characteristics can reduce the risk of a portfolio. Note that if the correlation of the returns between Southwest Airlines and Wal-Mart stock equaled one, holding these two stocks would not reduce risk because their prices would always move up or down together. Also, the standard deviation of the returns on the portfolio would equal the average of the standard deviations of the returns on the individual stocks.[6]

As we add more and more assets to a portfolio, calculating the variance using the approach illustrated in Equation 7.9 becomes increasingly complex. The reason for this is that we have to account for the covariance between each pair of assets. These more extensive calculations are beyond the scope of this book, but they are conceptually the same as those for a portfolio with two assets. **Learning by Doing Application 7.6** illustrates another calculation of the variance for a two asset portfolio.

LEARNING BY DOING

WileyPLUS

Need more help? Visit your WileyPLUS course.

APPLICATION 7.6 | Calculating the Variance of a Two-Asset Portfolio

Problem You are still planning to sell 45 percent of your pizza restaurant in order to diversify your personal portfolio. However, you have now decided to invest all of the proceeds in the stock market index fund. After you diversify, you will have 55 percent of your wealth invested in the restaurant and 45 percent invested in the stock market index fund. You have estimated the variances of the returns for these two investments and the covariance between their returns to be as follows:

$$\sigma^2_{R_{\text{Restaurant}}} = 0.0625$$
$$\sigma^2_{R_{\text{Stock market index}}} = 0.0400$$
$$\sigma_{R_{\text{Restaurant, Stock market index}}} = 0.0250$$

[6]You can see this by using Equation 7.11 to solve for $\sigma_{R_{1,2}} = \rho_{R_{1,2}}\sigma_{R_1}\sigma_{R_2}$, substituting for $\sigma_{R_{1,2}}$ in Equation 7.9, and then solving for $\sigma_{R_{2\text{Asset portfolio}}}$ by using algebra to solve for the square root of $\sigma^2_{R_{2\text{Asset portfolio}}}$.

What will be the variance and standard deviation of returns in your portfolio after you have sold the ownership interest in your restaurant and invested in the stock market index fund?

Approach Use Equation 7.9 to calculate the variance of the portfolio returns and then take the square root of this value to obtain the standard deviation.

Solution The variance of the portfolio returns is:

$$\begin{aligned}\sigma^2_{R_{\text{Portfolio}}} &= x^2_{R_{\text{Restaurant}}}\sigma^2_{R_{\text{Restaurant}}} + x^2_{R_{\text{Stock market index}}}\sigma^2_{R_{\text{Stock market index}}} \\ &\quad + 2x_{\text{Restaurant}}x_{\text{Stock market index}}\sigma_{R_{\text{Restaurant Stock market index}}} \\ &= [(0.55)^2 \times 0.0625] + [(0.45)^2 \times 0.0400] + (2 \times 0.55 \times 0.45 \times 0.0250) \\ &= 0.0394\end{aligned}$$

and the standard deviation is $(0.0394)^{1/2} = 0.1985$, or 19.85 percent.

Comparing the variance of the portfolio returns of 0.0394 with the variances of the restaurant returns, 0.0625, and the stock market index fund returns, 0.0400, shows that a portfolio with two or more assets can actually have a smaller variance of returns (and thus a smaller standard deviation of returns) than any of the individual assets in the portfolio.

The Limits of Diversification

In the sample calculations for the portfolio containing Southwest Airlines and Wal-Mart stock, we saw that the standard deviation of the returns for a portfolio consisting of equal investments in those two stocks was 16.9 percent from February 2012 through January 2017 and that this figure was lower than the average of the standard deviation of returns for the individual stocks. You might wonder how the standard deviation for the portfolio is likely to change if we increase the number of assets in the portfolio. The answer is simple. If the returns on the individual stocks added to our portfolio do not all change in the same way, then increasing the number of stocks in the portfolio will reduce the standard deviation of the portfolio returns even further.

Building Intuition

Diversified Portfolios are Less Risky

Diversified portfolios generally have less risk for a given level of return than the individual risky assets in the portfolio. This is because the values of individual assets rarely change by the same amount and in the same direction at the same time. As a result, some of the variation in an asset's value can be diversified away by owning another asset at the same time. This is important because it tells us that investors can eliminate some of the risk associated with individual investments by holding them in a diversified portfolio.

Let's consider a simple example to illustrate this point. Suppose that all assets have a standard deviation of returns that is equal to 40 percent and that the covariance between the returns for each pair of assets is 0.048. If we form a portfolio in which we have an equal investment in two assets, the standard deviation of returns for the portfolio will be 32.25 percent. If we add a third asset, the portfolio standard deviation of returns will decrease to 29.21 percent. It will be even lower, at 27.57 percent, for a four-asset portfolio. **Exhibit 7.8** illustrates how the standard deviation for the portfolio declines as more stocks are added.

In addition to showing how increasing the number of assets decreases the overall risk of a portfolio, Exhibit 7.8 illustrates three other very important points. First, the decrease in the standard deviation for the portfolio gets smaller and smaller as more assets are added. You can see this effect by looking at the distance between the straight horizontal line and the plot of the standard deviation of the portfolio returns.

The second important point is this: as the number of assets becomes very large, the portfolio standard deviation does not approach zero; it decreases only so far. In the example in Exhibit 7.8, it approaches 21.9 percent. The standard deviation does not approach zero because we are assuming that the variations in the asset returns do not completely cancel each other out. This is a realistic assumption because in practice investors cannot diversify away all risk. They can diversify away risk that is unique to the individual assets, but they cannot diversify away risk that is common to all assets. The risk investors can diversify away is called **unsystematic or diversifiable risk**, and the risk they cannot diversify away is called **systematic or nondiversifiable risk**. In the next section, we will discuss systematic risk in detail.

unsystematic or diversifiable risk risk that can be eliminated through diversification

systematic or nondiversifiable risk risk that cannot be eliminated through diversification

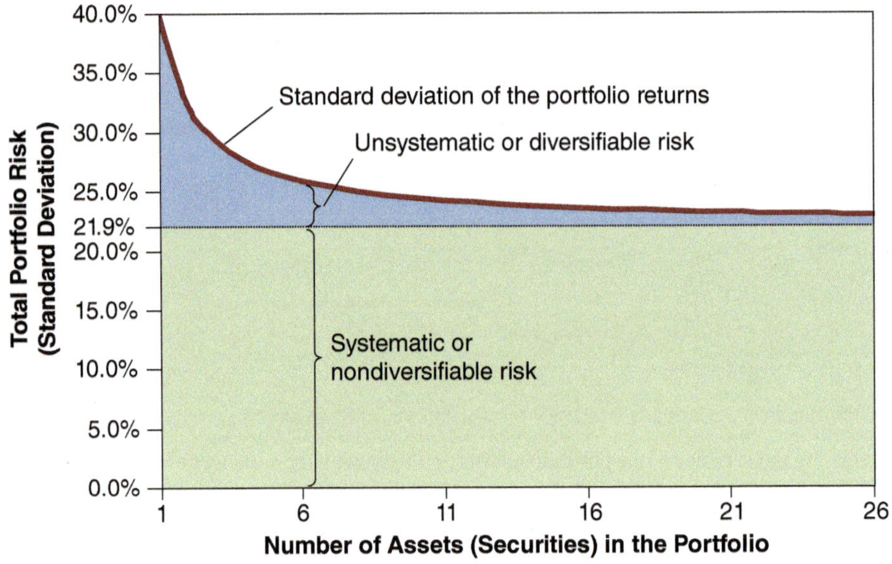

EXHIBIT 7.8 Total Risk in a Portfolio as the Number of Assets Increases

The total risk of a portfolio decreases as the number of assets increases. This is because the amount of unsystematic risk in the portfolio decreases. The diversification benefit from adding another asset declines as the total number of assets in the portfolio increases and the unsystematic risk approaches zero. Most of the diversification benefit can often be achieved with as few as 15 or 20 assets.

The third key point illustrated in Exhibit 7.8 is that most of the risk-reduction benefits from diversification can be achieved in a portfolio with 15 to 20 assets. Of course, the number of assets required to achieve a high level of diversification depends on the covariances between the assets in the portfolio. However, in general, it is not necessary to invest in a very large number of different assets.

Before You Go On

1. What does the coefficient of variation tell us, and how is it related to the Sharpe Ratio?
2. How would we expect the standard deviation of the return on an individual stock to compare with the standard deviation of the return on a stock index?
3. What are the two components of total risk?
4. Why does the total risk of a portfolio not approach zero as the number of assets in a portfolio becomes very large?

7.5 Systematic Risk

LEARNING OBJECTIVE

7. Discuss which type of risk matters to investors and why.

The objective of diversification is to eliminate variation in returns that is unique to individual assets. We diversify our investments across a number of different assets in the hope that these unique variations will cancel each other out. With complete diversification, all of the unsystematic risk is eliminated from the portfolio. An investor with a diversified portfolio still faces systematic risk, however, and we now turn our attention to that form of risk.

Why Systematic Risk Is All That Matters

The idea that unsystematic risk can be diversified away has direct implications for the relation between risk and return. If the transaction costs associated with constructing a diversified portfolio are relatively low, then rational, informed investors, such as the students who are taking this class, will prefer to hold diversified portfolios.

Diversified investors face only systematic risk, whereas investors whose portfolios are not well diversified face systematic risk plus unsystematic risk. Because they face less risk, the diversified investors will be willing to pay higher prices for individual assets than the other investors. Therefore, expected returns on individual assets will be lower than the total risk (systematic plus unsystematic risk) of those assets suggests they should be.

To illustrate, consider two individual investors, Emily and Jane. Each of them is trying to decide if she should purchase stock in your pizza restaurant. Emily holds a diversified portfolio and Jane does not. If your restaurant's stock has systematic and unsystematic risk, Emily faces less risk than Jane (Emily can diversify away the unsystematic risk while Jane cannot) and will require a lower expected rate of return. Consequently, Emily will be willing to pay a higher price than Jane.

If the market includes a large number of diversified investors such as Emily, competition among these investors will drive the price of your restaurant's shares up further. This competition will ultimately push the price up to the point where the expected return just compensates all investors for the systematic risk associated with your stock. The bottom line is this: because of competition among diversified investors, all investors are only rewarded for bearing systematic risk in asset markets. For this reason, we are concerned only about systematic risk when we think about the relation between risk and return in finance.

Building Intuition

Systematic Risk Is the Risk That Matters

The required rate of return on an asset depends only on the systematic risk associated with that asset. Because unsystematic risk can be diversified away, investors can and will eliminate their exposure to this risk. Competition among diversified investors will drive the prices of assets to the point where the expected returns will compensate investors for only the systematic risk that they bear.

Measuring Systematic Risk

If systematic risk is all that matters when we think about expected returns, then we cannot use the standard deviation of returns as a measure of risk.[7] The standard deviation is a measure of total risk. We need a way of quantifying the systematic risk of individual assets.

A natural starting point for doing this is to recognize that the most diversified portfolio possible will come closest to eliminating all unsystematic risk. Such a portfolio provides a natural benchmark against which we can measure the systematic risk of an individual asset. What is the most diversified portfolio possible? The answer is simple. It is the portfolio that consists of all assets, including stocks, bonds, real estate, precious metals, commodities, art, baseball cards, and so forth from all over the world. In finance, we call this the **market portfolio**.

market portfolio the portfolio of all assets

Unfortunately, we do not have very good data for most of these assets for most of the world, so we use the next best thing: the U.S. public stock market. A large number of stocks from a broad range of industries trade in this market. The companies that issue these stocks own a wide range of assets all over the world. These characteristics, combined with the facts that the U.S. market has been operating for a very long time and that we have very reliable and detailed information on prices for U.S. stocks, make the U.S. stock market a natural benchmark for estimating systematic risk.

Since systematic risk is, by definition, risk that cannot be diversified away, the systematic risk of an individual asset is really just a measure of the relation between the returns on the individual asset and the returns on the market. In fact, systematic risk is often referred to as

[7]This statement is true in the context of how expected returns are determined. However, the standard deviation is still a very useful measure of the risk faced by an individual investor who does not hold a diversified portfolio. For example, the owners of most small businesses have much of their personal wealth tied up in their businesses. They are certainly concerned about the total risk because it is directly related to the probability that they will go out of business and lose much of their wealth.

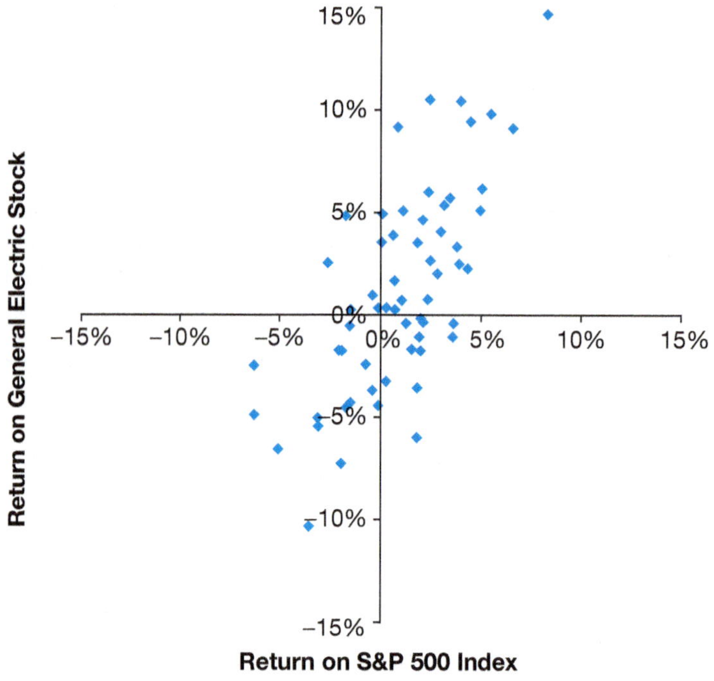

EXHIBIT 7.9 Plot of Monthly General Electric Company Stock and S&P 500 Index Returns: February 2012 through January 2017
The monthly returns on General Electric stock are positively related to the returns on the S&P 500 Index. In other words, the return on General Electric's stock tends to be higher when the return on the S&P 500 Index is higher and lower when the return on the S&P 500 Index is lower.

market risk a term commonly used to refer to nondiversifiable, or systematic, risk

market risk. To see how we might use data from the U.S. public stock market to estimate the systematic risk of an individual asset, look at **Exhibit 7.9**, which plots 60 historical monthly returns for General Electric Company (GE) against the corresponding monthly returns for the S&P 500 Index (a proxy for the U.S. stock market). In this plot, you can see that returns on GE stock tend to be higher when returns on the S&P 500 tend to be higher. The measure of systematic risk that we use in finance is a statistical measure of this relation.

We quantify the relation between the returns on GE stock and the market by finding the slope of the line that best represents the relation illustrated in Exhibit 7.9. Specifically, we estimate the slope of the *line of best fit.* We do this using the statistical technique called regression analysis. If you are not familiar with regression analysis, don't worry; the details are beyond the scope of this course. All you have to know is that this technique gives us the line that fits the data best.

Exhibit 7.10 illustrates the line that was estimated for the data in Exhibit 7.9 using regression analysis. Note that the slope of this line is 1.21. Recall from your math classes that the slope of a line equals the ratio of the rise (vertical distance) divided by the corresponding run (horizontal distance). In this case, the slope is the change in the return on GE stock divided by the change in the return on the U.S. stock market. A slope of 1.21 therefore means that, on average, the change in the return on GE stock was 1.21 times as large as the change in the return on the S&P 500 Index. Thus, if the S&P 500 Index goes up 1 percent, the average increase in GE's stock is 1.21 percent. This is a measure of systematic risk because it tells us that the volatility of the returns on GE stock is 1.21 times as large as that for the S&P 500 as a whole.

To explore this idea more completely, let's consider another, simpler example. Suppose that you have data for Nike stock and for the U.S. stock market (S&P 500 Index) for each of the past two years. In the first year, the return on the market was 10 percent, and the return on Nike stock was 15 percent. In the second year, the return on the market was 12 percent, and the return on Nike stock was 19 percent. From this information, we know that the return on Nike stock increased by 4 percent while the return on the market increased 2 percent. If we plotted the returns for Nike stock and for the market for each of the last two periods, as we did for GE stock and the market in Exhibits 7.9 and 7.10, and estimated the line that best fit

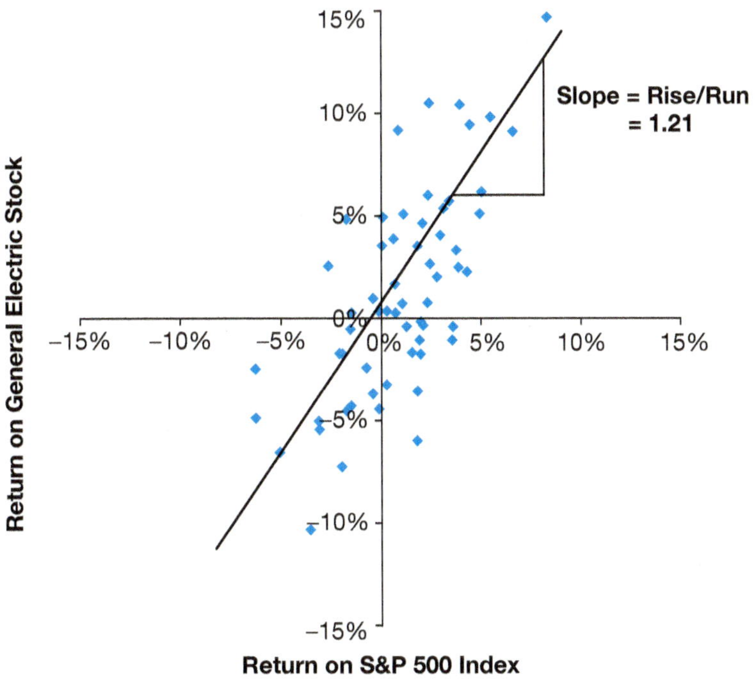

EXHIBIT 7.10 **Slope of Relation between General Electric Company Monthly Stock Returns and S&P 500 Index Returns: February 2012 through January 2017**

The line shown in the exhibit best represents the relation between the monthly returns on General Electric stock and the returns on the S&P 500 Index. The slope of this line, which equals 1.21, indicates that the return on General Electric stock tends to equal about 1.21 times the return on the S&P 500 Index.

the data, it would be a line that connected the dots for the two periods. The slope of this line would equal 2, calculated as follows:

$$\text{Slope} = \frac{\text{Rise}}{\text{Run}} = \frac{\text{Change in Nike return}}{\text{Change in market return}} = \frac{19\% - 15\%}{12\% - 10\%} = \frac{4\%}{2\%} = 2$$

Although we have to be careful about drawing conclusions when we have only two data points, we might interpret the slope of 2 to indicate that new information that causes the market return to increase by 1 percent will tend to cause the return on Nike stock to increase by 2 percent. Of course, the reverse might also be true. That is, new information that causes the market return to decrease by 1 percent may also cause the return on Nike stock to go down by 2 percent. To the extent that the same information is driving the changes in returns on Nike stock and on the market, it would not be possible for an investor in Nike stock to diversify this risk away. It is nondiversifiable, or systematic, risk.

In finance, we call the slope of the line of best fit **beta**. Often we simply use the corresponding Greek letter, β, to refer to this measure of systematic risk. As shown below, a beta of 1 tells us that an asset has just as much systematic risk as the market. A beta higher than or lower than 1 tells us that the asset has more or less systematic risk than the market, respectively. A beta of 0 indicates a risk-free security, such as a U.S. Treasury bill.

beta (β) a measure of nondiversifiable, systematic, or market, risk

$\beta = 1$	Same systematic risk as market
$\beta > 1$	More systematic risk than market
$\beta < 1$	Less systematic risk than market
$\beta = 0$	No systematic risk

Now you might ask yourself what happened to the unsystematic risk of GE or Nike stock. This is best illustrated by the GE example, where we have more than two observations. As you can see in Exhibit 7.10, the line of best fit does not go through each data point. That is because some of the change in GE's stock price each month reflected information that did not affect

Weblink

A convenient place to find betas for individual companies is MSN Money Central at http://moneycentral.msn.com. Just enter the stock symbol in the "Get Quote" box near the top of the page and hit "Enter" on your computer (try the railroad company CSX, for example). You will get prices, an estimate of the beta, and other financial information.

the S&P 500 as a whole. That information is the unsystematic component of the risk of GE's stock. The vertical distance between each data point and the line of best fit represents variation in GE's stock return that can be attributed to this unsystematic risk.

The positive slope (β) of the regression line in Exhibit 7.10 tells us that returns for the S&P 500 and for GE stock will tend to move in the same direction. The return on the S&P 500 and the return on GE's stock will not always change in the same direction, however, because the unsystematic risk associated with GE stock can more than offset the effect of the market in any particular period. In the next section, we will discuss the implications of beta for the level (as opposed to the change) in the expected return for a stock such as GE.

Before You Go On

1. Why are returns on the stock market used as a benchmark in measuring systematic risk?
2. How is beta estimated?
3. How would you interpret a beta of 1.5 for an asset? A beta of 0.75?

7.6 Compensation for Bearing Systematic Risk

Now that we have identified the measure of the risk that diversified investors care about—systematic risk—we are in a position to examine how this measure relates to expected returns. Earlier, in our discussion of the coefficient of variation and the Sharpe Ratio, we asserted that the expected return over and above the risk-free rate is the return that investors expect to earn for bearing risk. To see why this must be true, think about the rate of return that you would require for an investment. First, you would want to make sure that you were compensated for inflation. It would not make sense to invest if you expected the investment to return an amount that did not at least allow you to have the same purchasing power that the money you invested had when you made the investment. Second, you would want some compensation for the fact that you are giving up the use of your money for a period of time. This compensation may be very small if you are forgoing the use of your money for only a short time, such as when you invest in a 30-day Treasury bill, but it might be relatively large if you are investing for several years. Finally, you would also require compensation for the systematic risk associated with the investment.

When you invest in a U.S. government security such as a Treasury bill, note, or bond, you are investing in a security that has no risk of default. After all, the U.S. government can always increase taxes or print more money to pay you back. Changes in economic conditions and other factors that affect the returns on other assets do not affect the default risk of U.S. government securities. As a result, these securities do not have systematic risk, and their returns can be viewed as risk free. In other words, returns on government bonds reflect the compensation required by investors to account for the impact of inflation on purchasing power and for their inability to use the money during the life of the investment.

It follows that the difference between required returns on government securities and required returns for risky investments represents the compensation investors require for taking risk. Recognizing this allows us to write the expected return for an asset i as:

$$E(R_i) = R_{rf} + \text{Compensation for taking risk}_i$$

where R_{rf} is the return on a security with a risk-free rate of return, which analysts typically estimate by looking at returns on government securities. The compensation for taking risk, which varies with the risk of the asset, is added to the risk-free rate of return to get an estimate of the expected rate of return for an asset. If we recognize that the compensation for taking risk varies with asset risk and that systematic risk is what matters, we can write the preceding equation as follows:

$$E(R_i) = R_{rf} + (\text{Units of systematic risk}_i \times \text{Compensation per unit of systematic risk})$$

where units of systematic $risk_i$ is the number of units of systematic risk associated with asset *i*. Finally, if beta, β, is the appropriate measure for the number of units of systematic risk, we can also define compensation for taking risk as follows:

$$\text{Compensation for taking risk}_i = \beta_i \times \text{Compensation per unit of systematic risk}$$

where β_i is the beta for asset *i*.

Remember that beta is a measure of systematic risk that is directly related to the risk of the market as a whole. If the beta for an asset is 2, that asset has twice as much systematic risk as the market. If the beta for an asset is 0.5, then the asset has half as much systematic risk as the market. Recognizing this natural interpretation of beta suggests that the appropriate "unit of systematic risk" is the level of risk in the market as a whole and that the appropriate "compensation per unit of systematic risk" is the expected return required for the level of systematic risk in the market as a whole. The required rate of return on the market, over and above that of the risk-free return, represents compensation required by investors for bearing a market (systematic) risk. This suggests that:

$$\text{Compensation per unit of systematic risk} = E(R_m) - R_{rf}$$

where $E(R_m)$ is the expected return on the market. The term $E(R_m) - R_{rf}$ is called the *market risk premium*. Consequently, we can now write the equation for expected return as:

$$E(R_i) = R_{rf} + \beta_i[E(R_m) - R_{rf}] \quad (7.12)$$

7.7 The Capital Asset Pricing Model

LEARNING OBJECTIVE

8. Describe what the Capital Asset Pricing Model (CAPM) tells us and how to use it to evaluate whether the expected return of an asset is sufficient to compensate an investor for the risks associated with that asset.

In deriving Equation 7.12, we intuitively arrived at the **Capital Asset Pricing Model (CAPM)**. Equation 7.12 is the CAPM, a model that describes the relation between risk and expected return. We will discuss the predictions of the CAPM in more detail shortly, but first let's look more closely at how it works.

Capital Asset Pricing Model (CAPM) a model that describes the relation between risk and expected return

Suppose that you want to estimate the expected return for a stock that has a beta of 1.5 and that the expected return on the market and risk-free rate are 10 percent and 4 percent, respectively. We can use Equation 7.12 (the CAPM) to find the expected return for this stock:

$$\begin{aligned} E(R_i) &= R_{rf} + \beta_i[E(R_m) - R_{rf}] \\ &= 0.04 + [1.5 \times (0.10 - 0.04)] = 0.13, \text{ or } 13\% \end{aligned}$$

Note that we must have three pieces of information in order to use Equation 7.12: (1) the risk-free rate, (2) beta, and (3) either the market risk premium or the expected return on the market. Recall that the market risk premium is the difference between the expected return on the market and the risk-free rate $[E(R_m) - R_{rf}]$, which is 6 percent in the above example.

While the expected return on the market is known in the above example, we actually cannot observe it in practice. For this reason, financial analysts estimate the market risk premium using historical data. We discuss how they do this in Chapter 13.

The Security Market Line

Security Market Line (SML) a plot of the relation between expected return and systematic risk

Exhibit 7.11 displays a plot of Equation 7.12 to illustrate how the expected return on an asset varies with systematic risk. This plot shows that the relation between the expected return on an asset and beta is positive and linear. In other words, it is a straight line with a positive slope. The line in Exhibit 7.11 is known as the **Security Market Line (SML)**.

In Exhibit 7.11 you can see that the expected rate of return equals the risk-free rate when beta equals 0. This makes sense because when investors do not face systematic risk, they will only require a return that reflects the expected rate of inflation and the fact that they are giving up the use of their money for a period of time. Exhibit 7.11 also shows that the expected return on an asset equals the expected return on the market when beta equals 1. This is not surprising given that both the asset and the market would have the same level of systematic risk if this were the case.

It is important to recognize that the SML illustrates what the CAPM predicts the expected total return should be for various values of beta. The actual expected total return depends on the price of the asset. You can see this from Equation 7.1:

$$R_T = \frac{\Delta P + CF_1}{P_0}$$

where P_0 is the price that the asset is currently selling for. If an asset's price implies that the expected return is greater than that predicted by the CAPM, that asset will plot above the SML in Exhibit 7.11. This means that the asset's price is lower than the CAPM suggests it should be. Conversely, if the expected return on an asset plots below the SML, this implies that the asset's price is higher than the CAPM suggests it should be. The point at which a particular asset plots relative to the SML, then, tells us something about whether the price of that asset might be low or high. Recognizing this fact can be helpful in evaluating the attractiveness of an investment such as the General Electric stock in **Learning by Doing Application 7.7**.

Decision Making Example 7.2 further illustrates application of the concepts discussed in this section to the selection of investments.

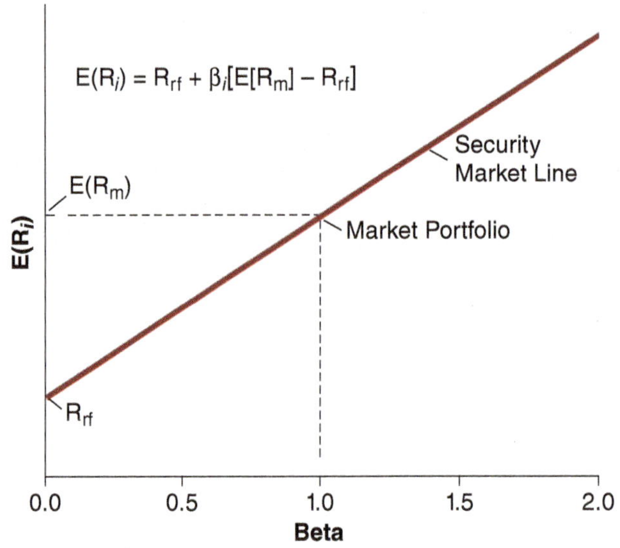

EXHIBIT 7.11 The Security Market Line

The Security Market Line (SML) is the line that shows the relation between expected return and systematic risk, as measured by beta. When beta equals 0 and there is no systematic risk, the expected return equals the risk-free rate. As systematic risk (beta) increases, the expected return increases. This is an illustration of the positive relation between risk and return. The SML shows that it is systematic risk that matters to investors.

APPLICATION 7.7 | Expected Returns and Systematic Risk

LEARNING BY DOING

Problem You are considering buying 100 shares of General Electric stock. The Yahoo Finance Web site reports that the beta for General Electric is 1.21. The risk-free rate is 4 percent, and the market risk premium is 6 percent. What is the expected rate of return on General Electric stock according to the CAPM?

Approach Use Equation 7.12 to calculate the expected return on General Electric stock.

Solution The expected return is:

$$\begin{aligned} E(R_{GE}) &= R_{rf} + \beta_{GE}[E(R_m) - R_{rf}] \\ &= 0.04 + (1.21 \times 0.06) = 0.1126, \text{ or } 11.26\% \end{aligned}$$

EXAMPLE 7.2 | Choosing between Two Investments

DECISION MAKING

Situation You are trying to decide whether to invest in one or both of two different stocks. Stock 1 has a beta of 0.8 and an expected return of 7.0 percent. Stock 2 has a beta of 1.2 and an expected return of 9.5 percent. You remember learning about the CAPM in school and believe that it does a good job of telling you what the appropriate expected return should be for a given level of risk. Since the risk-free rate is 4 percent and the market risk premium is 6 percent, the CAPM tells you that the appropriate expected rate of return for an asset with a beta of 0.8 is 8.8 percent. The corresponding return for an asset with a beta of 1.2 is 11.2 percent. Should you invest in either or both of these stocks?

Decision You should not invest in either stock. The expected returns for both of them are below the values predicted by the CAPM for investments with the same level of risk. In other words, both would plot below the line in Exhibit 7.11. This implies that they are both overpriced.

The Capital Asset Pricing Model and Portfolio Returns

The expected return for a portfolio can also be estimated using the CAPM. The expected return on a portfolio with n assets is calculated using the relation:

$$E(R_{n\text{ Asset portfolio}}) = R_{rf} + \beta_{n\text{ Asset portfolio}}[E(R_m) - R_{rf}]$$

Of course, this should not be surprising since investing in a portfolio is simply an alternative to investing in a single asset.

The fact that the SML is a straight line turns out to be rather convenient if we want to estimate the beta for a portfolio. Recall that the equation for the expected return for a portfolio with n assets was given by Equation 7.8:

$$\begin{aligned} E(R_{\text{Portfolio}}) &= \sum_{i=1}^{n} [x_i \times E(R_i)] \\ &= [x_1 \times E(R_1)] + [x_2 \times E(R_2)] + \cdots + [x_n \times E(R_n)] \end{aligned}$$

If we substitute Equation 7.12 into Equation 7.8 for each of the n assets and rearrange the equation, we find that the beta for a portfolio is simply a weighted average of the betas for the individual assets in the portfolio. In other words:

$$\beta_{n\text{ Asset portfolio}} = \sum_{i=1}^{n} x_i\beta_i = x_1\beta_1 + x_2\beta_2 + x_3\beta_3 + \cdots + x_n\beta_n \qquad (7.13)$$

where x_i is the proportion of the portfolio value that is invested in asset i, β_i is the beta of asset i, and n is the number of assets in the portfolio. This formula makes it simple to calculate the beta of any portfolio of assets once you know the betas of the individual assets. As an exercise, you might prove this to yourself by using Equations 7.8 and 7.12 to derive Equation 7.13.

Let's consider an example to see how Equation 7.13 is used. Suppose that you invested 25 percent of your wealth in a fully diversified market fund, 25 percent in risk-free Treasury bills, and 50 percent in a house with twice as much systematic risk as the market. What is the beta of your overall portfolio? What rate of return would you expect to earn from this portfolio if the risk-free rate is 4 percent and the market risk premium is 6 percent?

We know that the beta for the market must equal 1 by definition and that the beta for a risk-free asset equals 0. The beta for your home must be 2 since it has twice the systematic risk of the market. Therefore, the beta of your portfolio is:

$$\begin{aligned}\beta_{\text{Portfolio}} &= x_{\text{Fund}}\beta_{\text{Fund}} + x_{\text{TB}}\beta_{\text{TB}} + x_{\text{House}}\beta_{\text{House}}\\ &= (0.25 \times 1.0) + (0.25 \times 0.0) + (0.50 \times 2.0)\\ &= 1.25\end{aligned}$$

Your portfolio has 1.25 times as much systematic risk as the market. Based on Equation 7.12, you would, therefore, expect to earn a return of 11.5 percent, calculated as follows:

$$\begin{aligned}E(R_{\text{Portfolio}}) &= R_{\text{rf}} + \beta_{\text{Portfolio}}[E(R_m) - R_{\text{rf}}]\\ &= 0.04 + (1.25 \times 0.06) = 0.115, \text{ or } 11.5\%\end{aligned}$$

Learning by Doing Application 7.8 illustrates another calculation of the expected return for a portfolio.

LEARNING BY DOING

WileyPLUS

Need more help? Visit your WileyPLUS course.

APPLICATION 7.8 | Portfolio Risk and Expected Return

Problem You have recently become very interested in real estate. To gain some experience as a real estate investor, you have decided to get together with nine of your friends to buy three small cottages near campus. If you and your friends pool your money, you will have just enough to buy the three properties. Since each investment requires the same amount of money and you will have a 10 percent interest in each, you will effectively have one-third of your portfolio invested in each cottage.

While the cottages cost the same, they are different distances from campus and in different neighborhoods. You believe that this causes them to have different levels of systematic risk, and you estimate that the betas for the individual cottages are 1.2, 1.3, and 1.5. If the risk-free rate is 4 percent and the market risk premium is 6 percent, what will be the expected return on your real estate portfolio after you make all three investments?

Approach There are two approaches that you can use to solve this problem. First, you can estimate the expected return for each cottage using Equation 7.12 and then calculate the expected return on the portfolio using Equation 7.8. Alternatively, you can calculate the beta for the portfolio using Equation 7.13 and then use Equation 7.12 to calculate the expected return.

Solution Using the first approach, we find that Equation 7.12 gives us the following expected returns:

$$\begin{aligned}E(R_i) &= R_{\text{rf}} + \beta_i[E(R_m) - R_{\text{rf}}]\\ &= 0.04 + (1.2 \times 0.06) = 0.112, \text{ or } 11.2\%, \text{ for cottage 1}\\ &= 0.04 + (1.3 \times 0.06) = 0.118, \text{ or } 11.8\%, \text{ for cottage 2}\\ &= 0.04 + (1.5 \times 0.06) = 0.130, \text{ or } 13.0\%, \text{ for cottage 3}\end{aligned}$$

Therefore, from Equation 7.8, the expected return on the portfolio is:

$$\begin{aligned}E(R_{\text{Portfolio}}) &= [x_1 \times E(R_1)] + [x_2 \times E(R_2)] + [x_3 \times E(R_3)]\\ &= (1/3 \times 0.112) + (1/3 \times 0.118) + (1/3 \times 0.13) = 0.12, \text{ or } 12.0\%\end{aligned}$$

Using the second approach, from Equation 7.13, the beta of the portfolio is:

$$\beta_{\text{Portfolio}} = x_1\beta_1 + x_2\beta_2 + x_3\beta_3 = (1/3)(1.2) + (1/3)(1.3) + (1/3)(1.5) = 1.33333$$

and from Equation 7.12, the expected return is:

$$\begin{aligned}E(R_{\text{Portfolio}}) &= R_{\text{rf}} + \beta_{\text{Portfolio}}[E(R_m) - R_{\text{rf}}]\\ &= 0.04 + (1.33333 \times 0.06) = 0.120, \text{ or } 12.0\%\end{aligned}$$

Up to this point, we have focused on calculating the expected rate of return for an investment in any asset from the perspective of an investor, such as a stockholder. A natural question that might arise is how these concepts relate to the rate of return that should be used within a firm to evaluate a project. The short answer is that they are the same. The rate of return used to discount the cash flows for a project with a particular level of systematic risk is exactly the same as the rate of return that an investor would expect to receive from an investment in any asset having the same level of systematic risk. In Chapter 13 we will explore the relation between the expected return and the rate used to discount project cash flows in much more detail. By the time we finish that discussion, you will understand thoroughly how businesses determine the rate that they use to discount the cash flows from their investments.

Before You Go On

1. How is the expected return on an asset related to its systematic risk?
2. What name is given to the relation between risk and expected return implied by the CAPM?
3. If an asset's expected return does not plot on the line in question 2 above, what does that imply about its price?

Summary of Learning Objectives

1 Explain the relation between risk and return.

Investors require higher returns for taking greater risk. They prefer the investment with the highest possible return for a given level of risk or the investment with the lowest risk for a given level of return.

2 Describe the two components of a total holding period return, and calculate this return for an asset.

The total holding period return on an investment consists of a capital appreciation component and an income component. This return is calculated using Equation 7.1. It is important to recognize that investors do not care whether they receive a dollar of return through capital appreciation or as a cash dividend. Investors value both sources of return equally.

3 Explain what an expected return is and calculate the expected return for an asset.

The expected return is a weighted average of the possible returns from an investment, where each of these returns is weighted by the probability that it will occur. It is calculated using Equation 7.2.

4 Explain what the standard deviation of returns is and why it is very useful in finance, and calculate it for an asset.

The standard deviation of returns is a measure of the total risk associated with the returns from an asset. It is useful in evaluating returns in finance because the returns on many assets tend to be normally distributed. The standard deviation of returns provides a convenient measure of the dispersion of returns. In other words, it tells us about the probability that a return will fall within a particular distance from the expected value or within a particular range. To calculate the standard deviation, the variance is first calculated using Equation 7.3. The standard deviation of returns is then calculated by taking the square root of the variance.

5 Explain what an arithmetic average return is and what a geometric return is, and calculate these returns for an asset.

The arithmetic average return is the return earned in an average period while the geometric average return is the average compounded return earned by an investor. Equations 7.4 and 7.5 are used to calculate these returns.

6 Explain the concept of diversification.

Diversification entails reducing risk by investing in two or more assets whose values do not always move in the same direction at the same time. Investing in a portfolio containing assets whose prices do not always move together reduces risk because some of the changes in the prices of individual assets offset each other. This can cause the overall variance in the returns of an investor's portfolio to be lower than if it consisted of only a single asset.

7 Discuss which type of risk matters to investors and why.

Investors care about only systematic risk. This is because they can eliminate unsystematic risk by holding a diversified portfolio. Diversified investors will bid up prices for assets to the point at which they are just being compensated for the systematic risks they must bear.

8 Describe what the Capital Asset Pricing Model (CAPM) tells us and how to use it to evaluate whether the expected return of an asset is sufficient to compensate an investor for the risks associated with that asset.

The CAPM tells us that the relation between systematic risk and return is linear and that the risk-free rate of return is the appropriate return for an asset with no systematic risk. From the CAPM we know what rate of return investors will require for an investment with a particular amount of systematic risk (beta). This means that we can use the expected return predicted by the CAPM as a benchmark for evaluating whether expected returns for individual assets are sufficient. If the expected return for an asset is less than that predicted by the CAPM, then the asset is an unattractive investment because its expected return is lower than the CAPM indicates it should be. By the same token, if the expected return for an asset is greater than that predicted by the CAPM, then the asset is an attractive investment because its return is higher than it should be.

Summary of Key Equations

Equation	Description	Formula
7.1	Total holding period return	$R_T = R_{CA} + R_I = \frac{P_1 - P_0}{P_0} + \frac{CF_1}{P_0} = \frac{\Delta P + CF_1}{P_0}$
7.2	Expected return on an asset	$E(R_{Asset}) = \sum_{i=1}^{n} (p_i \times R_i)$
7.3	Variance of return on an asset	$Var(R) = \sigma_R^2 = \sum_{i=1}^{n} \{p_i \times [R_i - E(R)^2]\}$
7.4	Arithmetic average return	$R_{Arithmetic\ average} = \frac{\sum_{i=1}^{n} R_i}{n}$
7.5	Geometric (compounded) average return	$R_{Geometric\ average} = [(1 + R_1) \times (1 + R_2) \times \cdots \times (1 + R_n)]^{1/n} - 1$
7.6	Coefficient of variation	$CV_i = \frac{\sigma_{R_i}}{E(R_i)}$
7.7	Sharpe Ratio	$S = \frac{E(R_i) - R_{rf}}{\sigma_{R_i}}$
7.8	Expected return for a portfolio	$E(R_{Portfolio}) = \sum_{i=1}^{n} [x_i \times E(R_i)]$
7.9	Variance for a two-asset portfolio	$\sigma^2_{R_{2Asset\ portfolio}} = x_1^2\sigma^2_{R_1} + x_2^2\sigma^2_{R_2} + 2x_1x_2\sigma_{R_{1,2}}$
7.10	Covariance of returns between two assets	$\sigma_{R_{1,2}} = \sum_{i=1}^{n} \{p_i \times [R_{1,i} - E(R_1)] \times [R_{2,i} - E(R_2)]\}$
7.11	Correlation between the returns on two assets	$\rho_{R_{1,2}} = \frac{\sigma_{R_{1,2}}}{\sigma_{R_1}\sigma_{R_2}}$
7.12	Expected return and systematic risk	$E(R_i) = R_{rf} + \beta_i[E(R_m) - R_{rf}]$
7.13	Portfolio beta	$\beta_{n\ Asset\ portfolio} = \sum_{i=1}^{n} x_i\beta_i$

Self-Study Problems

7.1 Kaaran made a friendly wager with a colleague that involves the result from flipping a coin. If heads comes up, Kaaran must pay her colleague \$15; otherwise, her colleague will pay Kaaran \$15. What is Kaaran's expected cash flow, and what is the variance of that cash flow if the coin has an equal probability of coming up heads or tails? Suppose Kaaran's colleague is willing to handicap the bet by paying her \$20 if the coin toss results in tails. If everything else remains the same, what are Kaaran's expected cash flow and the variance of that cash flow?

7.2 You know that the price of CFI, Inc., stock will be \$12 exactly one year from today. Today the price of the stock is \$11. Describe what must happen to the price of CFI, Inc., today in order for an investor to generate a 20 percent return over the next year. Assume that CFI does not pay dividends.

7.3 The expected value of a normal distribution of prices for a stock is \$50. If you are 90 percent sure that the price of the stock will be between \$40 and \$60, then what is the variance of the stock price?

7.4 During the period from 2011 through 2015 the annual returns on small U.S. stocks were −3.26 percent, 18.23 percent, 45.07 percent, 2.92 percent, and −3.60 percent, respectively. What would a \$1 investment, made at the beginning of 2011, have been worth at the end of 2015? What average annual return would have been earned on this investment?

7.5 You must choose between investing in Stock A or Stock B. You have already used CAPM to calculate the rate of return you should expect to receive for each stock given each one's systematic risk and decided that the expected return for both exceeds that predicted by CAPM by the same amount. In other words, both are equally attractive investments for a diversified investor. However, since you are still in school and do not have a lot of money, your investment portfolio is not diversified. You have decided to invest in the stock that has the highest expected return per unit of total risk. If the expected return and standard deviation of returns for Stock A are 10 percent and 25 percent, respectively, and the expected return and standard deviation of returns for Stock B are 15 percent and 40 percent, respectively, which should you choose? Assume that the risk-free rate is 5 percent.

7.6 CSB, Inc., stock has a beta of 1.35. If the expected market return is 14.5 percent and the risk-free rate is 5.5 percent, what does CAPM indicate the appropriate expected return for CSB stock is?

Solutions to Self-Study Problems

7.1 Part 1: $E(\text{cash flow}) = (0.5 \times -\$15) + (0.5 \times \$15) = 0$

$$\sigma^2_{\text{Cash flow}} = [0.5 \times (-\$15 - \$0)^2] + [0.5 \times (\$15 - \$0)^2] = 225$$

Part 2: $E(\text{cash flow}) = (0.5 \times -\$15) + (0.5 \times \$20) = \$2.50$

$$\sigma^2_{\text{Cash flow}} = [0.5 \times (-\$15 - \$2.50)^2] + [0.5 \times (\$20 - \$2.50)^2] = 306.25$$

7.2 The expected return for CFI based on today's stock price is (\$12 − \$11)/\$11 = 9.09 percent, which is lower than 20 percent. Since the stock price one year from today is fixed, the only way that you will generate a 20 percent return is if the price of the stock drops today. Consequently, the price of the stock today must drop to \$10. It is found by solving the following: $0.2 = (\$12 - x)/x$, or $x = \$10$.

7.3 Since you know that 1.645 standard deviations around the expected return captures 90 percent of the distribution, you can set up either of the following equations:

$$\$40 = \$50 - 1.645\sigma \quad \text{or} \quad \$60 = \$50 + 1.645\sigma$$

and solve for σ. Doing this with either equation yields:

$$\sigma = \$6.079 \text{ and } \sigma^2 = 36.954$$

7.4 The value in 2015 is:

$$V_{2015} = \$1 \times (1 + -0.0326) \times (1 + 0.1823) \times (1 + 0.4507) \times (1 + 0.0292) \times (1 + -0.0360)$$
$$= \$1.646$$

Substituting into Equation 7.4 and solving for the geometric average yields:

$$R_{\text{Geometric average}} = [(1 + R_1) \times (1 + R_2) \times \cdots \times (1 + R_n)]^{1/n} - 1$$
$$= [\$1.646]^{1/5} - 1$$
$$= 0.1048, \text{ or } 10.48 \text{ per year}$$

7.5 A comparison of the Sharpe Ratios for the two stocks will tell you which has the higher expected return per unit of total risk.

$$S_A = \frac{E(R_A) - R_{rf}}{\sigma_{R_A}} = \frac{0.10 - 0.05}{0.25} = 0.20$$

$$S_B = \frac{E(R_B) - R_{rf}}{\sigma_{R_B}} = \frac{0.15 - 0.05}{0.40} = 0.25$$

You should invest in Stock B because it has the highest expected return per unit of risk.

7.6 $E(R_{CSB}) = R_{rf} + \beta_{CSB}[E(R_M) - R_{rf}] = 0.055 + [1.35 \times (0.145 - 0.055)] = 0.1765$ or, 17.65%

WileyPLUS

Questions and Problems, Solution Walkthrough Videos, Learning by Doing Tutorials, and additional study tools and resources are available in WileyPLUS.

Discussion Questions

7.1 Suppose that you know the risk and the expected return for two stocks. Discuss the process you might utilize to determine which of the two stocks is a better buy. You may assume that the two stocks will be the only assets held in your portfolio.

7.2 What is the difference between the expected rate of return and the required rate of return? What does it mean if they are different for a particular asset at a particular point in time?

7.3 Suppose that the standard deviation of the returns on the shares of stock at two different companies is exactly the same. Does this mean that the required rate of return will be the same for these two stocks? How might the required rate of return on the stock of a third company be greater than the required rates of return on the stocks of the first two companies even if the standard deviation of the returns of the third company's stock is lower?

7.4 The correlation between Stocks A and B is 0.50, while the correlation between Stocks A and C is −0.5. You already own Stock A and are thinking of buying either Stock B or stock C. If you want your portfolio to have the lowest possible risk, would you buy Stock B or C? Would you expect the stock you choose to affect the return that you earn on your portfolio?

7.5 The idea that we can know the return on a security for each possible outcome is overly simplistic. However, even though we cannot possibly predict all possible outcomes, this fact has little bearing on the risk-free return. Explain why.

7.6 Which investment category included in Exhibit 7.3 has shown the greatest degree of risk in the United States since 1926? Explain why that makes sense in a world where the value of an asset in this investment category is likely to be more sensitive to changes in market conditions than is the price of a corporate bond.

7.7 You are concerned about one of the investments in your fully diversified portfolio. You just have an uneasy feeling about the CFO, Iam Shifty, of that particular firm. You do believe, however, that the firm makes a good product and that it is appropriately priced by the market. Should you be concerned about the effect on your portfolio if Shifty embezzles a portion of the firm's cash?

7.8 The CAPM is used to price the risk (estimate the expected return) for any asset. Our examples have focused on stocks, but we could also use CAPM to estimate the expected rate of return for bonds. Explain why.

7.9 In recent years, investors have agreed that the market portfolio consists of more than just a group of U.S. stocks and bonds. If you are an investor who invests in only U.S. stocks and bonds, describe the effects on the risk in your portfolio.

7.10 You may have heard the statement that you should not include your home as an asset in your investment portfolio. Assume that your house will comprise up to 75 percent of your assets in the early part of your investment life. Evaluate the implications of omitting it when calculating the risk of your overall investment portfolio.

Questions and Problems

Excel *Excel templates and resources available in* **WileyPLUS**

Basic

7.1 **Returns:** Describe the difference between a total holding period return and an expected return.

7.2 **Expected returns:** John is watching an old game show rerun on television called *Let's Make a Deal* in which the contestant chooses a prize behind one of two curtains. Behind one of the curtains is a gag prize worth \$150, and behind the other is a round-the-world trip worth \$7,200. The producer of the game show has placed a subliminal message on the curtain containing the gag prize, which makes the probability of choosing the gag prize equal to 75 percent. What is the expected value of the selection, and what is the standard deviation of that selection?

7.3 **Expected returns:** You have chosen biology as your college major because you would like to be a medical doctor. However, you find that the probability of being accepted to medical school is about 10 percent. If you are accepted to medical school, then your starting salary when you graduate will be \$300,000 per year. However, if you are not accepted, then you would choose to work in a zoo, where you will earn \$40,000 per year. Without considering the additional years you would spend in school if you study medicine or the time value of money, what is your expected starting salary as well as the standard deviation of that starting salary?

7.4 **Historical market:** Describe the general relation between risk and return that we observe in the historical bond and stock market data.

7.5 **Single-asset portfolios:** Stocks A, B, and C have expected returns of 15 percent, 15 percent, and 12 percent, respectively, while their standard deviations are 45 percent, 30 percent, and 30 percent, respectively. If you were considering the purchase of each of these stocks as the only holding in your portfolio and the risk-free rate is 0 percent, which stock should you choose?

7.6 **Arithmetic average:** Tanner invested \$1,000 in large U.S. stocks at the beginning of 2012. This investment earned 15.98 percent in 2012, 32.41 percent in 2013, 13.69 percent in 2014, and 1.41 percent in 2015. What return did he earn in the average year during the 2012–2015 period?

7.7 **Geometric average:** What was the average annual return that Tanner earned over the 2012–2015 period in Problem 7.6?

7.8 **Diversification:** Describe how investing in more than one asset can reduce risk through diversification.

7.9 **Systematic risk:** Define systematic risk.

7.10 **Measuring systematic risk:** Susan is expecting the returns on the market portfolio to be negative in the near term. Since she is managing a stock mutual fund, she must remain invested in a portfolio of stocks. However, she is allowed to adjust the beta of her portfolio. What kind of beta would you recommend for Susan's portfolio?

7.11 **Measuring systematic risk:** Describe and justify what the value of the beta of a U.S. Treasury bill should be.

7.12 Measuring systematic risk: If the expected rate of return for the market is not much greater than the risk-free rate of return, what does this suggest about the general level of compensation for bearing systematic risk?

7.13 CAPM: Describe the Capital Asset Pricing Model (CAPM) and what it tells us.

7.14 The Security Market Line: If the expected return on the market is 10 percent and the risk-free rate is 4 percent, what is the expected return for a stock with a beta equal to 1.5? What is the market risk premium?

Intermediate

7.15 Expected returns: José is thinking about purchasing a soft drink machine and placing it in a business office. He knows that there is a 5 percent probability that someone who walks by the machine will make a purchase from the machine, and he knows that the profit on each soft drink sold is $0.10. If José expects a thousand people per day to pass by the machine and requires a complete return of his investment in one year, then what is the maximum price that he should be willing to pay for the soft drink machine? Assume 250 working days in a year, and ignore taxes and the time value of money.

7.16 Interpreting the variance and standard deviation: The distribution of grades in an introductory finance class is normally distributed, with an expected grade of 75. If the standard deviation of grades is 7, in what range would you expect 95 percent of the grades to fall?

7.17 Calculating the variance and standard deviation: Kate recently invested in real estate with the intention of selling the property one year from today. She has modeled the returns on that investment based on three economic scenarios. She believes that if the economy stays healthy, then her investment will generate a 30 percent return. However, if the economy softens, as predicted, the return will be 10 percent, while the return will be −25 percent if the economy slips into a recession. If the probabilities of the healthy, soft, and recessionary states are 0.4, 0.5, and 0.1, respectively, then what are the expected return and the standard deviation of the return on Kate's investment?

7.18 Calculating the variance and standard deviation: Barbara is considering investing in a company's stock and is aware that the return on that investment is particularly sensitive to how the economy is performing. Her analysis suggests that four states of the economy can affect the return on the investment. Using the table of returns and probabilities that follows, find the expected return and the standard deviation of the return on Barbara's investment.

	Probability	Return
Boom	0.1	25.00%
Good	0.4	15.00%
Level	0.3	10.00%
Slump	0.2	−5.00%

7.19 Calculating the variance and standard deviation: Ben would like to invest in gold and is aware that the returns on such an investment can be quite volatile. Use the following table of states, probabilities, and returns to determine the expected return and the standard deviation of the return on Ben's gold investment.

	Probability	Return
Boom	0.1	40.00%
Good	0.2	30.00%
OK	0.3	15.00%
Level	0.2	2.00%
Slump	0.2	−12.00%

7.20 Single-asset portfolios: Using the information from Problems 7.17, 7.18, and 7.19, calculate the coefficient of variation for each of the investments in those problems.

7.21 Portfolios with more than one asset: Emmy is analyzing a two-stock portfolio that consists of a utility stock and a commodity stock. She knows that the return on the utility stock has a standard deviation of 40 percent and the return on the commodity stock has a standard deviation of 30 percent. However, she does not know the exact covariance in the returns of the two stocks. Emmy would like to plot the variance of the portfolio for each of three cases—covariance of 0.12, 0, and −0.12—in order to understand what the variance of the portfolio would be for a range of covariances. Do the calculation for all three cases (0.12, 0, and −0.12), assuming an equal proportion of each stock in the portfolio.

7.22 Portfolios with more than one asset: Given the returns and probabilities for the three possible states listed below, calculate the covariance between the returns of Stock A and Stock B. For convenience, assume that the expected returns of Stock A and Stock B are 11.75 percent and 18 percent, respectively.

	Probability	Return on Stock A	Return on Stock B
Good	0.35	0.30	0.50
OK	0.50	0.10	0.10
Poor	0.15	−0.25	−0.30

7.23 Compensation for bearing systematic risk: You have constructed a diversified portfolio of stocks such that there is no unsystematic risk. Explain why the expected return of that portfolio should be greater than the expected return of a risk-free security.

7.24 Compensation for bearing systematic risk: Write out the equation for the covariance in the returns of two assets, Asset 1 and Asset 2. Using that equation, explain the easiest way for the two asset returns to have a covariance of zero.

7.25 Compensation for bearing systematic risk: Evaluate the following statement: "By fully diversifying a portfolio, such as by buying every asset in the market, we can completely eliminate all types of risk, thereby creating a synthetic Treasury bill."

7.26 CAPM: Damien knows that the beta of his portfolio is equal to 1, but he does not know the risk-free rate of return or the market risk premium. He also knows that the expected return on the market is 8 percent. What is the expected return on Damien's portfolio?

7.27 CAPM: In February 2017 the risk-free rate was 2.97 percent, the market risk premium was 6 percent, and the beta for Twitter stock was 0.99. What is the expected return that was consistent with the systematic risk associated with the returns on Twitter stock?

7.28 CAPM: The market risk premium is 6 percent, and the risk-free rate is 5 percent. If the expected return on a bond is 6.5 percent, what is its beta?

Advanced

7.29 David is going to purchase two stocks to form the initial holdings in his portfolio. Iron stock has an expected return of 15 percent, while Copper stock has an expected return of 20 percent. If David plans to invest 30 percent of his funds in Iron and the remainder in Copper, what will be the expected return from his portfolio? What if David invests 70 percent of his funds in Iron stock?

7.30 Peter knows that the covariance in the return on two assets is −0.0025. Without knowing the expected return of the two assets, explain what that covariance means.

7.31 In order to fund her retirement, Glenda needs her portfolio to have an expected return of 12 percent per year over the next 30 years. She has decided to invest in Stocks 1, 2, and 3, with 25 percent in Stock 1, 50 percent in Stock 2, and 25 percent in Stock 3. If Stocks 1 and 2 have expected returns of 9 percent and 10 percent per year, respectively, then what is the minimum expected annual return for Stock 3 that is likely to enable Glenda to achieve her investment requirement?

7.32 Tonalli is putting together a portfolio of 10 stocks in equal proportions. What is the relative importance of the variance for each stock versus the covariance for the pairs of stocks in her portfolio? For this exercise, ignore the actual values of the variance and covariance terms and explain their importance conceptually.

7.33 Explain why investors who have diversified their portfolios will determine the price and, consequently, the expected return on an asset.

7.34 Brad is about to purchase an additional asset for his well-diversified portfolio. He notices that when he plots the historical returns of the asset against those of the market portfolio, the line of best fit tends to have a large amount of prediction error for each data point (the scatter plot is not very tight around the line of best fit). Do you think that this will have a large or a small impact on the beta of the asset? Explain your opinion.

7.35 Draw the Security Market Line (SML) for the case where the market risk premium is 5 percent and the risk-free rate is 7 percent. Now suppose an asset has a beta of −1.0 and an expected return of 4 percent. Plot it on your graph. Is the security properly priced? If not, explain what we might expect to happen to the price of this security in the market. Next, suppose another asset has a beta of 3.0 and an expected return of 20 percent. Plot it on the graph. Is this security properly priced? If not, explain what we might expect to happen to the price of this security in the market.

7.36 If the CAPM describes the relation between systematic risk and expected returns, can both an individual asset and the market portfolio of all risky assets have negative expected real rates of return? Why or why not?

7.37 You have been provided the following data on the securities of three firms and the market:

Security	$E[R_i]$	σ_{R_i}	ρ	β_i
Stock A	0.15		1.0	1.5
Stock B	0.15	0.18	0.5	
Stock C	0.10	0.02		0.5
Market portfolio	0.10	0.04		
Treasury bills	0.05	0		

Assume the CAPM and SML are true and fill in the missing values in the table. Would you invest in the stock of any of the three firms? If so, which one(s) and why?

Sample Test Problems

7.1 Given the following information from Capstone Corporation, what price would the CAPM predict that the company's stock will trade for one year from today?

Risk free rate: 3%

Market risk premium: 8%

Beta: 0.65

Current stock price: $64.61

Annual dividend: $1.92

7.2 You are considering investing in a mutual fund. The fund is expected to earn a return of 15 percent in the next year. If its annual return is normally distributed with a standard deviation of 6.5 percent, what return can you expect the fund to beat 95 percent of the time?

7.3 You have just invested in a portfolio of three stocks. The amount of money that you invested in each stock and its beta are summarized below. Calculate the beta of the portfolio and use the Capital Asset Pricing Model (CAPM) to compute the expected rate of return for the portfolio. Assume that the expected rate of return on the market is 15 percent and that the risk-free rate is 7 percent.

Stock	Investment	Beta
A	$200,000	1.50
B	300,000	0.65
C	500,000	1.25

7.4 What would you recommend to an investor who is considering making an investment in a stock that plots *below* the Security Market Line (SML)? Explain.

7.5 Why does an investor want a diversified portfolio? Can an investor eliminate all risk?

CHAPTER 8

Bond Valuation and the Structure of Interest Rates

Matthew Henry/Unsplash

LEARNING OBJECTIVES

1. Describe the market for corporate bonds and three types of corporate bonds.
2. Explain how to calculate the value of a bond and why bond prices vary negatively with interest rate movements.
3. Distinguish between a bond's coupon rate, yield to maturity, and effective annual yield.
4. Explain why investors in bonds are subject to interest rate risk and why it is important to understand the bond theorems.
5. Discuss the concept of default risk and know how to compute a default risk premium.
6. Describe the factors that determine the level and shape of the yield curve.

As of January 2017, debt holders of Energy Future Holdings were wrangling with the company in court over what they believed was owed to them. The Texas-based utility company was formed in October 2007 when a group of private investors borrowed more than $40 billion to buy TXU Corp. Just six years later, Energy Future Holdings was struggling to make its debt payments. And in the first week of February 2013, when investors learned that the company had hired advisors who specialized in restructuring and bankruptcy, the firm's debt claims lost almost half a billion dollars of value. The debt holders' concerns were realized in April 2014 when Energy Future Holdings filed for bankruptcy protection under Chapter 11 of the U.S. bankruptcy code.

Chapter 11 is the part of the bankruptcy code that companies can use to restructure operations and debts when the debts are so large that the company cannot reasonably expect to pay them in full. In a situation such as that faced by Energy Future Holdings, a debt restructuring involves developing a plan that repays the creditors as much as possible while allowing the company to continue its operations. Many creditors in a restructuring are forced to "forgive" some of the value they are owed so that the company has the necessary breathing room to continue to function.

The value of all Energy Future Holdings' bonds fell when investors realized that the bankruptcy filing was coming, but the amount by which the values of different types of debt fell varied with the characteristics of those issues. Energy Future Holdings' debts were not all the same. For example, in the first week of February 2013, a term loan sold at 69 cents for each dollar that had been borrowed, an amount in line with estimates of what the debt holders would ultimately receive on this portion of the firm's debt. However, other debts were selling for only 15 cents per dollar. These debts were much riskier because they were essentially unsecured (not backed by valuable assets or guarantees). The declines in the values of Energy Future Holdings' debts were smallest for the safest debts and greatest for the riskiest debts.

The firm's debt values fell because the prices that investors pay for debts reflect the value of the interest and principal payments that ownership of the debts entitles them to receive.

When a debt issuer gets into financial difficulty, investors are less likely to receive the interest and principal payments that they have been promised, and so they place less value on them. Specifically, investors require higher rates of return for riskier debts and, as you might recall from Chapters 5 and 6, when required rates of return go up, the present value of future cash flows, such as interest and principal payments from debts, go down. The weaker the security underlying the interest and principal payments from a debt, the more the interest rates increase. This chapter discusses the characteristics of bonds, a common form of debt financing used by businesses, how bonds are valued, and the factors that determine bond prices and yields.

Chapter Preview

This chapter is all about bonds and how they are valued, or priced, in the marketplace. As you might suspect, the bond valuation models presented in this chapter are derived from the present value concepts discussed in Chapters 5 and 6. The market price of a bond is simply the present value of the promised cash flows (interest and principal payments), discounted at the current market rate of interest for bonds of similar risk.

In this chapter we first discuss the corporate bond market, bond price information that is available, and the types of bonds found in the market. Then we develop the basic equation used to calculate bond prices and show how to compute the following characteristics of a bond: (1) yield to maturity and (2) effective annual yield. We next discuss interest rate risk and identify three bond theorems that describe how bond prices respond to changes in interest rates. Finally, we explain why firms have different borrowing costs. We find that four factors affect a firm's cost of borrowing: (1) the debt's marketability, (2) default risk, (3) call risk, and (4) term to maturity.

8.1 Corporate Bonds

LEARNING OBJECTIVE

1. Describe the market for corporate bonds and three types of corporate bonds.

In this section we discuss the market for corporate bonds and some of the types of bonds that firms issue.

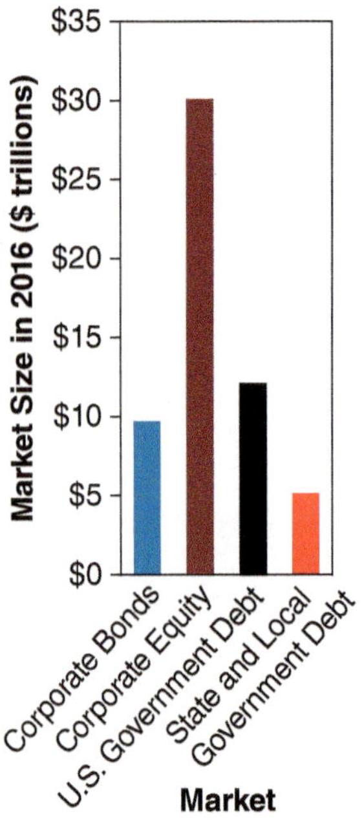

Market for Corporate Bonds

The market for corporate bonds is enormous. At the beginning of December 2016, for example, the value of corporate bonds outstanding in the United States was $9.7 trillion, almost 52 percent as large as the total U.S. gross domestic product in 2016 of $18.6 trillion. By comparison, the market for corporate equity was the largest part of the U.S. capital market with a value of $30.1 trillion and U.S. government long-term Treasury securities totaled $12.1 trillion. State and local government debt markets were much smaller at $3.1 trillion. The most important investors in corporate bonds are big institutional investors such as life insurance companies, pension funds, and mutual funds. Because the primary investors are so big, trades in this market tend to involve very large blocks of securities.

Most secondary market transactions for corporate bonds take place through dealers in the over-the-counter (OTC) market. An interesting characteristic of the corporate bond market is that there is a large number of different bond issues that trade in the market. The reason is that while a corporation typically has a single issue of common stock outstanding, it may have a dozen or more different notes and bonds outstanding. Therefore, despite the large overall trading volume of corporate bonds, the bonds from any particular issue will not necessarily trade on a given day. As a result, the market for corporate bonds is thin compared to the market for corporate stocks or money market securities. On Wall Street, the term *thin* means that secondary market trades of individual securities are relatively infrequent. Thus, corporate bonds are less marketable than the securities that have higher daily trading volumes.

Prices in the corporate bond market also tend to be more volatile than prices of securities sold in markets with greater trading volumes. This is because a few large trades can have a larger impact on a security's price than numerous trades of various sizes. The result of this is that the market for corporate bonds is not as efficient (new information does not get incorporated into corporate bond prices as efficiently) as those for highly marketable stocks or money market instruments, such as U.S. Treasury securities.

Bond Price Information

The corporate bond market also has little *transparency* because it is almost entirely an OTC market. A financial market is transparent if it is easy to view prices and trading volume. An example of a transparent market is the New York Stock Exchange (NYSE), where price information on every trade and trade size is available for every transaction during the day. In contrast, corporate bond market transactions are widely dispersed, with dealers located all over the country, and there is an enormous number of different securities. While trade prices are available for some debt securities, many corporate bond transactions are negotiated directly between the buyer and the seller and there is limited centralized reporting of these sales. As a result, information on individual corporate bond transactions is not widely published as the transactions occur. This is another reason that the corporate bond market is not as efficient as the stock or money markets.

Weblink

For a Web site providing educational information about bonds and their markets, go to http://www.investinginbonds.com. The trades and prices for debt in the Financial Industry Regulatory Authority's (FINRA's) Trade Reporting and Compliance Engine (TRACE) system can be viewed at FINRA's Market Data Center Web site: http://finra-markets.morningstar.com/BondCenter/.

Types of Corporate Bonds

Corporate bonds are long-term IOUs that represent claims against a firm's assets. Unlike stockholders' returns, most bondholders' returns are *fixed*; they receive only the interest payments that are promised plus the repayment of the loan amount when the bond matures. Debt instruments where the interest paid to investors is fixed for the life of the contract are called **fixed-income securities**. We examine three types of fixed-income securities in this section.

fixed-income securities debt instruments that pay interest in amounts that are fixed for the life of the contract

Vanilla Bonds

The most common bonds issued by corporations have coupon payments that are fixed for the life of the bond, and at maturity the entire original principal is paid and the bonds are retired. These bonds are known as vanilla bonds if they have no special characteristics, such as a conversion feature (discussed below).

The time line above shows the cash payments for a three-year vanilla bond with a $1,000 face value and an 8 percent coupon (interest) rate. P_B is the price (value) of the bond, which will be discussed in the next section. The $80 cash payments ($1,000 × 8 percent = $80) made each year are called the coupon payments. **Coupon payments** are the interest payments made to bondholders. These payments are usually made annually or semiannually, and the payment amount (or rate) remains fixed for the life of the bond contract, which for our example is three years. The **face value**, or **par value**, for most corporate bonds is $1,000, and it is the principal amount owed to the bondholder at maturity. Finally, the bond's **coupon rate** is the annual coupon payment (C) divided by the bond's face value (F). Our vanilla bond pays $80 of coupon interest annually and has a face value of $1,000. The coupon rate is thus:

coupon payments the interest payments made to bondholders

face value, or **par value** the amount on which interest is calculated and that is owed to the bondholder when a bond reaches maturity

coupon rate the annual coupon payment of a bond divided by the bond's face value

$$\text{Coupon rate} = \frac{C}{F} = \frac{\$80}{\$1{,}000} = 0.08, \text{ or } 8\%$$

Zero Coupon Bonds

Some bonds have no coupon payments but promise a single payment at maturity. The interest paid to a bondholder is the difference between the price paid for the bond and the face value received at maturity. These bonds are sold at a price below the amount that the investor receives at maturity because all of the interest is paid when the bonds are retired at maturity rather than in semiannual or yearly coupon payments. The face value of a zero coupon bond is different from that of a vanilla bond in that it includes both the interest and principal.

The most frequent and regular issuer of zero coupon securities is the U.S. Department of the Treasury, and perhaps the best-known zero coupon bond is a United States Saving Bond. Corporations also issue zero coupon bonds from time to time. Firms that are expanding operations but have little cash available to make interest payments are especially likely to use zero coupon bonds for funding. In the 1990s, the bond market was flooded with zero coupon bonds issued by telecommunications firms. These firms were spending huge amounts to build fiber-optic networks, which generated few cash inflows until they were completed.

Convertible Bonds

Corporate convertible bonds can be converted into shares of common stock at some predetermined ratio at the discretion of the bondholder. For example, a $1,000 face-value bond may be convertible into 100 shares of common stock. A conversion feature is valuable to bondholders because it allows them to share in the good fortunes of the firm if the firm's stock price rises above a certain level. Specifically, the bondholders profit if they exchange their bonds for the company's stock when the market value of the stock they receive exceeds the market value of the bonds.

Typically, the conversion ratio is set so that the firm's stock price must appreciate at least 15 to 20 percent before it is profitable to convert the bonds into stock. As you would expect from our discussion, since a conversion feature is valuable to bondholders, firms that issue convertible bonds can do so at a lower interest rate. This reduces the amount of cash that the firms must use to make interest payments.

Before You Go On

1. What are the main differences between the corporate bond markets and stock markets?
2. A bond has a 7 percent coupon rate, a face value of $1,000, and a maturity of four years. On a time line, lay out the cash flows for the bond.
3. Explain what a convertible bond is.

8.2 Bond Valuation

LEARNING OBJECTIVE

2. Explain how to calculate the value of a bond and why bond prices vary negatively with interest rate movements.

We turn now to the topic of bond valuation—how bonds are priced. Throughout this book, we have stressed that the value, or price, of any asset is the present value of its future cash flows. The steps necessary to value an asset are as follows:

1. Estimate the expected future cash flows.
2. Determine the required rate of return, or discount rate. This rate depends on the riskiness of the future cash flows.
3. Compute the present value of the future cash flows. This present value is what the asset is worth at a particular point in time.

For bonds, the valuation procedure is relatively easy. The cash flows (coupon and principal payments) are contractual obligations of the firm and are known by market participants, since they are stated in the bond contract. Thus, market participants know the magnitude and timing of the expected cash flows as promised by the borrower (the bond issuer). The required rate of return, or discount rate, for a bond is the market interest rate, called the bond's *yield to maturity* (or more commonly, simply its *yield*). This rate is determined from the market prices of bonds that have features similar to those of the bond being valued; by *similar*, we mean bonds that have the same term to maturity, have the same bond rating (default risk class), and are similar in other ways.

Notice that the required rate of return is the **opportunity cost** for the investors who purchase the bond. An opportunity cost is the highest alternative return that is given up when an investment is made. For example, if bonds identical to the bond being valued—having the same risk—yield 9 percent annually, the threshold yield or required return on the bond being valued is 9 percent. Why? An investor would not buy a bond with an 8 percent yield when an identical bond yielding 9 percent is available.

opportunity cost the return from the best alternative investment with similar risk that an investor gives up when he or she makes a certain investment

Given the above information, we can compute the current value, or price, of a bond (P_B) by calculating the present value of the bond's expected cash flows:

$$P_B = \text{PV(Coupon payments)} + \text{PV(Principal payment)}$$

Next, we examine this calculation in detail.

The Bond Valuation Formula

To begin, refer to **Exhibit 8.1**, which shows the cash flows for a three-year corporate bond (a bond with three years to maturity) with an 8 percent coupon rate and a $1,000 face value. If the market rate of interest on similar bonds is 10 percent and interest payments are made annually, what is the market price of the bond? In other words, how much should you be willing to pay for the promised cash flow stream?

To value (or price) the bond, we can discount each of the payments back to time zero one at a time, and add those values up. We can also view the bond payments as being made up of a regular annuity of three annual payments of $80 each and a final lump sum payment of $1,000. Thus, the price of the bond (P_B) is the sum of the present value calculations for the coupon payments (C) and the principal amount (F), discounted at the required rate (i). That calculation is:

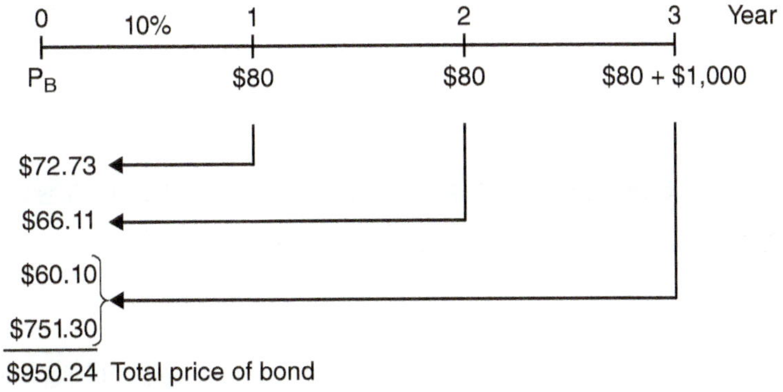

EXHIBIT 8.1 **Cash Flows for a Three-Year Bond**

The exhibit shows a time line for a three-year bond that pays an 8 percent coupon rate and has a face value of $1,000. How much should we pay for such a bond if the market rate of interest is 10 percent? To solve this problem, we discount the promised cash flows to the present and then add them up.

$$
\begin{aligned}
P_B &= \text{PV (Each coupon payment)} + \text{PV (Principle payment)} \\
&= \left[\frac{C_1}{(1+i)}\right] + \left[\frac{C_2}{(1+i)^2}\right] + \left[\frac{C_3}{(1+i)^3}\right] + \left[\frac{F_3}{(1+i)^3}\right] \\
&= \left[\frac{\$80}{1.10}\right] + \left[\frac{\$80}{(1.10)^2}\right] + \left[\frac{\$80}{(1.10)^3}\right] + \left[\frac{\$1{,}000}{(1.10)^3}\right] \\
&= \left[\frac{\$80}{1.10}\right] + \left[\frac{\$80}{1.21}\right] + \left[\frac{\$80}{1.331}\right] + \left[\frac{\$1{,}000}{1.331}\right] \\
&= \$72.73 + \$66.11 + \$60.10 + \$751.30 \\
&= \$950.24
\end{aligned}
$$

Notice that you could have simplified the calculation by combining the final coupon payment and the principal payment ($C_3 + F_3$), since both cash flows occur at time $t = 3$.

The above calculation suggests that the general equation for the price of the bond can be written as:

$$
\begin{aligned}
P_B &= \left[\frac{C_1}{(1+i)}\right] + \left[\frac{C_2}{(1+i)^2}\right] + \cdots + \left[\frac{C_n}{(1+i)^n}\right] + \left[\frac{F_n}{(1+i)^n}\right] \\
&= \left[\frac{C_1}{(1+i)}\right] + \left[\frac{C_2}{(1+i)^2}\right] + \cdots + \left[\frac{(C_n + F_n)}{(1+i)^n}\right]
\end{aligned}
$$

Or:

$$
P_B = \frac{C_1}{1+i} + \frac{C_2}{(1+i)^2} + \cdots + \frac{C_n + F_n}{(1+i)^n} \qquad (8.1)
$$

where:

P_B = the price of the bond, or present value of the stream of cash payments
C_t = the coupon payment in period t, where $t = 1, 2, 3, \ldots, n$
F_n = par value or face value (principal amount) to be paid at maturity
i = market interest rate (discount rate or yield)
n = number of periods to maturity

Note that there are five variables in the bond pricing equation. If we know any four of them, we can solve for the fifth.

Calculator Tip: Bond Valuation Problems

We can easily calculate bond prices using a financial calculator or a spreadsheet program. We solve for bond prices and bond yields in exactly the same way we solved for the present value (bond price) and discount rate (bond yield) in Chapter 6. We solve our example problem on a financial calculator as follows:

Enter	3	10		80	1,000
	N	i	PV	PMT	FV
Answer			**−950.26**		

Several points are worth noting:

1. Always draw a time line for the cash flows. This simple step will significantly reduce mistakes.
2. The PMT key enters the dollar amount of an ordinary annuity for n periods. In our example, keying in 3 with the N key and $80 with the PMT key enters an $80 annuity with the final payment made at the end of Year 3.
3. Be sure that you enter the coupon and the principal payments separately. Do not enter the final coupon payment ($80) and principal amount ($1,000) as a single entry of

$1,080 on the FV key. The reason is that the PMT key is the annuity key, and when you enter N = 3, the $80 is entered in the calculator as a three-year ordinary annuity with a final payment of $80 in period $t = 3$. If you then enter $1,080 on the FV key, you will have an extra $80 in the final period ($t = 3$). For the example problem, we correctly entered the $80 coupon payments with the PMT key and the $1,000 principal payment with the FV key.

4. Finally, as we have mentioned in earlier chapters, you must be consistent throughout a problem in how you enter the signs (positive or negative) for cash inflows and cash outflows. For example, if you are a bond investor and decide to enter all cash inflows with a positive sign, then you must enter all coupon and principal payments with a positive sign. The price you paid for the bond, which is a cash outflow, must be entered as a negative number. This is the convention we will follow.

Learning by Doing Application 8.1 illustrates another example of the use of a calculator to value a bond and the **Using Excel Example** at the top of the next page illustrates the use of a spreadsheet program to solve this problem.

Par, Premium, and Discount Bonds

One of the mathematical properties of the bond pricing equation is that whenever a bond's coupon rate is equal to the market rate of interest on similar bonds (the bond's yield), the bond will sell at par value. We call such bonds **par-value bonds**. For example, suppose that you own a three-year bond with a face value of $1,000 and an annual coupon rate of 5 percent, when the yield or market rate of interest on similar bonds is 5 percent. The price of your bond, based on Equation 8.1, is:

par-value bonds bonds that sell at par value, or face value; whenever a bond's coupon rate is equal to the market rate of interest on similar bonds, the bond will sell at par (face) value

$$\begin{aligned} P_B &= \frac{\$50}{1.05} + \frac{\$50}{(1.05)^2} + \frac{\$1{,}050}{(1.05)^3} \\ &= \$47.62 + \$45.35 + \$907.03 \\ &= \$1{,}000 \end{aligned}$$

As predicted, thc bond's price equals its par value.

LEARNING BY DOING

APPLICATION 8.1 | Pricing a Bond

Problem Your stockbroker is trying to sell you a 15-year bond with a 7 percent coupon, and the interest, or yield, on similar bonds is 10 percent. Is the bond selling for a premium, at par, or at a discount? Answer the question without making any calculations, and then prove that your answer is correct. The time line is as follows:

0 (10%)	1	2	…	14	15 Year
P_B	$70	$70		$70	$70 + $1,000

Approach Since the market rate of interest is greater than the coupon rate ($i >$ coupon rate), the bond must sell at a discount.

Solution To prove the answer is correct (or wrong), we can compute the bond's price with a financial calculator.

	N	i	PV	PMT	FV
Enter	15	10		70	1,000
Answer			−771.82		

The bond is selling at a discount, and it should. Why? The market rate of interest is 10 percent, and the bond is paying only 7 percent. Since the bond's coupon rate is fixed, the only way we can bring the bond's yield up to the current market rate of 10 percent is to reduce the price of the bond to $771.82.

Using Excel

Bond Prices and Yields

Calculating bond prices and yields using a spreadsheet may seem daunting at first. However, understanding the terminology used in the formulas will make the calculations a matter of common sense:

Settlement date—the date a buyer purchases the bond.

Maturity date—the date the bond expires. If you know only the "*n*" (number of years remaining) of the bond, use a date that is *n* years in the future in this field.

Redemption—the security's redemption value per $10 face value. In other words, if the bond has a par value of $1,000, you enter 100 in this field.

Frequency—the number of coupon payments per year.

Here is a spreadsheet showing the setup for calculating the price of the discount bond described in Learning by Doing Application 8.1.

	A	B	C	D
1				
2	Bond Price Calculations			
3	Inputs			
4	Settlement date	1/1/17		
5	Maturity date	1/1/32		
6	Rate	0.07		
7	Yield	0.10		
8	Redemption (% of par)	100		
9	Frequency	1		
10				
11	Bond Price			Formulas Used
12	Bond price as % of par	77.18		=PRICE(B4,B5,B6,B7,B8,B9)
13	Par value	$1,000.00		
14	Bond price	$771.82		=B12%*B13
15				

We first use the =PRICE(settlement, maturity, rate, yield, redemption, frequency) formula in Excel to calculate the bond price as a percentage of par. We then multiply this percentage (77.18 percent in the above example) by $1,000 to obtain the bond price in dollars. A bond yield, which is discussed in the next section, is calculated in a similar manner, using the "=YIELD (settlement, maturity, rate, price, redemption, frequency)" formula.

Now assume that the market rate of interest rises overnight to 8 percent. What happens to the price of the bond? Will the bond's price be below, above, or at par value?

$$
\begin{aligned}
P_B &= \frac{\$50}{1.08} + \frac{\$50}{(1.08)^2} + \frac{\$1{,}050}{(1.08)^3} \\
&= \$46.30 + \$42.87 + \$833.52 \\
&= \$922.69
\end{aligned}
$$

discount bonds bonds that sell at prices below par (face) value

When i is equal to 8 percent, the price of the bond declines to $922.69. The bond sells at a price below par value; such bonds are called **discount bonds**.

Whenever a bond's coupon rate is lower than the market rate of interest on similar bonds, the bond will sell at a discount. This is true because of the fixed nature of a bond's coupon payments. Let's return to our 5 percent coupon bond. If the market rate of interest is 8 percent and our bond pays only 5 percent, no economically rational person would buy the bond at its par value. This would be like choosing a bond with a 5 percent yield over one with an 8 percent yield. We cannot change the coupon rate to 8 percent because it is fixed for the life of the bond. That is why bonds are referred to as fixed-income securities. The only way to increase our bond's yield to 8 percent is to reduce the price of the bond to $922.69. At this price, the bond's yield will be precisely 8 percent, which is the current market rate for similar bonds. Through the price reduction of $77.31 ($1,000 – $922.69 = $77.31), the seller provides the new owner with additional "interest" in the form of a capital gain.

premium bonds bonds that sell at prices above par (face) value

What would happen to the price of the bond if interest rates on similar bonds declined to 2 percent and the coupon rate remained at 5 percent? The price would rise to $1,086.52. At this price, the bond's yield would be precisely 2 percent, which is the current market yield. The $86.52 ($1,086.52 – $1,000 = $86.52) premium adjusts the bond's yield to 2 percent, which is the current market yield for similar bonds. Bonds that sell at prices above par are called **premium bonds**. Whenever a bond's coupon rate is higher than the market rate of interest, the bond will sell at a premium.

Our discussion of bond pricing can be summarized as follows, where i is the market rate of interest:

1. $i >$ coupon rate—the bond sells for a discount
2. $i <$ coupon rate—the bond sells for a premium
3. $i = 5$ coupon rate—the bond sells at par value

This negative relation between changes in the level of interest rates and changes in the price of a bond (or any fixed-income security) is one of the most fundamental relations in corporate finance. The relation exists because the coupon payments on most bonds are fixed and the only way bonds can pay the current market rate of interest to investors is through an adjustment in the price of the bond. This is exactly what happened to Energy Future Holdings' bonds discussed at the beginning of this chapter. As the risk of those bonds increased, their prices declined so that investors received a market rate of interest that reflected the bond's higher risk.

Semiannual Compounding

In Europe, bonds generally pay coupon interest on an annual basis. In contrast, in the United States, most bonds pay coupon interest semiannually—that is, twice a year. Thus, if a bond has an 8 percent coupon rate (paid semiannually), each year the bondholder will receive two coupon payments of \$40 each, totaling \$80 (\$40 × 2 = \$80). We can modify Equation 8.1 as follows to adjust for coupon payments made more than once a year:

$$P_B = \frac{C/m}{1 + i/m} + \frac{C/m}{(1 + i/m)^2} + \frac{C/m}{(1 + i/m)^3} + \cdots + \frac{C/m + F_{mn}}{(1 + i/m)^{mn}} \qquad (8.2)$$

where C is the annual coupon payment, m is the number of times coupon payments are made each year, n is the number of years to maturity, and i is the annual market interest rate. In the case of a bond with semiannual coupon payments, m equals 2.

Whether we are computing bond prices annually, semiannually, quarterly, or for some other period, the computation is the same. We need only be sure that the bond's yield, coupon payment, and maturity are adjusted to be consistent with the bond's stated compounding period. Once that information is converted to the correct compounding period, it can simply be entered into Equation 8.1. Thus, there is really no need to memorize or use Equation 8.2 unless you find it helpful. Let's work an example to demonstrate.

Earlier we determined that a three-year, 5 percent coupon bond will sell for \$922.69 when the market rate of interest is 8 percent. Our computation assumed that coupon payments were made annually. What is the price of the bond if the coupon payments are made semiannually? The time line for the semiannual bond situation follows:

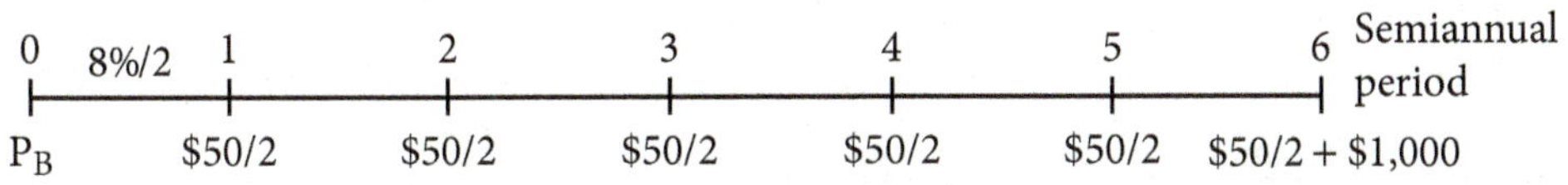

We convert the bond data to semiannual compounding as follows: (1) the market yield is 4 percent semiannually (8 percent per year/2 = 4 percent), (2) the coupon payment is \$25 semiannually (\$50 per year/2 = \$25), and (3) the total number of coupon payments is 6 (2 payments per year × 3 years = 6 payments). Plugging the data into Equation 8.1, we find that the bond price is:

$$P_B = \frac{\$25}{1.04} + \frac{\$25}{(1.04)^2} + \frac{\$25}{(1.04)^3} + \frac{\$25}{(1.04)^4} + \frac{\$25}{(1.04)^5} + \frac{\$1,025}{(1.04)^6}$$
$$= \$921.37$$

Notice that the price of the bond is slightly less with semiannual compounding than with annual compounding (\$921.37 < \$922.69). The slight difference in price reflects the change in the timing of the cash flows and the interest rate adjustment.[1]

[1] If the bond sold at a premium, the reverse would be true; that is, the price with semiannual compounding would be slightly more than the price with annual compounding.

Learning by Doing Application 8.2 illustrates the use of a calculator to value a bond with semiannual coupon payments.

LEARNING BY DOING

Application 8.2 | Bond Pricing with Semiannual Coupon Payments

Problem A corporate treasurer decides to purchase a 20-year Treasury bond with a 4 percent coupon rate. If the current market rate of interest for similar Treasury securities is 4.5 percent, what is the price of the bond?

Approach Treasury securities pay interest semiannually, so this problem is best worked on a financial calculator because of the large number of compounding periods. We can convert the bond data to semiannual compounding as follows: (1) the bond's semiannual yield is 2.25 percent (4.5 percent per year/2 = 2.25 percent), (2) the semiannual coupon payment is \$20 [(\$1,000 × 4 percent)/2 = \$40/2 = \$20], and (3) the total number of compounding periods is 40 (2 periods per year × 20 years = 40 periods). Note that at maturity, the bond principal, or face value, of \$1,000 is paid to the investor. Thus, the bond's time line for the cash payments is as follows:

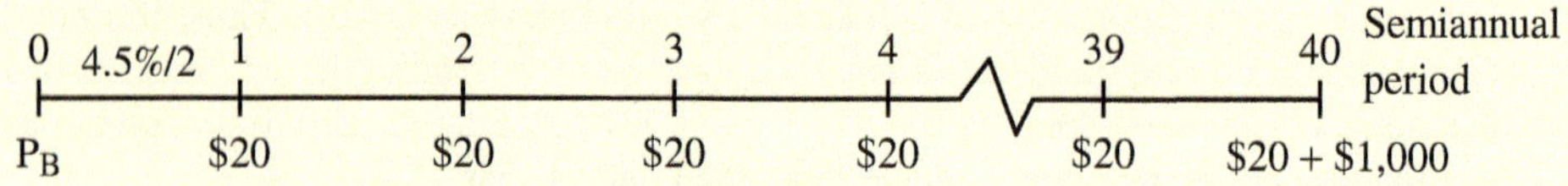

Solution We can enter the appropriate values on the financial calculator and solve for the present value:

Enter	40	2.25		20	1,000
	N	i	PV	PMT	FV
Answer			**−934.52**		

The bond sells for a discount, and its price is \$934.52.

Zero Coupon Bonds

As previously mentioned, zero coupon bonds have no coupon payments but promise a single payment at maturity. The price (or yield) of a zero coupon bond is simply a special case of Equation 8.2 in which all the coupon payments are equal to zero.

Hence, the pricing equation for a zero coupon bond is:

$$P_B = \frac{F_{mn}}{(1 + i/m)^{mn}} \tag{8.3}$$

where:

P_B = the price of the bond
F_{mn} = the amount of the cash payment at maturity (face value)
i = annual market interest rate (discount rate or yield)
n = number of years until the payment is due
m = number of times interest is compounded each year

Notice that if a zero coupon bond compounds annually, $m = 1$ and Equation 8.3 becomes:

$$P_B = \frac{F_n}{(1 + i)^n}$$

Now let's work an example. What is the price of a zero coupon bond with a \$1,000 face value, 10-year maturity, and semiannual compounding when the market interest rate is 12 percent? Since the bond compounds interest semiannually, the number of compounding periods is 20 ($m \times n = 2 \times 10 = 20$). The semiannual interest is 6 percent (12 percent/2 = 6 percent). The time line for the cash flows is as follows:

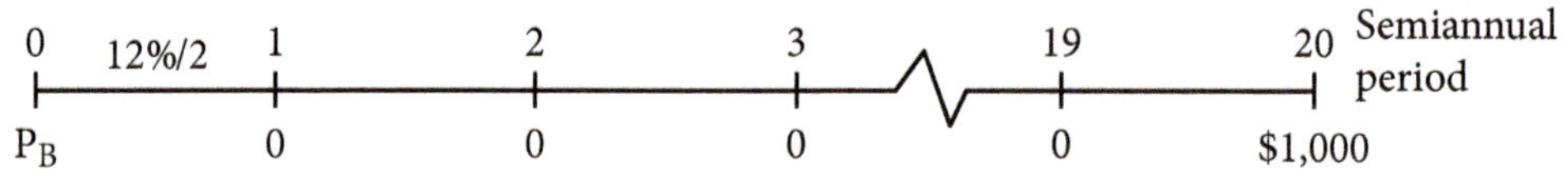

Plugging the data into Equation 8.3, we find that the price of the bond is:

$$P_B = \frac{\$1{,}000}{(1.06)^{20}}$$
$$= \$1{,}000 \times 0.3118 = \$311.80$$

Notice that the zero coupon bond is selling at a very large (deep) discount. This should come as no surprise, since the bond has no coupon payment and all the dollars paid to investors are paid at maturity. Why are zero coupon bonds so heavily discounted compared with similar bonds that do have coupon payments? From Chapter 5, we know that because of the time value of money, dollars to be received in the future have less value than current dollars. Thus, zero coupon bonds, for which all the cash payments are made at maturity, must sell for less than similar bonds that make coupon payments before maturity.

Learning by Doing Application 8.3 illustrates another example of a bond valuation.

APPLICATION 8.3 | Pricing a Corporate Bond

LEARNING BY DOING

Problem An investor is considering buying a U.S. corporate bond with an eight-year maturity and a coupon rate of 6 percent. Similar bonds in the marketplace yield 14 percent. How much should the investor be willing to pay for the bond? Using Equation 8.1 (or 8.2), set up the equation to be solved, and then solve the problem using your financial calculator. Note that the discount rate used in the problem is the 14 percent market yield on similar bonds (bonds of similar risk), which is the investor's opportunity cost.

Approach Since U.S. corporate bonds pay coupon interest semiannually, we first need to convert all of the bond data to reflect semiannual compounding: (1) the annual coupon payment is \$60 per year (6 percent × \$1,000 = \$60) and the semiannual payment is \$30 per period (\$60 per year/2 = \$30); (2) the appropriate semiannual yield is 7 percent (14 percent/2 = 7 percent); and (3) the total number of compounding periods is 16 (2 periods per year × 8 years = 16 periods). The time line for the semiannual cash flows is as follows:

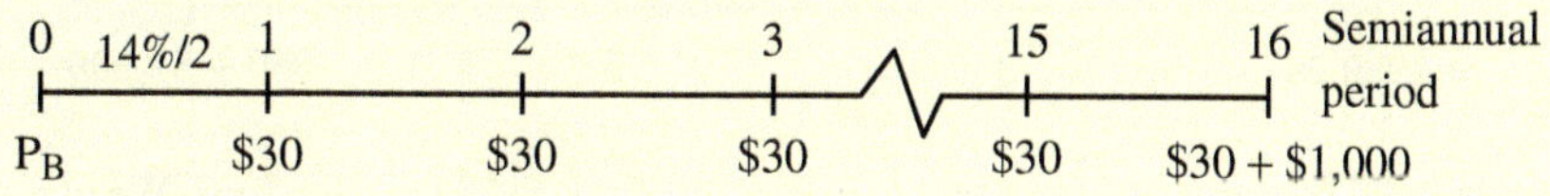

Solution Using Equation 8.1 (or 8.2), the setup is as follows:

$$P_B = \frac{\$30}{1.07} + \frac{\$30}{(1.07)^2} + \cdots + \frac{\$1{,}030}{(1.07)^{16}}$$

To solve the problem using a financial calculator, we enter the appropriate values and solve for PV:

Enter	16	7		30	1,000
	N	i	PV	PMT	FV
Answer			**−622.13**		

The investor should be willing to pay \$622.13 because the bond's yield at this price would be exactly 14 percent, which is the current market yield on similar bonds. If the bond price was more than \$622.13, the investment would yield a return of less than 14 percent. In this situation an investor would be better off buying the similar bonds in the market that yield 14 percent. Of course, if the investor can buy the bond for less than \$622.13, the price is a bargain, and the return on investment will be greater than the market yield.

WileyPLUS

Need more help? Visit your WileyPLUS course.

Before You Go On

1. Explain conceptually how bonds are priced.
2. What is the compounding period for most bonds sold in the United States?
3. What are zero coupon bonds, and how are they priced?

8.3 Bond Yields

LEARNING OBJECTIVE

3. Distinguish between a bond's coupon rate, yield to maturity, and effective annual yield.

We frequently know a bond's price from an offer to sell it, but not its yield to maturity. In this section, we discuss how to compute the yield to maturity and some other important bond yields.

Yield to Maturity

yield to maturity for a bond, the discount rate that makes the present value of the coupon and principal payments equal to the price of the bond

The **yield to maturity** of a bond is the discount rate that makes the present value of the coupon and principal payments equal to the price of the bond. The yield to maturity can be viewed as a *promised yield* because it is the annual yield that the investor earns if the bond is held to maturity and all the coupon and principal payments are made as promised. A bond's yield to maturity changes daily as interest rates increase or decrease, but its calculation is always based on the issuer's promise to make interest and principal payments as stipulated in the bond contract.

Let's work through an example to see how a bond's yield to maturity is calculated. Suppose you decide to buy a three-year bond with a 6 percent coupon rate for $960.99. For simplicity, we will assume that the coupon payments are made annually. The time line for the cash flows is as follows:

To compute the yield to maturity, we apply Equation 8.1 and solve for i. We can set up the problem using Equation 8.1 as follows:

$$960.99 = \frac{\$60}{1+i} + \frac{\$60}{(1+i)^2} + \frac{\$1{,}060}{(1+i)^3}$$

As we discussed in Chapter 6, we cannot solve for i mathematically; we must find it by trial and error. We know that the bond is selling for a discount because its price is below par, so the yield must be higher than the 6 percent coupon rate. Let's try 7 percent.

$$\$973.76 = \frac{\$60}{1.07} + \frac{\$60}{(1.07)^2} + \frac{\$1{,}060}{(1.07)^3}$$

The computed price of $973.76 is still greater than our market price of $960.99; thus, we need to use a slightly larger discount rate. Let's try 7.7 percent.

$$\$955.95 = \frac{\$60}{1.077} + \frac{\$60}{(1.077)^2} + \frac{\$1{,}060}{(1.077)^3}$$

Our computed value of $955.95 is now less than the market price of $960.99, so we need a lower discount rate. We'll try 7.5 percent.

$$\$960.99 = \frac{\$60}{1.075} + \frac{\$60}{(1.075)^2} + \frac{\$1{,}060}{(1.075)^3}$$

At a discount rate of 7.5 percent, the price of the bond is exactly equal to the market price, and thus, the bond's yield to maturity is 7.5 percent.

We can, of course, also compute the bond's yield to maturity using a financial calculator. Computing the yield in this way is no different from computing the price, except that the unknown is the bond's yield. As with calculating the price of a bond, the major source of computational errors is failing to make sure that all the bond data are consistent with the bond's compounding period. The three variables that may require adjustment are (1) the coupon payment, (2) the yield, and (3) the bond maturity.

For the three-year corporate bond discussed earlier, the bond data are already in a form that is consistent with the annual compounding period, so we enter it into the calculator and solve for *i*, which is the yield to maturity:

Enter	3		−960.99	60	1,000
	N	i	PV	PMT	FV
Answer		**7.5**			

The bond's yield to maturity is 7.5 percent, which is identical to the answer from our hand calculation.

Effective Annual Yield

Up to now, when pricing a bond with a semiannual compounding period, we assumed the bond's annual yield to be twice the semiannual yield. This is the convention used on Wall Street and by other practitioners who deal in bonds. However, notice that bond yields quoted in this manner are just like the APRs discussed in Chapter 6. For example, in Section 6.4 we showed that the APR for a bank credit card with a 1 percent monthly interest rate is simply the monthly interest rate multiplied by the number of months in a year, or 12 percent. As you recall, interest rates (or yields) annualized in this manner do not take compounding into account. Hence, the values calculated are not the true cost of funds, and their use can lead to decisions that are economically incorrect.

As a result, annualized yields calculated by multiplying a yield per period by the number of compounding periods are only acceptable for decision-making purposes when comparing bonds that have the same compounding frequencies. For example, an investor must be careful when comparing yields of European and U.S. bonds, since interest on a European bond is compounded annually while interest on a U.S. bond compounds twice a year.

The correct way to annualize an interest rate to make an economic decision is to compute the effective annual interest rate (EAR). On Wall Street, the EAR is called the **effective annual yield (EAY)**; thus, EAR = EAY. Drawing on Equation 6.7 (see Chapter 6), we find that the correct way to annualize the yield on a bond is as follows:

effective annual yield (EAY) the annual yield that takes compounding into account; another name for the *effective annual interest rate (EAR)*

$$\text{EAY} = \left(1 + \frac{\text{Quoted interest rate}}{m}\right)^m - 1$$

where: Quoted interest rate = simple annual yield (semiannual yield × 2)
m = the number of compounding periods per year

Let's work through an example to see how the EAY differs from the yield to maturity. Suppose an investor buys a 30-year bond with a $1,000 face value for $800. The bond's coupon rate is 8 percent, and interest payments are made semiannually. What is the bond's yield to maturity, and what is its EAY? To find out, we first need to convert the bond's annual data into semiannual data: (1) the 30-year bond has 60 compounding periods (30 years × 2 periods per year = 60 periods) and (2) the bond's semiannual coupon payment is $40 [($1,000 × 0.08)/2 = $80/2 = $40]. The time line for this bond is:

Semiannual period	0	1	2	3	…	59	60
$i = ?$	−$800	$40	$40	$40		$40	$40 + $1,000

We can set up the problem using Equation 8.1 (or 8.2) as:

$$\$800 = \frac{\$40}{1 + i/2} + \frac{\$40}{(1 + i/2)^2} + \frac{\$40}{(1 + i/2)^3} + \cdots + \frac{\$40}{(1 + i/2)^{59}} + \frac{\$1{,}040}{(1 + i/2)^{60}}$$

However, solving an equation with so many terms can be time consuming. Therefore, we will solve for the yield to maturity using the yield function in a financial calculator as follows:

Enter	60		−800	40	1,000
	N	i	PV	PMT	FV
Answer		**5.07**			

The answer is 5.07 percent. We then multiply the semiannual yield by 2 to convert it to an annual yield: 2 × 5.07 percent = 10.14 percent. This is the bond's yield to maturity.

If, instead of multiplying 5.07 percent by 2 we calculate the EAY for the semiannual yield of 5.07 percent, we will get:

$$\begin{aligned}\text{EAY} &= \left(1 + \frac{\text{Quoted interest rate}}{m}\right)^m - 1\\ &= \left(1 + \frac{0.1014}{2}\right)^2 - 1\\ &= (1.0507)^2 - 1 = 0.1040, \text{ or } 10.40\%\end{aligned}$$

The EAY of 10.40 percent is greater than the annual yield to maturity of 10.14 percent because the EAY takes into account the effects of compounding—earning interest on interest.

Learning by Doing Application 8.4 illustrates use of the EAY concept in choosing between different investments.

LEARNING BY DOING

WileyPLUS

Need more help? Visit your WileyPLUS course.

APPLICATION 8.4 | Choosing between Bonds with Different Coupon Payment Frequencies

Problem You can purchase a U.S. corporate bond from your broker for $1,099.50. The bond has six years to maturity, and an annual coupon rate of 5 percent. Another broker offers you a dollar Eurobond (a dollar-denominated bond sold overseas) with a yield of 3.17 percent, which is denominated in U.S. dollars and has the same maturity and credit rating as the U.S. corporate bond. Which bond should you buy?

Approach Solving this problem involves two steps. First, we must compute the U.S. bond's yield to maturity. The bond pays coupon interest semiannually, so we have to convert the bond data to semiannual periods: (1) the number of compounding periods is 12 (6 years × 2 periods per year = 12 periods) and (2) the semiannual coupon payment is $25 [($1,000 × 0.05)/2 = $50/2 = $25]. Second, we must annualize the yield for the U.S. bond so that we can compare its yield with that of the Eurobond.

Solution We can solve for the yield to maturity using a financial calculator:

Enter	12		−1,099.50	25	1,000
	N	i	PV	PMT	FV
Answer		**1.5831**			

The answer, 1.5831 percent, is the semiannual yield. Since the Eurobond's yield, 3.17 percent, is an annualized yield because of that bond's yearly compounding, we must annualize the yield on the U.S. bond in order to compare the two.[2] We annualize the yield on the U.S. bond by computing its effective annual yield:

$$\begin{aligned}\text{EAY} &= \left(1 + \frac{\text{Quoted interest rate}}{m}\right)^m - 1\\ &= \left(1 + \frac{0.031662}{2}\right)^2 - 1\\ &= (1.015831)^2 - 1 = 0.03191, \text{or } 3.191\%\end{aligned}$$

The U.S. corporate bond is a better deal because of its higher EAY (3.191 percent > 3.170 percent). Notice that if we had just annualized the yield on the U.S. bond by multiplying the semiannual yield by 2 (1.5831 percent × 2 = 3.1661 percent) and compared the simple yields for the Eurobond and the U.S. bond (3.170 percent > 3.1661 percent), we would have selected the Eurobond. This would have been the wrong economic decision.

[2]Notice that, for annual compounding, the yield to maturity equals the EAY; for the Eurobond, the yield to maturity = 3.17 percent and EAY = $(1 + \text{Quoted interest rate}/m)^m - 1 = (1 + 0.0317/1)^1 - 1 = (1 + 0.0317) - 1 = 0.0317$, or 3.17 percent.

As mentioned earlier, calculating the EAY is the economically correct way to annualize a bond's yield because it takes compounding into account.

Realized Yield

The yield to maturity (or promised yield) tells the investor the return on a bond if the bond is held to maturity and all the coupon and principal payments are made as promised. Quite often, however, the investor will sell the bond before maturity. The **realized yield** is the return earned on a bond given the cash flows *actually received* by the investor. More formally, it is the interest rate at which the present value of the actual cash flows from the investment equal the bond's price. The realized yield allows investors to see the return they actually earned on their investment. It is the same as the holding period return discussed in Chapter 7.

realized yield for a bond, the interest rate at which the present value of the actual cash flows from a bond equals the bond's price

Let's return to the situation involving a three-year bond with a 6 percent coupon that was purchased for \$960.99 and had a promised yield of 7.5 percent. Suppose that interest rates increased sharply and the price of the bond plummeted. Disgruntled, you sold the bond for \$750.79 after having owned it for two years. The time line for the realized cash flows looks like this:

0	$i = ?$	1	2	3 Year
−\$960.99		\$60	\$60 + \$750.79	\$60 + \$1,000

Relevant cash flows for computing realized yield (Years 0–2)

Substituting the cash flows into Equation 8.1 yields the following:

$$P_B = \$960.99 = \frac{\$60}{1+i} + \frac{\$60}{(1+i)^2} + \frac{\$750.79}{(1+i)^2}$$

We can solve this equation for i either by trial and error or with a financial calculator, as described earlier. Using a financial calculator, the solution is as follows:

	N	i	PV	PMT	FV
Enter	2		−960.99	60	750.79
Answer		**−4.97**			

The result is a realized yield of negative 4.97 percent. The difference between the promised yield of 7.50 percent and the realized yield of negative 4.97 percent is 12.47 percent [7.50 percent − (−4.97 percent) = 12.47 percent], which can be accounted for by the capital loss of \$210.20 (\$960.99 − \$750.79 = \$210.20) from the decline in the bond price.

Before You Go On

1. Explain how bond yields are calculated.

8.4 Interest Rate Risk

LEARNING OBJECTIVE

4. Explain why investors in bonds are subject to interest rate risk and why it is important to understand the bond theorems.

As discussed previously, the prices of bonds fluctuate with changes in interest rates, giving rise to **interest rate risk**. Anyone who owns bonds is subject to interest rate risk because interest rates are always changing in financial markets. A number of relations exist between bond

interest rate risk uncertainty about future bond values that is caused by the unpredictability of interest rates prices and changes in interest rates. These are often called the bond theorems, but they apply to all fixed-income securities. It is important that investors and financial managers understand these theorems.

Bond Theorems

1. **Bond prices are negatively related to interest rate movements.** As interest rates decline, the prices of bonds rise; and as interest rates rise, the prices of bonds decline. As mentioned earlier, this negative relation exists because the coupon rate on most bonds is fixed at the time the bonds are issued. Note that this negative relation is observed not only for bonds but also for all other financial claims that pay a fixed rate of interest to investors, such as bank loans and home mortgages.
2. **For a given change in interest rates, the prices of long-term bonds will change more than the prices of short-term bonds.** In other words, long-term bonds have greater price volatility (risk) than short-term bonds because, all other things being equal, long-term bonds have greater interest rate risk than short-term bonds. Exhibit 8.2 illustrates the fact that bond values are not equally affected by changes in market interest rates. The exhibit shows how the prices of a 1-year bond and a 30-year bond change with changing interest rates. As you can see, the long-term bond has much wider price swings than the short-term bond. Why? The answer is that long-term bonds receive most of their cash flows farther into the future, and because of the time value of money, these cash flows are heavily discounted. This makes the 30-year bond riskier than the 1-year bond.
3. **For a given change in interest rates, the prices of lower-coupon bonds change more than the prices of higher-coupon bonds.** Exhibit 8.3 illustrates the relation between bond price volatility and coupon rates. The exhibit shows the prices of three 10-year bonds: a zero coupon bond, a 5 percent coupon bond, and a 10 percent coupon bond.

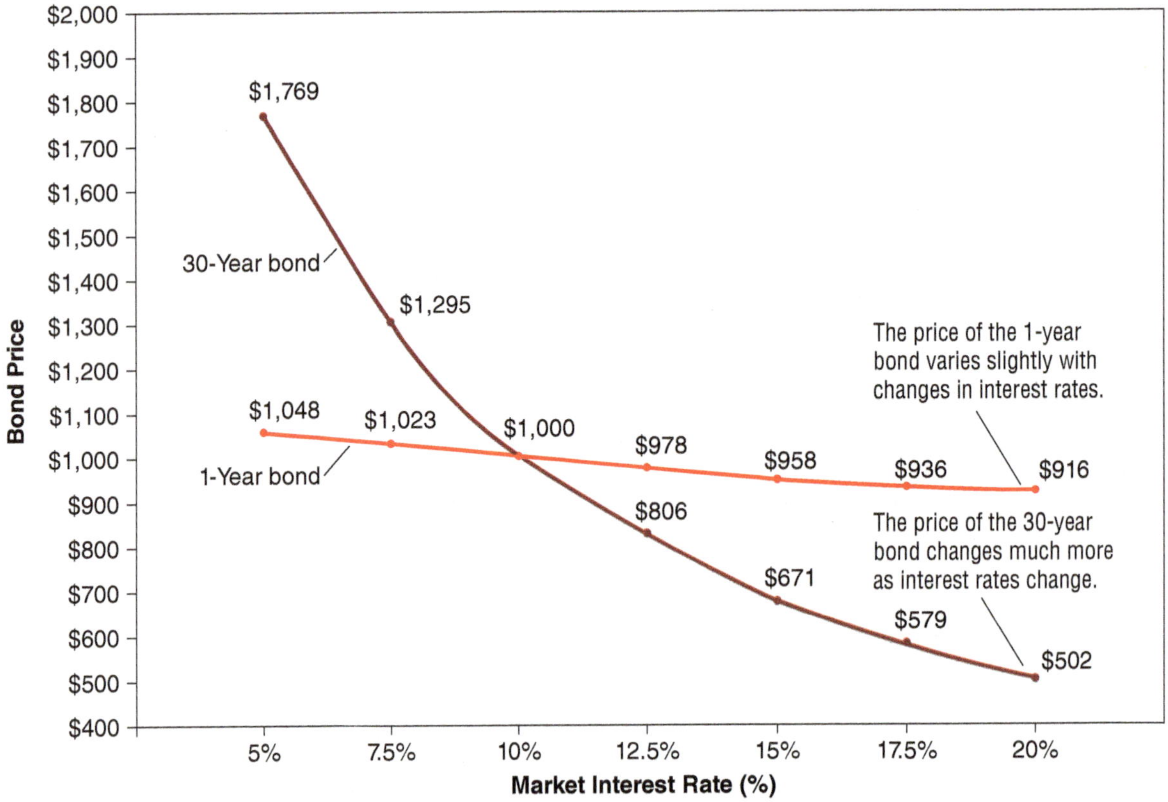

Note: Plots are for a 1-year bond and a 30-year bond with a 10 percent coupon rate and annual payment

EXHIBIT 8.2 Relation between Bond Price Volatility and Maturity

The prices of a 1-year and a 30-year bond respond differently to changes in market interest rates. The long-term bond has much wider price swings than the short-term bond, as predicted by the second bond theorem.

EXHIBIT 8.3 **Relation between Bond Price Volatility and the Coupon Rate**

The exhibit shows the prices of three 10-year bonds: a zero coupon bond, a 5 percent coupon bond, and a 10 percent coupon bond. Initially, the bonds are priced at a 5 percent yield (column 2). The bonds are then priced at yields of 6 and 4 percent (columns 3 and 6). The price changes shown are consistent with the third bond theorem: the smaller the coupon rate, the greater the percentage price change for a given change in interest rates.

		Price Change If Yield Increases from 5% to 6%			Price Change If Yield Decreases from 5% to 4%		
(1)	(2)	(3)	(4)	(5)	(6)	(7)	(8)
Coupon Rate	Bond Price at 5% Yield	Bond Price at 6%	Loss from Increase in Yield	% Price Change	Bond Price at 4%	Gain from Decrease in Yield	% Price Change
0%	$ 613.91	$ 588.39	$25.52	−9.04%	$ 675.56	$61.65	10.04%
5%	$1,000.00	$ 926.40	$73.60	−7.36%	$1,081.11	$81.11	8.11%
10%	$1,386.09	$1,294.40	$91.69	−6.62%	$1,486.65	$100.56	7.25%

Note: Calculations are based on a bond with a $1,000 face value and a 10-year maturity and assume annual compounding.

Initially, the bonds are priced to yield 5 percent (see column 2). The bonds are then priced at yields of 6 and 4 percent (see columns 3 and 6). The dollar price changes for each bond given the appropriate interest rate change are recorded in columns 4 and 7, and percentage price changes (price volatilities) are shown in columns 5 and 8.

As shown in column 5, when interest rates increase from 5 to 6 percent, the zero coupon bond experiences the greatest percentage price decline, and the 10 percent bond experiences the smallest percentage price decline. Similar results are shown in column 8 for interest rate decreases. In sum, the lower a bond's coupon rate, the greater its price volatility, and hence, lower-coupon bonds have greater interest rate risk.

The reason for the higher interest rate risk for low-coupon bonds is essentially the same as the reason for the higher interest rate risk for long-term bonds. The lower the bond's coupon rate, the greater the proportion of the bond's total cash flows investors will receive at maturity. This is clearly seen with a zero coupon bond, where all of the bond's cash flows are received at maturity. The farther into the future the cash flows are to be received, the greater the impact of a change in the discount rate on their present value. Thus, all other things being equal, a given change in interest rates will have a greater impact on the price of a low-coupon bond than a higher-coupon bond with the same maturity.

Bond Theorem Applications

The bond theorems provide important information about bond price behavior for financial managers. For example, if you are the treasurer of a firm and are investing cash temporarily—say, for a few days—the last security you want to purchase is a long-term zero coupon bond. In contrast, if you are an investor and you expect interest rates to decline, you may well want to invest in a long-term zero coupon bond. This is because as interest rates decline, the prices of long-term zero coupon bonds will increase more than those of any other type of bond.

Make no mistake, forecasting interest rate movements and investing in long-term bonds is a very high-risk strategy. In 1990, for example, executives at Shearson Lehman Hutton (predecessor to Lehman Brothers, the firm that famously went bankrupt in 2008, the beginning of the Great Recession) made a huge bet on interest rate movements and lost. Specifically, over a number of months, the firm made investments in long-term bonds that totaled $480 million. The bet was that interest rates would decline. When interest rates failed to decline and losses mounted, the Shearson team sold the bonds at a loss totaling $115 million. The executives responsible were fired for "lack of judgment."

Decision Making Example 8.1 illustrates another application of the bond theorems.

DECISION MAKING

EXAMPLE 8.1 | Risk Taking

Situation You work for the treasurer of a large manufacturing corporation where earnings are down substantially for the year. The treasurer's staff is convinced that interest rates are going to decline over the next three months, and they want to invest in fixed-income securities to make as much money as possible for the firm. The staff recommends investing in one of the following securities:

- 3-month Treasury bill
- 20-year corporate bond
- 20-year zero coupon Treasury bond

The treasurer asks you to answer the following questions about the staff's plan: (1) What is the underlying strategy of the proposed plan? (2) Which investment should be selected if the plan were to be executed? (3) What should the treasurer do?

Decision First, the staff's strategy is based on the negative relation between interest rates and bond prices. Thus, if interest rates decline, bond prices will rise, and the firm will earn a capital gain. Second, to maximize earnings, the treasurer should select bonds that will have the largest price swing for a given change in interest rates. Bond theorems 2 and 3 suggest that for a given change in interest rates, low-coupon, long-term bonds will have the largest price swing. Thus, the treasurer should invest in the 20-year zero coupon Treasury bond. With respect to the plan's merits, the intentions are good, but the investment plan is pure folly. Generating "earnings" from risky financial investments is not the firm's line of business or one of its core competencies. As was discussed in Chapter 1, the treasurer's primary investment function is to invest idle cash in safe investments such as money market instruments that have very low default and interest rate risk.

The moral of the story is simple. Long-term bonds carry substantially more interest rate risk than short-term bonds, and investors in long-term bonds need to fully understand the magnitude of the risk involved. Furthermore, no one can predict interest rate movements consistently, including the Federal Reserve Bank (Fed)—and it controls the money supply.

Before You Go On

1. What is interest rate risk?
2. Explain why long-term bonds with zero coupons are riskier than short-term bonds that pay coupon interest.

8.5 The Structure of Interest Rates

LEARNING OBJECTIVES

5. Discuss the concept of default risk and know how to compute a default risk premium.
6. Describe the factors that determine the level and shape of the yield curve.

In Chapter 2 we discussed the economic forces that determine the level of interest rates, and so far in this chapter, we have discussed how to price various types of debt securities. Armed with this knowledge, we now explore why, on the same day, different business firms have different borrowing costs. As you will see, market analysts have identified four risk characteristics of debt instruments that are responsible for most of the differences in corporate borrowing costs: the security's marketability, call provision, default risk, and term to maturity.

Marketability

The interest rate, or yield, on a security varies with its degree of marketability. Recall from Chapter 2 that marketability refers to the ease with which an investor can sell a security quickly at a low transaction cost. The transaction costs include all fees and the cost of searching for information. The lower the costs, the greater a security's marketability. Because investors prefer marketable securities, they must be paid a premium to purchase otherwise similar securities that are less marketable. The difference in interest rates or yields between a highly marketable security and a less marketable security is known as the *marketability risk premium* (MRP) and can be defined as follows:

$$MRP = i_{\text{low mkt}} - i_{\text{high mkt}} > 0$$

where $i_{\text{low mkt}}$ is the yield on a low or less marketable security and $i_{\text{high mkt}}$ is the yield on a more highly marketable security.

U.S. Treasury bills have the largest and most active secondary market and are considered to be the most marketable of all securities. Investors can sell virtually any dollar amount of Treasury securities quickly without disrupting the market. Similarly, the securities of many well-known businesses enjoy a high degree of marketability, especially firms whose securities are traded on the major exchanges. For thousands of other firms whose securities are not traded actively, marketability can pose a problem and can raise borrowing costs substantially.

Call Provision

Most corporate bonds contain a call provision in their contract. A call provision gives the firm issuing the bonds the option to purchase the bond from an investor at a predetermined price (the call price). The investor must sell the bond at that price to the firm when the firm exercises this option. Bonds with a call provision pay higher yields than comparable noncallable bonds. Investors require the higher yields because call provisions work to the benefit of the borrower and the detriment of the investor. For example, if interest rates decline after the bond is issued, the issuer can call (retire) the bonds at the call price and refinance with a new bond issued at the lower prevailing market rate of interest. The issuing firm is delighted because the refinancing has lowered its interest expense. However, investors are less gleeful. When bonds are called following a decline in interest rates, investors suffer a financial loss because they are forced to surrender their high-yielding bonds and reinvest their funds at the lower prevailing market rate of interest.

The difference in interest rates between a callable bond and a comparable noncallable bond is called the *call interest premium* (CIP) and can be defined as follows:

$$CIP = i_{\text{call}} - i_{\text{ncall}} > 0$$

where CIP is the call interest premium, i_{call} is the yield on a callable bond, and i_{ncall} is the yield on a noncallable bond of the same marketability, default risk, and term to maturity. Thus, the more likely a bond is to be called, the higher the CIP and the higher the bond's market yield. Bonds issued during periods when interest rates are high are likely to be called when interest rates decline, and as a result, these bonds have a large CIP. Conversely, bonds sold when interest rates are relatively low are less likely to be called and have a smaller CIP.

Default Risk

Recall that any debt, such as a bond or a bank loan, is a formal promise by the borrower to make periodic interest payments and pay the principal as specified in the debt contract. Failure on the borrower's part to meet any condition of the debt or loan contract constitutes default. As discussed in Chapter 4, default risk refers to the risk that the borrower will not be able to pay its debt obligations as they come due.

The Default Risk Premium

Because investors are risk averse, they must be paid a premium to purchase a security that exposes them to default risk. The size of the premium has two components: (1) compensation for the expected loss if a default occurs and (2) compensation for bearing the risk that a default could occur. The degree of default risk for a security can be measured as the difference between the interest rate on the risky security and the interest rate on a default-free security—all other factors, such as marketability, the existence of a call provision, or term to maturity, are held constant. The *default risk premium* (DRP) is defined as follows:

$$\text{DRP} = i_{\text{dr}} - i_{\text{rf}} > 0$$

where i_{dr} is the interest rate (yield) on the security that has default risk and i_{rf} is the interest rate (yield) on a risk-free security. U.S. Treasury securities are the best proxy measure for the risk-free rate. The larger the default risk premium, the higher the probability of default, and the higher the security's market yield.

Weblink

Fidelity Investment Company's Web site provides information on bond ratings at https://www.fidelity.com/learning-center/investment-products/fixed-income-bonds/overview.

investment-grade bonds bonds with low risk of default that are rated Baa (BBB) or above

noninvestment-grade bonds bonds rated below Baa (or BBB) by rating agencies; often called speculative-grade bonds, high-yield bonds, or junk bonds

Bond Ratings

Many investors, especially individuals and smaller businesses, do not have the expertise to formulate the probabilities of default themselves, so they must rely on credit rating agencies to provide this information. The three most prominent credit rating agencies are Moody's Investors Service (Moody's), Standard & Poor's (S&P), and Fitch. All three credit rating services rank bonds in order of their expected probability of default and publish the ratings as letter grades. The rating schemes used are shown in **Exhibit 8.4**. The highest-grade bonds, those with the lowest default risk, are rated Aaa (or AAA). The default risk premium on corporate bonds increases as the bond rating becomes lower.

Exhibit 8.4 also shows that bonds in the top four rating categories are called **investment-grade bonds**. Moody's calls bonds rated below Baa (or BBB) **noninvestment-grade bonds**, but most Wall Street practitioners refer to them as *speculative-grade bonds*, *high-yield bonds*, or *junk bonds*. The distinction between investment-grade and noninvestment-grade bonds is important because state and federal laws typically require commercial banks, insurance

EXHIBIT 8.4 Corporate Bond Rating Systems

Moody's has a slightly different notation in its ratings of corporate bonds than do Standard & Poor's and Fitch, but the interpretation is the same. Bonds with the highest credit standing are rated Aaa (or AAA) and have the lowest default risk. The credit rating declines as the default risk of the bonds increases.

Explanation	Moody's	Standard & Poor's/Fitch	Default Risk Premium	Regulatory Designation
Best quality, smallest degree of risk	Aaa	AAA	Lowest	Investment Grade
High quality, slightly more long-term risk than top rating	Aa	AA		
Upper-medium grade, possible impairment in the future	A	A		
Medium grade, lacks outstanding investment characteristics	Baa	BBB		
Speculative, protection may be very moderate	Ba	BB		Noninvestment Grade
Very speculative, may have small assurance of interest and principal payments	B	B		
Issues in poor standing, may be in default	Caa	CCC		
Speculative to a high degree, with marked shortcomings	Ca	CC		
Lowest quality, poor prospects of attaining real investment standing	C	C	Highest	

EXHIBIT 8.5 **Default Risk Premiums for Selected Bond Ratings**

The default risk premium (DRP) measures the yield difference between the yield on Treasury securities (the risk-free rate) and the yields on riskier securities of the same maturity.

Security: Credit Rating	Security Yield (%) (1)	Risk-Free Rate[a] (%) (2)	Default Risk: Premium (%) (1) − (2)
Aaa/AAA	3.77	2.79	0.98
Aa/AA	3.87	2.79	1.08
A/A	4.41	2.79	1.62
Baa/BBB	6.29	2.79	3.50

[a]20-year Treasury bond yield as of January 27, 2017.

Sources: U.S. Department of the Treasury (https://www.treasury.gov/resource-center/data-chart-center/interest-rates/Pages/TextView.aspx?data=yield) and Fidelity (https://fixedincome.fidelity.com/ftgw/fi/FILanding).

companies, pension funds, other financial institutions, and government agencies to purchase securities rated only as investment grade.

Exhibit 8.5 shows default risk premiums associated with selected bonds with investment-grade bond ratings in January 2017. The premiums are the differences between yields on Treasury securities—which, as mentioned, are the proxy for the risk-free rate—and yields on riskier securities of similar maturity. The 0.98 percent default risk premium on Aaa-rated corporate bonds represents the market consensus of the amount investors must be compensated to induce them to purchase typical Aaa-rated bonds instead of a risk-free security. As credit quality declines from Aaa to Baa, the default risk premiums increase from 0.98 percent to 3.50 percent.

The Term Structure of Interest Rates

The term to maturity of a loan is the length of time until the principal amount is payable. The relation between yield to maturity and term to maturity is known as the **term structure of interest rates**. We can view the term structure visually by plotting the **yield curve**, a graph with term to maturity on the horizontal axis and yield to maturity on the vertical axis. Yield curves show graphically how market yields vary as term to maturity changes.

term structure of interest rates the relation between yield to maturity and term to maturity

yield curve a graph representing the term structure of interest rates, with the term to maturity on the horizontal axis and the yield on the vertical axis

For yield curves to be meaningful, the securities used to plot the curves should be similar in all features (for example, marketability, call provisions, and default risk) except for maturity. We do not want to confound the relation of yield and term to maturity with other factors that also affect interest rates. We can see the term structure relation by examining yields on U.S. Treasury securities with different maturities because their other features are similar.

Exhibit 8.6 shows data and yield curve plots for Treasury securities at various points in time in the 2000s. As you can see, the shape of the yield curve is not constant over time. As the general level of interest rises and falls, the yield curve shifts up and down and has different slopes.

Weblink

Stockcharts.com has an animation of how the yield curve has changed over time. Go to http://stockcharts.com/freecharts/yieldcurve.php.

Note that the yield curve as of January 2017 is lower than the other two yield curves. Also short-term rates in January 2017 were less than 1 percent, which is very low by historical standards. In fact, in some European countries short-term rates have even been negative in recent years. A negative rate means that rather than earning interest, investors are effectively paying to lend money! Additionally, with interest rates at low levels, bond investors might be concerned about potential interest rate increases. As we know, when interest rates rise, bond prices fall and bondholders can face capital losses. A broader implication is that bond investors might start looking for higher returns elsewhere, which in turn likely involves different and riskier investments, a topic we will discuss further in later chapters.

We can observe three basic shapes (slopes) of yield curves in the marketplace. First is the ascending, or upward-sloping, yield curve (January 2017 and March 2008), which is the yield curve most commonly observed. Second, descending, or downward-sloping, yield curves (February 2007) appear periodically and are characterized by short-term yields (for

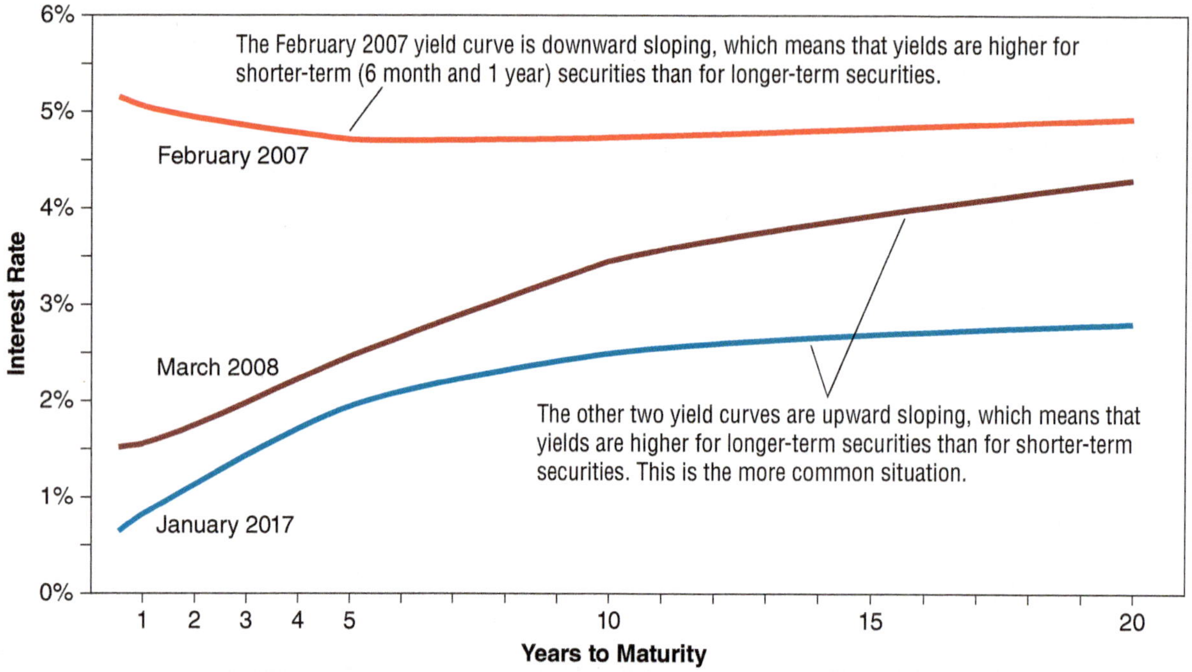

	Interest Rate (%)		
Terms to Maturity	January 2017	March 2008	February 2007
6 months	0.63	1.51	5.16
1 year	0.82	1.55	5.06
5 year	1.94	2.46	4.72
10 years	2.49	3.45	4.74
20 years	2.80	4.30	4.94

EXHIBIT 8.6 Yield Curves for Treasury Securities at Three Different Points in Time

The shape, or slope, of the yield curve is not constant over time. The exhibit shows two shapes: (1) the curves for March 2008 and January 2017 are upward sloping, which is the shape most commonly observed, and (2) the curve for February 2007 is downward sloping for maturities out to seven years.

example, the six-month yield) exceeding long-term yields (for example, the 20-year yield). Downward-sloping yield curves often appear before the beginning of a recession. Finally, relatively flat yield curves are not common but do occur from time to time. Three factors affect the level and the shape (the slope) of the yield curve over time: the real rate of interest, the expected rate of inflation, and interest rate risk.

The real rate of interest is the base interest rate in the economy and is determined by individuals' time preference for consumption; that is, it tells us how much individuals must be paid to forgo spending their money today. The real rate of interest varies with the business cycle, with the highest rates seen at the end of a period of business expansion and the lowest at the bottom of a recession. The real rate is not affected by the term to maturity. Thus, the real rate of interest affects the level of interest rates but not the shape of the yield curve.

The expected rate of inflation can influence the shape of the yield curve. If investors believe that inflation will increase in the future, the yield curve will be upward sloping because long-term interest rates will contain a larger inflation premium than short-term interest rates. The inflation premium is the market's best estimate of future inflation. Conversely, if investors believe inflation will subside in the future, the prevailing yield will be downward sloping.

Finally, the presence of interest rate risk affects the shape of the yield curve. As discussed earlier, long-term bonds have greater price volatility than short-term bonds. Because investors are aware of this risk, they demand compensation in the form of an interest rate premium. It follows that the longer the maturity of a security, the greater its interest rate risk, and the higher the interest rate. It is important to note that the interest rate risk premium always adds an upward bias to the slope of the yield curve.

In sum, the cumulative effect of three economic factors determines the level and shape of the yield curve: (1) the cyclical movements of the real rate of interest affect the level of the yield curve, (2) the expected rate of inflation can bias the slope of the yield curve either positively or negatively, depending on market expectations of inflation, and (3) interest rate risk always provides an upward bias to the slope of the yield curve.

Before You Go On

1. What are default risk premiums, and what do they measure?
2. Describe the three most prominent bond rating systems.
3. What are the key factors that most affect the level and shape of the yield curve?

Summary of Learning Objectives

1 Describe the market for corporate bonds and three types of corporate bonds.

The market for corporate bonds is a very large market in which the most important investors are large institutions. Most trades take place through dealers in the OTC market, making the corporate bond market relatively thin. Prices of corporate bonds tend to be more volatile than prices of securities that trade more frequently, such as stock and money market instruments, and the corporate bond market tends to be less efficient than markets for these other securities.

A vanilla bond pays fixed regular coupon payments over the life of the bond, and the entire principal is repaid at maturity. A zero coupon bond pays all interest and all principal at maturity. Since there are no payments before maturity, zero coupon bonds are issued at prices below their face value. Convertible bonds can be exchanged for common stock at a predetermined ratio.

2 Explain how to calculate the value of a bond and why bond prices vary negatively with interest rate movements.

The value of a bond is equal to the present value of the future cash flows (coupon payments and principal repayment) discounted at the market rate of interest for bonds with similar risk. Bond prices vary negatively with interest rates because the coupon rate on most bonds is fixed at the time the bond is issued. As market interest rates go up, the prices of bonds with fixed coupon payments will be bid down by investors, driving up the yields of those bonds to market levels. When interest rates decline, the yield on fixed-income securities will be higher relative to the yield on similar securities in the market; the favorable yield will increase investor demand for these securities, increasing their price and lowering their yield to the market yield.

3 Distinguish between a bond's coupon rate, yield to maturity, and effective annual yield.

A bond's coupon rate is the interest rate on the bond, relative to its face value. U.S. bonds typically pay interest semiannually, whereas European bonds pay once a year. The yield to maturity is the expected return on a bond if it is held to its maturity date. The effective annual yield is the yield an investor actually earns in one year, adjusting for the effects of compounding. If the bond pays coupon payments more often than annually, the effective annual yield will be higher than the simple annual yield because of compounding. Work through Learning by Doing Applications 8.2, 8.3, and 8.4 to master these calculations.

4 Explain why investors in bonds are subject to interest rate risk and why it is important to understand the bond theorems.

Because interest rates are always changing in the market, all investors who hold bonds are subject to interest rate risk. Interest rate risk is uncertainty about future bond values caused by fluctuations in interest rates. Three of the most important bond theorems can be summarized as follows:

1. Bond prices are negatively related to interest rate movements.
2. For a given change in interest rates, the prices of long-term bonds will change more than the prices of short-term bonds.
3. For a given change in interest rates, the prices of lower-coupon bonds will change more than the prices of higher-coupon bonds.

Understanding these theorems is important because it helps investors better understand why bond prices change and, thus, make better decisions regarding the purchase or sale of bonds and other fixed-income securities.

5 Discuss the concept of default risk and know how to compute a default risk premium.

Default risk is the risk that the issuer will be unable to pay its debt obligation. Since investors are risk averse, they must be paid a premium to purchase a security that exposes them to default risk. The default risk premium has two components: (1) compensation for the expected loss if a default occurs and (2) compensation for bearing the risk that a default could occur. All factors held constant, the degree of default risk a security possesses can be measured as the difference between the interest rate on a risky security and the interest rate on a default-free security. The default risk is also reflected in the company's bond rating. The highest-grade bonds, those with the lowest default risk, are rated Aaa (or AAA). The default risk premium on corporate bonds increases as the bond rating becomes lower.

6 Describe the factors that determine the level and shape of the yield curve.

The level and shape of the yield curve are determined by three factors: (1) the real rate of interest, (2) the expected rate of inflation, and (3) interest rate risk. The real rate of interest is the base interest rate in the economy and varies with the business cycle. The real rate of interest affects only the level of the yield curve and not its shape. The expected rate of inflation does affect the shape of the yield curve. If investors believe inflation will increase in the future, for example, the curve will be upward sloping, as long-term rates will contain a larger inflation premium than short-term rates. Finally, interest rate risk, which increases with a security's maturity, adds an upward bias to the slope of the yield curve.

Summary of Key Equations

Equation	Description	Formula
8.1	Price of a bond	$P_B = \frac{C_1}{1+i} + \frac{C_2}{(1+i)^2} + \cdots + \frac{C_n + F_n}{(1+i)^n}$
8.2	Price of a bond making multiple payments each year	$P_B = \frac{C/m}{1+i/m} + \frac{C/m}{(1+i/m)^2} + \frac{C/m}{(1+i/m)^3} + \cdots + \frac{C/m + F_{mn}}{(1+i/m)^{mn}}$
8.3	Price of zero coupon bond	$P_B = \frac{F_{mn}}{(1+i/m)^{mn}}$

Self-Study Problems

8.1 Calculate the price of a five-year bond that has a coupon rate of 6.5 percent paid annually. The current market rate is 5.75 percent.

8.2 Bigbie Corp. issued a five-year bond one year ago with a coupon rate of 8 percent. The bond pays interest semiannually. If the yield to maturity on this bond is 9 percent, what is the price of the bond?

8.3 Rockwell Industries has a three-year bond outstanding that pays a 7.25 percent coupon rate and is currently priced at $913.88. What is the yield to maturity of this bond? Assume annual coupon payments.

8.4 Hindenberg, Inc., has a 10-year bond that is priced at $1,100.00. It has a coupon rate of 8 percent paid semiannually. What is the yield to maturity on this bond?

8.5 Highland Corp., a U.S. company, has a five-year bond whose yield to maturity is 6.5 percent. The bond has no coupon payments. What is the price of this zero coupon bond?

Solutions to Self-Study Problems

8.1 The time line and calculations for the five-year bond are as follows:

0 (5.75%)	1	2	3	4	5 Year
$P_B = ?$	\$65	\$65	\$65	\$65	\$1,065

$$P_B = \frac{C_1}{1+i} + \frac{C_2}{(1+i)^2} + \frac{C_3}{(1+i)^3} + \frac{C_4}{(1+i)^4} + \frac{C_5 + F_5}{(1+i)^5}$$

$$= \frac{\$65}{1.0575} + \frac{\$65}{(1.0575)^2} + \frac{\$65}{(1.0575)^3} + \frac{\$65}{(1.0575)^4} + \frac{\$65 + \$1{,}000}{(1.0575)^5}$$

$$= \$61.47 + \$58.12 + \$54.96 + \$51.95 + \$805.28$$

$$= \$1{,}031.81$$

8.2 We can find the price of Bigbie Corp.'s bond as follows:

0 (9%)	1	2	3	4	5	6	7	8	Semiannual period
$P_B = ?$	\$40	\$40	\$40	\$40	\$40	\$40	\$40	\$1,040	

$$P_B = \frac{C/m}{1 + i/m} + \frac{C/m}{(1 + i/m)^2} + \frac{C/m}{(1 + i/m)^3} + \cdots + \frac{C/m + F_8}{(1 + i/m)^8}$$

$$= \frac{\$40}{1.045} + \frac{\$40}{(1.045)^2} + \frac{\$40}{(1.045)^3} + \cdots + \frac{(\$40 + \$1{,}000)}{(1.045)^8}$$

$$= \$38.28 + \$36.63 + \$35.05 + \$33.54 + \$32.10 + \$30.72 + \$29.39 + \$731.31$$

$$= \$967.02$$

Alternatively, we can use the present value of an ordinary annuity equation (Equation 6.1 from Chapter 6) and the present value equation (Equation 5.4 from Chapter 5) to solve for the price of the bond.

$$P_B = C \times \left[\frac{1 - \dfrac{1}{(1 + i/m)^{mn}}}{i/m}\right] + \frac{F_n}{(1 + i/m)^{mn}} = \$40 \times \left[\frac{1 - \dfrac{1}{(1 + 0.045)^8}}{0.045}\right] + \frac{\$1{,}000}{(1.045)^8}$$

$$= \$263.84 + \$703.19 = \$967.03$$

8.3 We start with a time line for Rockwell's bond:

0 ($i = ?$)	1	2	3	Year
$P_B = -\$913.88$	\$72.50	\$72.50	\$1,072.50	

Use trial and error to solve for the yield to maturity (YTM). Since the bond is selling at a discount, we know that the yield to maturity is higher than the coupon rate.

Try YTM = 10%.

$$P_B = \frac{C_1}{1 + i} + \frac{C_2}{(1 + i)^2} + \frac{C_3 + F_3}{(1 + i)^3}$$

$$\$913.88 = \frac{\$72.50}{1.10} + \frac{\$72.50}{(1.10)^2} + \frac{\$72.50 + \$1{,}000}{(1.10)^3}$$

$$= \$65.91 + \$59.92 + \$805.79$$

$$\neq \$931.61$$

Try a higher rate, say YTM = 11%.

$$P_B = \frac{C_1}{1 + i} + \frac{C_2}{(1 + i)^2} + \frac{C_3 + F_3}{(1 + i)^3}$$

$$\$913.88 = \frac{\$72.50}{1.11} + \frac{\$72.50}{(1.11)^2} + \frac{\$72.50 + \$1{,}000}{(1.11)^3}$$

$$= \$65.32 + \$58.84 + \$784.20$$

$$\neq \$908.36$$

Since this is less than the price of the bond, we know that the YTM is between 10 and 11 percent and closer to 11 percent.

Try YTM = 10.75%.

$$P_B = \frac{C_1}{1 + i} + \frac{C_2}{(1 + i)^2} + \frac{C_3 + F_3}{(1 + i)^3}$$

$$\$913.88 = \frac{\$72.50}{1.1075} + \frac{\$72.50}{(1.1075)^2} + \frac{\$72.50 + \$1{,}000}{(1.1075)^3}$$

$$= \$65.46 + \$59.11 + \$789.53$$

$$\cong \$914.09$$

Alternatively, we can use Equation 6.1 and Equation 5.4 to solve for the price of the bond.

$$P_B = C \times \left[\frac{1 - \frac{1}{(1+i)^n}}{i}\right] + \frac{F_n}{(1+i)^n}$$

$$\$913.88 = \$72.50 \times \left[\frac{1 - \frac{1}{(1+0.1075)^3}}{0.1075}\right] + \frac{\$1{,}000}{(1.1075)^3}$$

$$= \$177.94 + \$736.15$$

$$\cong \$914.09$$

Thus, the YTM is approximately 10.75 percent. Using a financial calculator provides an exact YTM of 10.7594%.

8.4 The time line for Hindenberg's 10-year bond looks like this:

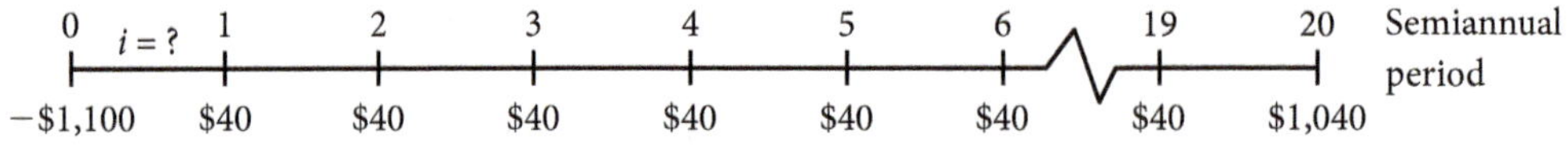

The easiest way to calculate the yield to maturity is with a financial calculator. The inputs are as follows:

	N	i	PV	PMT	FV
Enter	20		−1,100	40	1,000
Answer		**3.31**			

The answer we get is 3.31 percent, which is the semiannual interest rate. To obtain an annualized yield to maturity, we multiply this by two:

$$\text{YTM} = 3.31\% \times 2$$

$$\text{YTM} = 6.62\%$$

8.5 You have the following information about Highland's bonds:

YTM = 6.5%

No coupon payments

Most U.S. bonds pay interest semiannually. Thus $m \times n = 2 \times 5 = 10$ and $i/2 = 0.065/2 = 0.0325$. Using Equation 8.3, we obtain the following:

$$P_B = \frac{F_{mn}}{(1 + i/m)^{mn}}$$

$$= \frac{\$1{,}000}{(1 + 0.0325)^{10}}$$

$$= \$726.27$$

WileyPLUS

Questions and Problems, Solution Walkthrough Videos, Learning by Doing Tutorials, and additional study tools and resources are available in WileyPLUS.

Discussion Questions

8.1 Because the conversion feature in a convertible bond is valuable to bondholders, convertible bond issues have lower coupon payments than otherwise similar bonds that are not convertible. Does this mean that a company can lower its cost of borrowing by selling convertible debt? Explain.

8.2 What economic conditions would prompt investors to take advantage of a bond's convertibility feature?

8.3 We know that a vanilla bond with a coupon rate below the market rate of interest will sell for a discount and that a vanilla bond with a coupon rate above the market rate of interest will sell for a premium. What kind of bond or loan will sell at its par value regardless of what happens to the market rate of interest?

8.4 Define *yield to maturity*. Why is it important?

8.5 Define *interest rate risk*. How can CFOs manage this risk?

8.6 Explain why bond prices and interest rates are negatively related. What are the roles of the coupon rate and the term to maturity in this relation?

8.7 If interest rates are expected to increase, should investors look to long-term bonds or short-term bonds? Explain.

8.8 Explain what you would assume the yield curve would look like during economic expansion and why.

8.9 An investor holds a 10-year bond paying a coupon rate of 9 percent. The yield to maturity of the bond is 7.8 percent. Would you expect the investor to be holding a par-value, premium, or discount bond? What if the yield to maturity were 10.2 percent? Explain.

8.10 **a.** Investor A holds a 10-year bond, while investor B holds an 8-year bond. If the interest rate increases by 1 percent, which investor has the higher interest rate risk? Explain.

b. Investor A holds a 10-year bond paying 8 percent a year, while investor B also has a 10-year bond that pays a 6 percent coupon. Which investor has the higher interest rate risk? Explain.

Questions and Problems

Excel *Excel templates and resources available in* **WileyPLUS**

Basic

8.1 **Bond price:** BA Corp is issuing a 10-year bond with a coupon rate of 8 percent. The interest rate for similar bonds is currently 6 percent. Assuming annual payments, what is the value of the bond?

8.2 **Bond price:** Pierre Dupont just received a cash gift from his grandfather. He plans to invest in a five-year bond issued by Venice Corp. that pays an annual coupon rate of 5.5 percent. If the current market rate is 7.25 percent, what is the maximum amount Pierre should be willing to pay for this bond?

8.3 **Bond price:** Knight, Inc., has issued a three-year bond that pays a coupon rate of 6.10 percent. Coupon payments are made semiannually. Given the market rate of interest of 5.80 percent, what is the market value of the bond?

8.4 **Bond price:** Regatta Inc. has seven-year bonds outstanding that pay a 12 percent coupon rate. Investors buying these bonds today can expect to earn a yield to maturity of 8.875 percent. What is the current value of these bonds? Assume annual coupon payments.

8.5 **Bond price:** You are interested in investing in a five-year bond that pays a 7.8 percent coupon rate with interest to be received semiannually. Your required rate of return is 8.4 percent. What is the most you would be willing to pay for this bond?

8.6 **Zero coupon bonds:** Diane Carter is interested in buying a five-year zero coupon bond with a face value of $1,000. She understands that the market interest rate for similar investments is 9 percent. Assume annual coupon payments. What is the current value of this bond?

8.7 **Zero coupon bonds:** Ten-year zero coupon bonds issued by the U.S. Treasury have a face value of $1,000 and interest is compounded semiannually. If similar bonds in the market yield 10.5 percent, what is the value of these bonds?

8.8 **Zero coupon bonds:** Northrop Real Estate Company management is planning to fund a development project by issuing 10-year zero coupon bonds with a face value of $1,000. Assuming semiannual compounding, what will be the price of these bonds if the appropriate discount rate is 14 percent?

8.9 **Yield to maturity:** Ruth Hornsby is looking to invest in a three-year bond that makes semi-annual coupon payments at a rate of 5.875 percent. If these bonds have a market price of $981.13, what yield to maturity can she expect to earn?

8.10 **Yield to maturity:** Rudy Sandberg wants to invest in four-year bonds that are currently priced at $868.43. These bonds have a coupon rate of 6 percent and make semiannual coupon payments. What is the current market yield on this bond?

8.11 **Realized yield:** Josh Kavern bought 10-year, 12 percent coupon bonds issued by the U.S. Treasury three years ago at $913.44. If he sells these bonds, for which he paid the face value of $1,000, at the current price of $804.59, what is his realized yield on the bonds? Assume similar coupon-paying bonds make annual coupon payments.

8.12 **Realized yield:** Four years ago, Lisa Stills bought six-year, 5.5 percent coupon bonds issued by the Fairways Corp. for $947.68. If she sells these bonds at the current price of $894.52, what will be her realized yield on the bonds? Assume similar coupon-paying bonds make annual coupon payments.

Intermediate

8.13 **Bond price:** The International Publishing Group is raising \$10 million by issuing 15-year bonds with a coupon rate of 8.5 percent. Coupon payments will be made annually. Investors buying the bonds today will earn a yield to maturity of 8.5 percent. At what price will the bonds sell in the marketplace? Explain.

8.14 **Bond price:** Lopez Information Systems management is planning to issue 10-year bonds. The going market yield for such bonds is 8.125 percent. Assume that coupon payments will be made semiannually. Management is trying to decide between issuing an 8 percent coupon bond or a zero coupon bond. Lopez needs to raise \$1 million. What will be the price of an 8 percent coupon bond, and how many 8 percent coupon bonds will have to be issued? What will be the price of a zero coupon bond, and how many zero coupon bonds will have to be issued?

8.15 **Bond price:** Marshall Company is issuing eight-year bonds with a coupon rate of 6.5 percent and semiannual coupon payments. If the current market rate for similar bonds is 8 percent, what will the bond price be? If company management wants to raise \$1.25 million, how many bonds does the firm have to sell?

8.16 **Bond price:** Rockne, Inc., has outstanding bonds that will mature in six years and pay an 8 percent coupon semiannually. If you paid \$1,036.65 today and your required rate of return was 6.6 percent, did you pay the right price for the bond?

8.17 **Bond price:** Nanotech, Inc., has a bond issue maturing in seven years that is paying a coupon rate of 9.5 percent (semiannual payments). Management wants to retire a portion of the issue by buying the securities in the open market. If it can refinance at 8 percent, how much will Nanotech pay to buy back its current outstanding bonds?

8.18 **Zero coupon bonds:** Kintel, Inc., management wants to raise \$1 million by issuing six-year zero coupon bonds with a face value of \$1,000. The company's investment banker states that investors would use an 11.4 percent discount rate to value such bonds. At what price would these bonds sell in the marketplace? How many bonds would the firm have to issue to raise \$1 million? Assume semiannual coupon payments.

8.19 **Zero coupon bonds:** Rockinghouse Corp. management plans to issue seven-year zero coupon bonds. It has learned that these bonds will sell today at a price of \$439.76. Assuming annual coupon payments, what is the yield to maturity on these bonds?

8.20 **Yield to maturity:** Electrolex, Inc., has four-year bonds outstanding that pay a coupon rate of 6.6 percent and make coupon payments semiannually. If these bonds are currently selling at \$914.89, what is the yield to maturity that an investor can expect to earn on these bonds? What is the effective annual yield?

8.21 **Yield to maturity:** Serengeti Corp. has five-year bonds outstanding that pay a coupon rate of 8.8 percent. If these bonds are priced at \$1,064.86, what is the yield to maturity on these bonds? Assume semiannual coupon payments. What is the effective annual yield?

8.22 **Yield to maturity:** Adrienne Dawson is planning to buy 10-year zero coupon bonds issued by the U.S. Treasury. If these bonds have a face value of \$1,000 and are currently selling at \$404.59, what is the expected return on them? Assume that interest compounds semiannually on similar coupon paying bonds.

8.23 **Realized yield:** Brown & Co. issued seven-year bonds two years ago that can be called after two years. The bonds make semiannual coupon payments at a coupon rate of 7.875 percent. Each bond has a market value of \$1,053.40, and the call price is \$1,078.75. If an investor purchased the bonds at par value when they were originally issued and the bonds are called by the firm today, what is the investor's realized yield?

8.24 **Realized yield:** Trevor Price bought 10-year bonds issued by Harvest Foods five years ago for \$936.05. The bonds make semiannual coupon payments at a rate of 8.4 percent. If the current price of the bonds is \$1,048.77, what is the yield that Trevor would earn by selling the bonds today?

8.25 **Realized yield:** You bought a six-year bond issued by Runaway Corp. four years ago. At that time, you paid \$974.33 for the bond. The bond pays a coupon rate of 7.375 percent, and coupon payments are made semiannually. Currently, the bond is priced at \$1,023.56. What yield can you expect to earn on this bond if you sell it today?

Advanced

8.26 Pullman Corp issued 10-year bonds four years ago with a coupon rate of 9.375 percent. At the time of issue, the bonds sold at par. Today bonds of similar risk and maturity must pay an annual coupon of 6.25 percent to sell at par value. Assuming semiannual coupon payments:

a. What is the bond's yield to maturity?

b. What is the current market price of the firm's bonds?

8.27 Showbiz, Inc., has issued eight-year bonds with a coupon rate of 6.375 percent and semiannual coupon payments. The market's required rate of return on such bonds is 7.65 percent.

a. What is the market price of these bonds?

b. If the above bond is callable after five years at an 8.5 percent premium on the face value, what is the expected return on this bond?

8.28 Peabody Corp. has seven-year bonds outstanding. The bonds pay a coupon rate of 8.375 percent semiannually and are currently worth \$1,063.49. The bonds can be called in three years at a price of \$1,075.

a. What is the yield to maturity of these bonds?

b. What is the effective annual yield?

c. What is the realized yield on the bonds if they are called?

d. If you plan to invest in one of these bonds today, what is the expected yield on the investment? Explain.

8.29 The Maryland Department of Transportation has issued 25-year bonds that make semiannual coupon payments at a rate of 9.875 percent. The current market rate for similar securities is 11 percent.

a. What is the current market value of one of these bonds?

b. What will be the bond's price if rates in the market (i) decrease to 9 percent or (ii) increase to 12 percent?

c. Refer to your answers in part b. How do the interest rate changes affect premium bonds and discount bonds?

d. Suppose the bond were to mature in 12 years. How do the interest rate changes in part b affect the bond prices?

8.30 Rachette Corp. has 18-year bonds outstanding. These bonds, which pay interest semiannually, have a coupon rate of 9.735 percent and a yield to maturity of 7.95 percent.

a. Compute the current price of these bonds.

b. If the bonds can be called in five years at a premium of 13.5 percent over par value, what is the investor's realized yield?

c. If you bought one of these bonds today, what is your expected rate of return? Explain.

8.31 Zippy Corporation just sold $30 million of convertible bonds with a conversion ratio of 40. Each $1,000 bond is convertible into 25 shares of Zippy's stock.

a. What is the conversion price of Zippy's stock?

b. If the current price of Zippy's stock is $15 and the company's annual stock return is normally distributed with a standard deviation of $5, what is the probability that investors will find it attractive to convert the bond into Zippy stock in the next year?

Sample Test Problems

8.1 Seven years ago Eastern Corporation issued 20-year bonds that had a $1,000 face value, paid interest annually, and had a coupon rate of 7 percent. If the market rate of interest is 5.5 percent today, what is the current market price of an Eastern Corporation bond? Are these bonds selling at a premium or discount?

8.2 You are considering investing in a 10-year zero coupon bond that compounds interest semiannually. If the current market rate is 5.65 percent, what is the maximum price you should have to pay for this bond?

8.3 Bigbox, Inc., has bonds outstanding that will mature in eight years. These bonds pay interest semiannually and have a coupon rate of 4.6 percent. If the bonds are currently selling at $888.92, what is the yield to maturity that an investor who buys them today can expect to earn? What is the effective annual yield?

8.4 Given a change in market interest rates, which will change more: the market price of a bond with 20 years until maturity or the market price of a bond with five years until maturity? Assume all the characteristics of these bonds are identical except the maturity dates.

8.5 Which of the following classes of securities is likely to have the lowest corporate borrowing cost?

a. AAA rated bonds.

b. A rated bonds.

c. BB rated bonds.

d. C rated bonds.

e. All of the above will have the same corporate borrowing cost.

Ethics Case

The Subprime Mortgage Market Meltdown: How Did It Happen?

The U.S. economy appeared strong throughout the first half of 2007, but many observers saw clouds on the horizon in the form of trouble brewing in the subprime home mortgage market. Fear of the coming storm intensified as housing prices dropped, home foreclosures increased, major subprime mortgage lenders filed for bankruptcy, and investors took losses on mortgage-backed securities. By the end of the year, many were predicting a serious economic downturn.

Feverpitched/Getty Images

"It's not like a bottle of water," said Senator Charles E. Schumer, chairman of the Joint Economic Committee of the U.S. Congress. "It's much more like a pond where ripples start and can spread quickly. . . . The subprime ripple leads to another ripple of lower housing prices and a credit crunch for banks and financial markets. Another ripple driven by consumer anxiety causes lower consumer spending, which makes up nearly two-thirds of our economic growth, and leads to an even larger ripple that may end up causing a recession."[1]

What Are Subprime Mortgages?

The subprime mortgages at the center of all this turmoil were made to borrowers who had poor credit histories or who were considered high credit risks for other reasons. Subprime mortgages are a relatively recent phenomenon because, prior to the 1980s, usury laws limited the ability of lenders to charge interest rates that adequately compensated them for the risks associated with these loans. As a

[1] Senator Charles E. Schumer, "A Call to Action on the Subprime Mortgage Crisis," remarks on the state of the economy, as prepared for delivery to the Brookings Institution, December 19, 2007.

result, subprime mortgage loans were simply not made before the usury laws were relaxed.

Several new federal laws were passed in the 1980s that, among other things, eliminated interest rate caps and made it possible for high-risk borrowers to obtain home mortgages. The subprime market experienced ups and downs in the 1990s, but by the early 2000s it had become an important part of the broader mortgage market. Loans originated in the subprime market made up less than 5 percent of mortgage loans in 1994 but increased to 13 percent in 2000 and to more than 20 percent in 2005 and 2006.[2] The increase after 2000 accompanied a rapid rise in home prices in many real estate markets throughout the United States. Higher prices resulted in larger mortgage loans, which in turn increased the average risk of new loans, because incomes were not rising as quickly as home prices.

The emergence of the subprime market was accompanied by a number of changes in the structure of mortgage lending. Traditionally, a person who wanted a mortgage loan dealt with a bank or a savings and loan institution, which granted the loan (or refused to grant it), financed the loan with deposits, collected the payments, and foreclosed on the property if the payments weren't made. Today, these activities are much more likely to be carried out by separate institutions. For example, a majority of subprime mortgages are originated by mortgage brokers—intermediaries that earn a fee by bringing borrowers and lenders together. Once the loans are made, the lenders often resell the resulting mortgages.

Beginning in the 1990s, the *securitization* of mortgage loans became quite popular. This practice involves bundling groups of loans with similar characteristics and selling claims on the cash flows from these bundles, called mortgage-backed securities (MBSs). Most commonly, MBSs are sold to institutional investors by investment banks. Investors in mortgage-backed securities include insurance companies, mutual funds, pension funds, and hedge funds, among others. The securitization of subprime loans increased from about 32 percent of all such loans in 1994 to about 78 percent in 2006.[3] This development meant that much of the relatively high risk associated with subprime loans was spread among a large number of investors, rather than a relatively small number of lending institutions.

Over the same period a number of new kinds of mortgages were developed to supplement the traditional fixed-rate mortgage. Especially important in the subprime market are various kinds of adjustable-rate mortgages (ARMs). The interest rate in an ARM changes (resets) at regular intervals—once a year, for example—in response to changes in some index, such as the prime rate. Many subprime ARMs are hybrids that start with low "teaser" rates that remain constant for a certain period, typically two or three years. After that period is over, the mortgage "resets." Thereafter, it is adjusted periodically.

In addition, no-documentation loans appeared in the early 2000s as housing prices began their rapid rise. With these loans, lenders do not even ask for verification of the borrower's income.

What Went Wrong?

Many observers touted the benefits of subprime loans in enabling previously disadvantaged groups, such as those living in poor or minority neighborhoods, to become homeowners. In addition, lenders initially earned large profits by charging these borrowers high interest rates and, because so many of the mortgages were securitized, a relatively large number of investors earned high returns.

So how did this evidently great idea turn into an economic disaster? Remember that subprime borrowers are risky borrowers—they're considered more likely to default on their loans. And that's just what happened. Beginning in 2006, more and more subprime borrowers fell behind on their loan payments, and many of them ended up defaulting. This began a long upward trend in foreclosures that showed little sign of slowing even by the end of 2010. Several economic conditions contributed to the high rate of defaults. For one thing, the prime rate of interest, which had been declining or holding steady since 2001, began to rise in 2004, affecting the rate to which interest on ARMs was reset. To further complicate the situation, housing prices, which had been increasing steadily, began to drop in 2006, leaving some buyers owing more than the current value of their homes.

As a result of the large number of defaults, subprime lenders found themselves in deep financial trouble, and some top lenders filed for bankruptcy. Lenders were originating fewer loans and were finding it difficult to sell those that they had originated. Investment bankers who had purchased loans and securitized them, also suffered. In order to get the highest possible prices, they had retained some exposure to the riskiest parts of the loan bundles that they sold. As the default rates on loans underlying MBSs increased, the investment bankers suffered losses, as did the investors who bought the securities.

As investors in other types of fixed-income securities saw what was happening to the values of securitized subprime mortgages, they became concerned about the values of similar securitized debt instruments, such as collateralized loan obligations (CLOs). CLOs are securitized business loans, which included business loans that had been used to fund leveraged buyouts and were therefore also quite risky. Investors' concerns caused prices for CLOs to decline rapidly. In addition, banks and other lenders began to tighten their credit standards, which made it more difficult for businesses and individuals to get loans, further contributing to a general weakening of the economy.

Who's to Blame?

Inevitably, observers looked around for someone to blame for the subprime crisis. And they came up with a long list of candidates, from the homebuyers themselves (who should have been more prudent) to the SEC and the Federal Reserve (who should have been paying closer attention). Few disagree, though, that those promoting subprime mortgages—such as mortgage brokers and lenders—must bear at least a part of the blame.

Motivated by the potential to earn a lot of money in a rapidly expanding market, many of these players turned their backs on ethical standards. "In the feeding frenzy for housing loans," according to one writer, "basic quality controls were ignored in the mortgage business, while the big Wall Street investment banks that backed these firms looked the other way."[4] Problems existed at many levels, as a few examples show:

- Mortgage lenders did not adequately monitor what the mortgage brokers were doing. In fact, some allege that they were willing to make virtually any loan that brokers sent their way. With little oversight, the brokers did not have a strong incentive to carefully evaluate the ability of borrowers to repay the mortgages. They

[2]James R. Barth et al., "A Short History of the Subprime Mortgage Market Meltdown" (Milken Institute, January 2008), p. 3.

[3]Brenda B. White, "A Short History of Subprime (Mortgage Industry)," *Mortgage Banking*, March 1, 2006.

[4]David Cho, "Pressure at Mortgage Firm Led to Mass Approval of Bad Loans," *Washington Post*, May 7, 2007.

filled out the loan paperwork that they submitted to the lenders without verifying all of the information and, it has been alleged, in some cases actually misrepresented the facts.

- Appraisers inflated the market value of houses, causing consumers to take out mortgages that did not reflect their houses' true value. According to several national studies, lenders commonly pressured appraisers to value a property at whatever amount was needed to allow a high-priced sale to close.[5] Willingness to inflate appraisals also made some appraisers attractive to unscrupulous mortgage brokers, who were an important source of their business. The attorneys general of several states filed suit against mortgage and appraisal firms, claiming that they engaged in this practice.
- Mortgage companies lured buyers with teaser rates and other loan terms that appeared favorable but, in the longer run, were not. (Some have called these terms "toxic.") Mortgage agreements often included prepayment penalties that would make it very expensive for buyers to refinance later. Many subprime buyers weren't experienced or sophisticated enough to fully understand the terms, but lenders and brokers were interested in pushing through the loans—not in explaining the loan terms.
- Many subprime mortgages were "no-doc" loans, which required little or no documentation of income. These loans, claimed one observer, "were available to anyone with a pulse." Opportunities for abuse are obvious—and not restricted to borrowers. A former employee of Ameriquest Mortgage Corp. stated that it was "a common and open practice at Ameriquest for account executives to forge or alter borrower information or loan documents. . . . I saw account executives openly engage in conduct such as altering borrowers' W-2 forms or pay stubs, photocopying borrower signatures and copying them onto other, unsigned documents, and similar conduct."[6]
- As bonds backed by subprime mortgages became more popular and profitable, investment banks—eager to bundle more mortgages—loosened their standards. The quality of the loans being bundled began to slide as the popularity of subprime mortgages grew, according to the consultants (called due-diligence firms) hired by the bankers to evaluate loan quality. However, many investment banking firms overlooked the problem—and, as a result, passed ever-higher risk along to the investors who bought their mortgage-backed securities.
- Investors in the MBSs did not fully understand the risks associated with them. The way in which the mortgages were bundled made it difficult for investors to value the MBSs. They were so complex that many investors apparently relied on investment bankers to tell them what they were worth. The investment bankers apparently did not understand or simply failed to inform investors of all the risks. Some investors probably also got a bit greedy.

[5]Kenneth R. Harney, "Appraisal Inflation," *Washington Post*, April 21, 2007.
[6]Bob Irvy, "Subprime 'Liar Loans' Fuel Bust with $1 Billion Fraud (Update 1)," Bloomberg.com, updated April 25, 2007.

Discussion Questions

1. What were the responsibilities of the mortgage brokers to borrowers? To lenders? To investors? How well did they fulfill their responsibilities? Why?
2. Did some subprime lenders behave unethically? If so, how? Whose interests did the subprime lenders have a responsibility to represent? Did they adequately represent those interests?
3. What motivated the investment bankers to get involved in the subprime market? Did they behave appropriately? Why or why not?
4. Should the borrowers (homeowners) share in the blame? If so, how?
5. What about the investors in MBSs? What could they have done differently?
6. What can be done to prevent future blowups like the one that occurred in the subprime market?

Sources: Associated Press, "Regulators' Cases Targeting Wall Street's Role in Subprime Market," Boston.com, February 18, 2008; James R. Barth, Tong Li, Triphon Phumiwasana, and Glenn Yago, "A Short History of the Subprime Mortgage Market Meltdown" (Milken Institute, January 2008), p. 3; Souphala Chomsisengphet and Anthony Pennington-Cross, "The Evolution of the Subprime Mortgage Market," *Federal Reserve Bank of St. Louis Review*, January/February 2006; Patrick Rucker, "Wall Street Often Shelved Damaging Subprime Reports," *International Herald Tribune*, August 1, 2007; Robert J. Samuelson, "The Catch-22 of Economics," *Newsweek*, updated September 15, 2007; Time/CNN, "A Sub-Prime Primer," March 15, 2007; Faten Sabry and Thomas Schopflocher, "The Subprime Meltdown: A Primer," Part I of NERA Insights Series, June 21, 2007; Brenda B. White, "A Short History of Subprime (Mortgage Industry)," *Mortgage Banking*, March 1, 2006.

CHAPTER **9**

Stock Valuation

bunhill/Getty Images

LEARNING OBJECTIVES

1. List and describe the four types of secondary markets.
2. Explain why many financial analysts treat preferred stock as a special type of bond rather than as an equity security.
3. Describe how the general dividend-valuation model values a share of stock.
4. Discuss the assumptions that are necessary to make the general dividend-valuation model easier to use, and use the model to compute the value of a firm's stock.
5. Explain why *g* must be less than R in the constant-growth dividend model.
6. Explain how valuing preferred stock with a stated maturity differs from valuing preferred stock with no maturity, and calculate the price of a share of preferred stock under both conditions.

Finding the actual market price of a share of publicly traded stock is easy. You can just look it up online at a Web site such as Yahoo! Finance or MSN Money Central. But don't expect the market price to stay the same; stock prices change all the time—sometimes dramatically. For example, between the end of trading on March 2, 2017, and the end of trading on March 3, 2017, the price of Nutanix, Inc., stock dropped from $31.12 to $23.00 per share—a 26 percent decline. What caused this sudden drop in the company's share price? Investors decided that the value of the cash flows that they could expect to receive from ownership of the cloud computing company's shares was only about three-quarters of what they had thought those cash flows were worth on March 2.

Investors did not arbitrarily reduce their assessment of the value of the cash flows that Nutanix stockholders could expect to receive. They changed their assessment when company management announced, on the evening of March 2, earnings for the fiscal quarter that ended on January 31, 2017. While the revenues and earnings were higher than investors expected, management followed the announcement with discouraging comments about their expectations for the next quarter. These comments increased uncertainty in minds of investors about the ability of the company to produce the sales and earnings that investors were expecting in the future. In the context of the time value of money discussion in Chapter 6, investors revised downward their estimate of the size of the cash flows that the company would produce for stockholders and they revised upward the rate at which those cash flows should be discounted. The net effect of these revisions was the 26 percent drop in the company's stock price.

When stock prices rise or fall, how do investors or financial managers know when it is time to sell or buy? In other words, how can they tell if the market price of a stock reflects its value? One approach is to develop a stock-valuation model and compare the value estimate from the model with the market price. If the market price is below the estimate, the stock may be undervalued, in which case an investor might buy the stock. (Of course, other factors may also weigh into the final decision to buy.) In this chapter, we develop and apply stock-valuation models that enable us to estimate a stock's value. The models are very similar to those used by Wall Street firms.

Chapter Preview

This chapter focuses on equity securities (stocks) and how they are valued. We describe the market in which stocks trade and discuss several valuation models. These models tell us what a stock's price *should* be. We can compare our estimates from such models with the *actual* market price to better understand how the market is valuing an individual stock.

Why are stock-valuation formulas important for you to study in a corporate finance course? First, management may want to know if the firm's stock is undervalued or overvalued. This knowledge can affect the decisions that managers make. For example, if the stock is undervalued, management may want to repurchase shares of stock to reissue in the future or postpone an equity offering until the stock price increases. Second, as we mentioned in Chapter 1, the overarching goal of financial managers is to maximize the current value of the firm's stock. To make investment or financing decisions that increase stockholder wealth, you must understand the fundamental factors that determine the market value of the firm's stock.

We begin this chapter with a discussion of the secondary markets for stocks and their efficiency, describe the major U.S. stock market indexes, explain how to read stock market price listings in the newspaper or online, and introduce the types of equity securities that firms typically issue. We then develop a general valuation model and demonstrate that the value of a share of stock is the present value of *all* expected future cash dividends. We use some simplifying assumptions about dividend payments to implement this valuation model. These assumptions correspond to actual practice and allow us to develop several specific valuation models.

9.1 The Market for Stocks

Equity securities, which are certificates of ownership of a corporation, are the most visible securities on the financial landscape. In December 2016, $30.1 trillion worth of public equity securities were outstanding in the United States alone. Every day Americans eagerly track the ups and downs of the stock market. Most people instinctively believe that the performance of the stock market is an important barometer of the country's economic health. Also fueling interest is the large number of people who actually own equity securities through their pension or retirement plans. The stocks owned by households represent about 35 percent of the total value of all corporate equity.

Secondary Markets

LEARNING OBJECTIVE

1. List and describe the four types of secondary markets.

Recall from Chapter 2 that the stock market consists of primary and secondary markets. In the primary market, firms sell new shares of stock to investors to raise money. In secondary markets, outstanding shares of stock are bought and sold among investors. We will discuss the primary markets for stocks further in Chapter 15. Our focus here is on secondary markets.

Any trade of a security after its primary offering is said to be a secondary market transaction. Most secondary market transactions do not directly affect the firm that issues the securities. For example, when an investor buys 100 shares of AT&T stock on the New York Stock Exchange (NYSE), the exchange of money is only between the investors buying and selling the securities; no money flows into or out of AT&T.

The presence of a secondary market does, however, affect the issuer indirectly. As discussed in Chapter 2, investors will pay a higher price for primary securities that have an active secondary market. The reason is that, with an active secondary market, investors face lower transaction costs and are more likely to receive a price that reflects the true value of their securities when they sell them. As a result, firms whose securities trade on a secondary market can sell their new debt or equity issues at a lower cost than can firms selling similar securities that have no secondary market.

Secondary Markets and Their Efficiency

In the United States, most secondary market transactions take place on one of the many stock exchanges, the two most important being the NYSE and NASDAQ.

New York Stock Exchange

Chapter 2 described a traditional securities exchange as an organized market that provides a physical meeting place and communication facilities for members to buy and sell securities under a specific set of rules and regulations. The oldest, largest, and best-known exchange of this kind in the United States is the NYSE, which was founded in 1792. The exchange lists the common and preferred stocks of more than three thousand companies, as well as eight hundred bonds. Collectively, the companies whose securities are traded on the NYSE had a market capitalization (total stock value) of about $21.1 trillion in February 2017.

Stocks that are traded on an exchange are said to be *listed* on that exchange. For a firm's stocks to be listed on an exchange, the firm must pay a fee and meet the exchange's requirements for membership. Requirements include a minimum asset size, total stock value, a minimum number of shares of stock outstanding, and a minimum number of stockholders. Because of the prestige associated with being listed on the "big board," as the NYSE is known, it has the most stringent listing requirements. As a result, companies listed on the NYSE tend to be large, well-known firms.

Weblink

Learn more about the NYSE by visiting its Web site at http://www.nyse.com.

NASDAQ

The NASDAQ (pronounced "Naz-dak") is the world's largest electronic stock market, listing over three thousand companies. NASDAQ was created in 1971 by the National Association of Securities Dealers (NASD), and its odd name is an acronym for National Association of Securities Dealers Automated Quotation (NASDAQ) system.

NASDAQ is an OTC market because it does not have a physical location where trading takes place. Nevertheless, NASDAQ has achieved the stature of a major exchange. In fact, thanks to its sophisticated electronic trading system, NASDAQ is the second-largest stock market in the United States. The companies whose shares trade on NASDAQ had an aggregate market capitalization of $10.2 trillion in February 2017. Only the NYSE is larger. Although the OTC market has generally traded in the stocks of small firms that would not qualify to be listed on a major exchange, only 20 percent of the firms traded on NASDAQ are considered small.

Weblink

Find out about over-the-counter markets and NASDAQ at http://www.nasdaq.com.

The World's Stock Exchanges/Markets

Although we have focused on the NYSE and NASDAQ, it is important to recognize that there are approximately 100 equity stock exchanges/markets located throughout the world. The NYSE and NASDAQ are consistently two of the top three based on the market value of the shares that trade in them. The largest exchanges/markets outside the United States in 2017 were the Japan Exchange Group, the London Stock Exchange, Euronext, the Hong Kong Stock Exchanges and Clearing, the Shenzhen Stock Exchange, and the Shanghai Stock Exchange.

Furthermore, over the last decade there has been significant restructuring and consolidation of the exchanges and markets through mergers and acquisitions. Some examples are the purchase of Euronext by the NYSE, the merger of NASDAQ with the OMX Group, and the merger of the Chicago Mercantile Exchange with the Chicago Board of Trade. The consolidation among the world's major exchanges/markets is driven by (1) new technologies that provide faster executions of trades and access to more markets and more products, (2) increased competition, which has reduced profit margins, and (3) the need to increase size in order to achieve greater economies of scale and operational efficiencies.

The role of the NYSE, NASDAQ, and other secondary markets is to bring together buyers and sellers. Ideally, we would like them to do this as efficiently as possible. As discussed in Chapter 2, markets are efficient when the current market prices of securities that are trading reflect all available information relevant to the valuation of those securities. When this happens, security prices will be near or at their true (intrinsic) value. The more efficient the market, the more likely this is to happen.

There are four types of secondary markets, and each type differs according to the amount of price information available to investors, which in turn affects the efficiency of the market. We discuss the four types of secondary markets—direct search, broker, dealer, and auction—in the order from least to most efficient.

Direct Search

The secondary markets furthest from the ideal of complete availability of price information are those in which buyers and sellers must seek each other out directly. In these markets, individuals bear the full cost of locating and negotiating with a buyer or seller, and it is typically too costly for them to conduct a thorough search to locate the best price. Securities that sell in direct search markets are usually bought and sold so infrequently that few third parties, such as a brokers or dealers, find it profitable enough to serve the market. In these markets, sellers often rely on word-of-mouth communication to find interested buyers. The common stock of small private companies is a good example of a security that trades in this manner.

Broker

When trading in a security issue becomes sufficiently heavy, brokers find it profitable to offer specialized search services to market participants. Brokers bring together buyers and sellers to earn a fee, called a commission. To provide investors with an incentive to hire them, brokers may charge a commission that is less than the cost of a direct search. Brokers are not passive agents but aggressively seek out buyers or sellers and try to negotiate an acceptable transaction price for their clients. The presence of active brokers increases market efficiency because brokers are in frequent contact with market participants and are likely to know what constitutes a fair price for a security.

Dealer

If the trading in a given security has sufficient volume, market efficiency is improved when there is someone in the marketplace who provides continuous bidding (selling or buying) for the security. Dealers do this by holding inventories of securities, which they own, and then buying and selling from the inventory to earn a profit. Unlike brokers, dealers have capital at risk. Dealers earn their profits from the *spread* on the securities they trade—the difference between their **bid price** (the price at which they buy) and their **offer (ask) price** (the price at which they sell). NASDAQ is the best-known example of a dealer market in the United States.

bid price the price a securities dealer will pay for a given stock

offer (ask) price the price at which a securities dealer seeks to sell a given stock

The advantage of a dealer over a broker market is that brokers cannot guarantee that an order to buy or sell will be executed promptly. This uncertainty about the speed of execution creates price risk. During the time a broker is trying to sell a security, its price may change and the person trying to sell the security could suffer a loss. A dealer market eliminates the need for time-consuming searches for a fair deal because buying and selling take place immediately from the dealer's inventory of securities.

Dealers make markets in securities using electronic computer networks to quote prices at which they are willing to buy or sell a particular security. These networks enable dealers to electronically survey the prices quoted by different dealers to help establish their sense of a fair price and to trade. A major development in the 1990s was the opening of the so-called electronic communications network (ECN). An ECN is an electronic network that allows individual investors to trade securities directly with one another, much like dealers.

Auction

In an auction market, buyers and sellers interact directly with each other and bargain over price. The participants can communicate orally if they are located in the same place, or the information can be transmitted electronically. The NYSE is the best-known example of an auction market in the United States. In the NYSE, the auction for a security takes place at a specific location on the floor of the exchange, called a **post**. The auctioneer in this case is the **specialist**, who is designated by the exchange to represent orders placed by public customers. Specialists, as the name implies, specialize in orders for a small set of securities and are also allowed to act as dealers. Thus, in reality, the NYSE is an auction market that also has some features of a dealer market. Over the years, the NYSE has embraced electronic trading with the SuperDOT system (DOT stands for *designated order turnaround*), which allows orders to be transmitted electronically to specialists.

post a specific location on the floor of a stock exchange at which auctions for a particular security take place

specialist the trader designated by an exchange to represent orders placed by public customers at auctions of securities; specialists handle a small set of securities and are also allowed to act as dealers

Stock Market Indexes

Stock market indexes are used to measure the performance of the stock market—whether stock prices on average are moving up or down. The indexes are watched closely not only to track economic activity but also to measure the performance of specific firms. A wide variety of general and specialized indexes is available. Here, we discuss some of the better-known indexes.

- *Dow Jones Industrial Average*. The most widely quoted stock market index is the Dow Jones Industrial Average (DJIA), which was first published in 1896. The index consists of 30 companies that represent about 20 percent of the market value of all U.S. stocks. Dow Jones also publishes specialized indexes for industrial, transportation, and utility companies. These specialized indexes tell us how stocks in a particular segment of the economy are performing.
- *New York Stock Exchange Index*. The NYSE composite index, published since 1966, includes all of the common and preferred stocks listed on the NYSE. This index provides information on the performance of many of the largest and most well-known firms in the U.S. economy.
- *Standard and Poor's 500 Index*. The Standard and Poor's 500 Index, which consists of 500 stocks, was created in 1926 and is regarded as the best index for measuring the performance of the largest companies in the U.S. economy. The stocks in the S&P 500 are selected by the Standard and Poor's Index Committee and represent more than 70 percent of the total market capitalization (market value) of all stocks traded in the United States.
- *NASDAQ Composite Index*. The NASDAQ Composite Index consists of all of the common stocks listed on the NASDAQ stock exchange. Currently, the index includes more than three thousand firms, many of which are in the technology sector of the economy. Thus, the NASDAQ Composite Index is considered a barometer of performance in the high-tech sector.

Weblink

The Web site http://www.bigcharts.com offers a real-time summary of all the major market indexes.

Reading the Stock Market Listings

The *Wall Street Journal*, the *Financial Times*, and other newspapers provide stock listings for the major stock exchanges, such as the NYSE, NASDAQ, and the relevant regional exchanges. **Exhibit 9.1** shows a small section of a listing from the *Wall Street Journal* online (WSJ.com) for the NYSE on March 6, 2017.

In the exhibit, go to the entry for Adams Resources & Energy, which is highlighted. Adams is a Houston-based company that markets crude oil, natural gas, and petroleum products. Look at column 2, which provides the trading (ticker) symbol of the company—AE. The trading symbol is used in requesting price quotes or company information and in placing a trade. Columns 4 and 5 show the high price ($39.77 per share) and low price ($37.53 per share) for the day, and column 6 shows that AE's closing price at the end of the day was $37.53 per share. The closing price, which is the price at which the last trade took place, was a $2.12 decrease from the close on the previous day (column 7). The trading volume of shares for the day, which for AE is 4,279 shares of stock, is listed in column 9. Column 10 shows the firm's highest price ($44.27 per share) and column 11 its lowest price ($29.64 per share) over the past 52 weeks.

Column 12 shows AE's annual cash dividend per share, which is $0.88. Although the annual dividend is shown here, most firms, including AE, pay dividends quarterly, or four

Weblink

To monitor stocks trading on the New York Stock Exchange, visit the NYSE EURONEXT Web site at https://nyse.nyx.com/equities.

EXHIBIT 9.1 NYSE Stock Listings from the *Wall Street Journal*

Company Name (1)	Symbol (2)	Open (3)	High (4)	Low (5)	Close (6)	Net Chg (7)
Acme United	ACU	25.76	26.20	24.77	24.77	−0.62
ACRE Realty Investors	AIII	1.13	1.13	1.08	1.08	−0.06
Actinium Pharmaceuticals	ATNM	1.31	1.35	1.20	1.35	0.02
Adams Resources & Energy	AE	39.75	39.77	37.53	37.53	−2.12
AdCare Health Systems	ADK	1.35	1.35	1.21	1.24	−0.04
AeroCentury	ACY	9.95	9.95	9.60	9.65	−0.33
Air Industries Group	AIRI	3.67	3.85	3.62	3.85	0.13
Alexco Resource	AXU	1.47	1.57	1.47	1.55	0.05
Almaden Minerals	AAU	1.07	1.12	1.05	1.10	0.04
Alpha Pro Tech	APT	3.20	3.25	3.10	3.15	. . .
Altisource Asset Management	AAMC	79.05	85.90	78.75	85.90	6.90
AMCON Distributing	DIT	101.25	102.13	98.60	99.03	−1.02
American DG Energy	ADGE	0.32	0.34	0.32	0.34	0.01

SOURCE: Wall Street Journal Online, Monday, March 6, 2017.

dividend yield a stock's annual dividend divided by its current price

times a year. Column 13 shows AE's **dividend yield**, which is 2.34 percent. The dividend yield is calculated by dividing the annual dividend payout by the current market price. For AE, that calculation is $0.88/$37.53 = 0.0234, or 2.34 percent. If you scan the dividend yields, you will see that most of the firms pay no dividend at all; for those that pay dividends, the dividend yields range from 0.73 percent to 19.35 percent. Investors are willing to accept low dividend payouts, or none at all, as long as they expect higher cash dividends and/or a higher stock price in the future.

Column 14 shows AE's price-earnings (P/E) ratio, which—as you may recall from Chapter 4—is the stock's current price per share divided by its earnings per share. For AE, the P/E ratio is negative, which is indicated by . . . dd. This tells us that AE had negative earnings last year, making the P/E ratio a poor measure of value. In cases like this WSJ.com does not even report a value. Finally, column 15 shows the percentage change in price for the stock for the calendar year. In AE's case the price has gone down by 5.35 percent.

Common and Preferred Stock

common stock an equity share that represents the basic ownership claim in a corporation; the most common type of equity security

preferred stock an equity share in a corporation that entitles the owner to preferred treatment over owners of common stock with respect to dividend payments and claims against the firm's assets in the event of bankruptcy or liquidation, but that typically has no voting rights

Equity securities take several forms. The most prevalent type of equity security, as its name implies, is **common stock**. Common stock represents the basic ownership claim in a corporation. One of the basic rights of the owners is to vote on all important matters that affect the company, such as the election of the board of directors or a proposed merger or acquisition. Owners of common stock are not guaranteed any dividend payments and have the lowest-priority claim on the firm's assets in the event of bankruptcy. Legally, common stockholders enjoy limited liability; that is, their losses are limited to the original amount of their investment in the firm, and their personal assets cannot be taken to satisfy the obligations of the corporation. Finally, common stocks are perpetuities in the sense that they have no maturity. Common stock can be retired only if management buys it in the open market from investors or if the firm is liquidated, in which case its assets are sold, as described in the next section.

Like common stock, **preferred stock** represents an ownership interest in the corporation, but as the name implies, preferred stock receives preferential treatment over common

% Chg (8)	Volume (9)	52 Wk High (10)	52 Wk Low (11)	Div (12)	Yield (13)	P/E (14)	YTD % Chg (15)
−2.44	8,346	27.35	15.01	0.40	1.61	15.29	−3.13
−5.26	13,732	1.85	0.90	. . .	. . .	. . . dd	−2.70
1.50	1,230,368	2.36	0.86	. . .	. . .	. . . dd	54.29
−5.35	4,279	44.27	29.64	0.88	2.34	. . . dd	−5.35
−3.13	58,362	2.70	1.21	0.24	19.35	. . . dd	−15.07
−3.30	16,627	14.33	8.50	. . .	. . .	3.45	2.12
3.49	63,547	6.79	2.21	0.60	15.58	. . . dd	22.22
3.33	532,194	2.54	0.67	. . .	. . .	. . . dd	14.81
3.77	211,357	1.88	0.65	. . .	. . .	. . . dd	13.54
. . .	21,874	3.80	1.62	. . .	. . .	19.69	−10.00
8.73	20,256	85.90	11.40	. . .	. . .	. . . dd	60.56
−1.02	12,261	122.90	77.76	0.72	0.73	12.27	−14.12
1.61	14,314	0.65	0.22	. . .	. . .	. . . dd	19.75

stock. Specifically, preferred stockholders take precedence over common stockholders in the payment of dividends and in the distribution of corporate assets in the event of liquidation. Unlike the interest payments on bonds, which are contractual obligations, preferred stock dividends are declared by the board of directors, and if a dividend is not paid, the lack of payment is not legally viewed as a default.

Preferred stock is legally a form of equity. Thus, preferred stock dividends are paid by the issuer with after-tax dollars. Even though preferred stock is an equity security, the owners have no voting privileges unless the preferred stock is convertible into common stock. Preferred stocks are generally viewed as perpetuities because they have no maturity. However, most preferred stocks are not true perpetuities because their share contracts often contain call provisions and can even include *sinking fund* provisions, which require management to retire (purchase) a certain percentage of the stock issue annually until the entire issue is retired.

Preferred Stock: Debt or Equity?

LEARNING OBJECTIVE

2. Explain why many financial analysts treat preferred stock as a special type of bond rather than as an equity security.

An ongoing debate in finance is whether preferred stock is debt or equity. A strong case can be made that preferred stock is a special type of bond rather than equity. The argument behind this view is as follows. First, regular (nonconvertible) preferred stock confers no voting rights. Second, preferred stockholders receive a fixed dividend, regardless of the firm's earnings, and if the firm is liquidated, they receive a stated value (usually par) and not a residual value. Third, preferred stocks often have credit ratings that are similar in nature to those issued to bonds. Fourth, preferred stock is sometimes convertible into common stock. Finally, most preferred stock issues have a retirement date and, thus, are not true perpetuities.

Before You Go On

1. What is the NASDAQ?
2. How do dealers differ from brokers?
3. List the major stock market indexes and explain what they tell us.
4. What does the price-earnings ratio tell us?
5. Why do some people view preferred stock as a special type of bond rather than a stock?

9.2 Common Stock Valuation

In earlier chapters we emphasized that the value of any asset is the present value of its future cash flows. The steps in valuing an asset are as follows:

1. Estimate the expected future cash flows.
2. Determine the required rate of return, or discount rate, which reflects the riskiness of the future cash flows.
3. Compute the present value of the future cash flows to determine what the asset is worth.

It is relatively straightforward to apply these steps in valuing a bond because the cash flows are stated as part of the bond contract and the required rate of return or discount rate is just the yield to maturity on bonds with comparable risk. However, common stock valuation is more difficult for several reasons. First, while the expected cash flows for bonds are well documented and easy to determine, common stock dividends are much less certain. Dividends are declared by the board of directors, and a board may or may not decide to pay a cash dividend at a particular time. Thus, the size and the timing of dividend cash flows are less certain. Second, common stocks are true perpetuities in that they have no final maturity date. Thus, firms never have to redeem them. In contrast, with the exception of the consol bonds mentioned in Chapter 6, bonds have a finite maturity. Finally, unlike the rate of return, or yield, on bonds, the rate of return on common stock is not directly observable. Thus, grouping common stocks into risk classes is more difficult than grouping bonds. Keeping these complexities in mind, we now turn to a discussion of common stock valuation.

Weblink

You can read about stock-valuation models at the Motley Fool: http://www.fool.com/research/2000/features000406.htm.

A One-Period Model

Let's assume that you have a genie that can tell the future with perfect certainty. Also, suppose that you are thinking about buying a share of stock and selling it after a year. The genie volunteers that in one year the price (P_1) you can sell the stock for will be \$100 and it will pay an \$8 dividend (D_1) at the end of the year. The time line for the transaction is:

If you and the other investors require a 20 percent return on investments in securities in this risk class, what price would you be willing to pay for the stock today?

The value of the stock is the present value of the future cash flows you can expect to receive from it. The cash flows you will receive are as follows: (1) the \$8 dividend and (2) the \$100 sale price. Using a 20 percent rate of return, we see that the value of the stock equals the present value (PV) of the dividend plus the present value of the cash received from the sale of the stock:

$$\begin{aligned}\text{PV(stock)} &= \text{PV(dividend)} + \text{PV(sale price)}\\ &= \frac{\$8}{1+0.2} + \frac{\$100}{1+0.2}\\ &= \frac{\$8+\$100}{1.2} = \frac{\$108}{1.2}\\ &= \$90\end{aligned}$$

Thus, the value of the stock today is \$90. If you pay \$90 for the stock, you will have a one-year holding period return of exactly 20 percent. More formally, the time line and the current value of the stock for our one-period model can be as shown:

$$P_0 = \frac{D_1 + P_1}{1 + R}$$

where:

P_0 = the current value, or price, of the stock
D_1 = dividend paid at the end of the period
P_1 = price of the stock at the end of the period
R = required return on common stock, or discount rate, in a particular risk class

Note that P_0 denotes time zero, which is today; P_1 is the price one period later; P_2 is the price two periods in the future; and so on. Note also that when we speak of the price (P_t) in this context, we mean the value—what we have determined is what the price *should* be, given our model—not the actual market price. Our one-period model provides an estimate of what the market price should be.

Now, what if at the beginning of Year 2 we are again asked to determine the price of a share of common stock with the same dividend pattern and a one-year holding period. As in our first calculation, the current price (P_1) of the stock is the present value of the dividend and the stock's sale price, both received at the end of the year (P_2). Specifically, our time line and the stock pricing formula are as follows:

$$P_1 = \frac{D_2 + P_2}{1 + R}$$

If we repeat the process again at the beginning of Year 3, the result is similar:

$$P_2 = \frac{D_3 + P_3}{1 + R}$$

and at the beginning of Year 4:

$$P_3 = \frac{D_4 + P_4}{1 + R}$$

Each single-period model discounts the dividend and sale price at the end of the period by the required return.

A Perpetuity Model

Unfortunately, although our one-period model is correct, it is not very realistic. We need a stock-valuation formula for a perpetuity, not for one or two periods. However, we can string together a series of one-period stock pricing models to arrive at a stock perpetuity model. Here is how we do it.

First, we construct a two-period stock-valuation model. The time line for the two-period model is:

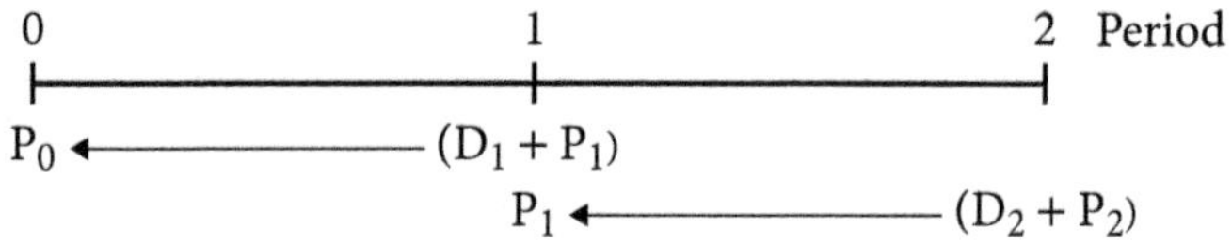

To construct our two-period model, we start with our initial single-period valuation model:

$$P_0 = \frac{D_1 + P_1}{1 + R}$$

Now we substitute into this equation the expression derived earlier for P_1 [$P_1 = (D_2 + P_2)/(1 + R)$] and obtain the following:

$$P_0 = \frac{D_1 + [(D_2 + P_2)/(1 + R)]}{1 + R}$$

Rearranging this equation results in a stock-valuation model for two periods:

$$P_0 = \frac{D_1}{1 + R} + \frac{D_2}{(1 + R)^2} + \frac{P_2}{(1 + R)^2}$$

Finally, we combine the second-period terms to obtain:

$$P_0 = \frac{D_1}{1 + R} + \frac{D_2 + P_2}{(1 + R)^2}$$

This equation shows that the price of a share of stock that is held for two periods is the present value of the dividend in period 1 (D_1) plus the present value of the dividend and sale price in period 2 (D_2 and P_2).

Now let's construct a three-period model. The time line for the three-period model is:

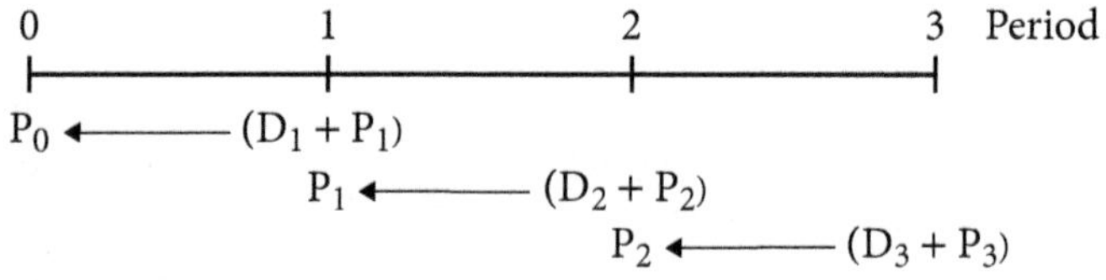

If we substitute the equation for P_2 into the two-period valuation model shown above, we have a three-period model, which is as follows. Recall that $P_2 = (D_3 + P_3)/(1 + R)$.

$$\begin{aligned} P_0 &= \frac{D_1}{1 + R} + \frac{D_2}{(1 + R)^2} + \frac{P_2}{(1 + R)^2} \\ &= \frac{D_1}{1 + R} + \frac{D_2}{(1 + R)^2} + \frac{(D_3 + P_3)/(1 + R)}{(1 + R)^2} \\ &= \frac{D_1}{1 + R} + \frac{D_2}{(1 + R)^2} + \frac{D_3}{(1 + R)^3} + \frac{P_3}{(1 + R)^3} \\ &= \frac{D_1}{1 + R} + \frac{D_2}{(1 + R)^2} + \frac{D_3 + P_3}{(1 + R)^3} \end{aligned}$$

By now, it should be clear that we could go on to develop a four-period model, a five-period model, a six-period model, and so on, ad infinitum. The ultimate result is the following equation:

$$P_0 = \frac{D_1}{1 + R} + \frac{D_2}{(1 + R)^2} + \frac{D_3}{(1 + R)^3} + \cdots + \frac{D_t}{(1 + R)^t} + \frac{P_t}{(1 + R)^t}$$

Here, t is the time period, which can be any number from one to infinity (∞). We will use t, instead of n, to denote the time period from this point forward because it is more commonly used in pricing equations; n will still be used to denote the number of periods.

In summary, we have developed a model showing that the value, or price, of a share of stock today (P_0) is the present value of all future dividends and the stock's sale price in the future. Although theoretically sound, this model is not practical to apply because the number of dividends could be infinite. It is unlikely that we can successfully forecast an infinite number of dividend payments or a stock's sale price far into the future. What we need are some realistic simplifing assumptions.

The General Dividend-Valuation Model

LEARNING OBJECTIVE

3. Describe how the general dividend-valuation model values a share of stock.

In the preceding equation, notice that the final term, as in the earlier stock valuation models, is always the sale price of the stock in period t (P_t) and that t can be any number, including infinity. The model assumes that we can forecast the sale price of the stock far into the future, which does not seem very likely in real life. However, as a practical matter, as P_t moves further out in time toward infinity, the value of the P_t approaches zero. Why? No matter how large the sale price of the stock, the present value of P_t will approach zero because the discount factor approaches zero. Therefore, if we go out to infinity, we can ignore the $P_t/(1 + R)^t$ term and write our final equation as:

$$P_0 = \frac{D_1}{1 + R} + \frac{D_2}{(1 + R)^2} + \frac{D_3}{(1 + R)^3} + \frac{D_4}{(1 + R)^4} + \frac{D_5}{(1 + R)^5} + \cdots + \frac{D_\infty}{(1 + R)^\infty}$$

$$= \sum_{t=1}^{\infty} \frac{D_t}{(1 + R)^t} \tag{9.1}$$

where:

P_0 = the current value, or price, of the stock
D_t = the dividend received in period t, where $t = 1, 2, 3, \ldots, \infty$
R = the required return on the common stock or discount rate

Equation 9.1 is a general expression for the value of a share of stock. It says that the price of a share of stock is the present value of *all* expected future dividends:

$$\text{Stock price} = \text{PV(All expected dividends)}$$

The formula does not assume any specific pattern for future dividends, such as a constant growth rate. Nor does it make any assumption about when the share of stock is going to be sold in the future. Furthermore, the model says that to compute a stock's current value, we need to forecast an infinite number of dividends, which is a daunting task.

Equation 9.1 provides some insights into why stock prices are changing all the time and why, at certain times, price changes can be dramatic. Equation 9.1 implies that the underlying value of a share of stock is determined by the market's expectations of the future cash flows (from dividends) that the firm can generate. In efficient markets, stock prices change constantly as new information becomes available and is incorporated into the firm's market price. For publicly traded companies, the market is inundated with facts and rumors, such as when a firm fails to meet sales projections, the CEO resigns or is fired, or a class-action suit is filed against the firm because of a defect in one of its products. Some events may have little or no impact on the firm's expected cash flows and, hence, its stock price. Others can have very large effects on expected cash flows. Examples include the effects of the subprime mortgage market collapse in 2007, which led to a sharp slowdown in the economy in 2008, or the effect of the 2010 Gulf oil spill on the cash flows of BP p.l.c., the large oil company.

The Growth Stock Pricing Paradox

An interesting issue concerning growth stocks arises out of the fact that the stock-valuation equation is based on dividend payments. *Growth stocks* are typically defined as the stocks of companies whose earnings are growing at above-average rates and are expected to continue to do so for some time. A company of this type typically pays little or no dividends on its stock because management believes that the company has a number of high-return investment opportunities and that both the company and its investors will be better off if earnings are reinvested rather than paid out as dividends.

To illustrate the problem with valuing growth stocks, let's suppose that the earnings of Acme Corporation are growing at an exceptionally high rate. The company's stock pays no dividends, and management states that there are no plans to pay any dividends. Based on our stock-valuation equation, what is the value of Acme's stock?

Obviously, since all the dividend values are zero, the value of our growth stock is zero!

$$P_0 = \frac{0}{1 + R} + \frac{0}{(1 + R)^2} + \frac{0}{(1 + R)^3} + \cdots = 0$$

How can the value of a growth stock be zero? What is going on here?

The problem is that our definition of growth stocks was less than precise. Our application of Equation 9.1 assumes that Acme will never pay a dividend. If Acme had a charter that stated it would *never* pay dividends and would *never* liquidate itself (unless it went bankrupt), the value of its stock would indeed be zero. Equation 9.1 predicts and common sense says that if you own stock in a company that will *never* pay you any cash, the market value of those shares of stock are worth absolutely nothing. As you may recall, this is a point we emphasized in Chapter 1.

What we should have said is that a growth stock is stock in a company that *currently* has exceptional investment opportunities and thus is not *currently* paying dividends because it is reinvesting earnings. At some time in the future, growth stock companies will pay dividends or will liquidate themselves (for example, by selling out to other companies) and pay a single large cash dividend. People who buy growth stocks expect rapid price appreciation because management reinvests the cash flows from earnings internally in investment projects believed to have high rates of return. If the internal investments succeed, the stock's price should go up significantly, and investors can sell their stock at a price that is higher than the price they paid.

Before You Go On

1. What is the general formula used to calculate the price of a share of a stock? What does it mean?
2. What are growth stocks, and why do they typically pay little or no dividends?

9.3 Stock Valuation: Some Simplifying Assumptions

LEARNING OBJECTIVE

4. Discuss the assumptions that are necessary to make the general dividend-valuation model easier to use, and use the model to compute the value of a firm's stock.

Conceptually, the general dividend-valuation model (Equation 9.1) is consistent with the notion that the value of an asset is the discounted value of future cash flows. Unfortunately, at a practical level, the model is not easy to use because of the difficulty of estimating future dividends over a long period of time. We can, however, make some simplifying assumptions about the pattern of dividends that make the model more manageable. Fortunately, these assumptions closely resemble the way many firms manage their dividend payments. We have a choice among three different assumptions: (1) Dividends remain constant over time; that is, they have a growth rate of zero. (2) Dividends grow at a constant rate; for example, they grow at 3 percent per year. (3) Dividends exhibit a mixed growth rate pattern; that is, dividends have one growth pattern and then switch to another. We discuss each of these assumptions in turn.

Zero-Growth Dividend Model

The simplest assumption is that dividends will have a growth rate of zero. Thus, the dividend payment pattern remains constant over time:

$$D_1 = D_2 = D_3 = \cdots = D_\infty$$

In this case the dividend-discount model (Equation 9.1) becomes:

$$P_0 = \frac{D}{1+R} + \frac{D}{(1+R)^2} + \frac{D}{(1+R)^3} + \frac{D}{(1+R)^4} + \frac{D}{(1+R)^5} + \cdots + \frac{D}{(1+R)^\infty}$$

This cash flow pattern is a perpetuity with a constant cash flow. You may recall that we developed an equation for such a perpetuity in Chapter 6. Equation 6.3 said that the present value of a perpetuity with a constant cash flow is CF/*i*, where CF is the constant cash flow and *i* is the interest rate. In terms of our stock-valuation model, we can present the same relation as follows:

$$P_0 = \frac{D}{R} \tag{9.2}$$

where:

P_0 = the current value, or price, of the stock
D = the constant cash dividend received in each time period
R = the required return on the common stock or discount rate

This model fits the dividend pattern for common stock of a company that is not growing and has little growth potential or for preferred stock, which we discuss in the next section.

For example, the Del Mar Corporation is a small printing company that serves a rural three-county area near San Diego, California. The county's economic base has remained constant over the years, and Del Mar's sales and earnings reflect this trend. The firm pays a $5 dividend per year, and the board of directors has no plans to change the dividend. If the firm's investors are mostly local businesspeople who expect a 20 percent return on their investment, what should be the price of the firm's stock?

Since the cash dividend payments are constant, we can use Equation 9.2 to find the price of the stock:

$$P_0 = \frac{D}{R} = \frac{\$5}{0.20} = \$25 \text{ per share}$$

Learning by Doing Application 9.1 illustrates use of Equation 9.2 in valuing the stock of another small business.

Constant-Growth Dividend Model

Under the next dividend growth assumption, cash dividends do not remain constant but instead grow at some average rate *g* from one period to the next forever. The rate of growth can be positive or negative. And, as it turns out, a constant-growth rate is not a bad approximation of the actual dividend pattern for some firms. Constant dividend growth is often an appropriate assumption for mature companies with a history of stable growth.

You may have concerns about the assumption of an infinite time horizon. In practice, though, it does not present a problem. It is true that most companies do not live on forever. We know, however, that the further in the future a cash flow will occur, the smaller its present value. Thus, far-distant dividends have a small present value and contribute very little to the price of the stock. For example, as shown in **Exhibit 9.2**, with constant dividends and a 15 percent discount rate, dividends paid during the first 10 years account for more than 75 percent of the value of a share of stock, while dividends paid after the twentieth year contribute only about 6 percent of the value.

LEARNING BY DOING

APPLICATION 9.1 | The Value of a Small Business

Problem For the past 15 years, a family has operated the gift shop in a luxury hotel near Rodeo Drive in Los Angeles. The hotel management wants to sell the gift shop to the family members rather than paying them to operate it. The family's accountant will incorporate the new business and estimates that it will generate an annual cash dividend of \$150,000 for the stockholders. The hotel will provide the family with an infinite guarantee for use of the space and a generous buyout plan in the unlikely event that the hotel closes its doors. The accountant estimates that a 20 percent discount rate is appropriate. What is the value of the stock?

Approach Assuming that the business will operate indefinitely, that its growth is constrained by its circumstances, and that inflation will be negligible, the zero-growth discount model can be used to value the stock. Thus, we can use Equation 9.2. Since the number of shares outstanding is not known, we can simply interpret P_0 as being the total value of the outstanding stock.

Solution Applying Equation 9.2:

$$P_0 = \frac{D}{R} = \frac{\$150{,}000}{0.20} = \$750{,}000$$

Identifying and applying the constant-growth dividend model is fairly straightforward. First, we need a model that can be used to compute the value of a dividend payment for any future period. If we assume that cash dividends grow at a constant rate g from one period to the next, we can use the future value formula, Equation 5.1, to obtain such a model:

$$FV_n = PV \times (1 + i)^n$$

To apply this formula to dividend payments, we replace FV_n with D_t, PV with D_0, i with g, and n with t:

$$D_t = D_0 \times (1 \times g)^t \tag{9.3}$$

where:

D_t = dividend payment in period t, where $t = 1, 2, 3, \ldots, \infty$
D_0 = dividend paid in the current period, $t = 0$
g = the constant-growth rate for dividends

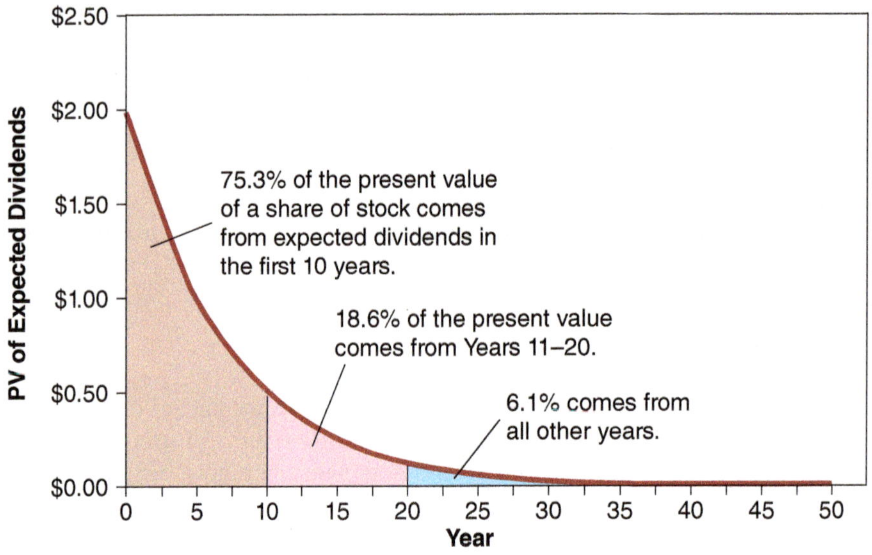

Note: Calculations based on discount rate of 15% and constant dividends.

EXHIBIT 9.2 Impact on Stock Prices of Near and Distant Future Dividends

Dividends expected far in the future have a smaller present value than dividends expected in the next few years, and so they have less effect on the price of the stock. As you can see in the exhibit, with constant dividends more than 75 percent of the current price of a share of stock comes from expected dividends in the first 10 years.

Equation 9.3 allows us to compute the dividend payment for any time period. For example, the next dividend, paid at time $t = 1$, is D_1, which is just the current dividend (D_0) multiplied by the growth factor, $(1 + g)$. Thus, $D_1 = D_0 \times (1 + g)$.

Notice that to compute the dividend payment for any future period, we multiply D_0 by the growth rate factor to some power, but we *always* start with D_0.

We can now develop the constant-growth dividend model, which is easy to do because it is just an application of Equation 6.6 from Chapter 6. Equation 6.6 says that the present value of a growing perpetuity (PVP) equals the cash flow value from period 1 (CF_1), divided by the difference between the discount rate (i) and the rate of growth (g) of the cash flow (CF_1):

$$\text{PVP} = \frac{CF_1}{i - g}$$

We can represent this same relation for stock valuation as follows:

$$P_0 = \frac{D_1}{R - g} \tag{9.4}$$

where:

P_0 = the current value, or price, of the stock
D_1 = the dividend paid in the next period ($t = 1$)
g = the constant-growth rate for dividends
R = the required return on the common stock or discount rate

In other words, the constant-growth dividend model tells us that the current price of a share of stock is the next period dividend divided by the difference between the discount rate and the dividend growth rate. Note that PVP is the current value of the stock (P_0), which equals the present value of the dividend cash flows.

As discussed in Chapter 6, the growing-perpetuity model is valid only if the growth rate is less than the discount rate, or required rate of return. In terms of Equation 9.4, then, the value of g must be less than the value of R ($g < R$). If the equation is used in situations where R is equal to or less than g ($R \leq g$), the computed results will be meaningless.

Finally, notice that if $g = 0$, there is no dividend growth and the dividend payment pattern is simply a constant no-growth dividend stream. In this case, Equation 9.4 becomes $P_0 = D/R$, which is precisely the same as Equation 9.2, the zero-growth dividend model. Thus, Equation 9.2 is just a special case of Equation 9.4 where $g = 0$.

Let's work through an example using the constant-growth dividend model. Big Red Automotive is a regional auto parts supplier based in Oklahoma City. At the firm's year-end stockholders' meeting, the CFO announces that this year's dividend will be \$4.81. The announcement conforms to Big Red's dividend policy, which sets dividend growth at a 4 percent annual rate. Investors who own stock in similar types of firms expect to earn a return of 18 percent. What is the value of the firm's stock?

First, we need to compute the cash dividend payment for next year (D_1). Applying Equation 9.3 for $t = 1$ yields the following:

$$D_1 = D_0 \times (1 + g) = \$4.81 \times (1 + 0.04) = \$4.81 \times 1.04 = \$5.00$$

Next, we apply Equation 9.4 to compute the value of the firm's stock, which is \$35.71 per share:

$$\begin{aligned} P_0 &= \frac{D_1}{R - g} \\ &= \frac{\$5.00}{0.18 - 0.04} \\ &= \frac{\$5.00}{0.14} \\ &= \$35.71 \end{aligned}$$

Learning by Doing Application 9.2 illustrates another application of Equation 9.4 to the valuation of a firm's stock.

LEARNING BY DOING

APPLICATION 9.2 | Big Red Grows Faster

Problem Using the information given in the text, compute the value of Big Red's stock if dividends grow at 6 percent rather than 4 percent and the discount rate remains 18 percent. Explain why the answer makes sense.

Approach First compute the cash dividend payment for next year (D_1) using the 6 percent growth rate (g) in Equation 9.3. Then apply Equation 9.4 to solve for the firm's stock price.

Solution

$$D_1 = D_0 \times (1 + g)$$

$$D_1 = \$4.81 \times 1.06 = \$5.10$$

$$P_0 = \frac{D_1}{R - g}$$

$$P_0 = \frac{\$5.10}{0.18 - 0.06} = \frac{\$5.10}{0.12} = \$42.50$$

The higher stock value of \$42.50 is no surprise because dividends are now growing at a rate of 6 percent rather than 4 percent and the discount rate has not changed. The value of the cash payments to investors (dividends) is expected to be larger.

Computing Future Stock Prices

The constant-growth dividend model (Equation 9.4) can be modified to determine the value, or price, of a share of stock at any point in time. In general, the price of a share of stock, P_t, can be expressed in terms of the dividend in the next period (D_{t+1}), g, and R, when the dividends from D_{t+1} forward are expected to grow at a constant rate. Thus, the price of a share of stock at time t is as follows:

$$P_t = \frac{D_{t+1}}{R - g} \tag{9.5}$$

Notice that Equation 9.4 is just a special case of Equation 9.5 in which $t = 0$. To be sure that you understand this, set up Equation 9.5 to compute a stock's current price at $t = 0$. When you are done, the resulting equation should look exactly like Equation 9.4.

An example will illustrate how Equation 9.5 is used. Suppose that a firm has a current dividend (D_0) of \$2.50, R is 15 percent, and g is 5 percent. What is the price of the stock today (P_0), and what will it be in five years (P_5)? To help visualize the problem, we will lay out a time line and identify some of the important variables necessary to solve the problem:

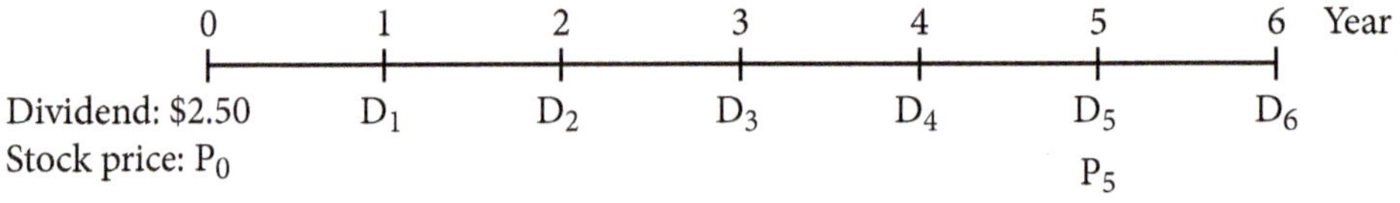

To find the current stock price, we can apply Equation 9.4, but we must first compute the dividend for the next period (D_1), which is at $t = 1$. Using Equation 9.3, we compute the firm's dividend for next year:

$$D_1 = D_0 \times (1 + g) = \$2.50 \times 1.05 = \$2.625$$

Now we can use Equation 9.4 to find the price of the stock today:

$$P_0 = \frac{D_1}{R - g} = \frac{\$2.625}{0.15 - 0.05} = \frac{\$2.625}{0.10} = \$26.25$$

We next find the value of the stock in five years. In this situation Equation 9.5 is expressed as:

$$P_5 = \frac{D_6}{R - g}$$

We need to compute D_6, and we do so by using Equation 9.3:

$$D_6 = D_0 \times (1 + g)^6 = 2.50 \times (1.05)^6 = 2.50 \times 1.34 = \$3.35$$

The price of the stock in five years is therefore:

$$P_5 = \frac{\$3.35}{0.15 - 0.05} = \frac{\$3.35}{0.10} = \$33.50$$

Finally, note that $\$33.50/(1.05)^5 = \$26.25$, which is the value today.

Learning by Doing Applications 9.3 and 9.4 illustrate additional examples of the use of Equations 9.3, 9.4, and 9.5 in stock valuation.

The Relation between R and *g*

LEARNING OBJECTIVE

5. Explain why *g* must be less than R in the constant-growth dividend model.

We previously mentioned that the dividend growth model provides valid solutions only when $g < R$. Students frequently ask what happens to Equation 9.4 or 9.5 if this condition does not

APPLICATION 9.3 | Procter & Gamble's Current Stock Price

LEARNING BY DOING

WileyPLUS

Need more help? Visit your WileyPLUS course.

Problem Suppose that the current cash dividend on Procter & Gamble's common stock is \$1.84. Financial analysts expect the dividends to grow at a constant rate of 5 percent per year, and investors require an 8 percent return on stocks with the same level of risk. What should be the current price of a share of Procter & Gamble stock?

Approach In this scenario, $D_0 = \$1.84$, $R = 0.08$, and $g = 0.05$. We first compute D_1 using Equation 9.3. We then calculate the value of a share using Equation 9.4.

Solution

$$\text{Dividend: } D_1 = D_0 \times (1 + g) = \$1.84 \times 1.05 = \$1.93$$

$$\text{Value of a share: } P_0 = \frac{D_1}{R - g} = \frac{\$1.93}{0.08 - 0.05} = \frac{\$1.93}{0.03} = \$64.33$$

APPLICATION 9.4 | Procter & Gamble's Future Stock Price

LEARNING BY DOING

WileyPLUS

Need more help? Visit your WileyPLUS course.

Problem Continuing the example in Learning by Doing Application 9.3, what should Procter & Gamble's stock price be seven years from now (P_7)?

Approach This is an application of Equation 9.5. We first must calculate Procter & Gamble's dividend in period 8, using Equation 9.3. Then we can apply Equation 9.5 to compute the estimated price of the stock seven years in the future.

Solution

$$\text{Dividend in period 8: } D_8 = D_0 \times (1 + g)^8 = \$1.93 \times (1.05)^8 = \$1.93 \times 1.477 = \$2.85$$

$$\text{Price of a share in 7 years: } P_7 = \frac{D_8}{R - g} = \frac{\$2.85}{0.08 - 0.05} = \frac{\$2.85}{0.03} = \$95.00$$

hold (if $g \geq R$). Mathematically, as g approaches R, the stock price becomes larger and larger, and when $g = R$, the value of the stock is infinite, which is, of course, nonsense. When the growth rate (g) is larger than the discount rate (R), the constant-growth dividend model tells us that the value of the stock is negative. However, this is not possible. The value of a share of stock can never be negative because, as we discussed in Section 1.2, stockholders have limited liability.

From a practical perspective, the growth rate in the constant-growth dividend model cannot be greater than the sum of the long-term rate of inflation and the long-term real growth rate of the economy. Since this model assumes that the firm will grow at a constant rate forever, any growth rate that is greater than this sum would imply that the firm will eventually take over the entire economy. Of course, we know this is not possible. Since the sum of the long-term rate of inflation and the long-term real growth rate has historically been less than 6 to 7 percent, the growth rate (g) is virtually always less than the discount rate (R) for the stocks that we would want to use the constant-growth dividend model to value.

It is possible for firms to grow faster than the long-term rate of inflation plus the real growth rate of the economy—just not forever. A firm that is growing at such a high rate is said to be growing at a supernormal growth rate. We must use a different model to value the stock of a firm like this. We discuss one such model next.

Mixed (Supernormal) Growth Dividend Model

For many firms, it is not appropriate to assume that dividends will grow at a constant rate. Firms typically go through life cycles and, as a result, exhibit different dividend patterns over time.

During the early part of their lives, successful firms experience a supernormal rate of growth in earnings. These firms tend to pay lower dividends or no dividends at all because many good investment projects are available to them and management wants to reinvest earnings in the firm to take advantage of these opportunities. If a growth firm does not pay regular dividends, investors receive their returns from capital appreciation of the firm's stock (which reflects increases in expected future dividends), from a cash or stock payout if the firm is acquired, or possibly from a large special cash dividend. As a firm matures, it will settle into a growth rate at or below the long-term rate of inflation plus the long-term real growth rate of the economy. When a firm reaches this stage, it will often be paying a fairly predictable regular dividend.

Exhibit 9.3 shows several dividend growth patterns. In the top curve, dividends exhibit a supernormal growth rate of 25 percent for four years, then a more sustainable nominal growth rate of 5 percent (this might, for example, be made up of 2.5 percent growth from inflation plus a 2.5 percent real growth rate). By comparison, the remaining curves show dividends with a constant nominal growth rate of 5 percent, a zero-growth rate, and a negative 10 percent growth rate. In addition to the constant growth rates illustrated in Exhibit 9.3, it is also possible for the dividend growth rate to vary during the early years. We refer to this as a mixed dividend growth pattern.

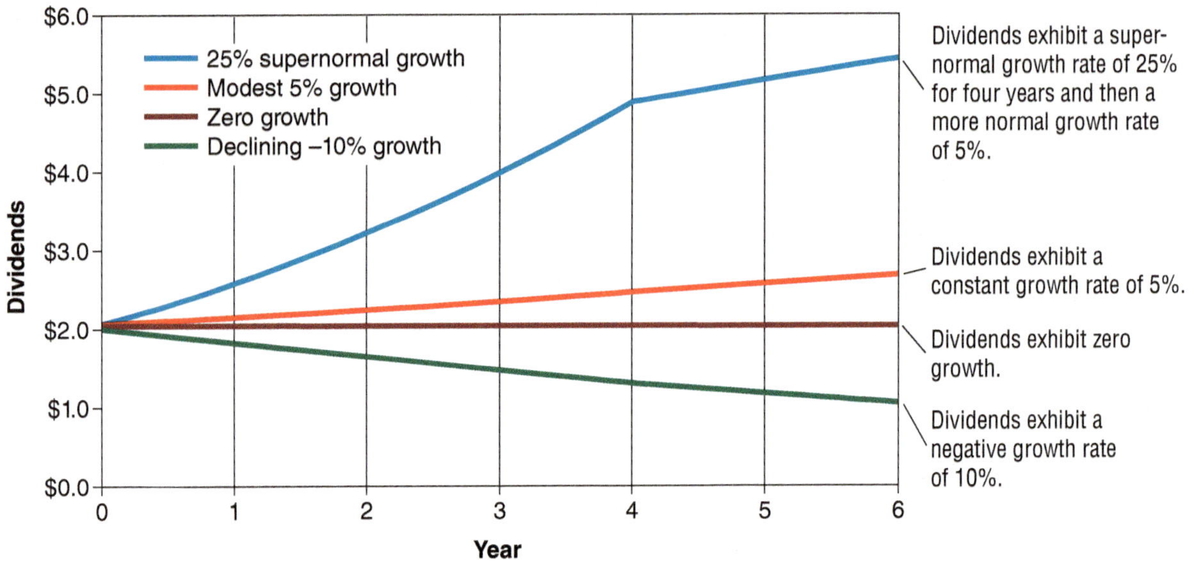

EXHIBIT 9.3 **Dividend Growth Rate Patterns**

As mentioned earlier, successful companies often experience supernormal growth early in their life cycles. During the last decade, for example, firms such as Google, Facebook, and Netflix have experienced supernormal growth. Older companies that reinvent themselves with new products or strategies may also experience periods of supernormal growth. In the early 2000s, Apple Inc. management repositioned the company from being primarily a manufacturer of computers into a firm that is now also a market leader in the manufacture of telecommunications devices and music players, and in the sale of digital music. Following this restructuring, Apple's stock generated huge returns for investors, rising from approximately \$1 per share in 2003 to \$153.18 per share on June 1, 2017.

To value a share of stock for a firm with a mixed (supernormal) dividend growth pattern, we do not have to develop any new equations. Instead, we can apply Equation 9.1, our general dividend model, and Equation 9.5, which gives us the price of a share of stock with constant dividend growth at any point in time.

We will illustrate with an example. Suppose a company's expected dividend pattern for three years is as follows: $D_1 = \$1$, $D_2 = \$2$, $D_3 = \$3$. After three years, the dividends are expected to grow at a constant rate of 6 percent a year. What should the current price (P_0) of the firm's stock be if the required rate of return demanded by investors is 15 percent?

We begin by drawing a time line, as shown in **Exhibit 9.4**. We recommend that you prepare a time line whenever you solve a problem with a complex dividend pattern so that you can be sure the cash flows are placed in the proper time periods. The critical elements in working these problems are to correctly identify when the constant growth starts and to value it properly.

Looking at Exhibit 9.4, it is easy to see that we have two different dividend patterns: (1) D_1 through D_3 represent a mixed dividend growth pattern, which can be valued using Equation 9.1, the general dividend-valuation model. (2) After the third year, dividends grow at a constant rate of 6 percent and can be valued using Equation 9.5, the constant-growth dividend-valuation model. Thus, our valuation model is:

$$P_0 = \text{PV(Mixed dividend growth)} + \text{PV(Constant dividend growth)}$$

Combining these present values yields the following formula:

$$P_0 = \underbrace{\frac{D_1}{(1+R)} + \frac{D_2}{(1+R)^2} + \frac{D_3}{(1+R)^3}}_{\substack{\text{PV of mixed-growth} \\ \text{dividend payments}}} + \underbrace{\frac{P_3}{(1+R)^3}}_{\substack{\text{Value of constant-growth} \\ \text{dividend payments}}}$$

The value of the constant-growth dividend stream is P_3, which is the value, or price, at time $t = 3$. More specifically, P_3 is the value of the future cash dividends discounted to time period $t = 3$. With a required rate of return of 15%, the value of these dividends is calculated as follows:

$$D_4 = D_3 \times (1 + g) = \$3.00 \times 1.06 = \$3.18$$

$$P_3 = \frac{D_4}{R - g} = \frac{\$3.18}{0.15 - 0.06}$$

$$= \frac{\$3.18}{0.09}$$

$$= \$35.33$$

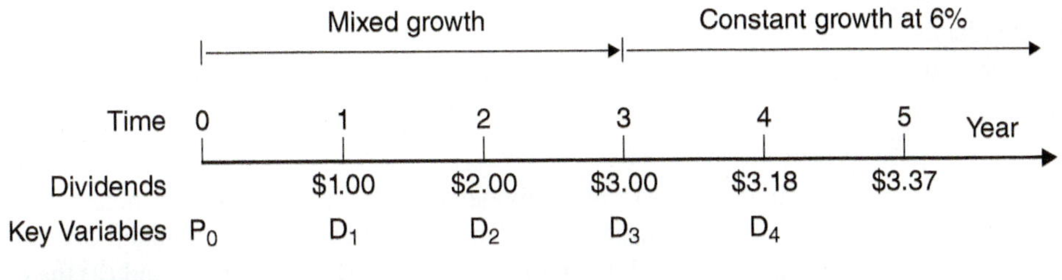

EXHIBIT 9.4 Time Line for Nonconstant Dividend Growth Pattern

The exhibit shows a time line for a nonconstant dividend growth pattern. The time line makes it easy to see that we have two different dividend growth patterns. For three years, the dividends are expected to grow at a mixed rate; after that, they are expected to grow at a constant rate of 6 percent.

We find the value of P_3 using Equation 9.5, which allows us to compute stock prices in the future for stocks with constant dividend growth. Note that the equation gives us the value, as of Year 3, of a constant-growth perpetuity that begins in Year 4. This formula always gives us the value as of one period before the first cash flow.

Now, since P_3 is at time period $t = 3$, we must discount it back to the present ($t = 0$). This is accomplished by dividing P_3 by $(1 + R)^3$.

Plugging the values for the dividends, P_3, and R into the above mixed-growth equation results in the following:

$$\begin{aligned} P_0 &= \frac{\$1.00}{1.15} + \frac{\$2.00}{(1.15)^2} + \frac{\$3.00}{(1.15)^3} + \frac{\$35.33}{(1.15)^3} \\ &= \$0.87 + \$1.51 + \$1.97 + \$23.23 \\ &= \$27.58 \end{aligned}$$

Thus, the value of the stock is \$27.58 per share.

We can write a general equation for the mixed (supernormal) growth situation, where dividends grow first at a mixed or high constant rate until period t, and then at a constant rate thereafter, as follows:

$$P_0 = \frac{D_1}{1 + R} + \frac{D_2}{(1 + R)^2} + \cdots + \frac{D_t}{(1 + R)^t} + \frac{P_t}{(1 + R)^t} \tag{9.6}$$

If the mixed- or high-growth period ends and dividends grow at a constant rate, g, then P_t can be calculated using Equation 9.5:

$$P_t = \frac{D_{t+1}}{R - g}$$

The two preceding equations can also be applied when dividends are constant over time, since we know that $g = 0$ is just a special case of the constant-growth dividend model ($g > 0$).

Let's look at another example, this time using Equation 9.6. Suppose that Redteck is a high-tech medical device firm located in Lincoln, Nebraska. The company is three years old and has experienced spectacular growth since its inception. You are a financial analyst for a stock brokerage firm and have just returned from a two-day visit to the company. You learned that Redteck plans to pay no dividends for the next five years. In Year 6, management plans to pay a large, special cash dividend, which you estimate to be \$25 per share. Then, beginning in Year 7, management plans to pay a constant annual dividend of \$6 per share for the foreseeable future. The appropriate discount rate for the stock is 12 percent, and the current market price is \$24 per share. Your boss doesn't think the stock is worth the price. You think that it's a bargain and that you should recommend it to the firm's clients. Who is right?

Our first step in answering this question is to lay out the expected dividend payments on a time line:

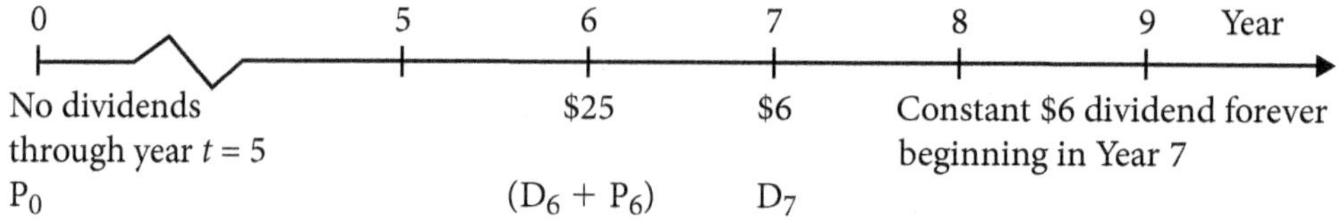

Equation 9.6, the mixed (supernormal) dividend model, can be used to determine the value of the stock. There are two different dividend cash streams: (1) the mixed dividends, which in this case comprise a single dividend paid in Year 6 (Equation 9.1), and (2) the constant dividend stream ($g = 0$) of \$6 per year forever (Equation 9.5). The value of the common stock can be computed as follows:

$$P_0 = \text{PV(Mixed dividend growth)} + \text{PV(Constant dividends with no growth)}$$

Applying Equation 9.6 to the cash flows presented in the problem yields:

$$P_0 = \frac{D_1}{1+R} + \frac{D_2}{(1+R)^2} + \cdots + \frac{D_t}{(1+R)^t} + \frac{P_t}{(1+R)^t}$$
$$= \frac{D_6}{(1+R)^6} + \frac{P_6}{(1+R)^6}$$
$$= \frac{D_6 + P_6}{(1+R)^6}$$

Note that the first term in the second line computes the present value of the large \$25 dividend paid in Year 6. In the second term, P_6 is the discounted value of the constant \$6 dividend payments made in perpetuity, as of period $t = 6$. To compute the present value of P_6, we divide it by the appropriate discount factor, which is $(1 + R)^6$.

Plugging the data given earlier into the above equation yields:

$$P_0 = \frac{\$25 + P_6}{(1.12)^6}$$

We can see from this relation that we still need to compute the value of P_6 using Equation 9.5:

$$P_t = \frac{D_{t+1}}{R - g}$$

Equation 9.5 is easy to apply since the dividend payments remain constant over time. Since $D_{t+1} = \$6$ and $g = 0$, P_6 is calculated as follows:

$$P_6 = \frac{D_7}{R - g} = \frac{\$6}{0.12 - 0} = \frac{\$6}{0.12}$$
$$= \$50$$

and the calculation for P_0 is, therefore:

$$P_0 = \frac{\$25 + \$50}{(1.12)^6}$$
$$= \frac{\$75}{1.9738}$$
$$= \$38.00$$

The stock's current market price is \$24, and if your estimates of dividend payments are correct, the stock's value is \$38 per share. This suggests that the stock is a bargain and that your boss is incorrect.

Before You Go On

1. What three different models are used to value stocks based on different dividend patterns?
2. Explain why the growth rate g must always be less than the rate of return R for the constant-growth dividend model.

9.4 Valuing Preferred Stock

LEARNING OBJECTIVE

6. Explain how valuing preferred stock with a stated maturity differs from valuing preferred stock with no maturity, and calculate the price of a share of preferred stock under both conditions.

As mentioned earlier in this chapter, preferred stocks are hybrid securities, falling someplace between bonds and common stock. For example, preferred stock has a higher-priority claim on the firm's assets than common stock but a lower-priority claim than the firm's creditors in the event of default. In computing the value of preferred stock, however, the critical issue is whether the preferred stock has a fixed maturity. If the preferred stock contract has a sinking fund that calls for the mandatory retirement of the stock over a scheduled period of time, financial analysts will tend to treat the stock as if it were a bond with a fixed maturity.

Weblink

Riskglossary.com offers a good discussion of preferred stock, including its valuation. Go to http://www.riskglossary.com/link/preferred_stock.htm.

The most significant difference between preferred stock with a fixed maturity and a bond is the risk of default. Bond coupon payments are a legal obligation of the firm, and failure to pay them results in default, whereas preferred stock dividends are declared by the board of directors, and failure to pay dividends does not result in default. Even though it is not a legal default, the failure to pay a preferred stock dividend as promised is not a trivial event. It is a noteworthy financial breach which can signal to the market that the firm is in serious financial difficulty. As a result, managers make every effort to pay preferred stock dividends as promised.

Preferred Stock with a Fixed Maturity

Because preferred stock with a fixed maturity is considered similar to a bond, we can use the bond valuation model developed in Chapter 8 to determine its price, or value. Applying Equation 8.2 requires only that we recognize that the coupon payments (C) are equivalent to dividend payments (D) and the preferred stock dividends are paid quarterly. Thus, Equation 8.2 can be restated as the price of a share of preferred stock (PS_0):

$$\text{Preferred stock price} = \text{PV(Dividend payments)} + \text{PV(Par value)}$$

$$PS_0 = \frac{D/m}{1 + i/m} + \frac{D/m}{(1 + i/m)^2} + \frac{D/m}{(1 + i/m)^3} + \cdots + \frac{D/m + P_{mn}}{(1 + i/m)^{mn}} \tag{9.7}$$

where:

D = the annual preferred stock dividend payment
P = the stated (par) value of the preferred stock
i = the yield to maturity of the preferred stock
m = the number of times dividend payments are made each year
n = the number of years to maturity

For preferred stock with quarterly dividend payments, m equals 4.

Consider an example of how this equation is used. Suppose that a utility company's preferred stock has an annual dividend payment of $10 (paid quarterly), a stated (par) value of $100, and a maturity of 20 years owing to a sinking fund requirement. If similar preferred stock issues have market yields of 8 percent, what is the value of the preferred stock?

First, we convert the data to quarterly compounding as follows: (1) the market yield is 2 percent quarterly (8 percent per year/4 quarters per year = 2 percent per quarter), (2) the dividend payment is $2.50 quarterly ($10 per year/4 quarters per year = $2.50 per quarter), and (3) the total number of dividend payments is 80 (4 payments per year × 20 years = 80 payments). Plugging the data into Equation 9.7, we find that the value of the preferred stock is:

$$PS_0 = \frac{\$2.50}{1.02} + \frac{\$2.50}{(1.02)^2} + \cdots + \frac{\$102.50}{(1.02)^{80}}$$
$$= \$119.87$$

We can, of course, also solve this problem on a financial calculator. The keystrokes are as follows:

Enter	80	2		2.50	100
	N	i	PV	PMT	FV
Answer			−119.87		

Learning by Doing Application 9.5 illustrates how Equation 9.7 or a calculator can be used to compute the yield to maturity of preferred stock.

APPLICATION 9.5 | Computing the Yield on Preferred Stock

LEARNING BY DOING

Problem San Diego Gas and Electric (SDG&E) has a preferred stock issue outstanding that has a stated value of $100, will be retired by the company in 15 years, and pays a $2 dividend each quarter. If the preferred stock is currently selling for $95, what is the stock's yield to maturity?

Approach We compute the yield to maturity on this preferred stock in exactly the same way we compute the yield to maturity on a bond. We already know that the quarterly dividend rate is $2, but we must convert the number of periods to allow for quarterly compounding. The total number of compounding periods is 60 (4 periods per year × 15 years = 60 periods). Using Equation 9.7, we can enter the data and find i, the stock's yield to maturity through trial and error. Alternatively, we can solve the problem easily on a financial calculator.

Solution Applying Equation 9.7:

$$\$95 = \frac{\$2}{1+i} + \frac{\$2}{(1+i)^2} + \frac{\$2}{(1+i)^3} + \cdots + \frac{\$102}{(1+i)^{60}}$$

Financial calculator steps:

	N	i	PV	PMT	FV
Enter	60		−95	2	100
Answer		**2.15**			

The preferred stock's yield is 2.15 percent per quarter, and the annual yield is 8.60 percent (2.15 percent per quarter × 4 quarters per year = 8.60 percent per year).

WileyPLUS

Need more help? Visit your WileyPLUS course.

Preferred Stock with No Maturity

Some preferred stock issues have no maturity. These securities have dividends that are constant over time ($g = 0$) and that go on forever. Thus, these preferred stocks can be valued as perpetuities, using Equation 9.2:

$$P_0 = \frac{D}{R}$$

where D is a constant cash dividend and R is the discount rate, or required rate of return.

Let's work an example. Suppose that Delta Air Lines has a perpetual preferred stock issue that pays a dividend of $5 per year and that investors require an 8 percent return on such an investment. What is the value of the preferred stock? Applying Equation 9.2, we find that the value is:

$$P_0 = \frac{D}{R} = \frac{\$5.00}{0.08} = \$62.50$$

Before You Go On

1. Why can skipping payment of a preferred dividend be a bad signal?
2. How is a preferred stock with a fixed maturity valued?

Summary of Learning Objectives

1 List and describe the four types of secondary markets.

The four types of secondary markets are (1) direct search, (2) broker, (3) dealer, and (4) auction. In direct search markets, buyers and sellers seek out each other directly. In broker markets, brokers bring together buyers and sellers for a fee. Trades in dealer markets go through dealers who buy securities at one price and sell at a higher price. The dealers face the risk that prices could decline while they own the securities. Auction markets have a fixed location where buyers and sellers confront each other directly and bargain over the transaction price.

2 Explain why many financial analysts treat preferred stock as a special type of bond rather than as an equity security.

Preferred stock represents ownership in a corporation and entitles the owner to a dividend, which must be paid before dividends are paid to common stockholders. Similar to bonds, preferred stock issues have credit ratings, are sometimes convertible to common stock, and are often callable. Unlike owners of common stock, owners of nonconvertible preferred stock do not have voting rights and do not participate in the firm's profits beyond the fixed dividends they receive. It is because of their strong similarity to bonds that many financial analysts treat preferred stocks which are not true perpetuities as a form of debt rather than equity.

3 Describe how the general dividend-valuation model values a share of stock.

The general dividend-valuation model values a share of stock as the present value of all future cash dividend payments, where the dividend payments are discounted using the rate of return required by investors for investments with a similar level of risk.

4 Discuss the assumptions that are necessary to make the general dividend-valuation model easier to use, and use the model to compute the value of a firm's stock.

The problems with the general dividend-valuation model are that future dividends are uncertain and some companies do not pay dividends at all. To make the model easier to apply, we make assumptions about the dividend payment patterns of firms. These simplifying assumptions allow the development of more manageable models, and they also conform with the actual dividend policies of many firms. Dividend patterns include the following: (1) Dividends are constant (zero growth), as computed in Learning by Doing Application 9.1. (2) Dividends have a constant-growth pattern (they grow forever at a constant rate g), as computed in Learning by Doing Application 9.2. (3) Dividends grow first at a nonconstant rate rather than at a constant rate, as computed in the Redteck example at the end of Section 9.3.

5 Explain why g must be less than R in the constant-growth dividend model.

The constant-growth dividend model assumes that dividends will grow at a constant rate forever. With the constant-growth model, if $g = R$, the value of the denominator is zero and the value of the stock is infinite, which of course is nonsense. If $g > R$, the value of the denominator is negative, as is the value of the stock, which also does not make economic sense since stockholders have limited liability. Thus, g must always be less than R ($g < R$).

6 Explain how valuing preferred stock with a stated maturity differs from valuing preferred stock with no maturity, and calculate the price of a share of preferred stock under both conditions.

When preferred stock has a stated maturity, financial analysts value it as they value any other fixed obligation—that is, like a bond. To value such preferred stock, we can use the bond valuation model from Chapter 8. Before using the model, we need to recognize that we will be using dividends in the place of coupon payments and that the stated (par) value of the preferred stock will replace the par value of the bond. In addition, while bond coupons are paid semiannually in the United States, preferred stock dividends are paid quarterly. When a preferred stock has no stated maturity, it becomes a perpetuity, with the dividend becoming a constant payment that goes on forever. We use the perpetuity valuation model represented by Equation 9.2 to price such stocks. The calculations appear in Learning by Doing Application 9.5 and the Delta Air Lines example at the end of Section 9.4.

Summary of Key Equations

Equation	Description	Formula
9.1	General dividend-valuation model	$P_0 = \frac{D_1}{1+R} + \frac{D_2}{(1+R)^2} + \frac{D_3}{(1+R)^3} + \frac{D_4}{(1+R)^4} + \frac{D_5}{(1+R)^5} + \cdots + \frac{D_\infty}{(1+R)^\infty} = \sum_{t=1}^{\infty} \frac{D_t}{(1+R)^t}$
9.2	Zero-growth dividend model	$P_0 = \frac{D}{R}$
9.3	Value of a dividend at time t with constant growth	$D_t = D_0 \times (1+g)^t$
9.4	Constant-growth dividend model	$P_0 = \frac{D_1}{R-g}$
9.5	Value of a stock at time t when dividends grow at a constant rate	$P_t = \frac{D_{t+1}}{R-g}$

continued

continued

Equation	Description	Formula
9.6	Mixed (supernormal) growth dividend model	$P_0 = \frac{D_1}{1+R} + \frac{D_2}{(1+R)^2} + \cdots + \frac{D_t}{(1+R)^t} + \frac{P_t}{(1+R)^t}$
9.7	Value of preferred stock with a fixed maturity	$PS_0 = \frac{D/m}{1+i/m} + \frac{D/m}{(1+i/m)^2} + \frac{D/m}{(1+i/m)^3} + \cdots + \frac{D/m + P_{mn}}{(1+i/m)^{mn}}$

Self-Study Problems

9.1 Ted McKay has just bought the common stock of Ryland Corp. Management of Ryland expects the company to grow at the following rates for the next three years: 30 percent, 25 percent, and 15 percent. Last year the company paid a dividend of \$2.50. Assume a required rate of return of 10 percent. Compute the expected dividends for the next three years and also the present value of these dividends if dividends grow at the same rate as the company.

9.2 Merriweather Manufacturing Company has been growing at a rate of 6 percent for the past two years, and the company's CEO expects it to continue to grow at this rate for the next several years. The company paid a dividend of \$1.20 last year. If your required rate of return is 14 percent, what is the maximum price that you would be willing to pay for this company's stock?

9.3 Clarion Corp. has been selling electrical supplies for the past 20 years. The company's product line has changed very little in the past five years, and the company's management does not expect to add any new items for the foreseeable future. Last year, the company paid a dividend of \$4.45 to its common stockholders. The company is not expected to increase its dividends in the future. If your required rate of return for such firms is 13 percent, what is the current value of this company's stock?

9.4 Barrymore Infotech is a fast-growing communications company. The company did not pay a dividend last year and is not expected to do so for the next two years. Last year the company's growth accelerated, and management expects to grow the business at a rate of 35 percent for the next five years before growth slows to a more stable rate of 7 percent. In the third year, management has forecasted a dividend payment of \$1.10. Dividends will grow with the company thereafter. Calculate the value of the company's stock at the end of its rapid growth period (i.e., at the end of five years). The required rate of return for such stocks is 17 percent. What is the current value of this stock?

9.5 You are interested in buying the preferred stock of a bank that pays a dividend of \$1.80 every quarter. If you discount such cash flows at 8 percent, what is the value of this stock?

Solutions to Self-Study Problems

9.1 Expected dividends for Ryland Corp and their present value:

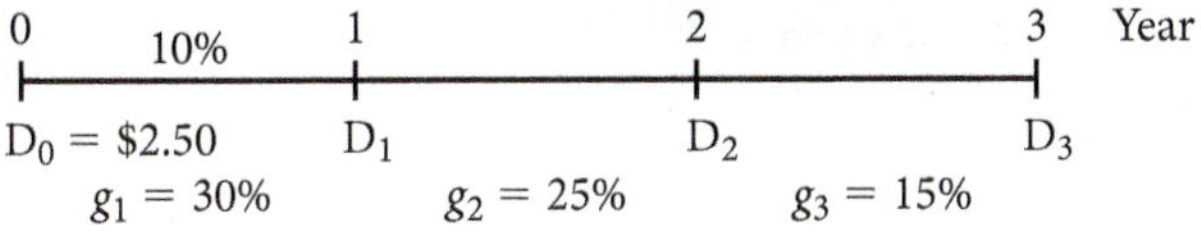

$D_1 = D_0 \times (1 + g_1) = \$2.50 \times (1 + 0.30) = \$3.25$
$D_2 = D_1 \times (1 + g_2) = \$3.25 \times (1 + 0.25) = \$4.06$
$D_3 = D_2 \times (1 + g_3) = \$4.06 \times (1 + 0.15) = \$4.67$

Present value of the dividends $= PV(D_1) + PV(D_2) + PV(D_3)$
$= \$2.96 + \$3.36 + \$3.51$
$= \$9.83$

9.2 Present value of Merriweather stock:

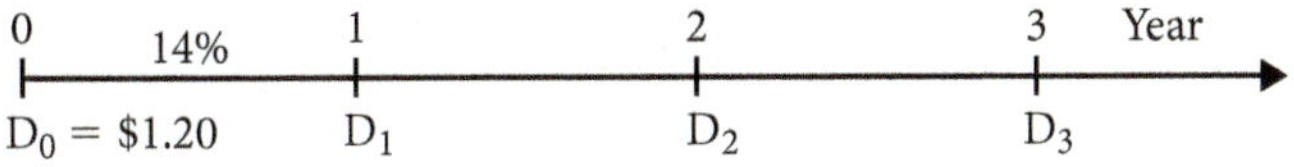

$g = 6\%$

$$\begin{aligned} D_1 &= D_0 \times (1 + g) \\ &= \$1.20 \times (1 + 0.06) \\ &= \$1.27 \end{aligned}$$

$$\begin{aligned} P_0 &= \frac{D_1}{R - g} \\ &= \frac{\$1.27}{0.14 - 0.06} \\ &= \$15.88 \end{aligned}$$

The maximum price you should be willing to pay for this stock is \$15.88.

9.3 Present value of Clarion Corp. stock:

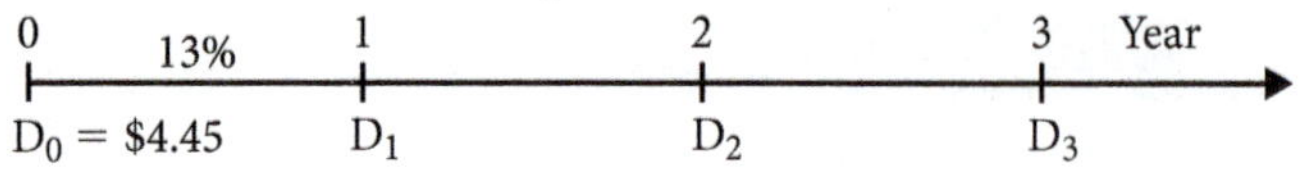

$g = 0\%$

Since the company's dividends are not expected to grow,

$D_0 = D_1 = D_2 = \cdots = D_\infty = \$4.45 = D$

$$\text{Current value of the stock} = \frac{D}{R}$$
$$= \$4.45/0.13$$
$$= \$34.23$$

9.4 Present value of Barrymore Infotech stock:

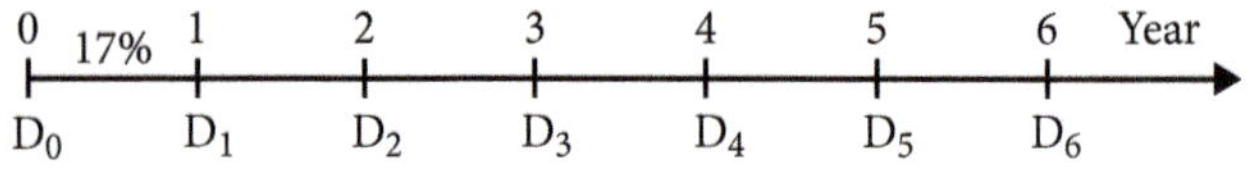

g_1 to $g_5 = 35\%$ $\qquad$ g_6 and beyond $= 7\%$

$D_0 = D_1 = D_2 = 0$

$D_3 = \$1.100$

$D_4 = D_3 \times (1 + g_4) = \$1.10 \times (1 + 0.35) = \$1.485$

$D_5 = D_4 \times (1 + g_5) = \$1.485 \times (1 + 0.35) = \$2.005$

$D_6 = D_5 \times (1 + g_6) = \$2.005 \times (1 + 0.07) = \$2.145$

Value of stock at $t = 5$:

$$P_5 = \frac{D_6}{R - g}$$
$$= \frac{\$2.145}{0.17 - 0.07}$$
$$= \$21.45$$

$$\text{Present value of the dividends in Years 1 to 5} = PV(D_1) + PV(D_2) + PV(D_3) + PV(D_4) + PV(D_5)$$
$$= \$0 + \$0 + \$0.69 + \$0.79 + \$0.91$$
$$= \$2.39$$

Current value of stock:

$$P_0 = PV(\text{Dividends}) + PV(P_5)$$
$$= \$2.39 + \frac{\$21.45}{(1.17)^5}$$
$$= \$2.39 + \$9.78$$
$$= \$12.17$$

9.5 Present value of bank preferred stock:

Quarterly dividend on preferred stock = D = $1.80

Required rate of return = 8%

Current value of stock:

$$P_0 = \frac{D}{R}$$
$$= \frac{\$1.80 \times 4}{0.08}$$
$$= \$90.00$$

WileyPLUS

Questions and Problems, Solution Walkthrough Videos, Learning by Doing Tutorials, and additional study tools and resources are available in WileyPLUS.

Discussion Questions

9.1 Why can the market price of a stock differ from its true (intrinsic) value?

9.2 Why are investors and managers concerned about stock market efficiency?

9.3 Why are common stockholders considered to be more at risk than the holders of other types of securities?

9.4 Under what conditions does it make sense to use the constant-growth dividend model to value a stock?

9.5 What does it mean when a company has a very high P/E ratio? Give examples of industries in which you believe high P/E ratios are justified.

9.6 Explain why preferred stock is considered to be a hybrid of equity and debt securities.

9.7 Why is stock valuation more difficult than bond valuation?

9.8 You are currently thinking about investing in a stock valued at $25.00 per share. The stock recently paid a dividend of $2.25 and its dividend is expected to grow at a rate of 5 percent for the foreseeable future. You normally require a return of 14 percent on stocks of similar risk. Is the stock overpriced, underpriced, or correctly priced?

9.9 Stock A and Stock B are both priced at $50 per share. Stock A has a P/E ratio of 17, while Stock B has a P/E ratio of 24. Which is the more attractive investment, considering everything else to be the same, and why?

9.10 Facebook does not pay dividends. How can it have a positive stock price?

Questions and Problems

Excel *Excel templates and resources available in* **WileyPLUS**

Basic

9.1 **Stock market index:** What is a stock market index?

9.2 **Stock market index:** What is the Dow Jones Industrial Average?

9.3 **Stock market index:** What does NASDAQ stand for? What is NASDAQ?

9.4 **Dividend yield:** What is a dividend yield? What does it tell us?

9.5 **Present value of dividends:** Fresno Corp. is a fast-growing company whose management expects it to grow at a rate of 30 percent over the next two years and then to slow to a growth rate of 18 percent for the following three years. If the last dividend paid by the company was $2.15, estimate the dividends for the next five years. Compute the present value of these dividends if the required rate of return is 14 percent.

9.6 **Zero growth:** Nynet, Inc., paid a dividend of $4.18 last year. The company's management does not expect to increase its dividend in the foreseeable future. If the required rate of return is 18.5 percent, what is the current value of the stock?

9.7 **Zero growth:** Knight Supply Corp. has not grown for the past several years, and management expects this lack of growth to continue. The firm last paid a dividend of $3.56. If you require a rate of return of 13 percent, what is the current value of this stock to you?

9.8 **Zero growth:** Ron Santana is interested in buying the stock of First National Bank. While the bank's management expects no growth in the near future, Ron is attracted by the dividend income. Last year the bank paid a dividend of $5.65. If Ron requires a return of 14 percent on such stocks, what is the maximum price he should be willing to pay for a share of the bank's stock?

9.9 **Zero growth:** The current stock price of Largent, Inc., is $44.72. If the required rate of return is 19 percent, what is the dividend paid by this firm if the dividend is not expected to grow in the future?

9.10 **Constant growth:** Moriband Corp. paid a dividend of $2.15 yesterday. The company's dividend is expected to grow at a steady rate of 5 percent for the foreseeable future. If investors in stocks of companies like Moriband require a rate of return of 15 percent, what should be the market price of Moriband stock?

9.11 **Constant growth:** Nyeil, Inc., is a consumer products firm that is growing at a constant rate of 6.5 percent. The firm's last dividend, which was just paid, was $3.36. If the required rate of return is 18 percent, what is the market value of this stock if dividends grow at the same rate as the firm?

9.12 **Constant growth:** Reco Corp. is expected to pay a dividend of $2.25 next year. The forecast for the stock price a year from now is $37.50. If the required rate of return is 14 percent, what is the current stock price? Assume constant growth.

9.13 **Constant growth:** Proxicam, Inc., is expected to grow at a constant rate of 7 percent. If the company's next dividend, which will be paid in a year, is $1.15 and its current stock price is $22.35, what is the required rate of return on this stock?

9.14 **Preferred stock valuation:** X-Centric Energy Company has issued perpetual preferred stock with a stated (par) value of $100 and a dividend of 4.5 percent. If the required rate of return is 8.25 percent, what is the stock's current market price?

9.15 **Preferred stock valuation:** The First Bank of Flagstaff has issued perpetual preferred stock with a $100 par value. The bank pays a quarterly dividend of $1.65 on this stock. What is the current price of this preferred stock given a required rate of return of 11.6 percent?

9.16 **Preferred stock valuation:** The preferred stock of Axim Corp. is currently selling at $47.13. If the required rate of return is 12.2 percent, what is the dividend paid by this stock?

9.17 **Preferred stock valuation:** Each quarter, Sirkota, Inc., pays a dividend on its perpetual preferred stock. Today the stock is selling at $63.37. If the required rate of return for such stocks is 15.5 percent, what is the quarterly dividend paid by Sirkota?

Intermediate

9.18 Constant growth: Kay Williams is interested in purchasing the common stock of Reckers, Inc., which is currently priced at $37.45. The company is expected to pay a dividend of $2.58 next year and to increase its dividend at a constant rate of 7 percent.

a. What should the market value of the stock be if the required rate of return is 14 percent?

b. Is this a good buy? Why or why not?

9.19 Constant growth: The required rate of return is 23 percent. Ninex Corp. has just paid a dividend of $3.12 and is expected to increase its dividend at a constant rate of 5 percent. What is the expected price of the stock three years from now?

9.20 Constant growth: Jenny Banks is interested in buying the stock of Fervan, Inc., which is increasing its dividends at a constant rate of 6 percent. Last year the firm paid a dividend of $2.65. The required rate of return is 16 percent. What is the current value of this stock? What should be the price of the stock in Year 5?

9.21 Constant growth: You own shares of Old World DVD Company and are interested in selling them. With so many people downloading music these days, sales, profits, and dividends at Old World have been declining 6 percent per year. The firm just paid a dividend of $1.15 per share. The required rate of return for a stock this risky is 15 percent. If dividends are expected to decline at 6 percent per year, what is a share of the stock worth today?

9.22 Nonconstant growth: You own a company that competes with Old World DVD Company (in the previous problem). Instead of selling DVDs, however, your company sells music downloads from a Web site. Things are going well now, but you know that it is only a matter of time before someone comes up with a better way to distribute music. Your company just paid a $1.50 per share dividend, and you expect to increase the dividend 10 percent next year. However, you then expect your dividend growth rate to begin going down—to 5 percent the following year, 2 percent the next year, and to −3 percent per year thereafter. Based on these estimates, what is the value of a share of your company's stock? Assume that the required rate of return is 12 percent.

9.23 Nonconstant growth: Tre-Bien, Inc., is a fast-growing technology company. Management projects rapid growth of 30 percent for the next two years, then a growth rate of 17 percent for the following two years. After that, a constant-growth rate of 8 percent is expected. The firm expects to pay its first dividend of $2.45 a year from now. If dividends will grow at the same rate as the firm and the required rate of return on stocks with similar risk is 22 percent, what is the current value of the stock?

9.24 Nonconstant growth: Management of ProCor, a biotech firm, forecasted the following growth rates for the next three years: 35 percent, 28 percent, and 22 percent. Management then expects the company to grow at a constant rate of 9 percent forever. The company paid a dividend of $1.75 last week. If the required rate of return is 20 percent, what is the value of this stock?

9.25 Nonconstant growth: Revarop, Inc., is a fast-growth company that is expected to grow at a rate of 23 percent for the next four years. It is then expected to grow at a constant rate of 6 percent. Revarop's first dividend, of $4.25, will be paid in Year 3. If the required rate of return is 17 percent, what is the current value of the stock if dividends are expected to grow at the same rate as the company?

9.26 Nonconstant growth: Quansi, Inc., management expects to pay no dividends for the next six years. It has projected a growth rate of 25 percent for the next seven years. After seven years, the firm will grow at a constant rate of 5 percent. Its first dividend, to be paid in Year 7, will be $3.25. If the required rate of return is 24 percent, what is the stock worth today?

9.27 Nonconstant growth: Staggert Corp. will pay dividends of $5.00, $6.25, $4.75, and $3.00 in the next four years. Thereafter, management expects the dividend growth rate to be constant at 6 percent. If the required rate of return is 18.5 percent, what is the current value of the stock?

9.28 Nonconstant growth: Diaz Corp. is expected to grow rapidly at a rate of 35 percent for the next seven years. The company's first dividend, to be paid three years from now, will be $5. After seven years, the company (and the dividends it pays) will grow at a rate of 8.5 percent. What is the value of Diaz stock with a required rate of return of 14 percent?

9.29 Nonconstant growth: Tin-Tin Waste Management, Inc., is growing rapidly. Dividends are expected to grow at rates of 30 percent, 35 percent, 25 percent, and 18 percent over the next four years. Thereafter, management expects dividends to grow at a constant rate of 7 percent. The stock is currently selling at $47.85, and the required rate of return is 16 percent. Compute the dividend for the current year (D_0).

Advanced

9.30 Equation 9.4 shows the relation between a stock's value and the dividend that is expected next year if dividends grow at a constant rate forever. If a firm pays all of its earnings as dividends, show how Equation 9.4 can be rearranged to calculate that firm's P/E ratio. What does this tell us about the factors that determine a firm's P/E ratio?

9.31 Riker Departmental Stores management has forecasted a growth rate of 40 percent for the next two years, followed by growth rates of 25 percent and 20 percent for the following two years. It then expects growth to stabilize at a constant rate of 7.5 percent forever. The firm paid a dividend of $3.50 recently. If the required rate of return is 18 percent, what is the current value of Riker's stock?

9.32 Courtesy Bancorp issued perpetual preferred stock a few years ago. The bank pays an annual dividend of $4.27 and your required rate of return is 12.2 percent.

a. What is the value of the stock given your required rate of return?

b. Should you buy this stock if its current market price is $34.41? Explain.

9.33 Rhea Kirby owns shares in Ryoko Corp. Currently, the market price of the stock is $36.34. Management expects dividends to grow at a constant rate of 6 percent for the foreseeable future. Its last dividend was $3.25. Rhea's required rate of return for such stocks is

16 percent. She wants to find out whether she should sell her shares or add to her holdings.

a. What is the value of this stock?

b. Based on your answer to part a, should Rhea buy additional shares in Ryoko Corp? Why or why not?

9.34 Perry, Inc., paid a dividend of $2.50 yesterday. You are interested in investing in this company, which has forecasted a constant-growth rate of 7 percent for its dividends, forever. The required rate of return is 18 percent.

a. Compute the expected dividends D_1, D_2, D_3, and D_4.

b. Compute the present value of these four dividends.

c. What is the expected value of the stock four years from now (P_4)?

d. What is the value of the stock today based on the answers to parts b and c?

e. Use the equation for constant growth (Equation 9.4) to compute the value of the stock today.

9.35 Zweite Pharma is a fast-growing drug company. Management forecasts that in the next three years, the company's dividend growth rates will be 30 percent, 28 percent, and 24 percent, respectively. Last week it paid a dividend of $1.67. After three years, management expects dividend growth to stabilize at a rate of 8 percent. The required rate of return is 14 percent.

a. Compute the dividends for each of the next three years, and calculate their present value.

b. Calculate the price of the stock at the end of Year 3, when the firm settles to a constant-growth rate.

c. What is the current price of the stock?

9.36 Triton Inc., is expected to grow at a rate of 22 percent for the next five years and then settle to a constant-growth rate of 6 percent. The company recently paid a dividend of $2.35. The required rate of return is 15 percent.

a. Find the present value of the dividends during the rapid-growth period if dividends grow at the same rate as the company.

b. What is the value of the stock at the end of Year 5?

c. What is the value of the stock today?

9.37 Ceebros Builders is expanding very fast and is expected to grow at a rate of 25 percent for the next four years. The company recently paid a dividend of $3.60 but is not expected to pay any dividends for the next three years. In Year 4, management expects to pay a $5 dividend and thereafter to increase the dividend at a constant rate of 6 percent. The required rate of return on such stocks is 20 percent.

a. Calculate the present value of the dividends during the fast-growth period.

b. What is the value of the stock at the end of the fast-growth period (P_4)?

c. What is the value of the stock today?

d. Would today's stock value be affected by the length of time you intend to hold the stock?

Sample Test Problems

9.1 Which type of secondary market provides the most efficient market for financial securities?

9.2 Is preferred stock a debt or an equity security?

9.3 Burnes, Inc., is a mature firm that is growing at a constant rate of 5.5 percent per year. The last dividend that the firm paid was $1.50 per share. If dividends are expected to grow at the same rate as the firm and the required rate of return on Burnes's stock is 12 percent, what is the market value of the company's stock?

9.4 Abacus Corporation will pay dividends of $2.25, $2.95, and $3.15 in the next three years. After three years, the dividends are expected to grow at a constant rate of 4 percent per year. If the required rate of return is 14.5 percent, what is the current value of the Abacus common stock?

9.5 The preferred stock of Wellcare Inc. is currently trading at $137.50 per share. If the required rate of return is 8 percent and this stock has no maturity date, what is the quarterly dividend paid by this stock? What is the quarterly dividend if the stock will mature in one year and it has a par value of $140?

Ethics Case

Insider Trading: Have I Got a Stock Tip for You!

Everyone would like to get a stock tip that will yield a huge return on a small investment. That's human nature. But stock tips can be mixed blessings. Consider the following example: Dr. Sam Waksal developed a promising cancer drug called Erbitux. As the CEO of ImClone, Waksal was an entrepreneur as well as an immunologist. Waksal sold an interest in Erbitux to the pharmaceutical company Bristol Myers for $42 million.

DON EMMERT/AFP/Getty Images

It was a Bristol Myers executive who informed Waksal that the Federal Drug Administration (FDA) was not going to approve the drug because there were insufficient data to determine its effectiveness; thus, new clinical trials were needed. Investors had expected approval, and once the FDA decision was made public, ImClone stock was certain to face a sharp decline in price. At least in the short term, some people were going to lose a lot of money.

One of those people was, of course, Waksal himself. He had millions of shares of ImClone. So did his family. Waksal told his daughter and father to sell their shares. In addition, Waksal transferred 79,000 of his own shares to his daughter to sell. Waksal knew that it was illegal under federal law for him or his family members to trade on inside information. And in the end, all three were indicted and later convicted of violating federal security laws.

Waksal was guilty of insider trading. As we pointed out in Chapter 1, insider trading results from information asymmetry, which arises when one party in a business transaction has information that is unavailable to the other parties in the transaction. To be legally actionable, insider trading must involve information that has not been publicly announced, as you might expect. In addition, the information must be material. *Material* means that the information will cause a significant change in the stock price—the price will go either up or down as a result of the event the information concerns. Examples of material corporate events include the introduction of a new product line, an acquisition, a divestiture, a key executive appointment, and the failure or success of a product under development.

Martha Stewart Enters the Picture

Waksal's conviction is not the only part of this story. Waksal was friends with the celebrity Martha Stewart, who also owned ImClone stock. On the day before the negative FDA announcement, Stewart sold 4,000 shares of ImClone worth $230,000. Did Stewart sell her shares on the basis of inside information regarding the FDA decision? Stewart's sale certainly looked suspicious, and the Securities and Exchange Commission (SEC) started an investigation and asked her to explain her sale. In her discussions with the SEC, Stewart did not admit to insider trading.

Stewart claimed that she had a prearranged order in place to sell her ImClone stock when it dipped below $60 per share. The stock did dip below $60 the day before the FDA announcement. Federal prosecutors, however, alleged that she and her broker, Peter Bacanovic, had doctored stock transaction records to support her story. In the SEC indictment, it was clear that they did not believe her explanation.

It is also interesting to note that Stewart is not alleged to have received a tip from Waksal himself. Indeed, she contacted Waksal only after the sale, when she called him to ask what was happening to the company. However, it is alleged that her broker, Bacanovic, received a tip that Waksal and his daughter had placed orders to sell shares of ImClone.

Martha Stewart was eventually convicted in a criminal trial, but convicted of what? The most serious charges, which involved securities fraud and insider trading, were thrown out of court. She was convicted only of lying to investigators. However, Stewart was also charged in a civil suit, and in that suit the insider trading charge would have been allowed in court. After serving a jail term, Stewart eventually reached an agreement with the SEC to settle the insider trading accusations. Under the agreement, she had to pay $195,000, covering her gains from the trading and penalties, although she did not admit to any wrongdoing.

Conclusions

What can we conclude about insider trading? The ethical issues can be analyzed at two levels: At the institutional level, we can ask whether the insider trading laws are ethical. At the individual level, we can ask why a person would engage in this illegal behavior.

Institutional Level. Fairness is the ethical basis of the insider trading laws. If the competitive system is to work, it must operate on an even playing field. If insiders have material financial information not available to the public, then the playing field is not level. Note what the SEC said in its press release: "It is fundamentally unfair for someone to have an edge on the market just because she has a stockbroker who is willing to break the rules and give her an illegal tip. It's worse still when the individual engaging in the insider trading is the Chairman and CEO of a public company." However, not everyone is convinced by this argument. Using a utilitarian framework, others argue that persons acting on insider information bring information to the market more quickly and thus make the market more efficient for the benefit of all.

Both sides have a point. One of the keystone propositions of efficient financial markets is that no participant should possess a significant *unfair* advantage over others. If you believe that the deck of cards is stacked against you and that some people who trade have access to inside information, you will collect your money and invest it elsewhere. Conversely, without inside information, there would be little reason for trading securities. Unless you know some information that affects securities' prices that others do not know, why trade? Furthermore, how would information relevant to security prices be released to the market unless some traded on that information?

The bottom line is that too much or too little inside information trading seems to be detrimental to financial markets. The critical question is how much inside information is optimal. There is no consensus among economists on an answer.

Individual Level. At the individual level, we must evaluate the motivation of the inside traders. Waksal, for example, knew that insider trading was illegal. Why did he do it? In an interview on CBS's *60 Minutes*, Waksal admitted that he did not think that he would get caught. Investigation showed that Waksal had been guilty of a number of ethical lapses in his life. He had been dismissed from a number of academic and research positions for questionable conduct. Aristotle would say he had a weak character. If Stewart had not tried to obscure what she did and simply told the truth to investigators, most legal experts are convinced she would not have been convicted of anything.

Discussion Questions

1. Discuss whether it would be unethical to buy a stock based on some information you found in the trash that had been thrown away by mistake.
2. Suppose you are the printer who has been given the job of preparing the official announcement of the FDA report. Can you use that information for personal gain? Why or why not?
3. Some argue that insider trading brings information to the market more quickly and thus is morally acceptable on the grounds of efficiency. Do you agree with that argument? Why or why not?

Sources: Press release from Securities and Exchange Commission, June 4, 2003; *CBS News*, www.cbsnews.com/2005/19/02/60minutes/main576328.shtml; CNNMoney.com, money.cnn.com/2004/03/05/news/companies/martha_verdict; Landon Thomas, Jr., "The Return of Martha Stewart, the Civil Case." *New York Times*, May 25, 2006, Section C, p. 1; and Landon Thomas, Jr., "Stewart Deal Resolves Stock Case," *New York Times*, August 8, 2006, www.nytimes.com/2006/08/08/business.

CHAPTER 10

The Fundamentals of Capital Budgeting

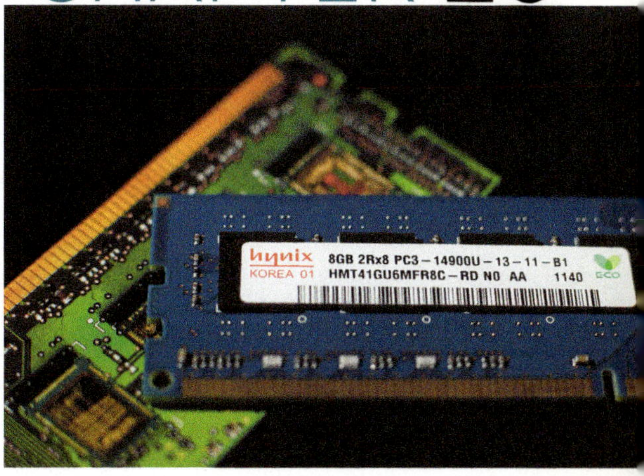

SeongJoon Cho/Bloomberg/Getty Images

LEARNING OBJECTIVES

1. Discuss why capital budgeting decisions are the most important investment decisions made by a firm's management.
2. Explain the benefits of using the net present value (NPV) method to analyze capital expenditure decisions and calculate the NPV for a capital project.
3. Describe the strengths and weaknesses of the payback period as a capital expenditure decision-making tool and compute the payback period for a capital project.
4. Explain why the accounting rate of return (ARR) is not recommended for use as a capital expenditure decision-making tool.
5. Compute the internal rate of return (IRR) for a capital project and discuss the conditions under which the IRR technique and the NPV technique produce different results.
6. Explain how the profitability index can be used to rank projects when a firm faces capital rationing and describe the limitations that apply to the profitability index.
7. Explain the benefits of postaudit and periodic reviews of capital projects.

In January 2017, managers of SK Hynix Inc., the second largest manufacturer of memory chips in the world, announced that the company would spend $6 billion in 2017 on projects ranging from additions to capacity, upgrades at existing plants, and maintenance. The 2017 capital expenditures at SK Hynix were part of a long-term, ongoing capital investment program through which the company had invested between $4.8 and $6.8 billion in each of the previous three years.

The decision to spend so much money on the renewal, replacement, and expansion of SK Hynix's infrastructure in a single year was undoubtedly based on a careful review of the firm's business strategy and detailed analyses of the specific investments that would best help SK Hynix achieve this strategy. Firms in capital-intensive industries, such as memory chip manufacturing, continually evaluate their capabilities in light of their business strategies, what their competitors are doing, and the environment in which they are competing. The capital budgeting process, through which firms decide in which real assets to invest, is an integral part of these evaluations.

Managers at SK Hynix had decided that 2017 was the appropriate year in which to build a new cleanroom at one of their plants, to increase their NAND flash manufacturing capacity, to expand their DRAM production capacity, and to begin mass-producing more sophisticated NAND and DRAM products. NAND flash memory is a type of nonvolatile storage technology that does not require power to retain data, while DRAM, or dynamic random-access memory, is a common type of memory found in computers. Managers apparently believed that each of these projects was necessary to pursue the company's business strategy. Similarly, each of the other capital investment decisions that contributed to the $6 billion total was likely based on an analysis of whether that decision made economic sense in light of the alternative choices.

While few companies have capital expenditure programs as large as those at SK Hynix, most companies must routinely invest capital in projects that are critical to their success. These investment opportunities must be carefully scrutinized and their costs and benefits carefully weighed. How do firms make these important capital budgeting decisions? In this chapter we examine this decision-making process and introduce some financial models used to make investment decisions.

Chapter Preview

This chapter is about capital budgeting, a topic we first visited in Chapter 1. Capital budgeting is the process of deciding which capital investments the firm should make.

We begin the chapter with a discussion of the types of capital projects that firms undertake and how the capital budgeting process is managed within the firm. When making capital investment decisions, management's goal is to select projects that will increase the value of the firm.

Next we examine some of the techniques used to evaluate capital budgeting decisions. We first discuss the net present value (NPV) method, which is the capital budgeting approach recommended in this book. The NPV method takes into account the time value of money and provides a direct measure of how much a capital project will increase the value of the firm.

We then examine the payback method and the accounting rate of return. As methods of selecting capital projects, both of these have some serious deficiencies. We also discuss the internal rate of return (IRR), which is the expected rate of return for a capital project when the project's NPV is equal to zero. The IRR is a very popular and important alternative to the NPV technique. However, in certain circumstances, the IRR can lead to incorrect decisions.

After discussing the above commonly used methods for selecting individual projects, we turn to the methods that financial managers use to select projects when there is not enough money to invest in all of the attractive ones. Finally, we present evidence on which techniques financial managers actually use when making capital budgeting decisions.

10.1 An Introduction to Capital Budgeting

LEARNING OBJECTIVE

1. Discuss why capital budgeting decisions are the most important investment decisions made by a firm's management.

We begin with an overview of capital budgeting, followed by a discussion of some important concepts you will need to understand in this and later chapters.

The Importance of Capital Budgeting

capital budgeting the process of choosing the productive assets in which the firm will invest

Capital budgeting decisions are the most important investment decisions made by management. The objective of these decisions is to select investments in productive assets that will increase the value of the firm. These investments *create value* when they are worth more than they cost. Capital investments are important because they can involve substantial cash outlays and, once made, are not easily reversed. They also define what the company is all about—the firm's lines of business and its inherent business risk. For better or worse, capital investments produce most of a typical firm's revenues for years to come.

Capital budgeting *techniques* help management systematically analyze potential business opportunities in order to decide which are worth undertaking. As you will see, not all capital budgeting techniques are equal. The best techniques are those that determine the value of a capital project by discounting all of the cash flows generated by the project and thus account for the time value of money.

In the final analysis, capital budgeting is really about management's search for the best capital projects—those that add the greatest value to the firm. Over the long term, the most successful firms are those whose managements consistently search for and find capital investment opportunities that increase firm value.

The Capital Budgeting Process

The capital budgeting process starts with a firm's strategic plan, which spells out its strategy for the next three to five years. Division managers then convert the firm's strategic objectives into business plans. These plans have a one- to two-year time horizon, provide a detailed description of what each division should accomplish during the period covered by the plan, and have quantifiable targets that each division is expected to achieve. Behind each division's business plan is a capital budget that details the resources management believes it needs to get the job done.

The capital budget is generally prepared jointly by the CFO's staff and financial staffs at the divisional and lower levels and reflects, in large part, the activities outlined in the divisional business plans. Many of these proposed expenditures are routine in nature, such as the repair or purchase of new equipment at existing facilities. Less frequently, firms face broader strategic decisions, such as whether to launch a new product, build a new plant, enter a new market, or buy a business. **Exhibit 10.1** identifies some reasons that firms initiate capital projects.

EXHIBIT 10.1 Key Reasons for Making Capital Expenditures

Capital budgeting decisions are the most important investment decisions made by management.Many of these decisions are routine in nature, but from time to time, managers face broader strategic decisions that call for significant capital investments.

Reason	Description
Renewal:	Over time, equipment must be repaired, overhauled, rebuilt, or retrofitted with new technology to keep the firm's manufacturing or service operations going. For example, a company that has a fleet of delivery trucks may decide to overhaul the trucks and their engines rather than purchase new trucks. Renewal decisions typically do not require an elaborate analysis and are made on a routine basis.
Replacement:	At some point, an asset will have to be replaced rather than repaired or overhauled. The major decision is whether to replace the asset with a similar piece of equipment or purchase equipment that would require a change in the production process. Sometimes, replacement decisions involve equipment that is operating satisfactorily but has become obsolete. The new or retrofitted equipment may provide cost savings with respect to labor or material usage and/or may improve product quality. These decisions typically originate at the plant level.
Expansion:	Strategically, the most important motive for capital expenditures is to expand the level of operating output. One type of expansion decision involves increasing the output of existing products. This may mean new equipment to produce more products or expansion of the firm's distribution system. These types of decisions typically require a more complex analysis than a renewal or replacement decision. Another type of expansion decision involves producing a new product or entering a new market. This type of expansion often involves large dollar amounts and significant business risk and requires the approval of the firm's board of directors.
Regulatory:	Some capital expenditures are required by federal and state regulations. These mandatory expenditures usually involve meeting workplace safety standards and environmental standards.
Other:	This category includes items such as parking facilities, office buildings, and executive aircraft. Many of these capital expenditures are hard to analyze because it is difficult to estimate their cash inflows. Ultimately, the decisions can be more subjective than analytical.

Sources of Information

Where does management get all of the information it needs to make capital budgeting decisions? Most of the information is generated within the firm, and, for expansion decisions, it often starts with sales representatives and marketing managers who are in the marketplace talking to potential and current customers on a day-to-day basis. For example, a sales manager with a new product idea might present the idea to management. If the product looks promising, the firm's marketing research group will estimate the size of the market and a market price. If the product requires new technology, the firm's research and development group must decide whether to develop the technology or to buy it. Next, cost accountants and production engineers will determine the cost of producing the product and any capital expenditures necessary to manufacture it. Finally, the CFO's staff will take the data and estimate the total cost of the project and the cash flows it will generate over time. The project is a viable candidate for the capital budget if the present value of the expected cash flows exceeds the present value of the project's cost.

Classification of Investment Projects

Potential capital budgeting projects can be classified into three types: (1) independent projects, (2) mutually exclusive projects, and (3) contingent projects.

Independent Projects

independent projects projects whose cash flows are unrelated

Projects are independent when their cash flows are unrelated. With **independent projects**, accepting or rejecting one project does not eliminate other projects from consideration (assuming the firm has unlimited funds to invest). For example, suppose a firm has unlimited funding and management wants to (1) build a new parking ramp at its headquarters; (2) acquire a small competitor; and (3) add manufacturing capacity to one of its plants. Since the cash flows for each project are unrelated, accepting or rejecting one of the projects will have no effect on the others.

Mutually Exclusive Projects

mutually exclusive projects projects for which acceptance of one precludes acceptance of the other

When projects are mutually exclusive, acceptance of one project precludes acceptance of others. Typically, **mutually exclusive projects** perform the same function, and thus only one project needs to be accepted. For example, when BMW decided to manufacture automobiles in the United States, it considered three possible manufacturing sites (or capital projects). Once BMW management selected the Spartanburg, South Carolina, site, the other two possible locations were out of the running. Since some projects are mutually exclusive, it is very important that a capital budgeting method allow us to choose the best project when we are faced with two or more alternatives.

Contingent Projects

contingent projects projects whose acceptance depends on the acceptance of other projects

With **contingent projects**, the acceptance of one project is contingent on the acceptance of another. There are two types of contingency situations. In the first type of situation, the contingent product is *mandatory*. For example, when a public utility company (such as your local electric company) builds a power plant, it must also invest in suitable pollution control equipment to meet federal environmental standards. The pollution control investment is a mandatory contingent project. When faced with mandatory contingent projects, it is best to treat all of the projects as a single investment for the purpose of evaluation. This provides management with the best measure of the value created by these projects.

In the second type of situation, the contingent project is *optional*. For example, suppose Lenovo invests in a new computer for the home market. This computer has a feature that allows Lenovo to bundle a proprietary gaming system. The gaming system is a contingent project but is an optional add-on to the new computer. In these situations, the optional contingent project should be evaluated *independently* and should be accepted or rejected on its own merits.

Basic Capital Budgeting Terms

In this section we briefly introduce two terms that you will need to be familiar with—*cost of capital* and *capital rationing.*

Cost of Capital

The **cost of capital** is the rate of return that a capital project must earn to be accepted by management. The cost of capital can be thought of as an opportunity cost. Recall from Chapter 8 that an *opportunity cost* is the value of the most valuable alternative given up if a particular investment is made.

cost of capital the required rate of return for a capital investment

Let's consider the opportunity cost concept in the context of capital budgeting decisions. When investors buy shares of stock in a company or loan money to a company, they are giving management money to invest on their behalf. Thus, when a firm's management makes capital investments in productive assets such as plant and equipment, they are investing *stockholders' and creditors' money* in *real assets*. Since stockholders and creditors could have invested their money in *financial assets,* the minimum rate of return they are willing to accept on an investment in a real asset is the rate they could have earned investing in financial assets that have similar risk. The rate of return that investors can earn on financial assets with similar risk is an *opportunity cost* because investors lose the opportunity to earn that rate if the money is invested in a real asset instead. It is therefore the rate of return that investors will require for an investment in a capital project. In other words, this rate is the cost of capital. It is also known as the **opportunity cost of capital**. Chapter 13 discusses how we estimate the opportunity cost of capital in practice. (See Building Intuition for more.)

opportunity cost of capital the return an investor gives up when his or her money is invested in one asset rather than the best alternative asset with the same risk

Building Intuition

Investment Decisions Have Opportunity Costs

When any investment is made, the opportunity to earn a return from an alternative investment is lost. The lost return can be viewed as a cost that arises from a lost opportunity. For this reason, it is called an *opportunity cost*. The opportunity cost of capital is the return an investor gives up when his or her money is invested in one asset rather than the best alternative asset with the same risk. For example, suppose that a firm invests in a piece of equipment rather than returning money to stockholders. If stockholders could have earned an annual return of 12 percent on a stock with cash flows that are as risky as the cash flows the equipment will produce, this is the opportunity cost of capital associated with the investment in the piece of equipment.

Capital Rationing

When a firm has all the money it needs to invest in all the capital projects that meet its capital selection criteria, the firm is said to be operating without a *funding constraint,* or *resource constraint.* Firms are rarely in this position, especially growth firms. Typically, a firm has a fixed number of dollars available for capital expenditures, and the number of qualified projects that need funding exceeds the funds that are available. This funding constraint on investments means that some projects will be mutually exclusive, since investing in one project exhausts resources that might otherwise be invested in another. When faced with a resource constraint, the firm must allocate its funds to the subset of projects that provides the largest increase in stockholder value. The process of limiting, or rationing, capital expenditures in this way is called **capital rationing**. Capital rationing and its implications for capital budgeting are discussed in Section 10.6.

capital rationing a situation where a firm does not have enough capital to invest in all attractive projects and must therefore ration capital

Before You Go On

1. Why are capital investments the most important decisions made by a firm's management?
2. What are the differences between capital projects that are independent, mutually exclusive, and contingent?
3. What is the cost of capital?
4. Describe the process of capital rationing.

10.2 Net Present Value

LEARNING OBJECTIVE

2. Explain the benefits of using the net present value (NPV) method to analyze capital expenditure decisions and calculate the NPV for a capital project.

net present value (NPV) method a method of evaluating a capital investment project that measures the difference between its cost and the present value of its expected cash flows

In this section we discuss a capital budgeting method that is consistent with this goal of financial management—to maximize the wealth of the firm's owners. It is called the **net present value (NPV) method**, and it is one of the most basic analytical methods underlying corporate finance. The NPV method tells us the amount by which the benefits from a capital expenditure exceed its costs. It is the capital budgeting technique recommended in this book.

Valuation of Real Assets

Throughout this book, we have emphasized that the value of any asset is the present value of its future cash flows. In Chapters 8 and 9, we developed valuation models for financial assets, such as bonds, preferred stock, and common stock. We now extend our discussion of valuation models from financial to real assets. The steps used in valuing an asset are the same whether the asset is real or financial:

1. Estimate the expected future cash flows.
2. Determine the required rate of return, or discount rate, which depends on the riskiness of the future cash flows.
3. Compute the present value of the future cash flows to determine what the asset is worth.

The valuation of real assets, however, is less straightforward than the valuation of financial assets, for several reasons.

First, in many cases, cash flows for financial assets are well documented in a legal contract. If they are not, we are at least able to make some reasonable assumptions about what they are. For real assets, much less information exists. Specialists within the firm, usually from the finance, marketing, and production groups, often prepare estimates of expected future cash flows for capital projects with only limited information.

Second, many financial securities are traded in public markets, and these markets are reasonably efficient. Thus, market data on rates of return are accessible. For real assets, no such markets exist. As a result, we must estimate required rates of return on real assets (opportunity costs) from market data on financial assets; this can be difficult to do.

NPV—The Basic Concept

The NPV of a project is the difference between the present value of the project's expected future cash flows and the present value of its cost. The NPV can be expressed as follows:

$$\text{NPV} = \text{PV(Project's expected future cash flows)} - \text{PV(Cost of the project)}$$

If a capital project has a positive NPV, the value of the cash flows the project is expected to generate exceeds the project's cost. Thus, a positive NPV project increases the value of the firm and, hence, stockholders' wealth. If a capital project has a negative NPV, the value of the expected cash flows from the project is less than its cost. If accepted, a negative NPV project will decrease the value of the firm and stockholders' wealth.

To illustrate these important points, consider an example. Suppose a firm is considering building a new marina for pleasure boats. The firm has a genie who can tell the future with perfect certainty. The finance staff estimates that the marina will cost \$3.50 million. The genie volunteers that the present value of the future cash flows from the marina is \$4.25 million.

Assuming this information is correct, the NPV for the marina project is a positive \$750,000 (\$4.25 million − \$3.50 million = \$0.75 million). Management should accept the project because the excess of the value of the cash flows over cost increases the value of the firm by \$750,000. Why is a positive NPV a *direct* measure of how much a capital project will increase the value of the firm? If management wanted to, the firm could sell the marina for \$4.25 million, pay the \$3.50 million in expenses, and deposit \$750,000 in the bank. The value of the firm would increase by the \$750,000 deposited in the bank. In sum, the NPV method tells us which capital projects to select and how much value they add to the firm.

NPV and Value Creation

We have just stated that any project with a positive NPV should be accepted because it will increase the value of the firm. Let's take a moment to think about this proposition. What makes a capital asset worth more than it costs? In other words, how does management create value with capital investments?

How Value Is Created

Suppose that when you were in college, you worked part time at a successful pizza parlor near campus. During this time, you learned a lot about the pizza business. After graduation, for \$100,000 you purchased a pizza parlor that was in a good location but had been forced to close because of a lack of business. The owners had let the restaurant and the quality of the pizzas deteriorate, and the wait staff had been rude to customers. Once you purchased the restaurant, you immediately invested \$40,000 to fix it up: you painted the building, spruced up the interior, replaced some of the dining room furniture, and added an eye-catching, 1950s-style neon sign to attract attention. You also spent \$15,000 for a one-time advertising blitz to quickly build a customer base. More important, you improved the quality of the pizzas you sold, and you built a profitable takeout business. Finally, you hired your wait staff carefully and trained them to be customer friendly.

Almost immediately the restaurant was earning a substantial profit and generating substantial cash flows. The really good news was that several owners of local pizzerias wanted to buy your restaurant. After intense negotiations with several of the potential buyers, you accepted a cash offer of \$475,000 for the business shortly after you purchased it.

What is the NPV for the pizza parlor? For this investment, the NPV is easy to calculate. We do not need to estimate future cash flows and discount them because we already have an estimate of the present value of the cash flows the pizza parlor is expected to produce—\$475,000. Someone is willing to pay you \$475,000 because he or she believes the future cash flows are worth that amount. The cost of your investment includes the purchase price of the restaurant, the cost to fix it up, and the cost of the initial advertising campaign, which totals \$155,000 (\$100,000 + \$40,000 + \$15,000 = \$155,000). Thus, the NPV for the pizza parlor is:

$$\begin{aligned}\text{NPV} &= \text{PV(Project's future cash flows)} - \text{PV(Cost of the project)}\\ &= \$475{,}000 - \$155{,}000\\ &= \$320{,}000\end{aligned}$$

The \$475,000 price paid for the pizza parlor exceeds the cost (\$155,000) by \$320,000. You have created \$320,000 in value. How did you do this? You did it by improving the food, customer service, and dining ambiance while keeping prices competitive. Your management skills and knowledge of the pizza business resulted in significant growth in the current year's cash flows and the prospect of even larger cash flows in the future.

Where did the \$320,000 in value you created go? The NPV of your investment is the amount that your personal net worth increased because of the investment. For an ongoing business, the result would have been a \$320,000 increase in the value of the firm.

How about the original owners? Why would they sell a business worth \$475,000 to you for \$100,000? The answer is simple; if they could have transformed the business as you did, they would have done so. Instead, when they ran the business, it lost money! They sold it to you because you offered them a price reflecting its value to them.

Market Data versus Discounted Cash Flows

Our pizza parlor example is greatly simplified by the fact that we can observe the price that someone is willing to pay for the asset. In most capital project analyses, we have to estimate the market value of the asset by forecasting its future cash flows and discounting them by the cost of capital. The discounted value of a project's future cash flows is an estimate of its value, or the market price for which it can be sold.

Framework for Calculating NPV

We now describe a framework for analyzing capital budgeting decisions using the NPV method. As you will see, the NPV technique uses the discounted cash flow technique developed in Chapters 5 and 6 and applied in Chapters 8 and 9. The good news, then, is that the NPV method requires only the application of what you already know.

The five-step framework discussed in this section and a cash flow worksheet like the one illustrated in **Exhibit 10.2** can help you systematically organize a project's cash flow data and compute its NPV. Most mistakes people make when working capital budgeting problems result from problems with cash flows: not identifying a cash flow, getting a cash flow in the wrong time period, or assigning the wrong sign to a cash flow. What can make cash flow analysis difficult in capital budgeting is that there are often multiple cash flows in a single time period, and some are cash inflows and others are cash outflows.

Weblink

Matt Evans's Web site has a lot of free worksheets that are useful to financial managers, including several related to capital budgeting. Go to http://www.exinfm.com/free_spreadsheets.html.

As always, we recommend that you prepare a time line when doing capital budgeting problems. Exhibit 10.2 shows a sample time line along with an identification of the cash flows for each period. Our goal is to compute the net cash flow (NCF) for each time period t, where NCF_t = Total cash inflows − Total cash outflows for the period t. For a capital project, the time periods (t) are usually in years, and t varies from the current period ($t = 0$) to some finite time period that is the estimated life of the project ($t = n$). Recall that getting the correct sign on each cash flow is critical to getting the correct answer to a problem. As you have seen in earlier chapters, the convention in finance problem solving is that cash inflows carry a positive sign and cash outflows carry a negative sign. Finally, note that all cash flows in this chapter are on an after-tax basis. We will make adjustments for tax consequences on specific transactions such as the calculation of a project's salvage value.

Our five-step framework for analysis is as follows:

1. **Determine the initial cost of starting the project.** We first need to identify and add up all the cash flows related to the initial cost of starting the project. In most cases, the initial cost of a project is incurred at the start; hence the cash flows are already in current dollars. These cash flows typically include any property, plant, and equipment outlays for

Time line	0	1	2	3	4	5 Year
Cash Flows:						
Initial cost	$-CF_0$					
Cash inflows (CIF)		CIF_1	CIF_2	CIF_3	CIF_4	CIF_5
Cash outflows (COF)		$-COF_1$	$-COF_2$	$-COF_3$	$-COF_4$	$-COF_5$
Salvage value (SV)						SV
Net cash flow	NCF_0	NCF_1	NCF_2	NCF_3	NCF_4	NCF_5

$$NPV = NCF_0 + \sum_{t=1}^{5} \frac{NCF_t}{(1 + k)^t}$$

EXHIBIT 10.2 Sample Worksheet for Net Present Value Analysis

In addition to following the five-step framework for solving NPV analysis problems, we recommend that you use a worksheet with a time line like the one shown here to help you determine the proper cash flows for each period.

production as well as employee hiring and training costs. In some cases, like those involving the construction of a manufacturing facility, these initial outlays can be made over several years before the project is up and running. Of course, any future cash flows must be discounted to obtain their present value. Turning to Exhibit 10.2, we have incurred a single negative cash flow ($-CF_0$) as our initial cost of starting the project; thus NCF_0 has a negative value.

2. **Estimate the project's future cash flows over its expected life.** Once they are up and running, capital projects typically generate some cash inflows from revenues (CIF_t) for each period, along with some cash outflows (COF_t) associated with costs incurred to generate the revenues. In most cases revenues exceed costs, and thus, NCF_t is positive. However, this may not always be the case. For example, if the project is the purchase of a piece of equipment, it is possible for NCF_3 to have a negative value ($CIF_3 < COF_3$) if the equipment is projected to need a major overhaul or must be replaced during the third year. Finally, you also need to pay attention to a project's final cash flow, which is $t = 5$ in Exhibit 10.2. There may be a salvage value (SV) at the end of the project, which is a cash inflow. In that case $NCF_5 = CIF_5 - COF_5 + SV$. The important point is that for each time period, we must identify all the cash flows that take place, assign each cash flow its proper sign, and add up all the cash flows.
3. **Determine the riskiness of the project and the appropriate cost of capital.** The third step is to identify for each project its risk-adjusted cost of capital, which takes into account the riskiness of the project's cash flows. The riskier the project, the higher its cost of capital. The cost of capital is the discount rate used in determining the present value of the future expected cash flows. In this chapter, the cost of capital and any risk adjustments will be supplied, and no calculations will be required for this step.
4. **Compute the project's NPV.** The NPV, as you know, is the present value of the net cash flows the project is expected to generate minus the cost of the project.
5. **Make a decision.** If the NPV is positive, the project should be accepted because all projects with a positive NPV will increase the value of the firm. If the NPV is negative, the project should be rejected; projects with negative NPVs will decrease the value of the firm.

You might be wondering about how to handle a capital project with an NPV of 0. Technically, management should be indifferent to accepting or rejecting projects such as this because they neither increase nor decrease the value of the firm. When the NPV = 0, the project is generating returns that are just equal to the opportunity cost of capital. At a practical level, projects rarely have an NPV equal to 0, and most firms have more good capital projects (with NPV > 0) than they can fund. Thus, this is not an issue that generates much interest among practitioners.

Net Present Value Techniques

The NPV of a capital project can be stated in equation form as the present value of all net cash flows (total cash inflows – total cash outflows) connected with the project, whether in the current period or in the future. The NPV equation can be written as follows:

$$NPV = NCF_0 + \frac{NCF_1}{1+k} + \frac{NCF_2}{(1+k)^2} + \cdots + \frac{NCF_n}{(1+k)^n} \tag{10.1}$$

$$= \sum_{t=0}^{n} \frac{NCF_t}{(1+k)^t}$$

where:

NCF_t = net cash flow (total cash inflows – total cash outflows) in period t, where $t = 0, 1, 2, 3, \ldots, n$

k = the cost of capital

n = the project's estimated life

Next, we will work an example to see how the NPV is calculated for a capital project. Suppose you are the president of a small regional firm located in Chicago that manufactures frozen pizzas which are sold to grocery stores and to firms in the hospitality and food service industry. Your market research group has developed an idea for a "pocket" pizza that can be used as an entrée with a meal or as an "on the go" snack. The sales manager believes that, with an aggressive advertising campaign, sales of the product will be about \$300,000 per year. The cost to modify the existing production line will also be \$300,000, according to the plant manager. The marketing and plant managers estimate that the cost to produce the pocket pizzas, to market and advertise them, and to deliver them to customers will be about \$220,000 per year. The product's life is estimated to be five years, and the specialized equipment necessary for the project has an estimated salvage value of \$30,000. The appropriate cost of capital is 15 percent.

When analyzing capital budgeting problems, we typically have a lot of data to sort through. The worksheet introduced in Exhibit 10.2 is helpful in keeping track of the data in an organized format. **Exhibit 10.3** shows the time line and relevant cash flows for the pocket pizza project. The steps in analyzing the project's cash flows and determining its NPV are as follows:

1. *Determine the initial cost of starting the project.* The cost of the project is the one-time cost to modify the existing production line, which is \$300,000. This is a cash outflow (negative sign).
2. *Estimate the project's future cash flows over its expected life.* The project's future cash inflows come from sales of the new product. Sales are estimated at \$300,000 per year (positive sign). The cash outflows are the costs to manufacture and distribute the new product, which are \$220,000 per year (negative sign). The life of the project is five years. The project has a salvage value of \$30,000, which is a cash inflow (positive sign). The net cash flow (NCF) in a particular time period is just the sum of the cash inflows and cash outflows for that period, including the cost of starting the project and any salvage value. For example, the NCF for period $t = 0$ is −\$300,000, the NCF for period $t = 1$ is \$80,000, and so on, as you can see in Exhibit 10.3.
3. *Determine the riskiness of the project and the appropriate cost of capital.* The discount rate is the cost of capital, which is 15 percent.
4. *Compute the project's NPV.* To compute the project's NPV, we apply Equation 10.1 by plugging in the NCF values for each time period and using the cost of capital, 15 percent, as the discount rate. The equation looks like this (the figures are in thousands of dollars):

$$\begin{aligned}
\text{NPV} &= \sum_{t=0}^{n} \frac{\text{NCF}_t}{(1+k)^t} \\
&= -\$300 + \frac{\$80}{1.15} + \frac{\$80}{(1.15)^2} + \frac{\$80}{(1.15)^3} + \frac{\$80}{(1.15)^4} + \frac{(\$80 + \$30)}{(1.15)^5} \\
&= -\$300 + \$69.57 + \$60.49 + \$52.60 + \$45.74 + \$54.69 \\
&= -\$300 + \$283.09 \\
&= -\$16.91
\end{aligned}$$

The NPV for the pocket pizza project is therefore −\$16,910.

Time line	0	1	2	3	4	5 Year
Cash Flows:						
Initial cost	−\$300					
Cash inflows		\$300	\$300	\$300	\$300	\$300
Cash outflows		−\$220	−\$220	−\$220	−\$220	−\$220
Salvage value						\$ 30
Net cash flow	−\$300	\$80	\$80	\$80	\$80	\$110

EXHIBIT 10.3 Pocket Pizza Project Time Line and Cash Flows (\$ thousands)

The worksheet introduced in Exhibit 10.2 is helpful in organizing the data given for the pocket pizza project.

5. *Make a decision.* The pocket pizza project has a negative NPV, which indicates that the project is not a good investment and should be rejected. If management undertook this project, the value of the firm would decrease by \$16,910; and, if the firm had 100,000 shares of stock outstanding, we can estimate that the project would decrease the value of each share by about 17 cents (\$16,910/100,000 shares = \$0.1691 per share).

Calculating NPV with a Financial Calculator

Using a financial calculator is an easier way to calculate the present value of the future cash flows. In this example you should recognize that the cash flow pattern is a five-year ordinary annuity with an additional cash inflow in the fifth year. This is exactly the cash pattern for a bond with annual coupon payments and payment of principal at maturity we saw in Chapter 8. We can find the present value using a financial calculator, with \$80 being the annuity stream for five years and \$30 the salvage value at Year 5:

	N	i	PV	PMT	FV
Enter	3	15		80	30
Answer			**−283.09**		

The PV of the future cash flows is −\$283.09. With that information, we can compute the NPV using Equation 10.1 as follows:

$$
\begin{aligned}
\text{NPV} &= \sum_{t=1}^{n} \frac{\text{NCF}_t}{(1+k)^t} - \text{NCF}_0 \\
&= \$283.09 - \$300.00 \\
&= -\$16.91
\end{aligned}
$$

Learning by Doing Application 10.1 and the following **Using Excel Example** illustrate another NPV calculation.

APPLICATION 10.1 | The Dough's Up: The Self-Rising Pizza Project

LEARNING BY DOING

WileyPLUS

Need more help? Visit your WileyPLUS course.

Problem Let's continue our frozen pizza example. Suppose the head of the research and development (R&D) group announces that R&D engineers have developed a breakthrough technology—self-rising frozen pizza dough that, when baked, rises and tastes exactly like fresh-baked dough.

The cost is \$300,000 to modify the production line and the modifications will have a five-year life. Sales of the new product are estimated at \$200,000 for the first year, \$300,000 for the next two years, and \$500,000 for the final two years. It is estimated that production, sales, and advertising costs will be \$250,000 for the first year and will then decline to a constant \$200,000 per year. There is no salvage value at the end of the product's life, and the appropriate cost of capital is 15 percent. Is the project, as proposed, economically viable?

Approach To solve the problem, work through the steps for NPV analysis given in the text.

Solution **Exhibit 10.4** shows the project's cash flows.

1. The cost to modify the production line is \$300,000, which is a cash outflow in Year 0 and the cost of the project.
2. The future cash flows over the expected life of the project are laid out on the time line in Exhibit 10.4. The project's life is five years. The NCFs for the capital project are negative at the beginning of the project and in the first year (−\$300,000 and −\$50,000) and thereafter are positive.
3. The appropriate cost of capital is 15 percent.

4. The values are substituted into Equation 10.1 to calculate the NPV:

$$\begin{aligned}
NPV &= NCF_0 + \frac{NCF_1}{1+k} + \frac{NCF_2}{(1+k)^2} + \cdots + \frac{NCF_n}{(1+k)^n} \\
&= -\$300{,}000 + \frac{-\$50{,}000}{1.15} + \frac{\$100{,}000}{(1.15)^2} + \frac{\$100{,}000}{(1.15)^3} + \frac{\$300{,}000}{(1.15)^4} + \frac{\$300{,}000}{(1.15)^5} \\
&= -\$300{,}000 - \$43{,}478 + \$75{,}614 + \$65{,}752 + \$171{,}526 + \$149{,}153 \\
&= \$118{,}567
\end{aligned}$$

5. The NPV for the self-rising pizza dough project is \$118,567. Because the NPV is positive, management should accept the project. The project is estimated to increase the value of the firm by \$118,567.

Time line	0	1	2	3	4	5 Year
Cash Flows:						
Initial cost	−\$300					
Cash inflows		\$200	\$300	\$300	\$500	\$500
Cash outflows		−\$250	−\$200	−\$200	−\$200	−\$200
Salvage value						
Net cash flow	−\$300	−\$50	\$100	\$100	\$300	\$300

EXHIBIT 10.4 Self-Rising Pizza Dough Project Time Line and Cash Flows (\$ thousands) The worksheet shows the time line and cash flows for the self-rising pizza dough project in Learning by Doing Application 10.1. As always, it is important to assign each cash flow to the appropriate year and to give it the proper sign. Once you have computed the net cash flow for each time period, solving for the NPV is just a matter of plugging the data into the NPV formula.

Using Excel

Net Present Value

Net present value problems are most commonly solved using a spreadsheet program. The program's design is good for keeping track of all the cash flows and the periods in which they occur. The spreadsheet setup for Learning by Doing Application 10.1, presented on the right, shows how to calculate the NPV for the self-rising pizza dough machine.

Notice that the NPV formula does not take into account the cash flow in year zero. Therefore, you only enter into the NPV formula the cash flows in Years 1 through 5, along with the discount rate. You then add the cash flow in Year zero to the total from the NPV formula calculation to get the NPV for the investment.

	A	B	C	D	E
1					
2		**Net Present Value Calculations**			
3					
4		**Year**		**Cash Flow**	
5		0		−\$300,000	
6		1		−50,000	
7		2		100,000	
8		3		100,000	
9		4		300,000	
10		5		300,000	
11					
12		Cost of capital		0.15	
13					
14		**NPV**		**\$118,567**	
15		Formula used	=NPV(D12, D6:D10)+D5		
16					

Mutually Exclusive Projects and NPV

Recall that investments are mutually exclusive if, by making one, another will not be undertaken. Projects may be mutually exclusive because they are substitutes for one another or because the firm has a funding constraint. A project's NPV provides an objective measure of its incremental value to the firm's investors, and thus makes it simple to choose between two or more mutually exclusive projects. When faced with such a choice, managers should allocate capital to the project that has the most positive dollar impact on the value of the firm—in other words, the project with the highest NPV.

Decision Making Example 10.1 illustrates how NPVs are used in project selection.

EXAMPLE 10.1 | The IS Department's Capital Projects

DECISION MAKING

Situation Suppose you are the manager of the information systems (IS) department of the frozen pizza manufacturer we have been discussing. Your department has identified four possible capital projects with the following NPVs: (1) $4,500, (2) $3,000, (3) $0.0, and (4) −$1,000. What should you decide about each project if the projects are independent? What should you decide if the projects are mutually exclusive?

Decision If the projects are independent, you should accept Projects 1 and 2, both of which have a positive NPV, and reject Project 4. Project 3, with an NPV of zero, could be either accepted or rejected without affecting the value of the firm. If the projects are mutually exclusive and you can accept only one of them, it should be Project 1, which has the largest NPV.

Concluding Comments on NPV

Some concluding comments about the NPV method are in order. First, as you may have noticed, the NPV computations are rather mechanical once we have estimated the cash flows and the cost of capital. The real difficulty is estimating or forecasting the future cash flows. Although this may seem to be a daunting task, managers with experience in producing and selling a particular type of product can usually generate fairly accurate estimates of sales volumes, prices, and production costs. Most business managers are routinely required to make decisions that involve expectations about future events. In fact, that is what business is really all about—dealing with uncertainty and making decisions that involve risk.

Second, estimating project cash flows over a long forecast period requires skill and judgment. There is nothing wrong with using estimates to make business decisions as long as they are based on informed judgments and not guesses. Problems can arise with the cash flow estimates when a project team becomes overly enamored with a project. In wanting a particular project to succeed, a project team can be too optimistic about the cash flow projections. It is therefore very important that capital budgeting decisions be subject to ongoing and postaudit review.

In conclusion, the NPV approach is the method we recommend for making capital investment decisions. It provides a direct (dollar) measure of how much a project will increase the value of the firm. NPV also makes it possible to correctly choose between mutually exclusive projects. The accompanying table summarizes NPV decision rules and the method's key advantages and disadvantages.

Summary of Net Present Value (NPV) Method

Decision Rule: NPV > 0 ⇨ Accept the project.
NPV < 0 ⇨ Reject the project.

Key Advantages	Key Disadvantage
1. Uses the discounted cash flow valuation technique to adjust for the time value of money.	**1.** Can be difficult to understand without an accounting and finance background.
2. Provides a direct (dollar) measure of how much a capital project will increase the value of the firm.	
3. Is consistent with the goal of maximizing stockholder value.	

Before You Go On

1. What is the NPV of a project?
2. If a firm accepts a project with a $10,000 NPV, what is the effect on the value of the firm?
3. What are the five steps used in NPV analysis?

10.3 The Payback Period

LEARNING OBJECTIVE

3. Describe the strengths and weaknesses of the payback period as a capital expenditure decision-making tool and compute the payback period for a capital project.

payback period the length of time required to recover a project's initial cost

The payback period is one of the most widely used tools for evaluating capital projects. The **payback period** is defined as the number of years it takes for the cash flows from a project to recover the project's initial investment. With the payback method for evaluating projects, a project is accepted if its payback period is below some specified threshold. Although it has serious weaknesses, this method does provide some insight into how quickly a firm will recover the cash that has been invested in a project.

Computing the Payback Period

To compute the payback period, we need to know the project's cost and estimate its future net cash flows. The net cash flows and the project cost are the same values that we use to compute the NPV. The payback (PB) equation can be expressed as follows:

$$\text{PB} = \text{Years before cost recovery} + \frac{\text{Remaining cost to recover}}{\text{Cash flow during the year}} \tag{10.2}$$

Exhibit 10.5 shows the net cash flows (row 1) and cumulative net cash flows (row 2) for a proposed capital project with an initial cost of \$70,000. The payback period calculation for our example is:

$$\begin{aligned}
\text{PB} &= \text{Years before cost recovery} + \frac{\text{Remaining cost to recover}}{\text{Cash flow during the year}} \\
&= 2 \text{ years} + \frac{\$70{,}000 - \$60{,}000}{\$20{,}000 \text{ per year}} \\
&= 2 \text{ years} + \frac{\$10{,}000}{\$20{,}000 \text{ per year}} \\
&= 2 \text{ years} + 0.5 \text{ year} \\
&= 2.5 \text{ years}
\end{aligned}$$

Let's look at this calculation in more detail. Note in Exhibit 10.5 that the firm recovers cash flows of \$30,000 in the first year and \$30,000 in the second year, for a total of \$60,000 over the two years. During the third year, the firm needs to recover only \$10,000 (\$70,000 – \$60,000 = \$10,000) to pay back the full cost of the project. The third-year cash flow is \$20,000, so we will have to wait 0.5 year (\$10,000/\$20,000 = 0.5) to recover the final amount. Thus, the payback period for this project is 2.5 years (2 years + 0.5 year = 2.5 years).

Time line	0	1	2	3	4 Year
Net cash flow (NCF)	–\$70,000	\$30,000	\$30,000	\$20,000	\$15,000
Cumulative NCF	–\$70,000	–\$40,000	–\$10,000	\$10,000	\$25,000

EXHIBIT 10.5 Payback Period Cash Flows and Calculations

The exhibit shows the net and cumulative net cash flows for a proposed capital project with an initial cost of \$70,000. The cash flow data are used to compute the payback period, which is 2.5 years.

The idea behind the payback period method is simple: the shorter the payback period, the faster the firm gets its money back and the more desirable the project. However, there is no economic rationale that links the payback method to stockholder value maximization. Firms that use the payback method accept all projects having a payback period under some threshold and reject those with a payback period over this threshold. If a firm has a number of projects that are mutually exclusive, the projects are selected in order of their payback rank: projects with the shortest payback period are selected first.

Learning by Doing Application 10.2 illustrates additional payback calculations.

How the Payback Period Performs

We have worked through some simple examples of how the payback period is computed. Now we will consider several more complex situations to see how well the payback period performs as a capital budgeting rule. **Exhibit 10.6** illustrates five different capital budgeting projects. The projects all have an initial investment of \$500, but each one has a different cash flow pattern. The bottom part of the exhibit shows each project's payback period, along with its net

APPLICATION 10.2 | A Payback Calculation

LEARNING BY DOING

WileyPLUS

Need more help? Visit your WileyPLUS course.

Problem A firm has two capital projects, A and B, which are under review for funding. Both projects cost \$500, and the projects have the following cash flows:

Year	Project A	Project B
0	–\$500	–\$500
1	100	400
2	200	300
3	200	200
4	400	100

What is the payback period for each project? If the projects are independent, which project should management select? If the projects are mutually exclusive, which project should management accept? The firm's payback cutoff point is two years.

Approach Use Equation 10.2 to calculate the number of years it takes for the cash flows from each project to recover the project's initial investment. If the two projects are independent, you should accept the projects that have a payback period that is less than or equal to two years. If the projects are mutually exclusive, you should accept the project with the shorter payback period if that payback period is less than or equal to two years.

Solution Computing the payback for Project A requires only that we calculate the first term in Equation 10.2—Years before recovery: the first year recovers \$100, the second year \$200, and the third year \$200, for a total of \$500 (\$100 + \$200 + \$200 = \$500). Thus, in three years, the \$500 investment is fully recovered, so $PB_A = 3.00$ years.

For Project B, the first year recovers \$400 and the second year \$300. Since we need only part of the second-year cash flow to recover the initial cost, we calculate both terms in Equation 10.2 to obtain the payback period.

$$PB = \text{Years before cost recovery} + \frac{\text{Remaining cost to recover}}{\text{Cash flow during the year}}$$

$$PB_A = 3 \text{ years}$$

$$PB_B = 1 \text{ year} + \frac{\$500 - \$400}{\$300 \text{ per year}}$$

$$= 1 \text{ year} + \frac{\$100}{\$300 \text{ per year}}$$

$$= 1.33 \text{ years}$$

Whether the projects are independent or mutually exclusive, management should accept only Project B since Project A's payback period exceeds the two-year cutoff point.

EXHIBIT 10.6 Payback Period with Various Cash Flow Patterns

Each of the five capital budgeting projects shown in the exhibit calls for an initial investment of $500, but all have different cash flow patterns. The bottom part of the exhibit shows each project's payback period, along with its net present value for comparison.

Year	A	B	C	D	E
0	–$500	–$500	–$500	–$500	–$500
1	200	300	250	500	200
2	300	100	250	0	200
3	400	50	–250	0	200
4	500	0	250	–5,000	5,000
Payback (years)	2.0	∞	2.0/4.0	1.0/∞	2.5
NPV	$450	–$131	–$115	–$2,924	$2,815
Cost of capital = 15%					

present value for comparison. We will assume that management has set a payback period of two years as the cutoff point for an acceptable project.

Project A: The cash flows for Project A are $200 in the first year and $300 in the second, for a total of $500; thus, the project's payback period is two years. Under our acceptance criterion, management should accept this project. Project A also has a positive NPV of $450, so the two capital budgeting decision rules agree.

Project B: Project B never generates enough cash flows to pay off the original investment of $500: $300 + $100 + $50 = $450. Thus, the project payback period is infinite. With an infinite payback period, the project should be rejected. Also, as you would expect, Project B's NPV is negative. So far, the payback period and NPV methods have agreed on which projects to accept.

Project C: Project C has a payback period of two years: $250 + $250 = $500. Thus, according to the payback criteria, it should be accepted. However, the project's NPV is a negative $115, which indicates that the project should be rejected. Why the conflict? Look at the cash flows after the payback period of two years. In Year 3 the project requires an additional investment of $250 (a cash outflow) and now is in a deficit position; that is, the cumulative net cash balance is now only $250 ($250 + $250 – $250 = $250). Then, in the final year, the project earns an additional $250, recovering the cost of the total investment. The payback period analysis can lead to erroneous decisions because the rule does not consider cash flows after the payback period.

Projects D and E: Projects D and E dramatically illustrate the problem when a capital budgeting evaluation tool fails to consider cash flows after the payback period. Project D has a payback period of one year, suggesting that it should be accepted, and Project E has a payback period of 2.5 years, suggesting that it should be rejected. However, a simple look at the future cash flows suggests otherwise. It is clear that Project D, with a negative $5,000 cash flow in Year 4, is a disaster and should be rejected, while Project E, with a positive $5,000 cash flow in Year 4, should be accepted. Indeed, the NPV analysis confirms these conclusions: Project D has a negative NPV of $2,924, and Project E has a positive NPV of $2,815. In both instances, the payback rule led to the wrong economic decision. These examples illustrate that a rapid payback does not necessarily mean a good investment.

Discounted Payback Period

discounted payback period the length of time required to recover a project's initial cost, accounting for the time value of money

Another weakness of the ordinary payback period criteria is that it does not take into account the time value of money. All dollars received before the cutoff period are given equal weight. To address this problem, some financial managers use a variant of the payback period called the **discounted payback period**. This payback calculation is similar to the ordinary payback calculation except that the future cash flows are discounted by the cost of capital.

Time line	0	1	2	3 Year
Net cash flow (NCF)	−\$40,000	\$20,000	\$20,000	\$20,000
Cumulative NCF	−\$40,000	−\$20,000	\$0	\$20,000
Discounted NCF (at 10%)	−\$40,000	\$18,182	\$16,529	\$15,026
Cumulative discounted NCF	−\$40,000	−\$21,818	−\$5,289	\$9,737

Payback period = 2 years + \$0/\$20,000 per year = 2 years

Discounted payback period = 2 years + \$5,289/\$15,026 year = 2.35 years

Cost of capital = 10%

NPV = \$49,737 − \$40,000 = \$9,737

EXHIBIT 10.7 Discounted Payback Period Cash Flows and Calculations

The exhibit shows the net and cumulative net cash flows for a proposed capital project with an initial cost of \$40,000. The cash flow data are used to compute the discounted payback period for a 10 percent cost of capital, which is 2.35 years.

The major advantage of the discounted payback approach is that it tells management how long it takes a project to reach an NPV of zero. Thus, any capital project that meets a firm's decision rule must also have a positive NPV. This is an improvement over the standard payback calculation, which can lead to accepting projects with negative NPVs. Regardless of the improvement, the discounted payback method is not widely used by businesses, and it also ignores all cash flows after the arbitrary cutoff period, which is a major flaw.

To see how the discounted payback period is calculated, turn to **Exhibit 10.7**. The exhibit shows the net cash flows for a proposed capital project along with both the cumulative and discounted cumulative cash flows; thus, we can compute both the ordinary and the discounted payback periods for the project and then compare them. The cost of capital is 10 percent.

The first two rows show the nondiscounted cash flows, and we can see by inspection that the ordinary payback period is two years. We do not need to make any additional calculations because the cumulative cash flows equal zero at precisely two years. Now let's turn our attention to the lower two rows, which show the project's discounted and cumulative discounted cash flows. Note that the first year's cash flow is \$20,000 and its discounted value is \$18,182 (\$20,000 × (1/1.1) = \$18,182), and the second year's cash flow is also \$20,000 and its discounted value is \$16,529 (\$20,000 × $(1/(1.1)^2)$ = \$16,529). Now, looking at the cumulative discounted cash flows row, notice that it turns positive between two and three years. This means that the discounted payback period is two years plus some fraction of the third year's discounted cash flow. The exact discounted payback period computed value is 2 years + \$5,289/\$15,026 year = 2 years + 0.35 year = 2.35 years.

As expected, the discounted payback period is longer than the ordinary payback period (2 years < 2.35 years), and in 2.35 years the project will reach a NPV of \$0. The project NPV is positive (NPV = \$9,737); therefore, we should accept the project. But notice that the payback decision criteria are ambiguous. If we use 2.0 years as the payback criterion, we reject the project, and if we use 2.5 or 3.0 years as criterion, the project is accepted. The lack of a definitive decision rule remains a major problem with the payback period as a capital budgeting tool.

Evaluating the Payback Rule

The standard payback period is often calculated for projects because it provides an intuitive and simple measure of a project's liquidity risk. This makes sense because there is a strong feeling in business that "getting your money back quickly" is an important standard when making capital investments. This intuition can be economically justified if the firm faces payments to creditors before the payback date, or if estimates of project cash flows beyond the payback date are very uncertain. Probably the greatest advantage of the payback period is its simplicity; it is easy to calculate and easy to understand.

When compared with the NPV method, however, the payback methods have some serious shortcomings. First, the standard payback calculation does not adjust or account for the timing or risk associated with future cash flows. Second, there is little economic justification for the choice of the payback cutoff criteria other than a liquidity motive. Who is to say that a particular cutoff, such as two years, is optimal with regard to maximizing stockholder value? Finally, perhaps the greatest shortcoming of the payback method is its failure to consider cash flows after the payback period. As a result, the payback method is biased toward shorter-term projects and may cause managers to reject important positive NPV projects where cash inflows tend to occur farther in the future, such as research and development investments, new product launches, and entry into new lines of business.

While the payback period is relatively simple to calculate, it is important to note that payback requires forecasts of future project cash flows up to the established cutoff period. Furthermore, discounted payback requires that managers identify a project's discount rate. Thus the inputs into the payback and NPV methods are virtually identical. Consequently, using a payback method may not even save much time and effort in evaluating a project. The table below summarizes key advantages and disadvantages of the payback method.

Summary of Payback Method

Decision Rule:

Payback period ≤ Payback cutoff point ⇨ Accept the project.
Payback period > Payback cutoff point ⇨ Reject the project.

Key Advantages	Key Disadvantage
1. Easy to calculate and understand for people without a strong accounting and finance background. 2. A simple measure of a project's liquidity risk.	1. Most common version does not account for time value of money. 2. Does not consider cash flows past the payback period. 3. Bias against long-term projects such as research and development and new product launches. 4. Arbitrary cutoff point.

Before You Go On

1. What is the payback period?
2. Why does the payback period provide a measure of a project's liquidity risk?
3. What are the main shortcomings of the payback method?

10.4 The Accounting Rate of Return

LEARNING OBJECTIVE

4. Explain why the accounting rate of return (ARR) is not recommended for use as a capital expenditure decision-making tool.

accounting rate of return (ARR) a rate of return on a capital project based on average net income divided by average book value over the project's life; also called the *book value rate of return*

We turn next to a capital budgeting technique based on the **accounting rate of return (ARR)**, sometimes called the *book value rate of return*. This method computes the return on a capital project using accounting numbers—the project's net income (NI) and book value (BV)—rather than cash flow data. The ARR can be calculated in a number of ways, but the most common definition is:

$$\text{ARR} = \frac{\text{Average net income}}{\text{Average book value}} \tag{10.3}$$

where:

Average net income = $(NI_1 + NI_2 + \cdots + NI_n)/n$
Average book value = $(BV_0 + BV_1 + BV_2 + \cdots + BV_n)/(n + 1)$
n = the project's estimated life
BV_0 = the original cost of the asset

Although ARR is fairly easy to understand and calculate, as you probably guessed, it has major flaws as a tool for evaluating capital expenditure decisions. Instead of discounting a project's cash flows over time, it simply gives us a number based on average figures from the income statement and balance sheet. Thus, the ARR is based on accounting numbers and ignores the time value of money. Also, as with the payback method, there is no economic rationale that links a particular acceptance criterion to the goal of maximizing stockholder value.

Because of these major shortcomings, the ARR technique should not be used to evaluate the viability of capital projects under any circumstances. You may wonder why we even included the ARR technique in this book if it is a poor criterion for evaluating projects. The reason is simply that we want to be sure that if you run across the ARR method at work, you will recognize it and be aware of its shortcomings.

Before You Go On

1. What are the major shortcomings of using the accounting rate of return (ARR) method as a capital budgeting method?

10.5 Internal Rate of Return

LEARNING OBJECTIVE

5. Compute the internal rate of return (IRR) for a capital project and discuss the conditions under which the IRR technique and the NPV technique produce different results.

The **internal rate of return**, known in practice as the **IRR**, is an important alternative to the NPV method. The NPV and IRR techniques are closely related in that both involve discounting the cash flows from a project; thus, both account for the time value of money. When we use the NPV method to evaluate a capital project, the discount rate is the rate of return required by investors for investments with similar risk, which is the project's opportunity cost of capital. When we use the IRR, we are looking for the rate of return associated with a project so that we can determine whether this rate is higher or lower than the project's discount rate.

internal rate of return (IRR) the discount rate at which the present value of a project's expected cash inflows equals the present value of the project's outflows; it is the discount rate at which the project's NPV equals zero

We can define the IRR as the discount rate that equates the present value of a project's cost to the present value of its expected cash inflows:

$$\text{PV(Cost of the project)} = \text{PV(Expected cash inflows)}$$

This means that we can also describe the IRR as the discount rate that causes the NPV to equal zero. This relation can be written in a general form as follows:

$$\text{NPV} = \text{NCF}_0 + \frac{\text{NCF}_1}{1 + \text{IRR}} + \frac{\text{NCF}_2}{(1 + \text{IRR})^2} + \cdots + \frac{\text{NCF}_n}{(1 + \text{IRR})^n} \qquad (10.4)$$

$$= \sum_{t=0}^{n} \frac{\text{NCF}_t}{(1 + \text{IRR})^t} = 0$$

Because of their close relation, it may seem that the IRR and the NPV are interchangeable—that is, either should tell you to accept or reject the same capital projects. After all, both methods are based on whether the project's return exceeds the cost of capital and, hence, whether the project will add value to the firm. In many circumstances, the IRR and NPV methods do give us the same answer. As you will see later, however, some of the properties of the IRR equation can lead to incorrect decisions concerning whether to accept or reject a particular capital project.

Calculating the IRR

The IRR is an expected rate of return much like the yield to maturity we calculated for bonds in Chapter 8. Thus, in calculating the IRR, we need to apply the same trial-and-error method we used in Chapter 8. We will begin by doing some IRR calculations by trial and error so that you understand the process, and then we will switch to the financial calculator and computer spreadsheets, which provide an answer more quickly.

Trial-and-Error Method

Suppose that Ford Motor Company has an investment opportunity with cash flows as shown in **Exhibit 10.8** and that the cost of capital is 12 percent. We want to find the IRR for this project. Using Equation 10.4, we will substitute various values for IRR into the equation to compute the project's IRR by trial and error. We continue this process until we find the IRR value that makes Equation 10.4 equal zero.

A good starting point is to use the cost of capital as the discount rate. Note that when we discount the NCFs by the cost of capital, we are calculating the project's NPV:

$$\text{NPV} = \text{NCF}_0 + \frac{\text{NCF}_1}{1 + \text{IRR}} + \frac{\text{NCF}_2}{(1 + \text{IRR})^2} + \cdots + \frac{\text{NCF}_n}{(1 + \text{IRR})^n}$$

$$\text{NPV}_{12\%} = -\$560 + \frac{\$240}{1.12} + \frac{\$240}{(1.12)^2} + \frac{\$240}{(1.12)^3} = \$16.44$$

Recall that the result we are looking for is zero. Because our result is greater than zero ($16.44), the discount rate of 12 percent is too low, and we must try a higher rate. Let's try 13 percent:

$$\text{NPV}_{13\%} = -\$560 + \frac{\$240}{1.13} + \frac{\$240}{(1.13)^2} + \frac{\$240}{(1.13)^3} = \$6.68$$

We are very close; let's try 14 percent:

$$\text{NPV}_{14\%} = -\$560 + \frac{\$240}{1.14} + \frac{\$240}{(1.14)^2} + \frac{\$240}{(1.14)^3} = -\$2.81$$

Because our result is now a negative number, we know the correct rate is between 13 percent and 14 percent, and looking at the magnitude of the numbers, we know that the answer is closer to 14 percent. Let's try 13.7 percent.

$$\text{NPV}_{13.7\%} = -\$560 + \frac{\$240}{1.137} + \frac{\$240}{(1.137)^2} + \frac{\$240}{(1.137)^3} = 0$$

Good guess! This means that the NPV of Ford's capital project is zero at a discount rate of 13.7 percent. The required rate of return is the cost of capital, which is 12.0 percent. Since the project's IRR of 13.7 percent exceeds the cost of capital, the IRR criterion indicates that the project should be accepted.

	0	1	2	3 Year
Time line				
Net cash flow	−$560	$240	$240	$240

Cost of capital = 12%

NPV = $576.44 – $560.00 = $16.44

EXHIBIT 10.8 Time Line and Expected Net Cash Flows for the Ford Motor Company Project ($ thousands)

The cash flow data in the exhibit are used to compute the project's IRR. The project's NPV is a positive $16,440, which indicates that the IRR is greater than the cost of capital of 12 percent.

The project's NPV is a positive $16,440, which also indicates that Ford should go ahead with the project. Thus, both the IRR and NPV suggest the same conclusion.

Learning by Doing Application 10.3 and the following **Using Excel Example** illustrate additional IRR calculations.

When the IRR and NPV Methods Agree

In the Ford example, the IRR and NPV methods agree. The two methods will *always* agree when you are evaluating *independent* projects and the projects' cash flows are *conventional*. As discussed earlier, an independent project is one that can be selected with no effect on the viability of any other project. A project with **conventional cash flows** is one with an initial cash outflow followed by one or more cash inflows. Put another way, after the initial

conventional cash flow a cash flow pattern consisting of an initial cash outflow that is followed by one or more cash inflows

APPLICATION 10.3 | Calculating the IRR at Larry's Homemade Ice Cream Shop

LEARNING BY DOING

WileyPLUS

Need more help? Visit your WileyPLUS course.

Problem Larry's Homemade Ice Cream Shop in the DuPont Circle area of Washington, D.C., is famous for its gourmet ice cream. However, some customers have asked for a healthy, low-cal, soft yogurt. The machine that makes this confection is manufactured in Italy and costs $5,000 plus $1,750 for installation. Larry estimates that the machine will generate a net cash flow of $2,000 a year. Larry also estimates the machine's life to be 10 years and that it will have a $400 salvage value. His cost of capital is 15 percent. Larry thinks the machine is overpriced. Is he right?

Approach The IRR for an investment is the discount rate at which the NPV is zero. Thus, we can use Equation 10.4 to solve for the IRR and then compare this value with Larry's cost of capital. If the IRR is greater than the cost of capital, the project has a positive NPV and should be accepted.

Solution The total cost of the machine is $6,750 ($5,000 + $1,750 = $6,750), and the final cash flow in Year 10 is $2,400 ($2,000 + $400 = $2,400).

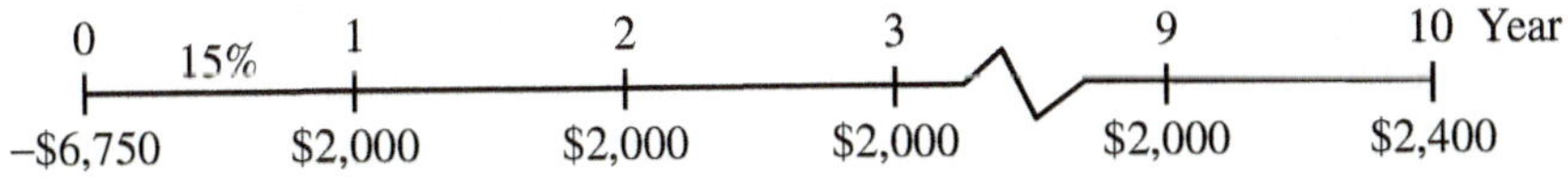

The hand trial-and-error calculations are shown below. The first calculation uses 15 percent, the cost of capital, our recommended starting point, and the answer is $3,386.41 (which is also the project's NPV). Because the value is a positive number, we need to use a discount rate larger than 15 percent. Our guess is 27.08 percent. At that value the NPV equals zero; thus, the IRR for the yogurt machine is 27.08 percent.

$$\text{NPV} = \text{NCF}_0 + \frac{\text{NCF}_1}{1 + \text{IRR}} + \frac{\text{NCF}_2}{(1 + \text{IRR})^2} + \cdots + \frac{\text{NCF}_n}{(1 + \text{IRR})^n} = 0$$

$$\text{NPV}_{15.00\%} = -\$6{,}750 + \frac{\$2{,}000}{1.15} + \frac{\$2{,}000}{(1.15)^2} + \cdots + \frac{\$2{,}400}{(1.15)^{10}} = \$3{,}386.41$$

$$\text{NPV}_{27.08\%} = -\$6{,}750 + \frac{\$2{,}000}{1.2708} + \frac{\$2{,}000}{(1.2708)^2} + \cdots + \frac{\$2{,}400}{(1.2708)^{10}} = \$0.00$$

Because the project's future cash flow pattern resembles that for a coupon bond, we can also solve for the IRR using a financial calculator, just as we would solve for the yield to maturity of a bond. Just enter the data directly into the corresponding keys on the calculator, press the interest key, and we have our answer: 27.08 percent.

	N	i	PV	PMT	FV
Enter	10		−6,750	2,000	400
Answer		**27.08**			

As with present value calculations, for projects with unequal cash flows, you should consult your financial calculator's manual.

Because the project's IRR exceeds Larry's cost of capital of 15 percent, the project should be accepted. Larry is wrong.

Using Excel

Internal Rate of Return

You know that calculating IRR by hand can be tedious. The trial-and-error method can take a long time and can be quite frustrating. Knowing all the cash flows and an approximate rate will allow you to use a spreadsheet formula to get an answer instantly.

The accompanying spreadsheet shows the setup for calculating the IRR for the low-cal yogurt machine at Larry's Homemade Ice Cream Shop that is described in Learning by Doing Application 10.3.

Here are a couple of important points to note about IRR calculations using spreadsheet programs:

1. Unlike the NPV formula, the IRR formula accounts for all cash flows, including the initial investment in Year 0, so there is no need to add this cash flow later.
2. The syntax of the IRR function requires that you first provide the project's cash flows in order beginning at time zero. To calculate the IRR, you will also need to provide a "guess" value, or a number you estimate is close to the IRR. A good value to start with is the cost of capital. To learn more about why this value is needed, you should go to your spreadsheet's help manual and search for "IRR."

◇	A	B	C	D	E
1					
2		IRR Calculations			
3					
4		Year		Cash Flow	
5		0		−$6,750	
6		1		2,000	
7		2		2,000	
8		3		2,000	
9		4		2,000	
10		5		2,000	
11		6		2,000	
12		7		2,000	
13		8		2,000	
14		9		2,000	
15		10		2,400	
16					
17		Cost of capital		0.15	
18					
19		IRR		27.08%	
20		Formula used		=IRR(D5:D15, D17)	
21					
22	Remember to keep track of signs—cash outflows are negative, and cash inflows are positive.				
23					
24					

investment is made (cash outflow), the net cash flow in each future year is positive (inflows). For example, the purchase of a bond involves conventional cash flows. You purchase the bond for a price (cash outflow), and in the future you receive coupon payments and a principal payment at maturity (cash inflows).

NPV profile a graph showing NPV as a function of the discount rate

Let's look more closely at the kinds of situations in which the NPV and the IRR methods agree. A good way to visualize the relation between the IRR and NPV methods is to graph NPV as a function of the discount rate. The graph, called an **NPV profile**, shows the NPV of the project at various costs of capital.

Exhibit 10.9 shows the NPV profile for the Ford Motor Company project. We have placed the NPVs on the vertical axis, or y-axis, and the discount rates on the horizontal axis, or x-axis. We used the calculations from our earlier example and made some additional NPV calculations at various discount rates as follows:

Discount Rate	NPV ($ thousands)
0%	$160
5	94
10	37
15	−12
20	−54
25	−92
30	−124

As you can see, a discount rate of 0 percent corresponds with an NPV of $160,000, a discount rate of 5 percent with an NPV of $94,000, and so forth. As the discount rate increases, the NPV curve declines smoothly. Not surprisingly, the curve intersects the x-axis at precisely the point where the NPV is 0 and the IRR is 13.7 percent.

The NPV profile in Exhibit 10.9 illustrates why the NPV and IRR methods lead to identical accept-reject decisions for the Ford Motor Company project. The IRR of 13.7 percent precisely marks the point at which the NPV changes from a positive to a negative value.

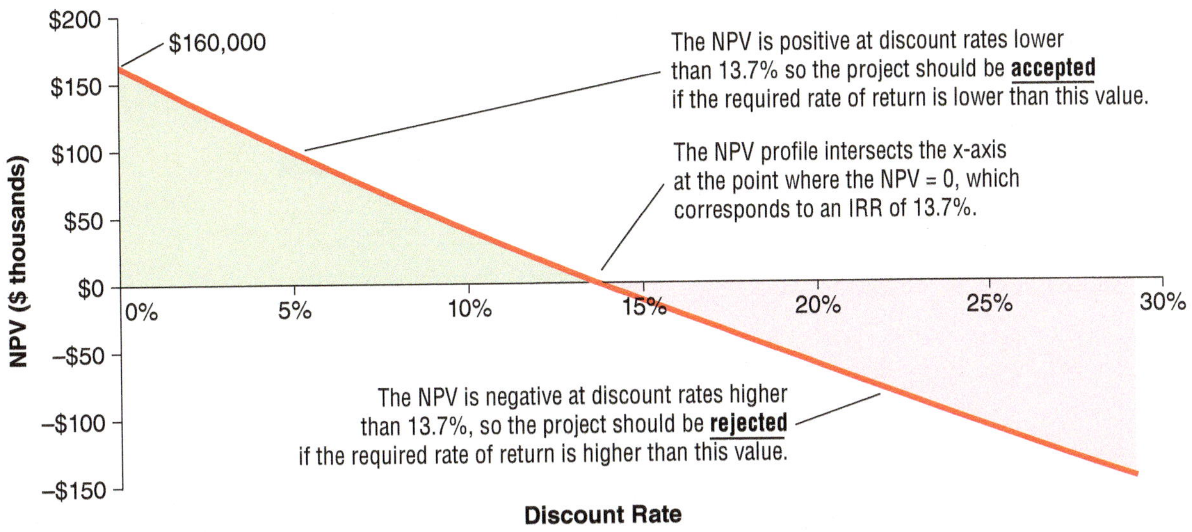

EXHIBIT 10.9 **NPV Profile for the Ford Motor Company Project**

In the NPV profile for the Ford Motor Company project, the NPV value is on the vertical (y) axis and the discount rate is on the horizontal (x) axis. You can see that as the discount rate increases, the NPV profile curve declines smoothly and intersects the x-axis at the point where the NPV is 0. The IRR of 13.7 percent is the point at which the NPV changes from a positive to a negative value. The NPV and IRR methods lead to identical accept-or-reject decisions for the Ford Motor Company project.

Whenever a project is independent and has conventional cash flows, the result will be as shown in the exhibit. The NPV will decline as the discount rate increases, and the IRR and the NPV methods will result in the same capital expenditure decision.

When the NPV and IRR Methods Disagree

We have seen that the IRR and NPV methods lead to identical investment decisions for capital projects that are independent and that have conventional cash flows. However, if either of these conditions is not met, the IRR and NPV methods can produce different accept-reject decisions.

Unconventional Cash Flows

Unconventional cash flows can cause a conflict between the NPV and IRR decision rules. In some instances the cash flows for an unconventional project are just the reverse of those of a conventional project: the initial cash flow is positive, and all subsequent cash flows are negative. In this case, we need only reverse the IRR decision rule and accept the project if the IRR is *less* than the cost of capital to make the IRR and NPV methods agree.

When a project's future cash flows include both positive and negative cash flows, the situation is more complicated. An example of such a project is an assembly line that will require one or more major renovations over its lifetime. Another common business situation is a project that has conventional cash flows except for the final cash flow, which is negative. The final cash flow might be negative because extensive environmental cleanup is required at the end of the project, such as the cost for decommissioning a nuclear power plant, or because the equipment originally purchased has little or no salvage value and is expensive to remove.

Consider an example. Suppose a firm invests in a gold-mining operation that costs $55 million and has an expected life of two years. In the first year, the project generates a cash inflow of $150 million. In the second year, extensive environmental and site restoration is required, so the expected cash flow is a negative $100 million. The time line for these cash flows follows.

	0	1	2 Year
Cash flow ($ millions)	−$55	$150	−$100

Once again, the best way to understand the effect of these cash flows is to look at an NPV profile. Shown here are NPV calculations we made at various discount rates to generate the data necessary to plot the NPV profile shown in **Exhibit 10.10**:

Discount Rate	NPV ($ millions)
0%	−$5.00
10	−1.28
20	0.56
30	1.21
40	1.12
50	0.56
60	−0.31
70	−1.37

Looking at the data in the table, you can probably spot a problem. The NPV is initially negative (−$5.00); then, at a discount rate of 20 percent, switches to positive ($0.56); and then, at a discount rate of 60 percent, switches back to negative (−$0.31).

The NPV profile in Exhibit 10.10 shows the results of this pattern: we have two IRRs, one at 16.05 percent and the other at 55.65 percent. Which is the correct IRR, or are both correct? Actually, there is no correct answer; the results are meaningless, and you should not try to interpret them. Thus, in this situation, the IRR technique provides information that should not be used for decision making.

How many IRR solutions can there be for a given cash flow? The maximum number of IRR solutions is equal to the number of sign reversals in the cash flow stream. For a project with a conventional cash flow, there is only one cash flow sign reversal; thus, there is only one IRR solution. In our mining example, there are two cash flow sign reversals; thus, there are two IRR solutions.

Finally, for some cash flow patterns, it is impossible to compute an IRR. These situations can occur when the initial cash flow ($t = 0$) is either a cash inflow or outflow and is followed by cash flows with two or more sign reversals. An example of such a cash flow pattern is $NCF_0 =$ $15, $NCF_1 = -\$25$, and $NCF_2 = \$20$. This type of cash flow pattern might occur on a building project where the contractor is given a prepayment, usually the cost of materials and supplies ($15); then does the construction and pays the labor cost ($25); and finally, upon completion

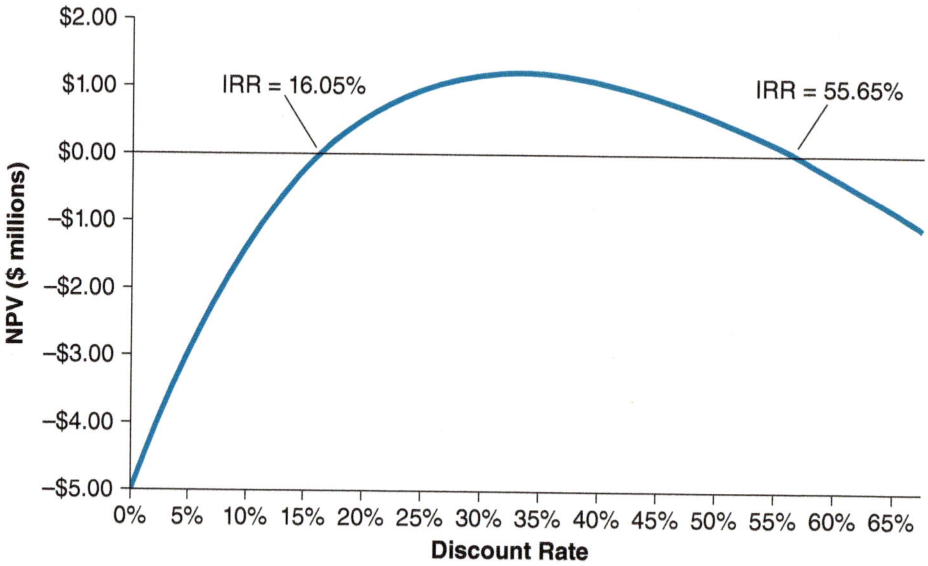

EXHIBIT 10.10 **NPV Profile for Gold-Mining Operation with Multiple IRR Solutions**

The gold-mining operation has unconventional cash flows. Because there are two cash flow sign reversals, we end up with two IRRs—16.05 percent and 55.65 percent—neither of them useful. In situations like this, the IRR provides a solution that is meaningless and, therefore, the results should not be used for capital budgeting decisions.

of the work, receives the final payment ($20). Note that when it is not possible to compute an IRR, the project either has a positive NPV or a negative NPV for all possible discount rates. In this example, the NPV is always positive.

Mutually Exclusive Projects

The other situation in which the IRR can lead to incorrect capital budgeting decisions is when projects are mutually exclusive—that is, when accepting one project means rejecting the other. For example, suppose you own a small store in the business district of Seattle that is currently vacant. You are looking at two business opportunities: opening an upscale coffee house or opening a copy center. Since you cannot pursue both projects at the same location, they are mutually exclusive.

When you have mutually exclusive projects, how do you select the best alternative? If you are using the NPV method, the answer is easy. You select the project that has the highest NPV because it will increase the value of the firm by the largest amount. If you are using the IRR method, it would seem logical to select the project with the highest IRR. In this case, though, the logic is wrong! You cannot tell which mutually exclusive project to select just by looking at the projects' IRRs.

Let's consider another example to illustrate the problem. The cash flows for two projects, A and B, are as follows:

Year	Project A	Project B
0	−$100	−$100
1	50	20
2	40	30
3	30	50
4	30	65

The IRR is 20.7 percent for Project A and 19.0 percent for Project B. Because the two projects are mutually exclusive, only one project can be accepted. If you were following the IRR decision rule, you would accept Project A. However, as you will see, it turns out that Project B might be the better choice.

The following table shows the NPVs for the two projects at several discount rates:

Discount Rate	NPV of Project A	NPV of Project B
0%	$50.0	$65.0
5	34.5	42.9
10	21.5	24.9
13	14.8	15.7
15	10.6	10.1
20	1.3	−2.2
25	−6.8	−12.6
30	−13.7	−21.3
IRR	20.7%	19.0%

Notice that the NPV of each project depends on the rate of return used to discount the cash flows. Our example shows a conflict in the ranking order between the IRR and NPV methods at discount rates between 0 percent and 13 percent. In this range, Project B has the lower IRR, but it has the higher NPV and should be the project selected. If the discount rate is 15 percent or above, however, Project A has the higher NPV as well as the higher IRR. In this range, there is no conflict between the two evaluation methods.

The relative IRR and NPV rankings change in this way because the larger cash inflows of Project B arrive later than the larger cash flows of Project A. Thus, higher discount rates have more of an impact on the value of Project B. In other words, changes in relative IRR and NPV rankings result from differences in the timing of project cash flows.

Now take a look at **Exhibit 10.11**, which shows the NPV profiles for Projects A and B. As you can see, there is a point, called the **crossover point**, at which the NPV profiles for Projects A and B intersect. The crossover point here is at a discount rate of 14.3 percent. For any cost

Weblink

To read an article that warns finance managers using the IRR about the method's pitfalls, visit www.cfo.com/printable/article.cfm/3304945?f=options.

crossover point the discount rate at which the NPV profiles of two projects cross and, thus, at which the NPVs of the projects are equal

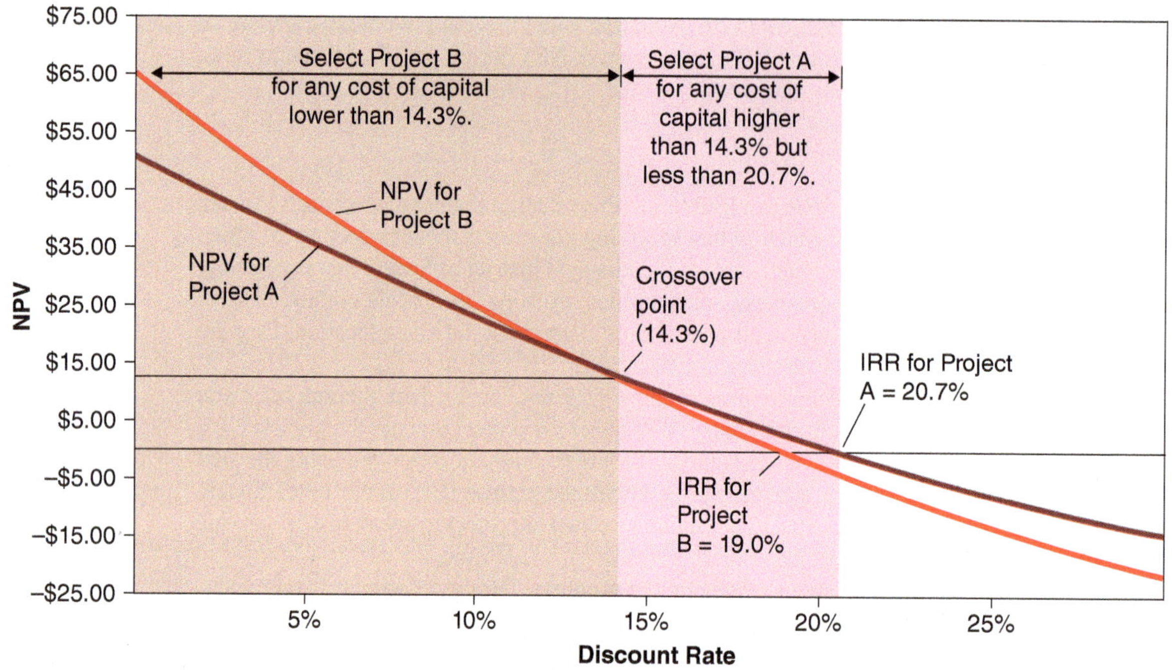

EXHIBIT 10.11 NPV Profiles for Two Mutually Exclusive Projects

The NPV profiles for two projects often cross over each other. When evaluating mutually exclusive projects, it is helpful to know where this crossover point is. For Projects A and B in the exhibit, the crossover point is at 14.3 percent. For any cost of capital above 14.3 percent but below 20.7 percent, the NPV for Project A is higher than that for Project B and is positive; thus, Project A should be selected. For any cost of capital below the crossover point, the NPV of Project B is higher, and Project B should be selected.

of capital above 14.3 percent, the NPV for Project A is higher than that for Project B; thus, Project A should be selected if its NPV is positive. For any cost of capital below the crossover point, Project B should be selected.

Another conflict involving mutually exclusive projects concerns comparisons of projects that have significantly different costs. The IRR does not adjust for these differences in the scale of projects. What the IRR gives us is a rate of return on each dollar invested. In contrast, the NPV method computes the total dollar value created by the project.

Decision Making Example 10.2 illustrates how this conflict can distort investment decisions when using the IRR criteria to evaluate mutually exclusive projects.

Modified Internal Rate of Return (MIRR)

A major weakness of the IRR method compared with the NPV method concerns the rate at which the cash flows generated by a capital project are reinvested. The NPV method assumes that cash flows from a project are reinvested at the cost of capital, whereas the IRR technique assumes they are reinvested at the IRR. Determining which is the better assumption depends on which rate better represents the rate that firms can actually earn when they reinvest a project's cash flows over time. It is generally believed that the cost of capital, which is often lower than the IRR, better reflects the rate that firms are likely to earn. Using the IRR may thus involve overly optimistic assumptions regarding reinvestment rates.

modified internal rate of return (MIRR) an internal rate of return (IRR) measure, which assumes that cash inflows are reinvested at the opportunity cost of capital until the end of the project

To eliminate the reinvestment rate assumption of the IRR, some practitioners prefer to calculate the **modified internal rate of return (MIRR)**. In this approach, each operating cash flow is converted to a future value at the end of the project's life, compounded at the cost of capital. These values are then summed up to get the *project's future value* (PFV). The MIRR is the interest rate that equates the project's cost (PV_{Cost}), or cash outflows, with the future value of the project's cash inflows at the end of the project (PV_{PFV}).[1] Because each future value is computed using the cost of capital as the interest rate, the reinvestment rate problem is eliminated.

[1] As we pointed out in Chapters 5 and 6, financial decision-making problems can be solved either by discounting cash flows to the beginning of the project or by using compounding to find the future value of cash flows at the end of a project's life.

EXAMPLE 10.2 | The Lemonade Stand versus the Convenience Store

DECISION MAKING

Situation Suppose you work for an entrepreneur who owns a number of small businesses in Fresno, California, as well as a small piece of property near California State University at Fresno, which he believes would be an ideal site for a student-oriented convenience store. His 7-year-old son, who happens to be in the office after school, says he has a better idea: his father should open a lemonade stand. Your boss tells you to find the NPV and IRR for both projects, assuming a 10 percent discount rate. After collecting data, you present the following analysis:

Year	Lemonade Stand	Convenience Store
0	−\$1,000	−\$1,000,000
1	850	372,000
2	850	372,000
3	850	372,000
4	850	372,000
IRR	76.2%	18.0%
NPV	\$1,694	\$179,190

Assuming the projects are mutually exclusive, which should be selected?

Decision Your boss, who favors the IRR method, looks at the analysis and declares his son a genius. The IRR decision rule suggests that the lemonade stand, with its 76.2 percent rate of return, is the project to choose! You point out that the goal of capital budgeting is to select projects, or combinations of projects, that maximize the value of the firm, his business. The convenience store adds by far the greater value: \$179,190 compared with only \$1,694 for the lemonade stand. Although the lemonade stand has a high rate of return, its small size precludes it from being competitive against the larger project.

We can set up the equation for the MIRR in the same way we set up Equation 10.4 for the IRR:

$$\text{PV(Cost of the project)} = \text{PV(Expected cash inflows)}$$

$$\text{PV}_{\text{Cost}} = \text{PV}_{\text{PFV}}$$

$$\text{PV}_{\text{Cost}} = \frac{\text{PFV}}{(1 + \text{MIRR})^n} \tag{10.5}$$

To compute the MIRR, we have to make two preliminary calculations. First, we calculate the value of PV_{Cost}, which is the present value of the cash outflows that make up the investment cost of the project. Since for most capital projects, the investment cost cash flows are incurred at the beginning of the project, $t = 0$, there is often no need to calculate a present value. If investment costs are incurred over time ($t > 0$), then the cash flows must be discounted at the cost of capital.

Second, we need to compute the project's future value (PFV). To do this, we find the future value of each operating cash flow at the end of the project's life, compounded at the cost of capital. We then sum up these future values to get the PFV. Mathematically, the PFV can be expressed as:

$$\begin{aligned}\text{PFV} &= [\text{CF}_1 \times (1 + k)^{n-1}] + [\text{CF}_2 \times (1 + k)^{n-2}] + \ldots + [\text{CF}_n \times (1 + k)^{n-n}] \\ &= \sum_{t=1}^{n} \text{CF}_t \times (1 + k)^{n-t}\end{aligned}$$

where:

PFV = the project's future value
CF_t = cash flow from operations in period t
k = the cost of capital
n = the project life

Once we have computed the values of PV_{Cost} and PFV, we use Equation 10.5 to compute the MIRR. Note that by combining intermediate cash flows into a single future value, MIRR has the added advantage of always yielding a conventional cash flow.

To illustrate, let's return to the Ford Motor Company example shown in Exhibit 10.8. Recall that the cost of the project is \$560, incurred at $t = 0$, and that the discount rate is 12 percent. To determine the MIRR for the project, we start by calculating the future value of the cash flows, as shown on the following time line:

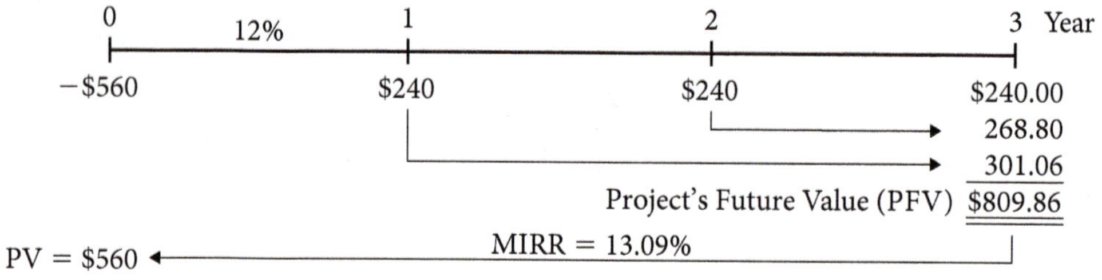

The project's future value of \$809.86 equals the sum of the \$240 in Year 1 compounded at 12 percent for two years plus the \$240 in Year 2 compounded at 12 percent for one year plus the \$240 in Year 3. Mathematically, this calculation is:

$$\begin{aligned} \text{PFV} &= [\text{CF}_1 \times (1 + k)^{n-1}] + [\text{CF}_2 \times (1 + k)^{n-2}] + \cdots + [\text{CF}_n \times (1 + k)^{n-n}] \\ &= [\$240 \times (1.12)^2] + [\$240 \times 1.12] + \$240 = \$809.86 \end{aligned}$$

With the information that the cost of the project is \$560 and the PFV is \$809.86, we can calculate the MIRR using Equation 10.5:

$$\begin{aligned} \text{PV}_{\text{Cost}} &= \frac{\text{PFV}}{(1 + \text{MIRR})^n} \\ \$560 &= \frac{\$809.86}{(1 + \text{MIRR})^3} \\ (1 + \text{MIRR})^3 &= \frac{\$809.86}{\$560} = 1.4462 \\ 1 + \text{MIRR} &= (1.4462)^{1/3} = 1.1309 \\ \text{MIRR} &= 1.1309 - 1 = 0.1309 \\ &= 13.09\% \end{aligned}$$

At 13.09 percent, the MIRR is higher than Ford's cost of capital of 12 percent, so the project should be accepted.

IRR versus NPV: A Final Comment

The IRR method, as noted, is an important alternative to the NPV method. As we have seen, it accounts for the time value of money, which is not true of methods such as the payback period and accounting rate of return. Furthermore, the IRR technique has great intuitive appeal. Many business practitioners are in the habit of thinking in terms of rates of return, whether the rates relate to their common-stock portfolios or their firms' capital expenditures. To these practitioners, the IRR method just seems to make sense. Indeed, we suspect that the IRR's popularity with business managers results more from its simple intuitive appeal than from its merit.

On the downside, we have seen that the IRR method has several flaws. For example, IRR can't be used effectively for projects with unconventional cash flows, and IRR can lead to incorrect investment decisions when it is used to choose between mutually exclusive projects. MIRR addresses some of the shortcomings of IRR; namely, it does not assume that project proceeds are reinvested at the IRR, and it eliminates issues associated with unconventional project cash flows. Nonetheless, we believe that NPV should be the primary method used to make capital budgeting decisions. Investment decisions made using NPV are always consistent with the goal of maximizing the value of the firm, even when discriminating between mutually exclusive projects. Finally, it is important to note that the IRR, MIRR, and NPV methods all require a set of projected cash flows over the life of the project and a discount rate. Thus, using IRR or MIRR, rather than NPV, does not require less effort from financial managers.

Summary of Internal Rate of Return (IRR) Method

Decision Rule: IRR > Cost of capital ⇨ Accept the project.
IRR < Cost of capital ⇨ Reject the project.

Key Advantages	Key Disadvantage
1. Intuitive and easy to understand. 2. Based on discounted cash flow technique.	1. With nonconventional cash flows, IRR approach can yield no usable answer or multiple answers. 2. A lower IRR can be better if a cash inflow is followed by cash outflows. 3. With mutually exclusive projects, IRR can lead to incorrect investment decisions. 4. IRR calculation assumes cash flows are reinvested at the IRR.

Before You Go On

1. What is the internal rate of return (IRR) method?
2. Under what circumstances do the NPV and IRR decision rules always yield the same decision?
3. In capital budgeting, what is a conventional cash flow pattern?
4. Why should the NPV method be the primary decision tool used in making capital investment decisions?

10.6 Investment Decisions with Capital Rationing

LEARNING OBJECTIVE

6. Explain how the profitability index can be used to rank projects when a firm faces capital rationing and describe the limitations that apply to the profitability index.

Our discussion of capital budgeting so far has focused on determining whether an individual project creates value for stockholders. Although the analytical methods we have discussed are critical components of the capital budgeting process, they do not tell us what to do when, as is often the case, a firm does not have enough money to invest in all available positive NPV projects. In other words, they do not tell us how to identify the *bundle* or combination of positive NPV projects that creates the greatest total value for stockholders when there are capital constraints or, as we called it earlier in this chapter, *capital rationing*.

In an ideal world we could accept all positive NPV projects because we would be able to finance them. If managers and investors agreed on which projects had positive NPVs, investors would provide capital to those projects because returns from them would be greater than the returns the investors could earn elsewhere in the capital markets. However, the world is not ideal, and firms often cannot invest in all of the available projects with positive NPVs. It can be difficult for outside investors to accurately assess the risks and returns associated with the firm's projects. Consequently, investors may require returns for their capital that are too high, and the firm may face capital constraints. Managers might be forced to reject some positive NPV projects because investors are not providing enough capital to fund those projects at reasonable rates.

Capital Rationing in a Single Period

profitability index (PI) a measure of the value a project generates for each dollar invested in that project

The basic principle that we follow in choosing the set of projects that creates the greatest value in a given period is to select the projects that yield the largest value *per dollar invested.* We can do this by computing the **profitability index (PI)** for each project and choosing the projects with the largest profitability indexes until we run out of money. The profitability index is computed as follows:

$$PI = \frac{\text{Benefits}}{\text{Costs}} = \frac{\text{Present value of future free cash flows}}{\text{Initial investment}} = \frac{\text{NPV} + \text{Initial investment}}{\text{Initial investment}} \quad (10.6)$$

where Initial investment is the up-front investment required to fund the project.

To illustrate, let's suppose you run a lawn mowing business and are considering buying a new lawn mower. Assume that the new mower would cost $2,000 and would bring in net cash flows of $7,000 for four years. With a discount rate of 10 percent, the NPV of this mower is $20,189 and its PI is calculated as follows:

$$PI = (\$20{,}189 + \$2{,}000)/\$2{,}000 = 11.09$$

This means that an investment in the new mower is expected to generate $11.09 of value for every dollar invested.

Now consider the case in which we have several projects to choose from in a given year but do not have enough money to invest in all of them. For example, suppose that we have identified the four positive NPV projects listed in **Exhibit 10.12** and have only $10,000 to invest. How do we choose from among the four projects when we cannot afford to invest in all of them?

Our objective in a case such as this is to identify the bundle or combination of positive NPV projects that creates the greatest total value for stockholders. The PI is helpful in such a situation because it helps us choose the projects that create the most value per dollar invested. We use the PI to do this by following a four-step procedure:

1. Calculate the PI for each project.
2. Rank the projects from highest PI to lowest PI.
3. Starting at the top of the list (the project with the highest PI) and working your way down (to the project with the lowest PI), select the projects that the firm can afford.
4. Repeat the third step by starting with the second project on the list, the third project on the list, and so on to make sure that a more valuable bundle cannot be identified.

Applying this process to the projects in Exhibit 10.12, we would choose to accept Projects A, B, and D. We would begin by choosing Projects A and B because they have the largest PIs and we have enough money to invest in both. Since choosing Projects A and B means we would no longer have enough money to invest in Project C, we would skip C and choose D, for which we do have enough money. Projects A, B, and D would generate a total of $7,500 in total value for stockholders. Following the fourth step reveals that no other combination of projects has a larger total NPV than Projects A, B, and D, so we would select these projects.

Learning by Doing Application 10.4 and **Decision Making Example 10.3** illustrate the calculation of PIs for projects and their use in making investment decisions.

EXHIBIT 10.12 Positive NPV Investments This Year

With only $10,000 to invest, how do we choose among these four positive NPV projects? The exhibit shows the yearly free cash flows, NPV, and profitability index (PI) for the projects. The PI values indicate the value of the expected future free cash flows per dollar invested in each project.

Project	Year 0	Year 1	Year 2	NPV @ 10%	PI
A	−$5,000	$5,500	$6,050	$5,000	2.000
B	−$3,000	$2,000	$3,850	$2,000	1.667
C	−$3,000	$4,400	$0	$1,000	1.333
D	−$2,000	$1,500	$1,375	$500	1.250

LEARNING BY DOING

APPLICATION 10.4 | Ranking Projects Using the Profitability Index

Problem You have identified the following seven positive NPV investments for your in-home computer-support business. If you have $50,000 to invest this year, which projects should you accept?

Project	Investment	NPV @ 10%
Buy new notebook computer	$ 3,000	$ 500
Buy employee training program	8,000	4,000
Buy new tool set	500	1,000
Buy office condo	40,000	5,000
Buy used car	12,000	4,000
Paint existing cars	4,000	2,000
Buy new test equipment	10,000	2,000

Approach Use the four-step procedure presented in the text to determine which projects you should accept.

Solution Calculating the PI and ranking the projects from highest to lowest PI yields the following:

Project	Investment	NPV @ 10%	PI
Buy new tool set	$ 500	$1,000	$1,500/$500 = 3.000
Buy employee training program	8,000	4,000	$12,000/$8,000 = 1.500
Paint existing cars	4,000	2,000	$6,000/$4,000 = 1.500
Buy used car	12,000	4,000	$16,000/$12,000 = 1.333
Buy new test equipment	10,000	2,000	$12,000/$10,000 = 1.200
Buy new notebook computer	3,000	500	$3,500/$3,000 = 1.167
Buy office condo	40,000	5,000	$45,000/$40,000 = 1.125

With $50,000 to invest, you should invest in all projects except the office condo. This strategy will require $37,500 and is expected to result in a total NPV of $13,500. The $12,500 that you have left over, which is not enough to buy the office condo, can be held in the business until an appropriate use for the money is identified, or it can be distributed to the stockholder (you).

DECISION MAKING

EXAMPLE 10.3 | Ranking Investment Alternatives

Situation The profitability index concept does not apply only to a firm's investments in projects. It can also apply to your personal investments. For example, suppose that you have just inherited $50,000 and want to invest it in ways that create as much value as possible. After researching investment alternatives, you have identified five investments that you believe will have positive NPVs. You estimate that the NPVs and PIs for these investments are as follows:

Project	Investment	NPV	PI
But a new car for your business	$20,000	$10,000	1.500
Buy a duplex apartment near campus	50,000	22,500	1.450
Start a small moving business	25,000	10,000	1.400
Invest in your roommate's Internet business	15,000	5,000	1.333
Buy a collection of old comic books	5,000	1,000	1.200

Which investment(s) should you choose?

Decision You should invest in the duplex apartment. If you began the selection process by choosing the new car because it has the largest PI and then work your way down the list until you reach a total investment of $50,000, you will see that you can invest in the car, the moving business, and the comic books. These three investments have a total NPV of $21,000. However, the investment in the duplex apartment alone has an NPV of $22,500. Investing in the duplex apartment will create more total value.

This problem illustrates why the procedure for using PI to choose projects has four steps. Without the fourth step, which tells us to repeat the third step beginning with the second project, the third project, and so on, we would not have identified the duplex apartment as the best alternative.

Capital Rationing across Multiple Periods

The PI concept is relatively straightforward and easy to apply if you are choosing among projects in a single period. However, if you are faced with capital rationing over several years, the investments you choose this year can affect your ability to make investments in future years. This can happen if you plan on reinvesting some or all of the cash flows generated by the projects you invest in this year. In such a situation, you cannot rely solely on the PI to identify the projects you should invest in this year. You must maximize the total NPV across all of the years in which you will be investing.

Let's look more closely at how multiperiod concerns can cause you to deviate from PI-based investment choices in a given year. Suppose you operate a business that will generate $10,000 per year for new investments. Furthermore, suppose that today (Year 0) you are choosing among Projects A, B, C, and D in **Exhibit 10.13** and that, based on the PIs of the individual projects, you choose to invest in Projects A, B, and D. The total NPV from these projects will be $7,500, and the total Year 1 cash flow from them will be $9,000 ($5,500 + $2,000 + $1,500 = $9,000).

Now suppose that you expect Projects F, G, and H to be available next year (Year 1). If other operations yield $10,000 for investments next year, you will have a total of $19,000 to invest in Year 1. With this amount of money, you can invest in Projects F and H, which require a total investment of $15,000 and have a combined NPV of $9,546 ($9,091 + $455 = $9,546). Therefore, in Year 0 dollars, the total value created from investing activities over the two years will be $17,046 ($7,500 + $9,546 = $17,046).

While $17,046 is a lot of value for a total investment of $25,000 ($10,000 today and $15,000 in Year 1), you could do better. Notice that if, instead of Projects A, B, and D, you invest in Projects A, C, and D today, you will have enough cash in Year 1 to invest in Projects F and G. This strategy would yield a total NPV of $21,955 ($5,000 + $1,000 + $500 + $9,091 + $6,364 = $21,955)! Ranking and selecting the projects today based on the PI would have yielded a bundle of projects over two years with a lower NPV. This illustrates an important limitation of the profitability index. It does not tell us enough to make informed decisions over multiple periods. Solving a multiple-period problem requires the application of more advanced analytical techniques, such as linear programming, that are beyond the scope of this book.

Weblink

If you have a strong math background and are interested, you can learn more about linear programming at http://www.purplemath.com/modules/linprog.htm.

EXHIBIT 10.13 **Positive NPV Investments for Two Years**

Investment decision making with capital rationing becomes more complex when multiple periods are involved. This exhibit shows the yearly free cash flows, NPV, and profitability index (PI) for the four positive NPV projects in Exhibit 10.12 and for three other positive-NPV projects that are expected to become available in Year 1.

Project	Year 0	Year 1	Year 2	Year 3	Year 0 NPV @ 10%	PI
A	−$5,000	$5,500	$6,050	$0	$5,000	2.000
B	−$3,000	$2,000	$3,850	$0	$2,000	1.667
C	−$3,000	$4,400	$0	$0	$1,000	1.333
D	−$2,000	$1,500	$1,375	$0	$500	1.250
F		−$10,000	$12,000	$11,000	$9,091	1.909
G		−$10,000	$8,000	$11,770	$6,364	1.636
H		−$5,000	$4,000	$2,255	$455	1.091

Before You Go On

1. What might cause a firm to face capital constraints?
2. What decision criteria should managers use in selecting projects when a firm faces capital constraints?
3. How can the profitability index (PI) help in choosing projects when a firm faces capital constraints? What are its limitations?

10.7 Capital Budgeting in Practice

LEARNING OBJECTIVE

7. Explain the benefits of postaudit and periodic reviews of capital projects.

Capital expenditures are big-ticket items in the U.S. economy. According to the World Bank, capital investment in the United States totaled $3.63 trillion in 2015. Capital investments also represent large expenditures for individual firms, though the amount spent can vary widely from year to year. For example, AT&T invested heavily in its network capabilities in 2016, and its $21.5 billion in capital expenditures that year exceeded those of all but a very small number of firms in the world. More typical are the capital expenditure totals for Caterpillar, Microsoft, and Kellogg Company, which are shown in the following table. Given the large dollar amounts and the strategic importance of capital expenditures, it is no surprise that corporate managers spend considerable time and energy analyzing capital projects.

Company	2016 Capital Expenditures ($ billions)	2016 Sales ($ billions)	Capital Expenditures as a Percentage of Sales
AT&T, Inc.	$21.5	$163.8	13.1%
Caterpillar, Inc.	2.9	38.5	7.5
Microsoft Corp.	8.3	85.3	9.7
Kellogg Company	0.5	13.0	3.8

Practitioners' Methods of Choice

Because of the importance of capital budgeting, over the years a number of surveys have asked financial managers what techniques they actually use in making capital investment decisions. Exhibit 10.14, which summarizes the results from two such studies, reveals significant changes over time. As shown, in 1981 only 16.5 percent of the financial managers surveyed frequently used the NPV approach, and the payback period and accounting rate of return approaches were used even less frequently. Most firms, 65.3 percent, used the IRR method. However, practices changed in the 1980s and 1990s. By 1999, 74.9 percent of the firms surveyed were frequently using the NPV technique, 75.7 percent were using the IRR, and 56.7 percent were using the payback period method. As you can see, the most recent findings reflect a much better alignment between what practitioners do and the theory discussed in this chapter. As you can also see, many financial managers use multiple capital budgeting tools.

Weblink

An article that surveys the use of capital budgeting techniques by the CFOs of Fortune 500 companies can be found at https://faculty.fuqua.duke.edu/~charvey/Research/Published_Papers/P76_How_do_CFOs.pdf.

EXHIBIT 10.14 Capital Budgeting Techniques Used by Business Firms

The exhibit summarizes evidence from two studies that examined the use of capital budgeting techniques by businesses. As you can see, over time more firms have come to use the NPV and IRR techniques. Surprisingly, though, even in 1999, 20.3 percent still computed the accounting rate of return.

	Percent of Surveyed Firms That Use the Technique Frequently	
Capital Budgeting Tool	1981	1999
Payback period	5.0%	56.7%
Accounting rate of return (ARR)	10.7	20.3
Internal rate of return (IRR)	65.3	75.7
Net present value (NPV)	16.5	74.9

Sources: Stanley, Marjorie T., and Stanley B. Block, "A Survey of Multinational Capital Budgeting," *The Financial Review*, March 1984. Graham, John R., and Campbell R. Harvey, "The Theory and Practice of Corporate Finance," *Journal of Financial Economics*, May/June 2001.

Postaudit and Periodic Reviews

postaudit review an audit to compare actual project results with the results projected in the capital budgeting proposal

Some firms have policies that require periodic reviews of the status of ongoing capital projects and postaudit reviews of completed capital projects. In a **postaudit review**, management compares the actual performance of a project with what was projected in the capital budgeting proposal. For example, suppose a new microchip production line was expected to earn a 20 percent IRR, but the project's actual IRR turned out to be 9 percent. A postaudit examination would determine why the project failed to achieve its expected financial goals. Project reviews keep all people involved in the capital budgeting process honest because they know that the project and their performance will be reviewed and that they will be held accountable for the results.

Periodic reviews of the status of ongoing capital projects provide useful information about a firm's business plan, including the cash flow projections and the operating cost assumptions. Business plans are management's best estimates of future events at the time they are prepared, but as new information becomes available, managers use this information to adjust their plans.

Managers also use information from periodic reviews to evaluate the people responsible for implementing a capital project. In doing this they determine whether the project's revenues and expenses are meeting projections. If the project is not proceeding according to plan, they try to determine whether the problem is a flawed plan or poor execution by the implementation team. If the problem is poor execution, the project's performance might be improved by putting a new team in place.

Before You Go On

1. What changes have taken place in the capital budgeting techniques used by U.S. companies?

Summary of Learning Objectives

1 Discuss why capital budgeting decisions are the most important investment decisions made by a firm's management.

Capital budgeting is the process by which management decides which productive assets the firm should invest in. Because capital expenditures involve large amounts of money, are critical to achieving the firm's strategic plan, define the firm's line of business over the long term, and determine the firm's profitability for years to come, they are the most important investment decisions made by management.

2 Explain the benefits of using the net present value (NPV) method to analyze capital expenditure decisions and calculate the NPV for a capital project.

The net present value (NPV) method leads to better investment decisions than other techniques because it (1) uses the discounted cash flow valuation approach, which accounts for the time value of money and (2) provides a direct measure of how much a capital project is expected to increase the dollar value of the firm. Thus, NPV is consistent with the top management goal of maximizing stockholder value. NPV calculations are described in Section 10.2 and Learning by Doing Application 10.1.

3 Describe the strengths and weaknesses of the payback period as a capital expenditure decision-making tool and compute the payback period for a capital project.

The payback period is the length of time it will take for the cash flows from a project to recover the cost of the project. The payback period is widely used, mainly because it is simple to apply and easy to understand. It also provides a simple measure of liquidity risk because it tells management how quickly the firm will get its money back. The payback period has a number of shortcomings, however. For one thing, the payback period, as most commonly computed, ignores the time value of money. We can overcome this objection by using discounted cash flows to calculate the payback period. Regardless of how the payback period is calculated, however, it fails to take account of cash flows recovered after the payback period. Thus, the payback period is biased in favor of short-lived projects. Also, the hurdle rate used to identify what payback period is acceptable is arbitrarily determined. Payback period calculations are described in Section 10.3 and Learning by Doing Application 10.2.

4 Explain why the accounting rate of return (ARR) is not recommended for use as a capital expenditure decision-making tool.

The ARR is based on accounting numbers, such as book value and net income, rather than cash flow data. As such, it is not a true rate of return. Instead of discounting a project's cash flows over time, it simply gives us a number based on average figures from the income statement and balance sheet. Furthermore, as with the payback method, there is no economic rationale for establishing the hurdle rate. Finally, the ARR does not account for the relative sizes of projects when a choice between projects of different sizes must be made.

5 Compute the internal rate of return (IRR) for a capital project and discuss the conditions under which the IRR technique and the NPV technique produce different results.

The IRR is the expected rate of return for a capital project; it is the discount rate that equates the present value of a project's expected cash inflows to the present value of the project's outflows—in other words, it is the discount rate at which the NPV is equal to zero. Calculations are shown in Section 10.5 and Learning by Doing Application 10.3. If a project's IRR is greater than the required rate of return, the cost of capital, the project is accepted. The IRR rule often gives the same investment decision for a project as the NPV rule. However, the IRR method does have operational pitfalls that can lead to incorrect decisions. Specifically, when a project's cash flows are unconventional, the IRR calculation may yield no IRR or more than one IRR. In addition, the IRR technique cannot be used to rank projects that are mutually exclusive because the project with the highest IRR may not be the project that would add the greatest value to the firm if accepted—that is, the project with the highest NPV.

6 Explain how the profitability index can be used to rank projects when a firm faces capital rationing and describe the limitations that apply to the profitability index.

The profitability index (PI) aids in the process of choosing the most valuable bundle of projects that the firm can afford. It is a measure of value received per dollar invested, which can be used to rank projects in a given period. The major limitation of the PI is that, although it can be used to rank projects in a given period, it can lead to less valuable project choices when considering capital investments over multiple years.

7 Explain the benefits of postaudit and periodic reviews of capital projects.

A postaudit review enables managers to determine whether a project's goals were met and to quantify the actual benefits or costs of the project. By conducting these reviews, managers can avoid making similar mistakes in future projects, learn to better recognize opportunities, and keep people involved in the budgeting process honest. A periodic review enables managers to assess the impact of changing information and market conditions on the value of a project that is already underway.

Summary of Key Equations

Equation	Description	Formula
10.1	Net present value	$\text{NPV} = \text{NCF}_0 + \frac{\text{NCF}_1}{1+k} + \frac{\text{NCF}_2}{(1+k)^2} + \cdots + \frac{\text{NCF}_n}{(1+k)^n} = \sum_{t=0}^{n} \frac{\text{NCF}_t}{(1+k)^t}$
10.2	Payback period	$\text{PB} = \text{Years before cost recovery} + \frac{\text{Remaining cost to recover}}{\text{Cash flow during the year}}$
10.3	Accounting rate of return	$\text{ARR} = \frac{\text{Average net income}}{\text{Average book value}}$
10.4	Internal rate of return	$\text{NPV} = \sum_{t=0}^{n} \frac{\text{NCF}_t}{(1+\text{IRR})^t} = 0$
10.5	Modified internal rate of return	$\text{PV}_{\text{Cost}} = \frac{\text{PFV}}{(1+\text{MIRR})^n}$
10.6	Profitability index	$\text{PI} = \frac{\text{NPV} + \text{Initial investment}}{\text{Initial investment}}$

Self-Study Problems

10.1 The management of Premium Manufacturing Company is evaluating two forklift systems to use in its plant that produces the towers for a windmill power farm. The costs and the cash flows from these systems are shown below. If the company uses a 12 percent discount rate for all projects, determine which forklift system should be purchased using the net present value (NPV) approach.

	Year 0	Year 1	Year 2	Year 3
Otis Forklifts	−$3,123,450	$979,225	$1,358,886	$2,111,497
Craigmore Forklifts	−$4,137,410	$875,236	$1,765,225	$2,865,110

10.2 Perryman Crafts Corp. management is evaluating two independent capital projects that will each cost the company $250,000. The two projects are expected to provide the following cash flows:

Year	Project A	Project B
1	$ 80,750	$ 32,450
2	93,450	76,125
3	40,235	153,250
4	145,655	96,110

Which project will be chosen if the company's payback criterion is three years? What if the company accepts all projects as long as the payback period is less than five years?

10.3 Terrell Corp. management is considering purchasing a machine that will cost $117,250 and will be depreciated on a straight-line basis over a five-year period. The sales and expenses (excluding depreciation) for the next five years are shown in the following table. The company's tax rate is 34 percent.

	Year 1	Year 2	Year 3	Year 4	Year 5
Sales	$123,450	$176,875	$242,455	$255,440	$267,125
Expenses	$137,410	$126,488	$141,289	$143,112	$133,556

Terrell will accept all projects that provide an accounting rate of return (ARR) of at least 45 percent. Should the company accept this project?

10.4 Refer to Problem 10.1. Compute the IRR for each of the two systems. Is the investment decision different from the one indicated by NPV?

10.5 You are considering a project that has an initial outlay of $1 million. The profitability index of the project is 2.24. What is the NPV of the project?

Solutions to Self-Study Problems

10.1 NPVs for two forklift systems:

NPV for Otis Forklifts:

$$NPV_{Otis} = \sum_{t=0}^{n} \frac{NCF_t}{(1+k)^t}$$

$$= -\$3,123,450 + \frac{\$979,225}{1.12} + \frac{\$1,358,886}{(1.12)^2} + \frac{\$2,111,497}{(1.12)^3}$$

$$= -\$3,123,450 + \$874,308 + \$1,083,296 + \$1,502,922$$

$$= \$337,076$$

NPV for Craigmore Forklifts:

$$NPV_{Craigmore} = \sum_{t=0}^{n} \frac{NCF_t}{(1+k)^t}$$

$$= -\$4,137,410 + \frac{\$875,236}{1.12} + \frac{\$1,765,225}{(1.12)^2} + \frac{\$2,865,110}{(1.12)^3}$$

$$= -\$4,137,410 + \$781,461 + \$1,407,227 + \$2,039,329$$

$$= \$90,607$$

Premium should purchase the Otis forklift since it has a larger NPV.

10.2 Payback periods for Perryman projects A and B:

Project A		
Year	**Cash Flow**	**Cumulative Cash Flows**
0	($250,000)	($250,000)
1	80,750	(169,250)
2	93,450	(75,800)
3	40,235	(35,565)
4	145,655	110,090

Project B		
Year	**Cash Flow**	**Cumulative Cash Flows**
0	($250,000)	($250,000)
1	32,450	(217,550)
2	76,125	(141,425)
3	153,250	11,825
4	96,110	107,935

Payback Period for Project A:

$$\text{Payback period}_A = \text{Years before cost recovery} + \frac{\text{Remaining cost to recover}}{\text{Cash flow during the year}}$$

$$= 3 \text{ years} + \frac{\$35{,}565}{\$145{,}655 \text{ per year}}$$

$$= 3.24 \text{ years}$$

Payback Period for Project B:

$$\text{Payback period}_B = \text{Years before cost recovery} + \frac{\text{Remaining cost to recover}}{\text{Cash flow during the year}}$$

$$= 2 \text{ years} + \frac{\$141{,}425}{\$153{,}250 \text{ per year}}$$

$$= 2.92 \text{ years}$$

If the payback period is three years, project B will be chosen. If the payback criterion is five years, both A and B will be chosen.

10.3 Evaluation of Terrell Corp. project:

	Year 1	Year 2	Year 3	Year 4	Year 5
Sales	$123,450	$176,875	$242,455	$255,440	$267,125
Expenses	137,410	126,488	141,289	143,112	133,556
Depreciation	23,450	23,450	23,450	23,450	23,450
EBIT	($ 37,410)	$ 26,937	$ 77,716	$ 88,878	$110,119
Taxes (34%)	12,719	9,159	26,423	30,219	37,440
Net Income	($ 24,691)	$ 17,778	$ 51,293	$ 58,659	$ 72,679
Beginning Book Value	117,250	93,800	70,350	46,900	23,450
Less: Depreciation	(23,450)	(23,450)	(23,450)	(23,450)	(23,450)
Ending Book Value	$ 93,800	$ 70,350	$ 46,900	$ 23,450	$ 0

$$\text{Average net income} = (-\$24{,}691 + \$17{,}778 + \$51{,}293 + \$58{,}659 + \$72{,}679)/5$$

$$= \$35{,}143.60$$

$$\text{Average book value} = (\$117{,}250 + \$93{,}800 + \$70{,}350 + \$46{,}900 + \$23{,}450 + \$0)/6$$

$$= \$58{,}625.00$$

$$\text{Accounting rate of return} = \$35{,}143.60/\$58{,}625.00$$

$$= 0.599, \text{ or } 59.9\%$$

The company should accept the project.

10.4 IRRs for two forklift systems:

Otis Forklifts:

First compute the IRR by the trial-and-error approach.

NPV (Otis) = \$337,075 > \$0

We should use a higher discount rate to get NPV = \$0.

At k = 15 percent:

$$NPV_{Otis} = -\$3,123,450 + \frac{\$979,225}{1.15} + \frac{\$1,358,886}{(1.15)^2} + \frac{\$2,111,497}{(1.15)^3}$$
$$= -\$3,123,450 + \$851,500 + \$1,027,513 + \$1,388,344$$
$$= \$143,907$$

Try a higher rate. At k = 17 percent:

$$NPV_{Otis} = -\$3,123,450 + \$836,944 + \$992,685 + \$1,318,357$$
$$= \$24,536$$

Try a higher rate. At k = 17.5 percent:

$$NPV_{Otis} = -\$3,123,450 + \$833,383 + \$984,254 + \$1,301,598$$
$$= -\$4,215$$

Thus, the IRR for Otis is less than 17.5 percent. Using a financial calculator, you can find the exact rate to be 17.43 percent.

Craigmore Forklifts:

First compute the IRR using the trial-and-error approach.

NPV (Craigmore) = \$90,606 > \$0

We should use a higher discount rate to get NPV = \$0.

At k = 15 percent:

$$NPV_{Craigmore} = -\$4,137,410 + \frac{\$875,236}{1.15} + \frac{\$1,765,225}{(1.12)^2} + \frac{\$2,865,110}{(1.12)^3}$$
$$= -\$4,137,410 + \$761,075 + \$1,334,764 + \$1,883,856$$
$$= -\$157,715$$

Try a lower rate. At k = 13 percent:

$$NPV_{Craigmore} = -\$4,137,410 + \$774,545 + \$1,382,430 + \$1,985,665$$
$$= \$5,230$$

Try a higher rate. At k = 13.1 percent:

$$NPV_{Craigmore} = -\$4,137,410 + \$773,860 + \$1,379,987 + \$1,980,403$$
$$= -\$3,161$$

Thus, the IRR for Craigmore is less than 13.1 percent. The exact rate is 13.06 percent. Based on the IRR, we would still choose the Otis system over the Craigmore system. The decision is the same as that indicated by NPV since both projects are conventional.

10.5 You can use Equation 10.6 to solve for the NPV:

$$PI = \frac{NPV + \text{Initial investment}}{\text{Initial investment}}$$

$$2.24 = \frac{NPV + \$1,000,000}{\$1,000,000}$$

Therefore:

$$NPV = \$1,240,000$$

WileyPLUS

Questions and Problems, Solution Walkthrough Videos, Learning by Doing Tutorials, and additional study tools and resources are available in WileyPLUS.

Discussion Questions

10.1 Explain why the cost of capital is referred to as the "hurdle" rate in capital budgeting.

10.2 **a.** Sykes, Inc., management is considering two projects: a plant expansion and a new computer system for the firm's production department. Classify these projects as independent, mutually exclusive, or contingent projects and explain your reasoning.

b. A company is building a new plant on the outskirts of Smallesville. The town has offered to donate the land, and as part of the agreement, the company will have to build an access road from the main highway to the plant. How will the project of building the road be classified in the capital budgeting analysis?

c. Management of your firm is currently considering upgrading the operating systems of all the firm's computers. One alternative is to choose the Linux operating system that a local computer services firm has offered to install and maintain. Microsoft has also put in a bid to install the new Windows operating system for businesses. How would these projects be classified?

10.3 In the context of capital budgeting, what is "capital rationing"?

10.4 Provide two conditions under which a set of projects might be characterized as mutually exclusive.

10.5 **a.** A firm invests in a project that is expected to earn a return of 12 percent. If the appropriate cost of capital is also 12 percent, did the firm make the right decision? Explain.

b. What is the impact on the firm if it accepts a project with a negative NPV?

10.6 Identify the weaknesses of the payback period method.

10.7 What are the strengths and weaknesses of the accounting rate of return approach?

10.8 Under what circumstances might the IRR and NPV approaches produce conflicting results?

10.9 The modified IRR (MIRR) alleviates two concerns with using the IRR method for evaluating capital investments. What are they?

10.10 Elkridge Construction Company has an average cost of capital of 12 percent. This cost of capital reflects the cost of capital for an Elkridge Construction project with average risk. However, the firm takes on projects of various risk levels. The company's experience suggests that low-risk projects have a cost of capital of 10 percent and high-risk projects have a cost of capital of 15 percent. Which of the following projects should the company reject?

Project	Expected Return	Risk
1. Single-family homes	13%	Low
2. Multifamily residential	12	Average
3. Commercial	18	High
4. Single-family homes	9	Low
5. Commercial	13	High

10.11 High Tech Monopoly Co. has plenty of cash to fund any conceivable positive NPV project. Can you describe a situation in which capital rationing could still occur?

10.12 The profitability index is a tool for measuring a project's benefits relative to its costs. How might this help to eliminate bias in project selection?

Questions and Problems

Excel *Excel templates and resources available in* **WileyPLUS**

Basic

10.1 **Net present value:** Riggs Corp. management is planning to spend $650,000 on a new marketing campaign. They believe that this action will result in additional cash flows of $325,000 over the next three years. If the discount rate is 17.5 percent, what is the NPV of this project?

10.2 **Net present value:** Kingston, Inc., management is considering purchasing a new machine at a cost of $4,133,250. They expect this equipment to produce cash flows of $814,322, $863,275, $937,250, $1,017,112, $1,212,960, and $1,225,000 over the next six years. If the appropriate discount rate is 15 percent, what is the NPV of this investment?

10.3 **Net present value:** Crescent Industries management is planning to replace some existing machinery in its plant. The cost of the new equipment and the resulting cash flows are shown in the accompanying table. If the firm uses an 18 percent discount rate for projects like this, should management go ahead with the project?

Year	Cash Flow
0	−$3,300,000
1	875,123
2	966,222
3	1,145,000
4	1,250,399
5	1,504,445

10.4 Net present value: Management of Franklin Mints, a confectioner, is considering purchasing a new jelly bean-making machine at a cost of $312,500. They project that the cash flows from this investment will be $121,450 for the next seven years. If the appropriate discount rate is 14 percent, what is the NPV for the project?

10.5 Net present value: Blanda Incorporated management is considering investing in two alternative production systems. The systems are mutually exclusive, and the cost of the new equipment and the resulting cash flows are shown in the accompanying table. If the firm uses a 9 percent discount rate for production system projects, in which system should the firm invest?

Year	System 1	System 2
0	–$15,000	–$45,000
1	15,000	32,000
2	15,000	32,000
3	15,000	32,000

10.6 Payback: Refer to Problem 10.5. What are the payback periods for Production Systems 1 and 2? If the systems are mutually exclusive and the firm always chooses projects with the lowest payback period, in which system should the firm invest?

10.7 Payback: Quebec, Inc., is purchasing machinery at a cost of $3,768,966. The company's management expects the machinery to produce cash flows of $979,225, $1,158,886, and $1,881,497 over the next three years, respectively. What is the payback period?

10.8 Payback: Northern Specialties just purchased inventory-management computer software at a cost of $1,645,276. Cost savings from the investment over the next six years will produce the following cash flow stream: $212,455, $292,333, $387,479, $516,345, $645,766, and $618,325. What is the payback period on this investment?

10.9 Payback: Nakamichi Bancorp has made an investment in banking software at a cost of $1,875,000. If management expects productivity gains and cost savings to generate additional cash flows of $586,212, $713,277, $431,199, and $318,697 over the next four years, what is the investment's payback period?

10.10 Average accounting rate of return (ARR): Capitol Corp. management is expecting a project to generate after-tax income of $63,435 in each of the next three years. The average book value of the project's equipment over that period will be $212,500. If the firm's investment decision on any project is based on an ARR of 37.5 percent, should this project be accepted?

10.11 Internal rate of return: Refer to Problem 10.4. What is the IRR that Franklin Mints management can expect on this project?

10.12 Internal rate of return: Hathaway, Inc., a resort management company, is refurbishing one of its hotels at a cost of $7.8 million. Management expects that this will lead to additional cash flows of $1.8 million for the next six years. What is the IRR of this project? If the appropriate cost of capital is 12 percent, should Hathaway go ahead with this project?

10.13 Profitability index: What is the profitability index, and why is it helpful in the capital rationing process?

Intermediate

10.14 Net present value: Champlain Corp. management is investigating two computer systems. The Alpha 8300 costs $3,122,300 and will generate cost savings of $1,345,500 in each of the next five years. The Beta 2100 system costs $3,750,000 and will produce cost savings of $1,125,000 in the first three years and then $2 million for the next two years. If the company's discount rate for similar projects is 14 percent, what is the NPV of each system? Which one should be chosen based on the NPV?

10.15 Net present value: Briarcrest Condiments is a spice-making firm. Recently, it developed a new process for producing spices. The process requires new machinery that would cost $1,968,450, have a life of five years, and would produce the cash flows shown in the following table. What is the NPV if the discount rate is 15.9 percent?

Year	Cash Flow
1	$512,496
2	–242,637
3	814,558
4	887,225
5	712,642

10.16 Net present value: Cranjet Industries is expanding its product line and its production capacity. The costs and expected cash flows of the two independent projects are given in the following table. The firm uses a discount rate of 16.4 percent for such projects.

a. What are the NPVs of the two projects?

b. Should both projects be accepted? or either? or neither? Explain your reasoning.

Year	Product Line Expansion	Production Capacity Expansion
0	–$2,575,000	–$8,137,250
1	600,000	2,500,000
2	875,000	2,500,000
3	875,000	2,500,000
4	875,000	3,250,000
5	875,000	3,250,000

10.17 Net present value: Emporia Mills management is evaluating two alternative heating systems. Costs and projected energy savings are given in the following table. The firm uses 11.5 percent to discount such project cash flows. Which system should be chosen?

Year	System 100	System 200
0	–$1,750,000	–$1735,000
1	275,223	750,000
2	512,445	612,500
3	648,997	550,112
4	875,000	384,226

10.18 Payback: Creative Solutions, Inc., has just invested $4,615,300 in new equipment. The firm uses a payback period criteria of rejecting any project that takes more than four years to recover its costs. Management anticipates cash flows of $644,386, $812,178, $943,279, $1,364,997, $2,616,300, and $2,225,375 over the next six years. Does this investment meet the firm's payback criteria?

10.19 Discounted payback: Timeline Manufacturing Co. management is evaluating two projects. The company uses payback criteria of three years or less. Project A has a cost of $912,855, and Project B's cost is $1,175,000. Cash flows from both projects are given in the following table. What are their discounted payback periods, and which will be accepted with a discount rate of 8 percent?

Year	Project A	Project B
1	$86,212	$586,212
2	313,562	413,277
3	427,594	231,199
4	285,552	

10.20 Payback: Regent Corp. management is evaluating three competing types of equipment. Costs and cash flow projections for all three are given in the following table. Which would be the best choice based on payback period?

Year	Type 1	Type 2	Type 2
0	−$1,311,450	−$1,415,888	−$1,612,856
1	212,566	586,212	786,212
2	269,825	413,277	175,000
3	455,112	331,199	175,000
4	285,552	141,442	175,000
5	121,396		175,000
6			175,000

10.21 Discounted payback: Nugent Communication Corp. is investing $9,365,000 in new technologies. The company's management expects significant benefits in the first three years after installation (as can be seen by the following cash flows) and smaller constant benefits in each of the next four years. What is the discounted payback period for the project assuming a discount rate of 10 percent?

	Year			
	1	2	3	4–7
Cash Flows	$2,265,433	$4,558,721	$3,378,911	$1,250,000

10.22 Modified internal rate of return (MIRR): Morningside Bakeries recently purchased equipment at a cost of $650,000. Management expects the equipment to generate cash flows of $275,000 in each of the next four years. The cost of capital is 14 percent. What is the MIRR for this project?

10.23 Modified internal rate of return (MIRR): Management of Sycamore Home Furnishings is considering acquiring a new machine that can create customized window treatments. The equipment will cost $263,400 and will generate cash flows of $85,000 over each of the next six years. If the cost of capital is 12 percent, what is the MIRR on this project?

10.24 Internal rate of return: Management of Great Flights, Inc., an aviation firm, is considering purchasing three aircraft for a total cost of $161 million. The company would lease the aircraft to an airline. Cash flows from the proposed leases are shown in the following table. What is the IRR of this project?

Year	Cash Flow
1–4	$23,500,000
5–7	72,000,000
8–10	80,000,000

10.25 Internal rate of return: Refer to Problem 10.5. Compute the IRR for both Production System 1 and Production System 2. Which has the higher IRR? Which production system has the higher NPV? Explain why the IRR and NPV rankings of Systems 1 and 2 are different.

10.26 Internal rate of return: Ancala Corporation management is considering investments in two new golf apparel lines for next season: golf hats and belts. Due to a funding constraint, these lines are mutually exclusive. A summary of each project's estimated cash flows over its three-year life, as well as the IRR and NPV of each, are outlined below. The CFO of the firm has decided to manufacture the belts; however, the CEO is questioning this decision given that the IRR is higher for manufacturing hats. Explain to the CEO why the IRRs and NPVs of the belt and hat projects disagree? Is the CFO's decision correct?

Year	Golf Belts	Golf Hats
0	−$1,000	−$500
1	1,000	500
2	500	300
3	500	300
NPV	$697.97	$427.87
IRR	54%	61%

10.27 Internal rate of return: Compute the IRR on the following cash flow streams:

a. An initial investment of $25,000 followed by a single cash flow of $37,450 in Year 6.

b. An initial investment of $1 million followed by a single cash flow of $1,650,000 in Year 4.

c. An initial investment of $2 million followed by cash flows of $1,650,000 and $1,250,000 in Years 2 and 4, respectively.

10.28 Internal rate of return: Compute the IRR for the following project cash flows:

a. An initial outlay of $3,125,000 followed by annual cash flows of $565,325 for the next eight years.

b. An initial investment of $33,750 followed by annual cash flows of $9,430 for the next five years.

c. An initial outlay of $10,000 followed by annual cash flows of $2,500 for the next seven years.

10.29 Profitability index: Suppose that you could invest in the following projects but have only $30,000 to invest. How would you make your decision and in which projects would you invest?

Project	Cost	NPV
A	$ 8,000	$4,000
B	11,000	7,000
C	9,000	5,000
D	7,000	4,000

10.30 Profitability index: Suppose that you could invest in the same projects as in the previous problem but have only $25,000 to invest. Which projects would you choose?

Advanced

10.31 Management of Draconian Measures, Inc., is evaluating two independent projects. The company uses a 13.8 percent discount rate for such projects. The costs and cash flows for the projects are shown in the following table. What are their NPVs?

Year	Project 1	Project 2
0	−$8,425,375	−$11,368,000
1	3,225,997	2,112,589
2	1,775,882	3,787,552
3	1,375,112	3,125,650
4	1,176,558	4,115,889
5	1,212,645	4,556,424
6	1,582,156	
7	1,365,882	

10.32 Refer to Problem 10.31.

a. What are the IRRs for the projects?

b. Does the IRR criterion suggest a different decision than the NPV criterion?

c. Explain how you would expect the management of Draconian Measures to decide which project(s) to invest in.

10.33 Management of Dravid, Inc., is currently evaluating three independent projects. The cost of funds can be either 13.6 percent or 14.8 percent depending on their financing plan. All three projects cost the same at $500,000. Expected cash flow streams are shown in the following table. Which projects would be accepted at a discount rate of 14.8 percent? What if the discount rate was 13.6 percent?

Year	Project 1	Project 2	Project 3
1	$ 0	$ 0	$245,125
2	125,000	$ 0	212,336
3	150,000	500,000	112,500
4	375,000	500,000	74,000

10.34 Management of Intrepid, Inc., is considering investing in three independent projects. The costs and the cash flows are given in the following table. The appropriate cost of capital is 14.5 percent. Compute the project IRRs and identify the projects that should be accepted.

Year	Project 1	Project 2	Project 3
0	−$275,000	−$312,500	−$500,000
1	63,000	153,250	212,000
2	85,000	167,500	212,000
3	85,000	112,000	212,000
4	100,000		212,000

10.35 Jekyll & Hyde Corp. management is evaluating two mutually exclusive projects. The cost of capital is 15 percent. Costs and cash flows for each project are given in the following table. Which project should be accepted?

Year	Project 1	Project 2
0	−$1,250,000	−$1,250,000
1	250,000	350,000
2	350,000	350,000
3	450,000	350,000
4	500,000	350,000
5	750,000	350,000

10.36 Management of Larsen Automotive, a manufacturer of auto parts, is considering investing in two projects. The company typically compares project returns to a cost of funds of 17 percent. Compute the IRRs based on the cash flows in the following table. Which project(s) will be accepted?

Year	Project 1	Project 2
0	−$475,000	−$500,000
1	300,000	117,500
2	110,000	181,300
3	125,000	244,112
4	140,000	278,955

10.37 Compute the IRR for each of the following projects:

Year	Project 1	Project 2	Project 3
0	−$10,000	−$10,000	−$10,000
1	4,750	1,650	800
2	3,300	3,890	1,200
3	3,600	5,100	2,875
4	2,100	2,750	3,400
5		800	6,600

10.38 Primus Corp. management is planning to convert an existing warehouse into a new plant that will increase its production capacity by 45 percent. The cost of this project will be $7,125,000. It will result in additional cash flows of $1,875,000 for the next eight years. The discount rate is 12 percent.

a. What is the payback period?

b. What is the NPV for this project?

c. What is the IRR?

10.39 Quasar Tech Co. management is investing $6 million in new machinery that will produce the next-generation routers. Sales to its customers will amount to $1,750,000 for the next three years and then increase to $2.4 million for three more years. The project is expected to last six years and operating costs, excluding depreciation, will be $898,620 annually. The machinery will be depreciated to a salvage value of $0 over six years using the straight-line method. The company's tax rate is 30 percent, and the cost of capital is 16 percent.

a. What is the payback period?

b. What is the average accounting return (ARR)?

c. Calculate the project NPV.

d. What is the IRR for the project?

10.40 Management of Skywards, Inc., an airline caterer, is purchasing refrigerated trucks at a total cost of $3.25 million. After-tax net income from this investment is expected to be $750,000 for the next five years. Annual depreciation expense will be $650,000. The cost of capital is 17 percent.

a. What is the discounted payback period?

b. Compute the ARR.

c. What is the NPV of this investment?

d. Calculate the IRR.

10.41 Trident Corp. management is evaluating two independent projects. The costs and expected cash flows are given in the following table. The cost of capital is 10 percent.

Year	Project A	Project B
0	−$312,500	−$395,000
1	121,450	153,552
2	121,450	158,711
3	121,450	166,220
4	121,450	132,000
5	121,450	122,000

a. Calculate the projects' NPV.

b. Calculate the projects' IRR.

c. Which project should be chosen based on NPV? Based on IRR? Is there a conflict?

d. If you are the decision maker for the firm, which project or projects will be accepted? Explain your reasoning.

10.42 Management of Tyler, Inc., is considering switching to a new production technology. The cost of the required equipment will be $4 million. The discount rate is 12 percent. The cash flows that management expects the new technology to generate are as follows.

Year	CF
1–2	0
3–5	$ 845,000
6–9	$1,450,000

a. Compute the payback and discounted payback periods for the project.

b. What is the NPV for the project? Should the firm go ahead with the project?

c. What is the IRR, and what would be the decision based on the IRR?

10.43 You are analyzing two proposed capital investments with the following cash flows:

Year	Project X	Project Y
0	−$20,000	−$20,000
1	13,000	7,000
2	6,000	7,000
3	6,000	7,000
4	2,000	7,000

The cost of capital for both projects is 10 percent. Calculate the profitability index (PI) for each project. Which project, or projects, should be accepted if you have unlimited funds to invest? Which project should be accepted if they are mutually exclusive?

CFA Problems

10.44 Given the following cash flows for a capital project, calculate the NPV and IRR. The required rate of return is 8 percent.

	Year 0	1	2	3	4	5
Cash Flow	−$50,000	$15,000	$15,000	$20,000	$10,000	$5,000

	NPV	IRR
a.	$1,905	10.9%
b.	$1,905	26.0%
c.	$3,379	10.9%
d.	$3,379	26.0%

10.45 Given the following cash flows for a capital project, calculate its payback period and discounted payback period. The required rate of return is 8 percent.

	Year 0	1	2	3	4	5
Cash Flow	−$50,000	$15,000	$15,000	$20,000	$10,000	$5,000

The discounted payback period is

a. 0.16 year longer than the payback period.

b. 0.80 year longer than the payback period.

c. 1.01 years longer than the payback period.

d. 1.85 years longer than the payback period.

10.46 An investment of $100 generates after-tax cash flows of $40 in Year 1, $80 in Year 2, and $120 in Year 3. The required rate of return is 20 percent. The net present value is closest to

a. $42.22 **b.** $58.33

c. $68.52 **d.** $98.95

10.47 An investment of $150,000 is expected to generate an after-tax cash flow of $100,000 in one year and another $120,000 in two years. The cost of capital is 10 percent. What is the internal rate of return?

a. 28.19 percent **b.** 28.39 percent

c. 28.59 percent **d.** 28.79 percent

10.48 An investment requires an outlay of $100 and produces after-tax cash flows of $40 annually for four years. A project enhancement increases the required outlay by $15 and the annual after-tax cash flows by $5. How will the enhancement affect the project's NPV profile? The vertical intercept of the NPV profile of the project shifts:

a. Up and the horizontal intercept shifts left.

b. Up and the horizontal intercept shifts right.

c. Down and the horizontal intercept shifts left.

d. Down and the horizontal intercept shifts right.

Sample Test Problems

10.1 Testco Corporation is considering adding a new product line. The cost of the factory and equipment to produce this product is \$1,780,000. Company management expects net cash flows from the sale of this product to be \$450,000 in each of the next eight years. If Testco uses a discount rate of 12 percent for projects like this, what is the net present value of this project? What is the internal rate of return?

10.2 Flowers Unlimited is considering purchasing an additional delivery truck that will have a seven-year useful life. The new truck will cost \$42,000. Cost savings with this truck are expected to be \$12,800 for the first two years, \$8,900 for the following two years, and \$5,000 for the last three years of the truck's useful life. What is the payback period for this project? What is the discounted payback period for this project with a discount rate of 10 percent?

10.3 What is the average accounting rate of return (ARR) on a piece of equipment that will cost \$1.2 million and that will result in pretax cost savings of \$380,000 for the first three years and then \$280,000 for the following three years? Assume that the machinery will be depreciated to a salvage value of 0 over six years using the straight-line method and the company's tax rate is 32 percent. If the acceptance decision is based on the project exceeding an ARR of 20 percent, should this machinery be purchased?

10.4 What do we know about that project's IRR if we know that it has a positive NPV?

10.5 West Street Automotive is considering adding state safety inspections to its service offerings. The equipment necessary to perform these inspections will cost \$557,000 and will generate cash flows of \$195,000 over each of the next five years. If the cost of capital is 14 percent, what is the MIRR on this project?

10.6 You are chairperson of the investment committee at your firm. Five projects have been submitted to your committee for approval this month. The investment required and the project profitability index for each of these projects are presented in the following table:

Project	Investment	PI
A	\$20,000	2.500
B	50,000	2.000
C	70,000	1.750
D	10,000	1.000
E	80,000	0.800

If you have \$500,000 available for investments, which of these projects would you approve? Assume that you do not have to worry about having enough resources for future investments when making this decision.

CHAPTER 11

Cash Flows and Capital Budgeting

LEARNING OBJECTIVES

1. Explain why incremental after-tax free cash flows are relevant in evaluating a project and calculate them for a project.
2. Discuss the five general rules for incremental after-tax free cash flow calculations and explain why cash flows stated in nominal (real) dollars should be discounted using a nominal (real) discount rate.
3. Describe how distinguishing between variable and fixed costs can be useful in forecasting operating expenses.
4. Explain the concept of equivalent annual cost and use it to compare projects with unequal lives, decide when to replace an existing asset, and calculate the opportunity cost of using an existing asset.
5. Determine the appropriate time to harvest an asset.

On January 25, 2017, managers of Johnson & Johnson, a large health care company that develops, manufacturers, and sells a wide range of consumer products, pharmaceuticals, and medical devices, announced that they had agreed to pay $30 billion in cash for the Swiss biotech company Actelion. This acquisition would add to Johnson & Johnson's drug portfolio and provide access to some high-margin products at a time that some of the company's existing drugs were facing competition from lower-priced alternatives. The press release announcing the acquisition stated that it was expected to immediately add to Johnson & Johnson's adjusted earnings per share and accelerate the company's revenue and earnings growth rates. Johnson & Johnson planned to pay for the acquisition using cash held in subsidiaries outside the United States.

Investors in the stock market appear to have initially been skeptical that the acquisition was good for Johnson & Johnson. The company's stock price declined 0.9 percent, from $112.80 to $111.84, in the first day following the announcement while the S&P stock market index was essentially unchanged. The decrease in the price of Johnson & Johnson stock suggests that investors thought that the company was overpaying for this acquisition. The decline in the stock price represented a $2.60 billion decrease ([$111.84 – $112.80] × 2.71 billion shares outstanding = –$2.60 billion) in the overall value of the company's shares. In contrast to the decline in the price of Johnson & Johnson's shares, Actelion's share price increased 22.1 percent in the first day following the announcement.

When the managers of Johnson & Johnson announced their plans to acquire Actelion, they were announcing a $30 billion investment. This investment was viewed by stock market investors from the same perspective as any capital project that a firm might pursue. Investors evaluated whether the net present value (NPV) of the cash flows from the acquisition of Actelion would be positive or negative. The financial model used to estimate this NPV is the same one you saw in Chapter 10. The decrease in the value of Johnson & Johnson's stock on the day of the announcement reflected investors' estimates of the NPV of the decision to purchase Actelion.

In Chapter 10 we stressed understanding the NPV concept and other project valuation models, as well as the mechanics of discounting project cash flows. This chapter focuses on what project cash flows are discounted and how they are calculated and used in practice. The topics covered in this chapter are central to the goal of value creation. It is necessary to understand them in order to determine which capital projects have positive NPVs and which projects have negative NPVs. Only if you can do this will you be able to choose projects that create value.

Chapter Preview

In Chapter 10 we saw that capital budgeting involves comparing the benefits and costs associated with a project to determine whether the project creates value for stockholders. These benefits and costs are reflected in the cash flows that the project is expected to produce. The NPV is a dollar measure of the amount by which the present value of the benefits exceeds the present value of the costs. Chapters 11 through 13 discuss how analysts actually apply the capital budgeting concepts introduced in Chapter 10. This chapter and Chapter 12 focus on cash flows, while Chapter 13 covers concepts related to the discount rate.

We begin this chapter with a discussion of how to calculate the cash flows used to compute the NPV of a project. We then present five rules to follow when you calculate cash flows. We also address some concepts that will help you better understand cash flow calculations.

Next, we discuss how analysts actually forecast a project's cash flows. Since the cash flows generated by a project will almost certainly differ from the forecasts, it is important to have a framework that helps minimize errors and ensures that forecasts are internally consistent. We discuss such a framework in this part of the chapter.

Finally, we examine some special cases that arise in capital budgeting problems. For example, we describe how analysts adjust cash flows to choose between projects that have different lives, how to determine when an existing piece of equipment should be replaced, how to determine the cost of using excess capacity for a project, and when to harvest (or sell) an asset.

11.1 Calculating Project Cash Flows

LEARNING OBJECTIVE

1. Explain why incremental after-tax free cash flows are relevant in evaluating a project and calculate them for a project.

We begin our discussion of cash flows in capital budgeting by describing the mechanics of cash flow calculations and the rules for estimating the cash flows for individual projects. You will see that the approach we use to calculate project cash flows is similar to that used to calculate the cash flow to investors discussed in Chapter 3. However, there are two very important differences:

1. Most important, the cash flows used in capital budgeting calculations are based on forecasts of *future* cash revenues, expenses, taxes, and investment outlays. In contrast, in Chapter 3 we focused on calculating historical cash flows to investors using accounting statements rather than the future cash flows that might be generated by the firm.

2. In capital budgeting we focus on estimating the cash flows we expect an individual project to produce in the future, which we refer to as incremental after-tax free cash flows. In contrast, the cash flow to investors in Chapter 3 is a measure of the cash flows generated by the entire firm.

Building Intuition

Capital Budgeting Is Forward Looking

In capital budgeting, we estimate the NPV of the cash flows that a project is *expected to produce in the future*. In other words, all of the cash flow estimates are forward looking. This is very different from using historical accounting statements to estimate cash flows.

Incremental After-Tax Free Cash Flows

The cash flows we discount in an NPV analysis are the **incremental after-tax free cash flows** that are expected from the project. The term *incremental* refers to the fact that these cash flows reflect how much the firm's total after-tax free cash flows will change if the project is adopted. Thus, we define the incremental after-tax free cash flows (FCF) for a project as the total after-tax free cash flows the firm would produce with the project, less the total after-tax free cash flows the firm would produce without the project.

incremental after-tax free cash flows the difference between the total after-tax free cash flows at a firm with a project and the total after-tax free cash flows at the same firm without that project; a measure of a project's total impact on the free cash flows at a firm

$$\text{FCF}_{\text{Project}} = \text{FCF}_{\text{Firm with project}} - \text{FCF}_{\text{Firm without project}} \tag{11.1}$$

In other words, $\text{FCF}_{\text{Project}}$ equals the net effect the project will have on the firm's cash revenues, costs, taxes, and investment outlays. These are the cash flows investors care about.

Throughout the rest of this chapter, we will refer to the total incremental after-tax free cash flows associated with a project simply as the FCF for the project. For convenience, we will drop the "Project" subscript from the FCF in Equation 11.1.

The FCF for a project is what we generically referred to as NCF in Chapter 10. The term *free cash flows,* which is commonly used in practice, refers to the fact that the firm is free to distribute these cash flows to creditors and stockholders because these are the cash flows that are left over after a firm has made necessary investments in working capital and long-term assets. The cash flows associated with financing a project (cash outflows or inflows to or from creditors or stockholders) are not included in the FCF calculation because, as we will discuss in Chapter 13, these are accounted for in the discount rate that is used in an NPV analysis. All of these points will become clearer as we discuss the FCF calculation next.

The FCF Calculation

The FCF calculation is illustrated in **Exhibit 11.1**. Let's begin with an overall review of how the calculation is done. After that, we will look more closely at details of the calculation.

When we calculate the FCFs for a project, we first compute the **incremental cash flow from operations (CF Opns)** for each year during the project's life. This is the cash flow that the project is expected to generate after all operating expenses and taxes have been paid. To obtain the FCF, we then subtract the **incremental capital expenditures (Cap Exp)** and the **incremental additions to working capital (Add WC)** required for the project. Cap Exp and Add WC represent the net investments in long-term assets, such as property, plant, and equipment, and in working capital items, such as cash and cash equivalents, accounts receivable, inventory, and accounts payable, which must be made if the project is pursued.

incremental cash flow from operations (CF Opns) the cash flow that a project generates after all operating expenses and taxes have been paid but before any cash outflows for investments

incremental capital expenditures (Cap Exp) the net investments in property, plant, and equipment and other long-term assets that must be made if a project is pursued

incremental additions to working capital (Add WC) the net investments in working capital items, such as cash and cash equivalents, accounts receivable, inventory, and accounts payable, that must be made if the project is pursued

As we noted earlier, the calculation of free cash flows for capital budgeting, which is summarized in Exhibit 11.1, is very similar to the calculation of the cash flows to investors that we discussed in Chapter 3. This should not be surprising since managers evaluate projects based on the present value of the cash flows they are expected to produce for their firms' investors. Nevertheless, there is an important computational difference between the cash flow calculations in Chapters 3 and 11. In Exhibit 11.1 the taxes for a project analysis are computed by multiplying the project's operating profit (EBIT) by the firm's marginal tax rate. This calculation gives us the taxes that the firm would owe on a project if no debt is used to finance that project. In contrast, the calculation in Chapter 3 uses the actual taxes paid by the firm, which includes the effect that interest deductions have on the taxes owed. It is true that interest payments will reduce the taxable income from a project if any debt financing is

EXHIBIT 11.1 The Free Cash Flow Calculation for a Project

This exhibit shows how the incremental after-tax free cash flow (FCF) for a project is calculated. The FCF equals the change in the firm's cash income, excluding interest expense, that the project is responsible for, plus depreciation and amortization for the project, minus all required capital expenditures and investments in working capital. FCF also equals the incremental after-tax cash flow from operations minus the net capital expenditures and investments in working capital required for the project.

Explanation	Calculation	Formula
The change in the firm's cash income, excluding interest expense, resulting from the project	Revenue	Revenue
	−Cash operating expenses	−Op Ex
	Earnings before interest, taxes, depreciation, and amortization	EBITDA
	−Depreciation and amortization	−D&A
	Operating profit	EBIT
	×(1 − Firm's marginal tax rate)	×(1 − t)
	Net operating profit after tax	NOPAT
Adjustments for the impact of depreciation and amortization and investments on FCF	+Depreciation and amortization	+D&A
	Cash flow from operations	CF Opns
	−Capital expenditures	−Cap Exp
	−Additions to working capital	−Add WC
	=Free cash flow	=FCF

Building Intuition

Incremental After-Tax Free Cash Flows Are What Stockholders Care About in Capital Budgeting

When evaluating a project, managers focus on the FCF that the project is expected to produce because that is what stockholders care about. The FCFs reflect the impact of the project on the firm's overall cash flows. They also represent the additional cash flows that can be distributed to security holders if the project is accepted. Only after-tax cash flows matter because these are the cash flows that are actually available for distribution after taxes are paid to the government.

used. However, we ignore this reduction when evaluating a project for two reasons. First, we want to exclude the effects associated with how the project is financed in order to isolate the cash flows from the project itself. Second, as we discuss in Chapter 13, the cost of both debt and equity financing for a project, including the impact of using debt financing on the firm's tax obligations, are reflected in the discount rate. Doing the calculation this way makes it easier to estimate the NPV of a project under alternative financial structures.

Since the FCF calculation gives us the after-tax cash flows from operations over and above what is necessary to make any required investments, the FCFs for a project are the cash flows that the firm's investors can expect to receive from the project. This is why we discount the FCFs when we compute the NPV.

The formula for the FCF calculation can also be written as:

$$\text{FCF} = [(\text{Revenue} - \text{Op Ex} - \text{D\&A}) \times (1 - t)] + \text{D\&A} - \text{Cap Exp} - \text{Add WC} \qquad (11.2)$$

where Revenue is the incremental revenue (net sales) associated with the project, D&A is the **incremental depreciation and amortization** associated with the project, and t is the **firm's marginal tax rate.**

incremental depreciation and amortization (D&A) the depreciation and amortization charges that are associated with a project

firm's marginal tax rate (t) the tax rate that is applied to each additional dollar of earnings at a firm

Let's use Equation 11.2 to work through an example. Suppose you are considering purchasing a new truck for your plumbing business. This truck will increase revenues \$50,000 and operating expenses \$30,000 in the next year. Depreciation and amortization charges for the truck will equal \$10,000 next year, and your firm's marginal tax rate will be 35 percent. Capital expenditures of \$3,000 will be required to offset wear and tear on the truck, but no additions to working capital will be required. To calculate the FCF for the project in the next year, you can simply substitute the appropriate values into Equation 11.2:

$$\begin{aligned}\text{FCF} &= [(\text{Revenue} - \text{Op Ex} - \text{D\&A}) \times (1 - t)] + \text{D\&A} - \text{Cap Exp} - \text{Add WC} \\ &= [(\$50{,}000 - \$30{,}000 - \$10{,}000) \times (1 - 0.35)] + \$10{,}000 - \$3{,}000 - \$0 \\ &= \$13{,}500\end{aligned}$$

The FCF calculated with Equation 11.2 equals the total annual cash flow the firm will produce with the project less the total cash flow the firm will produce without the project. Even so, it is important to note that it is not necessary to actually estimate the firm's total cash flows in an NPV analysis. We need only estimate the cash outflows and inflows that arise as a direct result of the project in order to value it. The idea that we can evaluate the cash flows from a project independently of the cash flows for the firm is known as the **stand-alone principle**. The stand-alone principle says that we can treat the project as if it were a stand-alone firm that has its own revenue, expenses, and investment requirements. NPV analysis compares the present value of the FCF from this stand-alone firm with the cost of the project.

stand-alone principle the principle that allows us to treat each project as a stand-alone firm when we perform an NPV analysis

To fully understand the stand-alone principle, it is helpful to consider an example. Suppose that you own shares of stock in Twitter Inc., and that Twitter's stock is currently selling for $19.00 per share. Now suppose that Twitter's management announces it will immediately invest $722 million in data centers that are expected to produce after-tax cash flows of $200 million per year forever. Since Twitter has 722 million shares outstanding and uses no debt, this means that the investment will equal $1.00 per share ($722 million/722 million shares = $1.00 per share). The annual increase in the cash flows for Twitter is expected to be $0.277 per share per year ($200 million/722 million shares = $0.277 per share). How should this announcement affect the value of a share of Twitter stock?

If the appropriate cost of capital for the project is 10 percent, then from Equation 9.2 and the discussion in Chapter 10, we know that the value of a share of Twitter's stock should increase by D/R = $0.277/0.10 = $2.77 less the $1.00 invested, or $1.77, making each share of Twitter stock worth $19.00 + $1.77 = $20.77 after the announcement. This example illustrates how the stand-alone principle allows us to simply add the value of a project's cash flows to the value of the firm's other cash flows to obtain the total value of the firm with the project.

Cash Flows from Operations

Let's examine Exhibit 11.1 in more detail to better understand why FCF is calculated as it is. First, note that the incremental cash flow from operations, CF Opns, equals the **incremental net operating profits after tax (NOPAT)** plus D&A.

incremental net operating profits after tax (NOPAT) a measure of the impact of a project on the firm's cash net income, excluding the effects of any interest expenses associated with financing the project

If you refer back to the discussion of the income statement in Chapter 3, you will notice that NOPAT is essentially a cash flow measure of the incremental net income from the project without interest expenses. In other words, it is the impact of the project on the firm's cash flow, excluding the effects of any interest expenses associated with financing the project. We exclude interest expenses when calculating NOPAT for an NPV analysis because, as we mentioned earlier, the cost of financing a project is reflected in the discount rate.

We use the firm's marginal tax rate, t, to calculate NOPAT because the profits from a project are assumed to be incremental to the firm. Since the firm already pays taxes, the appropriate tax rate for FCF calculations is the tax rate that the firm will pay on any *additional* profits that are earned because the project is adopted. You may recall from Chapter 3 that this rate is the marginal tax rate. We will discuss taxes in more detail later in this chapter.

We add incremental depreciation and amortization, D&A, to NOPAT when calculating CF Opns because, as in the accounting statement of cash flows, D&A represents a noncash charge that reduces the firm's tax obligation. Note that we subtract D&A before computing the taxes that the firm would pay on the incremental earnings for the project. This accounts for the ability of the firm to deduct D&A when computing taxes. However, since D&A is a noncash charge, we have to add it back to NOPAT in order to get the cash flow from operations right.

The net effect of subtracting D&A, computing the taxes, and then adding back D&A is to reduce the taxes attributable to earnings from the project. For example, suppose that EBITDA for a project is $100.00, D&A is $50.00, and t is 35 percent. If we did not subtract D&A before computing taxes and add it back to compute CF Opns, the taxes owed for the project would be $100.00 × 0.35 = $35.00 and CF Opns would be $100.00 − $35.00 = $65.00. This would understate CF Opns from this project by $17.50 since deducting D&A reduces the firm's tax obligation by this amount. With this deduction, the correct tax obligation is ($100.00 − $50.00) × 0.35 = $17.50 and the correct CF Opns is $100.00 − $17.50 = $82.50. We get exactly this value when we compute CF Opns as shown in Exhibit 11.1 and Equation 11.2:

$$\text{CF Opns} = [(\text{Revenue} - \text{Op Ex} - \text{D\&A}) \times (1 - t)] + \text{D\&A}$$

since Revenue − Op Ex = EBITDA, as shown in Exhibit 11.1, we can write:

$$\begin{aligned}\text{CF Opns} &= [(\text{EBITDA} - \text{D\&A}) \times (1 - t)] + \text{D\&A}\\ &= [(\$100.00 - \$50.00) \times (1 - 0.35)] + \$50.00\\ &= \$82.50\end{aligned}$$

Cash Flows Associated with Capital Expenditures and Net Working Capital

tangible assets physical assets such as property, plant, and equipment

intangible assets nonphysical assets such as patents, mailing lists, or brand names

current assets assets, such as cash and marketable securities, accounts receivable, and inventories, that are expected to be liquidated (collected or sold) within one year

Once we have estimated CF Opns, we simply subtract cash flows associated with the required investments to obtain the FCF for a project in a particular period. Investments can be required to purchase long-term **tangible assets**, such as property, plant, and equipment, to purchase **intangible assets**, such as patents, mailing lists, or brand names, or to fund **current assets**, such as cash and marketable securities, accounts receivables, and inventories.

It is important to recognize that all investments that are incremental to a project must be accounted for. The most obvious investments are those in the land, buildings, and machinery and equipment that are acquired for the project. However, investments in intangible assets can also be required. For example, a manufacturing firm may purchase the right to use a particular production technology. Incremental investments in long-term tangible assets and intangible assets are collectively referred to as incremental capital expenditures (Cap Exp).

In addition to tangible and intangible assets, such as those described earlier, it is also necessary to account for incremental additions to working capital (Add WC). For example, if a new project will require that the firm increase the amount of cash that it keeps on hand, this increase must be accounted for. If the product being produced is going to be sold on credit, thereby generating additional accounts receivable, the cost of providing that credit must also be accounted for. Similarly, if it will be necessary to hold product in inventory, the cost of financing that inventory must be considered. Finally, it is important to consider any incremental changes in current liabilities associated with the project.

The FCF Calculation: An Example

Let's work a more comprehensive example to see how FCF is calculated in practice. Suppose that you work at an outdoor performing arts center and are evaluating a project to increase the number of seats by building four new box seating areas and adding 5,000 seats for the general public. Each box seating area is expected to generate $400,000 in incremental annual revenue, while each of the new seats for the general public will generate $2,500 in incremental annual revenue. The incremental expenses associated with the new boxes and seating will amount to 60 percent of the revenues. These expenses include hiring additional personnel to handle concessions, ushering, and security. The new construction will cost $10 million and will be fully depreciated (to a value of zero dollars) on a straight-line basis over the 10-year life of the project. The center will have to invest $1 million in additional working capital immediately, but the project will not require any other working capital investments during its life. This working capital will be recovered in the last year of the project. The center's marginal tax rate is 30 percent. What are the incremental cash flows from this project?

EXHIBIT 11.2 **FCF Calculation Worksheet for the Performing Arts Center Project**

A free cash flow (FCF) calculation table is useful in evaluating a project. It helps organize the calculations and ensure that they are completed correctly.

	Year 0	Years 1 to 9	Year 10
Revenue			
−Op Ex	______	______	______
EBITDA			
−D&A	______	______	______
EBIT			
$\times(1-t)$	______	______	______
NOPAT			
+D&A	______	______	______
CF Opns			
−Cap Exp			
−Add WC	______	______	______
=FCF			

When evaluating a project, it is generally helpful to first organize your calculations by setting up a worksheet such as the one illustrated in **Exhibit 11.2**. A worksheet like this helps ensure that the calculations are completed correctly. The left-hand column in Exhibit 11.2 shows the actual calculations that will be performed. Other columns are included for each of the years during the life of the project, from Year 0 (today) through the last year in the life of the project (Year 10). In this example the cash flows will be exactly the same for Years 1 through 9; therefore, for illustration purposes, we will only include a single column to represent these years. If you were using a spreadsheet program, you would normally include one column for each year.

Unless there is information to the contrary, we can assume that the investment outlay for this project will be made today (Year 0). We do this because in a typical project, no revenue will be generated and no expenses will be incurred until after the investment has been made. Consequently, the only cash flows in Year 0 are those for new construction (Cap Exp = \$10,000,000) and additional working capital (Add WC = \$1,000,000). The FCF in Year 0 will therefore equal −\$11,000,000.

In Years 1 through 9, incremental revenue (Revenue) will equal:

Box seating (\$400,000 × 4)	\$ 1,600,000
Public seating (\$2,500 × 5,000)	\$12,500,000
Total incremental net revenue	\$14,100,000

Incremental Op Ex will equal 0.60 × \$14,100,000 = \$8,460,000. Finally, depreciation (there is no amortization in this example) is computed as:

$$\begin{aligned} \text{D\&A} &= (\text{Cap Exp} - \text{Salvage value of Cap Exp})/\text{Depreciable life of the investment} \\ &= (\$10{,}000{,}000 - \$0)/10 \text{ years} \\ &= \$1{,}000{,}000 \end{aligned}$$

Note that only the Cap Exp are depreciated and that these capital expenditures will be completely depreciated or written off over the 10-year life of the project because no salvage value is anticipated. Working capital is not depreciated because it will be recovered at the end of the project as the project's inventory is sold off, receivables are collected, and short-term liabilities are repaid.

The cash flows in Year 10 will be the same as those in Years 1 through 9 except that the \$1 million invested in additional working capital will be recovered in the last year.

EXHIBIT 11.3 **Completed FCF Calculation Worksheet for the Performing Arts Center Project**

The completed calculation table shows how the incremental after-tax free cash flows (FCF) for the performing arts center project are computed, along with the NPV for that project when the cost of capital is 10 percent.

	Year 0	Years 1 to 9	Year 10
Revenue		$14,100,000	$14,100,000
−Op Ex		8,460,000	8,460,000
EBITDA		$ 5,640,000	$ 5,640,000
−D&A		1,000,000	1,000,000
EBIT		$ 4,640,000	$ 4,640,000
$\times(1 - t)$		0.70	0.70
NOPAT		$ 3,248,000	$ 3,248,000
+D&A		1,000,000	1,000,000
CF Opns		$ 4,248,000	$ 4,248,000
−Cap Exp	$10,000,000	0	0
−Add WC	1,000,000	0	−1000,000
=FCF	−$11,000,000	$ 4,248,000	$ 5,248,000
NPV @ 10%	$15,487,664		

The $1 million is added back to (or a negative number is subtracted from) the incremental cash flows from operations in the calculation of the Year 10 cash flows.

The completed cash flow calculation worksheet for this example is presented in **Exhibit 11.3**. We could have completed the calculations without the worksheet. However, as mentioned, a cash flow calculation worksheet is a useful tool because it helps us make sure we don't forget anything. Once we have set up the worksheet, calculating the incremental cash flows is simply a matter of filling in the blanks. As you will see in the following discussion, correctly filling in some blanks can be difficult at times, but the worksheet keeps us organized by reminding us which blanks have yet to be filled in.

Notice that with a discount rate of 10 percent, the NPV of the cash flows in Exhibit 11.3 is $15,487,664. As in Chapter 10, the NPV is obtained by calculating the present values of all of the cash flows and adding them up. You might confirm this by doing this calculation yourself. The **Using Excel Example** on the next page illustrates the setup for the performing arts center project analysis in Excel.

FCF versus Accounting Earnings

It is worth stressing again that the FCF we have been discussing in this section is what matters to investors. The impact of a project on a firm's overall value or on its stock price does not depend on how the project affects the company's accounting earnings. It depends only on how the project affects the company's free cash flows.

Recall that accounting earnings can differ from cash flows for a number of reasons, making accounting earnings an unreliable measure of the costs and benefits of a project. For example, as soon as a firm sells a good or provides a service, its income statement will reflect the associated revenue and expenses, regardless of whether the customer has paid cash.

Accounting earnings also reflect noncash charges, such as depreciation and amortization, which are intended to account for the costs associated with deterioration of the assets in a business as those assets are used. Depreciation and amortization rules can cause substantial differences between cash flows and reported income because the assets acquired for a project are generally depreciated over several years, even though the actual cash outflow for their acquisition typically takes place at the beginning of the project.

Decision Making Example 11.1 illustrates how expected free cash flows can affect an investment decision.

Using Excel

Performing Arts Center Project

Cash flow calculations for capital budgeting problems are best set up and solved using a spreadsheet program. Here is the setup for the performing arts center project:

	A	B	D	F	H	J	L	N	P	R	T	V
1	**Key Assumptions:**											
2	Life of the project (Years)	10										
3	Number of new boxes	4										
4	Annual incremental revenue per box	$400,000										
5	Number of new seats	5,000										
6	Annual incremental revenue per seat	$2,500										
7	Incremental expense (% of revenue)	60%										
8	Construction cost (Cap Exp)*	$10,000										
9	Depreciation (per year)*	$1,000										
10	Additional investment in Year 0 (Add WC)*	$1,000										
11	WC to be recovered in Year 10*	($1,000)										
12	Tax rate	30%										
13	Cost of capital	10%										
14	Note: * denotes figures in thousands of dollars											
15												
16	**Cash Flow Calculations for Performing Arts Center Project ($ thousands)**											
17							Year					
18		0	1	2	3	4	5	6	7	8	9	10
19	Revenue		$14,100	$14,100	$14,100	$14,100	$14,100	$14,100	$14,100	$14,100	$14,100	$14,100
20	Operating Expenses		8,460	8,460	8,460	8,460	8,460	8,460	8,460	8,460	8,460	8,460
21	EBITDA		$5,640	$5,640	$5,640	$5,640	$5,640	$5,640	$5,640	$5,640	$5,640	$5,640
22	Less: Depreciation & Amortization		1,000	1,000	1,000	1,000	1,000	1,000	1,000	1,000	1,000	1,000
23	EBIT		$4,640	$4,640	$4,640	$4,640	$4,640	$4,640	$4,640	$4,640	$4,640	$4,640
24	Less Taxes		1,392	1,392	1,392	1,392	1,392	1,392	1,392	1,392	1,392	1,392
25	NOPAT		$3,248	$3,248	$3,248	$3,248	$3,248	$3,248	$3,248	$3,248	$3,248	$3,248
26												
27	Plus: Depreciation & Amortization		1,000	1,000	1,000	1,000	1,000	1,000	1,000	1,000	1,000	1,000
28	Cash Flows from Operations		$4,248	$4,248	$4,248	$4,248	$4,248	$4,248	$4,248	$4,248	$4,248	$4,248
29	Less: Capital Expenditures	$10,000	0	0	0	0	0	0	0	0	0	0
30	Less: Changes in Working Capital	$1,000	0	0	0	0	0	0	0	0	0	($1,000)
31												
32	**Free Cash Flow**	**($11,000)**	**$4,248**	**$4,248**	**$4,248**	**$4,248**	**$4,248**	**$4,248**	**$4,248**	**$4,248**	**$4,248**	**$5,248**
33												
34	**NPV**	**$15,488**										
35												

The following is the formula setup for the performing arts center project. As we did in Exhibit 11.3, we have combined Years 1 through 9 in a single column to save space. As mentioned in previous chapters, notice that none of the values in the actual worksheet are hard coded but instead use references from the key assumptions list, or specific formulas. This allows for an easy analysis of the impact of changes in the assumptions.

	A	B	C	D	E	V
1	**Key Assumptions:**					
2	Life of the project (Years)	10				
3	Number of new boxes	4				
4	Annual incremental revenue per box	400000				
5	Number of new seats	5000				
6	Annual incremental revenue per seat	2500				
7	Incremental expense (% of revenue)	0.6				
8	Construction cost (Cap Exp)*	10000				
9	Depreciation (per year)*	=B8/B2				
10	Additional investment in Year 0 (Add WC)*	1000				
11	WC to be recovered in Year 10*	(1000)				
12	Tax rate	0.3				
13	Cost of capital	0.1				
14	Note: * denotes figures in millions of dollars					
15						
16	**Cash Flow Calculations for Performing Arts Center Project ($ thousands)**					
17				Year		
18		0		1-9		10
19	Revenue			=($B$3*$B$4+$B$5*$B$6)/1000		=($B$3*$B$4+$B$5*$B$6)/1000
20	Operating Expenses			=$B$7*D19		=$B$7*V19
21	EBITDA			=D19-D20		=V19-V20
22	Less: Depreciation & Amortization			=$B$9		=$B$9
23	EBIT			=D21-D22		=V21-V22
24	Less Taxes			=D23*$B$12		=V23*$B$12
25	NOPAT			=D23-D24		=V23-V24
26						
27	Plus: Depreciation & Amortization			=$B$9		=$B$9
28	Cash Flows from Operations			=D25+D27		=V25+V27
29	Less: Capital Expenditures	=B8		0		0
30	Less: Changes in Working Capital	=B10		0		=B11
31						
32	**Free Cash Flow**	**=B28-B29-B30**		**=D28-D29-D30**		**=V28-V29-V30**
33						
34	**NPV**	**=NPV(B13, D32:V32)+B32**				
35						

DECISION MAKING

EXAMPLE 11.1 | Free Cash Flows

Situation You have saved $6,000 and plan to use $5,500 to buy a motorcycle. However, just before you go visit the motorcycle dealer, a friend of yours asks you to invest your $6,000 in a local pizza delivery business he is starting. Assuming he can raise the money, your friend has two alternatives regarding how to market the business. As illustrated below, both of these alternatives have an NPV of $2,614 with an opportunity cost of capital of 12 percent. You will receive all free cash flows from the business until you have recovered your $6,000 plus 12 percent interest. After that, you and your friend will split any additional cash proceeds. If you decide to invest, which alternative would you prefer that your friend choose?

	Alternative 1			Alternative 2		
	Year 0	Year 1	Year 2	Year 0	Year 1	Year 2
Revenue		$12,000	$12,000		$16,000	$8,000
−Op Ex		4,000	6,000		8,000	4,240
EBITDA		$ 8,000	$ 6,000		$ 8,000	$3,760
−D&A		2,500	2,500		2,500	2,500
EBIT		$ 5,500	$ 3,500		$ 5,500	$1,260
×(1 − t)		0.75	0.75		0.75	0.75
NOPAT		$ 4,125	$ 2,625		$ 4,125	$ 945
+D&A		2,500	2,500		2,500	2,500
CF Opns		$ 6,625	$ 5,125		$ 6,625	$3,445
−Cap Exp	$5,000	2,000	500	$5,000	500	500
−Add WC	1,000		(1,000)	1,000		(1,000)
=FCF	−$6,000	$ 4,625	$ 5,625	−$6,000	$ 6,125	$3,945
NPV @ 10%	$2,614			$2,614		

Decision If you expect no cash from other sources during the next year, you should insist that your friend choose Alternative 2. This is the only alternative that will produce enough FCF next year to purchase the motorcycle. Alternative 1 will produce $6,625 in CF Opns but will require $2,000 in capital expenditures. You will not be able to take more than $4,625 from the business in Year 1 under Alternative 1 without leaving the business short of cash.

Before You Go On

1. Why do we care about incremental cash flows at the firm level when we evaluate a project?
2. Why is D&A first subtracted and then added back in FCF calculations?
3. What types of investments should be included in FCF calculations?

11.2 Estimating Cash Flows in Practice

LEARNING OBJECTIVE

2. Discuss the five general rules for incremental after-tax free cash flow calculations and explain why cash flows stated in nominal (real) dollars should be discounted using a nominal (real) discount rate.

Now that we have discussed what FCFs are and how they are calculated, we are ready to focus on some important issues that arise when we estimate FCFs in practice. The first of these issues is determining which cash flows are incremental to the project and which are not. In this section we begin with a discussion of five general rules that help us do this. We then discuss why it is important to distinguish between nominal and real cash flows. Next, we discuss some concepts regarding tax rates and depreciation that are crucial to the calculation of FCF in practice. Finally, we describe and illustrate special factors that must be considered when calculating FCF for the final year of a project.

Five General Rules for Incremental After-Tax Free Cash Flow Calculations

As discussed earlier, we must determine how a project would change the after-tax free cash flows of the firm in order to calculate its NPV. This is not always simple to do, especially in a large firm that has a complex accounting system and many other projects that are not independent of the project being considered. Fortunately, there are five rules that can help us isolate the FCFs specific to an individual project even under the most complicated circumstances.

Rule 1: Include cash flows and only cash flows in your calculations. Do not include allocated costs unless they reflect cash flows. Examples of allocated costs are charges that accountants allocate to individual businesses to reflect their share of the corporate overhead (the costs associated with the senior managers of the firm, centralized accounting and finance functions, and so forth).

> **Weblink**
>
> You can learn more about incremental free cash flows at Investopedia.com, http://www .investopedia.com. Just enter "free cash flows" in the search box at the top of the page.

To see how allocated costs can differ from actual costs (and cash flows), consider a firm with $3 million of annual corporate overhead expenses and two identical manufacturing plants. Each of these plants would typically be allocated one-half, or $1.5 million, of the corporate overhead when their accounting profitability is estimated.

Suppose now that the firm is considering building a third plant that would be identical to the other two. If this plant is built, it will have no impact on the annual corporate overhead cash expense. Someone in accounting might argue that the new plant should be able to support its "fair share" of the $3 million overhead, or $1 million, and that this overhead should be included in the cash flow calculation. Of course, this person would be wrong. Since total corporate overhead costs will not change if the third plant is built, no overhead should be included when calculating the incremental FCFs for this plant.

Rule 2: Include the impact of the project on cash flows from other product lines. If the product associated with a project is expected to affect sales of one or more other products at the firm, you must include the expected impact of the new project on the cash flows from the other products when computing the FCFs. For example, consider the analysis that analysts at Apple Inc. would have done before giving the go-ahead for the development of the iPhone. Since, like iPods, the iPhone can store music, these analysts might have expected that the introduction of the iPhone would reduce annual iPod sales. If so, they would have had to account for the reduction in cash flows from lost iPod sales when they forecast the FCFs for the iPhone.

Similarly, if a new product is expected to boost sales of another, complementary, product, then the increase in cash flows associated with the new sales from that complementary product line should also be reflected in the FCFs. For example, consider how the introduction of the Apple iPad might affect music and video downloads from Apple iTunes. Many of the people who purchase an iPad and who have not previously downloaded songs and other content from iTunes will begin to do so. The cash flows from downloads by these new users are not directly tied to iPad sales, but they are incremental to those sales. If Apple had not introduced the iPad device, it would not have these iTunes sales. The analysis of the iPad project should have included the estimated impact of that project on cash flows from iTunes.

Rule 3: Include all opportunity costs. By opportunity costs, we mean the cost of giving up the next best opportunity.[1] Opportunity costs can arise in many different ways.

[1]The concept of opportunity cost here is similar to that discussed in Chapter 10 as it relates to the cost of capital.

For example, a project may require the use of a building or a piece of equipment that could otherwise be sold or leased to someone else. To the extent that selling or leasing the building or piece of equipment would generate additional cash flow for the firm and the opportunity to realize that cash flow must be forgone if the project is adopted, it represents an opportunity cost.

To see why this is so, suppose that a project will require the use of a piece of equipment that the firm already has and that can be sold for $50,000 on the used-equipment market. If the project is accepted, the firm will lose the opportunity to sell the piece of equipment for $50,000. This is a $50,000 cost that must be included in the project analysis. Accepting the project reduces the amount of money that the firm can realize from selling excess equipment by this amount.

Rule 4: Forget sunk costs. Sunk costs are costs that have already been incurred. All that matters when you evaluate a project at a particular point in time is how much you have to invest in the future and what you can expect to receive in return for that investment. Past investments are irrelevant.

To see this, consider the situation in which your company has invested $10 million in a project that has not yet generated any cash inflows. Also assume that circumstances have changed so the project, which was originally expected to generate cash inflows with a present value of $20 million, is now expected to generate cash inflows with a value of only $2 million. To receive this $2 million, however, your company will have to invest another $1 million. Should your firm do it? Of course it should!

The sunk cost for this investment is $10 million. That money has been spent and is therefore not relevant for the decision of whether to invest $1 million now. Since the $1 million of new spending generates new cash flows worth $2 million, this is a project with a positive NPV of $1 million and it should be accepted. Another way to think about it is that if your company stops investing now, it will have lost $10 million. If it makes the investment, its total loss will be $9 million. Although neither is an attractive alternative, it should be clear that it is better to lose $9 million than it is to lose $10 million. The point here is that, while it is often painful to do, you should ignore sunk costs when computing project FCFs.

Rule 5: Include only after-tax cash flows in the cash flow calculations. The incremental pretax earnings of a project matter only to the extent that they affect the after-tax cash flows that the firm's investors receive. For an individual project, as mentioned earlier, we compute the after-tax cash flows using the firm's marginal tax rate because this is the rate that will be applied against the incremental cash flows generated by the project.

Let's use the performing arts center project to illustrate how these rules are applied in practice. Suppose the following requirements and costs are associated with this project:

1. The chief financial officer requires that each project be assessed 5 percent of the initial investment to account for costs associated with the accounting, marketing, and information technology departments.
2. It is very likely that increasing the number of seats will reduce revenues next door at the cinema that your employer also owns. Attendance at the cinema is expected to be lower only when the performing arts center is staging a big event. The total impact is expected to be a reduction of $500,000 each year, before taxes, in the operating profits (EBIT) of the cinema. The depreciation of the cinema's assets will not be affected.
3. If the project is adopted, the new seating will be built in an area where exhibits have been placed in the past when the center has hosted guest lectures by well-known painters or sculptors. The performing arts center will no longer be able to host such events, and revenue will be reduced by $600,000 each year as a result.
4. The center has already spent $400,000 researching demand for new seating.
5. You have just discovered that a new salesperson will be hired if the center goes ahead with the expansion. This person will be responsible for sales and service of the four new luxury boxes and will be paid $75,000 per year, including salary and benefits. The $75,000 is not included in the 60 percent figure for operating expenses that was previously mentioned.

EXHIBIT 11.4 **Adjusted FCF Calculations and NPV for the Performing Arts Center Project**

The adjustments described in the text result in changes in the FCF calculations and a different NPV for the performing arts center project.

	Year 0	Years 1 to 9	Year 10
Revenue		$13,500,000	$13,500,000
−Op Ex		8,100,000	8,100,000
−New salesperson's salary		75,000	75,000
−Lost cinema EBIT		500,000	500,000
EBITDA		$ 4,825,000	$ 4,825,000
−D&A		1,000,000	1,000,000
EBIT		$ 3,825,000	$ 3,825,000
×(1 − *t*)		0.70	0.70
NOPAT		$ 2,677,500	$ 2,677,500
+D&A		1,000,000	1,000,000
CF Opns		$ 3,677,500	$ 3,677,500
−Cap Exp	$10,000,000	0	0
−Add WC	1,000,000	0	−1,000,000
=FCF	−$11,000,000	$ 3,677,500	$ 4,677,500
NPV @ 10%	$11,982,189		

What impact will these requirements and costs have on the FCFs for the project? **Exhibit 11.4** shows their impact on the FCFs and NPV presented in Exhibit 11.3.

1. The 5 percent assessment sounds like an allocated overhead cost. To the extent that this assessment does not reflect an actual increase in cash costs, it should not be included. It is not relevant to the project. The analysis should include only incremental cash flows.
2. The impact of the expansion on the operating profits of the cinema is an example of how a project can erode or cannibalize business in another part of a firm. The $500,000 reduction in EBIT is relevant and should be included in the analysis.
3. The loss of the ability to use the exhibits area, the next best alternative to the new seating plan, represents a $600,000 opportunity cost. The center is giving up revenue from guest lecturers that require exhibit space in order to build the additional seating. This opportunity cost will be partially offset by elimination of the operating expenses associated with the guest lectures.
4. The $400,000 for research has already been spent. The decision of whether to accept or reject the project will not alter the amount spent for this research. This is a sunk cost that should not be included in the analysis.
5. The $75,000 annual salary for the new salesperson is an incremental cost that should be included in the analysis. Even though the marketing department is a corporate overhead department, in this case the salesperson must be hired specifically because of the new project.

The specific changes in the analysis from Exhibits 11.3 to 11.4 are as follows. Revenue and Op Ex after Year 0 have been reduced from $14,100,000 and $8,460,000, respectively, in Exhibit 11.3 to $13,500,000 and $8,100,000, respectively, in Exhibit 11.4. These changes reflect the $600,000 loss of revenues and the reduction in costs (60 percent of revenue) associated with the loss of the ability to host guest lectures. The $75,000 expense for the new salesperson's salary and the $500,000 reduction in the EBIT of the cinema are then subtracted from Revenue, along with Op Ex. These changes result in EBITDA of $4,825,000 in Exhibit 11.4, compared with EBITDA of $5,640,000 in Exhibit 11.3. The net result is a reduction in the project NPV from $15,487,664 (in Exhibit 11.3) to $11,982,189 (in Exhibit 11.4).

Learning by Doing Application 11.1 provides more insights regarding application of the five rules for incremental after-tax free cash flow calculations.

LEARNING BY DOING

APPLICATION 11.1 | Using the General Rules for FCF Calculations

Problem You have owned and operated a pizza parlor for several years. The space that you lease for your pizza parlor is considerably larger than the space you need. To more efficiently utilize this space, you are considering subdividing it and opening a hamburger joint. You know that your analysis should consider the overall impact of the hamburger project on the total cash flows of your business, but beyond estimating revenues and costs from hamburger-related sales and the investment required to get the hamburger business started, you are unsure what else you should consider. Based on the five general rules for incremental after-tax cash flow calculations, what other factors should you consider?

Approach Careful consideration of each of the five rules provides insights concerning the other factors that should be considered.

Solution Rule 1 suggests that you should only consider the incremental impact of the hamburger stand on actual overhead expenses, such as the cost of additional accounting support. Rule 2 indicates that you should consider the potential for the hamburger business to take sales away from (or cannibalize) the pizza business. Rule 3 suggests that you should carefully consider the opportunity cost associated with the excess space or any excess equipment that might be used for the hamburger business. If you could lease the extra space to someone else, for example, then the amount that you could receive by doing so is an opportunity cost and should be included in the analysis. Similarly, the price for which any excess equipment could be sold represents an opportunity cost. Rule 4 reminds you to consider cash flows from this point forward only. Forget sunk costs. Finally, Rule 5 tells you not to forget to account for the impact of taxes in your cash flow calculations.

Nominal versus Real Cash Flows

nominal dollars dollar amounts that are not adjusted for inflation; the purchasing power of a nominal dollar amount depends on when that amount is received

real dollars inflation-adjusted dollars; the actual purchasing power of dollars stated in real terms is the same regardless of when those dollars are received

In addition to following the five rules for incremental after-tax cash flow calculations, it is very important to make sure that all cash flows are stated in either nominal dollars or real dollars—not a mixture of the two. The concepts of nominal and real dollars are directly related to the discussion in Chapter 2 that distinguishes between (1) the nominal rate of interest and (2) the real rate of interest. **Nominal dollars** are the dollars that we typically think of. They represent the actual dollar amounts that we expect a project to generate in the future, without any adjustments. To the extent that there is inflation, the purchasing power of each nominal dollar will decline over time. When prices are going up, a given nominal dollar amount will buy less and less over time. **Real dollars** represent dollars stated in terms of constant purchasing power. When we forecast in real dollars, the purchasing power of the dollars in one period is equal to the purchasing power of the dollars in any other period.

To illustrate the difference between nominal and real dollars, let's consider an example. Suppose that the rate of inflation is expected to be 5 percent next year and that you just lent \$100 to a friend for one year. If your friend is not paying any interest, the nominal dollar amount you expect to receive in one year is \$100. At that time, though, the purchasing power of this \$100 is expected to be only \$95.24: $\$100/(1 + \Delta P_e) = \$100/1.05 = \$95.24$, where ΔP_e is the expected rate of inflation as discussed in Chapter 2. In other words, if inflation is as expected, when your friend repays the \$100, it will buy only what \$95.24 would buy today. You will have earned a real return of $(\$95.24 - \$100)/\$100 = -0.0476$, or −4.76 percent, on this loan. Another way of thinking about this loan is that your friend is expected to repay you with dollars having a real value of only \$95.24.

To understand the importance of making sure that all cash flows are stated in either nominal dollars or real dollars, it is useful to write the cost of capital (k) from Chapter 10 as:

$$1 + k = (1 + \Delta P_e) \times (1 + r) \tag{11.3}$$

In Equation 11.3, k is the nominal cost of capital that is normally used to discount cash flows and r is the real cost of capital.[2] This equation tells us that the nominal cost of capital equals

[2]As discussed in Chapter 2, if we multiply the two terms on the right-hand side of Equation 11.3, we get $1 + k = 1 + \Delta P_e + r + \Delta P_e r$. Since the last term in this equation, $\Delta P_e r$, is the product of two fractions, it is a very small number and is often ignored in practice. Without this term, Equation 11.3 becomes $1 + k = 1 + \Delta P_e + r$ or $k = \Delta P_e + r$.

the real cost of capital, adjusted for the expected rate of inflation. This means that whenever we discount a cash flow using the nominal cost of capital, the discount rate we are using reflects both the expected rate of inflation (ΔP_e) and a real return (r). If, on the one hand, we discounted a *real cash flow* using the *nominal cost of capital,* we would be overcompensating for expected inflation in the discounting process. On the other hand, if we discounted a *nominal cash flow* using the *real cost of capital* (r), we would be undercompensating for expected inflation.

In capital budgeting, we normally forecast cash flows in nominal dollars and discount them using the nominal cost of capital.[3] As an alternative, we can state the cash flows in real terms and discount them using the real cost of capital. This alternative calculation will give us exactly the same NPV. To see this, consider a project that will require an investment of $50,000 in Year 0 and will produce FCFs of $20,000 a year in Years 1 through 4. With a 15 percent nominal cost of capital, the NPV for this project is:

$$\begin{aligned}
\text{NPV} &= \text{FCF}_0 + \frac{\text{FCF}_1}{1+k} + \frac{\text{FCF}_2}{(1+k)^2} + \frac{\text{FCF}_3}{(1+k)^3} + \frac{\text{FCF}_4}{(1+k)^4} \\
&= -\$50{,}000 + \frac{\$20{,}000}{1.15} + \frac{\$20{,}000}{(1.15)^2} + \frac{\$20{,}000}{(1.15)^3} + \frac{\$20{,}000}{(1.15)^4} \\
&= -\$50{,}000 + \$17{,}391 + \$15{,}123 + \$13{,}150 + \$11{,}435 \\
&= \$7{,}099
\end{aligned}$$

Equation 11.3 can be used to calculate the real cost of capital if we recognize that it can be rearranged algebraically as:

$$r = \frac{1+k}{1+\Delta P_e} - 1$$

With a 5 percent expected rate of inflation, the real cost of capital is therefore:

$$r = \frac{1+k}{1+\Delta P_e} - 1 = \frac{1.15}{1.05} - 1 = 0.09524\text{, or } 9.524\%$$

Discounting the nominal cash flows by the rate of inflation tells us that the real cash flows are:

Year 0	Year 1	Year 2	Year 3	Year 4
−$50,000	$\frac{\$20{,}000}{1+0.05}$	$\frac{\$20{,}000}{(1+0.05)^2}$	$\frac{\$20{,}000}{(1+0.05)^3}$	$\frac{\$20{,}000}{(1+0.05)^4}$
= −$50,000	= $19,048	= $18,141	= $17,277	= $16,454

Weblink

You can calculate the impact of inflation on purchasing power using the inflation calculator at http://www.westegg.com/inflation. This calculator tells you how much it would cost you, in nominal dollars, to buy the same goods in any two years, beginning in the year 1800.

Therefore, when we discount the real cash flows using the real cost of capital, we see that the NPV is:

$$\begin{aligned}
\text{NPV} &= -\$50{,}000 + \frac{\$19{,}048}{1.09524} + \frac{\$18{,}141}{(1.09524)^2} + \frac{\$17{,}277}{(1.09524)^3} + \frac{\$16{,}454}{(1.09524)^4} \\
&= -\$50{,}000 + \$17{,}391 + \$15{,}123 + \$13{,}150 + \$11{,}435 \\
&= \$7{,}099
\end{aligned}$$

Notice that the present value of each of the annual cash flows is exactly the same when we use nominal cash flows and when we use real cash flows. This has to be the case because when we stated the NPV calculation in real dollars, we first divided the discount rate by 1.05. We then reduced the value of the future cash flows by discounting them by 5 percent. This is equivalent to reducing the numerator and the denominator in each present value calculation by the same fraction, which must result in the same answer.

Learning by Doing Application 11.2 illustrates how nominal and real rates of return can be compared when evaluating investment opportunities.

[3]Note that when we use the term *cost of capital* without distinguishing between the nominal or real cost of capital, we are referring to the *nominal* cost of capital. This is the convention that is used in practice. In this example, we use the term *nominal* or *real* whenever we refer to the cost of capital for clarity. In the rest of this book, however, we follow convention by simply using the term *cost of capital* to refer to the nominal cost of capital.

LEARNING BY DOING

WileyPLUS

Need more help? Visit your WileyPLUS course.

APPLICATION 11.2 | The Investment Decision and Nominal versus Real Dollars

Problem You are trying to decide how to invest $25,000, which you just inherited from a distant relative. You do not want to take any risks with this money because you want to use it as a down payment on a home when you graduate in three years. Therefore, you have decided to invest the money in securities that are guaranteed by the U.S. government. You are considering two alternatives: a three-year Treasury note and an inflation-indexed Treasury security. If you invest in the three-year Treasury note, you will be paid 3 percent per year in interest and will get your $25,000 back at the end of three years. If you invest in the inflation-indexed security, you will be paid 1 percent per year plus an amount that reflects actual inflation in each of the next three years. For example, if inflation equals 2 percent per year for each of the next three years, you will receive 3 percent each year in total interest. This interest on the inflation-indexed security will compound, and you will receive a single payment at the end of three years. If you expect inflation to average 2.5 percent per year over the next three years, should you invest in the three-year Treasury note or in the inflation-indexed Treasury security?

Approach Compare the 3 percent return on the three-year Treasury note, which is a nominal rate of return, with the nominal rate of return that you can expect to receive from the inflation-indexed security and invest in the security with the highest rate. The nominal rate on the inflation-indexed security in each year equals the real rate of 1 percent plus the rate of inflation.

Solution Without doing any detailed calculations, it is apparent that you should invest in the inflation-indexed security. The reason is that if the rate of inflation turns out to be 2.5 percent, the inflation-indexed security will yield 3.5 percent (1 percent plus the 2.5 percent inflation adjustment) per year. With this investment, the real purchasing power of your money will increase by 1 percent per year. This will be true regardless of what inflation turns out to be during the three-year period. Assuming that you can reinvest the annual interest payments from the three-year Treasury note at 3 percent, if you buy this security, the real purchasing power of your money will increase by only 0.5 percent (3 percent interest rate less 2.5 percent inflation) per year.

Tax Rates and Depreciation

The United States has a very complicated corporate tax system. Corporations pay taxes at the federal, state, and local levels. Some governmental jurisdictions tax income, while others tax property or some other measure of value. Furthermore, a wide variety of deductions and adjustments are made to income or other measures of value when computing the actual taxes that a corporation owes. A detailed discussion of the different taxes that corporations pay and how they are computed is beyond the scope of this textbook. However, at this point, it is important for you to be familiar with the progressive tax system that we have in the United States and with the depreciation methods used for computing corporate tax obligations. These concepts are especially important in capital budgeting.

Marginal and Average Tax Rates

progressive tax system a tax system in which the marginal tax rate at low levels of income is lower than the marginal tax rate at high levels of income

A **progressive tax system**, which we have in the United States, is one in which taxpayers pay a progressively larger share of their income in taxes as their income rises. This happens in a progressive tax system because the marginal tax rate at low levels of income is lower than the marginal tax rate at high levels of income. Recall that the marginal tax rate is the rate paid on the last dollar earned. The tax system in the United States is progressive for both individuals and corporations. For example, **Exhibit 11.5** presents the 2016 federal tax rate schedule for single individuals. Notice that the percentage tax owed beyond the base amount in each row of Exhibit 11.5 increases as taxable income increases. In other words, the marginal tax rate, as well as the average tax rate, increases as an individual moves from one tax bracket to the next.

Exhibit 11.6 shows the 2016 tax rate schedule faced by a typical U.S. corporation (you may recall that a variation of this tax rate schedule is also presented in Exhibit 3.6). Notice that this schedule is also progressive. The U.S. corporate tax system in 2016 was structured

EXHIBIT 11.5 U.S. Tax Rate Schedule for a Single Individual in 2016

The income tax system for individuals in the United States is progressive in that the tax rate increases with income. For very low income levels—say, $20,000 per year—individuals pay only 15 percent on each additional dollar they earn. For individuals who earn more than $415,050, this rate is 39.6 percent.

Taxable Income		
More Than	But Not More Than	Tax Owed
$0	$9,275	10% of amount beyond $0
$9,275	$37,650	$927.50 + 15% of amount beyond $9,275
$37,650	$91,150	$5,183.75 + 25% of amount beyond $37,650
$91,150	$190,150	$18,558.75 + 28% of amount beyond $91,150
$190,150	$413,350	$46,278.75 + 33% of amount beyond $190,150
$413,350	$415,050	$119,934.75 + 35% of amount beyond $413,350
$415,050	no limit	$120,529.75 + 39.6% of amount beyond $415,050

EXHIBIT 11.6 U.S. Corporate Tax Rate Schedule in 2016

Just like the tax system for individuals, the tax system for corporations in the United States is progressive, with marginal tax rates ranging from 15 percent to as high as 39 percent.

Taxable Income		
More Than	But Not More Than	Tax Owed
$0	$50,000	15% of amount beyond $0
$50,000	$75,000	$7,500 + 25% of amount beyond $50,000
$75,000	$100,000	$13,750 + 34% of amount beyond $75,000
$100,000	$335,000	$22,250 + 39% of amount beyond $100,000
$335,000	$10,000,000	$113,900 + 34% of amount beyond $335,000
$10,000,000	$15,000,000	$3,400,000 + 35% of amount beyond $10,000,000
$15,000,000	$18,333,333	$5,150,000 + 38% of amount beyond $15,000,000
$18,333,333	————	35% on all income

so that the marginal rate exactly equals the average tax rate for all levels of income above $18,333,333. If the corporation's taxable income is below $18,333,333, the marginal tax rate will not necessarily be the same as the average tax rate. These rates differ in all tax brackets below $18,333,333, except the $335,000 to $10 million bracket. Remember that since we use marginal tax rates in capital budgeting, you cannot simply divide the dollar taxes paid by the taxable income for a company to estimate the tax rate. This calculation gives you the average, not the marginal, tax rate.

Learning by Doing Application 11.3 illustrates calculation of marginal and average tax rates.

LEARNING BY DOING

APPLICATION 11.3 | Calculating Marginal and Average Tax Rates

Problem Assume that you are operating the pizza parlor and hamburger joint described in Learning by Doing Application 11.1. Because the business has become complicated, you have incorporated. From now on, earnings are subject to the corporate tax rates presented in Exhibit 11.6. If your corporation's total taxable income is $200,000 in 2016, how much does it owe in federal taxes? What are the corporation's marginal and average federal tax rates? If you were considering buying a new oven, which tax rate would you use when computing the free cash flows?

Approach Use the rates presented in Exhibit 11.6 to calculate the total amount that your corporation owes. The marginal federal tax rate is the rate in the "Tax Owed" column in Exhibit 11.6 that corresponds to the row in which the total taxable income earned by your restaurant is found. The ratio of the total amount that you owe divided by your total taxable income equals the average federal tax rate. You would use the tax rate that would be applied to the incremental after-tax free cash flows associated with the new oven.

Solution From Exhibit 11.6, you can see that with a taxable income of \$200,000, your corporation will owe taxes of \$22,250 + (\$100,000 × 0.39) = \$61,250. The marginal tax rate is 39 percent, and the average tax rate is \$61,250/\$200,000 = 0.306, or 30.6 percent. You will use the marginal rate of 39 percent when computing the free cash flows for the new oven.

Taxes and Depreciation

Corporations keep two sets of books. One set is kept for preparing financial statements in accordance with generally accepted accounting principles (GAAP). These are the financial statements that appear in the annual report and other documents filed with the Securities and Exchange Commission (SEC). The other set is kept for computing the taxes that the corporation actually pays. Corporations must keep two sets of books because the GAAP rules for computing income are different from the rules that the IRS uses.

One especially important difference from a capital budgeting perspective is that the depreciation methods allowed by GAAP differ from those allowed by the IRS. The straight-line depreciation method illustrated earlier in this chapter in the performing arts center example is allowed by GAAP and is often used for financial reporting. In contrast, an "accelerated" method of depreciation, called the **Modified Accelerated Cost Recovery System (MACRS)**, has been in use for U.S. federal tax calculations since the Tax Reform Act of 1986 went into effect.[4] MACRS is an accelerated system in the sense that depreciation charges for all assets other than nonfarm real property (for example, buildings) are higher in the early years of an asset's life than with the straight-line method. MACRS thus enables a firm to deduct depreciation charges sooner, thereby realizing the tax savings sooner and increasing the present value of the tax savings. Since we want to estimate the actual incremental cash flows from a project in capital budgeting, we use the depreciation method allowed by the IRS in our calculations. This is the method that determines how much of a tax deduction a corporation actually receives for an investment.

Modified Accelerated Cost Recovery System (MACRS) the accelerated depreciation method that has been in use for U.S. federal taxes since the Tax Reform Act of 1986 went into effect

Exhibit 11.7 lists the percentage of the cost of an asset that can be depreciated in each year for assets with 3-, 5-, 7-, 10-, 15-, and 20-year allowable recovery periods. The recovery periods for specific types of assets are specified in the tax law that is passed by Congress and signed by the president. For instance, in 2016, the allowable recovery period was 5 years for computers and automobiles, 7 years for office furniture, 10 years for water transportation equipment such as barges, 15 years for railroad wharves and docks, 20 years for farm buildings, 27.5 years for residential rental property, and 39.5 years for nonresidential real property (such as manufacturing buildings). Residential rental and nonresidential real property are depreciated using the straight-line method. Depreciation charges are intended to represent the cost of wear and tear on assets in the course of business. However, since they are set through a political process, they may be greater than or less than the actual cost of this wear and tear.

Weblink

You can read more about tax rates and depreciation rules at the Internal Revenue Service Web site, http://www.irs.gov.

Note that the percentages in each column of Exhibit 11.7 add up to 100 percent. This is because the tax law allows firms to depreciate 100 percent of the cost of an asset regardless of the expected salvage value of that asset. Consequently, when we use the MACRS schedule to determine the tax depreciation, we do not have to worry about the expected salvage value for the asset.[5]

Let's consider an example to show how MACRS is applied. Suppose you are evaluating a project that will require the purchase of an automobile for \$25,000. Since an automobile is

[4]Although some assets that were acquired before 1986 are still being depreciated using earlier methods, the vast majority of depreciation for existing assets and all depreciation for new assets are based on MACRS.

[5]Under GAAP accounting rules, if the salvage value can be estimated with reasonable certainty, it should be used in computing depreciation. However, in practice the expected salvage value of a new capital asset is so often uncertain that it is typically assumed to equal \$0 even for financial reporting purposes.

EXHIBIT 11.7 MACRS Depreciation Schedules by Allowable Recovery Period

The MACRS schedule lists the tax depreciation rates that firms use for assets placed into service after the Tax Reform Act of 1986 went into effect. The table indicates the percentage of the cost of the asset that can be depreciated in each year during the period that it is being used. Year 1 is the year in which the asset is first placed into service.

Year	3-Year	5-Year	7-Year	10-Year	15-Year	20-Year
1	33.33%	20.00%	14.29%	10.00%	5.00%	3.75%
2	44.45	32.00	24.49	18.00	9.50	7.22
3	14.81	19.20	17.49	14.40	8.55	6.68
4	7.41	11.52	12.49	11.52	7.70	6.18
5		11.52	8.93	9.22	6.93	5.71
6		5.76	8.92	7.37	6.23	5.29
7			8.93	6.55	5.90	4.89
8			4.46	6.56	5.90	4.52
9				6.55	5.91	4.46
10				3.28	5.90	4.46
11					5.91	4.46
12					5.90	4.46
13					5.91	4.46
14					5.90	4.46
15					5.91	4.46
16					2.95	4.46
17						4.46
18						4.46
19						4.46
20						4.46
21						2.24
Total	100.00%	100.00%	100.00%	100.00%	100.00%	100.00%

a five-year asset under MACRS, you can use the percentages for a five-year asset in Exhibit 11.7 to calculate the annual depreciation deductions:

Year 1:	$25,000 × 0.2000 =	$5,000
Year 2:	$25,000 × 0.3200 =	$8,000
Year 3:	$25,000 × 0.1920 =	$4,800
Year 4:	$25,000 × 0.1152 =	$2,880
Year 5:	$25,000 × 0.1152 =	$2,880
Year 6:	$25,000 × 0.0576 =	$1,440
Total		$25,000

Notice that even though the automobile is a five-year asset, there is a depreciation charge in the sixth year. This is because MACRS assumes that the asset is placed in service in the middle of the first year. As a result, the firm is allowed a deduction for half of a year in Year 1, a full year in Years 2 through 5, and half of a year in Year 6.

Recall that the FCF calculation, Equation 11.1, included incremental depreciation along with incremental amortization (D&A). We put depreciation and amortization together in the calculation because amortization is a noncash charge (deduction) like depreciation. It is beyond the scope of this book to discuss amortization in detail because the rules that govern it are complex. However, you should know that, as was discussed in Chapter 3, amortization, like depreciation, is a deduction that is allowed under the tax law to compensate for the decline in value of certain, mainly intangible, assets used by a business.

Computing the Terminal-Year FCF

The FCF in the last, or terminal, year of a project's life often includes cash flows that are not typically included in the calculations for other years. For instance, in the final year of a project, the assets acquired during the life of the project may be sold and the working capital that has been invested may be recovered. The cash flows that result from the sale of assets and recovery of working capital must be included in the calculation of the terminal-year FCF.

You can see this in the performing arts center example discussed earlier. Note that the Year 10, or terminal year, cash flows in this example are different from those in the other years. They include both CF Opns and investment cash flows that reflect recovery of net working capital investments. Net incremental additions to working capital (Add WC) that are due to the project are calculated as follows:

$$\text{Add WC} = \text{Change in cash and cash equivalents} + \text{Change in accounts receivable} + \text{Change in inventories} - \text{Change in accounts payable} \quad (11.4)$$

where the changes in cash and cash equivalents (marketable securities), accounts receivable, inventories, and accounts payable represent changes in the values of these accounts that result from the adoption of the project.

Looking at the components of Add WC, we can see that cash and cash equivalents, accounts receivable, and inventories require the investment of capital, while accounts payable represent capital provided by suppliers. When a project ends, the cash and cash equivalents are no longer needed, the accounts receivable are collected, the inventories are sold, and the accounts payable are paid. In other words, the firm recovers the net working capital that has been invested in the project. To reflect this in the FCF calculation, the cash flow in the last year of the project typically includes a *negative investment in working capital* that equals the cumulative investment in working capital over the life of the project. It is very important to make sure that the recovery of working capital is reflected in the cash flows in the last year of a project. In some businesses, working capital can account for 20 percent or more of revenue, and excluding working capital recovery from the calculations can cause you to substantially understate the NPV of a project.

In some projects, there will also be incremental capital expenditures (Cap Exp) in the terminal year. This is because, for example, the assets acquired for the project are being sold or there are disposal costs associated with them. In the performing arts center example, Cap Exp is \$0 in Year 10. This is because we were assuming that, other than the working capital, the investments at the beginning of the project would have no salvage value, there would be no disposal costs associated with the assets, and there would be no clean-up costs associated with the project in Year 10. When an asset is expected to have a salvage value, we must include the salvage value realized from the sale of the asset and the impact of the sale on the firm's taxes in the terminal-year FCF calculations. Any costs that must be incurred to dispose of assets should also be included. Finally, clean-up costs, such as those associated with restoring the environment after a strip-mining project, also must be included in the terminal-year FCF.

The salvage value realized from the sale of the assets used in a project includes both the cash that is actually realized when they are sold and, if the salvage value of any asset differs from its depreciated book value, the tax implications from the sale. To better understand how taxes affect the terminal-year cash flows for a project, let's make the performing arts center example more realistic. Recall that the initial Cap Exp in the performing arts center example was \$10 million, that we used straight-line depreciation, and that we assumed that the salvage value would be \$0 in Year 10. Now that we know about MACRS, let's more realistically assume that the allowable recovery period for this investment under MACRS is 10 years.

Exhibit 11.8 presents the depreciation calculations for this investment under MACRS. Note that since the amount of depreciation now changes over time, we can no longer present Years 1 through 9 together as we did in Exhibit 11.3. Also note that because MACRS allows only a half year of depreciation in Year 1, the book value of the investment is greater than \$0 at the end of Year 10. In this case it is \$328,000.

If we still assume a salvage value of \$0 for this investment, the fact that the book value is positive means that the firm will have a tax loss when it writes off the remaining value of the investment at the end of the project. In other words, when the project ends, the firm will take a deduction when computing its taxes that equals the remaining \$328,000 book value of the asset. With a 30 percent tax rate, this will result in a tax savings of \$328,000 × 0.30 = \$98,400. This tax savings must be reflected in the cash flow calculations in Year 10. **Exhibit 11.9** illustrates the cash flow and NPV calculations for the performing arts center example with these changes. The \$98,400 tax savings is included as a negative capital

EXHIBIT 11.8 MACRS Depreciation Calculations for the Performing Arts Center Project ($ thousands)

Using the percentages from the 10-Year MACRS depreciation schedule in Exhibit 11.7, we can calculate the tax (MACRS) depreciation for each year during the life of the performing arts center project.

	Year 1	Year 2	Year 3	Year 4	Year 5	Year 6	Year 7	Year 8	Year 9	Year 10
Depreciation Calculations										
Beginning book value	$10,000	$9,000	$7,200	$5,760	$4,608	$3,686	$2,949	$2,294	$1,639	$983
MACRS percentage	10.00%	18.00%	14.40%	11.52%	9.22%	7.37%	6.55%	6.55%	6.56%	6.55%
MACRS depreciation	$1,000	$1,800	$1,440	$1,152	$922	$737	$655	$655	$656	$655
Ending book value	$9,000	$7,200	$5,760	$4,608	$3,686	$2,949	$2,294	$1,639	$983	$328

EXHIBIT 11.9 FCF Calculations and NPV for Performing Arts Center Project with MACRS Depreciation ($ thousands)

This exhibit shows the FCF calculations and the NPV for the performing arts center project when MACRS is used to compute depreciation. These calculations correspond to those in Exhibit 11.3, which reflect straight-line depreciation. Notice that the NPV is greater with the MACRS system because the tax shields from the depreciation are realized sooner.

	Year 0	Year 1	Year 2	Year 3	Year 4	Year 5	Year 6	Year 7	Year 8	Year 9	Year 10
Revenue		$14,100	$14,100	$14,100	$14,100	$14,100	$14,100	$14,100	$14,100	$14,100	$14,100
−Op Ex		8,460	8,460	8,460	8,460	8,460	8,460	8,460	8,460	8,460	8,460
EBITDA		$ 5,640	$ 5,640	$ 5,640	$ 5,640	$ 5,640	$ 5,640	$ 5,640	$ 5,640	$ 5,640	$ 5,640
−D&A		1,000	1,800	1,440	1,152	922	737	655	655	656	655
EBIT		$ 4,640	$ 3,840	$ 4,200	$ 4,488	$ 4,718	$ 4,903	$ 4,985	$ 4,985	$ 4,984	$ 4,985
$\times(1-t)$		0.70	0.70	0.70	0.70	0.70	0.70	0.70	0.70	0.70	0.70
NOPAT		$ 3,248	$ 2,688	$ 2,940	$ 3,142	$ 3,303	$ 3,432	$ 3,490	$ 3,490	$ 3,489	$ 3,490
+D&A		1,000	1,800	1,440	1,152	922	737	655	655	656	655
CF Opns		$ 4,248	$ 4,488	$ 4,380	$ 4,294	$ 4,225	$ 4,169	$ 4,145	$ 4,145	$ 4,145	$ 4,145
−Cap Exp	$10,000	0	0	0	0	0	0	0	0	0	−98
−Add WC	1,000	0	0	0	0	0	0	0	0	0	−1,000
=FCF	−$11,000	$ 4,248	$ 4,488	$ 4,380	$ 4,294	$ 4,225	$ 4,169	$ 4,145	$ 4,145	$ 4,145	$ 5,243
NPV @ 10%	$15,610										

expenditure in Year 10 (as −98 since we are rounding to thousands).[6] Notice that the NPV has increased from $15,487,664 in Exhibit 11.3 to $15,610,135. The $122,471 difference reflects the present value of the tax savings from using MACRS depreciation instead of straight-line depreciation plus the tax savings from the disposal of the asset.

If the salvage value is greater than $0 but less than the book value of $328,000, the tax savings will be smaller than $98,400, and if the salvage value exceeds the book value, the firm will actually have a gain on the sale of the asset that will increase its tax liability. In either of these cases, you must include the proceeds from the sale of the assets and the tax effects in your cash flow calculations.

The general formula for calculating the tax on the salvage value for an asset is:

$$\text{Tax on sale of an asset} = (\text{Selling price of asset} - \text{Book value of asset}) \times t$$

where t is the firm's marginal tax rate.

To make sure we know how we use this equation, suppose that the salvage value (selling price) in Year 10 of the $10,000,000 investment in the performing arts center project is expected to be $1,000,000 and that the book value remains $328,000. In this case the firm will pay additional taxes of ($1,000,000 − $328,000) × 0.30 = $201,600 on the sale of the assets. Deducting this amount from the $1,000,000 that the firm receives from the sale of the assets yields after-tax proceeds of $798,400 and the cash flows illustrated in **Exhibit 11.10**. This $798,400 is greater than the $98,000 in Exhibit 11.9 and therefore the NPV for the project is greater.

Learning by Doing Application 11.4 illustrates calculation of the after-tax proceeds from the sale of an asset.

[6]Including the tax savings as negative capital expenditure increases the FCF in Year 10 since we subtract all capital expenditures.

EXHIBIT 11.10 **FCF Calculations and NPV for the Performing Arts Center Project with a $1 Million Salvage Value in Year 10 ($ thousands)**

This exhibit shows the FCF calculations and NPV for the performing arts center project assuming that the salvage value of the $10 million capital investment is $1 million in Year 10. All other assumptions are the same as in Exhibit 11.9.

	Year 0	Year 1	Year 2	Year 3	Year 4	Year 5	Year 6	Year 7	Year 8	Year 9	Year 10
CF Opns		$4,248	$4,488	$4,380	$4,294	$4,225	$4,169	$4,145	$4,145	$4,145	$4,145
−Cap Exp	$10,000	0	0	0	0	0	0	0	0	0	−798
−Add WC	1,000	0	0	0	0	0	0	0	0	0	−1,000
=FCF	−$11,000	$4,248	$4,488	$4,380	$4,294	$4,225	$4,169	$4,145	$4,145	$4,145	$5,943
NPV @ 10%	$15,880										

LEARNING BY DOING

WileyPLUS

Need more help? Visit your WileyPLUS course.

APPLICATION 11.4 | Accounting for Taxes When Assets Are Sold

Problem You have decided to replace an oven in your pizza parlor. The old oven originally cost $20,000. Depreciation charges of $15,000 have been taken since you acquired it, resulting in a current book value of $5,000. The owner of a restaurant down the street has offered you $3,000 for the old oven. If you accept this offer, how will the sale affect the cash flows from your business? Assume the marginal tax rate for your business is 39 percent.

Approach First use the general formula presented above to calculate the tax on the salvage value. Then subtract (add) any tax obligation (savings) from (to) the amount that you will receive for the oven to obtain the total impact of the sale on the cash flows to your business.

Solution If you sell the old oven, you will receive a cash inflow of $3,000 from the purchaser in return for an asset with a book value of $5,000. With a 39 percent marginal tax rate, this will result in a tax of:

$$\text{Tax on sale of an asset} = (\text{Selling price of asset} - \text{Book value of asset}) \times t$$
$$= (\$3{,}000 - \$5{,}000) \times 0.39 = -\$780$$

Since you are selling the oven for less than its book value, you will realize a tax savings of $780. Therefore, the total impact of the sale on the cash flows from your business will be $3,000 + $780 = $3,780. Of course, the purchase price of the new oven will probably more than offset this amount.

Note that if the sale price exceeded the book value of the oven by $2,000, you would have a taxable gain and would have to pay $780. In this case, the cash flows received from the purchaser would be reduced, rather than increased, by $780.

Expected Cash Flows

It is very important to realize that in an NPV analysis we use the *expected* FCF for each year of the life of the project. Similar to the expected values calculated in Chapter 7, the expected FCF for a particular year equals the sum of the products of the possible outcomes (FCFs) and the probabilities that those outcomes will be realized.

To better illustrate this point, suppose that you have just invented a new board game and are trying to decide whether you should produce and sell it. If you decide to go ahead with this project, you estimate that it will cost you $100,000 for the equipment necessary to produce and distribute the game. Also suppose you think there are three possible outcomes if you make this investment—the game is very successful, game sales are acceptable but not exceptional, and game sales are poor—and that the probabilities associated with these outcomes are 25 percent, 50 percent, and 25 percent, respectively. If the FCFs under each of these three outcomes are as illustrated in Exhibit 11.11, then the expected values that you would discount in your NPV analysis are −$100.00, $48.75, $53.75, and

Building Intuition

We Discount *Expected* Cash Flows in an NPV Analysis

Not only are the FCFs that we discount forward looking, but they also reflect *expected* FCFs. Each FCF is a weighted average of the cash flows from each possible future outcome, where the cash flow from each outcome is weighted by the estimated probability that the outcome will be realized. The expected FCF represents the single best estimate of what the actual FCF will be.

EXHIBIT 11.11 **Expected FCFs for New Board Game ($ thousands)**

The expected FCF for each year during the life of the board game project equals the weighted average of the possible FCFs in that year.

		Year			
Outcome	**Probability**	**0**	**1**	**2**	**3**
Game is very successful	0.25	−$100	$70	$90	$60
Game sales are acceptable	0.50	−100	50	55	40
Game sales are poor	0.25	−100	25	15	0
Expected FCF		−$100.00	$48.75	$53.75	$35.00

$35.00 for years 0, 1, 2, and 3, respectively.[7] You should confirm that each of these values is correct to make sure that you understand how to calculate an expected FCF.

With these FCF estimates, we can now calculate the NPV of the board game project. For instance, if your cost of capital is 10 percent, the NPV is:

$$\begin{aligned} \text{NPV} &= \text{FCF}_0 + \frac{\text{FCF}_1}{1+k} + \frac{\text{FCF}_2}{(1+k)^2} + \frac{\text{FCF}_3}{(1+k)^3} \\ &= -\$100 + \frac{\$48.75}{1.10} + \frac{\$53.75}{(1.10)^2} + \frac{\$35.00}{(1.10)^3} \\ &= -\$100 + \$44.32 + \$44.42 + \$26.30 \\ &= \$15.04 \end{aligned}$$

Since the project has a positive NPV, you should accept it.

We use *expected* FCFs in an NPV analysis because uncertainties regarding project cash flows that are unique to the project should be reflected in the cash flow forecasts. In Chapter 13 we will discuss why analysts who try to account for such uncertainties by adjusting the discount rate, rather than the cash flows, are wrong.

Before You Go On

1. What are the five general rules for calculating FCF?
2. What is the difference between nominal and real dollars? Why is it important not to mix them in an NPV analysis?
3. What is a progressive tax system? What is the difference between a firm's marginal and average tax rates?
4. How can FCF in the terminal year of a project's life differ from FCF in the other years?
5. Why is it important to understand that cash flow forecasts in an NPV analysis are expected values?

11.3 Forecasting Free Cash Flows

LEARNING OBJECTIVE

3. Describe how distinguishing between variable and fixed costs can be useful in forecasting operating expenses.

Earlier, we discussed how to calculate the incremental free cash flows (FCFs) for a project. Of course, when we evaluate a project, we do not know exactly what the cash flows will be, and so we must forecast them. As the performing arts center example suggests, analysts do this

[7]For simplicity, the dollar values in Exhibit 11.11 and the associated calculations are reported in thousands.

for each line item in the FCF calculation for each year during the life of a project. We are now ready to discuss how these forecasts are prepared.

Cash Flows from Operations

To forecast the incremental cash flows from operations (CF Opns) for a project, we must forecast the incremental net revenue (Revenue), operating expenses (Op Ex), and depreciation and amortization (D&A) associated with the project, as well as the firm's marginal tax rate. To forecast Revenue, analysts typically estimate the number of units that will be sold and the per-unit sales price for each year during the life of the project. The product of the number of units sold and the per-unit sales price equals the Revenue (assuming that the project does not affect other product lines). Separating the Revenue forecast into incremental unit sales and price forces the analyst to think clearly about how well the project has to perform in terms of actual unit sales in order to achieve the forecasted Revenue.

variable costs costs that vary directly with the number of units sold

fixed costs costs that do not vary directly with the number of units sold

When forecasting Op Ex, analysts often distinguish between **variable costs**, which vary directly with unit sales, and **fixed costs**, which do not. To illustrate the difference, consider a situation in which the managers of a firm plan to introduce a video game player that uses virtual reality technology. An overseas design and manufacturing company will produce the components and ship them to the company, which will assemble, package, and ship the finished product. The main variable costs will be those associated with purchasing the components; the labor required for assembling the players; packaging materials; shipping; and perhaps sales and marketing. These variable costs will rise in direct proportion to the number of units produced. If the number of units doubles, for example, we would expect these costs to approximately double. Fixed costs, such as the costs associated with assembly space (assuming output can be increased by adding shifts rather than obtaining additional space) and administrative expenses, will not increase directly with the number of units sold.[8]

Distinguishing between variable and fixed costs simplifies the forecasting problem. If company analysts estimate Revenue for a project from unit sales and price forecasts, as described earlier, then the analysts can forecast variable costs by multiplying the variable cost per unit by the number of units expected to be sold each year. Fixed cost forecasts, in contrast, will not typically vary as closely with unit sales. They tend to be based on explicit estimations of the cost of manufacturing (assembly) space, salaries and number of people required for administration of the project, and so forth.

Since D&A is determined by the amounts invested in depreciable assets and the lives over which these assets can be depreciated, this line item in the CF Opns calculation is computed based on the incremental capital expenditures (Cap Exp) associated with the project, the allowable recovery period, and the depreciation method used. Consequently, it is very important to carefully think through the size and timing of the Cap Exp and the nature of those assets to properly estimate the D&A deductions.

As discussed earlier, the tax rate that should be used when forecasting CF Opns is the marginal rate the firm expects to pay on the incremental cash flows generated by the project *in the future*. Past tax rates are relevant only to the extent that they tell us something about future tax rates. Federal, state, and local officials can change tax rates in the future, and to the extent that such changes can be predicted, they should be reflected in the cash flow forecasts. Unfortunately, such changes are difficult to predict. As a result, analysts normally use the firm's current marginal tax rate.

Cash Flows Associated with Capital Expenditures and Net Working Capital

As discussed earlier, we must consider two general classes of investments when calculating FCF: incremental capital expenditures (Cap Exp) and incremental additions to working capital

[8]In some instances, costs are "fixed" in the short run but variable in the long run. For example, if a firm leases manufacturing space under a long-term contract, it may not be possible to reduce the lease expense immediately if demand for the firm's products falls. However, it will be possible to do so at the expiration of the lease or by sub-leasing excess space.

(Add WC). Each presents its own special challenges in the preparation of forecasts. In this section, we consider several issues related to forecasting Cap Exp and Add WC.

Capital Expenditures

Cap Exp forecasts in an NPV analysis reflect the expected level of investment during each year of the project's life, including any inflows from salvage values and any tax costs or benefits associated with asset sales. As illustrated in the performing arts center example, capital expenditures are typically required at the beginning of a project. Many projects require an initial investment for the assets necessary to produce a product and then little or no investment until the end of the project, when the assets are sold for their salvage value.

Some projects, however, require substantial periodic investments to replace or refurbish assets or to shut down operations (clean-up costs) at the end of the project's life. For example, a chemical plant project might require a substantial investment every few years to refurbish worn equipment. In addition, environmental regulations are likely to require that the property on which a chemical plant is built be restored to its previous condition when it is dismantled. These are like the clean-up costs for the strip mine that we mentioned earlier. Investments such as these should be included in cash flow forecasts wherever appropriate.

Weblink

You can find a number of free Excel spreadsheets that can be used to forecast free cash flows and use these cash flows to value projects and entire firms at Matt Evans's Web site, http://www.exinfm.com/free_spreadsheets.html. Follow the links to the Web sites of the individual contributors, and you will find even more free cash flow models and related information.

Net Working Capital

As shown in Equation 11.4, cash flow forecasts in an NPV analysis include four working capital items: (1) cash and cash equivalents, (2) accounts receivable, (3) inventories, and (4) accounts payable.

Requirements for cash and cash equivalents and accounts receivable are typically forecast as constant percentages of revenue. The cash and cash-equivalent requirements represent the amount of cash needed to make timely payments to suppliers and employees, as well as for other ongoing expenses. This amount tends to vary with the nature of the project, but analysts can gain insights into the required level of cash, as a percentage of revenue, by examining the cash-to-revenue ratios for companies that operate comparable businesses. For example, if you are forecasting cash flows for a hotel project, you might look at the ratio of cash to revenue at public companies that are focused on the hotel business for an indication of how much cash is required per dollar of revenue.

Forecasting accounts receivable is relatively straightforward. If customers will be given 30 days to pay for purchases and, on average, are expected to take 30 days to pay, the average accounts receivable balance will equal 30 days' worth of revenue or 30 days/365 days per year = 0.0822, or 8.22 percent of annual revenue. This represents the amount of money that must be set aside to finance purchases by customers. For example, a company with $100 million in annual revenue can expect to have $8.22 million invested in accounts receivable at any point in time if its customers take an average of 30 days to pay for their purchases.

Inventories and accounts payable are generally forecast as a percentage of the cost of goods sold. Inventories are forecast this way because the cost of goods sold represents a measure of the amount of money actually invested in inventories. Accounts payable are forecast this way because the cost of goods sold is a measure of the amount of money actually owed to suppliers.

Before You Go On

1. What is the difference between variable and fixed costs, and what are examples of each?
2. How are working capital items forecast? Why are accounts receivable typically forecast as a percentage of revenue and accounts payable and inventories as percentages of the cost of goods sold?

11.4 Special Cases (Optional)

LEARNING OBJECTIVE

4. Explain the concept of equivalent annual cost and use it to compare projects with unequal lives, decide when to replace an existing asset, and calculate the opportunity cost of using an existing asset.

Now that we have discussed the fundamental concepts underlying NPV analysis (in Chapter 10) and how cash flows are calculated (in this chapter), we can turn our attention to some special cases that arise in capital budgeting. As you will see, dealing with these special cases generally involves the application of concepts that we have already discussed, along with a dose of common sense.

Projects with Different Lives

One problem that arises quite often in capital budgeting involves choosing between two mutually exclusive investments. Recall from Chapter 10 that if investments are mutually exclusive, the manager can choose one investment or the other, but not both. This choice is simple if the expected lives of the two investments are the same. We choose the investment with the larger NPV. This type of problem was illustrated in Chapter 10.

The analysis becomes more complicated, however, if the investments have different lives. For example, suppose that you run a lawn-mowing service and have to replace one of your mowers. Further suppose that you have two options: mower A, which costs \$250 and is expected to last two years, and mower B, which costs \$360 and is expected to last three years.

If the mowers are identical in every other way and you expect to be in the mowing business for a long time (in other words, you are going to continue to replace mowers as they wear out for the foreseeable future), then you cannot decide which mower to buy simply by comparing the \$250 cost of mower A with the \$360 cost of mower B. Mower A will provide two years of service, while mower B will provide three years of service.[9]

You might be tempted to choose the mower with the lower initial investment per year of service. For example, you might choose mower B because the initial investment is \$120 per year of service (\$360/3 years = \$120 per year) while mower A requires an initial investment of \$125 per year of service (\$250/2 years = \$125 per year). As you will see, however, this reasoning can get you into trouble.

In this situation, we can effectively make the lives of the mowers the same by assuming repeated investments over some identical period and comparing the NPVs of their costs. We can do this by considering a six-year investment period. We determine the six-year period by multiplying the life of mower A by the life of mower B (2 × 3 = 6). In six years you would buy mower A three times—in Years 0, 2, and 4—or mower B twice—in Years 0 and 3. If we assume that the cost of each mower will remain the same over the next six years, and if we use a 10 percent opportunity cost of capital, the NPVs of the *costs* of the two alternatives are:

$$\text{NPV} = \text{FCF}_0 + \frac{\text{FCF}_1}{1+k} + \frac{\text{FCF}_2}{(1+k)^2} + \cdots + \frac{\text{FCF}_n}{(1+k)^n}$$

$$\text{NPV}_\text{A} = -\$250 + \frac{-\$0}{1.10} + \frac{-\$250}{(1.10)^2} + \frac{-\$0}{(1.10)^3} + \frac{-\$250}{(1.10)^4} + \frac{-\$0}{(1.10)^5} + \frac{-\$0}{(1.10)^6}$$
$$= -\$627.36$$

$$\text{NPV}_\text{B} = -\$360 + \frac{-\$0}{1.10} + \frac{-\$0}{(1.10)^2} + \frac{-\$360}{(1.10)^3} + \frac{-\$0}{(1.10)^4} + \frac{-\$0}{(1.10)^5} + \frac{-\$0}{(1.10)^6}$$
$$= -\$630.47$$

[9]If you don't expect to replace the machines as they wear out (for instance, if you plan to quit the mowing business in one year), then you can calculate the NPV of each mower, including the salvage values that you expect to realize for each at the end of the year, and choose the mower with the larger NPV.

Notice that mower A is actually cheaper over a six-year investment cycle. Over this period, it costs $627.36/6 = $104.56 per year in today's dollars, while mower B costs $630.47/6 = $105.08 per year.

Often, a much more efficient way of solving a problem of this nature is to compute the **equivalent annual cost (EAC)**. The EAC can be calculated as follows:

equivalent annual cost (EAC) the annual dollar amount of an annuity that has a life equal to that of a project and that also has a present value equal to the present value of the cash flows from the project; the term comes from the fact that the EAC calculation is often used to calculate a constant annual cost associated with projects in order to make comparisons

$$EAC_i = k\,NPV_i\left[\frac{(1+k)^t}{(1+k)^t - 1}\right] \tag{11.5}$$

where k is the opportunity cost of capital, NPV_i is the NPV of the investment i, and t is the life of the investment.

Using Equation 11.5, we find that the EACs for mowers A and B are:

$$EAC_A = (0.1)(-\$250)\left[\frac{(1+0.1)^2}{(1+0.1)^2 - 1}\right] = -\$144.05$$

and

$$EAC_B = (0.1)(-\$360)\left[\frac{(1+0.1)^3}{(1+0.1)^3 - 1}\right] = -\$144.76$$

We can see that the EAC gives us the same answer as equating the lives of the investments and calculating the NPVs over a six-year investment cycle. This is to be expected, since the EAC simply reflects the annuity that has the same present value as the cost of an investment over the investment period we are considering. For instance, the NPV of the EAC for mower A over a six-year period is

$$NPV_A = \frac{-\$144.05}{1.1} + \frac{-\$144.05}{(1.1)^2} + \frac{-\$144.05}{(1.1)^3} + \frac{-\$144.05}{(1.1)^4} + \frac{-\$144.05}{(1.1)^5} + \frac{-\$144.05}{(1.1)^6}$$
$$= -\$627.38$$

This is the same NPV we obtained earlier (allowing for rounding differences).

The problem is similar but a bit more complicated if the revenues or operating costs associated with the two mowers differ. For simplicity, let's continue to assume that the mowers will generate the same revenue per year, but let's also assume that mower A will cost $50 per year to maintain and mower B will cost $55 per year to maintain. The NPVs of the two mowers in this case are:

$$NPV_A = -\$250 + \frac{-\$50}{1.10} + \frac{-\$50}{(1.10)^2} = -\$336.78$$

$$NPV_B = -\$360 + \frac{-\$55}{1.10} + \frac{-\$55}{(1.10)^2} + \frac{-\$55}{(1.10)^3} = -\$496.78$$

The EACs are:

$$EAC_A = (0.1)(-\$336.78)\left[\frac{(1+0.1)^2}{(1+0.1)^2 - 1}\right] = -\$194.05$$

and

$$EAC_B = (0.1)(-\$496.78)\left[\frac{(1+0.1)^3}{(1+0.1)^3 - 1}\right] = -\$199.76$$

Of course, we still want to choose mower A in this case since all that has really happened is that the EAC of mower A has gone up by $50 and the EAC of mower B has gone up by $55. In contrast, if the annual cost of maintaining mower A is $50 and the annual cost of maintaining mower B is $49, we would choose mower B. As confirmation, you should try the calculations for this example.

One other point should be made about the EAC concept. Despite its name, it does not apply only to costs. If we included revenues in the above analysis and both mowers had positive NPVs, we could still use the EAC formula to compare the two alternatives. The only difference in this case is that the decision criteria would be to choose the most positive EAC instead of the least negative.

Learning by Doing Application 11.5 illustrates another example of how EAC can be used to compare projects with different lives.

LEARNING BY DOING

APPLICATION 11.5 | Using EAC to Compare Projects with Different Lives

Problem You are looking at new ovens for your pizza parlor, and you see two models that would work equally well. Model A would cost $40,000 and last 10 years. Model B would cost $50,000 but would last 12 years and would require $500 less electricity per year than model A. Which model is less expensive? Assume a 10 percent opportunity cost of capital.

Approach Use the EAC formula, Equation 11.5, to calculate the EAC of the initial investment for each model of oven. Add the annual electricity savings to the EAC of the initial investment for Model B. Choose the model with the smaller total EAC.

Solution The EACs for the initial investments in the two ovens are as follows:

$$EAC_A = (0.1)(-\$40{,}000)\left[\frac{(1+0.1)^{10}}{(1+0.1)^{10}-1}\right] = -\$6{,}509.82$$

$$EAC_B = (0.1)(-\$50{,}000)\left[\frac{(1+0.1)^{12}}{(1+0.1)^{12}-1}\right] = -\$7{,}338.17$$

Now since the electricity savings would be $500 per year in nominal dollars, we can simply add this amount to the EAC calculated for Model B above to get the true $EAC_B = -\$7{,}338.16 + \$500 = -\$6{,}838.16$.[10] Since the EAC for Model B is still more negative than that for Model A, we would conclude that Model A would be less expensive over its expected useful life.

When to Replace an Existing Asset

Occasionally, financial managers are asked to determine the appropriate time to replace an existing piece of equipment that is still operating. In these situations they must answer two fundamental questions: Do the benefits of replacing the existing machine exceed the costs, and if they do not now, when will they?

Let's examine how these questions can be answered for a situation that commonly arises in the lawn-mowing business. Suppose you have an old mower that is working perfectly well, but you are considering upgrading to a faster model. The old mower will run for another three years before it has to be replaced and will generate cash inflows, net of costs, of $6,500 for each of the next three years. The new mower costs $2,000 and would bring in net cash flows of $7,000 for four years. When should you replace the old mower?

Solving this problem is simply a matter of computing the EAC for the new mower and comparing it with the annual cash inflows from the old mower. With a 10 percent opportunity cost of capital, the NPV of the new mower is:

$$\begin{aligned} NPV_{\text{New mower}} &= -\$2{,}000 + \frac{\$7{,}000}{1.1} + \frac{\$7{,}000}{(1.1)^2} + \frac{\$7{,}000}{(1.1)^3} + \frac{\$7{,}000}{(1.1)^4} \\ &= -\$2{,}000 + \$6{,}364 + \$5{,}785 + \$5{,}259 + \$4{,}781 \\ &= \$20{,}189 \end{aligned}$$

Therefore, the EAC is:

$$EAC_{\text{New mower}} = (0.1)(\$20{,}189)\left[\frac{(1+0.1)^4}{(1+0.1)^4-1}\right] = \$6{,}369$$

In this example, the old mower should not be replaced until it wears out because it will generate net cash inflows of $6,500 for each of the next three years, while the EAC for the new mower is only $6,369.

Now suppose that, instead of remaining constant at $6,500, cash inflows from the old mower will decline from $6,500 in Year 1, to $6,000 in Year 2, and to $5,500 in Year 3 as

[10] We could have also calculated the NPV for Model B by discounting the $500 annual electricity savings by 10 percent and adding the present value of that savings stream to the $50,000 initial cost. Using this NPV in the EAC formula would also yield −$6,838.16.

DECISION MAKING

EXAMPLE 11.2 | Deciding When to Replace an Asset

Situation You are trying to decide when to replace your car. It is already five years old, and maintenance costs keep increasing each year as more and more parts wear out and need to be replaced. You do not really care whether or not your car is new. You just want a car that gets you around at the lowest cost. You expect maintenance costs for your car over the next five years to increase by \$500 per year from \$500 this past year. Your car will be worthless in five years. As an alternative, you can buy a new car with a five-year warranty that will cover all maintenance costs. The new car will cost \$15,000, and you expect to be able to sell it for \$10,000 in five years. The gas mileage for both cars is the same. Remembering what you learned in corporate finance, you calculate the EAC for each option using a 10 percent opportunity cost of capital. The NPV for your old car is:

$$\begin{aligned} \text{NPV}_{\text{Old car}} &= \frac{-\$1{,}000}{1.1} + \frac{-\$1{,}500}{(1.1)^2} + \frac{-\$2{,}000}{(1.1)^3} + \frac{-\$2{,}500}{(1.1)^4} + \frac{-\$3{,}000}{(1.1)^5} \\ &= -\$7{,}221.69 \end{aligned}$$

and the EAC is –\$1,905.06. The NPV for the new car is:

$$\begin{aligned} \text{NPV}_{\text{New car}} &= -\$15{,}000 + \frac{\$10{,}000}{(1.1)^5} \\ &= -\$8{,}790.79 \end{aligned}$$

and the EAC is –\$2,318.99. When should you replace your old car?

Decision The EAC for the new car is more negative than the EAC for your old car, suggesting that you should not replace your old car. However, if you compare the EAC for the new car with the annual maintenance costs you expect for your old car, you will see that the annual maintenance costs rise above the EAC of the new car in Year 4. Assuming that the economics of the new car remain the same, you should replace your car after Year 3.

maintenance expenditures and downtime increase near the end of the old mower's useful life. If the EAC for the new mower is \$6,369, the old machine should be replaced after the first year.

Decision Making Example 11.2 illustrates another example of how EAC can be used to decide when to replace an asset.

The Cost of Using an Existing Asset

In Section 11.2 we discussed five general rules for calculating the incremental after-tax free cash flows associated with a project. The third rule is *to include all opportunity costs.* Unfortunately, opportunity costs are not always directly observable. Sometimes they have to be computed. This is particularly true when the opportunity cost relates to the use of excess capacity associated with an existing asset.

To see how we can evaluate opportunity costs of this kind, consider an example. Suppose you run a plant that mixes, bags, and ships potting soil—the soil often used for potted plants kept in people's homes. The bagging machine at your plant has sufficient excess capacity to handle forecasted increases in sales for the next five years if you stick to the potting-soil business. However, one of your managers has proposed that your plant diversify into the mulch business. If you began using the existing bagging machine to bag mulch, you would have to purchase a second bagging machine in three years instead of in five years. The cost of a second, identical machine would be \$100,000, and this machine would have a five-year life. If the appropriate opportunity cost of capital is 10 percent, how should you account for the opportunity cost of using the bagging machine when computing the NPV of the mulch project?

The first step is to compute the EAC for the second bagging machine. It is:

$$\text{EAC}_{\text{Bagging machine}} = (0.1)(-\$100{,}000)\left[\frac{(1 + 0.1)^5}{(1 + 0.1)^5 - 1}\right] = -\$26{,}380$$

This tells us that the bagging machine costs \$26,380 per year. If you decide to get into the mulch business, this cost, which would not otherwise be incurred until Year 5, will also be incurred in Years 3 and 4. Therefore, the opportunity cost of using the excess bagging capacity equals the present value of the additional cost incurred in Years 3 and 4:

$$NPV_{\text{Bagging machine opportunity cost}} = \frac{-\$26,380}{(1.1)^3} + \frac{-\$26,380}{(1.1)^4} = -\$37,838$$

This cost should be included in the incremental cash flows for the mulch business. If the mulch project has a negative NPV with this cost, you might consider examining whether it has a positive NPV if you run the mulch business for only the next three years, while there is no constraint on the bagging capacity. A positive NPV in this latter analysis would indicate that the project should be pursued for three years and then abandoned.

When to Harvest an Asset

LEARNING OBJECTIVE

5. Determine the appropriate time to harvest an asset.

Another problem that arises from time to time involves deciding when to harvest an investment. A classic example occurs in the timber industry, where a decision must be made about when to harvest timber. The longer the harvest is delayed, the greater the number of board feet that can be obtained (since trees grow) and, assuming the price of lumber is constant, the greater the value of the harvested lumber. If the number of board feet that will be realized in the harvest and the price per board foot at any point in time is known, making the right decision involves a relatively straightforward application of concepts that we have already discussed.

For example, suppose that you own some land on which you planted pine trees 10 years ago. The trees can be harvested and sold to a pulp mill at any time now, but you want to make sure that you choose the point in time that maximizes the NPV of your investment in the trees. You have estimated the NPV (which equals the after-tax cash flow *at the time of the harvest*) of harvesting the trees today (Year 10) and for each of the next four years to be as follows:

$$NPV_{10} = \$35,000$$
$$NPV_{11} = \$40,250$$
$$NPV_{12} = \$45,483$$
$$NPV_{13} = \$49,576$$
$$NPV_{14} = \$52,550$$

If each of these NPVs is stated in dollars as of the time when the harvest would take place, we cannot compare them directly. They must first be restated in dollars adjusted to the same point in time. If the opportunity cost of capital is 10 percent, we can make this adjustment simply by discounting each of the NPV values to Year 10. The discounted values are as follows:

$$NPV_{10,\,10} = \$35,000$$
$$NPV_{10,\,11} = \$40,250/1.1 = \$36,591$$
$$NPV_{10,\,12} = \$45,483/(1.1)^2 = \$37,589$$
$$NPV_{10,\,13} = \$49,576/(1.1)^3 = \$37,247$$
$$NPV_{10,\,14} = \$52,550/(1.1)^4 = \$35,892$$

where $NPV_{x,y}$ refers to the NPV in Year x dollars if the trees are harvested in Year y. From these numbers, we can see that harvesting at the end of Year 12 will produce the largest NPV in today's dollars.

If you calculate the percentage increase in the nominal NPV values above, you can see that they increase by 15 percent from Year 10 to 11, by 13 percent from Year 11 to 12, by 9 percent from Year 12 to 13, and by 6 percent from Year 13 to 14. The optimal time to harvest is at the end of the year before the first year in which the rate of increase is no longer greater than or equal to the cost of capital. At this time it becomes optimal to harvest the trees and invest the proceeds in alternative investments that yield the opportunity cost of capital because you can earn more from the alternative investments. An alternative way of thinking about this is that you do not want to harvest as long as the asset is earning a return that is greater than or equal to the opportunity cost of capital. This general principle applies to all problems of this kind.

In our example, we are ignoring the fact that the sooner we harvest the trees, the sooner we can plant the next crop. In this sense the solution is somewhat simplistic—we should really be considering the NPVs for a series of crops—but it illustrates the key points that (1) you must state all NPV values as of the same point in time and (2) the optimal time to harvest an asset is when it is no longer earning at least the opportunity cost of capital.

Outside of the timber industry, these ideas are widely used to decide when to exit investments. For example, leveraged-buyout specialists, who buy companies with the intention of improving and then selling them within a few years, perform a very similar type of analysis when choosing the appropriate time to sell a company.

Before You Go On

1. When can we not simply compare the NPVs of two mutually exclusive projects?
2. When choosing between mutually exclusive projects with unequal lives, how can we ensure the best decision is made?
3. Under what circumstance would you replace an old machine that is still operating with a new one?
4. How do we decide when to harvest an asset?

Summary of Learning Objectives

1 Explain why incremental after-tax free cash flows are relevant in evaluating a project and calculate them for a project.

The incremental after-tax free cash flows, FCFs, for a project equal the expected change in the total after-tax free cash flows of the firm if the project is adopted. The impact of a project on the firm's total cash flows is the appropriate measure of cash flows because these are the cash flows that reflect all of the costs and benefits from the project and only the costs and benefits from the project. The incremental after-tax free cash flows are calculated using Equation 11.2. This calculation is also illustrated in Exhibit 11.1.

2 Discuss the five general rules for incremental after-tax free cash flow calculations and explain why cash flows stated in nominal (real) dollars should be discounted using a nominal (real) discount rate.

The five general rules are as follows:

Rule 1: *Include cash flows and only cash flows in your calculations.* Stockholders care about only the impact of a project on the firm's cash flows.

Rule 2: *Include the impact of the project on cash flows from other product lines.* If a project affects the cash flows from other projects, we must take this into account in NPV analysis in order to fully capture the impact of the project on the firm's total cash flows.

Rule 3: *Include all opportunity costs.* If an asset is used for a project, the relevant cost for that asset is the value that could be realized from its most valuable alternative use. By including this cost in the NPV analysis, we capture the change in the firm's cash flows that is attributable to the use of this asset for the project.

Rule 4: *Forget sunk costs.* The only costs that matter are those to be incurred from this point on.

Rule 5: *Include only after-tax cash flows in the cash flow calculations.* Since stockholders receive cash flows after taxes have been paid, they are concerned only about after-tax cash flows.

Since a nominal discount rate reflects both the expected rate of inflation and a real return, we would be overadjusting for inflation if we discounted a real cash flow with a nominal rate. Similarly, if we discounted a nominal cash flow using a real discount rate, we would be undercompensating for expected inflation in the discounting process. This is why we discount nominal cash flows using only a nominal discount rate and we discount real cash flows using only a real discount rate.

3 Describe how distinguishing between variable and fixed costs can be useful in forecasting operating expenses.

Variable costs vary directly with the number of units sold, while fixed costs do not. When forecasting operating expenses, it is often useful to treat variable and fixed costs separately. We can forecast variable costs by multiplying unit variable costs by the number of units sold. Fixed costs are more accurately based on the specific characteristics of those costs, rather than as a function of sales. Separating fixed costs from the variable also makes it easier to identify the factors that will cause them to change over time and therefore easier to forecast them.

4 Explain the concept of equivalent annual cost and use it to compare projects with unequal lives, decide when to replace an existing asset, and calculate the opportunity cost of using an existing asset.

The equivalent annual cost (EAC) is the annualized cost of an investment that is stated in nominal dollars. In other words, it is the annual payment from an annuity that has the same NPV and the same life as the project. Since it is a measure of the annual cost, or cash inflow from a project, the EAC for one project can be compared directly with the EAC from another project, regardless of the lives of those two projects. Application of the EAC concept is illustrated in Section 11.4.

5 Determine the appropriate time to harvest an asset.

The appropriate time to harvest an asset is that point in time where harvesting the asset yields the largest present value, in today's dollars, of the project NPV.

Summary of Key Equations

Equation	Description	Formula
11.1	Incremental free cash flow definition	$FCF_{Project} = FCF_{Firm\ with\ project} - FCF_{Firm\ without\ project}$
11.2	Incremental free cash flow calculation	$FCF = [(Revenue - Op\ Ex - D\&A) \times (1 - t)] + D\&A - Cap\ Exp - Add\ WC$
11.3	Inflation and real components of cost of capital	$1 + k = (1 + \Delta P_e) \times (1 + r)$
11.4	Incremental additions to working capital	Add WC = Change in cash and cash equivalents + Change in accounts receivable + Change in inventories − Change in accounts payable
11.5	Equivalent annual cost	$EAC_i = k\,NPV_i\left[\frac{(1+k)^t}{(1+k)^t - 1}\right]$

Self-Study Problems

11.1 Explain why the announcement of a new investment is usually accompanied by a change in the firm's stock price.

11.2 In calculating the NPV of a project, should we use all of the after-tax cash flows associated with the project or incremental after-tax free cash flows from the project? Why?

11.3 You are considering opening another restaurant in the TexasBurgers chain. The new restaurant will have annual revenue of $300,000 and operating expenses of $150,000. The annual depreciation and amortization for the assets used in the restaurant will equal $50,000. An annual capital expenditure of $10,000 will be required to offset wear and tear on the assets used in the restaurant, but no additions to working capital will be required. The marginal tax rate will be 40 percent. Calculate the incremental annual after-tax free cash flow for the project.

11.4 Sunglass Heaven, Inc., is launching a new store in a shopping mall in Houston. The annual revenue of the store depends on the weather conditions in the summer in Houston. The annual revenue will be $240,000 in a sizzling summer with a probability of 0.3, $80,000 in a cool summer with a probability of 0.2, and $150,000 in a normal summer with a probability of 0.5. What is the expected annual revenue for the store?

11.5 Sprigg Lane Manufacturing, Inc., needs to purchase a new central air-conditioning system for a plant. There are two choices. The first system costs $50,000 and is expected to last 10 years, and the second system costs $72,000 and is expected to last 15 years. Assume that the opportunity cost of capital is 10 percent. Which air-conditioning system should Sprigg Lane purchase?

Solutions to Self-Study Problems

11.1 A firm's investments cause changes in its future after-tax free cash flows, and stockholders are the residual claimants (owners) of those cash flows. Therefore, the stock price should increase when stockholders expect an investment to have a positive NPV and decrease when they expect it to have a negative NPV.

11.2 We should use incremental after-tax free cash flows from the project. Incremental after-tax free cash flows reflect the amount by which the firm's total cash flows will change if the project is adopted. In other words, they represent the net difference in cash revenues, costs, taxes, and investment outlays (for net working capital and capital expenditures) at the firm level with and without the project, which is precisely what the stockholders care about.

11.3 The incremental annual after-tax free cash flow is calculated as follows:

$$\text{FCF} = [(\$300{,}000 - \$150{,}000 - \$50{,}000) \times (1 - 0.4)] + \$50{,}000 - \$10{,}000 = \$100{,}000$$

11.4 The expected annual revenue is:

$$\text{E(Revenue)} = (0.3 \times \$240{,}000) + (0.2 \times \$80{,}000) + (0.5 \times \$150{,}000) = \$163{,}000$$

11.5 The equivalent annual cost for each system is as follows:

$$\text{EAC}_1 = (0.1)(\$50{,}000)\left[\frac{(1.1)^{10}}{(1.1)^{10} - 1)}\right] = \$8{,}137.27$$

$$\text{EAC}_2 = (0.1)(\$72{,}000)\left[\frac{(1.1)^{15}}{(1.1)^{15} - 1)}\right] = \$9{,}466.11$$

Therefore, Sprigg Lane should purchase the first system.

WileyPLUS

Questions and Problems, Solution Walkthrough Videos, Learning by Doing Tutorials, and additional study tools and resources are available in WileyPLUS.

Discussion Questions

11.1 Do you agree or disagree with the following statement given the discussion in this chapter? We can calculate future cash flows precisely and obtain an exact value for the NPV of an investment.

11.2 What are the differences between cash flows used in capital budgeting calculations and past accounting earnings?

11.3 Suppose that FRA Corporation already has divisions in both Dallas and Houston. FRA is now considering setting up a third division in Austin. This expansion will require that one senior manager from Dallas and one from Houston relocate to Austin. Ignore relocation expenses. Is their annual compensation relevant to the decision to expand?

11.4 MusicHeaven, Inc., is a producer of media players, which currently have either 20 gigabytes or 30 gigabytes of storage. Now the company is considering launching a new production line making mini media players with 5 gigabytes of storage. Analysts forecast that MusicHeaven will be able to sell 1 million such mini media players if the investment is made. In making the investment decision, discuss what the company should consider other than the sales of the mini media players.

11.5 QualityLiving Trust is a real estate investment company that builds and remodels apartment buildings in northern California. It is currently considering remodeling a few idle buildings that it owns in San Jose into luxury apartment buildings. The company bought those buildings eight months ago. How should the market value of the buildings be treated in evaluating this project?

11.6 High-End Fashions, Inc., bought a production line for ankle-length skirts last year at a cost of $500,000. This year, however, miniskirts are in and ankle-length skirts are completely out of fashion. High-End has the option to rebuild the production line and use it to produce miniskirts with an annual operating cost of $300,000 and expected revenue of $700,000. How should the company treat the $500,000 cost of the old production line in evaluating the rebuilding plan?

11.7 How is the MACRS depreciation method under IRS rules different from the straight-line depreciation allowed under GAAP rules? What is the implication on incremental after-tax free cash flows from firms' investments?

11.8 Explain the difference between marginal and average tax rates, and identify which of these rates is used in capital budgeting and why.

11.9 Under what circumstances will the sale of an asset result in a taxable gain? How do you estimate the taxes or tax benefit associated with the sale of an asset?

11.10 When two mutually exclusive projects have different lives, how can an analyst determine which is better? What is the underlying assumption in this method?

11.11 What is the opportunity cost of using an existing asset? Give an example of the opportunity cost of using the excess capacity of a machine.

11.12 You are providing financial advice to a shrimp farmer who will be harvesting his last crop of farm-raised shrimp. His current shrimp crop is very young and will, therefore, grow and become more valuable as their weight increases. Describe how you would determine the appropriate time to harvest the entire crop of shrimp.

Questions and Problems

Excel *Excel templates and resources available in* **WileyPLUS**

Basic

11.1 Calculating project cash flows: Why do we use forecasted incremental after-tax free cash flows instead of forecasted accounting earnings in estimating the NPV of a project?

11.2 The FCF calculation: How do we calculate incremental after-tax free cash flows from forecasted earnings of a project? What are the common adjustment items?

11.3 The FCF calculation: How do we adjust for depreciation when we calculate incremental after-tax free cash flow from EBITDA? What is the intuition for the adjustment?

11.4 Nominal versus real cash flows: What is the difference between nominal and real cash flows? Which rate of return should we use to discount each type of cash flow?

11.5 Taxes and depreciation: What is the difference between average tax rate and marginal tax rate? Which one should we use in calculating incremental after-tax cash flows?

11.6 Computing terminal-year FCF: Healthy Potions, Inc., a pharmaceutical company, bought a machine at a cost of $2 million five years ago that produces pain-reliever medicine. The machine has been depreciated over the past five years, and the current book value is $800,000. The company decides to sell the machine now at its market price of $1 million. The marginal tax rate is 30 percent. What are the relevant cash flows? How do they change if the market price of the machine is $600,000 instead?

11.7 Cash flows from operations: What are variable costs and fixed costs? What are some examples of each? How are these costs estimated in forecasting operating expenses?

11.8 Cash flows from operations: When forecasting operating expenses, explain the difference between a fixed cost and a variable cost.

11.9 Investment cash flows: Zippy Corporation just purchased computing equipment for $20,000. The equipment will be depreciated using a five-year MACRS depreciation schedule. If the equipment is sold at the end of its fourth year for $12,000, what are the after-tax proceeds from the sale, assuming the marginal tax rate is 35 percent?

11.10 Investment cash flows: Six Twelve, Inc., is considering opening up a new convenience store in downtown New York City. The expected annual revenue at the new store is $800,000. To estimate the increase in working capital, analysts estimate the ratio of cash and cash equivalents to revenue to be 0.03 and the ratios of receivables, inventories, and payables to revenue to be 0.05, 0.10, and 0.04, respectively, in the same industry. What is the expected incremental cash flow related to working capital when the store is opened?

11.11 Investment cash flows: Keswick Supply Company wants to set up a division that provides copy and fax services to businesses. Customers will be given 20 days to pay for such services. The annual revenue of the division is estimated to be $25,000. Assuming that the customers take the full 20 days to pay, what is the incremental cash flow associated with accounts receivable?

11.12 Expected cash flows: Define *expected cash flows,* and explain why this concept is important in evaluating projects.

11.13 Projects with different lives: Explain the concept of equivalent annual cost and how it is used to compare projects with different lives.

11.14 Replace an existing asset: Explain how we determine the optimal time to replace an existing asset with a new one.

11.15 Projects with different lives: If you had to choose between one project with an expected life of five years and a second project with an expected life of six years, how could you do this without using the equivalent annual cost concept?

Intermediate

11.16 Nominal versus real cash flows: You are buying a sofa. You will pay $200 today and make three consecutive annual payments of $300 in the future. The real rate of return is 10 percent, and the expected inflation rate is 4 percent. What is the actual price of the sofa?

11.17 Nominal versus real cash flows: You are graduating in two years. You want to invest your current savings of $5,000 in bonds and use the proceeds to purchase a new car when you graduate and start to work. You can invest the money in either Bond A, a two-year bond with a 3 percent annual interest rate, or Bond B, an inflation-indexed two-year bond paying 1 percent real interest above the inflation rate (assume this bond makes annual interest payments). The inflation rate over the next two years is expected to be 1.5 percent. Assume that both bonds are default free and have the same market price. Which bond should you invest in?

11.18 Marginal and average tax rates: Given the U.S. Corporate Tax Rate Schedule in Exhibit 11.6, what was the marginal tax rate and average tax rate of a corporation that had a taxable income of $12 million in 2016?

11.19 Investment cash flows: Healthy Potions, Inc., is considering investing in a new production line for eye drops. Other than investing in the equipment, the company needs to increase its cash and cash equivalents by $10,000, increase the level of inventory by $30,000, increase accounts receivable by $25,000, and increase accounts payable by $5,000 at the beginning of the project. Healthy Potions will recover these changes in working capital at the end of the project 10 years later. Assume the appropriate discount rate is 12 percent. What are the present values of the relevant investment cash flows?

11.20 Cash flows from operations: Given the soaring price of gasoline, Ford is considering introducing a new production line of gas-electric hybrid sedans. The expected annual unit sales of the hybrid cars is 30,000; the price is $22,000 per car. Variable costs of production are $10,000 per car. The fixed overhead including salary of top executives is $80 million per year. However, the introduction of the hybrid sedan will decrease Ford's sales of regular sedans by 10,000 cars per year; the regular sedans have a unit price of $20,000, a unit variable cost of $12,000, and fixed costs of $250,000 per year. Depreciation costs of the production plant are $50,000 per year. The marginal tax rate is 40 percent. What is the incremental annual cash flow from operations?

11.21 **FCF and NPV for a project:** Archer Daniels Midland Company is considering buying a new farm that it plans to operate for 10 years. The farm will require an initial investment of $12 million. This investment will consist of $2 million for land and $10 million for trucks and other equipment. The land, all trucks, and all other equipment are expected to be sold at the end of 10 years for a price of $5 million, which is $2 million above book value. The farm is expected to produce revenue of $2 million each year, and annual cash flow from operations equals $1.8 million. The marginal tax rate is 35 percent, and the appropriate discount rate is 10 percent. Calculate the NPV of this investment.

11.22 **Projects with different lives:** You are trying to choose between purchasing one of two machines for a factory. Machine A costs $15,000 to purchase and has a three-year life. Machine B costs $17,700 to purchase but has a four-year life. Regardless of which machine you purchase, it will have to be replaced at the end of its operating life. Which machine should you choose? Assume a marginal tax rate of 35 percent and a discount rate of 15 percent.

11.23 **Projects with different lives:** You are starting a family pizza parlor and need to buy a motorcycle for delivery orders. You have two models in mind. Model A costs $9,000 and is expected to run for 6 years; Model B is more expensive, with a price of $14,000, and has an expected life of 10 years. The annual maintenance costs are $800 for Model A and $700 for Model B. Assume that the opportunity cost of capital is 10 percent. Which one should you buy?

11.24 **When to harvest an asset:** Predator LLC, a leveraged-buyout specialist, recently bought a company and wants to determine the optimal time to sell it. The partner in charge of this investment has estimated the after-tax cash flows from a sale at different times to be as follows: $700,000 if sold one year later; $1,000,000 if sold two years later; $1,200,000 if sold three years later; and $1,300,000 if sold four years later. The opportunity cost of capital is 12 percent. When should Predator sell the company? Why?

11.25 **Replace an existing asset:** Bell Mountain Vineyards is considering updating its current manual accounting system with a high-end electronic system. While the new accounting system would save the company money, the cost of the system continues to decline. Bell Mountain's opportunity cost of capital is 10 percent, and the costs and values of investments made at different times in the future are as follows:

Year	Cost	Value of Future Savings (at time of purchase)
0	$5,000	$7,000
1	4,500	7,000
2	4,000	7,000
3	3,600	7,000
4	3,300	7,000
5	3,100	7,000

When should Bell Mountain buy the new accounting system?

11.26 **Replace an existing asset:** You have a 2000 Nissan that is expected to run for another three years, but you are considering buying a new Hyundai before the Nissan wears out. You will donate the Nissan to Goodwill when you buy the new car. The annual maintenance cost is $1,500 per year for the Nissan and $200 for the Hyundai. The price of your favorite Hyundai model is $18,000, and it is expected to run for 15 years. Your opportunity cost of capital is 3 percent. Ignore taxes. When should you buy the new Hyundai?

11.27 **Replace an existing asset:** Assume that you are considering replacing your old Nissan with a new Hyundai, as in the previous problem. However, the annual maintenance cost of the old Nissan increases as time goes by. It is $1,200 in the first year, $1,500 in the second year, and $1,800 in the third year. When should you replace the Nissan with the new Hyundai in this case?

11.28 **When to harvest an existing asset:** Anaconda Manufacturing Company currently owns a mine that is known to contain a certain amount of gold. Since Anaconda does not have any gold-mining expertise, the company plans to sell the entire mine and base the selling price on a fixed multiple of the spot price for gold at the time of the sale. Analysts at Anaconda have forecast the spot price for gold and have determined that the price will increase by 14 percent, 12 percent, 9 percent, and 6 percent during the next one, two, three, and four years, respectively. If Anaconda's opportunity cost of capital is 10 percent, what is the optimal time for Anaconda to sell the mine?

11.29 **Replace an existing asset:** You are thinking about delivering pizzas in your spare time. Since you must use your own car to deliver the pizzas, you will wear out your current car one year earlier, which is one year from today, than if you did not take on the delivery job. You estimate that when you purchase a new car, regardless of when that occurs, you will pay $20,000 for the car and it will last you five years. If your opportunity cost of capital is 7 percent, what is the opportunity cost of using your car to deliver pizzas?

Advanced

11.30 You are the CFO of SlimBody, Inc., a retailer of the exercise machine Slimbody6 and related accessories. Your firm is considering opening a new store in Los Angeles. The store will have a life of 20 years. It will generate annual sales of 5,000 exercise machines, and the price of each machine is $2,500. The annual sales of accessories will be $600,000, and the operating expenses of running the store, including labor and rent, will amount to 50 percent of the revenues from the exercise machines. The initial investment in the store will equal $30 million and will be fully depreciated on a straight-line basis over the 20-year life of the store. Your firm will need to invest $2 million in additional working capital immediately and recover it at the end of the investment. Your firm's marginal tax rate is 30 percent. The opportunity cost of opening up the store is 10 percent. What are the incremental free cash flows from this project at the beginning of the project as well as in Years 1–19 and 20? Should you approve it?

11.31 Merton Shovel Corporation has decided to bid for a contract to supply shovels to the Honduran Army. The Honduran Army intends to buy 1,000 shovels per year for the next three years. To supply these shovels, Merton will have to acquire manufacturing equipment at a cost of $150,000. This equipment will be depreciated on a straight-line basis over its five-year lifetime. At the end of the third year, Merton can sell the equipment for exactly its book value ($60,000). Additional fixed costs will be $36,000 per year, and variable costs will be $3.00 per shovel. An additional investment of $25,000 in net working capital will be required when the project is initiated. This investment will be recovered at the end of the third year. Merton Shovel has a 35 percent marginal tax rate and a 17 percent required rate of return on the project. What is the lowest possible per shovel price that Merton can offer for the contract and still create value for its stockholders?

11.32 Rocky Mountain Lumber, Inc., is considering purchasing a new wood saw that costs $50,000. The saw will generate revenues of $100,000 per year for five years. The cost of materials and labor needed to generate these revenues will total $60,000 per year, and other cash expenses will be $10,000 per year. The machine is expected to sell for $1,000 at the end of its five-year life and will be depreciated on a straight-line basis over five years to zero. Rocky Mountain's tax rate is 34 percent, and its opportunity cost of capital is 10 percent. Should the company purchase the saw? Explain why or why not.

11.33 A beauty product company is developing a new fragrance named Happy Forever. There is a probability of 0.5 that consumers will love Happy Forever, and in this case, annual sales will be 1 million bottles; a probability of 0.4 that consumers will find the smell acceptable and annual sales will be 200,000 bottles; and a probability of 0.1 that consumers will find the smell unpleasant and annual sales will be only 50,000 bottles. The selling price is $38, and the variable cost is $8 per bottle. Fixed production costs will be $1 million per year, and depreciation will be $1.2 million. Assume that the marginal tax rate is 40 percent. What are the expected annual incremental after-tax free cash flows from the new fragrance?

11.34 Great Fit, Inc., is a company that manufactures clothing. The company has a production line that produces women's tops of regular sizes. The same machine could be used to produce petite sizes as well. However, the remaining life of the machines will be reduced from four years to two years if the petite size production is added. The cost of identical machines with a life of eight years is $2 million. Assume the opportunity cost of capital is 8 percent. What is the opportunity cost of adding petite sizes?

11.35 Biotech Partners LLC has been farming a new strain of radioactive-material-eating bacteria that the electrical utility industry can use to help dispose of its nuclear waste. Two opposing factors affect Biotech's decision of when to harvest the bacteria. The bacteria are currently growing at a 22 percent annual rate, but due to known competition from other top firms, Biotech analysts estimate that the price for the bacteria will decline according to the schedule below. If the opportunity cost of capital is 10 percent, then when should Biotech harvest the entire bacteria colony at one time?

Year	Change in Price Due to Competition (%)
1	5%
2	−2
3	−8
4	−10
5	−15
6	−25

11.36 ACME Manufacturing management is considering replacing an existing production line with a new line that has a greater output capacity and operates with less labor than the existing line. The new line would cost $1 million, have a five-year life, and be depreciated using MACRS over three years. At the end of five years, the new line could be sold as scrap for $200,000 (in Year 5 dollars). Because the new line is more automated, it would require fewer operators, resulting in a savings of $40,000 per year before tax and unadjusted for inflation (in today's dollars). Additional sales with the new machine are expected to result in additional net cash inflows, before tax, of $60,000 per year (in today's dollars). If ACME invests in the new line, a one-time investment of $10,000 in additional working capital will be required. The tax rate is 35 percent, the opportunity cost of capital is 10 percent, and the annual rate of inflation is 3 percent. What is the NPV of the new production line?

11.37 The alternative to investing in the new production line in Problem 11.36 is to overhaul the existing line, which currently has both a book value and a salvage value of $0. It would cost $300,000 to overhaul the existing line, but this expenditure would extend its useful life to five years. The line would have a $0 salvage value at the end of five years. The overhaul outlay would be capitalized and depreciated using MACRS over three years. Should ACME replace or renovate the existing line?

CFA Problems

11.38 FITCO is considering the purchase of new equipment. The equipment costs $350,000, and an additional $110,000 is needed to install it. The equipment will be depreciated straight-line to zero over a five-year life. The equipment will generate additional annual revenues of $265,000, and it will have annual cash operating expenses of $83,000. The equipment will be sold for $85,000 after five years. An inventory investment of $73,000 is required during the life of the investment. FITCO is in the 40 percent tax bracket, and its cost of capital is 10 percent. What is the project NPV?

a. $47,818.

b. $63,658.

c. $80,189.

d. $97,449.

11.39 After estimating a project's NPV, the analyst is advised that the fixed capital outlay will be revised upward by $100,000. The fixed capital outlay is depreciated straight-line over an eight-year life. The tax rate is 40 percent, and the required rate of return is 10 percent. No changes in cash operating revenues, cash operating expenses, or salvage value are expected. What is the effect on the project NPV?

a. $100,000 decrease.

b. $73,325 decrease.

c. $59,988 decrease.

d. No change.

11.40 When assembling the cash flows to calculate an NPV or IRR, the project's after-tax interest expenses should be subtracted from the cash flows for:

a. The NPV calculation, but not the IRR calculation.

b. The IRR calculation, but not the NPV calculation.

c. Both the NPV calculation and the IRR calculation.

d. Neither the NPV calculation nor the IRR calculation.

Sample Test Problems

11.1 You purchased 100 shares of stock in an oil company, Texas Energy, Inc., at $50 per share. The company has 1 million shares outstanding. Ten days later, Texas Energy announced an investment in an oil field in east Texas. The probability that the investment will be successful and generate an NPV of $10 million is 0.2; the probability that the investment will be a failure and generate an NPV of negative $1 million is 0.8. How would you expect the stock price to change upon the company's announcement of the investment?

11.2 A division of Virginia City Highlands Manufacturing is considering purchasing for $1,500,000 a machine that automates the process of inserting electronic components onto computer motherboards. The annual cost of operating the machine will be $50,000, but it will save the company $370,000 in labor costs each year. The machine will have a useful life of 10 years, and its salvage value in 10 years is estimated to be $300,000. Straight-line depreciation will be used in calculating taxes for this project, and the marginal corporate tax rate is 32 percent. If the appropriate discount rate is 12 percent, what is the NPV of this project?

11.3 After examining the NPV analysis for a potential project that would increase the firm's output by 5 percent, an analyst's manager tells the analyst to increase the initial fixed capital outlay in the analysis by $480,000. The initial fixed capital outlay would be fully depreciated on a straight-line basis over a 12-year life, regardless of whether it is increased. If the firm's average tax rate is 28 percent, its marginal tax rate is 35 percent, and the required rate of return is 10 percent, what is the effect of the adjustment on the project NPV?

11.4 Which of the following are relevant cash flows in the evaluation of a proposal to produce a new product?

a. Decrease in the cash flows of a substitute product.

b. Alternative of leasing an existing building that will be used for manufacturing this product.

c. The cost of a new machine required to produce this product.

d. Salvage value of the new machine at the end of its useful life.

e. Increase in net working capital at the beginning of the project's life.

f. Cost to develop a product prototype last year.

11.5 Managers of Central Embroidery have decided to purchase a new monogram machine and are considering two alternative machines. The first machine costs $100,000 and is expected to last five years. The second machine costs $160,000 and is expected to last eight years. Assume that the opportunity cost of capital is 8 percent. Which machine should Central Embroidery purchase?

11.6 You have inherited an apple orchard and want to sell it in the next four years. An expert in apple orchard valuation has estimated the after-tax cash flow you would receive if you sold at the end of each of the next four years as follows: $1,000,000 if you sell in one year; $1,300,000 if you sell in two years; $1,500,000 if you sell in three years; and $1,600,000 if you sell in four years. Your opportunity cost of capital is 10 percent. When should you sell the orchard?

Ethics Case

Unilever's Sustainable Living Plan

Sustainability is all the buzz in business and is quickly becoming a mainstream topic. Governments as well as customers have been urging corporations to make themselves sustainable, but what does that mean?

What Is Sustainability?

Sustainability is acting to meet the needs of the present generation without compromising the ability of future generations to meet their own needs. For individuals it is a lifestyle that attempts to reduce an individual's or society's use of Earth's natural resources. The European Union has adopted sustainability as an official policy, urging companies to follow sustainable practices as a means of achieving their corporate social responsibility goals to contribute to a better society and a cleaner environment.

LEX VAN LIESHOUT/AFP/Getty Images

Unilever's Sustainability Plan

Talking about sustainability is one thing; doing it is another. In late 2010 Unilever took action by unveiling its global Sustainable Living Plan. Launched simultaneously in London, New York, Amsterdam, and New Delhi, the plan would affect all of Unilever's stakeholders worldwide—customers, suppliers, investors, employees, and the local communities where Unilever products are sold. It's not unusual for a company to try to reduce its CO_2 emissions or to reduce waste and water usage in its own manufacturing facilities. But Unilever's plan goes far beyond its plants. According to the company's management, more than two-thirds of greenhouse emissions and half the water in Unilever products' life cycles come from consumer use. Therefore, extending the plan to include consumers is a commitment on an unprecedented scale.

Accomplishing the Company's *Sustainability Goals*

Technological advances would enable the firm to achieve some of its sustainability goals. The company was developing products such as laundry detergents that work at lower temperatures and bath soaps that reduce the amount of hot water needed in showers and baths.

Company management intended to accomplish other parts of its plan by requiring that suppliers meet sustainability goals.

Finally, Unilever management planned to meet some goals by changing consumers' habits. For example, by 2015 Unilever aimed to change the hygiene behavior of 1 billion consumers across Asia, Africa, and Latin America by promoting the benefits of hand washing with soap at key times. Though this may seem rudimentary by Western standards, every year more than 3.5 million children die before age five due to diarrhea and acute respiratory infections. Much of this is from poor hygiene habits.[1]

Overall, through its ambitious sustainability plan, Unilever management intended to (1) improve the health and well-being of more than 1 billion people; (2) purchase 100 percent of its agricultural raw material from sustainable businesses; and (3) reduce the environmental impact of everything it sells by one-half over the following 10 years while doubling its revenue. The major challenge the company faced was to increase sales without also increasing its environmental footprint. Dave Lewis, president of Unilever America, recognized this dilemma: "We cannot choose between growth and sustainability. We have to do both."

Critics of the plan pointed out that much of its success depended on changing consumer behavior, which was largely beyond Unilever's control. Probably more important, critics questioned whether the adoption of the plan would contribute to Unilever's bottom line. Being green and socially responsible are all well and good, but a public company needs to make money. A company that is not financially successful is not sustainable, good intentions notwithstanding.

Integrating Business Strategy and Sustainability Strategy

What makes Unilever's plan so intriguing to many is the way it integrates business strategy and sustainability strategy. Let's take one example: health and hygiene. Unilever claimed it would use its Lifebuoy brand soap to encourage more hand washing in an effort to reduce diarrhea and respiratory diseases spread by germs. It would use its fluoride toothpaste and toothbrush brands to encourage brushing twice a day, which would reduce tooth decay in children by 50 percent compared to brushing once. It would make safe drinking water available to 500 million people through its affordable Pureit in-home water purifier. Through its Dove Social Mission, Unilever intended to use one of its best-known brands to enhance the self-esteem and thus improve the mental health of young women around the world.

Large companies are often criticized by nongovernmental organizations (NGOs). In the past, as a company headquartered in Europe where NGOs are particularly active, Unilever has been a target of such criticism. A common corporate strategy is to fight back. However, with its Sustainable Living Plan, Unilever endorsed many NGO recommendations. For example, Unilever would use eggs from 100 percent cage-free chickens in all of its products—a common demand from animal rights NGOs. All Lipton tea would be purchased from Rainforest Alliance certified suppliers. Even Ben and Jerry's ice cream would be made from ingredients that are fair-trade certified.

In rural India, Unilever planned to link 500,000 small farmers into a unified supply network to improve their farming practices. The farmers would be required to adhere to Unilever's Sustainable Agriculture Code and for the first time would benefit from economies of scale that could improve their lives. What's in it for Unilever? Relationships with a vastly expanded network of sustainable suppliers producing products at competitive prices. Building an adequate source of supplies is especially critical in a world where food shortages may become more common.

Critical Concerns and Responses

Is Unilever simply using the sustainability mantra as a device to increase its profits? To its critics, Unilever's motives are suspect. They claim it is pursuing sustainability, not because it is the right thing to do, but because it is good business. But are these two goals mutually exclusive? Can a firm's strategy seek to be profitable and sustainable? What's wrong with doing well by doing good? Nothing, according to Unilever management. They intend to lead the way in being a profitable, sustainable corporation.

Discussion Questions

1. Should Unilever's stockholders endorse its sustainability plan? Why or why not?
2. Are there business advantages to using sustainable or green suppliers? If so, what are they? If not, do you think a traditional return on investment analysis captures all possible benefits of going green?
3. Are there any ethical criticisms of Unilever's sustainable living strategy? If so, what are they?

[1]Studies by Unilever have shown that hand washing at key hygienic occasions can reduce diarrheal disease by 25 percent, respiratory infection by 19 percent, and eye infections by 46 percent.

Sources: (1) http://www.sustainable-living.unilever.com/, (2) http://www.sustainable-living.unilever.com/the-plan/health-hygiene, (3) http://en.wikipedia.org/wiki/Sustainable_living, (4) http://www.epa.gov/sustainability

CHAPTER 12

Evaluating Project Economics

Richard Levine/Alamy Stock Photo

LEARNING OBJECTIVES

1. Explain and demonstrate how variable costs and fixed costs affect the volatility of pretax operating cash flows and accounting operating profits.
2. Calculate and distinguish between the degree of pretax cash flow operating leverage and the degree of accounting operating leverage.
3. Define and calculate the pretax operating cash flow and accounting operating profit break-even points and the crossover levels of unit sales for a project.
4. Define the economic break-even point and be able to calculate it for a project.
5. Define sensitivity analysis, scenario analysis, and simulation analysis and describe how they are used to evaluate the risks associated with a project.

On March 17, 2017, the enterprise software company MuleSoft went public and shares of its stock began trading on the New York Stock Exchange under the ticker symbol MULE. At the beginning of that day, the company sold 13 million shares at a price of $17 each. The public offering was the culmination of tremendous success for the company over a relatively short period. MuleSoft had grown rapidly since its founding in 2006. By 2014, the company had revenues of $57.6 million and two years later this figure had grown to $187.7 million—an average annual growth rate of 80.5 percent in the two years before the public offering. During the day of the public offering, MuleSoft's stock price increased sharply to $24.75 per share, implying a value of just over $3.1 billion for the company as a whole.

As with any other capital investment, starting a business involves a great deal of uncertainty. If you put yourself in the shoes of the founders of MuleSoft, you can imagine the questions and concerns they had about the market they were entering and their ability to compete in that market. How large would the market be for the software platform that they were developing to connect applications, data sources, and devices? Which features would enable them to most quickly grow their user base? What market share could MuleSoft reasonably expect to capture? How likely was it that someone would develop a competing product or technology that would make theirs obsolete?

As the founders of MuleSoft contemplated starting the company, they probably also asked themselves more questions regarding the economics of this business: What level of unit sales would be required to cover costs? What would happen to the viability of the business if it did not earn enough to cover these costs quickly? How would competitors respond if the business was initially successful, and what effect would competitors' responses have on MuleSoft's revenues and profits over the long run? If the company was successful, how much value would be created for investors? Answering such questions is part of any thorough project analysis. This chapter discusses some of the tools and methods used to obtain the answers.

Chapter Preview

Financial analysts who forecast the free cash flows used in an NPV analysis realize that actual cash flows will almost certainly differ from their forecasts. No one can predict what will happen in the future! For this reason, it is important to understand the economic characteristics of a project and the implications of being wrong. This chapter discusses key tools and methods that analysts use to develop this understanding.

We first discuss how a project's cost structure affects its risk and how analysts measure this effect. We then describe break-even analysis, which is used to determine how many units must be sold in order for a project to break even. These concepts help analysts better understand the economic characteristics of projects and provide insights into how projects can be structured to maximize their value.

We end with a discussion of how financial analysts evaluate the uncertainties associated with cash flow forecasts. These techniques allow analysts to determine which characteristics of a project have the greatest impact on the level of the cash flows, how market or economic conditions affect the cash flows of the business, and the probability that certain levels of cash flows will be realized.

12.1 Variable Costs, Fixed Costs, and Project Risk

LEARNING OBJECTIVE

1. Explain and demonstrate how variable costs and fixed costs affect the volatility of pretax operating cash flows and accounting operating profits.

Two questions are always on the mind of a financial analyst evaluating a project: "How wrong can my free cash flow forecasts be?" and "What are the implications if my forecasts are wrong?" It is natural to ask these questions, since the actual incremental after-tax free cash flows (FCF) for a project will almost certainly differ from the forecasted FCF. This chapter discusses some important tools that help provide answers.

To fully understand how to evaluate project risk, you must first understand how variable costs and fixed costs affect the risk of a business. Recall from Chapter 11 that variable costs are costs that vary directly with the number of units sold. An example of a variable cost is the cost of the ingredients that a pizza parlor uses to make its pizzas. The total cost of these ingredients increases or decreases as the number of pizzas sold increases or decreases. Fixed costs, in contrast, do not vary with unit sales—at least in the short run. An example of a fixed cost in a pizza parlor is the salary of the manager. As pizza sales go up and down from month to month, the cost of the manager's salary remains constant.

The cash flows and accounting profits for a project are sensitive to the proportion of its costs that is variable and the proportion that is fixed. A project with a higher proportion of fixed costs will have cash flows and accounting profits that are more sensitive to changes in revenues than an otherwise identical project with a lower proportion of fixed costs. This is because the costs of a project with a higher proportion of fixed costs will not change as much when revenue changes.

To illustrate this point, we can represent the incremental cash operating expenses, Op Ex, from Equation 11.2 as

$$\text{Op Ex} = \text{VC} + \text{FC} \tag{12.1}$$

where VC is the incremental variable costs associated with a project and FC is the incremental fixed costs. Equation 12.1 simply says that all cash operating expenses are either variable costs or fixed costs.

Let's carry this equation a bit further. We know from Exhibit 11.1 that

$$\text{EBITDA} = \text{Revenue} - \text{Op Ex}$$

Thus, Equation 12.1 suggests that we can write EBITDA as

$$\text{EBITDA} = \text{Revenue} - \text{VC} - \text{FC}$$

You might recall from Chapter 11 that EBITDA is the incremental earnings before interest, taxes, depreciation, and amortization and Revenue is the incremental revenue from a project. EBITDA is often called **pretax operating cash flow** because it equals the incremental pretax *cash* operating profits from a project. Strictly speaking, EBITDA is not a complete measure of operating cash flow because it does not include the effects of working capital requirements on cash flows. Nevertheless, it is a very commonly used measure.

pretax operating cash flow earnings before interest, taxes, depreciation, and amortization, or EBITDA

Cost Structure and Sensitivity of EBITDA to Revenue Changes

To see how writing the calculation of EBITDA in terms of fixed and variable costs can be helpful, consider this situation: You have been trying to decide whether to buy a hammock-manufacturing business in which hammocks are currently made by hand.[1] Now you have become aware of the existence of an automated hammock-manufacturing system. This means that, in addition to deciding whether to go into the hammock business, you must choose between two manufacturing alternatives: (1) investing in manufacturing equipment that will largely automate the production process and (2) relying on the current manufacturing method in which hammocks are produced by hand. Assume that the per-unit variable costs (Unit VC) and the total FC and depreciation and amortization (D&A) for the two alternatives are as presented in **Exhibit 12.1**. How would you evaluate the relative advantages and disadvantages of the automated and the manual production alternatives?

One thing you might do is compare the sensitivity of EBITDA to changes in revenue for the two alternatives. This can help you better understand the risks and returns for the alternatives. To see why, assume that the sensitivity of EBITDA to changes in revenue is higher for one alternative than for the other. This means that EBITDA for the more sensitive alternative will decline more when revenue is lower than expected. A larger decline in EBITDA can cause problems not only because it reduces the value of the project more, but also because it has a greater impact on the amount of cash that the firm has available to fund other positive NPV projects. In an extreme case, a drop in EBITDA can unexpectedly force the firm to invest

EXHIBIT 12.1 Unit and Annual Costs for Hammock Project

To evaluate the automated and manual production alternatives in our hammock-manufacturing example, we start with information about the variable costs per unit (Unit VC), fixed costs (FC), and depreciation and amortization (D&A).

	Automated Production	Manual Production
Unit VC:		
Labor	$1	$5
Rope	5	5
Spacer bars	2	2
Hardware	2	2
Packaging	2	2
Shipping and other	4	4
Total	$16	$20
FC	$35,000	$4,000
D&A	$10,000	$1,000

[1]A hammock is a bed which is typically made of canvas or rope mesh and which is suspended by cords at each end. Hammocks are often used as garden furniture or on board ships.

EXHIBIT 12.2 EBITDA under Alternative Production Technologies

Here we calculate EBITDA for the automated and manual production alternatives in the hammock-manufacturing example. The calculations use the information provided in Exhibit 12.1 and assume that 10,000 units are sold at a price of $25 per unit.

	Automated Production	Manual Production
Units sold	10,000	10,000
Unit price	$25	$25
Unit VC	$16	$20
Revenue	$250,000	$250,000
– VC	160,000	200,000
– FC	35,000	4,000
= EBITDA	$ 55,000	$ 46,000

additional money into the project. On the positive side, EBITDA will increase more when revenue is greater than expected if the level of sensitivity is higher. Whether this potential benefit justifies the risks is a decision that you would have to make when choosing between the two alternatives. Comparing the sensitivity of EBITDA to changes in revenue for the two alternatives will at least help you better understand the trade-offs.

Distinguishing between fixed and variable costs enables us to calculate the sensitivity of EBITDA to changes in revenue. For example, suppose you expect to sell 10,000 hammocks next year at an average price of $25 each. Based on the costs in Exhibit 12.1, you would forecast EBITDA to be $55,000 under the automated production alternative and $46,000 under the manual production alternative.[2] These calculations are presented in **Exhibit 12.2**.

Although selling 10,000 units represents your best estimate of what you can expect, you might also envision a situation in which demand would be poor and sales would equal only 8,000 units, 20 percent less than your best estimate of 10,000 units. Distinguishing between fixed and variable costs makes it relatively straightforward to determine how EBITDA would be affected if only 8,000 units were sold. This "Poor Demand" scenario is illustrated in columns 2 and 4 of **Exhibit 12.3** for the automated production and manual production

EXHIBIT 12.3 Changes in EBITDA under Alternative Production Technologies

EBITDA for the automated and manual production alternatives in the hammock-manufacturing example declines by different amounts when the number of units sold declines 20 percent and the unit price remains the same.

	Automated Production		Manual Production	
	Expected Demand (1)	Poor Demand (2)	Expected Demand (3)	Poor Demand (4)
Units sold	10,000	8,000	10,000	8,000
Unit price	$25	$25	$25	$25
Unit VC	$16	$16	$20	$20
Revenue	$250,000	$200,000	$250,000	$200,000
– VC	160,000	128,000	200,000	160,000
– FC	35,000	35,000	4,000	4,000
= EBITDA	$ 55,000	$ 37,000	$ 46,000	$ 36,000
Percent change in revenue[a]		−20.0%		−20.0%
Percent change in EBITDA		−32.7%		−21.7%

[a]The percent change in revenue is calculated as:

Percent change = $(\text{Revenue}_{\text{Poor}} - \text{Revenue}_{\text{Expected}})/\text{Revenue}_{\text{Expected}}$

= ($200,000 − $250,000)/$250,000 = −0.20, or −20%

All other percent changes are calculated this way in the exhibits.

[2]VC equals Unit VC (or cost per unit) times the number of units sold. If we know Unit VC, we can therefore calculate VC for different levels of unit sales.

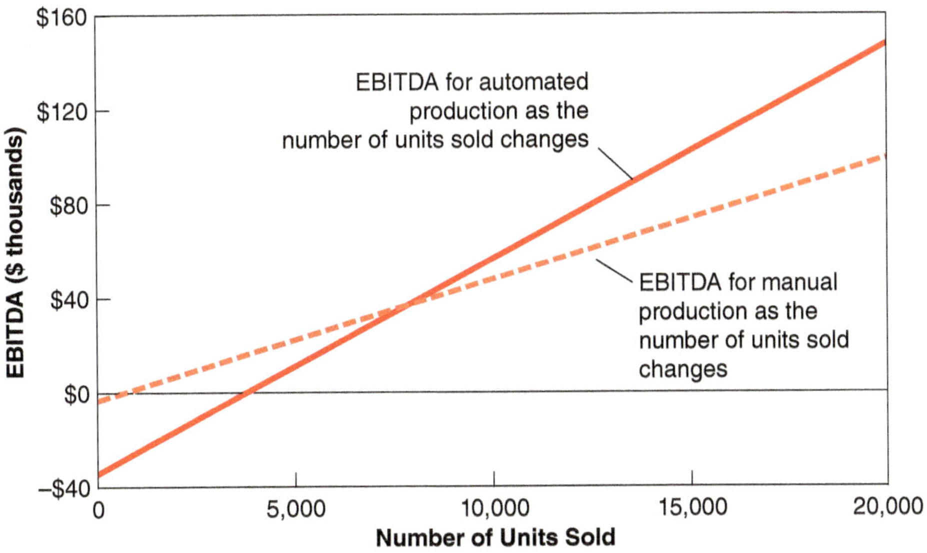

EXHIBIT 12.4 EBITDA for Different Levels of Unit Sales

The sensitivity of EBITDA to changes in unit sales differs for the automated and manual production alternatives in the hammock-manufacturing example. The steeper line for the automated production alternative means that EBITDA for this alternative is more sensitive to changes in the number of units sold.

alternatives (assuming that Unit VC does not change with unit sales). Columns 1 and 3 are identical to the two columns in Exhibit 12.2.

Exhibit 12.3 shows that EBITDA is much more sensitive to changes in revenue with the automated production process than with the manual process. A 20 percent decline in revenue results in a 32.7 percent decline in EBITDA with the automated production process, but only a 21.7 percent decline in EBITDA with the manual production process—an 11 percentage point difference. The reason for the difference is that more of the total costs are fixed with the automated process, making it more difficult to adjust costs when revenue changes. Because of this difference, the difference in EBITDA under the two production alternatives shrinks from $9,000 ($55,000 – $46,000 = $9,000) to only $1,000 ($37,000 – $36,000 = $1,000) when unit sales are 8,000 instead of 10,000.

You can see how the difference in EBITDA shrinks as the number of units sold decreases in **Exhibit 12.4**, which shows how EBITDA changes as the number of units sold changes for both the manual and the automated production process. Notice that the relation between EBITDA and the number of units sold is steeper with the automated production process, where there are more fixed costs. A steeper line indicates that EBITDA for the automated production process is more sensitive to changes in the number of units sold.

Note also that the effect of changes in the number of units sold is symmetrical because the relation between EBITDA and the number of units sold is linear. This means that the automated production process will produce larger declines in EBITDA when unit sales are lower than expected as well as larger increases in EBITDA when unit sales are higher than expected. This is exactly what we were referring to earlier when we said that when pretax operating cash flows are more sensitive to changes in revenue, they will decline more when revenue is lower than expected and increase more when revenue is greater than expected.

Cost Structure and Sensitivity of EBIT to Revenue Changes

Exhibit 12.5 expands the analysis in Exhibit 12.3 to illustrate how the sensitivity of accounting operating profits (EBIT) to changes in revenue differs under the two hammock-manufacturing

EXHIBIT 12.5 Changes in EBITDA and EBIT under Alternative Production Technologies

The EBIT values for the automated and manual production alternatives in the hammock-manufacturing example decline more than the EBITDA values when the number of units sold declines 20 percent and the unit price remains the same. This occurs because the fixed nature of depreciation and amortization (D&A) charges has the same effect as other fixed costs. When D&A is greater than zero, the percentage change in EBIT is greater than the percentage change in EBITDA.

	Automated Production		Manual Production	
	Expected Demand (1)	Poor Demand (2)	Expected Demand (3)	Poor Demand (4)
Units sold	10,000	8,000	10,000	8,000
Unit price	$25	$25	$25	$25
Unit VC	$16	$16	$20	$20
Revenue	$250,000	$200,000	$250,000	$200,000
– VC	160,000	128,000	200,000	160,000
– FC	35,000	35,000	4,000	4,000
= EBITDA	$ 55,000	$ 37,000	$ 46,000	$ 36,000
– D&A	10,000	10,000	1,000	1,000
= EBIT	$ 45,000	$ 27,000	$ 45,000	$ 35,000
Percent change in revenue		–20.0%		–20.0%
Percent change in EBITDA		–32.7%		–21.7%
Percent change in EBIT		–40.0%		–22.2%

alternatives. The sensitivity of EBIT to changes in revenue is of concern to managers because EBIT is a performance measure that is of interest to investors.

In Exhibit 12.5 you can see that the 20 percent decline in revenue results in a 40 percent decline in EBIT with the automated production process but only a 22.2 percent decline in EBIT with the manual production process. The difference in the decline in EBIT is 17.8 percentage points! This difference is larger than the 11 percentage point difference for EBITDA because the EBITDA calculation does not include D&A. Depreciation and amortization acts just like a fixed cost when we include it in the calculation because it is based on the amount that was invested in the project rather than in unit sales. Therefore, when we include D&A in the EBIT calculation, we effectively increase the proportion of costs that is fixed. Note that, since D&A is larger for the automated production alternative, including it in the calculation has a greater impact on the sensitivity of EBIT to changes in revenue for the automated production alternative than for the manual alternative. This is why the difference in the decline in EBIT is so much larger than the corresponding difference for EBITDA.

Building Intuition

High Fixed Costs Mean Larger Fluctuations in Cash Flows and Profits

The higher the proportion of fixed costs to variable costs in a project, the more pretax operating cash flows (EBITDA) and accounting operating profits (EBIT) will vary as revenue varies. This is true because it is more difficult to change fixed costs than to change variable costs when unit sales change. If unit sales decline, EBITDA and EBIT will decrease more in a business where fixed costs represent a larger proportion of total costs. Conversely, if unit sales increase, EBITDA and EBIT will increase more in a business with higher fixed costs.

If we recreated Exhibit 12.4 for EBIT, the lines would also be linear and the slope would be steeper for the automated production process than for the manual production process. As was the case with EBITDA, the linear relation between changes in revenue and EBIT indicates that there are benefits and costs associated with using the automated production process. When deciding whether to use the automated process, you must weigh the prospect of higher accounting operating profits if unit sales exceed expected levels against concerns about lower accounting operating profits if unit sales are below expectations. In other words, you must decide whether the potential for earning a higher return with the automated manufacturing process justifies the risks. In Chapter 16 we will discuss how greater volatility in operating profits increases the chances that a firm will be forced into bankruptcy.

Learning by Doing Applications 12.1 and 12.2 illustrate calculation of an EBIT forecast and examination of its sensitivity to changes in the inputs. The **Using Excel Example** that follows shows the spreadsheet setup for the sensitivity analysis.

APPLICATION 12.1 | Forecasting EBIT

LEARNING BY DOING

WileyPLUS

Need more help? Visit your WileyPLUS course.

Problem You have decided to start a business that provides in-home technical computer support to people in the community near your university. You have seen national advertisements for a company that provides these services in other communities. You would run this business out of your dorm room, and you know plenty of students who have the necessary technical skills and would welcome the opportunity to earn more than the university pays under its work-study programs. To get up and running quickly, you would have to invest in a computer system, an advertising campaign, three vehicles, and tools. You would also want to have enough cash to keep the business going until it began to generate positive cash flows. All of this would require about $100,000, which is about all that you think you can borrow on your credit cards, against your car, and from friends and family.

You are now working on the financial forecasts for the business. You plan to charge $45 for house calls lasting up to 30 minutes and $25 for each additional 30 minutes. Since you expect that the typical house call will require 60 minutes, you expect it to result in revenue of $70. You also estimate that monthly fixed operating costs (FC), which include an advertising contract with a local radio station and a small salary for you, will total $3,000. Unit VC, including the technicians' pay, gas, and so forth, will total $20 for the typical house call. Monthly depreciation and amortization charges (D&A) will be $1,000. Finally, you expect that after six months the business will average 120 house calls per month. Given this information, what do you expect the monthly EBIT to be in six months?

Approach Since EBIT = Revenue − VC − FC − D&A (see, for example, the calculation in Exhibit 12.5), you can forecast the expected monthly EBIT in six months by using this equation and the values for Revenue, VC, FC, and D&A that you expect in six months.

Solution The calculation is as follows:

Revenue	$70 per house call × 120 house calls =	$8,400
− VC	$20 per house call × 120 house calls =	2,400
− FC		3,000
− D&A		1,000
= EBIT		$2,000

APPLICATION 12.2 | Fixed Costs and Fluctuations in EBIT

LEARNING BY DOING

WileyPLUS

Need more help? Visit your WileyPLUS course.

Problem As you prepare the financial forecast for your computer-support business, you worry about the impact of fluctuations in the number of house calls on EBIT. You decide to examine how converting some fixed costs to variable costs will affect the sensitivity of EBIT to changes in the number of house calls. In a conversation with the manager at the radio station where you would be advertising, you discover that instead of paying $1,500 per month under a long-term advertising contract, you can get the same level of advertising for $1,600, where $1,000 of the total cost is fixed and $600 is variable. That is, in a given month, if you used the full level of advertising, you would pay $1,600, but you would also have the ability to reduce advertising costs to $1,000 by cutting back on the number of advertisements. You wonder how this contract would affect the sensitivity of EBIT to a decrease in the monthly number of house calls—say, from 120 to 90.

Approach To determine how the sensitivity of EBIT differs between the $1,500 per month long-term contract and the contract that has only $1,000 of fixed costs, you must calculate EBIT under each alternative contact for 120 house calls and for 90 house calls. Using these EBIT values, you must next calculate the percentage decrease in EBIT if the number of monthly house calls declines from 120 to 90 for each alternative. You can then compare the percentage decreases to see the difference in the sensitivity of EBIT to the decrease in the number of house calls.

Solution *$1,500 monthly fixed contract:* As we determined in Learning by Doing Application 12.1, EBIT is $2,000 with 120 house calls per month. With 90 house calls per month instead of 120, revenue would be $6,300 per month ($70 per house call × 90 house calls = $6,300) instead of $8,400 ($70 per house call × 120 house calls = $8,400) and EBIT would decline to $500:

$$\begin{aligned}\text{EBIT} &= \text{Revenue} - \text{VC} - \text{FC} - \text{D\&A}\\ &= \$6{,}300 - (\$20 \times 90) - \$3{,}000 - \$1{,}000\\ &= \$500\end{aligned}$$

This represents a 75 percent decrease in EBIT ([\$500 – \$2,000]/\$2,000 = –0.75, or –75 percent).

\$1,600 monthly contract with \$1,000 fixed: Switching to the alternative advertising arrangement would increase unit variable costs by \$5 (\$600/120 house calls = \$5 per house call) but would decrease fixed costs by \$500 (\$3,000 – \$2,500 = \$500). EBIT with 120 house calls per month would equal \$1,900:

$$\begin{aligned} \text{EBIT} &= \text{Revenue} - \text{VC} - \text{FC} - \text{D\&A} \\ &= \$8{,}400 - (\$25 \times 120) - \$2{,}500 - \$1{,}000 \\ &= \$1{,}900 \end{aligned}$$

With 90 house calls, EBIT would decline to \$550:

$$\text{EBIT} = \$6{,}300 - (\$25 \times 90) - \$2{,}500 - \$1{,}000 = \$550$$

This represents a 71 percent decrease in EBIT [(\$550 – \$1,900)/\$1,900 = –0.71, or –71 percent].

If the business averaged 120 house calls per month, EBIT under the alternative advertising arrangement would be \$100 lower than EBIT under the original advertising arrangement. However, it would actually be \$50 higher if the business averaged only 90 house calls per month because you would be able to cut back on advertising expenses under the alternative agreement if demand were poor.[3]

Using Excel

Examining the Impact of Changes in Your Assumptions

One of the main advantages of using a spreadsheet program for financial analysis is that it enables us to perform a sensitivity analysis in a matter of seconds. Once the spreadsheet is carefully set up with all the relevant key assumptions and calculations, we can change any one of the assumptions and immediately see the effect on the bottom line.

Below is a setup for Learning by Doing Applications 12.1 and 12.2 that analyzes the impact of the alternative advertising schemes on the EBIT of the in-home technical computer-support business.

Notice that the actual EBIT calculation is entirely derived from formulas utilizing inputs from the key assumptions. To use the model for sensitivity analysis, all you have to do is change the values for the volume of calls per month for the two advertising alternatives (in cell B11 and D11). For example, when you change the volume number for the alternative advertising scenario back to 120, EBIT equals \$1,900, just as it does in Learning by Doing Application 12.2.

	A	B	C	D	E	F	G	H	I	J
1										
2	**Key Assumptions:**	**Fixed Advertising Contract with More House Calls**		**Alternative Advertising Contract with Fewer House Calls**						
3	House call up to 30 minutes	\$45		\$45						
4	Each additional 30 minutes	\$25		\$25						
5	Revenue from typical call - unit (60 min.)	\$70		\$70						
6	FC	\$3,000		\$2,500						
7	VC/unit (technician's pay, gas, etc.)	\$20		\$20						
8	Alternative advertising option VC			\$600						
9	VC/unit of alternative advertising option			\$5	=D8/B11					
10	Monthly D&A	\$1,000		\$1,000						
11	Volume of calls per month	120		90						
12										
13										
14	**Fixed Advertising Contract:**						**Alternative Advertising Contract:**			
15	Revenue	\$8,400		=B11*B5			Revenue	\$6,300	=D11*D5	
16	Less: Variable cost (VC)	\$2,400		=B11*B7			Less: Variable cost (VC)	\$2,250	=D11*(D7+D9)	
17	Less: Fixed cost (FC)	\$3,000		=B6			Less: Fixed cost (FC)	\$2,500	=D6	
18	Less: Depreciation and Amortization	\$1,000		=B10			Less: Depreciation and Amortization	\$1,000	=D10	
19	**EBIT**	**\$2,000**		=B15-B16-B17-B18			**EBIT**	**\$550**	=H15-H16-H17-H18	
20										
21										

[3]We are assuming here that you will cut back on advertising expenditures if revenue declines and that a modest decrease in advertising will not adversely affect demand for your services. Of course, under certain circumstances, you might actually increase advertising expenditures if demand for your service declines.

Before You Go On

1. Why do analysts care about how sensitive EBITDA and EBIT are to changes in revenue?
2. How is the proportion of fixed costs in a project's cost structure related to the sensitivity of EBITDA and EBIT to changes in revenue?

12.2 Calculating Operating Leverage

LEARNING OBJECTIVE

2. Calculate and distinguish between the degree of pretax cash flow operating leverage and the degree of accounting operating leverage.

The examples in Section 12.1 illustrate the impact of **operating leverage** on pretax operating cash flows and on accounting operating profits when revenue changes. Operating leverage is a measure of the relative amounts of fixed and variable costs in a project's cost structure. It is the major factor that determines the sensitivity of EBITDA or EBIT to changes in revenue. The higher a project's operating leverage, the greater these sensitivities. Two measures of operating leverage often used by analysts are the degree of pretax cash flow operating leverage and the degree of accounting operating leverage.

operating leverage a measure of the relative amounts of fixed and variable costs in a project's cost structure; operating leverage is higher with more fixed costs

Degree of Pretax Cash Flow Operating Leverage

The **degree of pretax cash flow operating leverage (Cash Flow DOL)** provides us with a measure of how sensitive pretax operating cash flows are to changes in revenue. It is calculated using the following formula:

degree of pretax cash flow operating leverage (Cash Flow DOL) a measure of the sensitivity of cash flows from operations (EBITDA) to changes in revenue

$$\text{Cash Flow DOL} = 1 + \frac{\text{Fixed costs}}{\text{Pretax operating cash flows}} = 1 + \frac{\text{FC}}{\text{EBITDA}} \qquad (12.2)$$

Using the FC and EBITDA values in Exhibit 12.2, we can calculate Cash Flow DOL for the automated production alternative in the hammock-manufacturing example as follows:

$$\text{Cash Flow DOL}_{\text{Automated}} = 1 + \frac{\text{FC}}{\text{EBITDA}} = 1 + \frac{\$35{,}000}{\$55{,}000} = 1.64$$

This indicates that a 1 percent change in revenue will change pretax operating cash flow, EBITDA, by 1.64 percent. A measure such as this provides analysts with a convenient way of summarizing how much pretax operating cash flow will differ from forecasts if revenue is below or above the expected level.

You should be aware of one limitation to this measure: Cash Flow DOL changes with the level of revenue. In other words, the sensitivity is not the same for all levels of revenue. As a result, a particular Cash Flow DOL measure is only useful for modest changes in revenue. To understand why this limitation exists, notice that the numerator in the fraction in Equation 12.2, FC, does not vary with revenue. In contrast, the denominator, EBITDA, varies directly with revenue if the pretax operating cash flow margin is positive. If revenue is larger, the denominator in Equation 12.2 will be larger for any project that has a positive pretax operating cash flow margin. This, in turn, will cause Cash Flow DOL to become smaller as revenue increases. Alternatively, if revenue is lower, the denominator in the fraction will be smaller, and Cash Flow DOL will be larger.

Consider, for example, how Cash Flow DOL changes for the automated production alternative if unit sales are 20,000 instead of 10,000. **Exhibit 12.6** shows us that EBITDA will

EXHIBIT 12.6 EBITDA with Unit Sales of 10,000 and 20,000 for the Automated Production Alternative

For the automated production alternative in the hammock-manufacturing example, EBITDA increases from \$55,000 to \$145,000 when unit sales increase from 10,000 to 20,000 units.

Units sold	10,000	20,000
Unit price	\$25	\$25
Unit VC	\$16	\$16
Revenue	\$250,000	\$500,000
– VC	160,000	320,000
– FC	35,000	35,000
= EBITDA	\$ 55,000	\$145,000

equal \$145,000 with unit sales of 20,000. Therefore, Cash Flow DOL under the automated production alternative would be only 1.24:

$$\text{Cash Flow DOL}_{\text{Automated}} = 1 + \frac{\$35{,}000}{\$145{,}000} = 1.24$$

Degree of Accounting Operating Leverage

degree of accounting operating leverage (Accounting DOL) a measure of the sensitivity of accounting operating profits (EBIT) to changes in revenue

While Cash Flow DOL is a measure of the sensitivity of pretax operating cash flows to changes in revenue, the **degree of accounting operating leverage (Accounting DOL)** is a measure of how sensitive accounting operating profits (EBIT) are to changes in revenue. The formula for Accounting DOL is as follows:

$$\begin{aligned}\text{Accounting DOL} &= 1 + \frac{\text{Fixed charges}}{\text{Accounting operating profits}} \qquad (12.3)\\ &= 1 + \frac{\text{FC} + \text{D\&A}}{\text{EBITDA} - \text{D\&A}}\\ &= 1 + \frac{\text{FC} + \text{D\&A}}{\text{EBIT}}\end{aligned}$$

In this formula, D&A is treated as a fixed cost and is added to FC to obtain the total of the cash and noncash fixed costs on the income statement if the project were adopted. This total is then divided by total accounting operating profits (EBIT).[4]

The only difference between Accounting DOL and Cash Flow DOL is that Accounting DOL focuses on EBIT, whereas Cash Flow DOL focuses on EBITDA. This means that the calculations differ only in the way that D&A is treated, since EBIT = EBITDA – D&A. Note that Accounting DOL will always be larger than Cash Flow DOL if D&A is greater than zero. This is because, compared with the calculation in Equation 12.2, the calculation in Equation 12.3 will have a larger numerator and a smaller denominator when D&A is greater than zero.

Let's apply the Accounting DOL formula to the automated production alternative in the hammock example. Using the values of FC, D&A, and EBIT from column 1 in Exhibit 12.5, we get:

$$\begin{aligned}\text{Accounting DOL}_{\text{Automated}} &= 1 + \frac{\text{FC} + \text{D\&A}}{\text{EBIT}}\\ &= 1 + \frac{\$35{,}000 + \$10{,}000}{\$45{,}000}\\ &= 2.00\end{aligned}$$

This tells us that a 1 percent change in revenue will result in a 2 percent change in EBIT. In other words, EBIT will change by twice as much, in percentage terms, as revenue with the automated production alternative!

[4]The term *accounting operating profits* is used here to refer to EBIT, even though EBIT is not actually computed using accounting numbers when we forecast cash flows for a financial analysis. The term is used to refer to the fact that noncash charges, D&A, are subtracted when computing this measure of earnings, just as is done in the calculation of accounting operating profits.

In comparison, the Accounting DOL for the manual production alternative (column 3 in Exhibit 12.5) is only 1.11:

$$\text{Accounting DOL}_{\text{Manual}} = 1 + \frac{\$4{,}000 + \$1{,}000}{\$45{,}000} = 1.11$$

A 1 percent change in revenue will result in only a 1.11 percent change in EBIT with the manual production alternative.

One important insight that you should take away from this discussion is that the volatility of pretax operating cash flows (EBITDA) and accounting operating profits (EBIT) is strongly influenced by two factors: (1) volatility in revenue and (2) operating leverage. If there is no uncertainty regarding what the different costs associated with a project will be, these are the only two factors that determine volatility in EBITDA and EBIT. It is always a good idea to pay special attention to these two factors when you are evaluating the uncertainty associated with the cash flows or the accounting profits from a project.

Learning by Doing Application 12.3 illustrates other Cash Flow and Accounting DOL calculations.

Building Intuition

Revenue Changes Drive Profit Volatility Through Operating Leverage

If there is no uncertainty about costs, volatility in pretax operating cash flows (EBITDA) and accounting operating profits (EBIT) will be driven entirely by changes in revenue and operating leverage. If a project has any fixed costs associated with it, operating leverage will magnify changes in revenue. The degree of operating leverage is a direct measure of how much more volatile EBITDA and EBIT will be than revenue.

LEARNING BY DOING

APPLICATION 12.3 | Calculating Cash Flow and Accounting DOL

Problem You have decided to calculate the operating leverage for the in-home computer-support business you are thinking about starting. What will Cash Flow DOL and Accounting DOL be in six months if EBIT is $2,000, FC is $3,000, and D&A is $1,000?

Approach Use Equations 12.2 and 12.3 to calculate Cash Flow DOL and Accounting DOL, respectively.

Solution From Equation 12.2, Cash Flow DOL is:

$$\text{Cash Flow DOL} = 1 + \frac{\text{FC}}{\text{EBIT} + \text{D\&A}} = 1 + \frac{\$3{,}000}{\$2{,}000 + \$1{,}000} = 2.00$$

From Equation 12.3, Accounting DOL is:

$$\text{Accounting DOL} = 1 + \frac{\text{FC} + \text{D\&A}}{\text{EBIT}} = 1 + \frac{\$3{,}000 + \$1{,}000}{\$2{,}000} = 3.00$$

WileyPLUS

Need more help? Visit your WileyPLUS course.

Before You Go On

1. How does operating leverage change when there is an increase in the proportion of a project's costs that are fixed?
2. What do the degree of pretax cash flow operating leverage (Cash Flow DOL) and the degree of accounting operating leverage (Accounting DOL) tell us?

12.3 Break-Even Analysis

LEARNING OBJECTIVE

3. Define and calculate the pretax operating cash flow and accounting operating profit break-even points and the crossover levels of unit sales for a project.

A question that naturally comes to mind when we consider operating leverage is this: What level of unit sales or revenue is necessary for a project to break even? This is an important

break-even analysis an analysis that tells us how many units must be sold in order for a project to break even on a cash flow or accounting profit basis

question because it helps us better understand how successful the project will have to be in order to succeed. In this section, we discuss **break-even analysis,** which tells us how many units must be sold in order for a project to break even on a cash flow or accounting profit basis. Break-even analysis also helps us understand how sensitive cash flows and accounting profits are to changes in the number of units that will be sold.

Pretax Operating Cash Flow Break-Even

pretax operating cash flow (EBITDA) break-even point the number of units that must be sold for pretax operating cash flow to equal $0

When evaluating a project, we might want to know what level of unit sales is necessary for the project to break even on operations from a pretax operating cash flow perspective. In other words, how many units must be sold for pretax operating cash flow to equal $0? This is a very important question; if the project fails to break even from a pretax operating cash flow perspective, the firm will have to put more cash into the project to keep it going. The **pretax operating cash flow (EBITDA) break-even point** is calculated as follows:

$$\text{EBITDA Break-even} = \frac{\text{FC}}{\text{Price} - \text{Unit VC}} \tag{12.4}$$

For our hammock-manufacturing example, we can calculate the EBITDA break-even points for the automated and manual production alternatives as follows:

$$\text{EBITDA Break-even}_{\text{Automated}} = \frac{\$35{,}000}{\$25 - \$16} = 3{,}889 \text{ units}$$

$$\text{EBITDA Break-even}_{\text{Manual}} = \frac{\$4{,}000}{\$25 - \$20} = 800 \text{ units}$$

per-unit contribution the dollar amount that is left over from the sale of a single unit after all the variable costs associated with that unit have been paid; this is the amount that is available to help cover FC for the project

In each of these calculations, we are simply dividing the fixed costs, FC, by the **per-unit contribution** (Price – Unit VC). The per-unit contribution is how much money is left from the sale of a single unit after all the variable costs associated with that unit have been paid. This is the amount that is available to help cover FC for the project.

In the hammock-manufacturing example, we see that if the automated production alternative is selected instead of the manual production alternative, almost five times as many units (3,889 versus 800 units) will have to be sold before the project breaks even on a pretax operating cash flow basis in a particular year. This is because the automated production alternative has much higher fixed costs ($35,000 versus $4,000) than the manual production alternative, but its per-unit contribution is not proportionately higher (only $9 versus $5).

Learning by Doing Application 12.4 illustrates another EBITDA Break-even point calculation.

Because the pretax operating cash flow break-even points are the unit sales levels at which EBITDA equals $0, they are the unit sales levels at which the lines in Exhibit 12.4 cross the $0 point. You can see this in **Exhibit 12.7**, which is the same as Exhibit 12.4, except that, for simplicity, it plots EBITDA only from 0 to 10,000 units.

LEARNING BY DOING

APPLICATION 12.4 | Calculating the EBITDA Break-Even Point

Problem Calculate the expected pretax operating cash flow (EBITDA) break-even number of house calls per month for the in-home computer-support business after six months.

Approach Use Equation 12.4 to calculate the EBITDA break-even point.

Solution From Learning by Doing Application 12.1, we know that the monthly fixed costs (FC) are $3,000, the average revenue per house call (Price) is $70, and the variable cost per house call (Unit VC) is $20. Therefore, using Equation 12.4, we can calculate the EBITDA break-even point as follows:

$$\text{EBITDA Break-even} = \frac{\text{FC}}{\text{Price} - \text{Unit VC}} = \frac{\$3{,}000}{\$70 - \$20} = 60 \text{ house calls per month}$$

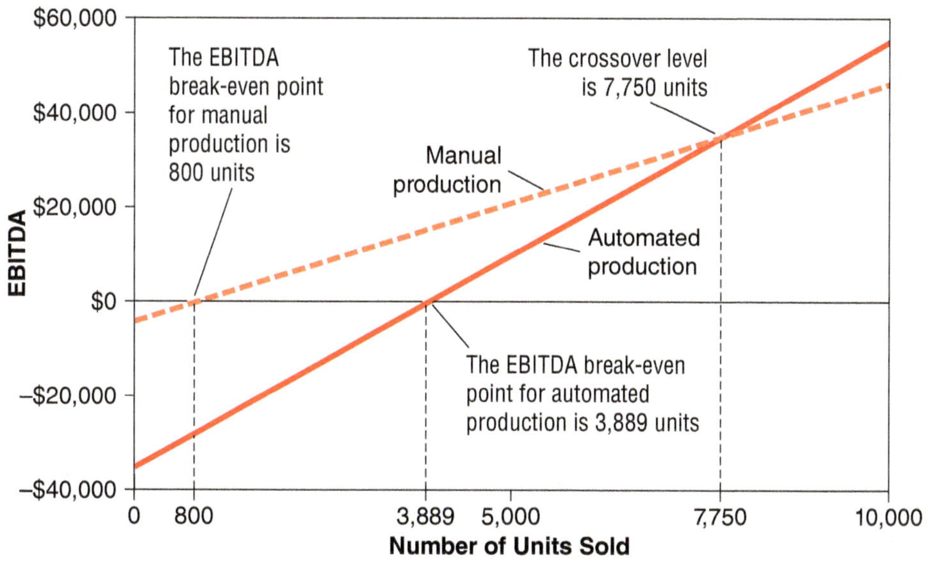

EXHIBIT 12.7 EBITDA Break-Even Points and Crossover Level of Unit Sales

The EBITDA break-even points for the automated and manual production alternatives in the hammock-manufacturing example tell us the unit sales at which pretax operating cash flows equals \$0. The crossover level of unit sales for EBITDA (CO_{EBITDA}) tells us the number of units at which the pretax operating cash flows become higher for the automated process than for the manual process.

Weblink

Learn more about fixed and variable costs and how they relate to break-even analysis from the Knowledge Dynamics Web site at http://www.knowledgedynamics.com/demos/Breakeven/.

In addition to illustrating the operating cash flow break-even points, Exhibit 12.7 shows that the automated production alternative has a larger EBITDA than the manual production alternative if sales exceed 7,750 units. This is because the larger per-unit contribution of the automated production alternative more than makes up for the higher fixed charges at this level of unit sales. We can compute the EBITDA **crossover level of unit sales (CO)**—the level above which the automated production alternative has higher pretax operating cash flows—as follows:

crossover level of unit sales (CO) the level of unit sales at which cash flows or profitability for one project alternative switches from being lower than that of another alternative to being higher

$$CO_{EBITDA} = \frac{FC_{\text{Alternative 1}} - FC_{\text{Alternative 2}}}{\text{Unit contribution}_{\text{Alternative 1}} - \text{Unit contribution}_{\text{Alternative 2}}} \tag{12.5}$$

where Unit contribution stands for the per-unit contribution. The calculation for our example is as follows:

$$\begin{aligned} CO_{EBITDA} &= \frac{FC_{\text{Automated}} - FC_{\text{Manual}}}{\text{Unit contribution}_{\text{Automated}} - \text{Unit contribution}_{\text{Manual}}} \\ &= \frac{\$35{,}000 - \$4{,}000}{\$9 - \$5} \\ &= 7{,}750 \text{ units} \end{aligned}$$

Equation 12.5 can be used to calculate the crossover level of unit sales for any two alternatives that differ in the amount of operating leverage they employ.

Accounting Operating Profit (EBIT) Break-Even

We might also be interested in determining what level of unit sales is necessary for the project to break even on operations from an accounting operating profit perspective. This is called the **accounting operating profit (EBIT) break-even point.** It is calculated using Equation 12.6:

accounting operating profit (EBIT) break-even point the number of units that must be sold for accounting operating profit to equal \$0

$$\text{EBIT Break-even} = \frac{FC + D\&A}{\text{Price} - \text{Unit VC}} \tag{12.6}$$

When we calculate the accounting operating profit break-even point, we are calculating how many units must be sold to avoid an accounting operating loss. This is important to know because an accounting operating loss indicates that the project might not be able to cover its cash expenses and the wear and tear on physical assets as reflected in D&A.

For the automated production alternative in the hammock-manufacturing business, the break-even point is calculated as follows:

Weblink

See what the U.S. Small Business Administration has to say about break-even analysis at http://www.sba.gov/starting-business/business-financials/breakeven-analysis.

$$\text{EBIT Break-even}_{\text{Automated}} = \frac{\text{FC}_{\text{Automated}} + \text{D\&A}_{\text{Automated}}}{\text{Price} - \text{Unit VC}_{\text{Automated}}}$$
$$= \frac{\$35{,}000 + \$10{,}000}{\$25 - \$16}$$
$$= 5{,}000 \text{ units}$$

Similarly, for the manual production alternative:

$$\text{EBIT Break-even}_{\text{Manual}} = \frac{\$4{,}000 + \$1{,}000}{\$25 - \$20} = 1{,}000 \text{ units}$$

The accounting operating profit break-even points for the automated and manual production alternatives are 5,000 and 1,000 units, respectively.

The accounting operating profit break-even points are larger than the corresponding pretax operating cash flow break-even points because in Equation 12.6 we are including the noncash D&A charges in the numerator in the calculation. Since the denominator of the fraction is the same in Equations 12.4 and 12.6, the accounting operating profit break-even points will always be larger when D&A is positive.

Learning by Doing Application 12.5 illustrates one more EBIT Break-even point calculation and **Decision Making Example 12.1** illustrates the use of break-even numbers in decision making.

LEARNING BY DOING

APPLICATION 12.5 | Calculating the EBIT Break-Even Point

Problem Calculate the expected accounting operating profit break-even number of house calls per month for the in-home computer-support business after six months of operation.

Approach Use Equation 12.6 to calculate the EBIT break-even point for the business.

Solution From Learning by Doing Application 12.1, we know that the monthly fixed cost (FC) is \$3,000, the monthly D&A is \$1,000, the average revenue per house call (Price) is \$70, and the variable cost per house call (Unit VC) is \$20. Therefore, using Equation 12.6, we find that the accounting operating profit break-even point after six months is:

$$\text{EBIT Break-even} = \frac{\text{FC} + \text{D\&A}}{\text{Price} - \text{Unit VC}} = \frac{\$3{,}000 + \$1{,}000}{\$70 - \$20} = 80 \text{ house calls per month}$$

Your company must make 80 house calls per month to break even on an accounting operating profit basis.

By comparing this calculation and the calculation in Learning by Doing Application 12.4, you can see that the accounting operating profit break-even point (80 house calls) is higher than the pretax operating cash flow break-even point (60 house calls). As we explained in the text, this is because D&A is included in the accounting operating profit break-even calculation.

DECISION MAKING

EXAMPLE 12.1 | Using Break-Even Numbers

Situation You have just finished calculating the pretax operating cash flow and accounting operating profit break-even numbers for the in-home computer-support business. These numbers are as follows:

- Pretax operating cash flow break-even point: 720 house calls per year (60 per month)
- Accounting operating profit break-even point: 960 house calls per year (80 per month)

You have also just heard that the national company that provides these services is going to move to the town in which you are located. This has caused you to reduce your estimate of the annual number of house calls you can expect for your business in half, from 1,440 (120 per month) to 720. How will this affect your decision to enter this business?

Decision With annual unit sales of 720, EBIT will be negative and EBITDA will equal \$0. With EBITDA of \$0, the business will not generate any cash flows that can be used to make necessary investments, let alone enable you to earn the opportunity cost of capital on the money you invest in this business. You can see this by referring back to the FCF calculation in Equation 11.2 or Exhibit 11.1. This is a case where you do not even need to calculate the NPV to know that it is negative.

In addition to the accounting operating profit break-even points for two alternatives, we can also calculate the crossover level of unit sales for EBIT. The equation that we use to do this is:

$$CO_{EBIT} = \frac{(FC + D\&A)_{Alternative\ 1} - (FC + D\&A)_{Alternative\ 2}}{\text{Unit contribution}_{Alternative\ 1} - \text{Unit contribution}_{Alternative\ 2}} \tag{12.7}$$

Notice that the only difference between Equations 12.5 and 12.7 is that D&A is included in the numerator in Equation 12.7.

The calculation for our hammock-manufacturing example is as follows:

$$\begin{aligned} CO_{EBIT} &= \frac{(FC + D\&A)_{Automated} - (FC + D\&A)_{Manual}}{\text{Unit contribution}_{Automated} - \text{Unit contribution}_{Manual}} \\ &= \frac{(\$35{,}000 + \$10{,}000) - (\$4{,}000 + \$1{,}000)}{\$9 - \$5} \\ &= 10{,}000 \text{ units} \end{aligned}$$

The cash flow and accounting break-even calculations are useful in helping us understand how many units must be sold to break even in a particular period of time, such as a month or a year. However, they are not comprehensive calculations in that they do not tell us what it takes for a project to break even in an economic sense—in other words, how many units must be sold over the life of a project to achieve an NPV of \$0. We discuss this more comprehensive break-even analysis in the next section.

Before You Go On

1. How is the per-unit contribution related to the pretax operating cash flow break-even point?
2. How is the per-unit contribution related to the accounting operating profit break-even point?
3. What is the difference between the pretax operating cash flow break-even point and the accounting operating profit break-even point?

12.4 The Economic Break-Even Point

LEARNING OBJECTIVE

4. Define the economic break-even point and be able to calculate it for a project.

Knowing the pretax operating cash flow and accounting operating profit break-even points on a year-by-year basis over the life of a project can help a financial manager ensure that sufficient cash is allocated to fund a project and to understand the impact of a project on the firm's accounting operating profits. The **economic break-even point** is a more comprehensive break-even measure that can help a financial manager assess the overall economic viability of a project. This measure tells the manager how low unit sales can get before a project destroys stockholder value. It is the number of units that must be sold each year over the life of a project in order for the NPV of that project to equal \$0.

economic break-even point the number of units that must be sold each year during the life of a project so that the NPV of the project equals \$0

The economic break-even point is a more comprehensive measure in a couple of ways. First, it considers the entire life of the project, rather than a single year. Second, it focuses on the after-tax free cash flows associated with the project rather than only on the cash flows or profits from operations. Unlike the other measures, the economic break-even point accounts for both the taxes and investments associated with a project.

We calculate the economic break-even point for a project using the following four step procedure:

1. Identify the present value of the net nonrecurring investments in real assets and working capital that are required for the project (this is the present value of the initial investment plus the after-tax cash flow associated with the salvage value and the recovery of working capital at the end of the project), the life of the project, and the opportunity cost of capital for the project. Use the above information in the present value of an ordinary annuity formula (Equation 6.1) to calculate the annual incremental after-tax free cash flow (FCF), that would make the project NPV equal $0.
2. Use the FCF formula (Equation 11.2) to solve for the EBIT that corresponds to the FCF value calculated in Step 1. Note that this calculation requires estimates of annual depreciation and amortization (D&A), capital expenditures (Cap Exp), and additions to working capital (Add WC), as well as the firm's marginal tax rate (t).
3. Add the EBIT calculated in Step 2 to the annual D&A and fixed costs (FC). This calculation gives you the annual total contribution of the project (Revenue − VC) that is associated with an NPV of $0.
4. Divide the annual total contribution by the unit contribution to obtain the number of units that would have to be sold annually for the project to have an NPV of $0.

To see how this four-step procedure works, let's use it to calculate the economic break-even point for the automated production alternative for the hammock-manufacturing business.

In addition to the information previously given about the automated production alternative, we will assume that the project has a four-year life, that the initial investment is $40,000, that the salvage value is expected to equal $0, that the annual capital expenditures will equal $0, that annual additions to working capital will equal $2,000, that the firm's marginal tax rate is 35 percent, and that the opportunity cost of capital for the project is 10 percent.

1. From the above assumptions, we know that the initial investment is $40,000, no salvage value is expected, and that additions to working capital will equal $2,000 per year. If we assume that all $8,000 of the working capital ($2,000 per year × 4 years = $8,000) will be recovered at the end of the project, the present value of the net nonrecurring investments is:

$$\begin{aligned}\text{PV(Net nonrecurring investments)} &= \$40{,}000 + \$8{,}000/(1.1)^4 \\ &= \$45{,}464\end{aligned}$$

In the capital budgeting calculations we discussed in Chapters 10 and 11, the NPV of a project will equal $0 when the present value of the annual FCFs from the project, PV(FCF), equals the present value of the net nonrecurring investments. If we assume, for simplicity, that the FCF will be the same each year over the four-year life of the project, we can compute the annual FCF (FCF_t) at which the project will have an NPV of $0 using the present value of an ordinary annuity formula. With a 10 percent discount rate, this calculation is (Note that this is equivalent to using the equivalent annual cost formula, Equation 11.5.):

$$\text{PV(FCF)} = \frac{\text{FCF}_t}{k}\left[1 - \frac{1}{(1+k)^n}\right]$$

$$\$45{,}464 = \frac{\text{FCF}_t}{0.10}\left[1 - \frac{1}{(1+0.10)^4}\right]$$

$$\text{FCF}_t = \frac{\$45{,}464 \times 0.10}{\left[1 - \frac{1}{(1+0.10)^4}\right]} = \$14{,}343$$

2. Knowing that FCF_t = \$14,343, Cap Exp_t = \$0, Add WC_t = \$2,000, $D\&A_t$ = \$10,000 (from Exhibit 12.1), and t = 35 percent, we can use Equation 11.2 to calculate $EBIT_t$ for the manufacturing alternative. Since:

$$\begin{aligned} FCF_t &= [(Revenue_t - Op\ Ex_t - D\&A_t) \times (1 - t)] + D\&A_t - Cap\ Exp_t - Add\ WC_t \\ &= [EBIT_t \times (1 - t)] + D\&A_t - Cap\ Exp_t - Add\ WC_t, \end{aligned}$$

solving for $EBIT_t$ yields:

$$\begin{aligned} EBIT_t &= (FCF_t - D\&A_t + Cap\ Exp_t + Add\ WC_t)/(1 - t) \\ &= (\$14{,}343 - \$10{,}000 + \$0 + \$2{,}000)/(1 - 0.35) = \$9{,}758. \end{aligned}$$

This is the EBIT that corresponds to the FCF at which the project NPV = \$0.

3. We next use $EBIT_t$ to calculate the amount by which revenue exceeds VC. Recall from our discussion of variable and fixed costs that:

$$EBIT = Revenue - VC - FC - D\&A$$

Rearranging this formula and solving for Revenue minus VC yields:

$$Revenue - VC = EBIT + D\&A + FC = \$9{,}758 + \$10{,}000 + \$35{,}000 = \$54{,}758$$

where the FC of \$35,000 is from Exhibit 12.1. The difference between Revenue and VC is the **total contribution** of the project. This is the amount that the project contributes to help pay its fixed costs, after covering all of its variable costs.

total contribution the total amount that a project contributes to help pay its fixed costs after covering all of its variable costs

4. Finally, to compute the economic break-even point, we simply divide the total contribution by the per-unit contribution that we previously calculated to be \$9. Doing this, we find that the economic break-even point is

$$\begin{aligned} \text{Economic Break-even}_{\text{Automated}} &= (Revenue - VC)/\text{Unit contribution} \\ &= \$54{,}758/\$9 \text{ per unit} = 6{,}084 \text{ units} \end{aligned}$$

This value tells us that if 6,084 units are sold each year over the life of the automated production alternative for the hammock-manufacturing business and the unit price and cost estimates are correct, the NPV of the project will equal \$0. Any unit sales above this amount will result in an **economic profit**—a profit that exceeds the opportunity cost of the capital invested in a project.

economic profit a profit that exceeds the opportunity cost of the capital invested in a project

To make sure we understand the economic break-even point calculation, let's also do it for the manual production alternative for the hammock-manufacturing business.

For this calculation, we will assume that the project has a four-year life, that the initial investment is \$4,000, that the salvage value is expected to equal \$0, that the annual capital expenditures will equal \$0, that annual additions to working capital will equal \$2,000, that the firm's marginal tax rate is 35 percent, and that the opportunity cost of capital for the project is 10 percent.

1. $$\begin{aligned} \text{PV(Net nonrecurring investments)} &= \$4{,}000 + \$8{,}000/(1.1)^4 \\ &= \$9{,}464 \end{aligned}$$

The life of the project is four years, and the opportunity cost of capital is 10 percent. Therefore the annual FCF at which the manual alternative would have an NPV of \$0 is:

$$\$9{,}464 = \frac{FCF_t}{0.10}\left[1 - \frac{1}{(1 + 0.10)^4}\right]$$
$$FCF_t = \$2{,}986$$

2. $$\begin{aligned} EBIT_t &= (FCF_t - D\&A_t + Cap\ Exp_t + Add\ WC_t)/(1 - t) \\ &= (\$2{,}986 - 1{,}000 + \$0 + \$2{,}000)/(1 - 0.35) = \$6{,}132 \end{aligned}$$

3. $$\begin{aligned} Revenue_t - VC_t &= EBIT_t + D\&A_t + FC_t \\ &= \$6{,}132 + \$1{,}000 + \$4{,}000 = \$11{,}132 \end{aligned}$$

4. $$\begin{aligned} \text{Economic Break-even}_{\text{Manual}} &= (Revenue - VC)/\text{Unit contribution} \\ &= \$11{,}132/\$5 \text{ per unit} = 2{,}226 \text{ units} \end{aligned}$$

The number of units that must be sold in order for investors to earn the opportunity cost of capital (i.e., to achieve a \$0 NPV) with the manual production alternative is substantially smaller than the number of units that must be sold if the automated production alternative is chosen (2,226 units versus 6,084 units). Of course, as we discussed earlier, the automated production alternative has the potential to generate substantially higher profits and greater value for investors with high levels of unit sales because it has greater operating leverage.

Learning by Doing Application 12.6 illustrates another economic break-even point calculation.

LEARNING BY DOING

APPLICATION 12.6 | Calculating the Economic Break-Even Point

Problem The opportunity cost of capital for the in-home computer support business you are starting is 8 percent, and you expect to operate the business for five years before shutting it down. Assume that the assets you acquire with the \$100,000 initial investment will have no salvage value in five years and that annual capital expenditures and additions to working capital will both equal \$0 in each of the next five years. In other words, the business will not require any investment beyond the initial \$100,000. Finally, assume that you expect your marginal tax rate to be 20 percent over the next five years. What is the economic break-even number of house calls per year?

Approach Follow the four-step procedure described in the text.

Solution

1. The present value of the net nonrecurring investments required for the business is \$100,000, the life of the business is five years, and the opportunity cost of capital is 8 percent. Using the formula for the present value of an annuity, the annual FCF at which the business will have an NPV of \$0 is:

$$\text{PV(FCF)} = \frac{\text{FCF}_t}{k}\left[1 - \frac{1}{(1+k)^n}\right]$$

$$\$100{,}000 = \frac{\text{FCF}_t}{0.08}\left[1 - \frac{1}{(1+0.08)^5}\right]$$

$$\text{FCF}_t = \$25{,}046$$

2. With FCF_t of \$25,046, annual D&A of \$12,000, annual FC of \$36,000 (monthly D&A and FC are given in Learning by Doing Application 12.1), Cap Expt of \$0, Add WC_t of \$0, and a marginal tax rate of 20 percent, the break-even EBIT_t is:

$$\text{EBIT}_t = (\text{FCF}_t - \text{D\&A}_t + \text{Cap Exp}_t + \text{Add WC}_t)/(1 - t)$$
$$= (\$25{,}046 - \$12{,}000 + \$0 + \$0)/(1 - 0.20) = \$16{,}308$$

3. The total contribution is therefore:

$$\text{Revenue}_t - \text{VC}_t = \text{EBIT}_t + \text{D\&A}_t + \text{FC}_t$$
$$= \$16{,}308 + \$12{,}000 + \$36{,}000 = \$64{,}308$$

4. The economic break-even level of unit sales is calculated by dividing the total contribution by the contribution per house call of \$50 (\$70 of Revenue per house call − \$20 unit VC):

$$\text{Economic Break-even} = (\text{Revenue} - \text{VC})/\text{Unit contribution}$$
$$= \$64{,}308/\$50 = 1{,}286.2 \text{ house calls per year}$$

If your business makes 1,286.2 house calls per year, it will earn the 8 percent opportunity cost of capital and have an NPV of \$0. The NPV will be positive if the annual number of house calls is greater than 1,286.2 and negative if the number of house calls is smaller.

Before You Go On

1. How is the economic break-even point a more comprehensive measure of the impact of a project on a firm's financial performance than the pretax operating cash flow break-even point or the accounting operating profit break-even point?

12.5 Risk Analysis

LEARNING OBJECTIVE

5. Define sensitivity analysis, scenario analysis, and simulation analysis and describe how they are used to evaluate the risks associated with a project.

In the preceding sections, we noted that two key factors—(1) the volatility of revenue and (2) operating leverage—determine the volatility of pretax operating cash flows (EBITDA) and operating profits (EBIT) when there is no uncertainty regarding costs. We also discussed how changes in unit sales affect the volatility of EBITDA and EBIT.

Unit sales is only one of many factors that an analyst must predict when forecasting the cash flows associated with a project. As with forecasts of unit sales, forecasting the values of these other factors involves a high degree of uncertainty. For example, the price of a product depends on the supply and demand for the product, which are often difficult to predict. Similarly, future values of operating expenses, capital expenditures, and additions to working capital can be very uncertain. Financial analysts often resort to sensitivity analysis, scenario analysis, and simulation analysis to obtain a better understanding of how errors in forecasting these factors affect the attractiveness of a project. In other words, these analyses help answer the questions "How wrong can I be?" and "What are the implications of being wrong?"

In this section we illustrate the application of sensitivity, scenario, and simulation analysis using the automated production alternative from our hammock-manufacturing example. With expected unit sales of 10,000 per year and the other indicated assumptions, the yearly free cash flows and NPV for this alternative are calculated in **Exhibit 12.8**.

EXHIBIT 12.8 **Incremental Free Cash Flows and NPV for the Automated Production Alternative for the Hammock-Manufacturing Business**

This exhibit shows the calculation of the yearly incremental pretax free cash flows (FCF) and the NPV of the automated production alternative in the hammock-manufacturing example assuming the project has a four-year life. The FCF calculation is illustrated in Exhibit 11.1.

Assumptions:

Opportunity cost of capital	10%	Initial investment	$40,000
Unit sales	10,000	D&A	$10,000
Unit price	$25	Annual Cap Exp	$8,000
Unit VC	$16	Add WC	$2,000
FC	$35,000	Tax Rate	35%

	Year 0	1	2	3	4
Revenue		$250,000	$250,000	$250,000	$250,000
– VC		160,000	160,000	160,000	160,000
– FC		35,000	35,000	35,000	35,000
EBITDA		$ 55,000	$ 55,000	$ 55,000	$ 55,000
– D&A		10,000	10,000	10,000	10,000
EBIT		$ 45,000	$ 45,000	$ 45,000	$ 45,000
– Taxes		15,750	15,750	15,750	15,750
NOPAT		$ 29,250	$ 29,250	$ 29,250	$ 29,250
+ D&A		10,000	10,000	10,000	10,000
CF Opns		$ 39,250	$ 39,250	$ 39,250	$ 39,250
– Cap Exp	$40,000	8,000	8,000	8,000	8,000
– Add WC		2,000	2,000	2,000	2,000
= FCF	($40,000)	$ 29,250	$ 29,250	$ 29,250	$ 29,250
NPV	$52,719				

Sensitivity Analysis

sensitivity analysis examination of the sensitivity of the results from a financial analysis to changes in individual assumptions

Sensitivity analysis involves examining the sensitivity of the output from an analysis, such as the NPV estimate in Exhibit 12.8, to changes in *individual* assumptions. In a sensitivity analysis, an analyst might examine how a project's NPV changes if there is a decrease in the value of individual cash inflow assumptions or an increase in the value of individual cash outflow assumptions. For example, if unit sales are 10 percent lower than expected, if FC is 10 percent higher than expected, or if annual Cap Exp is 10 percent higher than expected, then an analyst could calculate that the NPV of the automated production alternative in Exhibit 12.8 declines by 35.2 percent, 13.7 percent, and 4.8 percent, respectively, when these values are changed one at a time. These numbers would tell the analyst that the NPV for the automated production alternative is much more sensitive to the unit sales assumption than to the assumptions regarding FC or Cap Exp.

This information is very useful because it helps the analyst identify critical assumptions. These are the assumptions the analyst should pay special attention to when evaluating the project. It does not make sense to allocate substantial analytical resources to investigating assumptions that are of little importance. In our example, the numbers suggest that the analyst should be especially careful when developing the unit sales forecasts.

Scenario Analysis

As we have just seen, sensitivity analysis is a form of "what if" analysis that is very useful in identifying key assumptions. However, the individual assumptions in a financial analysis are often related to each other; their values do not tend to change one at a time. As a result, sensitivity analysis is not very useful in examining how the attractiveness of a project might vary under different economic scenarios. An analyst who wants to examine how the results from a financial analysis will change under alternative scenarios will thus perform a **scenario analysis**.

scenario analysis an analytical method concerned with how the results from a financial analysis will change under alternative scenarios

Suppose, for example, that the forecasted cash flows in Exhibit 12.8 represent the performance of the automated production alternative for the hammock-manufacturing business under expected future economic conditions. Let's consider how these cash flows might change if economic conditions turn out to be weaker or stronger than expected. In a scenario in which economic conditions are weaker than in the most likely case, we would expect unit sales to be less than 10,000 because overall demand for hammocks will be lower. The price at which the firm sells its hammocks is also likely to be lower because the firm will probably reduce prices in an effort to boost sales. On the bright side, unit variable costs might also be lower because the demand for rope, spacer bars, hardware, and so forth will decline in a weak market and producers of those products may reduce the prices they charge the firm. In contrast to the weak economic scenario, stronger economic conditions might result in higher-than-expected unit sales, prices, and unit variable costs. **Exhibit 12.9** illustrates how these assumptions and the resulting project NPV might vary under the alternative scenarios.

EXHIBIT 12.9 **NPV Values for the Automated Production Alternative for the Hammock-Manufacturing Business for Three Scenarios**

Different economic scenarios result in different NPV estimates for the automated production alternative in the hammock-manufacturing example. The expected unit sales, unit prices, and unit variable costs vary depending on economic conditions.

Economic Conditions	Unit Sales	Unit Price	Unit Variable Costs	NPV
Strong	12,000	$28	$17	$139,256
Expected	10,000	$25	$16	$52,719
Weak	8,000	$22	$15	($17,335)

In Exhibit 12.9 we can see that the project will have a negative NPV if economic conditions are weak. Furthermore, the decline in NPV if economic conditions are weaker than expected ($70,054, the difference between $52,719 and negative $17,335) is less than the increase in NPV if economic conditions are stronger than expected ($86,537, the difference between $139,256 and $52,719). The range of NPV values under the three scenarios is $156,591 (the range between negative $17,335 and $139,256).

Although this analysis can help us better understand how much uncertainty is associated with an NPV estimate, it is important to remember that *there is only one NPV value for a project* and that the FCF values we use in an NPV analysis represent the expected incremental free cash flows. For instance, in our example, suppose there is a 50 percent chance that the most likely economic conditions will occur, a 25 percent chance that economic conditions will be weak, and a 25 percent chance that economic conditions will be strong. The NPV calculation would be based on the expected values for unit sales, the unit price, and unit variable costs.

Recall that an expected value represents the sum of the products of the possible outcomes and the probabilities that those outcomes will be realized. Therefore, the expected values for unit sales, the unit price, and unit variable costs in this example are calculated as follows:

$$\text{Expected unit sales} = (0.25 \times 12{,}000) + (0.50 \times 10{,}000) + (0.25 \times 8{,}000) = 10{,}000 \text{ units}$$

$$\text{Expected unit price} = (0.25 \times \$28) + (0.50 \times \$25) + (0.25 \times \$22) = \$25$$

$$\text{Expected unit variable costs} = (0.25 \times \$17) + (0.50 \times \$16) + (0.25 \times \$15) = \$16$$

Therefore, the NPV of the project would equal $52,719, as illustrated in Exhibit 12.8.

Simulation Analysis

Simulation analysis is like scenario analysis except that in simulation analysis an analyst uses a computer to examine a large number of scenarios in a short period of time. Rather than selecting individual values for each of the assumptions—such as unit sales, unit price, and unit variable costs—the analyst assumes that those assumptions can be represented by statistical distributions. For instance, unit sales might be assumed to have a normal distribution with a mean value of 10,000 units and a standard deviation of 1,500 units, while prices might be assumed to follow a related normal distribution with a mean of $25 and a standard deviation of $5. A computer program then calculates the free cash flows associated with a large number of scenarios by repeatedly drawing numbers for the distributions for various assumptions plugging them into the free cash flow model, and computing the yearly free cash flows. This technique is referred to as Monte Carlo simulation when the numbers drawn from the distributions are independent of each other across different scenarios. It is not uncommon to compute 10,000 alternative sets of free cash flows. The average of the annual free cash flows generated in this way is then computed to obtain the expected free cash flows for each year during the life of the project. These expected free cash flows can then be discounted using the opportunity cost of capital to obtain the NPV for the project.

simulation analysis an analytical method that uses a computer to quickly examine a large number of scenarios and obtain probability estimates for various values in a financial analysis

Weblink

Monte Carlo simulations can be performed with relative ease using a spreadsheet program. An introduction to the process using Excel can be found at http://www.riskamp.com/how-to.

Weblink

You can download a trial version of an Excel add-in program for sensitivity analysis and simulation analysis at http://simquick.net.

In addition to providing an estimate of the expected free cash flows, simulation analysis provides information on the distribution of the free cash flows that the project is likely to produce in each year. For example, if simulation analysis is used to compute 10,000 alternative sets of free cash flows, there will be 10,000 cash flow estimates for each year. From these estimates, an analyst can estimate the probability that the free cash flows in a given year will be greater than $0, greater than $1,000, or greater than any other number. By summing up the free cash flows over time within each alternative set of cash flows, the analyst can also estimate the probability of recovering the initial investment in the project by any particular point in the project's life.

A discussion of the actual techniques used in simulation analysis is beyond the scope of this book. However, you should be aware that sophisticated financial analysts commonly use simulation analysis to evaluate the riskiness of projects. You are likely to see it in practice if you are ever involved with project analysis.

Before You Go On

1. How is a sensitivity analysis used in project analysis?
2. How does a scenario analysis differ from a sensitivity analysis?
3. What is a simulation analysis, and what can it tell us?

Summary of Learning Objectives

1 Explain and demonstrate how variable costs and fixed costs affect the volatility of pretax operating cash flows and accounting operating profits.

Because the fixed costs associated with a project do not change as revenue changes, when a project has fixed costs, fluctuations in revenue are magnified so that pretax operating cash flows and accounting operating profits fluctuate more than revenue in percentage terms. The greater the proportion of total costs that are fixed, the more the fluctuations in revenue will be magnified. To demonstrate this, you can perform calculations like those in the hammock-manufacturing example and in Learning by Doing Applications 12.1 and 12.2.

2 Calculate and distinguish between the degree of pretax cash flow operating leverage and the degree of accounting operating leverage.

The degree of pretax cash flow operating leverage (Cash Flow DOL) is a measure of how much pretax operating cash flow will change in relation to a change in revenue. Similarly, the degree of accounting operating leverage (Accounting DOL) is a measure of how much accounting operating profits will change in relation to a change in revenue. The only difference between cash flow operating leverage and accounting operating leverage is that the accounting measure treats incremental depreciation and amortization charges as a fixed cost in the calculation. These charges are excluded from the cash flow operating leverage measure because they do not reflect actual cash expenses and, therefore, do not affect pretax cash flows. Equations 12.2 and 12.3 are used to calculate these two measures.

3 Define and calculate the pretax operating cash flow and accounting operating profit break-even points and the crossover levels of unit sales for a project.

The pretax operating cash flow break-even point is the number of units that must be sold in a particular year to break even on a pretax operating cash flow (EBITDA) basis. It is calculated using Equation 12.4.

The accounting operating profit break-even point is the number of units that must be sold in a particular year to break even on an accounting operating profit basis. A project breaks even on an accounting operating profit basis when it produces exactly $0 in incremental operating profits (EBIT). It is calculated using Equation 12.6.

The crossover level of unit sales is the level of unit sales at which the pretax operating cash flows or accounting operating profits for one project alternative switches from being lower than that of another alternative to being higher. The EBITDA and EBIT crossover levels of unit sales are calculated using Equations 12.5 and 12.7, respectively.

4 Define the economic break-even point and be able to calculate it for a project.

The economic break-even point is the number of units that must be sold each year during the life of a project so that the NPV of the project equals $0. Section 12.4 illustrates how the economic break-even point is calculated.

5 Define sensitivity analysis, scenario analysis, and simulation analysis and describe how they are used to evaluate the risks associated with a project.

Sensitivity analysis is concerned with how sensitive the output from a financial analysis, such as the NPV, is to changes in an individual assumption. It helps identify which assumptions have the greatest impact on the output and, therefore, on the value of a project. Knowing this helps an analyst identify which assumptions are especially important to that analysis. Scenario analysis is used to examine how the output from a financial analysis changes under alternative scenarios. This type of analysis recognizes that changing economic and market conditions affect more than one variable at a time and tries to account for how each of the different variables will change under alternative scenarios. Simulation analysis is like scenario analysis except that in simulation analysis a computer is used to examine a large number of scenarios in a short period of time.

Summary of Key Equations

Equation	Description	Formula
12.1	Op Ex in terms of incremental variable and fixed costs	$\text{Op Ex} = \text{VC} + \text{FC}$
12.2	Degree of pretax cash flow operating leverage	$\text{Cash Flow DOL} = 1 + \dfrac{\text{FC}}{\text{EBITDA}}$
12.3	Degree of accounting operating leverage	$\text{Accounting DOL} = 1 + \dfrac{\text{FC} + \text{D\&A}}{\text{EBIT}}$
12.4	Pretax operating cash flow (EBITDA) break-even point	$\text{EBITDA Break-even} = \dfrac{\text{FC}}{\text{Price} - \text{Unit VC}}$
12.5	Crossover level of unit sales for EBITDA	$\text{CO}_{\text{EBITDA}} = \dfrac{\text{FC}_{\text{Alternative 1}} - \text{FC}_{\text{Alternative 2}}}{\text{Unit contribution}_{\text{Alternative 1}} - \text{Unit contribution}_{\text{Alternative 2}}}$
12.6	Accounting operating profit (EBIT) break-even point	$\text{EBIT Break-even} = \dfrac{\text{FC} + \text{D\&A}}{\text{Price} - \text{Unit VC}}$
12.7	Crossover level of unit sales of EBIT	$\text{CO}_{\text{EBIT}} = \dfrac{(\text{FC} + \text{D\&A})_{\text{Alternative 1}} - (\text{FC} + \text{D\&A})_{\text{Alternative 2}}}{\text{Unit contribution}_{\text{Alternative 1}} - \text{Unit contribution}_{\text{Alternative 2}}}$

Self-Study Problems

12.1 The Yellow Shelf Company sells all of its shelves for $100 per shelf and incurs $50 in variable costs to produce each. If the fixed costs for the firm are $2,000,000 per year, what will the EBIT for the firm be if it produces and sells 45,000 shelves next year? Assume that depreciation and amortization is included in the fixed costs.

12.2 Hydrogen Batteries sells its specialty automobile batteries for $85 each, while its current variable cost per unit is $65. Total fixed costs (including depreciation and amortization expense) are $150,000 per year. Management expects to sell 10,000 batteries next year but is concerned that variable cost will increase next year due to material cost increases. What is the maximum variable cost per unit increase that will keep the EBIT from becoming negative?

12.3 The Vinyl CD Co. is going to take on a project that is expected to increase its EBIT by $90,000, its fixed cost cash expenditures by $100,000, and its depreciation and amortization by $80,000 next year. If the project yields an additional 10 percent in revenue, what percentage increase in the project's EBIT will result from the additional revenue?

12.4 You are considering investing in a business that has monthly fixed costs of $5,500 and sells a single product that costs $35 per unit to make. This product sells for $90 per unit. What is the annual pretax operating cash flow break-even point for this business?

12.5 Belt Bottoms, Inc., is considering a five-year project with an initial investment of $20,000. What annual free cash flow (FCF) would be required for this project to have an NPV of $0 if the opportunity cost capital is 11 percent?

Solutions to Self-Study Problems

12.1 The calculations for Yellow Shelf are as follows:

Revenue	$100 × 45,000 =	$4,500,000
VC	$50 × 45,000 =	2,250,000
FC + D&A		2,000,000
EBIT		$ 250,000

12.2 The forecasted EBIT for Hydrogen Batteries is:

Revenue	$85 × 10,000 =	$850,000
VC	$65 × 10,000 =	650,000
FC + D&A		150,000
EBIT		$ 50,000

Therefore, total variable cost may increase by $50,000, which means that if the firm produces and sells 10,000 batteries, then the variable cost per unit may increase by $5 ($50,000/10,000 units = $5 per unit).

12.3 Accounting DOL $= 1 + \frac{\text{FC} + \text{D\&A}}{\text{EBIT}}$

$$= 1 + \frac{\$100{,}000 + \$80{,}000}{\$90{,}000}$$

$$= 3$$

Therefore, a 10 percent additional increase in revenue should result in approximately a 30 percent increase in EBIT.

12.4 You can solve for the *monthly* pretax operating cash flow break-even point using Equation 12.4:

$$\text{EBITDA Break-even} = \frac{\text{FC}}{\text{Price} - \text{Unit VC}} = \frac{\$5{,}500}{\$90 - \$35}$$

$$= 100 \text{ units per month}$$

Therefore, the annual EBITDA break-even point is 100 units per month × 12 months per year = 1,200 units.

12.5 If the FCF is equal in each of the five years, then we can solve for FCF using the present value of an ordinary annuity formula:

$$\$20{,}000 = \frac{\text{FCF}_t}{0.11} \times \left(1 - \frac{1}{(1.11)^5}\right) \Rightarrow \text{FCF} = \$5{,}411.41$$

WileyPLUS

Questions and Problems, Solution Walkthrough Videos, Learning by Doing Tutorials, and additional study tools and resources are available in WileyPLUS.

Discussion Questions

12.1 You are involved in the planning process for a firm that is expected to have a large increase in sales next year. Which type of firm would benefit more from that sales increase: a firm with low fixed costs and high variable costs or a firm with high fixed costs and low variable costs?

12.2 You own a firm with a single new product that is about to be introduced to the public for the first time. Your marketing analysis suggests that the annual demand for this product could be anywhere between 500,000 units and 5,000,000 units. Given such a wide range, discuss the safest cost structure alternative for your firm.

12.3 Discuss the interpretation of the degree of accounting operating leverage and degree of pretax cash flow operating leverage.

12.4 Explain how EBITDA differs from incremental after-tax free cash flows (FCF) and discuss the types of businesses for which this difference would be especially small or large.

12.5 Describe how the pretax operating cash flow break-even point is related to the economic break-even point.

12.6 Is it possible to have a crossover point where the accounting break-even point is the same for two alternatives—that is, above the break-even point for a low-fixed-cost alternative but below the break-even point for a high-fixed-cost alternative? Explain.

12.7 What is the fundamental difference between a sensitivity analysis and a scenario analysis?

12.8 The economic break-even calculation assumes that the number of units sold is the same each year during the life of the project. Is it possible for the NPV of a project to be negative if unit sales are not the same each year and the average unit sales are higher than that estimated using the economic break-even calculation? Explain.

12.9 How does the pretax operating cash flow for a project differ from the economic profit for the project?

12.10 What is the advantage of using a simulation analysis instead of a scenario analysis to assess the risk of a project?

Questions and Problems

Excel *Excel templates and resources available in* **WileyPLUS**

Basic

12.1 **Fixed and variable costs:** Define *variable costs* and *fixed costs,* and give an example of each.

12.2 **EBIT:** Describe the role that the mix of variable versus fixed costs has in the variation of earnings before interest and taxes (EBIT) for a firm.

12.3 **EBIT:** The Generic Publications Textbook Company sells all of its books for $100 per book, and it currently costs $50 in variable costs to produce each text. The fixed costs, which include depreciation and amortization for the firm, are currently $2 million per year. Management is considering changing the firm's production technology, which will increase the fixed costs for the firm by 50 percent but decrease the variable costs per unit by 50 percent. If management expects to sell 45,000 books next year, should they switch technologies?

12.4 EBIT: WalkAbout Kangaroo Shoe Stores management forecasts that it will sell 9,500 pairs of shoes next year. The firm buys its shoes for $50 per pair from the wholesaler and sells them for $75 per pair. If the firm will incur fixed costs plus depreciation and amortization of $100,000, then what is the percent increase in EBIT if the actual sales next year equal 11,500 pairs of shoes instead of 9,500?

12.5 Cash Flow DOL: The law firm of Dewey, Cheatem, and Howe has monthly fixed costs of $100,000, EBIT of $250,000, and depreciation charges on its office furniture and computers of $5,000. Calculate the Cash Flow DOL for this firm.

12.6 Cash Flow DOL: The degree of pretax cash flow operating leverage at Rackit Corporation is 2.7 when it sells 100,000 units of its new tennis racket and its EBITDA is $95,000. Ignoring the effects of taxes, what are the fixed costs for Rackit Corporation?

12.7 Accounting DOL: Explain how the value of the degree of accounting operating leverage can be used.

12.8 Accounting DOL: Caterpillar, Inc., is a manufacturer of large earth-moving and mining equipment. This firm and other heavy equipment manufacturers have degrees of accounting operating leverage that are relatively high. Explain why.

12.9 Break-even analysis: Why is the per-unit contribution important in a break-even analysis?

12.10 Break-even analysis: Calculate the accounting operating profit break-even point and pretax operating cash flow break-even point for each of the three production choices outlined below.

Choice	Price	Unit VC	FC	D&A
A	$250	$160	$15,000	$3,000
B	$55	$10	$1,100	$200
C	$10	$1.50	$100	$100

12.11 Break-even point: The accounting operating profit break-even point tells us the number of units that must be sold for a firm to break even in a given year from an accounting operating profit perspective. What measure tells us the number of units that must be sold each year during the life of a project in order for the project to break even with regard to its opportunity cost of capital?

12.12 Simulation analysis: What is simulation analysis, and how is it used?

Intermediate

12.13 EBIT: If a manufacturing firm and a service firm have identical cash fixed costs, but the manufacturing firm has much higher depreciation and amortization, then which firm is more likely to have a large discrepancy between its FCF and its EBIT?

12.14 EBIT: Duplicate Footballs, Inc., management expects to sell 15,000 balls this year. The balls sell for $110 each and have a variable cost per unit of $80. Fixed costs, including depreciation and amortization, are currently $220,000 per year. How much can either the fixed costs or the variable cost per unit increase before the company has a negative EBIT?

12.15 EBIT: Specialty Light Bulbs management anticipates selling 3,000 light bulbs this year at a price of $15 per bulb. It costs Specialty $10 in variable costs to produce each light bulb, and the fixed costs for the firm are $10,000. Specialty has an opportunity to sell an additional 1,000 bulbs next year at the same price and variable cost, but by doing so the firm will incur an additional fixed cost of $4,000. Should Specialty produce and sell the additional bulbs?

12.16 Cash Flow DOL: The pretax operating cash flow of Memphis Motors declined so much during the recession of 2008 and 2009 that the company almost defaulted on its debt. The owner of the company wants to change the cost structure of his business so that this does not happen again. He has been able to reduce fixed costs from $500,000 to $300,000 and, in doing so, reduce the Cash Flow DOL for Memphis Motors from 3.0 to 2.2 with sales of $1,000,000 and pretax operating cash flow of $250,000. If sales declined by 20 percent from this level, how much more pretax operating cash flow would Memphis Motors have with the new cost structure than under the old?

12.17 Cash Flow DOL: For the Vinyl CD Co. in Self-Study Problem 12.3, what percentage increase in pretax operating cash flow will be driven by the additional revenue?

Use the following information for Problems 12.18, 12.19, and 12.20:

Dandle's Candles will be producing a new line of dripless candles in the coming year and has the choice of producing the candles in a large factory with a small number of workers or a small factory with a large number of workers. Each candle will be sold for $10. If the large factory is chosen, the cost per unit to produce each candle will be $2.50. The cost per unit will be $7.50 in the small factory. The large factory would have fixed cash costs of $2 million and a depreciation expense of $300,000 per year, while those expenses would be $500,000 and $100,000, respectively, in the small factory.

12.18 Accounting operating profit break-even: Calculate the accounting operating profit break-even point for both factory choices for Dandle's Candles.

12.19 Crossover level of unit sales: Calculate the number of candles for which the accounting operating profit at Dandle's Candles is the same regardless of the factory choice.

12.20 Pretax operating cash flow break-even: Calculate the pretax operating cash flow break-even point for both factory choices for Dandle's Candles.

12.21 Accounting and cash flow break-even: Your analysis tells you that at a projected level of sales, a project your firm is considering will be below accounting break-even but above cash flow break-even. Explain why this might still be a viable project or firm.

12.22 Economic break-even point: Management of March and Dine Inc. has estimated that the firm's new TV dinner project must generate $10,200 in FCF during each of the next six years to have an NPV of $0. Management anticipates that depreciation and amortization charges will equal $3,000, capital expenditures will equal

$2,000, and additions to working capital will equal $500 during each of those years. What level of EBIT corresponds to an annual FCF of $10,200 if the firm is subject to the 30 percent marginal tax rate?

12.23 **Economic break-even point:** Rose Weiser Company management is considering a project that will require an initial investment of $50,000 and will last for 10 years. No other capital expenditures or increases in working capital are anticipated during the life of the project. What is the annual EBIT that will make the project economically viable if the cost of capital for the project is 9 percent and the firm will depreciate the investment using straight-line depreciation and a salvage value of $0? Assume that the marginal tax rate is 40 percent.

12.24 **Economic break-even point:** The BowGus Archery Company management estimates that its new Galactically Flexible Bow project will have to generate EBIT of $20,000 each year to be viable. The project's fixed cash expenses are expected to equal $8,000, and its depreciation and amortization expenses are expected to be $5,000 each year. If the Galactically Flexible bows are expected to sell for $150 each and the variable cost to produce each bow is expected to be $100, then how many of these bows must the firm produce and sell each year to generate annual EBIT of $20,000?

12.25 **Sensitivity and scenario analyses:** Sensitivity analysis and scenario analysis are somewhat similar. Describe which is a more realistic method of analyzing the impact of different scenarios on a project.

12.26 **Sensitivity analysis:** Describe the circumstances under which sensitivity analysis might be a reasonable basis for determining changes to a firm's EBIT or FCF.

12.27 **Scenario analysis:** Chip's Home Brew Whiskey management forecasts that if the firm sells each bottle of Snake-Bite for $20, then the demand for the product will be 15,000 bottles per year. Sales will equal only 90 percent of this amount if the price is raised 10 percent. Chip's variable cost per bottle is $10, and the total fixed cash cost for the year is $100,000. Depreciation and amortization charges are $20,000, and the firm has a 30 percent marginal tax rate. Management anticipates an increased working capital need of $3,000 for the year. What will be the effect of a 10 percent price increase on the firm's FCF for the year?

12.28 **Sensitivity, scenario, and simulation analysis:** If you were interested in calculating the probability that a project will have a positive FCF, what type of risk analysis tool would you most likely use?

Advanced

12.29 Mick's Soft Lemonade is starting to develop a new product for which the cash fixed costs are expected to be $80,000. The projected EBIT is $100,000, and the Accounting DOL is expected to be 2.0. What is the Cash Flow DOL?

12.30 If a firm has a fixed asset base, meaning that its depreciation and amortization for any year is positive, discuss the relation between its Accounting DOL and its Cash Flow DOL.

12.31 Silver Polygon, Inc. management has determined that if revenues were to increase by 10 percent, then EBIT would increase by 25 percent to $100,000. The fixed costs (cash only) for the firm are $100,000. Given the same 10 percent increase in revenues, what would be the corresponding change in EBITDA?

12.32 If a firm's costs (both variable as well as fixed) are known with certainty, then what are the only two sources of volatility for the firm's operating profits or its operating cash flows?

12.33 In most circumstances, given the choice between a higher fixed-cost structure and a lower fixed cost structure, which of the two would generate a larger contribution margin?

12.34 Using the same logic as with the accounting break-even calculation in Problem 12.19, adapt the formula for the crossover level of unit sales to find the number of units sold where the pretax operating cash flow is the same whether the firm chooses the large or small factory.

12.35 You are the project manager for Eagle Golf Corporation. You are considering manufacturing a new golf wedge with a unique groove design. You have put together the estimates in the following table about the potential demand for the new club and the associated selling and manufacturing prices. You expect to sell the club for five years. The equipment required for the manufacturing process can be depreciated using straight-line depreciation over five years and will have a zero salvage value at the end of the project's life. No additional capital expenditures are required. No new working capital is needed for the project. The required return for projects of this type is 12 percent and the company has a 35 percent marginal tax rate. You estimate that there is a 50 percent chance the project will achieve the expected sales and a 25 percent chance it will achieve either the weak or strong sales outcomes. Should you recommend the project?

	Strong Sales	Expected Sales	Weak Sales
Units sold	15,000	10,000	7,000
Selling price per unit	$130	$120	$110
Variable costs per unit	$70	$65	$60
Fixed costs	$1,290,000	$1,290,000	$1,290,000
Initial investment	$1,400,000	$1,400,000	$1,400,000

12.36 Commodore Motors management is considering a project to produce toy cars. The project would require an initial outlay of $100,000 and have an expected life of 10 years. Management estimates that each year during the life of the project depreciation and amortization would be $8,000, capital expenditures would be $4,000, additions to working capital would be $2,000, and fixed costs would be $3,000. Also, each toy car would sell for $15 and cost $7 to produce. Finally, the cost of capital for the project would be 12 percent, cash flow from the project would be taxed at a 25 percent rate, and the assets would be depreciated to a salvage value of $0. How many units must be sold each year in order for this project to break even from an economic standpoint?

CFA Problems

12.37 Operating leverage is a measure of the:

a. Sensitivity of net earnings to changes in operating earnings.

b. Sensitivity of net earnings to changes in sales.

c. Sensitivity of fixed operating costs to changes in variable costs.

d. Sensitivity of earnings before interest and taxes to changes in the number of units produced and sold.

12.38 The Fulcrum Company produces decorative swivel platforms for home televisions. If Fulcrum produces 40 million units, it estimates that it can sell them for $100 each. The variable production costs are $65 per unit, whereas the fixed production costs are $1.05 billion. Which of the following statements is true?

a. The Fulcrum Company produces a positive operating income if it produces and sells more than 25 million swivel platforms.

b. The Fulcrum Company's degree of operating leverage is 1.333.

c. If the Fulcrum Company increases production and sales by 5 percent, its operating earnings are expected to increase by 20 percent.

d. Increasing the fixed production costs by 10 percent will result in a lower sensitivity of operating earnings to changes in units produced and sold.

Sample Test Problems

12.1 Retro Inc. sells vintage football jerseys for $72 each. Variable costs are $58 per unit and total fixed costs (including depreciation and amortization expense) are $84,000 per year. If sales for next year are expected to equal 8,000 jerseys, how much can variable costs per unit increase without EBIT becoming negative?

12.2 How would a capital-intensive company fare during good and poor economic times as compared with less capital-intensive companies? Explain.

12.3 The manager of Roy's Restaurant has determined that if revenues were to increase by 20 percent, then EBIT would increase by 45 percent to $87,000. What would be the corresponding change in EBITDA if revenues increased 20 percent and cash fixed costs are $35,000?

12.4 Luminosity Inc. produces modern light fixtures that sell for $150 per unit. The firm's management is considering purchasing a high-capacity manufacturing machine. If the high-capacity machine is purchased, then the firm's annual cash fixed costs will be $60,000 per year, variable costs will be $55 per unit, and annual depreciation and amortization expenses will equal $30,000. If the machine is not purchased, annual cash fixed costs will be $25,000, variable costs will be $105 per unit, and annual depreciation and amortization expenses will equal $10,000. What is the minimum level of unit sales necessary in order for EBIT with the high-capacity machine to be higher than EBIT without that machine?

12.5 Paper Christmas Trees Inc. management is considering introducing a new line of inexpensive Christmas trees. The initial outlay for the project is $175,000, and the company will have to invest $5,000 in working capital and $10,000 in fixed assets each year during the six-year life of the project. The initial outlay will be depreciated assuming a salvage value of $0. Annual depreciation and amortization charges for the project will be $15,000, and cash-related fixed costs will be $6,000 per year. The firm will sell each tree for $75, and the variable cost to produce each tree will be $40. Calculate the number of trees that the firm must produce and sell in order to break even economically. Assume that the appropriate cost of capital for the project is 15 percent and that the marginal tax rate for the firm is 40 percent.

CHAPTER 13

The Cost of Capital

Robert Parrino

LEARNING OBJECTIVES

1. Explain what the weighted average cost of capital for a firm is and why it is often used as a discount rate to evaluate projects.
2. Calculate the cost of debt for a firm.
3. Calculate the cost of common stock and the cost of preferred stock for a firm.
4. Calculate the weighted average cost of capital for a firm, explain the limitations of using a firm's weighted average cost of capital as the discount rate when evaluating a project, and discuss the alternatives to the firm's weighted average cost of capital.

In early 2017 a new 37-story Fairmont hotel rapidly approached completion next to the convention center in downtown Austin, Texas. The $370 million Fairmont Austin Hotel was being developed by Manchester Texas Financial Group (Manchester Texas). When finished later that year, the hotel would have 1.4 million square feet of space with 1,068 hotel rooms and 106,500 square feet of meeting space, restaurants, bars, and other public areas. It would employ approximately 900 people and would be operated by Manchester Texas.

Manchester Texas is part of Manchester Financial Group, a sophisticated real estate development and management firm based in San Diego, California. Before the company announced the construction of the Fairmont Austin Hotel, you can be sure that the managers at Manchester carefully considered the financial aspects of the project. They evaluated the required investment, the revenues the new hotel was likely to generate, and how much it would cost to operate and maintain. They also estimated what it would cost to finance the project—how much they would pay for the debt and the equity used to finance it, given the associated risks. This "cost of capital" would be incorporated into their NPV analysis through the discounting process.

Accurately estimating the cost of capital is especially important for a capital-intensive project such as a hotel. The cost of financing a hotel like the Fairmont Austin can easily total \$100 per nightly room rental. In other words, if an average room rents for \$300, the cost of financing the project can consume one-third or more of the revenue the hotel receives from renting a room.

From this example, you can see how important it is to get the cost of capital right. If managers of Manchester Financial Group had estimated the cost of capital to be 6 percent when it was really 8 percent, they might have ended up investing in a project with a large negative NPV. In this chapter we discuss the tools and concepts that managers use to estimate the cost of capital when they evaluate a project.

Chapter Preview

Chapter 7 discussed the general concept of risk and described what financial analysts mean when they talk about the risk associated with a project's cash flows. It also explained how this risk is related to expected returns. With this background, we are ready to discuss the methods that financial managers use to estimate discount rates, the reasons they use these methods, and the key characteristics of each method.

We begin this chapter by introducing the weighted average cost of capital and explaining how this concept is related to the discount rates that many financial managers use to evaluate projects. Then we describe various methods that are used to estimate the costs of the three general types of financing that firms use to acquire assets—debt, common stock, and preferred stock—as well as the overall weighted average cost of capital for the firm.

We next discuss the circumstances under which it is appropriate to use the weighted average cost of capital for a firm as the discount rate for a project and outline the types of problems that can arise when the weighted average cost of capital is used inappropriately. Finally, we examine alternatives to using the weighted average cost of capital as a discount rate.

13.1 The Firm's Overall Cost of Capital

LEARNING OBJECTIVE

1. Explain what the weighted average cost of capital for a firm is and why it is often used as a discount rate to evaluate projects.

Our discussions of capital budgeting up to this point have focused on evaluating individual projects. We have assumed that the rate used to discount the cash flows for a project reflects the risks associated with the incremental after-tax free cash flows from that project. In Chapter 7, we saw that *unsystematic risk* can be eliminated by holding a diversified portfolio. Therefore, *systematic risk* is the only risk that investors require compensation for bearing. With this insight, we concluded that we can use Equation 7.12 to estimate the expected rate of return for a particular investment:

$$E(R_i) = R_{rf} + \beta_i[E(R_m) - R_{rf}]$$

where $E(R_i)$ is the expected return on project i, R_{rf} is the risk-free rate of return, β_i is the beta for project i, and $E(R_m)$ is the expected return on the market. Recall that the difference between the expected return on the market and the risk-free rate $[E(R_m) - R_{rf}]$ is known as the *market risk premium*.

Although these ideas help us better understand the discount rate on a conceptual level, they can be difficult to implement in practice. Firms do not issue publicly traded shares for individual projects. This means that analysts do not have the stock returns necessary to use a regression analysis like that illustrated in Exhibit 7.10 to estimate the beta (β) for an individual project. As a result, they have no way to directly estimate the discount rate that reflects the systematic risk of the incremental after-tax free cash flows from a particular project.

In many firms, senior financial managers deal with this problem by estimating the cost of capital for the firm as a whole and then requiring analysts within the firm to use this cost of capital to discount the free cash flows for all projects.[1] A problem with this approach is that it ignores the fact that a firm is really a collection of projects with different levels of risk. A firm's overall cost of capital is actually a weighted average of the costs of capital for these projects, where the weights reflect the relative values of the projects.

To see why a firm is a collection of projects, consider The Boeing Company. Boeing manufactures a number of different models of civilian and military aircraft. If you have ever flown on a commercial airline, chances are that you have been on a Boeing 737, 747, 757, 767, 777, or 787 aircraft. Boeing manufactures several versions of each of these aircraft models to meet the needs of its customers. These versions have different ranges, seat configurations, numbers of seats, and so on. Some are designed exclusively to haul freight for companies such as UPS and FedEx. Every version of every model of aircraft at Boeing was, at some point in time, a new project. The assets owned by Boeing today and its expected cash flows are just the sum of the assets and cash flows from all of these individual projects plus the other projects at the firm, such as those involving military aircraft.[2] This means that the overall systematic risk associated with Boeing's expected cash flows and the company's cost of capital are weighted averages of the systematic risks and the costs of capital for its individual projects.

If the risk of an individual project differs from the average risk of the firm, the firm's overall cost of capital is not the ideal discount rate to use when evaluating that project. Nevertheless, since this is the discount rate that is commonly used, we begin by discussing how a firm's overall cost of capital is estimated. We then discuss alternatives to using the firm's cost of capital as the discount rate in evaluating a project.

The Finance Balance Sheet

To understand how financial analysts estimate their firms' costs of capital, it is helpful to be familiar with a concept that we call the **finance balance sheet**. The finance balance sheet was referred to as the market-value balance sheet in Chapter 3. The main difference between the finance balance sheet and the accounting balance sheet is that the finance balance sheet is based on market values rather than book values. Recall that the total book value of the assets reported on an accounting balance sheet does not necessarily reflect the total market value of those assets. This is because the book value is largely based on historical costs, while the total market value of the assets equals the present value of the total cash flows that those assets are expected to generate in the future. The market value can be greater than or less than the book value but is rarely the same.

finance balance sheet
a balance sheet that is based on market values of expected cash flows

While the left-hand side of the accounting balance sheet reports the book values of a firm's assets, the right-hand side reports how those assets were financed. Firms finance the purchase of their assets using debt and equity.[3] Since the cost of the assets must equal the total value of the debt and equity that were used to purchase them, the book value of the assets

[1]Surveys of capital budgeting practices at major public firms in the United States indicate that a large percentage (possibly as high as 80 percent) of firms use the cost of capital for a firm or a division in capital budgeting calculations. For a discussion of this evidence, see the article titled "Best Practices in Estimating the Cost of Capital: Survey and Synthesis," by R. F. Bruner, K. M. Eades, R. S. Harris, and R. C. Higgins, which was published in the Spring/Summer 1998 issue of *Financial Practice and Education.*

[2]The total expected cash flows at Boeing also include cash flows from projects that the firm is expected to undertake in the future, or what are often referred to as *growth opportunities.*

[3]We will discuss how firms finance their assets in more detail in Chapters 15 and 16. For the time being, we will simply assume that a firm uses some combination of debt and equity. Here we use the term *debt* in the broadest sense to refer to all liabilities, including liabilities on which the firm does not pay interest, such as accounts payable. As is common practice, we focus only on long-term interest-bearing debt, such as bank loans and bonds, in the cost of capital calculations. The reason for this is discussed in the next section.

must equal the book value of the liabilities plus the book value of the equity on the accounting balance sheet. In Chapter 3 we called this equality the *balance sheet identity.*

Just as the total book value of the assets at a firm does not generally equal the total market value of those assets, the book value of total liabilities plus stockholders' equity does not usually equal the market value of these claims. In fact, the total market value of the debt and equity claims differs from their total book value by exactly the same amount that the total market value of a firm's assets differs from its total book value. This is because the total market value of the debt and the equity at a firm equals the present value of the cash flows that the debt holders and the stockholders have the right to receive. These cash flows are the cash flows that the assets in the firm are expected to generate. In other words, the people who have lent money to a firm and the people who have purchased the firm's stock have the right to receive all of the cash flows that the firm is expected to generate in the future. The value of the claims they hold must equal the value of the cash flows that they have a right to receive.

The fact that the market value of the assets must equal the value of the cash flows that these assets are expected to generate, combined with the fact that the value of the expected cash flows also equals the total market value of the firm's total liabilities and equity, means that we can write the market value (MV) of assets as follows:

$$\text{MV of assets} = \text{MV of liabilities} + \text{MV of equity} \quad (13.1)$$

Equation 13.1 is just like the accounting balance sheet identity. The only difference is that Equation 13.1 is based on market values. This relation is illustrated in **Exhibit 13.1**.

To better understand why the market value of the assets must equal the total market value of the liabilities and equity, consider a firm whose only business is to own and manage an apartment building that was purchased 20 years ago for \$1,000,000. Suppose that there is currently a \$300,000 mortgage on the building, the firm has no other liabilities, and the current market value of the building, based on the expected free cash flows from future rents, is \$4,000,000. What is the market value of all of the equity (stock) in this firm?

The fact that you paid \$1,000,000 20 years ago is not relevant to this question. What matters in finance is the value of the expected free cash flows from future rents, the \$4,000,000. This is the market value of the firm's assets—the left-hand side of the balance sheet in Exhibit 13.1. Since we know that the firm owes \$300,000, we can substitute into Equation 13.1 and solve for the market value of the equity:

$$\begin{aligned}\text{MV of assets} &= \text{MV of liabilities} + \text{MV of equity}\\ \$4{,}000{,}000 &= \$300{,}000 + \text{MV of equity}\\ \text{MV of equity} &= \$4{,}000{,}000 - \$300{,}000 = \$3{,}700{,}000\end{aligned}$$

If the free cash flows that the apartment building is expected to produce are worth \$4,000,000, then investors would be willing to pay \$3,700,000 for the equity in the firm. This is the value

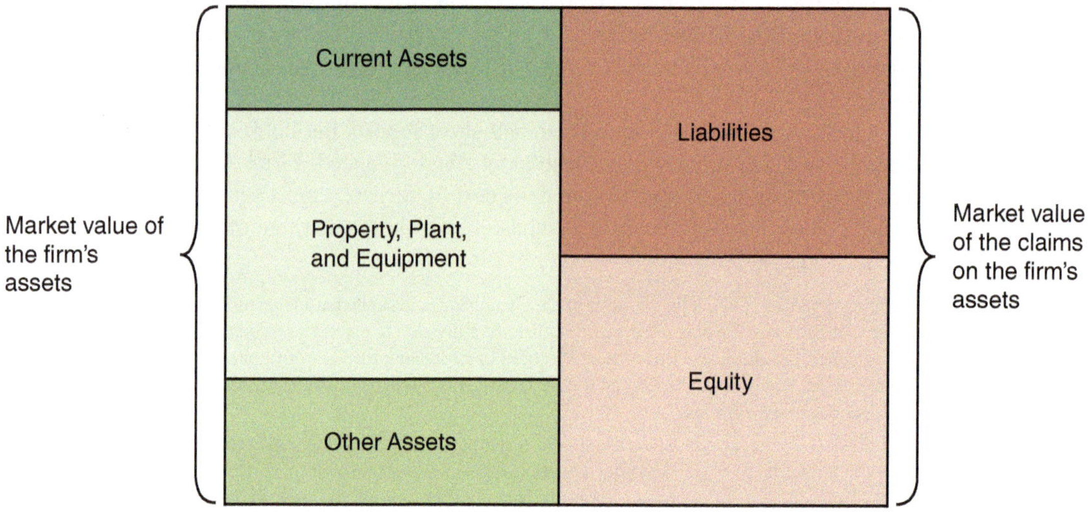

EXHIBIT 13.1 The Finance Balance Sheet

The market value of a firm's assets, which equals the present value of the cash flows those assets are expected to generate in the future, must equal the market value of the claims on those cash flows—the firm's liabilities and equity.

of the cash flows that they would expect to receive after making the interest and principal payments on the mortgage. Furthermore, since, by definition, the mortgage is worth \$300,000, the value of the debt plus the value of the equity is \$300,000 + \$3,700,000 = \$4,000,000—which is exactly equal to the market value of the firm's assets.

As suggested at the beginning of this discussion, the idea of a balance sheet based on market values was discussed in Chapter 3. In that chapter we pointed out that a market-value balance sheet would be more useful to financial decision makers than would the ordinary accounting balance sheet. Financial managers are much more concerned about the future than the past when they make decisions. You might revisit the discussion of sunk costs in Chapter 11 to remind yourself of why this is true.

Building Intuition

The Market Value of a Firm's Assets Equals the Market Value of the Claims on Those Assets

The market value of the debt and equity claims against the cash flows of a firm must equal the present value of the cash flows that the firm's assets are expected to generate. This is because, between them, the debt holders and the stockholders have the legal right to receive all of those cash flows.

Estimating a Firm's Cost of Capital

Now that we have discussed the basic idea of the finance balance sheet, consider the challenge that financial analysts face when they want to estimate the cost of capital for a firm. If analysts at a firm could estimate the betas for each of the firm's individual projects, they could estimate the beta for the entire firm as a weighted average of the betas for the individual projects. They could do this because, as we discussed earlier, the firm is simply a collection (portfolio) of projects. This calculation would just be an application of Equation 7.13:

$$\beta_{n\ \text{Asset portfolio}} = \sum_{i=1}^{n} x_i\beta_i = x_1\beta_1 + x_2\beta_2 + x_3\beta_3 + \cdots + x_n\beta_n$$

where β_i is the beta for project i and x_i is the fraction of the total firm value represented by project i.

The analysts could then use the beta for the firm in Equation 7.12:

$$E(R_i) = R_{rf} + \beta_i[E(R_m) - R_{rf}]$$

to estimate the expected return on the firm's assets, which is also the firm's cost of capital. Unfortunately, because analysts are not typically able to estimate betas for individual projects, they generally cannot use this approach.

Instead, analysts must use their knowledge of the finance balance sheet, along with the concept of market efficiency, which we discussed in Chapter 2, to estimate the cost of capital for the firm. Rather than using Equations 7.13 and 7.12 to perform the calculations for the *individual projects* represented on the left-hand side of the finance balance sheet, analysts perform a similar set of calculations for the *different types of financing* (debt and equity) on the right-hand side of the finance balance sheet. They can do this because, as we said earlier, the people who finance the firm have the right to receive all of the cash flows on the left-hand side. This means that the systematic risk associated with the total assets on the left-hand side is the same as the systematic risk associated with the total financing on the right-hand side. In other words, the weighted average of the betas for the different claims on the assets must equal a weighted average of the betas for the individual assets (projects).

Analysts do not need to estimate betas for each type of financing that the firm has. As long as they can estimate the cost of each type of financing—either directly, by observing that cost in the capital markets, or by using Equation 7.12—they can compute the cost of capital for the firm using the following equation:

$$k_{\text{Firm}} = \sum_{i=1}^{n} x_i k_i = x_1 k_1 + x_2 k_2 + x_3 k_3 + \cdots + x_n k_n \tag{13.2}$$

In Equation 13.2, k_{Firm} is the cost of capital for the firm, k_i is the cost of financing type i, and x_i is the fraction of the total market value of the financing (or of the assets) of the firm represented by financing type i. This formula simply says that the overall cost of capital for the firm is a weighted average of the cost of each different type of financing used by the firm.[4] Note

[4]As we will discuss in Section 13.2, if markets are efficient, the prices we observe in the markets will reflect the true costs of the different securities that the firm has outstanding.

Building Intuition

A Firm's Cost of Capital is a Weighted Average of All of Its Financing Costs

The cost of capital for a firm is a weighted average of the costs of the different types of financing used by the firm. The weights are the proportions of the total firm value represented by the different types of financing. By weighting the costs of the individual financing types in this way, we obtain the overall average opportunity cost of each dollar invested in the firm.

that since we are specifically talking about the cost of capital, we use the symbol k_i to represent this cost, rather than the more general notation $E(R_i)$ that we used in Chapter 7.

The similarity between Equation 13.2 and Equation 7.13 is not an accident. Both are applications of the basic idea that the systematic risk of a portfolio of assets is a weighted average of the systematic risks of the individual assets. Because R_{rf} and $E(R_m)$ in Equation 7.12 are the same for all assets, when we substitute Equation 7.12 into Equation 13.2 (remember that $E(R_i)$ in Equation 7.12 is the same as k_i in Equation 13.2) and cancel out R_{rf} and $E(R_m)$, we get Equation 7.13. We will not prove this here, but you might do so to convince yourself that what we are saying is true.

To see how Equation 13.2 is applied, let's return to the example of the firm whose only business is to manage an apartment building. Recall that the total value of this firm is $4,000,000 and that it has $300,000 in mortgage debt. If the firm has only one mortgage loan and one type of stock, then the fractions of the total value represented by those two types of financing are as follows:

$$x_{\text{Debt}} = \$300{,}000/\$4{,}000{,}000 = 0.075, \text{ or } 7.5\%$$
$$x_{\text{Equity}} = \$3{,}700{,}000/\$4{,}000{,}000 = 0.925, \text{ or } 92.5\%$$
$$\text{where } x_{\text{Debt}} + x_{\text{Equity}} = 0.075 + 0.925 = 1.000$$

This tells us that the value of the debt claims equals 7.5 percent of the value of the firm and that the value of the equity claims equals the remaining 92.5 percent of the value of the firm. If the cost of the debt for this business is 6 percent and the cost of the equity is 10 percent, the cost of capital for the firm can be calculated as a weighted average of the costs of the debt and equity:[5]

$$k_{\text{Firm}} = x_{\text{Debt}}k_{\text{Debt}} + x_{\text{Equity}}k_{\text{Equity}} = (0.075)(0.06) + (0.925)(0.10) = 0.097, \text{ or } 9.7\%$$

weighted average cost of capital (WACC) the weighted average of the costs of the different types of capital (debt and equity) that have been used to finance a firm; the cost of each type of capital is weighted by the proportion of the total capital that it represents

Notice that we have used Equation 13.2 to calculate a **weighted average cost of capital (WACC)** for the firm in this example. In fact, this is what people typically call the firm's cost of capital, k_{Firm}. From this point on, we will use the abbreviation WACC to represent the firm's overall cost of capital.

Learning by Doing Application 13.1 illustrates another WACC calculation.

LEARNING BY DOING

WileyPLUS

Need more help? Visit your WileyPLUS course.

APPLICATION 13.1 | Calculating the Cost of Capital for a Firm

Problem You are considering purchasing a rug cleaning company that will cost $2,000,000. You plan to finance the purchase with a $1,500,000 loan from Bank of America (BofA) that has a 6.5 percent interest rate, a $300,000 loan from the seller of the company that has an 8 percent interest rate, and $200,000 of your own money. You will own all of the equity (stock) in the firm. You estimate that the opportunity cost of your $200,000 investment—that is, what you could earn on an investment of similar risk in the capital market—is 12 percent with that much debt. What is the cost of capital for this investment?

Approach You can use Equation 13.2 to calculate the WACC for this firm. Since you are planning to finance the purchase using capital from three different sources—two loans and your own equity investment—the right-hand side of Equation 13.2 will have three terms.

Solution We begin by calculating the weights for the different types of financing:

$$x_{\text{BofA Loan}} = \$1{,}500{,}000/\$2{,}000{,}000 = 0.75$$
$$x_{\text{Seller loan}} = \$300{,}000/\$2{,}000{,}000 = 0.15$$
$$x_{\text{Equity}} = \$200{,}000/\$2{,}000{,}000 = 0.10$$

where $x_{\text{BofA loan}} + x_{\text{Seller loan}} + x_{\text{Equity}} = 0.75 + 0.15 + 0.10 = 1.00.$

[5]We are ignoring the effect of taxes on the cost of debt financing for the time being. This effect is discussed in detail in Section 13.2 and explicitly incorporated into subsequent calculations.

We can then calculate the WACC using Equation 13.2:

$$\begin{aligned}\text{WACC} = k_{\text{Firm}} &= x_{\text{BofA loan}}k_{\text{BofA loan}} + x_{\text{Seller loan}}k_{\text{Seller loan}} + x_{\text{Equity}}k_{\text{Equity}} \\ &= (0.75)(0.065) + (0.15)(0.08) + (0.10)(0.12) \\ &= 0.728, \text{ or } 7.28\%\end{aligned}$$

On average, you would be paying 7.28 percent per year on every dollar you invested in the firm. This is the opportunity cost of capital for the firm. It is the rate that you would use to discount the cash flows associated with the rug cleaning business in an NPV analysis.

Before You Go On

1. Why does the market value of the claims on the assets of a firm equal the market value of the assets?
2. How is the WACC for a firm calculated?
3. What does the WACC for a firm tell us?

13.2 The Cost of Debt

LEARNING OBJECTIVE

2. Calculate the cost of debt for a firm.

In our discussion of how the WACC for a firm is calculated, we assumed that the costs of the different types of financing were known. This assumption allowed us to simply plug those costs into Equation 13.2 once we had calculated the weight for each type of financing. Unfortunately, life is not that simple. In the real world, analysts have to estimate each of the individual costs. In other words, the discussion in the preceding section glossed over a number of concepts and issues that you should be familiar with. This section and Section 13.3 discuss those concepts and issues and show how the costs of the different types of financing can be estimated.

Before we move on to the specifics of how to estimate the costs of different types of financing, we must stress an important point: All of these calculations depend in some part on financial markets being efficient. We suggested this in the last section when we mentioned that analysts have to rely on the concept of market efficiency to estimate the WACC. The reason is that analysts often cannot directly observe the rate of return that investors require for a particular type of financing. Instead, analysts must rely on the security prices they can observe in the financial markets to estimate the required rate.

It makes sense to rely on security prices only if you believe that the financial markets are reasonably efficient at incorporating new information into these prices. If the markets were not efficient, estimates of expected returns that were based on market security prices would be unreliable. Of course, if the returns that are plugged into Equation 13.2 are bad, the resulting estimate for WACC will also be bad. With this caveat, we can now discuss how to estimate the costs of the various types of financing.

Key Concepts for Estimating the Cost of Debt

Virtually all firms use some form of debt financing. The financial managers at firms typically arrange for revolving lines of credit to finance working capital items such as inventories or accounts receivable. These lines of credit are very much like the lines of credit that come with your credit cards. Firms also obtain private fixed-term loans, such as bank loans, or sell bonds to the public to finance ongoing operations or the purchase of long-term assets—just as you would finance your living expenses while you are in school with a student loan or a car with a car loan. For example, an energy firm such as Next Era Energy Resources in Florida, will sell bonds to finance a new power plant, and a rapidly growing retailer, such as Target, will use debt to finance new stores and distribution centers. As mentioned earlier, we will discuss how firms finance themselves in more detail in Chapters 15 and 16, but for now it is sufficient to recognize that firms use these three general types of debt financing: lines of credit, private fixed-term loans, and bonds that are sold in the public markets.

There is a cost associated with each type of debt that a firm uses. However, when we estimate the cost of capital for a firm, we are particularly interested in the cost of the firm's long-term debt. Firms generally use long-term debt to finance their long-term assets, and it is the long-term assets that concern us when we think about the value of a firm's assets. By long-term debt, we usually mean the debt that, when it was borrowed, was set to mature in more than one year. This typically includes fixed-term bank loans used to finance ongoing operations or long-term assets, as well as the bonds that a firm sells in the public debt markets.

Although one year is not an especially long time, debt with a maturity of more than one year is typically viewed as permanent debt. This is because firms often borrow the money to pay off this debt when it matures. Doing this replaces maturing debt with new debt, thereby leaving the amount of debt at the firm unchanged.

We do not normally worry about revolving lines of credit when calculating the cost of debt because these lines tend to be temporary. Banks typically require that the outstanding balances be periodically paid down to $0 (just as we are sure you pay your entire credit card balance from time to time).

When analysts estimate the cost of a firm's long-term debt, they are estimating the cost on a particular date—the date on which they are doing the analysis. This is a very important point to keep in mind because the interest rate that the firm is paying on its outstanding debt does not necessarily reflect its current cost of debt. Interest rates change over time, and so does the cost of debt for a firm. The rate a firm was charged three years ago for a five-year loan is unlikely to be the same rate that it would be charged today for a new five-year loan. For example, suppose that Next Era Energy Resources issued bonds five years ago for 7 percent. Since then, interest rates have fallen, so the same bonds could be sold at par value today for 6 percent. The cost of debt today is 6 percent, not 7 percent, and 6 percent is the cost of debt that management will use in WACC calculations. If you looked in the firm's financial statements, you would see that the firm is paying an interest rate of 7 percent. This is what the financial managers of the firm agreed to pay five years ago, not what it would cost to sell the same bonds today. The accounting statements reflect the cost of debt that was sold at some time in the past.

Building Intuition

The Current Cost of Long-Term Debt Is What Matters When Calculating WACC

The current cost of long-term debt is the appropriate cost of debt for WACC calculations. This is because the WACC we use in capital budgeting is the opportunity cost of capital for the firm's investors as of today. This means we must use today's costs of debt and equity when we calculate the WACC. Historical costs do not belong in WACC calculations.

Estimating the Current Cost of a Bond or an Outstanding Loan

We have now seen that we should not use historical costs of debt in WACC calculations. Let's discuss how we can estimate the current costs of bonds and other fixed-term loans by using market information.

The Current Cost of a Bond

You may not realize it, but we have already discussed how to estimate the current cost of debt for a publicly traded bond. This cost is estimated using the yield to maturity calculation. Recall that in Chapter 8 we defined the yield to maturity as the discount rate that makes the present value of the coupon and principal payments equal to the price of the bond.

For example, consider a 10-year bond with a \$1,000 face value that was issued five years ago. This bond has five years remaining before it matures. If the bond has an annual coupon rate of 7 percent, pays coupon interest semiannually, and is currently selling for \$1,042.65, we can calculate its yield to maturity by using Equation 8.1 and solving for i or by using a financial calculator. Let's use Equation 8.1 for this example.

To do this, as was discussed in the section on semiannual compounding in Chapter 8, we first convert the bond data to reflect semiannual compounding: (1) the total number of coupon payments is 10 (2 payments per year × 5 years = 10 payments), and (2) the semiannual coupon payment is \$35 [(\$1,000 × 7 percent per year)/2 periods per year = \$70/2 = \$35]. We can now use Equation 8.1 and solve for i to find the yield to maturity:

$$P_B = \frac{C_1}{1+i} + \frac{C_2}{(1+i)^2} + \cdots + \frac{C_n + F_n}{(1+i)^n}$$

$$\$1{,}042.65 = \frac{\$35}{1+i} + \frac{\$35}{(1+i)^2} + \frac{\$35}{(1+i)^3} + \cdots + \frac{\$35}{(1+i)^9} + \frac{\$1{,}035}{(1+i)^{10}}$$

By trial and error or with a financial calculator, we solve for i and find:

$$i = k_{\text{Bond}} = 0.0300, \text{ or } 3.00\%$$

This semiannual rate would be quoted as an annual rate of 6 percent (2 periods per year × 0.03 per period = 0.06, or 6 percent) in financial markets. However, as explained in Chapter 8, this annual rate fails to account for the effects of compounding. We must therefore use Equation 6.7 to calculate the effective annual interest rate (EAR) in order to obtain the actual current annual cost of this debt:

$$\text{EAR} = \left(1 + \frac{\text{Quoted interest rate}}{m}\right)^m - 1 = \left(1 + \frac{0.06}{2}\right)^2 - 1$$

$$= (1.03)^2 - 1 = 0.0609, \text{ or } 6.09\%$$

If this bond was sold at par value, it paid 7 percent when it was issued five years ago. Someone who buys it today will expect to earn only 6.09 percent per year. This is the annual rate of return required by the market on this bond, which is known as the effective annual yield.

Notice that the above calculation takes into account the interest payments, the face value of the debt (the amount that will be repaid in five years), and the current price at which the bond is selling. It is necessary to account for all of these characteristics of the bond. The return received by someone who buys the bond today will be determined by both the interest income and the capital appreciation (or capital depreciation in this case, since the price is higher than the face value).

We must account for one other factor when we calculate the current cost of bond financing to a company—the cost of issuing the bond. In the above example, we calculated the return that someone who buys the bond can expect to receive. Since a company must pay fees to investment bankers, lawyers, and accountants, along with various other costs, to actually issue a bond, the cost to the company is higher than 6.09 percent.[6] Therefore, in order to obtain an accurate estimate of the cost of a bond to the issuing firm, analysts must incorporate *issuance costs* into their calculations. Issuance costs are an example of *direct out-of-pocket costs*, the actual out-of-pocket costs that a firm incurs when it raises capital.

The way in which issuance costs are incorporated into the calculation of the cost of a bond is straightforward. Analysts use the *net proceeds* that the company receives from the bond, rather than the price that is paid by the investor, on the left-hand side of Equation 8.1. Suppose the company in our example sold five-year bonds with a 7 percent coupon today and paid issuance costs equal to 2 percent of the total value of the bonds. After paying the issuance costs, the company would receive only 98 percent of the price paid by the investors. Therefore,

[6]These types of costs are incurred by firms whenever they raise capital. We only show how to include them in the cost of bond financing and, later, in estimating the cost of preferred stock, but they should also be included in calculations of the costs of capital from other sources, such as bank loans and common equity.

the company would actually receive only $1,042.65 × (1 − 0.02) = $1,021.80 for each bond it sold and the semiannual cost to the company would be:

$$P_B = \frac{C_1}{1+i} + \frac{C_2}{(1+i)^2} + \cdots + \frac{C_n + F_n}{(1+i)^n}$$

$$\$1{,}021.80 = \frac{\$35}{1+i} + \frac{\$35}{(1+i)^2} + \frac{\$35}{(1+i)^3} + \cdots + \frac{\$35}{(1+i)^9} + \frac{\$1{,}035}{(1+i)^{10}}$$

$$i = k_{Bond} = 0.0324, \text{ or } 3.24\%$$

Converting the adjusted semiannual rate to an EAR, we see that the actual annual cost of this debt financing is:

$$\text{EAR} = (1.0324)^2 - 1 = 0.0658, \text{ or } 6.58\%$$

In this example the issuance costs increase the effective cost of the bonds from 6.09 percent to 6.58 percent per year.

The Current Cost of an Outstanding Loan

Conceptually, calculating the current cost of long-term bank or other private debt is not as straightforward as estimating the current cost of a public bond because financial analysts cannot observe the market price of private debt. Fortunately, analysts do not typically have to do this. Instead, they can simply call their banker and ask what rate the bank would charge if they decided to refinance the debt today. A rate quote from a banker provides a good estimate of the current cost of a private loan.

Taxes and the Cost of Debt

It is very important that you understand one additional concept concerning the cost of debt: In the United States, *firms can deduct interest payments for tax purposes.* In other words, every dollar a firm pays in interest reduces the firm's taxable income by one dollar. Thus, if the firm's marginal tax rate is 35 percent, the firm's total tax bill will be reduced by 35 cents for every dollar of interest it pays. A dollar of interest would actually cost this firm only 65 cents because the firm would save 35 cents on its taxes.

More generally, the after-tax cost of interest payments equals the pretax cost times 1 minus the tax rate. This means that the after-tax cost of debt is:

$$k_{\text{Debt after-tax}} = k_{\text{Debt pretax}} \times (1 - t) \qquad (13.3)$$

This after-tax cost of debt is the cost that firms actually use to calculate the WACC. The reason is that investors care only about the after-tax cost of capital—just as they care only about after-tax cash flows. Managers are concerned about what they actually have to pay for capital, and the actual cost is reduced if the government subsidizes debt by providing a tax break.

Taxes affect the cost of debt in much the same way that the interest tax deduction on a home mortgage affects the cost of financing a house. For example, assume that you borrow $200,000 at 6 percent to buy a house on January 1 and your interest payments total $12,000 in the first year. Under the tax law, you can deduct this $12,000 from your taxable income when you calculate your taxes for the year.[7]

Suppose that your taxable income before the interest deduction is $75,000 and, for simplicity, that both your average and marginal tax rates are 20 percent. Without the interest deduction, you would pay taxes totaling $15,000 ($75,000 × 0.20 = $15,000). However, because the interest payments reduce your taxable income, your taxes with the interest deduction will be only $12,600 [($75,000 − $12,000) × 0.20 = $12,600]. The ability to deduct the interest payments you made saved you $2,400 ($15,000 − $12,600 = $2,400)! This savings is exactly equal to the interest payment you make times your marginal tax rate: $12,000 × 0.20 = $2,400. Since you are saving $2,400, the after-tax cost of your interest payments is $9,600 ($12,000 − $2,400 = $9,600), which means that the after-tax cost of this debt is 4.80 percent

[7]There is a limit on the total amount of home loan interest payments that you can deduct when you calculate your taxable income. For instance, in 2016 you could deduct interest payments on loans with a total face value of $1,100,000 ($1,000,000 mortgage plus $100,000 home equity loan).

($9,600/$200,000 = 0.0480, or 4.80 percent). This is exactly what Equation 13.3 tells us. With $k_{\text{Debt pretax}}$ at 6 percent and t at 20 percent, Equation 13.3 gives us:

$$k_{\text{Debt after-tax}} = k_{\text{Debt pretax}} \times (1 - t) = 0.06 \times (1 - 0.2) = 0.0480, \text{ or } 4.80\%$$

Estimating the Cost of Debt for a Firm

Most firms have several different debt issues outstanding at any particular point in time. Just as you might have both a car loan and a school loan, a firm might have several bank loans and bond issues outstanding. To estimate the firm's overall cost of debt when it has several debt issues outstanding, we must first estimate the costs of the individual debt issues and then calculate a weighted average of these costs.

To see how this is done, let's consider an example. Suppose that your pizza parlor business has grown dramatically in the past three years from a single restaurant to 30 restaurants. To finance this growth, two years ago you sold $25 million of five-year bonds. These bonds pay interest annually and have a coupon rate of 8 percent. They are currently selling for $1,026.24 per $1,000 bond. Just today, you also borrowed $5 million from your local bank at an interest rate of 6 percent. Assume that this is all the long-term debt that you have and that there are no issuance costs. What is the overall average after-tax cost of your debt if your business's marginal tax rate is 35 percent?

The pretax cost of the bonds as of today is the effective annual yield on those bonds. Since the bonds were sold two years ago, they will mature three years from now. Using Equation 8.1, we find that the effective annual yield (which equals the yield to maturity in this example) for these bonds is:

$$P_B = \frac{C_1}{1+i} + \frac{C_2}{(1+i)^2} + \cdots + \frac{C_n + F_n}{(1+i)^n}$$

$$\$1{,}026.24 = \frac{\$80}{1+i} + \frac{\$80}{(1+i)^2} + \frac{\$1{,}080}{(1+i)^3}$$

$$i = k_{\text{Bond pretax}} = 0.0700, \text{ or } 7.00\%$$

The pretax cost of the bank loan that you took out today is simply the 6 percent rate that the bank is charging you, assuming that the bank is charging you the market rate.

Now that we know the pretax costs of the two types of debt that your business has outstanding, we can calculate the overall average cost of your debt by calculating the weighted average of their two costs. Since the weights for the two types of debt are based on their current market values we must first determine these values. Because the bonds are currently selling above their par value, we know that their current market value is greater than their $25 million face value. In fact, it equals:

$$(\$1{,}026.24/\$1{,}000) \times \$25{,}000{,}000 = \$25{,}656{,}000$$

Since the bank loan was just made today, its value simply equals the amount borrowed or $5 million. The weights for the two types of debt are therefore:

$$x_{\text{Bonds}} = \$25{,}656{,}000/(\$25{,}656{,}000 + \$5{,}000{,}000) = 0.8369$$

$$x_{\text{Bank debt}} = \$5{,}000{,}000/(\$25{,}000{,}000 + \$5{,}000{,}000) = 0.1631$$

$$\text{where } x_{\text{Bonds}} + x_{\text{Bank debt}} = 0.8369 + 0.1631 = 1.000$$

The weighted average pretax cost of debt is:

$$\begin{aligned} k_{\text{Debt pretax}} &= x_{\text{Bonds}} k_{\text{Bonds pretax}} + x_{\text{Bank debt}} k_{\text{Bank debt pretax}} \\ &= (0.8369 \times 0.07) + (0.1631 \times 0.06) = 0.0586 + 0.0098 \\ &= 0.0684, \text{ or } 6.84\% \end{aligned}$$

The after-tax cost of debt is therefore:

$$k_{\text{Debt after-tax}} = k_{\text{Debt pretax}} \times (1 - t) = 6.84\% \times (1 - 0.35) = 4.45\%$$

Learning by Doing Application 13.2 and **Decision Making Example 13.1** provide more examples of cost of debt calculations and their application.

LEARNING BY DOING

WileyPLUS

Need more help? Visit your WileyPLUS course.

APPLICATION 13.2 | Calculating the After-Tax Cost of Debt for a Firm

Problem You have just successfully completed a leveraged buyout of the firm that you have been working for. To finance this $35 million transaction, you and three partners put up a total of $10 million in equity capital, and you borrowed $25 million from banks and other investors. The bank debt consists of $10 million of secured debt borrowed at a rate of 6 percent from Bank of America and $7 million of senior unsecured debt borrowed at a rate of 7 percent from JPMorgan Chase. The remaining $8 million was borrowed from an investment group managed by a private equity firm. The rate on this subordinated (junior) unsecured debt is 9.5 percent. What is the overall after-tax cost of the debt financing used to buy the firm if you expect the firm's average and marginal tax rates to both be 25 percent?

Approach The overall after-tax cost of debt can be calculated using the following three-step process: (1) Calculate the fraction of the total debt (weight) for each individual debt issue. (2) Using these weights, calculate the weighted average pretax cost of debt. (3) Use Equation 13.3 to calculate the after-tax average cost of debt.

Solution

(1) The weights for the three types of debt are as follows:

$$x_{\text{Secured debt}} = \$10{,}000{,}000/\$25{,}000{,}000 = 0.40$$
$$x_{\text{Senior unsecured debt}} = \$\ 7{,}000{,}000/\$25{,}000{,}000 = 0.28$$
$$x_{\text{Subordinated unsecured debt}} = \$\ 8{,}000{,}000/\$25{,}000{,}000 = 0.32$$

$$\text{where } x_{\text{Secured debt}} + x_{\text{Senior unsecured debt}} + x_{\text{Subordinated unsecured debt}} = 0.40 + 0.28 + 0.32 = 1.00$$

(2) The weighted average pretax cost of debt is:

$$\begin{aligned} k_{\text{Debt pretax}} &= x_{\text{Secured debt}}k_{\text{Secured debt pretax}} + x_{\text{Senior unsecured debt}}k_{\text{Senior unsecured debt pretax}} \\ &\quad + x_{\text{Subordinated unsecured debt}}k_{\text{Subordinated unsecured debt pretax}} \\ &= (0.40)(0.06) + (0.28)(0.07) + (0.32)(0.095) \\ &= 0.0740, \text{ or } 7.40\% \end{aligned}$$

(3) The after-tax cost of debt is therefore:

$$k_{\text{Debt after-tax}} = k_{\text{Debt pretax}} \times (1 - t) = 7.40\% \times (1 - 0.25) = 5.55\%$$

DECISION MAKING

EXAMPLE 13.1 | Using the Cost of Debt in Decision Making

Situation Your pizza parlor business has developed such a strong reputation that you have decided to take advantage of the restaurant's name recognition by selling frozen pizzas through grocery stores. In order to do this, you will have to build a manufacturing facility. You estimate that this will cost you $10 million. Since your business currently has only $2 million in the bank, you will have to borrow the remaining $8 million. You have spoken with two bankers about possible loan packages. The banker from Easy Money Financial Services offered you a loan for $6 million with a 6 percent rate and $2 million with a 7.5 percent rate. You calculate the pretax cost of debt for this package to be:

$$\begin{aligned} k_{\text{Loans pretax}} &= (\$6{,}000{,}000/\$8{,}000{,}000)(0.06) + (\$2{,}000{,}000/\$8{,}000{,}000)(0.075) \\ &= 0.0450 + 0.0188 \\ &= 0.0638, \text{ or } 6.38\% \end{aligned}$$

Your local banker offered you a single $8 million loan for 6.35 percent. Which financing should you choose if all terms on all of the loans, other than the interest rates, are the same?

Decision This is an easy decision. You should choose the less expensive alternative—the loan from your local bank. In this example, you can directly compare the pretax costs of the two alternatives. You do not need to calculate the after-tax costs because multiplying each pretax cost by the same number, $1 - t$, will not change your decision.

Before You Go On

1. Why do analysts care about the *current* cost of long-term debt when estimating a firm's cost of capital?
2. How do you estimate the cost of debt for a firm with more than one type of debt?
3. How do taxes affect the cost of debt?

13.3 The Cost of Equity

LEARNING OBJECTIVE

3. Calculate the cost of common stock and the cost of preferred stock for a firm.

The cost of equity (stock) for a firm is a weighted average of the costs of the different types of stock that the firm has outstanding at a particular point in time. We saw in Chapter 9 that some firms have both preferred stock and common stock outstanding. In order to calculate the cost of equity for these firms, we have to know how to calculate the cost of both common stock and preferred stock. In this section, we discuss how financial analysts can estimate the costs associated with these two different types of stock.

Common Stock

Just as information about market rates of return is used to estimate the cost of debt, market information is also used to estimate the cost of equity. There are several ways to do this. The particular approach a financial analyst chooses will depend on what information is available and how reliable the analyst believes it is. In this section we discuss three alternative methods for estimating the cost of common equity (stock). It is important to remember throughout this discussion that the "cost" we are referring to is the rate of return that investors require for investing in the stock at a particular point in time, given its systematic risk.

Method 1: Using the Capital Asset Pricing Model (CAPM)

The first method for estimating the cost of common equity is one that we discussed in Chapter 7. This method uses Equation 7.12:

$$E(R_i) = R_{rf} + \beta_i [E(R_m) - R_{rf}]$$

In this equation, the expected return on an asset is a linear function of the systematic risk associated with that asset.

If we recognize that $E(R_i)$ in Equation 7.12 is the cost of the common stock (equity) used to finance the firm (k_{cs}) when we are calculating the cost of common equity and that $[E(R_m) - R_{rf}]$ is the market risk premium, we can rewrite Equation 7.12 as follows:

$$k_{cs} = R_{rf} + (\beta_{cs} \times \text{Market risk premium}) \tag{13.4}$$

Equation 13.4 is just another way of writing Equation 7.12. It tells us that the cost of common stock equals the risk-free rate of return plus compensation for the systematic risk associated with the common stock. You already saw some examples of how to use this equation to calculate the cost of equity in the discussion of the Capital Asset Pricing Model (CAPM) in Chapter 7. In those examples you were given the current risk-free rate, the beta for the stock, and the market risk premium and were asked to calculate k_{cs} using the equation. Now we turn our attention to some practical considerations that you must be concerned with when choosing the appropriate risk-free rate, beta, and market risk premium for this calculation.

Weblink

You can find current yields on Treasury bills, notes, and bonds at the Web site of the U.S. Federal Reserve Bank at http://www.federalreserve.gov/releases/H15/update.

The Risk-Free Rate First, let's consider the risk-free rate. The current effective annual yield on a risk-free asset should always be used in Equation 13.4.[8] This is because the risk-free rate at a particular point in time reflects the rate of inflation that the market expects in the future. Since the expected rate of inflation changes over time, an old risk-free rate might not reflect current inflation expectations.

When analysts select a risk-free rate, they must choose between using a short-term rate, such as that for Treasury bills, or a longer-term rate, such as those for Treasury notes or bonds. Which of these choices is more appropriate? This question has been hotly debated by finance professionals for many years. We recommend that you use the risk-free rate on a long-term Treasury security when you estimate the cost of equity capital because the equity claim is a long-term claim on the firm's cash flows. As you saw in Chapter 9, the stockholders have a claim on the cash flows of the firm in perpetuity. By using a long-term Treasury security, you are matching a long-term risk-free rate with a long-term claim. A long-term risk-free rate better reflects long-term inflation expectations and the cost of getting investors to part with their money for a long period of time than does a short-term rate.

Weblink

Companies with publicly traded stock usually provide a lot of information about their businesses and financial performance on their Web sites. The Domino's Pizza Web site is a good example. Go to http://phx.corporate-ir.net/phoenix.zhtml?c=135383&p=irol-irhome.

The Beta If the common stock of a company is publicly traded, then you can estimate the beta for that stock using a regression analysis similar to that illustrated in Exhibit 7.10. However, identifying the appropriate beta is much more complicated if the common stock is not publicly traded. Since most companies in the United States are privately owned and do not have publicly traded stock, this is a problem that arises quite often when someone wants to estimate the cost of common equity for a firm.

Financial analysts often overcome this problem by identifying a "comparable" company with publicly traded stock that is in the same business and that has a similar amount of debt. For example, suppose you are trying to estimate the beta for your pizza business. The company has now grown to include more than 2,000 restaurants throughout the world. The frozen-foods business, however, was never successful and had to be shut down. You know that Domino's Pizza, Inc., one of your major competitors, has publicly traded equity and that the proportion of debt to equity for Domino's is similar to the proportion for your firm. Since Domino's overall business is similar to yours, in that it is only in the pizza business and competes in similar geographic areas, it would be reasonable to consider Domino's a comparable company.

The systematic risk associated with the stock of a comparable company is likely to be similar to the systematic risk for the stock of the private firm because a stock's systematic risk is determined by the nature of the firm's business and the amount of debt that it uses. If you are able to identify a good comparable company, such as Domino's Pizza, you can use its beta in Equation 13.4 to estimate the cost of equity capital for your firm. Even when a good comparable company cannot be identified, it is sometimes possible to use an average of the betas for the public firms in the same industry.

The Market Risk Premium It is not possible to directly observe the market risk premium. We just do not know what rate of return investors expect for the market portfolio, $E(R_m)$, at a particular point in time. Therefore, we cannot simply calculate the market risk premium as the difference between the expected return on the market and the risk-free rate, $[E(R_m) - R_{rf}]$. For this reason, financial analysts generally use a measure of the average risk premium investors have actually earned in the past as an indication of the risk premium they might require today.

For example, from 1926 through the end of 2015, actual returns on the U.S. stock market exceeded actual returns on long-term U.S. government bonds by an average of 5.92 percent per year (11.95 percent − 6.03 percent = 5.92 percent from Exhibit 7.3). If, on average, investors earned the risk premium that they expected, this figure reflects the average market risk premium over the period from 1926 to 2015. If a financial analyst believes that the market risk premium in the past is a reasonable estimate of the risk premium today, then he or she might use 5.92 percent as the market risk premium in Equation 13.4.

[8]We use the term *risk-free* here to refer to assets that have no default risk. Investors in such assets can still face interest rate risk as described in Chapter 8.

With this background, let's work an example to illustrate how Equation 13.4 is used in practice to estimate the cost of common stock for a firm. Suppose that it is December 20, 2016, and we want to estimate the cost of the common stock for the oil company ConocoPhillips. Using yields reported in the *Wall Street Journal* on that day, we determine that 30-day Treasury bills have an effective annual yield of 0.48 percent and that 20-year Treasury bonds have an effective annual yield of 2.88 percent. From the MSN Money Web site (http://moneycentral.msn.com), we find that the beta for ConocoPhillips stock is 1.19. We know that the market risk premium averaged 5.92 percent from 1926 to 2015. What is the expected rate of return on ConocoPhillips common stock?

Since we are estimating the expected rate of return on common stock, and common stock is a long-term asset, we use the long-term Treasury bond yield of 2.88 percent in the calculation. Notice that the Treasury bill and Treasury bond rates differed by 2.40 percent (2.88 percent − 0.48 percent = 2.40 percent) on December 20, 2016. They often differ by this amount or more, so the choice of which rate to use can make quite a difference in the estimated cost of equity.

Once we have selected the appropriate risk-free rate, we can plug it, along with the beta and market risk premium values, into Equation 13.4 to calculate the cost of common stock for ConocoPhillips:

$$\begin{aligned} k_{cs} &= \mathrm{R}_{rf} + (\beta_{cs} \times \text{Market risk premium}) \\ &= 0.0288 + (1.19 \times 0.0592) = 0.0992, \text{ or } 9.92\% \end{aligned}$$

This example illustrates how Equation 13.4 is used to estimate the cost of common stock for a company. How would the analysis differ for a private company? The only difference is that we would not be able to estimate the beta directly. We would have to estimate the beta using betas for similar public companies.

Learning by Doing Application 13.3 shows another example of the calculation of a firm's cost of common stock.

Method 2: Using the Constant-Growth Dividend Model

In Chapter 9 we noted that if the dividends received by the owner of a share of common stock are expected to grow at a constant rate in perpetuity, then the value of that share today can be calculated using Equation 9.4:

$$\mathrm{P}_0 = \frac{\mathrm{D}_1}{\mathrm{R} - g}$$

where D_1 is the dividend expected to be paid one period from today, R is the required rate of return, and g is the annual rate at which the dividends are expected to grow in perpetuity.

APPLICATION 13.3 | Calculating the Cost of Common Stock Using a Stock's Beta

LEARNING BY DOING

Problem You have decided to estimate the cost of the common stock in your pizza business on December 20, 2016. As noted earlier, the risk-free rate and the market risk premium on that day were 2.88 percent and 5.92 percent, respectively. Since you have already decided that Domino's Pizza is a reasonably comparable company, you obtain Domino's beta from the Google Finance Web site (http://www.google.com/finance). This beta is 0.60. What do you estimate the cost of common stock in your pizza business to be?

Approach The problem statement provides us with the information necessary to use the Capital Asset Pricing Model (CAPM). Therefore, in this example we will use Equation 13.4.

Solution

$$k_{cs} = \mathrm{R}_{rf} + (\beta_{cs} \times \text{Market risk premium}) = 0.0288 + (0.60 \times 0.0592) = 0.0643, \text{ or } 6.43\%$$

We can replace the R in Equation 9.4 with k_{cs} since we are specifically estimating the expected rate of return for investing in common stock (also the cost of equity if the firm has no other types of stock outstanding). We can then rearrange this equation to solve for k_{cs}:

$$k_{cs} = \frac{D_1}{P_0} + g \tag{13.5}$$

While Equation 13.5 is just a variation of Equation 9.4, it is important enough to identify as a separate equation because it provides a direct way of estimating the cost of equity under certain circumstances. If we can estimate the dividend that stockholders will receive next period, D_1, and we can estimate the rate at which the market expects dividends to grow over the long run, g, then we can use today's market price, P_0, in Equation 13.5 to tell us what rate of return investors in the firm's common stock are expecting to earn.

Consider an example. Suppose that the current price for the common stock at Sprigg Lane Company is \$20, that the firm is expected to pay a dividend of \$2 per share to its common stockholders next year, and that the dividend is expected to grow at a rate of 3 percent in perpetuity after next year. Equation 13.5 tells us that the required rate of return for Sprigg Lane's stock is:

$$k_{cs} = \frac{D_1}{P_0} + g = \frac{\$2}{\$20} + 0.03 = 0.1300, \text{ or } 13.00\%$$

This approach can be useful for a firm that pays dividends when it is reasonable to assume dividends will grow at a constant rate and when the analyst has a good idea what that growth rate will be. An electric utility firm is an example of this type of firm. Some electric utility firms pay relatively high and predictable dividends that increase at a fairly consistent rate. In contrast, this approach would not be appropriate for use by a high-tech firm that pays no dividends or that pays a small dividend that is likely to increase at a high rate in the short run. Equation 13.5, like any other equation, should be used only if it is appropriate for the particular stock.

You might be asking yourself at this point where you would get P_0, D_1, and g in order to use Equation 13.5 for a particular stock. You can get the current price of a share of stock as well as the dividend that a firm is expected to pay next year quite easily from many different Web sites on the Internet—for example, MSN Money and Google Finance, which were both mentioned earlier. The financial information includes the dollar value of dividends paid in the past year and the dividend that the firm is expected to pay in the next year.

Weblink

You can obtain recent stock prices and financial information for a large number of firms from MSN Money at http://moneycentral.msn.com or from Yahoo! Finance at http://finance.yahoo.com/.

Estimating the long-term rate of growth in dividends is more difficult, but there are some guidelines that can help. As we discussed in Chapter 9, the first rule is that dividends cannot grow faster than the long-term growth rate of the economy in a perpetuity model such as Equation 9.4 or 13.5. Assuming dividends will grow faster than the economy is the same as assuming that dividends will eventually become larger than the economy itself! We know this is impossible.

What is the long-term growth rate of the economy? Well, historically it has been the rate of inflation plus about 3 percent. This means that if inflation is expected to be 3 percent in the long run, then a reasonable estimate for the long-term growth rate in the economy is 6 percent (3 percent inflation + 3 percent real growth = 6 percent). This tells us that g in Equation 13.5 will not be greater than 6 percent. What exactly it will be depends on the nature of the business and the industry it is in. If it is a declining industry, then g might be negative. If the industry is expected to grow with the economy and the particular firm you are evaluating is expected to retain its market share, then a reasonable estimate for g might be 5 or 6 percent.

multistage-growth dividend model a model that allows for varying dividend growth rates in the near term, followed by a constant long-term growth rate; another term used to describe the mixed (supernormal) growth dividend model discussed in Chapter 9

Method 3: Using a Multistage-Growth Dividend Model

Using a **multistage-growth dividend model** to estimate the cost of equity for a firm is very similar to using a constant-growth dividend model. The difference is that a multistage-growth dividend model allows for faster dividend growth rates in the near term, followed by a constant long-term growth rate. If this concept sounds familiar, that is because it is the idea behind the *mixed (supernormal) growth dividend model* discussed in Chapter 9. In Equation 9.6 this model was written as:

$$P_0 = \frac{D_1}{1+R} + \frac{D_2}{(1+R)^2} + \cdots + \frac{D_t}{(1+R)^t} + \frac{P_t}{(1+R)^t}$$

where D_i is the dividend in period i, P_t is the value of constant-growth dividend payments in period t, and R is the required rate of return.

To refresh your memory of how this model works, let's consider a three-stage example. Suppose that a firm will pay a dividend one year from today (D_1) and that this dividend will increase at a rate of g_1 the following year, g_2 the year after that, and g_3 per year thereafter. The value of a share of this stock today thus equals:

$$P_0 = \frac{D_1}{1+k_{cs}} + \frac{D_1(1+g_1)}{(1+k_{cs})^2} + \frac{D_1(1+g_1)(1+g_2)}{(1+k_{cs})^3} + \left[\frac{D_1(1+g_1)(1+g_2)(1+g_3)}{k_{cs}-g_3}\right]\left[\frac{1}{(1+k_{cs})^3}\right]$$

In this equation, we have replaced the R in Equation 9.6 with k_{cs} since we are specifically estimating the expected rate of return for common stock. We have also written all of the dividends in terms of D_1 to illustrate how the different growth rates will affect the dividends in each year. Finally, we have written P_t in terms of the constant-growth model. If we substitute D_1, D_2, D_3, and D_4 where appropriate, you can see that this is really just Equation 9.6, where we have replaced R with k_{cs} and written P_t in terms of the constant-growth model:

$$P_0 = \frac{D_1}{1+k_{cs}} + \frac{D_2}{(1+k_{cs})^2} + \frac{D_3}{(1+k_{cs})^3} + \left[\frac{D_4}{k_{cs}-g_3}\right]\left[\frac{1}{(1+k_{cs})^3}\right]$$

All this equation does is add the present values of the dividends that are expected in each of the next three years and the present value of a growing perpetuity that begins in the fourth year. **Exhibit 13.2** illustrates how cash flows relate to the four terms in the equation.

Note that the fourth term in Exhibit 13.2 is discounted only three years because, as we saw in Chapters 6 and 9, the constant-growth model gives you the present value of a growing perpetuity as of the year before the first cash flow. In this case since the first cash flow is D_4, the model gives you the value of the growing perpetuity as of Year 3.

A multistage-growth dividend model is much more flexible than the constant-growth dividend model because we do not have to assume that dividends grow at the same rate forever.

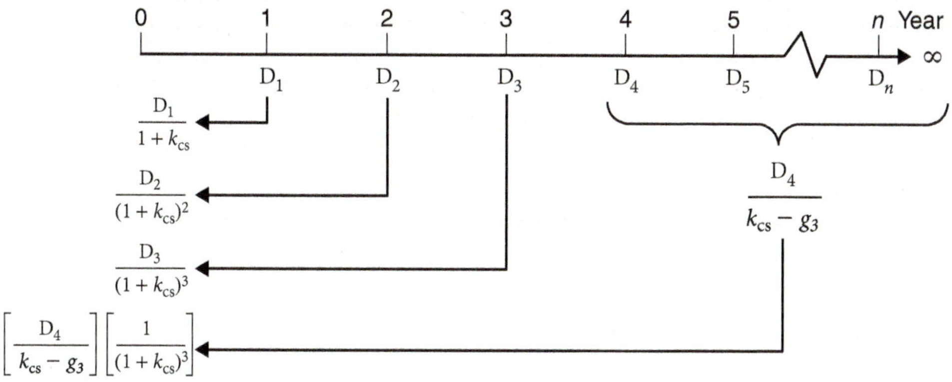

$$P_0 = \frac{D_1}{1+k_{cs}} + \frac{D_2}{(1+k_{cs})^2} + \frac{D_3}{(1+k_{cs})^3} + \left[\frac{D_4}{k_{cs}-g_3}\right]\left[\frac{1}{(1+k_{cs})^3}\right]$$

EXHIBIT 13.2 The Three-Stage Dividend Growth Equation

In the three-stage dividend growth equation shown here, the price of a share of stock is equal to the present value of dividends expected to be received at the end of Years 1, 2, and 3, plus the present value of a growing perpetuity that begins in Year 4 and whose dividends are assumed to grow at a constant rate g_3 forever.

We can use a model such as this to estimate the cost of common stock, k_{cs}, by plugging P_0, D_1, and the appropriate growth rates into the model and solving for k_{cs} using trial and error—just as we solved for the yield to maturity of bonds in Chapter 8 and earlier in this chapter. The major issues we have to be concerned about when we use a multistage-growth dividend model are (1) that we have chosen the right model, meaning that we have included enough stages or growth rates, and (2) that our estimates of the growth rates are reasonable.

Let's work an example to illustrate how this model is used to calculate the cost of common stock. Suppose that we want to estimate the cost of common stock for a firm that is expected to pay a dividend of \$1.50 per share next year. This dividend is expected to increase 15 percent the following year, 10 percent the year after that, 7 percent the year after that, and 5 percent annually thereafter. If the firm's common stock is currently selling for \$24 per share, what is the rate of return that investors require for investing in this stock?

Because there are four different growth rates in this example, we have to solve a formula with five terms:

$$P_0 = \frac{D_1}{1 + k_{cs}} + \frac{D_2}{(1 + k_{cs})^2} + \frac{D_3}{(1 + k_{cs})^3} + \frac{D_4}{(1 + k_{cs})^4} + \left[\frac{D_5}{k_{cs} - g_4}\right]\left[\frac{1}{(1 + k_{cs})^4}\right]$$

From the information given in the problem statement, we know the following:

$$\begin{aligned} D_1 &= \$1.50 \\ D_2 &= D_1 \times (1 + g_1) = \$1.500 \times 1.15 = \$1.725 \\ D_3 &= D_2 \times (1 + g_2) = \$1.725 \times 1.10 = \$1.898 \\ D_4 &= D_3 \times (1 + g_3) = \$1.898 \times 1.07 = \$2.031 \\ D_5 &= D_4 \times (1 + g_4) = \$2.031 \times 1.05 = \$2.133 \end{aligned}$$

Substituting these values into the above equation gives us the following, which we solve for k_{cs}:

$$\$24 = \frac{\$1.50}{1 + k_{cs}} + \frac{\$1.73}{(1 + k_{cs})^2} + \frac{\$1.90}{(1 + k_{cs})^3} + \frac{\$2.03}{(1 + k_{cs})^4} + \left[\frac{\$2.13}{k_{cs} - g_4}\right]\left[\frac{1}{(1 + k_{cs})^4}\right]$$

Using Excel

Solving for k_{cs} Using a Multistage-Growth Dividend Model

Because trial-and-error calculations can be somewhat tedious when you perform them by hand, you may find it helpful to use a spreadsheet program. If you would like to use a spreadsheet program to solve the preceding problem yourself, the output from the spreadsheet below shows you how to do it using trial and error.

Once you input the indicated numbers and formulas into cells B3 through B14, you can then vary the number in cell B2 until the number in cell B8 equals \$24. Once you have built the model, you can also use the "goal seek" or "solver" functions in Excel to avoid having to manually solve the problem by trial and error. See the "Help" feature in Excel for information on how to use these functions.

	A	B	C	D
1				**Comment**
2	k_{cs} =	0.1220		Change this number until the P_0 equals \$24.00
3	g_1 =	0.15		Growth rate in year 1
4	g_2 =	0.10		Growth rate in year 2
5	g_3 =	0.07		Growth rate in year 3
6	g_4 =	0.05		Growth rate for perpetuity
7				
8	P_0 =	\$24.00		Formula: =NPV(B2,B11:B14) - This formula calculates the present value of the
9				future dividends in cells B11 to B14 using the discount rate in cell B2.
10	Year			
11	1	\$1.500		D_1
12	2	\$1.725		D_2 = B11*(1+B3)
13	3	\$1.898		D_3 = B12*(1+B4)
14	4	\$31.619		D_4 = [B13*(1+B5)] + [B13*(1+B5)*(1+B6)]/(B2-B6) - This formula calculates the
15				value of D_4 plus the present value of all the cash flows after year 4 in year 4 dollars.
16				

As mentioned earlier, we can solve this equation for k_{cs} using trial and error. When we do this, we find that k_{cs} is 12.20 percent. This is the rate of return at which the present value of the cash flows equals $24. Therefore, it is the rate that investors currently require for investing in this stock.

The **Using Excel Example** illustrates how a spreadsheet program can make it easier to solve trial and error problems.

Which Method Should We Use?

We now have discussed three methods of estimating the cost of common equity for a firm. You might be asking yourself how you are supposed to know which method to use. The short answer is that, in practice, most people use the CAPM (Method 1) to estimate the cost of common equity if the result is going to be used in the discount rate for evaluating a project. One reason is that, assuming the theory is valid, CAPM tells managers what rate of return investors should require for equity having the same level of systematic risk that the firm's equity has. This is the appropriate opportunity cost of equity capital for an NPV analysis if the project has the same risk as the firm and will have similar leverage. Furthermore, CAPM does not require financial analysts to make assumptions about future growth rates in dividends, as Methods 2 and 3 do.

Used properly, Methods 2 and 3 provide an estimate of the rate of return that is implied by the current price of a firm's stock at a particular point in time. If the stock markets are efficient, then this should be the same as the number that we would estimate using CAPM. However, to the extent that the firm's stock is mispriced—for example, because investors are not informed or have misinterpreted the future prospects for the firm—deriving the cost of equity from the price at one point in time can yield a bad estimate of the true cost of equity.

Preferred Stock

As we discussed in Chapter 9, preferred stock is a form of equity that has a stated value and specified dividend rate. For example, a share of preferred stock might have a stated value of $100 and a 5 percent dividend rate. The owner of such a share would be entitled to receive a dividend of $5 ($100 × 0.05 = $5) each year. Another key feature of preferred stock is that it does not have an expiration date. In other words, preferred stock continues to pay the specified dividend in perpetuity, unless the firm repurchases it or goes out of business.

These characteristics of preferred stock allow us to use the perpetuity model, Equation 6.3, to estimate the cost of preferred equity. For example, suppose that investors would pay $85 for a share of the preferred stock mentioned above. We can rewrite Equation 6.3:

$$\text{PVP} = \frac{\text{CF}}{i}$$

as:

$$\text{P}_{\text{ps}} = \frac{\text{D}_{\text{ps}}}{k_{\text{ps}}}$$

where P_{ps} is the present value of the expected dividends (the current preferred stock price), D_{ps} is the annual preferred stock dividend, and k_{ps} is the cost of the preferred stock. Rearranging the formula to solve for k_{ps} yields:

$$k_{\text{ps}} = \frac{\text{D}_{\text{ps}}}{\text{P}_{\text{ps}}} \qquad (13.6)$$

Plugging the information from our example into Equation 13.6, we see that k_{ps} for the preferred stock in our example is:

$$k_{\text{ps}} = \frac{\text{D}_{\text{ps}}}{\text{P}_{\text{ps}}} = \frac{\$5}{\$85} = 0.0588, \text{ or } 5.88\%$$

This is the rate of return at which the present value of the annual $5 cash flows equals the market price of $85. Therefore, 5.88 percent is the rate that investors currently require for investing in this preferred stock.

It is easy to incorporate issuance costs into the above calculation to obtain the cost of the preferred stock to the firm that issues it. As in the earlier bond calculations, we use the net proceeds from the sale rather than the price that is paid by the investor in the calculation. For example, suppose that in order for a firm to sell the above preferred stock, it must pay an investment banker 5 percent of the amount of money raised. If there are no other issuance costs, the company would receive $85 × (1 – 0.05) = $80.75 for each share sold, and the total cost of this financing to the firm would be:

$$k_{ps} = \frac{D_{ps}}{P_{ps}} = \frac{\$5}{\$80.75} = 0.0619, \text{ or } 6.19\%$$

You may recall from the discussion in Chapter 9 that certain characteristics of preferred stock look a lot like those of debt. The equation $P_{ps} = D_{ps}/k_{ps}$ shows that the value of preferred stock also varies with market rates of return in the same way as debt. Because k_{ps} is in the denominator of the fraction on the right-hand side of the equation, whenever k_{ps} increases, P_{ps} decreases, and whenever k_{ps} decreases, P_{ps} increases. That is, the value of preferred stock is negatively related to market rates.

It is also important to recognize that the CAPM can be used to estimate the cost of preferred equity, just as it can be used to estimate the cost of common equity. A financial analyst can simply substitute k_{ps} for k_{cs} and β_{ps} for β_{cs} in Equation 13.4 and use it to estimate the cost of preferred stock. Remember from Chapter 7 that the CAPM does not apply only to common stock; rather, it applies to any asset. Therefore, we can use it to calculate the rate of return on any asset if we can estimate the beta for that asset.

Learning by Doing Application 13.4 illustrates another calculation of the cost of preferred stock.

LEARNING BY DOING

APPLICATION 13.4 | Estimating the Cost of Preferred Stock

Problem You work in the treasury department at Wells Fargo & Company, and your manager has asked you to estimate the cost of each of the different types of stock that Wells Fargo has outstanding. One of these issues is an 8 percent noncumulative preferred stock that has a stated value of $1,000 and is currently selling for $927.90. Although this preferred stock is publicly traded, it does not trade very often. This means that you cannot use the CAPM to estimate k_{ps} because you cannot get a good estimate of the beta using regression analysis. How else can you estimate the cost of this preferred stock, and what is this cost?

Approach You can also use Equation 13.6 to estimate the cost of preferred stock.

Solution First, you must find the annual dividend that someone who owns a share of this stock will receive. This preferred stock issue pays an annual dividend (for simplicity we are assuming one dividend payment per year) that equals 8 percent of $1,000, or $1,000 × 0.8 = $80. Substituting the annual dividend and the market price into Equation 13.6 yields:

$$k_{ps} = \frac{D_{ps}}{P_{ps}} = \frac{\$80}{\$927.90} = 0.0862, \text{ or } 8.62\%$$

Before You Go On

1. What information is needed to use the CAPM to estimate k_{cs} or k_{ps}?
2. Under what circumstances can you use the constant-growth dividend formula to estimate k_{cs}?
3. What is the advantage of using a multistage-growth dividend model, rather than the constant-growth dividend model, to estimate k_{cs}?

13.4 Using the WACC in Practice

LEARNING OBJECTIVE

4. Calculate the weighted average cost of capital for a firm, explain the limitations of using a firm's weighted average cost of capital as the discount rate when evaluating a project, and discuss the alternatives to the firm's weighted average cost of capital.

We have now covered the basic concepts and computational tools that are used to estimate the WACC. At this point, we are ready to talk about some of the practical issues that arise when financial analysts calculate the WACC for their firms.

When financial analysts think about calculating the WACC, they usually think of it as a weighted average of the firm's after-tax cost of debt, cost of preferred stock, and cost of common equity. Equation 13.2 is usually written as:

$$\text{WACC} = x_{\text{Debt}}k_{\text{Debt pretax}}(1 - t) + x_{\text{ps}}k_{\text{ps}} + x_{\text{cs}}k_{\text{cs}} \tag{13.7}$$

where $x_{\text{Debt}} + x_{\text{ps}} + x_{\text{cs}} = 1$. If the firm has more than one type of debt outstanding or more than one type of preferred or common stock, analysts will calculate a weighted average for each of those types of securities and then plug those averages into Equation 13.7. Financial analysts will also use the *market values*, rather than the accounting book values, of the debt, preferred stock, and common stock to calculate the weights (the x's) in Equation 13.7. This is because, as we have already seen, the theory underlying the discounting process requires that the costs of the different types of financing be weighted by their relative market values. Accounting book values have no place in these calculations unless they just happen to equal the market values.

Calculating WACC: An Example

An example provides a useful way of illustrating how the theories and tools that we have discussed are used in practice. Assume that you are a financial analyst at a manufacturing company that has used three types of debt, preferred stock, and common stock to finance its investments.

Debt The debt includes a \$4 million bank loan that is secured by machinery and equipment. This loan has an interest rate of 6 percent, and your firm could expect to pay the same rate if the loan were refinanced today. Your firm also has a second bank loan (a \$3 million mortgage on your manufacturing plant) with an interest rate of 5.5 percent. The rate would also be 5.5 percent today if you refinanced this loan. The third type of debt is a bond issue that the firm sold two years ago for \$11 million. The market value of these bonds today is \$10 million. Using the approach we discussed earlier, you have estimated that the effective annual yield on the bonds is 7 percent.

Preferred Stock The preferred stock pays an annual dividend of 4.5 percent on a stated value of \$100. A share of this stock is currently selling for \$60, and there are 100,000 shares outstanding.

Common Stock There are 1 million shares of common stock outstanding, and they are currently selling for \$21 each. Using a regression analysis, you have estimated that the beta of these shares is 1.1.

The 20-year Treasury bond rate is currently 2.88 percent, and you have estimated the market risk premium to be 5.92 percent using the returns on stocks and Treasury bonds from the 1926 to 2015 period. Your firm's marginal tax rate is 35 percent. What is the WACC for your firm?

Weblink

You can see real-world WACC calculations at the New Zealand Web site for Pricewaterhouse-Coopers, the international accounting and consulting firm, at http://www.pwc.co.nz/appreciating-value/edition-6-march-2015-deal-activity-ipo-and-listed-share-price-performance.

The first step in computing the WACC is to calculate the pretax cost of debt. Since the market value of the firm's debt is \$17 million (\$4 million + \$3 million + \$10 million = \$17 million), we can calculate the pretax cost of debt as follows:

$$\begin{aligned} k_{\text{Debt pretax}} &= x_{\text{Bank loan 1}}k_{\text{Bank loan 1 pretax}} + x_{\text{Bank loan 2}}k_{\text{Bank loan 2 pretax}} + x_{\text{Bonds}}k_{\text{Bonds pretax}} \\ &= (\$4/\$17)(0.06) + (\$3/\$17)(0.055) + (\$10/\$17)(0.07) \\ &= 0.0650, \text{ or } 6.50\% \end{aligned}$$

Note that because the \$4 million and \$3 million loans have rates that equal what it would cost to refinance them today, their market values equal the amount that is owed. Since the \$10 million market value of the bond issue is below the \$11 million face value, the rate that firm is actually paying must be lower than the 7 percent rate you estimated to reflect the current cost of this debt. Recall that as interest rates increase, the market value of a bond decreases. This is the negative relation that we referred to earlier in this chapter.

We next calculate the cost of the preferred stock using Equation 13.6, as follows:

$$\begin{aligned} k_{ps} &= \frac{D_{ps}}{P_{ps}} = \frac{0.045 \times \$100}{\$60} \\ &= \frac{\$4.5}{\$60} = 0.0750, \text{ or } 7.50\% \end{aligned}$$

From Equation 13.4, we calculate the cost of the common equity to be:

$$\begin{aligned} k_{cs} = R_{rf} + (\beta_{cs} \times \text{Market risk premium}) &= 0.0288 + (1.1 \times 0.0592) \\ &= 0.0939, \text{ or } 9.39\% \end{aligned}$$

We are now ready to use Equation 13.7 to calculate the firm's WACC. Since the firm has \$17 million of debt, \$6 million of preferred stock (\$60 per share × 100,000 shares = \$6 million), and \$21 million of common equity (\$21 per share × 1,000,000 shares = \$21 million), the total market value of its capital is \$44 million (\$17 million + \$6 million + \$21 million = \$44 million). The firm's WACC is therefore:

$$\begin{aligned} \text{WACC} &= x_{\text{Debt}}k_{\text{Debt pretax}}(1 - t) + x_{ps}k_{ps} + x_{cs}k_{cs} \\ &= (\$17/\$44)(0.0650)(1 - 0.35) + (\$6/\$44)(0.0750) + (\$21/\$44)(0.0939) \\ &= 0.0714, \text{ or } 7.14\% \end{aligned}$$

Learning by Doing Application 13.5 and **Decision Making Example 13.2** provide more examples of WACC calculations and their application.

LEARNING BY DOING

WileyPLUS

Need more help? Visit your WileyPLUS course.

APPLICATION 13.5 | Calculating the WACC with Equation 13.7

Problem After calculating the cost of the common equity in your pizza business to be 6.43 percent (see Learning by Doing Application 13.3), you have decided to estimate the WACC. You recently hired a business appraiser to estimate the value of your stock, which includes all of the outstanding common equity. His report indicates that it is worth \$500 million.

In order to finance the 2,000 restaurants that are now part of your company, you have sold three different bond issues. Based on the current prices of the bonds from these issues and the issue characteristics (face values and coupon rates), you have estimated the market values and effective annual yields to be:

Bond Issue	Value (\$ millions)	Effective Annual Yield
1	\$100	4.50%
2	187	4.90
3	154	5.40
Total	\$441	

Your company has no other long-term debt or any preferred stock outstanding. Both the marginal and average tax rates for your company are 20 percent. What is the WACC for your pizza business?

Approach You can use Equation 13.7 to solve for the WACC for your pizza business. To do so, you must first calculate the weighted average cost of debt. You can then plug the weights and costs for the debt and common equity into Equation 13.7. Since your business has no preferred stock, the value for this term in Equation 13.7 will equal \$0.

Solution The weighted average cost of the debt is:

$$
\begin{aligned}
k_{\text{Debt pretax}} &= x_1 k_{1\text{ Debt pretax}} + x_2 k_{2\text{ Debt pretax}} + x_3 k_{3\text{ Debt pretax}} \\
&= (\$100/\$441)(0.0450) + (\$187/\$441)(0.0490) + (\$154/\$441)(0.0540) \\
&= 0.0498, \text{ or } 4.98\%
\end{aligned}
$$

and the WACC is:

$$
\begin{aligned}
\text{WACC} &= x_{\text{Debt}} k_{\text{Debt pretax}}(1 - t) + x_{\text{ps}} k_{\text{ps}} + x_{\text{cs}} k_{\text{cs}} \\
&= (\$441/[\$441 + \$500])(0.0498)(1 - 0.20) + 0 + (\$500/[\$441 + \$500])(0.0643) \\
&= 0.0528, \text{ or } 5.28\%
\end{aligned}
$$

EXAMPLE 13.2 | Interpreting the WACC

DECISION MAKING

Situation You are a financial analyst for the company whose WACC of 7.14 percent we just calculated in the main text. One day, your manager walks into your office and tells you that she is thinking about selling $23 million of common stock and using the proceeds from the sale to pay back both of the firm's loans and to repurchase all of the outstanding bonds and preferred stock. She tells you that this is a smart move because if she does this, the beta of the firm's common stock will decline to 0.90 and the overall k_{cs} will decline from 9.39 percent to 8.21 percent:

$$
\begin{aligned}
k_{\text{cs}} &= \text{R}_{\text{rf}} + (\beta_{\text{cs}} \times \text{Market risk premium}) = 0.0288 + (0.90 \times 0.0592) \\
&= 0.0821, \text{ or } 8.21\%
\end{aligned}
$$

What do you tell your manager?

Decision You should politely point out that she is making the wrong comparison. Since the refinancing will result in the firm being financed entirely with equity, k_{cs} will equal the firm's WACC. Therefore, the 8.21 percent should really be compared with the 7.14 percent WACC. If your manager goes through with the refinancing, she will be making a bad decision. The average after-tax cost of the capital that your firm uses will *increase* from 7.14 percent to 8.21 percent.

Limitations of WACC as a Discount Rate for Evaluating Projects

At the beginning of this chapter, we told you that financial managers often require analysts within the firm to use the firm's current cost of capital to discount the cash flows for individual projects. They do so because it is very difficult to directly estimate the discount rate for individual projects. You should recognize by now that the WACC is the discount rate that analysts are often required to use. Using the WACC to discount the cash flows for a project can make sense under certain circumstances. However, in other circumstances, it can be very dangerous. The rest of this section discusses when it makes sense to use the WACC as a discount rate and the problems that can occur when the WACC is used incorrectly.

Chapter 11 discussed how an analyst forecasting the cash flows for a project is forecasting the incremental after-tax free cash flows at the firm level. These cash flows represent the difference between the cash flows that the firm will generate if the project is adopted and the cash flows that the firm will generate if the project is not adopted.

Financial theory tells us that the rate that should be used to discount these incremental cash flows is the rate that reflects their systematic risk. This means that the WACC is going to be the appropriate discount rate for evaluating a project only when the project has cash flows with systematic risks that are exactly the same as those for the firm as a whole. Unfortunately, this is not true for most projects. The firm itself is a portfolio of projects with varying degrees of risk.

When a single rate, such as the WACC, is used to discount cash flows for projects with varying levels of risk, the discount rate will be too low in some cases and too high in others. When the discount rate is too low, the firm runs the risk of accepting a negative NPV project. To see how this might happen, assume that you work at a company that manufactures soft drinks and that the managers at your company are concerned about all the competition in the core soft drink business. They are thinking about expanding into the manufacture and sale of exotic tropical beverages. The managers believe that entering this market would allow the firm to better differentiate its products and earn higher profits. Suppose also that the appropriate beta for soft drink projects is 1.2, while the appropriate beta for tropical beverage projects is 1.5. Since your firm is only in the soft drink business right now, the beta for its overall cash flows is 1.2. **Exhibit 13.3** illustrates the problem that could arise if your firm's WACC is used to evaluate a tropical beverage project.

In Exhibit 13.3, you can see that since the beta of the tropical beverage project is larger than the beta of the firm as a whole, the expected return (or discount rate) for the tropical beverage project should be higher than the firm's WACC. The Security Market Line indicates what this expected return should be. Now, if the firm's WACC is used to discount the expected cash flows for this project, and the expected return on the project is above the firm's WACC, then the estimated NPV will be positive. So far, so good. However, as illustrated in Exhibit 13.3, some projects may have an expected return that is above the WACC but below the SML. For projects such as those, using the WACC as the discount rate may actually cause the firm to accept a negative NPV project! The estimated NPV will be positive even though the true NPV is negative. The negative NPV projects that would be accepted in those situations have returns that fall in the red shaded area below the SML, above the WACC line, and to the right of the firm's beta.

In Exhibit 13.3 you can also see that using the WACC to discount expected cash flows for low-risk projects can result in managers at the firm rejecting projects that have positive NPVs. This problem is, in some sense, the mirror image of the case where the WACC is lower than the correct discount rate. Financial managers run the risk of turning down positive NPV projects whenever the WACC is higher than the correct discount rate. The positive NPV projects that would be rejected are those that fall into the green shaded area that is below the WACC but above the SML and to the left of the firm's beta.

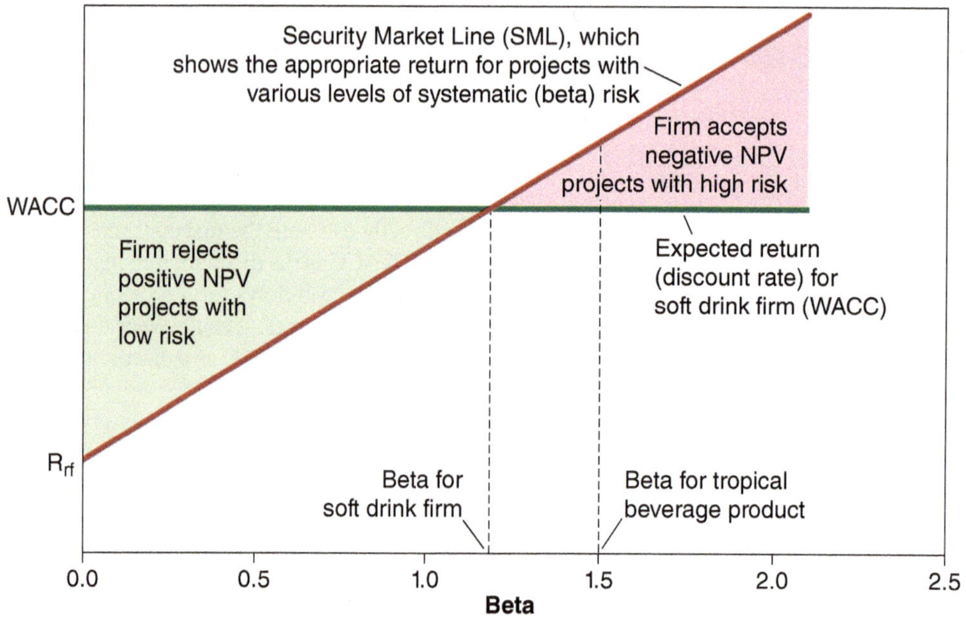

EXHIBIT 13.3 Potential Errors When Using the WACC to Evaluate Projects

Two types of problems can arise when the WACC for a firm is used to evaluate individual projects: positive NPV projects may be rejected or negative NPV projects may be accepted. For the tropical beverage example, if the expected return on that project was below the level indicated by the SML, but above the firm's WACC, the project might be accepted even though it would have a negative NPV.

To see how these types of problems arise, consider a project that requires an initial investment of \$100 million and that is expected to produce cash inflows of \$40 million per year for three years. If the correct discount rate for this project is 8 percent, its NPV will be:

$$\begin{aligned}\text{NPV} &= \text{FCF}_0 + \frac{\text{FCF}_1}{1+k} + \frac{\text{FCF}_2}{(1+k)^2} + \frac{\text{FCF}_3}{(1+k)^3} \\ &= -\$100 + \frac{\$40}{1+0.08} + \frac{\$40}{(1+0.08)^2} + \frac{\$40}{(1+0.08)^3} \\ &= \$3.08\end{aligned}$$

This is an attractive project because it returns more than the investors' opportunity cost of capital.

Suppose, however, that the financial managers of the firm considering this project require that all projects be evaluated using the firm's WACC of 11 percent. When the cash flows are discounted using a rate of 11 percent, the NPV is:

$$\text{NPV} = -\$100 + \frac{\$40}{1+0.11} + \frac{\$40}{(1+0.11)^2} + \frac{\$40}{(1+0.11)^3} = -\$2.25$$

As you can see, when the WACC is used to discount the cash flows, the firm will end up rejecting a positive NPV project. The firm will be passing up an opportunity to create value for its stockholders. As an exercise, you might try constructing a numerical example in which a firm accepts a negative NPV project.

It is also important to recognize that when a firm uses a single rate to evaluate all of its projects, there will be a bias toward accepting more risky projects. The average risk of the firm's assets will tend to increase over time. Furthermore, because some positive NPV projects are likely to be rejected and some negative NPV projects are likely to be accepted, new projects on the whole will probably create less value for stockholders than if the appropriate discount rate had been used to evaluate all projects. This, in turn, can put the firm at a disadvantage when compared with its competitors and adversely affect the value of its existing projects.

The key point to take away from this discussion is that it is only correct to use a firm's WACC to discount the cash flows for a project if the expected cash flows from that project have the same systematic risk as the expected cash flows from the firm as a whole. You might be wondering how you can tell when this condition exists. The answer is that we never know for sure. Nevertheless, there are some guidelines that you can use when assessing whether the systematic risk for a particular project is similar to that for the firm as a whole.

The systematic risk of the cash flows from a project depend on the nature of the business. Revenues and expenses in some businesses are affected more by changes in general economic conditions than revenues and expenses in other businesses. For example, consider the differences between a company that makes bread and a company that makes recreational vehicles. The demand for bread will be relatively constant in good economic conditions and in bad. The demand for recreational vehicles will be more volatile. People buy fewer recreational vehicles during recessions than when the economy is doing well.

While total volatility is not the same as systematic volatility, businesses with more total volatility (uncertainty or risk) typically have more systematic volatility. Since beta is a measure of systematic risk, and systematic risk is a key factor in determining a firm's WACC, this suggests that the firm's WACC should be used only for projects with business risks similar to those for the firm as a whole. Since financial managers usually think of systematic risk when they think of underlying business risks, we can restate this condition as follows:

Condition 1 A firm's WACC should be used to evaluate the cash flows for a new project only if the level of systematic risk for the project is the same as that for the portfolio of projects that currently comprise the firm.

You have to consider one other factor when you decide whether it is appropriate to use a firm's WACC to discount the cash flows for a project. That is the way in which the project will be financed and how this financing compares with the way the firm's assets are financed. To better understand why this is important, consider Equation 13.7:

$$\text{WACC} = x_{\text{Debt}}k_{\text{Debt pretax}}(1-t) + x_{\text{ps}}k_{\text{ps}} + x_{\text{cs}}k_{\text{cs}}$$

This equation provides a measure of the firm's cost of capital that reflects both how the firm's assets have been financed—that is, the mix of debt and preferred and common stock that was used to acquire those assets—and the current cost of each type of financing. In other words, the WACC reflects both the x's and the k's associated with the firm's financing. Why is this important? Because the costs of the different types of capital depend on the fraction of the total firm financing that each represents. If the firm uses more or less debt, the cost of debt will be higher or lower. In turn, the cost of both preferred stock and common stock will be affected. This means that even if the underlying business risk of the project is the same as that for the firm as a whole, if the project is financed differently than the firm as a whole the appropriate discount rate for the project analysis will be different from that for the firm as a whole.

Condition 2 A firm's WACC should be used to evaluate a project only if that project uses the same financing mix—the same proportions of debt, preferred shares, and common shares—used to finance the firm as a whole.

In summary, WACC is a measure of the current cost of the capital that the firm is using to finance its projects. It is an appropriate discount rate for evaluating projects only if (1) the project's systematic risk is the same as that of the firm's current portfolio of projects and (2) the project will be financed with the same mix of debt and equity as the firm's current portfolio of projects. If either of these two conditions does not hold, then managers should be careful in using the firm's current WACC to evaluate a project.

Alternatives to Using WACC for Evaluating Projects

Financial managers understand the limitations of using a firm's WACC to evaluate projects, but they also know that there are no perfect alternatives. As we noted earlier in this chapter, there is no publicly traded common stock for most individual projects within a firm. It is, therefore, not possible to directly estimate the beta for the common stock used to finance an individual project.[9] Although it might be possible to obtain an estimate of the cost of debt from the firm's bankers, without an estimate of the common stock beta—and, therefore, the cost of common stock—it is not possible to obtain a direct estimate of the appropriate discount rate for a project using Equation 13.7.

If the discount rate for a project cannot be estimated directly, a financial analyst might try to find a public firm that is in a business that is similar to that of the project. For example, in our exotic tropical beverage example, an analyst at the soft drink company might look for a company that produces only exotic tropical beverages and that also has publicly traded stock. This public company would be what financial analysts call a **pure-play comparable** because it is exactly like the project. The returns on the pure-play comparable company's stock could be used to estimate the expected return on the equity that is used to finance the project. Unfortunately, this approach is generally not feasible due to the difficulty of finding a public firm that is only in the business represented by the project. If the public firm is in other businesses as well, then we run into the same sorts of problems that we face when we use the firm's WACC.

pure-play comparable a comparable company that is in exactly the same business as the project or business being analyzed

From a practical standpoint, financial managers, such as company treasurers and chief financial officers, do not like letting analysts estimate the discount rates for their projects. Different analysts tend to make different assumptions or use different approaches, which can lead to inconsistencies that make it difficult to compare projects. In addition, analysts may be tempted to manipulate discount rates in order to make pet projects look more attractive.

In an effort to use discount rates that reflect project risks better than the firm's WACC, while retaining control of the process through which discount rates are set, financial managers sometimes classify projects into categories based on their systematic risks. They then specify a discount rate that is to be used to discount the cash flows for all projects within each category. The idea is that each category of projects has a different level of systematic risk and therefore a different discount rate should be used for each. **Exhibit 13.4** illustrates such a classification scheme.

[9]A few U.S. firms have issued a type of stock that has an equity claim on only part of their business. If a project is similar to the part of the business for which "tracking stock" like this has been sold, the returns on the tracking stock can be used to estimate the beta for the common stock used to finance the project.

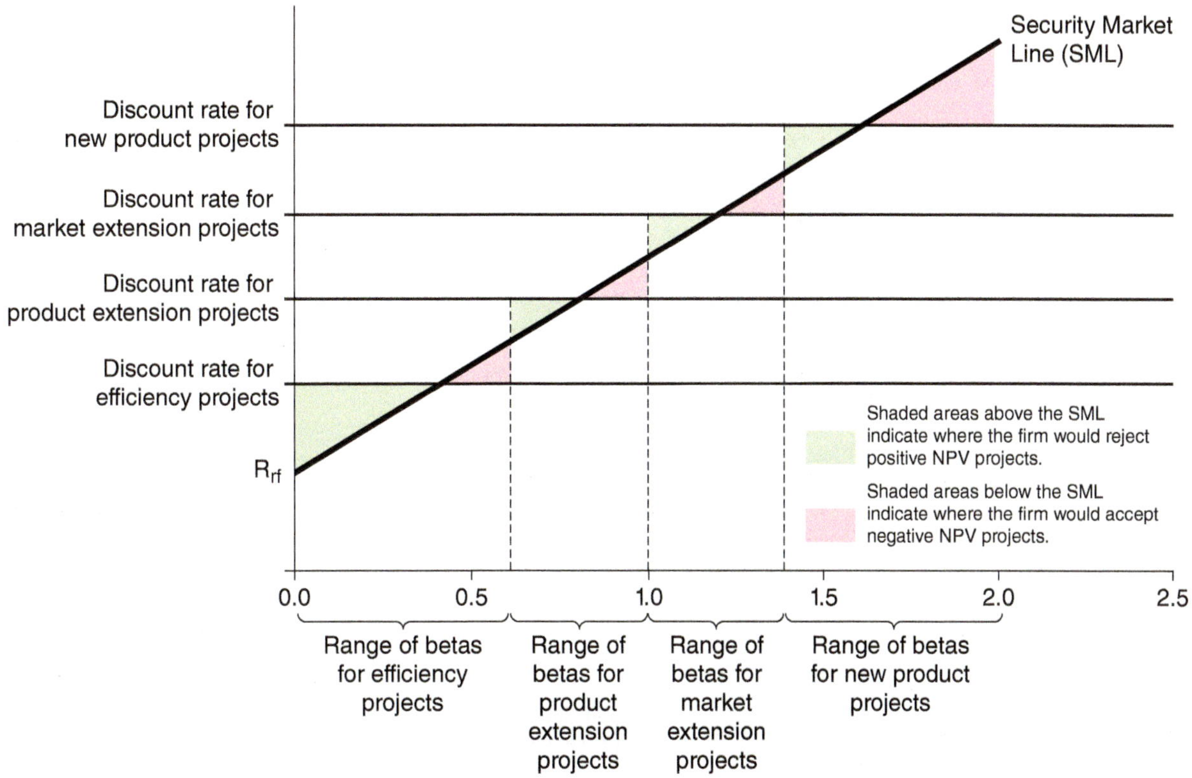

EXHIBIT 13.4 Potential Errors When Using Multiple Discount Rates to Evaluate Projects

The potential for errors—either rejecting a positive NPV project or accepting a negative NPV project—is smaller when discount rates better reflect the risk of the projects that they are used to evaluate. You can see this by noting that the total size of the shaded areas in this figure is smaller than the size of the shaded areas in Exhibit 13.3. In the ideal situation, where the correct discount rate is used for each project, there would be no shaded area at all in a figure like this.

The scheme illustrated in Exhibit 13.4 includes four project categories:

1. *Efficiency projects*, such as the implementation of a new production technology that reduces manufacturing costs for an existing product.
2. *Product extension projects*, such as those in which Boeing created variations of its aircraft, such as the Boeing 737, to help meet customer needs.
3. *Market extension projects*, in which existing products are sold in new markets, such as when Texas Instruments considers selling a new version of a computer chip that has been used in digital phones to digital camera manufacturers.
4. *New product projects*, in which entirely new products are being considered.

When using the scheme illustrated in Exhibit 13.4, the financial manager would assign a discount rate for each category that reflects the typical beta in the indicated range of betas. Such an approach is attractive because it is not generally difficult for analysts to figure out in which of the four categories particular projects belong, and it limits their discretion in choosing discount rates. Most important, it can reduce the possibility of accepting negative NPV projects or rejecting positive NPV projects. We can see the latter benefit by comparing the shaded areas in the figures in Exhibits 13.3 and 13.4. The total size of the shaded areas, which represents the possibility of making an error, is much smaller in Exhibit 13.4.

Before You Go On

1. Do analysts use book values or market values to calculate the weights when they use Equation 13.7? Why?
2. What kinds of errors can be made when the WACC for a firm is used as the discount rate for evaluating all projects in the firm?
3. Under what conditions is the WACC the appropriate discount rate for a project?

Summary of Learning Objectives

1 Explain what the weighted average cost of capital for a firm is and why it is often used as a discount rate to evaluate projects.

The weighted average cost of capital (WACC) for a firm is a weighted average of the current costs of the different types of financing that a firm has used to finance the purchase of its assets. When the WACC is calculated, the cost of each type of financing is weighted according to the fraction of the total firm value represented by that type of financing. The WACC is often used as a discount rate in evaluating projects because it is not possible to directly estimate the appropriate discount rate for many projects. As we also discuss in Section 13.4, having a single discount rate reduces inconsistencies that can arise when different analysts in the firm use different methods to estimate the discount rate and can also limit the ability of analysts to manipulate discount rates to favor pet projects.

2 Calculate the cost of debt for a firm.

The cost of debt can be calculated by solving for the yield to maturity of the debt using the bond pricing model (Equation 8.1), computing the effective annual yield, and adjusting for taxes using Equation 13.3.

3 Calculate the cost of common stock and the cost of preferred stock for a firm.

The cost of common stock can be estimated using the CAPM, the constant-growth dividend model, or a multistage-growth dividend model. The cost of preferred stock can be calculated using the perpetuity model for the present value of cash flows.

4 Calculate the weighted average cost of capital for a firm, explain the limitations of using a firm's weighted average cost of capital as the discount rate when evaluating a project, and discuss the alternatives to the firm's weighted average cost of capital.

The weighted average cost of capital is estimated using either Equation 13.2 or Equation 13.7, with the cost of each individual type of financing estimated using the appropriate method.

When a firm uses a single rate to discount the cash flows for all of its projects, some project cash flows will be discounted using a rate that is too high and other project cash flows will be discounted using a rate that is too low. This can result in the firm rejecting some positive NPV projects and accepting some negative NPV projects. It will bias the firm toward accepting more risky projects and can cause the firm to create less value for stockholders than it would have if the appropriate discount rates had been used.

One alternative to using the WACC as a discount rate is to identify a firm that engages in business activities that are similar to those associated with the project under consideration and that has publicly traded stock. The returns from this pure-play comparable firm's stock can then be used to estimate the common stock beta for the project. In instances where pure-play comparable firms are not available, another alternative is for the financial manager to classify projects according to their systematic risks and use a different discount rate for each class of project. This is the type of classification scheme illustrated in Exhibit 13.4.

Summary of Key Equations

Equation	Description	Formula
13.1	Finance balance sheet identity	MV of assets = MV of liabilities + MV of equity
13.2	General formula for weighted average cost of capital (WACC) for a firm	$k_{\text{Firm}} = \sum_{i=1}^{n} x_i k_i = x_1k_1 + x_2k_2 + x_3k_3 + \cdots + x_nk_n$
13.3	After-tax cost of debt	$k_{\text{Debt after-tax}} = k_{\text{Debt pretax}} \times (1 - t)$
13.4	CAPM formula for the cost of common stock	$k_{\text{cs}} = \text{R}_{\text{rf}} + (\beta_{\text{cs}} \times \text{Market risk premium})$
13.5	Constant-growth dividend formula for the cost of common stock	$k_{\text{cs}} = \frac{\text{D}_1}{\text{P}_0} + g$
13.6	Perpetuity formula for the cost of preferred stock	$k_{\text{ps}} = \frac{\text{D}_{\text{ps}}}{\text{P}_{\text{ps}}}$
13.7	Traditional WACC formula	$\text{WACC} = x_{\text{Debt}}k_{\text{Debt pretax}}(1 - t) + x_{\text{ps}}k_{\text{ps}} + x_{\text{cs}}k_{\text{cs}}$

Self-Study Problems

13.1 The market value of a firm's assets is $3 billion. If the market value of the firm's liabilities is $2 billion, what is the market value of the stockholders' investment and why?

13.2 Berron Comics, Inc., has borrowed $100 million and is required to pay its lenders $8 million in interest this year. If Berron is in the 35 percent marginal tax bracket, then what is the after-tax cost of debt (in dollars as well as in annual interest percentage) to Berron?

13.3 Explain why the after-tax cost of equity (common or preferred) does not have to be adjusted by the marginal income tax rate for the firm.

13.4 Mike's T-Shirts, Inc., has debt claims of $400 (market value) and equity claims of $600 (market value). If the after-tax cost of debt financing is 11 percent and the cost of equity is 17 percent, what is Mike's weighted average cost of capital?

13.5 You are analyzing a firm that is financed with 60 percent debt and 40 percent equity. The current cost of debt financing is 10 percent, but due to a recent downgrade by the rating agencies, the firm's cost of debt is expected to increase to 12 percent immediately. How will this increase change the firm's weighted average cost of capital if you ignore taxes? If you consider taxes and the firm is subject to a 40 percent marginal tax rate?

Solutions to Self-Study Problems

13.1 Since the identity that Value of assets = Value of liabilities + Value of equity holds for market values as well as book values, we know that the market value of the firm's equity is $3 billion − $2 billion = $1 billion.

13.2 Because Berron enjoys a tax deduction for its interest charges, the after-tax interest expense for Berron is $8 million × (1 − 0.35) = $5.2 million, which translates into an annual after-tax interest percentage of $5.2/$100 = 0.052, or 5.2 percent.

13.3 The U.S. tax code allows a deduction for interest expense incurred on borrowing. Preferred and common shares are not considered debt and, thus, do not benefit from an interest deduction. As a result, there is no distinction between the before-tax and after-tax cost of equity capital.

13.4 Mike's T-Shirts' total firm value = $400 + $600 = $1,000. Therefore,

Debt = 40% of financing

Equity = 60% of financing

$$\text{WACC} = x_{\text{Debt}}k_{\text{Debt}}(1 - t) + x_{\text{ps}}k_{\text{ps}} + x_{\text{cs}}k_{\text{cs}}$$

$$\text{WACC} = (0.4 \times 0.11) + (0.6 \times 0.17) = 0.146, \text{ or } 14.6\%$$

13.5 The pretax debt contribution to the cost of capital is $x_{\text{Debt}} \times k_{\text{Debt}}$, and since the firm's pretax cost of debt is expected to increase by 2 percent, we know that the effect on WACC (pretax) will be 0.6 × 0.02 = 0.012, or 1.2 percent. If we assume that the firm is subject to the 40 percent marginal tax rate, then the after-tax increase in the cost of capital for the firm would be 0.012 × (1 − 0.4) = 0.0072, or 0.72 percent.

WileyPLUS

Questions and Problems, Solution Walkthrough Videos, Learning by Doing Tutorials, and additional study tools and resources are available in WileyPLUS.

Discussion Questions

13.1 Explain why the required rate of return on a firm's assets must be equal to the weighted average cost of capital associated with its liabilities and equity.

13.2 Which is easier to calculate directly, the expected rate of return on the assets of a firm or the expected rate of return on the firm's debt and equity? Assume that you are an outsider to the firm.

13.3 With respect to the level of risk and the required return for a firm's portfolio of projects, discuss how the market and a firm's management can have inconsistent information and expectations.

13.4 Your friend has recently told you that the federal government effectively subsidizes the use of debt financing (vs. equity financing) for corporations. Do you agree with that statement? Explain.

13.5 Your firm will have a fixed interest expense for the next 10 years. You recently found out that the marginal income tax rate for the firm will change from 30 percent to 40 percent next year. Describe how the change will affect the cash flow available to investors.

13.6 Describe why it is not usually appropriate to use the coupon rate on a firm's bonds to estimate the pretax cost of debt for the firm.

13.7 Maltese Falcone, Inc., has not checked its weighted average cost of capital for four years. Firm management claims that since Maltese has not had to raise capital for new projects in four years, they should not have to worry about their current weighted average cost of capital. They argue that they have essentially locked in their cost of capital. Critique management's statements.

13.8 Ten years ago, the Edson Water Company issued preferred stock at a price equal to the par value of $100. If the dividend yield on that issue was 12 percent, explain why the firm's current cost of preferred capital is not likely to equal 12 percent.

13.9 Discuss under what circumstances you might be able to use a model that assumes constant growth in dividends to calculate the current cost of equity capital for a firm.

13.10 Your boss just finished computing your firm's weighted average cost of capital. He is relieved because he says that he can now use that cost of capital to evaluate all projects that the firm is considering for the next four years. Evaluate that statement.

Questions and Problems

Excel *Excel templates and resources available in* **WileyPLUS**

Basic

13.1 **Finance balance sheet:** KneeMan Markup Company has total debt obligations with book and market values equal to $30 million and $28 million, respectively. It also has total equity with book and market values equal to $20 million and $70 million, respectively. If you were going to buy all of the assets of KneeMan Markup today, how much should you be willing to pay?

13.2 **WACC:** What is the weighted average cost of capital for a firm?

13.3 **Taxes and the cost of debt:** How are taxes accounted for when we calculate the cost of debt?

13.4 **Cost of common stock:** List and describe each of the three methods used to calculate the cost of common stock.

13.5 **Cost of common stock:** Whitewall Tire Co. just paid an annual dividend of $1.60 on its common shares. If Whitewall is expected to increase its annual dividend by 2 percent per year into the foreseeable future and the current price of Whitewall's common shares is $11.66, what is the cost of common stock for Whitewall?

13.6 **Cost of common stock:** Seerex Wok Co. is expected to pay a dividend of $1.10 one year from today on its common shares. That dividend is expected to increase by 5 percent every year thereafter. If the price of Seerex common stock is $13.75, what is the cost of its common equity capital?

13.7 **Cost of common stock:** Two-Stage Rocket paid an annual dividend of $1.25 yesterday, and it is commonly known that the firm's management expects to increase its dividend by 8 percent for the next two years and by 2 percent thereafter. If the current price of Two-Stage's common stock is $17.80, what is the cost of common equity capital for the firm?

13.8 **Cost of preferred stock:** Fjord Luxury Liners has preferred shares outstanding that pay an annual dividend equal to $15 per year. If the current price of Fjord preferred shares is $107.14, what is the after-tax cost of preferred stock for Fjord?

13.9 **Cost of preferred stock:** Kresler Autos has preferred shares outstanding that pay annual dividends of $12, and the current price of the shares is $80. What is the after-tax cost of new preferred shares for Kresler if the flotation (issuance) costs for preferred shares are 5 percent?

13.10 **WACC:** Describe the alternatives to using a firm's WACC as a discount rate when evaluating a project.

13.11 **WACC:** Capital Co. has a capital structure, based on current market values, that consists of 50 percent debt, 10 percent preferred stock, and 40 percent common stock. If the returns required by investors are 8 percent, 10 percent, and 15 percent for the debt, preferred stock, and common stock, respectively, what is Capital's after-tax WACC? Assume that the firm's marginal tax rate is 40 percent.

13.12 **WACC:** What are direct out-of-pocket costs?

Intermediate

13.13 **Finance balance sheet:** Explain why the total value of all of the securities used to finance a firm must be equal to the value of the firm.

13.14 **Finance balance sheet:** Explain why the cost of capital for a firm is equal to the expected rate of return to the investors in the firm.

13.15 **Current cost of a bond:** You know that the after-tax cost of debt capital for Bubbles Champagne Company is 7 percent. If the firm has only one issue of five-year bonds outstanding, what is the current price of the bonds if the coupon rate on those bonds is 10 percent? Assume the bonds make semiannual coupon payments and the marginal tax rate is 30 percent.

13.16 **Current cost of a bond:** Perpetual Ltd. has issued bonds that never require the principal amount to be repaid to investors. Correspondingly, Perpetual must make interest payments into the infinite future. If the bondholders receive annual payments of $75 and the current price of the bonds is $882.35, what is the after-tax cost of this debt for Perpetual if the firm is subject to a 40 percent marginal tax rate?

13.17 **Current cost of a bond:** You are analyzing the cost of debt for a firm. You know that the firm's 14-year maturity, 8.5 percent coupon bonds are selling at a price of $823.48. The bonds pay interest semiannually. If these bonds are the only debt outstanding, what is the after-tax cost of debt for this firm if it is subject to 30 percent marginal and average tax rates?

13.18 **Taxes and the cost of debt:** Holding all other things constant, does a decrease in the marginal tax rate for a firm provide incentive for the managers of a firm to increase or decrease its use of debt?

13.19 **Cost of debt for a firm:** You are analyzing the after-tax cost of debt for a firm. You know that the firm's 12-year maturity, 9.5 percent semiannual coupon bonds are selling at a price of \$1,200. If these bonds are the only debt outstanding for the firm, what is the after-tax cost of debt for this firm if it has a marginal tax rate of 34 percent? What if the bonds are selling at par?

13.20 **Cost of common stock:** Underestimated Inc.'s common shares currently sell for \$36 each. The firm's management believes that its shares should really sell for \$54 each. If the firm just paid an annual dividend of \$2 per share and management expects those dividends to increase by 8 percent per year forever (and this is common knowledge to the market), what is the current cost of common equity for the firm and what does management believe is the correct cost of common equity for the firm?

13.21 **Cost of common stock:** Write out the general equation for the price of the stock for a firm that will grow dividends very rapidly at a constant rate for the four years after the next dividend is paid and will grow dividends thereafter at a constant, but lower rate. Discuss the problems in estimating the cost of equity capital for such a stock.

13.22 **Cost of common stock:** You have calculated the cost of common stock using all three methods described in this chapter. Unfortunately, all three methods have yielded different answers. Describe which answer (if any) is most appropriate.

13.23 **WACC:** The managers of a firm financed entirely with common stock are evaluating two distinct projects. The first project has a large amount of unsystematic risk and a small amount of systematic risk. The second project has a small amount of unsystematic risk and a large amount of systematic risk. Which project, if taken, is more likely to increase the firm's cost of capital?

13.24 **WACC:** The Imaginary Products Co. currently has debt with a market value of \$300 million outstanding. The debt consists of 9 percent coupon bonds (semiannual coupon payments) that have a maturity of 15 years and are currently priced at \$1,440.03 per bond. The firm also has an issue of 2 million preferred shares outstanding with a market price of \$12.00 per share. The preferred shares pay an annual dividend of \$1.20. Imaginary also has 14 million shares of common stock outstanding with a price of \$20.00 per share. The firm is expected to pay a \$2.20 common dividend one year from today, and that dividend is expected to increase by 5 percent per year forever. If Imaginary is subject to a 40 percent marginal tax rate, then what is the firm's weighted average cost of capital?

13.25 **Choosing a discount rate:** For the Imaginary Products firm in Problem 13.24, calculate the appropriate cost of capital for a new project that is financed with the same proportion of debt, preferred shares, and common shares as the firm's current capital structure. Also assume that the project has the same degree of systematic risk as the average project that the firm is currently undertaking (the project is also in the same general industry as the firm's current line of business).

13.26 **Choosing a discount rate:** If a firm's management anticipates financing a project with a capital mix that is different from its current capital structure, describe how the firm is subjecting itself to a calculation error if its historical WACC is used to evaluate the project.

Advanced

13.27 You are analyzing the cost of capital for MacroSwift Corporation, which develops software operating systems for computers. The firm's dividend growth rate has been a very constant 3 percent per year for the past 15 years. Competition for the firm's current products is expected to develop in the next year, and MacroSwift is currently expanding its revenue stream into the multimedia industry. Evaluate the appropriateness of continuing to use a 3 percent growth rate in dividends for MacroSwift in your cost of capital model.

13.28 You are an external financial analyst evaluating the merits of a stock. Since you are using a dividend discount model approach to evaluate a cost of equity capital, you need to estimate the dividend growth rate for the firm in the future. Describe how you might go about doing this.

13.29 You know that the return of Momentum Cyclicals common shares is 1.6 times as sensitive to macroeconomic information as the return of the market. If the risk-free rate of return is 2.88 percent and market risk premium is 5.92 percent, what is Momentum Cyclicals' cost of common equity capital?

13.30 In your analysis of the cost of capital for a common stock, you calculate a cost of capital using a dividend discount model that is much lower than the calculation for the cost of capital using the CAPM model. Explain a possible source for the discrepancy.

13.31 RetRyder Hand Trucks has a preferred share issue outstanding that pays a dividend of \$1.30 per year. The current cost of preferred equity for RetRyder is 9 percent. If RetRyder issues additional preferred shares that pay exactly the same dividend and the investment banker retains 8 percent of the sale price, what is the cost of the new preferred shares for RetRyder?

13.32 Enigma Corporation's management believes that the firm's cost of capital (WACC) is too high because the firm has been too secretive with the market concerning its operations. Evaluate that statement.

13.33 Discuss what valuable information would be lost if you decided to use book values in order to calculate the cost of each of the capital components within a firm's capital structure.

13.34 Hurricane Corporation is financed with debt, preferred equity, and common equity with market values of \$20 million, \$10 million, and \$30 million, respectively. The betas for the debt, preferred stock, and common stock are 0.2, 0.5, and 1.1, respectively. If the risk-free rate is 2.88 percent, the market risk premium is 5.92 percent, and Hurricane's average and marginal tax rates are both 30 percent, what is the company's weighted average cost of capital?

13.35 You are working as an intern at Coral Gables Products, a privately owned manufacturing company. Shortly after you read Chapter 13 in this book, you got into a discussion with the chief financial officer (CFO) at Coral Gables about weighted average cost of capital calculations. She pointed out that, just as the beta of the assets of a firm equals a weighted average of the betas for the individual assets, as shown in Equation 7.13:

$$\beta_{n \text{ Asset portfolio}} = \sum_{i=1}^{n} x_i\beta_i = x_1\beta_1 + x_2\beta_2 + x_3\beta_3 + \cdots + x_n\beta_n$$

the beta of the assets of a firm also equals a weighted average of the betas for the debt, preferred stock, and common stock of a firm:

$$\beta_{n \text{ Asset portfolio}} = \sum_{i=1}^{n} x_i\beta_i = x_{\text{Debt}}\beta_{\text{Debt}} + x_{\text{ps}}\beta_{\text{ps}} + x_{\text{cs}}\beta_{\text{cs}}$$

Why must this be true?

13.36 The CFO described in Problem 13.35 asks you to estimate the beta for Coral Gables' common stock. Since the common stock is not publicly traded, you do not have the data necessary to estimate the beta using regression analysis. However, you have found a company with publicly traded stock that has operations exactly like those at Coral Gables. Using stock returns for this pure-play comparable firm, you estimate the beta for the comparable company's stock to be 1.06. The market value of that company's common equity is $45 million, and it has one debt issue outstanding with a market value of $15 million and an annual pretax cost of 4.85 percent. The comparable company has no preferred stock.

a. If the risk-free rate is 2.88 percent and the market risk premium is 5.92 percent, what is the beta of the assets of the comparable company?

b. If the total market value of Coral Gables' financing consists of 35 percent debt and 65 percent equity (this is what the CFO estimates the market values to be) and the pretax cost of its debt is 5.45 percent, what is the beta for Coral Gables' common stock?

13.37 Estimate the weighted average cost of capital for Coral Gables using your estimated beta and the information in the problem statement in Problem 13.36. Assume that the average and marginal tax rates for Coral Gables are both 25 percent.

CFA Problems

13.38 The cost of equity is equal to the:

a. Expected market return.

b. Rate of return required by stockholders.

c. Cost of retained earnings plus dividends.

d. Risk the company incurs when financing.

13.39 Dot.Com has determined that it could issue $1,000 face value bonds with an 8 percent coupon paid semiannually and a five-year maturity at $900 per bond. If Dot.Com's marginal tax rate is 38 percent, its after-tax cost of debt is closest to:

a. 6.2 percent. **c.** 6.6 percent.

b. 6.4 percent. **d.** 6.8 percent.

13.40 Morgan Insurance Ltd. issued a fixed-rate perpetual preferred stock three years ago and placed it privately with institutional investors. The stock was issued at $25.00 per share with a $1.75 dividend. If the company were to issue preferred stock today, the yield would be 6.5 percent. The stock's current value is:

a. $25.00. **c.** $37.31.

b. $26.92. **d.** $40.18.

13.41 The Gearing Company has an after-tax cost of debt capital of 4 percent, a cost of preferred stock of 8 percent, a cost of equity capital of 10 percent, and a weighted average cost of capital of 7 percent. Gearing intends to maintain its current capital structure as it raises additional capital. In making its capital-budgeting decisions for the average-risk project, the relevant cost of capital is:

a. 4 percent. **c.** 8 percent.

b. 7 percent. **d.** 10 percent.

13.42 Suppose the cost of capital of the Gadget Company is 10 percent. If Gadget has a capital structure that is 50 percent debt and 50 percent equity, its before-tax cost of debt is 5 percent, and its marginal tax rate is 20 percent, then its cost of equity capital is closest to:

a. 10 percent. **c.** 14 percent.

b. 12 percent. **d.** 16 percent.

Sample Test Problems

13.1 Howard Power and Telecommunications Corporation has three divisions. The names of these divisions, along with the after-tax cost of capital for each division and the market value of the assets in each division, are as follows:

Division Name	Cost of Capital	MV of Assets
Infrastructure development	8.75	$250,000,000
Power	7.50	$325,000,000
Telecommunications	8.25	$675,000,000

What is the overall after-tax cost of capital for Howard Power and Telecommunications?

13.2 Quarri Industries has 8 percent coupon bonds outstanding. These bonds have a market price of $954.41, pay interest semiannually, and will mature in six years. If the tax rate is 35 percent, what are the pretax cost and after-tax cost of this debt?

13.3 Quarri Industries common stock has a beta of 1.6. If the market risk-free rate is 4 percent and the expected return on the market is 9 percent, what is Quarri's cost of common stock?

13.4 Miron's Copper Corp. management expects its common stock dividends to grow 1.5 percent per year for the indefinite future. The firm's shares are currently selling for $18.45, and the firm just paid a dividend of $3.00 yesterday. What is the cost of common stock for Miron?

13.5 Use the information in Questions 13.2 and 13.3 as well as the following information to compute the WACC for Quarri Industries. In addition to common stock, Quarri has 500,000 preferred shares outstanding that pay a quarterly dividend of $0.50 per share and are currently trading for $20.00 a share. The company's outstanding bonds have a face value of $209,553,546. There are 2 million shares of common stock outstanding with a current market price of $98.00 per share.

13.6 Staunton Energy Corporation managers are considering a capital budgeting project to replace some machinery used in one of the company's oil refineries. Is the company's WACC the appropriate discount rate to use in the NPV analysis of this project? Explain.

CHAPTER 14

Working Capital Management

Thomas Trutschel/Photothek/Getty Images

LEARNING OBJECTIVES

1. Define net working capital, discuss the importance of working capital management, and compute a firm's net working capital.
2. Define the operating and cash conversion cycles, explain how they are used, and compute their values for a firm.
3. Discuss the relative advantages and disadvantages of pursuing (1) flexible and (2) restrictive current asset management strategies.
4. Explain how accounts receivable are created and managed, and compute the cost of trade credit.
5. Explain the trade-off between carrying costs and reorder costs, and compute the economic order quantity for a firm's inventory orders.
6. Define cash collection time, discuss how a firm can minimize this time, and compute the economic costs and benefits of a lockbox.
7. Describe three current asset financing strategies and discuss the main sources of short-term financing.

Since its founding in 1976 by partners Steve Jobs, Ronald Wayne, and Steve Wozniak, Apple Inc. has been a cutting-edge retailer of consumer electronics and computing software. With hardware products that include the Mac line of computers, Beats headphones, the iPhone and iPad tablet, and online retail businesses including iTunes and Apple music, Apple Inc. has grown to become the largest publicly traded corporation in the world with a market capitalization of approximately $635 billion in January 2017.

Although much of Apple's success can be attributed to its innovative designs and strong worldwide demand for its products, the firm's sophisticated approach to managing supply chain and hardware production is seen by many analysts and investors as a critical component of the firm's success. Apple's focus on managing these aspects of its operations is driven by former chief operating officer, and current chief executive officer, Tim Cook, who has often publicly related the mantra that "Inventory is evil" because of its high cost and rapid depreciation.

Mr. Cook shut down the company's manufacturing businesses, opting instead to work with contract manufacturers around the world who build to order with customer demand. This in turn reduces Apple's need to stock inventories of components and finished hardware, allowing the firm to virtually eliminate its warehouses while keeping only a limited number of products on hand in its Apple retail stores. Apple continues to streamline its production and inventory practices. When a consumer places a hardware order online today, assembly and shipping typically originate directly from a manufacturing facility in China. This allows Apple to minimize inventory in its supply chain.

The focus of this chapter is on working capital management—which deals with the management of current assets, including cash, accounts receivable, and inventory—and how these assets are financed. In managing its working capital, Apple has concentrated on its inventory policies because inventory can comprise a significant portion of a firm's balance sheet and can be subject to periodic write-downs. As we will discuss, Apple is an industry leader in working capital management efficiency, and its working capital management policies contribute significantly to the returns it earns on the capital invested in its businesses.

Chapter Preview

The previous chapters dealt with long-term investment decisions and their impact on firm value. These capital investment decisions typically commit a firm to a course of action for a number of years and are difficult to reverse. In contrast, this chapter focuses on short-term activities that involve cash inflows and outflows that occur within a year or less. Examples include purchasing and paying for raw materials, managing the firm's investment in finished inventory, and collecting cash for sales made on credit. These types of activities comprise what is known as *working capital management*.

The term *working capital* refers to the short-term assets necessary to run a business on a day-to-day basis. These assets include cash, accounts receivable, and inventory and are typically funded by short-term liabilities such as accounts payable. Because of the short-term nature of these assets and liabilities, decisions involving them are more flexible and easily reversed than capital investment decisions. The greater flexibility associated with working capital management does not mean that these activities are not important, however. The management of short-term assets and liabilities can have a significant impact on the cash flow available to a firm's investors. In extreme cases, poor working capital management can result in severe financial consequences, including bankruptcy.

We begin the chapter by reviewing some basic definitions and concepts. Next, we examine the individual working capital accounts and discuss how to determine and analyze the operating and cash conversion cycles. Then we explain how to manage the different working capital accounts: the cash account, accounts receivable, and inventory. We finish by considering alternative means of financing short-term assets and the risks associated with each.

14.1 Working Capital Basics

LEARNING OBJECTIVE

1. Define net working capital, discuss the importance of working capital management, and compute a firm's net working capital.

Weblink

A video discussion of the importance of working capital management can be found at http://www.youtube.com/watch?v=bHK77lbdyWA.

Working capital management involves two fundamental questions: (1) What is the appropriate amount and mix of short-term assets for the firm to hold? (2) How should these short-term assets be financed? Firms must carry a certain amount of short-term assets to be able to operate smoothly. For example, without sufficient cash on hand, a company facing an unexpected expense might not be able to pay its bills on time. Without an inventory of raw materials, production might be subject to costly interruptions or shutdowns. Without an inventory of finished goods, sales might be lost because a product is out of stock.

To provide a background for the discussion of working capital management, we first briefly review some important terminology and ideas. Throughout the chapter, we use

EXHIBIT 14.1 **Apple Inc. Financial Statements, Fiscal Year Ended September 24, 2016 ($ millions)**

This exhibit shows the balance sheet and income statement for Apple Inc. for the fiscal year ended September 24, 2016. We use this information in illustrating various elements of working capital management.

Balance Sheet as of September 24, 2016				Income Statement for the fiscal year ended September 24, 2016	
Assets		**Liabilities and equity**			
Cash	$ 20,484	Accounts payable	$ 37,294	Net sales	$215,639
Short-term investments	46,671	Deferred revenue	8,080	Cost of goods sold	131,376
Accounts receivable	15,754	Accrued expenses	22,027	Operating expenses	24,239
Inventory	2,132	Other current liabilites	11,605	Earnings before	
Other current assets	21,828	Total current liabilities	$ 79,006	interest and taxes (EBIT)	$ 60,024
Total current assets	$106,869	Long-term debt	75,427	Interest and other income	1,348
Property, plant, and equipment	61,245	Other noncurrent liabilities	39,004	Earnings before taxes (EBT)	$ 61,372
Less: Accum. depreciation	34,235	Total liabilities	$193,437	Taxes	15,685
Net plant and equipment	27,010	Preferred stock	0	Net income	$ 45,687
Investments	170,430	Common stock	31,251		
Other noncurrent assets	17,377	Retained earnings	96,364	Common stock dividend	$ 12,188
Total Assets	$321,686	Other stockholder equity	634	Stock repurchases	29,000
		Less: Treasury stock	0	Addition to retained earnings	$ 4,080
		Total common equity	$128,249		
		Total liabilities and stockholder's equity	$321,686		

financial statements and supporting data from Apple Inc. to illustrate our discussions. Exhibit 14.1 presents Apple's balance sheet and income statement for the fiscal year that ended September 24, 2016.

Working Capital Terms and Concepts

In earlier chapters, we discussed the basic terms associated with working capital management. Here, we provide a brief review:

1. *Current assets* are cash and other assets that the firm expects to convert into cash in a year or less. These assets are usually listed on the balance sheet in order of their liquidity. Typical current assets include cash, short-term investments (sometimes also called marketable securities or cash equivalents because of their liquidity), accounts receivable, inventory, and others, such as prepaid expenses. At the end of its 2016 fiscal year, Apple's total current assets were $106,869 million.
2. *Current liabilities* (or short-term liabilities) are obligations that the firm expects to repay in a year or less. They may be interest bearing, such as short-term notes and current maturities of long-term debt, or noninterest bearing on such as accounts payable, deferred revenue, or accrued expenses. On September 24, 2016, Apple's total current liabilities were $79,006 million.
3. *Working capital* (also called *gross working capital*) includes the funds invested in a company's cash and short-term investment accounts, accounts receivable, inventory, and other current assets. All firms require a certain amount of current assets to operate smoothly and to carry out day-to-day operations. Note that working capital is defined in terms of current assets, so the two terms are one and the same. Thus, Apple's working capital was $106,869 million on September 24, 2016.

4. *Net working capital (NWC)* refers to the difference between current assets and current liabilities.[1]

$$\text{NWC} = \text{Total current assets} - \text{Total current liabilities}$$

NWC is important because it is a measure of a firm's liquidity. It is a measure of liquidity because it is the amount of working capital a firm would have left over after it paid off all of its short-term liabilities. The larger the firm's net working capital, the greater its liquidity. Most firms have more current assets than current liabilities and therefore their net working capital is positive. Apple's net working capital on September 24, 2016, was $27,863 million ($106,869 million – $79,006 million = $27,863 million).

5. *Working capital management* involves management of current assets and their financing. The financial manager's responsibilities include determining the optimum balance for each of the current asset accounts and deciding what mix of short-term debt, long-term debt, and equity to use in financing working capital. Working capital management decisions are usually fast paced as they reflect the pace of the firm's day-to-day operations.

6. *Working capital efficiency* is a term that refers to how efficiently working capital is used. It is most commonly measured by a firm's cash conversion cycle, which reflects the time between the point at which raw materials are paid for and the point at which finished goods made from those materials are converted into cash. The shorter a firm's cash conversion cycle, the more efficient is its use of working capital.

7. *Liquidity* is the ability of a company to convert assets—real or financial—into cash quickly without suffering a financial loss.

Working Capital Accounts and Trade-Offs

Short-term cash inflows and outflows do not always match in their timing or magnitude, creating a need to manage the working capital accounts. The objective of the managers of these accounts is to enable the company to operate effectively with the smallest possible net investment in working capital. To do this managers must make cost/benefit trade-offs. The trade-offs arise because it is easier to run a business with a generous amount of net working capital, but it is also more costly to do so. Let's briefly look at each working capital account to see what the basic trade-offs are. Keep in mind as you read the discussion that working capital assets are costly for the firm to hold because they must be financed by borrowing or selling equity or by using cash from operations that could otherwise be paid out to the firm's investors. The working capital accounts that are the focus of most working capital management activities are as follows:

1. *Cash (including short-term investments):* The more cash a firm has on hand, the more likely it will be able to meet its financial obligations if an unexpected expense occurs or take advantage of an unexpected investment opportunity. If cash balances become too small, the firm runs the risk that it will be unable to pay its bills; and if this condition becomes chronic, creditors could force the firm into bankruptcy. The downside of holding too much cash is that the returns on cash are low even when it is invested in an interest-paying bank account or highly liquid short-term money market instruments, such as U.S. government Treasury securities.

trade credit credit extended by one business to another

consumer credit credit extended by a business to a consumer

2. *Receivables:* The accounts receivable at a firm represent the total unpaid credit that the firm has extended to its customers. Accounts receivable can include **trade credit** (credit extended to another business) or **consumer credit** (credit extended to a consumer), or both. Businesses provide trade and consumer credit because doing so increases sales and

[1]Note that this is just Equation 3.2. For comparison, also note that the *incremental additions to working capital* (Add WC) in Equations 11.2 and 11.4 is a measure of the additional NWC that will be required to fund a project. Equation 11.4 does not include prepaid or accrued expenses because analysts do not typically forecast these items when they estimate Add WC. Prepaid and accrued expenses tend to be difficult to forecast and, to the extent that they cancel each other out in the calculation, are often quite small. All interest-bearing debt is also excluded from the calculation in Equation 11.4 because these sources of financing are either assumed to be temporary (for short-term notes) or, for current maturities of long-term debt, are assumed to be refinanced with new long-term debt and are therefore accounted for in the WACC calculation discussed in Chapter 13.

because it is often a competitive necessity to match the credit terms offered by competitors. The downside to granting such credit is that it is expensive to evaluate customers' credit applications to ensure that they are creditworthy and then to monitor their ongoing credit performance. Firms that are not diligent in managing their credit operations can suffer large losses from bad debts, especially during a recession when customers may have trouble paying their bills.

3. *Inventory:* Customers want firms to maintain large finished goods inventories because when they go to make a purchase, the item they want will likely be in stock. Similarly, large raw material inventories reduce the chance that the firm will not have access to raw materials when they are needed, which can cause costly interruptions in the manufacturing process. At the same time, large inventories are expensive to finance, can require warehouses that are expensive to build and maintain, must be protected against breakage and theft, and run a greater risk of obsolescence.
4. *Payables:* Accounts payable are trade credits provided to firms by their suppliers. Because suppliers typically grant a grace period before payables must be repaid, and firms do not have to pay interest during this period, trade credit is an attractive source of financing. For this reason, financial managers do not hurry to pay their suppliers when bills arrive. Of course, suppliers recognize that they provide attractive financing to their customers and that trade credit is expensive for them. Consequently, suppliers tend to provide strong incentives (either by providing discounts for paying on time or charging penalties for late payment) for firms to pay on time. As you might expect, firms typically wait until near the end of the grace period to repay trade credit. The financial manager at a firm that is having serious financial problems may have no choice but to delay paying its suppliers. However, besides incurring monetary penalties, a manager who is consistently late in making payments runs the risk that the supplier will no longer sell to his or her firm on credit.

When the financial manager makes a decision to increase working capital, good things are likely to happen to the firm—sales should increase, relationships with vendors and suppliers should improve, and work or manufacturing stoppages should be less likely. Unfortunately, the extra working capital costs money, and there is no simple algorithm or formula that determines the optimal level of working capital the firm should hold. The choice depends on management's strategic preferences, its willingness to bear risk, and the firm's line of business.

Before You Go On

1. How do you calculate net working capital, and why is it important?
2. What are some of the trade-offs required in the management of working capital accounts?

14.2 The Operating and Cash Conversion Cycles

LEARNING OBJECTIVE

2. Define the operating and cash conversion cycles, explain how they are used, and compute their values for a firm.

A very important concept in working capital management is known as the **cash conversion cycle**. This is the length of time from the point at which a company actually pays for raw materials until the point at which it receives cash from the sale of finished goods made from those materials. This is an important concept because the length of the cash conversion cycle is directly related to the amount of money that a firm needs to finance its working capital.

cash conversion cycle the length of time from the point at which a company pays for raw materials until the point at which it receives cash from the sale of finished goods made from those materials

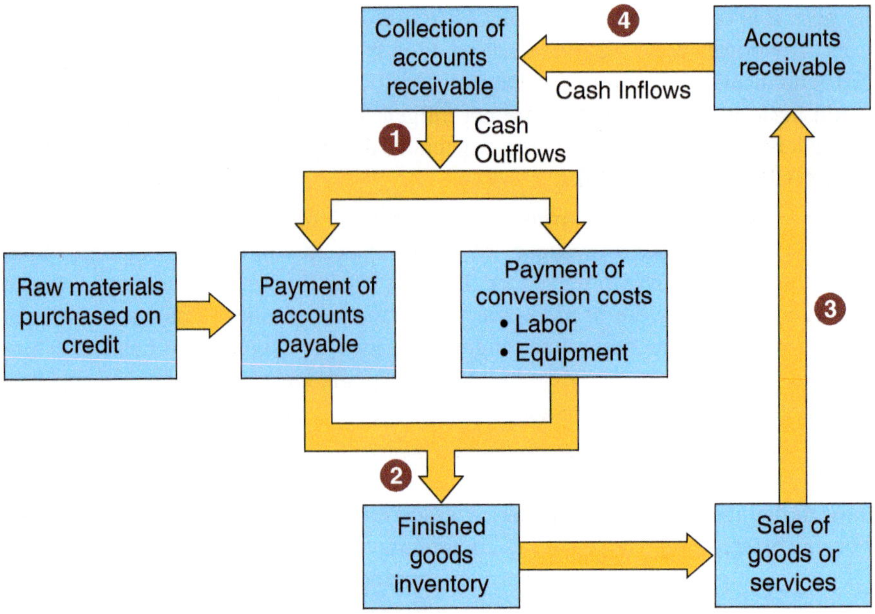

EXHIBIT 14.2 The Cash Conversion Cycle

A typical cash conversion cycle begins with cash outflows for raw materials and conversion costs and goes through several stages before these resources are turned back into cash. The cash conversion cycle reflects the average time from the point that cash is used to pay for raw materials until cash is collected on the accounts receivable associated with the product produced with those raw materials. One of the main goals of a financial manager is to optimize the time between the cash outflows and the cash inflows.

The sequence of events that occurs from the point in time that a firm actually pays for its raw materials to the point that it receives cash from the sale of finished goods is as follows: (1) the firm uses cash to pay for raw materials and the cost of converting them into finished goods (conversion costs), (2) finished goods are held in finished goods inventory until they are sold, (3) finished goods are sold on credit to the firm's customers, and finally, (4) customers repay the credit the firm has extended them and the firm receives the cash. The cash is then reinvested in raw materials and conversion costs, and the cycle is repeated. **Exhibit 14.2** shows a schematic diagram of the cash conversion cycle.

Financial managers generally want to achieve several goals in managing this cycle:

- Delay paying accounts payable as long as possible without suffering any penalties.
- Maintain the minimum level of raw material inventories necessary to support production without causing manufacturing delays.
- Use as little labor and other inputs to the production process as possible while maintaining product quality.
- Maintain the level of finished goods inventory that represents the best trade-off between minimizing the amount of capital invested in finished goods inventory and the desire to avoid lost sales.
- Offer customers terms on trade credit that are sufficiently attractive to support sales and yet minimize the cost of this credit, both the financing cost and the risk of nonpayment.
- Collect cash payments on accounts receivable as quickly as possible to close the loop.

All of these goals have implications for the firm's efficiency and liquidity. It is the financial manager's responsibility to ensure that he or she makes decisions that maximize the value of the firm. Managing the length of the cash conversion cycle is one aspect of managing working capital to maximize the value of the firm.[2] Next, we discuss two simple tools to measure working capital efficiency. As you read the discussion, refer to **Exhibit 14.3**.

[2]It is not usually in the best interest of the firm's stockholders for managers to simply minimize the cash conversion cycle. If it were, firms would stretch out repayment of their payables and not give credit to customers. Of course, this would upset suppliers, cause the firm to incur late-payment penalties, and result in lost sales.

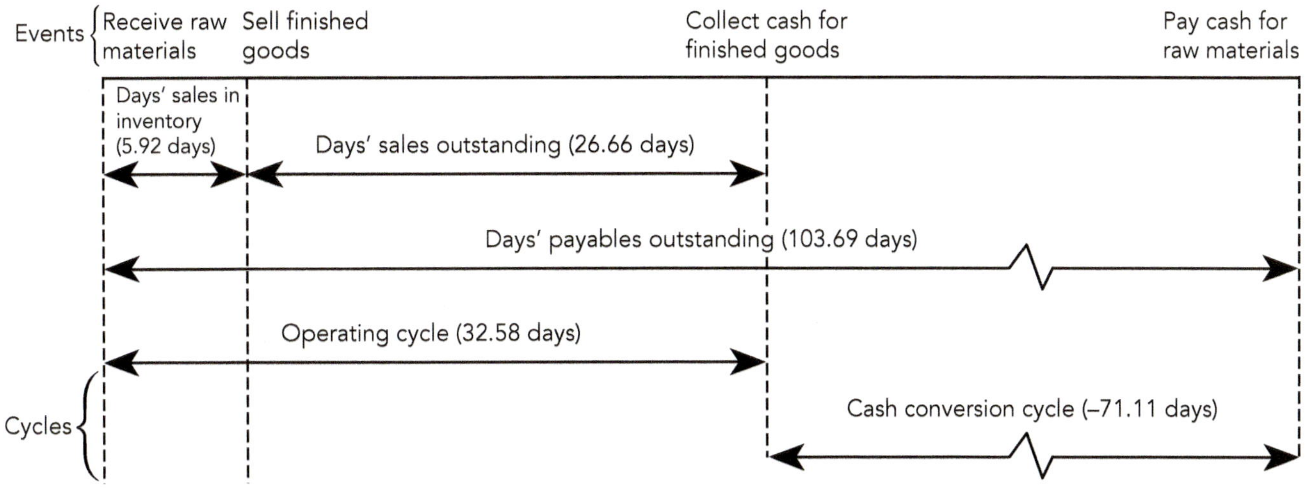

EXHIBIT 14.3 **Time Line for Operating and Cash Conversion Cycles for Apple Inc. in 2016**

The exhibit shows the cash inflows and outflows and other key events in a firm's operating cycle and cash conversion cycle, along with computed values for Apple. Both of these cycles are used for measuring working capital efficiency.

Operating Cycle

The **operating cycle** starts with the receipt of raw materials and ends with the collection of cash from customers for the sale of finished goods made from those materials. The operating cycle can be described in terms of two components: days' sales in inventory and days' sales outstanding. The formulas for these efficiency ratios were developed in Chapter 4. Apple's ratios and the average industry ratios are shown in **Exhibit 14.4**.

operating cycle the average time between receipt of raw materials and receipt of cash for the sale of finished goods made from those materials

Days' sales in inventory (DSI) shows, on average, how long a firm holds inventory before selling it. Recall from Chapter 4 that it is calculated by dividing 365 days by the firm's inventory turnover and that inventory turnover equals cost of goods sold (COGS) divided by inventory. Equation 4.4 and the formula for DSI, along with a calculation for Apple in 2016, are as follows:

$$\begin{aligned}\text{Days' sales in inventory} = \text{DSI} &= \frac{365 \text{ days}}{\text{Inventory turnover}}\\ &= \frac{365 \text{ days}}{\text{COGS/Inventory}}\\ &= \frac{365 \text{ days}}{\$131{,}376/\$2{,}132}\\ &= 5.92 \text{ days}\end{aligned}$$

EXHIBIT 14.4 **Selected Financial Ratios for Apple Inc. and the Computer Industry in 2016**

When we compare working capital ratios for Apple with average ratios for the computer industry, we see that Apple is outperforming its peers on all metrics. Apple holds less inventory, collects on its outstanding balances more quickly than competitors, and is able to defer its cash payments to suppliers longer than competitors. These three facts combined ensure that Apple's operating and cash conversion cycles are significantly shorter than is the norm in the computer industry. Note that a negative cash conversion cycle of −71.11 days means that Apple collects cash from its customers before it has to pay its suppliers. Thus, Apple's suppliers are financing all of Apple's working capital and then some.

Financial Ratio	Apple	Computer Industry
Days' sales in inventory (DSI)	5.92	54.25
Days' sales outstanding (DSO)	26.66	58.10
Days' payables outstanding (DPO)	103.69	72.41
Operating cycle (days)	32.58	112.35
Cash conversion cycle (days)	−71.11	39.93

As shown in Exhibit 14.4, the computer industry average for days' sales in inventory is 54.25 days, while for Apple it is 5.92 days. Inventory management has long been a critical factor in Apple's success, as discussed in the chapter opener. For the most part, Apple first takes the order from the customer and then routes the order to a contract manufacturer. According to the DSI ratio, it takes Apple a little less than six days to complete this process, whereas the average competitor takes almost eight weeks to complete the same task.

Days' sales outstanding (DSO) indicates how long it takes, on average, for the firm to collect its outstanding accounts receivable. Recall from Chapter 4 that DSO is calculated by dividing 365 days by accounts receivable turnover and that accounts receivable turnover equals net sales divided by accounts receivable. Sometimes this ratio is called the average collection period. An efficient firm with good working capital management should have a low average collection period compared with that of its industry. Equation 4.6, the DSO formula, and the calculation for Apple are as follows:

$$\begin{aligned}\text{Days' sales outstanding} = \text{DSO} &= \frac{365 \text{ days}}{\text{Accounts receivable turnover}}\\ &= \frac{365 \text{ days}}{\text{Net sales/Accounts receivable}}\\ &= \frac{365 \text{ days}}{\$215{,}639/\$15{,}754}\\ &= 26.66 \text{ days}\end{aligned}$$

Again, referring to Exhibit 14.4 we see that the average firm in the computer industry has 58.10 days of sales outstanding, while Apple's figure is 26.66 days. In 2016, Apple was doing a good job of quickly collecting the cash it was owed by its customers. This ratio helps to explain why Apple does not have as much money invested in current assets as some of its competitors do.

We can now calculate the operating cycle simply by summing the days' sales in inventory and the days' sales outstanding.

$$\text{Operating cycle} = \text{DSI} + \text{DSO} \qquad (14.1)$$

Apple's operating cycle for 2016 is 32.58 days (5.92 days + 26.66 days = 32.58 days), and the industry average is 112.35 days (54.25 days + 58.10 days = 112.35 days). Apple manages to complete its operating cycle in less than one third the time it takes the average computer firm, which means Apple has far less invested in working capital.

Cash Conversion Cycle

The cash conversion cycle is related to the operating cycle, but the cash conversion cycle does not begin until the firm actually pays for its raw materials. In other words, the cash conversion cycle is the length of time between the actual cash outflow for materials and the actual cash inflow from sales. To calculate this cycle, we need all of the information used to calculate the operating cycle plus one additional measure: days' payables outstanding.

Days' payables outstanding (DPO) tells us how long, on average, a firm takes to pay its suppliers. Recall that it is calculated by dividing 365 days by accounts payable turnover and that accounts payable turnover equals COGS divided by accounts payable. The DPO formula and the calculation for Apple are:

$$\begin{aligned}\text{Days' payables outstanding} = \text{DPO} &= \frac{365 \text{ days}}{\text{Accounts payable turnover}}\\ &= \frac{365 \text{ days}}{\text{COGS/Accounts payable}}\\ &= \frac{365 \text{ days}}{\$131{,}376/\$37{,}284}\\ &= 103.69 \text{ days}\end{aligned}$$

The industry average DPO is 72.41 days, and the DPO for Apple is 103.69 days. Apple takes an average of just over 30 days longer than its competitors to make payments to its suppliers.

We can now calculate the cash conversion cycle by summing the days' sales in inventory and the days' sales outstanding and subtracting the days' payables outstanding:

$$\text{Cash conversion cycle} = \text{DSI} + \text{DSO} - \text{DPO} \quad (14.2)$$
$$= 5.92 \text{ days} + 26.66 \text{ days} - 103.69 \text{ days}$$
$$= -71.11 \text{ days}$$

Apple's cash conversion cycle is −71.11 days. Another way to calculate the cash conversion cycle is to notice that it is simply the operating cycle minus the days' payables outstanding, as can be seen in Exhibit 14.3:

$$\text{Cash conversion cycle} = \text{Operating cycle} - \text{DPO} \quad (14.3)$$

Thus, Apple's cash conversion cycle for 2016 can be calculated as 32.58 days − 103.69 days = −71.11 days.

A negative cash conversion cycle of −71.11 days means that Apple receives cash from its customers an average of about 71 days before it pays its suppliers. In other words, instead of Apple having to invest in inventories and receivables, its suppliers finance all of these current assets and then some. A direct comparison of the accounts receivable and inventory balances ($15,754 and $2,132, respectively) with the accounts payable balance ($37,294) in Exhibit 14.1 reveals that the financing provided by Apple's suppliers is more than twice the amount the firm has invested in accounts receivable and inventories.

Apple has been able to achieve a negative cash conversion cycle through careful management of its accounts receivable and payable. In addition, the company outsources much of its manufacturing, which reduces its days' sales in inventory to just under six days. We discuss just-in-time inventory systems in more detail later in this chapter.

By now, it should be clear that the computer industry as a whole has a much longer cash conversion cycle than Apple. The industry average is 39.93 days, and Apple's is −71.11 days. While Apple receives financing from its negative cash cycle, the average computer firm has to provide financing for 39.93 days to support its operations. Apple has built its reputation and overall firm strategy on being an efficient quality provider and has historically enjoyed great success. But, Apple is not very representative of the average firm. A more typical manufacturing firm is shown in **Exhibit 14.5** and is the subject of **Learning by Doing Application 14.1**.

EXHIBIT 14.5 Kernel Mills Financial Statements, Fiscal Year Ended December 31, 2017 ($ millions)

The exhibit shows the balance sheet and income statement for Kernel Mills for the fiscal year ended December 31, 2017, as well as some ratios from the food industry. Use the data to work through and support your analysis in Learning by Doing Application 14.1.

Balance Sheet as of December 31, 2017				Income Statement	
Assets		**Liabilities and equity**			
Cash	$ 175,000	Accounts payable	$ 550,000	Net sales	$5,200,000
Short-term investments	165,000	Notes payable	400,000	Cost of goods sold	3,325,000
Accounts receivable	690,000	Accrued expenses	85,000	Operating expenses	1,500,000
Inventory	660,000	Taxes payable	80,000	Earnings before interest and taxes (EBIT)	$ 375,000
Total current assets	$1,690,000	Total current liabilities	$1,115,000	Investment and other income	40,000
Plant and equipment	2,400,000	Long-term debt	1,100,000	Interest expense	116,500
Less: Accum. depreciation	(800,000)	Total liabilities	$2,215,000	Earnings before taxes (EBT)	$ 298,500
Net plant and equipment	1,600,000	Common stock	600,000	Taxes	148,000
Investments	210,000	Retained earnings	685,000	Net income	$ 150,500
Total assets	$3,500,000	Total common equity	$1,285,000		
		Total liabilities and stockholder's equity	$3,500,000	Common stock dividend	$ 15,500
				Addition to retained earnings	$ 135,000

Selected food industry ratios: Days' sales in inventory = 71.59, Days' sales outstanding = 44.77, Days' payables outstanding = 58.33, Cash conversion cycle = 58.03 days

LEARNING BY DOING

APPLICATION 14.1 | Measuring Kernel Mills's Working Capital Efficiency

WileyPLUS

Need more help? Visit your WileyPLUS course.

Problem Kernel Mills is a manufacturing firm in the food industry. The board of directors would like to know how efficiently the firm's working capital is being managed. They are particularly interested in the cash conversion cycle. Exhibit 14.5 shows the financial statements for Kernel Mills, as well as some data from the food industry for comparison.

Approach Calculating the cash conversion cycle will answer the directors' question. This will require first calculating the days' sales in inventory (DSI), days' sales outstanding (DSO), and days' payables outstanding (DPO).

Solution

$$\text{DSI} = \frac{365 \text{ days}}{\$3{,}325{,}000/\$660{,}000} = 72.45 \text{ days}$$

It takes Kernel Mills more than 72 days to transform the raw material into finished goods and sell them, which is slightly higher than the industry average of 71.59 days.

$$\text{DSO} = \frac{365 \text{ days}}{\$5{,}200{,}000/\$690{,}000} = 48.43 \text{ days}$$

It takes Kernel Mills more than 48 days to collect cash from its customers. The industry average is 44.77. Kernel Mills could stand to improve the collection time of its accounts receivable.

$$\text{DPO} = \frac{365 \text{ days}}{\$3{,}325{,}000/\$550{,}000} = 60.38 \text{ days}$$

Kernel Mills does not pay cash to its suppliers for more than 60 days. The industry average is a little lower at 58.33.

Kernel Mills's cash conversion cycle for 2017 is 72.45 + 48.43 − 60.38 = 60.50 days. Thus, about two months pass between the time Kernel Mills pays for its raw materials (cash outflow) and the time it collects cash for the sales of finished goods (cash inflow). In other words, Kernel Mills has to finance its operations for over two months. Although this may seem like a long time, compared with the food industry's average cash conversion cycle of 58.03 days, Kernel Mills is not doing very badly in this area. Two to three days is a small difference.

Before You Go On

1. What is the operating cycle, and how is it related to the cash conversion cycle?

14.3 Working Capital Management Strategies

LEARNING OBJECTIVE

3. Discuss the relative advantages and disadvantages of pursuing (1) flexible and (2) restrictive current asset management strategies.

One of the financial manager's key decisions with regard to working capital is to determine how much money should be invested in current assets for a given level of sales. To the extent that managers have only limited control over their ability to increase days' payables outstanding without the risk of incurring high costs (losing discounts or having to pay penalties), choosing the level of current assets that the firm holds is essentially the same as choosing the amount of net working capital. Since more net working capital provides a firm with greater financial flexibility, but at a higher cost than a more restrictive (less flexible) strategy, choosing the appropriate amount of net working capital involves making trade-offs.

Flexible Current Asset Management Strategy

A firm that follows a **flexible current asset management strategy** might hold large balances of cash, short-term investments, and inventory. It might also offer liberal credit terms to customers, which results in high levels of accounts receivable. A flexible strategy is generally perceived to be a low-risk and low-return course of action. A principal benefit of such a strategy is that large working capital balances improve the firm's ability to survive unforeseen threats. This reduces the size of the firm's exposure to fluctuations in business conditions.

flexible current asset management strategy current asset management strategy that involves keeping high balances of current assets on hand

The downsides of such a strategy can include low returns on current assets, potentially high **inventory carrying costs**, and the cost of financing liberal credit terms. As discussed earlier, returns on cash and short-term investments can be low. Other current assets also usually earn lower returns than long-term assets. For example, inventory sitting on the shelf earns no interest income. Thus, by investing in current assets, management foregoes the higher rate of return it could have earned by investing in long-term assets. This is an opportunity cost. Furthermore, large investments in some types of inventory can require significant storage, tax, and insurance costs.

inventory carrying costs expenses associated with maintaining inventory, including interest forgone on money invested in inventory, storage costs, taxes, and insurance

Although a flexible current asset management strategy is a low-return strategy on average, it can yield large payoffs under certain circumstances. For example, having enough cash to weather a severe credit crunch that puts a firm's major competitors out of business can yield very large long-run returns. Similarly, having sufficient cash to take advantage of an unforeseen acquisition opportunity can be very valuable.

Restrictive Current Asset Management Strategy

A firm that follows a **restrictive current asset management strategy** keeps levels of current assets at a minimum. The firm invests the minimum possible in cash, marketable securities, and inventory and has strict terms of sale intended to limit credit sales and accounts receivable. A restrictive strategy is a high-return, high-risk alternative to a flexible strategy. A restrictive strategy enables the firm to invest a larger fraction of its money in higher-yielding assets. The high risk comes in the form of exposure to **shortage costs**, which can be either operating or financial costs.

restrictive current asset management strategy current asset management strategy that involves keeping the level of current assets at a minimum

shortage costs costs incurred because of lost production and sales or illiquidity

Operating shortage costs result from lost production and sales. If the firm does not hold enough raw materials in inventory, precious hours may be wasted by a halt in production. If the firm runs out of finished goods, sales may also be lost, and customer satisfaction may be damaged. Having restrictive credit policies, such as allowing no credit sales, will also result in lost sales. Overall, operating shortage costs can be substantial, especially if the product markets are competitive.

Financial shortage costs arise mainly from illiquidity. Firms become illiquid when unforeseen circumstances cause them to run out of cash. If bills come due, the firm can be forced to use expensive external emergency borrowing. Worse yet, if outside funding cannot be secured, the firm may default on some current liability and run the risk of being forced into bankruptcy by creditors.

The Working Capital Trade-Off

To determine the optimal management strategy for current assets, the financial manager must balance shortage costs against carrying costs. This is the *working capital trade-off.* If the costs of running short of working capital (shortage costs) dominate the costs of carrying extra working capital (carrying costs), a firm will move toward a more flexible policy. Alternatively, if carrying costs are greater than shortage costs, then the firm will maximize value by adopting a more restrictive strategy. Overall, management will try to find the level of current assets that minimizes the sum of the carrying costs and shortage costs.

Decision Making Example 14.1 illustrates additional applications of the concepts discussed in this section.

DECISION MAKING

EXAMPLE 14.1 | Managing Working Capital

Situation You are the CFO of Cornet Construction Supply Company, a wholesale building supplies retailer in the United States Pacific Northwest. Cornet caters to a wide range of customers, from professional building and remodeling contractors to weekend do-it-yourself homeowners. A financial analyst for the firm has reported the following data for the working capital position of Cornet and the average working capital position of competing firms as of the end of fiscal year 2017.

	Cornet Construction Supply	Industry Average
DSI	58 days	75 days
DSO	30 days	45 days
DPO	25 days	30 days

During the last year, Cornet realized sales growth of only 1.5 percent while the average annual sales growth rate for other firms in the industry was 4.8 percent. Given Cornet's relatively weak growth rate, you decide to do everything possible to improve the company's return on assets. As part of this effort, you ask a team of financial analysts for options on how to improve the efficiency with which net working capital is used at Cornet.

Your team recommends the following three actions:

i. Reduce inventory to 50 DSI
ii. Reduce receivables to 25 DSO
iii. Increase payables to 30 DPO

Which, if any, of these recommendations would you choose and why?

Decision All the recommendations will reduce the net working capital needs of Cornet. However, it is possible that more restrictive working capital management policies will do more harm than good. Cornet's average cash conversion cycle of 63 days (58 days + 30 days − 25 days = 63 days) is much less than the 90-day average conversion cycle for the industry. Cornet is already pursuing a relatively restrictive current asset management strategy.

The first two recommendations should probably not be pursued because the operating shortage costs associated with a more restrictive current asset strategy can outweigh the benefits. Cornet maintains a restrictive inventory policy relative to its competitors, and since retail customers rely on in-stock inventory, further tightening might lead to deterioration in sales if it results in stock-outs that drive customers away. With a DSO of 30 days, it appears that Cornet is requiring customers to pay for purchases in 30 days. The industry average is a more lax 45 days for customer receivables. If Cornet tightens its credit policies, it might lose sales as customers switch to other firms that provide longer credit. In fact, it is possible that the lagging sales growth for the firm is a by-product of its restrictive credit terms.

The third recommendation makes the most sense for Cornet. Its current DPO is less than both the industry average and the typical 30 days of credit provided by trade creditors. Increasing DPO to 30 will reduce the cash conversion cycle to 58 days and help improve return on assets.

Before You Go On

1. What are the two general current asset management strategies discussed in this section, and how do they differ?
2. What are the types of costs associated with each of these strategies?

14.4 Accounts Receivable

LEARNING OBJECTIVE

4. Explain how accounts receivable are created and managed, and compute the cost of trade credit.

We will now consider the components of the operating cycle, starting with accounts receivable, which are at the end of the cash conversion cycle (see Exhibit 14.2). Companies frequently make sales to customers on credit by delivering the goods in exchange for the promise of a future payment. The promise is an account receivable from the firm's point of view. The amount of credit offered to various customers and the terms of the credit are important decisions for the financial manager. Offering credit can help a firm attract customers by differentiating the firm and its products from its competitors, or it might be necessary to offer credit simply to match similar offers by competitors.

Terms of Sale

Whenever a firm sells a product, the seller spells out the terms and conditions of the sale in a document called the *terms of sale*. The simplest alternative is cash on delivery (COD)—that is, no credit is offered. Most firms would prefer to get cash from all sales immediately on delivery, but as mentioned before, being competitive often requires offering credit.

When credit is part of the sale, the terms of sale spell out the credit agreement between the buyer and seller. The agreement specifies when the cash payment is due and the amount of any discount if early payment is made. Trade credit, which is short-term financing, is typically made with a discount for early payment rather than an explicit interest charge. For example, suppose a firm offers terms of sale of "3/10, net 40." This firm will grant a 3 percent discount if the buyer pays the full amount of the purchase in cash within 10 days of the invoice date. Otherwise, the buyer has 40 days to pay the balance in full from the date of delivery.

In this case, the seller is offering to lend the buyer money for an additional 30 days. How expensive is it to the buyer to take advantage of this financing? To calculate the cost, we need to determine the interest rate the buyer is paying. In this case, the buyer pays 97 percent of the purchase price if it pays within 10 days. Otherwise, the buyer pays the full price within 40 days. The increase in the payment (and therefore the interest implicit in the loan) is 3/97 = 0.0309, or 3.09 percent. This is the interest for 30 days (40 days − 10 days = 30 days). To find the annual interest rate, we need to compute the effective annual interest rate (EAR), which was introduced in Section 6.4 of Chapter 6. As you recall, the EAR conversion formula accounts for the number of compounding periods and thereby annualizes the interest rate.

The formula for calculating the EAR for an accounts receivable (EARR) is shown in Equation 14.4, together with the calculation for our example. Notice that to annualize the interest rate, we compound the per-period rate by the number of periods in a year, which is 12.1667 (365 days per year/30 days per period = 12.1667 periods per year).

$$\text{EAR for accounts receivable} = \text{EARR} = \left(1 + \frac{\text{Discount}}{\text{Discounted price}}\right)^{365/\text{days credit}} - 1 \quad (14.4)$$

$$\begin{aligned} &= (1 + 3/97)^{365/30} - 1 \\ &= (1.0309)^{12.1667} - 1 \\ &= 1.4486 - 1 \\ &= 0.4486, \text{ or } 44.86\% \end{aligned}$$

By not paying on Day 10, but instead waiting until Day 40, the firm is paying an effective annual interest rate of 44.86 percent for the use of the money provided by the seller. The rate seems high, but these terms are not unusual for trade credit. Generally speaking, firms do not want to be in the short-term lending business and would prefer to be paid promptly. The terms of sale reflect this preference. If customers need short-term credit, most sellers would prefer

LEARNING BY DOING

APPLICATION 14.2 | Cost of Trade Credit

Problem Suppose that a firm sells its goods with terms of 4/10 EOM, net 30. What is the implicit cost of the trade credit?

Approach The terms of sale say that the buyer will receive a 4 percent discount if the full amount is paid in cash within 10 days of the end of the month; otherwise, the buyer must pay the full amount in 20 days. Once we have determined the cost of credit for 20 days, we can use Equation 14.4 to find the annualized rate.

Solution The cost of the credit for 20 days is 4/96 = 4.17 percent.

$$\begin{aligned}\text{EARR} &= \left(1 + \frac{\text{Discount}}{\text{Discounted price}}\right)^{365/\text{days credit}} - 1\\ &= (1 + 4/96)^{365/20} - 1\\ &= (1.0417)^{18.2500} - 1\\ &= 2.10064 - 1\\ &= 1.10064, \text{ or } 110.064\%\end{aligned}$$

That is pretty expensive credit when annualized!

that the customers go to firms that specialize in business lending, such as a commercial bank or commercial finance company. An important point to notice in the above example is that trade credit is a loan from the supplier and, as you can see, it can be a very costly form of credit.

Learning by Doing Application 14.2 presents one more example of an EARR calculation.

Another common credit term is *end-of-month payment* (EOM). If a firm makes several deliveries to the same customer over the course of a month, it often makes sense to send a single bill at the end of the month for the full amount. Of course, this can be combined with a discount for quick payment. For example, if the terms are "4/10 EOM, net 30," the buyer receives a 4 percent discount for paying within 10 days of the end of the month in which the delivery was made. Otherwise, the customer has an additional 20 days in which to make the payment. We can calculate the cost of credit in this situation using Equation 14.4, just as we did in the earlier example.

How do firms determine their terms of sale? One factor is the industry in which the firm operates. For example, purchases of some consumer products, such as cars and consumer durables, involve much larger amounts of money than others. Sales of relatively expensive products can be very sensitive to the availability of credit. The manufacturers of these types of products are therefore usually liberal with their terms of sale and frequently are in the business of offering short- to medium-term financing. Ford Motor Credit Company, Ford Motors' credit division, exists for exactly this purpose. In contrast, companies selling lower-cost perishable products, such as food companies, might ask for payment in full in less than 10 days.

The terms of sale are also affected by the customer's creditworthiness. If the firm's managers are confident that a customer will pay, they are far more likely to extend credit than if they have some doubt about receiving payment. If the customer is a particularly wealthy individual or a large firm or if there is a likelihood of repeat business, then extending credit may be part of the marketing effort to secure the order.

Aging Accounts Receivable

It would be nice if all customers paid their bills when they came due, but we all know that is not what happens. As a result, firms that offer sales on credit need tools to identify and monitor slow payers so that they can be prompted to pay. In credit circles, it is well documented that creditors that identify slow payers early and establish contact with them are more likely to be paid in full than those who do not monitor their receivables carefully. A tool that credit managers commonly use for this purpose is an *aging schedule*, which organizes the firm's accounts receivable by their age. Its purpose is to identify and track delinquent accounts and to see that they are paid. Aging schedules are also an important financial tool for analyzing the quality of a company's receivables. The aging schedule reveals patterns of delinquency and shows where collection efforts should be concentrated. Exhibit 14.6 shows aging schedules for three different firms.

EXHIBIT 14.6 **Aging Schedule of Accounts Receivable**

An aging schedule shows the breakdown of a firm's accounts receivable by their date of sale; it tells managers how long the accounts have gone unpaid. This exhibit shows the aging schedules for three different firms: Minnow, which is extremely effective in collecting on its accounts receivable, and Rooney and Hastings, which are not performing as well.

	Minnow Corporation		Rooney, Inc.		Hastings Corporation	
Age of Account (days)	Value of Account	% of Total Value	Value of Account	% of Total Value	Value of Account	% of Total Value
0–10	$436,043	60%	$363,370	50%	$319,765	44%
11–30	290,696	40	218,022	30	181,685	25
31–45	0	0	109,011	15	116,278	16
46–60	0	0	36,336	5	72,674	10
Over 60	0	0	0	0	36,337	5
Total	$726,739	100%	$726,739	100%	$726,739	100%

The first schedule belongs to the Minnow Corporation, which is extremely effective in collecting its accounts receivable. Sixty percent of Minnow's total accounts receivable are no more than 10 days old, and the remaining 40 percent are between 11 and 30 days old. Minnow does not have any open accounts receivable older than 30 days. Minnow's *effective DSO* can be calculated as follows:

$$\begin{aligned}\text{Effective DSO} &= \sum(\text{Age of account category in days} \times \text{Percent of total accounts receivable outstanding for the account category})\\ &= (10 \text{ days} \times 0.6) + (30 \text{ days} \times 0.4)\\ &= 6 \text{ days} + 12 \text{ days}\\ &= 18 \text{ days}\end{aligned}$$

The effective DSO is simply a weighted-average measure of DSO where the weights equal the percentage of total accounts receivable outstanding in each account category.

Rooney, Inc., and Hastings Corporation are identical to Minnow in that they sell the same amount of goods for the same price and have the same terms of sale. However, neither company is able to collect all of its accounts receivable on time, which makes their aging schedules different from Minnow's.

Rooney collects only 50 percent of its receivables in 10 days or less and 30 percent in 30 days or less. Of the remaining 20 percent, it collects 15 percent in 45 days or less and 5 percent in 60 days or less. Rooney's effective DSO is 23.75 days [(10 days × 0.50) + (30 days × 0.30) + (45 days × 0.15) + (60 days × 0.05) = 23.75 days], compared with Minnow's 18 days.

Things look even worse for Hastings. It collects 44 percent of its receivables in 10 days or less, 25 percent in 30 days or less, 16 percent in 45 days or less, and 10 percent in 60 days or less. As for the remaining 5 percent, they may never be collected. All we know is that these accounts receivable are over 60 days old. The worst-case scenario would be for Hastings to write these off as bad debt. Let's assume that Hastings can collect the remaining 5 percent in a year. In that case, Hastings's effective DSO becomes 43.35 days [(10 days × 0.44) + (30 days × 0.25) + (45 days × 0.16) + (60 days × 0.10) + (365 days × 0.05) = 43.35 days]. It takes Hastings more than twice as many days as Minnow to collect its accounts receivable.

Financial managers keep close track of both the aging schedule and the effective DSO. If either or both show consistent deterioration, it may be time to reconsider the firm's credit policy or the characteristics of its customers. Note that in some industries, sales vary by season. Managers must be aware of seasonal patterns and make the necessary adjustments before drawing conclusions about a firm's accounts receivable.

Weblink

Some steps a firm can take to monitor and collect on its accounts receivable are discussed at http://www.moneyinstructor.com/art/accountsreceivable.asp.

Before You Go On

1. What does "4/15, net 30" mean?
2. What is an aging schedule, and what is its purpose?

14.5 Inventory Management

LEARNING OBJECTIVE

5. Explain the trade-off between carrying costs and reorder costs, and compute the economic order quantity for a firm's inventory orders.

We have discussed the management of accounts receivable, which represents one end of the operating cycle. We now turn to a discussion of inventory management, which starts with the purchase of raw material and extends through the sale of finished goods inventory. Inventory management is largely a function of operations management, not financial management. For that reason, we touch briefly on a few major points related to operations.

Economic Order Quantity

Manufacturing companies generally carry three types of inventory: raw materials, work in process, and finished goods. We have already discussed some of the trade-offs a firm must consider in deciding how much inventory to hold. On the one hand, as explained earlier, a firm that carries too much inventory may incur high inventory carrying costs. On the other hand, a firm that does not carry enough inventory may incur high shortage costs.

Closely related to the decision of how much inventory to hold is the decision of how much inventory to order. The more of a particular type of inventory a firm orders, the larger the firm's inventory will be immediately after the order is received. A larger inventory means that the time before inventory must be ordered again will be greater, and so fewer orders will be required over the course of a year.

economic order quantity (EOQ) order quantity that minimizes the total costs incurred to order and hold inventory

Weblink

For a more detailed discussion of the drawbacks of using the EOQ model, go to http://yourbusiness.azcentral.com/advantages-disadvantages-economic-order-quantity-eoq-28712.html.

The **economic order quantity (EOQ)** model helps managers choose the appropriate quantity of a particular type of inventory to order. This model mathematically determines the order quantity that minimizes the total costs incurred to order and hold inventory. This model accounts for both inventory *reorder costs* and inventory *carrying costs*. Reorder costs are the fixed costs associated with ordering inventory. The trick in determining the optimal amount of inventory to order is to find the trade-off between these two costs. This trade-off exists because as a firm increases the size of its orders, the number of orders declines, and thus total reorder costs decline. However, larger order sizes increase the average inventory size, and therefore, the carrying cost of inventory increases. The optimal order size strikes the balance between these two costs.

The EOQ model makes the following assumptions: (1) that a firm's sales are made at a constant rate over a period, (2) that the cost of reordering inventory is a fixed cost, regardless of the number of units ordered, and (3) that inventory has carrying costs, which includes items such as the cost of space, taxes, insurance, the cost of capital invested in the inventory, and losses due to spoilage and theft. Under these assumptions, the formula for the economic order quantity is:

$$\text{EOQ} = \sqrt{\frac{2 \times \text{Reorder costs} \times \text{Sales per period}}{\text{Carrying costs}}} \tag{14.5}$$

Let's look at an example. Suppose that Best Buy sells Hewlett-Packard color printers at the rate of 2,200 units per year. The total cost of placing an order is \$750, and it costs \$120 per year to carry a printer in inventory. Using the EOQ formula, what is the optimal order size? Substituting the values into Equation 14.5 yields this result:

$$\text{EOQ} = \sqrt{\frac{2 \times \$750 \times 2{,}200}{\$120}} = 165.83\text{, or 166 printers per order}$$

Given Best Buy's cost structure, it should order 166 printers per order. This means that Best Buy should place about 13 orders per year (2,200 printers per year/166 printers

APPLICATION 14.3 | Economic Order Quantity

LEARNING BY DOING

Problem Gator Marine and Supply, one of the largest boat dealers in the South, sells about 1,500 pontoon boats a year. The cost of placing an order with its supplier is $500, the inventory carrying costs are $100 for each boat, and the safety stock is 20 boats. As you would expect, boat sales are very seasonal; thus, all of Gator's sales are made during a four-month period (summer and early fall). What should the average inventory be in boating season? How many orders should the firm place this year?

Approach The key to this problem is to recognize that it is an application of the EOQ formula and that the sales period is four months and not one year. Recognizing these facts, we can apply Equation 14.5 to solve for EOQ:

Solution

$$\text{EOQ} = \sqrt{\frac{2 \times \$500 \times 1{,}500}{\$100}} = 122.47\text{, or 123 boats per order}$$

Gator should order 123 boats per order, and over the four-month boating season, the firm should place 12 orders (1,500 boats per season/123 boats per order = 12.20 orders per season). The average inventory will then be 81.5 boats [(123 boats − 0 boats)/2 + 20 boats in safety stock = 81.5 boats] during the boating season.

per order = 13.25 orders per year). The EOQ formula also assumes that the firm uses up its entire inventory before the next inventory order is placed. Thus, over time, the average inventory is about 83 printers [(166 printers − 0 printers)/2 = 83 printers], with the inventory varying from a minimum of zero to a maximum of 166 printers.

The assumption of reordering inventory when it declines to zero is not very realistic. Most firms maintain a buffer or safety stock. The size of the safety stock depends on factors such as the carrying cost of inventory, seasonal sales variation, the reliability of suppliers, and the accuracy of the firm's sales projections. In our example, suppose that Best Buy's financial analysts determine that because of future demand uncertainty, the buffer stock should be 15 printers. In that case, the average inventory would be 98 printers (83 printers + 15 printers = 98 printers).

Learning by Doing Application 14.3 illustrates another EOQ calculation.

Just-in-Time Inventory Management

An important development in the management of raw material inventories is *just-in-time inventory management,* pioneered by Japanese firms such as Toyota Motor Company. Today, much of the auto industry and many other manufacturing companies have moved to just-in-time or nearly just-in-time supply delivery. In this system, based on the manufacturer's day-by-day or even hour-by-hour needs, suppliers deliver raw materials just in time for them to be used on the production line. A firm using a just-in-time system has essentially no raw material inventory costs and no risk of obsolescence or loss to theft. On the downside, the firm is heavily dependent on its suppliers. If a supplier fails to make the needed deliveries, then production shuts down. When such systems work, they can reduce working capital requirements dramatically.

Before You Go On

1. What is the economic order quantity model?
2. Why can investments in inventory be costly?

14.6 Cash Management and Budgeting

LEARNING OBJECTIVE

6. Define cash collection time, discuss how a firm can minimize this time, and compute the economic costs and benefits of a lockbox.

Next, we turn to the cash component of working capital. While most firms hold some cash, these balances earn little or no interest in a commercial bank account. Thus, many firms also invest their cash in short-term investments consisting of very liquid stocks and bonds that are expected to be converted into cash within one year. Corporate holdings of cash and short-term investments can be quite large. For example, at the end of its fiscal year 2016, Cisco reported holdings of over $65 billion. There is a variety of reasons why firms hold cash and short-term investments. We discuss these reasons next and then cover the issue of cash collection.

Reasons for Holding Cash

There are three main reasons for holding cash. The first is to facilitate transactions. Operational activities usually require cash. Cash collections from customers generate cash inflows, whereas payments for raw materials and payments to employees and to the government generate cash outflows. Because these cash inflows and outflows often do not occur simultaneously, firms hold positive cash balances to facilitate transactions. If a firm runs out of cash, it might have to sell some of its other investments or borrow, either of which will result in the firm incurring transaction costs.

The second reason for holding cash is to ensure that the firm has sufficient cash to make it through unexpected crises or to take advantage of unexpected investment opportunities. In other words, firms might hold larger cash balances for precautionary or strategic reasons.

The third reason for holding cash is that banks often require firms to hold minimum cash balances as partial compensation for the loans and other services the banks provide. These are known as **compensating balances**. The bank is, in part, compensated for the loans or services it provides by getting the use of the deposits interest free.

compensating balances bank balances that firms must maintain to at least partially compensate banks for loans or services rendered

In deciding how much cash to keep on hand, managers concentrate on the transaction and precautionary motives. Once an appropriate amount of cash is determined, the manager checks to see if the amount also satisfies any compensating balance requirements set by the bank. If it does, then all is well. If not, then the firm must hold the minimum compensating balance. The compensating balance thus forms a lower boundary on the amount of cash a firm will hold.

Of course, firms may hold more cash than required by the transaction and precautionary motives. There are two common explanations for why firms hold excess cash. The first is a by-product of the agency conflict we discussed in Chapter 1. Cash holdings can be used by managers to pursue their own self-interest in conflict with their stockholders. For example, managers can use excess cash to make unwise acquisitions or to invest in their own pet projects. When the interests of managers and stockholders are poorly aligned, managers have an incentive to hoard discretionary cash balances.

A second explanation for excess cash holdings is attributable to differences in the tax rates applied to the earnings of multinational firms. When a U.S.-based firm transacts in a foreign country, the earnings are taxed at the local rate. A U.S. multinational wishing to return these after-tax profits to the U.S.-based parent (commonly referred to as repatriation), however, must pay the difference between the U.S. corporate tax and the local tax paid on the original transaction. The U.S. federal corporate tax rate of 35 percent is the highest among developed nations, and this difference creates a disincentive for managers to repatriate profits earned outside of the United States, causing some corporate cash to be "trapped" overseas.

Cash Collection

The way in which a firm collects payments affects its cash needs. **Collection time**, or **float**, is the time between when a customer makes a payment and when the cash becomes available to the firm. Collection time can be broken down into three components. First is delivery or mailing time. When a customer mails a payment, it may take several days before that payment arrives at the firm. Second is processing delay. Once the payment is received, it must be opened, examined, accounted for, and deposited at the firm's bank. Finally, there is a delay between the time of the deposit and the time the cash is available for withdrawal. For example, if the customer writes a check on an out-of-state (or foreign) bank, the delay may be several days while the availability of the funds is confirmed.

collection time (float) the time between when a customer makes a payment and when the cash becomes available to the firm

Different forms of payment have different cash collection cycles. Cash payments made at the point of sale are the simplest, with a cash collection time of zero. If a firm takes checks or credit cards at the point of sale, then mailing time is eliminated, but processing and availability delays will still exist. Anything the firm can do to reduce the total collection time will reduce its total cash requirements, so firms spend time evaluating their cash collection procedures. A firm can reduce its total cash collection time in several ways, but as always, the firm's ability to implement them will vary according to its industry and its customers' expectations. A few restaurants manage to accept only cash, for example, but most find that such a policy hurts their sales.

One way a firm can reduce its collection time is through the use of lockboxes or concentration accounts. A **lockbox** system allows geographically dispersed customers to send their payments to a post office box close to them. For example, a New York customer would send payments to an East Coast post office box and a California customer to a West Coast post office box. The firm's bank then checks the box daily (or even several times a day) and processes the payments. A *concentration account* system replaces the post office box with a local branch of the company. The local branch receives the mailings, processes the payments, and makes the deposits. With either system, mailing time is reduced because the mailing has less distance to travel and availability delay is often reduced because the checks are more frequently drawn on local banks.

lockbox a system that allows geographically dispersed customers to send their payments to a post office box near them

Another popular means of reducing cash collection time is through the use of electronic funds transfers. Electronic payments reduce cash collection time in every phase. First, mailing time is eliminated. Second, processing time is reduced or eliminated, since no data entry is necessary. Finally, there is little or no delay in funds availability. From the firm's point of view, electronic funds transfers offer a perfect solution. For that reason, many firms encourage (and sometimes require) their customers to pay in this way.

How much is it worth to reduce cash collection time? If a firm that has daily sales of $1 million can reduce its total collection time by even one day, then at 5 percent interest per year, the savings amount to about $50,000 per year. This is not a huge amount to a firm with $365 million in annual sales, but it is certainly worth consideration.

Learning by Doing Application 14.4 illustrates another calculation of the savings from using a lockbox.

Weblink

To learn more about the use of lockboxes, visit http://www.ckfraud.org/lockbox.html.

APPLICATION 14.4 | When Is a Lockbox Worth Keeping?

LEARNING BY DOING

Problem Simon Electronics is evaluating whether a lockbox it is currently using is worth keeping. Management acknowledges that the lockbox reduces the mail float by 1.5 days and processing time by half a day. The remittances average $100,000 a day for Simon Electronics, with the average check being $1,000. The bank charges $0.30 per processed check. Assume that there are 270 business days in a year and that it costs Simon 5 percent to finance accounts receivable. Should Simon Electronics keep the lockbox?

Approach To solve this problem, we first calculate how much Simon is paying the bank per year to manage the lockbox. Then we can calculate the savings the lockbox provides to Simon by reducing the processing and mail floats.

Solution The average number of checks processed per day is:

$$\text{Average daily remittance/Average check size} = \frac{\$100{,}000}{\$1{,}000} = 100$$

Thus, the cost of a lockbox is:

$$100 \text{ checks} \times \$0.30 \text{ per check} \times 270 \text{ days} = \$8{,}100$$

Next we calculate the savings the lockbox provides:

$$\$100{,}000/\text{day} \times (1.5 \text{ day} + 0.5 \text{ day}) \times 0.05 = \$10{,}000$$

The annual savings are therefore $10,000, which is more than the $8,100 cost of the lockbox. Simon should keep the lockbox.

Before You Go On

1. What is float?
2. Explain how lockboxes are used.

14.7 Financing Working Capital

LEARNING OBJECTIVE

7. Describe three current asset financing strategies and discuss the main sources of short-term financing.

So far, we have been discussing the investment side of working capital management. As with other assets, working capital must be funded in some way. Financial managers can finance working capital with short-term debt, long-term debt, equity, or a mixture of all three. We next explore the main strategies used by financial managers to finance working capital, along with their benefits and costs.

Strategies for Financing Working Capital

In order to fully understand the strategies that might be used to finance working capital, it is important to recognize that some working capital needs are short term in nature and that others are long term, or permanent, in nature. As suggested earlier, the amount of working capital at a firm tends to fluctuate over time as its sales rise and fall with the business season. For example, a toy company might build up finished goods inventories in the spring and summer as it prepares to ship its products to retailers in the early fall for the holiday season. Working capital will remain high through the fall as finished goods inventories are sold and converted into accounts receivable but will then decline in January as receivables are collected—at which point the seasonal pattern begins again. These fluctuations reflect seasonal working capital needs.

Even during the slowest part of the year the typical firm will hold some inventory, have some outstanding accounts receivable, and have some cash and prepaid expenses. This minimum level of working capital can be viewed as **permanent working capital** in the sense that it reflects a level of working capital that will always be on the firm's books.

permanent working capital the minimum level of working capital that a firm will always have on its books

Exhibit 14.7 shows three basic strategies that a firm can follow to finance its working capital and fixed assets. The wavy line in each figure indicates the total financing needed for (1) seasonal working capital needs and (2) permanent working capital and fixed assets. The wavy line is upward sloping because we are assuming that the business represented in the figures is a going concern that is growing over time. As businesses grow, they need more working capital as well as more long-term productive assets. We next discuss each of the three strategies illustrated in the exhibit.

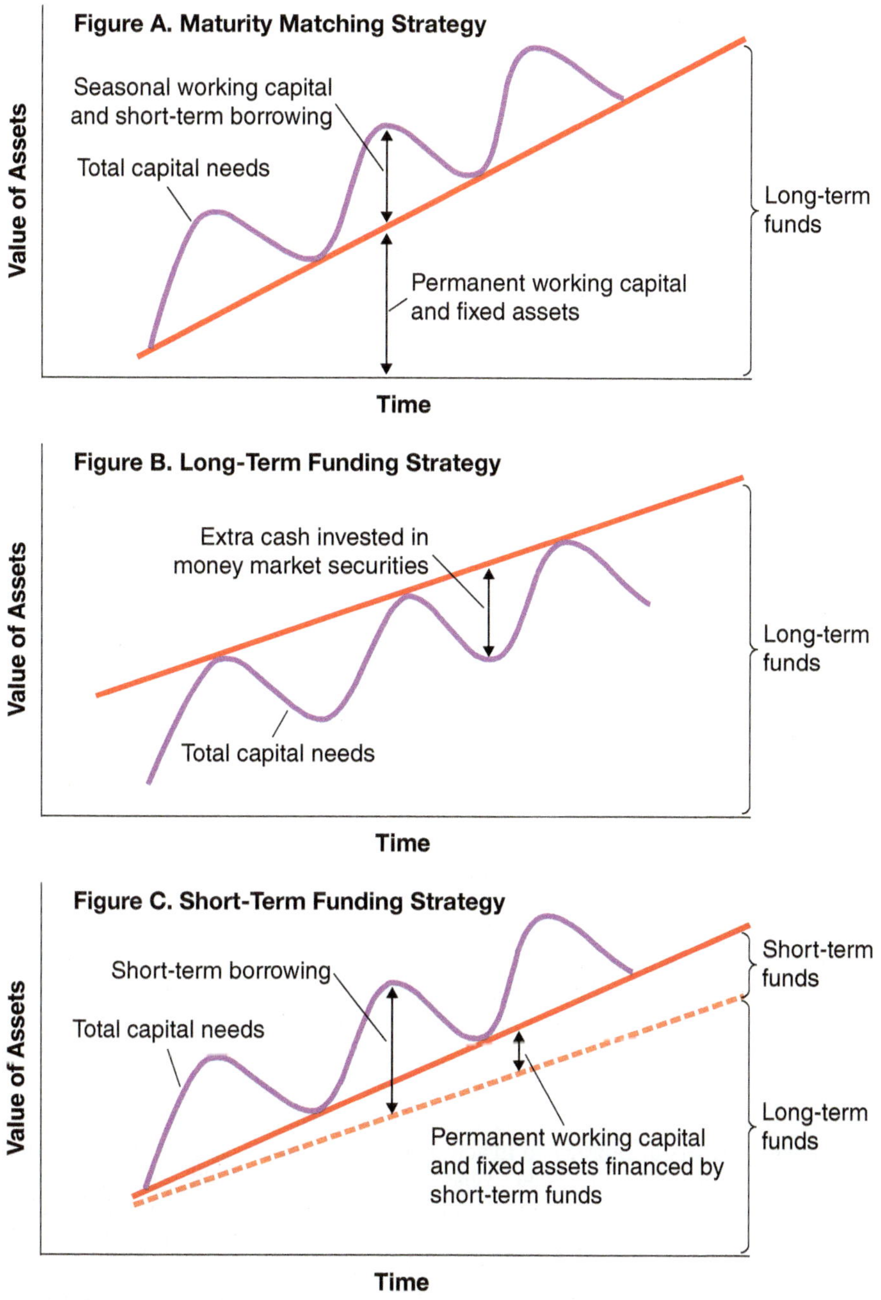

EXHIBIT 14.7 Working Capital Financing Strategies

Three alternative strategies for financing working capital and fixed assets are (1) a maturity matching strategy, which matches the maturities of assets and the sources of funding; (2) a long-term funding strategy, which relies on long-term debt to finance both working capital and fixed assets; and (3) a short-term funding strategy, which uses short-term debt to finance all seasonal working capital needs and a portion of permanent working capital and fixed assets.

The **maturity matching strategy** is shown in Figure A in Exhibit 14.7. Here, all seasonal working capital needs are funded with short-term borrowing. As the level of sales varies seasonally, short-term borrowing fluctuates with the level of seasonal working capital. Furthermore, all permanent working capital and fixed assets are funded with long-term financing. The principle underlying this strategy is very intuitive: the maturity of a liability should match the maturity of the asset that it funds. The "matching of maturities" is one of the most basic techniques used by financial managers to reduce risk when financing assets.

maturity matching strategy
financing strategy that matches the maturities of liabilities and assets

The **long-term funding strategy** is shown in Figure B in the exhibit. This strategy relies on long-term debt and equity to finance fixed assets, permanent working capital, and seasonal working capital. As shown, when the need for working capital is at its peak, it is funded

long-term funding strategy
financing strategy that relies on long-term debt and equity to finance both fixed assets and working capital

entirely by long-term funds. As the need for working capital diminishes over the seasonal cycle and cash becomes available, the excess cash is invested in short-term money market instruments to earn interest until the funds are needed again.

short-term funding strategy financing strategy that relies on short-term debt to finance all seasonal working capital and a portion of permanent working capital and fixed assets

Figure C shows a **short-term funding strategy**, whereby all seasonal working capital and a portion of the permanent working capital and fixed assets are funded with short-term debt. The benefit of using this strategy is that it can take advantage of an upward-sloping yield curve and lower a firm's overall cost of funding. Recall from Chapter 8 that yield curves are typically upward sloping, which means that short-term borrowing costs are lower than long-term rates. The downside to this strategy is that a portion of a firm's long-term assets must be periodically refinanced over their working lives, which can pose a significant refinancing risk (the firm might not be able to obtain new financing when it is needed). Also, as discussed in Chapter 8, the yield curve can become inverted, making short-term funds more expensive than long-term funds.

Financing Working Capital in Practice

Each working capital funding strategy has its costs and benefits. A financial manager will typically use some variation of one of the strategies discussed here to achieve his or her risk and return objectives.

Matching Maturities

Many financial managers try to match the maturities of assets and liabilities when funding the firm. That is, short-term assets are funded with short-term financing, and long-term assets are funded with long-term financing. As suggested in the discussion of the three financing strategies, managers have very sound reasons for matching assets and liabilities.

Suppose a firm buys a manufacturing plant with an estimated economic life of 15 years. If short-term rates are lower than long-term rates, short-term financing can look like a good deal. However, if the firm finances the project with short-term funds and interest rates increase substantially, the firm could find its borrowing cost skyrocketing when it refinances short-term debt at the new market interest rate. If the firm cannot pay the rising interest costs, it could be forced into bankruptcy. Even without bankruptcy, the project NPV could become negative. Managers therefore like to finance capital assets and other long-term assets with long-term debt or equity to lock in the cost of funds for the life of the project.

When they finance seasonal working capital requirements for inventory and receivables, most financial managers also prefer to match maturities of assets and liabilities by financing these investments with short-term debt. As a firm's sales rise and fall seasonally, a financial manager can expand or contract working capital by borrowing short term when more assets are needed and, as cash becomes available, using it to pay off the short-term obligations as they mature.

Permanent Working Capital

Many financial managers prefer to fund permanent working capital with long-term funds, as shown in Figure A in Exhibit 14.7. They prefer to do this in order to limit the risks associated with a short-term financing strategy. To the extent that permanent working capital is financed with long-term funds, the ability of the firm to finance this minimum level of working capital is not subject to short-term credit market conditions.

As illustrated in Figure C of Exhibit 14.7, other managers use short-term debt to finance at least some permanent working capital requirements. These managers subject their firms to more risk in the hope that they will realize higher returns.

Sources of Short-Term Financing

Now that we have discussed working capital financing strategies, let's turn our attention to the most important types of short-term financing instruments used in practice: accounts payable, bank loans, and commercial paper.

Accounts Payable (Trade Credit)

Accounts payable (trade credit) deserve special attention because they comprise a large portion of the current liabilities of many businesses. For example, accounts payable constitute about 35 percent of total current liabilities at publicly traded manufacturing firms. Accounts payable arise, of course, when managers do not pay for purchases with cash on delivery, but instead carry the amount owed as an account payable. If a firm orders $1,000 of a certain raw material daily and the supplier extends a 30-day credit policy, the firm will be receiving $30,000 of financing from this supplier in the form of trade credit.

We already discussed the cost of extending credit and offering discounts from the seller's point of view. We also discussed from a buyer's point of view that, if a discount is offered, the buyer needs to figure out whether it makes financial sense to pay early and take advantage of the discount or to wait and pay in full when the account is due. Taking advantage of a discount reduces cost of goods sold, but it also increases the amount of financing that must be raised from other sources.

Short-Term Bank Loans

Short-term bank loans are also important financing tools. They account for about 20 percent of total current liabilities for publicly traded manufacturing firms. When securing a loan, the firm and the bank negotiate the amount, the maturity, and the interest rate, as well as any binding covenants that might be included. After an agreement is reached, both parties sign the debt contract, which is sometimes referred to as a *promissory note.*

The firm may also have additional borrowing capacity with a bank through a line of credit. Lines of credits are advantageous because they provide easy access to additional financing without requiring a commitment to borrow unnecessary amounts. Lines of credit can be informal or formal.

An **informal line of credit** is a *verbal agreement* between the firm and the bank, allowing the firm to borrow up to an agreed-upon limit. For example, an informal credit line of $1 million for three years allows the firm to borrow up to $1 million within the three-year period. If it borrows $600,000 the first year, it will still have a limit of $400,000 for the remaining two years. The interest rate on an informal credit line depends on the borrower's credit standing. In exchange for providing the line of credit, a bank may require that the firm hold a compensating balance.

informal line of credit a verbal agreement between a bank and a firm under which the firm can borrow an amount of money up to an agreed-on limit

We mentioned compensating balances earlier as a possible reason for firms to hold cash. In exchange for providing a line of credit (or other loan or service), a bank may require a firm to maintain a compensating balance. When required for a loan, a compensating balance represents an implicit cost that must be included in an analysis for the cost of the loan. If a bank requires a compensating balance as a condition for making a loan, the firm must keep a predetermined percentage of the loan amount in a money market account, which can pay negligible interest. If the rate of return is low, the firm is subject to opportunity costs, which make the effective borrowing rate higher than the percentage stated in the promissory note. For example, suppose Virginia City Bank requires borrowers to hold a 10 percent compensating balance in an account that pays no interest. If Zortac Corporation borrows $120,000 from Virginia City at a 9 percent stated rate, it will have to maintain a compensating balance of $0.1 \times \$120{,}000 = \$12{,}000$. Because Zortac cannot use this money, the effective amount borrowed is equal to only $\$120{,}000 - \$12{,}000 = \$108{,}000$. However, since Zortac still must pay interest on the entire loan amount, the firm's interest expense is $0.09 \times \$120{,}000 = \$10{,}800$ and the effective rate on the loan is $\$10{,}800/\$108{,}000 = 0.1$, or 10 percent, rather than 9 percent.

A **formal line of credit** is also known as *revolving credit.* Under this type of agreement, the bank has a *contractual obligation* to lend funds to the firm up to a preset limit. In exchange, the firm pays a yearly fee, in addition to the interest expense on the amount borrowed. The yearly fee is commonly a percentage of the unused portion of the entire credit line.

formal line of credit a contractual agreement between a bank and a firm under which the bank has a legal obligation to lend funds to the firm up to a preset limit; also known as revolving credit

We can illustrate the mechanics of a formal credit line with an example. Higgins Ltd. has a formal credit line of $20 million for five years with First Safety Bank. The interest rate on the loan is 6 percent. Under the agreement, Higgins has to pay 75 basis points

(0.75 percent) on the unused amount as the yearly fee. If Higgins does not borrow at all, it will still have to pay First Safety 0.0075 × \$20,000,000 = \$150,000 for each year of the agreement. Suppose Higgins borrows \$4 million the first day of the agreement. Then the fee drops to 0.0075 × (\$20,000,000 − \$4,000,000) = \$120,000. Of course, Higgins will also have to pay an annual interest expense of 0.06 × \$4,000,000 = \$240,000. The effective interest rate on the loan for the first year is (\$240,000 + \$120,000)/\$4,000,000 = 0.09, or 9 percent.

Another important loan characteristic is whether the loan is secured or unsecured. If the firm backs the loan with an asset, called *collateral*, the loan is *secured*; otherwise, the loan is *unsecured*. Firms often use current assets such as inventory or accounts receivable as collateral when borrowing short term. These types of working capital tend to be highly liquid and therefore are attractive as collateral to lenders. Secured loans allow the borrower to borrow at a lower interest rate, all else being equal. The reason is, of course, that if the borrower defaults, the lender can liquidate the collateral and use the cash generated from their sale to pay off at least part of the loan. The more valuable and liquid the asset pledged as security, the lower the interest rate on the loan.

Commercial Paper

commercial paper short-term debt in the form of promissory notes issued by large, financially secure firms with high credit ratings

Commercial paper is short-term debt in the form of promissory notes issued by large, financially secure firms with high credit ratings. Currently, 600 to 800 firms issue significant quantities of commercial paper. The precise number of firms varies depending on the state of the economy. When market conditions and the economy are weak, firms of lesser credit quality are unable to borrow in the commercial paper market.

Most large companies sell commercial paper on a regular basis. Some large firms, such as GE Capital Corporation, transact in the market on a daily basis—they issue their own commercial paper as a source of funds or buy the commercial paper of other firms for their short-term investment portfolios. A firm's demand for commercial paper financing depends on the commercial paper interest rate relative to other borrowing rates and the firm's need for short-term funds at the time.

Weblink

The commercial paper market is monitored by the U.S. Federal Reserve Bank. For a description of this market and updated data, go to: http://www.federalreserve.gov/releases/CP/default.htm.

In dollars, the commercial paper market is as large, if not larger, than the short-term loan market. The buyers of commercial paper are businesses such as banks, insurance companies, mutual funds, and corporations. The maturity of commercial paper ranges from 1 day to 270 days, which is the maximum legal maturity. Most commercial paper has a maturity of less than 60 days. Commercial paper does not have an active secondary market, as nearly all investors hold commercial paper to maturity.

Commercial paper is not secured, which means that the lender does not have a claim on any specific assets of the issuer in the event of default. However, some commercial paper is backed by a credit line from a commercial bank. If the company does not have the money to pay off the paper at maturity, the bank will pay it. Therefore, the default rate on commercial paper is very low, usually resulting in an interest rate that is lower than the rate a bank would charge on a direct loan.

Accounts Receivable Financing

For medium-size and small businesses, accounts receivable financing is an important source of funds. Accounts receivable can be financed in two ways. First, a company can secure a bank loan by pledging (assigning) the firm's accounts receivable as security. Then, if the firm fails to pay the bank loan, the bank can collect the cash shortfall from the receivables as they come due. If for some reason the assigned receivables fail to yield enough cash to pay off the bank loan, the firm is still legally liable to pay the remaining bank loan. During the pledging process, the company retains ownership of the accounts receivable.

factor an individual or a financial institution, such as a bank or a business finance company, that buys accounts receivable without recourse

Second, a company can *sell* the receivables to a **factor** at a discount. A factor is an individual or a financial institution, such as a bank or a business finance company, that buys accounts receivable *without recourse*. "Without recourse" means that once the receivables are sold, the factor bears all of the risk of collecting the money due from the receivables. The firm that sells the receivables has no further legal obligation to the factor. The advantage of selling receivables to a factor is that the firm gets money from the receivables immediately rather than waiting for them to be paid as they come due. Factoring is just a specialized type of financing. The "discount" is the factor's compensation (in the trade, it is called a "haircut"), which typically ranges from 2 to 5 percent of the face value of the receivable sold.

In computing the cost of financing from a factor, it is helpful to analyze the transaction on a per-dollar basis. For example, suppose that a firm sells its accounts receivable to a factor for a 2 percent discount and that the average collection period is one month. This means that for every dollar of receivables sold to the factor today, the firm receives 98 cents today; one month later, the factor collects the one-dollar receivable. The cost to the firm of receiving the dollar one month earlier is 2 cents ($1 – $0.98 = $0.02). The monthly cost in percentage terms is $2/$98 = 0.0204, or 2.04 percent. This translates to a simple annual rate of 24.48 percent (12 months per year × 2.04 percent per month = 24.48 percent) and, from Equation 6.7, an effective annual rate (EAR) of:

$$\text{EAR} = \left(1 + \frac{\text{Quoted interest rate}}{m}\right)^m - 1$$

$$= (1 + 0.0204)^{12} - 1 = (1.0204)^{12} - 1 = 0.2742, \text{ or } 27.42\%$$

This is the loan-equivalent cost of obtaining financing from the factor.

Learning by Doing Application 14.5 illustrates another EAR calculation.

LEARNING BY DOING

APPLICATION 14.5 | Effective Annual Interest Rate for Financing from a Factor

Problem Kirby Manufacturing sells $100,000 of its accounts receivable to a factor at a 5 percent discount. The firm's average collection period is one month. What is the simple annual cost of the financing provided by the factor, and what is the effective annual loan-equivalent cost?

Approach We must first compute the cost on a per-dollar basis, which will enable us to compute the monthly cost in percentage terms. The key to solving the problem, however, is to realize that we must then calculate the EAR by using Equation 6.7, in order to account for the effect of compounding and therefore the true economic cost.

Solution The discount is 5 percent, and the average collection period is one month. Therefore, in one month, the factor should be able to collect one dollar for every 95 cents paid today. The dollar cost to the company of receiving cash one month earlier is 5 cents ($1 × 0.05 = $0.05), and the amount received is 95 cents ($1 × 0.95 = $0.95). Thus, the monthly cost is $0.05/$0.95 = 0.0526, or 5.26 percent. Plugging the appropriate values into Equation 6.7 and solving for the EAR yields:

$$\text{EAR} = \left(1 + \frac{\text{Quoted interest rate}}{m}\right)^m - 1$$

$$= (1 + 0.0526)^{12} - 1 = (1.0526)^{12} - 1 = 0.8500, \text{ or } 85.00\%$$

The annualized cost of the financing from the factor is 85.00 percent.

Before You Go On

1. List and briefly describe the three main strategies a firm may use to finance its working capital and fixed assets.
2. What are the advantages and disadvantages of short-term financing?
3. Give some examples of sources of short-term financing.

Summary of Learning Objectives

1 Define net working capital, discuss the importance of working capital management, and compute a firm's net working capital.

Net working capital is the difference between total current assets and total current liabilities. Working capital management refers to the decisions made regarding the use of current assets and how they are financed. The goal of working capital management is to maintain the optimal mix of current assets and liabilities that enables the firm to continue its day-to-day operations and pay its short-term debt obligations. The computation of net working capital is illustrated in Section 14.1.

2 Define the operating and cash conversion cycles, explain how are they used, and compute their values for a firm.

The operating cycle is the period starting with the receipt of raw materials and ending with the receipt of cash for finished goods made from those raw materials. It can be divided into two components: (1) days' sales in inventory, which shows how long a firm keeps its inventory before selling it, and (2) days' sales outstanding, which indicates how long it takes on average for the firm to collect its outstanding accounts receivable. Related to the operating cycle is the cash conversion cycle, which is the length of time between the cash outflow for materials and the cash inflow from sales. An additional measure, days' payables outstanding, is required to calculate the cash conversion cycle. Financial managers compute these cycles to help them monitor the efficiency with which working capital is being managed. The computations are illustrated in Section 14.2.

3 Discuss the relative advantages and disadvantages of pursuing (1) flexible and (2) restrictive current asset management strategies.

A flexible strategy involves maintaining relatively high levels of cash, short-term investments, and inventory, while a restrictive strategy keeps the levels of current assets relatively low. In general, a flexible strategy is thought to be low risk and low return; its downsides include low returns on current assets, potentially high inventory carrying costs, and the cost of the money necessary to provide liberal credit terms. The restrictive strategy involves higher risk and return, with higher potential financial and operating shortage costs as its major drawbacks.

4 Explain how accounts receivable are created and managed, and compute the cost of trade credit.

Accounts receivable are promises of future payment from customers that buy goods or services on credit. The details of trade credit agreements are defined in the terms of sale, which include the due date, the interest rate charged, and any discounts for early payment. The terms of sale are affected by the practice in the industry and the creditworthiness of the customer. To manage accounts receivable, a financial manager keeps close track of both days' sales outstanding and the aging schedule and takes necessary actions to ensure that neither goes outside the range that is acceptable to senior management.

5 Explain the trade-off between carrying costs and reorder costs, and compute the economic order quantity for a firm's inventory orders.

The trade-off between carrying costs and reorder costs exists because as the size of a firm's orders for materials increases, the number of orders and total reorder costs decline. At the same time, larger order sizes increase the average inventory size and, therefore, average inventory carrying costs. The economic order quantity (EOQ) calculation enables us to mathematically find the combination of the two costs that minimizes the firm's total inventory cost. Learning by Doing Application 14.3 offers practice in computing a firm's EOQ.

6 Define cash collection time, discuss how a firm can minimize this time, and compute the economic costs and benefits of a lockbox.

The cash collection time is the time between when a customer makes a payment and when the cash becomes available to the firm. It has three components: (1) delivery or mailing time, (2) processing delay, and (3) delay between deposit time and availability. A firm can minimize this time through lockboxes, concentration accounts, electronic funds transfers, and other methods. Learning by Doing Application 14.4 illustrates the computations necessary to decide whether a lockbox is worth keeping.

7 Describe three current asset financing strategies and discuss the main sources of short-term financing.

Three current asset financing strategies are (1) the maturity matching strategy, which matches the maturities of assets with the maturities of liabilities; (2) the long-term funding strategy, which finances both seasonal working capital needs and long-term assets with long-term funds; and (3) the short-term funding strategy, which uses short-term debt for both seasonal working capital needs and some permanent working capital and long-term assets. Sources of short-term financing include accounts payable, short-term bank loans, lines of credit, and commercial paper.

Summary of Key Equations

Equation	Description	Formula
14.1	Operating cycle	Operating cycle = DSI + DSO
14.2	Cash conversion cycle	Cash conversion cycle = DSI + DSO − DPO
14.3	Cash conversion cycle	Cash conversion cycle = Operating cycle − DPO
14.4	Effective annual rate (EAR) for accounts receivable	$\text{EARR} = \left(1 + \frac{\text{Discount}}{\text{Discounted price}}\right)^{365/\text{days credit}} - 1$
14.5	Economic order quantity (EOQ)	$\text{EOQ} = \sqrt{\frac{2 \times \text{Reorder costs} \times \text{Sales per period}}{\text{Carrying costs}}}$

Self-Study Problems

14.1 You are provided the following working capital information for the Blue Ridge Company for the most recent fiscal year:

Account	Beginning Balance	Ending Balance
Inventory	$ 2,600	$2,890
Accounts receivable	$ 3,222	$2,800
Accounts payable	$ 2,500	$2,670
Net sales	$24,589	
Cost of goods sold	$19,630	

What are the firm's operating and cash conversion cycles?

14.2 Merrifield Cosmetics management calculates that their firm's operating cycle for last year was 76 days. The company had $230,000 in its accounts receivable account and sales of $1.92 million. Approximately how many days does it take from the time raw materials are received at Merrifield until the finished products they are used to produce are sold?

14.3 Below is a partial aging of accounts receivable for Bitar Roofing Services. Fill in the rest of the information and determine Bitar's days' sales outstanding. How does it compare to the industry average of 40 days?

Age of Account (days)	Value of Account	% of Total Value
0–10	$211,000	
11–30	120,360	
31–45	103,220	
46–60	72,800	
Over 60	23,740	
Total	$531,120	

14.4 By obtaining a lockbox, Nizam's Manufacturing was able to reduce its total cash collection time by two days. The firm has annual sales of $570,000 and can earn 4.75 percent annual interest. Assuming that the lockbox costs $50 per year, calculate the savings that can be attributed to the lockbox.

14.5 Rockville Corporation is going to borrow $250,000 from its bank at an APR of 8.5 percent. The bank requires its customers to maintain a 10 percent compensating balance. What is the effective interest rate on this bank loan?

Solutions to Self-Study Problems

14.1 We calculate the operating and cash conversion cycles for Blue Ridge Company as follows:

Inventory = $2,890

Accounts receivable = $2,800

Accounts payable = $2,670

Net sales = $24,589

Cost of goods sold = $19,630

$$\text{DSI} = \frac{\text{Inventory}}{\text{COGS}/365} = \frac{\$2,890}{\$19,630/365} = 53.7 \text{ days}$$

$$\text{DSO} = \frac{\text{Accounts receivables}}{\text{Credit sales}/365} = \frac{\$2,800}{\$24,589/365} = 41.6 \text{ days}$$

$$\text{DPO} = \frac{\text{Accounts payable}}{\text{COGS}/365} = \frac{\$2,670}{\$19,630/365} = 49.6 \text{ days}$$

$$\begin{aligned}\text{Operating cycle} &= \text{DSI} + \text{DSO}\\ &= 53.7 \text{ days} + 41.6 \text{ days}\\ &= 95.3 \text{ days}\end{aligned}$$

$$\begin{aligned}\text{Cash conversion cycle} &= \text{DSI} + \text{DSO} - \text{DPO}\\ &= 53.7 \text{ days} + 41.6 \text{ days} - 49.6 \text{ days}\\ &= 45.7 \text{ days}\end{aligned}$$

14.2 Merrifield's days' sales in inventory is calculated as follows:

Operating cycle = 76 days
Accounts receivable = $230,000
Net sales = $1,920,000

$$\text{DSO} = \frac{\text{Accounts receivable}}{\text{Credit sales}/365} = \frac{\$230{,}000}{\$1{,}920{,}000/365} = 43.7 \text{ days}$$

$$\text{Operating cycle} = \text{DSI} + \text{DSO}$$
$$76 \text{ days} = \text{DSI} + 43.7 \text{ days}$$
$$\text{DSI} = 32.3 \text{ days}$$

Merrifield Cosmetics holds inventory an average of 32.3 days before selling it.

14.3 The missing information for Bitar Roofing and its days' sales outstanding are as follows:

Bitar Roofing		
Age of Account (days)	Value of Account	% of Total Value
0–10	$211,000	39.7%
11–30	120,360	22.7
31–45	103,220	19.4
46–60	72,800	13.7
Over 60	23,740	4.5
Total	$531,120	100.0%

$$\begin{aligned}\text{Effective DSO} &= (0.397 \times 10 \text{ days}) + (0.227 \times 30 \text{ days}) \\ &\quad + (0.194 \times 45 \text{ days}) + (0.137 \times 60 \text{ days}) \\ &\quad + (0.045 \times 365 \text{ days}) \\ &= 3.97 \text{ days} + 6.81 \text{ days} + 8.73 \text{ days} + 8.22 \text{ days} \\ &\quad + 16.43 \text{ days} \\ &= 44.2 \text{ days}\end{aligned}$$

Bitar takes about 4 days longer than the industry average of 40 days to collect on its receivables. The firm should focus collection efforts on all credit sales that take 60 days or more to collect.

14.4 The savings that can be attributed to Nizam's lockbox are:

Annual sales = $570,000
Annual interest rate = 4.75%
Collection time saved = 2 days

$$\text{Average daily sales} = \frac{\$570{,}000}{365} = \$1{,}561.64$$

$$\text{Savings} = (\$1{,}561.64 \times 0.0475 \times 2) - \$50 = \$98.36$$

The firm saves $98.36 each year by using the lockbox.

14.5 The effective rate on Rockville Corporation's loan is calculated as follows:

Amount to be borrowed = $250,000
Stated annual interest rate = 8.5%
Compensating balance = 10%

$$\text{Amount deposited as compensating balance} = \$250{,}000 \times 0.10 = \$25{,}000$$

$$\text{Effective amount borrowed} = \$250{,}000 - \$25{,}000 = \$225{,}000$$

$$\text{Interest expense} = \$250{,}000 \times 0.085 = \$21{,}250$$

$$\text{Effective interest rate} = \frac{\$21{,}250}{\$225{,}000} = 9.44\%$$

A compensating balance of 10 percent, or $25,000, on the loan increases the effective interest rate to 9.44 percent.

WileyPLUS

Questions and Problems, Solution Walkthrough Videos, Learning by Doing Tutorials, and additional study tools and resources are available in WileyPLUS.

Discussion Questions

14.1 What factors must a financial manager consider when making decisions about accounts receivable?

14.2 List some of the working capital management practices you would expect to see in a manufacturing company following just-in-time inventory practices.

14.3 What costs would a firm following a flexible current asset management strategy consider, and why?

14.4 How are customers and suppliers affected by a firm's working capital management decisions?

14.5 A beverage bottling company in Vermont has days' sales outstanding of 23.7 days. Is this good? Explain.

14.6 How do the following circumstances affect the cash conversion cycle: (a) favorable credit terms allow the firm to pay its accounts payable slower, (b) inventory turnover increases, and (c) accounts receivable turnover decreases?

14.7 What are some industries in which the use of lockboxes would especially benefit companies? Explain.

14.8 Suppose you are a financial manager at a big firm and you expect interest rates to decline in the near future. What current asset investment strategy would you recommend that the company pursue?

14.9 Why is the commercial paper market available only to the most creditworthy companies?

14.10 Explain what a negative cash conversion cycle means.

Questions and Problems

Excel *Excel templates and resources available in* **WileyPLUS**

Basic

14.1 Cash conversion cycle: Wolfgang's Masonry management estimates that it takes the company 27 days on average to pay its suppliers. Management also knows that the company has days' sales in inventory of 64 days and days' sales outstanding of 32 days. How does Wolfgang's cash conversion cycle compare with the industry average of 75 days?

14.2 Cash conversion cycle: Northern Manufacturing Company management found that during the last year it took an average of 47 days to pay its suppliers, whereas it took 63 days to collect its receivables. The company's days' sales in inventory was 49 days. What was Northern's cash conversion cycle?

14.3 Cash conversion cycle: Devon Automotive management estimates that it takes the company 62 days to collect cash from customers on finished goods from the day it receives raw materials, and it takes 65 days to pay its suppliers. What is the company's cash conversion cycle? Interpret your answer.

14.4 Operating cycle: Lilly's Bakery distributes its products to more than 75 restaurants and delis. The company's average collection period is 27 days, and it keeps its inventory for an average of four days. What is Lilly's operating cycle?

14.5 Operating cycle: NetSpeed Technologies is a telecom component manufacturer. The firm typically has a collection period of 44 days and days' sales in inventory of 29 days. What is the operating cycle for NetSpeed?

14.6 Operating cycle: Devlin Construction, Inc., reported the following balance sheet information for the last fiscal year. Devlin also reported net sales of $980,770 and days' sales in inventory of 48.90 days.

Devlin Construction Inc.	
Assets	
Cash and marketable securities	$ 15,032
Accounts receivable	$140,500
Inventories	$289,809
Other current assets	$ 12,647
Total current assets	$457,988

Calculate the firm's operating cycle.

14.7 Current asset management strategy: Describe the risks that are associated with a restrictive current asset management strategy.

14.8 Cost of trade credit: Sybex Corp. sells its goods with terms of 2/10 EOM, net 30. What is the implicit cost of the trade credit?

14.9 Cost of trade credit: Mill Street Corporation sells its goods with terms of 4/10 EOM, net 60. What is the implicit cost of the trade credit?

14.10 Lockbox: Rosenthal Design has daily sales of $59,000. The financial management team has determined that a lockbox would reduce the collection time by 1.6 days. Assuming the company can earn 5.2 percent interest per year, what are the savings from the lockbox?

14.11 Lockbox: Pacific Traders has annual sales of $1,895,000. The firm's financial manager has determined that using a lockbox will reduce collection time by 2.3 days. If the firm's opportunity cost on savings is 5.25 percent, what are the savings from using the lockbox?

14.12 Effective interest rate: The Kellogg Bank requires borrowers to keep an 8 percent compensating balance. Gorman Jewels borrows $340,000 at a 7 percent stated APR. What is the effective interest rate on the loan?

14.13 Effective interest rate: Morgan Contractors borrowed $1.75 million at an APR of 10.2 percent. The loan called for a compensating balance of 12 percent. What is the effective interest rate on the loan?

14.14 Factoring: Maltz Landscaping has an average collection period of 38 days for its accounts receivable. Currently, Maltz factors all of its receivables at a 2 percent discount. What is the effective annual interest rate on the financing from the factor?

14.15 Formal line of credit: Winegartner Cosmetics management is setting up a line of credit at the company's bank for $5 million for up to two years. The interest rate is 5.875 percent and the loan agreement calls for an annual fee of 40 basis points on any unused balance for the year. If the firm borrows $2 million on the day the loan agreement is signed, what is the effective rate for the line of credit?

Intermediate

14.16 Cash conversion cycle: Your boss asks you to compute your company's cash conversion cycle. Looking at the financial statements, you see that the average inventory for the year was $26,300, accounts receivable averaged $17,900, and accounts payable averaged $15,100. You also see that the company had sales of $154,000 and that cost of goods sold was $122,000. Calculate and interpret your firm's cash conversion cycle.

14.17 Cash conversion cycle: Blackwell Automotive, Inc., reported the following financial information for the last fiscal year.

Blackwell Automotive, Inc.			
Assets		**Liabilities and Equity**	
Cash and marketable securities	$ 23,015	Accounts payable and accruals	$163,257
Accounts receivable	$141,258	Notes payable	$ 21,115
Inventories	$212,444	Total current liabilities	$184,372
Other current assets	$ 11,223		
Total current assets	$387,940	**Sales and Costs**	
		Net sales	$912,332
		Cost of goods sold	$547,400

Calculate the firm's cash conversion cycle and operating cycle.

14.18 Cash conversion cycle: Elsee, Inc., has net sales of $13 million, and 75 percent of these are credit sales. Its cost of goods sold is 65 percent of annual net sales. The firm's cash conversion cycle is 41.3 days. The inventory balance at the firm is $1,817,344, while its accounts payable balance is $2,171,690. What is the firm's accounts receivable balance?

14.19 Cash conversion cycle: Joanna Handicrafts, Inc., has net sales of $4.23 million with 50 percent being credit sales. Its cost of goods sold is $2.54 million. The firm's cash conversion cycle is 47.9 days, and its operating cycle is 86.3 days. What is the firm's accounts payable?

14.20 Operating cycle: Aviva Technology's operating cycle is 81 days. Its inventory was $134,000 at the end of last year, and the company had cost of goods sold of $1.1 million. How long does it take Aviva to collect its receivables on average?

14.21 Operating cycle: Premier Corp. has net sales of $812,344, and cost of goods sold equal to 70 percent of net sales. If the firm's accounts receivable total $113,902 and its operating cycle is 81.6 days, how much inventory does the firm have?

14.22 Operating cycle: Telecraft Enterprises carries 45 days of inventory in its stores. Last year Telecraft reported net sales of $1,400,000 and the company had receivables of $325,000 at the end of the year. What is the operating cycle at Telecraft?

14.23 Operating cycle: Given the data for Telecraft Enterprises in Problem 14.22, re-estimate the firm's operating cycle if days' sales outstanding decreased to 75 days. For the same level of net sales, what is the implied dollar value of receivables with 75 days' sales outstanding?

14.24 Days' sales outstanding: Sliver Computing, Inc., reported the following balance sheet information for the last fiscal year. Sliver Computing also reported cost of goods sold of $291,240 for the same period. Internal auditors state that the firm's cash conversion cycle is 21.53 days.

Sliver Computing Inc.			
Assets		**Liabilities**	
Cash and marketable securities	$ 94,032	Accounts payable	$ 68,561
Accounts receivable	$160,684	Notes payable	$136,320
Inventories	$ 19,809	Total current liabilities	$204,881
Other current assets	$ 647		
Total current assets	$275,172		

Calculate the firm's days' sales outstanding.

14.25 Economic order quantity: Longhorn Traders is one of the largest RV dealers in Austin, Texas, and sells about 2,800 recreational vehicles a year. The cost of placing an order with Longhorn's supplier is $800, and the inventory carrying costs are $150 for each RV. Management likes to maintain safety stock of 12 RVs. Most of its sales are made in either the spring or the fall. How many orders should the firm place this year?

14.26 Effective interest rate: The Clarkson Designer Company management wants to borrow $750,000. The bank will provide the loan at an APR of 6.875. Since the loan calls for a compensating balance, the effective interest rate is actually 9.25 percent. What is the compensating balance on this loan?

14.27 Effective interest rate: The Colonial Window Treatments Company is borrowing $1.5 million. The loan requires a 10 percent compensating balance, and the effective interest rate on the loan is 9.75 percent. What is the stated APR on this loan?

14.28 Formal line of credit: Gruppa, Inc., has just set up a formal line of credit of $10 million with First Community Commercial Bank. The line of credit is good for up to five years. The bank will charge Gruppa an interest rate of 6.25 percent on any amount borrowed, and the firm will pay an annual fee of 60 basis points on the unused balance. The firm borrowed $7.5 million on the first day the credit line became available. What is the effective interest rate on this line of credit?

14.29 Formal line of credit: Lansdowne Electronics has a formal line of credit of $1 million for up to three years with HND Bank. The interest rate on the loan is 5.3 percent, and under the agreement, Lansdowne has to pay an annual fee of 50 basis points on the unused amount. Suppose the firm borrows $675,000 the first day of the agreement. What is the fee the company must pay on the unused balance? What is the effective interest rate?

14.30 Lockbox: Jennifer Electrical is evaluating whether a lockbox it is currently using is worth keeping. Management estimates that the lockbox reduces the mail float by 1.8 days and the processing by half a day. The remittances average $50,000 a day for Jennifer Electrical, with the average check being for $500. The bank charges $0.34 per processed check. Assume that there are 270 business days in a year and that the firm's opportunity cost for these funds is 6 percent. What will the firm's savings be from using the lockbox?

14.31 Lockbox: Hazel Corp. has just signed up for a lockbox. Management expects the lockbox to reduce the mail float by 2.1 days. Hazel Corp.'s remittances average $37,000 a day, and the average check is $125. The bank charges $0.37 per processed check. Assume that there are 270 business days in a year. What will the firm's savings be from using the lockbox if the opportunity cost for these funds is 12 percent?

14.32 Aging schedule: Ginseng Company collects 50 percent of its receivables in 10 days or fewer, 31 percent in 11 to 30 days, 7 percent in 31 to 45 days, 7 percent in 46 to 60 days, and 5 percent in more than 60 days. The company has $1,213,000 in accounts receivable. Prepare an aging schedule for Ginseng Company.

14.33 Aging schedule: A partial aging of accounts receivable for Lincoln Cleaning Services is given in the accompanying table. What percent of receivables is in the 45-day range? Determine the firm's effective days' sales outstanding. How does it compare with the industry average of 35 days?

Age of Account (days)	Value of Account	% of Total Value
10	$271,000	
30	$145,220	
45		
60	$ 53,980	
75	$ 31,245	
Total	$589,218	100.0%

14.34 Aging schedule: Keswick Fencing Company collects 45 percent of its receivables in 10 days or fewer, 34 percent in 10 to 30 days, 12 percent in 31 to 45 days, 5 percent in 46 to 60 days, and 4 percent in more than 60 days. The company has $937,000 in accounts receivable. Prepare an aging schedule for Keswick Fencing.

14.35 Factoring: Zenex, Inc., sells $250,000 of its accounts receivable to factors at a 3 percent discount. The firm's average collection period is 90 days. What is the dollar cost of the factoring service? What is the simple annual interest cost of the factors loan?

14.36 Factoring: A firm sells $100,000 of its accounts receivable to factors at a 2 percent discount. The firm's average collection period is one month. What is the dollar cost of the factoring service?

Advanced

14.37 What impact would the following actions have on the operating and cash conversion cycles? Would the cycles increase, decrease, or remain unchanged?

a. More raw material than usual is purchased.

b. The company enters into an off season, and finished goods inventory builds up.

c. Better terms of payment are negotiated with suppliers.

d. The cash discounts offered to customers are decreased.

e. All else remaining the same, an improvement in manufacturing technique decreases the cost of goods sold.

14.38 What impact would the following actions have on the operating and cash conversion cycles? Would the cycles increase, decrease, or remain unchanged?

a. Less raw material than usual is purchased.

b. The company encounters unseasonable demand, and inventory declines rapidly.

c. Tighter terms of payment are demanded by suppliers.

d. The cash discounts offered to customers are increased.

e. All else remaining the same, due to labor turnover and poor efficiency, the cost of goods sold increases.

14.39 Morgan Sports Equipment Company just reported the following financial information.

Morgan Sports Equipment Company			
Assets		**Liabilities and Equity**	
Cash	$ 677,423	Accounts payable	$1,721,669
Accounts receivable	$1,845,113	Notes payable	2,113,345
Inventories	1,312,478	Total current liabilities	$3,835,014
Total current assets	$3,835,014	**Sales and Costs**	
		Net sales	$9,912,332
		Cost of goods sold	$5,947,399

a. Calculate the firm's days' sales outstanding.

b. What is the firm's days' sales in inventory?

c. What is the firm's days' payables outstanding?

d. What is the firm's operating cycle? How does it compare with the industry average of 72 days?

e. What is the firm's cash conversion cycle? How does it compare with the industry average of 42 days?

14.40 Jackson Electrical, one of the largest generator dealers in Phoenix, sells about 2,000 generators a year. The cost of placing an order with its supplier is $750, and the inventory carrying costs are $170 for each generator. Jackson likes to maintain safety stock of 15 generators at all times.

a. What is the firm's EOQ?

b. How many orders will the firm need to place this year?

c. What is the average inventory for the season?

14.41 Tanzaniqe, Inc., sells $200,000 of its accounts receivable to factors at a 5 percent discount. The firm's average collection period is 90 days.

a. What is the dollar cost of the factoring service?

b. What is the simple annual interest cost of the loan?

c. What is the effective annual interest cost of the loan?

CFA Problems

14.42 A company increasing its credit terms for customers from 1/10, net 30 to 1/10, net 60 will likely experience:

a. An increase in cash on hand.

b. An increase in the average collection period.

c. Higher net income.

d. A higher level of uncollectible accounts.

14.43 Suppose a company uses trade credit with the terms of 2/10, net 50. If the company pays its account on the 50th day, the effective borrowing cost of skipping the discount on Day 10 is closest to

a. 14.6 percent.

b. 14.9 percent.

c. 15.0 percent.

d. 20.2 percent.

The following information relates to Problems 14.44 through 14.46.

Mary Gonzales is evaluating companies in the office supply industry and has compiled the following information:

	2016		2017	
Company	**Credit Sales**	**Average Receivables Balance**	**Credit Sales**	**Average Receivables Balance**
A	$ 5.0 million	$1.0 million	$ 6.0 million	$1.2 million
B	$ 3.0 million	$1.2 million	$ 4.0 million	$1.5 million
C	$ 2.5 million	$0.8 million	$ 3.0 million	$1.0 million
D	$ 0.5 million	$0.1 million	$ 0.6 million	$0.2 million
Industry	$25.0 million	$5.0 million	$28.0 million	$5.4 million

14.44 Which of the companies has the lowest accounts receivable turnover in 2017?

a. Company A.

b. Company B.

c. Company C.

d. Company D.

14.45 The industry average receivables collection period:

a. Increased from 2016 to 2017.

b. Decreased from 2016 to 2017.

c. Did not change from 2016 to 2017.

d. Increased along with the increase in the industry accounts receivable turnover.

14.46 Which of the companies reduced the average time it took to collect on accounts receivable from 2016 to 2017?

a. Company A.

b. Company B.

c. Company C.

d. Company D.

Sample Test Problems

14.1 The Whole Foods Market, Inc., balance sheet for the fiscal year ending September 25, 2016 included the following: total current assets of $1,975 million, total assets of $6,341 million, total current liabilities of $1,341 million, and total liabilities of $3,117 million. What was the company's net working capital on September 25, 2016? What does this tell us?

14.2 Last year Perpetual Plastics Company took an average of 46 days to pay suppliers and 38 days to collect its receivables. The company's average days' sales in inventory was 52 days. What was Perpetual's operating cycle and cash conversion cycle last year?

14.3 Montrose, Inc., sells its products with terms of 3/15 EOM, net 30. What is the cost of the trade credit it provides its customers?

14.4 FRA Manufacturing Company purchases 9,000 units of Part 3BX each year. The cost of placing an order is $5 and the cost of carrying one part in inventory for a year is $1. What is the economic order quantity (EOQ) for part 3BX if the company carries a safety stock of 200 units? How many orders will the company need to place each year?

14.5 Rosemary Corporation has daily sales of $139,000. The financial manager at the firm has determined that a lockbox would reduce collection time by 2.2 days. Assuming the company can earn 5.5 percent interest per year, what are the potential annual savings from the lockbox?

14.6 Sunny Way Landscaping has a formal line of credit of $500,000 with First Commerce Bank. The interest rate on the loan is 6 percent, and under the agreement Sunny Skies must pay an annual fee of 75 basis points on the unused amount. The amount currently outstanding on the loan is $325,000. What is the annual fee the company must pay on the current unused balance? What is the effective interest rate?

CHAPTER 15

How Firms Raise Capital

DWD-Media/Alamy Stock Photo

LEARNING OBJECTIVES

1. Explain what is meant by bootstrapping when raising seed financing and why bootstrapping is important.
2. Describe the role of venture capitalists in the economy and discuss how they reduce their risk when investing in start-up businesses.
3. Discuss the advantages and disadvantages of going public and compute the net proceeds from an IPO.
4. Explain why, when underwriting new security offerings, investment bankers prefer that the securities be underpriced. Compute the total cost of an IPO.
5. Discuss the costs of bringing a general cash offer to market.
6. Explain why a firm that has access to the public markets might elect to raise money through a private placement.
7. Review some advantages of borrowing from a commercial bank rather than selling securities in financial markets and discuss bank term loans.

Snap Inc., the owner of the Snapchat camera application used to communicate through videos and pictures, sold shares in a public offering for the first time on March 2, 2017. Snap had come a long way in the short period since its Snapchat application was introduced to the public under the name Picaboo in 2011. By March 2017, Snapchat had more than 150 million daily active users across the globe and Snap's common stock was valued at approximately $25 billion.

Snap's founders had to raise a lot of capital in a short period to grow the company so rapidly. They had raised a total of $2.7 billion by December 31, 2016, the date of the last balance sheet prepared before the public offering, through private sales of at least 11 different issues of stock. Of this amount, $1.7 billion had already been spent to cover $1.2 billion of operating losses and purchase $0.5 billion of long-term assets.

Snap had roughly $1.0 billion of cash and investments in marketable securities remaining at the end of December 2016, so the public offering was not made because the company was in imminent danger of running out of cash. The $1.0 billion was sufficient to cover foreseeable operating losses and investment requirements for roughly a year. Snap management said that the $2.465 billion raised by the company in the public offering would provide greater financial flexibility and create a public market for its Class A common stock.

Founders of companies such as Snap are constantly thinking about how to fund their businesses. Initial financing often comes from the founders themselves and from family members and friends. However, these sources often cannot provide all of the capital that a growing firm requires, and the founders in such cases will eventually begin to sell shares through private offerings to outsiders, such as angel investors and venture capitalists. Snap's founders obtained most of their financing prior to the public offering through such private sales.

While some firms can be funded through the private markets indefinitely, others obtain the resources they need by merging into another firm or, like Snap, by going public. The path that each firm follows depends on its needs and the objectives of its owners. Snap had such large ongoing capital requirements in 2017 that its owners decided to raise $2.465 billion through a public offering. Public markets provide access to large amounts of capital at reasonable prices. By establishing a public market for Snap shares, the March 2, 2017, offering also provided the liquidity necessary for the company's early investors to sell their shares and realize the returns that they had earned. In fact, these investors sold $0.935 billion of their stock along with the $2.465 billion offering by the company. This chapter discusses how firms such as Snap raise capital to finance their business activities and the costs and benefits associated with various public and private financing alternatives.

Chapter Preview

This chapter is about how firms raise capital so that they can acquire the productive assets needed to grow and remain profitable. To raise money, a firm can borrow, sell stock, or both. How a firm actually raises capital depends on factors such as where the firm is in its life cycle, its expected cash flows, and its risk characteristics. Management's goal is to raise the amount of money necessary to finance the business at the lowest possible cost.

We start the chapter by examining how many new businesses acquire their first equity funding through "bootstrapping" and the role venture capitalists play in providing equity to help firms get started. Once a firm is successfully launched, the venture capitalists' job is done and they exit the scene. At this juncture, management has a number of other funding options, and we discuss those options in the remainder of this chapter.

We explain how firms sell their first issue of common stock in the public markets and the work of investment banks in completing these sales. First-time equity sales are known as initial public offerings, or IPOs. We then discuss the role that private markets play in funding business firms and describe factors that managers consider when deciding between a public and a private market sale. We close the chapter with a discussion of the importance of commercial banks in providing short-term and intermediate-term financing.

15.1 Bootstrapping

LEARNING OBJECTIVE

1. Explain what is meant by bootstrapping when raising seed financing and why bootstrapping is important.

New business start-ups are an important factor in determining and sustaining long-term economic growth. This fact explains why state and local governments invest heavily in industrial parks, new business incubators, and technology and entrepreneurial programs at state universities and two-year colleges. Although governments can do a lot to foster new business development, they generally can do little to provide the equity capital and the initial support that new businesses need during their start-up phase.

How New Businesses Get Started

Most businesses are started by an entrepreneur who has a vision for a new business or product and a passionate belief in the concept's viability. New businesses are seldom started in large corporations. In fact, entrepreneurs regularly leave large companies to start businesses, often using technology developed by these firms. Large companies are efficient at producing goods and services and bringing them to market, but they generally do not excel at incubating new businesses.

The entrepreneur often fleshes out his or her ideas and makes them operational through informal discussions with people whom the entrepreneur respects and trusts, such as friends and early investors. These discussions may involve issues related to technology, manufacturing, personnel, marketing, and finance. The discussions are far from glamorous. They are usually low-budget affairs that take place around a kitchen table with lots of coffee. The founder and his or her advisers often have a common bond that has drawn them together. They may have graduated from the same college, have worked for the same company, or have some fraternal or family ties.

Initial Funding of the Firm

The process by which many entrepreneurs raise seed money and obtain other resources necessary to start their businesses is often called **bootstrapping**. The term bootstrapping comes from the old expression "pull yourself up by your bootstraps," which means to accomplish something on your own.

bootstrapping the process by which many entrepreneurs raise seed money and obtain other resources necessary to start their businesses

The ways in which entrepreneurs bootstrap their businesses vary greatly. The initial seed money usually comes from the entrepreneur or other founders. Until the business gets started, entrepreneurs often work regular full-time jobs. The job provides some of the cash flow needed to launch the business and to support the entrepreneur's family (although not always in that order of priority). Other cash may come from personal savings, the sale of assets such as cars and boats, borrowing against the family home, loans from family members and friends, and loans obtained through credit cards. At this stage of business development, venture capitalists or banks are not normally willing to fund the business.

Where does the seed money go? In most cases, it is spent on developing a prototype of the product or service and a business plan. The deliverables at this stage are whatever it takes to satisfy investors that the new business concept can become a viable business and deserves their financial support.

The movie producer Spike Lee offers a classic example of bootstrapping. After graduating from New York University's Tisch School of the Arts with a master's degree, he launched his film production company on money earned from his first feature movie, *She's Gotta Have It.* The film was shot in four days to hold costs down, and most of the cast and crew were former classmates of Lee's who worked for little or no wages. The film's out-of-pocket cost of $125,000 was financed by credit card loans and money from family and friends. The film went on to gross $8.5 million.

Before You Go On

1. Explain bootstrapping, and list common sources of seed money.

15.2 Venture Capital

LEARNING OBJECTIVE

2. Describe the role of venture capitalists in the economy and discuss how they reduce their risk when investing in start-up businesses.

The bootstrapping period usually lasts no more than one or two years. At some point, the founders will have developed a prototype of the product and a business plan, which they use to obtain venture capital funding to grow the business.[1] For most entrepreneurs, this is a critical time that determines whether they have a viable business concept that will be funded or will disband because of the lack of investor interest.

venture capitalists individuals or firms that invest by purchasing equity in new businesses and often provide entrepreneurs with business advice

angels (angel investors) wealthy individuals who invest their own money in new ventures

Venture capitalists are individuals or firms that help new businesses get started and provide much of their early-stage financing. Individual venture capitalists, so-called **angels** (or **angel investors**), are typically wealthy individuals who invest their own money in emerging businesses at the very early stages. In contrast, venture capital firms typically pool money from various sources to invest in new businesses. The primary sources of funds for venture capital firms include financial and insurance firms, private and public pension funds, wealthy individuals and families, corporate investments not associated with employee pensions, and endowments and foundations.

The Venture Capital Industry

Venture capitalists have always operated in the United States in one form or another. The venture capital industry, as we know it today, emerged after venture capital firms began raising capital through venture capital limited partnerships (funds) in the late 1960s. These funds revolutionized the industry and the annual flow of capital into venture capital firms increased greatly after they first appeared. **Exhibit 15.1** shows that at the end of 2016, there were 898 venture capital firms and 1,562 separate venture capital funds in the United States—many firms are managing more than one fund at a given time. The funds had access to an average of $213.5 million of capital. Venture capital firms invested a total of $69.0 billion in 8,136 deals during 2016, for an average of $8.5 million per deal ($69.0 billion/8,136 deals = $8.5 million).

Today, the venture capital industry employs several thousand professionals, with the biggest concentrations of firms in California and Massachusetts. Other areas of concentration are the Research Triangle in North Carolina; Austin, Texas; the New York City/New Jersey area; and the Dulles Airport corridor near Washington, D.C. Modern venture capital firms tend to specialize in a specific line of business, such as clean energy, business software, hospitality (lodging, restaurants, and related services), or medical devices. A significant number of these firms focus on high-technology investments.

Weblink

Visit the National Venture Capital Association's Web site at http://www.nvca.org for information on venture capital funding.

Why Venture Capital Funding Is Different

Venture capital is important because entrepreneurs have only limited access to traditional sources of funding. In general, there are three reasons why traditional sources of funding do not work for new or emerging businesses:

1. *The high degree of risk involved.* Starting a new business is a risky proposition. The fact is that most new businesses fail, and it is difficult to identify which firms will be successful. Most suppliers of capital, such as banks, pension funds, and insurance companies, are averse to undertaking high-risk investments, and much of their risk-averse behavior is mandated in regulations that restrict their conduct.

[1]A business plan is like a road map for a business. It presents the results from a strategic planning process that focuses on how the business will be developed over time. Business plans are discussed in more detail in Chapter 18.

EXHIBIT 15.1 Venture Capital Industry Characteristics, 2009–2016

At the end of 2016, there were 898 venture capital firms and 1,562 separate venture capital funds in the United States. The funds had an average of $213.5 million of investable capital. Venture capital firms invested a total of $69.0 billion in 8,136 deals during 2016. The number of firms and funds, and the level of investment activity, increased over the 2009–2016 period.

	Venture Capital Firms and Funds			Investments by Venture Capital Firms	
Year	Number of firms[a]	Total Number of Existing Funds	Average Fund Size ($ millions)	Number of Deals	Total Dollar Value ($ billions)
2009	791	1,276	$204.8	4,458	$26.0
2010	791	1,294	194.3	5,411	31.0
2011	815	1,344	202.6	6,771	44.0
2012	844	1,372	194.7	7,987	41.0
2013	869	1,408	190.3	9,326	45.0
2014	898	1,481	194.8	10,550	69.0
2015	906	1,528	206.3	10,468	79.0
2016	898	1,562	213.5	8,136	69.0
Average	852	1,408	$200.2	7,888	$50.5

[a]Number of firms that had raised funds in the previous eight years.
Source: National Venture Capital Association 2017 Yearbook.

2. *Types of productive assets.* Most commercial loans are made to firms that have tangible assets, such as machinery, equipment, and physical inventory. Lenders understand the operations of these firms and their inherent risks; thus, they are comfortable making loans to them. New firms whose primary assets are often intangibles, such as patents or trade secrets, find it difficult to secure financing from traditional lending sources.
3. *Information asymmetry problems.* Recall from Chapter 1 that information asymmetry arises when one party to a transaction has knowledge that the other party does not. An entrepreneur knows more about his or her company's prospects than a lender does. Also, when dealing with highly specialized technologies, or companies emerging in new business areas, most investors do not have the expertise to distinguish between competent and incompetent entrepreneurs. As a result, they are reluctant to invest in these firms.

For these reasons, investors such as financial and insurance firms, pension funds, endowment funds, and university foundations find it difficult to participate *directly* in the venture capital market. Instead, they invest in venture capital funds that specialize in identifying attractive investments in new businesses, managing those investments, and selling (exiting) them at the appropriate time.

The Venture Capital Funding Cycle

To illustrate how venture capitalists help launch new business firms, we next examine the venture capital funding cycle, which is summarized in Exhibit 15.2. You may want to refer to the exhibit from time to time as we discuss the funding cycle.

Starting a New Business—The Tuscan Pizzeria

Suppose you have been in the pizza business for several years and have developed a concept for a high-end pizzeria that you believe has the potential to grow into a national chain. The shops will have an Italian ambiance: a Tuscan facade with an Old World Italian interior decor. They will feature pizzas with all-natural ingredients that will be baked in wood-burning ovens. The interior will be designed so that customers can watch their pizzas being prepared

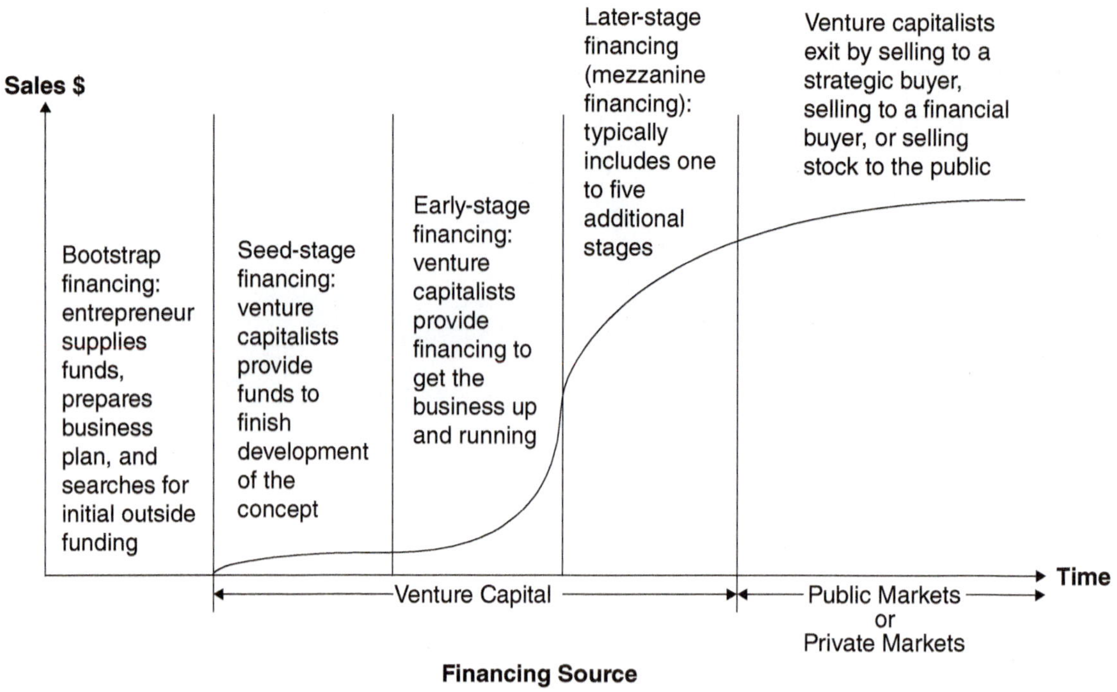

EXHIBIT 15.2 The Venture Capital Funding Cycle

The typical venture capital funding cycle begins when the entrepreneur runs low on bootstrap financing. Venture capitalists then provide equity financing. They will later exit through a private or public sale of their equity. The duration of the cycle is typically three to seven years, and only a small percentage of new ventures make it all the way to the end.

and baked. The dough is slow rising and, after baking, is good enough to eat by itself. In addition, the pizzerias will feature *panzanella* salads of diced raw vegetables and Italian cold cuts, modestly priced wines, and sandwiches made from crackly loaves of bread baked in the wood-burning oven. You are planning to name your firm "The Tuscan Pizzeria."

The Business Plan

You have spent nearly six months of evenings and weekends developing a business plan. You received help from an attorney and consultants at a regional business incubator. In addition, several people who have started successful restaurants have read and commented on your plan. As a result of your efforts, your business plan is well thought out and well executed. The business plan describes what you want the business to become, why consumers will find your pizzerias attractive (the *value proposition*), how you are going to accomplish your objectives, and what resources you will need. You presented your finished business plan to a venture capitalist at a regional venture capital firm, and she expressed an interest in it. This is a serious inquiry, because venture capital firms receive many unsolicited business plans, but respond to very few.

First-Stage Financing

After a number of meetings with you and your management team, the venture capitalist agrees to fund the project, but only in stages, and for less than the full amount you requested. At this time, the firm is willing to fund $1.6 million of the $6 million you estimate is necessary to build a successful business. In addition, you will have to come up with $400,000 on your own. You plan to do this by using $200,000 of your own money and obtaining the remaining $200,000 from family members and key employees. Financially, you will be stretched to the limit.

How Venture Capitalists Reduce Their Risk

Venture capitalists know that only a handful of new companies will survive to become successful firms. To reduce their risk, they use a number of tactics when they invest in new ventures, including funding the ventures in stages, requiring entrepreneurs to make personal investments, syndicating investments, and maintaining in-depth knowledge about the industry in which they specialize.

Staged Funding The key idea behind staged funding is that each stage gives the venture capitalist an opportunity to reassess the management team and the firm's financial performance. If the performance does not meet expectations, the venture capitalists can bail out and cut their losses, or, if they still have confidence in the project, they can help management make some midcourse corrections so that the project can proceed. Companies typically go through three to seven funding stages, and each stage passed is a vote of confidence for that project. For example, each of the 11 stock offerings that Snap completed in the years before its IPO was one of these stages. (As you can see in Exhibit 15.2, the later stages of financing are sometimes called mezzanine financing because these investors did not get in on the ground floor.)

In our example, the \$2 million (\$1.6 million + \$0.4 million = \$2 million) with which you are starting your business makes up the first, or seed-stage, financing. It will be enough to build the prototype pizzeria, make it operational, and test the concept's viability in the marketplace. Based on the prototype's success, additional financing (such as the other \$4 million you need) may be allocated to build two additional pizzerias and develop the operating and financial systems needed to operate a chain of Tuscan pizzerias. Later stages of financing will fund more new restaurants.

The venture capitalists' investments give them an equity interest in the company. Typically, this is in the form of preferred stock that is convertible into common stock at the discretion of the venture capitalist. Preferred stock ensures that the venture capitalists have the most senior claim among the stockholders if the firm fails, while the conversion feature enables the venture capitalists to share in the gains if the business is successful.

Personal Investment Venture capitalists often require the entrepreneur to make a substantial personal investment in the business. In our example, by investing \$400,000 of your money and money from friends and employees, you confirm that you are confident in the business and highly motivated to make it succeed. Note that it is unlikely that the venture capitalists will allow you to pay yourself a large salary as manager of the business. They want your financial rewards to come from building a successful business, not from your salary.

Syndication It is a common practice to syndicate seed- and early-stage venture capital investments. Syndication occurs when the originating venture capitalist sells a percentage of a deal to other venture capitalists. Syndication reduces risk in two ways. First, it increases the diversification of the originating venture capitalist's investment portfolio, since other venture capitalists now own a portion of the deal and the originating venture capitalist has less money invested. Second, the willingness of other venture capitalists to share in the investment provides independent corroboration that the investment is a reasonable decision.

In-Depth Knowledge Another factor that reduces risk is the typical venture capitalist's in-depth knowledge of the industry and technology. The specialization we mentioned earlier gives the venture capitalist a comparative advantage over other investors or lenders who are generalists.

The Exit Strategy

Venture capitalists are not long-term investors in the companies they back. Typically, they stay with a new firm until it is a successful going concern, which usually takes three to seven years; then they exit by selling their equity position. Every venture capital agreement includes provisions identifying who has the authority to make critical decisions concerning the exit process. Those provisions usually include the following: (1) timing (when to exit), (2) the method of exit, and (3) what price is acceptable. Exit strategies can be controversial, because the venture capitalist and the other owners may not agree on these important details.

There are three principal ways in which venture capital firms exit venture-backed companies: selling to a strategic buyer, selling to a financial buyer, and offering stock to the public.

Strategic Buyer A common way for venture capitalists to exit is to sell the firm's equity to a strategic buyer in the private market. An example of a strategic buyer for the Tuscan Pizzeria would be a restaurant firm such as McDonald's Corporation. McDonald's might view the purchase as a strategic acquisition because one of the company's goals is to move into the nonhamburger food market with new brands, as it did when it acquired Chipotle Mexican Grill. The strategic buyer is looking to create value through synergies between the acquisition and the firm's existing productive assets.

Financial Buyer Sales to financial buyers are another way for venture capitalists to exit a firm. This type of sale occurs when a financial group—often a private equity (leveraged buyout) firm—buys the new firm with the intention of holding it for a period of time, usually three to five years, and then selling it for a higher price. (Private equity firms are discussed in more detail in Section 15.6.) The difference between a strategic and a financial buyout is that a financial buyer does not expect to gain from operating or marketing synergies. In a financial sale, the firm operates independently, and the buyer focuses on creating value by improving operations as much as possible. If the firm is performing poorly, the buyer will likely bring in a new management team.

Initial Public Offering A venture capitalist may also exit an investment by taking the company public through an initial public offering (IPO). To obtain the highest price possible in the IPO, a venture capitalist will not sell all of the shares he or she holds at the time of the IPO. Selling everything would send a bad signal to investors. Once the firm's shares are publicly traded, however, he or she can sell the remaining shares in the public market. **Exhibit 15.3** shows the number of strategic and financial sales and ventured-backed IPOs of new businesses in the United States between 2003 and 2016. As you can see, the majority of venture capitalists exit through strategic and financial sales rather than IPOs.

Venture Capitalists Provide More Than Financing

A common misconception about venture capitalists is that their sole function is to provide financing for new firms. One of their most important roles is to provide advice to entrepreneurs. Because of their industry knowledge and their general knowledge about what it takes for a business to succeed, they are able to provide counsel to entrepreneurs when a business is being started and during the early period of the business's operation. At these points in the development of a business, the people managing it (including the entrepreneur) often are long on technical skills, but short on the skills necessary to successfully manage growth.

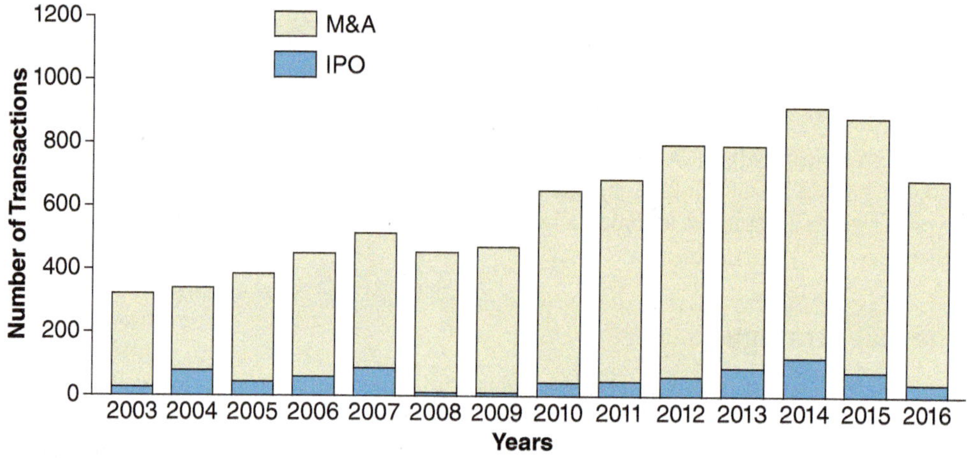

EXHIBIT 15.3 Strategic and Financial Sales and Venture-Backed IPO Exits in the United States, 2003–2016

Comparing the number of strategic and financial (M&A) sales of new businesses with the number of venture-backed IPOs from 2003 through 2016 shows that strategic and financial sales were far more common than IPOs during this period.

Source: National Venture Capital Association 2017 Yearbook.

The extent of the venture capitalists' involvement in the management of the firm depends on the experience and depth of the management team. Venture capital investors may want a seat on the board of directors. At a minimum, they will want an agreement that gives them unrestricted access to information about the firm's operations and financial performance and the right to attend and observe any board meeting. Finally, venture capitalists will insist on a mechanism giving them the authority to assume control of the firm if the firm's performance is poor, as well as the authority to install a new management team if necessary.

The Cost of Venture Capital Funding

The cost of venture capital funding is very high, but the high rates of return earned by venture capitalists are not unreasonable. First, venture capitalists bear a substantial amount of risk when they fund a new business. On average, for every ten businesses backed by venture capitalists, only one or two will prove successful. The winners have to cover the losses on businesses that fail. Second, venture capitalists spend a considerable amount of their time monitoring the progress of businesses they fund and intervening when a business's management team needs help. If a venture capital–financed new business is successful, more than likely the venture capitalists will have made a substantial contribution to creating value for the other owners.

Just what returns do venture capitalists earn on their investments in new businesses? As you might expect, the annual rate of return varies substantially from year to year, and the returns earned by different venture capitalists can differ considerably. It is difficult to generalize; however, a typical venture capital fund may generate annual returns of 15 to 25 percent on the money that it invests, compared with an average annual return for the S&P 500 of 11.95 percent over the 1926 to 2015 period (see Exhibit 7.3). The bottom line is that venture capital investing involves very high risk and is not for the faint of heart.

Before You Go On

1. Who are venture capitalists, and what do they do?
2. How is venture capital financing different from traditional sources of financing?
3. How do venture capitalists reduce the risk of their investments?
4. Explain the venture capital funding cycle.

15.3 Initial Public Offering

LEARNING OBJECTIVE

3. Discuss the advantages and disadvantages of going public and compute the net proceeds from an IPO.

If a business is very successful, at some point it will outgrow the ability of private sources of equity, such as family and friends and venture capitalists, to fund its growth. More money will be needed for investments in plant and equipment, working capital, and research and development (R&D) than these sources of capital will provide. One way to raise larger sums of cash or to facilitate the exit of a venture capitalist is through an initial public offering, or IPO, of the company's common stock.

As the name implies, an IPO is a company's first sale of common stock in the public market. First-time stock issues are given a special name because the marketing and pricing of these issues are distinctly different from those of seasoned offerings. A **seasoned public offering** is a sale of securities (either stock or bonds) by a firm that already has similar

seasoned public offering the sale of securities to the public by a firm that already has publicly traded securities outstanding publicly traded securities. The term *public offering* means that the securities being sold are registered with the Securities and Exchange Commission and, thus, can legally be sold to the public at large. Only registered securities can be sold to the public. Alternatively, securities can be sold directly to institutional investors in the private market, which we discuss in Section 15.6.

Advantages and Disadvantages of Going Public

When large sums of capital are necessary to fund a business or when the entrepreneur or venture capitalists are ready to sell some or all of their investment in a business, the entrepreneur and the venture capitalists may decide that an IPO, rather than the sale of the business to a strategic or financial buyer, is the appropriate way to achieve their goals. The decision to go public depends on an assessment of whether the advantages outweigh the disadvantages.

Advantages of Going Public

Weblink

For information on recent and forthcoming initial public offerings, go to http://www.ipoboutique.com.

Going public has a number of potential advantages. First, the amount of equity capital that can be raised in the public equity markets is typically larger than the amount that can be raised through private sources. There are millions of investors in public stock markets, and it is easier for firms to reach these investors through public markets. Second, after a firm has completed an IPO, additional equity capital can usually be raised through follow-on seasoned public offerings at a low cost. This is because the public markets are highly liquid and investors are willing to pay higher prices for more liquid shares of public firms than for the relatively illiquid shares of private firms. Third, going public can enable an entrepreneur to fund a growing business without giving up control. The entrepreneur does not have to sell the entire business but only what is needed to raise the necessary funds. Fourth, once a company has gone public, there is an active secondary market in which stockholders can buy and sell its shares. This enables the entrepreneur and other managers to more easily diversify their personal portfolios or to just sell shares in order to enjoy some of the rewards of having built a successful business. Of course, it also provides a way for venture capitalists to sell their shares.

Another potential advantage of having an active market for a firm's shares is that it can make it easier for the firm to attract top management talent and to better motivate current managers. This is true because senior managers generally own equity in the firm, and some part of their compensation is tied to the firm's stock performance. Recall that this aligns management's behavior with the objective of maximizing stockholder value. For publicly traded companies, it is easy to offer incentives tied to stock performance because market information about the value of a share of stock is readily available. For privately held companies, market transactions are infrequent, and thus the market value of a firm's equity must be estimated.

Disadvantages of Going Public

One disadvantage of going public is the high cost of the IPO itself. This cost is partly due to the fact that the stock is not seasoned. A seasoned stock, which is traded in a public secondary market, has an established record. Investors can observe how many shares trade on a regular basis (a measure of the liquidity for the shares) and the prices at which the trades take place. In contrast, the likely liquidity of a stock that is sold in an IPO is less well known and its value is more uncertain. For this reason investors are less comfortable buying a stock sold in an IPO and thus will not pay as high a price for it as for a similar seasoned stock. In addition, out-of-pocket costs such as legal fees, accounting expenses, printing costs, travel expenses, SEC filing fees, consultant fees, and taxes can add substantially to the cost of an IPO.

The costs of complying with ongoing SEC disclosure requirements also represent a disadvantage of going public. Once a firm goes public, it must meet a myriad of filing and other requirements imposed by the SEC. For larger firms, these regulatory costs are not terribly important because they represent a relatively small fraction of the total equity value. However, regulatory costs can be significant for small firms.

In addition to the out-of-pocket costs of complying with SEC requirements, the transparency that results from this compliance can be costly for some firms. The requirement that firms provide the public with detailed financial statements, detailed information on executive compensation, information about the firm's strategic initiatives, and so forth can put the firm at a competitive disadvantage relative to private firms that are not required to disclose such information.

Finally, some investors argue that the SEC's requirement of quarterly earnings estimates and quarterly financial statements encourages managers to focus on short-term profits rather than long-term value maximization. Managers who fail to meet their quarterly earnings projections often see their firm's stock price drop significantly.

Building Intuition

Investors View Seasoned Securities as Less Risky Than Unseasoned Securities

Investors will pay higher prices (or accept lower yields) for seasoned stock than for otherwise similar stock from an IPO. This is true because the liquidity and value of a seasoned stock are better known. The same is true for other types of securities, such as bonds.

Investment Banking Services

To complete an IPO, a firm will need the services of investment bankers, who are experts in bringing new securities to market. From Chapter 2, recall that investment bankers provide three basic services when bringing securities to market: (1) *origination*, which includes giving the firm financial advice and getting the issue ready to sell; (2) *underwriting*, which is the risk-bearing part of investment banking; and (3) *distribution*, which involves reselling the securities to the public.

Smaller firms such as The Tuscan Pizzeria will probably use the full range of services provided by the investment banker because they have little or no experience in issuing new securities. In contrast, larger firms that go to the seasoned public markets on a regular basis have experienced financial staffs and may provide some or all of the origination services themselves.

Identifying the investment banking firm that will manage the IPO process is an important task for the management of a firm because not all investment banks are equal. Top investment banking firms do not want to tarnish their reputation by bringing bad deals to market. Their willingness to underwrite a firm's IPO is an implicit seal of approval. Thus, securing the services of an investment banking firm with a reputation for quality and honesty will improve the market's receptivity and help ensure a successful IPO. Let's walk through the steps that a business takes in bringing a common-stock IPO to market. Note that the steps are nearly the same for debt issues.

Origination

During the origination phase, the investment banker helps management determine whether the firm is ready for an IPO. That requires determining whether the management team, the firm's historical financial performance, and the firm's expected future performance are strong enough to merit serious consideration by sophisticated investors. If the answer to any of these questions is no, the investment banker might help the firm find private capital to see it through until all of the answers are yes. Other issues that must be decided are how much money the firm needs to raise and how many shares must be sold.

Once the decision to sell stock is made, the firm's management must obtain a number of approvals. The firm's board of directors must approve all security sales, and stockholder approval is required if the number of shares of stock is to be increased.

Since securities sold to the public must be registered in advance with the SEC, the first step in this process is to file a registration statement with the SEC.[2] A portion of this statement, called the **preliminary prospectus**, contains detailed information about the type of business activities in which the firm is engaged and its financial condition, a description of the management team and their experience, a competitive analysis of the industry, a range within which the issuer expects the initial offering price for the stock to fall, the number of shares that the firm plans to sell, an explanation of how the proceeds from the IPO will be used, and a detailed discussion of the risks associated with the investment opportunity. While the SEC is reviewing the preliminary prospectus, the firm may distribute copies of it to potential customers, but by law no sales can be made from this document.

preliminary prospectus the initial registration statement filed with the SEC by a company preparing to issue securities in the public market; it contains detailed information about the issuer and the proposed issue

[2]There are two notable exemptions from this requirement: (1) an exemption for commercial paper with maturities up to 270 days and (2) a small-issue exemption for security issues of less than $5 million.

The information in a prospectus is designed to allow investors to make intelligent decisions about investing in a security issue and the risks associated with it. SEC approval is not an endorsement of the wisdom or desirability of making a particular investment. Approval means only that the firm has followed various rules and regulations required to issue securities and that the information is complete and accurate.

Underwriting

Once the origination work is complete, the security issue can be sold to investors. The securities can be underwritten in two ways: (1) on a firm-commitment basis or (2) on a best-effort basis.

Firm-Commitment Underwriting

firm-commitment underwriting underwriting agreement in which the underwriter purchases securities for a specified price and resells them

In the typical underwriting arrangement, called **firm-commitment underwriting**, the investment banker guarantees the issuer a fixed amount of money from the stock sale. The investment banker actually buys the stock from the firm at a fixed price and then resells it to the public. The underwriter bears the risk that the resale price might be lower than the price the underwriter pays—this is called *price risk*. The resale price can be lower if the underwriter overestimates the value of the stock when determining how much to pay the firm or if the value of the stock declines before it is resold to the public.

The investment banker's compensation is called the *underwriter's spread.* In a firm-commitment offering, the spread is the difference between the investment banker's purchase price and the offer price. The underwriter's spread in the vast majority of initial public stock offerings in the United States is 7 percent. The spread covers the investment banker's expenses, compensation for bearing risk, and profit. For example, suppose an investment banker buys a firm's stock for \$46.50 per share and the offer price is \$50.00. The gross underwriter's spread is \$3.50 per share (\$50.00 − \$46.50 = \$3.50), or 7 percent of the offer price. If the underwriter's total expenses for the offering are \$1.50 per share, the underwriter's net profit is \$2.00 per share (\$3.50 − \$1.50 = \$2.00).

Best-Effort Underwriting

best-effort underwriting underwriting agreement in which the underwriter does not agree to purchase the securities at a particular price but promises only to make its "best effort" to sell as much of the issue as possible above a certain price

With **best-effort underwriting**, the investment banking firm makes no guarantee to sell the securities at a particular price. It promises only to make its "best effort" to sell as much of the issue as possible at a certain price. In best-effort offerings, the investment banker does not bear the price risk associated with underwriting the issue, and compensation is based on the number of shares sold. Not surprisingly, most corporations issuing stock prefer firm-commitment arrangements to best-effort contracts. In fact, more than 95 percent of all underwritten offerings involve firm-commitment contracts. Best-effort offerings arise when underwriters do not want to accept the risk of guaranteeing the offering price.

Underwriting Syndicates

underwriting syndicate a group of underwriters that joins forces to reduce underwriting risk

To share the underwriting risk and to sell a new security issue more efficiently, underwriters may combine to form a group called an **underwriting syndicate**. Each member of the syndicate is responsible for selling some of the securities being issued. Participating in the syndicate entitles each underwriter to receive a portion of the underwriting fee as well as a proportionate allocation of the securities to sell to its own customers.

To broaden the search for potential investors, underwriting syndicates may enlist other investment banking firms in a syndicate known as a *selling group*, which assists in the sale of the securities. These firms receive a commission for each security they sell and bear none of the risk of underwriting the issue.

Determining the Offer Price

One of the investment banker's most difficult tasks is to determine the highest price at which the bankers will be able to quickly sell all of the shares being offered and that will result in a stable secondary market for the shares. One step in determining this price is to consider the value of the firm's expected future cash flows; the analysis and formulas used are like those presented in Chapter 9. In addition, the investment bankers will consider the stock price implied by multiples of total firm value to EBITDA or stock price to earnings per share for similar firms that are already public. Finally, the investment banker will conduct a *road show* in which management makes presentations about the firm and its prospects to potential investors. The road show is the key marketing and information-gathering event for an IPO. It generates interest in the offering and helps the investment banker determine the number of shares that investors are likely to purchase at different prices.

Due Diligence Meeting

Before the shares are sold, representatives from the underwriting syndicate hold a due diligence meeting with representatives of the issuer. The purpose of the meeting is to list, gather, and authenticate matters such as articles of incorporation, by-laws, patents, important contracts, and corporate minutes. In addition, the investment bankers have a final opportunity to ask management questions about the firm's financial integrity, intended use of the proceeds, and any other issues deemed relevant to the pending security sale.

Investment bankers hold due diligence meetings to protect their reputations and to reduce the risk of investors' lawsuits in the event the investment goes sour later on. The due diligence meetings are serious in that they ensure that all material issues about the firm and the offering are discovered and, subsequently, fully disclosed to investors.

Distribution

Once the due diligence process is complete, the underwriters and the issuer determine the final offer price in a *pricing call*. The pricing call typically takes place after the market has closed for the day. During this call, the lead underwriter (also known as the book runner because this underwriter assembles the book of orders for the offering) makes its recommendation concerning the appropriate price, and the firm's management decides whether that price is acceptable. By either accepting or rejecting the investment banker's recommendation, management ultimately makes the pricing decision. If management finds the price acceptable, the issuer files an amendment to the registration statement with the SEC, which contains the terms of the offering and the final prospectus. Once the securities are registered with the SEC, they can be sold to investors.

The First Day of Trading

The underwriter then typically sells the shares to investors when the market opens on the next day. The syndicate's primary concern is to sell the securities as quickly as possible at the offer price. Speed of sale is important because the offer price reflects market conditions at the end of the previous day and these conditions can change quickly. In successful offerings, most of the securities will have been presold to investors prior to delivery, and if the issue is not entirely presold, it will be sold out within a few hours. If the securities are not sold within a few days, the underwriting syndicate disbands, and members sell the securities at whatever price they can get.

The Closing

At the *closing* of a firm-commitment offering, the issuing firm delivers the security certificates to the underwriter and the underwriter delivers the payment for the securities, net of the underwriting fee, to the issuer. The closing usually takes place on the third business day after trading has started.

The Proceeds

We now arrive at the bottom line: How much money does the firm, and the underwriter, make from the sale of the new stock? Let's look at an example to see how to answer this question. Suppose a small manufacturing firm is doing a stock IPO with an investment banking firm on a firm-commitment basis. The firm plans to issue 2 million shares of common stock, and the gross underwriting spread is 7 percent. Following the road show, the CFO accepts a $20 per-share offering price that has been proposed by the underwriter. Based on this information, consider the following questions:

1. What are the total expected proceeds from the common-stock sale?
2. How much money does the issuer expect to get from the offering?
3. What is the investment bank's expected compensation from the offering?

The best approach to calculating these amounts is to first work through the funding allocations on a per-share basis and then compute the total dollar amounts. We know that the IPO's offer price is $20 per share and the underwriter's spread is 7 percent; thus, the issuer's expected net proceeds are $18.60 per share [$20 per share − ($20 per share × 0.07) = $18.60 per share]. The total proceeds from the sale of the stock are expected to equal $40 million ($20 per share × 2 million shares = $40 million). The total proceeds will be shared by (1) the firm, with $37.2 million ($18.60 per share × 2 million shares = $37.2 million) and (2) the underwriter, with $2.8 million ($1.40 per share × 2 million shares = $2.8 million). If the syndicate sells the stock at the offering price of $20, the sale will be deemed successful, and both the underwriter and the issuer will receive their expected proceeds.

Learning by Doing Applications 15.1 and **15.2** illustrate additional IPO calculations.

LEARNING BY DOING

APPLICATION 15.1 | An Unsuccessful IPO

Problem Let's continue with our IPO example from the text. Suppose that the stock sale is not successful and the underwriter is able to sell the stock, on average, for only $19 per share. If the underwriter buys the stock from the issuer for $18.60, what will be the proceeds for each party from the sale?

Approach Because the underwriting is a firm-commitment offering, the underwriter guarantees that the issuer will receive the full expected amount, as calculated in the text. The underwriter will have to absorb the entire loss.

Solution The total proceeds from the sale are $19 per share. Since the issuer still receives $18.60 per share because of the firm-commitment offering, the issuer receives total proceeds of $18.60 per share × 2 million shares = $37.2 million. By comparison, underwriter receives $0.40 per share. Its total proceeds from the sale are $0.8 million ($0.40 per share × 2 million shares = $0.8 million) rather than the expected $2.8 million. The total proceeds for the IPO sale are $38 million ($37.2 million + $0.8 million = $38.0 million).

LEARNING BY DOING

APPLICATION 15.2 | A Best-Effort IPO

Problem Now let's assume that the stock in our IPO is sold on a best-effort basis and that the underwriter agrees to a spread of 7 percent of the selling price. The average selling price remains at $19 per share. What are the net proceeds for the issuer and the underwriter in this best-effort offering?

Approach The key to working this problem is recognizing that in a best-effort IPO, the underwriter bears no risk. The risk of an unsuccessful sale is borne entirely by the issuing firm. Thus, the underwriter is paid first, and the residual goes to the issuer.

Solution Since the underwriter agreed to a spread of 7 percent of the price at which each share of stock is sold, the distribution of the proceeds can be calculated as follows: The underwriter's spread for each share sold is $1.33 per share ($19.00 per share × 0.07 = $1.33 per share). The firm's total net proceeds are $35.34 million [($19.00 per share × 0.93) × 2 million shares = $35.34 million], and the underwriter's total proceeds are $2.66 million ($1.33 per share × 2 million shares = $2.66 million). The total proceeds from the IPO sale are still $38 million, but are distributed differently.

Before You Go On

1. What is a seasoned offering, and why are seasoned securities valued more highly than securities sold in an IPO?
2. Explain the two ways in which a security issue can be underwritten.
3. List the steps in the IPO process.

15.4 IPO Pricing and Cost

LEARNING OBJECTIVE

4. Explain why, when underwriting new security offerings, investment bankers prefer that the securities be underpriced. Compute the total cost of an IPO.

In the preceding section, we mentioned that pricing an IPO is one of the underwriter's most difficult tasks. In this section, we discuss an important pricing issue, underpricing, and then turn once again to the costs of issuing an IPO.

The Underpricing Debate

As you might expect, tension arises between the issuer and the underwriters when the final offer price for the stock is being determined. Clearly, the issuer prefers the stock price to be as high as realistically possible. In contrast, the underwriters prefer some degree of underpricing. **Underpricing** is defined as offering new securities for sale at a price below their true value. The lower the offering price, the more likely the securities will sell out quickly—and the less likely the underwriters will end up with unsold inventory. Investment bankers will also argue that some underpricing helps attract long-term institutional investors who help provide stability for the stock price once the secondary market for the shares is established. Because these investors will not sell, or *flip,* the shares as quickly, their presence reduces price volatility.

underpricing offering new securities for sale at a price below their true value

Although the issuer and the underwriters may disagree on pricing, in reality both face potential costs if the stock price is too high or too low. On the one hand, if the stock is priced too high, the entire issue will not sell at the proposed offer price. Furthermore, there can be considerable uncertainty about what the true value of the shares is since they have not yet traded in the public market. This uncertainty also contributes to the pressure to set a lower price. In a firm-commitment offering, the underwriters will suffer a financial loss if the offer price is set too high; under a best-effort agreement, the issuing firm will raise less money than expected.

On the other hand, if the stock is priced below its true value, the firm's existing stockholders will experience an opportunity loss; that is, the firm will receive less money for the stock than it is worth. In addition, if the underpricing is significant, the investment banking firm will suffer a loss of reputation for failing to price the new issue correctly and raising less money for its client than it could have. In practice, most market participants agree that some underpricing is good for both the issuer and the underwriter. However, the question of *how much* underpricing is appropriate is open for debate.

IPOs Are Consistently Underpriced

Data from the marketplace show that the shares sold in an IPO are typically priced between 10 and 15 percent below the price at which they close at the end of the first day of trading. This implies that underwriters tend to sell shares of stock in IPOs to investors for between 90 and 85 percent of their true market value.

The real costs of underpricing can be staggering. For example, when Snap went public on March 2, 2017, the company and its early investors sold 200 million shares of stock at a price of \$17.00 per share, raising \$3.4 billion in total. At the end of the first day of trading, the stock closed at \$24.48 per share. This means that Snap stock was underpriced by \$7.48 per share (\$24.48 − \$17.00 = \$7.48). Thus, the Snap stock might have sold for \$1.496 billion (\$7.48 per share × 200 million shares = \$1.496 billion) more. Who received this \$1.496 billion of value? It went into the pockets of the new investors who bought the shares allocated by the underwriters of the IPO.

Exhibit 15.4 shows data for the number of IPOs per year and the average first-day return to investors for the years 1997–2016. The average first-day return is a measure of the amount of underpricing. Excluding 1999 and 2000, the weighted average first-day return over the 1997–2016 period is about 13.1 percent, although there is considerable variation on a

EXHIBIT 15.4 Initial Public Offerings, Gross Proceeds, and Returns, 1997–2016

This exhibit summarizes the number of IPOs per year, the gross proceeds, and the average first-day returns to investors from all IPOs for the 1997–2016 period. The average first-day return represents the amount of underpricing. The exhibit illustrates the substantial variation in IPO activity and underpricing in the U.S. public equity markets during this period.

Year	Number of IPOs	Gross Proceeds ($ billions)	Avg First Day Return (%)[a]
1997	474	$31.8	14.4%
1998	281	33.7	15.6
1999	477	65.0	57.1
2000	381	64.9	46.0
2001	79	34.2	8.7
2002	66	22.0	5.1
2003	63	9.5	10.4
2004	173	31.2	12.4
2005	159	28.2	9.3
2006	157	30.5	13.0
2007	159	35.7	13.9
2008	21	22.8	24.8
2009	41	13.2	11.1
2010	91	29.8	6.2
2011	81	27.0	13.0
2012	93	31.1	8.9
2013	157	38.8	20.5
2014	206	42.2	12.8
2015	115	21.7	18.7
2016	74	12.1	14.4
Average	167	$31.3	21.1%

[a]Average returns are calculated as the weighted average where the dollar amount of each issue is the weight.
Source: Jay R. Ritter, Table 1 in unpublished note titled "Initial Public Offerings: Updated Statistics," dated February 20, 2017.

year-by-year basis. The average underpricing of issues during the last 16 years, from 2001 through 2016, was 13.1 percent, while the average during the 1999 to 2000 period was 63.7 percent. Some 858 total IPO offerings were sold during 1999 and 2000, and in both years the total amount of money raised through IPOs was unusually high. Because of the underpricing, however, about $66.9 billion was left on the table (not received by the companies making the offerings or their selling shareholders) during these two years.

The Cost of an IPO

As we have already mentioned, the cost of going public is high. Bringing our previous discussions together, we can identify three basic costs associated with issuing stock in an IPO:

1. **Underwriting spread.** The underwriting spread is the difference between the proceeds the issuer receives and the total amount raised in the offering.
2. **Out-of-pocket expenses.** Out-of-pocket expenses include other investment banking fees, legal fees, accounting expenses, printing costs, travel expenses, SEC filing fees, consultant fees, and taxes. All of these expenses are reported in the prospectus.
3. **Underpricing.** Underpricing is typically defined as the difference between the offering price and the closing price at the end of the first day of trading in the public market. It is the opportunity loss that the issuer's stockholders incur from selling the security below its true market value.

EXHIBIT 15.5 Costs of Issuing an IPO, 2001–2016

This exhibit shows IPO costs in the United States for the period from 2001 to 2016, by the total value of the shares issued. IPO costs include the direct costs associated with the underwriter's spread and out-of-pocket expenses plus the costs of underpricing (represented by the average first-day return). As you can see, underpricing costs tend to be higher in larger issues, while direct costs decline as the size of the issue increases.

Value of Issue ($ millions)	Number of IPOs	Direct Cost[a] (%)	Average First-Day Return[b] (%)
$2–9.99	24	16.46%	−0.27%
$10–19.99	65	11.37	10.20
$20–39.99	126	9.18	6.40
$40–59.99	190	8.28	9.65
$60–79.99	216	7.88	11.74
$80–99.99	199	7.70	19.78
$100–199.99	402	7.56	17.84
$200–499.99	306	6.47	12.72
$500 and over	127	5.35	11.44
All issues	1,655	8.92%	11.06%

[a]Direct costs (underwriting spread plus out-of pocket expenses).
[b]Average first-day returns are reported as a percent of the issue price.
Source: Securities Data Corporation and author estimates.

Exhibit 15.5 presents some market data on the cost of issuing an IPO. The first column shows the size (value of the shares sold) of the IPO; the second column presents the total direct costs to the issuer, which equals the underwriter's spread plus out-of-pocket expenses; and the third column shows the average first-day returns to investors, which represents the amount by which the issue was underpriced.

For a smaller IPO (less than $40 million), the costs associated with underpricing are relatively small; however, direct costs comprise a much larger fraction of the total value of the issue. In deals valued at less than $10 million, for example, average direct costs are 16.46 percent of the value of the issue, while underpricing is negligible. In contrast, underpricing of IPOs is more pronounced for larger issues, but there are significant economies of scale in direct costs.

Decision Making Example 15.1 and **Learning by Doing Application 15.3** illustrate additional IPO calculations and analyses.

EXAMPLE 15.1 | Pricing an IPO

DECISION MAKING

Situation You are the CFO of a small firm that is planning an IPO. You are meeting with your investment banker to discuss the offer price for your common-stock issue. The investment banker tells you that an IPO pricing model indicates that the current value of your stock is $20 per share. Furthermore, a firm with similar risk characteristics completed an IPO two months ago, and its stock price suggests a current market price of $21 per share. The investment banker says that the offer price should be set at $15 per share. What decision should you make with regard to the investment bank's offer price?

Decision Given the available information, you should be cautious about accepting the proposed offer price of $15 per share. The investment bank's IPO pricing model estimates that your stock's current market value is $20 per share. This estimate is validated by the fact that it is very close to the price of the similar firm's stock. If you sold the stock for $15 and the closing price at the end of the first day was $20, the first-day return would be 33.3 percent [($20 − $15)/$15 = 0.333, or 33.3 percent], which is on the upper end of the first-day returns in Exhibit 15.4. Unless your IPO is unusual in some way—for example, you are issuing a large number of shares or the stock price is highly uncertain—a more reasonable price might be $18 per share. With a price of $18 you would expect a first-day return of 11.1 percent [($20 − $18)/$18 = 0.111, or 11.1 percent].

LEARNING BY DOING

APPLICATION 15.3 | The Cost of an IPO

Problem Suppose that Madrid Electronics from Madrid, New Mexico, sells $70 million of stock at $50 per share in an IPO. The underwriter's spread is 7 percent, and the firm's legal fees, SEC registration fees, and other out-of-pocket costs are $200,000. The firm's stock price increases 15 percent on the first day of trading. In dollars, what is the total cost to the firm of issuing the stock?

Approach To calculate the total cost to the firm of issuing the stock, we must consider all three major costs associated with bringing it to market: underwriting spread, out-of-pocket expenses, and underpricing.

Solution

1. *Underwriting spread:* The underwriter's spread is $3.50 per share ($50.00 per share × 0.07 = $3.50 per share). The number of shares sold is 1.4 million ($70 million/$50.00 per share = 1.4 million shares). Thus, the underwriting cost is $4.9 million ($3.50 per share × 1.4 million shares = $4.9 million).
2. *Out-of-pocket expenses:* The out-of-pocket expenses are $200,000.
3. *Underpricing:* The dollar amount of underpricing is computed as follows. The firm's stock was offered at $50.00 and increased to $57.50 per share ($50.00 per share × 1.15 = $57.50 per share) during the first day of trading; thus, the first-day underpricing is $7.50 per share ($57.50 per share − $50.00 per share = $7.50 per share). The total underpricing is $10.5 million ($7.50 per share × 1.4 million shares = $10.5 million).

The total cost to the firm of the IPO is $15.6 million, which consists of the following: (1) $4.9 million in underwriting fees, (2) $0.2 million out-of-pocket expenses, and (3) $10.5 million in underpricing.

Before You Go On

1. What is underpricing, and why is it a cost to the stockholders?
2. What are the components of the cost associated with an IPO?

15.5 General Cash Offer by a Public Company

LEARNING OBJECTIVE

5. Discuss the costs of bringing a general cash offer to market.

The need for funding does not end when a company goes public. Most companies continually make new investments in real assets and working capital. If they do not generate enough cash from operations to fund these investments, their managers must raise capital from outside the firm.

Managers of every business want to fund the business at the lowest possible cost. If a public firm is financially sound, the lowest-cost source of external funds is often a **general cash offer**, also referred to as a *registered public offering*. A general cash offer is a sale of debt or equity, open to all investors, by a registered public company that has previously sold stock to the public. The procedures involved in a general cash offer are summarized here. You will see that there are some similarities between these procedures and those involved in an IPO.

general cash offer a sale of debt or equity, open to all investors, by a company that has previously sold stock to the public

1. *Type of Security and Amount to Be Raised.* Management decides how much money the firm needs to raise and what type of security to issue, such as debt, common stock, or preferred stock.

2. *Approvals.* Approval is obtained from the board of directors to issue securities. If the size of a stock issue exceeds the previously authorized number of shares of common or preferred stock, approval from stockholders is required as well.
3. *Registration Statement.* The issuer files a registration statement and satisfies all of the securities laws enforced by the SEC. For a debt issue, the registration statement must contain a bond indenture which specifies the details of the issue.
4. *Offer Price.* After assessing demand, the underwriter and the issuer agree on an offer price.
5. *Closing.* At the closing of a firm-commitment offering, the issuer delivers the securities to the underwriter, and the underwriter pays for them, net of its fees. The securities are then sold to investors.

The issuer has flexibility in the method of sale and the way the securities are registered. Both of these factors can affect the issuer's funding cost. Next we consider methods of sale and registration and discuss the costs of general cash offers.

Competitive versus Negotiated Sale

In a general cash offer, management must decide whether to sell the securities on a competitive or a negotiated basis. In a *competitive sale,* the issuer specifies the type and number of securities it wants to sell and hires an investment banking firm to do the origination work. Once the origination work is completed, the issuer invites underwriters to bid competitively to buy the issue.[4] The investment banking firm that offers the highest price for the securities wins the bid. The winning underwriter then pays for the securities and makes them available to investors at the offer price.

In a *negotiated sale,* the issuer selects the underwriter at the beginning of the origination process. At that time, the scope of the work is defined, and the issuer negotiates the origination and underwriter's fees to be charged. The issuer and underwriter then work closely to design the issue and determine the most favorable time to take the securities to market. Following an assessment of demand, the offer price is set and the underwriter pays the issuer for the securities and sells them to individual investors.

Lower Cost Method of Sale

Which method of sale—competitive or negotiated—results in the lower funding cost for the issuing firm? This question has been hotly debated, and the results from empirical studies are mixed.

The argument for competitive bidding is straightforward: competition keeps everyone honest. That is, the greater the number of bidders, the greater the competition for the security issue, and the lower the cost to the issuer. Negotiated sales lack competition and therefore should be the more costly method of sale.

Not everyone agrees with this argument, however. Proponents of negotiated sales argue that in a negotiated sale the investment banker works closely with the issuer and thus has intimate knowledge of the firm and its problems. As a result, the investment banker is in a better position to reduce uncertainty surrounding the issue and tell the firm's story to potential investors, resulting in a lower issue cost. Proponents also argue that negotiated sales involve *potential competition.* The potential competitors are the other investment banks that were not chosen to underwrite the current issue but would like to underwrite the firm's next issue. These investment bankers will not hesitate to drop by and tell the issuer's CFO how much better they could have done than the underwriter that was chosen. Thus, the threat of potential competition provides many of the same benefits as direct competition.

[4]The investment banking firm that does the origination work is excluded from bidding on the issue because its intimate knowledge of the deal would be considered an unfair advantage by other bidders and thus would discourage them from bidding.

Selecting the Better Method

In the end, the better method of sale depends on the complexity of the sale and the market conditions at the time of sale. It also depends on the type of securities being offered.

For debt issues, most experts believe that competitive sales are the less costly method of selling so-called *vanilla bonds* when market conditions are stable. Recall from Chapter 8 that vanilla bonds are bonds with no unusual features. Their terms and conditions are standardized and well-known to market participants, and they lack complex features. These securities are like commodities because market participants understand the risks of investing in them and are comfortable buying them. In contrast, when there are complex circumstances to explain or when market conditions are unstable, negotiated sales provide the less costly method of sale for debt issues. In these situations, a negotiated sale allows the underwriter to better manage uncertainty and explain the firm's situation, which results in the lower funding cost.

For equity securities, negotiated sales generally provide the lower-cost method of sale. Equity issues by their very nature tend to be complex, and for the reasons just mentioned, complexities are better handled when sales are negotiated. Thus, it is no surprise that virtually all equity issues, including IPOs, involve negotiated sales.

Decision Making Example 15.2 illustrates choices between competitive and negotiated sales of securities.

Shelf Registration

shelf registration a type of SEC registration that allows firms to register to sell securities over a two-year period and, during that time, take the securities "off the shelf" and sell them as needed

As mentioned earlier, the preparation of an SEC registration statement is a costly undertaking. Since November 1983, the SEC has allowed some two thousand large corporations the option of using **shelf registration**. Shelf registration allows a firm to register an inventory of securities for a two-year period. During that time, the firm can take the securities "off the shelf" and sell them as needed. Costs associated with selling the securities are reduced because only a single registration statement is required. A shelf registration statement can cover multiple securities, and there is no penalty if authorized securities are not issued.

In addition to reducing costs, corporations gain two important benefits from shelf registration. First is the greater flexibility in bringing securities to market. Securities can be taken off the shelf and sold within minutes. Thus, firms can sell their securities when market conditions are more favorable. Second, shelf registration allows firms to periodically sell small amounts of securities, raising money as it is actually needed, rather than banking a large amount of money from a single security sale and spending it over time.

DECISION MAKING

EXAMPLE 15.2 | Method of Sale

Situation You are the CFO of a firm that plans to issue a number of securities during the upcoming year. You expect market conditions to remain stable during this period. To obtain the lower funding costs, which method of sale—competitive or negotiated—will you choose for the issues listed in the following?

a. An issue of common stock.
b. A 20-year bond with a fixed-rate coupon.
c. A 20-year revenue bond to fund a manufacturing facility in Brazil; payment of interest and principal is tied to revenues earned by the new facility.
d. A 10-year fixed-rate bond sold from a shelf registration issue.

Decision The method of sale that would more likely achieve the lower funding cost for each of the proposed security issues is as follows:

a. Negotiated sale, because negotiated sales are generally better for equity issues.
b. Competitive sale, because this is a vanilla bond, and competitive sales are more cost-effective for these standardized bond issues.
c. Negotiated sale, because this bond issue involves several complexities.
d. Competitive sale, because this is another vanilla bond.

EXHIBIT 15.6 **Average Gross Underwriting Spread and Out-of-Pocket Expenses as a Percentage of Amount Raised for Public Offerings, 1977–2001**

You can see from this exhibit that issuing common stock is the most expensive method of obtaining funds, while issuing corporate bonds (debt) is the least expensive. The higher cost for the stock issues reflects the greater underwriting risk (higher sales commissions) and the higher out-of-pocket expenses required to bring equity securities to market. For all three types of securities shown—common stock, preferred stock, and bonds—there are economies of scale; as issue size increases, total issue cost, as a percent of the amount raised, declines.

	Common Stock			Preferred Stock			Bonds		
Principal Amount ($ millions)	Gross Under-writing Spread (%)	Out-of-Pocket Expenses (%)	Total (%)	Gross Under-writing Spread (%)	Out-of-Pocket Expenses (%)	Total (%)	Gross Under-writing Spread (%)	Out-of-Pocket Expenses (%)	Total (%)
$0.0–$9.9	7.69%	5.94%	13.63%	4.69%	3.65%	8.34%	2.04%	1.91%	3.95%
$10.0–$24.9	5.99	2.70	8.69	3.05	1.24	4.29	1.29	1.11	2.40
$25.0–$49.9	5.52	1.57	7.09	2.33	0.57	2.90	0.95	0.68	1.63
$50.0–$99.9	5.13	0.89	6.02	2.06	0.28	2.34	0.96	0.43	1.39
$100.0–$199.9	4.68	0.59	5.27	2.76	0.28	3.04	0.90	0.30	1.20
$200.0–$499.9	4.16	0.41	4.57	2.63	0.17	2.80	0.84	0.16	1.00
$500.0 and over	3.49	0.14	3.63	2.62	0.10	2.72	0.57	0.08	0.65

Excludes rights issues, issues callable or putable in under one year, and issues that are not underwritten.
Source: Thomson Reuters.

The Cost of a General Cash Offer

Even though a general cash offer is a *wholesale market* transaction, the cost of raising money through such an offer is not trivial. **Exhibit 15.6** shows the average underwriting spread, out-of-pocket expenses, and total cost for common stock, preferred stock, and corporate bond issues of various sizes. Note that this exhibit does not include data on underpricing; total cost includes only underwriting spread and out-of-pocket expenses.

As you can see from the exhibit, issuing common stock is the most costly alternative, and issuing corporate bonds (nonconvertible) is the least costly. For example, for a large security issue ($500 million and over), the total cost of issuing common stock is 3.63 percent of the amount raised, whereas the total cost for a corporate bond issue is 0.65 percent of the amount raised. The higher cost for the equity issues reflects the greater underwriting risk, the higher sales commissions for those involved in selling the issue, and the higher administrative expenses required to bring equity securities to market.

Exhibit 15.6 also reveals significant economies of scale in both underwriting spreads and out-of-pocket expenses. Look at the "Total" column for common stock, for example. The cost for a small equity issue (with a principal amount of less than $10 million) is 13.63 percent of the amount raised, whereas the cost for large equity issues ($500 million and over) is only 3.63 percent.

Finally, let's compare this exhibit with Exhibit 15.5, which gives the costs associated with issuing an IPO. In comparing the exhibits, we need to compare the direct costs from Exhibit 15.5 with the total costs from Exhibit 15.6, since Exhibit 15.6 includes no underpricing costs. As you can see, the cost of an IPO is significantly higher than the cost of a general cash offer of equity—even when the cost of underpricing for the IPO is not included in the total. The total direct cost of selling a large ($500 million and over) equity IPO is 5.51 percent, while the total cost for a general cash offer of the same size is 3.63 percent. This reflects the greater risk involved in underwriting an IPO and the higher cost of distributing the shares in an IPO.

Before You Go On

1. Explain why firms generally sell their equity and complicated debt issues through negotiated sales.
2. Explain the importance of shelf registration.

15.6 Private Markets and Bank Loans

LEARNING OBJECTIVE

6. Explain why a firm that has access to the public markets might elect to raise money through a private placement.

As we have noted, the public markets for debt and equity are wholesale markets where firms can often sell securities at the lowest possible cost. For various reasons, however, firms may sometimes need—or prefer—to sell their securities in private markets. In this section, we first consider various aspects of the private securities markets and then briefly discuss private placements of equity and debt.

Private versus Public Markets

Firms that sell securities in the public markets are typically large, well-known firms with high credit quality and sustainable profits. Of course, not every firm reaches these levels of achievement. As a result, many smaller firms and firms of lower credit standing have limited access, or no access, to the public markets. Their cheapest source of external funding is often the private markets.

Market conditions also affect whether a firm can sell its securities in the public markets. When market conditions are unstable, some smaller firms that were previously able to sell securities in the public markets no longer can do so at a reasonable price. The reason for this is that during periods of market instability, investors seek to hold high-quality securities, and they are reluctant to purchase or hold high-risk securities in their portfolios. On Wall Street, this phenomenon is called *flight to quality* and refers to moving capital to the safest possible investments to protect oneself during unsettled periods in the market.

A number of sizable companies of high credit quality prefer to sell their securities in the private markets even though they can access public markets. Many of these private companies are owned by entrepreneurs, families, or family foundations. Two examples of large "family" businesses that avoid public markets and fund themselves privately are the Cargill Company and the Carlson Companies, both located in Minneapolis, Minnesota. Such firms elect to avoid the public markets for different reasons. Some wish to avoid the regulatory costs and transparency requirements that come with public sales of securities, as discussed in Section 15.3. Others believe that their firms have intricate business structures or complex legal or financial structures that can best be explained to a small group of sophisticated investors rather than to the public at large.

We should mention that bootstrapping and venture capital financing are part of the private market as well. We discussed these two processes at the beginning of the chapter because they are primary sources of funding for new businesses.

Private Placements

As you may recall from Chapter 2, a *private placement* occurs when a firm sells unregistered securities directly to investors such as insurance companies, commercial banks, or wealthy individuals. Most private placements involve the sale of debt issues, but equity issues can also be privately placed. About half of all corporate debt is sold through the private placement market.

Investment banks and money center banks often assist firms with private placements. They help the issuer locate potential buyers for their securities, put the deal together, and do the necessary origination work. They may also help negotiate the terms and price of the sale, but they do not underwrite the issue. In a traditional private placement, the issuer sells the securities directly to investors.

Private placements have a number of advantages, relative to public offerings, for certain issuers. The cost of funds, net of transaction costs, may be lower, especially for smaller firms and those with low credit ratings. Also, private lenders, because of their intimate knowledge of the firm and its management, are more willing to negotiate changes to a bond contract, if changes are needed. Furthermore, if a firm suffers financial distress, the problems are more likely to be resolved without going to a bankruptcy court. Other advantages include the speed at which private placements can be completed and flexibility in issue size. If the issuer and the investor already have a relationship, a sale can be completed in a few days, and small issues of a few million dollars are not uncommon.

Weblink

Visit this small-business information Web site for more about private placements and other topics: http://sbinformation.about.com/cs/creditloans/a/prplacemt.htm.

The biggest drawback of private placements involves restrictions on the resale of the securities. Private placements do not have to be registered with the SEC as long as the securities are purchased for investment and not for resale. In practice, securities laws in the United States limit the sale of private placements to investors who have the capacity to evaluate the securities' investment potential and risk. These are generally high income investors or investors with large investment portfolios. Thus, private placement securities have limited marketability unless the firm subsequently registers the issue. To address their concern about the lack of marketability, investors in private placements require a higher yield relative to a comparable public offering or that the firm agree to register the securities shortly after the transaction is completed.

In April 1990, the SEC adopted Rule 144A, which allows large financial institutions to trade unregistered securities among themselves. This rule dramatically improved the marketability of privately placed securities. The rule also allows issuers to sell unregistered securities to investment banking firms, which can then resell the securities to qualified institutional buyers (QIBs). Since 1995, about half of all private placement deals have been conducted under Rule 144A.

Private Equity Firms

Like venture capitalists, private equity firms pool money from financial and insurance firms, pension funds, individuals and families, corporations, foundations and endowments, and other sources to make investments. Unlike venture capitalists, private equity firms invest in more mature companies, and they often purchase 100 percent of a business. Private equity managers look to increase the value of the firms they acquire by closely monitoring their performance and providing better management. Once value is increased, they sell the firms for a profit. Private equity firms generally hold investments for three to five years.

While private equity firms often purchase 100 percent of a business, they also represent a potential source of capital for large public firms that have businesses—such as divisions or individual plants—that they are interested in selling. Large public firms often sell businesses when they no longer fit the firms' strategies or when they are offered a price they cannot refuse. Selling such businesses is an alternative to selling equity or debt as a means of raising new capital.

Private equity firms establish *private equity funds* to make investments. These funds are usually organized as limited partnerships (or more recently as limited liability companies), which consist of (1) general partners who manage the firm's investments and (2) limited partners who invest money in the firm, but have limited liability and are not involved in the day-to-day activities of the firm.[5] As owners, the limited partners share in the income, capital gains, and tax benefits from the private equity funds. The general partners, who also invest in the funds, receive income, capital gains, and tax benefits that are proportionate to their investments. In addition, as compensation for managing the funds, general partners collect management fees and receive a percentage of the income and capital gains that are earned with the limited partners' money.

Private equity funds have historically focused on investments in small and medium-size firms that have stable cash flows and where there is the potential to improve cash flows substantially. In recent years, however, private equity firms have been able to raise so much capital

[5]Limited liability companies are discussed in Chapter 1. The same forms of organization are used by venture capital funds.

that they have started doing large deals. In fact, nine of the ten largest private equity transactions in U.S. history have been completed in the last eight years. One transaction, involving the Texas utility company TXU, had a total price tag of $44 billion.

Private equity investors focus on firms that have stable cash flows because they use a lot of debt to finance their acquisitions. A firm must have stable positive cash flows in order to make the interest and principal payments. A private equity firm may borrow as much as $3 or $4 for every dollar it invests. By adding more debt, the private equity firm frees up its own cash, allowing it to make additional investments and increasing the return on its equity investments. When a large amount of leverage is used to take over a company, the transaction is called a *leveraged buyout.*[6]

How do private equity firms improve the performance of firms in which they invest? First, they make sure that the firms have the best possible management teams. Since a private equity firm typically owns 100 percent of the equity in a firm it invests in, its general partners have the ability to replace the management team when necessary. Second, private equity investors closely monitor each firm's performance and provide advice and counsel to the firm's management team. General partners have in-depth knowledge of the industries in which they invest, and some have been CEOs of similar firms. Third, private equity investors often facilitate mergers and acquisitions that help improve the competitive positions of the companies in which they invest.

Agency problems tend to be smaller in firms owned by private equity investors than in public firms. In public firms, stockholders are the owners. However, we know that it is not practical for dispersed stockholders to be actively engaged in managing the firm. Day-to-day decision-making responsibilities are delegated to the firm's managers. Managers are stock-holders' agents and are supposed to act in the best interest of stockholders. Yet, as we discussed in Chapter 1, managers tend to pursue their own self-interest instead of the interests of stockholders. The misalignment between the owners' best interests and the manager's self-interest results in agency costs. Private equity funds have much lower agency costs than the average publicly held firm. Since the general partners in a private equity fund are owners and benefit greatly from the value they create, they have every incentive to act in a manner consistent with maximizing the value of limited partners' investments.

Finally, we should note that private equity firms carry a much smaller regulatory burden and fewer financial reporting requirements than do public firms. Specifically, private equity firms are able to avoid most of the SEC's registration and compliance costs and other regulatory burdens, such as compliance with the Sarbanes-Oxley Act.

Private Investments in Public Equity

As we have already noted, small- and medium-size companies can find it difficult and costly to raise money in the public markets. In these circumstances, it can be more efficient or cost effective to sell stock privately, even if the company's stock is already publicly traded. *Private investment in public equity,* or PIPE, transactions are transactions in which a public company sells unregistered stock to an investor—often a hedge fund or some other institutional investor. PIPE transactions have been around for a long time, but the number of these transactions has increased greatly since the late 1990s.

In a PIPE transaction, investors purchase securities (equity or debt) directly from a publicly traded company in a private placement. The securities are virtually always sold to the investors at a discount to the price at which they would sell in the public markets. This discount compensates the buyer for limits on the marketability of these securities and, often, for being able to provide capital quickly.

Because the securities sold in a PIPE transaction are not registered with the SEC, they are restricted securities in the sense that, under federal securities law, they cannot be resold to investors in the public markets for one year unless the company registers them. As a result, as part of the PIPE contract, the company often agrees to register the restricted securities with the SEC, usually within 90 days of the PIPE closing. Once the securities are registered, they

[6]In a leveraged buyout, a private equity firm takes over a company by using a high proportion of borrowed funds. The target company's assets provide security for the loans taken out by the acquiring firm.

can be resold freely in the secondary markets. In the event that the issuer is unable to register the securities or the registration is delayed past a deadline date, the issuer might be required to pay the investor liquidity damages, usually 1 or 1.5 percent per month, as compensation for the loss of liquidity.

The major advantages of a PIPE transaction to issuers are that it gives them faster access to capital and a lower funding cost than a registered public offering. A PIPE transaction can be completed in a few days, whereas a typical public offering underwritten by an investment bank takes much longer. PIPE transactions involving a healthy firm can also be executed without the use of an investment bank, resulting in a cost saving of as much as 7 or 8 percent of the proceeds raised. Finally, a PIPE transaction can be the only way for a small financially distressed company to raise equity capital.

Commercial Bank Lending

LEARNING OBJECTIVE

7. Review some advantages of borrowing from a commercial bank rather than selling securities in financial markets and discuss bank term loans.

The previous sections have discussed long-term debt and equity funding that is obtained in private and public financial markets. Commercial banks are another important source of funds for businesses. Almost every company has a working relationship with at least one bank, and smaller companies depend on them for funding and for financial advice. Next, we review some of the most common types of bank loans used by businesses. Most small and medium-size firms borrow from commercial banks on a regular basis.

Prime-Rate Loans

The most common type of business loan is a *prime-rate loan*. These are loans in which the borrowing rate is based on the *prime rate of interest*, which is historically the loan rate that banks charge their most creditworthy customers. In practice, some customers are able to borrow below the prime rate. Prime-rate loans are often used to finance working capital needs such as inventory purchases. To ensure that prime-rate borrowing is not used as long-term financing, banks often require that the loan balance be brought to zero for a short time each year.

The prime rate charged by a bank might be higher than other market borrowing rates. This is because banks provide a range of services with these loans, much as venture capitalists provide services to start-up businesses. For example, small and medium-size firms often rely on the bank's lending officer to serve as the firm's financial adviser and to keep the CFO abreast of current developments and trends in financing. Thus, the cost of a prime-rate loan can include the cost of the advisory services as well as the cost of the financing.

Bank Term Loans

Term loans are defined as business loans with maturities greater than one year. Term loans are the most common form of intermediate-term financing provided by commercial banks, and there is wide variation in how these loans are structured. In general, they have maturities between one and fifteen years, but most are in the one-to-five-year range. Bank term loans may be secured or unsecured, and the funds can be used to buy inventory or to finance plant and equipment. As in all bank commercial lending, banks maintain close relationships with borrowers, and bank officers closely monitor borrower performance.

term loan a business loan with a maturity greater than one year

The Loan Pricing Model

We have mentioned that the prime rate is the rate banks historically charge their most credit worthy customers. The prime rate is not a market-determined interest rate, since bank management sets it. However, the prime rate is subject to market forces that affect the bank's cost of funds and the rate the bank's customers are willing to accept. Thus, as the general level of interest rates in the economy increases or decreases, bank management raises or lowers the prime rate to adjust for the bank's cost of funds and to respond to competitive conditions.

In determining the interest rate to charge on a loan, the bank takes the prime rate plus two other factors into account. The calculation, called the bank loan pricing model, is as follows:

$$k_l = \text{PR} + \text{DRP} + \text{MAT} \qquad (15.1)$$

where:

k_l = the loan rate (%)
PR = the prime rate (%)
DRP = adjustment for default risk above the prime rate (%)
MAT = adjustment for the yield curve for term loans (%)

Weblink

You can read an article on bank loan pricing at the Web site of the Minneapolis Fed at https://www.minneapolisfed.org/publications/community-dividend/how-do-lenders-set-interest-rates-on-loans.

Before making a loan, the bank conducts a credit analysis of the customer. The first step is to determine the customer's credit category. Banks usually have five to seven credit risk categories, which look very much like bond ratings. If the customer is of the highest credit standing, it is classified as a prime-rate customer and, thus, borrows at the prime rate (or below if it does not require substantial services). For all other customers, there is some markup above the prime rate, which is a default risk premium (DRP). For example, if a bank customer is "prime + 2," the customer borrows at the prevailing prime rate plus 2 percent.

The second step, if the customer wants a term loan, is to adjust for the term to maturity (MAT). MAT is defined as the difference between the yield on a Treasury security with the same maturity as the term loan and the yield on a three-month Treasury bill. Mathematically, that can be expressed as follows:

$$\text{MAT} = y_n - y_{3\text{-mo}}$$

where y_n is the yield on a Treasury security with n years to maturity and $y_{3\text{-mo}}$ is the yield on a three-month Treasury security. (As a practical matter, most financial analysts treat the prime rate as a three-month interest rate.) Suppose, for example, that a customer wants a two-year term loan. If the yield on a two-year Treasury security is 4.00 percent and the yield on a three-month Treasury is 3.70 percent, then the appropriate MAT is 0.30 percent (4.00 percent − 3.70 percent = 0.30 percent).

Let's consider an example of credit analysis for a short-term loan, which requires consideration of only the prime rate and the DRP. Suppose a bank has two customers that are medium-size business firms. Firm A has the bank's highest credit standing, and Firm B's credit standing is prime + 3. The bank prime rate is 4.25 percent. What is the appropriate loan rate for each customer, assuming the loan is not a term loan?

Firm A, with its high credit standing, is clearly a prime customer, so its borrowing rate is the prime rate, 4.25 percent. Firm B's credit rating is prime + 3, or prime plus 3 percent, so its borrowing cost is 7.25 percent (4.25 percent + 3.00 percent = 7.25 percent). Note that the prime rate is a floating rate. Thus, if the bank raises its prime rate by 25 basis points, both firms' borrowing costs increase by 25 basis points, firm A's to 4.5 percent and firm B's to 7.5 percent.

Learning by Doing Application 15.4 illustrates the pricing of a term loan.

LEARNING BY DOING

APPLICATION 15.4 | Pricing a Term Loan

Problem In our text example, Firm B's borrowing cost for a short-term loan is 7.25 percent. Suppose, however, that Firm B's CFO would like to lock in the borrowing cost for five years and asks for a quote on a five-year term loan. The lending officer has access to the following information: a three-month Treasury bill yields 1.00 percent, and five-year Treasury notes yield 2.80 percent. What loan rate should the bank quote?

Approach We first need to find the appropriate MAT, which in this case is the difference between the five-year and three-month Treasury rates. Then, by applying Equation 15.1, we can calculate the five-year term loan rate.

Solution First, we find the MAT:

$$\begin{aligned} \text{MAT} &= \text{5-year Treasury note rate} - \text{3-month Treasury bill rate} \\ &= 2.80\% - 1.00\% \\ &= 1.80\% \end{aligned}$$

We can now apply Equation 15.1:

$$\begin{aligned} k_l &= \text{PR} + \text{DRP} + \text{MAT} \\ &= 4.25\% + 3.00\% + 1.80\% \\ &= 9.05\% \end{aligned}$$

Concluding Comments on Funding the Firm

This chapter has focused on how firms raise capital to fund their current operations and growth. How a firm raises capital depends on the firm's stage in its life cycle, its expected cash flows, and its risk characteristics. For new businesses, funding comes from friends, family, credit cards, and venture capitalists. More mature firms rely heavily on (1) public markets, (2) private markets, and (3) bank loans. Each market has particular characteristics, and firms select the method of financing that provides the best combination of low-cost borrowing and favorable terms and conditions. There are no simple rules or formulas on how to fund the enterprise. Chapter 16 tackles a number of important questions regarding a firm's capital structure and the use of financial leverage.

Before You Go On

1. What are the disadvantages of a private placement sale compared with a public sale?
2. Why do companies engage in PIPE transactions?

Summary of Learning Objectives

1 Explain what is meant by bootstrapping when raising seed financing and why bootstrapping is important.

Bootstrapping is the process by which many entrepreneurs raise seed money and obtain other resources necessary to start new businesses. Seed money often comes from the entrepreneur's savings and credit cards and from family and friends. Bootstrapping is important because business start-ups are a significant factor in determining and sustaining long-term economic growth in an economy. Many state and local governments have invested heavily in business incubators, hoping to foster new business formation.

2 Describe the role of venture capitalists in the economy and discuss how they reduce their risk when investing in start-up businesses.

Venture capitalists specialize in helping businesses get started by providing early-stage financing and advising management. Because of the high risk of investing in start-up businesses, venture capitalists finance projects in stages and often require the owners to make a significant personal investment in the firm. The owners' equity stake signals their belief in the viability of the business and ensures that management actions are focused on building a successful business. Risk is also reduced through syndication and because of the venture capitalist's in-depth knowledge of the industry and technology.

3 Discuss the advantages and disadvantages of going public and compute the net proceeds from an IPO.

The major advantages of entering public markets are that they provide firms with access to large quantities of money at relatively low cost, enable firms to attract and motivate good managers, and provide liquidity for existing stockholders, such as entrepreneurs, other managers, and venture capitalists. Disadvantages include the high cost of the IPO, the cost of ongoing SEC disclosure requirements, the need to disclose sensitive information, and possible incentives that focus on short-term profits rather than on long-term value maximization. Section 15.3 and Learning by Doing Applications 15.1 and 15.2 provide practice in computing net IPO proceeds.

4 Explain why, when underwriting new security offerings, investment bankers prefer that the securities be underpriced. Compute the total cost of an IPO.

When underwriting new securities, investment bankers prefer that the issue be underpriced because it increases the likelihood of a successful offering. The lower the offering price, the more likely that the securities will sell out quickly—and the less likely that the underwriters will end up with unsold inventory. Furthermore, many investment bankers will argue that some underpricing helps attract long-term institutional investors who help provide stability for the stock price.

The total cost of issuing an IPO includes three elements: (1) the underwriter's spread; (2) out-of-pocket expenses, which include legal fees, SEC filing fees, and other expenses; and (3) the cost of underpricing. For calculations of these costs, see Section 15.4, including Learning by Doing Application 15.3. Exhibit 15.5 shows average costs for IPOs in recent years.

5 Discuss the costs of bringing a general cash offer to market.

The total cost of bringing a general cash offer to market is lower than the cost of issuing an IPO because these seasoned offerings do not include a large underpricing cost and underwriting spreads are smaller. Section 15.5 explains how to compute the total cost of a general cash offer. Some average costs are listed in Exhibit 15.6.

6 Explain why a firm that has access to the public markets might elect to raise money through a private placement.

There are a number of advantages to private placement, even for companies with access to the public markets. A private placement may be more cost-effective and can be accomplished much more quickly. In addition, some larger companies, especially those owned by entrepreneurs or families, may not wish to be exposed to the public scrutiny that comes with public sales of securities.

7 Review some of the advantages of borrowing from a commercial bank rather than selling securities in financial markets and discuss bank term loans.

Most small and medium-size firms borrow from commercial banks on a regular basis. Small and medium-size firms may have limited access to the financial markets. For these firms, banks provide not only funds but also a full range of services, including financial advice. Furthermore, if a firm's financial circumstances change over time, it is much easier for the firm to borrow or renegotiate the debt contract with a bank than with other lenders. For many companies, bank borrowing may be the lowest-cost source of funds.

Bank term loans are business loans with maturities greater than one year. Most bank term loans have maturities from one to five years, though the maturity may be as long as fifteen years. The cost of the loans depends on three factors: the prime rate, an adjustment for default risk, and an adjustment for the term to maturity.

Summary of Key Equations

Equation	Description	Formula
15.1	Bank Loan Pricing Model	$k_l = \text{PR} + \text{DRP} + \text{MAT}$

Self-Study Problems

15.1 Management of Oakley, Inc., is planning to raise $1 million in new equity through a private placement. If the sale price is $18 per share, how many shares does the company have to issue?

15.2 Suppose a firm is doing an IPO and the investment bank offers to buy the securities for $39 per share with an offering price of $42. What is the underwriter's spread? Assume that the underwriter's cost of bringing the security to the market is $1 per share. What is its net profit per share?

15.3 Management of The Stride Rite Corporation, designer and marketer of athletic apparel, is planning an expansion into foreign markets and needs to raise $10 million to finance this move. Management anticipates raising the money through a general cash offering for $13 a share. If the underwriters charge a 5 percent spread, how many shares will the company have to sell to achieve its goal?

15.4 Dean Foods Co. needs to borrow $23 million for a factory equipment upgrade. Management decides to sell 10-year bonds. They determine that the 3-month Treasury bill yields 4.32 percent, the firm's credit rating is AA, and the yield on 10-year Treasury bonds is 1.06 percent higher than that for 3-month bills. Right now, AA bond rates are 1.35 percent above the 10-year Treasury bond rate. What is the borrowing cost for this transaction?

15.5 You are considering starting a new online dating service, but you lack the initial capital. What are your options for obtaining the necessary financing?

Solutions to Self-Study Problems

15.1 To raise $1 million, Oakley will have to issue 55,556 shares ($1,000,000/$18 per share = 55,556 shares).

15.2 Underwriter's spread: $42 − $39 = $3, or 7.1% ($3/$42 = 0.071, or 7.1%)

Net profit per share: $3 − $1 = $2

15.3 Underwriter's spread = 5%

Proceeds per share to the firm = [$13.00 × (1 − 0.05)] = $12.35

To raise $10 million, the company will have to issue 809,717 new shares ($10,000,000/$12.35 per share = 809,717 shares).

15.4 The borrowing cost for Dean Foods can be calculated as follows:

$$k_l = 4.32\% + 1.35\% + 1.06\%$$
$$= 6.73\%$$

The approach used here is similar to that used in the bank loan pricing model.

15.5 Possible sources of capital include your own savings, friends and family, wealthy individuals, venture capital firms, and financial institutions such as banks.

WileyPLUS

Questions and Problems, Solution Walkthrough Videos, Learning by Doing Tutorials, and additional study tools and resources are available in WileyPLUS.

Discussion Questions

15.1 Assume you work for a venture capital firm and have been approached by a couple of recent college graduates with a request to fund their new business. If you are interested in the idea, what process will you follow?

15.2 Identify the three basic services investment bankers provide to help firms bring new security issues to the market. During which stage of the typical IPO does the investment banker take on the risk of the offering? Is there an alternative in which the risk remains with the company going public?

15.3 Define *underpricing*, and explain why the majority of IPOs are underpriced. What role do investment banks play in the price-setting process?

15.4 Explain why the owners of a company might choose to keep it private.

15.5 Identify the three cost components that make up the total cost of issuing securities for a company. Briefly describe each.

15.6 What are the characteristics of a public bond? (Think in terms of comparing it to private placement and bank term loans.)

15.7 Discuss the advantages of shelf registration. What kinds of securities are most likely to be registered this way?

15.8 Identify whether each of the following factors implies a lower or higher price for a bond.

a. Low marketability of the security.

b. Short term to maturity.

c. Low credit rating of the issuer.

d. No call provision.

15.9 Explain why time might play a significant role during low-interest periods in a decision of whether to choose a private placement or public sale.

15.10 Managers at a large firm are looking for a medium-size loan with a long term to maturity and low liquidity. Which of the following types of debt would be the most appropriate?

a. Public bond.

b. Private placement.

c. Bank term loan.

Questions and Problems

Excel *Excel templates and resources available in* **WileyPLUS**

Basic

15.1 **Venture capital:** What items in a business plan does a venture capitalist look for in deciding whether to provide initial financing?

15.2 **Venture capital:** You finally decide to act on your brilliant idea and start an online textbook rental company. You develop a detailed business plan and calculate that you will need about $350,000 of initial funding to get the business going. Luckily for you, you have lined up two venture capital firms offering to supply the funding. What criteria should guide your decision to select one firm over the other?

15.3 **Venture capital:** What are some viable exit strategies for investors in a start-up company?

15.4 **IPO:** Briefly describe the IPO process.

15.5 **IPO:** Based on your knowledge from this and previous chapters, what are some methods an investment banker uses to determine an IPO price? What factors will play a significant role in the calculation?

15.6 **IPO:** A majority of firms choose a firm-commitment underwriting arrangement rather than a best-effort arrangement for their IPO. Explain why.

15.7 **Competitive versus negotiated sale:** Why might a negotiated sale be the lowest-cost means of issuing a complex debt security?

15.8 **IPO pricing:** Trajax, Inc., a high-technology firm in Portland, raised a total of $90 million in an IPO. The company received $27 of the $30 per share offering price. The firm's legal fees, SEC registration fees, and other out-of-pocket costs were $450,000. The firm's stock price increased 17 percent on the first day of trading. What was the total cost to the firm of issuing the securities?

15.9 **IPO pricing:** Myriad Biotech management plans a $114 million IPO in which the offering price to the public will be $51 per share. The company will receive $47.50 per share. The firm's legal fees, SEC registration fees, and other out-of-pocket costs will total $525,000. If the stock price increases 14 percent on the first day of trading, what will be the total cost of issuing the securities?

15.10 **Shelf registration:** Are the following statements true or false?

a. Shelf registration allows firms to register an inventory of securities for an unlimited time.

b. The securities can be taken off the shelf at any time and sold to the public.

c. Shelf registration reduces flotation and other expenses associated with registration.

d. There is a large penalty if the authorized securities are not issued.

e. A shelf registration can cover multiple securities.

15.11 **General cash offer:** What are the steps in a general cash offering? Explain each of them.

15.12 **General cash offer:** Explain the difference between a competitive and negotiated cash sale. Which method of sale is likely to yield the lower funding cost for firms selling plain vanilla bonds in stable markets?

15.13 **Issuing securities:** Explain what is meant by economies of scale in issuing securities.

15.14 **Bank term lending:** Explain how term to maturity affects the price of a bank loan.

15.15 **Private placement versus public debt offering:** Nalco Holding is an international company that operates in 130 countries, has a market capitalization (market value of equity) of $2.3 billion, and reported net income of $45 million on $3.3 billion in revenues last year. The company needs to raise $200 million in debt, and management is deciding between private placement and public offering. What are the advantages and disadvantages of the two alternatives, and which is likely to be the better choice?

15.16 **Prime-rate lending:** Suppose two firms want to borrow money from a bank for a period of one year. Firm A has excellent credit, whereas Firm B's credit standing is such that it would pay prime + 2 percent. The current prime rate is 6.75 percent, the 30-year Treasury bond yield is 4.35 percent, the 3-month Treasury bill yield is 3.54 percent, and the 10-year Treasury note yield is 4.22 percent. What are the appropriate loan rates for each firm?

15.17 **Prime-rate lending:** Now suppose that Firm B from Problem 15.16 decides to get a term loan for 10 years. How does this affect the company's borrowing cost?

15.18 **Prime-rate lending:** Cartco needs to borrow $5 million for an upgrade to its headquarters and manufacturing facility. Management has decided to borrow using a five-year term loan from its existing commercial bank. The prime rate is 3.25 percent, and Cartco's current rating is prime + 2.48 percent. The yield on a five-year U.S. Treasury note is 2.01 percent, and the three-month U.S. Treasury bill rate is 0.09 percent. What is the estimated loan rate for the five-year bank loan?

Intermediate

15.19 **Venture capital:** You work for a venture capital firm and are approached to finance a new high-tech start-up. While you believe in the business idea, you also believe it is very risky. What strategies can help to mitigate the risk of the invsetment to your firm? Explain how these measures would work.

15.20 **IPO:** On August 19, 2004, Google completed its IPO of 19.6 million shares to the initial investors at $85.00 per share. The closing price of the stock that same day was $100.34. What was the dollar value of the underpricing associated with the Google IPO?

15.21 **IPO:** Deere and Bros. is a broker that brings new issues of small firms to the public market. Its most recent deal for Dextra, Inc., had the following characteristics:

Number of shares: 1,000,000 Price to public: $15 per share
Proceeds to Dextra: $13,500,000

The legal fees were $150,000, printing costs were $56,000, and all the other expenses were $72,000. What is the profit or loss for Deere and Bros.?

15.22 **IPO:** When Global Partners went public in September 2016, the offer price was $22.00 per share and the closing price at the end of the first day was $23.90. The firm issued 4.9 million shares. What was the loss to the company due to underpricing?

15.23 **IPO:** Bellex Technologies agreed to complete its IPO on a best-effort basis. The company's investment bank demanded a spread of 17 percent of the offer price, which was set at $30 per share. Three million shares were issued; however, the bank's management was overly optimistic and eventually was able to sell all of the stock for only $28 per share. What were the proceeds for the issuer and the underwriter?

15.24 **IPO:** Suppose a biotech company in Boston, Massachusetts, completes an $85 million IPO priced to the public at $75 per share. The firm receives $72 per share, and the out-of-pocket expenses are $340,000. The stock's closing price at the end of the first day is $84. What is the total cost to the firm of issuing the securities?

15.25 **IPO:** An online medical advice company just completed an IPO with an investment bank on a firm-commitment basis. The firm issued 5 million shares of common stock, and the underwriting fees were $1.90 per share. The offering price was $26 per share.

a. What were the total proceeds from the common-stock sale?

b. How much money did the company receive?

c. How much money did the investment bank receive in fees?

15.26 **IPO underpricing:** Suppose that a biotech firm in Pittsburgh raised $120 million in an IPO. The firm received $23 per share, and the stock sold to the public for $25 per share. The firm's legal fees, SEC registration fees, and other out-of-pocket costs were $270,000. The firm's stock price increased 17.5 percent on the first day. What was the total cost to the firm of issuing the securities?

15.27 **Long-term corporate debt:** The 20-year Treasury rate is 4.67 percent, and a firm's credit rating is BB. Suppose management of the firm decides to raise $20 million by selling 20-year bonds. Management determines that since it has plenty of experience, it will not need to hire an investment banker. At present, 20-year BB bonds are selling for 185 basis points above the 20-year Treasury rate, and it is forecast that interest rates will not stay this low for long. What is the cost of borrowing? What role does timing play in this situation?

Sample Test Problems

15.1 Why are traditional sources of funding not usually available for new or emerging businesses?

15.2 A firm is making an initial public offering. The investment bankers agree to a firm-commitment underwriting for 500,000 shares that would be priced to the public at $36 per share. The underwriter's spread is 7 percent. What will be the proceeds for the issuer and the underwriter?

15.3 Hilton Worldwide Holdings Inc. completed an initial public offering on December 12, 2013. The offer price was $20.00 per share, and the closing price at the end of the first day was $21.50. The firm issued 117.6 million shares. What was the loss to Hilton stockholders due to underpricing? Who received this value?

15.4 SMA Inc. is considering issuing the following securities. For which security would a competitive sale be less costly than a negotiated sale under stable market conditions? Why?

a. Plain vanilla bonds.

b. IPO of common stock.

c. Secondary offering of common stock.

d. Convertible bonds.

15.5 Management of Southern Parts Company has decided to sell 10-year bonds to finance expansion into the Pacific Northwest. The market rate on these bonds is 8 percent, and the 3-month Treasury bill rate is 2.1 percent. The firm's credit rating is B, and the yield on 10-year Treasury bonds is 2.5 percent higher than that on 3-month Treasury bills. How much of a premium over the 10-year Treasury bond will these Southern Parts bonds sell for?

Ethics Case

Profiting from Death: "Janitor's Insurance"

teekid/Getty Images

Companies often provide life insurance to employees as a benefit. Several decades ago, a new twist was developed: corporate-owned life insurance (COLI). A COLI policy is taken out by a company on the life of an employee. The company pays the premium on the insurance but also owns the policy's cash value and is its primary beneficiary.

Historically, companies were able to purchase insurance on an employee only if they had a significant financial or emotional stake in the person's survival, known as an "insurable interest." Thus, a company could buy life insurance on key executives, and partners in accounting and law firms could buy life insurance on each other.

In the 1980s, however, insurance companies convinced the insurance regulators in most states to change the rules to allow companies to buy life insurance policies on any and all employees. As firms became aware of the tax advantages associated with these plans, there was an explosion in the number of COLI programs that covered rank-and-file workers. These programs became known in the industry as "janitor's insurance" because everyone "including the janitor" was covered.

How COLI Programs Work

Companies have earned millions of dollars on broad-based COLI programs because of the favorable tax treatment of life insurance policies. The policies yield tax-free income as the investment value of the insurance policy rises; companies can also borrow against the policies to raise cash. Moreover, any interest payments on money borrowed against these policies are tax deductible, and the premium payments are tax deductible as well. If the employee dies prematurely, the death benefits are also exempt from taxation. Thus, on an after-tax basis, on average the value of the cash benefits will exceed the cash value of the premiums. The implication of these tax advantages is that in certain cases, from a purely financial perspective, some employees are worth more to their company dead than alive.

Broad-based COLI programs soon became widespread. Firms like Wal-Mart, Nestlé, Pitney Bowes, Procter & Gamble, Winn-Dixie, and Dow Chemical instituted such programs. For example, in the 1990s, Wal-Mart took out COLI on 350,000 of its workers. Janitor's insurance was also big business for life insurance companies. Hartford Life, a major COLI provider, had $4.3 billion in force at the end of 2001.

Public Outcry against COLI Programs

When the existence of COLI became public knowledge in 2002, there was a tremendous outcry. Some argued that it was unseemly for a company to profit from the death of its employees. To the families of dead employees who could not afford to own much, if any, insurance on their loved ones, the whole scheme was unfair. For example, CM Holdings, Inc., had a COLI policy on its employee Felipe Tillman. When Tillman died at 29 from complications of AIDS in 1992, CM Holdings received a death benefit of $339,302. But since Felipe had no policy on his own life, there was no death benefit for his family. When Felipe's brother Anthony learned how his brother's death benefited CM Holdings, his response was "it isn't fair.

Is janitor's insurance unfair, and is it unseemly to profit from the death of employees? People do not always object to profiting from death. The funeral business, for example, is highly profitable, as is the life insurance business. And defense is a very big industry. In fact, lots of industries profit from death in one way or another. Perhaps what seems morally wrong in the case of COLI policies is profiting from the death of one's own employees—especially when the benefits do not work in the interest of the employees. Interestingly, though, most companies claim that the death benefits are used to help finance general employee benefits, including health insurance. Procter & Gamble uses the death benefits in this way. Pitney Bowes and Nestlé make the same point: the death benefits are used to help finance general employee benefits. It is hard to see why janitor's insurance used for such purposes is wrong. Perhaps one could fault Public Service of New Mexico for using the death benefits from its employees to help put a nuclear power plant out of service. But even here, the moral case is not clear. Although the death benefits were not used directly to help employees, they did benefit stockholders. Moreover, some might argue that phasing out nuclear power plants benefits customers and society at large.

Some cynical people might see a conflict of interest here. If an employee really is worth more to a company dead than alive, then a company has an interest in hastening that employee's death. That may be technically true, but it does seem a bit of a stretch to think that an executive would do away with an employee for financial gain.

COLI Programs Often Lack Transparency

Other issues arise with respect to COLI policies, however. In many cases, employees were never told about the policies. It came as a surprise to them or to their families when the existence of the policies became public knowledge. In one poignant case, an employee of Advantage Medical Services, Inc., Peggy Stillwagoner, was killed in a car accident. Before succumbing to her injuries, she ran up tens of thousands of dollars in medical bills. The Stillwagoner family asked the owner of the company if it provided life insurance. The owner of the company said it did not. A few months later, the family discovered that the company had a $200,000 policy on Peggy Stillwagoner.

Clearly, the owner of Advantage Medical Services was wrong to have lied. And it does seem an abuse of informational asymmetry when employees are not told about the company's COLI policies on them. However, suppose the existence of such policies was completely transparent? Would there be anything wrong then?

Societal Responses

In 1996, in reaction to society's strong objections to companies that may profit from death unfairly, Congress passed a law phasing out the tax-deductible insurance payments. Still, it preserved many of the financial benefits for companies. More recently, federal appeals courts in the Sixth and Tenth Circuits have determined that companies do not have an insurable interest in most of their employees. In addition, some courts have explicitly mentioned the lack of transparency around COLI. Thus, the attitude of the courts has changed since many states changed their regulations in the 1980s.

Companies that do not change their policies in accordance with current laws and court decisions can be hit financially. For example, Dow Chemical was charged $22.2 million in back taxes from losses created by COLI. The National Association of Insurance Commissioners has developed transparency guidelines that require the consent of individuals if insurance is to be purchased on their behalf. Most states have enacted similar guidelines. Such revised laws and professional guidelines speak to some of the examples mentioned earlier. Even so, COLI policies on executives remain a booming business and for the same reason that COLI boomed: significant tax advantages.

Discussion Questions

1. Is COLI unethical? If you think there is something unethical about the practice, what is it? If you do not think so, why do you think so many people find it unethical?
2. Suppose a company provided life insurance to each employee and also had a COLI policy on each employee? Would that settle the fairness question?
3. Does the fact that from a financial perspective some employees are worth more dead than alive represent a genuine conflict of interest?

Sources: Ellen E. Schultz and Theo Francis, "Valued Employees: Worker Dies, Firm Profits—Why?" *Wall Street Journal*, April 19, 2002; "U.S. Court: Employers Can't Write COLI Policies on Rank-and-File Employees," *Best Wire*, May 23, 2005; "Dow Chemical Is Ordered to Pay in Janitor's Case," *Wall Street Journal*, January 26, 2006; and Warren S. Hersch, "The Market for COLI—Still Strong and Robust," *National Underwriter: Life & Health Financial Services Division*, June 12, 2006.

CHAPTER 16

Capital Structure Policy

iCreative3D/Shutterstock

LEARNING OBJECTIVES

1. Describe the two Modigliani and Miller propositions, the key assumptions underlying them, and their relevance to capital structure decisions. Use Proposition 2 to calculate the return on equity.
2. Discuss the benefits and costs of using debt financing and calculate the value of the income tax benefit associated with debt.
3. Describe the trade-off and pecking order theories of capital structure choice and explain what the empirical evidence tells us about these theories.
4. Discuss some of the practical considerations that managers are concerned with when they choose a firm's capital structure.

At the end of 2016, the average publicly traded firm in the U.S. technology industry had debt obligations that represented less than 15 percent of the market value of its total capital. Some well-known technology firms, such as Alphabet, Facebook, GoPro, and Square, actually had more cash than debt. In other words, these companies could have paid off all their debt and still had cash left over!

The capital structure policies at these technology firms stood in stark contrast to the corresponding policies of firms in most other industries. The average U.S. public firm had debt obligations that represented about 25 percent of the market value of its total capital and were far greater than the firm's cash balance. In fact, debt represented over 30 percent of the total capital at the average firm in a number of industries, such as building construction; air transportation; financial services (including banking); printing, publishing, and related industries; and paper and allied product manufacturers.

The capital structure policies at firms reflect trade-offs between the benefits and the costs of using debt financing. For example, because interest payments are deductible when a firm calculates its taxable income, the low debt levels at technology firms means that they pay higher income taxes than they would if they had more debt. On the other hand, these companies have more flexibility in reacting to changing economic or industry conditions because they have the ability to borrow more money. Such flexibility can help their managers reduce the impact of economic recessions on their businesses. It can also enable them to take advantage of unexpected opportunities and to survive unexpected competitive threats.

What is apparent from the wide range of capital structures that we observe in public firms is that the appropriate capital structure for a particular firm depends on that firm's characteristics. When it comes to capital structure policy, one size does not fit all. The appropriate mix of debt and equity financing differs across firms and, even within the same firm, it can change over time. We discuss the factors that affect a firm's capital structure policy in this chapter.

Chapter Preview

In Chapter 15 we discussed how firms raise debt and equity capital to finance their investments. That discussion focused on individual sources of capital. In this chapter, we focus on the choice between various types of financing. In particular, we examine how a firm's value is affected by the mix of debt and equity used to finance its investments and the factors that managers consider when choosing this mix. Managers use the concepts and tools discussed in this chapter to make financing decisions that create value for their stockholders.

We begin with a discussion of two propositions that provide valuable insights into how the choice between debt and equity financing can affect the value of a firm and its cost of equity. These insights provide a framework that we then use to examine the benefits and costs associated with using debt financing. We next describe and evaluate two theories of how managers choose the appropriate mix of debt and equity financing. Finally, we discuss some of the practical considerations that managers say influence their choices.

16.1 Capital Structure and Firm Value

LEARNING OBJECTIVE

1. Describe the two Modigliani and Miller propositions, the key assumptions underlying them, and their relevance to capital structure decisions. Use Proposition 2 to calculate the return on equity.

As you know, a firm's capital structure is the mix of debt and equity used to finance its activities. This mix will always include common stock and will often include debt and preferred stock. In addition, the same firm can have different types of common stock, debt, and preferred stock. The firm may have several classes of common stock, for example, with different voting rights and, possibly, different claims on the cash flows available to stockholders. The debt at a firm can be long term or short term, secured or unsecured, convertible or not convertible into common stock, and so on. Preferred stock can be cumulative or noncumulative and convertible or not convertible into common stock.[1]

The fraction of the total financing that is represented by debt is a measure of the *financial leverage* in the firm's capital structure. A higher fraction of debt indicates a higher degree of financial leverage. The amount of financial leverage in a firm's capital structure is important because, as we discuss next, it affects the value of the firm.

The Optimal Capital Structure

When managers at a firm choose a capital structure, their challenge is to identify the mix of securities that minimizes the cost of financing the firm's activities. We refer to this mix as the **optimal capital structure** because the capital structure that minimizes the cost of financing the firm's projects is also the capital structure that maximizes the total value of those projects and, therefore, the overall value of the firm.

Building Intuition

The Optimal Capital Structure Minimizes the Cost of Financing a Firm's Activities

The optimal capital structure for a firm is the capital structure that minimizes the overall cost of financing the firm's portfolio of projects. Minimizing the overall cost of financing the firm's projects maximizes the value of the firm's free cash flows.

optimal capital structure the capital structure that minimizes the cost of financing a firm's projects and thus maximizes the value of the firm

[1]These are the types of securities that firms issue to finance the assets that they purchase. However, it is important to recognize that firms do not purchase all assets they use. Many assets that businesses use are leased (rented). A lease (rental) agreement can enable a business to obtain the use of an asset without purchasing it and, consequently, the asset and its associated lease financing might not show up on the company's balance sheet. Also, since business lease agreements generally require no deposit, they essentially represent 100 percent debt financing. For these reasons, the decision to purchase or lease an asset is directly related to the capital structure choices that managers make. The appendix to this chapter discusses lease agreements and how managers choose between buying and leasing an asset.

You can see why the optimal capital structure maximizes the value of the firm if you think back to our discussions of NPV analysis for a single project. Recall that the incremental after-tax free cash flows we discount in an NPV analysis are not affected by the way a project is financed. There is no interest or principal payment in Equation 11.2:

$$\text{FCF} = [(\text{Revenue} - \text{Op Ex} - \text{D\&A}) \times (1 - t)] + \text{D\&A} - \text{Cap Exp} - \text{Add WC}$$

Recall also that the discount rate, or weighted average cost of capital (WACC), for a project accounts for the way that it is financed. The lower the cost of financing a project, the lower the discount rate and, therefore, the larger the present value of the free cash flows. This same idea applies for the total portfolio of projects in a firm. If the overall cost of financing those projects is lower, the present value of the total free cash flows they produce is larger.

The Modigliani and Miller Propositions

To understand what determines the optimal capital structure for a particular firm, it is necessary to be familiar with the mechanisms through which financing decisions affect financing costs. The Modigliani and Miller (M&M) propositions provide essential insights into these mechanisms. These propositions, originally developed by Franco Modigliani and Merton Miller more than 50 years ago, are still very relevant today.[2] We discuss them in this section and explore their implications throughout much of this chapter.

M&M Proposition 1

Modigliani and Miller's Proposition 1, which we will denote as M&M Proposition 1, states that the capital structure decisions a firm makes will have no effect on the value of the firm if (1) there are no taxes, (2) there are no information or transaction costs, and (3) the real investment policy of the firm is not affected by its capital structure decisions. The **real investment policy** of the firm includes the criteria it uses in deciding which real assets (projects) to invest in. A policy to invest in all positive NPV projects is an example of a real investment policy. We will discuss each of the three conditions in detail later, but let's first discuss the intuition behind M&M Proposition 1.

real investment policy the policy relating to the criteria the firm uses in deciding which real assets (projects) to invest in

Assume that a firm pays no taxes and that the present value of the free cash flows produced by the assets of the firm can be represented as a pie that is divided between the stockholders and the debt holders, as illustrated in **Exhibit 16.1**. The slice of the pie labeled V_{Equity}

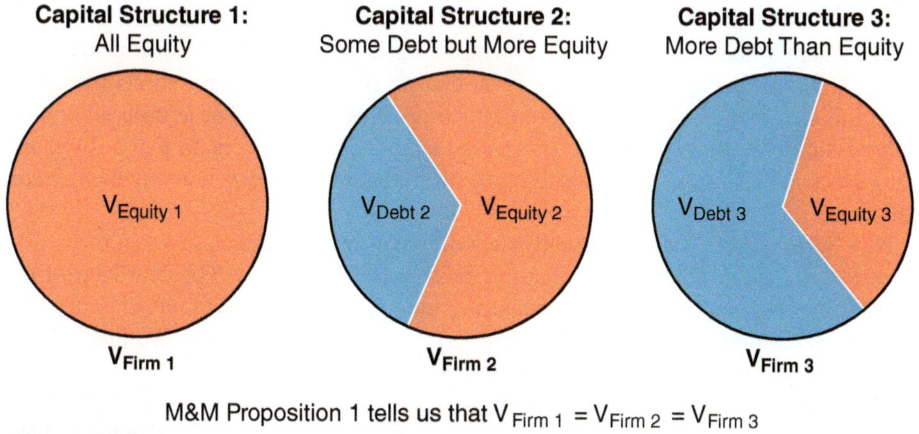

EXHIBIT 16.1 Capital Structure and Firm Value under M&M Proposition 1

The size of the pie represents the present value of the free cash flows that the assets of a firm are expected to produce in the future (V_{Firm}). The sizes of the slices reflect the value of the total cash flows that the debt holders (V_{Debt}) or stockholders (V_{Equity}) are entitled to receive for three different capital structures. Under the three conditions identified by M&M, the total value of the cash flows to the debt holders and stockholders does not change, regardless of which capital structure the firm uses.

[2]The Nobel Prize Committee cited the M&M propositions when it awarded Nobel Prizes in Economics to Professor Modigliani in 1985 and to Professor Miller in 1990.

firm value, or enterprise value the total value of the firm's assets; it equals the value of the equity financing plus the value of the debt financing used by the firm

represents the value of the cash flows to be received by the stockholders, and the slice labeled V_{Debt} represents the value to be received by the debt holders.

From the discussion of the finance balance sheet in Chapter 13, we know that the market value of the debt plus the market value of the equity must equal the market value of the cash flows produced by the firm's assets (V_{Assets}). In practice, we also refer to V_{Assets} as the **firm value** or the firm's **enterprise value** (V_{Firm}), which means that we can write Equation 13.1 as:

$$V_{Firm} = V_{Assets} = V_{Debt} + V_{Equity} \tag{16.1}$$

Building Intuition

Capital Structure Choices Do not Affect Firm Value If They Do not Affect the Value of the Free Cash Flows to Investors

Capital structure choices will not affect a firm's value if all of the following three conditions exist: (1) there are no taxes, (2) there are no information or transaction costs, and (3) the way in which the firm is financed does not affect its real investment policy. This is M&M Proposition 1.

M&M Proposition 1 says that if the size of the pie (representing the present value of the free cash flows the firm's assets are expected to produce in the future) is fixed, and no one other than the stockholders and the debt holders is getting a slice of the pie, then the combined value of the equity and debt claims does not change when you change the capital structure. You can see this in Exhibit 16.1, where each of the three pies represents a different capital structure. No matter how you slice the pie, the total value of the debt plus the equity remains the same. If the three conditions specified by M&M hold, the capital structure of the firm specifies how that pie is to be sliced, but it does not change the overall size of the pie or the combined size of the debt and equity slices.

Understanding M&M Proposition 1 To help you better understand M&M Proposition 1, let's consider its implications in the context of an example. Assume that the three conditions identified by M&M apply and consider a company, Millennium Motors, that is financed entirely with equity. Millennium Motors produces annual cash flows of \$100, which are expected to continue forever. If the appropriate discount rate for Millennium's cash flows is 10 percent, we can use the perpetuity model, Equation 6.3, to calculate the value of the firm:

$$V_{Firm} = PVP = \frac{CF}{i} = \frac{\$100}{0.1} = \$1{,}000$$

Since the firm is financed entirely with equity, the equity is also worth \$1,000. Suppose that the management of Millennium Motors is considering changing its capital structure from \$1,000 (100 percent) equity to \$800 (80 percent) equity and \$200 (20 percent) debt. The company would accomplish this change by selling \$200 worth of perpetual bonds and paying the \$200 to stockholders through a one-time special dividend.

financial restructuring a combination of financial transactions that changes the capital structure of the firm without affecting its real assets

The change that Millennium is contemplating is an example of a **financial restructuring**. A financial restructuring is a combination of financial transactions that changes the capital structure of the firm without affecting its real assets. These transactions might involve issuing debt and using the proceeds to repurchase stock or to pay a dividend, or selling stock and using the proceeds to repay debt. No new money is actually being invested in the firm.

Now suppose that you are currently the only investor in Millennium—you own 100 percent of the outstanding stock—and that the firm would have to pay 5 percent interest on the debt after the restructuring. If the restructuring took place, you would immediately receive a \$200 special dividend. After that, each year you would be entitled to the \$90 that is left over after the \$10 interest payment on the bonds.[3]

M&M showed that if you, as an investor, decide that you do not like the effect the restructuring would have on your cash flows, management could go ahead with the restructuring and you could undo its effect on the cash flows you receive by making offsetting trades in your personal investment account. To undo the effects of Millennium's proposed financial restructuring, you would simply use the entire \$200 special dividend to buy all of the perpetual bonds the firm issues. From that point forward, you would receive the first \$10 that the firm earns each year as an interest payment on your bonds. In addition, you would receive any remaining cash flows because you would still own 100 percent of the stock. Just as before the

[3]Since we are assuming that there are no taxes, the after-tax cost of the interest is \$10.

restructuring, you would be receiving all of the cash flows generated by the firm. Only now, instead of receiving all of those cash flows as dividends, you would receive some cash in the form of interest payments.

What if Millennium Motors had more than one stockholder? It wouldn't matter—the result would be the same. For instance, if you owned only 10 percent of the firm's equity before the restructuring, you could still undo the change by using your special dividend to purchase 10 percent of the bonds. You would receive the same cash flows after the restructuring as you did before.

Furthermore, M&M Proposition 1 suggests that transactions such as those we have described need not be used to undo a financial restructuring that the firm undertakes—investors can also use them to create their own restructuring. For example, as before, suppose you own 100 percent of the stock in Millennium Motors. This time, however, let's assume that management has no intention of adding debt to the firm's capital structure, but that you wish they would. You would like management to alter the capital structure so that it would include 80 percent equity and 20 percent debt and pay you a \$200 special dividend.

You could easily produce the same effect by making trades in your investment account that would alter your cash flows. You could borrow \$200 at a 5 percent interest rate and pay the interest on the debt out of the annual cash flows you receive from the company. Of course, in order for this transaction to exactly duplicate a similar restructuring by the firm, you would have to be able to borrow at the same interest rate as the firm.[4] If you borrowed at the same rate, your cash flows would be exactly the same as if Millennium Motors had borrowed the money and paid you the special dividend. You would receive \$200 from the loan today, and you would have \$90 left over each year after you paid interest on that loan.

Learning by Doing Application 16.1 illustrates another example of how an investor can undo the effects of a financial restructuring.

APPLICATION 16.1 | Undoing the Effects of a Financial Restructuring on Your Own

LEARNING BY DOING

WileyPLUS

Need more help? Visit your WileyPLUS course.

Problem You own 5 percent of the stock in a company that is financed with 80 percent equity and 20 percent debt. Like Millennium Motors, the company generates cash flows of \$100 per year before any interest payments and has a total value of \$1,000. Management has announced plans to increase the proportion of debt in the firm's capital structure from 20 percent to 30 percent by borrowing \$100 and paying a special dividend equal to that amount. Assume that the interest rate on debt is 5 percent regardless of how much debt the company has. How can you undo the effect of the financial restructuring on the cash flows that you receive in your personal account? Show that when you do this, your cash flows after the restructuring are the same as they were before.

Approach As illustrated in the example in the text, you can undo the effect of this restructuring by using all of the money you receive from the special dividend to purchase some of the firm's debt. To show that the cash flows you are entitled to receive remain unchanged, you must calculate the dividends and interest you are entitled to receive before the financial restructuring and afterward.

Solution Since the company currently has \$200 of debt (20 percent × \$1,000 = \$200), it pays \$10 in interest annually (5 percent interest rate × \$200 = \$10). Therefore, the stockholders receive \$90 in dividends each year, and you receive an annual dividend of 5 percent × \$90.00 = \$4.50 for your 5 percent of the total stockholdings.

When the restructuring takes place, you will receive a special dividend equal to 5 percent of the \$100 total special dividend, or \$5. Since the company will then have to pay interest of \$15 each year

[4]In order for this transaction to have precisely the same effect as if Millennium's capital structure had been altered by management, you would also have to use the firm's stock as the only collateral for this borrowing. That way, if you failed to pay the interest, you would forfeit the equity to the lender and have no further obligation. The assumption that you can borrow at the same rate as the firm and use the stock as collateral is implied by the M&M condition that there are no information or transaction costs. If you paid a higher interest rate than the firm, then some of the value you are entitled to receive from the firm would be transferred from you to the lender.

(5 percent interest rate × \$300 = \$15), the total regular dividend after the restructuring will be \$85. Your portion of the total regular dividend will be 0.05 × \$85.00 = \$4.25. Therefore, you will receive \$5 up front and a dividend of \$4.25 per year thereafter.

If you use the \$5 that you receive from the special dividend to buy \$5 (5 percent) of the new debt issue, you will receive \$4.25 per year in regular dividends and 5 percent × \$5.00 = \$0.25 in interest, for a total of \$4.50. This is exactly what you were receiving before the company restructured.

Conclusion from M&M Proposition 1 As our examples illustrate, in perfect financial markets—markets in which the three conditions specified in M&M Proposition 1 hold—investors can make changes in their own investment accounts that will replicate the cash flows for any capital structure that the firm's management might choose or that they might desire. Since investors can do this on their own, they are not willing to pay more for the stock of a firm that does it for them. Therefore, the value of the firm will be the same regardless of its capital structure. This is true because changes in capital structure will not change the total value of the claims that debt holders and stockholders have on the cash flows—which is the point of M&M Proposition 1 and is illustrated in the pie diagrams of Exhibit 16.1.

M&M Proposition 2

Under the three conditions outlined in M&M Proposition 1, a firm's capital structure does not affect the value of the firm's real assets. That's because capital structure decisions do not affect the level, timing, or risk of the cash flows produced by those assets. Although the risk of the cash flows produced by the assets does not change with changes in the firm's capital structure, the risk of the equity claims on those cash flows—and therefore the required return on equity—does change. M&M's Proposition 2 states that the cost of (required return on) a firm's common stock is directly related to the debt-to-equity ratio.[5] To see why, let's return to the WACC formula, Equation 13.7:

$$\text{WACC} = x_{\text{Debt}} k_{\text{Debt pretax}} (1 - t) + x_{\text{ps}} k_{\text{ps}} + x_{\text{cs}} k_{\text{cs}}$$

If there are no taxes, as M&M Proposition 1 assumes, then $t = 0$ and Equation 13.7 is:

$$\text{WACC} = x_{\text{Debt}} k_{\text{Debt}} + x_{\text{ps}} k_{\text{ps}} + x_{\text{cs}} k_{\text{cs}}$$

Furthermore, if we assume (for simplicity) that the firm has no preferred stock, then this equation can be simplified further:

$$\text{WACC} = x_{\text{Debt}} k_{\text{Debt}} + x_{\text{cs}} k_{\text{cs}} \tag{16.2}$$

where $x_{\text{Debt}} + x_{\text{cs}} = 1$.

Since, under the M&M Proposition 1 conditions, capital structure choices do not affect the risk of the cash flows produced by a firm's assets, the WACC does not change with the firm's capital structure. The reason is that, as a weighted average of the cost of debt and the cost of equity, the WACC reflects the riskiness of the cash flows generated by the firm's assets (k_{Assets}). Now if we recognize that the proportions of debt and equity in the firm's capital structure are calculated as:

$$x_{\text{Debt}} = \frac{V_{\text{Debt}}}{V_{\text{Debt}} + V_{\text{cs}}}$$

and

$$x_{\text{cs}} = \frac{V_{\text{cs}}}{V_{\text{Debt}} + V_{\text{cs}}}$$

where V_{Debt} is the dollar value of the debt and V_{cs} is the dollar value of the common stock, we can write Equation 16.2 as follows:

$$\text{WACC} = k_{\text{Assets}} = \frac{V_{\text{Debt}}}{V_{\text{Debt}} + V_{\text{cs}}} k_{\text{Debt}} + \frac{V_{\text{cs}}}{V_{\text{Debt}} + V_{\text{cs}}} k_{\text{cs}}$$

[5] In finance, we use the terms *cost* of debt or equity interchangeably with *required return* on debt or equity because, by definition, the *pretax* cost of a particular type of capital to a firm equals the rate of return that investors require. Note that since firms can deduct interest payments, the *after-tax* cost of debt to the firm will be lower than the rate of return required by its creditors.

Finally, using basic algebra, we can rearrange this equation to solve for k_{cs} in terms of k_{Assets} and k_{Debt}. We find that:

$$k_{cs} = k_{Assets} + \left(\frac{V_{Debt}}{V_{cs}}\right)(k_{Assets} - k_{Debt}) \tag{16.3}$$

Equation 16.3 is M&M's Proposition 2, which shows that the cost of (required return on) a firm's common stock is directly related to the debt-to-equity ratio. You can see this in the equation by noting that as the ratio V_{Debt}/V_{cs} increases on the right-hand side, k_{cs} will increase on the left-hand side. We have demonstrated this relation assuming that a firm has only common stock outstanding. However, you can rest assured that it also holds if the firm also has preferred stock outstanding.[6]

> **Building Intuition**
>
> **The Cost of Equity Increases with Financial Leverage**
>
> The required rate of return on a firm's equity (cost of equity) increases as its debt-to-equity ratio increases. This is M&M Proposition 2.

Understanding M&M Proposition 2 We can think of the two terms on the right-hand side of Equation 16.3 as reflecting two sources of risk in the cash flows to which stockholders have a claim. The first source of risk is the underlying risk of the assets. This risk is reflected in the required return on the firm's assets (k_{Assets}) and is known as the **business risk** of the firm. It is the risk associated with the characteristics of the firm's assets (projects).

business risk the risk in the cash flows to stockholders that is associated with uncertainty due to the characteristics of the firm's assets

financial risk the risk in the cash flows to stockholders that is due to the way in which the firm's assets have been financed

The second source of risk, which is reflected in the second term, is the capital structure of the firm. The capital structure determines the **financial risk**, which reflects the effect that financing decisions have on the riskiness of the cash flows that the stockholders will receive. The more debt financing a firm uses, the greater the financial risk. As you know from our earlier discussions, debt holders have the first claim on the cash flows produced by the assets. Interest and principal payments must be made before any cash can be distributed to the stockholders. Therefore, the larger the proportion of debt in a firm's capital structure, the larger the interest and principal payments, and the greater the uncertainty associated with the cash flows to which the stockholders have a claim.

If we assume that a firm's net income is a reasonable measure of the cash flows to which stockholders have a claim, then we can use the simple income statement in **Exhibit 16.2** to illustrate the distinction between business and financial risk.[7] The exhibit shows that business

EXHIBIT 16.2 Relations between Business Risk, Financial Risk, and Total Equity Risk

The total risk associated with the cash flows that stockholders are entitled to receive reflects the risk related to the firm's assets (business risk) and the risk related to the way those assets are financed (financial risk). (We assume here that net income is a reasonable measure of these cash flows.)

Income statement	Risk
Revenue	
– Cost of goods sold	
Gross profit	Business risk (Revenue through Operating profit)
– Selling, general & admin. expenses	
Operating profit	×
– Interest expense	
Earnings before tax	Financial risk (Operating profit through Net income)
– Income tax	=
= Net income	Total equity risk

[6]M&M assumed that the cost of debt was constant and equal to the risk-free rate when they derived their Proposition 2. Of course, we know that the rate of return required by investors increases with risk and that the riskiness of the interest and principal payments on debt increases with leverage. Therefore, the cost of debt must also increase with leverage. If you look carefully at Equation 16.3, you will notice that $(k_{Assets} - k_{Debt})$ gets smaller as leverage increases because, although k_{Debt} gets larger, k_{Assets} does not change. Although this suggests that k_{cs} can get smaller as leverage increases (specifically, the decrease in $k_{Assets} - k_{Debt}$ might more than offset the increase in V_{Debt}/V_{cs}), this never happens in practice. The cost of common stock always increases with leverage.

[7]In previous chapters, we discussed a number of reasons that net income might differ from the cash flows to which stockholders have a claim. For example, accounting accruals may cause net income to differ from cash flows, or depreciation charges might not equal actual cash expenditures on capital equipment or working capital in a particular year. For the time being, we will ignore these potential complications.

EXHIBIT 16.3 **Illustration of Relations between Business Risk, Financial Risk, and Total Risk**

The exhibit shows how a decrease in revenue affects net income (total equity risk) for four different combinations of debt financing (financial risk) and operating leverage (business risk). In columns 1 and 2, we see the effect on a firm with no debt and low operating leverage; in columns 3 and 4, no debt and high operating leverage; in columns 5 and 6, debt and low operating leverage; and in columns 7 and 8, debt and high operating leverage. As you can see, total equity risk, represented by the percent drop in net income, is greater when operating leverage is higher (for example, compare columns 1 and 2 with columns 3 and 4) and when a firm has financial risk (for example, compare columns 1 and 2 with columns 5 and 6). Furthermore, financial risk magnifies operating risk (for example, compare columns 3 and 4 with columns 7 and 8).

	No Financial Risk				Financial Risk			
	Low Operating Leverage		High Operating Leverage		Low Operating Leverage		High Operating Leverage	
Column	1	2	3	4	5	6	7	8
Fixed costs as a percent of total costs	20%		60%		20%		60%	
Interest expense	$0.00		$0.00		$15.00		$15.00	
	Before	**After**	**Before**	**After**	**Before**	**After**	**Before**	**After**
Revenue	$100.00	$80.00	$100.00	$80.00	$100.00	$80.00	$100.00	$ 80.00
– Cost of goods sold (VC)	60.00	48.00	30.00	24.00	60.00	48.00	30.00	24.00
Gross profit	$ 40.00	$32.00	$ 70.00	$56.00	$ 40.00	$32.00	$ 70.00	$ 56.00
– Selling, general, & admin. (FC)	15.00	15.00	45.00	45.00	15.00	15.00	45.00	45.00
Operating profits	$ 25.00	$17.00	$ 25.00	$11.00	$ 25.00	$17.00	$ 25.00	$ 11.00
– Interest expense	0.00	0.00	0.00	0.00	15.00	15.00	15.00	15.00
Earnings before tax	$ 25.00	$17.00	$ 25.00	$11.00	$ 10.00	$ 2.00	$ 10.00	–$4.00
– Income taxes (35%)	8.75	5.95	8.75	3.85	3.50	0.70	3.50	– 1.40
Net income	$ 16.25	$11.05	$ 16.25	$ 7.15	$ 6.50	$ 1.30	$ 6.50	–$2.60
Percent change in net income		–32%		–56%		–80%		–140%

risk is associated with the operations of the business. If you think of business risk as the systematic risk associated with operating profits, and you recall the discussion of operating leverage in Chapter 12, you can see that a firm's business risk reflects the systematic variation in (1) unit sales, (2) unit prices, (3) the costs of producing and selling the firm's products, and (4) the degree of operating leverage in the production process.[8] Financial risk, in contrast, is associated with required payments to a firm's lenders. The total risk of the cash flows that the stockholders have a claim to depends on both the business risk and the financial risk.

The numerical example in **Exhibit 16.3** illustrates the distinction between business risk and financial risk and shows how they combine to determine total equity risk. Consider a firm that sells recreational vehicles and that has the income statement illustrated in column 1. The firm has $100 in revenue; costs of goods sold of $60; and selling, general, and administrative expenses of $15. If we assume that costs of goods sold are all variable costs (VC) and that selling, general, and administrative expenses are all fixed costs (FC), 80 percent [$60/($60 + $15) = 0.80, or 80 percent] of the total costs at this firm are variable costs and 20 percent [$15/($60 + $15) = 0.20, or 20 percent] are fixed. This cost structure, combined with variation in unit sales, the unit pricing, and the costs of producing and selling the firm's products, determines the business risk of the firm. Looking farther down the income statement in column 1, we can see that the firm has no interest expense, which means that it has no debt. In other words, this firm has no leverage and therefore no financial risk.

Now suppose that the price of gasoline increases significantly, causing a drop in the demand for recreational vehicles and a 20 percent decline in revenue, from $100 to $80. Column 2 in Exhibit 16.3 shows that net income would decline to $11.05 (you should verify

[8]Recall from Chapter 12 that operating leverage is a measure of the relative amounts of fixed and variable costs in a project's cost structure. The greater the proportion of total costs that are fixed, the higher the operating leverage. Operating leverage is the major factor that determines the sensitivity of operating profit (EBIT) to changes in revenue. The higher a project's operating leverage, the greater this sensitivity.

this calculation), which is a 32 percent decrease [($11.05 − $16.25)/$16.25 = −0.32, or −32 percent] from the net income in column 1. Since the firm has no debt, and we are assuming that the only change in costs is the reduction in variable costs that occurs when fewer units are sold, this change reflects only the decrease in revenue and the operating leverage of the firm.

If the firm had greater operating leverage, the decline in net income would be even larger. For example, in columns 3 and 4, we show the income statements for a company that has fixed costs representing only 60 percent [$45/($30 + $45) = 0.60, or 60 percent] of total costs and that has no debt. In this case, a 20 percent decline in net revenue results in a 56 percent [($7.15 − $16.25)/$16.25 = −0.56, or −56 percent] decline in net income, illustrating how greater operating leverage magnifies changes in revenue even more.

Next, consider a firm with the income statement presented in column 5. This firm is exactly like the one in column 1 except that it uses some debt financing. You can see that it has an annual interest expense of $15. If revenue drops by 20 percent, the net income of the firm in column 5 will drop by 80 percent [($1.30 − $6.50)/$6.50 = −0.80, or −80 percent]. Thirty-two percent of the decline is due to the nature of the business (remember that it is just like the business in columns 1 and 2), and the remaining 48 percent is due to the use of debt financing. The financial risk magnifies the effect of the operating leverage on net income.

Weblink

An Excel model called "Leverage" will help you calculate the impact of leverage on a company's earnings. Find this model on Matt Evans's Web site at http://www.exinfm.com/free_spreadsheets.html.

Columns 7 and 8 show that if a firm with the same cost structure as the firm in column 3 had to make a $15 interest payment, the decline in net income would increase from 56 percent to 140 percent—a difference of 84 percent! The examples in columns 5 through 8 illustrate why the proportion of debt in a firm's capital structure is called financial leverage.[9] Just as fixed operating costs create operating leverage, fixed-interest costs create financial leverage, which magnifies the effect of changes in revenue on the bottom line of the income statement. This is why the risk and, as M&M told us in their Proposition 2, the cost of common stock increases with financial leverage.

Using M&M Proposition 2 to Calculate the Return on Equity M&M Proposition 2 can be used to calculate the cost of common stock following a financial restructuring. To see how this is done, let's return to the Millennium Motors example.

Before the restructuring, the return on equity for Millennium Motors was the same as the return on assets, 10 percent. We know this because the firm used 100 percent equity financing, which means that the stockholders received all of the cash flows produced by the assets.

After the proposed restructuring, however, the firm would be financed with 20 percent debt and 80 percent common equity. The return on assets would still be 10 percent, and as noted earlier, the return on the debt would be 5 percent. From Equation 16.3, we know that the cost of equity will be:

$$\begin{aligned} k_{cs} &= k_{Assets} + \left(\frac{V_{Debt}}{V_{cs}}\right)(k_{Assets} - k_{Debt}) \\ &= 0.10 + \left(\frac{0.2}{0.8}\right)(0.10 - 0.05) \\ &= 0.1125, \text{ or } 11.25\% \end{aligned}$$

The financial restructuring would increase the cost of equity from 10 percent to 11.25 percent.

Note, too, that if you (as the only investor in Millennium Motors) had offset the effect of the restructuring by using the $200 special dividend to purchase all of the bonds, then the expected return on your combined portfolio would be (0.2 × 0.05) + (0.8 × 0.1125) = 0.10, or 10 percent, just as it was before the restructuring. Again, the restructuring would not change the riskiness of the firm's real assets or the value of those assets.

Learning by Doing Application 16.2, on the next page, presents another example of calculating the cost of common stock using M&M Proposition 2.

How the Costs of Assets, Debt, and Equity Change with Leverage Exhibit 16.4 illustrates M&M Proposition 2 by plotting the cost of common stock (k_{cs}) against the debt-to-equity ratio. Recall from Equation 16.3 that k_{cs} equals k_{Assets} if the firm uses no debt

[9]In Exhibit 16.3, the percentage decrease in net income is 1.75 times as large in the firm with financial leverage as it is in the firm without financial leverage, regardless of whether the firm has low or high operating leverage (−56.00 percent/−32.00 percent = 1.75 and −140.00 percent/−80.00 percent = 1.75). This is because the fixed-interest expense in this example is the same percentage of revenue in both businesses.

LEARNING BY DOING

APPLICATION 16.2 | Using M&M Proposition 2 to Calculate k_{cs}

Problem The required rate of return on the assets of Tempe Technologies is 8 percent, the firm has a debt-to-common-stock ratio of 30 percent, and the cost of debt is 5 percent. If the firm has no preferred stock and the three conditions specified by M&M hold, what is the expected rate of return on the firm's common stock?

Approach The expected return on the firm's common stock can be calculated using Equation 16.3.

Solution

$$k_{cs} = k_{Assets} + \left(\frac{V_{Debt}}{V_{cs}}\right)(k_{Assets} - k_{Debt})$$
$$= 0.08 + (0.30)(0.08 - 0.05)$$
$$= 0.089\text{, or } 8.9\%$$

financing ($V_{Debt}/V_{cs} = 0$) and has no preferred stock. In Figure A of the exhibit, you can see that these costs both equal 10 percent if the firm has no leverage in this example. Equation 16.3 also tells us that as the debt-to-equity ratio increases from zero, the cost of equity will increase by $(V_{Debt}/V_{cs})(k_{Assets} - k_{Debt})$. This increase is illustrated by the blue upward-sloping line.

Figure A. Constant Cost of Debt

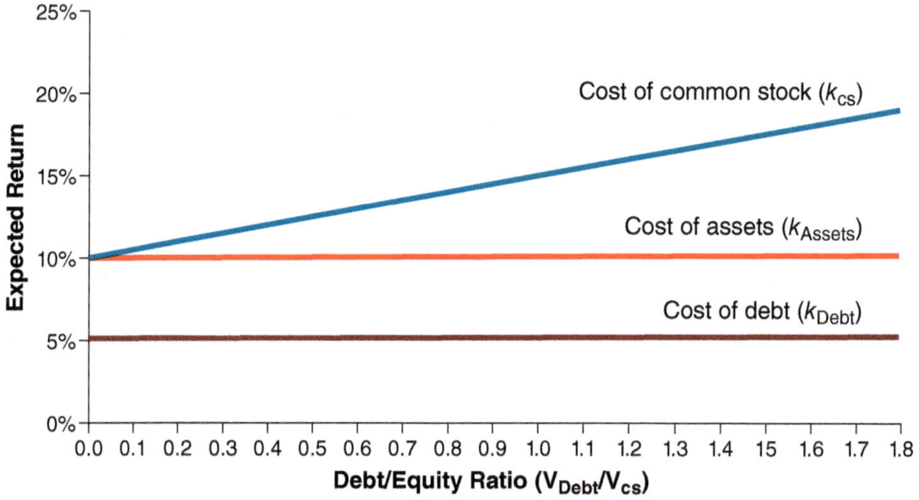

Figure B. Changing Cost of Debt

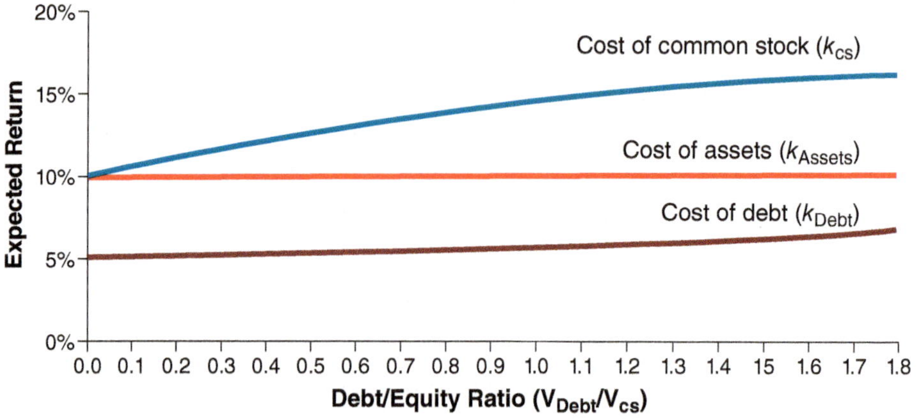

EXHIBIT 16.4 Illustrations of M&M Proposition 2

The costs of assets, common stock, and debt for different debt-to-equity ratios. Figure A assumes that the cost of debt remains constant, and Figure B assumes that the cost of debt increases with leverage. The cost of assets, which is the return that investors require to compensate them for business risk, does not change with leverage. As M&M Proposition 2 tells us, the cost of common stock increases with leverage.

Figure A in Exhibit 16.4 assumes that the cost of debt will remain 5 percent regardless of the amount of debt financing that the firm uses. Figure B in the exhibit shows a more realistic plot of how the costs of assets, debt, and equity change with the debt-to-equity ratio. The key things to understand about the plot in Figure B are that (1) *both* the cost of debt and the cost of equity increase as the debt-to-equity ratio increases and (2) the cost of debt increases at an increasing rate. We explain why the cost of debt increases as it does in the next section.

What the M&M Propositions Tell Us

M&M provided elegant analyses of how capital structure choices are related to firm value and how financial leverage affects the cost of equity. They recognized, however, that the three conditions underlying their analyses are unrealistic. Firms do pay taxes, there are information and transaction costs, and as you will see soon, financing decisions do affect the real investment policies of firms. The value of the M&M analysis is that it tells us exactly where we should look if we want to understand how capital structure affects firm value and the cost of equity. If financial policy matters, it must be because (1) taxes matter, (2) information or transaction costs matter, or (3) capital structure choices affect a firm's real investment policy. We discuss each of these possibilities in the next section.

Weblink

You can see what the Nobel Prize selection committee said about Professors Modigliani and Miller if you visit the economics page on the Nobel Prize Web site at http://www.nobelprize.org.

Before You Go On

1. What is the optimal capital structure for a firm?
2. What is M&M Proposition 1? M&M Proposition 2?
3. What is the difference between business risk and financial risk?
4. How can the three conditions specified by M&M help us understand how the capital structure of a firm affects its value?

16.2 The Benefits and Costs of Using Debt

LEARNING OBJECTIVE

2. Discuss the benefits and costs of using debt financing and calculate the value of the income tax benefit associated with debt.

There are both benefits and costs associated with using debt to finance the purchase of assets. Studies suggest that for very low levels of debt (relative to equity), the marginal benefits of adding more debt outweigh the marginal costs, and the use of more debt reduces the firm's WACC. However, as the amount of debt in the firm's capital structure increases, the marginal costs become greater and eventually begin to outweigh the marginal benefits. The point at which the marginal costs just equal the marginal benefits is the point at which the WACC is minimized. Understanding the location of this point requires an understanding of the costs and benefits and how they change with the amount of debt used by a firm. In this section, we use the framework provided by the three M&M conditions to discuss the benefits and costs of debt.

The Benefits of Debt

We have noted that including debt in the capital structure has advantages for a firm. We now discuss these benefits in detail.

Interest Tax Shield Benefit

The most important benefit from including debt in a firm's capital structure stems from the fact that, as we discussed in Chapter 13, firms can deduct interest payments for tax purposes, but cannot deduct dividend payments.[10] This makes it less costly to distribute cash to investors through interest payments than through dividends.

To understand the implications of the tax deductibility of interest payments for firm value, let's return to the pie analogy in Exhibit 16.1. If we relax the M&M assumption that firms pay no taxes, while assuming that the other two M&M conditions still apply, the pie is now cut into three slices instead of two. In addition to the slices for debt holders and stockholders, there is now a tax slice for the government.

Exhibit 16.5 illustrates the new situation. As shown in the pie on the left, if the firm is financed entirely with equity, there is no interest expense, the firm pays taxes on all of the income from operations, and the value of the firm equals the present value of the after-tax cash flows that the stockholders have a right to receive. Now if the firm uses debt, some of the income from operations will be tax deductible, and the tax slice—the present value of the taxes the firm must pay—will be smaller than in the first pie. This is illustrated for one level of debt in the second pie and for an even greater level of debt in the third pie. Note that the value of the firm, which equals the combined values of the debt and equity slices, increases as the tax slice gets smaller.

Just how large is the value of the interest tax shield? Suppose a firm has fixed perpetual debt equal to D dollars, on which it pays an annual interest rate of k_{Debt}. The total dollar amount of interest paid each year—and, therefore, the amount that will be deducted from the firm's taxable income—is $D \times k_{Debt}$. This will result in a reduction in taxes paid of $D \times k_{Debt} \times t$, where t is the firm's marginal tax rate that applies to the interest expense deduction.

To put this tax reduction in perspective, consider a firm that has no debt and annual earnings before interest and taxes, EBIT, of \$100, which is expected to remain constant in perpetuity. Because the firm has no debt, it currently pays taxes equal to 35 percent of EBIT. Management is considering borrowing \$1,000 at an interest rate of 5 percent. If the firm borrows the money, it will thus pay interest of \$50 each year.

The after-tax earnings for the firm without the debt equal \$65 [\$100 × (1 − 0.35) = \$65], and the taxes paid by the firm equal \$35 (\$100 × 0.35 = \$35). If the firm borrows the \$1,000, its after-tax earnings will be \$32.50 [(\$100 − \$50) × (1 − 0.35) = \$32.50], and it will pay

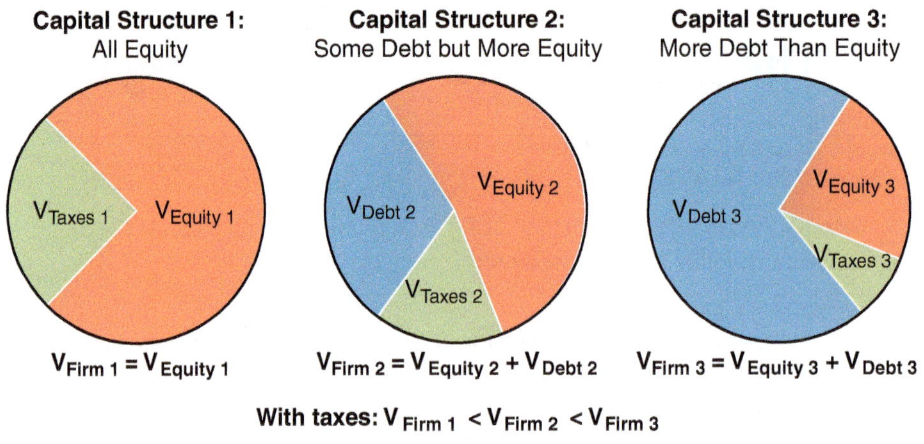

EXHIBIT 16.5 Capital Structure and Firm Value with Taxes

Leverage can increase the value of a firm when interest payments are tax deductible but dividend payments are not. The pie on the left represents a firm financed entirely with equity. The slice labeled $V_{Taxes\ 1}$ reflects the proportion of the cash flows from operations that this firm pays in taxes. The two pies to the right illustrate how the value of the cash flows paid in taxes decreases as leverage is increased. By reducing the fraction paid in taxes, leverage increases the value of the firm in these examples.

[10]This effect is offset somewhat by the fact that dividends and capital gains are taxed at a lower rate than interest income in individual income tax returns. This effect is secondary to the corporate income tax effect because it is smaller in magnitude and because many investors, such as pension funds, endowments, and foundations, pay no taxes at all.

taxes of \$17.50 [(\$100 – \$50) × 0.35 = \$17.50]. The new debt will reduce the taxes that the firm pays each year by \$17.50 ($D \times k_{\text{Debt}} \times t$ = \$1,000 × 0.05 × 0.35 = \$17.50). The total cash flows to the government, the stockholders, and the debt holders in each situation are as follows:

	No Debt	After \$1,000 Loan
Government (taxes)	\$ 35.00	\$ 17.50
Stockholders	65.00	32.50
Debt holders	0.00	50.00
Total	\$100.00	\$100.00

How much is the reduction in taxes worth? If we assume the annual dollar value of the tax reduction will continue in perpetuity, we can use Equation 6.3, the perpetuity model, to calculate the present value of the tax savings from debt:

$$V_{\text{Tax-savings debt}} = \text{PVP} = \frac{\text{CF}}{i} = \frac{D \times k_{\text{Debt}} \times t}{i}$$

All we need now is the appropriate discount rate. In this case, it is reasonable to assume that the appropriate discount rate equals the 5 percent cost of debt. This is a reasonable assumption because we know that the discount rate should reflect the risk of the cash flow stream that is being discounted. Since the firm will benefit from the interest tax shield only if it is able to make the required interest payments, the cash savings associated with the tax shield are about as risky as the cash flow stream associated with the interest payments. This implies that the value of the future tax savings is:

$$V_{\text{Tax-savings debt}} = \frac{D \times k_{\text{Debt}} \times t}{k_{\text{Debt}}} = \frac{\$17.5}{0.05} = \$350$$

If you look closely at this calculation, you will see that \$350 is exactly equal to the product of the \$1,000 that the firm would borrow and its 35 percent tax rate ($D \times t$). In other words:

$$V_{\text{Tax-savings debt}} = D \times t \qquad (16.4)$$

This is because k_{Debt} is in both the numerator and the denominator in the formula and cancels out.

You can see in the above example that the value of the interest tax shield increases with the amount of the debt that a firm has outstanding and with the size of the corporate tax rate. More debt or a higher tax rate implies a larger benefit.

It is important to recognize that the income tax benefit we calculated using the perpetuity model is an upper limit for this value. This is true for several reasons. The perpetuity model assumes that (1) the firm will continue to be in business forever, (2) the firm will be able to realize the tax savings in the years in which the interest payments are made (the firm's EBIT will always be at least as great as the interest expense), and (3) the firm's tax rate will remain at 35 percent.

In the real world, each of these conditions is likely to be violated. While a corporation has an indefinite life, the fact is that corporations go out of business. Of course, at that point the tax benefit ends. Even firms that do not go out of business are unlikely to realize the full benefit of the tax shield. Firms occasionally have poor operating performance, which can prevent them from realizing the benefit of the interest deduction in the year when the payment is made. In such cases, firms often must carry the tax loss forward and apply it to earnings in a future year. Carrying a tax deduction forward reduces its value by pushing it further into the future. Finally, even if the firm is profitable, the effective tax rate can fall below 35 percent because earnings are lower than expected or the firm has other deductions that reduce the value of the interest tax shield.

You might be asking yourself, too, whether it is reasonable to assume that a firm will borrow money forever. The *consols* that we discussed in Chapter 6 are the only perpetual bonds that we know of that have been issued. Nevertheless, it is reasonable to assume that the long-term borrowings by firms will be in place as long as the firm is in business. While the specific debt instruments used by firms are not perpetuities, firms do tend to roll over their maturing debt by borrowing new money to make required principal payments.

As long as a firm does not shrink, prompting it to pay down some of its debt, and as long as the firm does not currently have too much debt, long-term debt can be considered permanent.

The value of the interest tax shield adds to the total value of a firm. In other words, the value of a firm with debt equals the value of that firm without debt plus the present value of the interest tax shield. If only the tax condition, from among the three conditions identified by M&M, is violated, the more debt a firm has, the more it will be worth. This is illustrated in **Exhibit 16.6**, where we plot the value of a firm with debt, a financially leveraged firm, against the proportion of the firm's total capital represented by debt.

In a research paper published in the October 2000 issue of the *Journal of Finance,* John Graham from Duke University estimated that the tax benefit of debt realized by the average firm equals 9.7 percent of *firm* value. When we look at the actual capital structures of public firms, we find that the average firm has debt that is worth about 25 percent of firm value. If we consider a firm with a total value of $100, this implies that tax benefits from debt represent $9.70 of this $100 and that the firm's outstanding debt is worth $25.0. Using Equation 16.4 to solve for t implies a tax rate of:

$$V_{\text{Tax-savings debt}} = D \times t$$

$$t = \frac{V_{\text{Tax-savings debt}}}{D} = \frac{\$9.7}{\$25.0} = 0.388, \text{ or } 38.8\%$$

This tax rate is pretty consistent with U.S. corporate tax rates when we consider both federal and state taxes, along with tax credits that are provided to corporations in the tax laws. It suggests that Equation 16.4 provides a reasonable ballpark estimate for the value of the interest tax shield.

To illustrate how taxes affect firm value, let's return to the initial Millennium Motors example. This time, we will assume that the company must pay corporate taxes equal to 35 percent of its taxable income. As before, the firm is financed entirely with common stock, and management is considering changing its capital structure by selling a $200 perpetual bond with an interest rate of 5 percent and paying a one-time special dividend of $200. The firm produces annual cash flows of $100, and the appropriate discount rate for these cash flows is 10 percent. What is the value of the firm without any debt, and what will the value be if the restructuring is completed?

We begin by calculating the value of Millennium Motors without any debt. If the entire $100 in pretax cash flows that the firm generates is taxable, Millennium's after-tax cash flows will equal $65 per year [$100 × (1 − 0.35) = $65]. Using the perpetuity formula, we find that the value of the unleveraged firm is $650 ($65/0.10 = $650) with a 10 percent discount rate.

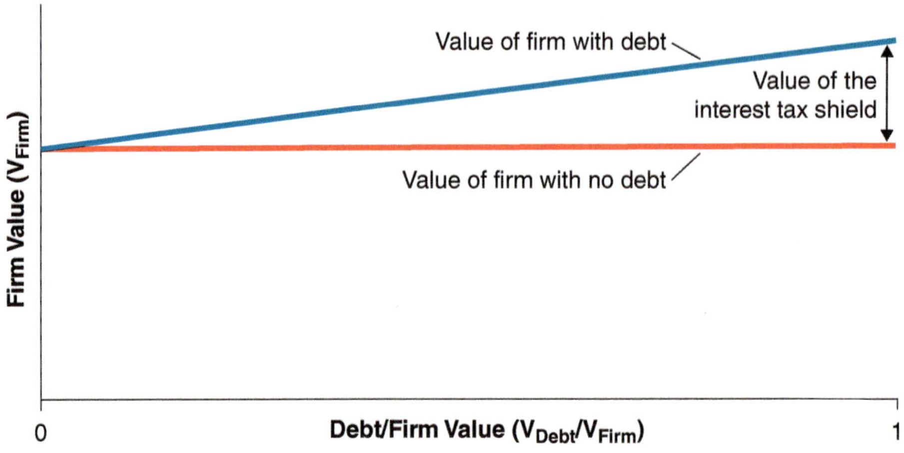

EXHIBIT 16.6 How Firm Value Changes with Leverage When Interest Payments Are Tax Deductible and Dividends Are Not

The value of a firm increases with leverage when interest payments are tax deductible and dividend payments are not, and when the second and third M&M conditions—that there are no information or transaction costs and that the real investment policy of the firm is not affected by its capital structure decisions—apply.

We next calculate the value of the interest tax shield that would accompany the new debt. This value is \$70 ($D \times t = \$200 \times 0.35 = \$70$). The total value of the firm after the restructuring is equal to the value of the unleveraged firm plus the value of the tax shield. In this case, that is \$720 (\$650 + \$70 = \$720).

We can also calculate the WACC for Millennium Motors after the financial restructuring using Equation 13.7. To do so, we must first calculate the value of the equity (V_{Equity}). In this case, since we know from Equation 16.1 that $V_{Firm} = V_{Equity} + V_{Debt}$, we can calculate the value of the equity to be \$520 ($V_{Equity} = V_{Firm} - V_{Debt} = \$720 - \$200 = \$520$). Since we also know that the cash flows available to stockholders after the restructuring will equal \$58.50 [(\$100 – \$10) × (1 – 0.35) = \$58.50], we can calculate the required return on equity to be 11.25 percent (\$58.50/\$520 = 0.1125). This is the same number we got when we used Equation 16.3. With these values, we are now ready to calculate the WACC:

$$\text{WACC} = x_{\text{Debt}} k_{\text{Debt pretax}}(1 - t) + x_{\text{ps}} k_{\text{ps}} + x_{\text{cs}} k_{\text{cs}}$$

$$= \left(\frac{\$200}{\$720}\right)(0.05)(1 - 0.35) + 0 + \left(\frac{\$520}{\$720}\right)(0.1125) = 0.0903, \text{ or } 9.03\%$$

As Exhibit 16.4 illustrates, the cost of common stock increases with the amount of debt in the firm's capital structure. In this example, it goes from 10 percent to 11.25 percent. However, with the interest tax deduction, the WACC actually decreases from 10 percent (recall that the cost of equity equals the WACC for a firm with no debt) to 9.03 percent.

When we perform the same calculations for other potential debt levels at Millennium, we see how the value of the firm increases and the WACC decreases as the amount of debt in the capital structure increases. This is illustrated in **Exhibit 16.7** for levels of debt ranging from \$0 to \$800.

You should note several other points concerning Exhibit 16.7. First, we do not show the calculations for a firm with 100 percent debt because all firms must have some common equity. Second, the payments to investors and the firm value increase as the amount of debt financing increases. This is because the size of the government's slice of the pie gets smaller. Third, for simplicity, we assume that the cost of debt remains constant. However, even though the cost of equity increases, the WACC decreases. This decrease is entirely due to the interest tax shield. Finally, while the value of the firm under each scenario is calculated as we have illustrated, you can confirm the answer by noting that the firm value for each capital structure equals the payments to investors for the unleveraged firm, \$65, divided by the WACC. The payments to investors for the unleveraged firm are used in this calculation, regardless of the firm's capital structure, because, as was the case for project analysis, the effects of capital structure choices are reflected in the discount rate rather than the cash flows.

EXHIBIT 16.7 The Effect of Taxes on the Firm Value and WACC of Millennium Motors

The value of Millennium Motors increases and its WACC decreases with the amount of debt in the capital structure. The calculations assume that the cost of debt remains constant regardless of the amount of leverage and that the second and third M&M conditions apply.

	Total debt				
	\$0	\$200	\$400	\$600	\$800
Cost of debt	5.00%	5.00%	5.00%	5.00%	5.00%
EBIT	\$100.00	\$100.00	\$100.00	\$100.00	\$100.00
Interest expense	—	10.00	20.00	30.00	40.00
Earnings before taxes	\$100.00	\$ 90.00	\$ 80.00	\$ 70.00	\$ 60.00
Taxes (35%)	35.00	31.50	28.00	24.50	21.00
Net income	\$ 65.00	\$ 58.50	\$ 52.00	\$ 45.50	\$ 39.00
Dividends	\$ 65.00	\$ 58.50	\$ 52.00	\$ 45.50	\$ 39.00
Interest payments	—	10.00	20.00	30.00	40.00
Payments to investors	\$ 65.00	\$ 68.50	\$ 72.00	\$ 75.00	\$ 79.00
Value of equity	\$650.00	\$520.00	\$390.00	\$260.00	\$130.00
Cost of equity	10.00%	11.25%	13.33%	17.50%	30.00%
Firm value	\$650.00	\$720.00	\$790.00	\$860.00	\$930.00
WACC	10.00%	9.03%	8.23%	7.56%	6.99%

Learning by Doing Application 16.3 presents another example of how debt affects firm value and WACC.

LEARNING BY DOING

WileyPLUS

Need more help? Visit your WileyPLUS course.

APPLICATION 16.3 | Calculating the Effect of Debt on Firm Value and WACC

Problem Up to this point, you have financed your pizza chain entirely with equity. You have heard about the tax benefit associated with using debt financing and are considering borrowing $1 million at an interest rate of 6 percent to take advantage of the interest tax shield. You do not need the extra money in the business, so you will distribute it to yourself through a special dividend. You are the only stockholder.

Your pizza business generates taxable (pretax) cash flows of $300,000 each year and pays taxes at a rate of 25 percent; the cost of assets, k_{Assets} (which equals k_{cs} for your unleveraged firm), is 10 percent. What is the value of your firm without debt, and how much would $1 million of debt increase its value if you assume that all cash flows are perpetuities and that the second and third M&M conditions hold (that is, there are no information or transaction costs and the real investment policy of the firm is not affected by its capital structure decisions)? Also, what would the WACC for your business be before and after the proposed financial restructuring?

Approach The value of your restaurant chain equals the present value of the after-tax cash flows that the stockholders and debt holders expect to receive in the future. Without debt, this value equals the present value of the dividends that you can expect to receive as the only stockholder. The value with debt equals the value without debt plus the value of the interest tax shield.

The WACC before the financial restructuring equals k_{cs}, since your firm currently has no preferred stock or debt. Equation 13.7 can be used to calculate the WACC with debt.

Solution The value of your business without debt can be calculated using the perpetuity model as follows:

$$V_{Firm} = [\$300{,}000 \times (1 - 0.25)]/0.10 = \$2{,}250{,}000$$

The value of the tax shield is:

$$D \times t = \$1{,}000{,}000 \times 0.25 = \$250{,}000$$

Therefore, after the restructuring, the value of the firm would be $2.5 million ($2,250,000 + $250,000 = $2,500,000).

The WACC before the financial restructuring equals:

$$\text{WACC} = k_{cs} = 10\%$$

To calculate the WACC after the restructuring, we must first calculate the cost of the common stock. Since the values of the firm and debt will be $2.5 million and $1 million, respectively, the value of the equity must equal $1.5 million. The after-tax cash flows to stockholders will equal $180,000 {[$300,000 − ($1,000,000 × 0.06)] × [1 − 0.25] = $180,000}. Therefore, k_{cs} equals 12 percent ($180,000/$1,500,000 = 0.12, or 12 percent). We can now calculate the WACC using Equation 13.7 as follows:

$$\begin{aligned}\text{WACC} &= x_{Debt}k_{Debt\ pretax}(1-t) + x_{ps}k_{ps} + x_{cs}k_{cs}\\ &= \left(\frac{\$1{,}000{,}000}{\$2{,}500{,}000}\right)(0.06)(1-0.25) + 0 + \left(\frac{\$1{,}500{,}000}{\$2{,}500{,}000}\right)(0.12)\\ &= 0.090, \text{ or } 9.0\%\end{aligned}$$

We can also show that, *with taxes* the cost of equity can be written as:

$$k_{cs} = k_{Assets} + (V_{Debt}/V_{cs}) \times (k_{Assets} - k_{Debt})(1 - t) \quad (16.5)$$

From Learning by Doing Application 16.3, we would calculate the k_{cs} as

$$k_{cs} = k_{Assets} + (V_{Debt}/V_{cs}) \times (k_{Assets} - k_{Debt})(1 - t)$$

$$k_{cs} = 0.10 + (\$1{,}000{,}000/\$1{,}500{,}000) \times (0.10 - 0.06)(1 - 0.25)$$

$$k_{cs} = 0.12 \text{ or } 12\%$$

which is the same value that we had previously.

Decision Making Example 16.1 shows how a change in the tax rate can affect a firm's capital structure.

DECISION MAKING

EXAMPLE 16.1 | Capital Structure and Tax Rates

Situation You are the chief financial officer at Maricopa Manufacturing Company in Phoenix, Arizona. The company is currently financed with 30 percent debt and 70 percent equity. Maricopa's chief lobbyist in Washington, D.C., just told you that he expects the federal government to reduce the top corporate income tax rate from 35 percent to 28 percent beginning next year. What action should you take with regard to Maricopa's capital structure?

Decision Assuming that state and local taxes are not also expected to change next year, the reduction in the top federal corporate income tax rate means that the interest tax shield benefit your company receives from its outstanding debt will decline. If the current capital structure maximizes Maricopa's value when the federal income tax rate is 35 percent and you expect all of the other costs and benefits of debt to remain the same, you should reduce the amount of debt that is used to finance Maricopa when the new tax rate goes into effect. This is because the smaller benefits from debt will be offset by the costs of debt at a lower debt level. Precisely how much you should reduce the company's debt will depend on exactly how large the total benefits and costs will be next year.

Other Benefits

Any firm that must pay taxes can benefit from the interest tax shield. Not surprisingly, most financial managers cite it as a major benefit from using debt in a firm's capital structure.

Although the tax benefit is important, you should be aware of other benefits. For example, it is less expensive to issue debt than to issue stock. Underwriting spreads and out-of-pocket costs are more than three times as large for stock sales as they are for bond sales. Recall from Chapter 15 (in Exhibit 15.6) that a firm raising between $25.0 million and $49.9 million will typically pay 7.09 percent of the amount raised to sell stock, but only 1.63 percent of the amount raised to sell bonds—a substantial difference. This benefit is related to the second of the three conditions identified by M&M. Issuance costs are a form of transaction costs. If there were no transaction costs, then debt issues would not have this cost advantage.

Another benefit associated with using debt financing is that debt provides managers with incentives to focus on maximizing the firm's cash flows. Unlike dividends, which are discretionary, interest and principal payments must be made when they are due. Because managers must make these payments or face the prospect of bankruptcy, the use of debt puts more pressure on managers to focus on the efficiency of the business. Because a bankruptcy filing can destroy a manager's career, managers will work very hard to avoid letting this happen. Providing managers with these incentives can increase the overall value of the firm.

Finally, debt can be used to limit the ability of bad managers to waste the stockholders' money on things such as fancy jet aircraft, plush offices, and other negative NPV projects that benefit the managers personally. It does this by forcing managers to distribute excess cash to the investors. In some very famous cases, such as General Motors in the 1980s and WorldCom in the 1990s, managers wasted large amounts of corporate assets on negative NPV projects. Clearly, the managers at these firms had a great deal of discretion over the use of the large sums of cash generated by their businesses. If the firms had been more highly leveraged, the managers would have had less discretion.

The benefits arising from providing managers with incentives to focus on the cash flows generated by their firms and limiting their ability to make poor investments are related to the second and third conditions identified by M&M. These benefits are related to information and transaction costs because if investors had enough information to know whether managers were doing the right thing, or if it were reasonably inexpensive to provide the managers with pay packages that gave them incentives to do the right thing on their own, there would be no such benefits from debt. The benefits also relate directly to the M&M condition that capital structure decisions do not affect the real investment policies of the firm. The whole point of using debt to limit the investments managers can make is to change firms' real investment policies so that managers focus on investing in only positive NPV projects.

The Costs of Debt

We have discussed several benefits associated with using debt. If this were the whole story, choosing the optimal capital structure would be straightforward. More debt would imply a higher firm value, and financial managers would use as much debt as possible. In other words, a plot of a firm's value against the proportion of debt in its capital structure would look like the upward-sloping line in Exhibit 16.6. Managers would try to move their firms' capital structures as far to the right as possible, and we would expect to see firms using as close to 100 percent debt financing as possible.

Recall, however, that the debt of the average public firm represents only about 25 percent of the value of the firm. The fact that this number is so much lower than 100 percent raises a question: Is it just that financial managers do not understand the benefits of debt, or is something else going on? As you might suspect, the answer to this question is that financial managers are pretty smart and are limiting the amount of debt in their firms' capital structures for some very good reasons. Offsetting the benefits of debt are costs, and these costs can be quite substantial at high levels of debt.

Exhibit 16.8 illustrates how the costs of using debt combine with the benefits to result in an optimal capital structure that includes less than 100 percent debt. At low levels of debt, the benefits are greater than the costs, and adding more debt increases the overall value of the firm. However, at some point the costs begin to exceed the benefits, and adding more debt financing destroys firm value. Financial managers want to add debt just to the point at which the value of the firm is maximized.

The costs of using debt fall into two general categories: bankruptcy costs and agency costs.

Bankruptcy Costs

bankruptcy costs, or costs of financial distress costs associated with financial difficulties a firm might experience because it uses debt financing

Bankruptcy costs, also referred to as **costs of financial distress**, are costs associated with financial difficulties that a firm might get into because it uses debt financing. The term *bankruptcy costs* is used rather loosely in capital structure discussions to refer to costs incurred when a firm gets into financial distress. Financial distress occurs when a firm is not able to make all of the interest and principal payments that it owes its lenders.

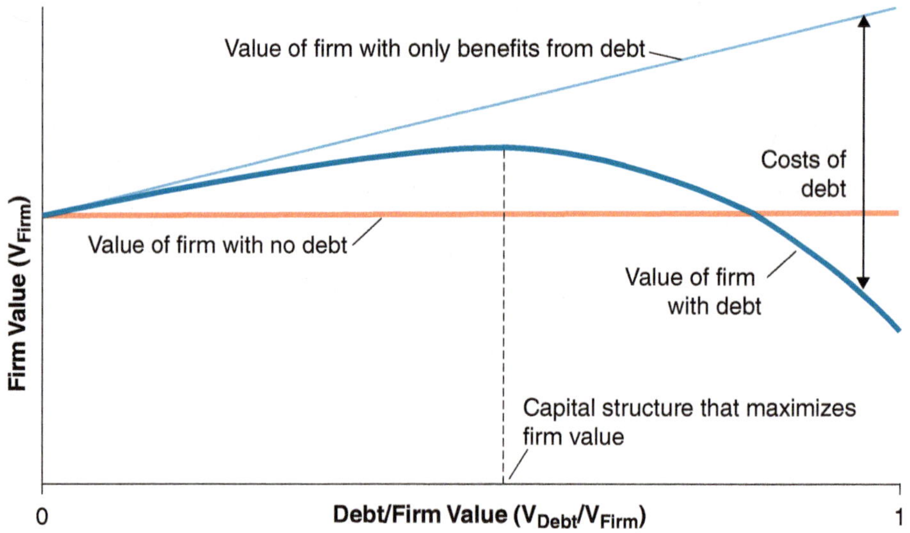

EXHIBIT 16.8 Trade-Off Theory of Capital Structure

The benefits and costs of debt combine to affect firm value. For low levels of debt, adding more debt to a firm's capital structure increases firm value because the additional (marginal) benefits are greater than the additional (marginal) costs. However, at some point, which is the point at which the value of the firm is maximized, the costs of adding more debt begin to outweigh the benefits, and the value of the firm decreases as more debt is added. The difference between the upward-sloping line and the curved line reflects the costs associated with debt.

A financially distressed firm might subsequently enter into a formal legal bankruptcy process, such as those under Chapter 11 or Chapter 7 of the U.S. bankruptcy code, but not all financially distressed firms will do this. Consequently, as you will see shortly, firms can incur the bankruptcy costs discussed in this section even if they never actually file for bankruptcy.

Direct Bankruptcy Costs **Direct bankruptcy costs** are out-of-pocket costs that a firm incurs as a result of financial distress. These costs include fees paid to lawyers, accountants, and consultants. One of the first actions a firm's management takes when the firm gets into financial distress is to initiate negotiations with its lenders to defer its interest and principal payments. This deferment can give management more time to correct whatever went wrong with the firm's operations that made it difficult to make interest and principal payments in the first place. Lawyers are experienced in assisting in these negotiations and in writing the necessary legal documents. Additional accounting support often becomes necessary to satisfy demands for information from lenders and to help management figure out what went wrong. Consultants might be hired to help identify and implement changes to improve the firm's performance. The costs of hiring all of these people are included in direct bankruptcy costs. For example, accountants, lawyers, and other professionals providing services in the Lehman Brothers bankruptcy were reportedly paid more than $2.2 billion in fees, while for the General Motors bankruptcy it was $110 million (which one expert suggested was astonishingly low given the size of the company!). Since the probability of financial distress increases with the amount of debt that a firm uses, the expected size of these costs increases with leverage, driving up the interest rate that investors charge the firm for its debt. Investors charge a higher interest rate when the expected value of direct bankruptcy costs increases because the payment of these costs is likely to come out of the cash flows that they would otherwise receive.

direct bankruptcy costs out-of-pocket costs that a firm incurs when it gets into financial distress

You might be asking yourself why the lenders to a firm would defer interest and principal payments. After all, pushing these payments further into the future reduces the present value of the payments that the lenders are promised. The reason is simple: it can cost lenders even more if they refuse to work with management and the firm is forced to file for bankruptcy. Once a firm files for bankruptcy, legal fees increase because the firm must hire attorneys to help with the bankruptcy process, and accounting fees increase because the bankruptcy process will require the firm to generate even more information. In addition, the firm must reimburse the court for the costs that it incurs. By negotiating with management up front, the lenders might be able to help the firm avoid incurring the costs associated with the formal bankruptcy process. This leaves more value in the firm, which can be used to satisfy the lenders' claims.

Direct bankruptcy costs are a form of transaction costs that must be incurred to facilitate negotiations with lenders and to navigate the bankruptcy process. The second condition identified by M&M—that there are no transaction and information costs—assumes that these transaction costs do not exist. Because the costs do exist, they tend to offset, at least to some extent, the benefits associated with debt. In fact, researchers have estimated that direct bankruptcty costs can amount to as much as 3 to 5 percent of firm value. Although these costs are substantial, they are not large enough on their own to cause the firm value curve to turn downward in the manner illustrated in Exhibit 16.8.

Indirect Bankruptcy Costs **Indirect bankruptcy costs** are costs associated with changes in the behavior of people who deal with a firm when it becomes financially distressed. The interests of many people who deal with a firm are normally similar to those of the stockholders—they all want to maximize the firm's value. However, when a firm gets into financial distress, the interests of these people begin to differ, and the actions they take to protect their interests often reduce firm value.

indirect bankruptcy costs costs associated with changes in the behavior of people who deal with a firm when the firm gets into financial distress

For example, suppose a firm's products come with warranties or require after-sales service or parts (automobiles, for example) and it becomes known that the firm is having financial difficulties. Some of this firm's potential customers will decide to purchase a competitor's products because of concerns that the firm will not be able to honor its warranties or that parts or service will not be available in the future. Other customers will demand a lower price to compensate them for these risks. In either case, the firm's revenues will decline below what they would otherwise have been. Indeed, when automaker SAAB was about to file for bankruptcy, new SAAB vehicles were being offered at record-low prices as dealers struggled to sell their inventory.

When suppliers learn that a firm is in financial distress, they worry about not being paid. They can do little about goods they have already shipped, but to protect against losses for future shipments, they often begin to require cash on delivery. In other words, they will deliver supplies only if the firm pays cash for them. This requirement can be devastating for a financially distressed firm because such a firm typically does not have much cash. For example, if a retailer, like a department store, cannot pay cash for its merchandise, the amount of merchandise on the shelves in its stores will decline over time. Customers will not be able to find what they want, and they will respond by shopping at competitors' stores. This will cause revenues to decline even faster than they might otherwise have. In the worst case, suppliers' demands for cash payments can force a firm to stop operating altogether.

Employees at a distressed firm worry that their jobs or benefits are in danger, and some start looking for new jobs. The loss of highly skilled employees can reduce the value of the firm, especially if they take jobs with direct competitors. Even when employees do not leave, their productivity will often decline because the firm's problems lead to lower morale and distractions.

Like direct bankruptcy costs, indirect bankruptcy costs are transaction costs that would not exist under the second condition identified by M&M. They are transaction costs because they represent costs incurred in the course of contracting with the people who deal with the firm.

If the firm enters into the formal bankruptcy process, it incurs another indirect bankruptcy cost. This cost stems from the fact that the bankruptcy judge must approve all of the firm's major investments. Bankruptcy judges are responsible for representing the interests of the creditors and tend to be more conservative than the stockholders would like. This results in a change in the firm's real investment policy and a violation of the third M&M condition.

The nature of indirect bankruptcy costs differs from company to company. For example, loss of skilled workers is more damaging to a technology firm than to a retailer. Potential customers of an auto manufacturer worry a lot more about the implications of financial distress than potential customers of a company that makes T-shirts, whereas suppliers are concerned in both of these cases. In spite of these differences, indirect bankruptcy costs are often very substantial and are reflected in the interest rates that firms must pay. Researchers have estimated that indirect bankruptcy costs range from 10 to 23 percent of firm value, suggesting that they can be large enough to offset the interest tax shield benefit of debt.

It is worth stressing that indirect bankruptcy costs occur at absolutely the worst time for a firm. The point at which a firm gets into financial distress is the point at which it can benefit most from the support of people who deal with it. However, this is exactly when it is often in the best interests of those people to provide less support and, in many cases, abandon the firm. The associated changes in behavior can accelerate the firm's deterioration and push it into formal bankruptcy.

Building Intuition

People Behave Differently toward a Firm in Financial Distress, and This Increases Bankruptcy Costs

When a firm gets into financial distress, the people who deal with the company take actions to protect their interests. These actions often contribute to the firm's problems because when the firm is financially distressed, the interests of customers, suppliers, and employees, among others, differ from those of stockholders.

Agency Costs

The managers and stockholders of a firm also often behave in ways that reduce a firm's value when the firm becomes financially distressed. The resulting costs are a type of *agency cost.* You may recall from Chapter 1 that agency costs result from conflicts of interest between principals and agents. In agency relationships, one party, known as the *principal,* delegates decision-making authority to another party, known as the *agent.* The agent is expected to act in the interest of the principal. However, agents' interests sometimes conflict with those of the principal.

To better understand agency costs, consider the following example. Suppose that you have a newspaper route and you want to go out of town for a week. You offer a friend $100 to deliver your papers while you are gone. If your friend agrees to the arrangement, you will have entered into a principal–agent relationship. Now assume that you deliver the *Wall Street Journal* and that all papers are supposed to be on your customers' doorsteps by 6:00 A.M., before they leave home for work. You tell this to your friend before you leave town, but he likes to sleep late in the morning, so he doesn't get all the papers delivered until 9:00 A.M. Because the papers are late for five days in a row, a few customers complain, and some don't give you a tip at the end of the year as they have in the past. Any problems that arise because of the complaints and the lost tips are examples of agency costs. These costs arose because you delegated decision-making authority to your friend and he acted in his best interest rather than yours.

Stockholder–Manager Agency Costs Stockholders hire managers to manage the firm on their behalf. In this relationship, managers receive considerable decision-making authority. While the board of directors approves major decisions and monitors the performance of the managers on behalf of the stockholders, managers still make many decisions that the board never observes. To the extent that the managers' incentives are not perfectly identical to those of the stockholders, managers will make some decisions that benefit themselves at the expense of the stockholders.

As we saw in our discussion of the benefits of debt, a firm's use of debt financing can help align the interests of managers with those of stockholders. Using debt financing provides managers with incentives to focus on maximizing the firm's cash flows and limits the ability of bad managers to waste the stockholders' money on negative NPV projects. These benefits amount to reductions in the agency costs associated with the principal–agent relationship between stockholders and managers.

Although the use of debt financing can reduce agency costs, it can also increase these costs by altering the behavior of managers. Managers often have a high proportion of their wealth riding on the success of the firm, through their stockholdings, future income, and reputations. Consequently, they tend to prefer less risk than stockholders who hold more diversified portfolios. As you know, the use of debt increases the volatility of a firm's earnings and the probability that the firm will get into financial difficulty. This increased risk causes managers to make more conservative decisions. For example, managers of firms with more financial leverage will have greater incentives to turn down positive NPV projects with high risk than otherwise similar managers at firms with less leverage. Similarly, managers at highly financially leveraged firms will prefer to distribute fewer profits to stockholders because earnings retained as cash provide a buffer against possible bankruptcy. These types of actions reduce the overall value of the firm and are examples of agency costs associated with the use of debt financing.

Recall that the third M&M condition is that the use of debt financing does not affect the firm's real investment policy. To the extent that using debt financing causes managers to turn down high-risk positive NPV projects and distribute fewer earnings, however, financing decisions do affect real investment policies. Leverage provides managers with incentives to invest in lower-risk positive NPV projects rather than in all positive NPV projects. It also provides them with incentives to retain excess earnings. They might even have incentives to invest some of the excess retained earnings in low-risk negative NPV projects. The fact that managers may act in this way is another reason that debt financing affects the value of the firm.

Stockholder–Lender Agency Costs A principal–agent relationship also exists between lenders and stockholders. When investors lend money to a firm, they delegate authority to the stockholders to decide how that money will be used. The lenders expect that the stockholders, through the managers they appoint, will invest the money in a way that enables the firm to make all of the interest and principal payments that have been promised. However, stockholders may have incentives to use the money in ways that are not in the best interests of the lenders.

For example, stockholders might decide that instead of investing the money to grow the firm, they will distribute it to themselves as a dividend. In the U.S. corporate system, the liability of stockholders is limited to the amount of money they have invested in the firm. Since loans that are made to a corporation are contracts between the lenders and the corporation, not the stockholders, paying such a dividend reduces the resources in the firm that are available to repay the lenders and therefore the value of the lender's claims. Unless the dividend violates the loan agreement or otherwise violates the law, the lenders have no way to get that money back. This is an example of what we call a *wealth transfer* from the lenders to the stockholders. Wealth has been transferred because the stockholders have made themselves better off at the expense of the lenders.

Lenders know that stockholders have incentives to distribute some or all of the funds that they borrow as dividends. To protect themselves against this sort of behavior, lenders often include provisions in loan agreements that limit the ability of stockholders to pay dividends. However, these provisions are not entirely foolproof. Stockholders can be very innovative in transferring wealth from lenders to themselves.

For example, in October 1992 Marriott Corporation had a substantial amount of debt that had been borrowed to build new hotels. The economy was in a recession, and there was growing concern about the ability of Marriott to make all of its promised interest and principal payments. If the company defaulted, the stockholders stood to lose a good deal of the value of their stock.

In response to this situation, Marriott management announced a *spin-off* in which the company would be split into two separate companies. After the spin-off, stockholders would own one share of stock in each of the two new companies for every share that they had owned in the original company. While spin-offs are quite common, this one was unique in that the company was spinning off its most profitable businesses into one company and leaving much of its debt, some real estate, and a small operating business in the other. The spin-off effectively reduced the value of the assets that the lenders would have to rely on to receive their interest and principal payments while reducing the assets that the stockholders could lose if there was a default. When the spin-off was announced, the market value of Marriott's public bonds decreased 16.51 percent, or \$333.3 million, while the market value of Marriott's outstanding stock increased by \$236.3 million.[11] The increase in the value of the stock represented a wealth transfer from the lenders to the stockholders. In addition, the fact that the value of the debt went down more than the value of the equity increased suggests that the capital markets did not like this transaction: the total value of the firm (debt plus equity) went down.

Notice that when we talk about stockholder–lender agency costs, we assume that managers do exactly what the stockholders would like them to do. However, in the discussion of stockholder–manager agency costs, we saw that managers are not always so cooperative. This results in some conflicting possibilities with respect to how financial leverage affects a managers' decisions. For example, in a firm that uses debt financing, managers prefer to invest in low-risk projects, whereas diversified stockholders prefer high-risk projects. Stockholders will pressure managers to invest in riskier projects, but whether stockholders get what they want will depend on how strong the corporate governance system is in the firm.

To better understand the nature of the conflict between stockholders and lenders, consider the following example. Suppose a firm has \$50 million invested in 10 percent risk-free bonds that will pay \$55 million in one year. The firm also has one-year debt on which \$50 million of interest and principal will be due when it matures in a year. In other words, this firm is solvent and will be able to repay its debt, but the equity will be worth only \$5 million at the end of the year, since this is all that will be left over after the lenders are paid.

Now suppose that the stockholders decide to sell the risk-free bonds and invest in a project that has a 50 percent chance of returning \$95 million in one year and a 50 percent chance of returning only \$15 million. Instead of receiving \$50 million with no risk, the lenders now face a 50 percent chance of receiving the \$50 million they are owed, and a 50 percent chance of receiving only \$15 million. The value that the lenders expect to receive is \$32.5 million:

$$E(V_{\text{Bonds}}) = (0.50 \times \$50) + (0.50 \times \$15) = \$32.5 \text{ million}$$

This amount is \$17.5 million less than the \$50 million that the lenders expected to receive when the firm held the risk-free bonds. The value that the stockholders expect to receive, on the other hand, has increased by \$17.5 million, from \$5 million to \$22.5 million:

$$E(V_{\text{Stock}}) = [0.50 \times (\$95 - \$50)] + (0.50 \times \$0) = \$22.5 \text{ million}$$

asset substitution problem the incentive that stockholders in a financially leveraged firm have to substitute more risky assets for less risky assets

The change to riskier assets has resulted in a \$17.5 million wealth transfer. This is known as the **asset substitution problem**. Once a loan has been made to a firm, the stockholders have an incentive to substitute more risky assets for less risky assets.

[11]R. Parrino, "Spin-offs and Wealth Transfers: The Marriott Case," *Journal of Financial Economics* 43 (1997), 241–274.

Under certain circumstances, stockholders will actually have incentives to invest in risky *negative* NPV projects. To see how this can happen, assume that the stockholders in our example sell the $50 million of risk-free bonds and invest the proceeds in a project that has a 50 percent chance of returning $70 million and a 50 percent chance of returning $10 million. The expected return on the $50 million investment is $40 million [(0.50 × $70) + (0.50 × $10) = $40 million]. This is a negative NPV project. However, the value that the stockholders can expect to receive is $10 million—twice as much as the $5 million they could expect to receive when the firm owned the risk-free bonds:

$$E(V_{Stock}) = [0.50 \times (\$70 - \$50)] + (0.50 \times \$0) = \$10 \text{ million}$$

The lenders bear the $15 million loss in firm value ($55 million – $40 million = $15 million), and they pay for the $5 million gain to the stockholders. The lenders now expect to receive $20 million less than the $50 million they would have received if the risk-free bonds had not been sold:

$$E(V_{Bonds}) = (0.50 \times \$50) + (0.50 \times \$10) = \$30 \text{ million}$$

A situation similar to that just described confronted stockholders of firms in the U.S. savings and loan industry in the mid-1980s. Many small savings and loan firms had a very high ratio of debt to equity and faced the possibility that they would have to file for bankruptcy. With little to lose, managers at savings and loan firms, who were often also large stockholders, started making very risky real estate loans with high rates of interest. They knew that if the loans were repaid, their firms would avoid bankruptcy and the stockholders would realize much of the benefit. If the loans were not repaid, the government, which insured all of the deposits used to finance the loans, would have to bear the loss. Ultimately, these sorts of investments led to what became known as the savings and loan crisis.

Weblink

Learn more about the savings and loan crisis of the 1980s at http://www.fdic.gov/bank/historical/s&l and http://www.fdic.gov/bank/analytical/banking/2000dec/brv13n2_2.pdf.

Stockholders of financially distressed firms can also have incentives to turn down positive NPV projects. This situation is known as the **underinvestment problem**. It occurs in a financially distressed firm when the value that is created by investing in a positive NPV project is likely to go to the lenders instead of the stockholders. For example, as of 2017 some companies in the oil industry with very high debt levels needed more cash to explore for, and extract from, potentially profitable oil and gas reserves. Given their poor financial condition, they could not raise more debt and stockholders would not provide more equity to fund these investments as any profits would go to paying the debt holders.

underinvestment problem the incentive that stockholders in a financially leveraged firm have to turn down positive NPV projects when the firm is in financial distress

To see how this can happen, suppose that a company has debt with a face value of $50 million outstanding and that the value of the company's assets is $32.5 million. If the assets of this financially distressed firm were sold today, the lenders would receive $32.5 million, and the stockholders would receive nothing. Now suppose that the managers of the firm identify a project that requires a $5 million investment and will return $17.5 million tomorrow with no risk. Since the firm is distressed, management will have to sell stock to raise the $5 million required for this investment. Does it make sense for the stockholders to make the investment?

The answer is no, because if the stockholders invest the $5 million, they can expect to get nothing back if the firm is subsequently sold. Both the $5 million that the stockholders invest and the $12.5 million NPV ($17.5 million – $5 million = $12.5 million) from the project will go to the lenders. Instead of receiving $32.5 million, the lenders will receive $50 million, and the stockholders will be out $5 million. This example illustrates why, in the real world, financially distressed businesses have a very difficult time raising equity capital.

It is important to note that without financial leverage, there would be no asset substitution or underinvestment problems. Stockholders would always want to invest in positive NPV projects and reject negative NPV projects regardless of their risk.

Lenders know that debt provides stockholders with incentives to alter their firms' investment policies to engage in asset substitution and to turn down positive NPV projects. However, it is difficult to write contracts that protect lenders against this sort of behavior. Therefore, as with any other risk that they cannot eliminate, lenders compensate by increasing the interest rate that they charge. This increases the cost of adding more debt to a firm's capital structure.

The fact that there are a number of different benefits and costs associated with the use of debt financing suggests that managers will balance, or trade off, the benefits against the costs when they choose a firm's capital structure. We discuss this idea along with an alternative theory for how managers choose their firms' capital structures in the next section.

Before You Go On

1. What are some benefits of using debt financing?
2. What are bankruptcy costs, and what are the two types of bankruptcy costs?
3. What are agency costs, and how are they related to the use of debt financing?

16.3 Two Theories of Capital Structure

LEARNING OBJECTIVE

3. Describe the trade-off and pecking order theories of capital structure choice and explain what the empirical evidence tells us about these theories.

How do managers choose the capital structures for their firms? Next, we consider two theories that attempt to explain how this choice is made: the trade-off theory and the pecking order theory.

The Trade-Off Theory

trade-off theory the theory that managers trade off the benefits against the costs of using debt to identify the optimal capital structure for a firm

The **trade-off theory** of capital structure states that managers choose a specific target capital structure based on the trade-offs between the benefits and the costs of debt. This target capital structure is the capital structure that maximizes the value of the firm, as illustrated in Exhibit 16.8.

Underlying the trade-off theory is the idea that when a firm uses a small amount of debt financing, it receives the interest tax shield and possibly some of the other benefits we discussed. Since leverage is low and the chances that the firm will get into financial difficulties are also low, the costs of debt are small relative to the benefits, and firm value increases. However, as more and more debt is added to the firm's capital structure, the marginal costs of debt increase and eventually reach the point where the cost associated with the next dollar that is borrowed equals the benefit. Beyond this point, the costs of adding additional debt exceed the benefits, and any additional debt reduces firm value. The trade-off theory of capital structure says that managers will increase debt to the point at which the costs and benefits of adding another dollar of debt are exactly equal because this is the capital structure that maximizes firm value.

The Pecking Order Theory

pecking order theory the theory that when financing projects, managers first use retained earnings, which they view as the least expensive form of capital, then debt, and finally externally raised equity, which they view as the most expensive

The trade-off theory makes intuitive sense, but there is another popular theory of how the capital structures of firms are determined. This is known as the **pecking order theory**. The pecking order theory recognizes that different types of capital have different costs and that this leads to a pecking order in the financing choices that managers make. Managers choose the least expensive capital first then move to increasingly costly capital when the lower-cost sources of capital are no longer available.

Under the pecking order theory, managers view internally generated funds, or cash on hand, as the cheapest source of capital.[12] Debt is more costly to obtain than internally generated

[12]Since internally generated funds are reinvested on behalf of the stockholders, the true cost of these funds equals the cost of equity. However, using internally generated funds enables the firm to avoid the issuance costs associated with borrowing or selling stock, which, in turn, can make internal funds most attractive.

funds, but is still relatively inexpensive. In contrast, raising money by selling stock can be very expensive. As we saw in Exhibit 15.6, the out-of-pocket costs of selling equity are much higher than the comparable costs for bonds. In addition, the filings required by government agencies, such as the SEC, are greater, and the stock market tends to react negatively to announcements that firms are selling stock. When firms announce that they will sell stock, their stock prices often decline because such sales can be interpreted as evidence that the firms are not profitable enough to fund their investments internally. Of course, a lower stock price reduces the value of everyone's shares and makes future stock issues even more costly, since more shares will have to be sold to raise the same dollar amount.

The pecking order theory says that firms use internally generated funds as long as they are available. Following that, they tend to borrow money to finance additional projects until they are no longer able to do so because of restrictions in loan agreements or until high interest rates make debt unattractive. Only then will managers choose to sell equity. Notice that the pecking order theory does not assume that managers have a target capital structure. Rather, it implies that the capital structure of a firm is, in some sense, a by-product of the firm's financing history.

The Empirical Evidence

At this point, you might be asking yourself what we actually know about how capital structures are determined in the real world. A great deal of research has been done in this area, and the evidence supports both of the theories we have just described. When researchers compare the capital structures in different industries, they find evidence that supports the trade-off theory. Industries with a great many tangible assets, such as the building construction, air transportation, and printing, publishing, and related industries, typically use relatively large amounts of debt. In contrast, industries with more intangible assets and numerous growth opportunities, such as the computer and drug industries, use relatively little debt. What accounts for this difference? At least in part, the difference exists because indirect bankruptcy costs and stockholder–lender agency costs tend to be lower in industries with more tangible assets. The assets in these industries have higher liquidation values, and it is more difficult for stockholders to engage in asset substitution. Exhibit 16.9 shows the variation in capital structures across a sample of industries.

EXHIBIT 16.9 Average Capital Structures for Selected Industries in 2016

This table shows average capital structures for different U.S. industries in 2016. The industries are arranged in order of declining debt-to-firm value ratios, where firm value is estimated as the market value of equity plus the book value of debt. Industries with a great many tangible assets, such as the building construction, air transportation, and printing, publishing, and related industries, tend to have larger debt-to-firm value ratios.

Industry Description	Number of Firms	Debt/Firm Value
Building construction	23	0.46
Gas, electric, and sanitary services	126	0.38
Communications (including telephone companies)	79	0.37
Financial services	500	0.35
Air transportation	19	0.34
Paper and allied product manufacturesrs	25	0.33
Printing, publishing, and related industries	22	0.30
Transportation equipment (including automobiles)	77	0.25
Food stores	12	0.24
Food manufacturers	61	0.19
Business service companies	366	0.14
Electronic and other electrical equipment (including computer) manufacturers	193	0.14
Furniture and fixture manufacturers	19	0.11
Chemicals and allied products (including drug companies)	460	0.11

Source: Estimated by authors using data from the Standard and Poor's Compustat database.

Some researchers argue that, on average, debt levels appear to be lower than the trade-off theory suggests they should be. Firms pay large amounts of taxes that could be reduced through the use of more debt financing, even though their current capital structures are such that they face little possibility of financial distress. For example, in 2016 the technology firms listed in the opener to this chapter each held cash and short-term securities that exceeded the face value of all of their interest-bearing debt. These firms pay out a great deal of money each year in taxes and yet do not use long-term debt to reduce their tax liability.

More general evidence also indicates that the more profitable a firm is, the less debt it tends to have. This is exactly opposite what the trade-off theory suggests we should see. Under the trade-off theory, more profitable firms pay more taxes, so they should use more debt to take advantage of the interest tax shield. Instead, this evidence is consistent with the pecking order theory. Highly profitable firms have plenty of cash on hand that can be used to finance their projects and this reduces their need for debt financing.

The pecking order theory is also supported by the fact that, in an average year, public firms actually repurchase more shares than they sell. Moreover, in the United States, internally generated funds represent the largest source of financing for new investments, and debt represents the largest source of external financing.

Both the trade-off theory and the pecking order theory offer some insights into how managers choose the capital structures for their firms. However, neither of them is able to explain all of the capital structure choices that we observe. The truth is that capital structure decisions are very complex, and it is difficult to characterize them with a single general theory. In the next section, we briefly discuss some of the practical issues that managers say they consider when they make capital structure decisions.

Before You Go On

1. What is the trade-off theory of capital structure?
2. What is the pecking order theory of capital structure?
3. What does the empirical evidence tell us about the two theories?

16.4 Practical Considerations in Choosing a Capital Structure

LEARNING OBJECTIVE

4. Discuss some of the practical considerations that managers are concerned with when they choose a firm's capital structure.

When managers talk about capital structure choices, their comments are sprinkled with terms such as *financial flexibility, risk,* and *earnings impact.* Managers don't think only in terms of a trade-off or a pecking order. Rather, they are concerned with how their financing decisions will influence the practical issues that they must deal with when managing a business.

For example, *financial flexibility* is an important consideration in many capital structure decisions. Managers must ensure that they retain sufficient financial resources in the firm to take advantage of unexpected opportunities and to overcome unforeseen problems. In theory, if a positive NPV investment becomes available, managers should be able to obtain financing for it. Unfortunately, financing might not be available at a reasonable price for all positive NPV projects at all times. For example, it might be difficult to convince investors that a project is as good as management thinks it is. As a result, investors may require too high a return, making the project's NPV negative and causing the firm to pass up a good opportunity. Similarly, if the firm does not have enough financial flexibility, an unforeseen problem might end up being more costly than it should be. To see how this might happen, suppose that a firm's major manufacturing facility is destroyed by a hurricane. Insurance would eventually cover much of the loss, but by the time the insurance settlement is received, the company might be out of business. In such a case, cash is needed immediately to help employees so that key skills are not lost and to relocate or start rebuilding as quickly as possible.

Managers are also concerned about the impact of financial leverage on the volatility of the firm's net income. Most businesses experience fluctuations in their operating profits over time, and we know that fixed-interest payments magnify fluctuations in operating profits, thereby causing even greater variation in net income. Managers do not like volatility in reported net income because it causes problems in their relationships with outside investors, who do not like unpredictable earnings. Furthermore, as we have seen, if a firm is too highly leveraged, it runs a greater risk of defaulting on its debt, which can lead to all sorts of bankruptcy and agency costs. Managers use the term *risk* to describe the possibility that normal fluctuations in operating profits will lead to financial distress. They try to manage their firms' capital structures in a way that limits the risk to a reasonable level—one that allows them to sleep at night.

A third factor that managers think about when they choose a capital structure is the impact of financial leverage on the size of the firm's earnings per share. The interest expense associated with debt financing reduces the reported *dollar value of net income.* However, depending on the market value of the firm's stock, using debt instead of equity to finance a project can increase the reported *dollar value of earnings per share.* Many managers are very concerned about the earnings per share that their firms report because they believe that it affects the stock price. Financial theory states that managers should not be so concerned about accounting earnings because cash flows are what really matter. Whether they are right or wrong, if managers believe that accounting earnings matter to investors, their capital structure decisions will reflect this belief.

Another factor that managers consider when making capital structure decisions is the *control implications* of their decisions. The choice between equity and debt financing affects the control of the firm. For example, suppose that a firm is controlled by the founding family, which owns 55 percent of the common stock, and that the firm must raise capital to fund a large project. The project has a zero NPV and the capital raised to finance it will result in a 20 percent increase in the value of the firm. On the one hand, using equity financing will drop the founding family's ownership (voting rights) below 50 percent if the family does not buy some of the new shares. In fact, they will end up with 45.8 percent of the stock [55/(100 + 20) = 0.458, or 45.8 percent]. On the other hand, their ownership will remain at 55 percent, and they will retain absolute control of the firm if the project is financed entirely with debt. In such a situation, the founding family is likely to prefer debt financing. Of course, although debt can help a controlling stockholder retain control of a firm, too much debt can cause that stockholder to lose control. This can happen if the firm uses so much debt that fluctuations in business conditions put the firm in financial distress. When this happens, the ability of the creditors to control what happens to the firm can overwhelm the ability of the controlling stockholder to do so.

These are just some examples of practical considerations that managers must deal with when choosing the appropriate capital structure for a firm. There is no set formula that they can follow in making financing decisions because many of these considerations are difficult to quantify and their relative importance is unique to each firm. Nevertheless, it is safe to say that the ultimate objective of a firm's stockholders—and of managers who have the stockholders' interests in mind—is to choose the capital structure that maximizes the value of the firm.

Before You Go On

1. Why is financial flexibility important in the choice of a capital structure?
2. How can capital structure decisions affect the risk associated with net income?
3. How can capital structure decisions affect the control of a firm?

Summary of Learning Objectives

1 Describe the two Modigliani and Miller propositions, the key assumptions underlying them, and their relevance to capital structure decisions. Use Proposition 2 to calculate the return on equity.

M&M Proposition 1 states that the value of a firm is unaffected by its capital structure if the following three conditions hold: (1) there are no taxes, (2) there are no information or transaction costs, and (3) capital structure decisions do not affect the real investment policies of the firm. This proposition tells us the three reasons that capital structure choices affect firm value.

M&M Proposition 2 states that the expected return on a firm's equity increases with the amount of debt in its capital structure. This proposition also shows that the expected return on equity can be separated into two parts—a part that reflects the risk of the underlying assets of the firm and a part that reflects the risk associated with the financial leverage used by the firm. This proposition helps managers understand the implications of financial leverage for the cost of the equity used to finance the firm's investments. Equation 16.3 can be used to calculate the cost of equity for common stock.

2 Discuss the benefits and costs of using debt financing and calculate the value of the income tax benefit associated with debt.

Using debt financing provides several benefits. A major benefit arises from the deductibility of interest payments. Since interest payments are tax deductible and dividend payments are not, distributing cash to investors through interest payments can increase the value of a firm. Debt is also less expensive to issue than equity. Finally, debt can benefit stockholders in certain situations by providing managers with incentives to maximize the cash flows produced by the firm and by reducing their ability to invest in negative NPV projects.

The costs of debt include bankruptcy and agency costs. Bankruptcy costs arise because financial leverage increases the probability that a firm will get into financial distress. Direct bankruptcy costs are the out-of-pocket costs that a firm incurs when it gets into financial distress, while indirect bankruptcy costs are associated with actions the people who deal with the firm take to protect their own interests when the firm is in financial distress. Agency costs are costs associated with actions taken by managers and stockholders who are acting in their own interests rather than in the best interests of the firm. When a firm uses financial leverage, managers have incentives to take actions that benefit themselves at the expense of stockholders, and stockholders have incentives to take actions that benefit themselves at the expense of lenders. To the extent that these actions reduce the value of lenders' claims, the expected losses will be reflected in the interest rates that lenders require.

Equation 16.4 can be used to calculate the value of the income tax benefit associated with debt.

3 Describe the trade-off and pecking order theories of capital structure choice and explain what the empirical evidence tells us about these theories.

The trade-off theory says that managers balance, or trade off, the benefits of debt against the costs of debt when choosing a firm's capital structure in an effort to maximize the value of the firm. The pecking order theory says that managers raise capital as they need it in the least expensive way available, starting with internally generated funds, then moving to debt, then to the sale of equity. In contrast to the trade-off theory, the pecking order theory does not imply that managers have a particular target capital structure. There is empirical evidence that supports both theories, suggesting that each helps explain the capital structure choices made by managers.

4 Discuss some of the practical considerations that managers are concerned with when they choose a firm's capital structure.

Practical considerations that concern managers when they choose a firm's capital structure include the impact of the capital structure on financial flexibility, risk, net income, and the control of the firm. Financial flexibility involves having the necessary financial resources to take advantage of unforeseen opportunities and to overcome unforeseen problems. Risk refers to the possibility that normal fluctuations in operating profits will lead to financial distress. Managers are also concerned with the impact of financial leverage on their reported net income, especially on a per-share basis. Finally, the impact of capital structure decisions on who controls the firm is also a concern.

Summary of Key Equations

Equation	Description	Formula
16.1	Value of the firm as the sum of the debt and equity values	$V_{Firm} = V_{Assets} = V_{Debt} + V_{Equity}$
16.2	Formula for the weighted average cost of capital (WACC) for a firm with only debt and common stock and no taxes	$WACC = x_{Debt}k_{Debt} + x_{cs}k_{cs}$
16.3	Cost of common stock in terms of financial leverage, the required return on assets, and the required return on debt	$k_{cs} = k_{Assets} + \left(\frac{V_{Debt}}{V_{cs}}\right)(k_{Assets} - k_{Debt})$

continued

continued

Equation	Description	Formula
16.4	Value of the tax savings from debt (upper bound)	$V_{\text{Tax-savings debt}} = D \times t$
16.5	Cost of common stock with taxes	$k_{cs} = k_{\text{Assets}} + \left(\frac{V_{\text{Debt}}}{V_{cs}}\right)(k_{\text{Assets}} - k_{\text{Debt}})(1 - t)$

Self-Study Problems

16.1 If any of the three assumptions in Modigliani and Miller Proposition 1 are relaxed, which has the most predictably quantifiable impact on the value of the firm?

16.2 If we assume that the cash flows for a firm with financial leverage are equal to the cash flows for the same firm without financial leverage, what can we say about the value of this firm if its cost of capital also does not vary with the degree of leverage utilized?

16.3 Are taxes necessary for the cost of debt financing to be less than the cost of equity financing?

16.4 You are offered jobs with identical responsibilities by two different firms in the same industry. One has no debt in its capital structure, and the other has 99 percent debt in its capital structure. Will you require a higher level of compensation from one firm than from the other? If so, which firm will have to pay you more?

16.5 You are valuing two otherwise identical firms in the same industry. One firm has a corporate jet for every executive at the vice president level and above, while the other does not have a single corporate jet. More than likely, which firm has the greater stockholder–manager agency costs?

Solutions to Self-Study Problems

16.1 The assumption with the most measurable impact is that involving taxes. We can calculate the present value of the tax shield generated by the interest costs of borrowing. The impacts of the other two assumptions, though real, are more difficult to predict.

16.2 If the cash flows produced by the firm and the cost of capital for the firm are the same, regardless of the amount of leverage utilized, we can say that the value of the firm is also the same, regardless of the amount of financial leverage.

16.3 The deduction for interest expense does make debt borrowing more attractive than it would otherwise be. However, even without the interest deduction benefit, the cost of debt is less than the cost of equity because equity is a riskier investment than debt. This means that the pretax cost to the firm for debt is still lower than the cost of equity.

16.4 The firm with the large amount of debt financing (the firm with 99 percent debt) has a higher probability of becoming financially distressed. Therefore, you should require greater compensation from that firm because your income is less certain and working at that firm poses a greater risk to your career.

16.5 While corporate jets can make economic sense because they enable managers to use their time more efficiently, one jet per vice president is very unlikely to be cost-effective. The multijet firm most likely has higher stockholder–manager agency costs than the no-jet firm. It is probably spending too much on jets. The cash that is being spent on excess jets could be invested in positive NPV projects or returned to the firm's stockholders.

WileyPLUS

Discussion Questions

16.1 List and briefly describe the three key assumptions in Modigliani and Miller's Proposition 1 that are required for total firm value to be independent of capital structure.

16.2 Evaluate the statement that the weighted average cost of capital (WACC) for a firm (assuming that all three assumptions of Modigliani and Miller's propositions hold) is always less than or equal to the cost of equity for the firm.

16.3 If the value of the firm remains constant as a function of its capital structure and the three Modigliani and Miller assumptions apply, why might the overall cost of capital change or not change as capital structure changes?

16.4 Consider the WACC for a firm that pays taxes. Explain what the best course of action would be to minimize the firm's WACC and thereby maximize its value. Use the WACC formula for your explanation.

16.5 The Modigliani and Miller propositions, when the no-tax assumption is relaxed, suggest that the firm should finance itself with as much debt as possible. Taking this suggestion to the extreme, is it even possible to finance a firm with 100 percent debt and no equity? Why or why not?

16.6 Crossler Automobiles sells autos in a market where the standard auto comes with a 10-year/100,000-mile warranty on all parts and labor. Describe how an increased probability of bankruptcy could affect sales of autos by Crossler.

16.7 Agency problems occur because the nonowner managers and stockholders of a firm have different interests. Propose a capital structure change that might help better align these different interests.

16.8 If a firm increases its debt to a very high level, then the positive effect of debt in aligning the interests of management with those of stockholders tends to become negative. Explain why this occurs.

16.9 Using the Modigliani and Miller framework, but excluding the assumptions that there are no taxes and no information or transaction costs, describe the value of the firm as a function of the proportion of debt in its capital structure.

16.10 When we observe the capital structure of many firms, we find that they tend to utilize lower levels of debt than that predicted by the trade-off theory. Offer an explanation for this.

Questions and Problems

Excel *Excel templates and resources available in* **WileyPLUS**

Basic

16.1 **M&M Proposition 1:** The Modigliani and Miller theory suggests that the value of the firm's assets is equal to the value of the claims on those assets and is not dependent on how the asset claims are divided. The common analogy to the theorem is that the total amount of pie available to be eaten (the firm) does not depend on the size of each slice of pie. If we continue with that analogy, then what if we cut up the pie with a very dull knife such that the total amount of pie available to be eaten is less after it is cut than before it was cut. Which of the three Modigliani and Miller assumptions, if relaxed, is analogous to the dull knife? *Hint:* Think about the process by which investors could undo the effects of a firm's capital structure decisions.

16.2 **M&M Proposition 1:** Describe what exactly is meant when someone is distinguishing between the value of the firm and the value of the equity of the firm.

16.3 **M&M Proposition 1:** Under Modigliani and Miller's Proposition 1, where all three of the assumptions remain in effect, explain how the value of the firm changes due to changes in the proportion of debt and equity utilized by the firm.

16.4 **M&M Proposition 1:** Cerberus Security Company produces a cash flow of $200 per year and is expected to continue doing so in the infinite future. The cost of equity capital for Cerberus is 20 percent, and the firm is financed entirely with equity. Management would like to repurchase $100 in shares by borrowing $100 at a 10 percent annual rate (assume that the debt will also be outstanding into the infinite future). Using Modigliani and Miller's Proposition 1, what is the value of the firm today, and what will be the value of the claims on the firm's assets after the stock repurchase? What will be the rate of return on common stock required by investors after the stock repurchase?

16.5 **M&M Proposition 1:** A firm that is financed completely with equity currently has a cost of capital equal to 15 percent. Assume that the assumptions in Modigliani and Miller's Proposition 1 hold and that the firm's management plans to change its capital structure to 50 percent debt and 50 percent equity. What will be the cost of equity after the change if the cost of debt is 10 percent?

16.6 **M&M Proposition 1:** Swan Specialty Cycles is currently financed with 50 percent debt and 50 percent equity. The firm pays $125 each year to its debt investors (at a 10 percent cost of debt), and the debt has no maturity date. What will be the value of the equity if the firm repurchases all of its debt and raises the funds to do this by issuing equity? Assume that all of the assumptions in Modigliani and Miller's Proposition 1 hold.

16.7 **M&M Proposition 1:** The weighted average cost of capital for a firm, assuming all three Modigliani and Miller assumptions hold, is 10 percent. What is the current cost of equity capital for the firm if the cost of debt for the firm is 8 percent, and the firm is 80 percent financed with debt?

16.8 **Interest tax shield benefit:** Legitron Corporation has $350 million of debt outstanding at an interest rate of 9 percent. What is the dollar value of the tax shield on that debt, just for this year, if Legitron is subject to a 35 percent marginal tax rate?

16.9 **Interest tax shield benefit:** FAJ, Inc., has $500 million of debt outstanding at an interest rate of 9 percent. What is the present value of the tax shield on that debt if it has no maturity and if FAJ is subject to a 30 percent marginal tax rate?

16.10 **Interest tax shield benefit:** Springer Corp. has $250 million of debt outstanding at an interest rate of 11 percent. What is the present value of the interest tax shield if the debt has no maturity and if Springer is subject to a 40 percent marginal tax rate?

16.11 **Interest tax shield benefit:** Structural Corp. currently has a cost of equity capital equal to 15 percent. Assume that the Modigliani and Miller Proposition 1 assumptions hold, with the exception of the assumption that there are no taxes, and that the firm's capital structure consists of 50 percent debt and 50 percent equity. What is the weighted average cost of capital for the firm if the cost of debt is 10 percent and the firm is subject to a 40 percent marginal tax rate?

16.12 **Practical considerations in capital structure choice:** List and describe three practical considerations that concern managers when they make capital structure decisions.

Intermediate

16.13 M&M Proposition 1: Keyboard Chiropractic Clinic produces $300,000 of cash flow each year. The firm has no debt outstanding, and its cost of equity capital is 25 percent. The firm's management would like to repurchase $600,000 of its equity by borrowing $600,000 at a rate of 8 percent per year. If we assume that the debt will be perpetual, find the cost of equity capital for Keyboard after it changes its capital structure. Assume that the Modigliani and Miller Proposition 1 assumptions hold.

16.14 M&M Proposition 1: Marx and Spender Corp. currently has a WACC of 21 percent. If the cost of debt capital for the firm is 12 percent and the firm is currently financed with 25 percent debt, then what is the current cost of equity capital for the firm? Assume that the assumptions in Modigliani and Miller's Proposition 1 hold.

16.15 M&M Proposition 1: What is the effect on Modigliani and Miller's Proposition 1 of relaxing the assumption that there are no information or transaction costs?

16.16 M&M Proposition 1: The weighted average cost of capital for a firm (assuming all three Modigliani and Miller Proposition 1 assumptions apply) is 15 percent. What is the current cost of equity capital for the firm if its cost of debt is 10 percent and the proportion of debt to total firm value for the firm is 0.5?

16.17 M&M Proposition 2: Mikos Processed Foods is currently valued at $500 million. Mikos will repurchase $100 million of its equity by issuing perpetual debt at an annual interest rate of 10 percent. Mikos is subject to a 30 percent marginal tax rate. If the Modigliani and Miller assumptions apply, except the assumption that there are no taxes, what will the value of Mikos be after the recapitalization?

16.18 M&M Proposition 2: Backwards Resources Company has a WACC of 12.6 percent, and it is subject to a 40 percent marginal tax rate. Backwards has $250 million of debt outstanding at an interest rate of 9 percent and $750 million of equity (at market value) outstanding. What is the expected return on the equity with this capital structure?

16.19 The costs of debt: Briefly discuss costs of financial distress to a firm that may arise when employees believe it is highly likely that the firm will declare bankruptcy.

16.20 The costs of debt: Santa's Shoes is a retailer that has just begun having financial difficulty. Santa's suppliers are aware of the increased possibility of bankruptcy. What might Santa's suppliers do based on this information?

16.21 Stockholder–manager agency costs: Deficit Corp. management has determined that the firm will be $50 million short of being able to pay its debt obligations at the end of this year. Management has identified a positive NPV project that will require a great deal of effort on its part. However, this project is expected to generate only $40 million at the end of the year. Assume that all the members of Deficit's management team will lose their jobs if the firm goes into bankruptcy at the end of the year. How likely is management to take the positive NPV project? If management declines the project, what kind of cost will Deficit's stockholders incur?

16.22 Two theories of capital structure: Use the information in the following table to make a suggestion concerning the proportion of debt that the firm should utilize in its capital structure.

Benefit or (Cost)	No Debt	25% Debt	50% Debt	75% Debt
Tax shield	$ 0	$10	$20	$30
Agency cost	–$10	–$ 5	–$ 5	–$20
Financial distress cost	–$ 1	–$ 3	–$10	–$10

16.23 Two theories of capital structure: Problem 16.22 introduces taxes and information and transaction costs to the simplified Modigliani and Miller model. If the marginal tax rate for the firm were to suddenly increase by a material amount, would the capital structure that maximizes the firm include less or more debt?

16.24 Two theories of capital structure: Describe how managers who subscribe to the pecking order theory of financing would rank the alternative sources of financing. Evaluate that ranking in terms of the costs of each source relative to the costs of other sources.

16.25 Two theories of capital structure: The pecking order theory suggests that managers prefer to first use internally generated equity to finance new projects. Does this preference mean that these funds represent an even cheaper source of funds than debt? Justify your answer.

16.26 The costs of debt: Discuss how the legal costs of financial distress may increase with the probability that a firm will formally declare bankruptcy, even if the firm has not reached that point yet.

Advanced

16.27 Operating a firm without debt is generally considered to be a conservative practice. Discuss how such a conservative approach to a firm's capital structure is good or bad for the value of the firm in the absence of information or transaction costs and any effect of debt on the real investment policy of the firm.

16.28 Finite Corp. has $250 million of debt outstanding at an interest rate of 11 percent. What is the present value of the debt tax shield if the debt will mature in five years (and no new debt will replace the old debt), assuming that Finite is subject to a 40 percent marginal tax rate?

16.29 The Boring Corporation is currently valued at $900 million, but management wants to completely pay off its perpetual debt of $300 million. Boring is subject to a 30 percent marginal tax rate. If Boring pays off its debt, what will the total value of its equity be?

16.30 If we drop the assumption that there are no information or transaction costs, in addition to dropping the no-tax assumption, then will the Modigliani and Miller model still suggest that the firm should take on a greater proportion of debt in its capital structure? Explain.

16.31 PolyAna Corporation has such high cash flow that the company's managers take Fridays off for a weekly luncheon in Cancun using the corporate jet. Describe how altering the capital structure of the firm might make the management of this firm stay in the office on Fridays in order to work on new positive NPV projects.

16.32 **M&M Proposition 2 with taxes:** Forwards Resources Company is currently an all-equity firm with a WACC of 14 percent and a 40 percent marginal tax rate. Forwards wants to move to a capital structure with $250 million of debt outstanding at an interest rate of 9 percent and a market value of equity equal to $750 million outstanding. Using M&M Proposition 2 with taxes, Equation 16.5, what is the expected return on equity at the new capital structure?

16.33 **M&M Proposition 2 with taxes:** You own all of the equity in a debt-free app development business that generates cash flows of $400,000 each year in perpetuity. The cost of assets, k_{Assets}, is 10 percent and the tax rate is 25 percent. What is the value of your all-equity firm? If you decide to replace $1 million of equity by borrowing $1 million at an interest rate of 6 percent, how much would the value of the firm increase? What would the k_{cs} and WACC for your business be before and after the proposed financial restructuring? Use M&M Proposition 2 with taxes, Equation 16.5, to determine the expected return on the equity for input to the WACC calculation. Assume that all cash flows are perpetuities and that the second and third M&M conditions hold.

CFA Problems

16.34 Consider two companies that operate in the same line of business and have the same degree of operating leverage: the Basic Company and the Grundlegend Company. The Basic Company has no debt in its capital structure, but the Grundlegend Company has a capital structure that consists of 50 percent debt. Which of the following statements is true?

a. The Grundlegend Company has a degree of total leverage that exceeds that of the Basic Company by 50 percent.

b. The Grundlegend Company has the same sensitivity of net earnings to changes in earnings before interest and taxes as the Basic Company.

c. The Grundlegend Company has the same sensitivity of earnings before interest and taxes to changes in sales as the Basic Company.

d. The Grundlegend Company has the same sensitivity of net earnings to changes in sales as the Basic Company.

16.35 According to the pecking order theory:

a. New debt is preferable to new equity.

b. New equity is preferable to internally generated funds.

c. New debt is preferable to internally generated funds.

d. New equity is always preferable to other sources of capital.

16.36 According to the trade-off theory:

a. The amount of debt a company has is irrelevant.

b. Debt should be used only as a last resort.

c. Debt will not be used if a company's tax rate is high.

d. Companies have an optimal level of debt.

Sample Test Problems

16.1 Central Grocers Inc. produces annual cash flows of $175,000, which are expected to continue indefinitely. The company is financed entirely with equity capital at an annual cost of 12 percent. Management is considering borrowing $400,000 at an annual interest rate of 6 percent to repurchase $400,000 of the company's outstanding stock. (You can assume that the debt will be outstanding into the indefinite future.) What is the total value of Central Grocers' stock before the stock repurchase? Under the assumptions in Modigliani and Miller's Proposition 1, what would be the value of the total claims on the company's assets after the stock repurchase? What will be the rate of return on common stock required by investors after the repurchase?

16.2 The required rate of return on the assets of a firm is 12 percent. The firm has a debt-to-common-stock ratio of 40 percent and a cost of debt of 6 percent. If the firm has no preferred stock and the three conditions specified by M&M hold, what is the expected rate of return on the firm's common stock?

16.3 Your boss at Box and Freight Company asks you how much additional debt the company would have to add through a capital restructuring in order to create $9 million in present value from the resulting interest tax shields. What would you tell your boss if the debt will have no maturity and if Box and Freight is subject to a 32 percent marginal tax rate?

16.4 Southwest Airlines has substantial cash reserves and an investment-grade bond rating. How would the trade-off theory predict that managers of Southwest would raise capital and choose the company's capital structure if they were planning an expansion into Mexico? What would the pecking order theory suggest?

16.5 What control implications do a firm's capital structure decisions have?

Appendix: Leasing

LEARNING OBJECTIVE

A1. Describe what a lease is and discuss the motivations for leasing, what types of assets are more or less likely to be leased, and conflicts that arise in lease agreements and how the costs of these conflicts are reduced by lessors. Evaluate the choice between leasing and purchasing an asset.

Leasing is an alternative way of financing the acquisition of an asset. When the managers of a firm decide to acquire an asset, they can often choose between (1) purchasing the asset with a combination of debt and equity or (2) leasing it. A **lease** (or **rental agreement**) is a financial arrangement in which the user of an asset (the **lessee**) pays the owner of that asset (the **lessor**) to use it for a period of time.[1]

lease (rental agreement) a financial arrangement in which the user of an asset pays the owner of the asset to use it for a period of time

lessee the user of a leased asset

lessor the owner of a leased asset

A lease divides the right to use an asset into two parts: (1) the right to use it during the term of the lease and (2) the right to use it after the lease ends—the *salvage rights*. The **lessee** pays for the right to use the asset during the term of the lease while the **lessor**, who owns the asset, receives the lease payments in return for giving up the right to use the asset during the term of the lease. As an example, consider a rental agreement through which an oil company leases an oil drilling rig for six months. This lease gives the oil company (the lessee) the right to use the rig for six months in return for payments to the owner of the rig (the lessor). The owner retains all rights to use the rig after the agreement expires in six months.

Virtually all firms lease some of their assets. Commonly leased assets include office space, furniture, computers, copy machines, cars, trucks, rail cars, airplanes, ships, and oil drilling rigs. The length of a lease can be as short as a few minutes (for example, when someone leases the use of a supercomputer to run a simulation) or as long as many years (as is common with leases involving office space).

Since leasing is an alternative means of financing the acquisition of an asset, whether leasing is more or less attractive than purchasing the asset depends on the same factors that affect the choice of how much debt and equity should be used to purchase an asset. In other words, the same three M&M conditions that affect the choice between debt and equity also affect the choice between leasing and purchasing an asset. If this choice affects firm value, it must be because of (1) taxes, (2) information or transaction costs, or (3) because it affects the real investment policy of the firm.

Building Intuition

Leasing is an Alternative Means of Financing the Acquisition of an Asset

When managers in a firm decide to acquire an asset, they often have a choice between purchasing the asset using debt and equity or leasing the asset. The firm gets the use of the asset in either case, but the ownership rights are different.

In this Appendix we first describe the two general types of lease agreements that businesses enter into. We then use the M&M conditions to provide a framework for understanding why leasing can be more attractive than purchasing an asset and what types of assets are more likely to be leased versus owned. We next examine the types of conflicts that arise between lessees and lessors and the different ways in which lessors limit the cost of these conflicts. Finally, we discuss how managers choose between purchasing and leasing an asset.

Two Types of Leases

The value of an asset to a lessor is equal to the sum of the present value of the lease payments that the lessor will receive plus the salvage value of the asset at the end of the lease. The present value of the lease payments, as a percentage of the total value of an asset, varies with the length of a lease agreement. For example, consider a rental company that both rents cars by the day and leases them for up to seven years. The value of a one-day rental fee will be very small compared to the total value of the car. If the daily rental fee for a $20,000 car is $50, this

[1] A rental agreement is a lease that involves tangible property.

fee represents only 0.25 percent ($50/$20,000 = 0.0025, or 0.25 percent) of the total value. On the other hand, the lease payments on a seven-year lease might have a present value that equals the entire $20,000 value of the car. In such a lease, the lessee is effectively paying as much as it would cost to buy the car and, since the salvage value is likely to be quite small after seven years, the lease payments represent most of the value that the lessor will receive from the car. Note that the seven-year lease is pretty close to an outright sale in which the lessor is selling the car to the lessee and providing 100 percent debt financing.

The fact that a lease can look like a sale is of concern to accountants and the IRS because accounting rules and tax laws treat leases and asset sales differently. Generally accepted accounting principles (GAAP) and the IRS distinguish between leases that are truly rentals (known as **operating leases**) and leases that have the key elements of an outright sale (known as **capital leases**). Specifically, a lease is considered to be a capital lease if any of the following four conditions hold: (1) the lease transfers ownership of the asset to the lessee at the end of the lease term; (2) the lease contains a bargain purchase option;[2] (3) the lease cannot be canceled for a period that is greater than 75 percent of the estimated economic life of the asset; or (4) the present value of the minimum lease payments is greater than 90 percent of the fair market value of the asset. If none of these conditions holds, then a lease is classified as an operating lease.

operating lease a lease which does not have the characteristics of a sale

capital lease a lease that has the characteristics of a sale

The accounting and tax treatments of assets under capital leases are like those for assets that are purchased by the user. Specifically, with a capital lease, the asset is recorded on the balance sheet of the lessee, along with an offsetting liability that equals the present value of the lease payments. The lessee must depreciate the asset and can only deduct, when calculating its income taxes, the portion of the lease payments that the lessee would have paid as interest on a loan used to purchase the asset. In contrast, with an operating lease, the asset is recorded on the books of the lessor and is depreciated by the lessor. With an operating lease, the lessee is able to deduct the entire lease payments when calculating income taxes.

Weblink

You can read more about the accounting treatment of operating and capital leases at http://www.investopedia.com/study-guide/cfa-exam/level-1/liabilities/cfa16.asp.

While this represents the current state of lease accounting, we note that, depending on the type of organization and when it reports its financial statements, new lease accounting rules will be implemented between 2018 and 2020.

Motivations for Leasing

The primary motivation for leasing an asset is that doing so is a less-expensive way of obtaining the use of the asset than purchasing it. We will use the M&M conditions to frame our discussion of how leasing can create value for stockholders.

Taxes

Let's first consider how relaxing the M&M assumption that there are no taxes affects the choice between purchasing and leasing an asset. Suppose that you need a new delivery truck for your pizza restaurant business and that you can either (1) buy the truck outright using a loan or (2) lease the truck from a truck leasing company. Assume that the truck will cost $30,000 and will be depreciated for tax purposes using straight-line depreciation over three years to a salvage value of $0. Also assume that your business pays a marginal tax rate of 10 percent on its taxable income and that the truck leasing company, which is larger and more profitable, pays a marginal tax rate of 35 percent on its taxable income. Finally, assume that both you and the truck leasing company can finance the entire $30,000 purchase price with a 5 percent three-year "balloon" loan from a bank. The entire face value of a balloon loan is repaid at the end of the life of the loan, which in this case is the end of the three-year life of the truck.

If you purchased the truck, you would receive a deduction of $10,000 per year for depreciation and this would save you $10,000 × 0.10 = $1,000 per year in taxes. You would also save $150 each year in taxes because of the interest deduction ($30,000 × 0.05 × 0.10 = $150), for a total tax saving of $1,150. By comparison, if the truck leasing company purchased the truck, it would save $3,500 on its taxes each year because of the depreciation tax shield ($10,000 × 0.35 = $3,500) and $525 because of interest the interest deduction ($30,000 × 0.05 × 0.35 = $525). The truck leasing company's total tax savings would be $3,500 + $525 = $4,025.

[2]A bargain purchase option is an option to buy the asset at a price that is so low, relative to the expected fair market value of the property, that exercise of the option is reasonably assured.

The difference between your total tax savings and that of the truck leasing company, \$4,025 − \$1,150 = \$2,875, is a potential tax benefit that can be realized if you let the truck leasing company purchase the truck and lease it to you. Furthermore, if the monthly lease payments are set so that you and the truck leasing company split this \$2,875 tax benefit, the leasing arrangement is a win-win situation. You get the use of the truck for less than it would cost you to buy it, and the truck leasing company profits from its share of the tax savings.

Reducing the combined tax obligations of two companies can provide an important motivation for leasing. The delivery truck example illustrates how a lease contract can increase stockholder value when a company that uses an asset has a lower marginal tax rate than another company. These types of tax differences, which exist between companies within countries as well as between companies in different countries, contribute to the wide range of leasing opportunities that exist today.

Information and Transaction Costs

Tax savings represent only one potential source of savings from lease contracts. A lease can also be used to reduce information and transaction costs. Furthermore, differences across types of assets in the extent to which information and transaction costs can be reduced provide us with insights as to what types of assets are more or less likely to be leased.

Information and Transaction Cost Motivations for Leasing To see how leasing can reduce information and transaction costs, consider the choice between buying and leasing a car. The cost of acquiring a car and of selling it after you have finished using it can be quite high. When individuals purchase a car, they typically spend a considerable amount of time learning about the alternative makes and models that are being offered for sale, visiting dealerships, taking test drives, negotiating the price, and so on. Similarly, selling a car can require spending time searching for a buyer and negotiating and completing the sale. While it can make sense to incur such information and transaction costs if you are going to keep a car for several years, it makes no sense to do this if you only plan to use the car for a few days. This is the main reason that there is such a large car rental industry. Car rental companies incur the information and transaction costs associated buying and selling a car and spread them across a large number of short-term renters, thereby reducing the cost of obtaining the use of a car for a few days. The same motivation explains the short-term rental agreements for assets like power tools, moving trucks, and aircraft.

Of course, individuals and businesses also often lease cars for several years at a time. While the information and transaction costs associated with purchasing and selling a car are spread out (amortized) over a longer period and are therefore smaller on a per-day basis, there are circumstances under which it can still make sense to enter into a leasing contract. For example, a company can find it less costly to lease the cars in its fleet because a leasing company is able to manage the fleet, including activities such as providing regular maintenance, more efficiently. Furthermore, because the leasing company buys and sells a lot of cars in the ordinary course of its business, it is likely to be able to acquire cars at a lower price and to realize a higher value from used car sales. Cost reductions such as these contribute to the prevalence of long-term lease agreements on assets like copiers, computers, and office space, as well as vehicles.

Finally, lease agreements in business are often written with clauses that allow the lessee to terminate the agreement before the end of the lease term by providing 60 or 90 days' notice to the lessor. Early termination provisions like these provide the lessee with operational flexibility. For example, in the airline industry early termination provisions enable managers to rapidly, and at relatively low cost, adjust fleet sizes during economic downturns by reducing the number of leased aircraft. This flexibility is valuable to airlines because the opportunity cost of the capital tied up in an idle airplane is high. For example, if the cost of capital for an airline is 10 percent, the opportunity cost of capital that is tied up in a \$150 million aircraft is \$15 million per year.

Why Certain Types of Assets Are Leased Information and transaction costs can also help to explain what types of assets are leased rather than owned by companies. In order to see why this is true, you must be familiar with the concepts of a firm-specific asset and a general-use asset. A **firm-specific asset** is an asset that is substantially more valuable to a particular

firm-specific asset an asset that is substantially more valuable to a particular firm than to any other firm

firm than to any other firm. For example, the big signs with company names that you often see on the top of office buildings are firm-specific assets. They are valuable to the company whose name is on them, but virtually worthless to any other firm. Similarly, a company that has a proprietary manufacturing process might use custom-made equipment in that process that would be of little value to any other company. In contrast to firm-specific assets, **general-use assets** are of similar value to potential users, such as office buildings or office equipment.

general-use asset an asset that is of similar value to potential users

Firm-specific assets are leased less frequently than general-use assets because it is easier for one party to engage in opportunistic behavior that harms the other party when a firm-specific asset is leased. To see why this is the case, suppose that managers at Pfizer Inc., the pharmaceutical firm, have decided to replace an old manufacturing plant. Instead of owning the new plant, they are in discussions with potential investors who would build the plant to Pfizer's specifications using their own money and then lease it to Pfizer.

Assume that the plant will cost \$50 million and will have a useful life of 20 years. Also assume that while it will be worth \$50 million to Pfizer, the highest price anyone else would pay for the plant is \$40 million. In other words, the plant is a firm-specific asset in which \$10 million of the value can only be realized by Pfizer. Finally, assume that the firm-specific and general-use values of the plant both decline in a straight line over its 20-year life as illustrated in the following table:

	Value		
Value component	**Year 0**	**Year 10**	**Year 20**
Pfizer-specific	\$10 mil	\$ 5 mil	\$ 0 mil
General	\$40 mil	\$20 mil	\$ 0 mil

Pfizer managers do not want to include the plant on their company's balance sheet, so they decide to propose a leasing arrangement that avoids any possibility of the transaction being classified as a capital lease. In particular, they decide to propose paying the investors for making the investment using two consecutive 10-year operating leases. In order to avoid capital lease treatment (which can negate some of the benefits from leasing), both Pfizer management and the investors know that the first agreement cannot specify any of the conditions in the second lease. In other words, all of the terms of the second lease will be negotiated in 10 years. The Pfizer managers propose to the investors that the value of the lease payments over the first 10-year lease should be \$25 million since the lease will cover half of the life of the \$50 million facility.

This proposal concerns the investors. They worry that at the end of the first lease, Pfizer managers won't agree to lease payments in the second lease that have a value equal to the remaining \$25 million that they invested. Since Pfizer managers know that the plant will be worth only \$20 million to another user in Year 10, the investors are afraid that if they accept \$25 million in the first lease that Pfizer managers will offer them only \$20 million for the second lease and that they will end up losing \$5 million (\$50 million invested − \$25 million from first lease − \$20 million from second lease = \$5 million). This is what economists call a hold-up problem.

To avoid being held up like this, the investors respond to Pfizer management by proposing that the payments for the first lease be set so that their total present value equals \$30 million. This way, regardless of whether Pfizer leases the plant in the last 10 years the investors will recover their investment. Unfortunately, while protecting the investors from the hold-up problem, this proposal subjects Pfizer to a hold-up problem. Specifically, in Year 10 when it is time to renew the lease, the investors will know that use of the plant in the last 10 years of its life will be worth \$25 million to Pfizer and that Pfizer would have to pay \$25 million to obtain a comparable plant. Knowing this, the investors are likely to demand more than \$20 million in the second lease. In fact, they would be able to charge Pfizer up to \$25 million. If they did this, use of the plant for 20 years would end up costing Pfizer \$55 million (\$30 million + \$25 million = \$55 million). Pfizer would be better off building the plant itself for \$50 million.

There is no easy solution to the hold-up problem in the Pfizer example. Both parties will be concerned about being held up because they cannot agree, in writing, on the terms for the second lease without the overall transaction being classified as a capital lease. The potential for this sort of problem arises whenever someone considers leasing a firm-specific asset. As a result, because the firm-specific component in the value of firm-specific assets creates such a costly bargaining environment, firm-specific assets are rarely leased. Because general-use assets tend to have a similar value to a number of users, they are not as subject to hold-up problems and therefore are more likely to be leased. Examples of commonly leased assets include transportation equipment, such as cars, trucks, rail cars, and planes, office furniture and equipment, such as copiers and computers, buildings with general office space, and other assets with a relatively large number of similar users, such as construction and oil drilling equipment.

Real Investment Policy

Even in the absence of taxes and information and transaction cost considerations, having the ability to structure lease agreements can affect stockholder value by changing the real investment opportunities that are available to a firm. For example, managers at manufacturing firms can sometimes use lease contracts to maximize the value of a product line by charging a higher price to customers who are willing to pay more and yet still making their products accessible to customers who are not willing to pay as much.

To see how this might be done, consider a manufacturing company that has developed a new product for which there is limited direct competition in the market. The manufacturer can choose whether to sell the product or just make it available through lease contracts.[3] Leasing provides more flexibility in setting prices than selling the product. For example, suppose a manufacturing firm has two types of customers. One type of customer is not willing to pay much more than the marginal cost to the manufacturing firm of producing its product because these customers won't be using it very intensively. The other type of customer is willing to pay considerably more than the marginal cost because these customers will get a lot of use out of the asset. In a situation like this, the company can set a lease price that provides the company a modest return on producing an additional unit of the product but that limits its use. The high-volume users who are willing to pay more can be charged higher prices based on their usage levels. Products such as office copiers, telephones, and TV cable boxes have all been made available to consumers with such leasing schemes at one time or another.

It is worth noting that a firm can also achieve similar results by using a combination of sales and leasing. This is done by setting a high sales price and a lower lease price for modest useage. The high-volume users will pay a high price to purchase the product, and low-volume users will lease.

Regardless of which strategy is used, using leases to charge different prices to different customers affects the mix of real assets within a firm. A firm that leases the products it manufactures will have different assets than a firm that only sells its products. The former will be in both the manufacturing and leasing businesses while the latter will be only in manufacturing.

Conflicts between Lessees and Lessors

Separating the right to use an asset during the term of a lease from the right to use the asset afterward creates two natural conflicts of interest between lessees and lessors. These conflicts concern how intensely the asset is used and how well it is maintained during the term of the lease. The intensity of use and maintenance conflicts lead to what we refer to as the *asset abuse problem* in leasing. The asset abuse problem can increase the cost of leasing for the lessor when it is not controlled.

Intensity of Use Conflict This conflict arises because the lessee can have an incentive to use a leased asset more intensely than the lessor would prefer. As long as using the asset more intensely does not significantly affect the lessee's ability to use it during the lease term, the lessee does not have an incentive to be concerned about how intensely the asset is used. To the extent that more intense use reduces the value of the asset, this reduction is borne by the lessor. For example, if you rent a car for a week you are unlikely to be concerned about driving it too many miles. On the other hand, the company that leases it to you is likely to be

[3]In practice, the leasing alternative would be accomplished by setting up a leasing subsidiary that is owned by the manufacturer.

concerned. If rental car customers average 1,000 miles a week instead of 500 miles a week, the value of a rental fleet will decline more rapidly.

Maintenance Conflict To the extent that cutting back on maintenance expenditures does not significantly affect a lessee's ability to use a leased asset, the lessee has an incentive to spend less on maintenance than the lessor would like. Spending less on maintenance, or avoiding it altogether, can save the lessee money and time, but it can also reduce the asset's salvage value and increase the out-of-pocket maintenance costs for the lessor.

> **Building Intuition**
>
> **Splitting the Rights to an Asset Between the Lessee and Lessor Can Create Costly Conflicts**
>
> Separating the right to use an asset during the term of a lease from the right to use the asset afterward creates conflicts concerning how intensely the asset is used and how well it is maintained during the term of the lease. These conflicts can increase the cost of leasing.

The intensity of use and maintenance conflicts are related. The quantity of services that an asset will provide over its life is generally related to how well it is maintained. Cutting back on maintenance can magnify the negative effects of using an asset more intensely.

Lessors know all about the intensity of use and maintenance conflicts and do a number of different things to protect themselves. It is important to recognize that it only makes sense to lease an asset if these actions are able to reduce the cost of the asset abuse problem so that it is smaller than the benefits of leasing. The things that lessors do to limit the cost of the asset abuse problem include:

1. **Invest in assets that are less subject to abuse:** For example, hotel operators invest in room furniture that is durable and less likely to show abuse. They know that people tend to take better care of their own furniture than furniture in hotels, and so they tend to avoid purchasing furniture that shows wear and tear or breaks easily. This is why, even in some of the best hotels, the furniture is made of veneer-covered particle board.

2. **Price the lease so that the expected return on invested capital is equal to its opportunity cost:** In doing this, lessors factor in the expected costs associated with asset abuse and under-maintenance. A higher rental price compensates the lessor for the greater susceptibility to asset abuse. This is the reason that the lease prices are so high for assets that are more subject to abuse. You will see this if you ever rent an exotic sports car. The rental price for just a few hours can easily be several hundred dollars. Unfortunately, pricing the lease to compensate for asset abuse costs can also make the problem worse because it discourages people who are less likely to abuse an asset from leasing it.

3. **Track the total services obtained from the asset and charge the lessee based on useage:** This reduces the incentive for the lessee to use the asset intensively and compensates the lessor if the lessee does this. An example of tracking usage and pricing based on it is seen in Ryder or U-Haul truck rental agreements. In these agreements, the base rental price includes a prespecified number of miles that the truck can be driven. The lessee must pay an additional per-mile charge for each mile the truck is driven over that limit.

4. **Require a damage deposit:** Such deposits are commonly required in lease agreements involving apartments or other assets where it is easy to observe abuse. They provide an incentive for the lessee not to abuse the asset and make it easier for the lessor to recover the cost if the asset is abused.

5. **Bundle the lease contract with a service contract:** Where under-maintenance is of particular concern, lessors often bundle a maintenance (service) contract with the lease contract. In other words, the lessee must purchase a maintenance contract along with the lease. Since the lessee simply has to make a phone call (or for a vehicle, bring it to the shop) in order to have maintenance performed, he or she is more likely to do so.

6. **Place explicit restrictions on how an asset may be used:** Bundling a maintenance contract with a lease might work well with an asset such as a copier where you are dealing with ordinary maintenance. However, it will be less effective with an asset like a car where you are also concerned about how it is used. For this reason auto leasing companies often place restrictions on the use of leased vehicles. For example, they might prohibit driving the vehicle off-road or hauling a trailer with a weight in excess of a prespecified limit. Restrictions on use also take other forms, such as prohibitions on the commercial use of a

piece of equipment that is designed for home use or limits on sub-leasing office space or an apartment.

7. **Provide the lessee with the right to buy the asset when the lease expires:** Having the right to buy the asset gives the lessee an option on the salvage rights. This reduces his incentive to abuse the asset during the lease term.

Evaluating a Leasing Opportunity

As we stated earlier, the primary motivation for leasing an asset is that doing so is a less-expensive way of obtaining the use of the asset than purchasing it. In other words, despite the intensity of use and maintenance conflicts, leasing an asset can create more value for stockholders than can purchasing it. This value can come from larger tax shields, the flexibility that short-term leasing can provide, and reduced contracting costs, among other benefits.

The analytical techniques that are used to choose between buying and leasing an asset are identical to those used in capital budgeting. Analysts typically use NPV analysis. Since the asset that would be purchased is often exactly the same as the asset that would be leased, many of the cash flows associated with the use of the asset are the same regardless of whether the asset is owned or leased. These identical cash flows, which often include the revenues and costs of goods sold associated with the sale of products produced using the leased asset, can be ignored when comparing the two alternatives. For this reason, the NPV values in a buy versus lease analysis only reflect cash flows that are not the same between the two alternatives. To see how this analysis is done, consider the following example.

The owner of a small furniture manufacturing company in Athens, Ohio, has to replace an old wood lathe that has reached the end of its useful life. She is considering either buying or leasing a replacement lathe. Under either alternative, she plans to use the lathe in her business for only six years, even though its economic life is expected to be considerably longer. Assume that the furniture manufacturing company has a marginal tax rate of 25 percent.

Lease alternative: The company that manufactures the lathe offers a leasing option under which the furniture manufacturing company can lease the lathe for an annual lease payment of $3,400 per year. With this option, the lessor will be responsible for maintenance of the lathe and will take it back after six years. The lease will be classified as an operating lease under the accounting and tax rules.

Purchase alternative: It would cost $20,000 to purchase the replacement lathe, and a local bank has offered to lend the entire amount to the company at an interest rate of 8 percent. The loan would be a six-year balloon loan in which the company would not have to repay any of the principal until the loan matures in six years. The lathe would be depreciated using the five-year MACRS depreciation method shown in Exhibit 11.7. As a percentage of the purchase price, the annual depreciation deductions would be 20 percent, 32 percent, 19.2 percent, 11.52 percent, 11.52 percent, and 5.76 percent in Years 1 through 6, respectively. Maintenance of the lathe would cost $500 per year, and the lathe is expected to have a salvage value of $10,000 after six years.

Analysis: We can assume that the revenues and cost of goods sold associated with the use of the lathe are the same under either alternative and ignore these cash flows in comparing the two alternatives. In making this assumption we are also assuming that the asset abuse problem is not an important concern with this lease. There are two reasons this is reasonable in this situation. First, the manufacturing company is unlikely to significantly alter its production rates just to use this one machine more intensely. Second, the maintenance arrangement, which bundles a service contract with the lease contract, will limit the maintenance conflict.

With the above information, the analysis of the lease versus purchase options involves calculating the present value of the after-tax cash flows that are unique to each of them.

Exhibit A16.1 shows the annual after-tax cash flows and the NPV for the lease alternative. Since the lease is an operating lease, the furniture manufacturing company will be able to deduct the entire lease payment when calculating its taxes each year. Furthermore, since the lathe will be owned, maintained, and depreciated by the lessor, the lessee does not have to worry about

EXHIBIT A16.1 NPV of the Cash Flows for Leasing the Wood Lathe

This table shows the cash flows and the NPV of the cash flows associated with leasing the wood lathe. This analysis excludes cash flows that would be the same under both the purchase and lease alternatives.

Year	Pre-Tax Lease Payment (1)	After-Tax Lease Payment (1) × (1 − 0.25) (2)
1	−$3,400	−$2,550
2	−$3,400	−$2,550
3	−$3,400	−$2,550
4	−$3,400	−$2,550
5	−$3,400	−$2,550
6	−$3,400	−$2,550
After-tax cost of debt = 0.08 × (1 − 0.25) = 0.06, or 6%		
NPV of total after-tax cash flows at 6 percent = −$12,539.18		

the cash flows associated with the purchase or sale of the lathe, maintenance, or depreciation deductions. The NPV of the after-tax cash flows associated with the lease is −$12,539.18.[4]

The cash flows that are unique to the purchase option are the interest and principal payments associated with the loan, the tax savings associated with the depreciation of the lathe, the cost of the maintenance, and the salvage value of the lathe after six years. **Exhibit A16.2** illustrates how the annual after-tax value of these cash flows and their NPV are calculated and shows that the present value of these cash flows is −$12,904.97. This NPV represents the total cost of obtaining the use of this machine for six years if it is purchased.

Since the after-tax cost of owning the wood lathe for six years is greater than the after-tax cost of leasing it for six years (the NPV is more negative), the owner of the furniture manufacturing company should lease the lathe.

Decision Making Example A16.1 illustrates another lease or purchase decision.

DECISION MAKING

EXAMPLE A16.1 | Lease or Purchase Decision

Situation You work for a courier firm that offers fast physical delivery of packages in downtown New York City (Manhattan). If someone wants to have a package delivered before the postal service or one of the big courier firms, such as FedEx or UPS, can deliver it, he or she will call your office and you will send a courier on a bicycle to pick up the package and make the delivery. Your couriers have used their own bicycles up to this point, but you have decided that it conveys a more professional image if they use identical bicycles with your company's logo on them. A bicycle manufacturing company has offered to lease or sell you the bicycles that you want. After performing an NPV analysis, you find that the NPV associated with leasing a bicycle for two years is −$545.12 and that the NPV associated with purchasing and maintaining the same bicycle is −$515.00. Should you purchase or lease the bicycles?

Decision The NPV analysis suggests that you should purchase the bicycles because it is less expensive to purchase them than to lease them. Of course, this assumes that all the relevant costs are reflected in your analysis.

Before You Go On

1. What is a lease? What are the two types of leases?
2. What is the most common motivation for leasing?
3. What types of conflicts arise with leases, and why?

[4]Note that we used the after-tax cost of the 8 percent loan as the discount rate. We did this because the bank has agreed to lend the company the entire $20,000 purchase price at that rate and the lease is effectively 100 percent debt financing. We can assume that the risk associated with the lease cash flows is the same as that associated with the loan cash flows. It only makes sense to do this if the bank would lend the entire amount at that rate without any guarantees from the furniture manufacturing company or its owner. If there were such guarantees, using the 8 percent stated cost of debt would understate the true cost of 100 percent debt financing.

EXHIBIT A16.2 NPV of the Cash Flows for Purchasing the Wood Lathe

This table shows the cash flows and the NPV of the cash flows associated with purchasing the wood lathe. This analysis excludes cash flows that would be the same under both the purchase and lease alternatives.

	Loan			Depreciation					
		Interest							
Year	Principal Repayment (1)	Pre-Tax (8% × \$20,000) (2)	After-Tax (2) × (1 − 0.25) (3)	Percent of Asset Cost (4)	Depreciation Deduction (4) × \$20,000 (5)	Tax Savings (5) × 0.25 (6)	After-Tax Maintenance Cost \$500 × (1 − 0.25) (7)	After-Tax Salvage value[a] \$10,000 × (1 − 0.25) (8)	Total After-Tax Cash Flows (1) + (3) + (6) + (7) + (8) (9)
1		−\$1,600	−\$1,200	20.00%	\$4,000	\$800.00	−\$375		−\$775
2		−\$1,600	−\$1,200	32.00%	\$6,400	\$2,048.00	−\$375		\$473
3		−\$1,600	−\$1,200	19.20%	\$3,840	\$737.28	−\$375		−\$838
4		−\$1,600	−\$1,200	11.52%	\$2,304	\$265.42	−\$375		−\$1,310
5		−\$1,600	−\$1,200	11.52%	\$2,304	\$265.42	−\$375		−\$1,310
6	−\$20,000	−\$1,600	−\$1,200	5.76%	\$1,152	\$66.36	−\$375	\$7,500	−\$14,009

After-tax cost of debt = 0.08 × (1 − 0.25) = 0.06, or 6%

NPV of total after-tax cash flows at 6 percent = −\$12,904.97

[a]Since the lathe will be fully depreciated at the end of the sixth year, the entire salvage value will be taxable.

Summary of Learning Objective

A1 Describe what a lease is and discuss the motivations for leasing, what types of assets are more or less likely to be leased, and conflicts that arise in lease agreements and how the costs of these conflicts are reduced by lessors. Evaluate the choice between leasing and purchasing an asset.

A lease is a financial contract that divides the right to use an asset into two parts: (1) the right to use it during the term of the lease and (2) the right to use it after the lease expires (the salvage rights). Leasing is an alternative to purchasing an asset when someone wants to obtain the right to use the asset for a period of time. The primary motivation for leasing an asset is that it is less expensive than purchasing the asset. Leasing can provide larger tax shields, greater flexibility, and reduced contracting costs. General-use assets are more likely to be leased because the hold-up problem will be less severe with them than with firm-specific assets. Because of the way a lease divides the right to use an asset, it leads to conflicts concerning how intensely it is used and how well it is maintained. Ways in which lessors limit the costs of these conflicts include (1) investing in assets that are less subject to abuse, (2) pricing leases to reflect expected abuse, (3) tracking how intensely the leased assets are used and charging based on that intensity of use, (4) requiring damage deposits, (5) bundling lease and service contracts, (6) restricting how the assets can be used, and (7) offering the lessees the right to purchase the assets at the end of the lease. The analytical techniques that are used to choose between buying and leasing an asset are identical to those used in capital budgeting.

Self-Study Problem

A16.1 You own a real estate investment firm and have been asked by the owner of Big Box Shipping Company if you would be willing to construct an office building and lease it to Big Box. The owner of Big Box has some very unusual requirements for the interior layout of the building and is only willing to commit to leasing the building for 10 years, even though the life of the building is likely to be many times that long. What should concern you about this proposal?

Solution to Self-Study Problem

A16.1 Assuming that there is likely to be sufficient demand for office space in the same area by other businesses at the end of the 10 years, the biggest concern would be the interior layout requirements. If the owner of Big Box wants permanent interior walls for this layout and future potential tenants are likely to demand costly changes, this building would be a firm-specific asset and might not be a good investment for you. You should consider making the investment only if the lease payments include the cost of reconfiguring the space when Big Box moves out. Avoiding this sort of problem is a major reason that modern office buildings are often built without permanent interior walls and tenants use moveable cubicles instead.

WileyPLUS

Questions and Problems, Solution Walkthrough Videos, Learning by Doing Tutorials, and additional study tools and resources are available in WileyPLUS.

Discussion Questions

A16.1 Your boss just read an article about the tax benefits of leasing. He states that your firm should lease all of its assets since it faces a low tax rate. How would you respond?

A16.2 You have decided to open a Segway Personal Transporter (PT) rental shop on your campus. A Segway PT is a two-wheeled electric personal transportation system that enables a person to move around more efficiently in urban settings. If you plan to rent Segway PTs by the day, what sort of asset abuse problem(s) are you likely to be concerned about and how might you control it/them?

Questions and Problems

Excel *Excel templates and resources available in* **WileyPLUS**

Basic

A16.1 **Leasing:** What characteristic of a lease leads to conflicts between the lessee and the lessor?

Intermediate

A16.2 **Leasing:** Fresno Machine Shop management has decided to acquire a new machine that costs $3,000. The machine will be worthless after three years. Only straight-line depreciation is allowed by the IRS for this type of machine. ABC Leasing, Inc., offers to lease the same machine to Fresno under an operating lease. Annual lease payments are $1,200 per year and are due at the end of each of the three years. The market-wide borrowing rate is 8 percent for loans on assets such as this. Fresno's marginal tax rate is 35 percent. Should Fresno lease the machine or buy it? Assume that Fresno would not borrow to purchase the machine.

Advanced

A16.3 Your firm is considering leasing a Chrome® computer. The lease would last for three years and require four payments of $100 per year, with the first payment due immediately. The computer would cost $360 to buy and would be depreciated using straight-line depreciation over three years to a salvage value of zero. The actual salvage value is expected to be $100 after three years. The borrowing rate is 10 percent for loans on assets such as this, and your firm's marginal tax rate is 25 percent. Should your firm lease or buy the computer?

CHAPTER 17

Dividends, Stock Repurchases, and Payout Policy

Karen Desjardin/Moment Mobile ED/Getty Images

LEARNING OBJECTIVES

1. Explain what a dividend is, and describe the different types of dividends and the dividend payment process. Calculate the expected change in a stock's price around an ex-dividend date.
2. Explain what a stock repurchase is and how companies repurchase their stock. Calculate how taxes affect the after-tax proceeds that a stockholder receives from a dividend and from a stock repurchase.
3. Discuss the benefits and costs associated with dividend payments and compare the relative advantages and disadvantages of dividends and stock repurchases.
4. Define stock dividends and stock splits and explain how they differ from other types of dividends and from stock repurchases.
5. Describe factors that managers consider when setting the dividend payouts for their firms.

On February 24, 2017, managers at Hilton Worldwide Holdings Inc., the international hotel company, announced that Hilton's board of directors had authorized payment of a cash dividend of \$0.15 per share in the first quarter of 2017. The value of this dividend was similar to the value of the quarterly cash dividends the company had been paying in recent years, after adjusting for a recent stock split. The February 24 announcement also stated that the Hilton board of directors had authorized a new stock repurchase program under which the company's managers were authorized to use up to \$1 billion of excess cash to buy Hilton stock on the open market.

The dividend and stock repurchase announcements came nine days after Hilton had reported a substantial decline in earnings per share in the recently completed 2016 fiscal year. This decline was partly due to one-time restructuring charges associated with recent divestitures of two of Hilton's businesses: Park Hotel & Resorts Inc. and Hilton Grand Vacations Inc. With these charges behind them, Hilton managers indicated that they expected earnings per share to rebound from \$1.05 in 2016 to between \$1.60 and \$1.71 in 2017. The 2017 values corresponded to total earnings of between \$555 million and \$592 million.

The decision to keep the level of the quarterly cash dividend flat at \$0.15, or \$0.60 per year, while initiating a stock repurchase program most likely reflected uncertainty Hilton managers faced regarding future profitability and capital requirements. With regular cash dividends already equal to 57.1 percent (\$0.60/\$1.05 = 0.571, or 57.1 percent) of earnings, committing to a higher regular cash dividend might have placed Hilton managers in a bind if earnings did not recover as expected or an investment opportunity arose that required substantial capital. The stock repurchase program would enable Hilton management to distribute excess cash to stockholders without committing to making regular distributions. The repurchase program also had some tax advantages over regular cash dividends.

The trade-off between regular cash dividends and stock repurchases is one that is faced by managers whenever they must decide how to distribute value to stockholders. Dividends have historically been a more popular means of distributing value, but this is not always the case. In the period leading up to the great recession of 2008, the total dollar value distributed by U.S. public firms through stock repurchases exceeded that distributed through dividends for several years. This chapter discusses concepts that help us understand why managers make the dividend and stock repurchase decisions that they make. It also helps us understand why firms distribute capital to stockholders and the implications of such distributions.

Chapter Preview

In Chapter 16, we discussed factors that influence capital structure decisions at firms. In this chapter we look at some different but related financing decisions—those concerning how and when to return value (cash or other assets) to stockholders.

We begin by describing the various types of dividends and the dividend payment process. We then discuss stock repurchases as an alternative to dividends. Stock repurchases are a potential component of any payout policy because, like dividends, they are a means of distributing value to stockholders.

We next examine the benefits and costs associated with making dividend payments and describe how stock prices react when a company makes an announcement about future dividend payments. These discussions provide insights into the ways in which payout policies affect firm value. We end this part of the chapter by directly comparing the benefits and costs of dividends with those of stock repurchases.

We then describe stock splits and stock dividends and discuss the reasons managers might want to split their company's stock or pay a stock dividend. Finally, we conclude the chapter with a discussion of factors that managers and their boards of directors consider when they set payout policies.

17.1 Dividends

LEARNING OBJECTIVE

1. Explain what a dividend is, and describe the different types of dividends and the dividend payment process. Calculate the expected change in a stock's price around an ex-dividend date.

payout policy the policy concerning the distribution of value from a firm to its stockholders

dividend something of value distributed to a firm's stockholders on a pro-rata basis—that is, in proportion to the percentage of the firm's shares that they own

Decisions concerning whether to distribute value to stockholders, how much to distribute, and how best to distribute it are very important financing decisions that have implications for a firm's future investment and capital structure policies. Any time value is distributed to a firm's stockholders, the amount of equity capital invested in the firm is reduced. Unless the firm raises additional equity by selling new shares, distributions to stockholders reduce the availability of capital for new investments and increase the firm's financial leverage.

The term **payout policy** refers to a firm's overall policy regarding distributions of value to stockholders. In this section, we discuss the use of dividends to distribute this value. A **dividend** is something of value that is distributed to a firm's stockholders on a pro-rata basis—that is, *in proportion to the percentage of the firm's shares that they own.* A dividend can involve the distribution of cash, assets, or something else, such as discounts on the firm's products that are available only to stockholders.

When a firm distributes value through a dividend, it reduces the value of the stockholders' claims against the firm. To see this, consider a firm that has $1,000 in cash plus other assets that have a market value of $9,000. If the firm has no debt and 10,000 shares are outstanding, what is the value of each share? Each share of this firm is worth $1, since the total value of the cash and the other assets is $10,000 and the stockholders own it all.

> **Building Intuition**
>
> **Dividends Reduce the Stockholders' Investment in a Firm**
>
> A dividend reduces the stockholders' investment in a firm by distributing some of that investment to them. The value that stockholders receive through a dividend was already theirs. A dividend simply takes this value out of the firm and returns it to them.

Now, suppose management distributes the $1,000 of cash as a dividend. Each stockholder receives 10 cents ($1,000/10,000 shares = $0.10) for each share that he or she owns, and the value of each share declines to 90 cents. This is true because the firm is now worth $9,000 and there are still 10,000 shares. Note that each stockholder still has $1 of value for each share owned, but the share represents only 90 cents of the total. The other 10 cents is in the hands of the stockholder, who can spend or reinvest it.[1]

Types of Dividends

As mentioned, dividends can take various forms. The most common form is the **regular cash dividend**, which is a cash dividend that is paid on a regular basis. These dividends are generally paid quarterly and are a common means by which firms return some of their profits to stockholders. By one estimate, more than 1,850 U.S. firms paid cash dividends during the year 2000.[2] The dividend payments made by the vast majority of these firms were part of regular cash dividend payment programs.

regular cash dividend a cash dividend that is paid on a regular basis, typically quarterly

In the chapter opener, you saw that in 2017 Hilton was paying a regular cash dividend of $0.15 each quarter. The size of a firm's regular cash dividend is typically set at a level that management expects the company to be able to maintain in the long run. This is because, barring some major change in the fortunes of the company, management does not want to have to reduce the dividend. As we will discuss later, stock market investors often view a dividend reduction negatively.

Management can afford to err on the side of setting the regular cash dividend too low because it always has the option of paying an **extra dividend** if earnings are higher than expected. Extra dividends are often paid at the same time as regular cash dividends, and some companies use them to ensure that a minimum portion of earnings is distributed to stockholders each year. For example, suppose that the management of a company wants to distribute 40 percent of the company's net income to stockholders each year. If the company earns $2 per share in a particular year and the regular cash dividend is 60 cents per share, management can pay an extra 20-cent dividend at the end of the year to ensure that the company hits its 40 percent payout target [($0.60 + $0.20)/$2.00 = 0.40, or 40 percent].

extra dividend a dividend that is generally paid at the same time as a regular cash dividend to distribute additional value

A **special dividend**, like an extra dividend, is a one-time payment to stockholders. However, special dividends tend to be considerably larger than extra dividends. They are normally used to distribute unusually large amounts of cash. For instance, a company might use a special dividend to distribute excess cash from operations that has accumulated over time. Microsoft did this in a very dramatic way in 2004 when it paid a $32.4 billion special dividend. A special dividend might also be used to distribute the proceeds from the sale of a major asset or business or as a means of altering a company's capital structure.

special dividend a one-time payment to stockholders that is normally used to distribute a large amount of value

Sealed Air Corporation, the company that first produced those plastic sheets of packaging materials with the air bubbles, provides a good example of how a special dividend can be used to dramatically change a company's capital structure. In April 1989, Sealed Air borrowed $306.7 million, which it combined with cash it already had on hand to pay a $40 per share ($329.8 million) dividend. Since the price of Sealed Air's stock was only about $45 before

[1]The investors will actually have less than 10 cents per share to invest if they are required to pay taxes on the dividend. Later in this chapter, we discuss how tax laws affect the attractiveness of dividends to investors and the dividend decisions made by firms.

[2]Harry DeAngelo, Linda DeAngelo, and Douglas J. Skinner, "Are Dividends Disappearing? Dividend Concentration and the Consolidation of Earnings," *Journal of Financial Economics* 72 (2004), 425–456.

the dividend, most of the equity was distributed to stockholders. The net effect of borrowing the money to pay a large dividend like this was to substantially increase the debt-to-total-capital ratio at Sealed Air—from 8.1 percent to more than 76.2 percent.[3] Sealed Air senior management increased the company's leverage so dramatically in order to provide managers at all levels with incentives to focus on maximizing the firm's cash flows. We discussed this potential benefit from using debt financing in Chapter 16.

liquidating dividend the final dividend that is paid to stockholders when a firm is liquidated

A **liquidating dividend** is a dividend that is paid to stockholders when a firm is liquidated. When we say that a firm is liquidated, we mean that its assets are sold; the proceeds from the sale of the assets are distributed to creditors, stockholders, and others who have a claim on the firm's assets; and the firm ceases to exist. In the United States, the proceeds from the sale of a company's assets are first used to pay all wages owed to employees and the company's obligations to suppliers, lenders, the various taxing authorities, and any other party that has a claim on those assets. Only after all of these obligations are satisfied can the company pay a liquidating dividend to the stockholders. These priorities highlight the fact that the stockholders are truly the residual claimants to a firm's assets.

Distributions of value to stockholders can also take the form of discounts on the company's products, free samples, and the like. Often, these noncash distributions are not thought of as dividends, in part because the value received by stockholders is not in the form of cash and in part because the value received by individual stockholders does not often reflect their proportional ownership in the firm.

For example, CSX Corporation used to own a swanky resort in West Virginia called the Greenbrier. CSX stockholders received a discount on the cost of their hotel room when they stayed at the Greenbrier. For a three- or four-day stay, this discount could easily equal the value of the regular cash dividend for someone who owned 200 shares. However, the value of the discount was exactly the same for someone who owned 1 million shares. Obviously, for this large stockholder the value of the discount would be small compared with the value of the cash dividend. Note that the discount could actually exceed the total value of the shares owned by a stockholder who only had five or ten shares.

The discounts offered to CSX stockholders were true distributions of noncash value. Because the resort could rent the discounted rooms at full price, there was a very real opportunity cost associated with these discounts.

The Dividend Payment Process

A relatively standard sequence of events takes place before a dividend is paid. This process is more easily defined for companies with publicly traded stock than for private companies. For this reason, we first focus on the process for public companies and then discuss how it differs for private companies. The time line for the sequence of events in the dividend payment process at a public company is illustrated in **Exhibit 17.1**.

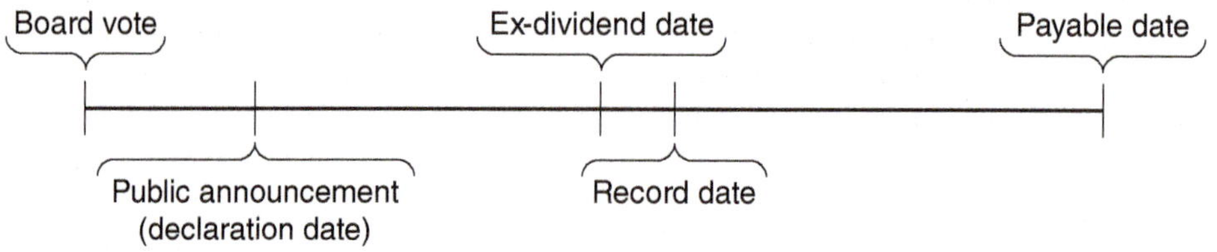

EXHIBIT 17.1 The Dividend Payment Process Time Line for a Public Company

The dividend payment process begins when the board votes to pay a dividend. Shortly afterward, the firm publicly announces its intent to pay a dividend, along with, typically, the amount of the dividend, the ex-dividend date, and the record date. The record date is the date by which an investor must be a stockholder of record in order to receive the dividend. The ex-dividend date, which is set by the stock exchange, normally precedes the record date by two days and is the date before which an investor must buy the stock to be a stockholder of record on the record date. The payable date is the date on which the firm actually pays the dividend.

[3] This was the increase in the debt-to-total-capital ratio from the day before the initial public announcement of the restructuring to the ex-dividend date. For a detailed discussion of the Sealed Air restructuring, see Karen Hooper Wruck, "Financial Policy, Internal Control, and Performance: Sealed Air Corporation's Leveraged Special Dividend," *Journal of Financial Economics* 36 (1994), 157–192.

The Board Vote

The process begins with a vote by a company's board of directors to pay a dividend. As stockholder representatives, the board must approve any distribution of value to stockholders.

The Public Announcement

After the board vote, the company announces to the public that it will pay the dividend. The date on which this announcement is made is known as the **declaration date**, or announcement date, of the dividend. The announcement typically includes the amount of value that stockholders will receive for each share of stock that they own, as well as the other dates associated with the dividend payment process.

declaration date the date on which a dividend is publicly announced

The price of a firm's stock often changes when a dividend is announced. This happens because the public announcement sends a signal to the market about what management thinks the future performance of the firm will be. If the signal differs from what investors expected, they will adjust the prices at which they are willing to buy or sell the company's stock accordingly. For example, the announcement that a company will pay an unexpectedly large dividend can indicate that management is optimistic about future profits—suggesting that future cash flows are higher than expected. This, in turn, can result in an increase in the company's stock price. In contrast, the decision to cut or eliminate a dividend can send a signal that management is pessimistic and can cause the stock price to go down. We have more to say about how stock prices react to dividend announcements later in this chapter. For now, it is important to remember that a dividend decision sends information to investors and that information is incorporated into stock prices at the time of the public announcement.

Building Intuition

Dividend Announcements Send Signals to Investors

A dividend announcement reveals information about management's view of a company's prospects. Investors use this information to refine their expectations concerning future cash flows from the company. A change in investor expectations will cause the company's stock price to change at the time of the public announcement.

The Ex-Dividend Date

An important date included in the public announcement is the **ex-dividend date**—the first date on which the stock will trade without rights to the dividend. An investor who buys shares before the ex-dividend date will receive the dividend, while an investor who buys the stock on or after the ex-dividend date will not. Before the ex-dividend date, a stock is said to be trading *cum dividend,* or with dividend. On or after the ex-dividend date, the stock is said to trade *ex dividend.*

ex-dividend date the first day on which a stock trades without the rights to a dividend

It is important for investors to know the ex-dividend date because it can have significant implications for the taxes and transaction costs they pay. If an investor purchases the company's shares before the ex-dividend date, the investor knows that he or she will soon receive a dividend on which taxes will have to be paid. (Dividends received by investors are taxed by state and federal governments unless the investor is a tax-exempt organization, such as a university endowment.) In addition, a dividend can create difficulties for a stockholder who wants to have a specific amount of money invested in the firm. By returning value to the stockholder, a firm that pays a dividend may reduce the stockholder's investment below the level preferred by the stockholder, thereby making it necessary for the stockholder to purchase additional shares and incur the associated brokerage fees and possibly other transaction costs.

As you might suspect, the price of the firm's shares changes on the ex-dividend date even if there is no new information about the firm. This drop simply reflects the difference in the value of the cash flows that the stockholders are entitled to receive before and after the ex-dividend date. To see how this works, consider a company that recently announced a $1 per share dividend. The company's stock is currently trading for $10 per share, and the ex-dividend date is tomorrow. In this example, the $10 price includes the value of the dividend because an investor who purchases this company's stock before the ex-dividend day will receive the dividend. You can think of the $10 as consisting of a $1 dividend plus the value of the stock on the ex-dividend date.[4] Since an investor who buys the stock tomorrow will receive only the stock, and not the dividend, the price of the stock will certainly be below $10 tomorrow.

Weblink

You can read more about the ex-dividend date and the dividend payment process on the SEC Web site at http://www.sec.gov/answers/dividen.htm.

Does it follow that the stock price will drop by $1 tomorrow? No. Research has shown that stock prices drop on the ex-dividend date but that this drop is smaller than the full amount

[4]We do not have to worry about the time value of money in this example since we are assuming that the ex-dividend date is tomorrow.

of the dividend. In our example, this means that the drop will be less than $1. Why would the price not drop by the full $1? Because the dividend will be taxed. If you knew that you would have to pay a 23.8 percent tax on a dividend that you received (this became the maximum tax rate for dividends in 2013), would you pay 100 percent of the value of that dividend? We hope not. By this point in the book, you should realize that a $1 dividend has an after-tax value of only $0.762 if you have to pay a 23.8 percent tax on it [$\$1.00 \times (1 - 0.238) = \$0.762$]. If investors pay a 23.8 percent tax on dividends, the $10 price of the stock in our example should include $0.762 for the dividend and $9.238 ($\$10.00 - \$0.762 = \$9.238$) for other cash flows, so the stock price should drop to $9.238 on the ex-dividend date.

Learning by Doing Application 17.1 illustrates another example of how stock prices change around the ex-dividend date.

The Record Date

record date the date by which an investor must be a stockholder of record in order to receive a dividend

The **record date** typically follows the ex-dividend date by two business days. The record date is the date on which an investor must be a *stockholder of record* (that is, officially listed as a stockholder) in order to receive the dividend. The board specifies the record date when it votes to make the dividend payment. Once the company informs the exchange on which its stock is traded what the record date is, the exchange sets the ex-dividend date. The ex-dividend day precedes the record date because it takes time to update the stockholder list when someone purchases shares. If you buy the shares before the ex-dividend date, the exchange will ensure that you are listed as a stockholder of record for that company as of the record date.

The Payable Date

payable date the date on which a company pays a dividend

The final date in the dividend payment process is the **payable date**, when the stockholders of record actually receive the dividend. The payable date is typically a couple of weeks after the record date.

An Example of the Dividend Payment Process

We can use Wal-Mart Stores, Inc., to illustrate the dividend payment process. In early 2017, the board of directors of Wal-Mart approved an increase in the company's regular cash dividend to $2.04 per share per year. As is commonly done, Wal-Mart pays its regular cash dividend quarterly. In other words, after the board vote, its stockholders could expect to receive dividends of $0.51 per share each quarter.[5] The dividend increase was announced on February 21, 2017, and so this was the declaration, or announcement, date. **Exhibit 17.2** summarizes the full sequence of events for Wal-Mart's dividend.

LEARNING BY DOING

WileyPLUS

Need more help? Visit your WileyPLUS course.

APPLICATION 17.1 | Stock Prices and Dividend Payments

Problem It is January 20, 2018, and J&W Corporation's stock is trading at $23.50 per share. Earlier today, J&W announced that the record date for its next regular cash dividend will be Wednesday, February 15, 2018, and that the dividend payment will be $0.40 per share. The stock exchange has just announced that the ex-dividend date will be Monday, February 13, 2018. If all investors pay taxes of 20 percent on dividends (this became the top rate for all but the highest earners in 2013), what do you expect to happen to J&W's stock price between the time the market closes on Friday, February 10, 2018, and the time it opens on Monday, February 13, 2018?

Approach The stock price should decline by an amount that equals the after-tax value of the dividend; you can therefore answer this question by calculating this after-tax value.

Solution You would expect the price of J&W's stock to decrease by $\$0.40 \times (1 - 0.20) = \$0.32$. You cannot say what the actual stock price will be after this decrease because you do not know what the price will be beforehand. The $23.50 price is for January 20, 2018, not for February 10, 2018, the day immediately before the ex-dividend date.

[5]Note that this announcement does not obligate Wal-Mart to continue paying quarterly dividends at that level. In fact, Wal-Mart has increased its dividend payment on a regular basis, but there is no reason that the board could not reduce the quarterly dividend payment at some point in the future.

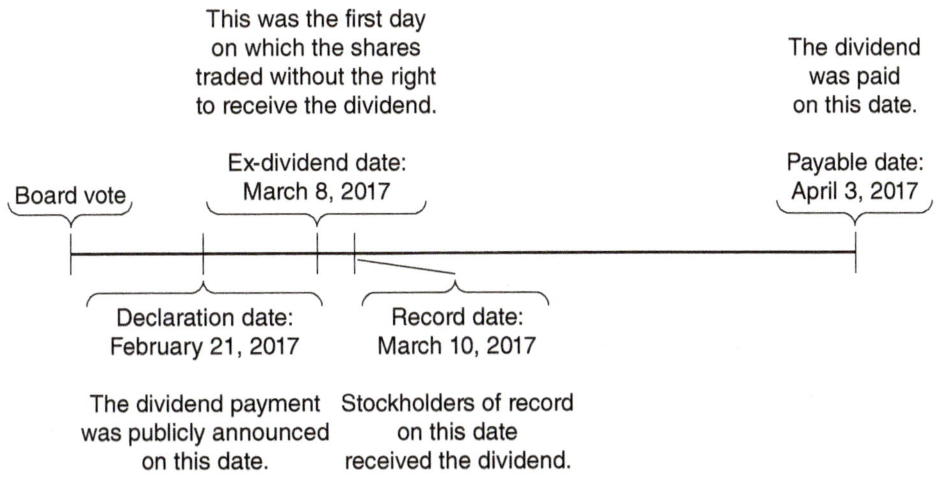

EXHIBIT 17.2 **Key Dates for Wal-Mart's First Quarter 2017 Dividend**

This exhibit summarizes the key dates and time line for the regular cash dividend that Wal-Mart paid on April 3, 2017.

Wal-Mart's announcement also specified the other key dates in Exhibit 17.2. The next regular cash dividend would be paid to investors of record as of Friday, March 10, 2017. This was the record date. The ex-dividend date was Wednesday, March 8, 2017—two trading days earlier—and the payable date was Monday, April 3, 2017.

The Dividend Payment Process at Private Companies

The dividend payment process is not as well defined for private companies as it is for public companies, because in private companies shares are bought and sold less frequently, there are fewer stockholders, and no stock exchange is involved in the dividend payment process. The board members know the identities of the stockholders when they vote to authorize a dividend—generally, the list of stockholders is relatively short and the largest stockholders are on the board. As a result, it is easy to inform all stockholders of the decision to pay a dividend, and it is easy to actually pay it. There is no public announcement, and there is no need for an ex-dividend date. Consequently, the record date and payable date can be any day on or after the day that the board approves the dividend.

Before You Go On

1. How does a dividend affect the size of a stockholder's investment in a firm?
2. List and define four types of dividends.
3. What are the key events and dates in the dividend payment process?

17.2 Stock Repurchases

LEARNING OBJECTIVE

2. Explain what a stock repurchase is and how companies repurchase their stock. Calculate how taxes affect the after-tax proceeds that a stockholder receives from a dividend and from a stock repurchase.

stock repurchase the purchase of stock by a company from its stockholders; an alternative way for the company to distribute value to the stockholders

Stock repurchases are another popular method of distributing value to stockholders. With a **stock repurchase**, a company buys some of its shares from stockholders.

How Stock Repurchases Differ from Dividends

Stock repurchases differ from dividends in a number of important ways. First, they do not represent a pro-rata distribution of value to the stockholders, because not all stockholders participate. Individual stockholders decide whether they want to participate in a stock repurchase. Some stockholders participate, while others do not. In contrast, in a dividend distribution, all stockholders receive the dividend.

Second, when a company repurchases its own shares, it removes them from circulation. This reduces the number of shares of stock held by investors. Removing a large number of shares from circulation can change the ownership of the firm. It can increase or decrease the fraction of shares owned by the major stockholders and thereby diminish their ability to control the company. Also, if a company with a relatively small number of shares in the public market distributes a lot of cash to investors through a stock repurchase, there will be less liquidity for the remaining shares. An extreme example of this occurs when a public company repurchases most of its outstanding shares and "goes private." Since a dividend does not affect who owns the shares or the number of shares outstanding, it does not have these effects on ownership and liquidity.

Third, stock repurchases are taxed differently than dividends. As we saw in the discussion of the ex-dividend date, the total value of dividends is normally taxed.[6] In contrast, when a stockholder sells shares back to the company, the stockholder is taxed only on the profit from the sale. For example, suppose a stockholder purchased 100 shares for \$150 and then sold them to the company for \$200 a year later. In this example, the \$50 profit (\$200 − \$150 = \$50) that the stockholder earned on the sale would be treated as a capital gain and would be taxed at no more than a 23.8 percent rate (the maximum rate on capital gains in 2013), depending on the stockholder's income. The maximum total tax on the sale of the stock would be \$11.90 (\$50 × 0.238 = \$11.90). In contrast, if the company had distributed the \$200 as a dividend, the tax would have been \$47.60 (\$200 × 0.238 = \$47.60)—four times as much! Of course, this difference is even more significant when you remember that stockholders who receive dividends have no choice as to when they must pay the tax because a dividend is not optional. In contrast, since stockholders choose whether to participate in a repurchase plan, they are able to choose when they pay taxes on the profits from selling their stock.

Finally, dividends and stock repurchases are accounted for differently on the balance sheet. For example, when a company pays a cash dividend, the cash account on the assets side of the balance sheet and the retained earnings account on the liabilities and stockholders' equity side of the balance sheet are reduced. In contrast, when a company uses cash to repurchase stock, the cash account on the assets side of the balance sheet is reduced, while the treasury stock account on the liabilities and stockholders' equity side of the balance sheet is increased (becomes more negative). The balance sheet in Exhibit 3.1 includes a treasury stock account, indicating that Diaz Manufacturing repurchased 571,320 shares for \$23.3 million in 2017.

Learning by Doing Application 17.2 illustrates calculations associated with a stock repurchase.

LEARNING BY DOING

WileyPLUS

Need more help? Visit your WileyPLUS course.

APPLICATION 17.2 | Stock Repurchases and Taxes

Problem Your pizza parlor business has been doing very well, and, as a result, you have more cash than you can productively reinvest in the business. You have decided to distribute this cash to yourself, the only stockholder, through a stock repurchase. When you started the business, you invested \$300,000 and received 10,000 shares of stock. In other words, each share cost you \$30. There are no other shares outstanding, and your business valuation adviser tells you that the stock is worth \$800,000 today. If you want to distribute \$80,000 through a stock repurchase, how many shares will the company have to repurchase? If you pay taxes of 20 percent on capital gains, how much money will you have left over after paying taxes on the proceeds from the sale of your stock?

[6] An exception is when the dividend is viewed as a return of the capital that the stockholders have invested in the firm, rather than a distribution of profits. Dividends generally are not a return of capital unless they are very large or when they are liquidating dividends.

Approach First calculate the current share price. Next, divide the amount of cash that you want to distribute by the share price to obtain the number of shares the company will have to repurchase. To calculate the amount of money you would have left over after paying taxes, first compute the capital gain (profit) per share on the stock and multiply this amount by the tax rate and the number of shares the company will have to repurchase to obtain the total tax. Then, subtract the total tax from $80,000 to obtain the answer.

Solution Each share of stock is worth $80 ($800,000/10,000 shares = $80 per share) today. This means that the company would have to repurchase 1,000 shares ($80,000/$80 per share = 1,000 shares) in order to distribute $80,000.

The capital gain per share from the sale would be $50 ($80 – $30 = $50). With a 20 percent tax rate, you would pay taxes of $10,000 ($50 × 0.20 × 1,000 shares = $10,000) on the capital gain, leaving you with gross proceeds from the sale of $70,000 ($80,000 – $10,000 = $70,000).

How Stock Is Repurchased

Companies repurchase stock in three general ways. First, they can simply purchase shares in the market, much as an individual would. These kinds of purchases are known as **open-market repurchases** and are a very convenient way of repurchasing shares on an ongoing basis. For example, a company might use such repurchases to distribute some of its profits instead of paying a regular cash dividend.

open-market repurchase the repurchase of shares by a company in the open market

When a company has a large amount of cash to distribute, open-market repurchases can be cumbersome because the government limits the number of shares that a company can repurchase on a given day. These limits, which are intended to restrict the ability of firms to influence their stock price through trading activity, mean that it could take months for a company to distribute a large amount of cash using open-market repurchases.

When the management of a company wants to distribute a large amount of cash at one time and does not want to use a special dividend, it can repurchase shares using a **tender offer**. A tender offer is an open offer by a company to purchase shares.[7] There are two types of tender offers: *fixed-price* and *Dutch auction*. With a fixed-price tender offer, management announces the price that will be paid for the shares and the maximum number of shares that will be repurchased. Interested stockholders then tender their shares by letting management know how many shares they are willing to sell. If the number of shares tendered exceeds the announced maximum, then the maximum number of shares are repurchased, and each stockholder who tendered shares participates in the repurchase in proportion to the fraction of the total shares that he or she tendered.

tender offer an open offer by a company to purchase shares

With a Dutch auction tender offer, the firm announces the number of shares that it would like to repurchase and asks the stockholders how many shares they would sell at a series of prices, ranging from just above the price at which the shares are currently trading to some higher price. The alternative prices are set higher than the market price to make the offer attractive to stockholders. Stockholders then tell the company how many of their shares they would sell at the various offered prices. Once these offers to sell have been collected, management determines the price that would allow them to repurchase the number of shares that they want. All of the tendering stockholders who indicate a willingness to sell at or below this price will then receive this price for their shares.

Weblink

Go to Thomas Bulkowski's thepatternsite.com Web site at http://www.thepatternsite.com/dutch.html to read more about the Dutch auction tender offers.

The third general way in which shares are repurchased is through direct negotiation with a specific stockholder. These **targeted stock repurchases** are typically used to buy blocks of shares from large stockholders. Such repurchases can benefit stockholders who are not selling because managers may be able to negotiate a per-share price that is below the current market price. This is possible because the only alternative for a stockholder who owns a large block of shares and wants to sell them at one time often involves offering the shares for a below-market price in the open market. Of course, targeted stock repurchases can also be attractive to managers for other reasons—notably, if the company repurchases the block of shares, there is less chance that the shares will fall into the hands of an unfriendly investor.

targeted stock repurchase a stock repurchase that targets a specific stockholder

Exhibit 17.3 presents statistics for the different types of stock repurchases from a sample of repurchases involving public U.S. firms over the 1984–2001 period. The exhibit indicates

[7]The term *tender offer* is commonly used to refer to any open offer to purchase any shares, not just the shares of the firm making the announcement. For example, when a company tries to take over another company, it might begin by announcing a tender offer for that other company's shares.

EXHIBIT 17.3 Descriptive Statistics for Stock Repurchases in the United States, 1984–2001

Open-market repurchase programs are the most common means of repurchasing shares. However, managers tend to use other methods when they want to repurchase a large percentage of their firm's total shares.

	Open-Market Repurchase Programs	Fixed-Price Tender Offers	Dutch Auction Tender Offers	Targeted Stock Repurchases
Average percentage of shares repurchased	7.37%	29.46%	15.88%	13.00%
Average premium paid over market price	NA	20.74%	14.72%	1.92%
Percentage of cases where repurchase price was below market price	NA	0.00%	0.40%	44.78%
Average market-adjusted stock price change following repurchase announcement	2.39%	7.68%	7.60%	−1.81%
Number of observations	6,470	303	251	737

Source: Information from *Journal of Financial Economics*, 75(2), Urs C. Peyer and Theo Vermaelen, "The Many Facets of Privately Negotiated Stock Repurchases," 361–395, Copyright 2005, with permission from Elsevier.

that the most common way to repurchase shares is through open-market repurchases (6,470 observations versus 737 for targeted stock repurchases, the second most common method). However, the average percentage of shares repurchased, at 7.37 percent, is considerably smaller for open-market repurchase programs than for the other repurchase methods. This confirms what we stated earlier—managers tend to use methods other than open-market repurchases when they want to distribute a large amount of cash at one time. Finally, Exhibit 17.3 shows that almost half of the targeted stock repurchases involve a purchase price that is below the stock's price in the open market. This is consistent with the idea that managers can often negotiate discounts when making such purchases. Interestingly, the average stock price reaction to a targeted stock repurchase is negative. The reason for this is not obvious. In some cases, investors may think that managers are repurchasing shares to entrench themselves to the detriment of the stockholders. In other cases, a large stockholder's willingness to sell his or her shares may signal this investor's pessimism about the firm's prospects, thereby causing other market participants to drive down the stock price.

Before You Go On

1. What is a stock repurchase?
2. How do stock repurchases differ from dividends?
3. In what ways can a company repurchase its stock?

17.3 Dividends and Firm Value

LEARNING OBJECTIVE

3. Discuss the benefits and costs associated with dividend payments and compare the relative advantages and disadvantages of dividends and stock repurchases.

One reason that we devote so much space in this book to dividends is that they can affect the value of a firm. In this section, we explain why. The best way to begin is by recalling, from Chapter 16, the general conditions under which capital structure policy does *not* affect firm value:

1. There are no taxes.
2. There are no information or transaction costs.
3. The real investment policy of the firm is fixed.

These are the three conditions identified by Modigliani and Miller (M&M). Since a dividend payment has implications for a firm's capital structure, as illustrated earlier in the Sealed Air example, the factors that cause dividends to affect firm value are very closely related to the conditions identified by M&M. In fact, if the above conditions hold, then the dividends a firm pays will not affect its value.

Dividends do not matter under these conditions because a stockholder can "manufacture" any dividends he or she wants at no cost, and the total cash flows a firm produces from its real assets are not affected by the dividends that it pays. To see how a stockholder can manufacture dividends, consider a retired stockholder who owns 50,000 shares of a company's stock and needs to receive a $1 per share dividend each year on this investment to cover his or her living expenses. If the company pays such a dividend, there is no problem. But what if the company does not pay such a dividend? Well, under the above conditions, the stockholder could "manufacture" his or her own dividend by selling $50,000 worth of stock each year. This would reduce the total value of this investor's stock by $50,000, just as a $50,000 dividend would. Remember that we are assuming that no taxes must be paid, so the decline in the value of the shares would exactly equal the value of the dividend if one were paid.

A stockholder could also undo the dividend decisions made by managers by simply reinvesting the dividends that the company pays in new shares. For instance, if a company paid a $50,000 dividend, thereby reducing the value of a stockholder's shares, that stockholder could increase his or her ownership in the company's shares to its previous level by purchasing $50,000 worth of shares.

Just as with changes in capital structure policy, if investors could replicate the dividends paid by a company on their own at no cost and the managers' dividend decisions do not affect the total cash flows the firm produces, investors would not care whether or not the company paid a dividend. In other words, they would not be willing to pay more or less for the stock of a firm that pays a dividend than for the stock of a firm that does not pay a dividend.

Benefits and Costs of Dividends

Of course, we know that the M&M assumptions do not apply in the real world. But that is good news in the sense that the imperfect world we live in provides companies with the opportunity to create value through their dividend decisions. Doing so involves balancing benefits and costs, just as we do in choosing a capital structure. We now turn our attention to a discussion of the benefits and costs associated with paying dividends.

Benefits of Dividends

One benefit of paying dividends is that it attracts investors who prefer to invest in stocks that pay dividends. For example, consider the retired stockholder we discussed earlier. While he or she could simply sell some stock each month to cover expenses, in the real world it may be less costly—and it is certainly less trouble—to simply receive regular cash dividend payments instead. Recall that under the M&M conditions, there are no transaction costs. In the real world, though, the retiree will have to pay brokerage commissions each time he or she sells stock. The dividend check, in contrast, simply arrives each quarter. Of course, the retiree will have to consider the impact of taxes on the value of dividends versus the value of proceeds from the sale of stock; but it is quite possible that receiving dividends might, on balance, be more appealing.

Another type of investor that might prefer income-paying stocks is an institutional investor, such as an endowment or a foundation. Because of their investment guidelines, some institutional investors are only allowed to spend proceeds that are received as income from their investments. These institutions face limitations on their ability to sell shares to replicate a dividend.

Unfortunately, the ability to appeal to certain investors is not a very compelling reason for paying dividends. While retirees and some institutional investors might prefer dividends, investors with no current need for income from their investment portfolios might prefer not to receive dividends. Those investors might actually choose to avoid stocks that pay high dividends, since they might have to pay taxes on the dividends and would face transaction costs when they reinvest the dividends they receive.

Furthermore, the fact that some investors prefer to receive dividends does not necessarily mean that an individual company can increase the value of its stock by paying dividends. After all, a wide range of dividend-paying stocks is already available on the market. The addition of one more such stock is unlikely to markedly increase the options available for investors looking for dividends. Therefore, these investors will not be willing to pay a higher price for that stock.

Some people have argued that a large regular dividend indicates that a company is financially strong. This "signal" of strength, they say, can result in a higher stock price. This argument is based on the assumption that a company that is able to pay a large dividend, rather than holding on to cash for future investments, is a company that is doing so well that it has more money than it needs to fund its available investments. The problem with this line of reasoning is that such a company might have more than enough money for all its future investment opportunities because it does not have many future investment opportunities. In this situation, the fact that the company does not need the cash would be a bad signal, not a good one.

Another benefit of paying dividends is suggested by the fact that many companies pay regular cash dividends on the one hand while routinely selling new shares on the other. For example, FPL Group pays a regular dividend and occasionally raises capital by issuing new equity. Why might FPL reduce its equity by paying a dividend and then turn around and increase it by selling new shares? One possible explanation is that management is just trying to appeal to investors who prefer dividends, as we discussed earlier. But another explanation is that this practice helps to align the incentives of managers and stockholders.

Let's look more closely at this second explanation. Consider a company that is so profitable that it never has to go to the debt or equity markets to raise external capital. This company can pay for all of its needs with earnings from operations. The managers in charge of the company might have incentives to operate the business less efficiently than the stockholders would like. For example, they might invest in negative NPV assets—such as corporate jets, plush offices, or a company apartment in Manhattan—that benefit them but do not create value for the stockholders. These managers might also spend more time than they should away from the office, perhaps serving on the boards of other companies or golfing, letting the operating performance of the company fall below the level that could be achieved if they focused on running the business. Stockholders understand that managers at highly profitable firms have these incentives. Thus, they are likely to reduce the price that they are willing to pay for this company's stock to reflect the loss of value associated with the managers' unproductive behaviors.

Now suppose that the company's board of directors votes to pay dividends that amount to more than the excess cash that the company is producing from its operations. Since the money to pay the dividends will have to come from somewhere, the board is effectively forcing management to sell equity periodically in the public markets. The need to raise equity in the capital markets will help align the incentives of managers with those of stockholders. Why? Because it increases the cost to managers of operating the business inefficiently. In order to raise equity at a reasonable cost, the managers must be careful how efficiently they are operating the business. The process of raising new equity involves a special audit that is more detailed than an annual audit and invites the close attention of lawyers, investment bankers, and outside experts. These outside parties provide a certification function that increases the amount of public information about the firm's activities. Voluntarily submitting to such outside certification—by paying a dividend and issuing equity rather than just keeping cash inside the firm—can ultimately lead to better company performance and the willingness of investors to pay a higher price for the company's stock.

One last potential benefit of paying dividends is that dividends can be useful in managing the capital structure of a company. The trade-off theory of capital structure, which we discussed in Chapter 16, tells us that there is an optimal mix of debt and equity that maximizes the value of a firm. To the extent that a company is internally generating more equity than it can profitably invest, the fraction of debt in its capital structure will always be decreasing over time unless the company borrows more money (which it doesn't need) or distributes cash to stockholders. Paying dividends can help keep the firm's capital structure near its optimal mix.

Costs of Dividends

In addition to benefits, there are costs associated with dividends. Taxes are among the most important of these costs. As we discussed earlier, dividends are taxable, and the stockholders of firms that pay dividends have no choice but to receive the dividends and pay the associated taxes if they want to own the stock. Before 2003, dividends were taxed as ordinary income by the federal government in the United States. This meant that, depending on the stockholder's income, as much as 39.6 percent of the dividend would be paid to the federal government in taxes. Tax law changes made in 2003 lowered this top rate to 15 percent, making it the same as the top rate on capital gains. The top rates on both dividends and capital gains were increased to 23.8 percent in 2013, but some government officials are working to make the rate for dividends once again be the same as that for ordinary income. Since, dividends are also taxed by a number of states, depending on where you live, the total tax rate can be even higher.

Stockholders can always sell some of their shares to "manufacture" their own dividends, as we discussed earlier. If they do this, they pay taxes only on the profit on the sale. Unless the stockholder received the stock for free, this profit is a smaller amount than the amount the dividend would be. Furthermore, the U.S. tax system has typically treated capital gains differently from dividends. If you own a stock for some specified period of time, currently 12 months, any gain on the sale of that stock is treated as a capital gain. Until 2003, as mentioned, dividends were taxed as ordinary income, and the ordinary income tax rate for most taxpayers was higher than the capital gains tax rate. Thus, before 2003, if you sold shares rather than receiving dividends, you not only paid taxes on a smaller amount, but you also paid a lower rate on the amount that was taxable. Since 2003, the tax rates have been the same for dividends and capital gains. If history is any indication, however, tax rates on dividends will be higher again in the not-too-distant future.

In addition to paying taxes on dividends, owners of stocks that pay dividends often have to pay brokerage fees if they want to reinvest the proceeds. To eliminate this cost, some companies offer **dividend reinvestment programs (DRIPs)**. Through a DRIP, a company sells new shares, commission free, to dividend recipients who elect to automatically reinvest their dividends in the company's stock. While DRIPs eliminate transaction costs, they do not affect the taxes that must be paid on the dividends. Also, since it is costly to administer a DRIP, these programs effectively transfer the cost from the stockholders who want to reinvest to the firm (which means all stockholders).

dividend reinvestment program (DRIP) a program in which a company sells new shares, commission free, to dividend recipients who elect to automatically reinvest their dividends in the company's stock

It is worth remembering that the total value of the assets in a company goes down when a dividend is paid. To the extent that a company uses a lot of debt financing, paying dividends can increase the cost of debt. This will happen if the payment of dividends reduces the value of the assets underlying debt holder claims on the cash flows from the firm. With less valuable assets, the debt holders face greater risk of default. To compensate for this greater risk, they will charge the company a higher rate on its debt.

Stock Price Reactions to Dividend Announcements

In the earlier discussion of the dividend payment process, we stated that the price of a company's stock often changes when a dividend is announced. We also noted that this happens because the public announcement sends a signal to the market about what management thinks the future performance of the firm will be. Let's consider this issue in more detail.

We can think about the market's reaction to a dividend announcement in the context of what we call the *cash flow identity,* a term which means that, during any period, the *sources* of cash must equal the *uses* of cash in a firm:

$$\begin{array}{ccc}\textbf{Sources} & = & \textbf{Uses}\\ \text{CFOA}_t + \text{Equity}_t + \text{Debt}_t & = & \text{Div}_t + \text{Repurchases}_t + \text{Interest}_t + \text{Principal}_t + \text{Inv}_t\end{array}$$

where:

$$\begin{aligned}
\text{CFOA}_t &= \text{cash flow to investors from operating activity in period } t\\
\text{Equity}_t &= \text{proceeds from the sale of stock in period } t\\
\text{Debt}_t &= \text{proceeds from the sale of debt in period } t\\
\text{Div}_t &= \text{dividends paid in period } t\\
\text{Repurchases}_t &= \text{cash used to repurchase stock in period } t\\
\text{Interest}_t &= \text{interest payments to debt holders in period } t\\
\text{Principal}_t &= \text{principal payments on debt in period } t\\
\text{Inv}_t &= \text{investments in net working capital and fixed assets period } t
\end{aligned}$$

How can this identity help us to understand how investors use dividend announcements to infer what management thinks the firm's future performance will be? Let's consider an example.

Assume that a company has just announced an increase in its dividend payments that investors did not expect. If the company is not selling new equity or debt, not repurchasing stock, and its investment in fixed assets and net working capital does not change, this means that Div_t is going up and that Equity_t, Debt_t, Repurchases_t, Interest_t, Principal_t, and Inv_t are not changing. Since investors know that the cash flow identity must hold, CFOA_t, the cash flow to investors from operating activity, must be expected to increase. This situation can be illustrated as follows:

$$\begin{array}{ccccccccccccccc} \text{CFOA}_t & + & \text{Equity}_t & + & \text{Debt}_t & = & \text{Div}_t & + & \text{Repurchases}_t & + & \text{Interest}_t & + & \text{Principal}_t & + & \text{Inv}_t \\ \uparrow & & \rightarrow & & \rightarrow & & \uparrow & & \rightarrow & & \rightarrow & & \rightarrow & & \rightarrow \end{array}$$

An expected increase in the cash flow to investors from operating activity is a good signal, and investors will interpret it as suggesting that cash flows to stockholders will increase in the future. As a result, the stock price should go up.

Evidence from studies of stock price reactions to dividend announcements is generally consistent with this theory. This evidence indicates that when a company announces it will begin paying a regular cash dividend, its stock price increases by an average of about 3.5 percent. Similarly, announcements of increases in regular cash dividends are associated with an average stock price increase of 1 to 2 percent. In contrast, the announcement that a company will reduce its regular cash dividend is associated with a 3.5 percent decrease in its stock price, on average. An announcement that a company will pay a special dividend is associated with an average stock price increase of about 2 percent.

It is important to recognize that we cannot interpret these studies as proof that changes in dividends *cause* changes in stock prices. Rather, the cash flow identity suggests that managers change dividends when something fundamental has changed in the business. It is this fundamental change that causes the stock price to change. The dividend announcement is really just the means by which investors find out about the fundamental change. Although there are benefits and costs associated with dividend payments, the sizes of these benefits and costs tend to be relatively small compared with the changes in value associated with the fundamental changes that take place in firms. By the same token, there is no evidence that it is possible to increase firm value by increasing dividends. Again, dividend changes only provide a signal concerning a fundamental change at the firm. In this sense, they are only by-products of the change.

Dividends versus Stock Repurchases

As we noted earlier, stock repurchases are an alternative to dividends as a way of distributing value. Our discussion has already suggested that stock repurchases have some distinct advantages over dividends. They give stockholders the ability to choose when they receive the distribution, which affects the timing of the taxes they must pay as well as the cost of reinvesting funds that are not immediately needed. In addition, stockholders who sell shares back to a company pay taxes only on the gains they realize, and historically these capital gains have been taxed at a lower rate than dividends.

From management's perspective, stock repurchases provide greater flexibility in distributing value. We have already discussed how stock prices react to announcements of changes in dividend payments. We can therefore imagine why managers might find stock repurchases relatively more attractive. Even when a company publicly announces an ongoing open-market stock repurchase program, as opposed to a regular cash dividend, investors know that management can always quietly cut back or end the repurchases at any time. In contrast, dividend programs represent a stronger commitment to distribute value in the future because they cannot be quietly ended. For this reason, investors know that managers will initiate regular cash dividends only when they are quite confident that they will be able to continue them for the long run.

Thus, if future cash flows are not certain, managers are likely to prefer to distribute extra cash today by repurchasing shares through open-market purchases because this enables them to preserve some flexibility. If cash flows decline in the future, management can reduce the repurchases without a pronounced effect on the company's stock price.

Potentially offsetting the advantages of stock repurchases are a few notable disadvantages. One of these disadvantages is the flip side of the signaling benefit discussed in the previous paragraph. Since most ongoing stock repurchase programs are not as visible as dividend programs, they cannot be used as effectively to send a positive signal about the company's prospects to investors.

A more subtle issue concerns the fact that managers can choose when to repurchase shares in a stock repurchase program. Just like other investors, managers prefer purchasing shares when they believe that the shares are undervalued in the market. The problem is that since managers have better information about the company's prospects than do other investors, they can take advantage of this information to the detriment of other investors. If managers are taking advantage of superior information, their repurchases are effectively transferring value from stockholders who choose to sell their shares (perhaps because they simply need money to live on) to stockholders who choose to remain invested in the company. A transfer of wealth from one group of stockholders to another is a problem. Remember that management is supposed to act in the best interest of *all* of the firm's stockholders.

Companies in the United States have historically distributed more value through dividend payments than through stock repurchases. This suggests that managers have, on balance, found dividends more attractive. However, in recent years the popularity of stock repurchases has increased. From 2005 to 2007, the total dollar value distributed through stock repurchases exceeded the value distributed through dividends for the first time. While the dollar value of stock repurchases has been below that of dividends since 2008, it has remained at historically high levels. At the same time, the way companies pay dividends and how much they pay have changed substantially. Between 1978 and 2000, the number of public industrial companies in the United States that paid dividends declined from approximately 2,250 to 926.[8] Interestingly, the companies that stopped paying dividends were primarily those that had paid small dividends. The total value of dividends paid has actually increased since 1978 even after adjusting for inflation. The net result is that the firms that pay dividends are, on average, paying larger dividends.

Weblink

To read more about the increasing popularity of stock repurchases, see the discussion of recent research at http://www.ur.umich.edu/0405/Dec13_04/14.shtml.

These trends are illustrated in **Exhibit 17.4**, which shows the total dollar value of dividends paid and stock repurchased by public U.S. firms from 1980 to 2016. The exhibit also

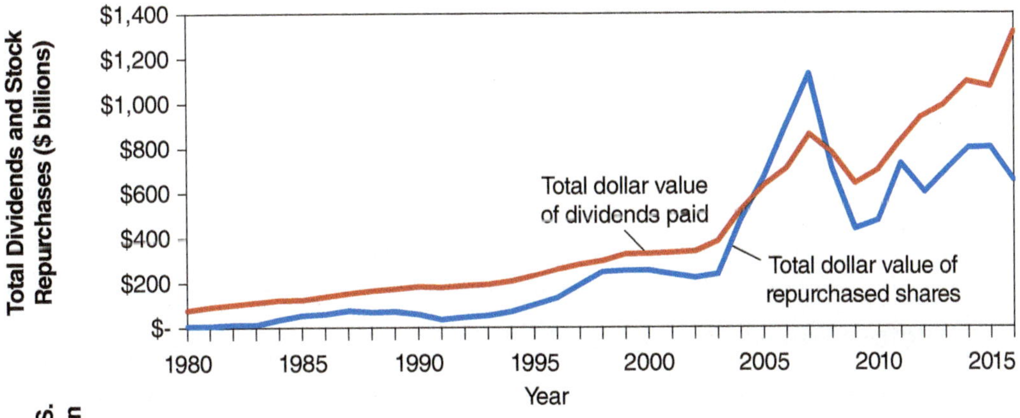

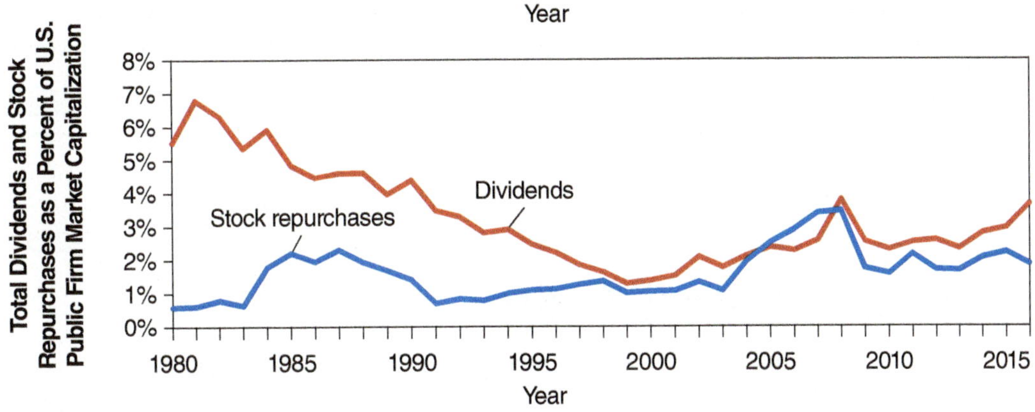

EXHIBIT 17.4 Dividend Payments and Stock Repurchases by U.S. Public Firms, 1980–2016

Both the dollar value of dividends paid by U.S. public firms and the dollar value of stock repurchases increased over the period from 1980 to 2016, as shown in the top figure. However, the increase was more pronounced for stock repurchases. Despite these increases in dollar values, total distributions of value as a percentage of the total market capitalization (total equity value) of U.S. firms actually decreased, as shown in the bottom figure.

Source: Estimated by authors using data from the Standard and Poors' Compustat database.

[8]DeAngelo, DeAngelo, and Skinner. See full reference in footnote 2. Section 17.1 reported that an estimated 1,850 companies paid dividends in 2000; that figure includes all public companies, not just industrial companies.

DECISION MAKING

EXAMPLE 17.1 | Choosing a Payout Method

Situation You are the chief executive officer of San Marcos Pharmaceuticals, a generic drug manufacturing firm. With patents on a lot of brand-name drugs sold by other pharmaceutical firms expiring, San Marcos has been doing very well manufacturing generic copies of those drugs. In fact, business has been going so well that San Marcos is generating more cash flow than is required for investment in the positive NPV projects that are available to the company.

You have decided that you want to distribute the excess (free) cash flow to stockholders rather than accumulate it in the company's cash accounts. You expect the company to continue to generate free cash flow in the future, but the amount is likely to vary considerably as the new national health law goes into effect. You want to be able to adjust distributions as free cash flows rise and fall but do not want to make San Marcos's stock price any more volatile than it already is. Furthermore, relatively few of the company's shares are held by investors that do not pay taxes, such as pension funds and university endowments, so you would prefer that the distributions be as tax efficient as possible.

Your chief financial officer tells you that the most feasible means of distributing the excess cash on an ongoing basis is to pay a regular cash dividend or to repurchase shares through open-market repurchases. Which of these two options should you choose?

Decision As long as the ownership structure of the company or the liquidity of its shares is not severely altered or impaired, the open-market repurchase alternative is the better choice. Open-market repurchases can easily be adjusted to accommodate changes in the amount of free cash flow that San Marcos generates without adding to stock price volatility. In contrast, increasing and decreasing a regular cash dividend as free cash flows rise and fall would most likely add to the volatility of the company's stock price. Since an open-market repurchase program is more tax efficient than a regular cash dividend, it will also enable stockholders to keep more of the money that is distributed to them. Finally, it will let individual stockholders choose whether they want to participate in the program in the first place.

shows the total value of dividends and of stock repurchases as a percentage of the total market capitalization (total equity value) of public U.S. firms. You can see that the fraction of total equity value that is being distributed to stockholders has declined.

Decision Making Example 17.1 illustrates the choice of a payout method.

Before You Go On

1. What are the benefits and costs associated with dividends?
2. How do stock prices react to dividend announcements?
3. Why might stock repurchases be preferred to dividends?

17.4 Stock Dividends and Stock Splits

LEARNING OBJECTIVE

4. Define stock dividends and stock splits and explain how they differ from other types of dividends and from stock repurchases.

Recall that earlier we defined a dividend as something of value distributed to a firm's stockholders on a pro-rata basis The term *dividend* is not always used so precisely. In this section, we discuss actions taken by financial managers that are associated with dividends but that do not involve a distribution of value and are, therefore, not really dividends.

Stock Dividends

One type of dividend that does not involve the distribution of value is known as a **stock dividend**. When a company pays a stock dividend, it distributes new shares of stock on a pro-rata basis to existing stockholders. For example, if a company pays a 10 percent stock dividend, it gives each stockholder a number of new shares equal to 10 percent of the number of shares the stockholder already owns.[9] If an investor owns 100 shares, that investor receives 10 additional shares. An investor that owns 500 shares receives 50 additional shares, and so on. Although stock dividends are not as common as regular cash dividends, a number of companies pay stock dividends. For example, Enbridge Energy Management, Tootsie Roll Industries, and United Security Bancshares all paid stock dividends in 2017.

stock dividend a distribution of new shares to existing stockholders in proportion to the percentage of shares that they own (pro rata); the value of the assets in a company does not change with a stock dividend

To understand why no value is distributed when a stock dividend is paid, consider again a company that pays a 10 percent stock dividend. Assume that the company has total assets with a market value of $11,000, that it has 10,000 shares of stock outstanding, and that it has no debt. Since there is no debt, the stockholders own all of the assets in the firm and each share is worth $1.10 ($11,000/10,000 shares = $1.10 per share).

When the 10 percent stock dividend is paid, the number of shares outstanding increases by 10 percent, from 10,000 to 11,000. Notice that this is really just an accounting change, since no assets are going out of the company. As a result, the value of the total assets in the company does not change, and the value of each share decreases from $1.10 to $1.00 ($11,000/11,000 shares = $1.00 per share). All that happens when the stock dividend is paid is that the number of shares each stockholder owns increases and their value goes down proportionately. The stockholder is left with exactly the same value as before. In our example, a stockholder who owned 100 shares worth $110 ($1.10 per share × 100 shares = $110) before the stock dividend will own 110 shares worth $110 ($1.00 per share × 110 shares = $110) afterward.

Stock Splits

A **stock split** is quite similar to a stock dividend, but it involves the distribution of a larger multiple of the outstanding shares.[10] As the name suggests, we can think of a stock split as an actual division of each share into more than one share. For example, in a stock split, stockholders frequently receive one additional share for each share they already own. This is known as a two-for-one stock split. Stock splits can also involve even larger ratios. For example, there might be a three-for-one stock split in which each stockholder receives two additional shares for each share of stock he or she owns. Besides their size, a key distinction between stock dividends and stock splits is that stock dividends are typically regularly scheduled events, like regular cash dividends, whereas stock splits tend to occur infrequently during the life of a company.

stock split a pro-rata distribution of new shares to existing stockholders that is not associated with any change in the assets held by the firm; stock splits involve larger increases in the number of shares than stock dividends

An example of a stock split is the two-for-one stock split that Comcast Corporation announced on January 26, 2017. In this stock split, each Comcast stockholder received one additional share for each share that he or she owned on February 17, 2017.

As with a stock dividend, nothing substantial changes when a stock split takes place. A stockholder might own twice as many shares after the split, but because the split does not change the nature of the company's assets, those shares represent the same proportional ownership in the company as the original shares. In the Comcast example, the prices per share at the close of trading on Friday February 17 and Monday February 21, the next trading day, were $75.32 and $37.89, respectively. This 49.7 percent [($37.89 – $75.32)/$75.32 = –0.497, or –49.7 percent] price decline was almost equal to the 50 percent decline that you would expect from a two-for-one stock split.[11] The number of shares doubled, while the value of the expected cash flows against which stockholders had claims remained largely unchanged.

[9]Fractional shares are generally made up for by a small cash payment.

[10]Note that for accounting purposes, a stock split and a stock dividend are treated differently. From a finance point of view, however, they are similar events.

[11]If nothing else happened, and the split had none of the effects discussed in the following section, we would expect the Comcast stock price to drop by exactly 50 percent. However, changes in market conditions and other circumstances at the firm, as well as possible effects of the split on the attractiveness of Comcast's stock, apparently combined to cause a price decline of slightly less than 50 percent.

Reasons for Stock Dividends and Splits

At this point, you might be asking why companies pay stock dividends or split their stock. The most often cited reason is known as the *trading range* argument. This argument proposes that successful companies use stock dividends or stock splits to make their shares more attractive to investors. Why would stock dividends or splits have this effect? Suppose the price of the stock of a successful company was allowed to continue to increase over a long time. Eventually, few investors would be able to afford to purchase a *round lot* of 100 shares. This, in turn, could affect the company's stock price.

To understand this argument, you must know that it has historically been more expensive for investors to purchase *odd lots*, which consist of less than 100 shares, than round lots, which are multiples of 100 shares. Odd lots are less liquid than round lots because more investors want to buy round lots. Furthermore, it is relatively expensive for companies to service odd-lot owners. (Consider, for example, the cost per share of sending stockholders annual reports and prospectuses or writing and mailing quarterly dividend checks.) Because of these disadvantages, investors tend to be less than enthusiastic about purchasing odd lots of less than 100 shares and managers prefer that they do not. According to the trading range argument, when buying a round lot becomes too expensive, investors might avoid buying the stock at all. Stock dividends and splits offer ways to bring the price of the stock down to the appropriate "trading range."

Although the trading range argument may be appealing to some, researchers have found little support for it. After a stock split, the stock's dollar trading volume does not appear to be higher than it was before the split. Also, the transaction costs argument no longer carries much weight, as there is now little difference in the costs of purchasing round lots and odd lots.

In fact, shares of some companies trade at per-share prices that are far above what is typically thought of as a *normal* trading range. The most famous of these companies is Berkshire Hathaway, Inc. Its class A shares were trading for $250,660 per share on March 27, 2017, with no apparent negative effects.[12]

One real benefit of stock splits is that they can send a positive signal to investors about management's outlook for the future. This, in turn, can lead to a higher stock price. After all, management is unlikely to want to split the stock of a company two-for-one or three-for-one if it expects the stock price to decline. It is only likely to split the stock when it is confident that the stock's current market price is not too high. A number of research studies have reported evidence indicating that investors tend to interpret stock splits as good news.[13]

Companies occasionally do *reverse* stock splits, in which case the number of shares owned by each stockholder is reduced. For example, in a 1-for-10 reverse split, a stockholder receives one share in exchange for each ten shares he or she owned before. If you owned 1,000 shares of the stock of such a company, you would have only 100 (1,000/10 = 100) shares after the reverse stock split.

Reverse stock splits may be undertaken to satisfy exchange requirements. For example, the New York Stock Exchange generally requires listed shares to trade for more than $5, and the NASDAQ requires shares to trade for at least $1. Being removed from the NYSE or NAS DAQ can dramatically reduce the liquidity of the company's stock and harm management's ability to raise capital in the future. A reverse stock split can help avoid these negative effects by keeping the per-share price above the required thresholds.

Before You Go On

1. What is a stock dividend?
2. How does a stock dividend differ from a stock split?
3. How does a stock dividend differ from other types of dividends?

[12]In 1996, Berkshire Hathaway issued a second class of stock, which was trading at $167.42 on March 27, 2017, but which had no voting rights. Until 2010, when these shares were split 50-to-1, even they were trading for as much as $4,500 per share.

[13]For an example of such a study, see R. M. Conroy and R. S. Harris, "Stock Splits and Information: The Role of Share Price," *Financial Management* 28 (Autumn 1999), 28–40.

17.5 Setting a Dividend Payout

LEARNING OBJECTIVE

5. Describe factors that managers consider when setting the dividend payouts for their firms.

An important question that you may be asking yourself is exactly how managers set the dividend payouts for their firms. In this section, we discuss the results from two important surveys. These surveys deal with how managers select their dividend payouts and what practical considerations managers must balance when they choose a dividend payout.

What Managers Tell Us

The best known survey of dividend decisions was published in 1956, more than 60 years ago, by John Lintner.[14] The survey asked managers at 28 industrial firms how they set their firms' dividend payouts. The key conclusions from the Lintner study are as follows:

1. Firms tend to have long-term target payout ratios.
2. Dividend changes follow shifts in long-term sustainable earnings.
3. Managers focus more on dividend changes than on the level (dollar amount) of the dividend.
4. Managers are reluctant to make dividend changes that might have to be reversed.

These results are consistent with the idea that managers tend to use dividends to distribute excess earnings and that they are concerned about unnecessarily surprising investors with bad news.

A more recent study, published in 2005, updates Lintner's findings.[15] The authors conducted a survey of 384 financial executives and personally interviewed 23 other managers. They found that managers continue to be concerned about surprising investors with bad news. Indeed, maintaining level dividend payouts is as important to executives as the investment decisions they make. The authors also found, as Lintner did, that the expected stability of future earnings affects dividend decisions. However, the link between earnings and dividends is weaker today than when Lintner conducted his survey.

In response to the increased use of stock repurchases, the authors of the 2005 study asked managers about their views on repurchases. They found that rather than setting a target level for repurchases, managers tend to repurchase shares using cash that is left over after investment spending. In addition, many managers prefer repurchases because repurchase programs are more flexible than dividend programs and because they can be used to time the market by repurchasing shares when management considers a company's stock price too low. Finally, the managers who were interviewed appeared to believe that institutional investors do not prefer dividends over repurchases or vice versa. In other words, the choice between these two methods of distributing value has little effect on who owns the company's stock.

Practical Considerations in Setting a Dividend Payout

In this chapter, we have discussed a wide range of factors that enter into managers' decisions regarding the selection of their firms' dividend payouts. While the details are important, it is

[14]J. Lintner, "Distribution of Incomes of Corporations among Dividends, Retained Earnings, and Taxes," *American Economic Review* 46 (1956), 97–113.

[15]A. Brav, J. R. Graham, C. R. Harvey, and R. Michaely, "Payout Policy in the 21st Century," *Journal of Financial Economics* 77 (2005), 483–527.

easy to get caught up in them and to lose sight of the big picture. A company's dividend payout decision is largely about how the excess value in a company is distributed to its stockholders. Central to choosing this payout is the question of how much value should be distributed. It is extremely important that managers choose their firms' dividend payouts in a way that enables them to continue to make the investments necessary for the firm to compete in its product markets. With this in mind, managers should consider several practical questions when selecting a dividend payout, including the following:

1. Over the long term, how much does the company's level of earnings (cash flows from operations) exceed its investment requirements? How certain is this level?
2. Does the firm have enough financial reserves to maintain dividend payouts in periods when earnings are down or investment requirements are up?
3. Does the firm have sufficient financial flexibility to maintain dividends if unforeseen circumstances wipe out its financial reserves when earnings are down?
4. Can the firm quickly raise equity capital if necessary?
5. If the company chooses to finance dividends by selling equity, will changes in the number of stockholders have implications for control of the company?

Before You Go On

1. How are dividend payouts affected by expected earnings?
2. What did the 2005 study conclude about how managers view stock repurchases?
3. List three practical considerations managers should take into account when setting a dividend payout.

Summary of Learning Objectives

1 Explain what a dividend is, and describe the different types of dividends and the dividend payment process. Calculate the expected change in a stock's price around an ex-dividend date.

A dividend is something of value that is distributed to a firm's stockholders on a pro-rata basis—that is, in proportion to the percentage of the firm's shares that they own. There are four types of dividends: (1) regular cash dividends, (2) extra dividends, (3) special dividends, and (4) liquidating dividends. Regular cash dividends are the cash dividends that firms pay on a regular basis (typically quarterly). Extra dividends are paid, often at the same time as a regular cash dividend, when a firm wants to distribute additional cash to its stockholders. Special dividends are one-time payments that are used to distribute large amounts of cash. A liquidating dividend is the dividend that is paid when a company goes out of business and is liquidated.

The dividend payment process begins with a vote by the board of directors to pay a dividend. This vote is followed by public announcement of the dividend on the declaration date. On the ex-dividend date, the shares begin trading without the right to receive the dividend. The record date, which follows the ex-dividend date by two days, is the date on which an investor must be a stockholder of record in order to receive the dividend. Finally, the payable date is the date on which the dividend is paid.

Learning by Doing Application 17.1 shows how to calculate the expected change in a stock's price around the ex-dividend date.

2 Explain what a stock repurchase is and how companies repurchase their stock. Calculate how taxes affect the after-tax proceeds that a stockholder receives from a dividend and from a stock repurchase.

A stock repurchase is a transaction in which a company purchases some of its own shares from stockholders. Like dividends, stock repurchases are used to distribute value to stockholders. The three ways in which stock is repurchased are (1) open-market repurchases, (2) tender offers, and (3) targeted stock repurchases. With open-market repurchases, the company purchases stock on the open market, just like any investor does. A tender offer is an open offer by a company to purchase shares. Finally, targeted stock repurchases are used to purchase shares from specific stockholders.

The calculation of the after-tax proceeds that a stockholder receives is illustrated in the text and in Learning by Doing Application 17.2.

3 Discuss the benefits and costs associated with dividend payments and compare the relative advantages and disadvantages of dividends and stock repurchases.

The potential benefits from paying dividends include (1) attracting investors who prefer dividends, (2) sending a positive signal to the market concerning the company's prospects, (3) helping to provide managers with incentives to manage the company more efficiently, and (4) helping to manage the company's capital structure. One cost of dividends is the fact that a stockholder must take a dividend, and pay taxes on the dividend, whether or not he or she wants the dividend. Stockholders who want to reinvest the dividend in the company must, unless there is a dividend reinvestment program (DRIP), pay brokerage fees to reinvest the money. Finally, paying a dividend can increase a company's leverage and thereby increase its cost of debt.

With a stock repurchase program, investors can choose whether they want to sell their shares back to the company. Stock repurchases also receive more favorable tax treatment. From management's point of view, stock repurchase programs offer more flexibility than dividends and can have less of an effect on the company's stock price. One disadvantage of stock repurchases involves an ethical issue: Managers have better information than others about the prospects of their companies, and a stock repurchase can enable them to take advantage of this information in a way that benefits the remaining stockholders at the expense of the selling stockholders.

4 Define stock dividends and stock splits and explain how they differ from other types of dividends and from stock repurchases.

Stock dividends involve the pro-rata distribution of additional shares in a company to its stockholders. Stock splits are much like stock dividends but involve larger distributions of shares than stock dividends. Stock dividends and stock splits differ from other types of dividends because they do not involve the distribution of value to stockholders. The total value of each stockholder's shares is largely the same after a stock dividend or stock split as it was before the distribution. Since they do not involve the distribution of value, stock dividends are not really dividends at all.

5 Describe factors that managers consider when setting the dividend payouts for their firms.

A company's dividend payout decision is largely about how excess value in the company is distributed to its stockholders. Setting the payout depends on several factors: the expected level and certainty of the firm's future profitability, the firm's future investment requirements, the firm's financial reserves and financial flexibility, the firm's ability to raise capital quickly if necessary, and the control implications of financing dividends by selling equity.

Self-Study Problems

17.1 You would like to own a common stock that has a record date of Friday, September 8, 2017. What is the last date that you can purchase the stock and still receive the dividend?

17.2 You believe that the average investor is subject to a 20 percent tax rate on dividend payments. If a firm is going to pay a $0.30 dividend, by what amount would you expect the stock price to drop on the ex-dividend date?

17.3 Management of the Veil Acts Company just announced that instead of a regular dividend this quarter, the company will repurchase shares using the same amount of cash that would have been paid in the suspended dividend. Should this be a positive or negative signal from the firm?

17.4 Management of the Bernie Rubbel Company has just declared a three-for-one stock split. If you own 12,000 shares before the split, how many shares will you own after the split? What if it were a one-for-three reverse stock split?

17.5 Two publicly traded companies in the same industry are similar in all respects except one. Whereas Publicks has issued debt in the public markets, Privicks has never borrowed from any public source. In fact, Privicks always uses private bank debt for its borrowing. Which firm is likely to have a more aggressive regular dividend payout? Explain.

Solutions to Self-Study Problems

17.1 The ex-dividend date is the first day that the stock will be trading without the rights to the dividend, and that occurs two days before the record date, or on Wednesday, September 6, 2017. Therefore, the last day that you can purchase the stock and still receive the dividend will be the day before the ex-dividend date, or Tuesday, September 5, 2017.

17.2 If the tax rate of the average investor is reflected in the stock price change, we would expect investors to receive 80 percent (1.0 – 0.20 = 0.80, or 80 percent) of the dividend after paying taxes. This implies a $0.24 ($0.80 \times \$0.30 = \$0.24$) drop in the stock price of the firm on the ex-dividend date.

17.3 Veiled Acts has replaced a commitment to distribute cash with a stated intention to distribute cash that does not have to be acted on. The signal would be negative if the announcement was interpreted to suggest that management is concerned about the level of cash flows from operations this quarter.

17.4 You will own three shares of Bernie Rubbel for every one share that you currently own. Therefore, you will own $3 \times 12{,}000$ shares = 36,000 shares of the company. In the case of the reverse split, you will own $1/3 \times 12{,}000$ shares = 4,000 shares of the company.

17.5 If all other characteristics of the two companies are the same, then Publicks could be expected to have a more aggressive dividend payout. Since Publicks has issued debt in the past, while Privicks has not, Publicks is likely to have greater access to the capital markets than Privicks. Firms with greater access to capital markets can be more aggressive in their dividend payouts to the extent that they can raise capital more easily (cheaply) if necessary.

WileyPLUS

Questions and Problems, Solution Walkthrough Videos, Learning by Doing Tutorials, and additional study tools and resources are available in WileyPLUS.

Discussion Questions

17.1 Suppose that you live in a country where it takes 10 days to settle a stock purchase. By how many days will the ex-dividend date precede the record date?

17.2 The price of a share of stock is $15.00 on Tuesday, November 14, 2017. The record date for a $0.50 dividend is Friday, November 17, 2017. If there are no taxes on dividends, what would you expect the price of a share to be on each day from November 14 through 17 if no other information relevant to the price of the shares becomes public?

17.3 You find that you are the only investor in a particular stock who is subject to a 15 percent tax rate on dividends (all other investors are subject to a 5 percent tax rate on dividends). Is there greater value to you in holding the stock beyond the ex-dividend date or selling the stock and then repurchasing it on or after the ex-dividend date? Assume that the stock is currently selling for $10.00 per share and the dividend will be $0.25 per share.

17.4 Discuss why the dividend payment process is so much simpler for private companies than for public companies.

17.5 You are the CEO of a firm that appears to be the target of a hostile takeover attempt. Thibeaux Piques has been accumulating the shares of your stock and now holds a substantial percentage of the outstanding shares. You would like to purchase the shares that he owns. What method of stock repurchase will you choose?

17.6 You have accumulated stock in a firm that does not pay cash dividends. You have read that, according to Modigliani and Miller, you can create a "homemade" dividend should you require cash. Discuss why this choice may not be very good for the overall value of your position.

17.7 You have just read a press release in which a firm claims that it will be able to generate a higher level of cash flows for its investors going forward. Justify the choice of a dividend payout that could credibly convey that information to the market.

17.8 Some people argue that a high tax rate on dividends creates incentives for managers to go about their business without credibly convincing investors that the firm is doing well, even when it is. Discuss why this may be true.

17.9 Fred Flightstone Mining Co. management does not like to pay cash dividends due to the volatility of the company's cash flows. Management has found, however, that when the company does not pay dividends, its stock price becomes too high for individual investors to afford round lots. What course of action could management take to get the stock price down without dissipating firm value for stockholders?

17.10 The Lintner study found that firms are reluctant to make dividend changes that might have to be reversed. Discuss the rationale for that behavior.

Questions and Problems

Excel *Excel templates and resources available in* **WileyPLUS**

Basic

17.1 **Dividends:** The Poseidon Shipping Company has paid a $0.25 dividend per quarter for the past three years. Poseidon just lowered its declared dividend to $0.20 for the next dividend payment. Discuss what this new information might convey concerning Poseidon management's belief about the future of the company.

17.2 **Dividends:** Marx Political Consultants management has decided to discontinue all of the firm's business operations. The firm has total debt of $7 million, and the liquidation value of its assets is $10 million. If the book value of the firm's equity is $5 million, then what will be the amount of the liquidating dividend when the firm liquidates all of its assets?

17.3 **Dividends:** Place the following in the proper chronological order, and describe the purpose of each: ex-dividend date, record date, payment date, and declaration date.

17.4 **Dividends and firm value:** Explain how the issuance of new securities by a firm can produce useful information about the issuing firm. How can this information make the shares of the firm more valuable, even if it only confirms existing information about the firm?

17.5 **Dividends:** Explain why holders of a firm's debt should insist on a covenant that restricts the amount of cash dividends the firm pays.

17.6 **Stock splits and stock dividends:** Explain why managers of firms might prefer that their firms' shares trade in a moderate per-share price range rather than in a high per-share price range. How do managers of firms keep their shares trading in a moderate price range?

17.7 **Dividends:** Scintilla, Inc., stock is trading for $10.00 per share on the day before the ex-dividend date. If the dividend is $0.25 and there are no taxes, what should the price of the shares be on the ex-dividend date?

17.8 **Dividends:** A company's management announces a $1.00 per share dividend payment. Assuming all investors are subject to a 15 percent tax rate on dividends, how much should the company's share price drop on the ex-dividend date?

Intermediate

17.9 **Dividends and firm value:** Explain how a stock repurchase is different from a dividend payment.

17.10 **Dividends and firm value:** You have just encountered two identical firms with identical investment opportunities, as well as the ability to fund these opportunities. One of the firms has just announced that it will pay a dividend, while the other has continued to pay no dividend. Which of the two firms is worth more? Explain.

17.11 **Dividends and firm value:** Explain what the introduction of transaction costs does to the Modigliani and Miller assumption that dividends are irrelevant. Start with a firm that pays dividends to investors that do not want to receive dividend payments. Do not consider taxes.

17.12 **Dividends and firm value:** CashCo increased its cash dividend each quarter for the past eight quarters. While this may signal that the firm is financially very healthy, what else could we conclude from these actions?

17.13 **Dividends and firm value:** In 2013 the maximum tax rate on dividends increased from 15 percent to 23.8 percent. How would you expect this increase to affect the prices of dividend-paying stocks versus those of nondividend-paying stocks?

17.14 **Dividends:** Undecided Corp. has excess cash on hand right now, although management is not sure about the level of cash flows going forward. If management would like to put cash in stockholders' hands, what kind of dividend should the firm pay, and why?

17.15 **Dividends and firm value:** A firm can deliver a negative signal to stockholders by increasing the level of dividends or by reducing the level of dividends. Explain why this is true.

17.16 **Dividends and firm value:** A commentator on a financial talk show on TV says that "On average, firms pay out too little to stockholders. This is why stock prices go up with dividend increases and down with dividend decreases." Is the commentator right?

17.17 **Dividends and firm value:** You own shares in a firm that has extra cash on hand to distribute to stockholders. You do not want the cash. What course of action would you prefer the firm take?

17.18 **Dividends and firm value:** Stock repurchases, once announced, do not actually have to occur in total or in part. From a signaling perspective, why would a special dividend be better than a stock repurchase?

17.19 **Dividends and firm value:** Consider a firm that repurchases shares from its stockholders in the open market, and explain why this action might be detrimental to the stockholders from whom the firm buys shares.

17.20 **Dividends and firm value:** You read that a number of public companies have been financing their dividend payments in recent years entirely through equity issues. A colleague of yours argues that this only increases taxes paid by individual stockholders and boosts underwriting and other transactions costs for the company. He says that such a policy cannot make sense. What do you say?

17.21 **Stock repurchases:** Briefly discuss the methods available for a firm to repurchase its shares and explain why you might expect the stock price reaction to the announcement of each of these methods to differ.

17.22 **Stock repurchases:** What is an advantage of a Dutch auction over a fixed-price tender offer?

Advanced

17.23 In the early 1990s, the amount of time that elapsed between purchasing a stock and actually obtaining that stock was five business days. This period was known as the settlement period. The settlement period for stock purchases is now two business days. Describe what should have happened to the number of days between the ex-dividend date and the record date at the time of this change.

17.24 Dividend reinvestment programs (DRIPs) sometimes sell shares at a discount to stockholders who reinvest their dividends through such plans. Your boss tells you that such plans are just a scheme to transfer wealth from nonparticipating to participating stockholders and that they should be stopped. Do you agree? Why or why not?

17.25 WeAreProfits, Inc., has not issued any new debt securities in 10 years. It will begin paying cash dividends to its stockholders for the first time next year. Explain how a dividend might help the firm get closer to its optimal capital structure of 50 percent debt and 50 percent equity.

17.26 Shadows, Inc., had shares outstanding that were valued at $120 per share before a two-for-one stock split. After the stock split, the shares were valued at $62 per share. If we accept that the firm's financial maneuver did not create any new value, then why might the market value of the shares increase?

17.27 Saguaro Company currently has 30,000 shares outstanding. Each share has a market value of $20. If the firm pays $5 per share in dividends, what will each share be worth after the dividend payment? Ignore taxes.

17.28 Cholla Company currently has 30,000 shares outstanding. Each share has a market value of $20. If the firm repurchases $150,000 worth of shares, then what will be the value of each share outstanding after the repurchase? Ignore taxes.

17.29 You purchased 1,000 shares of Koogal stock five years ago for $30 per share. Today Koogal is repurchasing your shares through a fixed-price tender offer for $80 per share. What are the after-tax proceeds to you if only your capital gain is taxed at a 15 percent rate?

17.30 You purchased 1,000 shares of Zebulon Copper Co. five years ago for $50 per share. Today Zebulon management is trying to decide whether to repurchase shares for $70 per share through a fixed-price tender offer or pay a $70 cash dividend per share. If capital gains are taxed at a 15 percent rate, then at what rate must dividends be taxed for you to be indifferent between receiving the dividend and selling your shares back to Zebulon?

17.31 Llama Wool Company management is doing some financial planning for the coming year. Llama plans to raise $10,000 in new equity this year and wants to pay a dividend to stockholders of $30,000. The firm must pay $20,000 of interest during the year and will also pay down principal on its debt obligations by $10,000. Its capital budgeting plan calls for $100,000 of capital expenditures during the year. Given the above information, how much cash must be provided from operations for the firm to meet its plan?

17.32 You are the chief financial officer (CFO) of a large publicly traded company. You would like to convey positive information about the firm to the market. If you agree with the conclusions from the Lintner study, will you keep paying your currently high dividend or raise that dividend by a small amount? Explain.

17.33 You are the CFO of a public company that advises distressed companies about how to manage their businesses. Your company has been performing extremely well. In fact, it has earned so much money that the increase in its retained earnings has resulted in a decline in the firm's debt to total capital ratio from 30 percent to 15 percent. Much of the retained earnings is sitting in a cash account because your firm does not need the money to fund investments. You would like to increase the debt-to-total capital ratio to 30 percent, which you view as optimal for your firm. How would you recommend doing this if you want to complete the adjustment as soon as possible?

Sample Test Problems

17.1 Shares of Convoy West, Inc. are trading for $55.45 on the day before the ex-dividend date. If the quarterly dividend is $0.16 per share and there are no taxes, how will the share price change on the ex-dividend date?

17.2 Three years ago, you purchased 4,000 shares of Metwa Inc. for $17 per share. Today Metwa is repurchasing its shares through a fixed-price tender offer at a price of $45 per share. What are the after-tax proceeds that you will receive if capital gains are taxed at a rate of 20 percent?

17.3 Why does an ongoing stock repurchase program offer management greater flexibility in distributing value to stockholders than a regular cash dividend?

17.4 Why would management of a company undertake a reverse stock split?

17.5 Mastercard, Inc., completed a ten-for-one stock split on January 22, 2014. Immediately before the stock split there were 120.38 million shares outstanding at a price of $826.00 per share. After the split how many shares were outstanding, and at what price would you expect them trade? Did the stock split cause any substantial change for Mastercard or the investors? Why would Mastercard management choose to split the company's stock?

CHAPTER 18

Business Formation, Growth, and Valuation

Daniel Schweinert/Shutterstock

LEARNING OBJECTIVES

1. Explain why the choice of organizational form is important, and describe two financial considerations that are especially important in starting a business.
2. Describe the key components of a business plan and explain what a business plan is used for.
3. Explain the three general approaches to valuation and value a business using common business valuation approaches.
4. Explain how valuations can differ between public and private companies and between young and mature companies, and discuss the importance of control and key person considerations in valuation.

Clinc, an artificial intelligence (A.I.) start-up based in Ann Arbor, Michigan, closed on a $6.3 million round of venture capital financing in mid-February 2017. Drive Capital, Hyde Park Venture Partners, Cahoots Holdings, and Stuart Porter were among the group of investors that provided Clinc with this first round of financing.

This financing closely followed important milestones in the introduction of Finie, an advanced voice-controlled A.I. platform for banking. In 2016, Clinc had signed a number of deals with financial institutions and Finie had won the "Best-of-Show" award at Finovate New York, a leading conference for financial technology companies and financial institutions. Prior to the February 2017 financing, Clinc had also developed a suite of A.I. engines, called Clinc Eco, which can be used to develop A.I. applications in other areas.

Raising venture capital financing required a great deal of careful management by Clinc's founders and managers, not only of the business but also of the fundraising activities. They had to prove the viability of their A.I. products in a highly technical and competitive market. Of course, Clinc would have never even been in a position to raise venture capital financing if its managers had not made good decisions early in the life of the company. They also had to put together a compelling story that would help them to convince investors that their products would stand out in a crowded field, that they could overcome obstacles to building and marketing A.I. and financial technology products, that there would be sufficient demand for their products, and that the Clinc team had the skills necessary to develop and market products that would earn attractive returns for investors.

This chapter discusses some financial aspects of forming, growing, and financing a new business. It also discusses, in detail, the methods used to value both small and large businesses. Business valuation concepts were certainly on the minds of Clinc's managers when they were raising capital and had to decide exactly how much of the company's equity they would have to sell to obtain the funds they needed to grow the business. These concepts are also on their minds every day as they make business decisions that create value for the company's investors.

Chapter Preview

In earlier chapters, we discussed how businesses are organized and how financial managers make long-term investment decisions, manage working capital, and finance the investments and activities of their businesses. In this chapter, we reexamine these concepts in the context of a discussion of business formation, growth, and valuation. The chapter provides an integrated perspective on how the decisions that financial managers make affect firm value.

We begin by considering the decision by an entrepreneur to start a business and the choice of how the business should be organized. The organizational form of a business affects many important financial decisions through its impact on the availability and cost of capital, the control of the business, the ability to attract and retain high-quality managers, the taxes that must be paid, and the agency problems that might arise in the business, among other factors. We then discuss financial considerations that are important to managers of young, rapidly growing firms.

Next we focus on the role that a carefully prepared business plan plays in raising capital for a young, rapidly growing business and in providing a road map of where the business is going for use in managerial decision making. The importance of a business plan cannot be understated. The act of preparing a business plan forces an entrepreneur to think carefully about the aspects of the business that are crucial to its success. This helps him or her better communicate to others what the prospects for the business are and to manage the business more effectively.

The last two sections of the chapter address business valuation concepts. These sections provide a broad overview of the business valuation approaches used by financial managers and describe how differences in the characteristics of companies affect valuation analyses. The impact of control considerations and key people on business valuations are also discussed.

18.1 Starting a Business

LEARNING OBJECTIVE

1. Explain why the choice of organizational form is important, and describe two financial considerations that are especially important in starting a business.

People start their own business for a wide variety of reasons. Some have an idea for a new product or service that they think will revolutionize an industry and make them rich. Others live in an area where there are no attractive employment opportunities for them, and starting a business is the only way to earn a living. Others simply want to be their own boss.

Weblink

To learn more about starting a business, see the U.S. Small Business Administration Web site at http://www.sba.gov/content/follow-these-steps-starting-business.

Regardless of their motives, all of these people face the decision of whether to start their own business or purchase an already established business. Starting your own business can provide greater potential rewards but is inherently more risky than buying and growing a business that someone else has already built. The founder of a company must start from scratch by choosing the products to sell, the markets to sell them in, and the best strategy for selling them. He or she must then raise the money necessary to develop the products, acquire the necessary assets, and hire the right people. Of course, as the business is being built, the founder must also manage the day-to-day operations to ensure that his or her overall plan is being implemented as well as possible.

In this section, we discuss factors that entrepreneurs consider when deciding to launch a new business, factors that affect the form of organization that they choose, and financial considerations associated with starting a business.

Making the Decision to Proceed

Hundreds of thousands of new businesses are started in the United States each year, but many do not succeed. The U.S. Department of Labor Bureau of Labor Statistics estimates that 679,072 new firms were formed in 2015. However, statistical analyses of earlier business formations suggest that only about 53 percent of these firms will still be in business in 2020 (see https://www.bls.gov/bdm/entrepreneurship/entrepreneurship.htm). Among those that do survive, only a few will provide high returns to their founders.

Businesses fail for many reasons. Some fail because consumers do not accept their products. Others fail because the founder pursues a poorly thought-out strategy or does not have the management skills to properly execute a good strategy. Another common reason for new business failures is that founders underestimate how much money it will take to get their businesses up and running. For example, they underestimate the amount of money that will be needed to cover cash outflows until cash inflows from sales are large enough to do so. These founders fail to ensure that they have enough money to give the business a fighting chance.

The fact that many new businesses fail does not mean that you should not start a business if you believe that you have a good idea. It simply means that you should carefully think through your new business idea before you make the decision to proceed. Not thinking carefully about your idea can lead you to pursue a poor strategy, fail to realize that you might need help in executing your strategy, or underestimate how much money you will need.

It is beyond the scope of this book to tell you how to properly evaluate a business idea, a strategy for pursuing it, or your management abilities. Fortunately, a lot has been written on these topics by others. For example, you can find useful readings on these topics on the U.S. Small Business Administration Web site (see the earlier margin reference).

The only advice that we can give you in these areas is to be careful and realistic in assessing your opportunities. On the one hand, don't jump into a business without careful thought. On the other hand, don't overanalyze opportunities to the point where you are just convincing yourself not to proceed. Taking calculated risks is part of business. The important thing to remember is that the risks you take should be "calculated." Also, don't think that failure will ruin your chances of ultimately achieving business success. Many successful entrepreneurs and executives have failed more than once in their careers. Successful people learn from both their failures and their successes.

Choosing the Right Organizational Form

Once you have made the decision to start a business, you must decide what form of organization will work best. Chapter 1 discussed some of the more common basic forms of business organization—sole proprietorships, partnerships, and corporations—and some of their advantages and disadvantages. In that discussion, you saw that there are variations in the basic forms of business organization. For example, Chapter 1 describes general, limited, and limited liability partnerships. There are also a number of different types of corporations, as well as hybrids between partnerships and corporations. The reason that so many different forms of organization exist is that the needs of businesses vary considerably. The wide range of choices has made the decision of how to organize a business so complex that many people don't even try to make this decision without the advice of an attorney. In this section, we extend the discussion begun in Chapter 1 by focusing, from a financial perspective, on factors that affect the choice of the appropriate organizational form for a new business.

As you can see in **Exhibit 18.1**, which is the same as Exhibit 1.3, a sole proprietorship is the least expensive type of business to start. To start a sole proprietorship, all you have to do is to obtain the business licenses required by your local and state governments. Partnerships are more costly to form because the partners must hire an attorney to draw up and maintain the

EXHIBIT 18.1 Characteristics of Different Forms of Business Organization

Choosing the appropriate form of business organization is an important step in starting a business. This exhibit compares key characteristics of the most popular forms of business organization in the United States.

	Sole Proprietorship	Partnership		Corporation		Limited Liability Partnership (LLP) or Company (LLC)
		General	Limited	S-Corp.	C-Corp.	
Cost to establish	Inexpensive	More costly	More costly	More costly	More costly	More costly
Life of entity	Limited	Flexible	Flexible	Indefinite	Indefinite	Flexible
Control by founder over business decisions	Complete	Shared	Shared	Depends on ownership	Depends on ownership	Shared
Access to capital	Very limited	Limited	Less limited	Less limited	Excellent	Less limited
Cost to transfer ownership	High	High	High	High	Can be low	High
Separation of management and investment	No	No	Yes	Yes	Yes	Yes
Potential owner/manager conflicts	No	No	Some	Potentially high	Potentially high	Some
Ability to provide incentives to attract and retain high-quality employees	Limited	Good	Good	Good	Good	Good
Liability of owners	Unlimited	Unlimited	Unlimited for general partner	Limited	Limited	Limited
Tax treatment of income	Flow-through	Flow-through	Flow-through	Flow-through	Double tax	As elected
Tax deductibility of owner benefits	Limited	Limited	Limited	Limited	Limited	Limited

partnership agreement, which specifies the nature of the relationships between the partners. Forming a corporation also requires hiring an attorney to draft a document that spells out things such as how many shares can be issued, what voting rights the stockholders will have, and who the board members are. Over the life of a successful business, these out-of-pocket costs are not very important. However, to a cash-strapped entrepreneur, they can seem substantial.

Because the life of a sole proprietorship is limited to the life of the proprietor, it ceases to exist when the proprietor gets out of the business. In contrast, the lives of all other forms of organization can be made independent of the life of the founder. Partnership agreements, including the corresponding agreement in an LLC, can be amended to allow for the business to continue when the founders leave. Corporations, which are legal persons under state law, automatically have an indefinite life. You will notice that Exhibit 18.1 indicates that the lives of partnerships and LLCs are flexible. This is because, while partnership and LLC agreements can be written so that their lives are indefinite, they can also be written with a fixed life in mind. For example, private equity and venture capital limited partnerships and LLCs are typically structured so that they last only 10 years.

The ability to make the life of a business independent of that of the founder increases the liquidity of the ownership interests, making it easier for the business to raise capital or for investors to sell their interests at an attractive price. Since a sole proprietorship has no ownership interest that can be sold directly, the proprietor can sell only the assets of the business. There is no way to sell a partial ownership interest.

Even with partnerships and corporations, it can be quite expensive to raise capital for the business or for an investor to sell an ownership interest. Common restrictions in partnership and LLC agreements and the need to amend the partnership and LLC documents to reflect a change in ownership can make transferring ownership time consuming and costly. Selling shares in a corporation can be costly if that corporation is not publicly traded.

Making sure that a new business has access to enough capital is always an important concern for an entrepreneur. By their nature, sole proprietorships must rely on equity contributions from the proprietor and debt or lease financing. In contrast, partnerships can turn to all of the partners for additional capital, and corporations can sell shares to both insiders and outsiders. Limited partnerships and LLCs are less constrained than general partnerships because they can raise money from limited partners or from "members," as outside investors in LLCs are called, who are not directly involved in running the business. C-corporations can have a virtually unlimited number of potential stockholders.

The downside of being able to raise equity capital from other people is the need to share control. An entrepreneur who chooses a form of organization other than a sole proprietorship, and who does not retain 100 percent ownership, must give up some control. Of course, the entrepreneur may have little choice in this trade-off if the business requires more equity capital than he or she can personally provide.

It is important to recognize that investors, such as angel investors and venture capitalists, who are especially important sources of capital for young, rapidly growing firms, tend to prefer to only invest in C-corporations. Since venture capitalists do not typically want to become full operating partners in the businesses in which they invest and because the cost of transferring ownership interests can be much lower for C-corporations, they will generally invest only in businesses that are organized this way.

Chapter 1 discussed the concept of separation of ownership and control and how it is related to agency problems. This separation has benefits as well as costs. While it is true that agency problems can arise when owners delegate decision-making authority to professional managers, these costs might be smaller than the benefits. Specifically, the ability to separate ownership from management control enables a firm to raise capital from investors who have no interest in being directly involved in the business. This can greatly increase the number of potential investors. Another benefit is that an entrepreneur can turn over day-to-day control of a business to a more capable manager, become less involved in the business, and yet continue to benefit from its successes as an investor.

Another key concern of all entrepreneurs is being able to attract and retain high-quality employees. Being able to offer a current or potential employee an ownership interest in the business can help greatly in retention and recruiting. The inability to offer ownership interests is a major disadvantage of sole proprietorships.

Financial liabilities associated with a business are also an important consideration when choosing the form for a business. On this dimension, sole proprietorships, general partnerships, and limited partnerships are at a disadvantage. Sole proprietors and general partners face the possibility that their personal assets can be taken from them to satisfy claims on their businesses. In contrast, the liabilities of investors in corporations (both S-corporations and C-corporations) and LLPs and LLCs are limited to the money that they have invested in the business.

The choice of organizational form also affects how the business's operating profits will be taxed. More taxes mean that the owners get less. In each of the organizational forms in Exhibit 18.1, with the exception of C-corporations, all profits normally flow through to the owners in proportion to their ownership interests.[1] These owners pay taxes on the business profits when they file their personal tax returns. Profits earned in C-corporations are taxed at the corporate tax rate, and the after-tax profits are taxed a second time when they are distributed to stockholders in the form of dividends. On the bright side, because profits are taxed in the corporation, certain benefits, such as health insurance, that are paid to stockholders who work in a C-corporation are tax deductible. These benefits are not generally deductible with the other forms of organization.

Financial Considerations

The most important financial concern of any entrepreneur is making sure that the business has access to enough money to be successful. Unlike a successful mature company, which can rely on cash flows from sales of other products to fund new product introductions, an entrepreneur must obtain funding from outside the firm. This makes it especially important for the entrepreneur to understand the cash requirements of the business.

The margin for error is small. If the entrepreneur miscalculates how much money is necessary, it may be too late to raise more money by the time this error is recognized. Raising external capital can be a time-consuming process and becomes increasingly difficult as a firm becomes more and more cash constrained. Outside investors are especially careful about investing in businesses that have run short of cash. The fact that the business has gotten into such

[1]The owners of an LLC can elect for the LLC to be taxed as a C-corporation.

a position can suggest that the business idea might not be viable or that the entrepreneur may not be the right person to build it, or both.

Two tools are particularly useful in understanding the cash requirements of a business and in estimating how much financing a new business will require: (1) the cash flow break-even analysis discussed in Chapter 12 and (2) the cash budget.

Cash Flow Break-Even

Recall that pretax operating cash flow (EBITDA) break-even analysis is used to compute the level of unit sales that is necessary to break even on operations from a pretax operating cash flow perspective. It is calculated using Equation 12.4:

$$\text{EBITDA Break-even} = \frac{\text{FC}}{\text{Price} - \text{Unit VC}}$$

where FC is the fixed costs associated with the business and Price − Unit VC is the per-unit contribution.

It is important for an entrepreneur to understand the concept of EBITDA break-even and how to calculate this point for each product a business produces. This calculation focuses the entrepreneur's attention on the importance of maximizing a product's per-unit contribution and minimizing overhead costs. It also provides a means of estimating how long it will take for a product to reach the break-even point and, therefore, how much money will be needed to launch a new product or business.

Although it might seem obvious that an entrepreneur should want to maximize the per-unit contribution of each product and minimize total fixed costs, entrepreneurs often lose sight of these objectives. An entrepreneur can get so caught up in developing the best possible product that he or she does not adequately consider how much customers are willing to pay for that product. For example, adding another feature to a word-processing program can be expensive, and consumers might not be willing to pay the additional cost if they are unlikely to use that feature. Of course, being too sensitive to the possibility of overinvesting in new product development can harm a business by causing it to lose its competitive advantage. An entrepreneur should always be looking for ways to maximize the per-unit contribution of the firm's products while maintaining the firm's competitive position.

Many entrepreneurs also lose sight of the importance of controlling fixed costs. For example, several firms with virtually no sales have spent well over a million dollars each for short advertisements during Super Bowl football games. Many such firms also spend a great deal of money on extravagant fringe benefits or things like team-building activities in which they take their entire product development staffs on week-long trips to vacation resorts. Although expenses such as these might help to increase employee productivity or encourage more creativity and hard work among the development staff, they also increase the number of units that a business must sell to break even. Unfortunately, some companies run out of money before they ever break even.

Cash Inflows and Outflows

Weblink

The Cash Flow Template, Excel spreadsheet #60 on the Web site maintained by Matt H. Evans, is an example of a comprehensive Excel model for forecasting monthly cash flows. See the spreadsheet at http://www.exinfm.com/free_spreadsheets.html.

The cash budget is also a very useful planning tool for entrepreneurs. It summarizes the cash flows into and out of a firm over a period of time. Cash budgets often present the inflows and outflows on a monthly basis but can be prepared for any period, including daily or weekly. Preparing a cash budget helps an entrepreneur better understand where money is coming from, where it is going, how much external financing is likely to be needed, and when the need is likely to arise. Understanding where the money is coming from and where it is going helps an entrepreneur maintain control of the company's finances. Knowing how much external financing is likely to be needed and when helps the entrepreneur plan fundraising efforts before it is too late.

To better understand how a cash budget can help an entrepreneur, let's consider an example. Suppose that it is March 1, 2018, and that you are planning to open a new restaurant called the Pizza Palace. You have saved $25,000, which you intend to invest in the business, and you have obtained a five-year loan for $50,000 at an APR of 8 percent (8 percent/12 months per year = 0.667 percent per month). The loan principal will be repaid in five equal installments of $10,000 at the end of each of the next five years. **Exhibit 18.2** presents a monthly cash budget for your restaurant investment.

EXHIBIT 18.2 **Pizza Palace Monthly Cash Budget for the Period March 2018 through February 2019[a]**

A monthly cash budget summarizes the cash that management expects to flow into and out of a business each month. At a minimum, it presents the cash inflows and outflows for each of the next 12 months and for the entire 12-month period. Monthly cash budgets can extend beyond 12 months.

Row	Mar.	Apr.	May	June	July	Aug.	Sept.	Oct.	Nov.	Dec.	Jan.	Feb.	Total
1. Beginning cash balance	$75,000	$ 6,097	$ 5,000	$ 5,000	$ 5,000	$ 5,000	$ 5,000	$ 6,497	$ 7,993	$ 9,490	$10,987	$12,483	
2. Cash receipts:													
3. Cash sales	3,000	12,000	15,000	20,000	25,000	30,000	35,000	35,000	35,000	35,000	35,000	35,000	$315,000
4. Collections from credit accounts	–	–	–	–	–	–	–	–	–	–	–	–	–
5. Investments by owner	–	9,457	9,103	6,553	4,004	1,253	–	–	–	–	–	353	30,723
6. Total cash receipts	$ 3,000	$21,457	$24,103	$26,553	$29,004	$31,253	$35,000	$35,000	$35,000	$35,000	$35,000	$35,353	$345,723
7. Total cash available	$78,000	$27,554	$29,103	$31,553	$34,004	$36,253	$40,000	$41,497	$42,993	$44,490	$45,987	$47,836	
Cash payments:													
8. Operations													
9. Food purchases	$ 1,200	$ 4,800	$ 6,000	$ 8,000	$10,000	$12,000	$14,000	$14,000	$14,000	$14,000	$14,000	$14,000	$126,000
10. Gross wages	10,800	10,800	10,800	10,800	10,800	10,800	10,800	10,800	10,800	10,800	10,800	10,800	129,600
11. Payroll expenses	1,620	1,620	1,620	1,620	1,620	1,620	1,620	1,620	1,620	1,620	1,620	1,620	19,440
12. Misc. supplies	500	500	500	500	500	500	500	500	500	500	500	500	6,000
13. Repairs and maintenance	150	600	750	1,000	1,250	1,500	1,750	1,750	1,750	1,750	1,750	1,750	15,750
14. Advertising	1,000	1,000	1,000	1,000	1,000	1,000	1,000	1,000	1,000	1,000	1,000	1,000	12,000
15. Accounting and legal	3,000	200	200	200	200	200	200	200	200	200	200	200	5,200
16. Rent	1,500	1,500	1,500	1,500	1,500	1,500	1,500	1,500	1,500	1,500	1,500	1,500	18,000
17. Telephone and utilities	1,000	1,200	1,400	1,600	1,800	1,800	1,800	1,800	1,800	1,800	1,800	1,800	19,600
18. Other expenses	–	–	–	–	–	–	–	–	–	–	–	–	–
19. Operations total	$20,770	$22,220	$23,770	$26,220	$28,670	$30,920	$33,170	$33,170	$33,170	$33,170	$33,170	$33,170	$351,590
Financing and investments:													
20. Interest payments	$ 333	$ 333	$ 333	$ 333	$ 333	$ 333	$ 333	$ 333	$ 333	$ 333	$ 333	$ 333	$ 4,000
21. Principal payments on loans	–	–	–	–	–	–	–	–	–	–	–	10,000	10,000
22. Capital expenditures	50,000	–	–	–	–	–	–	–	–	–	–	–	50,000
23. Start–up costs	800	–	–	–	–	–	–	–	–	–	–	–	800
24. Withdrawals by owner	–	–	–	–	–	–	–	–	–	–	–	–	–
25. Total cash payments	$71,903	$22,553	$24,103	$26,553	$29,003	$31,253	$33,503	$33,503	$33,503	$33,503	$33,503	$43,503	$416,390
26. Ending cash balance	$ 6,097	$ 5,000	$ 5,000	$ 5,000	$ 5,000	$ 5,000	$ 6,497	$ 7,993	$ 9,490	$10,987	$12,483	$ 4,333	

[a]Some totals do not appear to add up precisely because the actual values computed in the model are rounded to the nearest whole number for presentation in this exhibit.

The initial cash balance in row 1 of the March column of your budget equals the $75,000 that you have raised to finance the project. You estimate that it will take two weeks to actually open the restaurant and, knowing that you will have to build a customer base from scratch, you expect to have only $3,000 in sales during the first month. You do not anticipate providing any credit to your customers, so all of the proceeds from the sales will be received in cash. As shown in rows 8 through 25 of Exhibit 18.2, you expect cash operating expenses to total $20,770 and interest expense, capital expenditures, and start-up costs to be $333, $50,000, and $800, respectively, during March. With only $3,000 in cash inflows, these expenditures will reduce the cash balance by the end of March to only:

$$\$75{,}000 + \$3{,}000 - \$20{,}770 - \$333 - \$50{,}000 - \$800 = \$6{,}097$$

While the restaurant is expected to have a positive cash balance at the end of March, the cash balance will be negative by the end of April if no additional financing is obtained. You can see this by noting that the beginning cash balance of $6,097 plus the cash sales of $12,000 would provide a total of only $18,097 with which to pay $22,220 in operating expenses and $333 of interest. This would result in an ending cash balance of:[2]

$$\$6{,}097 + \$12{,}000 - \$22{,}220 - \$333 = -\$4{,}457$$

Since a restaurant cannot operate without at least some cash for the cash register, you will have to invest more than $4,457 in the business during the month of April. For example, if you decide that you want to maintain a cash balance of at least $5,000, you will have to invest an additional $4,457 + $5,000 = $9,457. This investment is shown in row 5 of the April column in Exhibit 18.2. In this example, the investment is treated as an equity investment by the owner rather than as additional debt. You can tell this by the fact that there is no change in the interest payments in row 20. However, we could easily have treated this amount as a loan instead.

Notice that the cash budget tells you that if the cash forecasts in your budget are correct, you will have to raise a total of:

$$\$9{,}457 + \$9{,}103 + \$6{,}553 + \$4{,}004 + \$1{,}253 = \$30{,}370$$

by the end of August to ensure that your restaurant's cash balance does not fall below $5,000. Knowing this at the beginning of March can be very helpful in planning your fundraising activities for the year.

You might also note that the cash budget indicates that $353 will have to be invested in February 2019. This is because the first principal payment on the debt is due at the end of that month. If you plan to maintain total debt of $50,000 in this business, you could cover this requirement by obtaining a new $10,000 loan, which you would use to make the debt principal payment.

We can also calculate the pretax operating cash flow break-even point for the Pizza Palace restaurant. If, for simplicity, we assume that the average customer spends $10 for pizza and a drink and that the only unit variable costs are those associated with the food, then we can calculate that the unit contribution will be $6 per customer when the business is up and running in September 2018. We know that the unit contribution is $6 because food purchases represent $14,000/$35,000 = 0.40, or 40 percent of cash sales. This leaves 60 percent of cash sales, or $6 per customer, to cover fixed costs. Knowing the unit contribution and assuming all costs other than those associated with food purchases are fixed, we can calculate the pretax operating cash flow break-even point as follows:

$$\text{EBITDA Break-even} = \frac{\text{FC}}{\text{Price} - \text{Unit VC}} = \frac{\$33{,}170 - \$14{,}000}{\$10 - \$4} = 3{,}195 \text{ customers}$$

In other words, your restaurant will have to serve at least 3,195 customers per month (approximately 107 per day) in order to break even on a cash flow basis once it is up and running.

[2]The actual result of the calculation shown here is −$4,456, rather than −$4,457. The $1 difference is due to rounding. The interest expense is actually $333.33 [(0.08/12) × $50,000 = $333.33] and the beginning cash balance is $6,096.67, which yields −$4,456.66.

We have simplified our example by assuming that the restaurant does not provide credit to customers or hold any material inventories of food, supplies, and so forth. However, we could have incorporated these characteristics into our cash budget using the working capital management concepts discussed in Chapter 14.

Decision Making Example 18.1 illustrates the use of a cash budget.

EXAMPLE 18.1 | Using a Cash Budget

DECISION MAKING

Situation It is January 1, and you have prepared the following cash budget for the next four months for your new business venture:

Monthly Cash Budget

	Jan.	Feb.	Mar.	Apr.	Total
Beginning cash balance	$ 0	($ 18,510)	($ 25,270)	($ 28,530)	
Cash receipts:					
Cash sales	2,500	5,000	12,000	20,000	$39,500
Investments by owner	–	–	–	–	–
Total cash receipts	$ 2,500	$ 5,000	$ 12,000	$ 20,000	$39,500
Total cash available	$ 2,500	($ 13,510)	($ 13,270)	($ 8,530)	
Cash payments:					
Operations					
Merchandise purchases	$ 1,250	$ 2,500	$ 6,000	$ 10,000	$19,750
Gross wages and payroll	5,760	5,760	5,760	5,760	23,040
Advertising	1,000	1,000	1,000	1,000	4,000
Rent	1,500	1,500	1,500	1,500	6,000
Other expenses	1,000	1,000	1,000	1,000	4,000
Operations total	$ 10,510	$ 11,760	$ 15,260	$ 19,260	$56,790
Financing and investments					
Capital expenditures	$ 10,000	–	–	–	$10,000
Start-up costs	500	–	–	–	500
Withdrawals by owner	–	–	–	–	–
Total cash payments	$ 21,010	$ 11,760	$ 15,260	$ 19,260	$67,290
Ending cash balance	($18,510)	($25,270)	($ 28,530)	($27,790)	

If you plan to finance the business entirely with equity, how much money should you invest now to ensure that there is at least $1,000 still in the business at the end of April? How much will you have to invest each month after April to maintain a $1,000 cash balance if the cash inflows and outflows in the following months look like those for April?

Decision Assuming that your cash forecast is correct, you should invest $28,790 today. This will cover the $27,790 cash shortfall reflected in the ending cash balance for April while leaving $1,000 in the business. The ending cash balance for April reflects the cumulative cash shortfall over the four-month period because the beginning cash balance for January has been set to zero. You will not have to invest any money after April because the cash inflows exceed the cash outflows in April, and this is not expected to change in the following months.

Before You Go On

1. What are three general reasons that new businesses fail?
2. How do financing considerations affect the choice of organizational form?
3. How does a cash budget help an entrepreneur?

18.2 The Role of the Business Plan

LEARNING OBJECTIVE

2. Describe the key components of a business plan and explain what a business plan is used for.

In our discussion of the cash budget, we assumed that any cash required by the business would come from the owner or from a loan. Unfortunately, financing a business is not always so simple. An important tool in financing a young, rapidly growing business—as well as in managing it—is the business plan.

Why Business Plans Are Important

Recall from Chapter 15 that the equity capital used by entrepreneurs includes their own money, investments from friends and family, investments by venture capitalists, equity raised by selling shares in the stock market, and so on. Debt financing can also come from a wide variety of sources, including the entrepreneur, a bank, a local individual investor, another business, and the sale of debt in the public debt markets, among others.

Ensuring that a young, rapidly growing business has enough cash is a simple matter if the money comes from the entrepreneur. The entrepreneur only has to decide to make the investment. Things are more complicated when the money comes from elsewhere. The entrepreneur must convince potential investors that purchasing debt or equity in the firm will yield attractive returns. In other words, they must be persuaded that they will be adequately compensated for the risks they bear.

Convincing outsiders to invest in a company can be difficult enough if the business has a well-established track record. Raising money from outsiders can be immensely difficult for a young company. The entrepreneur often begins the process with little more than an idea of where the business is headed and some limited operating results in the form of unaudited and often incomplete financial statements. To overcome the skepticism of outside investors, many entrepreneurs prepare a business plan.

business plan a document that describes the details of how a business will be developed over time

A **business plan** is like a road map for a business. It presents the results from a strategic planning process that focuses on how the business will be developed over time. It describes where the company is going and what steps the company will follow to get there. A well-prepared business plan makes it easier for an entrepreneur to communicate to potential investors precisely what he or she expects the business to look like in the future, how he or she expects to get it to that point, and what returns an investor might expect to receive. The fact that an entrepreneur has prepared such a document also demonstrates to investors that the entrepreneur has carefully thought through the business idea. This is especially important when the business is in a very early stage of development and the entrepreneur must convince investors that he or she is capable of building it.

In addition to its usefulness in raising capital, a business plan can help an entrepreneur set the goals and objectives for the company, serve as a benchmark for evaluating and controlling the company's performance, and communicate the entrepreneur's ideas to managers, outside directors, customers, suppliers, and others. A thoroughly thought-out plan can help a business owner avoid problems and better deal with those that arise. In short, business planning is extremely important to the survival of a small and growing company.

The Key Elements of a Business Plan

The depth and scope of business plans vary widely, but most well-developed business plans include the following:

- An *executive summary*, which summarizes the key points made in the plan.
- A *company overview*, which describes what the company does and what its comparative advantages are.

- A detailed description of the *products and services* the company sells or plans to sell, their current state of development or market penetration, competitive advantages, product life cycle, and any patents or legal protections that might provide a competitive advantage.
- A *market analysis*, which discusses the markets for the firm's products and highlights the important characteristics of these markets as they relate to the company.
- A discussion of the *marketing and sales* activities that will enable the company to achieve the sales and profits reflected in the financial forecasts.
- A discussion of the *operations* of the business—how the product is (will be) produced and distributed, who the suppliers are, and any competitive advantages the business has in this area.
- A discussion of the *management team*, which includes the company's organizational structure and describes the talents and skills of the managers. The discussion of the managers should explain why they are especially well qualified to manage and grow this particular business. This is an especially important part of the business plan when it comes to raising capital. Investors in young businesses invest in the key people as much as in the business idea itself.
- A description of the *ownership* structure, including the types of securities the firm has issued and who owns them. Potential investors use this information when they value the securities they are considering purchasing and to help them understand the incentives that managers and other owners have to make the business a success.
- A discussion of *capital requirements and uses.* This section covers the current capital requirements of the business as well as capital requirements over the next five years and provides a detailed account of how the money will be used.
- Historical *financial results*, when they are available, along with *financial forecasts.* If sufficient historical results are available, this section will also include an analysis of those results using the financial statement analysis tools discussed in Chapter 4. The forecasts include a month-by-month cash budget for the next two or three years as well as yearly forecasts of operating results. The cash budget helps the reader understand what the cash inflows and outflows will be and their timing. The yearly results provide an indication of what types of returns might be expected from the business.
- *Appendixes* that contain detailed supporting information for the above discussions and analyses.

Weblink

To learn more about business plans and to see sample plans, visit the PlanWare Web site at http://www.planware.org or the Bplans Web site at http://www.bplans.com.

Before You Go On

1. Why is a business plan important in raising capital for a young company?
2. What else can a business plan be used for?
3. Why is it important to discuss the qualifications of the management team in a business plan?

18.3 Valuing a Business

LEARNING OBJECTIVE

3. Explain the three general approaches to valuation and value a business using common business valuation approaches.

Successful decision makers in both small and large firms must understand what determines the value of a business. It is not possible to consistently make investment and operating decisions that create value without knowing how to identify positive NPV projects or how operating decisions affect the value of a firm. This knowledge is also crucial when making financing decisions. In Chapters 16 and 17, we also saw how a firm's value is affected by capital structure and payout policies. Decision makers must understand business valuation concepts in order to be able to identify the optimal capital structure and payout policy.

In this section, we discuss fundamental business valuation concepts. You will see that financial analysts apply many of the concepts that have already been discussed in this book when they value a business. The reason is that a business is really just a bundle of related projects, and the value of the business equals the total value of this bundle. In other words, the value of a business is determined by the magnitude of the cash flows that it is expected to produce, the timing of those cash flows, and the likelihood that the cash flows will be realized.

Fundamental Business Valuation Principles

Before we discuss the specific ways in which businesses are valued, you should be aware of two important valuation principles.

The First Valuation Principle: The first valuation principle is that the value of a business changes over time. Changes in general economic and industry conditions, and decisions made by the managers, all affect the value of the cash flows that a business is expected to generate in the future. For example, changes in interest rates affect the firm's cost of capital and, therefore, the present value of future cash flows. A change in interest rates can also affect the demand for a firm's products if customers typically finance the purchases of those products with loans, as they often do for big-ticket items such as automobiles and houses. Similarly, competitors enter and exit industries, introduce new products, change prices, and so forth. These actions also affect the value of a business by altering its cash flows or risk. Finally, the value of a business is affected by managers' investment, operating, and financing decisions.

valuation date the date on which a value estimate applies

Because the value of a business changes over time, it is important to specify a **valuation date** when valuing a business. Normally, this date is the date on which you do the analysis, but it can be an earlier date in some situations. For example, when companies are sued or when stockholders are involved in a dispute with the Internal Revenue Service, the value of the business or its stock as of some date in the past must often be estimated. A stockholder may claim that managers sold stock for less than it was worth at some time in the past, or the IRS may claim that the value of shares passed to an heir was greater than claimed when the taxes were filed by the estate of a deceased stockholder. By specifying the valuation date, the person who values a business makes it clear to anyone who uses the value estimate precisely what economic, industry, and firm conditions are reflected in that estimate.

Building Intuition

The Value of a Business is Specific to a Point in Time

The value of a business is affected by general economic and industry conditions as well as the decisions made by managers. All of these factors affect the cash flows that a business is expected to produce in the future and the rate at which those cash flows should be discounted. Since all of these factors change over time, so will the value of the business.

The Second Valuation Principle: A second very important valuation principle is that there is no such thing as *the* value for a business. The value of a business can be different to different investors. To understand why, consider two different investors who are interested in purchasing a business that is for sale. Suppose that one investor is a competitor of the business that is for sale and the other is an individual who just wants to invest some money and plans to let the same management continue to operate the business independently. The competitor, who is what we call a *strategic investor*, might be willing to pay a higher price for the business than the other investor, who is what we call a *financial investor*, because the strategic investor might be able to combine the business with his or her current business in a way that reduces costs or increases revenues. The financial investor does not have the potential to benefit from these synergies.

Building Intuition

The Value of a Business is Not the Same to All Investors

The value of a business is not the same to all investors because different investors will obtain different cash flows from owning a business. For example, the cash flows to passive investors will differ from the cash flows to investors who are active in the management of the business. Cash flows will also differ among active investors because they will have different skill levels, operating preferences, and abilities to benefit from synergies.

The key implication of the idea that the value of a business can differ among investors is that the purpose of a valuation affects the way we do the analysis. If a valuation is being performed to determine what price a particular investor would be willing to pay for a business, the analysis must consider how that investor will operate the business. In the business valuation terminology, we would refer to this as an estimate of the **investment value** of the business to that investor.

investment value the value of a business to a specific investor

If, instead of estimating the value of a business to a particular investor, an analyst is trying to estimate the price that a typical investor would pay for a business, he or she would be estimating the **fair market value** of the business. The fair market value of a business is the value of that business to a hypothetical person who is knowledgeable about the business. It does not include the value of *synergies* or the effects of any investor-specific management style. For this reason, the fair market value can differ considerably from the investment value of a business.

fair market value the value of a business to a typical investor

Business Valuation Approaches

There is a wide variety of business valuation methods, but most can be classified into one of three general categories: (1) cost approaches, (2) market approaches, and (3) income approaches. Cost, market, and income valuation approaches can be used to value a wide range of assets. They do not apply only to business valuation.

For example, the house or apartment building you live in has at some point been valued using a cost, market, or income approach—possibly even all three. When the building was insured, the insurance company probably used a cost approach to estimate its replacement cost. The appraiser for the local taxing authority is likely to have used a market approach, in which the estimated value was based on recent prices paid for similar properties in the local real estate market. Finally, if your house or apartment building was ever evaluated as a potential rental property by an investor, the investor probably used an income approach. In this analysis, the investor estimated the present value of the cash flows that the property would produce if it were rented.

While the ways in which the cost, market, and income approaches are used to value a business differ from the ways they are used to value real estate, the basic principles are the same. We next describe how these approaches are used to value businesses.

Cost Approaches

Two cost approaches that are commonly used to value businesses or their individual assets are the replacement cost and adjusted book value approaches.

Replacement Cost The **replacement cost** of a business is the cost of duplicating the business's assets in their present form as of the valuation date. It thus reflects both the nature and condition of the assets. For example, the replacement cost of a 15-year-old electric wood saw that is in relatively good condition equals what it would cost to purchase an identical used saw in the same good condition.

replacement cost the cost of duplicating the assets of a business in their present form as of the valuation date

The replacement cost valuation approach is generally used to value individual assets within a business when they are being insured, but it is rarely used to value an entire business. Since investors are concerned with the value of the cash flows that the business can be expected to generate in the future, they use valuation approaches that reflect the value of these expected cash flows when deciding how much to pay for firms.

Although the replacement cost approach tends to be more useful for insurance purposes, it can be helpful in conducting a buy-versus-build analysis when managers are thinking about making a business acquisition. Before purchasing a business, it usually makes sense to ask if you could build the same business in a way that would result in a greater NPV—in other words, whether it is cheaper to build the business yourself or to buy one that already exists. Answering this question can serve as a useful sanity check on whether you might be paying too much for the business.

When using the replacement cost approach in a buy-versus-build analysis, you must be sure to include the cost of all tangible assets, such as property, plant, and equipment, and all intangible assets, such as brand names and customer lists. You must also include the cost of hiring the people necessary to run the business and account for the cash flows that you would not receive during the time that it would take to build the business. It can take a long time to build a business, and until the business is up and running it will produce smaller cash flows than a business you might acquire.

adjusted book value the sum of the fair market values of the individual assets in a business

Adjusted Book Value The **adjusted book value** approach involves estimating the market values of the individual assets in a business and adding them up. When this approach is used, the fair market value of each asset is estimated separately and the values are summed to arrive at the total value of the business. As with the replacement cost approach, an adjusted book value analysis should include all tangible and intangible assets, whether they are actually included on the accounting balance sheet or not.

The adjusted book value approach is useful in valuing holding companies whose main assets are publicly traded or other investment securities, but it is generally less applicable to operating businesses. The value of an operating business is usually greater than the sum of the values of its individual assets because the present value of the cash flows expected from the company is greater. The difference between the value of the expected cash flows and that of the assets is referred to as **going-concern value**.

going-concern value the difference between the value of a business as a going concern (the present value of the expected cash flows) and the adjusted book value

Going-concern value reflects the value associated with additional cash flows the business is expected to produce because of the way in which the individual assets are managed together. A lot of different factors determine the going-concern value of a business. For example, one business can have a larger going-concern value than another business because it has a stronger management team that is able to invest in and utilize the business's assets more efficiently. The going-concern value might also be larger because the employees of the company are more skilled or work better together or because the government provides some special benefit to a particular business.

To see how going-concern value might be created, suppose that you just obtained the exclusive right to produce and sell a patented type of specialty brick in the United States that has been very popular among homebuilders in Europe. Also suppose that you expect to be able to satisfy demand for this brick with a single manufacturing plant. No matter where you build this plant, its adjusted book value will be the same, assuming that the assets in the plant, such as kilns, forklifts, conveyer belts, and so forth, are commonly available and used all over the country. However, the actual value of the plant (business) will depend in part on where you decide to build it if transportation costs are an important component of the overall costs (bricks are heavy and cost a lot to transport). If you build the plant in Oklahoma (the middle of the country), it will be worth more than if you build it in one corner of the country, such as in Miami, because average transportation costs will be lower from Oklahoma. As a result, the going-concern value will be greater if you build it in Oklahoma.

Although the adjusted book value approach does not capture the going-concern value associated with a business, it is useful under certain circumstances. We might use this approach (1) when it is especially difficult to forecast a business's likely cash flows; (2) when we suspect that the going-concern value of the business is negative—in other words, the owners of the business would be better off if the business were simply shut down and its assets were sold off; or (3) if we are explicitly considering liquidation. The adjusted book value approach might also be used as a "sanity check" when using one of the other valuation approaches. If your value estimate is lower than the adjusted book value when you use another approach, it might indicate that there is an error in your analysis. Of course, if you find no errors, this might also be an indication that you would be better off shutting down the business and liquidating it.

When using the adjusted book value approach to estimate the liquidation value of a business, we must make sure to subtract liquidation-related expenses such as sales commissions, legal and accounting fees, and the cost of dismantling and hauling away the assets. To see how the adjusted book value approach might be used to estimate the liquidation value of a business, consider the following situation. Last year you started a business that prints custom logos on T-shirts for business clients. Unfortunately, the economy went into a recession shortly after you started your business, and it never got off the ground. You have virtually run out of cash and have decided to shut down the business rather than invest any more money. The current balance sheet of this business is as follows:

Assets:		Liabilities and Equity:	
Cash	$ 78	Accounts payable	$ 480
Accounts receivable	2,368	Loan balance	2,000
T-shirt inventory	1,600	Stockholders' equity	2,366
Printing press	800		
Total assets	$4,846	Total liab. & equity	$4,846

What is the liquidation value of your ownership interest in this business?

The first step in estimating the liquidation value of the business is to estimate how much value will be realized from the individual assets after accounting for liquidation costs. Let's begin with the cash. Since the objective of the liquidation process is to convert all assets into cash, the liquidation value of any cash on the balance sheet, $78 in this example, simply equals its face value. Assuming that your customers are reputable businesspeople, you expect to collect all of the receivables with little effort. However, since you will incur some expenses in the collection process, you estimate that you will actually receive a net amount that equals 95 percent of the face value of the receivables. A call to your T-shirt supplier reveals that you can return unused inventory to the supplier and receive an 80 percent refund. You do not believe that anyone else will pay you more for the T-shirts. Finally, a supplier of T-shirt printing equipment has offered to pay you $600, or 75 percent of the book value, for your printing press.

With this information, you estimate the liquidation value of the assets is $4,208:

Cash	$ 78	×	100%	=	$ 78
Accounts receivable	$2,368	×	95%	=	$2,250
T-shirt inventory	$1,600	×	80%	=	$1,280
Printing press	$ 800	×	75%	=	$ 600
Total assets	$4,846				$4,208

Therefore, after paying your accounts payable and the loan, your equity ownership interest has a liquidation value of $4,208 – $480 – $2,000 = $1,728.

Learning by Doing Application 18.1 illustrates use of the adjusted book value approach.

APPLICATION 18.1 | Using the Adjusted Book Value Approach

LEARNING BY DOING

Problem You are considering purchasing a company that manufactures specialized components for recreational vehicles. These components are sold to the companies that manufacture the vehicles. As part of your analysis of this opportunity, you decide to estimate the liquidation value of the company. Management has provided you with the following information about its assets. All values are in thousands of dollars.

Cash	$ 444
Accounts receivable	739
Inventory	1,436
Net PP&E	8,463
Total assets	$11,082

Management has also told you that you can reasonably expect to collect 93 percent of the receivables (accounting for collection expenses), that the inventory can be sold to realize 85 percent of its book value, and that sale of the property, plant, and equipment would yield $6,100. What is the liquidation value of this company?

Approach Calculate the value that will be realized for each of the individual types assets and sum those values to obtain the liquidation value of the company.

Solution The liquidation value is:

Cash	$ 444	×	100%	=	$ 444
Accounts receivable	$ 739	×	93%	=	$ 687
Inventory	$ 1,436	×	85%	=	$1,221
Net PP&E	$ 8,463				$6,100
Total assets	$11,082				$8,452

You can expect to realize $8,452 from the liquidation of this company if there are no liquidation expenses that are not accounted for in these numbers.

Market Approaches

multiples analysis a valuation approach that uses stock price or other value multiples for public companies to estimate the value of another company's stock or its entire business

transactions analysis a valuation approach that uses transactions data from the sale of similar companies to estimate the value of another company's stock or its entire business

Two market approaches are commonly used in business valuation. The first approach, which is often called **multiples analysis**, uses stock price or other value multiples that are observed for similar public companies to estimate the value of a company or its equity. The second approach, often called **transactions analysis**, uses information from transactions involving the sale of similar companies to estimate the value of a company or its stock.

Market approaches reflect prices that have actually been paid for a company's stock or for the entire company. While it is not always obvious why people pay a particular price, the information on what they pay can yield useful insights into how those people view the prospects for similar businesses. Market approaches can also provide useful benchmarks against which valuations based on other methodologies can be compared.

Multiples Analysis Multiples analysis is widely used in business valuation. This approach involves: (1) identifying publicly traded companies engaged in business activities that are similar to those of the company being analyzed and (2) using the prices at which shares of those *comparables* are trading, along with accounting data, to estimate the value of the equity of a company of interest or its entire value. Multiples analysis can be especially useful in estimating the price at which the stock of a private company can be sold. For example, this approach is often used to help identify the price at which shares can be sold when a company does its initial public offering (IPO) or when some or all of its shares are being sold privately to investors.

Price/earnings (P/E) and price/revenue multiples (ratios) are commonly used to directly estimate the value of the stock in a company. These ratios divide a measure of stock price by an accounting measure of profits and revenue, respectively. Analysts typically estimate one of these multiples using data from comparable public companies, and then they use an average or, if one comparable is clearly better than the others, a multiple from a single comparable company to estimate the value of the company of interest.

Suppose, for example, that we want to estimate the value of the equity of a private department store chain that we are considering purchasing. The chain earned net income of \$3.65 million last year. We have identified a publicly traded company that is very similar to the company we are valuing and notice in the *Wall Street Journal* that the P/E ratio for its common stock is 17.63. From this information, we can estimate that the market value of the equity (V_E) of the company that we are considering purchasing is:

$$\begin{aligned} V_E &= \left(\frac{P}{E}\right)_{\text{Comparable}} \times \text{Net income}_{\text{Company being valued}} \\ &= 17.63 \times \$3.65 \text{ million} \\ &= \$64.35 \text{ million} \end{aligned}$$

It is important to recognize that because the stock of the comparable companies is publicly traded and shares that are bought and sold in public markets are more liquid than shares that are not publicly traded, we must be careful when using multiples analysis to value a private company. The prices paid for shares that are not publicly traded can be considerably less than the prices paid for public shares. While the size of this *marketability discount* depends on many factors, such as the fraction of the total shares being bought or sold, it can amount to well more than 30 percent in some instances.[3]

A multiples analysis is conceptually straightforward but can be difficult in a real situation. One complicating factor is that truly comparable public companies are difficult to find. The ideal comparable company would match the company being valued on many dimensions. It would sell the same products, compete in the same markets, be of similar size, have similar revenue growth prospects, have similar profit margins, and have similar management quality, among other characteristics. In addition, if an equity ratio (such as price/earnings or price/revenue) is being used, the comparable should have a similar capital structure because, all else being equal, capital structure can have a dramatic impact on those ratios.

The importance of identifying comparable companies that are similar to the company being analyzed can be illustrated by considering the characteristics that determine a company's

[3]Marketability discounts are also sometimes called *discounts for lack of marketability* or *liquidity discounts*.

price/earnings multiple. Recall from Chapters 9 and 13 that the constant-growth dividend model, Equation 9.4, can be used to estimate the value of a share of stock. Using the notation from Chapter 13, this model can be written as:

$$P_0 = \frac{D_1}{k_{cs} - g}$$

where P_0 is the current stock price, D_1 is the dividend that is expected next year, k_{cs} is the required return on common stock, and g is the expected growth rate in dividends. If we recognize that dividends equal the fraction of earnings distributed to the stockholders times the earnings of the firm, we can rewrite Equation 9.4 as:

$$P_0 = \frac{E_1 b}{k_{cs} - g}$$

where E_1 is the earnings per share expected next year and b is the fraction of the firm's earnings that is paid out as dividends. (b, which is known as the dividend payout ratio, is referred to in the summary of the Lintner study in Section 17.5 of Chapter 17 and is discussed in more detail in Chapter 19). Finally, we can rearrange this equation to obtain the price/earnings multiple:

$$\frac{P_0}{E_1} = \frac{b}{k_{cs} - g} \quad (18.1)$$

This equation tells us that the P/E multiple can be thought of as equal to the dividend payout ratio over k_{cs} minus g.[4]

By focusing on the variables that drive the P/E multiple in this simple framework, we can see the importance of identifying comparable companies that are as similar to the company of interest as possible. For example, consider what company characteristics determine k_{cs}. The Capital Asset Pricing Model (CAPM) tells us that k_{cs} depends on beta, which is a measure of the systematic risk associated with a company's stock price. Since this systematic risk is closely related to the volatility of the earnings of the company, our discussion of total risk in Chapter 16 (see the discussion of Exhibit 16.3) suggests that the cost of equity depends on both business and financial risk. In other words, it depends on things such as the products the company sells, the markets it sells them in, its profit margins, and its operating and financial leverage. The growth rate of dividends, g, is determined by the same factors that affect k_{cs}. This means that if we cannot identify a comparable company that is similar to the company of interest in both its business and financial characteristics, the P/E multiple we obtain for the comparable company will not be a good measure for our analysis.

Because P/E ratios are sensitive to leverage, many analysts use ratios that divide the total value of a company's equity plus its debt by an accounting measure of cash flows available to all providers of capital (debt and equity). These ratios provide a direct measure of the total value of a company's equity plus its debt, which is known as its **enterprise value**.[5] The total value of the firm was written in Equation 16.1 as $V_{Firm} = V_{Debt} + V_{Equity}$. In the interest of brevity, we will write it in this chapter as:

$$V_F = V_D + V_E$$

where V_F is the value of the firm, V_D is the value of the debt, and V_E is the value of the equity. Multiples that are based on the total value of the firm are known as *enterprise multiples*. Examples include enterprise value/revenue and enterprise value/EBITDA.

To see how an enterprise multiple can be used to estimate the total value of a firm, let's return to the example in which we were valuing the department store chain. Assume that, in addition to the P/E ratio analysis, we want to estimate the enterprise value of the business using an enterprise value/EBITDA ratio. We have estimated that EBITDA last year was $8.67 million for the department store chain we are valuing. In the *Wall Street Journal*, we find that the current price of the comparable company's stock is $31.25, and, from the

Weblink

You can learn more about business valuation and find a wide range of Excel templates that can be used to value businesses and their securities on the Web site maintained by Aswath Damodaran at http://pages.stern.nyu.edu/~adamodar.

enterprise value the value of a company's equity plus the value of its debt; also the present value of the total free cash flows the company's assets are expected to generate in the future

[4]This is not strictly true for most firms because it assumes that the stock price can be estimated using a constant-growth perpetuity model and most firms either do not pay dividends at all or do not increase dividends at a constant rate. Nevertheless, this model does provide a useful way of thinking about P/E multiples.

[5]Enterprise value is typically defined as: Market value of common stock + Market value of preferred stock + Market value of debt – Excess cash and cash equivalents (also referred to as short-term investments or marketable securities).

balance sheet in the annual report, we observe that the comparable company has 3.67 million shares outstanding. We also estimate that the value of the comparable company's outstanding debt is \$19.46 million, and we note that EBITDA for this company was \$14.35 million last year. Using this information, we can calculate the enterprise value/EBITDA ratio for the comparable company as follows:

$$\begin{aligned}\text{Enterprise value} &= V_D + V_E \\ &= \$19.46 \text{ million} + (\$31.25 \times 3.67 \text{ million shares}) \\ &= \$134.15 \text{ million}\end{aligned}$$

$$\left(\frac{\text{Enterprise value}}{\text{EBITDA}}\right)_{\text{Comparable}} = \frac{\$134.15}{\$14.35} = 9.35$$

and we can estimate the enterprise value for the company we are valuing as:

$$\begin{aligned}V_F &= \left(\frac{\text{Enterprise value}}{\text{EBITDA}}\right)_{\text{Comparable}} \times \text{EBITDA}_{\text{Company being valued}} \\ &= 9.35 \times \$8.67 \text{ million} \\ &= \$81.06 \text{ million}\end{aligned}$$

Learning by Doing Application 18.2 presents another example of a Multiples Analysis.

LEARNING BY DOING

WileyPLUS

Need more help? Visit your WileyPLUS course.

APPLICATION 18.2 | Using Multiples Analysis

Problem In addition to performing the liquidation analysis in Learning by Doing Application 18.1, you have decided to estimate the enterprise value of the company that manufactures specialized components for recreational vehicles. You have collected the following information for a comparable company and for the company you are valuing:

Comparable company:	*Company you are valuing:*
Stock price = \$10.62	Value of debt = \$1.25 million
Number of shares outstanding = 9.55 million	EBITDA last year = \$2.37 million
Value of debt = \$11.67 million	Net income last year = \$0.45 million
EBITDA last year = \$10.85 million	
Net income last year = \$2.67 million	

Estimate the enterprise value of the company you are valuing using the P/E and enterprise value/EBITDA multiples.

Approach First, calculate the P/E and enterprise value/EBITDA multiples for the comparable company. Next, use these multiples to estimate the value of the company you are valuing. Multiply the P/E multiple for the comparable company by the net income of the company you are valuing to estimate the equity value. Add this equity value to the value of the debt to obtain an estimate of the enterprise value. Multiply the enterprise value/EBITDA multiple for the comparable company by the EBITDA for the company you are valuing to obtain a direct estimate of the enterprise value.

Solution The P/E and enterprise value/EBITDA multiples for the comparable company are:

$$\begin{aligned}\left(\frac{P}{E}\right)_{\text{Comparable}} &= \left(\frac{\text{Stock price}}{\text{Earnings per share}}\right)_{\text{Comparable}} \\ &= \frac{\$10.62 \text{ per share}}{\$2.67 \text{ million}/9.55 \text{ million shares}} = 38.0\end{aligned}$$

$$\begin{aligned}\left(\frac{\text{Enterprise value}}{\text{EBITDA}}\right)_{\text{Comparable}} &= \left(\frac{V_D + V_E}{\text{EBITDA}}\right)_{\text{Comparable}} \\ &= \frac{\$11.67 \text{ million} + (\$10.62 \text{ per share} \times 9.55 \text{ million shares})}{\$10.85 \text{ million}} \\ &= 10.42\end{aligned}$$

Using the P/E multiple, we calculate the value of the equity as:

$$V_E = \left(\frac{P}{E}\right)_{\text{Comparable}} \times \text{Net income}_{\text{Company being valued}}$$
$$= 38.0 \times \$0.45 \text{ million}$$
$$= \$17.1 \text{ million}$$

which suggests an enterprise value of:

$$V_F = V_D + V_E = \$1.25 \text{ million} + \$17.1 \text{ million} = \$18.35 \text{ million}$$

Using the enterprise/EBITDA multiple, we estimate the enterprise value to be:

$$V_F = \left(\frac{\text{Enterprise value}}{\text{EBITDA}}\right)_{\text{Comparable}} \times \text{EBITDA}_{\text{Company being valued}}$$
$$= 10.42 \times \$2.37 \text{ million}$$
$$= \$24.70 \text{ million}$$

Whenever we use multiples analysis, we must remember that we are estimating the *fair market value* of a company's equity or its enterprise value and that this value is based on transactions involving small ownership interests. The transaction prices that we observe in the stock market are typically based on trades that involve unknown investors buying small numbers of shares that do not give them the ability to control the business. In other words, a multiples analysis does not provide an estimate of *investment value* because the identities of the buyers are not known. This means that value estimates based on a multiples analysis do not reflect the synergies that might be realized by combining the company with another business. These estimates also do not include the value associated with being able to control a business, an important consideration that we discuss in more detail later.

When performing a multiples analysis, it is also important to make sure that the numerator and the denominator of the ratio we are using are consistent with each other. In other words, if stock price is in the numerator, some measure of cash flow to equity must be in the denominator. If enterprise value is in the numerator, a measure of total cash flows from the entire business must be in the denominator.

The exception to this rule is the price/revenue ratio. This ratio can be useful in valuing the stock of a relatively young company that is not yet generating profits. Shares in very young companies are often bought and sold based on multiples of their revenue. Implicit in those multiples are expectations about future margins, as well as growth in revenue. By using price to revenue, the analyst is effectively assuming that the company being analyzed will, over time, have profit margins similar to those that are anticipated by the market in pricing the publicly traded comparables.

Another important point to keep in mind when doing multiples analysis is that the data used to compute the multiple for the comparable company should include the stock price as of the valuation date and that accounting data for the two companies should be from the same period. Since any value estimate is specific to a particular date, we must be sure to use multiples for the appropriate point in time. Furthermore, if we use accounting data from the past 12 months to estimate the ratio for a comparable company, we must use accounting data from the same 12-month period to calculate the value of the company of interest.

Transactions Analysis The information used in a transactions analysis is typically obtained from Securities and Exchange Commission (SEC) filings of public companies that have acquired other companies or from commercial services that collect and sell this information. This information is used to compute the same types of multiples that are used in a multiples analysis, and these multiples are used in the same way to value a company. Transaction data reflect the price that a particular investor paid for an entire company. For this reason, it provides an estimate of the *investment value* to that investor.

Like multiples analysis, transactions analysis can be difficult to use in practice, although the reasons for the difficulty are different. One problem is that transactions data are not typically as reliable as the data available for multiples analysis, especially when the transactions involve private companies. For example, the available data on transactions might include revenues of the private company, but not data on its profitability. The data might include the net income but not enough information to estimate EBITDA. This can make it difficult to compute some multiples.

In addition, unlike stock market transactions, transactions involving the purchase or sale of an entire business occur relatively infrequently. This means that the data available for a transactions analysis often include only transactions that occurred months or even years earlier. Since the value of a business is specific to a particular point in time, the price that was paid for a business becomes less useful as an indicator of what the business is worth as time passes after the sale.

Finally, the terms of the transactions can be difficult to assess. While the P/E multiple for a publicly traded company is an indication of the price that might be obtained in a cash transaction, transactions involving the sale of an entire company often involve some combination of cash, debt, or equity payments. A whole package of such securities, some of which can be difficult to value, could be included in the reported transaction price, and this may not be apparent to the analyst. The value estimates for those securities and claims can also be distorted if the buyer or seller has a reason to prefer reporting a higher or lower price.

Income Approaches

At the beginning of this section, we said that the value of a business is determined by the magnitude of the cash flows that it is expected to produce, the timing of those cash flows, and the likelihood that the cash flows will be realized. The cost and market approaches are useful for estimating this value in certain situations—such as in doing a buy-versus-build analysis, estimating the liquidation value of a firm, or when good comparable firms or transactions are available. The most direct approaches for estimating the value of the cash flows a business is expected to produce, however, are the income approaches. Like NPV analysis, these approaches directly estimate the value of those cash flows.

Before we discuss specific income valuation approaches, we should note that the market and income approaches differ in one very important way. Because the market approaches rely on prices that have been paid for companies or their securities, the value estimates that they yield are estimates of *what people are willing to pay*. In contrast, the income approaches provide estimates of the *intrinsic, or true, value* of a company or its securities.

While the market value can equal the intrinsic value, the two values are not necessarily the same. For example, if you are valuing the company you work for, you might have better information about its prospects than do stock market investors. By using an income approach, you would be able to incorporate your superior information directly into the valuation analysis in a way that you would not be able to do with a market approach.

Using Income Approaches The life of a business is not usually known when it is valued. Whereas a project might be expected to last a specific number of years, a business can have an indefinite life. This makes it more difficult to use an income approach to value a business than a project. It is difficult enough to forecast cash flows for a relatively short period, such as three or five years, let alone for the indefinite future.

Another complication in business valuation is that businesses often have cash or other assets that are not necessary for operations. These can include cash that was earned in the past but has not been distributed to stockholders and assets that are left over from old projects. We call these **nonoperating assets (NOA)**. When we estimate the value of an individual project, we do not have to worry about NOA because there are none. However, when we value a business, NOA are an additional source of value. NOA can be distributed directly to stockholders or sold and the proceeds distributed to stockholders without affecting the cash flows that the operations of the business are expected to generate.

nonoperating assets (NOA) cash or other assets that are not required to support the operations of a business

In practice, we account for the indefinite life associated with a business and the possibility that it has NOA by estimating the value of the business as the sum of three numbers. This calculation can be represented as follows:

$$V_F = PV(FCF_T) + PV(TV_T) + NOA \qquad (18.2)$$

where V_F is the value of the firm, $PV(FCF_T)$ is the present value of the free cash flows (FCF) that the business is expected to produce over the next T years, $PV(TV_T)$ is the present value of all free cash flows after year T, and NOA is the value of all of the nonoperating assets in the firm. Note that the present value of all free cash flows after year T is generally known as the **terminal value**. Note also that if we only want to calculate the value of the equity, we can do this by first calculating the value of the firm using Equation 18.2 and then subtracting the value of the debt.

terminal value the value of the expected free cash flows beyond the period over which they are explicitly forecast

Free Cash Flow from the Firm Approach When using the **free cash flow from the firm (FCFF) approach**, an analyst values the free cash flows that the assets of the firm are expected to produce in the future. The present value of these free cash flows equals the total value of the firm, or its enterprise value.

free cash flow from the firm (FCFF) approach an income approach to valuation in which all free cash flows the assets are expected to generate in the future are discounted to estimate the enterprise value

The free cash flows used in a FCFF analysis are almost identical to the free cash flows from the left-hand side of the finance balance sheet that was illustrated in Exhibit 13.1. The only difference is that when we value a business, we do not include cash flows necessary to pay short-term liabilities that do not have interest charges associated with them, such as accounts payable and accrued expenses. The costs associated with these noninterest-bearing current liabilities, which are included in the firm's cost of sales and other operating expenses, are subtracted in the calculation of FCFF. **Exhibit 18.3** shows precisely what we are referring to when we refer to the value of FCFF.

The most common FCFF approach involves using the weighted-average cost of capital (WACC), which we discussed in Chapter 13, to discount the FCFF. This is often referred to as the WACC valuation method. In this approach, the total value of the firm (V_F) is computed as the present value of the FCFF, discounted by the firm's WACC:

$$V_F = \sum_{t=0}^{\infty} \frac{FCFF_t}{(1 + WACC)^t} \tag{18.3}$$

In this equation, t equals the period when the cash flow is produced.

We compute the FCFF using the same calculation that we used for the free cash flows for a project in Chapter 11. The only differences are (1) that since business valuation involves valuing all of the projects in the firm, we compute the total after-tax free cash flows the firm's assets are expected to produce rather than the incremental after-tax free cash flows from a project and (2) we use the average tax rate instead of the marginal tax rate. The FCFF calculation is shown in **Exhibit 18.4**. Notice that this calculation is just like the calculation in Exhibit 11.1.

Analysts typically estimate future FCFF by forecasting each of the individual components and then performing the calculation shown in Exhibit 18.4. Next, the resulting FCFF values

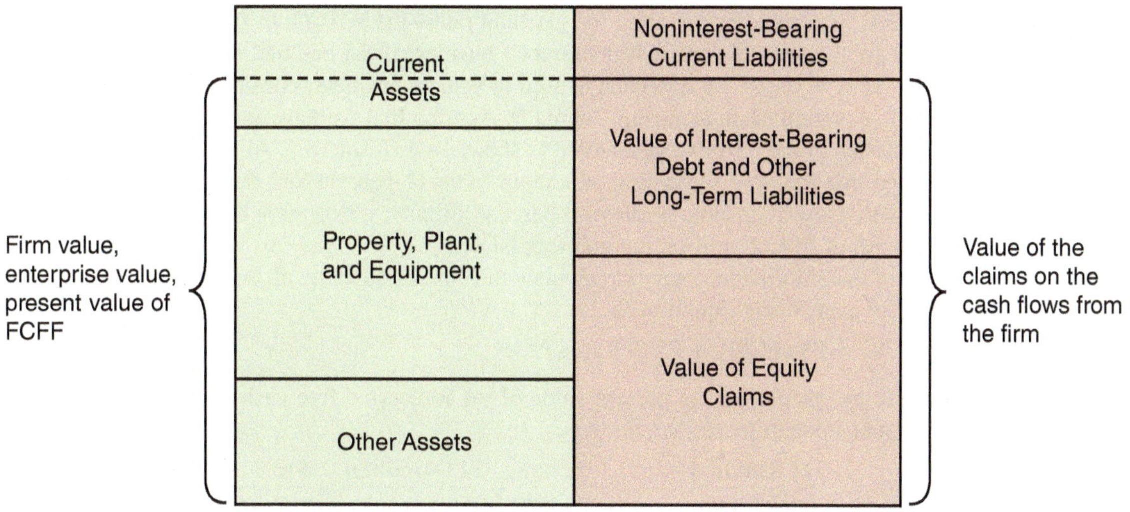

EXHIBIT 18.3 **The Finance Balance Sheet and Firm Value**

The value of a firm (enterprise value) equals the present value of the future free cash flows from the firm (FCFF). Since the owners of the interest-bearing debt and other long-term liabilities and the stockholders, collectively, have the right to receive all of the FCFF, the total value of those claims equals the value of the firm.

EXHIBIT 18.4 The FCFF Calculation

Free cash flows from the firm (FCFF) are calculated in the same way as the incremental after-tax free cash flows (FCF) that are expected from a project. The only differences between the FCFF calculation and the FCF calculation, which is illustrated in Exhibit 11.1, are that in the FCFF calculation (1) we use *total* cash flows rather than *incremental* cash flows, and (2) we use the *average* tax rate instead of the *marginal* tax rate when we are valuing a company that is operating independent of any other company.

Explanation	Calculation	Formula
The firm's cash income excluding interest expense	Revenue	Revenue
	− Cash operating expenses	− Op Ex
	Earnings before interest, taxes, depreciation and amortization	EBITDA
	− Depreciation and amortization	− D&A
	Operating profit	EBIT
	× (1 − Firm's average tax rate)	× (1 − *t*)
Adjustments for the impact of depreciation and amortization and investments on FCFF	Net operating profit after tax	NOPAT
	+ Depreciation and amortization	+ D&A
	Cash flow from operations	CF Opns
	− Capital expenditures	− Cap Exp
	− Additions to working capital	− Add WC
	= Free cash flow from the firm	= FCFE

are discounted back to the present using the WACC, as already mentioned. Recall that the WACC is calculated using Equation 13.7:

$$\text{WACC} = x_{\text{Debt}} k_{\text{Debt pretax}}(1 - t) + x_{\text{ps}} k_{\text{ps}} + x_{\text{cs}} k_{\text{cs}}$$

where $x_{\text{Debt pretax}} + x_{\text{ps}} + x_{\text{cs}} = 1$ and where $k_{\text{Debt pretax}}$, k_{ps}, and k_{cs} are the pretax cost of debt and the after-tax costs of preferred stock and common stock, respectively. Also, t is the tax rate that applies to interest deductions, and x_{Debt}, x_{ps}, x_{cs} are the proportions of the value of the firm that are represented by debt, preferred stock, and common stock.

When analysts use the WACC approach to value a business, they must make an assumption about how the firm's operations will be financed in the future. For example, the financing might be 80 percent equity and 20 percent debt. Or it might be 30 percent equity and 70 percent debt. These are very important assumptions because, as we saw in Chapter 16 (see Exhibit 16.8), the capital structure choice affects the value of the firm. The FCFF calculation is not affected by the firm's capital structure, but from Equation 18.3 we know that capital structure affects firm value by affecting the discount rate—the WACC. In fact, as we discussed in Chapter 16, the optimal capital structure for a business is the one that minimizes the WACC.

To see how the FCFF approach is used to value a business, consider an example involving Bell Mountain Manufacturing Company. Assume that we have forecast Bell Mountain's FCFF in each of the next five years to be as shown in **Exhibit 18.5**. Also assume that we have estimated that the WACC for Bell Mountain to be 11 percent and that the cash flows after Year 5 will grow at an annual rate of 3 percent. Finally, we observe that Bell Mountain has excess cash of \$14.68 million but no other NOA.

With this information, we can calculate the enterprise value of Bell Mountain Manufacturing Company using Equation 18.2:

$$V_F = PV(FCF_T) + PV(TV_T) + NOA$$

We begin by calculating the present value of the forecasted free cash flows in Exhibit 18.5. The present value of these cash flows is

$$PV(FCFF_5) = \frac{\$11.8 \text{ million}}{1+0.11} + \frac{\$13.1 \text{ million}}{(1+0.11)^2} + \frac{\$13.4 \text{ million}}{(1+0.11)^3} + \frac{\$13.7 \text{ million}}{(1+0.11)^4} + \frac{\$14.1 \text{ million}}{(1+0.11)^5}$$

$$= \$48.45 \text{ million}$$

In this example, we prepared cash flow forecasts for five years. The length of the period for which detailed projections are produced depends on the level of uncertainty surrounding the future of

EXHIBIT 18.5 **FCFF Forecasts for Bell Mountain Manufacturing Company ($ millions)**

This exhibit presents forecasts of free cash flow from the firm (FCFF) for Bell Mountain for each of the next five years.

	Year				
	1	2	3	4	5
Revenue	$100.0	$106.0	$112.4	$119.1	$126.3
– Cash operating expenses	70.0	74.2	78.7	83.4	88.4
Earnings before interest, taxes, depreciation and amortization	$ 30.0	$ 31.8	$ 33.7	$ 35.7	$ 37.9
– Depreciation and amortization	8.0	8.3	8.5	8.8	9.0
Operating profit	$ 22.0	$ 23.5	$ 25.2	$ 26.9	$ 28.9
– Taxes	7.7	8.2	8.8	9.4	10.1
Net operating profits after tax	$ 14.3	$ 15.3	$ 16.4	$ 17.5	$ 18.8
+ Depreciation and amortization	8.0	8.3	8.5	8.8	9.0
Cash flow from operations	$ 22.3	$ 23.6	$ 24.9	$ 26.3	$ 27.8
– Capital expenditures	10.0	10.0	11.0	12.0	13.0
– Additions to working capital	0.5	0.5	0.5	0.6	0.7
= Free cash flow from the firm	$ 11.8	$ 13.1	$ 13.4	$ 13.7	$ 14.1

the business. In general, we want to forecast the cash flows out to a point in time where we expect the business to reach a steady-state growth rate. We can then estimate the cash flows for the remainder of the business's life (the terminal value) by (1) calculating the present value of all cash flows after the final year of the detailed forecast using the formula for a growing perpetuity and (2) discounting this value to the present. For Bell Mountain, these calculations are as follows:

$$TV_5 = \frac{FCFF_5 \times (1 + g)}{WACC - g} = \frac{\$14.1 \text{ million} \times (1 + 0.03)}{0.11 - 0.03} = \$181.54 \text{ million}$$

and

$$PV(TV_5) = \frac{TV_5}{(1 + WACC)^5} = \frac{\$181.54 \text{ million}}{(1 + 0.11)^5} = \$107.74 \text{ million}$$

Finally, we can use Equation 18.2 to calculate the total value of Bell Mountain Manufacturing Company:

$$\begin{aligned} V_F &= PV(FCF_T) + PV(TV_T) + NOA \\ &= \$48.45 \text{ million} + \$107.74 \text{ million} + \$14.68 \text{ million} = \$170.87 \text{ million} \end{aligned}$$

Learning by Doing Application 18.3 presents another example of the application of the FCFF Income Approach.

APPLICATION 18.3 | Using the FCFF Income Approach

LEARNING BY DOING

WileyPLUS

Need more help? Visit your WileyPLUS course.

Problem You have decided to use the FCFF income approach to estimate the intrinsic value of the company that manufactures components for recreational vehicles. You expect the company's cash flows to grow very rapidly during the next five years and to level off after that. Based on this, you forecast the cash flows for each of the next five years to be:

	Year				
	1	2	3	4	5
FCFF ($ millions)	–$0.284	$0.108	$0.998	$2.110	$2.857

You expect cash flows to be constant after Year 5. There are no NOA in this firm. If the appropriate WACC is 9 percent, what is the enterprise value of this business? What is the value of the equity if the value of the company's debt equals $1.25 million?

Approach First calculate the total present value of the individual FCFF that you have forecast by discounting them to Year 0 using the WACC and summing them up. Next, calculate the terminal value, assuming no growth in the cash flows after Year 5, and discount this value to Year 0. The enterprise value equals the present value of the individual cash flows plus the present value of the terminal value. The value of the equity can then be calculated by subtracting the value of the debt.

Solution The present value of the cash flows in the first five years is:

$$PV(FCFF_5) = \frac{-\$0.284 \text{ million}}{1+0.09} + \frac{\$0.108 \text{ million}}{(1+0.09)^2} + \frac{\$0.998 \text{ million}}{(1+0.09)^3} + \frac{\$2.110 \text{ million}}{(1+0.09)^4} + \frac{\$2.857 \text{ million}}{(1+0.09)^5}$$
$$= \$3.95 \text{ million}$$

With no growth after Year 5, the present value of the terminal value is:

$$PV(TV_5) = \frac{TV_5}{(1+WACC)^5} = \frac{\$2.857 \text{ million}/(0.09-0)}{(1+0.09)^5} = \$20.63 \text{ million}$$

Therefore, the total enterprise value is:

$$V_F = PV(FCF_T) + PV(TV_T) + NOA = \$3.95 \text{ million} + \$20.63 \text{ million} + \$0 \text{ million}$$
$$= \$24.58 \text{ million}$$

and the value of the equity equals \$24.58 million − \$1.25 million = \$23.33 million.

free cash flow to equity (FCFE) approach an income approach to valuation in which all cash flows that are expected to be available for distribution to stockholders in the future are discounted to estimate the value of the equity

Free Cash Flow to Equity Approach The **free cash flow to equity (FCFE) approach** is very similar to the FCFF approach. However, instead of valuing the total cash flows the assets of the business are expected to generate, we value only the portion of the cash flows that are available for distribution to stockholders. To see how the FCFF and FCFE approaches are related, ask yourself the following question: If you wanted to value only the equity claims, how would you adjust the cash flows that are used in the FCFF approach? The answer is that you would simply strip out the cash flows to or from the people who lend money to the firm. Since the value of the firm equals the value of the debt plus the value of the equity, stripping out the cash flows to or from the lenders leaves the cash flows available to stockholders.

Exhibit 18.6 shows how FCFE is calculated. Notice that this calculation includes three cash flows that are not in the FCFF calculation. One is the interest expense, which is a cash

EXHIBIT 18.6 The FCFE Calculation

Free cash flow to equity (FCFE) equals free cash flow from the firm (FCFF) less any net cash outflows to debt holders. In the FCFE calculation, we subtract the interest and principal payments to the debt holders and add any proceeds from the sale of new debt.

Explanation	Calculation	Formula
The firm's cash income	Revenue	Revenue
	− Cash operating expenses	− Op Ex
	Earnings before interest, taxes, depreciation and amortization	EBITDA
	− Depreciation and amortization	− D&A
	Operating profit	EBIT
	− Interest	− Int
	Earnings before tax	EBT
	× (1 − Firm's average tax rate)	× (1 − *t*)
	Net income	NI
Adjustments for the impact of depreciation and amortization, investments on FCFF, and debt repayments and new issues	+ Depreciation and amortization	+ D&A
	Cash flow from operations	CF Opns
	− Capital expenditures	− Cap Exp
	− Additions to working capital	− Add WC
	− Repayment of debt principal	− Dept Pmt
	+ Proceeds from new debt issues	+ Debt Proc
	= Free cash flow to equity	= FCFE

flow to the lenders. The others are the cash flows associated with the repayment of debt principal and the proceeds from new debt issues. The FCFE approach takes the total after-tax free cash flows from the business and removes any cash flows to or from lenders, leaving the after-tax free cash flows available to the stockholders.

Because cash flows available to stockholders are residual cash flows, they are riskier than the total cash flows from the firm (assuming the firm has some debt). Consequently, in using the FCFE valuation approach, the cost of equity (k_E) is used to discount the cash flows:

$$V_E = \sum_{t=0}^{\infty} \frac{\text{FCFE}_t}{(1 + k_E)^t} \qquad (18.4)$$

Note that k_E equals k_{cs} if the firm has no preferred stock outstanding. Otherwise k_E is a weighted average of k_{cs} and k_{ps}. Other than the difference in the way that the cash flows are calculated, the procedure for estimating the value of a firm's equity using the FCFE approach is the same as that used to estimate the total value of the firm using the FCFF approach.

Dividend Discount Model Approach The **dividend discount model (DDM) approach** is very similar to the FCFE approach. In this approach, we estimate the value of equity directly by discounting cash flows to stockholders. However, there is a subtle difference. The DDM approach values the stream of cash flows that stockholders *expect to receive* through dividend payments. In contrast, the FCFE approach values cash flows that are *available for distribution* to stockholders. The firm may or may not be expected to distribute all available cash flows in any particular year.

dividend discount model (DDM) approach an income approach to valuation in which all dividends that are expected to be distributed to stockholders in the future are discounted to estimate the value of the equity

The constant-growth dividend model, Equation 9.4, is an example of a DDM:

$$P_0 = \frac{D_1}{k_{cs} - g}$$

Notice that in this model the price of a share of common stock is computed by discounting future dividends.

Since the constant-growth model assumes that the firm pays dividends and that these dividends will increase at a constant rate forever, this approach is really useful for only a limited number of mature firms that pay dividends. More often, use of the DDM approach involves discounting dividends that either will not begin until some point in the future or that are currently growing at a high rate that is not sustainable in the long run. In these cases, an approach such as that illustrated for the FCFF approach above must be used. The expected dividends must be individually discounted for some period, and then a terminal value must be estimated once the growth rate in dividends stabilizes at some level that is sustainable over the long run. This is the mixed (supernormal) growth dividend model from Chapter 9.

Decision Making Example 18.2 illustrates the choice of an appropriate valuation approach or approaches.

EXAMPLE 18.2 | Choosing an Appropriate Valuation Approach

DECISION MAKING

Situation You have decided to make an offer for the recreational vehicle manufacturing business that you evaluated in Learning by Doing Applications 18.1, 18.2, and 18.3. Your analysis yielded the following enterprise value estimates:

Liquidation value	$ 8.45 million
Value from multiples analysis	
P/E multiple	$18.35 million
Enterprise/EBITDA multiple	$24.70 million
FCFF value	$24.58 million

The seller of the company is asking for $18 million. Is this price reasonable?

Decision The price appears to be reasonable. It is almost $10 million greater than the liquidation value, but the liquidation value does not include the going-concern value associated with the business. The other three estimates, which all reflect the company's going-concern value, suggest that the fair market value of the business is greater than the seller's asking price.

Before You Go On

1. Why is it important to specify a valuation date when you value a business?
2. What is the difference between investment value and fair market value?
3. What are the two market approaches that can be used to value a business, and how do they differ?
4. What is a nonoperating asset, and how are such assets accounted for in business valuation?
5. What are three income approaches used to value a business?
6. What is the difference between FCFE and dividends?

18.4 Important Issues in Valuation

LEARNING OBJECTIVE

4. Explain how valuations can differ between public and private companies and between young and mature companies, and discuss the importance of control and key person considerations in valuation.

We conclude the chapter by discussing some important issues in valuing businesses. Whether a business is public or private, whether it is young or old, and whether a minority interest or a controlling interest is involved can make a difference in valuation. In addition, we may have to take account of the role of key employees.

Public versus Private Companies

The same valuation approaches are used to value both public and private companies. However, there are some important differences, which we consider next.

Financial Statements

While financial statements of public companies must be audited and filed with the Securities and Exchange Commission, there is no requirement that the financial statements of private companies be audited. As a result, the completeness and reliability of financial statements for private companies vary considerably. Some private companies have complete, audited financial statements, whereas others have incomplete financial statements that are not prepared in accordance with the generally accepted accounting principles (GAAP) discussed in Chapter 3. Incomplete and unreliable financial statements can complicate the process of valuing a private business, making it more difficult to accurately assess its value.

Financial statements of private companies also differ from those of public companies in some of the expense accounts. Owners of private businesses have incentives to pass some of their personal expenses through the business because this enables them to deduct the expenses on their taxes. Examples might include the owner's car, "business" trips to Hawaii or Europe, the company condominium in New York, or the sky box at the local football stadium. While there may be legitimate reasons for a business to incur expenses such as these—for example, entertaining important customers in the sky box—there are often more such expenses in private companies.

Owners of private companies can also have incentives to pay themselves more than it would cost to hire someone to do their job. If the income from the company is taxed before it is distributed to the owners (such as in a C-corporation), this *excess compensation* reduces the taxes that the company must pay. Compensation payments are deductible for the corporation and are therefore only taxed as income to the owner. If instead of paying themselves excess compensation, owners distributed the money as dividends, it would be taxed twice—once as income to the corporation and a second time as income to the owner. In addition to having incentives to pay themselves excess compensation, owners of private companies often put family members on the payroll at wages that are above what would ordinarily be paid for the services they provide. When valuing a private company, analysts typically adjust for excess compensation to the owner and family members by estimating what it would cost to hire other people to perform the services and, using this, change the actual expense reported in the income statement accordingly.

Marketability

In the discussion of multiples analysis, we mentioned that the prices paid for shares in a company whose stock is not publicly traded can be considerably less than the prices paid for publicly traded shares of a similar company. One reason is that stockholders of a public firm can generally sell their shares at close to their true value by simply going online or calling a broker and paying a small fee. In contrast, a stockholder in a private firm may have to spend considerable resources (both money and time) to sell his or her shares. An investor who is offered the opportunity to buy identical equity claims to the cash flows of a public and a private firm (that is, the cash flows have the same size, timing, and risk) will require different rates of return for the two investments. Because of the higher transaction costs associated with the stock of the private firm, the investor will not be willing to pay as much for that stock (and will therefore expect a higher return) as for the publicly traded shares. This must be taken into account in estimating the value of any claim to the cash flows of a firm. As we mentioned earlier, differences in marketability can result in discounts of 30 percent or more for shares of private companies. Where analysts are able to estimate the appropriate size of such a discount, they deduct the discount directly from the final value estimate that is obtained using the methods described in the preceding section.

Young (Rapidly Growing) versus Mature Companies

Another important issue that arises in business valuation concerns the fact that young, rapidly growing companies tend to be more difficult to value than mature, stable companies. Both entrepreneurs and investors in new businesses, such as venture capitalists, must deal with these difficulties when young companies seek financing. One factor that makes it more difficult to value a young company is that less reliable historical information is available. A company may have only two or three years of historical financial records, and those records may reflect the company at a different stage in its development.

In addition, the future of a young, rapidly growing company is often less certain than that of a mature company because much of the young company's future growth depends on investment, operating, and financing decisions that have not yet been made. This makes it much more complicated to identify appropriate comparable companies for a multiples or transactions analysis and more difficult to estimate expected cash flows for an income analysis.

Furthermore, many young, rapidly growing companies are not yet profitable. With no profits, it is difficult to use earnings multiples to value the business, leaving price/revenue or enterprise value/revenue multiples as the only viable alternatives for a multiples analysis. When analysts use these multiples, they are implicitly assuming that the business they are valuing will become as profitable (specifically, have the same profit margins) as the public companies that were used to estimate the multiples and that the risks of the business will also be similar. These can be very heroic assumptions when the company being valued is only a couple of years old.

Finally, many young companies invest a considerable amount of money in order to grow. This can make it very difficult to use an income valuation approach. The cash flows will be negative until the business becomes profitable and its profits exceed its investment expenditures. Since it can take several years for this to happen, expected cash flows are typically negative for several years. This means that positive cash flows, which represent the value that the business is expected to produce for its owners, are further in the future and are therefore less certain. The bottom line is that this increases the overall level of uncertainty associated with an income-based valuation.

Controlling Interest versus Minority Interest

Another important issue that we must consider when we value a business is whether we are valuing a controlling ownership interest or a minority interest. The amount of stock required for an investor to exercise control varies depending on the ownership structure of the company. For example, a stockholder with just 20 percent, or possibly even less, of the total votes in a public company can effectively control that company if there are no other large stockholders. Even if there are other large stockholders, that investor can control the public company if friendly stockholders provide enough additional votes. In private companies, which tend to have relatively few stockholders, a stockholder must generally control 50 percent of the shares, either directly or indirectly through friendly stockholders, to control the firm. A stockholder who has such control can run the business as he or she wants. He or she can select the board of directors, choose the business strategy, hire and fire managers, and approve or disapprove any investment, operating, or financing decisions.

Whether a controlling ownership interest is being valued has important implications for a valuation analysis. Recall that in the discussion of multiples analysis we noted that a multiples analysis does not reflect the value associated with being able to control a business. Thus, when we are using multiples computed using public stock market prices to estimate the value of a controlling interest, we must make adjustments to reflect the benefits of control. Similarly, when we use an income approach to value a business, the cash flow forecasts and discount rate assumptions we use will differ depending on whether we are valuing a *minority* or a *controlling* ownership interest.

Let's consider an example of how these differences arise when the income approach is used. Suppose we are valuing 100 shares of Hewlett-Packard (HP) stock. Since owning 100 shares of HP stock will not enable us to exercise any control, the expected cash flows that we should discount simply reflect the cash flows that we can expect HP to generate under its current management (assuming we know of no imminent management change). In contrast, if we are valuing a controlling interest in HP stock for a potential buyer, we would discount the cash flows that HP would be expected to generate if it were under the control of that buyer.

It is also important to note that the market rates of return that we use to calculate the cost of equity with the Capital Asset Pricing Model (CAPM) discussed in Chapter 7 are based on small stock transactions. If having control would enable an investor to better manage the systematic risk associated with a business, a discount rate based on small transactions would be higher than a discount rate estimated from a transaction that involves a controlling position. Therefore, a discount rate estimated using public stock market information and CAPM might be too high for a valuation that involves a controlling position.

Unfortunately, while the discount rate we estimate using CAPM might be too high when we value a controlling interest, the CAPM theory provides us with no insights concerning how we might adjust that rate. As a result, analysts typically adjust for the effects of an incorrect discount rate (as well as for any possible cash flows that are not reflected in an income-based valuation) by adding a **control premium**. For instance, if the value of a firm's equity is estimated to be \$100 million using an income approach, a 20 percent premium might be added to arrive at a final value of \$120 million. Of course, the magnitude of the adjustment depends on the situation.

control premium an adjustment that is made to a business value estimate to reflect value associated with control that is not already reflected in the analysis

Key People

If the cash flows that a business is expected to generate depend heavily on the retention of a particular individual or group of individuals, then the analyst must also consider whether it is appropriate to adjust the estimated value of the business for the likelihood that these "key people" may not remain with the firm as long as expected. An example of a key person might be the CEO of a service firm who has strong personal ties with the major customers. If an analyst believes that those customers might transfer their business to a competitor if the CEO departs, then a **key person discount** may be appropriate. The issue is similar to the one that arises when a firm receives a significant portion of its business from a small number of customers. In either case, it is difficult to forecast the cash flows for the firm.

key person discount an adjustment to a business value estimate that is made to reflect the potential loss of value associated with the unexpected departure of a key person

Before You Go On

1. How might financial statements for private companies differ from those for public companies?
2. Why is marketability an important issue in business valuation?
3. What is a key person?

Summary of Learning Objectives

1 Explain why the choice of organizational form is important, and describe two financial considerations that are especially important in starting a business.

The choice of organizational form is important because it affects the returns from a business in a number of ways. For example, it affects the cost of getting started, the life of the business, management's ability to raise capital and grow the business, the control of the business, the ability to attract and retain good managers, the exposure of the investors to liabilities, and the taxes that are paid on the earnings of the business.

Two especially important financial considerations are the pretax operating cash flow break-even point for the business and its overall cash inflows and outflows. The pretax operating cash flow break-even point represents the level of unit sales that must be achieved in order for the business to break even on a cash flow basis. Entrepreneurs must also understand where money is coming from, where it is going, and how much external financing is likely to be needed and when. The cash budget helps with this understanding.

2 Describe the key components of a business plan and explain what a business plan is used for.

The key components of a business plan include the executive summary, a company overview, a description of the company's products and services, a market analysis, a discussion of marketing and sales activities, a discussion of the business's operations, a discussion of the management team, the ownership structure of the firm, capital requirements and uses, and financial forecasts.

A business plan helps an entrepreneur set the goals and objectives for a company, serves as a benchmark for evaluating and controlling the company's performance, and helps communicate the entrepreneur's ideas to managers and others (including investors) outside the firm.

3 Explain the three general approaches to valuation and value a business using common business valuation approaches.

The three general valuation approaches are (1) cost approaches, (2) market approaches, and (3) income approaches. Cost approaches commonly used in business valuation are the replacement cost and adjusted book value approaches. The market approaches are multiples analysis and transactions analysis. Three key income approaches are the free cash flow from the firm, free cash flow to equity, and dividend discount approaches. The application of these approaches is discussed in Section 18.3.

4 Explain how valuations can differ between public and private companies and between young and mature companies, and discuss the importance of control and key person considerations in valuation.

Valuations differ between public and private companies for a number of reasons, including (1) the quality of the financial statements and (2) the marketability of the securities being valued. Marketability is important because it affects the price that investors are willing to pay for a security. The less marketable a security, the lower the price investors are willing to pay.

Young, rapidly growing companies are more difficult to value than mature companies because there is less reliable historical information on young companies and their futures tend to be less certain.

Control is an important consideration in business valuation because having control of a business provides an investor with more flexibility in managing the business. Investors value this flexibility and will, therefore, pay more for a controlling interest in a company.

If the cash flows that a business is expected to generate depend heavily on certain employees, those employees are key people. When valuing a business, an analyst must account for the possibility that the key people will unexpectedly leave the company and must consider the associated impact on the company's cash flows.

Summary of Key Equations

Equation	Description	Formula
18.1	Price/earnings multiple based on constant-growth model	$\frac{P_0}{E_1} = \frac{b}{k_{cs} - g}$
18.2	Implementing the income approach to business valuation	$V_F = PV(FCF_T) + PV(TV_T) + NOA$
18.3	FCFF approach	$V_F = \sum_{t=0}^{\infty} \frac{FCFF_t}{(1 + WACC)^t}$
18.4	FCFE approach	$V_E = \sum_{t=0}^{\infty} \frac{FCFE_t}{(1 + k_E)^t}$

Self-Study Problems

18.1 Your sister wants to open a store that sells antique-style jewelry and accessories. She has $15,000 of savings to invest, but opening the store will require an initial investment of $20,000. Net cash inflows will be −$2,000, −$1,000, and $0 in the first three months. As the store becomes better known, net cash inflows will become +$500 in the fourth month and grow at a constant rate of 5 percent in the following months. You want to help your sister by providing the additional money that she needs. How much money do you have to invest each month to start and to keep the store operating with a minimum cash balance of $1,000?

18.2 You have the following information for a company you are valuing and for a comparable company:

Comparable company	Company you are valuing
Stock price = $23.45	Value of debt = $3.68 million
Number of shares outstanding = 6.23 million	Est. EBITDA next year = $4.4 million
Value of debt = $18.45 million	Est. income next year = $1.5 million
Est. EBITDA next year = $17.0 million	
Est. income next year = $5.3 million	

Estimate the enterprise value of the company you are evaluating using the P/E and enterprise value/EBITDA multiples.

18.3 How do the cash flows that are discounted when the WACC approach (FCFF approach) is used to value a business differ from those that are discounted when the free cash flow to equity (FCFE) approach is used to value the equity in a business?

18.4 You are valuing a company using the WACC approach and have estimated that the free cash flows from the firm (FCFF) in the next five years will be $36.7, $42.6, $45.1, $46.3, and $46.6 million, respectively. Beginning in Year 6, you expect the cash flows to decrease at a rate of 3 percent per year for the indefinite future. You estimate that the appropriate WACC to use in discounting these cash flows is 10 percent. What is the value of this company?

18.5 You want to estimate the value of a local advertising firm. The earnings of the firm are expected to be $2 million next year. Based on expected earnings next year, the average price-to-earnings ratio of similar firms in the same industry is 48. Therefore, you estimate the value of the firm you are valuing to be $96 million.

Further investigation shows that a large portion of the firm's business is obtained through connections that John Smith, a senior partner of the firm, has with various advertising executives at customer firms. Mr. Smith only recently started working with his junior partners to establish similar relationships with these customers.

Mr. Smith is approaching 65 years of age and might announce his retirement at the next board meeting. If he does retire, revenues will drop significantly and earnings are estimated to shrink by 30 percent. You estimate that the probability that Mr. Smith will retire this year is 50 percent. If he does not retire this year, you expect that Mr. Smith will have sufficient time to work with his junior partners so his departure will not affect earnings when he departs. How does this information affect your estimate of the value of the firm?

Solutions to Self-Study Problems

18.1 You will have to invest $5,000 to open the store (the difference between $20,000 and $15,000). You will then have to invest an additional $3,000 during the first month to cover the cash flow of −$2,000 and to establish a cash balance of $1,000. Another $1,000 will be required in the second month to cover the negative cash flow during that month. Since cash flows will be $0 or positive beginning in the third month, you will not have to invest any additional funds after the second month.

18.2 The P/E and enterprise value/EBITDA multiples for the comparable company are:

$$\left(\frac{P}{E}\right)_{\text{Comparable}} = \left(\frac{\text{Stock price}}{\text{Earnings per share}}\right)_{\text{Comparable}}$$

$$= \frac{\$23.45 \text{ per share}}{\$5.3 \text{ million}/6.23 \text{ million shares}}$$

$$= 27.6$$

$$\left(\frac{\text{Enterprise value}}{\text{EBITDA}}\right)_{\text{Comparable}} = \left(\frac{V_D + V_E}{\text{EBITDA}}\right)_{\text{Comparable}}$$

$$= \frac{\$18.45 \text{ million} + (\$23.45 \text{ per share} \times 6.23 \text{ million shares})}{\$17.0 \text{ million}}$$

$$= 9.68$$

Using the P/E multiple, we can calculate the value of the equity as:

$$V_E = \left(\frac{P}{E}\right)_{\text{Comparable}} \times \text{Net income}_{\text{Company being valued}}$$

$$= 27.6 \times \$1.5 \text{ million}$$

$$= \$41.4 \text{ million}$$

which suggests an enterprise value of:

$$V_F = V_E + V_D = \$41.4 \text{ million} + \$3.68 \text{ million} = \$45.08 \text{ million}$$

Using the enterprise/EBITDA multiple, we obtain:

$$V_F = \left(\frac{\text{Enterprise value}}{\text{EBITDA}}\right)_{\text{Comparable}} \times \text{EBITDA}_{\text{Company being valued}}$$

$$= 9.68 \times \$4.4 \text{ million}$$

$$= \$42.59 \text{ million}$$

18.3 The cash flows that are discounted when the WACC approach is used to value a business are calculated in the same way that the cash flows are calculated for a project analysis. These cash flows represent the total after-tax free cash flows that the business is expected to generate from operations. The cash flows that are discounted when the FCFE approach is used are the total after-tax free cash flows from the business that are available for distribution to the stockholders. In other words, they equal the total cash flows that the business is expected to generate less the net cash flows to the debt holders. The net cash flows to the debt holders is equal to the interest and principal payments that the firm makes less any proceeds for the sale of new debt.

18.4 The present value of the cash flows expected over the next five years is:

$$PV(FCFF_5) = \frac{\$36.7 \text{ million}}{1 + 0.1} + \frac{\$42.6 \text{ million}}{(1 + 0.1)^2} + \frac{\$45.1 \text{ million}}{(1 + 0.1)^3}$$

$$+ \frac{\$46.3 \text{ million}}{(1 + 0.1)^4} + \frac{\$46.6 \text{ million}}{(1 + 0.1)^5}$$

$$= \$163.01 \text{ million}$$

The terminal value is:

$$TV_5 = \frac{FCFF_5 \times (1 + g)}{WACC - g} = \frac{\$46.6 \text{ million} \times (1 - 0.03)}{0.1 + 0.03} = \$347.71 \text{ million}$$

and the present value of the terminal value is:

$$PV(TV_5) = \frac{TV_5}{(1 + WACC)^5} = \frac{\$347.71 \text{ million}}{(1 + 0.1)^5} = \$215.90 \text{ million}$$

Therefore, if there are no nonoperating assets, the value of the firm is:

$$V_F = \$163.01 \text{ million} + \$215.90 \text{ million} = \$378.91 \text{ million}$$

18.5 Mr. Smith is a *key person* in this firm. An adjustment should be made to the valuation to account for his potential departure this year.

Taking the possibility that Mr. Smith will retire into account, the expected earnings next year will be:

$$(\$2{,}000{,}000 \times 0.5) + [\$2{,}000{,}000 \times (1 - 0.30) \times 0.5] = \$1{,}700{,}000$$

Therefore, the adjusted value for the firm is \$1.7 million × 48 = \$81.6 million. We can see that this implies a 15 percent key person discount from the original estimate of \$96 million [(\$81.6 million − \$96.0 million)/\$96.0 million = −0.15, or −15 percent].

WileyPLUS

Questions and Problems, Solution Walkthrough Videos, Learning by Doing Tutorials, and additional study tools and resources are available in WileyPLUS.

Discussion Questions

18.1 Given that many new businesses fail in the first few years after they are established, how should an entrepreneur think about the risk of failure associated with a new business? From what you have learned in this chapter, what can an entrepreneur do to increase the chance of success?

18.2 Explain how the taxation of a C-corporation differs from the taxation of the other forms of business organization discussed in this chapter.

18.3 What is a business plan? Explain how a business plan can help an entrepreneur succeed in building a business.

18.4 You are entering negotiations to purchase a business and are trying to formulate a negotiating strategy. You want to determine the minimum price you should offer and the maximum you should be willing to pay. Explain how the concepts of fair market value and investment value can help you do this.

18.5 You have just received a business valuation report that is dated six months ago. Describe the factors that might have changed during the past six months and, therefore, caused the value of the business today to be different from the value six months ago. Which of these changes affect the expected cash flows, and which affect the discount rate that you would use in a discounted cash flow valuation of this company?

18.6 Is the replacement cost of a business generally related to the value of the cash flows that the business is expected to produce in the future? Why or why not? Illustrate your answer with an example.

18.7 You want to estimate the value of a company that has three very different lines of business. It manufactures aircraft, is in the data processing business, and manufactures automobiles. How could you use an income approach to value a company such as this—one with three very distinct businesses that will have different revenue growth rates, profit margins, investment requirements, discount rates, and so forth?

18.8 Your boss has asked you to estimate the intrinsic value of the equity for Google, which does not currently pay any dividends. You are going to use an income approach and are trying to choose between the free cash flow to equity (FCFE) approach and the dividend discount model (DDM) approach. Which would be more appropriate in this instance? Why? What concerns would you have in applying either of these valuation approaches to a company such as this?

18.9 Explain how the financial statements of a private company might differ from those of a public company. What does this imply for valuing a private company?

18.10 Explain why it is difficult to value a young, rapidly growing company.

Questions and Problems

Excel *Excel templates and resources available in* **WileyPLUS**

Basic

18.1 **Organizational form:** List some common forms of business organization, and discuss how access to capital differs across these forms of organization.

18.2 **Starting a business:** What are some of the things that the founder of a company must do to launch a new business?

18.3 Organizational form: Explain how financial liabilities differ among different forms of business organization.

18.4 Cash requirements: List two useful tools to help an entrepreneur to understand the cash requirements of a business and to estimate the financing needs of that business.

18.5 Cash requirements: You believe you have a great business idea and want to start your own company. However, you do not have enough savings to finance it. Where can you get the additional funds you need?

18.6 Raising capital: Why is it especially difficult for an entrepreneur with a new business to raise capital? What tool can help him or her to raise external capital?

18.7 Replacement cost: What is the replacement cost of a business?

18.8 Multiples analysis: It is April 4, 2018, and your company is considering the possibility of purchasing the Chrysler automobile manufacturing business. Managers of Fiat Chrysler Automobiles N.V., the automobile manufacturer that owns Chrysler, have hinted that they might be interested in selling Chrysler. Since Chrysler does not have publicly traded shares of its own, you have decided to use Ford Motor Company as a comparable company to help you determine the market value of Chrysler.

This morning, Ford's common stock was trading at $11.75 per share, and the company had 3.9 billion shares outstanding. You estimated that the market value of all of the company's other outstanding securities (excluding the common stock but including special shares owned by the Ford family) is $35.0 billion and that its revenues from auto sales were $155.0 billion last year. Chrysler's revenue in 2017 was $50.0 billion. Based on the enterprise value/revenue ratio, what is the total value of Chrysler that is implied by the Ford market values?

18.9 Nonoperating assets: Why is excess cash a nonoperating asset (NOA)? Why does it make sense to add the value of excess cash to the value of the discounted cash flows when we use the WACC (FCFF) or FCFE approach to value a business?

18.10 Dividend discount approach: You want to estimate the total intrinsic value of a large gas and electric utility company. This company has publicly traded stock and has been paying a regular dividend for many years. You decide that, due to the predictability of the dividend that this company pays, you can use the dividend discount valuation approach. The company is expected to pay a dividend of $1.25 per share next year, and the dividend is expected to grow at a rate of 3 percent per year thereafter. You estimate that the appropriate rate for discounting future dividends is 12 percent. In addition, you know that the company has 46 million shares outstanding and that the market value of its debt is $350 million. What is the total enterprise value of the company?

18.11 Public versus private company valuation: You are considering investing in a private company that is owned by a friend of yours. You have read through the company's financial statements and believe that they are reliable. Multiples of similar publicly traded companies in the same industry suggest that the value of a share of stock in your friend's company is $12. Should you be willing to pay $12 per share?

18.12 Control: Does the expected rate of return that is calculated using CAPM, with a beta estimated from stock returns in the public market, reflect a minority or a controlling ownership position? How is it likely to differ between a minority and a controlling position?

Intermediate

18.13 Organizational form: Compare the characteristics of an LLC with those of a partnership and a C-corporation.

18.14 Organizational form: Discuss the pros and cons of an S-corporation compared with a C-corporation.

18.15 Break-even point: You have started a business that sells a home gardening system that allows people to grow vegetables on their kitchen countertop. You are considering two options for marketing your product. The first is to advertise on local TV. The second is to distribute flyers in the local community. The TV option, which costs $50,000 annually, will promote the product more effectively and create a demand for 1,200 units per year. The flyer advertisement option costs only $6,000 annually, but will create a demand for only 250 units per year. The price per unit of the indoor gardening system is $100, and the variable cost is $60 per unit. Assume that the production capacity is not limited and that the marketing cost is the only fixed cost involved in your business. What are the break-even points for both marketing options? Which one should you choose?

18.16 Going-concern value: Aggie Motors is a chain of used car dealerships that has publicly traded stock. Using the adjusted book value approach, you have estimated the value of Aggie Motors to be $45,646,000. The company has $40.5 million of debt outstanding. Its stock price is $5.5 per share, and there are 1,378,000 shares outstanding. What is the going-concern value of Aggie Motors?

Use the following information concerning Johnson Machine Tool Company in Problems 18.17, 18.18, and 18.19.

Johnson's income statement from the fiscal year that ended this past December is:

Revenue	$995
Cost of goods sold	652
Gross profit	$343
Selling, general, and administrative expenses	135
Operating profit (EBIT)	$208
Interest expense	48
Earnings before taxes	$160
Taxes	64
Net income	$ 96

All dollar values are in millions. Depreciation and amortization expenses last year were $42 million, and the company has $533 million of debt outstanding.

18.17 Multiples analysis: You are an analyst at a private equity firm that buys private companies, improves their operating performance, and sells them for a profit. Your boss has asked you to estimate the fair market value of the Johnson Machine Tool Company. Billy's Tools is a public company with business operations that are virtually identical to those at Johnson. The most recent income statement for Billy's Tools is as follows:

Revenue	$1,764
Cost of goods sold	1,168
Gross profit	$ 596
Selling, general, and administrative expenses	211
Operating profit (EBIT)	$ 385
Interest expense	12
Earnings before taxes	$ 373
Taxes	147
Net income	$ 226

All dollar values are in millions. Billy's had depreciation and amortization expenses of $71 million last year and had 200 million shares and $600 million of debt outstanding as of the end of the year. Its stock is currently trading at $12.25 per share.

Using the P/E multiple, what is the per share value of Johnson's stock? What is the total value of Johnson Machine Tool Company?

18.18 Multiples analysis: Using the enterprise value/EBITDA multiple, what is the total value of Johnson Machine Tool Company? What is the per share value of Johnson's stock?

18.19 Multiples analysis: Which of the above multiples analyses do you believe is more accurate for valuing the firm and its stock?

18.20 Income approaches: You are using the FCFF approach to value a business. You have estimated that the FCFF for next year will be $123.65 million and that it will increase at a rate of 8 percent for each of the following four years. After that point, the FCFF will increase at a rate of 3 percent forever. If the WACC for this firm is 10 percent and it has no NOA, what is it worth?

18.21 Valuing a private business: You want to estimate the value of a privately owned restaurant that is financed entirely with equity. Its most recent income statement is as follows:

Revenue	$3,000,000
Cost of goods sold	600,000
Gross profit	$2,400,000
Salaries and wages	1,400,000
Selling expenses	100,000
Operating profit (EBIT)	$ 900,000
Taxes	315,000
Net income	$ 585,000

You note that the profitability of this restaurant is significantly lower than that of comparable restaurants, primarily due to high salary and wage expenses. Further investigation reveals that the annual salaries for the owner and his wife, the firm's accountant, are $900,000 and $300,000, respectively. These salaries are much higher than the industry median salaries for these two positions of $100,000 and $50,000, respectively. Compensation for other employees ($200,000 in total) appears to be consistent with the market rates. The median P/E ratio of comparable restaurants with no debt is 10. What is the total value of this restaurant?

18.22 Valuing a private business: A few years ago, a friend of yours started a small business that develops gaming software. The company is doing well and is valued at $1.5 million based on multiples for comparable public companies after adjustments for their lack of marketability. With 300,000 shares outstanding, each share is estimated to be worth $5. Your friend, who has been serving as CEO and CTO (chief technology officer), has decided that he lacks sufficient managerial skills to continue to build the company. He wants to sell his 160,000 shares and invest the money in an MBA education. You believe you have the appropriate managerial skills to run the company. Would you pay $5 each for these shares? What are some of the factors you should consider in making this decision?

Advanced

18.23 You plan to start a business that sells waterproof sun block with a unique formula that reduces the damage of UVA radiation 30 percent more effectively than similar products on the market.

You expect to invest $50,000 in plant and equipment to begin the business. The targeted price of the sun block is $15 per bottle. You forecast that unit sales will total 1,500 bottles in the first month and will increase by 20 percent in each of the following months during the first year. You expect the cost of raw materials to be $3 per bottle. In addition, monthly gross wages and payroll are expected to be $13,000, rent is expected to be $3,000, and other expenses are expected to total $1,000. Advertising costs are estimated to be $35,000 in the first month, but to remain constant at $5,000 per month during the following eleven months.

You have decided to finance the entire business at one time using your own savings. Is an initial investment of $75,000 adequate to avoid a negative cash balance in any given month? If not, how much more do you need to invest up front? How much do you need to invest up front to keep a minimum cash balance of $5,000? What is the break-even point for the business?

18.24 For the previous question, assume that you do not have sufficient savings to cover the entire amount required to start your sun-block business. You are going to have to get external financing. A local banker whom you know has offered you a six-month loan of $20,000 at an APR of 12 percent. You will pay interest each month and repay the entire principal at the end of six months.

Assume that instead of making a single up-front investment, you are going to finance the business by making monthly investments as cash is needed in the business. If the proceeds from the loan go directly into the business on the first day and are therefore available to pay for some of the capital expenditures, how much money will you need to take from your savings account every month to run the business and keep the cash balances positive?

18.25 Your friend is starting a new company. He wants to write a business plan to clarify the company's business outlook and raise venture capital. Knowing that you have taken this course, he has asked you, as a favor, to help him prepare a template for a business plan. Prepare a template that includes the key elements of a business plan.

18.26 A friend of yours is trying to value the equity of a company and, knowing that you have read this book, has asked for your help. So far she has tried to use the FCFE approach. She estimated the cash flows to equity to be as follows:

Sales	\$ 800.0
– CGS	–450.0
– Depreciation	–80.0
– Interest	–24.0
Earning before taxes (EBT)	\$ 246.0
– Taxes (0.35 × EBT)	–86.1
= Cash flow to equity	\$159.9

She also computed the cost of equity using CAPM as follows:

$$k_E = k_F + \beta_E(\text{Risk premium}) = 0.06 + (1.25 \times 0.084)$$
$$= 0.165, \text{ or } 16.5\%$$

where the beta is estimated for a comparable publicly traded company.

Using this cost of equity, she estimates the discount rate as

$$\text{WACC} = x_{\text{Debt}} k_{\text{Debt pretax}}(1 - t) + x_{cs} k_{cs}$$
$$= [0.20 \times 0.06 \times (1 - 0.35)] + (0.80 \times 0.165)$$
$$= 0.14, \text{ or } 14\%$$

Based on this analysis, she concludes that the value of equity is \$159.9 million/0.14 = \$1,142 million.

Assuming that the numbers used in this analysis are all correct, what advice would you give your friend regarding her analysis?

18.27 Forever Youth Technology is a biochemical company that is two years old. Its main product, an antioxidant drink that is supposed to energize the consumer and delay aging, is still under development. The company's equity consists of \$5 million invested by its founders and \$5 million from a venture capitalist. The company has spent \$3 million in each of the past two years, mostly on lab equipment and R&D costs. The company has had no sales so far. What are the challenges associated with valuing such a young and uncertain company?

18.28 Mad Rock Inc. is a company that sells music online. It is expected to generate earnings of \$1 per share this year after its Web site is upgraded and online marketing is stepped up. The stock price of Mad Rock has rocketed from \$8 to \$95 per share in the past 12 months. The cost of capital for the company is 18 percent.

Of course, the future of a young Internet company such as Mad Rock is highly uncertain. Nevertheless, using the very limited information provided in this problem, do you think \$95 per share could be a fair price for its stock? Support your argument with a simple analysis.

18.29 At the end of 2016 the value of the S&P 500 Index divided by the estimated 2016 earnings for S&P 500 firms (the S&P 500 P/E multiple) was 25.54. Assume that the long-term Treasury bond yield was 2.88 percent, the market risk premium was 5.92 percent, and firms in the S&P 500 were expected to pay out an average of 40.2 percent of their earnings as dividends in the future. At what rate were dividends paid by S&P 500 firms expected to grow in the future?

18.30 The S&P 500 P/E multiple of 25.54 at the end of 2016 was higher than its historical average of approximately 15. Some financial commentators argued that this meant that the firms in the S&P 500 were, on average, overvalued at the end of 2016. Based on your analysis in Problem 18.29 and the concepts covered in this book, do you think that these commentators are right or wrong? Why or why not?

18.31 You own a company that produces and distributes course packets for classes at local universities via the Internet. You have asked a friend to invest \$35,000 in the business. Your friend wants to know what the business is worth so that he can determine how much of the equity (e.g., what percentage) he should expect to receive for his investment. You offer to help him value the business.

The business is expected to generate revenue of \$110,000 and incur cash operating expenses of \$70,000 next year. Over the following three years, revenue and cash operating expenses are expected to increase 15 percent, 10 percent, and 7 percent. After Year 4, they are expected to grow 2 percent per year forever. Depreciation and amortization, capital expenditures, and additions to working capital are expected to equal 5 percent, 6 percent, and 1 percent of revenue, respectively, in the future. You have determined that a target capital structure of 10 percent is reasonable for this business. With this capital structure, the pretax cost of debt will be 6 percent and the beta for the equity will be 1.30. The average tax rate for the business is 10 percent, and the marginal rate is 20 percent. The risk-free rate is 4.25 percent, and the market risk premium is 6.01 percent. What is a 100 percent equity interest in the business worth? What percentage of the equity should your friend get for his investment?

Sample Test Problems

18.1 You plan to start a business to produce and sell custom kitchen cabinets. The targeted price for each order of cabinets is \$10,000. You estimate that you will receive orders for cabinets for eight kitchens in each of the first two months, nine kitchens in the third month, and ten kitchens in the fourth month. The cost of the equipment necessary to produce the cabinets is \$105,000. You expect the cost of raw materials to be \$3,000 per order. In addition, you expect monthly gross wages and payroll to be \$27,000, rent to be \$8,000, and other expenses to total \$4,000. You also expect advertising costs to be \$10,000 in the first month but to remain constant at \$1,000 per month during the following three months. How much will you have to initially invest to ensure that you have a cash balance of \$10,000 at the beginning of the second month? If you invest this amount, what will be your cash balance at the end of the fourth month?

18.2 Which of the following is/are usually included in an entrepreneur's business plan?

a. Detailed description of the company's products and services.

b. Discussion of the management team, including organizational structure.

c. A listing of the types of securities that have been issued and who owns them.

d. A market analysis.

e. All of the above are typically included in a business plan.

18.3 Sessler Corporation is a private company that had EBIT of \$186 million and depreciation and amortization of \$22 million in the most recent fiscal year. At the end of that year, a similar, public firm has an enterprise value/EBITDA multiple of 4.3. What is the implied enterprise value of Sessler?

18.4 Winters Inc. management estimates that the company will generate after-tax free cash flows from the firm (FCFF) of \$12.5 million, \$16.8 million, and \$19.7 million, respectively, over the next three years. After that, FCFF are expected to grow at a constant 5 percent per year forever. The company has \$5 million in nonoperating assets. If the appropriate WACC is 8 percent, what is the enterprise value of this business?

18.5 Do private companies have audited financial statements prepared in accordance with GAAP?

CHAPTER 19

Financial Planning and Managing Growth

ANDREW KELLY/REUTERS/Newscom

LEARNING OBJECTIVES

1. Explain what a financial plan is and why financial planning is important.
2. Discuss how management uses financial planning models in the planning process, and explain the importance of sales forecasts in the construction of financial planning models.
3. Discuss how the relation between projected sales and the income statement and balance sheet accounts can be determined, and analyze a strategic investment decision using a percent of sales model.
4. Describe the conditions under which fixed assets vary directly with sales, and discuss the impact of so-called lumpy assets on this relation.
5. Explain what factors determine a firm's sustainable growth rate, discuss why it is of interest to management, and compute the sustainable growth rate for a firm.

On April 3, 2017, Kevin Johnson replaced Howard Schultz as chief executive officer (CEO) of Starbucks. At the time of Mr. Johnson's appointment, Starbucks management faced its greatest challenges since 2008, when Howard Schultz was forced out of retirement to help turn the company around. In 2008, Starbucks had lost its focus on product quality and the customer in-store experience and was struggling to attract customers who were willing to pay for its premium-priced products. Increased competition from brands such as McDonald's and Dunkin' Donuts, combined with the global economic downturn, had also hurt the Starbucks bottom line.

Mr. Schultz turned things around by cutting costs, shifting new store investment to more profitable foreign markets, improving product quality and the customer experience, and introducing a lower-cost brand to compete with value-based rivals. This restructuring was a great success, with the company experiencing six years of more than 5 percent annual growth in same-store sales. Earnings in 2015 were the highest in Starbucks's history and the company's stock price rose from a low of $7.17 per share on November 20, 2008, to a high of $97.92 per share on March 24, 2015.

However, by April 2017, the positive trajectory under Mr. Schultz was proving difficult to maintain. The rate at which Starbucks was growing had declined. Same-store sales failed to grow at an annual rate of 5 percent in 2016, the company failed to achieve management's earnings projections, and the stock price declined substantially. By April 3, 2017, Starbucks's stock price was $58.44 per share, a 40.3 percent decline from its peak in 2015. The decline was even worse when compared with the 12.8 percent increase in the S&P 500 Index over that same period.

When Kevin Johnson became CEO, he knew that he had to put the company back on the fast track by improving same-store sales, increasing profit margins, and taking advantage of new growth opportunities. He would have to pursue thoughtful corporate growth using feasible operating and financial strategies in order to succeed. This chapter explains how managers like Mr. Johnson plan for the future and manage growth to create value for their stockholders.

Chapter Preview

It is often said that a company that fails to plan for the future may have no future. In the short run, a firm may do well being opportunistic—reacting quickly to events as they unfold. To succeed over the long term, however, a firm must be innovative and must plan and employ a strategy that generates sustainable profits. Top executives spend a lot of time thinking about the types of investments the firm needs to make and how to finance them. The process that executives go through is called financial planning, and the result is called a financial plan.

This chapter focuses on long-term financial planning. We begin with a discussion of the firm's strategic plan and its components. We then discuss the preparation of a financial plan. Next, we turn our attention to financial planning models used in the preparation of financial plans. These models generate projected financial statements that estimate the amount of external funding needed and identify other financial consequences of proposed strategic investments. We end the chapter by examining the relation between a firm's growth and its need for external funding. Managing growth is an important topic, because growth without sufficient profits can lead to cash flow shortages and bankruptcy.

19.1 Financial Planning

LEARNING OBJECTIVE

1. Explain what a financial plan is and why financial planning is important.

financial planning the process by which management decides what types of investments the firm needs to make and how to finance those investments

financial plan a plan outlining the investments a firm intends to make and how it will finance them

Top management engages in long-term **financial planning** because experience has shown that having a well-articulated **financial plan** helps create value for stockholders. Planning is important for established businesses because it forces management to systematically think through the firm's strategies, much like preparing a business plan helps an entrepreneur. Not surprisingly, a lack of planning is a common reason for poor performance and bankruptcy. For example, the bankruptcy filing by Ronco Corporation in June 2007 was attributed to a failure to plan and recognize the importance of the firm's traditional distribution channels. Ronco was the manufacturer of the Veg-O-Matic vegetable slicer and other novelty gadgets, such as Mr. Microphone and a device that mixes eggs inside the shells.[1]

The Planning Documents

When top management begins to prepare a company's financial plan, it must answer four basic questions. First, where is the company headed? Second, what assets does it need to get there? Third, how is the firm going to pay for these assets? And, finally, does the firm have enough cash to pay its day-to-day bills as they come due?

These questions are answered in four important planning documents: (1) the *strategic plan*, which describes where the firm is headed and articulates the strategies that will be used

[1]Ronco's founder, Ron Popeil, became a minor household celebrity hawking the firm's products on late-night television.

to get it there; (2) the *investment plan*, which identifies the capital assets needed to execute the strategies; (3) the *financing plan*, which explains how the firm will raise the money to buy the assets; and (4) the *cash budget*, which determines whether the firm will have sufficient cash to pay its bills. These four planning documents provide the foundation for the firm's *financial plan*, which consolidates the documents into a single scheme. Thus, the financial plan is a blueprint for the firm's future.

Exhibit 19.1 shows the relations among the various plans and budgets. Notice that information from the strategic plan flows down to the financial plan and information from the other plans and the cash budget flows up to the financial plan.

strategic planning the process by which management establishes the firm's long-term goals, the strategies that will be used to achieve those goals, and the capabilities that are needed to sustain the firm's competitive position

The Strategic Plan

Strategic planning is the most crucial planning step. The strategic plan sets out the vision for the firm—what management wants the firm to become—and establishes the strategies that managers will use to achieve their vision. Overall, the strategic plan provides high-level direction to management for making business decisions and guidance about what the firm will and will not do.

Preparing the strategic plan is the responsibility of top management, with the financial manager as a key participant and the board of directors as approver of the plan. The strategic plan covers all areas in the firm, such as operations, marketing, finance, information systems, and human resource management. The plan determines the lines of business in which the firm will compete and the relative emphasis placed on each business activity. It also identifies major areas for investments in productive assets: capital expenditures, the acquisition of a firm, or the launch of a new line of business. When deemed necessary, the plan also identifies mergers, alliances, and divestitures that management may seek to strengthen the firm's business portfolio.

Building Intuition

A Firm's Strategy Drives Its Business Decisions

The firm's business strategy drives all of its decisions. It determines the firm's lines of business, the products it will sell, its method of producing them, and the geographic markets in which it will compete. Thus, a company's strategy defines its competitive position within its industry. To be successful, a firm must have a good strategy and a management team that can implement it. Management is always searching for a strategy that gives the firm a sustainable competitive edge.

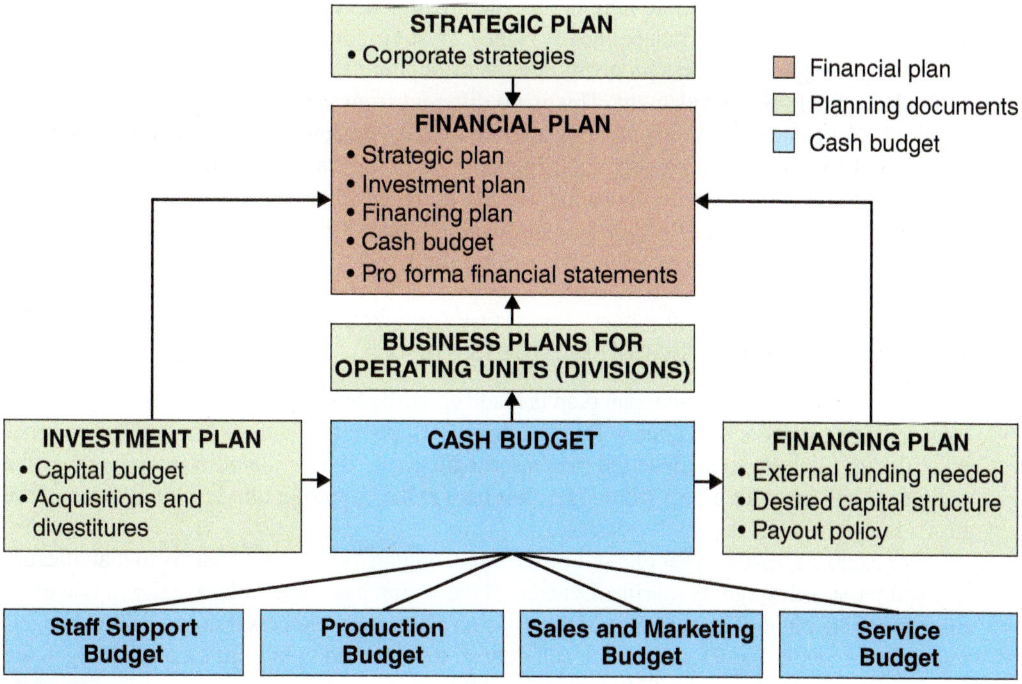

EXHIBIT 19.1 **The Financial Planning Process**

Various planning and budget documents flow into a financial plan and form its foundation. The completed financial plan articulates the firm's strategic goals and identifies what types of investments the firm should make to achieve its goals, as well as how to finance those investments.

The Investment Plan

The investment plan, also known as the capital budget, lays out the firm's proposed spending on capital assets for the year.[2] The capital expenditures support the firm's business strategy. Some capital expenditures pay for significant new additions, such as a new building, a new plant, or a new production line. Other capital expenditures are for more routine items, such as the replacement of old equipment and machinery. Once made, capital expenditures define a firm's line of business for years to come. For example, Ford Motor Company could not suddenly start making tennis shoes instead of cars because Ford's long-term assets hardly lend themselves to manufacturing shoes and the cost of conversion would be prohibitive. The preparation of the capital budget and the decision criteria for selecting capital projects are discussed in Chapters 10 through 13.

The Financing Plan

Once the capital budget is set, management must decide how to finance the assets. The simplest financing environment is one in which all capital projects are financed using *internally* generated funds. This means that the firm's earnings, less cash used to pay dividends or repurchase stock, provide the necessary capital. However, only rarely does a firm finance all its projects in this way, as most firms have more capital projects than they can fund internally. Thus, management must seek *external* funding from a variety of sources, such as bank borrowing, selling of long-term debt, and issuance of additional equity. Overall, the goal of the financing plan is to determine how much external funding the firm needs.

Weblink

A source for sample business plans, including financial plans, is the Center for Business Planning at http://www.businessplans.org/tabplan.html.

The financing plan has three components. First, a financing plan states the dollar amount of *external funding needed* and identifies the sources of funds available to the firm. Second, the plan states management's *desired capital structure* for the firm. This is important because it determines the relative amounts of debt and equity funds to be raised externally. Finally, the financing plan establishes the firm's *payout policy*, which is relevant because it directly affects the amount of funds available for new investment projects. That is, the more funds the firm pays out as cash dividends or uses to repurchase stock, the more external capital the firm must raise if its internally generated funds are not sufficient to fund its investments. Capital structure policy is discussed in Chapter 16, and payout policy in Chapter 17.

An important point to note here is that the investment (capital budgeting) and financing decisions *cannot* be made independently—they must be considered together. The reason is that when management makes an investment decision, it must already have identified a source of funds to pay for the investment. This is no different from what you would do in your personal life. For example, you would not walk into a BMW dealership to buy a high-priced new car without having lined up a source of financing. Nor, for that matter, would the dealer sell you the car without having the financing already arranged. The investment decision (buy the car) and the financing decision (get an auto loan) are made simultaneously and hence are not independent.

Operating Unit (Divisional) Business Plans

Another component of the financial plan is made up of the *business plans* prepared by the various operating units or divisions within the firm. Each operating unit business plan describes what the unit will do to achieve the firm's strategic goals. It also identifies the resources the unit needs and includes a detailed budget. It is here at the operating unit level that much of the firm's budget work is done.

For example, assume that one of Ford Motor Company's strategic goals is to manufacture and sell jet-skis through its marine division. The division has some idle capacity in one of its manufacturing plants. Thus, as part of the division's business plan, it submits a capital budgeting request to enter the jet-ski market. (Of course, to be included in Ford's capital budget, the jet-ski project must have an NPV greater than $0.)

[2]The investment plan consists of the capital budget plus any acquisitions or divestitures management plans to make. To simplify our discussion in this chapter, we treat the investment plan and capital budget as one and the same because, for most firms, acquisitions and divestitures are not regular events.

Cash Budget

The cash budget for the firm is the aggregation (adding up) of the cash budgets from all of the operating units plus the cash budget for the corporate offices. The cash budget focuses exclusively on when the firm actually receives and pays out cash. The firm's cash needs may vary weekly, monthly, and seasonally, as well as with predictable events such as payroll payments, payment of cash dividends, and debt retirements. If a shortfall of cash develops, the cash budget indicates the amount of money the firm needs to borrow and the anticipated borrowing cost.

As Exhibit 19.1 shows, the planning process drills down deep into the firm and gathers cash budget information on the myriad of activities that take place. If cash budgets are not well managed and monitored, serious cash shortages can occur. Tools used in cash management are discussed in Chapter 14 and the preparation of cash budgets is covered in Chapter 18.

Concluding Comments

The principal benefit of financial planning is that it establishes financial and operating goals for the firm and communicates them throughout the organization. The financial plan also helps to align the actions of managers and their operating units with the firm's strategic goals. Thus, the plan acts as a catalyst to get everyone in the firm moving in the same direction. To build support for the financial plan and energize people's actions, top management should involve managers and other leaders in the firm at all levels in the planning process. An old axiom in management says that people support plans when they have had meaningful involvement in the plans' preparation.

Before You Go On

1. What are the four planning documents on which the financial plan is based?
2. What is the strategic plan?
3. How are the investment decision and financing decision related?

19.2 Financial Planning Models

LEARNING OBJECTIVE

2. Discuss how management uses financial planning models in the planning process, and explain the importance of sales forecasts in the construction of financial planning models.

Financial planning models are used to analyze how proposed investments and financing alternatives affect a firm's financial statements. The models are usually run on computer spreadsheets, which reduce the drudgery of tracing investment, financing, and operating decisions through a company's accounting system. While commercial planning models have an aura of sophistication about them, most are built around the same basic concepts presented in this chapter.

In this section, we build a simple financial planning model to show how such models are constructed, how they work, and how their output is generated. Once you understand this model, you can easily step up to more advanced models.

The Sales Forecast

The sales forecast is the most important input for developing a financial planning model. Most firms generate their own sales forecasts. However, forecasting techniques vary widely, ranging from "seat-of-the-pants" forecasts—wherein the sales manager and key sales staff members talk it over and give their best estimate—to forecasts generated by complex statistical models. In addition, because the performance of the national and international economies have an effect on a company's sales volume, most companies use economic forecasts as part of their sales forecasting process. Large companies often hire consulting firms that specialize in forecasting to help prepare sales forecasts under different scenarios. As you would expect, their services are quite expensive; economic forecasts can also be obtained from many regional banks at modest prices.

Building a Financial Planning Model

A financial planning model is no more than a series of equations that is used to generate projected financial statements for a company, such as an income statement or a balance sheet. The three basic components of a financial planning model, shown in **Exhibit 19.2**, are (1) inputs to the model, (2) the model itself, and (3) outputs from the model—the projected financial statements. Let's discuss each component in turn.

Inputs to the Model

As shown in the exhibit, important inputs to the financial planning model include current financial statements, sales forecasts, and investment and financial policy decisions.

Weblink

You can find financial statements for publicly held firms online in the EDGAR database of the Securities and Exchange Commission: http://www.sec.gov.

Current Financial Statements The starting point for constructing a financial planning model is the firm's current income statement and balance sheet. These statements serve as a baseline.

Sales Forecasts For most financial planning models, the principal input variable is a forecast of the firm's sales or sales growth rate. The sales forecast is the key driver in financial models because so many items on the income statement and balance sheet vary with changes in the level of sales. For example, if sales increase, it stands to reason that the firm will use more labor and raw materials. Higher sales may also require additional investments in capital assets.

Sales forecasts are given for some time period, such as a quarter or a year, and are often expressed as percent change in sales:

$$\% \Delta S = \frac{(S_{t+1} - S_t)}{S_t} \tag{19.1}$$

where:

$\%\Delta S$ = percent change in net sales

S_t = level of net sales in period t

S_{t+1} = level of net sales in period $t + 1$

Sales are calculated as the number of units sold times the price at which they are sold. For an example of how Equation 19.1 is used, if the current year's sales (S_t) are \$100 million and the forecasted sales for next year (S_{t+1}) are \$120 million, applying Equation 19.1 yields the percent growth in sales over the coming year:

$$\% \Delta S = \frac{(S_{t+1} - S_t)}{S_t} = \frac{(\$120 - \$100)}{\$100} = 0.20, \text{ or } 20\%$$

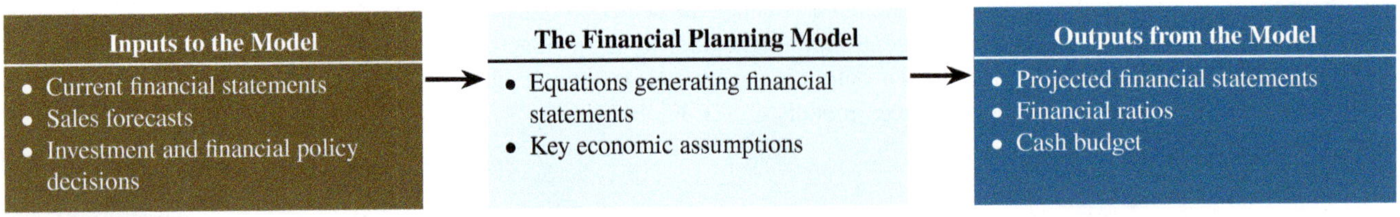

EXHIBIT 19.2 The Components of a Financial Planning Model

We can categorize the parts of a financial planning model as inputs, the model itself, and outputs. Models allow management to generate projected financial statements that enable them to see the financial impact of strategic initiatives.

Investment and Financial Policy Decisions Preparing a financial planning model requires top management to make a number of investment and financial policy decisions. These decisions impose constraints on the financial model's outputs that must be recognized during its preparation. Some important investment and financial policy decisions are:

- *Investment policy decisions:* Identify the investment decisions to be evaluated as part of the financial planning process. Typically, these are large capital expenditures such as building a new manufacturing facility, entering a new line of business, or acquiring another firm.
- *Financial policy decisions:*
  - *Capital structure decision:* Determines management's targeted capital structure—its willingness to use financial leverage.
  - *Financing decision:* Determines the acceptable type of financing—retained earnings, equity, preferred stock, and/or long-term debt.
  - *Payout decision:* Identifies the firm's dividend and stock repurchase policies for the sales period.

The Financial Planning Model

A financial planning model is a set of equations that generates projected financial statements. Along with the sales forecast and the investment and financial policy decisions, management must specify key assumptions regarding how the income statement and the balance sheet accounts vary with sales. For example, suppose that, based on historical data, a company finds that cost of goods sold is 80 percent of sales and inventory and accounts receivables are each 15 percent of sales. In such a case, it might be reasonable to assume that these relations will hold for the projected income statement and balance sheet. Thus, if sales are projected to be $100 million next year, the projected cost of goods sold will be $80 million ($100 million × 0.80 = $80 million), and inventory and accounts receivable will both be $15 million ($100 million × 0.15 = $15 million). This simple model, along with the other planning models presented in this chapter, is a **percent of sales model**, in which most of the variables vary directly with the level of sales.

percent of sales model a simple financial planning model that assumes that most income statement and balance sheet accounts vary proportionally with sales

Learning by Doing Application 19.1, at the top of the next page, illustrates how next year's accounts receivable and inventory can be calculated as a percent of sales.

Outputs from the Model: Projected Financial Statements

The outputs from the financial planning model are projected financial statements called **pro forma financial statements**. In finance and accounting, the term *pro forma* means forecasted or projected.[3] The statements produced by a financial planning model are forecasted based on the inputs and assumptions entered into the model. In addition to pro forma financial statements, computer-based planning models usually generate a set of financial ratios similar to those discussed in Chapter 4 and include features that enable management to prepare a cash budget.

pro forma financial statements projected financial statements that reflect a set of assumptions concerning investment, financing, and operating decisions

A Simple Planning Model

Let's work through a simple percent of sales example to see how a financial planning model generates pro forma financial statements and is used to analyze a strategic investment.[4] Keep in mind that more sophisticated planning models are built around the same basic concepts—there are just more assumptions to deal with. The important point here is to make sure you understand how the model is built on a set of assumptions and how it generates the pro forma financial statements.

[3]The phrase *pro forma* is a Latin term that literally means "as a matter of form." In its modern context in finance and accounting, *pro forma* refers to data that are hypothetical.

[4]Note that to simplify the analysis, some of the income statement and balance sheet accounts used in the planning model are aggregated. For example, in our initial planning model, the balance sheet lists only total assets, debt, and equity.

LEARNING BY DOING

APPLICATION 19.1 | Financial Statement Items Often Vary with Sales

Problem You have the following information: (1) sales this year are \$50 million; (2) sales are expected to grow by 20 percent next year; and (3) for the current year, accounts receivable are 7 percent of sales and inventory is 10 percent of sales. Your boss has asked you to estimate next year's sales, accounts receivable, and inventory.

Approach You can rearrange Equation 19.1 to find next year's sales level (S_{t+1}). Then, assuming accounts receivable and inventory grow proportionately with sales, you can use the result to calculate the expected levels of accounts receivable and inventory for next year.

Solution

$$\%\Delta S = \frac{(S_{t+1} - S_t)}{S_t}$$

$$0.2 = \frac{(S_{t+1} - \$50{,}000{,}000)}{\$50{,}000{,}000}$$

$$S_{t+1} = (0.2 \times \$50{,}000{,}000) + \$50{,}000{,}000$$

$$= \$60{,}000{,}000$$

$$\text{Accounts receivable} = \$60{,}000{,}000 \times 0.07 = \$4{,}200{,}000$$

$$\text{Inventory} = \$60{,}000{,}000 \times 0.10 = \$6{,}000{,}000$$

Generating Pro Forma Statements

Sleepy Hollow Corporation's financial statements for the year that just ended are shown in simplified form in the following table:

Sleepy Hollow Corporation Current Financial Statements (\$ millions)						
Income Statement		**Balance Sheet**				
Net sales	\$1,000	Assets	\$600	Debt	\$400
Costs	700			Equity	200
Net income	\$ 300	Total	\$600	Total	\$600

Sleepy Hollow's management expects sales to increase by 15 percent for the coming year. Assume that the financial statement accounts vary directly with changes in sales and that management has no financing plan at this time. Given this information, we can make the following calculations:

$$\text{Projected sales} = \$1{,}000 \text{ million} \times 1.15 = \$1{,}150 \text{ million}$$

$$\text{Projected costs} = \$700 \text{ million} \times 1.15 = \$805 \text{ million}$$

We now have the sales and cost figures for the firm's pro forma income statement:

Sleepy Hollow Corporation Pro Forma Income Statement (\$ millions)	
Net sales	\$1,150
Costs	805
Net income	\$ 345

Thus, the firm's projected net income is \$345 million.

Turning to the balance sheet, since we are assuming that all financial statement items vary with the change in sales, the projected values for the balance sheet accounts are:

$$\text{Projected assets} = \$600 \text{ million} \times 1.15 = \$690 \text{ million}$$

$$\text{Projected debt} = \$400 \text{ million} \times 1.15 = \$460 \text{ million}$$

$$\text{Projected equity} = \$200 \text{ million} \times 1.15 = \$230 \text{ million}$$

and the resulting pro forma balance sheet is:

Sleepy Hollow Corporation Pro Forma Balance Sheet ($ millions)					
Assets	$690	($90)	Debt	$460	($60)
			Equity	230	(30)
Total	$690	($90)	Total	$690	($90)

The numbers in parentheses are the changes between the current and projected dollar amounts. Notice that all the balance sheet figures have increased by 15 percent and that the balance sheet balances. This is because both the sources and use of funds have increased by 15 percent. The $90 million in new assets is being financed by $30 million from retained earnings (internal financing) and $60 million from new long-term debt (external funding).

The balance sheet balances, but if you look back at the income statement, you may notice that the equity account does not look right. Recall that Sleepy Hollow's projected net income was $345 million. Adding this amount to the initial equity account balance of $200 million yields a final equity balance of $545 million ($345 million + $200 million = $545 million). As you can see, the equity balance in the pro forma balance sheet is $230 million. Why the apparent conflict?

As a general rule, whenever account balances differ or there is some confusion about an account, the easiest way to determine what is going on is to reconcile the account. For the equity account, if the firm is not expected to sell new stock, there are two basic things that could take place during the year: (1) the firm could generate income that is added to retained earnings and (2) management could distribute value to stockholders by paying a cash dividend, repurchasing stock, or doing a combination of both. Dividends will be subtracted from retained earnings and stock repurchases will be reflected in the treasury share account. Since the pro forma equity balance is lower than the sum of the initial equity account balance plus Sleepy Hollow's net income, the forecasts assume the firm will pay a dividend, repurchase stock, or do a combination of both. We can calculate how large this dividend or repurchase is as follows:

Beginning equity balance	=	$200 million
+ Net income	=	345 million
− Dividend/repurchase	=	X
Ending equity balance	=	$230 million

Solving for X, we find that:

$$\text{Dividend/repurchase} = (\$200 \text{ million} + \$345 \text{ million}) - \$230 \text{ million} = \$315 \text{ million}$$

The reconciliation makes the dividend or repurchase transaction transparent. It is clear that with a net income of $345 million and the constraint that the ending equity balance is $230 million, the firm must pay a $315 million cash dividend, repurchase $315 million of shares, or distribute $315 million through a combination of a dividend and a stock repurchase.

Evaluating an Investment Opportunity

Now let's suppose that Sleepy Hollow is considering building a new manufacturing plant. The project is estimated to cost $200 million and is to be financed entirely with debt. As in the prior example, sales are expected to increase by 15 percent for the year, and the plant will be placed in service the following year. Finally, assume that all financial statement accounts vary directly with changes in sales and that the current payout policy is to pay a $315 million cash dividend.

To determine whether the project is feasible as planned, management needs to prepare a set of pro forma financial statements that includes the cost of the new facility. Sleepy Hollow's pro forma income statement will not change because of the building project. Thus, we can use

Sleepy Hollow's income statement shown earlier. The preliminary pro forma balance sheet for the project, which excludes external funding, is as follows:

Sleepy Hollow's Building Project Preliminary Pro Forma Balance Sheet ($ millions)					
Assets	$690	($90)	Debt	$400	
New facility	200	($200)	Equity	230	(30)
Total	$890		Total	$630	

We can see that total assets are $890 million, composed of the $690 million ($600 million × 1.15 = $690 million) we calculated earlier plus $200 million for the new facility. The value of the equity account remains unchanged at $230 million ($200 million × 1.15 = $230 million), because it is subject to the 15 percent growth limit, and management must pay the $315 million cash dividend. Since we do not know the amount of debt needed, we enter debt at the current balance sheet amount of $400 million.

Now, comparing the totals, we see that the balance sheet does not balance: total assets are $890 million, while total debt and equity equals $630 million. The difference between the two numbers is $260 million ($890 million – $630 million = $260 million). This "plug value" is the amount of **external funding needed (EFN)** by the firm. EFN is the additional debt or equity a firm needs to issue so that it can meet its total funding requirements. In this analysis, we refer to EFN as the plug value because it is the number we have to plug into the balance sheet to get it to balance. In our example, the firm must issue $260 million of debt because, as you recall, management made a decision to finance the new project entirely with debt.

external funding needed (EFN) the additional debt or equity a firm must raise from external sources to meet its total funding requirements

The final balance sheet, which includes the building project, is shown in the following table. Overall, the firm is financing $290 million of new assets: $200 million for the new facility and $90 million for new assets to support the increase in sales expected next year. The funding is a combination of internal and external funding, which totals $290 million: $260 million in debt (external) and $30 million in addition to retained earnings (internal). The firm is also able to pay the required $315 million of cash dividends. If the firm can borrow the $260 million at a reasonable rate, it will be able to generate sufficient funds to finance the $200 million capital project and pay the required cash dividend of $315 million.

Sleepy Hollow's Building Project Final Pro Forma Balance Sheet ($ millions)					
Assets	$690	($90)	Debt	$660	($260)
New facility	200	(200)	Equity	230	(30)
Total	$890	($290)	Total	$890	($290)

Decision Making Example 19.1 illustrates how pro forma financial information can be helpful in decision-making.

DECISION MAKING

EXAMPLE 19.1 | Informed Judgment about Risk

Situation You are given some additional information about Sleepy Hollow Corporation's use of financial leverage, as shown:

Debt to total assets before capital project = $400/$600 = 66.7%
Debt to total assets after capital project = $660/$890 = 74.2%
Industry average debt to total assets = 40.0%

What should management do in light of this information?

Decision Sleepy Hollow's current leverage ratio of 66.7 percent is already high compared with the industry average of 40 percent. If the firm goes ahead with the project, the leverage ratio will increase to 74.2 percent, which is even higher. The high debt ratio makes the firm's cash flows more risky and could negatively affect its stock price, its borrowing cost, and even its ability to borrow money. A more prudent alternative would be to fund at least part of the $290 million of new assets ($90 million + $200 million = $290 million) with internally generated funds by reducing dividends or with externally raised equity by selling new stock, or both.

The important point here is that financial planning models do not think for management. Even though the balance sheet balances and results are consistent with the firm's financing plan, management must apply informed judgment.

Before You Go On

1. Why is the sales forecast the key component of a financial model?
2. What are pro forma financial statements, and why are they an important part of the financial planning process?
3. What is the plug value in a financial model?

19.3 A Better Financial Planning Model

LEARNING OBJECTIVE

3. Discuss how the relation between projected sales and the income statement and balance sheet accounts can be determined, and analyze a strategic investment decision using a percent of sales model.

The preceding section presented a simple financial planning model that assumes *all* income and balance sheet accounts vary directly with sales. Although that assumption is helpful to simplify calculations, it does not reflect what happens in the real world. We now relax our assumptions so that our model is more realistic and generates more accurate forecasts. We assume that all working capital accounts—current assets and liabilities—vary directly with sales. For other accounts in the financial statements, independent forecasts may be required, or values may be set by management based on other criteria. To illustrate the process, we will work through an example.

The Blackwell Sales Company

The Blackwell Sales Company is a small, privately owned company located in College Station, Texas. The firm serves the oil and gas exploration industry in Texas and the adjoining states. It sells and does light manufacturing of rigging equipment for oil and gas exploration. The firm's management owns 75 percent of the stock, with the balance owned by friends and outside investors. Blackwell's management is projecting a banner year, as sales are expected to increase 30 percent. The reason for the large increase is an oil and gas shortage caused by political instability in the Middle East. Because of the high-risk nature of the business, management is very conservative with respect to any action that might materially increase the firm's risk. Some of the management team is concerned about the risk associated with increasing sales by 30 percent in a one-year period.

The financial manager looks at the firm's financial statements and provides the following information:

- Net sales during the fiscal year that just ended were $2 million.
- Historical financial data indicate that the total cost of producing the firm's services and products averages 85 percent of sales.
- The firm's average tax rate is 34.1 percent and is not expected to change.
- The firm's payout policy is to pay 33.5 percent of earnings as cash dividends.

EXHIBIT 19.3 Blackwell Sales: Current and Pro Forma Income Statements ($ thousands)

The pro forma income statement for Blackwell Sales assumes that the income statement items vary directly with sales.

	Current	Pro Forma	Assumptions
Net sales	$2,000	$2,600	Sales increase: 30%
Costs	1,700	2,210	Total costs = 85% of sales
Taxable income	$ 300	$ 390	
Taxes (34.1%)	102	133	
Net income	$ 198	$ 257	
Dividends	$ 66	$ 86	Dividend policy: 33.5% of net income
Addition to retained earnings	$ 132	$ 171	

The Income Statement

Exhibit 19.3 shows the firm's current (most recent) and pro forma income statements. Let's look at the calculations used to arrive at the pro forma income statement. Management expects sales to increase by 30 percent next year, and so projected sales are $2 million × 1.30 = $2.6 million. Since total costs have averaged 85 percent of sales, projected total costs are $2.6 million × 0.85 = $2.21 million. Projected taxes, which are 34.1 percent of taxable income, are 0.341 × $390,000 = $132,990, which we will round to $133,000 for simplicity. Subtracting taxes from taxable income, we arrive at the firm's projected net income of $257,000.

Blackwell's cash dividend is $86,000 (0.335 × $257,000 = $86,095, which we will round to $86,000), and the remaining $171,000 of net income (0.665 × $257,000 = $170,905) is retained in the firm as an addition to retained earnings.

dividend payout ratio the proportion of net income paid out (distributed) as dividends

retention (plowback) ratio the proportion of net income retained in the firm

These amounts relate to two ratios we will use in this chapter: the **dividend payout ratio** and the **retention ratio**, or **plowback ratio**. The formulas and calculations for Blackwell are as follows:

$$\text{Dividend payout ratio} = \frac{\text{Cash dividends}}{\text{Net income}} \tag{19.2}$$

$$= \frac{\$86{,}000}{\$257{,}000} = 0.335, \text{ or } 33.5\%$$

$$\text{Retention (plowback) ratio} = \frac{\text{Addition to retained earnings}}{\text{Net income}} \tag{19.3}$$

$$= \frac{\$171{,}000}{\$257{,}000} = 0.665, \text{ or } 66.5\%$$

The dividend payout ratio shows the percentage of the firm's earnings paid out as cash dividends to stockholders. Similarly, the retention ratio tells what percentage of the firm's earnings is retained in the firm. Generally speaking, smaller, fast-growing companies plow back all or most of their earnings into the business, whereas more established firms with slower growth rates and larger cash flows distribute more of their profits to stockholders. Notice that the sum of the retention ratio and the dividend payout ratio equals 1.000 (0.335 + 0.665 = 1.000). This is because every dollar of net income is either paid out as a cash dividend or retained in the firm.

The Balance Sheet

To generate a pro forma balance sheet, we start with the current balance sheet, as shown in Exhibit 19.4. For each account that varies directly with sales, the exhibit gives the relation as a percent of sales for the current year. Notice that these percentages differ among the accounts. How do we determine which accounts vary with sales, and how do we know the relevant percentages? Fortunately, the process is straightforward.

EXHIBIT 19.4 Blackwell Sales: Current Balance Sheet ($ thousands)

In this balance sheet for Blackwell Sales, many accounts vary directly with sales. The projected percent of sales is shown for each of these accounts. The accounts labeled "n/a" do not change proportionately with sales.

Assets			Liabilities and Stockholders' Equity		
	Current	Projected % of Sales		Current	Projected % of Sales
Current assets			Current liabilities		
Cash	$ 100	5%	Accounts payable	$ 60	4%
Accounts receivable	120	6	Notes payable	140	n/a
Inventory	140	7	Total	$ 200	n/a
Total	$ 360	18%	Long-term debt	$ 200	n/a
			Owner's equity		
			Common stock	$ 10	n/a
			Retained earnings	590	n/a
			Total equity	$ 600	n/a
Net fixed assets	640	32	Total liabilities and		
Total assets	$1,000	50%	stockholders' equity	$1,000	50%

Historical Trends

We begin by looking at balance sheet accounts that might vary with sales. To do this we gather four or five years of historical accounting data and express those data as a percent of sales. A trend may be self-evident, or some simple trend lines can be fit to the data to identify trends. In either case, this process allows the financial manager to decide which financial accounts can safely be estimated as a percent of sales and which must be forecast using other information.

The following table shows several years of historical data from Blackwell's balance sheet accounts, and the far-right column contains the final forecast values for 2018. We now discuss the rationale for assigning a percent of sales figure to each balance sheet account. We look first at the working capital accounts: cash, accounts receivable, inventory, and accounts payable.

	Percent of Sales				
	2014	2015	2016	2017	Forecast 2018
Cash	5%	5%	4%	5%	5%
Accounts receivable	10	9	9	9	6
Inventory	7	8	7	6	7
Accounts payable	4	4	4	3	4
Net fixed assets	30	32	34	32	32

Working Capital Accounts

The key working capital accounts tend to vary directly with sales. Take inventory as an example. As sales increase, the firm needs to increase the level of inventory proportionately to support the higher sales level. The historical data in the table support this view. Inventory levels have been a relatively constant percentage of sales, varying from 6 to 8 percent. In selecting the appropriate percentage for the planning process, management must consider what the firm's optimal inventory ratio is. On the one hand, as discussed in Chapter 14, management would like to minimize inventory levels, because inventory is expensive to finance. On the other hand, if inventory levels become too low, the firm may lose sales because of stockouts, which occur when an order comes in and there is no product to sell. Let's assume that Blackwell's management determines that 7 percent of projected sales is the right inventory-to-sales ratio for the firm.

The ratio of accounts receivable to sales has been 9 percent for the last several years. However, firms with similar credit policies operate with a receivables-to-sales ratio of 6 percent. As sales have increased, Blackwell has provided proportionately more credit to its customers. To improve the firm's performance to industry standards, management decides to collect receivables more aggressively and targets a ratio of 6 percent. Management has also targeted cash accounts totaling 5 percent of sales. Management believes that a 5 percent cash ratio provides adequate liquidity to fund ongoing operations and pay for unexpected emergencies yet does not tie up an excessive amount of cash in low-yielding assets.

On the liability side, the firm's historical data show that accounts payable vary with sales. This seems reasonable, since the greater a firm's sales, the more orders the firm will have to place with its suppliers. Management is satisfied with the firm's vendor relationships and the payment schedule for vendors. Hence, accounts payable are forecast to be 4 percent of sales.

Fixed Assets

We assume that the company's net fixed assets vary with the level of sales. An examination of historical data confirms that this is a reasonable assumption. Blackwell's management decides to use the firm's four-year historical average—32 percent—for the projected ratio of fixed assets to sales. Thus, for every \$100 in sales, the firm needs \$32 of fixed assets to support the sales.

We should note that such a relation between fixed assets and sales may not always hold. The reason is that fixed assets may vary directly with sales only when a firm is operating at full capacity and fixed assets can be added in small increments. For example, if a firm has a large amount of unused capacity, its sales could increase by 20 percent without adding any new fixed assets. We will come back to this issue in more detail later in the chapter. For Blackwell, the data support the proportional fixed assets-to-sales ratio, so we can proceed on that basis.

As a final comment, notice in Exhibit 19.4 on the asset side of the balance sheet that the total percent of sales for asset items adds up to 50 percent. This means that total assets are 50 percent of sales. The ratio of total assets to sales is called the *capital intensity ratio* and is calculated for Blackwell Sales as follows:

$$\text{Capital intensity ratio} = \frac{\text{Total assets}}{\text{Net sales}} \tag{19.4}$$

$$= \frac{\$1 \text{ million}}{\$2 \text{ million}} = 0.5, \text{ or } 50\%$$

The capital intensity ratio, which is the inverse of the total asset turnover ratio discussed in Chapter 4 (Equation 4.7), tells us something about the amount of assets the firm needs to generate \$1 in sales. The higher the ratio, the more capital the firm needs to generate sales—that is, the more *capital intensive* the firm. Firms that are highly capital intensive tend to be more risky than similar firms that use less fixed assets. High capital intensities are generally associated with high fixed assets and correspondingly high fixed costs. If there is a downturn in sales, profits decrease sharply for firms with high fixed costs because fixed costs cannot be reduced in the short term. This is the operating leverage concept that is illustrated in Exhibit 16.3 in Chapter 16. With a 50 percent capital intensity ratio, Blackwell Sales is not a highly capital-intensive firm. Examples of capital-intensive industries are the airline and the automobile industries; for example, both United Airlines and Ford Motor Company have capital intensity ratios greater than 100 percent.

Liabilities and Equity

For most firms, the remaining liability accounts on the balance sheet do not vary with sales. Their values typically change because of management decisions, such as the decision to pay off a loan or issue debt. Thus, each liability and equity account must be evaluated separately.

Turning to individual accounts, notes payable typically represent short-term borrowing. This account value will only change with some decision by Blackwell's management, such as making a payment on a note or borrowing more money from a bank. Thus, the account's value does not vary with sales, as indicated by the "n/a," or "not applicable," in Exhibit 19.4. Similarly, the account value for long-term debt changes only when management decides to issue or retire debt. The same argument holds for the common stock account, which changes only when management decides to sell or repurchase common shares. The last account is retained earnings. Retained earnings may or may not vary directly with sales. The reason for the ambiguity is that the amount of funds in retained earnings depends not only on the firm's earnings but also on the firm's payout policy, which is set by management. Thus, for now, both the common stock and the retained earnings accounts are entered as n/a in Exhibit 19.4.

The Preliminary Pro Forma Balance Sheet

We are now in a position to construct a preliminary pro forma balance sheet, as shown in Exhibit 19.5. The preliminary pro forma balance sheet is a first approximation in deciding how the firm should fund the assets it needs to support an increase in sales of 30 percent. Once it is constructed, management can develop a suitable financing plan.

To construct the preliminary pro forma balance sheet, we follow these steps:

1. We first calculate the projected values for all the accounts that vary with sales, and we enter these values into the preliminary pro forma balance sheet.
2. We then compute and enter the projected value of any other balance sheet accounts for which an end-of-period value can be forecast or otherwise determined.
3. For all the accounts for which end-of-period values could not be forecast or otherwise determined, we enter the current year's value.
4. Typically, the balance sheet will not balance at this point. We thus compute the plug value, which balances the balance sheet. The plug value will involve the accounts marked "n/a" in the initial balance sheet (Exhibit 19.4). We must analyze these accounts in light of the firm's capital structure and dividend policies. The plug value is usually the amount of external funding needed (EFN), because we are usually adding new assets to the balance sheet to support growth; thus, total assets exceed total liabilities plus equity.

Let's work through each step using numbers from the Blackwell case.

Step One. We calculate the projected balance sheet values for the accounts that vary with sales as follows (projected sales are $2.6 million):

- Cash is projected to be 5 percent of sales: $2.6 million × 0.05 = $130,000.
- Accounts receivable is projected to be 6 percent of sales: $2.6 million × 0.06 = $156,000.

EXHIBIT 19.5 **Blackwell Sales: Preliminary Pro Forma Balance Sheet ($ thousands)**

This preliminary pro forma balance sheet for Blackwell Sales is a first approximation in deciding how to fund anticipated growth. At this stage of the analysis, the balance sheet will not balance (Total Assets will not equal Liabilities and Stockholders' Equity), and the difference will be the plug value, which is usually the amount of external funding the firm will need in order to fund investments and operations.

Assets	Projected	Change	Liabilities and Stockholders' Equity	Projected	Change
Current assets			Current liabilities		
Cash	$ 130	$ 30	Accounts payable	$ 104	$ 44
Accounts receivable	156	36	Notes payable	140	0
Inventory	182	42	Total	$ 244	$ 44
Total	$ 468	$108	Long-term debt	$ 200	$ 0
			Owner's equity		
			Common stock	$ 10	$ 0
			Retained earnings	761	171
			Total equity	$ 771	$171
Net fixed assets	832	192	Total liabilities and		
Total assets	$1,300	$300	stockholders' equity	$1,215	$215
			External funding needed (EFN)	$ 85	

- Inventory is projected to be 7 percent of sales: \$2.6 million × 0.07 = \$182,000.
- Net fixed assets are projected to be 32 percent of sales: \$2.6 million × 0.32 = \$832,000.
- Accounts payable are projected to be 4 percent of sales: \$2.6 million × 0.04 = \$104,000.

These values, along with the differences between the current and forecast amounts, are shown in Exhibit 19.5.

Step Two. We now consider the balance sheet accounts that do not vary with sales. We can determine the value of retained earnings, since the firm has a policy of paying out 33.5 percent of earnings as dividends. Recall from our earlier discussion that projected net income is \$257,000 and the proportion of that amount going to retained earnings is \$171,000 (0.665 × \$257,000 = \$171,000). Thus, the end-of-year account balance is \$761,000 (\$590,000 + \$171,000 = \$761,000), where \$590,000 is the current retained earnings balance.

Step Three. The remaining accounts that do not vary with sales represent sources of financing for the firm: notes payable, long-term debt, and common stock. These accounts are entered into the preliminary pro forma balance sheet at their current values, as shown in Exhibit 19.5.

Step Four. As predicted, the preliminary pro forma balance sheet does not balance at this point: projected assets total \$1.3 million, and projected sources of funding (debt and equity) total \$1.215 million. The difference between these two values is our plug value. The plug value represents EFN, which is \$85,000 (\$1.3 million − \$1.215 million = \$85,000). Since we are dealing with a financing decision, all accounts with the n/a designation represent possible financing options. Management must use its judgment and its knowledge of Blackwell Sales to select the appropriate financing for the firm.

What the Findings Mean

What does all the information in Exhibit 19.5 tell management? First, if sales increase as projected, the firm's total assets will expand by \$300,000. Of that \$300,000 increase, \$108,000 will go to increase current assets and \$192,000 will go to increase the firm's fixed assets.

Second, the \$300,000 in additional assets could be financed as follows: \$171,000 from internally generated funds (the addition to retained earnings), \$44,000 from expanded trade credit (the increase in accounts payable), and \$85,000 of external funding from the sale of debt or equity or both.

Management's Decision

How should Blackwell Sales fund the \$300,000 to support the 30 percent increase in sales? The firm could issue debt, equity, or reduce dividends. Alternatively, the firm could rethink its strategy and scale back the 30 percent targeted growth figure. Suppose Blackwell's management team meets to discuss the findings from Exhibit 19.5. After much discussion, they reach a consensus on the following points:

1. The firm has a unique opportunity to ride a strong market for oil and gas development and wants to pursue the 30 percent sales growth targeted.
2. Management is concerned about issuing more debt because of the volatility of the oil and gas exploration business.
3. Management prefers not to issue more common stock for fear of diluting earnings.
4. Management would like to pay an annual dividend but only when justified.

What does management do? In the end, management decides to pay no cash dividend to stockholders for the coming year. Thus, the \$300,000 increase in assets is funded entirely from earnings. This decision is made to avoid the risks associated with additional debt and the dilution of earnings that would result from issuing additional common stock.

EXHIBIT 19.6 **Blackwell Sales: Final Pro Forma Balance Sheet ($ thousands)**

The final pro forma balance sheet reflects Blackwell management's decision to temporarily suspend dividends and fund its growth with internal funds (retained earnings). Although financial models can determine the amount of EFN needed, management must make the final decision about how to fund the firm's capital requirements.

Assets			Liabilities and Stockholders' Equity		
	Projected	Change		Projected	Change
Current assets			Current liabilities		
Cash	$ 130	$ 30	Accounts payable	$ 104	$ 44
Accounts receivable	156	36	Notes payable	139	−1
Inventory	182	42	Total	$ 243	$ 43
Total	$ 468	$108	Long-term debt	$ 200	$ 0
			Owner's equity		
			Common stock	$ 10	$ 0
			Retained earnings	847	257
			Total equity	$ 857	$257
Net fixed assets	832	192	Total liabilities and		
Total assets	$1,300	$300	stockholders' equity	$1,300	$300
			External funding needed (EFN)	$ 0	

The Final Pro Forma Balance Sheet

Exhibit 19.6 shows the final pro forma balance sheet reflecting the decision to temporarily suspend dividends and fund the expansion with internal funds (retained earnings). As you recall, Blackwell's net income is $257,000; and thus, the retained earnings account is increased by $257,000, making the final balance $847,000 ($590,000 + $257,000 = $847,000). Since the proposed dividend of $86,000 now goes entirely into retained earnings, a source of funds, and the firm's additional financing needs are $85,000, there is $1,000 ($86,000 − $85,000 = $1,000) available to reduce debt. The most likely course of action is to reduce notes payable by $1,000, making notes payable $139,000 rather than $140,000.[5]

Finally, it is important to note that financial models do not make decisions; only the firm's management can do that. Financial models can only generate numbers given the inputs and assumption made when constructing the model. Once constructed, financial models can help management evaluate strategic alternatives, assess their financial impact on the firm, and determine whether they are consistent with the firm's financial policies. In the Blackwell case, management suspended its dividend policy.

Learning by Doing Application 19.2 illustrates how restoring the dividend, but paying a smaller amount, affects the Blackwell retained earnings account.

LEARNING BY DOING

APPLICATION 19.2 | Blackwell's Alternative Plan

Problem Let's continue the Blackwell Sales example. Suppose that Blackwell's management now decides to pay a cash dividend, but to reduce the payout to 10 percent of net income. Reconcile Blackwell's retained earnings account.

Approach First, we must calculate the new dividend payout and the amount of funds going into retained earnings. Since net income remains unchanged at $257,000, we calculate the dividends and addition to retained earnings by multiplying the net income by the payout and the retention percentages.

[5]Alternatively, we could have redone the preliminary pro forma balance sheet and found: Total assets = $1.3 million and Total liabilities and stockholders' equity = $1.301 million ($244,000 + $200,000 + $857,000 = $1,301,000). Since Total liabilities and stockholders' equity is greater than Total assets, we have more funds than we need. To make the balance sheet balance, we elect to reduce the notes payable by $1,000.

Second, we must calculate the impact of the new dividend policy on the retained earnings account. An easy way to do this is to reconcile the retained earnings account.

Solution The calculations for the new dividend payout and the addition to retained earnings are:

(1) Cash dividends = 0.10 × \$257,000 = \$25,700.
(2) Addition to retained earnings = 0.90 × \$257,000 = \$231,300.

The calculations to reconcile the retained earnings account are:

Beginning retained earnings balance	\$590,000
+ Net income	257,000
− Dividends	25,700
Ending retained earnings balance	\$821,300

Thus, the new retained earnings balance is \$821,300.

Before You Go On

1. How are historical financial data used to determine the forecast values of balance sheet accounts?
2. Why might you expect accounts receivable to vary with sales?

19.4 Beyond the Basic Planning Models

LEARNING OBJECTIVE

4. Describe the conditions under which fixed assets vary directly with sales, and discuss the impact of so-called lumpy assets on this relation.

In this section, we tie up some important loose ends concerning financial planning models. We first consider some shortcomings of the simple models we have been discussing and describe how more sophisticated models address those shortcomings. We then discuss additional benefits of financial planning.

Improving Financial Planning Models

Much of the discussion concerning the planning models developed in this chapter focuses on the underlying process for generating pro forma statements. Our goal is to have you understand how planning models work so that when you move to more complex computer-based models, you will be an informed user capable of understanding the models' limitations and strengths. We now discuss some of the improvements you should expect to find incorporated in more sophisticated models.

Interest Expense

One omission from the models presented in this chapter is that they fail to account for interest expense in the financial statements. A problem we face in modeling is that interest expense cannot be estimated accurately until the cost and amount of borrowing have been determined, and the cost of borrowing depends in part on the amount of borrowing. Thus, we cannot accurately estimate one without the other. More sophisticated financial models estimate interest payments and borrowings simultaneously.

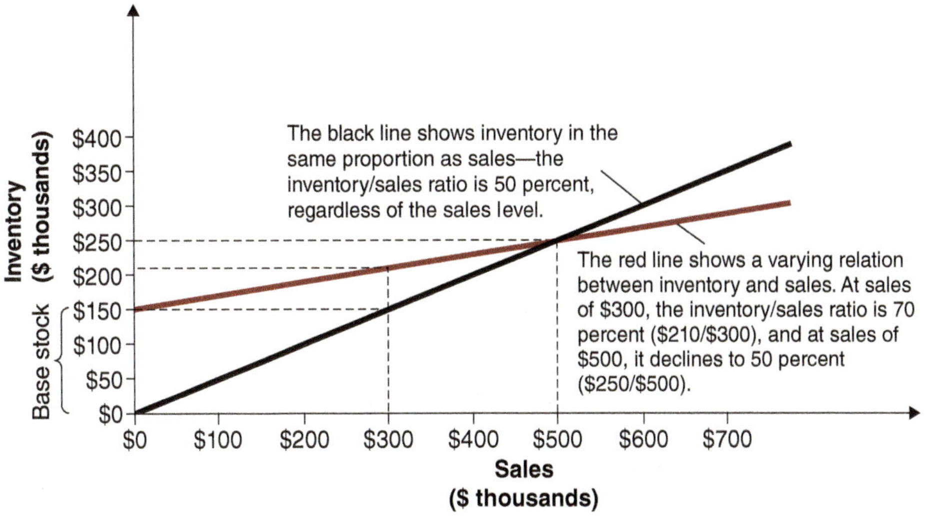

EXHIBIT 19.7 Relation between Inventory Levels and Changes in Sales

This graph shows inventory-to-sales ratios for two situations: one in which inventory varies directly with sales (black line) and one in which it does not (red line). Financial managers know from experience that most working capital accounts, such as inventory, do not increase directly with sales. Instead, they increase at a decreasing rate as sales increase.

Working Capital Accounts

Another weakness in our percent of sales model is the assumption that working capital increases proportionally with sales. Seasoned financial managers know that increases in some working capital accounts are not proportional to sales; this is particularly true for cash balances and inventory. Exhibit 19.7, for example, shows the inventory-to-sales ratios for two situations: one where inventory varies directly with sales and one where it does not. The black line illustrates the assumption that changes in inventory vary in proportion to changes in sales. Notice that inventory gets very small as sales approach zero. When inventory varies in proportion to sales, the inventory/sales ratio is 50 percent, regardless of the level of sales. The red line illustrates a different relation. Here, at sales of $300,000, the inventory/sales ratio is 70 percent ($210,000/$300,000 = 0.70, or 70 percent), and at sales of $500,000 it declines to 50 percent ($250,000/$500,000 = 0.50, or 50 percent). The important point here is not the ratio calculations but the fact that working capital does not increase directly with sales. Instead, it increases at a decreasing rate as sales increase. This is a common relation between inventory and sales and between cash and sales.

Fixed Assets

Another issue concerns the way we handled fixed assets. Specifically, we assumed that when sales increase, fixed assets are added in small increments and that production facilities are always operating near or at full capacity. This is not typically the case. In most instances, fixed assets are added as large discrete units, and much of a firm's capacity may not be utilized for some period of time. These types of assets are often called **lumpy assets**. Let's look at an example.

lumpy assets fixed assets added as large, discrete units; these assets may not be used to full capacity for some time, leaving the company with excess capacity

Suppose you and a group of investors decide to enter the market for frozen Mexican snack foods, which you believe is a growing market. You buy a small food-manufacturing facility that can easily be converted to manufacture Mexican snack foods. Exhibit 19.8 illustrates your initial situation. After you make the purchase, your sales are zero, and you have $100,000 in fixed assets, which will support sales of up to $150,000. Thus, the facility has $150,000 in excess capacity.

Over time, sales expand to $75,000. At this level, no additional assets are needed (Point A in the exhibit) because the firm still has excess capacity of $75,000 ($150,000 − $75,000 = $75,000). When the firm's sales expand to $150,000 (Point B), however, the firm no longer has idle capacity. You determine that a $200,000 addition to fixed assets is the most economical way to gain additional capacity. If you make this investment, the firm will have $300,000

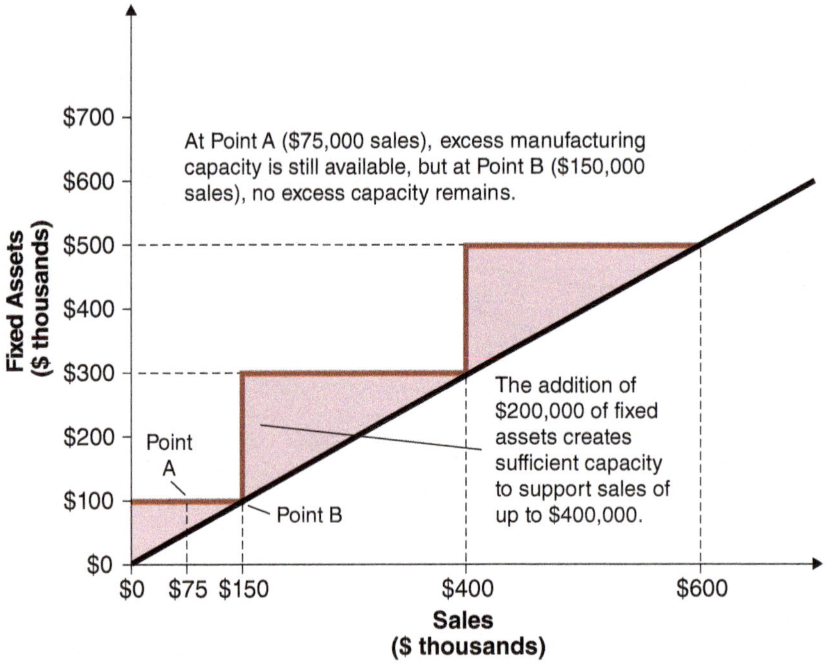

EXHIBIT 19.8 Fixed Assets Are Usually Acquired in Large, Discrete Units

In real-world situations, fixed assets usually do not vary directly with sales, as we assumed with our simplified financial models. Management often adds fixed assets in very large increments in order to add capacity in the most economical way.

($100,000 + $200,000 = $300,000) in fixed assets, which will support sales up to $400,000. Notice that when your firm is at Point B, the threshold point, even a small increase in sales results in more than doubling the firm's fixed assets.

In financial planning, management must account for the fact that investments in fixed assets often come in very large increments, or "lumps." Furthermore, a significant amount of lead time is often required to bring them on line. Thus, as a firm nears full manufacturing capacity, management should begin planning to acquire additional fixed assets in the future. In contrast, if a firm has considerable excess capacity, sales growth will not require additions to fixed assets.

Before You Go On

1. Why is it that some working capital accounts may not vary proportionately with sales?
2. What are lumpy assets, and how do these assets vary with sales?

19.5 Managing and Financing Growth

LEARNING OBJECTIVE

5. Explain what factors determine a firm's sustainable growth rate, discuss why it is of interest to management, and compute the sustainable growth rate for a firm.

We close the chapter with a discussion of how a business can grow and the need to manage growth. When companies add assets through acquisition or the capital budgeting process, they grow in size. If the rate of growth is rapid, much of the asset expansion will likely require external funding. Rapid growth is often a goal of management because it helps a company gain market share quickly and strengthens its competitive position in the marketplace. In addition, managers of companies with high growth rates often receive accolades and recognition from investors and their peers for their business acumen. Overall, rapid growth is considered a desirable achievement.

Rapid growth can have a dark side, however. As a firm grows rapidly, management might finance the growth with long-term debt in a way that increases the firm's overall financial leverage. Higher financial leverage increases the probability that a firm will face financial distress if business conditions deteriorate. If management is using a lot of debt financing and sales then unexpectedly plunge, causing cash flows to decline, the firm may not have enough cash to pay long-term debt holders and other creditors.

An example of a firm that used too much debt to finance growth is Boston Chicken, Inc., the former operator and franchiser of Boston Market, a chain of fast-food restaurants offering reasonably priced home-style meals. The firm burst onto the national scene in 1993 as one of the hottest initial public offerings (IPOs) of the year. The first day of trading, its stock price shot up 143 percent! Early successes allowed the firm to expand rapidly from an initial 33 stores to over 1,200.

Beginning in 1996, management decided to go head-to-head with McDonald's and Burger King in the highly competitive fast-food lunch market. Boston Chicken used a lot of debt to finance this effort, but the market proved to be difficult. As sales began to slow, management began to tinker with the menu. Management teams moved in and out, menus grew more complex, service and quality suffered, and sales continued to drop. By October 1998, poor sales and a debt load of over $900 million forced Boston Chicken into bankruptcy. In December 1999, McDonald's bought the firm for a bargain-basement price of $173.5 million.

How does rapid growth cause businesses like Boston Chicken to fail? The classic formula for business failure is rapid expansion, a lack of solid long-term planning, and an insufficient equity base or, put another way, the use of too much financial leverage.

External Funding Needed

When a firm expands rapidly, its operations might not be able to generate sufficient cash flows to meet all of its financial obligations. If this happens, management must look for outside funding—debt or equity. We now explore the factors affecting management's decision to seek external funding. We do so by developing some relations between a firm's growth rate and the amount of external funding needed (EFN).

Growth and External Funding

The best way to understand the relation between growth and external funding is in the context of a rapidly growing firm and its financial statements. The firm we use is called Empire Enterprises, which is a hypothetical real estate investment firm located in New York City that engages in real estate development and property management. Empire is a public company whose stock is listed on the NYSE.

Exhibit 19.9 shows the current income statement and balance sheet for Empire Enterprises. Last year Empire had total assets of $50 million, book equity of $30 million, and generated $10 million of earnings on $100 million in sales. Empire's management team believes the firm can increase sales by 20 percent for the coming year. All costs and assets are assumed to grow at the same rate as sales, 60 percent of earnings are paid as cash dividends, and the board of directors is reluctant to issue additional common stock.

Given this information, we can prepare the pro forma income statement and balance sheet for Empire Enterprises, which appear in **Exhibit 19.10**. The income statement shows both sales and costs increasing by 20 percent for the year: projected sales are $120 million ($100 million × 1.20 = $120 million), projected costs are $108 million ($90 million × 1.20 = $108 million), and thus, the firm's projected net income is $12 million ($120 million − $108 million = $12 million).

Turning to the pro forma balance sheet, we see that the total assets for the firm are $60 million ($50 million × 1.20 = $60 million). For the moment, we hold total debt constant at $20 million so that we can compute the EFN needed to support the 20 percent increase in sales. The firm's payout policy calls for 40 percent of earnings to be retained

EXHIBIT 19.9 Empire Enterprises: Income Statement and Balance Sheet ($ millions)

The exhibit shows the current income statement and balance sheet for Empire Enterprises. Management believes that the firm can increase sales by 20 percent for the coming year. All costs and assets are assumed to grow at the same rate as sales, 60 percent of earnings are paid out as dividends, and the directors do not want to issue additional common stock.

Income Statement

Net sales	$100.0
Costs	90.0
Net income	$ 10.0
Dividends	$ 6.0
Addition to retained earnings	$ 4.0

Balance Sheet

Assets		Projected % of Sales	Liabilities and Stockholders' Equity		Projected % of Sales
Assets	$50.0	50.0%	Total debt	$20.0	n/a
			Equity	30.0	n/a
Total assets	$50.0		Total liabilities and stickholders' equity	$50.0	

in the firm, since 60 percent will be paid to stockholders as a dividend. Thus, given net income of $12 million, the addition to retained earnings is $4.8 million (0.40 × $12 million = $4.8 million). The equity account is increased to $34.8 million ($30.0 million + $4.8 million = $34.8 million).

After these changes have been made, the pro forma balance sheet does not balance. Total assets equal $60.0 million, and total liabilities and equity equal $54.8 million. The difference, $5.2 million ($60.0 million − $54.8 million = $5.2 million), is the EFN. The $10 million ($4.8 million + $5.2 million = $10 million) investment is being financed from two sources: $4.8 million from the addition to retained earnings and $5.2 million from external funding. The EFN could be either debt or equity, but in Empire's case it will be long-term debt, since Empire's board is reluctant to issue equity.

EXHIBIT 19.10 Empire Enterprises: Pro Forma Income Statement and Balance Sheet ($ millions)

The pro forma balance sheet for Empire Enterprises does not balance, and the difference is the amount of EFN. Because the company's board does not wish to issue common stock, the funding will have to take the form of long-term debt.

Income Statement (Pro Forma)

Net sales	$120.0
Costs	180.0
Net income	$ 12.0
Dividends	$ 7.2
Addition to retained earnings	$ 4.8

Balance Sheet (Pro Forma)

Assets	Projected	Change	Liabilities and Stockholders' Equity	Projected	Change
Assets	$60.0	$10.0	Total debt	$20.0	$0.0
			Equity	34.8	4.8
Total assets	$60.0	$10.0	Total liabilities and stickholders' equity	$54.8	$4.8
			External funding needed (EFN)	$ 5.2	

So far, we have calculated EFN exactly as we did in the previous sections. However, we are now going to build a mathematical model to calculate EFN. The model will allow us to better understand the relation between a firm's growth ambitions and the amount of EFN.

A Mathematical Model

Looking at the pro forma balance sheet calculations for Empire Enterprises (Exhibit 19.10), we can see that new investments are determined by the firm's total assets and projected growth in sales:

$$\text{New investments} = \text{Growth rate} \times \text{Initial total assets}$$

For Empire, the calculation is \$10 million = 0.20 × \$50 million. Note that to calculate new investments, we multiply the firm's initial total assets by the expected growth rate in sales forecasted by management. The new investments are the capital expenditures and the increase in working capital necessary to sustain the increase in sales.

Conceptually, the new investments are funded first by internally generated funds, which come from earnings retained in the firm. Once those funds are exhausted, the remainder of new investments must be financed externally by the sale of debt or equity, or some combination of both. Thus, the amount of EFN can be expressed as:

$$\text{EFN} = \text{New investments} - \text{Addition to retained earnings} \tag{19.5}$$

Substituting Growth rate × Initial total assets for New investments in Equation 19.5 yields the following:

$$\text{EFN} = (\text{Growth rate} \times \text{Initial total assets}) - \text{Addition to retained earnings} \tag{19.6}$$

Applying Equation 19.6 to our Empire Enterprise situation, we get the following results:

$$\begin{aligned}\text{EFN} &= (0.20 \times \$50\text{ million}) - \$4.8\text{ million} = \$10\text{ million} - \$4.8\text{ million}\\ &= \$5.2\text{ million}\end{aligned}$$

The result, \$5.2 million, agrees with the financial planning model calculation for Empire Enterprises presented earlier.

Equation 19.6 highlights two important points. First, holding dividend policy constant, the amount of EFN depends on the firm's projected growth rate. The faster management expects the firm to grow, the more the firm needs to invest in new assets, and the more capital it has to raise. The potential sources of external capital are the sale of new stock and the sale of long-term debt. Second, the firm's payout policy also affects EFN. Holding the growth rate constant, the higher the firm's dividend payout ratio, the larger the amount of external debt or equity financing needed. Also, since EFN is the net amount of external funding needed, the more stock a firm repurchases, the more new capital it must raise to satisfy its EFN requirements if EFN is positive.

A Graphical View of Growth

Exhibit 19.11 illustrates Equation 19.6—the relation between sales growth rate and EFN—for Empire Enterprises. The horizontal axis plots the firm's projected growth rate, and the vertical axis plots EFN. The slope of the line illustrates how EFN increases with the growth rate, assuming that dividend policy is held constant. As you can see, the line is upward sloping. This means that as the growth rate increases, the amount of EFN increases.

As a reference point in the exhibit, we plotted Empire's EFN value of \$5.2 million when the firm's sales are growing at a 20 percent rate. If you want to generate the line yourself, all you need to do is make another calculation of EFN at a different growth rate, plot the points, and connect them with a straight line. However, the important point here is not the mechanics of generating the graph in Exhibit 19.11, but the interpretation of the line.

Turning to the exhibit, you can see that at low growth rates Empire Enterprises will generate more funds from earnings than it will spend on new investments. In these situations, the calculated value for EFN is negative ($\text{EFN} < 0$), and the firm has a surplus of funds. In other words, the internally generated funds exceed the firm's planned investments. With the surplus

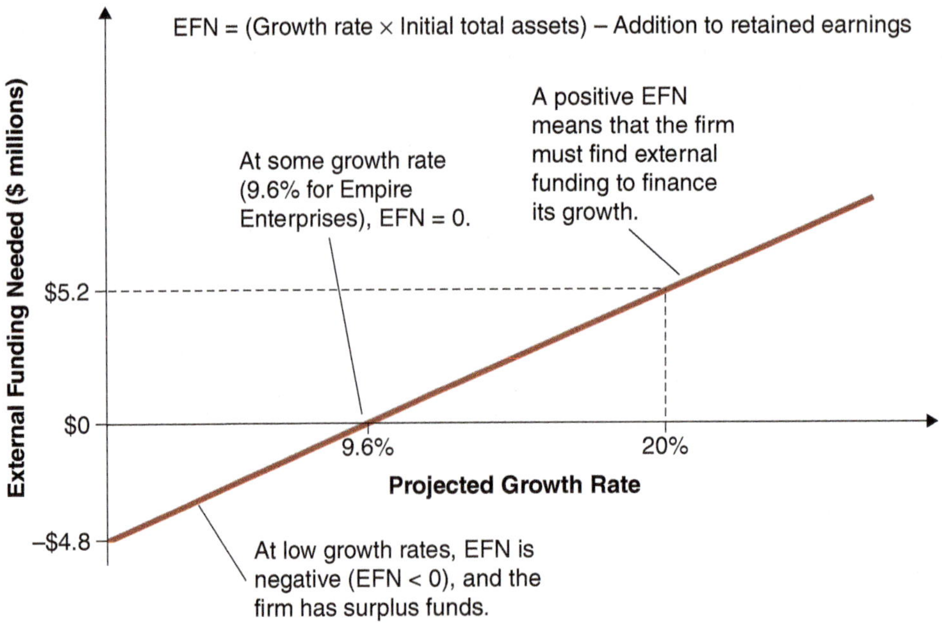

EXHIBIT 19.11 External Funding Needed (EFN) and Growth for Empire Enterprises

The exhibit graphically illustrates Equation 19.6, showing the connection between growth rate in sales and EFN. The horizontal axis plots the firm's projected growth rate, and the vertical axis plots EFN. The upward slope of the line illustrates how external funding increases with the growth rate, assuming that the dividend policy is held constant.

funds, management may elect to retire some debt or repurchase some common stock. For example, at a 0 percent rate of growth, no funds are needed for expansion, and all the retained earnings are surplus, as we can see by using Equation 19.6:

$$\begin{aligned}\text{EFN} &= (\text{Growth rate} \times \text{Initial total assets}) - \text{Addition to retained earnings}\\ &= (0.0 \times \$50 \text{ million}) - \$4.8 \text{ million}\\ &= -\$4.8 \text{ million}\end{aligned}$$

With a higher growth rate, the surplus becomes smaller and smaller as more and more funds are used to finance the new investments. At a growth rate of 9.6 percent, the surplus equals zero, as does the calculated value of EFN. Next we explain how to calculate the growth rate at which the surplus equals zero. The key point here is that the higher the rate at which a firm grows, the more external funding it requires.

The Internal Growth Rate

internal growth rate (IGR) the maximum growth rate that a firm can achieve without external funding

Management often has an interest in knowing the rate at which the firm can grow using just internally generated funds. This rate is called the **internal growth rate (IGR)**. The IGR is the maximum growth rate that a firm can achieve without external funding. To determine this rate, we set Equation 19.6 equal to zero (EFN = 0) and solve for the growth rate. Thus,

$$\text{EFN} = (\text{Growth rate} \times \text{Initial total assets}) - \text{Addition to retained earnings} = 0$$

Rearranging terms yields the internal growth rate:

$$\text{IGR} = \frac{\text{Addition to retained earnings}}{\text{Initial total assets}} \tag{19.7}$$

The managerial implications of the formula are straightforward. Firms that can generate a higher volume of retained earnings and/or use fewer assets can sustain a higher growth rate without raising more capital. For the Empire Enterprises example, the internal growth rate is calculated as:

$$\begin{aligned}\text{IGR} &= \frac{\text{Addition to retained earnings}}{\text{Initial total assets}}\\ &= \frac{\$4.8 \text{ million}}{\$50 \text{ million}} = 0.096, \text{ or } 9.6\%\end{aligned}$$

To gain more insight into what factors determine a firm's internal growth rate, we can manipulate Equation 19.7 by multiplying both the numerator and the denominator by net income and total equity, as follows:

$$\text{IGR} = \frac{\text{Addition to retained earnings}}{\text{Total assets}} \times \frac{\text{Net income}}{\text{Net income}} \times \frac{\text{Total equity}}{\text{Total equity}}$$

If we then rearrange terms, we arrive at the following expression:

$$\text{IGR} = \frac{\text{Addition to retained earnings}}{\text{Net income}} \times \frac{\text{Net income}}{\text{Total equity}} \times \frac{\text{Total equity}}{\text{Total assets}}$$

From the discussions in Chapter 4 and in this chapter, we know the following: (1) Plowback ratio = Addition to retained earnings/Net income; (2) Return on equity = Net income/Total equity; and (3) Equity multiplier = Total assets/Total equity.[6] This means that we can write the above equation as:

$$\text{IGR} = \text{Plowback ratio} \times \text{Return on equity} \times \text{Measure of leverage} \quad (19.8)$$

Equation 19.8 tells us that firms that achieve higher growth rates without seeking external funding tend to have one or more of the following characteristics:

- They have payout policies that retain a high proportion of earnings inside the firm—that is, they have a high plowback ratio.
- They are able to generate a high net income with a smaller amount of equity than other firms and hence have a high return on equity (ROE).
- They use low amounts of leverage; thus, their debt-to-equity ratios are low.

The Sustainable Growth Rate

Another growth rate helpful in long-term planning is the **sustainable growth rate (SGR)**, which is the rate of growth that the firm can sustain without selling additional equity while maintaining the same capital structure. You may wonder why management is interested in the sustainable growth rate. The sustainable growth rate is important to managers of firms that are likely to generate excess funds internally and who want to determine the payout ratio that enables them to fund their firms' growth while maintaining their current capital structures.

sustainable growth rate (SGR) the rate of growth that a firm can sustain without selling additional equity while maintaining the same capital structure

The sustainable growth rate is the rate at which a firm can grow using only (1) internally generated funds from earnings and (2) external funds from the sale of new debt while maintaining a constant debt equity ratio. As it turns out, SGR is a function of the firm's plowback ratio and the return on equity (ROE). SRG can be expressed as follows:

$$\text{SGR} = \text{Plowback ratio} \times \text{ROE} \quad (19.9)$$

For Empire Enterprises, the sustainable growth rate is:

$$\begin{aligned}\text{SGR} &= 0.4 \times \frac{\$10 \text{ million}}{\$30 \text{ million}} \\ &= 0.4 \times 0.333 \\ &= 0.133, \text{ or } 13.3\%\end{aligned}$$

The 13.3 percent rate is a fairly high SGR that is driven by the company's rather hefty 33.3 percent return on equity.

An analysis of a company's SGR relative to the company's actual growth rate can provide management with some insights into problems the firm may face in the future. For example, if a firm's actual growth rate consistently exceeds its SGR, managers know that unless they sell new equity, the firm will have a cash shortage problem in the future because of the need to purchase new assets to generate the growth. The SGR model does not, however, tell management how fast the firm should grow. That decision requires informed judgment about the attractiveness of the investment opportunities available to the firm.

[6]Note that the measure of leverage in Equation 19.8, Total equity/Total assets, is the inverse of the equity multiplier, Equation 4.11.

Decision Making Example 19.2 and **Learning by Doing Application 19.3** illustrate applications of the EFN, IGR, and SGR concepts.

DECISION MAKING

EXAMPLE 19.2 | Empire's Ambitious Growth Plan

Situation You are part of the Empire Enterprises finance team. The firm's strategic plan calls for revenues to grow at 20 percent next year. As mentioned, the board of directors is not interested in using any external equity funding. Some members of the team question whether these goals are realistic.

You have just been asked to comment on the proposed growth plan at a meeting. You have a little over an hour to prepare. During the time available, you completed the following calculations using data from the most recent and the pro forma income statements and balance sheets (Exhibits 19.9 and 19.10):

- EFN = (Growth rate × Initial total assets) − Addition to retained earnings = (0.20 × $50 million) − $4.8 million = $5.2 million
- IGR = Addition to retained earnings/Initial assets = $4.8 million/$50 million = 0.96, or 9.6%
- SGR = Plowback ratio × ROE = 0.40 × 0.333 = 13.3%

Given the above information, what can you say about this ambitious growth plan?

Decision You begin by applauding the visionary nature of the strategic plan. Clearly, you want to keep your job. You point out, however, that the firm is facing some challenges. First, Empire's IGR is 9.6 percent, which is the maximum growth rate the firm can achieve without any kind of external funding. This amount is substantially below the desired growth rate of 20 percent. Second, you note that Empire's EFN is $5.2 million. This means that $5.2 million of external capital will have to be raised by selling equity, debt, or some combination of the two. Finally, Empire's SGR is 13.3 percent—also below the 20 percent growth target. Empire cannot grow more than 13.3 percent without selling equity if management wants to keep the firm's capital structure at its current level.

LEARNING BY DOING

APPLICATION 19.3 | Sustainable Growth and Financial Statements

Problem Because of your presentation (see Decision Making Example 19.2), Empire's top management team has had second thoughts about its goal of growing the firm 20 percent during the next year. As a result, you must prepare pro forma financial statements at a sales growth rate equal to the firm's SGR of 13.3 percent.

Approach For the income statement, all costs grow at the same rate as revenues. Thus, you can multiply the current period's net sales and costs by 1.133 to calculate the projected values of sales and costs. To construct the balance sheet, you must first compute the values of accounts that vary with net sales. Since you have no information about how much of Empire's total debt is long-term debt, you should enter its total debt value of $20 million, along with all the information you have on the balance sheet accounts. Finally, to make the balance sheet balance, you should calculate the amount of EFN.

Solution

Net sales = $100 million × 1.133 = $113.30 million

Costs = $90 million × 1.133 = $101.97 million

The income statement is:

Empire Enterprises Pro Forma Income Statement ($ millions)	
Net sales	$113.30
Costs	101.97
Net income	$ 11.33

Dividend = Net income × Payout ratio = $11.33 million × 0.60 = $6.80 million

Addition to retained earnings = Net income × Plowback ratio = $11.33 million × 0.40
= $4.53 million

Forecast value of the assets: \$50 million × 1.133 = \$56.65 million

Value of the equity: \$30 million + \$4.53 million = \$34.53 million, where \$30 million is the initial value and \$4.53 million is the addition to retained earnings

Value of debt plus equity: \$20 million + 34.53 million = \$54.53 million

The balance sheet does not balance (\$56.65 million assets > \$54.53 million debt plus equity), and the difference (\$2.12 million) is the plug number, which is the EFN. Thus, to achieve the 13.3 percent rate of growth, Empire will need to issue \$2.12 million in long-term debt, which will bring the debt account to \$20 million + \$2.12 million = \$22.12 million. The resulting balance sheet is as follows:

Empire Enterprises Pro Forma Balance Sheet (\$ millions)

Assets		Liabilities and Stockholders' Equity	
Assets	\$56.65	Total debt	\$22.12
		Equity	34.53
Total assets	\$56.65	Total liabilities and stockholders' equity	\$56.65

Growth Rates and Profits

So far, we have focused on a firm's rate of growth. In the final analysis, however, the critical question in business is not how fast the firm can grow, but whether the firm can sustain rapid growth and maintain a satisfactory level of profits. In reality, it is very difficult to achieve and sustain rapid growth in a competitive market and remain profitable. The business arena is littered with failed growth firms like Boston Chicken.

To provide a reality check, only 7 percent of publicly traded U.S. companies increase both revenues and operating profits by an average of 10 percent a year. Experts generally agree that growth rates at or above 10 percent are very difficult to sustain for established companies.

Growth as a Planning Goal

The final question we address is whether growth by itself is an acceptable strategic goal. We pose this question because it is common for top management to set growth rates as goals for the firm or operating divisions. In fact, there is nothing a CEO likes to do better at the annual meeting than point out that "last year, under my leadership, Sleepy Hollow exceeded its goal of 10 percent growth," and have it followed by a hearty round of applause. Growth rate goals are popular because they are easy to communicate and understand. But are they appropriate goals for financial planning? The short answer is "no." Let's consider why this is the case.

As we discussed in Chapter 1, an appropriate goal for management is maximizing the market value of stockholders' equity. If management invests in productive assets with positive NPVs, finances them at the lowest possible cost, and skillfully manages these assets, the company should be profitable and grow in size. This growth results from making sound business decisions and executing strategies that create sustainable competitive advantages over the long term. Thus, growth is an acceptable goal as long as it is anchored to a sound business strategy that will generate an increase in stockholder value.

Before You Go On

1. What two factors determine the amount of EFN?
2. What is IGR, and why is it of interest to management?
3. If a firm continually exceeds its SGR, what problems may it face in the future?

Summary of Learning Objectives

1 Explain what a financial plan is and why financial planning is important.

A financial plan is a set of actionable goals derived from the firm's strategic plan and other planning documents, such as the investment and financing plans. The financial plan focuses on selecting the best investment opportunities and determining how they will be financed. The financial plan is a blueprint for the firm's future. Financial planning is important to management because the plan communicates the firm's strategic goals throughout the organization, builds support for the firm's strategies, and helps align operating unit goals with the firm's strategic goals.

2 Discuss how management uses financial planning models in the planning process, and explain the importance of sales forecasts in the construction of financial planning models.

Financial models are the analytical part of the financial planning process. A planning model is simply a series of equations that model a firm's financial statements, such as the income statement and balance sheet. Once the model is constructed, management can generate projected (pro forma) financial statements to determine the financial impact of proposed strategic initiatives on the firm.

For most financial planning models, a forecast of the firm's sales is the most important input variable. The sales forecast is the key driver in financial planning models because many items on the income statement and balance sheet vary directly with sales. Thus, once sales are forecasted, it is easy to generate projected financial statements using the historical relation between a particular account and sales.

3 Discuss how the relation between projected sales and the income statement and balance sheet accounts can be determined, and analyze a strategic investment decision using a percent of sales model.

Historical financial data can be examined to determine whether and how a variable changes with sales. One way to do this is to prepare a table that shows four or five years of historical financial statement account data as a percent of sales. Then fit trend lines to the data to see what type of relation exists between that variable and sales. Many income statement and balance sheet items vary directly with sales, but others may vary in a nonlinear manner. The analysis in the Blackwell Sales Company example illustrates how to analyze a strategic investment decision.

4 Describe the conditions under which fixed assets vary directly with sales, and discuss the impact of so-called lumpy assets on this relation.

Fixed assets vary directly with sales only when assets can be added in small increments and production facilities are operating near full capacity. This is typically not the case. In most situations, fixed assets are added in large, discrete units, and as a result, much of the new capacity may go unused for a period of time. These types of assets are often called lumpy assets. After lumpy assets are added, sales can increase for a period of time with no corresponding change in the level of fixed assets.

5 Explain what factors determine a firm's sustainable growth rate, discuss why it is of interest to management, and compute the sustainable growth rate for a firm.

A firm's sustainable growth rate (SGR) is the maximum rate at which the firm can grow without external equity funding and with leverage held constant. The determinants of a firm's SGR are (1) profit margins (the greater a firm's profit margin, the greater the firm's SGR); (2) asset utilization (the more efficiently a firm uses its assets, the higher its SGR); (3) financial leverage (as a firm increases its use of leverage, its SGR increases); (4) payout policy (as a firm decreases its payout ratio, its SGR increases); and (5) economic conditions (the more favorable the economic environment, the higher the firm's SGR). Management may be interested in knowing the SGR for two reasons. First, the SGR is the rate of growth at which a firm's capital structure (debt to equity) will remain constant without the firm selling or repurchasing stock. Second, if a firm's actual growth rate exceeds its SGR, the firm could face cash shortage problems in the future unless it can sell new equity. Learning by Doing Application 19.3 uses the SGR formula.

Summary of Key Equations

Equation	Description	Formula
19.1	Percent change in sales	$\% \Delta S = \frac{(S_{t+1} - S_t)}{S_t}$
19.2	Percent of net income paid out as dividends	$\text{Dividend payout ratio} = \frac{\text{Cash dividends}}{\text{Net income}}$

continued

continued

Equation	Description	Formula
19.3	Percent of net income retained (plowed back into the firm)	$\text{Retention (plowback) ratio} = \frac{\text{Addition to retained earnings}}{\text{Net income}}$
19.4	Amount of assets needed to generate \$1 of sales	$\text{Capital intensity ratio} = \frac{\text{Total assets}}{\text{Net sales}}$
19.5 & 19.6	External funding needed to support growth in sales	$\text{EFN} = \text{New investments} - \text{Addition to retained earnings}$ $= (\text{Growth rate} \times \text{Initial total assets}) - \text{Addition to retained earnings}$
19.7 & 19.8	Internal growth rate (level of growth that can be supported without raising external funds)	$\text{IGR} = \frac{\text{Addition to retained earnings}}{\text{Initial total assets}}$ $= \text{Plowback ratio} \times \text{Return on equity} \times \text{Measure of leverage}$
19.9	Sustainable growth rate (level of growth that can be supported without raising external equity or increasing current leverage)	$\text{SGR} = \text{Plowback ratio} \times \text{ROE}$

Self-Study Problems

19.1 The Starlight, Inc., financial statements for the fiscal year ended June 30, 2017, are presented below. The firm's sales are projected to grow at a rate of 20 percent next year, and all financial statement accounts will vary directly with sales. Based on that projection, develop a pro forma balance sheet and income statement for the fiscal year ending June 30, 2018.

Starlight, Inc., Balance Sheet as of June 30, 2017

Assets:		Liabilities and Stockholders' Equity:	
Cash	\$ 25,135	Accounts payable	\$ 67,855
Accounts receivable	43,758	Notes payable	36,454
Inventories	167,112		
Total current assets	\$236,005	Total current liabilities	\$104,309
Net fixed assets	325,422	Long-term debt	223,125
Other assets	13,125	Common stock	150,000
		Retained earnings	97,118
Total assets	\$574,552	Total liabilities and equity	\$574,552

Starlight, Inc., Income Statement for the Fiscal Year Ended June 30, 2017

Net sales	\$1,450,000
Costs	812,500
EBITDA	\$ 637,500
Depreciation	175,000
EBIT	\$ 462,500
Interest	89,575
EBT	\$ 372,925
Taxes (35%)	130,524
Net income	\$ 242,401

19.2 Use the financial information for Starlight from Self-Study Problem 19.1. Assume now that equity accounts do not vary directly with sales but change when retained earnings change or new equity is issued. The company pays 45 percent of its income as dividends every year. In addition, the company plans to expand production capacity by building a new facility that will cost \$225,000. The firm has no plans to issue new equity this year and any funds that need to be raised will be raised through the sale of long-term debt. Prepare a pro forma balance sheet using this information.

19.3 Use the financial statements from Self-Study Problem 19.1 and the information from Self-Study Problem 19.2 to calculate the company's retention (plowback) ratio, external funds needed (EFN), internal growth rate (IGR), and sustainable growth rate (SGR).

19.4 Northwood Corp. has a dividend payout ratio of 60 percent, return on equity of 14.5 percent, total assets of \$11,500,450, and equity of \$4,652,125. Calculate the firm's internal rate of growth (IGR).

19.5 Renewal Company has net income of \$1.25 million and a dividend payout ratio of 35 percent. It currently has equity of \$2,875,223. What is the firm's sustainable growth rate (SGR)?

Solutions to Self-Study Problems

19.1 The pro forma statements for Starlight are as follows:

Starlight, Inc., Balance Sheet as of June 30, 2018			
Assets:		Liabilities and Stockholders' Equity:	
Cash	$ 30,162	Accounts payable	$ 81,426
Accounts receivable	52,510	Notes payable	43,754
Inventories	200,534		
Total current assets	$283,206	Total current liabilities	$125,171
Net fixed assets	390,506	Long-term debt	267,750
Other assets	15,750	Common stock	180,000
		Retained earnings	116,542
Total assets	$689,462	Total liabilities and equity	$689,462

Starlight, Inc., Income Statement for the Fiscal Year Ended June 30, 2018	
Net sales	$1,740,000
Costs	975,000
EBITDA	$ 765,000
Depreciation	210,000
EBIT	$ 555,000
Interest	107,490
EBT	$ 447,510
Taxes (35%)	156,629
Net income	$ 290,882

19.2 The pro forma income statement is the same as that shown in the solution to Self-Study Problem 19.1. We now have to account for the payment of dividends. Since the company pays 45 percent of its net income as dividends, the retained earnings for 2018 is calculated as follows:

Retained earnings from 2018 income = $290,882 × (1 − 0.45) = $159,985.

- This is the amount by which retained earnings will increase in 2018, from $97,118 to $257,103.
- No new equity is added.
- The increase in assets is financed externally through the sale of long-term debt.

The pro forma balance sheet is as follows:

Starlight, Inc., Balance Sheet as of June 30, 2018			
Assets:		Liabilities and Stockholders' Equity:	
Cash	$ 30,162	Accounts payable	$ 81,426
Accounts receivable	52,510	Notes payable	43,754
Inventories	200,534		
Total current assets	$283,206	Total current liabilities	$125,171
Net fixed assets	390,506	Long-term debt	382,188
Addition to fixed assets	225,000	Common stock	150,000
Other assets	15,750	Retained earnings	257,103
Total assets	$914,462	Total liabilities and equity	$914,462

19.3 The retention (plowback) ratio, external funds needed, internal growth rate, and sustainable growth rate are calculated as follows:

$$\text{Retention ratio} = \frac{\text{Addition to retained earnings}}{\text{Net income}}$$

$$= \frac{\$159,985}{\$290,882}$$

$$= 0.55, \text{ or } 55\%$$

$$\begin{aligned} \text{EFN} &= (\text{Growth rate} \times \text{Initial total assets}) - \text{Addition to retained earnings} \\ &= (0.20 \times \$574{,}552) - \$159{,}985 \\ &= -\$45{,}075 \end{aligned}$$

Thus, without considering the investment of $225,000 for the new facility, the firm will not need any external funding. However, if you add the investment, then,

$$\begin{aligned} \text{EFN} &= \text{New investments} - \text{Addition to retained earnings} \\ &= (0.20 \times \$574{,}552) + \$225{,}000 - \$159{,}985 \\ &= \$179{,}925 \end{aligned}$$

$$\begin{aligned} \text{IGR} &= \frac{\text{Addition to retained earnings}}{\text{Initial total assets}} \\ &= \frac{\$159{,}985}{\$574{,}552} \\ &= 0.278, \text{ or } 27.8\% \end{aligned}$$

$$\begin{aligned} \text{SGR} &= \text{Plowback ratio} \times \text{ROE} \\ &= \frac{\text{Addition to retained earnings}}{\text{Net income}} \times \frac{\text{Net income}}{\text{Total equity}} \\ &= 0.55 \times 0.715 \\ &= 0.393, \text{ or } 39.3\% \end{aligned}$$

19.4 We calculate Northwood's internal growth rate as follows:

$$\begin{aligned} \text{IGR} &= \text{Plowback ratio} \times \text{ROE} \times \text{Measure of leverage} \\ &= 0.40 \times 0.145 \times \frac{\$4{,}652{,}125}{\$11{,}500{,}450} \\ &= 0.0235, \text{ or } 2.35\% \end{aligned}$$

19.5 Renewal's sustainable growth rate is:

$$\begin{aligned} \text{SGR} &= \text{Plowback ratio} \times \text{ROE} \\ &= 0.65 \times \frac{\$1{,}250{,}000}{\$2{,}875{,}223} \\ &= 0.283 = 28.3\% \end{aligned}$$

WileyPLUS

Questions and Problems, Solution Walkthrough Videos, Learning by Doing Tutorials, and additional study tools and resources are available in WileyPLUS.

Discussion Questions

19.1 What is financial planning? What four types of plans/budgets are involved in financial planning?

19.2 Why is the capital budget an important part of a firm's financial planning?

19.3 Why do financing and investment decisions have to be made concurrently?

19.4 Explain how sales can be used to develop pro forma financial statements.

19.5 Why is sales not always a good measure to use in forecasting fixed assets?

19.6 List all the accounts that can be affected by the "plug" value. How does this value help managers?

19.7 Explain why the fixed asset account may or may not vary with sales.

19.8 How does the dividend payout ratio affect the amount of funds needed to finance growth?

19.9 Define internal growth rate (IGR). Identify the characteristics of a high-growth firm that has no external funds needed.

19.10 What is the sustainable growth rate (SGR)? Why is it important?

Questions and Problems

Excel *Excel templates and resources available in* **WileyPLUS**

Basic

19.1 **Strategic plan:** Explain the importance of the strategic plan.

19.2 **Capital budget:** What are the various steps in preparing a capital budget?

19.3 **Financing plan:** What are the elements of a financing plan?

19.4 **Financial planning:** Identify the steps in the financial planning process.

19.5 **Financial modeling:** List the various elements of financial modeling.

19.6 **Payout ratio:** Define the retention (plowback) ratio and the dividend payout ratio.

19.7 **Addition to retained earnings:** Northwood, Inc., has revenue of $455,316, costs of $316,487, and a tax rate of 31 percent. If the firm pays out 45 percent of its earnings as dividends every year, how much earnings are retained and what is the firm's retention ratio?

19.8 **Payout and retention ratio:** Goodwin Corp. has revenues of $12,112,659, costs of $9,080,545, interest payments of $412,375, and a tax rate of 34 percent. It paid dividends of $1,025,000 to its stockholders. What are the firm's dividend payout ratio and retention ratio?

19.9 **Percent of sales:** Cattail Corporation's financial statements for the fiscal year just ended are shown below:

Cattail Corporation
Financial Statements for Fiscal Year Just Ended
($ thousands)

Income Statement		Balance Sheet			
Net sales	$1,500	Assets	$700	Debt	$600
Costs	350			Equity	100
Net income	$1,150	Total	$700	Total	$700

Cattail management expects sales to increase by 14 percent next year. Assume that the financial statement accounts vary directly with changes in sales and that management has no financing plan at this time. Given this information, develop a pro forma income statement for Cattail for the next fiscal year.

19.10 **Percent of sales:** Given the data for Cattail Corporation in Problem 19.9, if you assume that all balance sheet items also vary with the change in sales, develop a pro forma balance sheet for Cattail for the next fiscal year. Assuming that the firm did not sell or repurchase stock, what is the cash dividend implied by the pro forma income statement and balance sheet?

19.11 **Capital intensity ratio:** Define capital intensity ratio, and explain its significance.

19.12 **Capital intensity ratio:** Tantrix Confectioners has total assets of $3,257,845 and net sales of $5,123,951. What is the firm's capital intensity ratio?

19.13 **Capital intensity ratio:** McDonald Metal Works has been able to generate net sales of $13,445,196 on assets of $9,145,633. What is the firm's capital intensity ratio?

19.14 **Capital intensity ratio:** For McDonald Metal Works in Problem 19.13, how much must net sales grow if the capital intensity ratio has to drop to 60 percent? State your answer as both a percent of sales and a dollar sales increase.

19.15 **Internal growth rate:** Swan Supply Company has net income of $1,212,335, assets of $12,522,788, and retains 70 percent of its income every year. What is the company's internal growth rate?

19.16 **Sustainable growth rate:** If Newell Corp. has a ROE of 13.7 percent and a dividend payout ratio of 32 percent, what is its sustainable growth rate?

19.17 **EFN and growth:** Refer to Exhibits 19.10 and 19.11 in the text. The EFNs for several growth rates for Empire Enterprises are as follows:

Growth Rate (%)	EFN ($ millions)
0%	–$4.8
5	–2.3
9.6	0.0
10	0.2
15	2.7
20	5.2

Check the calculations and plot the line to replicate the graph in Exhibit 19.11.

Intermediate

19.18 Retention ratio: Refer to Problem 19.7. Northwood expects to increase its sales by 15 percent next year. All costs vary directly with sales. If Northwood wants to retain $65,000 of earnings next year, will it have to change its dividend payout ratio? If so, what will be the new dividend payout and retention ratios for the firm?

19.19 Capital intensity: Identify two industries (other than airlines) that are capital intensive. Using online or other data sources, compute the capital intensity ratio for the largest firm in each of the chosen industries.

19.20 Percent of sales: Tomey Supply Company's financial statements for the most recent fiscal year are shown below. Management projects that sales will increase by 20 percent next year. Assume that all costs and assets increase directly with sales. The company has a constant 33 percent dividend payout ratio and has no plans to issue new equity. Any financing needed will be raised through the sale of long-term debt. Prepare pro forma financial statements for the coming year based on this information, and calculate the EFN for Tomey.

Tomey Supply Company Income Statement and Balance Sheet

Income Statement		Balance Sheet	
Net sales	$1,768,121	Assets:	
Costs	1,116,487	Current assets	$280,754
EBT	$ 651,634	Net fixed assets	713,655
Taxes (35%)	228,072	Total assets	$994,409
Net income	$ 423,562		
		Liabilities and Equity:	
		Current liabilities	$167,326
		Long-term debt	319,456
		Common stock	200,000
		Retained earnings	307,627
		Total liabilities and equity	$994,409

19.21 Internal growth rate: Using the pro forma financial statements for Tomey Supply Company developed in Problem 19.20, find the internal growth rate for Tomey.

19.22 Sustainable growth rate: Use the following pro forma information for Tomey Supply Company for next year: net income = $508,275; addition to retained earnings = $340,544; common equity = $848,171; net sales = $2,121,745. Assume that management does not want the ratio of long-term debt to equity to exceed the current long-term debt-to-equity ratio of 63 percent and also does not want to issue new equity. What level of sales growth can Tomey Supply Company sustain? Calculate the new sales level.

19.23 Sustainable growth rate: Rowan Company has a net profit margin of 8.3 percent, debt ratio of 45 percent, total assets of $4,157,550, and sales of $6,852,654. If the company has a dividend payout ratio of 67 percent, what is its sustainable growth rate?

19.24 Sustainable growth rate: Refer to the information for Rowan Company in Problem 19.23. The firm's management desires a sustainable growth rate of 10 percent but does not wish to change the company's level of debt or its payout ratio. What will the firm's new net profit margin have to be in order to achieve the desired growth rate?

19.25 Sustainable growth rate: Rocky Sales, Inc., has current sales of $1,215,326 and net income of $211,253. It also has a debt ratio of 25 percent and a dividend payout ratio of 75 percent. The company's total assets are $712,455. What is its sustainable growth rate?

19.26 Sustainable growth rate: Ellicott Textile Mills management has reported the following financial information for the year ended September 30, 2017. The company generated a net income of $915,366 on a net profit margin of 6.4 percent. It has a dividend payout ratio of 50 percent, a capital intensity ratio of 62 percent, and a debt ratio of 45 percent. What is the company's sustainable growth rate?

19.27 Internal growth rate: Given the information in Problem 19.26, what is the internal growth rate of Ellicott Textile Mills?

19.28 Internal growth rate: Fantasy Travel Company has a return on equity of 17.5 percent, a total equity/total assets ratio of 65 percent, and a dividend payout ratio of 75 percent. What is the company's internal growth rate?

19.29 EFN: Maryland Micro Brewers generated revenues of $12,125,800 with a 72 percent capital intensity ratio during the year ended September 30, 2017. Its net income was $873,058. With the introduction of a half dozen new specialty beers, management expects to grow sales by 15 percent next year. Assume that all costs vary directly with sales and that the firm maintains a dividend payout ratio of 70 percent. What will be the EFN needed by this firm? If the company wants to raise no more than $750,000 externally and is not averse to adjusting its dividend payout policy, what will be the new dividend payout ratio?

19.30 EFN: Ritchie Marble Company has total assets of $12,899,450, sales of $18,174,652, and net income of $4,589,774. Management expects sales to grow by 25 percent next year. All assets and costs (including taxes) vary directly with sales, and management expects to maintain a payout ratio of 65 percent. Calculate Ritchie's EFN.

19.31 EFN: Norton Group, Inc., expects to add $1,213,777 to retained earnings and currently has total assets of $23,159,852. If the company has the ability to borrow up to $1 million, how much growth can the firm support if it is willing to borrow to its maximum capacity?

19.32 EFN: Capstone Marketing Group has total assets of $5,568,000, sales of $3,008,725, and net income of $822,000. The company expects its sales to grow by 12 percent next year. All assets and costs (including taxes) vary directly with sales, and the firm expects to maintain a payout ratio of 55 percent. Calculate Capstone's EFN.

19.33 Maximum sales growth: Given the data for Capstone Marketing Group in Problem 19.32, what would Capstone's payout ratio have to be for the firm's EFN to be zero?

19.34 Maximum sales growth: Rockville Consulting Group expects to add $271,898 to retained earnings this year. The company has total assets of $3,425,693 and wishes to add no new external funds for the coming year. If assets and costs vary directly with sales, how much sales growth can the company support while retaining an EFN of zero? What is the firm's internal growth rate?

Advanced

19.35 The financial statements for the year ended June 30, 2017, are given below for Morgan Construction Company. The firm's sales are projected to grow at a rate of 25 percent next year, and all financial statement accounts will vary directly with sales. Based on that projection, develop a pro forma balance sheet and an income statement for the 2018 fiscal year.

Morgan Construction Company Balance Sheet as of June 30, 2017

Assets:		Liabilities and Stockholders' Equity:	
Cash	$ 3,349,239	Accounts payable	$ 9,041,679
Accounts receivable	5,830,754	Notes payable	4,857,496
Inventories	22,267,674	Total current liabilities	$13,899,175
Total current assets	$31,447,667	Long-term debt	29,731,406
Net fixed assets	43,362,482	Common stock	19,987,500
Other assets	1,748,906	Retained earnings	12,940,974
Total assets	$76,559,055	Total liabilities and equity	$76,559,055

Morgan Construction Company Income Statement for the Fiscal Year Ended June 30, 2017

Net sales	$193,212,500
Costs	45,265,625
EBITDA	$ 47,946,875
Depreciation	23,318,750
EBIT	$ 24,628,125
Interest	11,935,869
EBT	$ 12,692,256
Taxes (35%)	4,442,290
Net income	$ 8,249,966

19.36 Use the financial information for Morgan Construction Company from Problem 19.35. Assume now that equity accounts do not vary directly with sales but change when retained earnings change or new equity is issued. The company pays 75 percent of its income as dividends every year. In addition, the company plans to expand production capacity by expanding the current facility and acquiring additional equipment. This will cost the firm $10 million. The firm has no plans to issue new equity this year. Prepare a pro forma balance sheet using this information. Any funds that need to be raised (in addition to changes in current liabilities) will be in the form of long-term debt. What is the external funding needed in this case?

19.37 Using the information for Morgan Construction Company in the preceding problem, calculate the firm's internal growth rate and sustainable growth rate.

19.38 Use the information for Morgan Construction Company from Problems 19.35 and 19.36. Assume that equity accounts do not vary directly with sales, but change when retained earnings change or new equity is issued. The company's long-term debt-to-equity ratio is approximately 90 percent, and its equity-to-total assets ratio is about 43 percent. The company management wishes to increase its equity-to-total assets ratio to at least 50 percent. Management is willing to reduce the company's payout ratio but will retain no more than 40 percent of earnings. The company will raise any additional funds needed, including funds for expansion, by selling new equity. No new long-term debt will be issued. Prepare pro forma statements to reflect this new scenario.

a. What is the external funding needed to accommodate the expected growth?

b. What is the firm's internal growth rate?

c. What is the firm's sustainable growth rate?

d. How much new equity will the firm have to issue?

e. What is the firm's new equity ratio and debt-to-equity ratio?

19.39 Munson Communications Company management has just reported earnings for the year ended June 30, 2017. Below are the firm's income statement and balance sheet. The company had a 55 percent dividend payout ratio for the last 10 years and management does not plan to change this policy. Based on internal forecasts, management expects sales growth in 2018 to be 20 percent. Assume that equity accounts and long-term debt do not vary directly with sales but change when retained earnings change or additional capital is issued.

Munson Communications Company Balance Sheet as of June 30, 2017

Assets:		Liabilities and Stockholders' Equity:	
Cash	$ 1,728,639	Accounts payable	$ 4,666,673
Accounts receivable	3,009,421	Notes payable	2,507,094
Inventories	11,492,993	Total current liabilities	$ 7,173,767
Total current assets	$16,231,054	Long-term debt	13,345,242
Net fixed assets	22,380,636	Common stock	10,165,235
Other assets	1,748,906	Retained earnings	9,676,351
Total assets	$40,360,595	Total liabilities and equity	$40,360,595

Munson Communications Company Income Statement for the Fiscal Year Ended June 30, 2017

Net sales	$79,722,581
Costs	59,358,499
EBITDA	$20,364,082
Depreciation	7,318,750
EBIT	$13,045,332
Interest	3,658,477
EBT	$ 9,386,855
Taxes (35%)	3,285,399
Net income	$ 6,101,456

a. What is the firm's internal growth rate (IGR)?

b. What is the firm's sustainable growth rate (SGR)?

c. What is the external funding needed (EFN) to accommodate the expected growth?

d. Construct the firm's 2018 pro forma financial statements under the assumption that long-term debt will provide all external funding.

Sample Test Problems

19.1 Mars Company had net sales of $18 million in the year that just ended. Next year, the company's management expects a 15 percent increase in sales. If cost of goods sold is 60 percent of sales and inventory is 25 percent of sales, what would you estimate sales, inventory, and cost of goods sold to be next year?

19.2 Lavaca Inc. management expects net sales to be $855,000, total costs to be $647,000, and to pay taxes at an average rate of 32 percent this year. If Lavaca pays out 38 percent of its earnings as dividends, what is its retention ratio? How much will Lavaca's retained earnings increase?

19.3 Spurlock Inc. had net income of $266,778 in its most recent fiscal year and total assets of $1,833,400 at the end of the year. The company's total debt ratio (total debt to total assets) is 35 percent, and Spurlock retains 60 percent of its income every year. What is Spurlock's internal growth rate? What is its sustainable growth rate?

19.4 Using the information in Sample Test Problem 19.3, what is Spurlock's capital intensity ratio if the company has net sales of $3,557,100? What does this ratio tell us?

19.5 Edgefield Excavation Company has total assets of $4,976,456, sales of $1,225,700, and net income of $587,000. The company's management expects sales to grow by 9 percent next year. All costs (including taxes) and assets vary directly with sales, and the firm expects to maintain a payout ratio of 35 percent. Calculate the external funds needed (EFN) by Edgefield. What would Edgefield's payout ratio have to be in order for the company's EFN to equal zero?

Options and Corporate Finance

CHAPTER **20**

Francesco Mocellin/Wikimedia Commons

LEARNING OBJECTIVES

1. Define a call option and a put option, and describe the payoff function for each of these options.
2. List and describe the variables that affect the value of an option. Calculate the value of a call option and of a put option.
3. Name some of the real options that occur in business and explain why traditional NPV analysis does not accurately incorporate their values.
4. Describe how the agency costs of debt and equity are related to options.
5. Explain how options can be used to manage a firm's exposure to risk.

On March 27, 2017, management of Uranium Resources Inc. announced that the company had acquired a one-year option, or right, to purchase mining claims covering an area of approximately 3,040 acres within the Columbus Salt Marsh area of west-central Nevada. These claims would expand the area encompassed by Uranium Resources' Columbus Basin project, in which the company was assembling mineral rights for lithium exploration, to more than 14,200 acres. Uranium Resources agreed to pay $75,000 to the owner of the mineral claims and $23,560 in mine claim maintenance fees to the Bureau of Land Management for the option.

Uranium Resources is an energy metals exploration and development company that was founded in 1977 and is headquartered in Centennial, Colorado. The company owns property with lithium and uranium exploration potential, a uranium development project, and idled uranium production properties in the United States and Turkey. Uranium Resources' objective is to become the leading producer of energy metals, specifically lithium and uranium.

Lithium is a soft, silver-white metal that is commonly obtained from brine, a naturally occurring fluid that is found in sedimentary rocks. In the Columbus Basin project, Uranium Resources was assembling mining claims for land that its management thought would contain lithium-enriched brines. Lithium extracted from these brines has a number of industrial uses, including the production of lithium batteries and lithium-ion batteries. The development of the Tesla "Gigafactory" near Sparks, Nevada, which, by itself, would produce more lithium-ion batteries each year than were produced worldwide in 2013, was a sign that demand for lithium would remain strong in the foreseeable future. Uranium Resources' management noted in the company's 2016 annual report that demand for lithium was expected to increase 6 percent per year through 2025.

Of course, Uranium Resources could have purchased the mineral rights for the 3,040 acres outright, but doing so would have required considerably more money and been a riskier strategy than purchasing the option. The option cost only a fraction of the cost of acquiring the rights outright, but gave the company the exclusive right to purchase the mineral rights at any time in the next year.

This gave Uranium Resources' managers time to investigate the economic viability of the mineral rights more thoroughly before making a final investment decision. Options such as those acquired by Uranium Resources are only one example of the many different types of options we see in the corporate world. This chapter explains what options are, some of their applications in corporate finance, how they can affect corporate decision making, and how they affect the value of a business.

Chapter Preview

Options and option-like payoffs complicate the analytical frameworks that we have discussed in this book. Financial options, such as the right to buy or sell the shares of a company at a prespecified price, are often found in financial securities that firms issue and therefore must be considered in the valuation of those securities. Real options, such as those acquired by Uranium Resources in the chapter opener, make calculation of the true NPV of a project more complex. In order to fully understand the implications of these complications for financial analyses, it is important that you understand what options are and the types of options that are available to managers or that they must contend with.

We begin with a discussion of financial options and how they are valued because financial options are, in many ways, simpler than real options to illustrate and value. Many financial options are traded independently in the financial markets while others are bundled with the financial instruments that managers issue and that also trade in the financial markets. Since financial options are commonly traded, we know a lot about how they are valued.

We then turn to real options, which affect the value of corporate investments. As illustrated in the chapter opener, managers often have options to delay investing in a project, expand a project, abandon a project, change the technology employed in a project, and so on. You will see that the value of these options is not adequately reflected in an NPV analysis.

We next revisit the agency costs of debt that we discussed in Chapter 16. In particular, we show how option-like payoffs contribute to the dividend payout, asset substitution, and underinvestment conflicts. We follow this discussion with a related discussion of how option-like payoffs contribute to conflicts between stockholders and the managers who work for them. We conclude the chapter with a discussion of the ways in which managers use financial options to alter their companies' exposures to various types of risks.

20.1 Financial Options

financial option the right to buy or sell a financial security, such as a share of stock, on or before a specified date for a specified price

derivative security a security that derives its value from the value of another asset; an option is an example of a derivative security

underlying asset the asset from which the value of an option is derived

exercise (expiration) date the last date on which an option can be exercised

exercise (strike) price the price at which the owner of an option has the right to buy or sell the underlying asset

LEARNING OBJECTIVE

1. Define a call option and a put option, and describe the payoff function for each of these options.

A **financial option** is a **derivative security** in that its value is derived from the value of another asset. The owner of a financial option has the right, but not the obligation, to buy or sell an asset on or before a specified date for a specified price. The asset that the owner has a right to buy or sell is known as the **underlying asset**. The last date on which an option can be exercised is called the **exercise date** or **expiration date**, and the price at which the option holder can buy or sell the asset is called the **exercise price** or **strike price**.

Call Options

Let's consider how the value of an option is derived from the value of an underlying asset. Suppose you own an option to buy one share of IBM stock for \$150 per share and today is the exercise date. If you don't exercise the option today, it will expire and become worthless. If the price of IBM's stock is less than \$150 per share, it does not make sense to exercise your option, because if you did, you would be paying $150 for something you could buy for less than $150 in the open market. Similarly, if the stock price is $150, there is no benefit to be had from exercising your option. If, however, the price is above $150, then you will benefit from exercising the option. Even if you do not want to own IBM stock, you can buy it for $150 and immediately turn around and sell it for a profit. The value of the option to you is the difference between the market price of IBM stock and the exercise price of the option. For example, if the IBM stock is trading for $160 per share in the market, then the option is worth $10 ($160 stock price − $150 exercise price = $10) to you. If the stock is trading for $170 per share, then the value of the option is $20 ($170 − $150 = $20), and so on.

The relation between the value of an option and the price (value) of the underlying asset, such as the IBM stock, is known as the **option payoff function**. Figure A in **Exhibit 20.1** illustrates the payoff function at expiration (actually, the instant before the option expires) for the owner of an option that is like the IBM stock option we just discussed. This option is known as a **call option** because it gives the owner the right to buy, or "call," the underlying asset.

option payoff function the function that shows how the value of an option varies with the value of the underlying asset

call option an option to buy the underlying asset

With an exercise price of $150, the value of the IBM call option equals $0 if the price of the underlying stock is $150 or less. As we noted earlier, it would not make sense to exercise the option if the price of the stock is not greater than $150. Since an option is the *right* to buy or sell an underlying asset, rather than an *obligation* to buy or sell, the owner of the option can simply let it expire if it does not make sense to exercise it. This limits the downside for the owner of the option to $0.

If the underlying asset price is above the exercise price, the value of the call option at exercise increases dollar for dollar with the price of the underlying asset. You can see this relation in Figure A of the exhibit. For every dollar that the asset price exceeds the exercise price, the value of the call option increases by one dollar. In other words, the slope of the payoff function equals one when the underlying asset price is above the exercise price.

Figure B of Exhibit 20.1 illustrates the payoff function for a person who sells a call option. Notice that the payoff function for the seller is the mirror image of that for the owner (buyer)

Figure A. Owner (buyer) of a call option

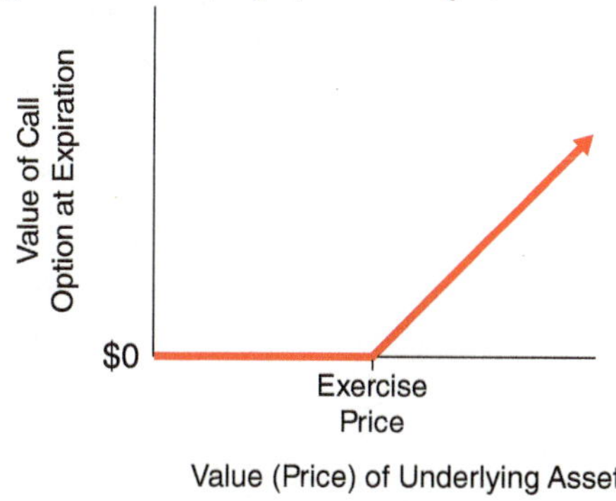

The value of a call option *increases* dollar for dollar with an *increase* in the value of the underlying asset when the value of that asset is above the exercise price.

At the instant before it expires, the value of a call option to the owner equals either (1) $0, if the value of the underlying asset is less than or equal to the exercise price, or (2) the value of the underlying asset minus the exercise price, if the value of the underlying asset is greater.

Figure B. Seller of call option

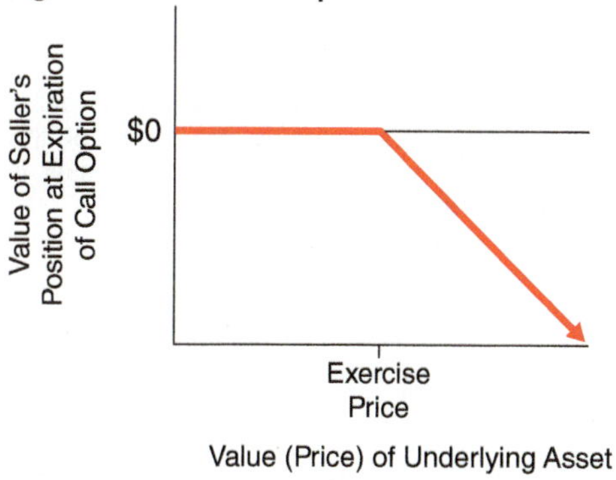

The value of the seller's position *decreases* dollar for dollar with an *increase* in the value of the underlying asset when the value of that asset is above the exercise price of a call option.

The value of the seller's position equals either (1) $0 if the value of the underlying asset is less than or equal to the exercise price or (2) the exercise price minus the value of the underlying asset if the value of the underlying asset is greater.

EXHIBIT 20.1 **Payoff Functions for a Call Option at Expiration**

of the call option. This makes sense, since any gain for the owner is a loss for the seller. To see why this is true, let's return to the IBM option example. Recall that if the stock is trading at $160 when the option expires, the call option is worth $10 to the owner, who can purchase the stock for $150 and then immediately sell it on the market for $160. The seller of the call option, though, must sell a share of stock that is worth $160 for $150, resulting in a $10 loss.

Figure B of Exhibit 20.1 shows that the payoff to the seller of the call option is never positive. It is negative when the price of the underlying asset is greater than the exercise price, and it equals zero when the price of the underlying asset is equal to or less than the exercise price. You may be wondering why anyone would ever sell a call option if the return is never positive. The reason is simply that the buyer pays the seller a fee to purchase the option. This fee, which is known as the **call premium**, makes the total return to the seller positive when the price of the underlying asset is near or below the exercise price.

call premium the price that the buyer of a call option pays the seller for that option

A call premium is just like the premium you pay when you purchase insurance for your car. In return for the insurance premium, the insurance company agrees to pay you if certain events occur, such as if you collide with another car or if a hailstorm damages the car. The seller of a call option is simply selling insurance to the buyer that pays the buyer when the value of the underlying asset is above the exercise price.

Put Options

While the owner of a *call option* has the right to *buy* the underlying asset at a prespecified price on or before the expiration date, the owner of a **put option** has the right to *sell* the underlying asset at a prespecified price. The payoff function for the owner of a put option is similar to that for a call option, but it is the reverse in the sense that the owner of a put option profits if the price of the underlying asset is *below* the exercise price. This is illustrated in **Exhibit 20.2**.

put option an option to sell the underlying asset

Figure A. Owner (buyer) of a put option

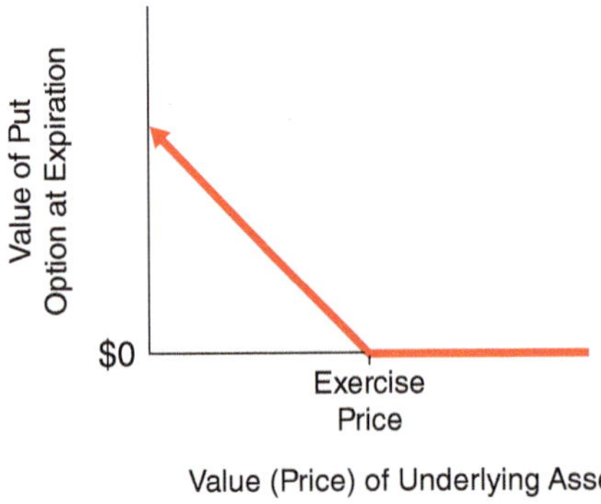

The value of an expiring put option *increases* dollar for dollar with a *decrease* in the value of the underlying asset when the value of that asset is below the exercise price.

At the instant before it expires, the value of a put option to the owner equals either (1) $0, if the value of the underlying asset is greater than or equal to the exercise price, or (2) the exercise price minus the value of the underlying asset, if the value of the underlying asset is less than the exercise price.

Figure B. Seller of a put option

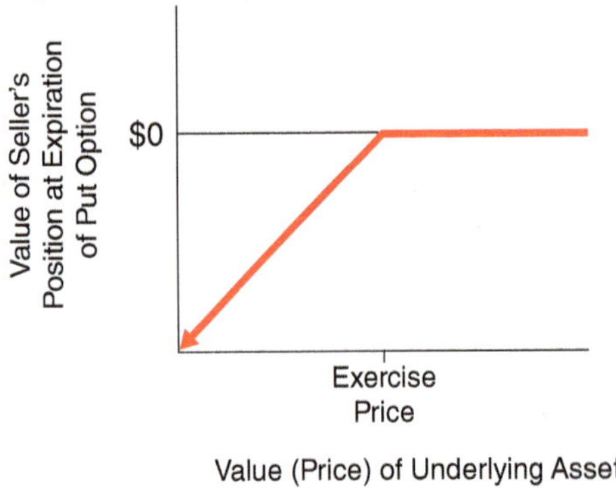

The value of the seller's position *decreases* dollar for dollar with a *decrease* in the value of the underlying asset, when the value of that asset is below the exercise price of a put option.

The value to the seller of a put option equals either (1) $0, if the value of the underlying asset is greater than or equal to the exercise price, or (2) the value of the underlying asset minus the exercise price, if the value of the underlying asset is smaller than the exercise price.

EXHIBIT 20.2 Payoff Functions for Put Option at Expiration

Figure A of the exhibit shows that the owner of a put option will not want to exercise that option if the price of the underlying asset is above the exercise price. Obviously, it does not make sense to sell an asset for less than you can get on the open market. When the value of the underlying asset is below the exercise price, however, the owner of the put option will find it profitable to exercise the option. For example, suppose that you own a put option that is expiring today and that entitles you to sell a share of IBM stock for $150. If the current price of IBM stock in the market is $145, the put option is worth $5 because exercising the option will enable you to buy a share of stock for $145 and then turn around and sell it for $150. Similarly, if the current price of IBM stock is $130, the put option is worth $20 because you can buy the stock for $130 and sell it for $150.

Figure B of Exhibit 20.2 shows that the payoff for the seller of the put option is negative when the price of the underlying asset is below the exercise price. This is because the seller of the put option is obligated to purchase the asset at a price that is higher than its market price. For instance, in the IBM put option example, if the exercise price is $150 and the current market price is $130, the seller of the put option must buy the stock for $150 but can only sell it for $130. This results in a $20 loss.

As with a call option, the payoff for the seller of a put option, which is illustrated in Figure B of Exhibit 20.2, is never positive. The seller of a put option hopes to profit from the fee, or **put premium,** that he or she receives from the buyer of the put option.

Decision Making Example 20.1 illustrates the decision of when to exercise an option.

put premium the price that the buyer of a put option pays the seller of that option

DECISION MAKING

EXAMPLE 20.1 | When It Makes Sense to Exercise an Option

Situation You own a call option and a put option on a share of Ford Motor Company stock. The exercise price for both of these options is $18 per share, and both options expire today. If the current price of Ford stock is $17, would you exercise either of these options? If so, which one?

Decision You should exercise the put option. It allows you to sell a share of Ford stock for $18 that would cost you only $17 to buy. It does not make sense to exercise the call option because the exercise price is greater than the market price of Ford stock.

American, European, and Bermudan Options

At the beginning of this section, we said that the owner of a financial option has the right to buy or sell a specific asset *on or before a specified date* for a specified price. In the real world, there are actually several different arrangements concerning when an option can be exercised. Some options can only be exercised on the expiration date. These are known as *European options*. Other options, known as *American options*, can be exercised at any point in time on or before the expiration date. There are also exotic options, such as so-called *Bermudan options*, which can be exercised only on specific dates during the life of the option. Most exchange-traded options (even in Europe) are American options.

Weblink

You can learn more about call options and put options on the Wikipedia Web site at http://en.wikipedia.org/wiki/Call_option and http://en.wikipedia.org/wiki/Put_option.

More on the Shapes of Option Payoff Functions

It is important to note that the payoff functions in Exhibits 20.1 and 20.2 illustrate the values of options to owners and sellers at the instant before they expire. These payoff functions have similar, but somewhat different, shapes at earlier points in time. We discuss why this is the case in the next section.

It is also important to recognize that the payoff functions in Exhibits 20.1 and 20.2 are not straight lines for all possible values of the underlying asset. Each payoff function has a "kink" at the exercise price. This kink exists because the

Building Intuition

Payoff Functions for Options are not Linear

Payoff functions for options are not straight lines. This is because the owners of options have the right, rather than the obligation, to buy or sell the underlying assets. If it is not in the owner's best interest to exercise an option, he or she can simply let it expire without exercising it. This limits the owner's potential loss to the value of the premium he or she paid for the option.

owner of the option has a right, not an obligation, to buy or sell the underlying asset. If it is not in the owner's interest to exercise the option, he or she can simply let it expire. Later, we will discuss how this feature of options causes agency problems and how it can be useful in managing the risks faced by a firm.

Before You Go On

1. What is a call option, and what do the payoff functions for the owner and seller of a call option look like?
2. What is a put option, and what do the payoff functions for the owner and seller of a put option look like?
3. Why does the payoff function for an option have a kink in it?

20.2 Option Valuation

LEARNING OBJECTIVE

2. List and describe the variables that affect the value of an option. Calculate the value of a call option and of a put option.

We saw in the preceding section that determining the value of a call or a put option at the instant before it expires is relatively simple. For a call option, if the value of the underlying asset is less than or equal to the exercise price, the value of the option to the owner is $0. If the value of the underlying asset is greater than the exercise price, the value to the owner is simply the value of the underlying asset minus the exercise price. For a put option, if the value of the underlying asset is greater than or equal to the exercise price, the value of the option is $0 to the owner. If the value of the underlying asset is less than the exercise price, the value to the owner is the exercise price minus the value of the underlying asset.

It is more complicated to determine the value of an option at a point in time before its expiration date. We don't know exactly how the value of the underlying asset will change over time, and therefore we don't know what value the owner will ultimately receive from the option. In this section, we discuss the key variables that affect the value of an option prior to expiration and describe one method that is commonly used to value options. Our objective is not to make you an expert in option valuation, but rather to help you develop some intuition about what makes an option more or less valuable. This intuition will help you better understand how options affect corporate finance decisions.

Limits on Option Values

Let's begin by using some common sense to put limits on what the value of a call option can possibly be prior to its expiration date. We focus on call options here because, as you will see, there is a simple relation that enables us to calculate the value of a put option once we know the value of a call option with the same exercise price.

We already know that the value of a call option can never be less than zero, since the owner of the option can always decide not to exercise it if doing so is not beneficial. A second limit on the value of a call option is that it can never be greater than the value of the underlying asset. It would not make sense to pay more for the right to buy an asset than you would pay for the asset itself. These two limits suggest that the value of a call option prior to expiration must be in the shaded area in Figure A of **Exhibit 20.3**. The shaded area is bounded below by the horizontal axis, because the value of the option must be greater than $0, and it is bounded above by the line that slopes upward at a 45-degree

Figure A. Possible values with first two limits

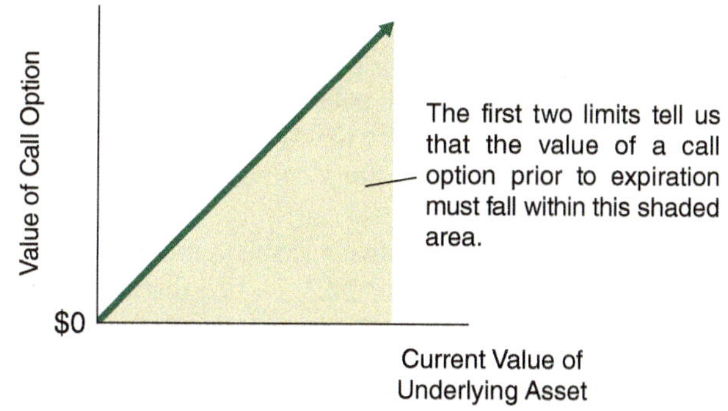

The value of a call option: (1) must be greater than or equal to $0 (horizontal axis) and (2) cannot be greater than the value of the underlying asset (45 degree line).

Figure B. Possible values with all four limits

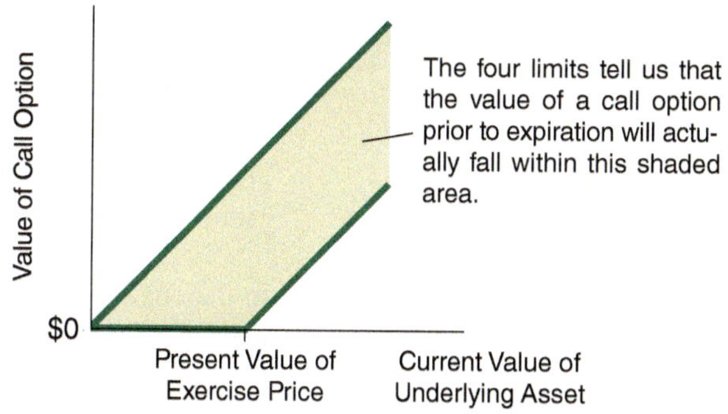

In addition to the two limits illustrated in Figure A, the value of a call option prior to expiration: (3) will never be less than the value of the option if it were exercised immediately where (4) the value of the option is calculated using the present value of the exercise price, discounted from the expiration date at the risk-free rate. These conditions are both illustrated by the lower 45, degree line.

Figure C. Typical payoff function for call option prior to expiration

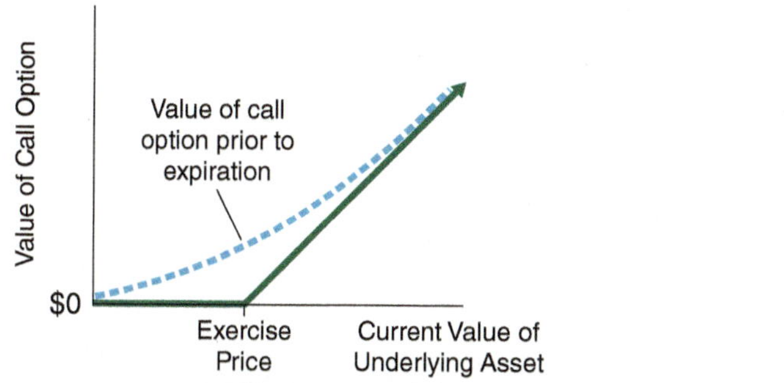

This figure shows the typical relation between the value of a call option prior to expiration and its value at expiration. The value of the option prior to expiration is farthest from the value of the option at expiration when the value of the underlying asset is near the exercise price.

EXHIBIT 20.3 Possible Values of a Call Option Prior to Expiration

angle, because an option value greater than this would exceed the value of the underlying asset.

There are two other limits on the value of a call option prior to expiration, and these limits are somewhat more subtle. First, the value of a call option prior to the expiration date will never be less than the value of that option if it had to be exercised immediately. This is true because there is always a possibility that the value of the underlying asset will be greater than it is today at some time before the option expires. Of course, it is possible that the value will be lower, but since the value of the option cannot be less than $0 and there is no limit on how high it can go, the expected effect of an increase in the value of the underlying asset on the value of the option is greater than the expected effect of a decrease. The bottom line is that, prior to expiration, the value of a call option will be greater than the value represented by the solid red line in Figure A of Exhibit 20.1 (in the preceding section of this chapter).[1]

The fourth and final limit arises because of the time value of money. When we consider the value of a call option at some time prior to expiration, we must compare the current value of the underlying asset with the *present value of the exercise price*, discounted at the *risk-free rate*. We would be comparing apples and oranges if we did not do this. The present value of

[1]Even if the value of the option ever fell below the line to the right of the exercise price in Figure A of Exhibit 20.1, it would not stay there. This is because investors would be able to make an instant profit by buying the option, exercising it to get the underlying asset, and then selling the underlying asset. Such trading by investors would drive the price of the option back above the line.

the exercise price is the amount that an investor would have to invest in risk-free securities at any point prior to the expiration date to ensure that he or she would have enough money to exercise the option when it expired. Thus, when we compare the value of a call option prior to expiration with the value at expiration, represented by the solid red line in Figure A of Exhibit 20.1, we must use the present value of the exercise price to draw the line. The shaded area in Figure B of Exhibit 20.3 illustrates the possible values for a call option prior to expiration under all four of the limits we have discussed.

In practice, we find that, prior to expiration, call options have a shape that is very similar to the one illustrated by the dotted line in Figure C of Exhibit 20.3. Notice that this dotted line approaches \$0 as the value of the underlying asset gets very small relative to the exercise price. This makes sense because, with a very low asset value, it becomes highly unlikely that the owner of the option will ever choose to exercise it.

On the right side of the dotted line, you can see that the value of a call option prior to expiration approaches the value of the call option at expiration. This is because when the current value of the underlying asset is far to the right of the kink in the option's payoff function, the probability that this value will fall below the exercise price is very small. In other words, the expected effect of an increase in the value of the underlying asset on the value of the option is no longer much greater than the expected effect of a decrease.

Finally, notice that the dotted line is furthest above the value of the call option at expiration when the price of the underlying asset is near the exercise price. At the exercise price, the expected effect of an increase in the value of the underlying asset on the value of the option exceeds the expected effect of a decrease by the greatest amount.

Variables That Affect Option Values

Five variables affect the value of a call option prior to expiration. Four of them are related to the following questions:

1. How likely is it that the value of the underlying asset will be higher than the exercise price the instant before the option expires?
2. How far above the exercise price might it be?

The first two variables are relatively easy to understand. They are the *current value of the underlying asset* and the *exercise price*. The higher the current value of the underlying asset, the more likely it is that the value of the asset will be above the exercise price when the call option nears expiration. Furthermore, the higher the current value of the asset, the greater the likely difference between the value of the asset and the exercise price. This means that, holding the exercise price constant, investors will pay more for a call option if the underlying asset value is higher, because the expected value of the option as it nears expiration is higher.[2] For example, suppose that you are considering purchasing a three-month American call option on a share of IBM stock with an exercise price of \$150. You should be willing to pay more for this option if the current price of IBM stock is \$155 than if it is \$150.

The opposite relation applies to the exercise price. That is, the lower the exercise price, the more likely that the value of the underlying asset will be higher than the exercise price when the option nears expiration. In addition, the lower the exercise price, the greater the likely difference between these two amounts. Thus, the lower the exercise price, the more valuable the option is likely to be at expiration. Of course, if the option is expected to be more valuable at expiration, it will also be more valuable at any point prior

[2]We are focusing in this discussion on what the value of the underlying asset is likely to be immediately before the option expires because it does not generally make sense to exercise an option before its expiration date as long as there is a chance that the value of the underlying asset could increase further. An exception is when the value of the underlying asset is not expected to be higher as the expiration of the option nears because value is being distributed to the owners of the underlying asset (for example, through dividend payments). In a situation like this, it can be appropriate to exercise a call option immediately before such a distribution. There are also situations where it is advantageous to exercise a put option early. Such situations can arise if the value of the underlying asset is \$0 before expiration. When this happens, the value received from exercising the option today can exceed the present value of the amount that is expected to be received if the option is exercised immediately before expiration.

to expiration. Returning to our IBM example, we see that a call option with an exercise price of $145 is worth more than a call option with an exercise price of $150.

We turn next to two variables that affect the value of call options in somewhat more subtle ways. These variables are the *volatility of the value of the underlying asset* and the *time until the expiration of the option*. To understand how these factors affect the value of a call option, recall from Figure C of Exhibit 20.3 that the payoff function for a call option prior to expiration is not symmetric. If the value of the underlying asset is well above the exercise price, then the value of the option varies in much the same way as the value of the underlying asset. However, if the value of the underlying asset is well below the exercise price, then the value of the option approaches $0, but changes at a much lower rate than the value of the underlying asset changes. It does not matter if the underlying asset value is just a little bit below the exercise price or is completely worthless—a call option cannot be worth less than $0.

To show how the volatility of the underlying asset value affects the value of an option, we will consider a call option on an underlying asset that has a value exactly equal to the exercise price of the option. The value of this option will increase more when the value of the underlying asset goes up than it will decrease when the value of the underlying asset goes down. Let's suppose that the value of the underlying asset is equally likely to go up or down. In this case, the further the value of the asset is likely to move (the greater its volatility), the higher the value of a call option on this asset will be. In other words, the greater the volatility of the underlying asset value, the higher the value of a call option on the asset prior to expiration.

In our IBM example, suppose the exercise price for a call option on IBM stock is $150, the current price of the stock is $150, and the option expires in one year. Further suppose that the standard deviation, σ, of the return on the IBM stock is 30 percent per year. Recall from the discussion in Chapter 7 that with a standard deviation of 30 percent, there is a 5 percent chance that the IBM stock price will change by more than 58.8 percent (1.96 standard deviations × 30 percent = 58.8 percent) by the time the option expires. In other words, there is a 5 percent chance that the IBM stock price will be less than $61.80 [$150 × (1 − 0.588) = $61.80] or greater than $238.20 [$150 × (1 + 0.588) = $238.20] in a year. If, instead of 30 percent, the standard deviation of IBM stock were 40 percent per year, there would be a 5 percent chance that the price would be below $32.40 or above $267.60. (You should check these numbers to make sure you know how they are calculated.) As you can see, this higher standard deviation means the stock price is more volatile. Investors will pay more for an option on a stock that has a more volatile price, because the potential change in the stock's price is greater.

Weblink

You can read about what affects the values of financial options and how they are traded at the Web sites for the Chicago Board Options Exchange (CBOE) at http://www.cboe.com/.

The time until the expiration affects the value of a call option through its effect on the volatility of the value of the underlying asset. The greater the time to maturity, the more the value of the underlying asset is likely to change by the time the option expires. For example, let's return once again to the IBM example. Suppose that the option expires in two years rather than in one year. People who study statistics have found that the standard deviation of the return on an asset increases over time by the square root of n, where n is the number of periods. Thus, if the standard deviation of the return on IBM stock is 30 percent per year, the standard deviation over two years will be:

$$\sigma_{2\text{ years}} = \sigma_{1\text{ year}} \times (n)^{1/2} = 30\% \times (2\text{ years})^{1/2} = 30\% \times 1.414 = 42.42\%$$

Clearly, then, a two-year option will be worth more than a one-year option if all other characteristics of the options are the same.

We've now discussed four of the five variables that affect the value of an option. The fifth variable is the *risk-free rate of interest*. The value of a call option increases with the risk-free rate. Exercising a call option involves paying cash in the future for the underlying asset. The higher the interest rate, the lower the present value of the amount that the owner of a call option will have to pay to exercise it.

The Binomial Option Pricing Model

In this section, we use a simple model to show how we can calculate the value of a call option at some point before the expiration date. This model assumes that the underlying asset will have one of only two possible values when the option expires. The value of the underlying asset will either increase to some value above the exercise price or decrease to some value below the exercise price.

arbitrage buying and selling assets in a way that takes advantage of price discrepancies and yields a profit greater than that which would be expected based solely on the systematic risk of the individual investments

To solve for the value of the call option using this model, we must assume that investors have no arbitrage opportunities with regard to this option. **Arbitrage** is the act of buying and selling assets in a way that yields a return above that suggested by the Security Market Line (SML), which we discussed in Chapter 7. In other words, the absence of arbitrage opportunities means that investors cannot earn a return that is greater than that justified by the systematic risk associated with an investment. As an example of an arbitrage opportunity, suppose that the stock of a particular company is being sold for a lower price in one country than in another country. An investor could simultaneously buy the stock in the country where it is less expensive and sell it in the country where it is more expensive. Assuming that the profit exceeds any transaction costs, the investor would earn an instantaneous risk-free profit. Since it is instantaneous, this profit would, by definition, be above the SML because the SML would predict that the expected return on a risk-free investment is zero if the holding period is zero.

To value the call option in our simple model, we will first create a portfolio that consists of the asset underlying the call option and a risk-free loan. The relative investments in these two assets will be selected so that the combination of the asset and the loan have the same cash flows as the call option, regardless of whether the value of the underlying asset goes up or down. This is called a *replicating portfolio*, since it replicates the cash flows of the option. The replicating portfolio must have the same value as the option today, since it has the same cash flows as the call option in all possible future outcomes. If the replicating portfolio did not have the same value as the option, an investor could construct an arbitrage portfolio by buying the cheaper of the two and selling the more expensive of the two. Such trading would eventually drive the values of the option and the replicating portfolio together.

To see how a replicating portfolio is constructed, consider an example. Suppose that the stock of ABC Corporation currently trades for \$50 and that its price will be either \$70 or \$40 in one year. We want to determine the value of a call option to buy ABC stock for \$55 in one year. First, notice that the value of this option is \$15 if the stock price goes up to \$70 (\$70 − \$55 = \$15) and that it is \$0 if the stock price goes down to \$40, since the option will not be exercised. Suppose also that the risk-free rate is 5 percent.

We can construct a portfolio consisting of x shares of ABC Corporation stock and a risk-free loan with a value of y dollars that produces a payoff of either \$70 or \$40. The risk-free loan may involve either borrowing or lending, as you will see. For each risk-free dollar we lend, we know that we will receive \$1.05 regardless of what happens to the price of ABC stock. In the same way, if we borrow \$1, we will owe \$1.05 at the end of the year. The value of the stock, the risk-free loan, and the option today and at expiration can be illustrated as follows.

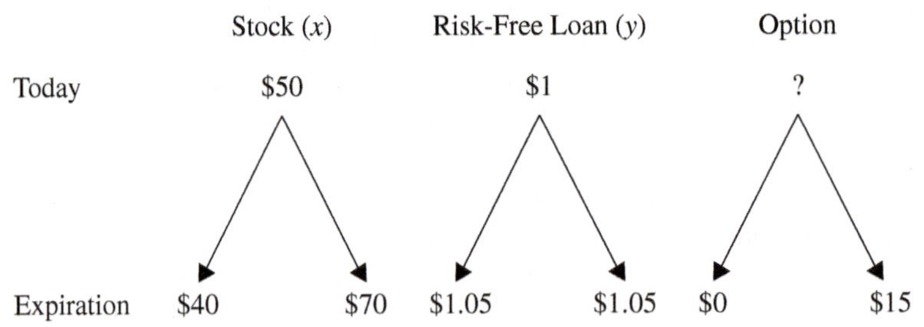

The value of each asset when the stock price goes up to \$70 is shown on the right arrow, and the value when the stock goes down to \$40 is shown on the left arrow. Notice that we do not know the value of the option today—that is what we are trying to calculate.

We can write two equations that define the replicating portfolio that we want to construct:

$$\$15 = (\$70 \times x) + (1.05 \times y)$$
$$\$0 = (\$40 \times x) + (1.05 \times y)$$

The first equation represents the case in which the stock price increases to \$70, and the second equation represents the case in which the stock price goes down to \$40. The first equation says that we want the portfolio to be worth \$15 when the stock price increases to \$70 and that the \$15 value will consist of x shares of stock worth \$70 and a risk-free loan with a face value of y and a value in one year of \$1.05 per dollar of face value. Similarly, the second equation says that if the stock price falls to \$40, we want the portfolio to be worth \$0. In this case, the portfolio will consist of x shares of stock worth \$40 and a risk-free loan with a face value of y and a value in one year of \$1.05 per dollar of face value.

Since we have two equations and there are two unknowns, *x* and *y*, we can solve for the values of the unknowns. Recall from your algebra class that we can solve for *x* and *y* by first writing one equation in terms of either *x* or *y* and then substituting the result into the second equation. For example, the first equation can be written in terms of *x* as follows:

$$x = \frac{\$15 - (1.05 \times y)}{\$70}$$

Now, substituting into the second equation gives us:

$$\$0 = \left(\$40 \times \frac{\$15 - (1.05 \times y)}{\$70}\right) + (1.05 \times y)$$

We can now solve this equation for *y* as follows:

$$\$0 = \left(\$40 \times \frac{\$15}{\$70}\right) - \left(\$40 \times \frac{1.05 \times y}{\$70}\right) + (1.05 \times y)$$

$$\$0 = \$8.5714 - (0.6 \times y) + (1.05 \times y)$$

$$\$0 = \$8.5714 + 0.45y$$

$$0.45y = -\$8.5714$$

Therefore:

$$y = \frac{-\$8.5714}{0.45} = -\$19.05$$

Finally, substituting this value back into the first equation gives us the value of *x*:

$$x = \frac{\$15 - (1.05 \times -\$19.05)}{\$70}$$

$$x = \frac{\$15 + \$20.00}{\$70}$$

$$x = 0.5$$

This tells us that the replicating portfolio consists of one-half share of ABC Corporation stock ($x = 0.50$) and a $19.05 risk-free loan ($y = -\$19.05$). The negative value for *y* tells us that we would borrow, rather than lend, $19.05 at the risk-free rate. If we buy one-half share of stock and borrow $19.05, then in one year our replicating portfolio will have exactly the same payoff as the call option with an exercise price of $55.

If the value of the stock declined to $40, we would own one-half share of stock worth $20, and we would owe $\$19.05 \times 1.05 = \$20$ on the loan. Since the value of the stock would exactly equal the amount owed on the loan, the portfolio would have a total value of exactly $0. In contrast, if the value of the stock increased to $70, the one-half share of stock would be worth $35. Since we would still owe only $20 in this case, the portfolio would have a total value of $15. Since these payoffs are exactly the same as those for the option, this portfolio must have the same value as the option.

At this point, we know what the replicating portfolio consists of, and we know that the replicating portfolio must have the same value as the call option. Now all we have to do to estimate the value of the call option is to figure out what the value of the replicating portfolio is. To do this, we simply determine how much of our own money we would actually have to invest to construct the replicating portfolio. In our example, we could use the $19.05 loan to help purchase the stock, so we would not have to come up with all the money for the stock on our own. In fact, since a share of ABC Corporation stock is currently worth $50, one-half share of this stock would cost only $25. Therefore, we would have to come up with only $5.95 ($25.00 − $19.05 = $5.95) over and above the amount received from the loan to buy the stock. Since $5.95 is the amount of money that we would actually have to invest to obtain the replicating portfolio, it is the value of this portfolio and therefore the value of the call option.

The equation for calculating the value of the replicating portfolio, and therefore the value of the call option, can be expressed as follows:

$$\begin{aligned}\text{Value of the call option today} = C &= (\$50 \times x) + (1 \times y)\\ &= (\$50 \times 0.5) + (1 \times -\$19.05)\\ &= \$5.95\end{aligned}$$

Notice, too, that the exercise price, the current price of the underlying stock, the possible future prices of the underlying stock, and the risk-free rate are all that entered into our calculations. We did not even mention the probabilities that the stock price would go up or down at any point. That is because the volatility of the underlying stock value is accounted for by how far apart the two possible future values are. Similarly, the time to expiration is not directly considered. However, the time to expiration affects how high and how low the stock price can be when the option expires.[3]

This model may seem surprisingly simple. However, that is largely because we chose to illustrate a simple example. The model can be extended in several ways. For example, we can incorporate possible prices for the underlying asset between now and the expiration date of the option. The underlying asset price might take one of two values one month (or day or hour) from now, and then for each of those values there might be two possible values in the following month (day or hour), and so on. Solving a model such as this requires us to work backwards from the expiration date to find the value of the option at each intermediate date and price until we finally arrive at the value of the option today. Most modern option pricing models are extensions of this type of model.

Learning by Doing Application 20.1 illustrates another example of a call option valuation.

Put-Call Parity

put-call parity the relation between the value of a call option on an asset and the value of a put option on the same asset that has the same exercise price

To this point, our discussion has focused on call options. As mentioned earlier, this is possible because there is a simple relation that enables us to calculate the value of a put option once we know the value of a call option with the same exercise price. This relation is called **put-call parity**. The formula for put-call parity is:

$$P = C + Xe^{-rt} - V \qquad (20.1)$$

LEARNING BY DOING

WileyPLUS

Need more help? Visit your WileyPLUS course.

APPLICATION 20.1 | Valuing a Call Option

Problem You are considering purchasing a call option on the stock of Grote Agricultural Company. Grote stock currently trades for \$35 per share, and you predict that its price will be either \$25 or \$50 in one year. The call option would enable you to buy a share of Grote stock in one year for \$30. What is this option worth if the risk-free rate is 4 percent?

Approach The value of the option can be determined by computing the cost of constructing a portfolio that replicates the payoffs from that option.

Solution With an exercise price of \$30, the option will be worth \$20 if the stock price rises to \$50 (\$50 − \$30 = \$20) and will be worth \$0 if the stock price declines to \$25. Therefore, the replicating portfolio for this option can be determined from the following two equations:

$$\$20 = (\$50 \times x) + (1.04 \times y)$$
$$\$0 = (\$25 \times x) + (1.04 \times y)$$

Solving for x and y, we find that $x = 0.80$ and $y = -\$19.23$. Therefore, the replicating portfolio consists of 0.8 share of Grote stock and a \$19.23 loan. Since a 0.8 share would cost \$28 (0.8 × \$35 = \$28), and \$19.23 of this amount would be covered by the loan, this replicating portfolio would cost \$8.77 (\$28.00 − \$19.23 = \$8.77) to construct. Therefore, the call option is worth \$8.77.

[3] There are other ways to solve the binomial pricing problem than by actually finding an equivalent portfolio. While they differ in their calculation, the underlying concepts are identical. See any advanced investments textbook for details.

where P is the value of the put option, C is the value of the call option, X is the exercise price, r is the risk-free rate, t is the amount of time before the option expires, and V is the current value of the underlying asset. The term e^{-rt} is the exponential function that you can calculate using the "e^x" key on your calculator; it is simply a discount factor that assumes continuous compounding. It is important to make sure that the r and t are both stated in the same units of time (for example, months or years).

To see how this formula works, let's consider the call option on the stock of ABC Corporation that we just valued. We know that C = \$5.95, X = \$55, $r = 0.05$, $t = 1$, and V = \$50. Substituting these values into the put-call parity formula and solving for P, we get

$$\begin{aligned} P &= \$5.95 + \$55e^{-(0.05)(1)} - \$50 \\ &= \$5.95 + \$52.32 - \$50 \\ &= \$8.27 \end{aligned}$$

Notice that the variables used in this calculation are the same variables that determine the value of a call option. This means that the same factors that affect the value of a call option also affect the value of a put option. Notice, too, that the value of the put option (\$8.27) is greater than the value of the call option (\$5.95) in this example. This will not always be true. However, it is true in our example because the current stock price of \$50 is below the \$55 exercise price.

Learning by Doing Application 20.2 illustrates another example of a put option valuation.

Valuing Options Associated with the Financial Securities That Firms Issue

In the chapter preview we stated that financial options are often included in the financial securities that firms issue and that they make the valuation of those securities more complicated. A detailed discussion of the valuation of financial securities with options is beyond the scope of this chapter. However, because such options are quite common, it is important that you have some intuition concerning how they affect security values. The key principle that we use in valuing securities with options is known as the principle of *value additivity*. It states that if two independent assets are bundled together, the total value of both assets equals the sum of their individual values. In other words, the value of a financial security with an option equals the value of the same security without the option, plus the value of the option. To illustrate this idea, let's consider a few of the many options that are commonly observed in financial securities.

APPLICATION 20.2 | Valuing a Put Option

LEARNING BY DOING

Problem In Learning by Doing Application 20.1, we found that a call option on a share of Grote Agricultural Company stock is worth \$8.77 when the stock price is \$35, the exercise price is \$30, the risk-free rate is 4 percent, and the time to maturity is one year. What is the value of a put option on a share of this stock if the exercise price and all other variables have the same values?

Approach Use the put-call parity relation, Equation 20.1, to calculate the value of a put option.

Solution The value of the put option is as follows:

$$\begin{aligned} P &= C + Xe^{-rt} - V \\ &= \$8.77 + \$30e^{-(0.04)(1)} - \$35 \\ &= \$8.77 + \$28.82 - \$35 \\ &= \$2.59 \end{aligned}$$

Note that the value of the put option is less than the value of the call option in this example. This is because the current price of the stock is above the exercise price.

Financial options are often added to the securities that firms issue because doing so is beneficial to the firm. For example, when the managers of a young, rapidly growing company issue debt, they must be concerned about the amount of cash required to make interest and principal payments. If these payments are too great, the company's operations might not generate enough cash to both service the debt and fund the company's growth. One way to reduce the interest payments on debt is to make it convertible into common stock.

To see how this works, consider the convertible bonds that we described in Chapter 8. Suppose that a 20-year vanilla bond issued by a particular company must have coupon payments of \$80 per year, or 8 percent, in order to sell for its par value of \$1,000. Further suppose that management of that company must raise \$50 million today and only expects to have enough cash to pay interest of \$3 million per year, or 6 percent, on the \$50 million.

One way to reduce the amount of interest that the firm must pay on the bonds is to make them convertible into the company's stock. For example, if the company's stock is currently trading at \$40 per share, the bond might be structured so that buyers have the option (right, but not obligation) to convert each bond into 20 shares of stock. With this arrangement, each bond includes a call (conversion) option with an exercise price of \$50 per share (\$1,000/20 shares = \$50 per share). The exercise price of the conversion option is above the current stock price. However, since there is a chance that the stock price will go above \$50 before the debt matures in 20 years, this call option has a value that can be calculated using the binomial option pricing model.

When a conversion option is included with a bond, investors will be willing to accept a lower interest rate. How much lower depends on the value of the option. If the company wants to sell the convertible bonds at their par value of \$1,000, the present value of the interest and principal payments *plus* the value of the conversion option must equal \$1,000. In the example above, if the bonds are going to pay 6 percent, the conversion option must be worth \$197.30. This is because the valuation methods discussed in Chapter 8 tell us that a 20-year bond paying a coupon of 6 percent is only worth \$802.70 if the market requires a coupon rate of 8 percent (you might check this number to confirm that you understand the bond valuation concepts from Chapter 8). If a conversion option with an exercise price of \$50 is worth more or less than \$197.30, then management will have to adjust the exercise price upward or downward until the total value of the 6 percent bond plus the conversion option equals \$1,000.

Convertible preferred stock provides another common example of a financial security that has an option associated with it. This type of preferred stock, which is typically sold to venture capitalists, for example, is convertible into the common stock of the company at a prespecified exercise price. Recall from Chapter 9 that regular preferred stock with no maturity can be valued using the zero-growth dividend model, Equation 9.2:

$$P_0 = \frac{D}{k_{ps}}$$

For example, if the preferred stock pays an annual dividend, D, of \$10 and the required rate of return, k_{ps}, is 10 percent, then the value of the preferred stock is \$100 (\$10/0.10 = \$100). If this preferred stock is made convertible into the company's common stock, its value will be greater than \$100 by an amount that equals the value of the conversion option. The company will get a higher price for convertible preferred stock because it is selling investors both regular preferred stock plus a conversion option.

Convertible bonds and preferred shares are not the only types of securities that firms issue with options attached to them. Another common transaction where managers sell financial securities with options is when they bundle options to purchase a company's common stock with common shares that are being sold in an initial public offering (IPO). When this happens, for each 100 shares that an investor purchases, he or she also receives options (which are called *warrants* in these instances) to purchase additional shares, on or before a specified future date, for a price that is higher than the IPO price. For example, if the shares are expected to sell for \$10 each in the IPO, the investor might have the option to purchase a certain number of shares at any time in the next five years for \$15 per share. Why would the managers of a firm bundle options with stock in an IPO? One reason is to reduce the number of common shares that must be sold at the IPO price in order to raise the amount of money that the firm needs. As was the case with convertible bonds and preferred stock, since the options have value, investors will pay a higher price for the package of stock plus options than they will for the stock alone.

Before You Go On

1. What are the limits on the value of a call option prior to its expiration date?
2. What variables affect the value of a call option?
3. Why are the variables that affect the value of a put option the same as those that affect the value of a call option?

20.3 Real Options

LEARNING OBJECTIVE

3. Name some of the real options that occur in business and explain why traditional NPV analysis does not accurately incorporate their values.

Many investments in business involve **real options**—options on real assets. Unfortunately, as we mentioned in the chapter preview, NPV analysis does not adequately reflect the value of these options. While it is not always possible to directly estimate the value of the real options associated with a project, it is important to recognize that they exist when we perform a project analysis. If we do not even consider them, we are ignoring potentially important sources of value. In this section, we provide an overview of the types of real options commonly associated with real investments. As you read this section you should note that the first three types of real options—options to defer investments, make follow-on investments, and change operations—are call options while the fourth type of real option—the option to abandon a project—is a put option.

real option an option for which the underlying asset is a real asset

Options to Defer Investment

In the chapter opener we used the example of Uranium Resources Inc. to illustrate a kind of real option that is commonly available to business managers. This is the option to defer making an investment decision. Recall that Uranium Resources obtained an option that gave the company the right to purchase mining claims in the Columbus Salt Marsh area of Nevada. This option gave the managers at Uranium Resources an opportunity to better assess the economic viability of the mining claims before committing the large amount of money that would be required to purchase them. Uranium Resources' managers must have thought that the price of the option was worth paying in order to be able to make more informed investment decisions. With this option, we can think of the underlying asset as being the stream of cash flows associated with owning the mining claims and the exercise price as being the cost of purchasing those claims. While it is too soon, at the time this discussion is being written, to tell how things will ultimately work out for Uranium Resources, you can be sure that its managers will be better informed when they do make the final investment decision regarding the option that they acquired.

Real estate developers often purchase deferral options on properties that they might want to develop in the near future. For example, a developer might pay a landowner $100,000 for a one-year option to purchase a property at a particular price. By accepting the payment, the landowner agrees not to sell the property to anyone else for a year. Like in the Uranium Resources example, such an option provides the developer with more time to make a final decision on whether it makes economic sense to purchase the land and proceed with a project.

With these options, the land is the underlying asset and the cost of purchasing it is the exercise price.

Another example of an option to defer investment is found in the oil industry. Many oil companies own drilling rights on properties that are expected to contain oil deposits but have not yet been developed. In these situations, the oil companies have the option to wait and see what happens to oil prices before deciding whether to invest in developing the deposits. The underlying asset in this case is the stream of cash flows that the developed oil field is expected to produce, whereas the exercise price is the amount of money that the company would have to spend to develop it (drill the well and build any necessary infrastructure). Just as the value of a share of stock might go up or down, the value of the cash flows produced by the oil field might increase or decrease with the price of oil.

Weblink

You can find a list of Web sites with information about real options at http://www.real-options.com/resources_links.htm.

The value of an option to defer investment is not reflected in an NPV analysis. Recall that the NPV rule tells us to accept a project with a positive NPV and to reject one with a negative NPV. NPV analysis does not allow for the possibility of deferring an investment decision (or deferring completion of a project once it is underway). It assumes that we invest either now or never. However, if we have the option of deferring an investment decision, it may make sense to do so. After all, a project that has a negative NPV today might have a positive NPV at some point in the future. The price of the product may increase, production costs may decline, or the cost of capital may go down, making the project attractive. We need not assume that an investment that is unattractive today will never be attractive.

Options to Make Follow-On Investments

Another very important type of real option is an *option to make follow-on investments*. Some projects open the door to future business opportunities that would not otherwise be available. For example, until the late 1990s, Dell, Inc., focused on selling computers to businesses. Although the company sold computers to individuals for home use, it did not focus on that market segment. In the late 1990s, Dell decided to target the home personal computer market and introduced a low-price, bare-bones computer. At first glance, this did not look like a very good move, because the low-end home computer business has small profit margins. However, the move created options for a wide range of follow-on investments. By moving into the home computer market, Dell established relationships with many individual consumers. These relationships, in turn, made it feasible for Dell to later move into new areas, such as the sale of cameras, TVs, MP3 players, and other consumer electronics goods. In other words, investing in the home computer business provided Dell with options to enter other consumer product markets.

Another example of an option to make follow-on investments concerns an investment in a new technology that can be extended to other products. For instance, in the early 1990s, Boeing Company invested in a computer-aided aircraft design system as part of the development of its Boeing 777 aircraft. This system allowed the company to complete much more of the design work for a new aircraft on a computer before building a prototype, thereby lowering the cost of designing and building a new aircraft. While the cost of the new system and the associated facilities—over $1 billion—was relatively high compared with the cost of the 777 project, the investment provided benefits that extended well beyond that project. For example, the technologies could be used in the design of other new aircraft, both civilian and military. By reducing the cost of developing new aircraft, the design system had the potential to make projects economically attractive that would not have been attractive otherwise.

Weblink

Real options are considered by NASA' when space systems and other investments are evaluated. See the following document on the NASA Web site for a discussion of this and references to additional readings in this area: https://trs.jpl.nasa.gov/bitstream/handle/2014/18213/99-1681.pdf?sequence=1.

Options to make follow-on investments are inherently difficult to value because, at the time we are evaluating the original project, it may not be obvious what the follow-on projects will be. Even if we know what the projects will be, we are unlikely to have enough information to estimate what they are worth. Of course, this makes it impossible to directly estimate the value of any option associated with them. Nevertheless, it is important for managers to consider options to make follow-on investments when evaluating projects. Doing so is a central part of the process of evaluating projects in the context of the overall strategy of the firm.

Projects that lead to investment opportunities that are consistent with a company's overall strategy are more valuable than otherwise similar projects that do not.

Options to Change Operations

In addition to options to defer investment and options to make follow-on investments, which are real options related to the investment decisions themselves, there are also real options that are related to the flexibility managers have once an investment decision has been made. These options, which include the options to change operations and to abandon a project, affect the NPV of a project and must be taken into account at the time the investment decision is made.

In an NPV analysis, we discount the expected cash flows from a project. We often consider several alternative scenarios and use our estimates of the probabilities associated with those scenarios to compute the expected cash flows. While this sort of analysis does consider alternative scenarios, it does not fully account for the fact that once a project has begun, the managers at a company have *options to change operations* as business conditions change. This means that there is value associated with being able to change operations that is not fully reflected in a scenario analysis.

The changes that managers might make can involve something as simple as reducing output if prices decline or increasing output if prices increase. Businesses do this all the time in response to changing demand for their goods and services. At the extreme, managers might temporarily suspend operations entirely if business conditions are weak. This is quite common in the auto industry, where we often hear of plants being temporarily shut down during periods of slow auto sales. Other changes in operations can involve fundamentally altering the way in which a product is produced, as when a new production technology becomes available, making the old technology uncompetitive.

Having the flexibility to react to changing business conditions can be very valuable. Since we do not know precisely how conditions are likely to change it can be difficult to estimate just how valuable this flexibility is. Nevertheless, we can see that managers do recognize the importance of flexibility by observing how they structure projects. For example, most modern office buildings do not have permanent internal walls. Not having permanent walls provides flexibility in configuring the offices and work spaces in the building. If more people must be put into a building than originally anticipated, the work spaces can be compressed to fit them. If the company finds that it does not need all of the space, having a flexible interior makes it easier to change things so that the excess space can be leased. Similarly, when a company plans to build a new manufacturing facility, it often acquires more land than is immediately needed and designs the facility to accommodate additional production capacity if demand for its products is greater than expected.

Building flexibility into a project costs money, but this can be money well spent if things change unexpectedly. The flexibility to expand, scale back, temporarily shut down, or change the methods or technology employed in a project are all real options that managers should consider when evaluating projects. Projects with more flexibility in these dimensions are inherently more valuable.

Options to Abandon Projects

A project can also be terminated if things do not go as well as anticipated.[4] In other words, management often has an *option to abandon a project*. The ability to choose to terminate a project is a bit like a put option. By shutting down the project, management is saving money that would otherwise be lost if the project kept going. The amount saved represents the gain from exercising this option.

As with flexibility, we can see that managers recognize the importance of having an option to abandon a project by observing the way they design projects. Consider, for

[4]An exception exists where a contractual agreement prevents the project from being terminated without payment of a penalty that is equivalent to the remaining value of the project.

DECISION MAKING

EXAMPLE 20.2 | The Value of Real Options

Situation You work for a company that manufactures cardboard packaging for consumer product companies under long-term contracts. For example, your company manufactures the boxes for several popular cereal and aspirin products. You have just won a large five-year contract to produce packaging materials for a company that sells furniture on the Internet. Since this contract will require you to produce much larger boxes than you currently can produce, you must purchase some new equipment. You have narrowed your choices to two alternatives. The first is a capital-intensive process that will cost more up front, but will be less expensive to operate. This process requires very specialized equipment that can be used only for the type of packaging that your furniture client needs. The second alternative is a labor-intensive process that will require a smaller up-front investment, but will have higher unit costs. This process involves equipment that can be used to produce a wide range of other packages. If the expected life of both alternatives is 10 years and you estimate the NPV to be the same for both, which should you choose?

Decision You should choose the labor-intensive alternative. Your contract is only for five years, and there is a chance that it will not be renewed before the equipment's useful life is over. If the contract is not renewed, it will be easier to convert the labor-intensive equipment to another use. In other words, the labor-intensive alternative gives you the added value of having the option to abandon producing packaging for furniture.

example, that most industrial buildings are built like big boxes that can be easily reconfigured as manufacturing spaces, warehouses, or even retail outlets, depending on which use is most valuable. Suppose a company is building a facility to use as a warehouse. If the building is only able to accommodate a warehouse, it might end up sitting empty for long periods of time—for example, if the area has excess warehouse space at some point in the future. Designing the building so that it can be reconfigured relatively inexpensively for some other use increases the likelihood that the building will remain fully utilized in the future.

Decision Making Example 20.2 presents an example of how real options affect investment decisions.

Concluding Comments on NPV Analysis and Real Options

We have stated that NPV analysis does not account for real options very well. This is true because the riskiness of a project that has real options associated with it varies with time, and the appropriate discount rate varies with the risk. For example, in order to use NPV analysis to value an option to expand operations, we would not only have to estimate the expected value of all the cash flows associated with the expansion but would also have to estimate the probability that we would actually undertake the expansion under alternative future scenarios and determine the appropriate rate(s) at which to discount the incremental cash flows from the expansion back to the present. Furthermore, the discount rate for the original project cash flows could change with the expansion.

In some cases, we can incorporate the value of a real option into an investment analysis by valuing the option separately and then adding this value to the NPV estimate. When we do this, we value the real option using valuation methods similar to those used to value financial options, as illustrated in Section 20.2.

Before You Go On

1. What is a real option?
2. What are four different types of real options commonly found in business?
3. Is it always possible to estimate the value of a real option? Why or why not?

20.4 Agency Costs

LEARNING OBJECTIVE

4. Describe how the agency costs of debt and equity are related to options.

Agency conflicts arise between stockholders and lenders (creditors and bondholders) and between stockholders and managers because the interests of stockholders, lenders, and managers are not perfectly aligned. In fact, their interests can differ greatly. One reason is that the claims that they have against the cash flows produced by the firm have payoff functions that look like different types of options. We now discuss how these payoff functions lead to agency conflicts and their related costs.

Agency Costs of Debt

In Chapter 16, we discussed agency costs that arise in a company that uses debt financing. We noted that these costs occur because the incentives of people who lend to a company differ from those of the stockholders. If you were to carefully reread those discussions now, you might notice that the problems we discussed arise because the payoff functions for stockholders and lenders differ like those for the different options we have been discussing in this chapter.

To understand why this is the case, consider a company that has a single loan outstanding. This loan will mature next year, and all of the interest and principal will be due at that time. Now, consider what happens when the debt matures. On the one hand, if the value of the company is less than the amount owed on the debt, the stockholders will simply default, and the lenders will take control of the assets of the company. The stockholder claims will be worth $0 in this case. If, on the other hand, the value of the company is greater than the amount owed on the loan, the stockholders will pay off the loan and retain control of the assets. In this case, the stockholder claims will be worth the difference between the value of the firm and the amount owed to the lenders.

In other words, the payoff function for the stockholders looks exactly like that for the owner of a call option, where the exercise price is the amount owed on the loan and the underlying asset is the firm itself. If the value of the firm exceeds the exercise price, the stockholders will choose to exercise their option; and if it does not exceed the exercise price, they will let their option expire unexercised. Figure A of **Exhibit 20.4** illustrates the payoff function for the stockholders in this simple example.

The payoff function for the lenders in our example is illustrated in Figure B of Exhibit 20.4. If the value of the firm is less than the amount owed, the lenders receive only the assets of the firm; and if the value of the firm is greater than the amount owed, the lenders receive only the amount owed. One way to think about the payoff function for the lenders is that when they lend money to the firm, they are essentially selling a put option to the stockholders.[5] This option gives the stockholders the right to "put" the assets to the lenders with an exercise price that equals the amount they owe. When the value of the firm is less than the exercise price, the stockholders will exercise their option by defaulting. Of course, the stockholders are able to default and walk away only because our bankruptcy laws limit their liability to the amount that they have invested in the company.

The Dividend Payout Problem

Knowing that debt and equity claims are like options in which the underlying asset is the firm, we can use the intuition gained from the discussion of the determinants of option value to

[5]This payoff function is actually like that from the combination of selling a put option and buying a risk-free loan. Lenders receive the face value of the loan from the risk-free bond, but they might have to pay some or all of that value in losses on the put option. Since the risk-free loan payout is unaffected by changes in the value of the firm, it does not affect the discussion above.

Figure A. Stockholder payoff function

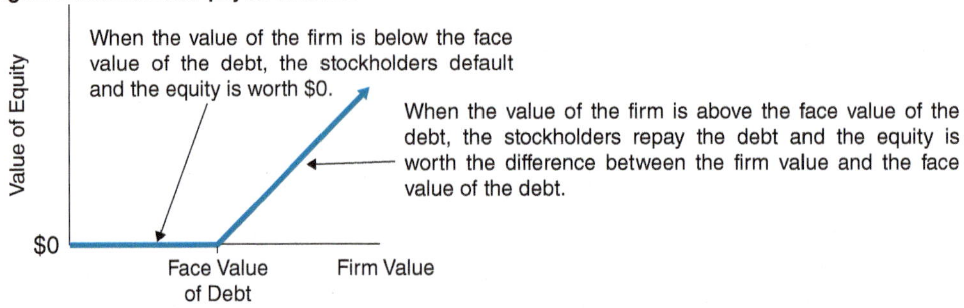

The equity in a leveraged corporation is like a call option on the underlying assets of the firm. The stockholders exercise their option by paying off the debt if the firm is worth more than the face value of the debt when the debt matures. If the value of the firm is lower than the face value of the debt, the stockholders can default (let their option expire) without incurring losses beyond their investment in the firm.

Figure B. Lender payoff function

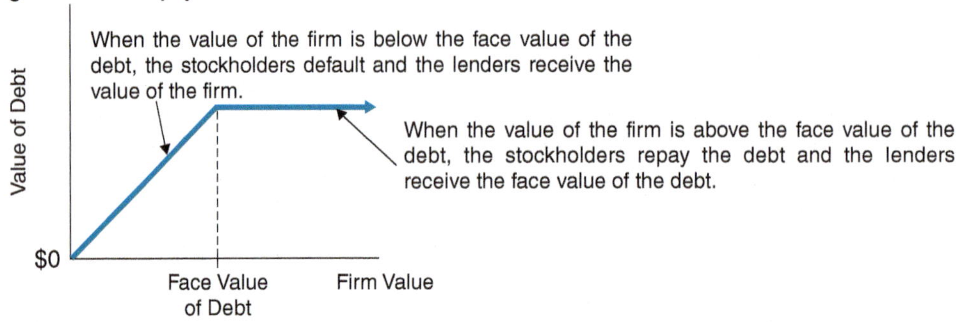

The lenders' payoff function is like that for the seller of a put option. They have effectively agreed to purchase the firm for an amount that equals the face value of the firm's debt, at the discretion of the stockholders.

EXHIBIT 20.4 Payoff Functions for Stockholders and Lenders

better understand the agency costs of debt. The incentives that stockholders of a leveraged firm have to pay themselves dividends arise because of their option to default. If a company faces some realistic risk of going bankrupt, the stockholders might decide that they are better off taking money out of the firm by paying themselves dividends. This situation can arise because the stockholders know that the bankruptcy laws limit their possible losses. If the firm goes bankrupt and the lenders end up receiving, for example, 50 percent rather than 80 percent of what they are owed, it will make no difference to the stockholders, who will get nothing from the liquidation of the company's assets in either case.

The Asset Substitution Problem

In Chapter 16, we saw that when bankruptcy is possible, stockholders have an incentive to invest in very risky projects, some of which might even have negative NPVs. Stockholders have this incentive because they receive all of the benefits if things turn out well, but do not bear all of the costs if things turn out poorly. Since equity claims are like call options on the assets of the firm, this *asset substitution problem* should not be surprising. We pointed out earlier in this chapter that the more volatile the value of the underlying asset, the more valuable a call option on that asset will be. Stockholders of leveraged firms know this and therefore have an incentive to invest in risky projects that increase the overall volatility of the value of their companies' assets.

Lenders, in contrast, do not want the firm to invest in high-risk projects. As you can see from their payoff function in Exhibit 20.4, the lenders bear costs as the value of the firm drops below the amount they are owed, but do not benefit at all as the value of the firm's assets increases above that amount. Lenders to companies that are worth more than they are owed can only expect to lose when a project increases the overall riskiness of a company's assets.

The Underinvestment Problem

Chapter 16 also explained that stockholders have incentives to turn down positive NPV projects when all of the benefits are likely to go to the lenders. You can see how this *underinvestment problem* arises from the differences in the payoff functions in Exhibit 20.4. Suppose that the company will owe $10 million when the loan matures, that the company is currently worth $5 million, and that the loan matures next week. This company is financially distressed because its assets are not even worth as much as its outstanding debt—so it is unlikely to have enough money to finance new investments. Now suppose that management identifies a positive NPV project that would require a $3 million investment and that has a positive NPV of $1 million that will be realized before the debt payment must be made. Management would have a hard time convincing the stockholders to invest an additional $3 million in the firm, because even if the investment turns out to be worth $4 million, all of the money will go to the lenders. The stockholders have a strong incentive to turn down this positive NPV project.

Agency Costs of Equity

Many of our discussions assume that managers act in the best interests of the stockholders. Since managers are hired to manage the firm on behalf of the stockholders, this might appear to be a reasonable assumption. However, as you already know, managers do not always act in the stockholders' best interest. This is because the payoff function for a manager can be quite different from that for stockholders. In fact, a manager's payoff function can look a lot like a lender's payoff function.

To see how this is possible, consider the connection between managers' personal wealth and the performance of the companies for which they work. The present value of a manager's future earnings is a large part of his or her overall wealth. If a company gets into financial distress and a manager is viewed as responsible, that manager could lose his or her job and find it difficult to obtain a similar job at another company. So as long as a company is able to avoid defaulting on its debt, a manager has a reasonable chance of retaining his or her job. Once the firm defaults, the chances of job loss increase dramatically. In addition, researchers have found that senior managers of financially distressed large public companies who lose their jobs find it difficult to obtain similar jobs afterward.[6] We might also expect that the worse the company's financial distress, the worse the manager's future employment prospects and the lower the present value of the compensation that he or she can expect to receive in the future. If this is so, when the value of a firm is less than the amount it owes, the payoff function for a manager will look something like that for the lender in Figure B of Exhibit 20.4—it will slope downward as the value of the firm decreases.

On the positive side, we would expect the present value of a manager's future earnings to increase with the value of the firm when this value is above the amount that the company owes to its lenders. Managers will receive larger bonuses and larger pay raises, and any stock or options that they receive will be more valuable. However, these increases will not be nearly as large as those for stockholders. The stockholders are not likely to give the managers a large proportion of any increase in firm value. The net result is that the payoff function for managers can look something like the one in **Exhibit 20.5**.

The fact that the payoff function for a manager resembles that for a lender means that managers, like lenders, have incentives to invest in less risky assets and to distribute less value through dividends and stock repurchases than the stockholders would like them to. Because the likelihood of financial distress increases with leverage, managers also have incentives to use less debt than stockholders would like them to. These tendencies are reinforced by the fact that managers are individuals who do not hold diversified portfolios, since most of their wealth is tied to the performance of their firms. Managers tend to make conservative investment, payout, and financing decisions because the cost to them of failure can be very large.

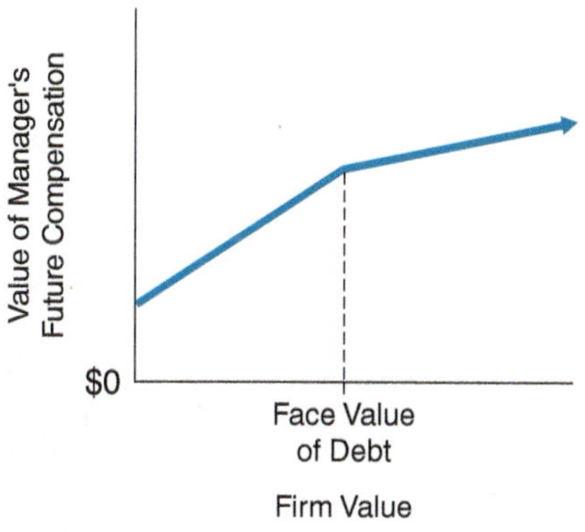

EXHIBIT 20.5 Representative Payoff Function for a Manager

The payoff function for a manager with a typical compensation arrangement is more similar in shape to the payoff function for a lender than for a stockholder. While a stockholder's payoff function is flat to the left of the face value of the debt, the value of the manager's compensation is downward sloping, much like the payoff for a lender. When the value of the firm is greater than the face value of the debt, the value of the manager's compensation does not increase as much as the value of the firm's shares (the line in the payoff function is not as steep). Because managers' payoff functions differ from those for stockholders, managers have incentives to take actions that are not in the best interests of stockholders.

[6] S. C. Gilson, "Management Turnover and Financial Distress," *Journal of Financial Economics* 25 (1989), 241–262.

Boards of directors understand how the incentives of managers differ from those of stockholders. Consequently, boards put a great deal of effort into designing compensation plans that make the payoff functions for managers look as much as possible like those of stockholders. Ultimately, this is a key to minimizing agency conflicts between stockholders and the managers who represent them.

Before You Go On

1. What do the payoff functions for stockholders and lenders look like?
2. What does the payoff function for a typical manager look like?

20.5 Options and Risk Management

LEARNING OBJECTIVE

5. Explain how options can be used to manage a firm's exposure to risk.

We have discussed options that are bundled with financial securities, how options found in real investments can have value, and how the option-like payoff functions of stockholders, lenders, and managers contribute to agency conflicts. Another place in which options are frequently encountered in corporate finance is in the management of risk. *Risk management* involves *hedging,* or reducing the financial risks faced by a firm. Options, along with other derivative securities, such as forwards, futures, and swaps, are used to reduce risks associated with commodity prices, interest rates, foreign exchange rates, and equity prices.

To see how risks can be managed using options, consider an oil company that is producing and selling oil to refiners. Suppose that the price of West Texas Intermediate (WTI) crude oil has recently risen above $90 per barrel and the company wants to make sure that, even if prices drop below $85 per barrel, it will receive at least $85 per barrel for each barrel of WTI that it sells during the next three months. If the company plans to sell 100,000 barrels of oil in the next three months, the financial managers can hedge the price risk by purchasing put options on 100,000 barrels of oil with an exercise price of $85 per barrel plus the cost of the options. The maturity dates on the options must be selected to match the timing of the company's oil output over the next three months. In addition, the actual exercise prices on the options must be slightly greater than $85 to account for the premiums that the company pays to purchase the options. This will ensure that the company actually receives $85 per barrel after paying for the options.

One interesting benefit of using options in this way is that they provide downside protection but do not limit the upside to the company if oil prices continue to increase. Put options give the company the right to sell its oil for the exercise price if WTI prices fall, but because there is no obligation to sell, the company can still benefit if oil prices increase. As discussed earlier, this is just like buying insurance. In fact, many insurance contracts are really little more than specialized put options.

In addition to using options and other derivative securities to manage commodity price risks, as in the oil company example, companies can use these securities to manage risks associated with changing interest rates. Large swings in interest rates can cause a great deal of volatility in the net income of a highly financially leveraged company whose managers rely on floating-rate debt. As interest rates go up and down, the company's interest expense also goes up and down. Furthermore, under certain circumstances, this volatility can actually increase the company's taxes.

Options can also be used to manage risks associated with foreign exchange rates. For example, as we discuss in Chapter 21, the revenues that a U.S. company reports can be affected by changes in exchange rates if the company manufactures products in the United States and has overseas sales. If the dollar strengthens against foreign currencies, for example, the company will have to increase the overseas prices of its products in order to maintain the same dollar prices per unit. This, in turn, can prompt consumers in overseas markets to purchase fewer of the company's products. By using options and other derivative securities to protect against exchange rate movements, managers can limit declines in revenues that occur because of such movements.

Finally, options can be used to manage risks associated with equity prices. This is especially important to companies that have traditional defined-benefit pension plans, which provide retirees with guaranteed retirement payments. Companies are required to put money aside to cover the costs of these payments, and this money is generally invested in stocks. When the stock market declines significantly, these companies must replace any lost value with new contributions, which must come from earnings. As you might expect, managers are very interested in managing the risk that they will have to make these contributions.

Before You Go On

1. What is hedging?
2. What types of risks can options be used to manage?

Summary of Learning Objectives

1 Define a call option and a put option, and describe the payoff function for each of these options.

An option is the right, but not the obligation, to buy or sell an asset for a given price on or before a specific date. The price is called the exercise or strike price, and the date is called the exercise date or expiration date of the option. The right to buy the asset is known as a call option. The payoff from a call option equals $0 if the value of the underlying asset is less than or equal to the exercise price at expiration. If the value of the underlying asset is greater than the exercise price at expiration, then the payoff from a call option is equal to the value of the underlying asset value minus the exercise price. The right to sell the asset is called a put option. The payoff from a put option is $0 if the value of the underlying asset is greater than or equal to the exercise price at expiration. If the value of the underlying asset is less than the exercise price, then the payoff from a put option equals the exercise price minus the value of the underlying asset.

2 List and describe the variables that affect the value of an option. Calculate the value of a call option and of a put option.

The value of an option is affected by five variables: the current price of the underlying asset, the exercise price of the option, the volatility of the value of the underlying asset, the time left until the expiration of the option, and the risk-free rate.

Section 20.2 describes how to calculate the values of call and put options, both at expiration and at some point before the expiration date.

3 Name some of the real options that occur in business and explain why traditional NPV analysis does not accurately incorporate their values.

Real options that are associated with investments include options to defer the investments, make follow-on investments, change operations, and abandon projects. Traditional NPV analysis is designed to make a decision to accept or reject a project at a particular point in time. It is not designed to incorporate potential value associated with deferring the investment decision. Incorporating the value of the other real options into an NPV framework is technically possible but would be very difficult to do because the rate used to discount the cash flows would change over time with their riskiness. In addition, the information necessary to value real options using the NPV approach is not always available.

4 Describe how the agency costs of debt and equity are related to options.

The chapter discusses two classes of agency conflicts. The first is between stockholders (owners) and lenders. When there is a risk of bankruptcy, stockholders may have incentives to increase the volatility of the firm's assets, turn down positive NPV projects, or pay out assets in the form of dividends. Stockholders have these incentives because their payoff functions look like those for the owner of a call option.

The other class of agency conflicts is between managers and stockholders. Managers tend to prefer less risk than stockholders. They have incentives to invest in less risky projects and use less debt financing than stockholders would like them to. Managers also prefer to distribute fewer assets in the form of dividends or through stock repurchases because their payoff functions are more like those of lenders than those of stockholders. These preferences are magnified by the fact that managers are risk-averse individuals whose portfolios are not well diversified.

5 Explain how options can be used to manage a firm's exposure to risk.

A company can adjust its exposure to risks associated with commodity prices, interest rates, foreign exchange rates, and equity prices by buying or selling options. For example, a company that is concerned about a decline in the prices it will receive for products that will be delivered in the future can purchase put options to partially or totally eliminate that risk.

Summary of Key Equations

Equation	Description	Formula
20.1	Put-call parity	$P = C + Xe^{-rt} - V$

Self-Study Problems

20.1 Of the two parties to an option contract, the buyer and the seller, who has a right and who has an obligation?

20.2 The stock of Augusta Light and Power is currently selling at \$12 per share. Over the next year the company is undertaking a new electricity production project. If the project is successful, the company's stock is expected to rise to \$24 per share. If the project fails, the stock is expected to fall to \$8 per share. The risk free rate is 6 percent. Calculate the value today of a one year call option on one share of Augusta Light and Power with an exercise price of \$20.

20.3 ADCAP International is a U.S.-based company that sells its products primarily in overseas markets. The company's stock is currently trading at \$50 per share. Depending on the outcome of U.S. trade negotiations with the countries to which ADCAP exports its products, the company's stock price is expected to be either \$65 or \$30 in six months. The risk free rate is 8 percent per year. What is the value of a put option on ADCAP stock that has an exercise price of \$40 per share?

20.4 Your company is considering opening a new factory in Europe to serve the growing demand for your product there. What real options might you want to consider in your capital budgeting analysis of the factory?

20.5 Your firm, which uses oil as an input to its production processes, hedges its exposure to changes in the price of oil by buying call options on oil at today's price. If the price of oil goes down by the time the contract expires, what effect will that have on your company?

Solutions to Self-Study Problems

20.1 The buyer (owner) of the option has the right to exercise the option but is not required to do so. The seller (or writer) of the option is obligated to take the other side of the transaction if the option owner decides to exercise it.

20.2 First determine the payoffs for the stock, a risk-free loan, and the call option under the two possible outcomes. In one year, the stock price is expected to be either \$8 or \$24. The loan will be worth \$1.06 regardless of whether the project is successful. If the project fails, the stock price will be less than the exercise price of the call option. The option will not be exercised and will be worth \$0. If the project is successful, the stock price will be higher than the exercise price of the call option. The option will be exercised and its value will be the difference between the stock price and the exercise price, \$4.

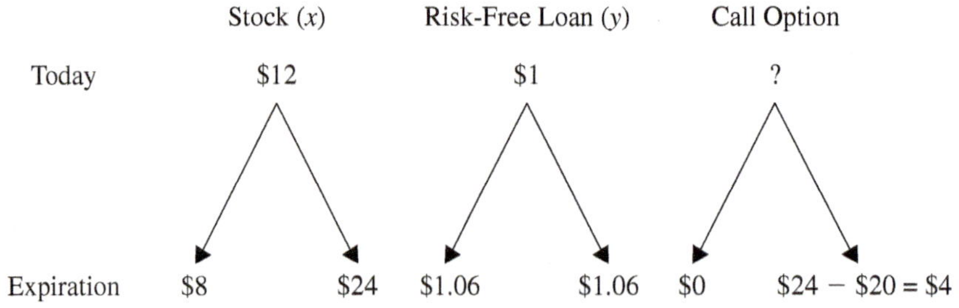

The stock and loan can be used to create a replicating portfolio, which has the same payoff as the call option:

$(\$8 \times x) + (1.06 \times y) = \$0$

$(\$24 \times x) + (1.06 \times y) = \$4$

Solving the two equations yields $x = 0.25$, $y = -1.887$.

The value of the call option is the same as the current value of this portfolio:

$(\$12 \times 0.25) + (\$1 \times -1.887) = \$1.11$

20.3 Here we solve directly for the value of the put option. First we determine the payoffs for the stock, a risk-free bond, and the put option under the two possible outcomes. To determine payoff of the bond six months from now, we must calculate the six-month, risk-free interest rate given the one-year, risk-free rate in the problem statement:

Six-month, risk-free rate = $(1 + 0.08)^{1/2} - 1 = 0.039$, or 3.9%

The payoffs are therefore:

	Stock (x)		Risk-Free Loan (y)		Put Option	
Today	$50		$1		?	
Expiration	$30	$65	$1.039	$1.039	$40 − $30 = $10	$0

Now we can use the stock and bond to create a replicating portfolio, which will give the same payoff as the put option:

$(\$30 \times x) + (1.039 \times y) = \$10$

$(\$65 \times x) + (1.039 \times y) = \$0$

Solving the two equations we determine $x = -0.286$, $y = 17.87$.

The value if the put option is the same as the current value of this portfolio:

$(\$50 \times -0.286) + (\$1 \times 17.87) = \$3.58$

Alternatively, you could solve this problem by calculating the value of a call option with an exercise price of $40 per share and then using the put-call parity relation. The value of the call option is $15.09 and value of the associated put option calculated using the put-call parity relation is $3.52. The difference ($3.58 vs. $3.52) is due to rounding and the compounding assumption for the discount rate.

20.4 Several significant real options might be associated with the factory. First, by having a factory in Europe, and the employees and management associated with it, your company might be better positioned to introduce products to the European markets. In addition, you will have options to change operations, to sell the factory, or to simply abandon the project.

20.5 The effect on your company of the decline in the price of oil will be to increase earnings. This is because the oil is an input to your production process, and a drop in prices will reduce your expenses. If the price of oil goes down, you would let the call option expire without exercising it. Of course, the benefit your company receives from the drop in oil prices would be reduced by the amount that you paid to purchase the option.

WileyPLUS

Questions and Problems, Solution Walkthrough Videos, Learning by Doing Tutorials, and additional study tools and resources are available in WileyPLUS.

Discussion Questions

20.1 Options can be combined to create more complicated payoff structures. Consider the combination of one put option and one call option with the same expiration date and the same strike price. Draw the payoff diagram and describe what the purchaser of such a combination thinks will happen before expiration.

20.2 A writer (seller) of a call option may or may not actually own the underlying asset. If he or she owns the asset, and therefore will have the asset available to deliver should the option be exercised, he or she is said to be writing a *covered call*. Otherwise, he or she is writing a *naked call* and will have to buy the underlying asset on the open market should the option be exercised. Draw the payoff diagram of a covered call (including the value of the owned underlying asset) and compare it with the payoff of other options.

20.3 An American option will never be worth less than a European option. Evaluate this statement.

20.4 Explain why, in the binomial pricing theory, the probabilities of an upward move versus a downward move are not important.

20.5 Like all other models, the binomial pricing model is a simplification of reality. In this model, how do we represent high volatility or low volatility of the value of the underlying asset?

20.6 What kinds of real options should be considered in the following situations?

a. Wingnuts R Us is considering two sites for a new factory. One is just large enough for the planned facility, while the other is three times larger.

b. Carousel Cruises is purchasing three new cruise ships to be built sequentially. The first ship will commence construction today and will take one year to build. The second will then be started. Carousel can cancel the order for a given cruise ship at any time before construction begins.

20.7 Future Enterprises is considering building a factory that will include an option to expand operations in three years. If things go well, the expansion will have an expected value of $10 million and will cost $2 million to undertake. Otherwise, the expansion will have an expected value of only $1 million and will not take place. What information would we need in order to analyze this capital budgeting problem using the traditional NPV approach that we would not need using option valuation techniques?

20.8 Corporations frequently include employee stock options as a part of the compensation for their managers and sometimes for all of their employees. These options allow the holder to buy the stock of the company for a prespecified price like any other option, but they are usually very long lived, with maturities of 10 years. The goal of stock option plans is to align the incentives of employees with those of stockholders. What are the implications of these compensation plans for current stockholders?

20.9 You own ABC Corp. bonds. Using option pricing theory, explain what agency concerns you would have if ABC were in danger of bankruptcy.

20.10 A bond covenant is a part of a bond contract that restricts the behavior of the firm, barring it from taking certain actions. Using the terminology of options, explain why a bond contract might include a covenant preventing the firm from making large dividend payments to its stockholders.

20.11 How can the insurance policy on a car be viewed as an option?

Questions and Problems

Excel *Excel templates and resources available in* **WileyPLUS**

Basic

20.1 **Option characteristics:** What is an option?

20.2 **Option characteristics:** Explain how the payoff functions differ for the owner (buyer) and the seller of a call option and of a put option.

20.3 **Option payoffs:** What is the payoff for a call option with a strike price of $50 if the stock price at expiration is $40? What if the stock price is $65?

20.4 **Option payoffs:** What is the payoff for a put option with a strike price of $50 if the stock price at expiration is $40? What if the stock price is $65?

20.5 **Option valuation:** What are the five variables that affect the value of an option, and how do changes in each of these variables affect the value of a call option?

20.6 **Option valuation:** Assuming nothing else changes, what happens to the value of an option as time passes and the expiration date gets closer?

20.7 **Option valuation:** What does the seller of a put option hope will happen?

20.8 **Option valuation:** What is the value of a call option or a put option if the stock price is zero? What if the stock price is extremely high (relative to the strike price)?

20.9 **Option valuation:** Like *owners* of stock, *owners* of options can lose no more than the amount they invested. They are far more likely to lose that full amount, but they cannot lose more. Do *sellers* of options have the same limitation on their losses?

20.10 **Option valuation:** What is the value at expiration of a call option with a strike price of $65 if the stock price is $1? $50? $65? $100? $1,000?

20.11 **Option valuation:** Suppose you have an option to buy a share of ABC Corp. stock for $100. The option expires tomorrow, and the current price of ABC Corp. is $95. How much is your option worth?

20.12 **Option valuation:** You hold an American option to sell one share of Zyther Co. stock. The option expires tomorrow. The strike price of the option is $50, and the current stock price is $49. What is the value of exercising the option today? If you wanted to sell the option instead, about how much would you expect to receive?

20.13 **Real options:** What is the difference between a financial option and a real option?

20.14 **Real options:** List and describe four different types of real options that are associated with investment projects.

20.15 **Agency costs:** How are options related to the agency costs of debt and equity?

Intermediate

20.16 Option valuation: Suppose that you own a call option and a put option on the same stock and that these options have the same exercise price. Explain how the relative values of these two options will change as the stock price increases or decreases.

20.17 Other options: A *callable bond* is a bond that can be bought back by the bond issuer before maturity for some prespecified price (normally a small amount above face value) at the discretion of the bond issuer. How would you go about finding the value of such a bond? Would the bond be worth more or less than an equivalent noncallable bond?

20.18 Other options: A *convertible bond* is a bond that can be exchanged for stock at the discretion of the bondholder. How would you go about finding the value of such a bond? Would the bond be worth more or less than an equivalent nonconvertible bond?

20.19 Option valuation: The seller of an option can never make any money from a change in the value of the underlying asset; he or she can only hope that the option will not be exercised and that and he or she will not lose any money. Given that this is the case, why do people sell options?

20.20 Option valuation: The stock of Socrates Motors is currently trading for $40 and will either rise to $50 or fall to $35 in one month. The risk-free rate for one month is 1.5 percent. What is the value of a one-month call option with a strike price of $40?

20.21 Option valuation: Assume that the price of Socrates Motors stock will either rise to $50 or fall to $35 in one month and that the risk-free rate for one month is 1.5 percent. How much is an option with a strike price of $40 worth if the current stock price is $45 instead of $40?

20.22 Option valuation: Assume that the stock of Socrates Motors is currently trading for $40 and will either rise to $50 or fall to $35 in one month. The risk-free rate for one month is 1.5 percent. What is the value of a one-month call option with a strike price of $25?

20.23 Option valuation: You are considering buying a three-month put option on Wing and a Prayer Construction stock. The company's stock currently trades for $10 per share and its price will either rise to $15 or fall to $7 in three months. The risk-free rate for three months is 2 percent. What is the appropriate price for a put option with a strike price of $9?

20.24 Option valuation: You hold a European put option on Tubes, Inc., stock, with a strike price of $100. Things haven't been going too well for Tubes. The current stock price is $2, and you think that it will either rise to $3 or fall to $1.50 at the expiration of your option. The appropriate risk-free rate is 5 percent. What is the value of the option? If this were an American option, would it be worth more?

20.25 Other options: A *golden parachute* is a part of a manager's compensation package that makes a large lump-sum payment in the event that the manager is fired or loses his or her job in a merger. Providing such payouts to managers seems ill advised to most people first hearing about it. Explain how a golden parachute can help reduce agency costs between stockholders and managers.

Advanced

20.26 Consider the following payoff diagram.

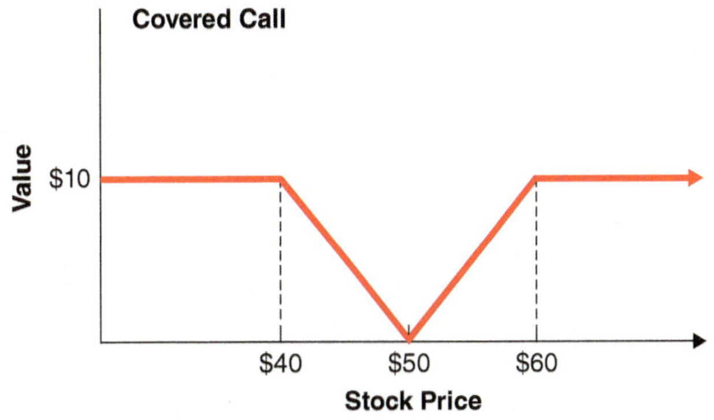

Find a combination of calls, puts, risk-free bonds, and stock that has this payoff. (You need not use all of these instruments, and there are many possible solutions.)

20.27 Consider the payoff structures of the following two portfolios:

a. Buying a one-month call option on one share of stock at a strike price of $50 and saving the present value of $50 (so that at expiration it will have grown to $50 with interest).

b. Buying a one-month put option on one share of stock at a strike price of $50 and buying one share of stock.

What conclusion can you draw about the relation between call prices and put prices from a comparison of these two portfolios?

20.28 One way to extend the binomial pricing model is by including multiple time periods. Suppose Splittime, Inc., is currently trading for $100 per share. In one month, the price will either increase by $10 (to $110) or decrease by $10 (to $90). The following month will be the same. The price will either increase by $10 or decrease by $10. Notice that in two months, the price could be $120, $100, or $80. The risk-free rate is 1 percent per month. Find the value today of an option to buy one share of Splittime in two months for a strike price of $105. (*Hint:* To do this, first find the possible values of the option at the end of the second month. Then use those values as the payoffs to find the value today.)

20.29 SpinTheWheel Co. has assets currently worth $10 million in the form of one-year, risk-free bonds that will return 10 percent. The company has debt with a face value of $5.5 million due in one year. (No interest payments will be made.) The stockholders decided to sell $8 million of the risk-free bonds and to invest the money in a very risky venture. This venture consists of giving Mr. William Kid the money now and, in one year, flipping a coin. If it comes up heads, Mr. Kid will pay SpinTheWheel $17.6 million. If it is tails, SpinTheWheel gets nothing. This investment has an NPV of zero.

a. What is the value of the debt and equity before the stockholders make this "investment"?

b. Using the binomial pricing model, with the payoff to the equity holders representing the option and the assets of the company representing the underlying asset, estimate the value of the equity after the stockholders make the investment.

c. What is the new value of the debt after the investment?

20.30 The price of a stock that does not pay dividends is currently $35, and the risk-free rate is 4 percent. A European call option on the stock, with a strike price of $35 and that expires in six months, sells for $3.04. A European put option on the same stock with the same strike price sells for $2.35. Is there an arbitrage opportunity here? If so, what is it?

20.31 Two call options have been written on the same underlying stock. Call #1 has a strike price of $42, and call #2 has a strike price of $52. Call #1 is selling for $5.00, and call #2 is selling for $6.00. What arbitrage opportunity do these prices present investors? Show the potential payoffs from this opportunity.

20.32 Husky Motors has two debt issues outstanding, both of which mature in five years. The senior debt issue, which has a face value of $10 million, must be paid in full before any of the principal for the junior debt issue is paid. The junior debt issue also has a face value of $10 million. Draw the payoff diagrams for Husky's equity and both debt issues as the value of the firm changes. Under what circumstances would you expect to see conflicts between the senior and junior debt holders?

20.33 The payoff function for the holder of straight debt looks like that for the seller of a put option. Convertible debt is straight debt plus a call option on a firm's stock. How does the addition of a call option to straight debt affect the concern that lenders have about the asset substitution problem, and why?

Sample Test Problems

20.1 You own a call option on Pepsico stock with a strike price of $60 per share that expires in 60 days. The current market price of Pepsico stock is $63.50 per share. What are the limits on the value of the call option you own?

20.2 Assume that the current market price of Montrose Industrials stock is $28 per share and will either rise to $38 per share or fall to $21 per share in one month. The risk-free rate for one month is 1 percent. What is the value of a one-month call option with a strike price of $24 per share?

20.3 The market value of Whole Foods stock is currently $53.73 per share, and the annual risk-free rate is 3 percent. A three-month call option on the stock with a strike price of $55 sells for $2.15. What is the value of a put option on Whole Foods stock that has the same strike price and expiration date if there are no arbitrage opportunities?

20.4 Why is it hard to account for real options in an NPV analysis?

20.5 Fuel costs are a significant fraction of total costs in the airline industry. How might airline managers use options to manage fuel costs? What is the downside of doing this?

CHAPTER 21

International Financial Management

TP/Alamy Stock Photo

LEARNING OBJECTIVES

1. Discuss how the basic principles of finance apply to international financial transactions.
2. Differentiate among the spot rate, the forward rate, and the cross rate in the foreign exchange markets, perform foreign exchange and cross rate calculations, and hedge an asset purchase where payment is made in a foreign currency.
3. Identify the major factors that distinguish international from domestic capital budgeting, explain how the capital budgeting process can be adjusted to account for these factors, and compute the NPV for a typical international capital project.
4. Discuss the importance of the Euromarkets to large U.S. multinational firms and calculate the cost of borrowing in the Eurobond market.
5. Explain how large U.S. money center banks make and price Eurocredit loans to their customers and compute the cost of a Eurocredit bank loan.

Founded in 1964, Nike Incorporated has grown to be one of the most recognizable consumer brands in the world. Many of the company's products are closely tied to sporting legends including Tiger Woods, who headlines their golf apparel line, and Michael Jordan and his famed "Air Jordan" basketball shoes. The company, based in Beaverton, Oregon, employs more than 70,000 people and is one of the largest retailers of athletic shoes, apparel, and sports equipment. In 2016 the company recorded over $32 billion in sales, and according to its annual report, $14.9 billion of those sales were to customers outside of the United States. To support its operations, Nike maintains branch offices in over three dozen countries.

Managing the financial aspects of such a large and complex multinational organization poses tremendous challenges. In 2016, the company's footwear was manufactured in 142 different factories in 15 different countries, while its apparel line was produced in 394 factories in 39 countries. Over 40 percent of its footwear is made by producers in Vietnam and much of the manufacturing and labor costs for this production is paid in the Vietnamese currency known as the dong. Most of these shoes, however, are sold outside Vietnam in a variety of different countries and currencies. As a result, the profitability of Nike can vary due to fluctuations in the exchange rates between the dong and various other currencies and also between the dong and the U.S. dollar, the currency in which Nike reports its financial results. If Nike executives don't take actions that limit the effects of changes in currency exchange rates on the company's profits, these changes can make financing the business more difficult and can adversely affect the company's stock price.

Capital budgeting is also more demanding in a multinational firm. Forecasting sales for numerous countries is much more difficult than forecasting only domestic demand for a company's products. An analyst must understand the key factors that will drive foreign product demand, including demographic, cultural, and regulatory factors as well as general economic conditions. In addition, production location decisions, supply chain considerations, and inventory management can be quite complex for firms with operations across the globe, making costs more difficult to estimate. Countries also have unique political and financial risk factors. For example, Singapore is widely recognized as a country with a very stable political system and a reliable rule of law. This makes it easier for businesses to make long-run investments in the country and to obtain capital from local banks. At the other end of the spectrum, countries with political conflict and economic discord such as Venezuela and Greece present extreme challenges for multinational firms.

Financing a multinational company like Nike is also complex. Multinational firms typically raise capital in different regions of the world. This requires that financial managers understand international finance and have a working knowledge of foreign financial markets. Financial managers must also maintain banking relationships in the various countries in which they operate to ensure that their firms have adequate working capital to support their operations. This chapter discusses these and other challenges associated with the financial management of multinational firms.

Chapter Preview

So far, we have focused on doing business in the United States, yet a large proportion of U.S. companies today engage in international business transactions. This chapter provides an introduction to international financial management.

The goal of financial management is the same abroad as it is at home—to maximize the value of the firm. Thus, the financial manager's job is to seek out international business opportunities in which the value of the expected cash flows exceeds their cost. If this is done, the firm's international activities will increase the overall value of the firm.

We start the chapter by providing some background information about the globalization of the world economy, the rise of multinational corporations, and the key factors that distinguish domestic from international business transactions. We emphasize that the basic principles of finance remain valid for international business transactions, even though some of the variables used in financial models change. We also introduce two risks that are not present in domestic business transactions: foreign exchange rate risk and country risk.

We follow this with discussions of markets for foreign currency exchange and how firms protect themselves from fluctuations in exchange rates. We then explain how multinational firms manage their overseas capital investments and compute the NPVs for these projects.

We next turn our attention to global money and capital markets. We pay particular attention to the Euromarket, where large multinational companies adjust their liquidity, borrow short term from banks in the Eurocredit market, and borrow long term in the international bond markets. Finally, we discuss how banks price and structure Eurocredits.

21.1 Introduction to International Financial Management

LEARNING OBJECTIVE

1. Discuss how the basic principles of finance apply to international financial transactions.

Businesses operate in a far different world today than they did only a generation or two ago. Because of the globalization of the world economy, management—including financial management—has changed in many respects. Yet, as you will see, the goals and principles of financial management remain essentially the same.

Globalization of the World Economy

Over the past 50 years, we have witnessed the globalization of business and financial markets. **Globalization** refers to the removal of barriers to free trade and the integration of national economies. Large corporations often generate more than half of their sales revenue in countries other than the one in which they are based. For example, almost two-thirds of McDonald's revenue is generated from countries other than the United States. As you read the *Wall Street Journal* or the business section of any major newspaper, you will see numerous reminders that we live in a globalized world economy.

globalization the removal of barriers to free trade and the integration of national economies

As *consumers,* Americans routinely purchase clothing and shoes made in China, oil from Saudi Arabia, automobiles from Germany, pasta and high-fashion shoes from Italy, wines from France, coffee from Brazil, TV sets from Japan, and textiles from India. Foreigners, in turn, purchase American-made aircraft, medical technology, software, movies, music CDs, wheat, beef, lumber, and numerous other products.

The *production* of goods and services has also become highly globalized. As large multinational companies have emerged, the economies of the world have become increasingly interdependent. Most multinational companies have integrated sales and production operations in a dozen or more countries. These firms seek to purchase components and locate production where costs are lower to generate higher margins. For example, personal computers manufactured by U.S.-based firms such as Dell and HP are sold worldwide and may be assembled in Malaysia or China, with monitors and hard drives made in Taiwan, computer chips made in the United States, keyboards made in Korea, and software packages produced in India.

Weblink

Read about current issues in international financial management in the International section of CNN News on: http://money.cnn.com/news/world.

Like product markets, the *financial system* has also become highly integrated. Much of the impetus for financial integration came from the governments of the major Asian and Western nations as they began deregulating their foreign exchange markets, money and capital markets, and banking systems.

The Rise of Multinational Corporations

A major factor driving globalization of the world economy is direct investment by multinational corporations. A **multinational corporation** is a business firm that operates in more than one country. These corporations engage in traditional lines of business such as manufacturing, mining, gas and oil, and agriculture, as well as consulting, accounting, law, telecommunications, and hospitality. They may purchase raw materials from one country, obtain financing from a capital market in another country, produce finished goods with labor and capital equipment from a third country, and sell finished goods in a number of other countries.

multinational corporation a business firm that operates in more than one country

Multinationals are owned by a mixture of domestic and foreign stockholders. In fact, the ownership of some firms is so widely dispersed that they are known as **transnational corporations**. Transnational corporations, regardless of the location of their headquarters, are managed from a global perspective rather than the perspective of a firm residing in a particular country. This fact has made them politically controversial because they are viewed as *stateless corporations* with no allegiance or social responsibility to any nation or region of the world. An example of a transnational firm is Royal Dutch Shell.

transnational corporation a multinational firm that has widely dispersed ownership and that is managed from a global perspective

Exhibit 21.1 lists the largest 15 multinational firms ranked by their total worldwide revenues in the year 2016. Royal Dutch Shell is the fifth largest of this group with $272.2 billion in revenue. As you can see, most of the firms on the list are household names. By country of origin, five of the largest 15 firms are headquartered in the United States, with the balance in China, Japan, Europe, and South Korea.

Weblink

Visit www.citigroup.com for an overview of a multinational banking institution.

Factors Affecting International Financial Management

As we suggested earlier, most of the basic finance principles discussed in this book apply to international financial management. However, six factors can cause international business transactions to differ from domestic transactions. We look at these factors next.

EXHIBIT 21.1 The World's Largest Multinational Firms Ranked by 2016 Revenue

Many of the world's 15 largest multinational firms are household names; five of the top 15 are based in the United States, with the balance located in China, Japan, Europe, and South Korea.

Rank	Company	Country	Revenue ($ billions)	Profits ($ billions)
1	Wal-Mart Stores	U.S.A.	$482.1	$14.7
2	State Grid	China	329.6	10.2
3	China National Petroleum	China	299.3	7.1
4	Sinopec	China	294.3	3.6
5	Royal Dutch Shell	Netherlands/U.K.	272.2	1.9
6	Exxon Mobil	U.S.A.	246.2	16.2
7	Volkswagen	Germany	236.6	(1.5)
8	Toyota Motor	Japan	236.6	19.3
9	Apple	U.S.A.	233.7	53.4
10	BP	U.K.	226.0	(6.5)
11	Berkshire Hathaway	U.S.A.	210.8	24.1
12	McKessen	U.S.A.	192.5	2.3
13	Samsung Electronics	South Korea	177.4	16.5
14	Glencore	Switzerland	170.5	(5.0)
15	Industrial and Commercial Bank of China	China	167.2	44.1

Source: http://beta.fortune.com/global500/.

Currency Differences

Most sovereign nations have their own currencies. Thus, businesses that engage in international transactions are likely to deal in two or more currencies. If this is the case, financial managers need to know how unexpected fluctuations in currency exchange rates can affect the firm's cash flows and, hence, the value of the firm. The uncertainty of future exchange rate movements is called **foreign exchange rate risk**, or just **exchange rate risk**, and we discuss it later in this chapter.

foreign exchange rate risk, or exchange rate risk the uncertainty associated with future currency exchange rate movements

Differences in Legal Systems and Tax Codes

Differences in legal systems and tax codes can also impact the way firms operate in foreign countries. Some countries, including the United States, Canada, and India, operate under legal systems derived from British common law, whereas Western European countries such as France, Germany, and Italy have legal systems derived from the French Napoleonic codes. Chinese law and other Asian legal systems evolved over centuries, with an emphasis on moral teaching and legally stipulated punishments.

What emerges from the world's legal systems and tax codes is a patchwork of different systems that can vary substantially from country to country and can affect how foreign business firms are treated within a particular country's borders. Legal systems can vary on simple matters, such as the requirements for opening a business, selecting a site location, and hiring employees, as well as more complex matters, such as the taxation of companies and dividends, the rights and legal liabilities of ownership, and the resolution of business conflicts. Thus, legal and tax differences can affect financial decisions concerning what assets to acquire, how to organize the firm, and what capital structure to use.

Language Differences

There are two important levels of communication in international business: business communication and social communication. Most multinational negotiations and legal contracts use English. English is the language of choice for international business throughout much of the world. Thus, reading and speaking fluent English are necessary skills for anyone planning to be a senior manager in a multinational corporation.

English is not, however, the world's social language—the language spoken when important social relationships that build trust are formed. Local languages are important for social relationships. For example, suppose that you are the CEO of an American food-processing firm and you are negotiating a deal to manufacture food products in Guangzhou, China (about 60 miles from Hong Kong). You are partnering with a Dutch firm that you know well. During the day, business and contract negotiations are conducted in English. Most members of the Chinese management team will probably speak English; indeed, some will have MBAs from U.S. or Hong Kong based business schools.

At the traditional Chinese business dinner banquets, however, the preferred social language will be Cantonese, a regional Chinese dialect, or French, which is a common second language spoken by educated Chinese in Southeast Asia. Needless to say, those who speak only English in this situation would be at a disadvantage. Historically, most U.S. business executives have spoken only English; however, this is changing rapidly as more U.S. executives receive overseas assignments and business students recognize the importance of a second language.

Cultural Differences

Culture is defined as the socially transmitted behavior patterns, beliefs, and attitudes of a group. Cultural views and attitudes are powerful forces that bind people together and define a particular society. The cultures of different countries, and even different regions within the same country, can vary considerably.

Cultural views also shape business practices and people's attitudes toward business. For example, in Germany business firms are generally expected to carry more equity and less debt in their capital structure than is typical for comparable firms in the United States. Other areas of business that differ by culture are willingness to assume risk, management style, tolerance for inflation, and attitude toward race, gender, and business failure.

Weblink

To learn about the business environment and other information about a country, you can explore the CIA Web site at https://www.cia.gov/library/publications/the-world-factbook/index.html.

Differences in Economic Systems

An economic system determines how a country mobilizes its resources to produce goods and services needed by society, as well as how the production is distributed. In the twentieth century, two basic economic systems competed for government endorsement: (1) centrally planned economies and (2) market economies.

In a centrally planned economy, resources are allocated, produced, and distributed under the direction of the central government, as in the former Soviet Union. These economies have no financial markets or banking systems to allocate capital flows. The central government sets interest rates and foreign exchange rates, and financial managers need not worry about capital budgeting decisions because capital resources are allocated centrally.

In market economies, resources are allocated, produced, and distributed by market forces rather than by government decree. Market economies have proven to be much more efficient in producing goods and services than traditional centrally planned economies. This fact is borne out by current trends in what once were the two largest communist countries in the world: the Soviet Union and China. Both China and the nations that formerly made up the Soviet Union are moving toward market-based economies.

Differences in Country Risk

Sovereign nations are usually free to place or remove constraints on businesses.[1] At the extreme, a country's government may even expropriate (take over) a business's assets within

[1]Sovereign nations are nations that have the right of self-rule, which includes the right to regulate commerce within their borders.

country risk the political uncertainty associated with a particular country

the country. These types of actions clearly can affect a firm's cash flows and, thus, the value of the firm. **Country risk** refers to political uncertainty associated with a particular country. We discuss country risk in more detail later in this chapter.

Goals of International Financial Management

Throughout this book, we have argued that maximization of firm value is the proper goal for management to pursue. Maximizing firm value will generate the greatest amount of wealth for a firm's stockholders, which is the accepted goal for firms in the United States, as well as in other countries that share a similar heritage, such as the United Kingdom, Australia, India, and Canada. However, it is not a widely embraced goal in other parts of the world. In Continental Europe, for example, countries such as France and Germany focus on maximizing corporate wealth. This means that stockholders are treated no differently from stakeholders, such as management, labor, suppliers, creditors, and even the government. The European manager's goal is to create as much wealth as possible while considering the overall welfare of both the stockholders and stakeholders. In Japan, companies form tightly knit, interlocking business groups called *keiretsu*, such as Mitsubishi, Mitsui, and Sumitomo, and the goal of the Japanese business manager is to increase the wealth and growth of the keiretsu. As a result, they might focus on maximizing market share rather than stockholder value.

In China, which is making a transition from a centrally planned economy to a market-based economy, there are sharp differences between state-owned companies and emerging private-sector firms. The large state-owned companies have an overall goal that can best be described as maintaining full employment in the economy. In contrast, private-sector firms fully embrace the standard of stockholder value maximization.

Basic Principles Remain the Same

In today's globalized environment, financial managers must be prepared to handle international transactions and all the complexities that those transactions involve. Fortunately, the basic principles of finance remain the same whether a transaction is domestic or international. The time value of money, for example, is not affected by whether a business transaction is domestic or international. Likewise, we use the same models for valuing capital assets, bonds, stocks, and entire firms.

The things that do change are some of the input variables used to make financial calculations. For example, required rates of return often differ between countries, and the appropriate rate must be used. Similarly, cash flows may be stated in terms of home or foreign currency. Tax codes and accounting standards also differ across countries. **Exhibit 21.2** lists some of the important finance concepts and procedures discussed in the first 20 chapters of this book and indicates where there are differences between domestic and international operations.

Building Intuition

The Basic Principles of Finance Apply No Matter Where You Do Business

The principles of finance do not stop at international borders. They apply no matter where the firm is headquartered or where it operates. Although basic finance principles do not change, international financial managers must contend with complications stemming from factors such as differences in accounting standards and tax codes, differences in interest rates, the presence of foreign exchange rate risk and country risk, and cultural differences.

Before You Go On

1. What is globalization?
2. What are multinational corporations?
3. Explain the difference between American and European views on wealth maximization.

EXHIBIT 21.2 The Basic Principles of Finance Apply in International Finance

Most of the basic finance principles discussed in this book remain unchanged in the international context. Where there are differences, they generally result from differences in accounting standards, tax codes, legal and regulatory systems, monetary systems, interest rates, and cultural norms.

Finance Concepts and Procedures	Differences Between Domestic and International Operations
Business risk	Foreign exchange rate and country risk must be taken into account
Form of business organization	Varies with countries' legal and regulatory systems
Ethical norms	Differ with countries' cultural norms
Nominal rate of interest	Affected by the rate of inflation in a given country
Accounting standards	Vary by country
Financial statement analysis	Financial statements must be adjusted for cross-country comparisons
Tax codes	Vary by country
Concept of cash flows	Cash is cash, but monetary units are different
Goal of maximizing shareholders' wealth	Proper goal for U.S.-based firms, but may vary by country
Time value of money	No difference
Bond valuation	Basic valuation concepts are the same, but market conditions differ
Valuation of equity	Basic valuation concepts are the same, but market conditions differ
Net present value analysis	No difference
Operating and financial leverage	No difference
Working capital management	Basic concepts are the same, but market conditions differ
Expected returns and variance	No difference
Cost of debt and equity	Basic concepts are the same, but market conditions and tax systems differ
Weighted average cost of capital	Basic concepts are the same, but market conditions and tax systems differ
Optimal capital structure	Basic concepts are the same, but market conditions and tax systems differ
Payout policy	Basic concepts are the same, but tax systems differ

21.2 Foreign Exchange Markets

LEARNING OBJECTIVE

2. Differentiate among the spot rate, the forward rate, and the cross rate in the foreign exchange markets, perform foreign exchange and cross rate calculations, and hedge an asset purchase where payment is made in a foreign currency.

The **foreign exchange markets** are international markets where currencies are bought and sold in wholesale amounts. Foreign exchange markets provide three basic economic benefits:

foreign exchange markets international markets where currencies are bought and sold in wholesale amounts

1. A mechanism to transfer purchasing power from individuals who deal in one currency to individuals who deal in a different currency, facilitating the import and export of goods and services.
2. A way for corporations to pass the risk associated with foreign exchange price fluctuations to professional risk-takers. This hedging function is particularly important to corporations in the present era of floating, or variable, exchange rates.
3. A channel for importers and exporters to acquire credit for international business transactions. The time span between the shipment of goods by exporters and their receipt by

importers can be considerable. While the goods are in transit, they must be financed. Foreign exchange markets provide a mechanism through which financing and currency conversions can be accomplished efficiently and at low cost.

The foreign exchange markets are very large, with an average daily volume of about \$5 trillion in 2016. This is more than the value of all the cars, wheat, oil, and other products sold daily in the real economy. London is by far the largest foreign exchange trading center, with New York City, Hong Kong, and Singapore being other important locations for foreign exchange trade. In this section, we examine how the foreign exchange markets are structured and how they work.

Market Structure and Major Participants

There is no single formal foreign exchange market. Rather, as suggested earlier, there are a group of informal markets closely interlocked through international banking relationships. Participants are linked by telephone and electronic networks. The market trades any time of day or night and every day of the year. Virtually every country has some type of active foreign exchange market.

The major participants in the foreign exchange markets are multinational commercial banks, large investment banking firms, and currency boutiques that specialize in foreign exchange transactions. In the United States, the market is dominated by money center banks including Citigroup, JP Morgan, and Bank of America. The other major participants are the central banks, which intervene in the markets primarily to smooth out fluctuations in the exchange rates for their countries' currencies.

Foreign Exchange Rates

Weblink

For foreign exchange rate data, go to http://www.x-rates.com.

When U.S.-based firms buy raw materials or finished goods, they want to get the best possible deal—the quality they need at the lowest price. When suppliers are located in the United States, comparisons of the alternatives are quite easy. Both the supplier and the customer keep their books and pay their bills in the same currency—U.S. dollars.

When the suppliers are not located in the United States, comparisons are more difficult. American buyers prefer to pay for purchases in dollars, but the foreign supplier must pay employees and other local expenses with its domestic currency. Hence, one of the two parties in the transaction will be forced to deal in a foreign currency and incur foreign exchange rate risk (recall that this risk arises because of the uncertainty associated with future exchange rate movements).

Fortunately, we can easily compare prices stated in different currencies by checking the foreign exchange rate quotes in major newspapers or on the Internet. A foreign exchange rate is the price of one monetary unit, such as the British pound, stated in terms of another currency, such as the U.S. dollar.

As an example, assume that you are the CFO of a U.S.-based manufacturing firm and you can buy American steel at \$660.00 per ton and British steel for £536 per ton. Furthermore, a Japanese company is willing to sell steel for ¥71,500 per ton. Which supplier should you choose? If the exchange rate between dollars and pounds is \$1.25/£, meaning that one British pound will cost \$1.25, the British steel will cost £536 × \$1.25/£ = \$670.00. At this dollar price, the American firm will prefer to buy steel from the American supplier at \$660.00 per ton. If the exchange rate between the yen and the dollar is ¥111/\$, which means that one dollar costs ¥111, the Japanese steel will cost ¥71,500/¥111/\$ = \$644.14 per ton. This price is \$15.86 per ton (\$660.00 − \$644.14 = \$15.86) less than the American supplier's price of \$660.00 per ton. If the price quotation of ¥71,500 includes all transportation costs and tariffs, or if the sum of those costs is less than \$15.86 per ton, the American manufacturer will find it cheaper to purchase steel from the Japanese supplier. The first three rows in **Exhibit 21.3** show the calculations used to reach this conclusion.

Now suppose that the exchange rate between the dollar and the pound falls from \$1.25/£ to \$1.15/£. Because the exchange rates for the world's major currencies float freely, based on market forces, such fluctuations occur continuously. At this point, the British steel can be bought for £536 × \$1.15/£ = \$616.40 (row 4 in Exhibit 21.3). The British firm has become the low-cost supplier, even though it has done nothing itself to lower its price.

EXHIBIT 21.3 **Foreign Exchange Rates and the Price of Steel in International Markets**

The exhibit shows the calculations necessary to decide which steel supplier offers the best price: American, British, or Japanese. If the exchange rate between the dollar and the pound is $1.25/£ and the exchange rate between the yen and the dollar is ¥111/$, it makes economic sense to select the Japanese supplier. The situation changes when the exchange rate between pound and dollar falls to $1.15/£.

Supplier	Price in Local Currency	Foreign Exchange Rate	Conversion to Price in U.S. Dollars	Price of Steel in U.S. Dollars
American	$660	–	–	$660.00
British	£536	$1.25/£	£536 × $1.25/£ =	$670.00
Japanese	¥71,500	¥111/$	¥71,500/¥111/$ =	$644.14
British	£536	$1.15/£	£536 × $1.15/£ =	$616.40

Notice that it now takes fewer dollars to buy one British pound and, conversely, more pounds to purchase one U.S. dollar. It is correct to say that the value of the pound has fallen against the dollar or that the value of the dollar has risen against the pound. Both statements indicate that goods and services priced in pounds are now cheaper to someone holding dollars and that purchases priced in dollars are now more expensive to someone holding pounds.

Also notice that, other things remaining equal, the demand for a country's products will be higher when the value of the country's currency declines relative to the value of other currencies. In our example, the change in the exchange rate led to a reversal of the U.S. company's purchase decisions; at $1.25/£, British steel was the most expensive, but when the exchange rate fell to $1.15/£, British steel was the cheapest.

Learning by Doing Application 21.1 and **Decision Making Example 21.1** present other examples that illustrate exchange rate calculations and the interpretation of exchange rates.

APPLICATION 21.1 | Exchange Rates and the Blue Sweater

LEARNING BY DOING

Problem While in a clothing store on Savile Row in London, you find the blue cashmere sweater of your dreams. The sweater is on sale at 50 percent off, priced at £250. "At 50 percent off, the sweater must be a bargain," you say to yourself. "In the states, a sweater like that costs about $300." If the current exchange rate is $1.38/£, is the sweater a bargain?

Approach Of course, the relevant question is, 50 percent off what? The shops on Savile Row in London are very pricey. You will need to use the exchange rate to calculate the price in dollars before comparing the price with that of a comparable sweater in the United States.

Solution The price of the sweater in dollars is £250 × $1.38/£ = $345, which is higher than the $300 price in the United States. It is not such a good deal.

EXAMPLE 21.1 | Exchange Rate Movement: Good or Bad News?

DECISION MAKING

Situation You are the purchasing agent for the U.S.-based firm buying steel in the example just discussed in the text. Your assistant, Omar, who is a British subject, runs into the office and breathlessly says, "The pound is stronger against the dollar! The new exchange rate is $1.32/£!" Is Omar's report good news or bad news?

Decision The fact that the pound has risen in value against the dollar is good news for Omar, because the British pounds he owns will now buy more U.S. goods. But for your firm, the news is bad. It now takes more U.S. dollars to purchase one British pound. At the new exchange rate, the British steel costs $707.52 per ton (£536 × $1.32/£ = $707.52).

The Equilibrium Exchange Rate

Exhibit 21.4 shows the supply and demand for British pounds and the equilibrium exchange rate between the U.S. dollar and the pound. As you can see, the supply of and demand for pounds move in opposite directions as the exchange rate changes. The demand for pounds increases as the U.S. dollar appreciates in value against the pound. In other words, as pounds become less expensive in relation to dollars, British products become less expensive for Americans to buy. We import more British goods; therefore, we demand more British pounds to pay for those goods. This is illustrated by the *downward-sloping demand curve* in Exhibit 21.4.

At the same time, the supply of pounds decreases as the dollar price of pounds declines. From the point of view of a British buyer, the lower the dollar price of pounds, the greater the number of pounds that must be given up to obtain dollars to buy foreign (e.g., U.S.) goods. Thus, the lower the dollar price of pounds, the more likely British residents are to switch from imported to domestic products. When purchases are diverted in this way to domestic goods, British residents will supply fewer pounds to the foreign exchange markets because they no longer want to buy as many imports. This is shown by the *upward-sloping supply curve* in the exhibit.

Exhibit 21.4 also shows the *equilibrium exchange rate* ($/£), which is at the point where the supply and demand curves intersect and the quantity of the currency demanded exactly equals the quantity supplied. At that rate of exchange, participants in the foreign exchange market will neither be accumulating nor divesting a currency.

The key to understanding movements in exchange rates, then, is to identify factors that cause shifts in the supply and demand curves for foreign currency. In general, whatever causes U.S. residents to buy more or fewer foreign goods shifts the demand curve for the foreign currency. Similarly, whatever causes foreigners to buy more or fewer U.S. goods shifts the supply curve for the foreign currency.

Major currencies such as the British pound and the U.S. dollar are referred to as "floating" currencies in that their exchange rates are allowed to freely fluctuate with supply and demand on the foreign exchange markets. In some cases, however, countries

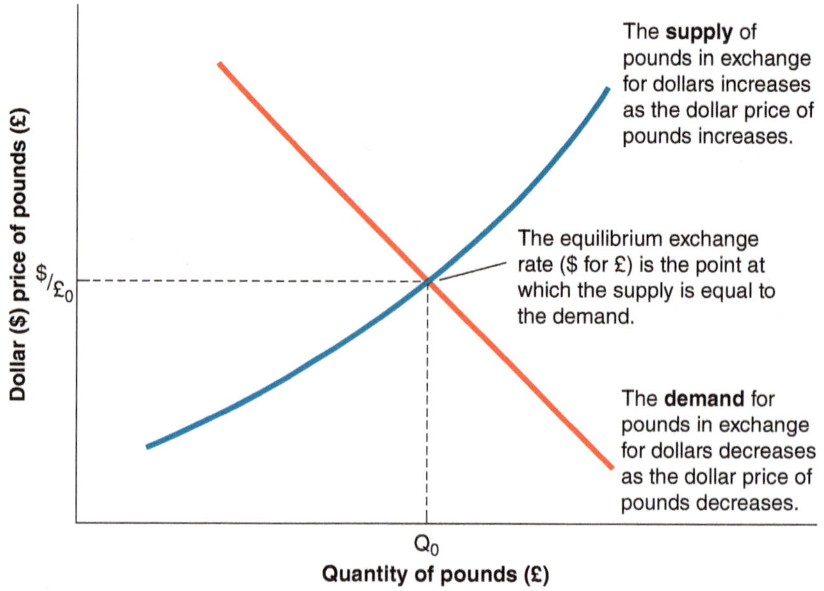

EXHIBIT 21.4 The Equilibrium Exchange Rate

The supply of and demand for pounds move in opposite directions. The equilibrium exchange rate occurs at the intersection of the supply and demand curves. At this point, the quantity of the currency demanded equals the quantity supplied.

elect to "peg" or fix their exchange rate to another major currency such as the U.S. dollar or the euro. Around the world, over two dozen countries including Denmark, Togo, and Bulgaria have opted to peg their currency exchange rate. For example, Bahrain maintains a fixed exchange rate between its dinar and the U.S. dollar of 0.376 dinar per U.S. dollar. Countries typically peg their currency to maintain stability in the exchange rate and to ensure that their goods and services remain competitively priced in export markets.

Weblink

To learn more about countries with pegged exchange rates, go to http://www.investmentfrontier.com/2013/02/19/investors-list-countries-with-fixed-currency-exchange-rates/.

Foreign Currency Quotations

Exhibit 21.5 shows selected exchange rate quotations from the *Wall Street Journal*. As you can see, there are several types of quotations, which we discuss next.

The Spot Rate

Look first at Panel B (on the next two pages) of the exhibit. The exchange rate quotations here (except the ones identified as "forward," which we discuss later) are spot rates. The **spot rate** is the cost of buying a foreign currency today "on the spot." In other words, it is the exchange rate that you would pay for immediate delivery of a currency.

spot rate the exchange rate for immediate delivery of a currency

In Panel B, the first column shows the name of the country and the name of its currency. The second and third columns, labeled "USD Equivalent," show how many U.S. dollars it takes to buy one unit of the foreign currency. Because this rate is the price in dollars for a foreign currency, it is often called the *American* or *direct* quote. For example, using the Tuesday quote, it takes $1.2154 to buy one British (UK) pound, 31.53 cents to buy one Brazilian real, and 1.520 cents to buy an Indian rupee.

The fourth and fifth columns in Panel B, labeled "Currency per USD," show how much foreign currency exchanges for one U.S. dollar. For example, $1 would get you 82.28 British pence, 3.1695 Brazilian reals, or 65.7705 Indian rupees. This quote is often called the *European* or *indirect* quote because it is the amount of foreign currency per U.S. dollar (although the foreign currency may not be European). As you may have noted, the second exchange rate is the reciprocal ($1/x$) of the first. For example, the American quote for the British pound

EXHIBIT 21.5 Spot Foreign Exchange Rates and Cross Rates

Panel A of the exhibit shows the cross rates for seven currencies commonly dealt with in the United States. Panel B lists spot and forward rates for selected currencies. Columns 2 and 3 in Panel B show how many U.S. dollars it takes to buy one unit of the foreign currency, and columns 4 and 5 show how much foreign currency it takes to purchase one U.S. dollar.

Panel A: Key Currency Cross Rates

March 14th, 2017. 5 p.m. Eastern Standard Time

	Dollar	Euro	Pound	SFranc	Peso	Yen	CdnDlr
Canada	1.3480	1.4294	1.6383	1.3343	0.0685	0.0117	...
Japan	114.7430	121.6792	139.4586	113.5844	5.8348	...	85.1241
Mexico	19.6652	20.8540	23.9011	19.4666	...	0.1714	14.5890
Switzerland	1.0102	1.0713	0.1228	...	0.0514	0.0088	0.7494
U.K.	0.8228	0.8725	...	0.8145	0.0418	0.0072	0.6104
Euro	0.9430	...	1.1461	0.9335	0.0480	0.0082	0.6996
U.S.	...	1.0605	1.2154	0.9899	0.0509	0.0087	0.7419

Source: Tullett Prebon

continued

EXHIBIT 21.5 Spot Foreign Exchange Rates and Cross Rates (*continued*)

Panel B: Foreign Exchange Data for Tuesday March 14, 2017

	USD Equivalent		Currency per USD	
Country/currency	**Tuesday**	**Monday**	**Tuesday**	**Monday**
Americas:				
Argentina peso	0.0644	0.0644	15.5385	15.5318
Brazil real	0.3155	0.3172	3.1695	3.1525
Canada dollar	0.7419	0.7437	1.3480	1.3447
Chile peso	0.001494	0.001500	669.4	666.7
Colombia peso	0.0003337	0.0003351	2,996.98	2,984.05
Ecuador U.S. dollar	1	1	1	1
Mexico peso	0.0509	0.0510	19.6652	19.6173
Peru new sol	0.3049	0.3046	3.2796	3.2835
Uruguay peso	0.03525	0.03527	28.37	28.35
Venezuela bolivar	0.10004952	0.10009960	9.9951	9.9901
Asia-Pacific:				
Australian dollar	0.7559	0.7571	1.3229	1.3208
1-mos forward	0.7650	0.7563	1.3072	1.3222
3-mos forward	0.7551	0.7558	1.3243	1.3231
6-mos forward	0.7540	0.7520	1.3263	1.3298
China yuan	0.1446	0.1446	6.9144	6.9145
Hong Kong dollar	0.1287	0.1288	7.7673	7.7647
India rupee	0.01520	0.01511	65.7705	66.1804
Indonesia rupiah	0.0000748	0.0000749	13371	13358
Japan yen	0.00872	0.00870	114.74	114.88
1-mos forward	0.008371	0.008713	119.4600	114.7710
3-mos forward	0.008754	0.008742	114.2335	114.3903
6-mos forward	0.008796	0.008780	113.6880	113.8952
Kazakhstan tenge	0.00314	0.00314	318.2	318.43
Macau pataca	0.1249938	0.1258986	8.000	7.943
Malaysia ringgit	0.2247	0.2249	4.4495	4.4465
New Zealand dollar	0.6919	0.6923	1.4453	1.4445
Pakistan rupee	0.00954	0.00954	104.8	104.8
Philippines peso	0.0199	0.0199	50.316	50.282
Singapore dollar	0.7064	0.7071	1.4156	1.4142
South Korea won	0.0008696	0.0008711	1149.97	1148
Sri Lanka rupee	0.0065854	0.0066636	151.85	150.07
Taiwan dollar	0.0323	0.03233	30.96	30.93
Thailand baht	0.02832	0.02834	35.31	35.29
Vietnam dong	0.00004385	0.00004406	22805	22695

Country/currency	USD Equivalent		Currency per USD	
	Tuesday	Monday	Tuesday	Monday
Europe:				
Bulgaria lev	0.54283	0.54469	1.842	1.836
Croatia kuna	0.1428	0.1434	7.0019	6.9732
Czech Rep. koruna	0.03924	0.03943	25.481	25.364
Denmark krone	0.1426	0.1433	7.0102	6.9783
Euro area euro	1.0605	1.0653	0.943	0.9387
Hungary forint	0.00340727	0.00341227	293.49	293.06
Iceland krona	0.009029	0.009020	110.76	110.86
Norway krone	0.1161	0.1167	8.6122	8.566
Poland zloty	0.2457	0.2462	4.0699	4.0621
Romania leu	0.2335	0.234	4.2832	4.2733
Russia ruble	0.0169	0.01699	59.183	58.843
Sweden krona	0.1115	0.1118	8.9712	8.9424
Switzerland franc	0.9899	0.9928	1.0102	1.0073
3-mos forward	0.9960	0.9988	1.0040	1.0012
Turkey lira	0.2672	0.2673	3.7425	3.7418
Ukraine hryvnia	0.0371	0.0375	26.9435	26.6470
UK pound	1.2154	1.2218	0.8228	0.8185
1-mos forward	1.2172	1.2232	0.8216	0.8175
3-mos forward	1.2190	1.2249	0.8203	0.8164
6-mos forward	1.2223	1.2279	0.8181	0.8144
Middle East/Africa:				
Bahrain dinar	2.6522	2.6539	0.3771	0.3768
Egypt pound	0.0554	0.0556	18.0485	17.9805
Israel shekel	0.2727	0.2729	3.667	3.6641
Kuwait dinar	3.272	3.2737	0.3056	0.3055
Oman sul rial	2.5975	2.59703	0.38	0.39
Qatar rial	0.2747	0.2746	3.6408	3.6410
Saudi Arabia riyal	0.2667	0.2667	3.7502	3.7496
South Africa rand	0.0760	0.0761	13.1527	13.1380

Sources: SIX Financial Information, Tullett Prebon, and the Wall Street Journal Market Data Group as reprinted in the *Wall Street Journal Online*, March 14, 2017.

is \$1.2154/£; the European exchange rate, which is the reciprocal, is 1/1.2154 = 0.8228, or £0.8228/\$; that is, \$1 equals £0.8228.

Bid and Ask Rate Quotations

The foreign exchange rate quotes given in the *Wall Street Journal* are provided by foreign exchange dealers, most of whom operate in large money center banks. Like all dealers in financial markets, foreign exchange dealers quote two prices: *bid* and *ask* quotes. The *bid* quote represents the rate at which the dealer will *buy* foreign currency, while the *ask* quote is the rate at which the dealer will *sell* foreign currency. The prices quoted in the *Wall Street Journal* are ask quotes for wholesale transactions ($1 million or more).

The difference between the bid and ask price is the dealer's spread, which is often calculated in percent form, as follows:

$$\text{Bid-ask spread} = \frac{\text{Ask rate} - \text{Bid rate}}{\text{Ask rate}} \tag{21.1}$$

Suppose a dealer is quoting a bid rate for euros (the currency of the European Union) of $1.0595/€ and an ask rate of $1.0681/€. The bid-ask spread is 0.805 percent [(1.0681 – 1.0595)/1.0681 = 0.00805, or 0.805 percent]. Now assume that ABC Corporation decides to buy €1,000,000 to use in a transaction. The dealer sells the euros to the company at the ask rate of $1.0681/€, and the firm pays the dealer a total of $1,068,100 (€1,000,000 × $1.0681/€ = $1,068,100). Later in the day, ABC Corporation finds it does not need the euros and decides to sell them back. The dealer buys the euros from the firm at the bid rate of $1.0595/€. The firm receives $1,059,500 (€1,000,000 × $1.0595/€ = $1,059,500). This represents a loss of $8,600 or 0.805 percent ($8,600/$1,068,100 = 0.00805, or 0.805 percent), which is exactly equal to the bid-ask spread quoted above.

Cross Rates

Weblink

To look up the current cross rates, go to: https://www.bloomberg.com/markets/currencies/cross-rates.

People who have to deal with more than one foreign currency often make use of a table of spot exchange rates called *cross rates,* which are simply exchange rates between two currencies. Panel A of Exhibit 21.5 shows cross rates for seven different currencies. Cross rate tables can be found in the *Wall Street Journal* and on many financial Web sites.

It is also possible to calculate cross rates, given enough information. Suppose, for example, that a dealer is interested in finding the exchange rate between the Canadian dollar and the euro but only knows the exchange rate between each of these currencies and the U.S. dollar: C$1.3480/$ and €0.9430/$. The dealer can calculate the desired cross rate as follows:

$$\frac{\text{C\$/U.S.\$}}{\text{€/U.S.\$}} = \frac{1.3480}{0.9430} = \text{C\$1.4294/€}$$

Turning to the cross rate table in Panel A of Exhibit 21.5, you can find exactly the same value—1.4294—by looking down the column for the euro and matching it with the Canadian dollar.

Learning by Doing Application 21.2 illustrates another application of cross exchange rates.

LEARNING BY DOING

APPLICATION 21.2 | Cross Exchange Rates

Problem An American executive is going on a business trip to Japan and England. Before she departs, the executive purchases $10,000 worth of Japanese yen at the prevailing rate of ¥114.74/$. After finishing her business in Japan, she departs for London, where she converts her remaining yen to British pounds. She sells ¥512,375 at a rate of ¥139.4586/£. She finally returns to the United States with £567.35, which she would like to convert to U.S. dollars. Based only on the rates given, how many dollars will she receive if she sells the pounds?

Approach To solve this problem, you need to know the exchange rate, or cross rate, between the U.S. dollar and the British pound. Given the other two exchange rates, you can calculate this rate by dividing the ¥/£ rate by the ¥/$ rate.

Solution

$$\text{Cross rate} = \frac{\text{¥139.4586/£}}{\text{¥114.74/\$}} = \text{\$1.2154/£}$$

$$\text{Amount of dollars received} = \text{£567.35} \times \text{\$1.2154/£} = \text{\$689.55}$$

Forward Rates

For the major world currencies, such as the U.S. dollar, the British pound, and the Japanese yen, the *Wall Street Journal* also lists the forward rates for one month, three months, and six months (see Panel B of Exhibit 21.5). Recall that the spot rate is what you pay to buy money today. The **forward rate**, as the name implies, is what you agree to pay for money in the future—that is, you sign a contract today to buy the money on a date in the future, such as one month, three months, or six months from now.

forward rate a rate agreed on today for an exchange to take place on a specified date in the future

Forward contracts are important because foreign business transactions may extend over long periods. This means that financial managers must anticipate their future needs for foreign currencies. By contracting now to buy or sell foreign currencies at some future date, managers can lock in the cost of foreign exchange at the beginning of a transaction, and do not have to worry about the possibility of an unfavorable movement in the exchange rate before the transaction is completed. This is one way that forward contracts are used by companies to manage risk.

Note that the forward rate is established at the date on which the agreement is made and defines the exchange rate to be used when the transaction is completed in the future. This characteristic is extremely important for facilitating international business transactions, because it permits the two parties to eliminate all uncertainty about the amount of currency to be delivered or received in the future.

The forward rate quoted on a particular day is seldom the same as the spot rate on the same day. Whether it is a one-month, three-month, or six-month quote, the forward rate is the market's best estimate of what the spot rate will be at that time in the future. The difference between the forward rate and the spot rate is called the *forward premium* or *forward discount*. For example, suppose the spot rate today on the British pound is \$1.2179/£, while the three-month forward rate is \$1.2105/£. According to the forward quote, the market expects the British pound to cost \$1.2105 three months in the future, a value that is less than today's spot rate of \$1.2179. Thus, we say that the British pound is at a forward discount against the U.S. dollar, or that the dollar is at a forward premium against the British pound.

This forward premium or discount can be measured as a percentage on an annualized basis. Equation 21.2 shows this relation:

$$\text{Forward premium (discount)} = \frac{\text{Forward rate} - \text{Spot rate}}{\text{Spot rate}} \times \frac{360}{n} \times 100 \qquad (21.2)$$

where n is the number of days in the forward agreement. Applying this equation to our example, the forward discount on the pound is equal to:

$$\text{Forward discount} = \frac{\$1.2105/£ - \$1.2179/£}{\$1.2179/£} \times \frac{360}{90} \times 100 = -2.43\%$$

where the negative sign indicates the discount on the pound.

Learning by Doing Application 21.3 illustrates another forward premium (discount) calculation.

Hedging a Currency Transaction

In finance, to **hedge** means to engage in a financial transaction to reduce risk. In the discussion of forward rates, we briefly described how firms can lock in (hedge) the cost of foreign exchange.

hedge a financial transaction intended to reduce risk

Let's take a look at an example of how a firm might hedge a transaction using a forward contract. Suppose an American exporter sells farm equipment to a British firm for £100,000; the equipment is to be delivered and paid for in 90 days. The English firm will pay for the purchase in pounds. The American exporter wants to hedge the transaction. How will this hedging work?

If, at the time of the sale, the spot rate is \$1.30/£, the farm equipment is worth \$130,000 (£100,000 × \$1.30/£ = \$130,000). However, the actual number of dollars to be received

LEARNING BY DOING

APPLICATION 21.3 | Forward Premium (Discount)

Problem Ian Chappell is planning a trip from Sydney, Australia, to visit his brother, who works in India. He plans to make the trip in six months. In preparing his budget for the trip, he finds that the spot rate for Indian rupees is Rs54.4811 per Australian dollar (A$). He also finds the six-month forward rate to be Rs50.9001/A$. What is the forward premium or discount on the Indian rupees against the Australian dollar?

Approach Recognize that the Australian dollar will buy fewer Indian rupees in six months than now. This means that the Indian rupee is at a forward premium against the Australian dollar or that the Australian dollar is at a discount against the rupee. To find out how much, we use Equation 21.2.

Solution Using Equation 21.2, we calculate the value as:

$$\text{Forward discount} = \frac{\text{Rs}50.9001/\text{A\$} - \text{Rs}54.4811/\text{A\$}}{\text{Rs}54.4811/\text{A\$}} \times \frac{360}{180} \times 100 = -13.15\%$$

Thus, the Australian dollar is at a forward discount of 13.15 percent against the Indian rupee.

for the machinery, which is the relevant price to the American firm, is not really certain. The American firm must wait 90 days to collect the £100,000 and then sell the pounds in the spot market for dollars. There is a risk that the dollar price of the pound might decline more than expected during that time. For instance, if in 90 days a pound is worth only $1.22, the American exporter will receive only $122,000 (£100,000 × $1.22/£ = $122,000), a loss of $8,000 ($130,000 − $122,000 = $8,000).

To eliminate this foreign exchange rate risk and ensure a certain future price, the American company can hedge by selling the £100,000 forward 90 days. If the forward rate at the time of sale is $1.28/£, the American exporter can enter into a forward contract in which it agrees to deliver the £100,000 to the bank in 90 days and receive $128,000 (£100,000 × $1.28/£ = $128,000) in return. Assume that the spot rate on the day of the delivery actually turns out to be $1.22/£. In this case, the "savings" from hedging is $6,000, since the firm will receive $128,000 instead of the $122,000 it would have received if it had not entered into the forward contract.

Notice that, even with hedging, the firm has "lost" $2,000, because at the time of the sale, when the exchange rate was $1.30/£, the machine was worth $130,000. Can this kind of loss be prevented? The answer is that forward contracts cannot protect against *expected* changes in exchange rates, only against *unexpected* changes. At the time of sale, the 90-day forward rate is $1.28/£, and this is the market's best estimate of what the rate will be in 90 days. Of course, in 90 days the spot rate for dollars may be actually $1.28/£, but there is a very good chance that it will be either more or less.

What would happen in our example if the spot rate in 90 days rose to $1.40/£? The unhedged transaction would yield $140,000. However, the forward contract would again provide exactly the number of dollars anticipated—$128,000. Although the company may have some regrets because the forward contract prevented it from receiving the benefits of the strengthening pound, most businesses would consider leaving the account receivable exposed (that is, unhedged) to be "speculation." It is generally believed that foreign exchange speculation is not a logical or legitimate function of nonfinancial businesses that import or export goods or services.

Before You Go On

1. What is foreign exchange rate risk?
2. How is the equilibrium exchange rate determined?
3. What does it mean to hedge a financial transaction?

21.3 International Capital Budgeting

LEARNING OBJECTIVE

3. Identify the major factors that distinguish international from domestic capital budgeting, explain how the capital budgeting process can be adjusted to account for these factors, and compute the NPV for a typical international capital project.

Multinational firms have operations outside of their home countries that range from simple sales offices to large manufacturing operations. As a legal and practical matter, most multinational firms set up separate foreign subsidiaries for each country in which they operate. When a multinational firm wants to consider overseas capital projects, the financial manager faces the decision of which capital projects should be accepted on a company-wide basis.

Fortunately, the overall decision-making framework and computational methods developed for domestic capital budgeting in Chapters 10 through 13 apply to international capital projects as well. Thus, the financial manager's goal is to seek out domestic and overseas capital projects whose cash flows yield a positive net present value (NPV). The decision to accept international projects with a positive NPV increases the value of the firm and is consistent with the fundamental goal of financial management, which is to maximize the value of stockholder equity.

Furthermore, when financial managers evaluate a capital project overseas, they must estimate the same inputs to compute the NPV for that project that they would for a domestic project: (1) the project's incremental after-tax free cash flows and (2) the appropriate discount rate. Although the same basic principles apply to both international and domestic capital budgeting, firms must deal with some differences. We now focus on those differences.

Determining Cash Flows

A number of issues complicate the determination of cash flows from overseas capital projects. First, it is often more difficult to estimate the incremental after-tax free cash flows for foreign projects. Some of the problems stem from the lack of firsthand knowledge by the parent company's financial staff of procedures and systems used at the overseas operations; other problems arise because of differences in the accounting and legal systems, language, and cultural differences.

Second, foreign subsidiaries can remit cash flows to the parent firm in a number of ways, including (1) cash dividends, (2) royalty payments or license agreement payments for use of patents or brand names, and (3) management fees for services the parent provides to a subsidiary. Problems with forecasting expected cash flows can arise when foreign governments restrict the amount of cash that can be repatriated, or returned to the parent company, and therefore moved out of the country. These **repatriation of earnings restrictions** may arise because foreign governments are politically sensitive to charges that large multinational companies are exploiting their countries and draining vital investment capital from their economies.

repatriation of earnings restrictions restrictions placed by a foreign government on the amount of cash that can be repatriated, or returned to a parent company by a subsidiary doing business in the foreign country

Repatriation of earnings restrictions usually take the form of a ceiling on the amount of cash dividends that a foreign subsidiary can pay to its parent. The ceiling is typically some percentage of the firm's net worth and is intended to force the parent to reinvest in the foreign subsidiary. The repatriation of the project cash flows can be a critical issue if there are significant delays in receiving the funds. From the parent firm's perspective, the relevant cash flow for analysis of foreign capital investment opportunities is the cash flow that the parent company expects to actually receive from its foreign subsidiary.

Exchange Rate Risk

The next issue that financial managers must deal with when evaluating international capital investments is foreign exchange rate risk. The cash flows from an overseas capital project will most likely be in a foreign currency that must eventually be converted to the parent company's home currency—the U.S. dollar in the case of an American firm. This is not a simple task because most of the cash flows from capital project are *future* cash flows. Thus, analysts cannot use the current spot rate to convert one currency to another. To convert the project's future cash flows into another currency, they must forecast exchange rates.

Where can firms secure forecasts for exchange rates? Forecasts for three or four years into the future can be obtained from most money center banks or from currency specialists on Wall Street. However, one of the problems with obtaining currency rate forecasts for use in analysis of capital projects is that many projects have lives of 20 years or more. Needless to say, it is difficult to forecast exchange rates far into the future.

Country Risk

Financial managers must also account for country risk when evaluating foreign business activities. If a firm is located in a country with a relatively unstable political environment, management will require a higher rate of return on capital projects as compensation for the additional risk. At the extreme, a local government could expropriate, or take over, the plant and equipment of the overseas operation without giving the company any compensation. This expropriation of assets is called *nationalization*. Sometimes, nations will expropriate the assets and offer some form of compensation. In other cases, they will offer no compensation. Other ways that a foreign government can affect the risk of a foreign project include:

- Change tax laws in a way that adversely impacts the firm.
- Impose laws related to labor, wages, and prices that are more restrictive than those applicable to domestic firms.
- Disallow any remittance of funds from the subsidiary to the parent firm for either a limited time, or the duration of the project.
- Require that the subsidiary be headed by a local citizen or have a local firm as a major equity partner.
- Impose tariffs and quotas on any imports.

Weblink

For country risk information, visit http://www.prsgroup.com.

To help firms assess country risk, some private firms and government agencies rate nations for their relative level of country risk. **Exhibit 21.6** shows one such ranking for country risk by a private firm for 2016. In addition, U.S. governmental agencies such as the Department of Commerce and Central Intelligence Agency (CIA) gather information on countries continuously and are able to provide information on country risk to businesses to help them make decisions regarding investing in, exporting to, or importing from a particular country.

Once management has gauged a capital project's country risk, that risk must be incorporated into the capital budgeting analysis. One way to do this is to adjust the firm's discount rate for the additional risk. For example, if the firm's cost of capital is 8 percent and the financial manager's staff estimates that investment in a particular country requires a 3 percent expected return to compensate for the additional risk, the appropriate discount rate is 11 percent. Of course, from Chapters 7 and 13, we know that adjustments like this should only be made to the discount rate to reflect country risk that is systematic. Unsystematic risk should be reflected in the expected cash flows.

The Barcelona Example

Suppose a U.S.-based manufacturing company is considering the possibility of establishing a manufacturing operation overseas in Barcelona, Spain. The U.S. firm wants overseas capital investment decisions to be based on the same criteria as domestic investment decisions. The firm's overseas financial staff forecasts the expected incremental after-tax free cash flows for the Barcelona project in millions of euros, as shown in the following time line:

Year	0	1	2	3	4
Cash flow	−€10.0	€3.00	€3.00	€3.00	€3.00

EXHIBIT 21.6 Composite Country Risk Ratings for Selected Countries in 2016

The composite risk for a country is determined by the country's political, financial, and economic risk. A higher number means lower risk. Are you surprised by the rank of the United States?

Rank	Country	Composite Risk	Rank	Country	Composite Risk
1	Switzerland	88.5	22	Australia	78.3
2	Norway	88.0	24	Israel	77.8
3	Luxembourg	87.0	26	United Kingdom	77.5
4	Singapore	86.3	33	Italy	75.3
5	Sweden	86.0	38	Spain	74.5
6	Germany	85.0	49	France	72.3
7	New Zealand	83.3	53	China, Peoples' Rep.	71.5
8	Taiwan	83.0	59	Cuba	70.3
9	Canada	82.8	66	India	69.8
10	Korea, Republic	82.5	70	Mexico	67.8
11	Netherlands	82.5	73	Russia	67.3
12	Ireland	82.0	78	Greece	66.8
13	Denmark	81.8	81	Indonesia	65.8
13	Japan	81.8	85	Brazil	64.8
15	Finland	81.3	94	Tanzania	63.8
16	Hong Kong	80.8	99	Turkey	63.3
17	Iceland	80.5	105	Kenya	62.5
18	Austria	79.5	119	Ukraine	59.8
19	Czech Republic	79.5	138	Syria	46.8
20	United States	79.3	140	Venezuela	41.0

Rankings are provided for the 140 surveyed countries. Composite scores range from 0 to 100 with countries broken into categories ranging from very low risk (80 to 100) to very high risk (0 to 49.9).
Source: PRS Group (www.prsgroup.com), July 2016.

Assume that the current spot rate between the euro (€) and the U.S. dollar ($) is \$1.20/€. The parent company's finance staff acquires forecasts from an analyst for the expected foreign exchange (EFX) rates between the euro and the dollar. These forecasts and calculations for the analysis of the project are shown in the following table:

Year (1)	Cash Flow (€ millions) (2)	EFX Rate (3)	Calculation (4)	Cash Flow ($ millions) (5)
0	−€10.00	\$1.20/€	−€10.00 × \$1.20/€	−\$12.00
1	3.00	1.25	3.00 × 1.25	3.75
2	3.00	1.30	3.00 × 1.30	3.90
3	3.00	1.32	3.00 × 1.32	3.96
4	3.00	1.35	3.00 × 1.35	4.05

Column (2) shows the project's cash flows in euros. Column (3) shows the current spot rate (Year 0) and the forecast foreign exchange rates (Years 1 to 4). In Column (4), the euro cash flows are multiplied by the appropriate exchange rate (spot or forecast) to convert to dollar cash flows, and the results are shown in Column (5).

The firm's cost of capital is 8 percent, and the financial manager estimates that the project in Barcelona carries a 2 percent country risk premium. Thus, the appropriate discount rate for the project is 10 percent.

With this information, the NPV for the project is computed by discounting the cash flows by the country-risk-adjusted discount rate of 10 percent, as follows:

$$\begin{aligned} \text{NPV} &= -\$12.00 + \frac{\$3.75}{1.10} + \frac{\$3.90}{(1.10)^2} + \frac{\$3.96}{(1.10)^3} + \frac{\$4.05}{(1.10)^4} \\ &= -\$12.00 + \$3.41 + \$3.22 + \$2.98 + \$2.77 \\ &= \$0.38 \end{aligned}$$

The project should be accepted because its NPV is positive.

Learning by Doing Application 21.4 presents another international capital budgeting example.

LEARNING BY DOING

APPLICATION 21.4 | International Capital Budgeting

Problem A U.S. electronics firm is establishing a manufacturing plant in Taiwan to produce components that will be sold to customers in Taiwan. The cost of the investment is $10 million. The project is expected to last five years and then shut down. The company usually uses a discount rate of 7.5 percent for domestic projects like this, but for this project, the financial manager adds a 2.5 percent country risk premium. The following time line shows the expected cash flows in millions of Taiwanese dollars (TWD) and the forecasted year-end exchange rates between the U.S. dollar and the Taiwanese dollar.

Year	1	2	3	4	5
Cash flows (millions of TWD)	64.3	71.2	93.6	121.8	109.6
Expected exchange rate (TWD/$)	32.031	33.632	36.155	32.221	33.670

What is the NPV of this project?

Approach Since we know the expected cash flows in the foreign currency and the expected exchange rates, we can calculate the expected cash flows to the parent firm in U.S. dollars by dividing the TWD cash flows by the appropriate exchange rate. We also must adjust the project discount rate for the 2.5 percent country risk premium.

Solution The following table shows the conversion of the cash flows the U.S. firm expects to receive from Taiwanese dollars to U.S. dollars.[2]

Year	Cash Flows (TWD millions)		Exchange Rate		Cash Flows ($ millions)
0					−$10.00
1	64.3 TWD	÷	32.031 TWD/$	=	2.01
2	71.2	÷	33.632	=	2.12
3	93.6	÷	36.155	=	2.59
4	121.8	÷	32.221	=	3.78
5	109.6	÷	33.670	=	3.26

[2]You may wonder why there was a currency conversion for the initial cash flow in the Barcelona example and no similar conversion for this problem. The reason is that for the current problem, the initial cash flow of −$10 million is already in U.S. dollars, and thus there is no need for a conversion. The remaining cash flows are in TWD.

The appropriate discount rate is 2.5 percent over the discount rate that the firm normally uses for domestic capital budgeting projects. Thus, the discount rate to be used is 10 percent (2.5 + 7.5 = 10). By discounting the cash flows at the risk-adjusted discount rate of 10 percent, we can compute the NPV for this project.

$$\begin{aligned} \text{NPV} &= -\$10.00 + \frac{\$2.01}{1.10} + \frac{\$2.12}{(1.10)^2} + \frac{\$2.59}{(1.10)^3} + \frac{\$3.78}{(1.10)^4} + \frac{\$3.26}{(1.10)^5} \\ &= -\$10.00 + \$1.83 + \$1.75 + \$1.95 + \$2.58 + \$2.02 \\ &= \$0.13 \text{ million} \end{aligned}$$

Since the NPV is positive, the project should be accepted.

Before You Go On

1. What difficulties do firms face in estimating cash flows from an overseas project?
2. Why is the repatriation of cash flows from an overseas project considered critical to the project's value?
3. When do companies have to consider country or political risk?

21.4 Global Money and Capital Markets

LEARNING OBJECTIVE

4. Discuss the importance of the Euromarkets to large U.S. multinational firms and calculate the cost of borrowing in the Eurobond market.

Next, we focus on how multinational business firms use global money and capital markets to adjust their liquidity, to finance their domestic and international operations, and to raise equity capital. The global financial markets operate and transact in securities denominated in all of the world's major currencies. However, the dollar portion of these global markets is the largest. This is because international business contracts all over the world commonly require payment in U.S. dollars.

The dollar has been a preferred medium of exchange because of the strength and size of the U.S. economy and the government's long history of political stability. As a result of these factors, businesses, governments, and individuals throughout the world often choose to hold and transact in dollars rather than their home currency.

The euro is now the main currency used in the 19 countries that are part of the Eurozone. (The Eurozone consists of 19 of the 28 member states of the European Union.) The euro is second only to the dollar in its popularity as a reserve currency and in its volume as a traded currency. The renminbi is the currency issued by the People's Republic of China and is denominated in yuan. The yuan is also an increasingly popular currency for worldwide exchange as the Chinese economy continues to grow.

The Emergence of the Euromarkets

Before World War II, dollar-denominated deposits of multinational corporations and governments were held in U.S. money center banks. When the cold war started in the 1950s, the Soviet Union feared that for political reasons the U.S. government might temporarily freeze or expropriate its deposits in the United States. Motivated by profits, a number of London-based

Eurodollar a U.S. dollar deposited in a bank outside the United States

banks responded to the Soviets' concern by offering to hold their dollar-denominated deposits in British banks. The new accounts became quite popular and were soon dubbed Eurodollars. A **Eurodollar** is defined as a U.S. dollar deposited in a bank outside the United States. The banks accepting these deposits are called *Eurobanks*.

Over time, other major currencies, such as the Japanese yen and British pound, were deposited offshore, and the Euromarkets emerged. Today, the Euromarkets are vast, largely unregulated money and capital markets. London and New York City are the two most important markets, but Euromarkets also exist in places like Tokyo, Hong Kong, and Singapore. Though many of the market centers are not in Europe, the term *Euromarket* has become a generic term.

The Eurocurrency Market

Eurocurrency a time deposit that is in a bank located in a country different from the country that issued the currency

The core of international financial markets is the *Eurocurrency market*, which is the short-term portion of the Euromarket. A **Eurocurrency** is a time deposit that is in a bank located in a country different from the country that issued the currency. For example, a Japanese yen or an American dollar account in a British bank is a Eurocurrency account.[3]

The largest segment of the Eurocurrency market is interbank transactions, in which banks borrow from and lend to one another overnight. Although short-term transactions dominate the market, there is an active market for loans with maturities of up to six months. The importance of the Eurocurrency market lies in its role in allocating funds on a global basis. This means that banks with strong loan demand can borrow Eurocurrencies, such as Eurodollars, and make loans to multinational corporations, sovereign governments, or other large international entities.

London Interbank Offer Rate (LIBOR) the interest rate British-based banks charge each other for short-term loans. Also, commonly used as the base rate for Eurodollar loans that are not between two banks

The most widely quoted Eurocurrency interest rate is the **London Interbank Offer Rate**, or **LIBOR**, which is the short-term interest rate that major banks in London charge one another. This rate is also commonly used as the base rate for Eurodollar loans other than those between two banks. If the lending bank is located in another Euromarket financial center, such as Singapore, the offer rate quoted is SIBOR, which is the Singapore Interbank Offer Rate; if the bank is based in Hong Kong, the offer rate is HKIBOR; and so on. Because the various Euromarkets are closely linked, the interbank rates for a particular Eurocurrency tend to be similar. The LIBOR is also similar to the Fed funds rate, which is the rate that large U.S. banks charge one another.

The Eurocredit Market

Eurocredits short- to medium-term loans of a Eurocurrency to multinational corporations and governments of medium to high credit quality

The international banking system gathers funds from businesses and governments in the Eurocurrency market and then allocates funds to banks that have the most profitable lending opportunities. These loans are called **Eurocredits**—short- to medium-term loans of a Eurocurrency to multinational corporations and governments of medium to high credit quality. Eurocredits are denominated in all major Eurocurrencies, although the dollar is the overwhelming favorite. An example of a Eurocredit transaction would be an American firm borrowing Eurodollars from a bank in Hong Kong.

International Bond Markets

International bonds fall into two generic categories: foreign bonds and Eurobonds.

Foreign Bonds

Foreign bonds are long-term debt sold by a foreign firm to investors in another country and denominated in that country's currency. They are called *foreign bonds* because the issuer is a foreigner in the country where the bonds are sold. Foreign bonds may have colorful nicknames: foreign bonds sold in the United States are called Yankee bonds, and yen-denominated bonds sold in Japanese financial markets by non-Japanese firms are called Samurai bonds.

[3]Note that an American dollar deposited overseas, which is a Eurodollar, is only one of many Eurocurrencies.

Firms sell foreign bonds when they need to finance projects in a particular foreign country. For example, the German car manufacturer BMW might decide to sell dollar-denominated bonds in the United States to build an assembly plant in South Carolina. Similarly, Amazon.com might need euros to build a new shipping depot in Germany. To raise the euros, Amazon.com could sell euro-denominated bonds in Germany to German and other European investors.

Eurobonds

Eurobonds are long-term debt instruments sold by firms to investors in countries other than the country in whose currency the bonds are denominated. Multinational firms can use Eurobonds to finance international or domestic projects. For example, suppose Ford Motor Company decides to sell U.S.-dollar denominated bonds in Europe. Investors would call the bonds Eurodollar bonds. What can Ford do with the dollars from the bond sales? It can spend them overseas to finance a project, or it can spend them in the United States—after all, a dollar is a dollar.

The fact that the proceeds from a Eurodollar bond issue can be spent in the United States raises an important point. During the 1980s, multinational firms discovered that they could sell Eurodollar bond issues at interest cost savings as large as 50 to 150 basis points (0.5 to 1.5 percent) annually compared with similar bond issues sold domestically. Needless to say, multinationals that needed to borrow dollars long term flocked to the Eurodollar bond market. Although the large interest cost spreads we have mentioned no longer exist, today any multinational firm that needs to borrow dollars long term routinely evaluates whether it makes more sense to sell the bond issue domestically or in the Eurodollar bond market.

Eurodollar and other Eurocurrency bonds have a number of characteristics that differ from similar U.S corporate bonds. Eurobonds are bearer bonds and do not have to be registered. Because the bonds are not registered, there is no record of who owns them. As a result, some Eurobond investors conveniently "forget" to pay taxes on the coupon income earned. This is no secret, of course, and there is growing pressure to eliminate bearer bonds.

Eurobonds also differ from domestic bonds in that they pay interest, in the form of coupon payments, annually, whereas U.S. corporate bonds make coupon payments twice a year. Thus, the interest rate on Eurodollar bonds is not directly comparable to similar domestic bonds because of the difference in compounding periods.

Finally, historically almost all Eurocurrency bonds were sold without credit ratings. The reason for this practice was that almost all bond issues sold in Europe were purchased by institutional investors who relied on their own credit analyses, so there was no reason for the issuer to purchase a credit rating for the bond issue. However, since the mid-1980s, the retail segment of the equity and bond markets in Western Europe has grown significantly. Individual investors typically prefer to purchase bonds that have credit ratings. Today, more than half of the Eurodollar bonds sold in Europe have credit ratings.

Learning by Doing Application 21.5 illustrates the comparison of returns on Eurodollar versus domestic bonds.

APPLICATION 21.5 | Eurodollar versus Domestic Bond Issue

LEARNING BY DOING

Problem Suppose Hewlett-Packard (HP) needs $350 million to build a new facility. The firm plans to finance the facility by selling bonds domestically or in the Eurodollar bond market. In either case, the bond issue will have a maturity of three years, a par value of $1,000, and coupon interest payments totaling $50 a year. After transaction costs and underwriters' fees, the domestic bond issue will net $951.90 per bond, and the Eurodollar bonds will net $948.00 per bond. Which bonds—domestic or Eurodollar—should HP issue?

Approach Fortunately, we know from Chapter 8 that the best deal is the alternative that offers the lowest interest cost. You may want to review the bond yield calculation formulas in Section 8.3 of Chapter 8. Drawing on those formulas, we calculate the yield to maturity for each alternative. Because bond issues pay coupon interest semiannually in the United States and annually in Europe, we must also compute the effective annual yield (EAY) for the domestic bonds in order to compare it with the yield on the Eurodollar bonds.

Solution For the Eurodollar bond, the annual coupon payment is $50 per year, and the yield calculation is:

$$\$948.00 = \frac{\$50}{1+i} + \frac{\$50}{(1+i)^2} + \frac{\$1{,}050}{(1+i)^3}$$

Using our financial calculator, we find that the Eurodollar bond issue's annual yield is 6.9808 percent.

For the domestic bond issue, the semiannual coupon payments are $25 ($50/2 = $25), and the semiannual bond yield calculation is:

$$\$951.90 = \frac{\$25}{1+i} + \frac{\$25}{(1+i)^2} + \cdots + \frac{\$1{,}025}{(1+i)^6}$$

The bond issue's semiannual yield is 3.3997 percent. We now apply the EAY formula from Chapter 8 to find the effective annual yield for the domestic bonds:

$$\begin{aligned} \text{EAY} &= (1 + \text{Quoted interest rate}/m)^m - 1 \\ &= (1 + 0.033997)^2 - 1 \\ &= 1.0691 - 1 \\ &= 6.91\% \end{aligned}$$

The domestic bond issue, with a 6.91 percent effective annual yield, will provide the lower interest cost, all other things being equal. Of course, the fact that the domestic bond nets a higher price per $1,000 owed tells us that this bond has a lower interest cost. We just did not know precisely how much lower without performing the calculations.

Before You Go On

1. Which currency is the most widely preferred currency of exchange in global financial markets? Why?
2. What is the difference between foreign bonds and Eurobonds?

21.5 International Banking

LEARNING OBJECTIVE

5. Explain how large U.S. money center banks make and price Eurocredit loans to their customers and compute the cost of a Eurocredit bank loan.

During the period when the major European countries were establishing their colonial empires, British, Dutch, and Belgian banks developed a worldwide presence, and London emerged as the center of international banking and finance. European governments fostered the growth of large international banks in their countries and viewed them as engines of territorial and economic expansion.

In the United States, it was quite a different story. National banks, which are chartered by the federal government, were not permitted to establish branches or accept bills of exchange outside the United States until passage of the Federal Reserve Act of 1913. However, even after the act was passed, American banks did not rush overseas. Not until after World War II did American banks begin to establish any significant foreign presence. The catalyst for growth was the ambition of American corporations as they established sales offices overseas, imported foreign goods, and acquired foreign manufacturing facilities. To accommodate their customers' needs, large U.S. banks established networks of foreign branches and affiliates.

Exhibit 21.7 shows the 15 largest banks in the world in 2016. These banks offer a full range of international and domestic banking services to businesses in their home countries

EXHIBIT 21.7 The World's Largest Banks in 2016

The exhibit lists the 15 largest banks in the world ranked on the basis of global sales, profits, assets, and market value. Industrial and Commercial Bank of China is the world's largest bank with total assets of $3,420.3 billion. By country, the majority of the top 15 banks are located in China and the United States.

Rank	Bank Name	Country	Total Assets ($ billions)	Revenue ($ billions)	Profits ($ billions)
1	Industrial and Commercial Bank of China	China	3,420.3	$171.1	$44.2
2	China Construction Bank	China	2,826.0	146.8	36.4
3	Agricultural Bank of China	China	2,739.8	131.9	28.8
4	JP Morgan Chase	U.S.A	2,423.8	99.9	23.5
5	Bank of China	China	2,589.6	122.0	27.2
6	Wells Fargo	U.S.A	1,849.2	91.4	22.7
7	Bank of America	U.S.A	2,185.5	91.5	15.8
8	Citigroup	U.S.A	1,801.0	85.9	15.8
9	HSBC Holdings	U.K.	2,409.7	70.3	13.5
10	BNP Paribas	France	2,166.3	74.9	7.4
11	Mitsubishi UFJ Financial	Japan	2,458.8	44.2	7.9
12	Bank of Communications	China	1,101.9	57.0	10.6
13	Banco Santander	Spain	1,455.9	49.8	6.6
14	China Merchants Bank	China	843.1	48.2	9.2
15	Royal Bank of Canada	Canada	853.0	33.1	7.7

Source: "The World's Biggest Companies," https://www.forbes.com/global2000/.

and to multinational firms overseas. The services include providing transaction accounts, commercial loans, foreign exchange, underwriting of debt and equity issues, and letters of credit.

Risks Involved in International Bank Lending

The principles of loan administration and credit analysis are similar for domestic and overseas loans. There are differences, however, including some additional risk exposures for overseas lending.

Credit Risk

Credit risk involves assessing the probability that some part of the interest or principal due to a lender will not be paid. The greater the probability of default, the higher the loan rate that the bank must charge the borrower. Credit risk is the same whether a loan is domestic or international. However, it may be more difficult to obtain or assess credit information abroad. U.S. banks are less familiar with local economic conditions and business practices than are domestic banks. It takes time and practice to develop appropriate sources of information and to understand how to evaluate such information. As a result, many U.S. banks tend to restrict their foreign lending to large, well-known companies or financial institutions.

Currency Risk

We have already discussed foreign exchange rate risk. Fluctuations in exchange rates can affect the cash flows associated with a loan or investment, and, hence, can affect their value.

Weblink

A discussion on managing foreign exchange rate risk is available at this New York University Web site: http://pages.stern.nyu.edu/~igiddy/fxrisk.htm.

Some loans made by U.S. banks are denominated in foreign currency rather than dollars, and if the foreign currency is expected to lose value against the dollar during the course of the loan, the repayment will be worth fewer dollars. Thus, bank loans that have foreign exchange rate risk will carry an additional risk premium; the greater the foreign exchange rate risk, the higher the loan rate the bank must charge the borrower.

Of course, if the foreign currency has a well-developed market and the maturity of the loan is relatively short, the loan may be hedged. However, many world currencies, particularly those in developing nations, do not have well-established foreign currency markets; consequently, these international loans cannot always be hedged at a reasonable price.

Country Risk

We have also discussed country risk, which is tied to political developments in a country that could affect the cash flows associated with a loan or investment in that country. If an international loan might suffer some loss in value due to political developments, the loan will carry an additional risk premium; the greater the country risk of a loan, the higher the rate the bank must charge the borrower.

Eurocredit Bank Loans

As noted earlier, Eurocredits are short- to medium-term loans of a Eurocurrency to multinational corporations or governments. The loans are denominated in a currency that is different from the bank's home currency. Eurocredits can have a high degree of credit risk and may be too large for a single bank to handle. As a result, the lending banks often form a syndicate to spread the risk. Each bank in the lending syndicate participates by taking a portion of the loan. One bank acts as the lead bank and is responsible for negotiating the price of the loan and its terms with the borrower.

The loan pricing for Eurocredits is similar to the loan pricing that U.S. money center banks use for their largest domestic customers. The loan rate (k) is equal to a base rate, such as LIBOR, which represents the bank's cost of funds, plus a markup, which is the bank's lending margin:

$$k = \text{Base rate} + X$$

where X is the lending margin. The lending margin depends on the borrower's credit risk; international risk factors, such as foreign exchange rate (currency) risk and country risk; and the bank's gross profit margin. From the gross profit margin, the bank must cover all its expenses in making the loan and earn a profit. The general equation for Eurocredit pricing can thus be expressed as follows:

$$k = \text{BR} + \text{DRP} + \text{FXR} + \text{CR} + \text{GPMAR} \tag{21.3}$$

where:

k = individual firm's loan rate
BR = Eurocurrency base rate, such as LIBOR
DRP = default risk premium
FXR = foreign exchange rate or currency risk premium
CR = country risk premium
GPMAR = bank's gross profit margin

Eurocredits typically are floating-rate loans structured as "rollovers." Rollover pricing was developed to protect banks against adverse interest rate movements so that lenders do not end up paying more on the Eurocurrency time deposit than they earn from the loan. Banks are vulnerable to taking such losses because the money to fund Eurocredits comes from short-term deposits. As a result, a Eurocredit can be viewed as a series of short-term loans, where at the end of each time period (three or six months), the loan is "rolled over" and repriced at the current market interest rate.

Suppose, for example, that Citibank is considering making a Eurocredit loan to a Mexican manufacturer that needs to borrow $1.5 million for three years. The bank lending officer wants the loan to be structured as a six-month, floating-rate loan. That means the loan is a three-year loan priced as six successive six-month loans. The bank's credit department believes the credit risk premium is 3 percent, the country risk for Mexico is an additional 1 percent, and the bank's gross profit margin is 0.125 percent. The bank can buy the funds in the Euromarket: the six-month LIBOR rate is 0.74 percent. Applying the loan pricing model (Equation 21.3), we find that the Eurocredit pricing for this loan is:

$$\begin{aligned} k &= \text{BR} + \text{DRP} + \text{CR} + \text{GPMAR} \\ &= 0.74\% + 3.00\% + 1.00\% + 0.125\% \\ &= 4.865\% \end{aligned}$$

Note that the loan involves no foreign exchange rate risk (FXR) for the bank, because the loan is in dollars.

We can also describe the loan rate in terms of the lending margin (X), which is the markup used to reprice the loan when it rolls over. For the Mexican loan, the lending margin is as follows:

$$\begin{aligned} X &= \text{DRP} + \text{CR} + \text{GPMAR} \\ &= 3.00\% + 1.00\% + 0.125\% \\ &= 4.125\% \end{aligned}$$

When the loan is repriced at the end of six months, if LIBOR at that point is 1.00 percent, the new loan rate will be 5.125 percent (1.00 percent + 4.125 percent = 5.125 percent).

Lending margins are quite small for North American and Western European multinational companies with good credit ratings. The margins are low because the credit risk and country risk for these companies are low.

Learning by Doing Application 21.6 illustrates a calculation of the interest cost on a Eurocredit loan.

LEARNING BY DOING

APPLICATION 21.6 | Interest on a Eurocredit Loan

Problem Siemens International can borrow \$5 million from HSBC at LIBOR plus a lending margin of 0.5 percent on a three-month rollover Eurocredit loan. Suppose that the prevailing annualized LIBOR rate is 1.1 percent and that over the next three-month period, the LIBOR rate is expected to increase to 1.25 percent. How much interest will Siemens have to pay HSBC for the Eurocredit loan for the first six months?

Approach The total expected interest cost of the Siemens loan is the sum of the interest paid for the first three months plus the expected interest paid over the next three months.

Solution Siemens's annualized borrowing cost is 1.6 percent (1.1 percent + 0.5 percent = 1.6 percent) for the first three-month period and is expected to be 1.75 percent (1.25 percent + 0.5 percent = 1.75 percent) for the next three-month period; thus, the total interest cost for the six-month period is as follows:

$$\begin{aligned} \text{Total interest cost} &= (\$5{,}000{,}000 \times 0.016 \times 0.25 \text{ year}) + (\$5{,}000{,}000 \times 0.0175 \times 0.25 \text{ year}) \\ &= \$20{,}000 + \$21{,}875 \\ &= \$41{,}875 \end{aligned}$$

Before You Go On

1. Why is credit risk higher in international markets?
2. List the inputs that are used in calculating a Eurocredit price.

Summary of Learning Objectives

1 Discuss how the basic principles of finance apply to international financial transactions.

The basic principles of finance remain the same whether a transaction is domestic or international. For example, the time value of money calculations remain the same, as do the models used to calculate asset values. What does change, however, are some of the input variables. These variables may be affected by cultural or procedural differences between countries or differences in tax and accounting standards. Exhibit 21.2 lists some of these changes.

2 Differentiate among the spot rate, the forward rate, and the cross rate in the foreign exchange markets, perform foreign exchange and cross rate calculations, and hedge an asset purchase where payment is made in a foreign currency.

The spot rate is the exchange rate at which one currency can be converted to another immediately, whereas the forward rate is a rate agreed on today for an exchange to take place at a specified point in the future. Forward rates are usually different from spot rates and are the market's best estimate of what a future spot rate will be. The cross rate is simply the exchange rate between two currencies. Learning by Doing Applications 21.1 through 21.3 illustrate foreign exchange rate problems that you should be able to solve.

3 Identify the major factors that distinguish international from domestic capital budgeting, explain how the capital budgeting process can be adjusted to account for these factors, and compute the NPV for a typical international capital project.

One issue that distinguishes international from domestic capital budgeting is the difficulty in estimating the incremental cash flows from an international project. These difficulties can stem from differences in operating, accounting, and legal practices, as well as from the variety of ways in which a multinational firm can transfer profits and funds from the subsidiary to the parent corporation. Furthermore, firms engaged in international capital budgeting face two risks that domestic firms do not have to deal with: foreign exchange rate risk and country risk. The Barcelona example in Section 21.3 and Learning by Doing Application 21.4 illustrate capital budgeting calculations.

4 Discuss the importance of the Euromarkets to large U.S. multinational firms and calculate the cost of borrowing in the Eurobond market.

The Eurocurrency markets are important to large multinational corporations. These corporations hold Eurocurrency time deposits as investments and finance much of their business activity by borrowing in the Eurocredit market and selling debt in the Eurobond market. The Euromarkets are popular with large multinational firms because they are largely unregulated; thus, they offer more attractive borrowing and lending rates and greater flexibility in conducting transactions. Learning by Doing Application 21.5 illustrates how to calculate the cost of issuing bonds in the domestic and Eurobond markets.

5 Explain how large U.S. money center banks make and price Eurocredit loans to their customers and compute the cost of a Eurocredit bank loan.

Eurocredit loans are made by large multinational banks. Eurocredits typically have fixed maturities and variable, or floating, rates of interest. The loan rate is tied to a base interest rate (BR), such as LIBOR. The total rate charged on a Eurocredit is BR + X, where X is the lending margin, which consists of risk premiums (credit, country, and currency risks) and the lender's profit margin. The Citibank example in Section 21.5 and Learning by Doing Application 21.6 illustrate how loan costs are computed.

Summary of Key Equations

Equation	Description	Formula
21.1	Bid-ask spread	$\text{Bid-ask spread} = \dfrac{\text{Ask rate} - \text{Bid rate}}{\text{Ask rate}}$
21.2	Forward premium or discount	$\text{Forward premium (discount)} = \dfrac{\text{Forward rate} - \text{Spot rate}}{\text{Spot rate}} \times \dfrac{360}{n} \times 100$
21.3	Eurocredit bank loan pricing	$k = \text{BR} + \text{DRP} + \text{FXR} + \text{CR} + \text{GPMAR}$

Self-Study Problems

21.1 If a Volkswagen Passat costs \$26,350 in Baltimore and €21,675 in Frankfurt, what is the implied exchange rate between the U.S. dollar and the euro?

21.2 Calculate the indicated exchange rates given the following information.

Given	Compute
a. ¥101.3500/\$	\$/¥
b. \$1.8694/£	£/\$
c. \$0.9981/C\$	C\$/\$

21.3 Management of Digital, Inc., an electronic games manufacturer, is planning to purchase flash memory from one of two sources. Kyoto, Inc., quotes a price of ¥6,800 per gigabyte. The current exchange rate is ¥102.30/\$. Another Japanese manufacturer offers to supply the same flash memory at a price of €58.46 per gigabyte. The spot rate available is ¥141.60/€. Which is the cheaper source of flash memory for Digital?

21.4 Columbia Corp. has just made a sale to a British customer. The sale was for a total value of £135,000 and is to be paid 60 days from now. Columbia management is concerned that the British pound will depreciate against the U.S. dollar and plans to hedge this risk. The company's bank informs management that the spot rate is \$1.2461/£ and the 60-day forward rate is \$1.2283/£. If Columbia sells its pounds receivable at the forward rate, what is the dollar value of its receivables? If it does not enter into a forward contract and the spot rate 60 days later is \$1.2107/£, how much would the company lose by not hedging?

21.5 American Bancorp management is planning to make a \$3.5 million loan to a French firm. Currently, LIBOR is at 1.5 percent. American management considers a default risk premium of 1.15 percent, a foreign exchange rate risk premium of 0.35 percent, and a country risk premium of 0.13 percent to be appropriate for this loan. What is the loan rate charged by American Bancorp?

Solutions to Self-Study Problems

21.1 Cost of the car in Baltimore = \$26,350

Cost of the car in Frankfurt = €21,675

$$\text{Dollar to euro exchange rate} = \frac{\$26{,}350}{€21{,}675} = \$1.2157/€$$

21.2
a. 1/¥101.3500/\$ = \$0.00987/¥
b. 1/\$1.8694/£ = £0.5349/\$
c. 1/\$0.9981/C\$ = C\$1.00190/\$

21.3 Cost from Vendor 1:

Flash memory price quote = ¥6,800 per gigabyte

Spot rate for U.S. dollar = ¥102.30/\$

$$\text{Cost to Digital in dollars} = \frac{¥6{,}800}{¥102.30/\$} = \$66.47 \text{ per gigabyte}$$

Cost from Vendor 2:

Flash memory price quote = €58.46 per gigabyte

Spot rate for U.S. dollar = ¥141.60/€

To compute the dollar cost, we need to compute the cross rate between the euro and the dollar.

$$\frac{¥141.60/€}{¥102.30/\$} = \$1.3842/€$$

Cost to Digital in dollars = €58.46 × \$1.3842/€
= \$80.92 per gigabyte

The first vendor has the cheaper quote for Digital.

21.4 Amount received by Columbia by selling at the forward rate:

= £135,000 × \$1.2283/£ = \$165,820.50

Amount received by Columbia by selling at the spot rate 60 days later:

= £135,000 × \$1.2107/£ = \$163,444.50

Loss incurred by not hedging = \$165,820.50 − \$163,444.50 = \$2,376.00

21.5 The loan rate charged by American Bancorp is calculated as follows:

$$k = \text{BR} + \text{DRP} + \text{FXR} + \text{CR}$$
$$= 1.5\% + 1.15\% + 0.35\% + 0.13\%$$
$$= 3.13\%$$

WileyPLUS

Questions and Problems, Solution Walkthrough Videos, Learning by Doing Tutorials, and additional study tools and resources are available in WileyPLUS.

Discussion Questions

21.1 Royal Dutch Shell, an oil company, has headquarters in both the Netherlands and the United Kingdom. What type of firm is it?

21.2 International economic integration and technological changes in the last couple of decades have dramatically increased globalization across many industries. Explain how a biotech firm or a medical firm (for example, a hospital) can take advantage of these changes.

21.3 In the United States, managers are asked to focus on maximizing stockholder value. Is this consistent with the goals of managers in Germany and Japan?

21.4 A Canadian cooperative of wheat farmers sold wheat to a grain company in Russia. Under what circumstances will the Canadian farmers be exposed to foreign exchange rate risk? When will the Russian importer be facing foreign exchange rate risk?

21.5 Stardust, Inc., is an exporter of plumbing fixtures. About 30 percent of its sales are made in Canada. The sales department just found out that the Canadian dollar is at a premium against the U.S. dollar based on the 90-day forward rate, while the 180-day forward rate indicates that the Canadian dollar is at a forward discount. What is the likely impact of these rates on the company's sales to Canada?

21.6 Mello Wines, a California winery, grows its grapes locally, uses local labor, and sells its wines only in the United States. Can this firm be exposed to foreign exchange rate risk?

21.7 A U.S. firm owns a subsidiary in Belgium. What kind of foreign exchange rate risk does the U.S. firm face?

21.8 Ray Corp. is a U.S. electronics manufacturer with a production plant in Turkey. This morning, the Turkish government introduced a new law prohibiting the repatriation of any funds from the country for two years. What type of risk does Ray Corp. face?

27.9 Suppose GE issues bearer bonds in France denominated in British pounds. What type of bonds are these?

21.10 Give examples of U.S. banks facing different risks in international lending.

Questions and Problems

Excel *Excel templates and resources available in* **WileyPLUS**

Basic

21.1 Spot rate: Ryan wants to buy a pair of leather shoes at Harrods in London that costs £113.60. If the exchange rate is $1.6177/£, what is Ryan's cost in U.S. dollars?

21.2 Spot rate: Crescent Corporation's recent sale to a firm in Mexico produced revenues of 13,144,800 Mexican pesos. If the firm sold the pesos to its bank and was credited with $1,077,873.60, what was the spot rate at which the pesos were converted?

21.3 Spot rate: Given the following direct quotes, calculate the equivalent indirect quotes.

- **a.** $0.0844/Mexican peso
- **b.** £0.8513/€
- **c.** Rs54.64/C$

21.4 Spot rate: Convert the following indirect quotes to the appropriate American quotes.

- **a.** £0.6917/$
- **b.** ¥104.28/$
- **c.** SF 1.0769/$

21.5 Spot rate: Suppose a BMW 528i is priced at $68,750 in New York and €50,267 in Berlin. In which place is the car more expensive if the spot rate is $1.1077/€?

21.6 Forward rate: Explain the relation between each pair of currencies.

Spot Rate	Forward Rate
a. $1.655/£	$1.6001/£
b. ¥104.45/$	¥102.33/$
c. C$1.1121/$	C$1.0940/$

21.7 Forward rate: If the spot rate was $1.0413/C$ and the 90-day forward rate was $1.0507/C$, how much more (in U.S. dollars) would you receive by selling C$1,000,000 at the forward rate than at the spot rate?

21.8 Forward rate: Crane, Inc., sold equipment to an Irish firm and will receive €1,319,405 in 30 days. If the company entered a forward contract to sell at the 30-day forward rate of $1.0812/€, what is the dollar revenue received?

21.9 Forward rate: Brilliant Equipment purchased machinery from a Japanese firm and must make a payment of ¥313.25 million in 45 days. The bank quotes a forward rate of ¥103.01/$ to buy the required yen. What is the cost to Brilliant in U.S. dollars?

21.10 Forward rate: Triumph Autos has contracted with an Indian software firm for design software. The payment of 22,779,750 rupees (Rs) is due in 30 days. What is the cost in dollars if the 30-day forward rate is Rs64.39/$.

21.11 Forward rate: Use the data in Exhibit 21.5 to answer these questions:

- **a.** What is the three-month forward rate (in U.S. dollars) for Swiss francs? Is the Swiss franc selling for a premium or a discount?
- **b.** What is the three-month forward rate (in U.S. dollars) for the Japanese yen? Is the Japanese yen selling for a premium or a discount?
- **c.** Given the information above, what do you think will happen to the value of the Swiss franc and the Japanese yen relative to the U.S. dollar?

21.12 Bid-ask spread: Nova Scotia Bank offers quotes on the Canadian dollar as shown below. What is the bid-ask spread based on these quotes?

Bid	Ask
C$1.3081/$	C$1.3087/$

21.13 Bid-ask spread: A local community bank has requested foreign exchange quotes for the Swiss franc from Citibank. Citibank quotes a bid rate of $1.0934/SF and an ask rate of $1.0997/SF. What is the bid-ask spread?

21.14 Bid-ask spread: A foreign exchange dealer is willing to buy the Danish krone (DKr) at $0.1556/DKr and will sell it at a rate of $0.1563/DKr. What is the bid-ask spread on the Danish krone?

21.15 Cross rate: Given the following quotes, calculate the €/£ cross rate.

Bank of America	$ 1.663/£
JP Morgan Chase	$1.3914/€

21.16 Cross rate: Barclays Bank of London has offered the following exchange rate quotes: ¥134.64/£ and Korean won 13.8374/¥. What is the cross rate between the Korean won and the British pound?

21.17 Cross rate: Bremer Corporation observes that the Swiss franc (SF) is being quoted at €0.7660/SF, while the Swedish krona (SK) is quoted at €0.1114/SK. What is the SK/SF cross rate?

21.18 Country risk: Ford Motor Company maintains production facilities in many different countries including Brazil, Taiwan, and the United States. Given the data in Exhibit 21.6, which production plant is likely to face the greatest country risk? How does country risk affect a firm's capital budgeting decisions?

21.19 Foreign exchange rate risk: How is transaction exposure different from operating exposure?

21.20 International debt: What are Yankee bonds?

Intermediate

21.21 Forward premium: The spot rate on the London market is £0.7531/$, while the 90-day forward rate is £0.7602/$. What is the annualized forward premium or discount on the British pound?

21.22 Forward premium: Bank of America quoted the 180-day forward rate on the Swiss franc at $1.0407/SF. The spot rate was quoted at $1.0268/SF. What is the forward premium or discount on the Swiss franc?

21.23 Forward premium: The foreign exchange department at Tokyo's Daiwa Bank quoted the spot rate on the euro at €0.007269/¥. The 90-day forward rate is quoted at a premium of 5.42 percent on the euro. What is the 90-day forward rate?

21.24 Forward premium: The spot rate of the Australian dollar (A$) is A$1.1667/$. The Australian dollar is quoted at a 30-day forward premium of 4.90 percent against the U.S. dollar. What is the 30-day forward quote?

21.25 Bid-ask spread: The foreign exchange department of Bank of America has a bid quote on Canadian dollars (C$) of C$1.0800/$. If the bank typically tries to make a bid-ask spread of 0.5 percent on these foreign exchange transactions, what will the ask rate have to be?

21.26 Bid-ask spread: Banco Santiago wants to make a bid-ask spread of 0.65 percent on its foreign exchange transactions. If the ask rate on the Mexican peso (MP) is MP18.3092/$, what does the bid rate have to be?

21.27 Cross rate: Alcor Pharma just received revenues of $3,165,300 in Australian dollars (A$). Management has the following exchange rates: A$1.8010/£ and $1.5906/£. What is the U.S. dollar value of the company's revenues?

21.28 Cross rate: Flint Corp. recently purchased auto parts worth 17.5 million Mexican pesos (MP) on credit. Management needs to find out the U.S. dollar cost of the purchase. It has access to two quotes for Canadian dollars (C$): C$1.0174/$ and C$0.0820/MP. What did it cost Flint to purchase the auto parts?

21.29 Hedging: Tricolor Industries has purchased equipment from a Brazilian firm for a total cost of 272,500 Brazilian reals. The firm has to pay in 30 days. Citibank has given the firm a 30-day forward quote of $0.3102/real. Assume that on the day the payment is due, the spot rate is $0.3417/real. How much would Tricolor save by hedging with a forward contract?

21.30 Eurocredit loan: A Swiss sporting goods company borrows in yen in the Eurocredit market at a rate of 4.35 percent from Bank of America using a three-month rollover loan. Bank of America assigns a default risk premium of 2 percent on the loan, and the country risk is an additional 0.75 percent. The bank can borrow funds in the Euromarket at the three-month LIBOR rate of 0.40 percent. What is Bank of America's gross profit margin on this loan?

Advanced

21.31 Covington Industries just sold equipment to a Mexican firm. Payment of 11,315,000 Mexican pesos (MP) will be due to Covington in 30 days. Covington has the option of selling the pesos today at a 30-day forward rate of $0.05139/MP. If it waits 30 days to sell the pesos, the expected spot rate is $0.04881/MP. In dollars, how much better off is Covington by selling the pesos in the forward market?

21.32 Barrington Fertilizers, Inc., exports its specialized lawn care products to Canada. It made a sale worth C$1,150,000, with the payment due in 90 days. Barrington's banker gave it a forward quote of $0.9021/C$. By using the forward rate, the firm gained an additional $8,433.25 over what it would have gotten if it had sold the Canadian dollars in the spot market 90 days later. What was the spot rate at the time the payment was received?

21.33 Moon Rhee Auto Supply, a Korean supplier of parts to Kia Motors, is evaluating an opportunity to set up a plant in Alabama, where Kia Motors has an auto assembly plant for its SUVs. The cost of this plant will be $13.5 million. The current spot rate is 1,120.318 Korean won per U.S. dollar. The firm is expected to use this plant for the next five years and is expecting to generate the following cash flows:

	Year				
	1	2	3	4	5
Cash flows ($ millions)	$2.3	$4.2	$3.6	$5.8	$7.6
Expected exchange rate (Korean won/$)	1,105.231	1,115.632	1,146.155	1,120.221	1,110.670

The firm uses a discount rate of 9 percent for projects like this in the United States.

What is the NPV of this project? Should Moon Rhee Auto Supply take on this project?

21.34 The Boeing Company has two different debt issues, both maturing four years from now. The domestic bond issue pays semiannual coupons and has a coupon rate of 4.80 percent. The current price on the bond is $962.75. The Eurobond issue is priced at $964.33 and pays an annual coupon of 4.95 percent. What is the yield to maturity for each bond?

21.35 Caterpillar, Inc., management is trying to decide between selling a new bond issue in the U.S. or the Eurodollar bond market. In either market the bonds will be denominated in dollars and will have a three-year maturity. The domestic bonds will have a coupon rate of 4.1 percent and sell at a market price of $1,034.25. The Eurobonds will have a coupon rate of 4 percent, paid annually, and will sell at $1,029.76. Which bond issue will have the lower cost to the firm?

21.36 IBM's German unit is looking to borrow €7.5 million from Deutsche Bank. Deutsche Bank quotes a rate of three-month LIBOR plus 0.25 percent for the 90-day loan. Currently, the three-month LIBOR is 3.875 percent. What is IBM's interest cost on the loan in euros? If the exchange rate on the payoff date is €0.8164/$, what is the dollar cost of the loan?

21.37 Toyota is interested in borrowing $5 million for 90 days. Bank of America has quoted a rate that is 1.125 percent under the prime rate of 6.25 percent. Daiwa Bank is offering Toyota a rate that is 0.75 percent over the three-month LIBOR of 4.2 percent. Which is the better deal for Toyota, and what is the lower interest cost in dollars?

Sample Test Problems

21.1 What are six factors that cause international transactions to differ from domestic transactions?

21.2 If a Dell Studio laptop sells for $999 in Austin, Texas, and £689 in London, what is the implied exchange rate between the U.S. dollar and the euro?

21.3 A bank in India has offered a spot rate quote on Indian rupees (Rs) of Rs62.2905/$. The Indian rupee is quoted at a 30-day forward premium of 5.22 percent against the dollar. What is the 30-day forward quote?

21.4 Technocorp has purchased industrial parts from a German company for a total cost of €1,225,000. The firm has 30 days to pay. A bank has given Technocorp a 30-day forward quote of $1.1278/€. Assume that on the day the payment is due, the spot rate is $1.1468/€. How much would Technocorp have saved by hedging with a forward contract?

21.5 Tass Co., Ltd, a Japanese electrical parts producer, is considering building a plant in the United States. The cost of this plant will be $20 million, and the current spot exchange rate between the yen and the U.S. dollar is ¥101.8/$. Tass management expects to use this plant for the next five years and expects it to generate the following cash flows during this period:

	Year				
	1	2	3	4	5
Cash flows ($ millions)	$2.0	$3.6	$5.0	$6.8	$8.0
Expected exchange rate (¥/$)	¥101.5/$	¥100.4/$	¥98.6/$	¥95.9/$	¥92.5/$

If Tass uses a discount rate of 8 percent for projects in the United States, what is the NPV of this project? Should Tass Co. take on this project?

Appendix A

Future Value and Present Value Tables

APPENDIX TABLES

TABLE A.1 **Future Value Factors for $1 Compounded at i Percent Per Period for N Periods**

	i									
N	1%	2%	3%	4%	5%	6%	7%	8%	9%	10%
1	1.010	1.020	1.030	1.040	1.050	1.060	1.070	1.080	1.090	1.100
2	1.020	1.040	1.061	1.082	1.103	1.124	1.145	1.166	1.188	1.210
3	1.030	1.061	1.093	1.125	1.158	1.191	1.225	1.260	1.295	1.331
4	1.041	1.082	1.126	1.170	1.216	1.262	1.311	1.360	1.412	1.464
5	1.051	1.104	1.159	1.217	1.276	1.338	1.403	1.469	1.539	1.611
6	1.062	1.126	1.194	1.265	1.340	1.419	1.501	1.587	1.677	1.772
7	1.072	1.149	1.230	1.316	1.407	1.504	1.606	1.714	1.828	1.949
8	1.083	1.172	1.267	1.369	1.477	1.594	1.718	1.851	1.993	2.144
9	1.094	1.195	1.305	1.423	1.551	1.689	1.838	1.999	2.172	2.358
10	1.105	1.219	1.344	1.480	1.629	1.791	1.967	2.159	2.367	2.594
11	1.116	1.243	1.384	1.539	1.710	1.898	2.105	2.332	2.580	2.853
12	1.127	1.268	1.426	1.601	1.796	2.012	2.252	2.518	2.813	3.138
13	1.138	1.294	1.469	1.665	1.886	2.133	2.410	2.720	3.066	3.452
14	1.149	1.319	1.513	1.732	1.980	2.261	2.579	2.937	3.342	3.797
15	1.161	1.346	1.558	1.801	2.079	2.397	2.759	3.172	3.642	4.177
16	1.173	1.373	1.605	1.873	2.183	2.540	2.952	3.426	3.970	4.595
17	1.184	1.400	1.653	1.948	2.292	2.693	3.159	3.700	4.328	5.054
18	1.196	1.428	1.702	2.026	2.407	2.854	3.380	3.996	4.717	5.560
19	1.208	1.457	1.754	2.107	2.527	3.026	3.617	4.316	5.142	6.116
20	1.220	1.486	1.806	2.191	2.653	3.207	3.870	4.661	5.604	6.727
21	1.232	1.516	1.860	2.279	2.786	3.400	4.141	5.034	6.109	7.400
22	1.245	1.546	1.916	2.370	2.925	3.604	4.430	5.437	6.659	8.140
23	1.257	1.577	1.974	2.465	3.072	3.820	4.741	5.871	7.258	8.954
24	1.270	1.608	2.033	2.563	3.225	4.049	5.072	6.341	7.911	9.850
25	1.282	1.641	2.094	2.666	3.386	4.292	5.427	6.848	8.623	10.835
30	1.348	1.811	2.427	3.243	4.322	5.743	7.612	10.063	13.268	17.449
35	1.417	2.000	2.814	3.946	5.516	7.686	10.677	14.785	20.414	28.102
40	1.489	2.208	3.262	4.801	7.040	10.286	14.974	21.725	31.409	45.259
45	1.565	2.438	3.782	5.841	8.985	13.765	21.002	31.920	48.327	72.890
50	1.645	2.692	4.384	7.107	11.467	18.420	29.457	46.902	74.358	117.390

i									
11%	12%	13%	14%	15%	20%	25%	30%	35%	40%
1.110	1.120	1.130	1.140	1.150	1.200	1.250	1.300	1.350	1.400
1.232	1.254	1.277	1.300	1.323	1.440	1.563	1.690	1.823	1.960
1.368	1.405	1.443	1.482	1.521	1.728	1.953	2.197	2.460	2.744
1.518	1.574	1.530	1.689	1.749	2.074	2.441	2.856	3.322	3.842
1.685	1.762	1.842	1.925	2.011	2.488	3.052	3.713	4.484	5.378
1.870	1.974	2.082	2.195	2.313	2.986	3.815	4.827	6.053	7.530
2.076	2.211	2.353	2.502	2.660	3.583	4.768	6.275	8.172	10.541
2.305	2.476	2.658	2.853	3.059	4.300	5.960	8.157	11.032	14.758
2.558	2.773	3.004	3.252	3.518	5.160	7.451	10.604	14.894	20.661
2.839	3.106	3.395	3.707	4.046	6.192	9.313	13.786	20.107	28.925
3.152	3.479	3.836	4.226	4.652	7.430	11.642	17.922	27.144	40.496
3.498	3.896	4.335	4.818	5.350	8.916	14.552	23.298	36.644	56.694
3.883	4.363	4.898	5.492	6.153	10.699	18.190	30.288	49.470	79.371
4.310	4.887	5.535	6.261	7.076	12.839	22.737	39.374	66.784	111.120
4.785	5.474	6.254	7.138	8.137	15.407	28.422	51.186	90.158	155.560
5.311	6.130	7.067	8.137	9.358	18.488	35.527	66.542	121.710	217.790
5.895	6.866	7.986	9.276	10.761	22.186	44.409	86.504	164.310	304.910
6.544	7.690	9.024	10.575	12.375	26.623	55.511	112.450	221.820	426.870
7.263	8.613	10.197	12.056	14.232	31.948	69.389	146.190	299.460	597.630
8.062	9.646	11.523	13.743	16.367	38.338	86.736	190.050	404.270	836.680
8.949	10.804	13.021	15.668	18.822	46.005	108.420	247.060	545.760	1171.300
9.934	12.100	14.714	17.861	21.645	55.206	135.520	321.180	716.780	1639.800
10.026	13.552	16.627	20.362	24.891	66.247	169.400	417.530	994.660	2297.800
12.239	15.179	18.788	23.212	28.625	79.497	211.750	542.800	1342.700	3214.200
13.585	17.000	21.231	26.462	32.919	95.396	264.690	705.640	1812.700	4499.800
22.892	29.960	39.116	50.950	66.212	237.370	807.790	2619.900	8128.500	24201.000
38.575	52.800	72.069	98.100	133.170	590.660	2465.100	9727.800	36448.000	130161.000
65.001	93.051	132.782	188.880	267.860	1469.700	7523.100	36118.000	163437.000	700037.000
109.530	163.980	244.641	363.670	538.760	3657.200	22958.000	134106.000	732857.000	
184.560	289.000	450.735	700.230	1083.600	9100.400	70064.000	497929.000		

TABLE A.2 **Present Value Factors for $1 Received at the End of N Periods, Discounted at *i* Percent Per Period**

	i									
N	1%	2%	3%	4%	5%	6%	7%	8%	9%	10%
1	.990	.980	.971	.962	.952	.943	.935	.926	.917	.909
2	.980	.961	.943	.925	.907	.890	.873	.857	.842	.826
3	.971	.942	.915	.889	.864	.840	.816	.794	.772	.751
4	.961	.924	.888	.855	.823	.792	.763	.735	.708	.683
5	.951	.906	.863	.822	.784	.747	.713	.681	.650	.621
6	.942	.888	.837	.790	.746	.705	.666	.630	.596	.564
7	.932	.871	.813	.760	.711	.665	.623	.583	.547	.513
8	.923	.853	.789	.731	.677	.627	.582	.540	.502	.467
9	.914	.837	.766	.703	.645	.592	.544	.500	.460	.424
10	.905	.820	.744	.676	.614	.558	.508	.463	.422	.386
11	.896	.804	.722	.650	.585	.527	.475	.429	.388	.350
12	.887	.788	.701	.625	.557	.497	.444	.397	.356	.319
13	.879	.773	.681	.601	.530	.469	.415	.368	.326	.290
14	.870	.758	.661	.577	.505	.442	.388	.340	.299	.263
15	.861	.743	.642	.555	.481	.417	.362	.315	.275	.239
16	.853	.728	.623	.534	.458	.394	.339	.292	.252	.218
17	.844	.714	.605	.513	.436	.371	.317	.270	.231	.198
18	.836	.700	.587	.494	.416	.350	.296	.250	.212	.180
19	.828	.686	.570	.475	.396	.331	.277	.232	.194	.164
20	.820	.673	.554	.456	.377	.312	.258	.215	.178	.149
21	.811	.660	.538	.439	.359	.294	.242	.199	.164	.135
22	.803	.647	.522	.422	.342	.278	.226	.184	.150	.123
23	.795	.634	.507	.406	.326	.262	.211	.170	.133	.112
24	.788	.622	.492	.390	.310	.247	.197	.158	.126	.102
25	.780	.610	.478	.375	.295	.233	.184	.146	.116	.092
30	.742	.552	.412	.308	.231	.174	.131	.099	.075	.057
35	.706	.500	.355	.253	.181	.130	.094	.068	.049	.036
40	.672	.453	.307	.208	.142	.097	.067	.046	.032	.022
45	.639	.410	.264	.171	.111	.073	.048	.031	.021	.014
50	.608	.372	.228	.141	.087	.054	.034	.021	.013	.009

					i				
11%	12%	13%	14%	15%	20%	25%	30%	35%	40%
.901	.893	.885	.877	.870	.833	.800	.769	.741	.714
.812	.797	.783	.769	.756	.694	.640	.592	.449	.510
.731	.712	.693	.675	.658	.579	.512	.455	.406	.364
.659	.636	.613	.592	.572	.482	.410	.350	.301	.260
.593	.567	.543	.519	.497	.402	.328	.269	.223	.186
.535	.507	.480	.456	.432	.335	.262	.207	.165	.133
.482	.452	.425	.400	.376	.279	.210	.159	.122	.095
.434	.404	.376	.351	.327	.233	.168	.123	.091	.068
.391	.361	.333	.308	.284	.194	.134	.094	.067	.048
.352	.322	.295	.270	.247	.162	.107	.073	.050	.035
.317	.287	.261	.237	.215	.135	.086	.056	.037	.025
.286	.257	.231	.208	.187	.112	.069	.043	.027	.018
.258	.229	.204	.182	.163	.093	.055	.033	.020	.013
.232	.205	.181	.160	.141	.078	.044	.025	.015	.009
.209	.183	.160	.140	.123	.065	.035	.020	.011	.006
.188	.163	.141	.123	.107	.054	.028	.015	.008	.005
.170	.146	.125	.108	.093	.045	.023	.012	.006	.003
.153	.130	.111	.095	.081	.038	.018	.009	.005	.002
.138	.116	.098	.083	.070	.031	.014	.007	.003	.002
.124	.104	.087	.073	.061	.026	.012	.005	.002	.001
.112	.093	.077	.064	.053	.022	.009	.004	.002	.001
.101	.083	.068	.056	.046	.018	.007	.003	.001	.001
.091	.074	.060	.049	.040	.015	.006	.002	.001	
.082	.066	.053	.043	.035	.013	.005	.002	.001	
.074	.059	.047	.038	.030	.010	.004	.001	.001	
.044	.033	.026	.020	.015	.004	.001			
.026	.019	.014	.010	.008	.002				
.015	.011	.008	.005	.004	.001				
.009	.006	.004	.003	.002					
.005	.003	.002	.001	.001					

TABLE A.3 **Future Value of Annuity Factors for $1 Received Per Period for Each of N Periods, Compounded at *i* Percent Per Period**

	i									
N	1%	2%	3%	4%	5%	6%	7%	8%	9%	10%
1	1.000	1.000	1.000	1.000	1.000	1.000	1.000	1.000	1.000	1.000
2	2.010	2.020	2.030	2.040	2.050	2.060	2.070	2.080	2.090	2.100
3	3.030	3.060	3.091	3.122	3.152	3.184	3.215	3.246	3.278	3.310
4	4.060	4.122	4.184	4.246	4.310	4.375	4.440	4.506	4.573	4.641
5	5.101	5.204	5.309	5.416	5.526	5.637	5.751	5.867	5.985	6.105
6	6.152	6.308	6.468	6.633	6.802	6.975	7.153	7.336	7.523	7.716
7	7.214	7.434	7.662	7.898	8.142	8.394	8.654	8.923	9.200	9.487
8	8.286	8.583	8.892	9.214	9.549	10.897	10.260	10.637	11.028	11.436
9	9.369	9.755	10.159	10.583	11.027	11.491	11.978	12.488	13.021	13.579
10	10.462	10.950	11.464	12.006	12.578	13.181	13.816	14.487	15.193	15.937
11	11.567	12.169	12.808	13.486	14.207	14.972	15.784	16.645	17.560	18.531
12	12.683	13.412	14.192	15.026	15.917	16.870	17.888	18.977	20.141	21.384
13	13.809	14.680	15.618	16.627	17.713	18.882	20.141	21.495	22.953	24.523
14	14.947	15.971	17.086	18.292	19.599	21.015	22.550	24.215	26.019	27.975
15	16.097	17.291	18.599	20.024	21.579	23.276	25.129	27.152	29.361	31.722
16	17.258	18.639	20.157	21.825	23.657	25.673	27.888	30.324	33.003	35.950
17	18.430	20.012	21.762	23.698	25.840	28.213	30.840	33.750	36.974	40.545
18	19.615	21.412	23.414	25.645	28.132	30.906	33.999	37.450	41.301	45.599
19	20.811	22.841	25.117	27.671	30.539	33.760	37.379	41.446	46.018	51.159
20	22.019	24.297	26.870	29.778	33.066	36.786	40.995	45.762	51.160	57.275
21	23.239	25.783	28.676	31.969	35.719	39.993	44.865	50.423	56.765	64.002
22	24.472	27.299	30.537	34.248	38.505	43.392	49.006	55.457	62.873	71.403
23	25.716	28.845	32.453	36.618	41.430	46.996	53.436	60.893	69.532	79.543
24	26.973	30.422	34.426	39.083	44.502	50.816	58.177	66.765	76.790	88.497
25	28.243	32.030	36.459	41.646	47.727	54.865	63.249	73.106	84.701	98.347
30	34.785	40.568	47.575	56.085	66.439	79.058	94.461	113.280	136.300	164.490
35	41.660	49.994	60.462	73.652	90.320	111.430	138.230	172.310	215.710	271.020
40	48.886	60.402	75.401	95.026	120.800	154.760	199.630	259.050	337.880	442.590
45	56.481	71.893	92.720	121.020	159.700	212.740	285.740	386.500	525.850	718.900
50	64.463	84.579	112.790	152.660	209.340	290.330	406.520	573.770	815.080	1163.900

				i					
11%	12%	13%	14%	15%	20%	25%	30%	35%	40%
1.000	1.000	1.000	1.000	1.000	1.000	1.000	1.000	1.000	1.000
2.110	2.120	2.130	2.140	2.150	2.200	2.250	2.300	2.350	2.400
3.342	3.374	3.407	3.440	3.472	3.640	3.813	3.990	4.172	4.360
4.710	4.779	4.850	4.921	4.993	5.368	5.766	6.187	6.633	7.104
6.228	6.353	6.480	6.610	6.742	7.442	8.207	9.043	9.954	10.196
7.913	8.115	8.232	8.536	8.754	9.930	11.259	12.756	14.438	16.324
9.783	10.089	10.405	10.730	11.067	12.916	15.073	17.583	20.492	23.853
11.859	12.300	12.757	13.233	13.727	16.499	19.842	23.858	28.664	34.395
14.164	14.776	15.416	16.085	16.786	20.799	25.802	32.015	39.696	49.153
16.722	17.549	18.420	19.337	20.304	25.959	33.253	42.619	54.590	69.814
19.561	20.655	21.814	23.045	24.349	32.150	42.566	56.405	74.697	98.739
22.713	24.133	25.650	27.271	29.002	39.581	54.208	74.327	101.840	139.230
26.212	28.029	29.985	32.089	34.352	48.497	68.760	97.625	138.480	195.920
30.095	32.393	34.883	37.581	40.505	59.196	86.949	127.910	187.950	275.300
34.405	37.280	40.417	43.842	47.580	72.035	109.680	167.280	254.730	386.420
39.190	42.753	46.672	50.980	55.717	87.442	138.100	218.470	344.890	541.980
44.501	48.884	53.739	59.118	65.075	105.930	173.630	285.010	466.610	759.780
50.396	55.750	61.725	68.394	75.836	128.110	218.040	371.510	630.920	1064.600
56.939	63.440	70.749	78.969	88.212	154.740	273.550	483.970	852.740	1491.500
64.203	72.052	80.947	91.025	102.440	186.680	342.940	630.160	1152.200	2089.200
72.265	81.699	92.470	104.760	118.810	225.020	429.680	820.210	1556.400	2925.800
81.214	92.503	105.491	120.430	137.630	271.030	538.100	1067.200	2102.200	4097.200
91.148	104.600	120.205	138.290	159.270	326.230	673.620	1388.400	2839.000	5737.100
102.170	118.150	136.831	158.650	184.160	392.480	843.030	1806.000	3833.700	8032.900
114.410	133.330	155.620	181.870	212.790	471.980	1054.700	2348.800	5176.500	11247.000
199.020	241.330	293.199	356.780	434.740	1181.800	3227.100	8729.900	23221.000	60501.000
341.590	431.660	546.681	693.570	881.170	2948.300	9856.700	32422.000	104136.000	325400.000
581.820	767.090	1013.704	1342.000	1779.000	7343.800	30088.000	120392.000	466960.000	
986.630	1358.200	1874.165	2490.500	3585.100	18281.000	91831.000	447019.000		
1668.700	2400.000	3459.507	4994.500	7217.700	45497.000	280255.000			

TABLE A.4 **Present Value of Annuity Factors for $1 Received Per Period for Each of N Periods, Discounted at *i* Percent Per Period**

	i									
N	1%	2%	3%	4%	5%	6%	7%	8%	9%	10%
1	0.990	0.980	0.971	0.962	0.952	0.943	0.935	0.926	0.917	0.909
2	1.970	1.942	1.913	1.886	1.859	1.833	1.808	1.783	1.759	1.736
3	2.941	2.884	2.829	2.775	2.723	2.673	2.624	2.577	2.531	2.487
4	3.902	3.808	3.717	3.630	3.546	3.465	3.387	3.312	3.240	3.170
5	4.853	4.713	4.580	4.452	4.329	4.212	4.100	3.993	3.890	3.791
6	5.795	5.601	5.417	5.242	5.076	4.917	4.767	4.623	4.486	4.355
7	6.728	6.472	6.230	6.002	5.786	5.582	5.389	5.206	5.033	4.868
8	7.652	7.325	7.020	6.733	6.463	6.210	5.971	5.747	5.535	5.335
9	8.566	8.162	7.786	7.435	7.108	6.802	6.515	6.247	5.995	5.759
10	9.471	8.983	8.530	8.111	7.722	7.360	7.024	6.710	6.418	6.145
11	10.368	9.787	9.253	8.760	8.306	7.887	7.499	7.139	6.805	6.495
12	11.255	10.575	9.954	9.385	8.863	8.384	7.943	7.536	7.161	6.814
13	12.134	11.348	10.635	9.986	9.394	8.853	8.358	7.904	7.487	7.103
14	13.004	12.106	11.296	10.563	9.899	9.295	8.745	8.244	7.786	7.367
15	13.865	12.849	11.938	11.118	10.380	9.712	9.108	8.559	8.061	7.606
16	14.718	13.578	12.561	11.652	10.838	10.106	9.447	8.851	8.313	7.824
17	15.562	14.292	13.166	12.166	11.274	10.477	9.763	9.122	8.544	8.022
18	16.398	14.992	13.754	12.659	11.690	10.828	10.059	9.372	8.756	8.201
19	17.226	15.678	14.324	13.134	12.085	11.158	10.336	9.604	8.950	8.365
20	18.046	16.351	14.877	13.590	12.462	11.470	10.594	9.818	9.129	8.514
21	18.857	17.011	15.415	14.029	12.821	11.764	10.836	10.017	9.292	8.649
22	19.660	17.658	15.937	14.451	13.163	12.042	11.061	10.201	9.442	8.772
23	20.456	18.292	16.444	14.857	13.489	12.303	11.272	10.371	9.580	8.883
24	21.243	18.914	16.936	15.247	13.799	12.550	11.469	10.529	9.707	8.985
25	22.023	19.523	17.413	15.622	14.094	12.783	11.654	10.675	9.823	9.077
30	25.808	22.396	19.600	17.292	15.372	13.765	12.409	11.258	10.274	9.427
35	29.409	24.999	21.487	18.665	16.374	14.498	12.948	11.655	10.567	9.644
40	32.835	27.355	23.115	19.793	17.159	15.046	13.332	11.925	10.757	9.779
45	36.095	29.490	24.519	20.720	17.774	15.456	13.606	12.108	10.881	9.863
50	39.196	31.424	25.730	21.482	18.256	15.762	13.801	12.233	10.962	9.915

i									
11%	**12%**	**13%**	**14%**	**15%**	**20%**	**25%**	**30%**	**35%**	**40%**
0.901	0.893	0.885	0.877	0.870	0.833	0.800	0.769	0.741	0.714
1.713	1.690	1.668	1.647	1.626	1.528	1.440	1.361	1.289	1.224
2.444	2.402	2.361	2.322	2.283	2.106	1.952	1.816	1.696	1.589
3.102	3.037	2.974	2.914	2.855	2.589	2.362	2.166	1.997	1.849
3.696	3.605	3.517	3.433	3.352	2.991	2.689	2.436	2.220	2.035
4.231	4.111	3.998	3.889	3.784	3.326	2.951	2.643	2.385	2.168
4.712	4.564	4.423	4.288	4.160	3.605	3.161	2.802	2.508	2.263
5.146	4.968	4.799	4.639	4.487	3.837	3.329	2.925	2.598	2.331
5.537	5.328	5.132	4.946	4.772	4.031	3.463	3.019	2.665	2.379
5.889	5.650	5.426	5.216	5.019	4.192	3.571	3.092	2.715	2.414
6.207	5.938	5.687	5.453	5.234	4.327	3.656	3.147	2.752	2.438
6.492	6.194	5.918	5.660	5.421	4.439	3.725	3.190	2.779	2.456
6.750	6.424	6.122	5.842	5.583	4.533	3.780	3.223	2.799	2.469
6.982	6.628	6.302	6.002	5.724	4.611	3.824	3.249	2.814	2.478
7.191	6.811	6.462	6.142	5.847	4.675	3.859	3.268	2.825	2.484
7.379	6.974	6.604	6.265	5.954	4.730	3.887	3.283	2.834	2.489
7.549	7.120	6.729	6.373	6.047	4.775	3.910	3.295	2.840	2.492
7.702	7.250	6.840	6.467	6.128	4.812	3.928	3.304	2.844	2.494
7.839	7.366	6.938	6.550	6.198	4.843	3.942	3.311	2.848	2.496
7.963	7.469	7.025	6.623	6.259	4.870	3.954	3.316	2.850	2.497
8.075	7.562	7.102	6.687	6.312	4.891	3.963	3.320	2.852	2.498
8.176	7.654	7.170	6.743	6.359	4.909	3.970	3.323	2.853	2.498
8.266	7.718	7.230	6.792	6.399	4.925	3.976	3.325	2.854	2.499
8.348	7.784	7.283	6.835	6.434	4.937	3.981	3.327	2.855	2.499
8.422	7.843	7.330	6.873	6.464	4.948	3.985	3.329	2.856	2.499
8.694	8.055	7.496	7.003	6.566	4.979	3.995	3.332	2.857	2.500
8.855	8.176	7.586	7.070	6.617	4.992	3.998	3.333	2.857	2.500
8.951	8.244	7.634	7.105	6.642	4.997	3.999	3.333	2.857	2.500
9.008	8.283	7.661	7.123	6.654	4.999	4.000	3.333	2.857	2.500
9.042	8.304	7.675	7.133	6.661	4.999	4.000	3.333	2.857	2.500

Solutions to Odd Problems

Chapter 1

1.1. The two basic sources of funds for all businesses are debt and equity.

1.3. A profitable firm is able to generate enough cash flows from productive assets to cover its operating expenses, payments to creditors, and taxes. Unprofitable firms fail to do this, and therefore they may be forced to declare bankruptcy.

1.5. A firm should undertake a capital project only if the value of its future cash flows exceeds the cost of the project. For example, a financial manager would not invest $10,000,000 in a new production line if the future cash flows from that line are expected to produce only $9,000,000 in future cash flows. That would be like throwing $1,000,000 away.

1.7. The financial manager must make working capital decisions regarding the levels of cash and inventory to hold, the terms of granting credit (account receivables), and the firm's policy on paying accounts payable.

1.9. *Advantages*: easiest business type to start; least regulated; owners have full control; all income is taxed as personal income. *Disadvantages*: unlimited liability of proprietor; equity capital is limited to proprietor's wealth; difficult to transfer ownership.

1.11. The owners of a corporation are its stockholders, and the evidence of their ownership is represented by shares of stock.

1.13. Double taxation occurs when earnings are taxed twice. The owners of a C-corporation are subject to double taxation—first at the corporate level when the firm's earnings are taxed and then again at a personal level when the dividends they receive are taxed.

1.15. The board of directors of a corporation is responsible for serving the interests of stockholders in managing the corporation. It is possible that the interests of managers may deviate from those of their stockholders. The board's objective is to ensure that managers are acting in the best interests of the stockholders. Board duties include hiring and firing the CEO, setting CEO pay, and monitoring the investment decisions of managers.

1.17. Drawbacks include: It is difficult to determine what is meant by profits; it does not address the size and timing of cash flows (it does not account for the time value of money); and it ignores the uncertainty (risk) of cash flows.

1.19. Factors that affect the stock price include: The characteristics of the firm, the general state of the economy, economic shocks, the business environment, expected cash flows from the firm, and current stock market conditions.

1.21. If a firm's stock price falls substantially below its maximum potential price, it might attract corporate raiders. These persons look for firms that are fundamentally sound but poorly managed, so that they can buy the firm, turn it around, and sell it for a profit.

1.23. A lack of business ethics can lead to corruption, which, in turn, creates inefficiencies in an economy, inhibits the growth of capital markets, and slows the rate of overall economic growth. For example, the Russian economy has had a relatively difficult time attracting foreign investment since the fall of the Soviet Union due, in part, to corruption in the business community and local and national governments. Lower foreign investment has led to slower overall economic growth than the country might otherwise have enjoyed.

1.25. An information asymmetry exists when one party to a business transaction possesses information that is not available to the other parties in the transaction. If the parties with less information understand their relative disadvantage, they are likely to pay lower prices for the goods or services they purchase, or charge higher prices for the goods and services that they sell. This will provide the parties that have more information with greater incentives to disclose information that is not available to the other parties.

Chapter 2

2.1. The role of the financial system is to gather money from businesses and individuals who have surplus funds and channel funds to those who need them. The financial system consists of financial markets and financial institutions.

2.3. Saver-lenders are those who have more money than they need right now. The principal saver-lenders in the economy are households. Borrower-spenders are those who need the money saver-lenders are offering. The main borrower-spenders in the economy are businesses and the federal government.

2.5. Your security is marketable, but not liquid. Liquidity implies that when a security is sold, its value will be preserved; marketability does not.

2.7. Trader, Inc., is more likely to go public because of its larger size. Though the cost of SEC registration and compliance is very high, larger firms can offset these costs by the lower funding cost in public markets. Smaller companies find the cost prohibitive for the dollar amount of securities they are likely to sell.

2.9. **a.** secondary; **b.** secondary; **c.** primary

2.11. **a.** $300,000; **b.** 3.05%; **c.** $9,850,000

2.13. Financial intermediaries allow smaller companies to access the financial markets. They do this by converting securities with one set of characteristics into securities with another set of characteristics that meets the needs of smaller companies. By repackaging securities, they are able to meet the needs of different clients.

2.15. Money markets are markets where short-term debt instruments with maturities of less than one year are bought and sold. Capital markets are markets where equity securities and debt instruments with maturities of more than one year are sold.

2.17. Treasury bills, bank negotiable CDs, and commercial paper.

2.19. The strong-form of market efficiency states that all information is reflected in the security's price. In other words, there is no private or inside information that, if released, would potentially change the price. The semistrong-form of market efficiency holds that all public information available to investors is reflected in the security's price. Therefore, insiders with access to private information could potentially profit from trading on this information before it becomes public. Finally, the weak-form of market efficiency holds that there is both public and private information that is not reflected in the security's price and having access to it can enable an investor to earn abnormal profits.

2.21. Yes. The last sentence in the Problem 2.20 problem statement suggests why this might happen. If, on the same day of the announcement, some very bad news about the future prospects for Zippy became public or if the market went down substantially, Zippy's stock price might also have gone down despite the positive sales and earnings announcement.

2.23. Public markets are organized financial markets where the public buys and sells securities through their stockbrokers or other brokers or dealers. The SEC regulates public securities markets in the United States. In contrast, private markets involve direct transactions between two parties. These transactions lack SEC regulation.

2.25. The real rate of interest measures the return earned on savings, and it represents the cost of borrowing to finance capital goods. The real rate of interest is determined by the interaction between firms that invest in capital projects and the rate of return they expect to earn on those investments, and individuals' time preference for consumption. The real rate of interest is determined when the desired level of savings equals the desired level of investments in the economy.

2.27. The Fisher equation is an equation that shows how the expected annualized change in prices (ΔP_e) is related to the nominal and real rates of interest. It is used to determine the nominal rate that protects the buying power of a lender's money from changes in inflation. It is also used to determine the interest rate, by subtracting ΔP_e from the nominal interest rate, that would exist in the absence of inflation.

2.29. Yes. The CD will be worth $1,067.50 at the end of the year, and the price of the trip will be $1,066.

Chapter 3

3.1. The balance sheet for Elkridge Sporting Goods is:

Assets	Book Value
Cash and marketable securities	$ 25,135
Accounts receivable	43,758
Inventories	167,112
Total current assets	$236,005
Net fixed assets	325,422
Other assets	13,125
Total assets	$574,552
Liabilities and Stockholders Equity	**Book Value**
Accounts payables	$ 67,855
Notes payables	36,454
Total current liabilities	$104,309
Long-term debt	223,125
Common stock	150,000
Retained earnings	97,118
Total liabilities and stockholders' equity	$574,552

The firm's retained earnings were $97,118.

3.3. FIFO makes sense during times of rising prices (inflationary times) because it allows the firm to eliminate the lower-priced inventory first, which results in higher profit margins.

3.5. $6,655,610

3.7. The company's net income is $242,401.25. The income statement is as follows:

Oakland Mills Company Income Statement For the period ended on March 31, 2017	
	Amount
Revenues	$1,450,000.00
COGS	812,500.00
EBITDA	$ 637,500.00
Depreciation	175,000.00
EBIT	$ 462,500.00
Interest	89,575.00
EBT	$ 372,925.00
Taxes (35%)	130,523.75
Net income	**$ 242,401.25**

3.9. –$132,085

3.11. Noncash expenses are expenses identified on income statement that did not result in cash flows. Depreciation and amortization are examples of such expenses. Other noncash expenses include deferred taxes, deferred wages, and prepaid expenses.

3.13. $284,115

3.15. The **average tax rate** is the total taxes paid divided by taxable income. The **marginal tax rate** is the tax rate that is paid on the last dollar of income earned, or the rate that will be paid on the next dollar earned.

3.17. $502,838

3.19. $153,470

3.21. $137,263

3.23. $1,804,546

3.25. $620,878

3.27. $218,364; 34%; 34%

3.29. $715,720

3.31. $198,152

3.33. CFNWC = –$16,467

CFLTA = $291,401

Chapter 4

4.1. The quick ratio provides a better measure of liquidity because it includes only the most liquid of the current assets.

4.3. $1,627,579

4.5. 2.873 times; 127.0 days

4.7. 2.65; 0.623; 29.9%

4.9. 29.93%

4.11. **a.** Trademark is not doing as well as its peers. The total asset and inventory turnover ratios indicate that the firm either needs to increase its sales relative to its level of total assets and inventory or reduce its total assets and inventory relative to its level of sales. In addition, the lower quick ratio indicates that Trademark has less liquidity. The higher DSO indicates that accounts receivable are relatively high.

b. Average industry ratios serve as benchmarks that management can use to assess a firm's performance. While no two firms are identical in any industry, the average ratios across an industry are generally good target ratios for a firm.

4.13. 1.34

4.15. $3,825,000

4.17. $843,863

4.19. 1.27; 2.27

4.21. 51.2%; 19.1%; 12.6%

4.23. 0.41; 36.02%; 18.32%; 25.84%

4.25. 34.4 times

4.27. $6,473,600; 5.7%

4.29. $10,226,559; $88,236,057; 81.6%

4.31. Current ratio = 0.77; quick ratio = 0.57; gross margin = 51.2%; net profit margin = 12.6%; debt ratio = 0.70; long-term debt to equity = 0.73; interest coverage = 20.6; ROA = 11.4%; ROE = 37.5%

4.33. Net profit margin = 12.61%; total asset turnover = 0.90; equity multiplier = 3.30; return on equity = 12.61% × 0.90 × 3.30 = 37.5%

4.35. $292,756.63

4.37. Current ratio = 1.81; quick ratio = 1.19; inventory turnover = 3.50; accounts receivable turnover = 5.16; DSO = 70.76; total asset turnover = 1.23; fixed asset turnover = 7.15; total debt ratio = 0.63; debt-to-equity ratio = 1.72; equity multiplier = 2.72; times interest earned = 17.56; cash coverage = 25.94, gross profit margin = 0.36; net profit margin = 0.08; ROA = 0.10; ROE = 0.27

Chapter 5

5.1. $53,973.12

5.3. $6,712.35

5.5. $3,289.69

5.7. **a.** $154,154.24; **b.** $154,637.37; **c.** $154,874.91; **d.** $154,883.03

5.9. $16,108.92

5.11. $6,507.05

5.13. $734.83

5.15. 7.42%; you should borrow from the bank.

5.17. 92,016 copies; 101,218 copies

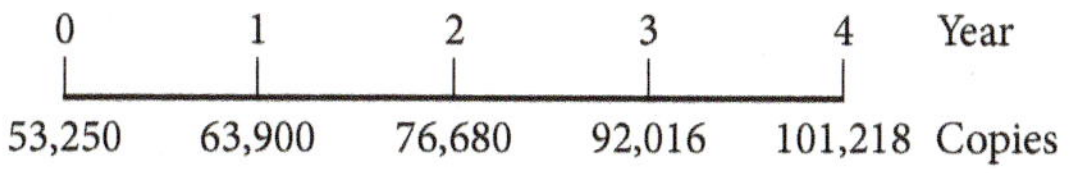

5.19. 1,045 members

5.21. **a.** $2,246.57; **b.** $2,073.16; **c.** $2,946.96; **d.** $2,949.88

5.23. 11 years

5.25. 3.8 years

5.27. 10.42%

5.29. The present value of $2,100 is $1,869. Since $1,869 is greater than $1,820, Caroline should wait two years unless she needs the money sooner.

5.31. 13.96%

5.33. Option 1 (mutual fund): $26,803.77; Option 2 (brother's business): $23,579.48; you should choose the mutual fund.

5.35. Option A: $6,922,647; Option B: $6,983,894; Option C: $7,083,096; Jared should choose Option C.

5.37. 13.14%

Chapter 6

6.1. $74,472.48

6.3. $3,185.40

6.5. $5,747.40

6.7. $5,652.06

6.9. $247,609.95

6.11. $1,361,642.36

6.13. $4,221.07

6.15. **a.** $15,000; **b.** $6,000; **c.** $10,000

6.17. 7%

6.19. $6,144,462.11

6.21. $1,496,377.71

6.23. $1,193,831.54

6.25. $7,000,000

6.27. $2,958,662.16

6.29. **a.** $17,857.14; **b.** $114,533.97; **c.** $4,250.00

6.31. **b.** has the highest EAR (8.57%)

6.33. $20,495.15

6.35. $3,971.94

6.37. 5%

6.39. **a.** $1,906,071.48; **b.** $2,272,554.25; **c.** $212,889.63; **d.** $181,804.34

6.41. $2,048.27

Chapter 7

7.1. A holding period return is the total return over some investment or "holding" period. It consists of a capital appreciation component and an income component. A holding period return reflects past performance. An expected return is the probability-weighted average of the possible returns from an investment. It describes a possible return (or even a return that may not be possible) for a yet-to-occur investment period.

7.3. Expected salary: $66,000; standard deviation: $78,000

7.5. Stock B

7.7. 0.1535

7.9. Risk that cannot be diversified away is *systematic risk*. It is the only type of risk that exists in a diversified portfolio, and it is the only type of risk that is rewarded in asset markets.

7.11. Since the beta of any asset is the slope of the line of best fit for the plot of the asset's return against the market return, we can use that relation to help us understand the beta of a T-bill. If we purchased a T-bill five years ago and held that T-bill through each of the last 60 months, then the return for each of those 60 months would be exactly the same. Therefore, the vertical axis coordinates of each of the monthly returns would have the same value, and the slope (beta) of the line of best fit would be zero. The meaning of a beta of zero means that our T-bill has no systematic risk. That makes sense given that we know that a T-bill has no risk at all since it is a riskless asset.

7.13. The CAPM is a model that describes the relation between systematic risk and the expected return. The model tells us that the expected return on an asset with no systematic risk equals the risk-free rate. As systematic risk increases, the expected return increases linearly with beta. The CAPM is written as $E(R_i) = R_{rf} + \beta_i[E(R_m) - R_{rf}]$.

7.15. $1,250

7.17. 0.145; 0.162

7.19. 0.125; 0.168

7.21. $\sigma_{1,2} = 0.12, 0.1225; \sigma_{1,2} = 0, 0.0625; \sigma_{1,2} = -0.12, 0.0025$

7.23. Your portfolio contains no unsystematic risk, but it does contain systematic risk. Therefore, the market should compensate the holder of this portfolio for the systematic risk that the investor bears. A risk-free security has no risk, and therefore requires no compensation for risk bearing. The expected return of your portfolio should therefore be greater than the return from the risk-free security.

7.25. The statement is false. Even if we could afford such a portfolio and thus completely diversify our portfolio, we would only be eliminating unsystematic risk. The systematic risk associated with the portfolio would remain. Otherwise, the expected rate of return on the market portfolio would be equal to the risk-free rate of return. We know that to be a false statement.

7.27. 0.0891

7.29. 0.185; 0.165

7.31. 0.19

7.33. If we assume that all investors will seek to be compensated (generate returns) for the level of risk that they are bearing, then we can see that undiversified investors will require a greater return for a given investment than diversified investors will. Given that, we can see that diversified investors will be willing to pay a greater price for an asset than undiversified investors. Therefore, the diversified investor is the marginal investor whose purchase will determine the equilibrium price, and therefore the equilibrium return for an asset.

7.35. The first security is underpriced, and the second is overpriced. With the underpriced security, investors will purchase the security until its price increases to the point where it is no longer underpriced. With the overpriced security, investors will sell the security and drive its price down.

7.37. $\sigma_{RA} = 0.06; \beta_B = 2.25; \rho_{RC,M} = 1.00; \rho_{RM,M} = 1.00; \beta_M = 1.00;$
$\rho_{RT\text{-bill},M} = 0; \beta_{T\text{-bill}} = 0$

$E(R_A) = 0.125; E(R_B) = 0.1625; E(R_C) = 0.075$

A comparison of the expected returns that are given in the problem statement, with the returns that CAPM predicts (which are presented above), indicates that you should buy stocks A and C and avoid stock B.

Chapter 8

8.1. $1,147.20

8.3. $1,008.15

8.5. $975.91

8.7. $359.38

8.9. 6.58%

8.11. 9.52%

8.13. $1,000

8.15. $912.61; 1,370 bonds

8.17. $1,079.23

8.19. 12.45%

8.21. 7.33%; 7.36%

8.23. 11.49% (EAY = 11.81%)

8.25. 8.65% (EAY = 8.84%)

8.27. **a.** $924.75; **b.** 9.67% (EAY = 9.90%)

8.29. **a.** $904.76; **b.** $1,086.46, $832.53
c. Bond prices decrease when interest rates go up and increase when interest rates go down.
d. $1,063.42, $866.65

8.31. **a.** $25
b. The stock price would have to increase by two standard deviations (2 × $5 = $10) for the price to increase to $25 and for conversion to become attractive to the investors. From Chapter 7 we know that 95% of possible outcomes fall within 1.96 standard deviations of the mean (average) value in a normal distribution. This means that there is approximately a 5 percent chance that the stock price will move up or down by $10 or more. Since the normal distribution is symmetric, this means that there is only a 2.5 percent chance that Zippy's stock price will increase enough for it to become attractive for the investors to exercise the conversion option in the next year.

Chapter 9

9.1. A stock market index is an index used to measure the performance of a stock market. These indexes reflect the value of stocks in a particular market, such as the NYSE or the NASDAQ, or across markets, and they increase and decrease as the values of the stocks go up and down. Examples of stock market indexes include the Dow Jones Industrial Average, the New York Stock Exchange Index, the Standard & Poor's 500 Index, and the NASDAQ Composite Index.

9.3. National Association of Securities Dealers Automated Quotation system. NASDAQ is one of the world's largest electronic markets, listing over three thousand companies.

9.5. $14.24

9.7. $27.38

9.9. $8.50

9.11. $31.12

9.13. 12.15%

9.15. $56.90

9.17. $2.46

9.19. $21.07

9.21. $5.15

9.23. $23.35

9.25. $32.34

9.27. $25.95

9.29. $2.15

9.31. $73.94

9.33. **a.** $34.45
b. No, she should not buy more shares. This stock is overpriced with the stock selling at a higher price than it is worth. She should sell her shares.

9.35. **a.** $6.37; **b.** $62.03; **c.** $48.24

9.37. **a.** $2.41; **b.** $37.86; **c.** $20.67
d. No, the length of the holding period has no bearing on today's stock price.

Chapter 10

10.1. $62,337

10.3. Yes; NPV = $134,986.

10.5. Blanda should invest in System 2. The NPV of System 1 is $22,969.42, and the NPV of System 2 is $36,001.43.

10.7. 2.87 years

10.9. 3.45 years

10.11. 33.8%

10.13. The profitability index is computed as the ratio of NPV plus initial investment divided by initial investment. In the capital rationing process, we can calculate the profitability index for each potential investment and choose the projects with the largest indexes until we run out of capital. This follows the basic principle that we need to choose the set of projects that creates the greatest value given the limited capital available.

10.15. −$351,223

10.17. System 200 should be chosen. NPV = $75,758 for System 200 and NPV = −$56,667 for System 100.

10.19. The discounted payback periods for the projects are: Project A = 4+ years; Project B = 3+ years. Since the firm's acceptance criteria is three years, neither project will be accepted.

10.21. 4.19 years

10.23. 17.4%

10.25. System 1 IRR = 83.93%; System 2 IRR 50.07%. System 1 NPV = $22,969.42; System 2 NPV = $36,001.43. System 1 delivers a higher IRR because it requires a lower initial investment and the cost is recovered the first year. Thus, even with lower cash inflows in the years after start-up, System 1 is able to deliver a higher return on the initial investment. System 2 has a higher initial investment but delivers a higher net cash flow for the firm.

10.27. **a.** 6.97%; **b.** 13.3%; **c.** 14.2%

10.29. Compute the profitability index for each of the projects. PI_A = 1.50; PI_B = 1.64; PI_C = 1.56; PI_D = 1.57. With $30,000, you should invest in B, D, and C. The total cost is $27,000, and the total NPV is $16,000.

10.31. NPV of Project 1 = −$668,283 (reject); NPV of Project 2 = $375,375 (accept)

10.33. At 14.8%, only Project 2 will be accepted (NPV = $118,353). At 13.6%, Projects 2 and 3 will be accepted (NPVs of $141,295 and $1,491, respectively).

10.35. Project 1 should be accepted. Its NPV = $186,683 and its IRR = 20.1%. Project 2 has NPV = −$76,796 and IRR = 12.4%.

10.37. Project 1 = 16.1%; Project 2 = 13.7%; Project 3 = 10.9%

10.39. **a.** 5.45 years; **b.** 4.1%; **c.** −$2,043,927; **d.** 3.1%

10.41. **a.** A = $147,891, B = $166,553; **b.** A = 27.2%, B = 26.1%; **c.** Both should be accepted under the NPV and IRR decision criteria; **d.** Both projects will be accepted. They are independent and both have a positive NPV.

10.43. NPV_x = $2,650.78; NPV_y = $2,189.06; PI_x = 1.1325; PI_y = 1.1095. Both methods rank Project X over Project Y. However, both projects should be accepted under the NPV criteria. Therefore, both should be accepted if they are independent and sufficient resources are available. If the projects are mutually exclusive, the project with the higher NPV or PI, which in this case is Project X, should be chosen.

10.45. **c.** Discounted payback period is 1.01 years longer than the payback period.

10.47. **d.** IRR = 28.79%

Chapter 11

11.1. The main reason is that accounting earnings generally differ from free cash flows, and free cash flows are what stockholders care about.

11.3. Subtract depreciation from EBITDA, multiply by (1 – tax rate), and add back depreciation. This enables us to account for the fact that depreciation reduces the taxes that must be paid.

11.5. The average tax rate is the total tax paid divided by total earnings, while the marginal tax rate is the rate paid on the last dollar earned. Use the marginal tax rate when calculating incremental after-tax free cash flows.

11.7. Variable costs vary directly with the number of units of output. Fixed costs do not vary with the number of units.

11.9. $9,009.60

11.11. $1,370

11.13. The equivalent annual cost (EAC) is the annual payment from an annuity that has a life equal to that of a project and that has the same NPV as the project. EAC values for two projects with different lives can be directly compared to determine which project has a lower cost per year.

11.15. The alternative to using the Equivalent Annual Cost concept is to assume that each of the projects is repeated the number of times necessary for the number of years they produce cash flows to be equal. In this problem you would assume that the five-year project was repeated six times and the six-year project was repeated five times. This effectively makes each of these projects a 30-year project. You then can use standard NPV analysis to choose between the two.

11.17. You should invest in Bond A because it pays a higher nominal interest rate.

11.19. The cash flow related to working capital at the beginning of the project is: $10,000 + $30,000 + $25,000 − $5,000 = $60,000.

The present value of the cash flow related to working capital at the end of the project is: $\$60{,}000/(1 + 0.12)^{10} = \$19{,}318.39$.

11.21. NPV = $718,056.94

11.23. You should buy Model A because it has a lower EAC (−$2,866.47 vs. −$2,978.44).

11.25. Bell Mountain should buy the system in Year 3.

11.27. The optimal time to replace the old car is at the end of Year 2.

11.29. −$4,558.70

11.31. P = $107.74 per shovel

11.33. $10,410,000

11.35. Biotech should sell its bacteria colony at the beginning of the third year (or at the end of the second year).

11.37. Renovating the old line is less costly.

Chapter 12

12.1. Variable costs vary with the number of units of output. Fixed costs do not vary with the number of units.

12.3. Yes. EBIT is $375,000 with the new technology and $250,000 with the old.

12.5. 1.392

12.7. The degree of accounting operating leverage can be used to tell us how much a firm's EBIT will change for a given change in revenue. For example, if the firm's accounting operating leverage is 3, then a 15 percent increase in revenue will result in a 45 percent (15 percent × 3 = 45 percent) increase in EBIT for the firm.

12.9. We must know the difference between unit price and unit variable cost (the per-unit contribution) in order to determine how many units must be sold to pay a firm's fixed costs.

12.11. The economic break-even point.

12.13. Since depreciation and amortization is a noncash item, the manufacturing firm is more likely to have a discrepancy between its FCF and EBIT.

12.15. Specialty should produce and sell the bulbs because EBIT for the additional bulbs is positive (EBIT = $1,000).

12.17. 15.9%

12.19. 340,000 candles

12.21. While the business may be expected to have an accounting operating loss, our focus should be on the expected operating cash flow. A business can produce an accounting operating loss at the same time it produces positive operating cash flow income because the depreciation and amortization charges are not subtracted in the calculation of operating cash flow. Since depreciation and amortization are noncash charges, the project could still be viable if it does not have negative operating cash.

12.23. $4,651.67

12.25. Scenario analysis is a more realistic method because it accounts for the fact that changes in key variables are often related and that they therefore can change at the same time.

12.27. A 10 percent increase in the price of a bottle will increase FCF from $38,000 to $46,400.

12.29. 1.67

12.31. A 10 percent increase in revenue will result in a 20 percent increase in EBITDA.

12.33. The firm with the higher fixed cost structure should have the lower variable cost per unit, assuming there is a trade-off. A lower variable cost per unit would result in a higher contribution margin.

12.35. No. The project NPV = −$298,110.03.

Chapter 13

13.1. $98 million

13.3. When we calculate the cost of debt for a U.S. firm, we must take into account the tax subsidy given in the United States for interest payments on debt. For every dollar the firm pays in interest, the firm's tax bill will decline by ($1 × t), where t is the firm's marginal tax rate. We adjust for this tax benefit by multiplying the pretax cost of debt by $(1 - t)$. This calculation gives us the after-tax cost of debt. We use the after-tax cost of debt for cost of capital calculations such as when we calculate the WACC.

13.5. 16%

13.7. 10%

13.9. 15.8%

13.11. 9.4%

13.13. The owners of all of the securities that have been sold to finance a firm, collectively, own all of the cash flows that the assets of the firm generate. The value of these securities must equal the value of these cash flows and, therefore, the value of the firm.

13.15. $1,000

13.17. 7.7%

13.19. 4.63%, 6.27%

13.21.
$$P_{cs} = \frac{D_1}{1 + k_{cs}} + \frac{D_1(1 + g_1)}{(1 + k_{cs})^2} + \frac{D_1(1 + g_1)^2}{(1 + k_{cs})^3} + \frac{D_1(1 + g_1)^3}{(1 + k_{cs})^4} + \frac{D_1(1 + g_1)^4}{(1 + k_{cs})^5} + \frac{D_1(1 + g_1)^4(1 + g_2)}{(k_{cs} - g_2)(1 + k_{cs})^5}$$

It is easy to see that in order to solve for a cost of capital, k_{cs}, you must have a good idea of what g_1 and g_2 are. If the estimates for those growth rates are poor, then the calculation for k_{cs}, will also yield a poor estimate.

13.23. Markets adjust the cost of capital according to the level of systematic risk in a project. Therefore, the project with the greatest level of systematic risk will have the greatest positive impact on the cost of capital for the firm, even if it has the lowest level of unsystematic risk.

13.25. Since Imaginary will be financing the project with the same mix of capital that the firm is currently utilizing for its projects, it will have satisfied the condition concerning financing mix. In addition, the new project will have the same degree of systematic risk (in addition to being in the same general line of business) as the average project in the firm. Therefore, Imaginary management can use the firm's 9.26 percent cost of capital to evaluate this project.

13.27. While the growth in dividends has been extremely constant for MacroSwift over the last 15 years, it is appropriate to assume a constant-growth rate only if that same rate is expected to continue in the future. Two factors will act to alter that growth in the future. MacroSwift will have competition for its current products in the near future, and that could alter the firm's growth rate. In addition, the firm is expanding its product line into an area that will probably not yield the same level of growth. It is, therefore, unlikely that MacroSwift's dividend growth rate will continue at a 3 percent annual rate. This suggests that you should consider something other than constant growth in your modeling.

13.29. 12.35%

13.31. 9.78%

13.33. Expected returns are impounded in market prices and reflect the information that investors have about the values of securities. Since the market adjusts security prices to reflect the expected returns for investing in securities, ignoring that information by using book values is the same as ignoring what the market deems to be an appropriate cost of capital for the firm.

13.35. Since, collectively, the debt and equity holders are entitled to receive all of the cash flows that the assets of the firm are expected to produce, the systematic risk of the cash flows that they are entitled to receive must be the same as the systematic risk of the cash flows the assets are expected to produce.

13.37. 7.60%

Chapter 14

14.1. Wolfgang's cash conversion cycle is 69 days. Since this is less than the industry average of 75 days, the firm is more efficient than the average firm in the industry in managing its working capital.

14.3. −3 days; the amount of time Devon takes to turn over its inventory and to collect its receivables is less than the amount of time Devon takes to pay its suppliers.

14.5. 73 days

14.7. Risks associated with a restrictive current asset management strategy arise from exposure to either financial or operating shortage costs. Financial costs are associated with a sudden and unforeseen loss of liquidity that makes it difficult for a firm to repay its current liabilities. In this situation, a firm may be forced to rely on costly external emergency borrowing, or if such funds can't be secured, the firm may default on its loan obligations. Operating shortage costs result from lost production or sales that occur if the firm does not have sufficient raw material or finished goods. Operating shortage costs can also occur if a firm's credit policies are too restrictive and discourage a significant number of potential customers from purchasing its products.

14.9. 34.72%

14.11. $626.91

14.13. 11.6%

14.15. 6.48%

14.17. 89.3 days, 198.2 days

14.19. $267,222

14.21. $47,361

14.23. $287,671

14.25. 16 orders

14.27. 8.775%

14.29. 5.54%

14.31. $9,324

14.33. 14.9%, 28.2 days. Lincoln's effective days' sales outstanding is approximately seven days less than the industry average.

14.35. $7,500; 37.1%

14.37. **a.** Increase, Increase; **b.** Increase, Increase; **c.** No change, Decrease; **d.** Increase, Increase; **e.** Increase, No change

14.39. **a.** 67.9 days; **b.** 80.6 days; **c.** 105.7 days; **d.** 148.5 days; **e.** 42.8 days

14.41. **a.** $30,000; **b.** 63.2%; **c.** 85.06%

Chapter 15

15.1. As noted in Footnote 1, business plans (and their contents) are discussed in detail in Chapter 18. As explained in this chapter, in general terms the business plan describes (1) what you want the business to become, (2) why consumers will find your product(s) attractive (the value proposition), (3) how you are going to accomplish your objectives, and (4) what resources you will need.

15.3. Sell the business to a strategic or financial buyer, take it public, or remain a private company and sell shares privately.

15.5. Examine comparable companies and see what prices their share are trading for; A discounted cash flow analysis.

15.7. Debt issues that are complex in nature or that are issued in uncertain times are often sold through negotiated sales. This allows the underwriter to better control the conditions of the sale and to better explain the firm to potential investors, thereby keeping issue costs relatively low.

15.9. $24,308,528

15.11. The steps in a general cash offering are: (1) Decide what type of security to issue and the amount to be raised, (2) Obtain approvals, (3) File registration statement, (4) Set offer price, and (5) Closing.

15.13. As the size of a securities issue increases, the total flotation costs per security (or dollar raised) decline.

15.15. Nalco is probably better off choosing to sell debt in the public market, given its size.

15.17. The borrowing cost will increase to 9.43%.

15.19. You can fund the project in stages. This will allow you to review the project's profitability before you commit to further financing. You can also require the entrepreneurs to invest some of their own capital, which will tie them to the project by making it more costly for them to abandon it. Finally, you can syndicate the deal. Doing this spreads the risk among multiple venture capital firms and provides corroboration regarding the reasonableness of the investment decision.

15.21. $1,220,000

15.23. $68,700,000; $15,300,000

15.25. **a.** $130,000,000; **b.** $120,500,000; **c.** $9,500,000

15.27. 6.52%; If the economy is supposed to improve (deteriorate), interest rates are likely to go up (down) in the near future. This could make the cost of borrowing more (less) expensive.

Chapter 16

16.1. The assumption that there are no information or transaction costs.

16.3. The value of the firm is independent of the proportion of debt and equity utilized to finance the firm under the Modigliani and Miller's Proposition 1 assumptions.

16.5. 20%

16.7. 18%

16.9. $150,000,000

16.11. 10.5%

16.13. 42%

16.15. Information or transaction costs would reduce the total value that is available for the debt holders and the stockholders and, therefore, the value of the firm.

16.17. $530,000,000

16.19. Lower productivity due to lower morale and job hunting and higher recruiting costs are among the costs of financial distress that the firm will incur.

16.21. The managers expect to lose their jobs in one year whether they take on the project and work hard or not. They have no incentive to take on the project. Declining it makes the shortfall to the debt holders greater, and any possible return to the stockholders smaller, than it would be if the firm followed the rule of always accepting positive NPV projects.

16.23. Given the information in the question we would expect that an increase in the marginal tax rate will increase the value of the tax shield and increase the amount of debt in the optimal capital structure.

16.25. That internally generated equity is utilized first as a source of financing does not mean that the internally generated funds are cheaper than debt. Internally generated funds belong to stockholders and are therefore really equity financing, which we know to be more expensive than debt.

16.27. Under these conditions, the value of the firm will increase with the amount of debt financing that is used due to the interest tax shields. The conservative approach will not maximize firm value.

16.29. $810,000,000

16.31. If enough debt is used to finance this firm, then the challenges of ensuring that the firm produces enough cash to make interest and principal payments would provide managers of the firm with incentives to work on new positive NPV projects rather than spend their Fridays in Cancun.

16.33. $3,000,000; $250,000; k_{cs} and WACC before restructuring both equal 10%; after restructuring $k_{cs} = 11.33\%$ and WACC = 9.23%.

Chapter 17

17.1. This reduction could indicate that management expects a lower level of profitability in the future (negative signal). It could also indicate that Poseidon requires additional money to invest in positive NPV projects that were not previously available (positive signal).

17.3. The proper chronological order is: (1) Declaration date, (2) Ex-dividend date, (3) Record date, (4) Payment date.

17.5. Any cash paid to stockholders through a dividend reduces the value of the assets that remain in the firm to secure the creditors' claims.

17.7. $9.75

17.9. With a stock repurchase, stockholders can decide whether to participate. It they choose to participate, there is a tax advantage for the stockholders, relative to the tax treatment of a dividend. A dividend payment forces the stockholders to receive cash and recognize associated tax implications. Also, with a stock repurchase the stockholder only pays tax on the gain from the sale. With a dividend the stockholder pays tax on the full amount of the dividend.

17.11. Relaxing the no transaction cost assumption increases the cost of producing a homemade dividend (or the cost of undoing unwanted dividends). This makes a firm's dividend policy a relevant factor when valuing its shares.

17.13. The value of dividend-paying stocks should decrease relative to the value of non-dividend-paying stocks because the after-tax cash flows from the dividend-paying stocks will go down.

17.15. Reducing a dividend may indicate that a firm does not have sufficient cash, which would be a negative signal. On the other hand, when a high-growth firm increases its dividend, the increase may be interpreted as indicating that the firm has fewer positive NPV projects and that its growth rate will decline, which is also a negative signal.

17.17. You would probably prefer that the firm initiate a stock repurchase. You can opt not to sell your shares to the firm but still participate in the increased value of the firm's shares since your pro-rata share of the expected future cash flows generated by the firm will increase. You would probably not prefer a dividend payment since you would then be required to receive the cash if you were the registered owner of the shares on the record date.

17.19. Assuming that managers are acting to maximize firm value, any time they are repurchasing shares they must be doing so because they believe that the firm's shares are undervalued and that repurchasing shares is a positive NPV project. In repurchasing the shares, management is utilizing inside information to take advantage of the sellers of those shares in a way that benefits the remaining stockholders of the firm. Consequently, management is not doing something in the interest of all stockholders. Stockholders who sell will be selling at a lower price than they could have realized had they held their shares until the inside information became public.

17.21. (1) Open-market purchase—the firm simply purchases the shares in the market, (2) Tender offer—the firm makes an offer through a general announcement, offering to buy up to a certain number of shares from anyone who wishes to sell, (3) Targeted stock repurchase—the firm directly negotiates with an individual stockholder to buy shares from that individual. Exhibit 17.3 presents data on stock price reactions.

17.23. The purpose of setting the ex-dividend date before the record date is to allow time for a sale of securities to be completed and recorded before the record date. Since the settlement period was reduced from five days to two days, we should also have seen the number of days between the ex-dividend date and the record date reduced, which we did.

17.25. Paying a dividend reduces the value of equity and thereby increases the debt-to-total-capital ratio in a levered firm.

17.27. $15

17.29. $72,500

17.31. $150,000

17.33. Ultimately, the best decision will depend on a comparison of the advantages and disadvantages of a special dividend and a share repurchase, in view of the characteristics of your company and your objectives. If speed is a primary concern, a special dividend is likely to be your only choice. On the other hand, if speed is not a primary concern, a share repurchase might be more appropriate.

Chapter 18

18.1. The forms of organizations discussed in this chapter include: Sole Proprietorship, Partnership (General Partnership and Limited Partnership), Corporation (S-Corporation and C-Corporation), and Limited Liability Partnership (LLP) and Company (LLC). The access to capital for each is summarized in Exhibit 18.1.

18.3. With sole proprietors and general partners, there is the possibility that personal assets can be taken to satisfy claims on the business. In contrast, the liabilities of investors in LLPs, LLCs, and corporations are generally limited to the money that they have invested in the business.

18.5. Equity capital can be obtained from friends and family, venture capitalists, or other potential investors that you know. Debt capital can be obtained from bank loans, cash advances on credit cards, or loans from other individual investors or other businesses. Once the company is large enough, equity and debt financing can be obtained in the public markets.

18.7. The replacement cost of a business is the cost of replacing the assets of the business in their present form.

18.9. Excess cash is a nonoperating asset because this cash can be distributed to stockholders without affecting the operations of the business and therefore the value of the expected free cash flows from the firm. It makes sense to add back the value of excess cash because it represents value over and above that which the operating assets of the business are expected to produce.

18.11. Probably not. The private shares are relatively illiquid and the value would be discounted for this lack of liquidity in the market.

18.13. A Limited Liability Company (LLC) is a hybrid of a C-corporation and a partnership. It has the limited liability of a C-corporation with the tax advantages of a partnership.

18.15. Break-even point for TV option = 1,250 units per year. Break-even point for flyer option = 150 units per year. Choose the flyer option.

18.17. $1,573.64 million

18.19. The enterprise value/EBITDA multiple is more appropriate since the capital structures of Johnson and Billy's differ considerably.

18.21. $12,675,000

18.23. It is not adequate. $9,400 of additional capital will be required up-front. $89,400 is needed to maintain a $5,000 cash balance. The monthly break-even points for the firm are: 4,333.3 bottles in the initial month and 1,833.3 bottles in the following months.

18.25. See the key elements of a business plan in Section 18.2.

18.27. The company has a short history, high investments, no sales, and highly uncertain future cash flows. The cost approach is not valid for such a young biochemical company; it is hard to value the company using multiples because of the lack of sales and negative earnings, and because of a lack of comparable public companies. The transaction approach is also likely to be difficult to apply due to the difficulty of finding a comparable transaction. Despite the many uncertainties, we should try to estimate the future free cash flows and the risks associated with these cash flows and use the FCFF approach to value it.

18.29. 7.115%

18.31. V_E = $354,849; Your friend should receive 9.88 percent of the equity.

Chapter 19

19.1. The strategic plan is the blueprint for a company's management that drives all decision making within the firm across all areas of its operations.

19.3. The financing plan identifies external funding needed, sources of funding, target capital structure, and payout policy.

19.5. The important elements of financial modeling are sales and cost forecasts, investment decisions, financing requirements and choices, and pro-forma statements.

19.7. $52,686; 55%

19.9. Net sales $1,710; Costs $399; Net income $1,311

19.11. The capital intensity ratio measures the amount of assets needed to generate $1 in sales. It tells us how much a firm must invest in assets to support a given level of sales.

19.13. 68.02%

19.15. 6.8%

19.17. Exhibit 19.11 gives you the plot.

19.19. The electric utilities industry and the aluminum processing industry are examples of capital-intensive industries.

19.21. 34.25%

19.23. 8.2%

19.25. 9.9%

19.27. 5.2%

19.29. $1,008,381; 44.27%

19.31. 9.6%

19.33. 27.4%

19.35.

Morgan Construction Company—Pro Forma Balance Sheet for June 30, 2018							
	2017		2018		2017		2018
Cash	$ 3,349,239	1.25	$ 4,186,548	Accounts payable	$ 9,041,679	1.25	$11,302,098
Accounts receivable	5,830,754	1.25	7,288,442	Notes payable	4,857,496	1.25	6,071,869
Inventories	22,267,674	1.25	27,834,593	Total current liabilities	$13,899,174		$17,373,968
Total current assets	$31,447,666		$39,309,583				
				Long-term debt	29,371,406		37,164,258
Net fixed assets	43,362,482	1.25	54,203,102	Common stock	19,987,500	1.25	24,984,375
Other assets	1,748,482	1.25	2,186,133	Retained earnings	12,940,974	1.25	16,176,217
Total assets	$76,559,054		$95,698,818	Total liabilities & equity	$76,559,054		$95,698,818

Morgan Construction Company Pro Forma Income Statement for the Fiscal Year Ended June 30, 2018			
	2017		2018
Net sales	$193,212,500	1.25	$241,515,625
Costs	145,265,625	1.25	181,582,031
EBITDA	$ 47,946,875		$ 59,933,594
Depreciation	23,318,750	1.25	29,148,438
EBIT	$ 24,628,125		$ 30,785,156
Interest	11,935,869	1.25	14,919,836
EBT	$ 12,692,256		$ 15,865,320
Taxes (35%)	4,442,290	1.25	5,552,862
Net income	$ 8,249,967		$ 10,312,458

19.37. 3.37%; 6.26%

19.39. **a.** 8.16%; **b.** 13.86%; **c.** $4,777,333;
d. See the following financial statements.

Munson Communications Company—Pro Forma Balance Sheet for June 30, 2018							
	2017		2018		2017		2018
Cash	$ 1,728,639	1.20	$ 2,074,367	Accounts payable	4,666,673	1.20	$ 5,600,007
Accounts receivable	3,009,421	1.20	3,611,305	Notes payable	2,507,094	1.20	3,008,513
Inventories	11,492,993	1.20	13,791,592	Total current liabilities	$ 7,173,767		$ 8,608,521
Total current assets	$16,231,054		$19,477,264				
				Long-term debt	13,345,242		16,687,821
Net fixed assets	22,380,635	1.20	26,856,763	Common stock	10,165,235		10,165,235
Other assets	1,748,906	1.20	2,098,688	Retained earnings	9,676,351		12,971,137
Total assets	$40,360,595		$48,432,714	Total liabilities & equity	$40,360,595		$48,432,714

Munson Communications Company Pro Forma Income Statement for the Fiscal Year Ended June 30, 2018			
	2017		2018
Net sales	$79,722,581	1.20	$95,667,097
Costs	59,358,499	1.20	71,230,199
EBITDA	$20,364,082		$24,436,898
Depreciation	7,318,750	1.20	8,782,500
EBIT	$13,045,332		$15,654,398
Interest	3,658,477	1.20	4,390,172
EBT	$ 9,386,855		$11,264,226
Taxes (35%)	3,285,399	1.20	3,942,479
Net income	$ 6,101,456		$ 7,321,747

Chapter 20

20.1. An option is the right to buy or sell an asset at a prespecified price on or before a prespecified date.

20.3. $0; $15

20.5. The value of a call option increases as: (1) Current value of the underlying asset increases; (2) Exercise price decreases; (3) Volatility of the value of the underlying asset increases; (4) Time until the expiration of the option increases; or (5) Risk-free rate of interest increases.

20.7. The seller of a put option hopes that the value of the underlying asset will remain at or above the exercise price, thereby making it worth-less to the owner (buyer) of the option.

20.9. No. The losses to the seller of a call option are only limited by the extent to which the value of the underlying asset can increase. There is no other limit.

20.11. Your option is worth very slightly more than zero. There is little chance that the stock price will move above $100 by tomorrow, but the chance is not zero, so the option still has some value.

20.13. The underlying asset of a financial option is a financial asset, such as a share of stock. The underlying asset of a real option is a nonfinancial (real) asset, such as a project.

20.15. The payoff functions for lenders and stockholders are like those for different types of options. Agency costs arise because these payoff functions are different from each other.

20.17. The purchaser of a callable bond is simultaneously buying a straight (noncallable) bond and selling the issuer a call option on that bond. The total value of the callable bond equals the value of the straight bond minus the value of the option. It would be lower than the value for a straight bond.

20.19. Because option buyers pay option sellers an amount that compensates sellers for the risks that they will lose money on the option. The amount that the seller receives is known as the option premium.

20.21. $7.01

20.23. $1.18

20.25. A golden parachute can help reduce agency problems by reducing the potential cost to a manager of making decisions that stockholders want, but that could harm the manager. For example, having a golden parachute can provide a manager with stronger incentives to invest in risky projects or approve a merger that could result in the loss of his or her job.

20.27. The payoffs from these two portfolios are identical.

20.29. **a.** Both the debt and equity are worth $5 million before the investment; **b.** $6.5 million; **c.** $3.5 million

20.31. Call option #1 has a lower strike price and costs less. In a situation like this you can earn arbitrage profits by purchasing the less expensive option (#1) and selling the more expensive option (#2).

20.33. It mitigates this concern because the lenders will benefit through the call option from increased volatility in the value of the firm. How much a conversion option mitigates this concern depends on the specific characteristics of the option.

Chapter 21

21.1. $183.77

21.3. **a.** MP11.8483/$; **b.** €1.1747/£; **c.** C$0.0183/Rs

21.5. It is more expensive in New York. The cost in Berlin is $55,680.76.

21.7. $9,400

21.9. $3,040,967

21.11. **a.** There is a forward premium of (0.9960 – 0.9899)/0.9899 = 0.62% on the Swiss franc.

b. There is a forward premium of (0.008754 – 0.00872)/0.00872 = 0.39% on the Japanese yen.

c. We can expect both the Swiss franc and the Japanese yen to appreciate relative to the U.S. dollar in the next three months.

21.13. 0.573%

21.15. €1.1952/£

21.17. SK6.8761/SF

21.19. Transaction exposure is related to foreign exchange risk faced by firms that are expecting revenues in foreign currency or have expenses in foreign currency that relate to transactions they have already entered into. As the exchange rate changes, the home currency value of these revenues or expenses changes. If exchange rate changes are more permanent in nature and modify the way a firm does its business, then we say that a firm is facing operating exposure.

21.21. 3.77%

21.23. €0.007171/¥

21.25. C$1.0854 is the ask rate that provides a 0.5 percent spread.

21.27. $4,657,593

21.29. $8,583.75

21.31. $29,192.70

21.33. 4,426,787 million won; yes, the project should be accepted.

21.35. 2.92%; 2.95%; The domestic bond issue will have the lowest cost to the firm.

21.37. $64,062.50; $61,875; Daiwa's offer has the lower interest cost.

Glossary

Accounting operating profit (EBIT) break-even point the number of units that must be sold for accounting operating profit to equal $0

accounting rate of return (ARR) a rate of return on a capital project based on average net income divided by average book value over the project's life; also called the *book value rate of return*

adjusted book value the sum of the fair market values of the individual assets in a business

agency conflicts conflicts of interest between a principal and an agent

agency costs the costs arising from conflicts of interest between a principal and an agent—for example, between a firm's owners and its managers

amortization schedule a table that shows the loan balance at the beginning and end of each period, the payment made during that period, and how much of that payment represents interest and how much represents repayment of principal

amortizing loan a loan for which each loan payment contains repayment of some principal and a payment of interest that is based on the remaining principal to be repaid

angels (angel investors) wealthy individuals who invest their own money in new ventures

annual percentage rate (APR) the simple interest rate charged per period multiplied by the number of periods per year

annuity a series of equally spaced and level cash flows extending over a finite number of periods

annuity due an annuity in which payments are made at the beginning of each period

arbitrage buying and selling assets in a way that takes advantage of price discrepancies and yields a profit greater than that which would be expected based solely on the systematic risk of the individual investments

arithmetic average return the return earned in an average period

asset substitution problem the incentive that stockholders in a financially leveraged firm have to substitute more risky assets for less risky assets

average tax rate total taxes paid divided by taxable income

balance sheet financial statement that shows a firm's financial position (assets, liabilities, and equity) at a point in time

bankruptcy legally declared inability of an individual or a company to pay its creditors

bankruptcy costs, or costs of financial distress costs associated with financial difficulties a firm might experience because it uses debt financing

benchmark a standard against which performance is measured

best-effort underwriting underwriting agreement in which the underwriter does not agree to purchase the securities at a particular price but promises only to make its "best effort" to sell as much of the issue as possible above a certain price

beta (β) a measure of nondiversifiable, systematic, or market risk

bid price the price a securities dealer will pay for a given stock

book value the net value of an asset or liability recorded on the financial statements—normally reflects historical cost

bootstrapping the process by which many entrepreneurs raise seed money and obtain other resources necessary to start their businesses

break-even analysis an analysis that tells us how many units must be sold in order for a project to break even on a cash flow or accounting profit basis

brokers market specialists who bring buyers and sellers together, usually for a commission

business plan a document that describes the details of how a business will be developed over time

business risk the risk in the cash flows to stockholders that is associated with uncertainty due to the characteristics of the firm's assets

call option an option to buy the underlying asset

call premium the price that the buyer of a call option pays the seller for that option

Capital Asset Pricing Model (CAPM) a model that describes the relation between risk and expected return

capital budgeting the process of choosing the productive assets in which the firm will invest

capital lease a lease which has the characteristics of a sale

capital markets financial markets where equity and debt instruments with maturities greater than one year are traded

capital rationing a situation where a firm does not have enough capital to invest in all attractive projects and must therefore ration capital

capital structure the mix of debt and equity that is used to finance a firm

cash conversion cycle the length of time from the point at which a company pays for raw materials until the point at which it receives cash from the sale of finished goods made from those materials

cash flow to investors the cash flow that a firm generates for its investors in a given period, excluding cash inflows from the sale of securities to investors

chief financial officer, or CFO the most senior financial manager in a company

coefficient of variation (CV) a measure of the risk associated with an investment for each 1 percent of expected return

collection time (float) the time between when a customer makes a payment and when the cash becomes available to the firm

commercial paper short-term debt in the form of promissory notes issued by large, financially secure firms with high credit ratings

common-size financial statement a financial statement in which each number is expressed as a percentage of a base number, such as total assets or net revenues (net sales)

common stock an equity share that represents the basic ownership claim in a corporation; the most common type of equity security

compensating balances bank balances that firms must maintain to at least partially compensate banks for loans or services rendered

compound annual growth rate (CAGR) the average annual growth rate over a specified period of time

compounding the process by which interest earned on an investment is reinvested, so in future periods interest is earned on the interest as well as the principal

compound interest interest earned both on the original principal amount and on interest previously earned

consumer credit credit extended by a business to a consumer

contingent projects projects whose acceptance depends on the acceptance of other projects

control premium an adjustment that is made to a business value estimate to reflect value associated with control that is not already reflected in the analysis

conventional cash flow a cash flow pattern consisting of an initial cash outflow that is followed by one or more cash inflows

corporation a legal entity formed and authorized under a state charter; in a legal sense, a corporation is a "person" distinct from its owners

cost of capital the required rate of return for a capital investment

country risk the political uncertainty associated with a particular country

coupon payments the interest payments made to bondholders

coupon rate the annual coupon payment of a bond divided by the bond's face value

covariance of returns a measure of how the returns on two assets covary, or move together

crossover level of unit sales (CO) the level of unit sales at which cash flows or profitability for one project alternative switches from being lower than that of another alternative to being higher

crossover point the discount rate at which the NPV profiles of two projects cross and, thus, at which the NPVs of the projects are equal

current assets assets, such as cash and marketable securities, accounts receivable, and inventories, that are expected to be liquidated (collected or sold) within one year

dealers market specialists who make markets for securities by buying and selling from their own inventories

declaration date the date on which a dividend is publicly announced

default (insolvency) risk the risk that a firm will not be able to pay its debt obligations as they come due

degree of accounting operating leverage (Accounting DOL) a measure of the sensitivity of accounting operating profits (EBIT) to changes in revenue

degree of pretax cash flow operating leverage (Cash Flow DOL) a measure of the sensitivity of cash flows from operations (EBITDA) to changes in revenue

depreciation the allocation of the cost of an asset over its estimated useful life to reflect the wear and tear on the asset as it is used to produce the firm's goods and services

derivative security a security that derives its value from the value of another asset; an option is an example of a derivative security

direct bankruptcy costs out-of-pocket costs that a firm incurs when it gets into financial distress

discount bonds bonds that sell at prices below par (face) value

discounted payback period the length of time required to recover a project's initial cost, accounting for the time value of money

discounting the process by which the present value of future cash flows is obtained

discount rate the interest rate used in the discounting process to find the present value of future cash flows

diversification reducing risk by investing in two or more assets whose values do not always move in the same direction at the same time

dividend something of value distributed to a firm's stockholders on a pro-rata basis—that is, in proportion to the percentage of the firm's shares that they own

dividend discount model (DDM) approach an income approach to valuation in which all dividends that are expected to be distributed to stockholders in the future are discounted to estimate the value of the equity

dividend payout ratio the proportion of net income paid out (distributed) as dividends

dividend reinvestment program (DRIP) a program in which a company sells new shares, commission free, to dividend recipients who elect to automatically reinvest their dividends in the company's stock

dividend yield a stock's annual dividend divided by its current price

earnings per share (EPS) net income divided by the number of common shares outstanding

economic break-even point the number of units that must be sold each year during the life of a project so that the NPV of the project equals $0

economic order quantity (EOQ) order quantity that minimizes the total costs incurred to order and hold inventory

economic profit a profit that exceeds the opportunity cost of the capital invested in a project

effective annual interest rate (EAR) the annual interest rate that reflects compounding within a year

effective annual yield (EAY) the annual yield that takes compounding into account; another name for the *effective annual interest rate* (EAR)

efficient market market where prices reflect the knowledge and expectations of all investors

efficient market hypothesis a theory concerning the extent to which information is reflected in security prices and how information gets incorporated into security prices

enterprise value the value of a company's equity plus the value of its debt; also the present value of the total free cash flows the company's assets are expected to generate in the future

equivalent annual cost (EAC) the annual dollar amount of an annuity that has a life equal to that of a project and that also has a present value equal to the present value of the cash flows from the project; the term comes from the fact that the EAC calculation is often used to calculate a constant annual cost associated with projects in order to make comparisons

Eurocredits short- to medium-term loans of a Eurocurrency to multinational corporations and governments of medium to high credit quality

Eurocurrency a time deposit that is in a bank located in a country different from the country that issued the currency

Eurodollar a U.S. dollar deposited in a bank outside the United States

ex-dividend date the first day on which a stock trades without the rights to a dividend

exercise (expiration) date the last date on which an option can be exercised

exercise (strike) price the price at which the owner of an option has the right to buy or sell the underlying asset

expected return an average of the possible returns from an investment, where each return is weighted by the probability that it will occur

external funding needed (EFN) the additional debt or equity a firm must raise from external sources to meet its total funding requirements

extra dividend a dividend that is generally paid at the same time as a regular cash dividend to distribute additional value

face value, or par value the amount on which interest is calculated and that is owed to the bondholder when a bond reaches maturity

factor an individual or a financial institution, such as a bank or a business finance company, that buys accounts receivable without recourse

fair market value the value of a business to a typical investor

finance balance sheet a balance sheet that is based on market values of expected cash flows

financial assets assets that are claims on the cash flows from other assets; business loans, stocks, and bonds are financial assets

financial intermediation conversion of securities with one set of characteristics into securities with another set of characteristics

financial leverage the use of debt in a firm's capital structure; the more debt, the higher the financial leverage

financial option the right to buy or sell a financial security, such as a share of stock, on or before a specified date for a specified price

financial plan a plan outlining the investments a firm intends to make and how it will finance them

financial planning the process by which management decides what types of investments the firm needs to make and how to finance those investments

financial ratio A number from a financial statement that has been scaled by dividing by another financial number

financial restructuring a combination of financial transactions that changes the capital structure of the firm without affecting its real assets

financial risk the risk in the cash flows to stockholders that is due to the way in which the firm's assets have been financed

financial statement analysis the use of financial statements to analyze a company's performance and assess its strengths and weaknesses

firm-commitment underwriting underwriting agreement in which the underwriter purchases securities for a specified price and resells them

firm-specific asset an asset that is substantially more valuable to a particular firm than to any other firm

firm's marginal tax rate (*t*) the tax rate that is applied to each additional dollar of earnings at a firm

firm value, or enterprise value the total value of the firm's assets; it equals the value of the equity financing plus the value of the debt financing used by the firm

fixed-income securities debt instruments that pay interest in amounts that are fixed for the life of the contract

fixed costs costs that do not vary directly with the number of units sold

flexible current asset management strategy current asset management strategy that involves keeping high balances of current assets on hand

foreign exchange markets international markets where currencies are bought and sold in wholesale amounts

foreign exchange rate risk, or exchange rate risk the uncertainty associated with future currency exchange rate movements

formal line of credit a contractual agreement between a bank and a firm under which the bank has a legal obligation to lend funds to the firm up to a preset limit; also known as revolving credit

forward rate a rate agreed on today for an exchange to take place on a specified date in the future

free cash flow from the firm (FCFF) approach an income approach to valuation in which all free cash flows the assets are expected to generate in the future are discounted to estimate the enterprise value

free cash flow to equity (FCFE) approach an income approach to valuation in which all cash flows that are expected to be available for distribution to stockholders in the future are discounted to estimate the value of the equity

future value (FV) the value of an investment after it earns interest for one or more periods

future value of an annuity (FVA) the value of an annuity at some point in the future

general-use asset an asset which is of similar value to potential users

general cash offer a sale of debt or equity, open to all investors, by a company that has previously sold stock to the public

generally accepted accounting principles (GAAP) a set of rules that defines how companies are to prepare financial statements

geometric (compounded) average return average compounded return earned by an investor

globalization the removal of barriers to free trade and the integration of national economies

going-concern value the difference between the value of a business as a going concern (the present value of the expected cash flows) and the adjusted book value

growing annuity an annuity in which the cash flows increase at a constant rate

growing perpetuity a cash flow stream that grows at a constant rate forever

hedge a financial transaction intended to reduce risk

income statement a financial statement that reports a firm's revenues, expenses, and profits or losses over a period of time

incremental additions to working capital (Add WC) the net investments in working capital items, such as cash and cash equivalents, accounts receivable, inventory, and accounts payable, that must be made if the project is pursued

incremental after-tax free cash flows the difference between the total after-tax free cash flows at a firm with a project and the total after-tax free cash flows at the same firm without that project; a measure of a project's total impact on the free cash flows at a firm

incremental capital expenditures (Cap Exp) the net investments in property, plant, and equipment and other long-term assets that must be made if a project is pursued

incremental cash flow from operations (CF Opns) the cash flow that a project generates after all operating expenses and taxes have been paid but before any cash outflows for investments

incremental depreciation and amortization (D&A) the depreciation and amortization charges that are associated with a project

incremental net operating profits after tax (NOPAT) a measure of the impact of a project on the firm's cash net income, excluding the effects of any interest expenses associated with financing the project

independent projects projects whose cash flows are unrelated

indirect bankruptcy costs costs associated with changes in the behavior of people who deal with a firm when the firm gets into financial distress

informal line of credit a verbal agreement between a bank and a firm under which the firm can borrow an amount of money up to an agreed-on limit

information asymmetry the situation in which one party in a business transaction has information that is unavailable to the other parties in the transaction

initial public offering (IPO) the first offering of a corporation's stock to the public

insolvency the inability to pay debts when they are due

intangible assets nonphysical assets such as patents, mailing lists, or brand names

interest on interest interest earned on interest that was earned in previous periods

interest rate risk uncertainty about future bond values that is caused by the unpredictability of interest rates

internal growth rate (IGR) the maximum growth rate that a firm can achieve without external financing

internal rate of return (IRR) the discount rate at which the present value of a project's expected cash inflows equals the present value of the project's outflows; it is the discount rate at which the project's NPV equals zero

inventory carrying costs expenses associated with maintaining inventory, including interest forgone on money invested in inventory, storage costs, taxes, and insurance

investment banks firms that specialize in helping companies sell new security issues

investment-grade bonds bonds with low risk of default that are rated Baa (BBB) or above

investment value the value of a business to a specific investor

key person discount an adjustment to a business value estimate that is made to reflect the potential loss of value associated with the unexpected departure of a key person

lease (rental agreement) a financial arrangement in which the user of an asset pays the owner of the asset to use it for a period of time

lessee the user of a leased asset

lessor the owner of a leased asset

limited liability the legal liability of an investor is limited to the amount of capital invested in the business

limited liability partnership (LLP) and limited liability company (LLC) hybrid business organizations that combine some of the advantages of corporations and partnerships; in general, income to the partners is taxed only as personal income, but the partners have limited liability

liquidating dividend the final dividend that is paid to stockholders when a firm is liquidated

liquidity the ability to convert an asset into cash quickly without loss of value

lockbox a system that allows geographically dispersed customers to send their payments to a post office box near them

London Interbank Offer Rate (LIBOR) the interest rate British-based banks charge each other for short-term loans. Also, commonly used as the base rate for Eurodollar loans that are not between two banks

long-term funding strategy financing strategy that relies on long-term debt and equity to finance both fixed assets and working capital

lumpy assets fixed assets added as large, discrete units; these assets may not be used to full capacity for some time, leaving the company with excess capacity

marginal tax rate the tax rate paid on the last dollar of income earned

marketability the ease with which a security can be sold and converted into cash

market informational efficiency the degree to which current market prices reflect relevant information and, therefore, the true value of the security

market operational efficiency the degree to which the transaction costs of bringing buyers and sellers together are minimized

market portfolio the portfolio of all assets

market risk a term commonly used to refer to nondiversifiable, or systematic, risk

market value the price at which an item can be sold

maturity matching strategy financing strategy that matches the maturities of liabilities and assets

Modified Accelerated Cost Recovery System (MACRS) the accelerated depreciation method that has been in use for U.S. federal taxes since the Tax Reform Act of 1986 went into effect

modified internal rate of return (MIRR) an internal rate of return (IRR) measure, which assumes that cash inflows are reinvested at the opportunity cost of capital until the end of the project

money center banks large commercial banks that provide both traditional and investment banking services throughout the world

money markets markets where short-term debt instruments are traded

multinational corporation a business firm that operates in more than one country

multiples analysis a valuation approach that uses stock price or other value multiples for public companies to estimate the value of another company's stock or its entire business

multistage-growth dividend model a model that allows for varying dividend growth rates in the near term, followed by a constant long-term growth rate; another term used to describe the mixed (supernormal) growth dividend model discussed in Chapter 9

mutually exclusive projects projects for which acceptance of one precludes acceptance of the other

net present value (NPV) method a method of evaluating a capital investment project that measures the difference between its cost and the present value of its expected cash flows

net working capital the dollar difference between total current assets and total current liabilities

nominal dollars dollar amounts that are not adjusted for inflation; the purchasing power of a nominal dollar amount depends on when that amount is received

nominal rate of interest the rate of interest that is unadjusted for inflation

noninvestment-grade bonds bonds rated below Baa (or BBB) by rating agencies; often called speculative-grade bonds, high-yield bonds, or junk bonds

nonoperating assets (NOA) cash or other assets that are not required to support the operations of a business

normal distribution a symmetric frequency distribution that is completely described by its mean and standard deviation; also known as a bell curve due to its shape

North American Industry Classification System (NAICS) a classification system for businesses introduced to refine and replace the older SIC system

NPV profile a graph showing NPV as a function of the discount rate

offer (ask) price the price at which a securities dealer seeks to sell a given stock

open-market repurchase the repurchase of shares by a company in the open market

operating cycle the average time between receipt of raw materials and receipt of cash for the sale of finished goods made from those materials

operating lease a lease which does not have the characteristics of a sale

operating leverage a measure of the relative amounts of fixed and variable costs in a project's cost structure; operating leverage is higher with more fixed costs

opportunity cost the return from the best alternative investment with similar risk that an investor gives up when he or she makes a certain investment

opportunity cost of capital the return an investor gives up when his or her money is invested in one asset rather than the best alternative asset with the same risk

optimal capital structure the capital structure that minimizes the cost of financing a firm's projects and thus maximizes the value of the firm

option payoff function the function that shows how the value of an option varies with the value of the underlying asset

ordinary annuity an annuity in which payments are made at the end of each period

par-value bonds bonds that sell at par value, or face value; whenever a bond's coupon rate is equal to the market rate of interest on similar bonds, the bond will sell at par (face) value

partnership two or more owners who have joined together legally to manage a business and share in its profits

payable date the date on which a company pays a dividend

payback period the length of time required to recover a project's initial cost

payout policy the policy concerning the distribution of value from a firm to its stockholders

pecking order theory the theory that when financing projects, managers first use retained earnings, which they view as the least expensive form of capital, then debt, and finally externally raised equity, which they view as the most expensive

per-unit contribution the dollar amount that is left over from the sale of a single unit after all the variable costs associated with that unit have been paid; this is the amount that is available to help cover FC for the project

percent of sales model a simple financial planning model that assumes that most income statement and balance sheet accounts vary proportionally with sales

permanent working capital the minimum level of working capital that a firm will always have on its books

perpetuity a series of equally spaced and level cash flows that continues forever

portfolio the collection of assets an investor owns

post a specific location on the floor of a stock exchange at which auctions for a particular security take place

postaudit review an audit to compare actual project results with the results projected in the capital budgeting proposal

preferred stock an equity share in a corporation that entitles the owner to preferred treatment over owners of common stock with respect to dividend payments and claims against the firm's assets in the event of bankruptcy or liquidation, but that typically has no voting rights

preliminary prospectus the initial registration statement filed with the SEC by a company preparing to issue securities in the public market; it contains detailed information about the issuer and the proposed issue

premium bonds bonds that sell at prices above par (face) value

present value (PV) the current value of a future cash flow discounted at the appropriate discount rate

present value of an annuity (PVA) the present value of the cash flows from an annuity, discounted at the appropriate discount rate

pretax operating cash flow (EBITDA) break-even point the number of units that must be sold for pretax operating cash flow to equal $0

pretax operating cash flow earnings before interest, taxes, depreciation, and amortization, or EBITDA

primary market a financial market in which new security issues are sold by companies directly to investors

principal the amount of money on which interest is paid

private information information that is not available to all investors

privately held, or closely held, corporations corporations whose stock is not traded in the public markets

private placement the sale of an unregistered security directly to an investor, such as an insurance company or a wealthy individual

productive assets the long-term tangible and intangible assets a firm uses to generate cash flows

profitability index (PI) a measure of the value a project generates for each dollar invested in that project

pro forma financial statements projected financial statements that reflect a set of assumptions concerning investment, financing, and operating decisions

progressive tax system a tax system in which the marginal tax rate at low levels of income is lower than the marginal tax rate at high levels of income

public information information that is available to all investors

public markets markets regulated by the Securities and Exchange Commission in which securities such as stocks and bonds are publicly traded

pure-play comparable a comparable company that is in exactly the same business as the project or business being analyzed

put-call parity the relation between the value of a call option on an asset and the value of a put option on the same asset that has the same exercise price

put option an option to sell the underlying asset

put premium the price that the buyer of a put option pays the seller of that option

quoted interest rate a simple annual interest rate, such as the APR

real assets nonfinancial assets such as plant and equipment; productive assets are real assets; many financial assets are claims on cash flows from real assets

real dollars inflation-adjusted dollars; the actual purchasing power of dollars stated in real terms is the same regardless of when those dollars are received

real investment policy the policy relating to the criteria the firm uses in deciding which real assets (projects) to invest in

real option an option for which the underlying asset is a real asset

real rate of interest the interest rate that would exist in the absence of inflation

realized yield for a bond, the interest rate at which the present value of the actual cash flows from a bond equals the bond's price

record date the date by which an investor must be a stockholder of record in order to receive a dividend

regular cash dividend a cash dividend that is paid on a regular basis, typically quarterly

repatriation of earnings restrictions restrictions placed by a foreign government on the amount of cash that can be repatriated, or returned to a parent company by a subsidiary doing business in the foreign country

replacement cost the cost of duplicating the assets of a business in their present form as of the valuation date

residual cash flows the cash remaining after a firm has paid operating expenses and what it owes creditors and in taxes; can be distributed to the owners as a cash dividend or by repurchasing some shares, or reinvested in the business

restrictive current asset management strategy current asset management strategy that involves keeping the level of current assets at a minimum

retention (plowback) ratio the proportion of net income retained in the firm

Rule of 72 a rule proposing that the time required to double money invested (TDM) approximately equals 72/*i*, where *i* is the rate of return expressed as a percentage

scenario analysis an analytical method concerned with how the results from a financial analysis will change under alternative scenarios

seasoned public offering the sale of securities to the public by a firm that already has publicly traded securities outstanding

secondary market a financial market in which the owners of outstanding securities can sell them to other investors

Security Market Line (SML) a plot of the relation between expected return and systematic risk

semistrong-form of the efficient market hypothesis the theory that security prices reflect all public information but not all private information

sensitivity analysis examination of the sensitivity of the results from a financial analysis to changes in individual assumptions

Sharpe Ratio a measure of the return per unit of risk for an investment

shelf registration a type of SEC registration that allows firms to register to sell securities over a two-year period and, during that time, take the securities "off the shelf" and sell them as needed

short-term funding strategy financing strategy that relies on short-term debt to finance all seasonal working capital and a portion of permanent working capital and fixed assets

shortage costs costs incurred because of lost production and sales or illiquidity

simple interest interest earned on the original principal amount only

simulation analysis an analytical method that uses a computer to quickly examine a large number of scenarios and obtain probability estimates for various values in a financial analysis

sole proprietorship a business owned by a single person

special dividend a one-time payment to stockholders that is normally used to distribute a large amount of value

specialist the trader designated by an exchange to represent orders placed by public customers at auctions of securities; specialists handle a small set of securities and are also allowed to act as dealers

spot rate the exchange rate for immediate delivery of a currency

stakeholder anyone other than an owner (stockholder) with a claim on the cash flows of a firm, including employees, suppliers, creditors, and the government

stand-alone principle the principle that allows us to treat each project as a stand-alone firm when we perform an NPV analysis

standard deviation (σ) the square root of the variance

Standard Industrial Classification (SIC) System a numerical system developed by the U.S. government to classify businesses according to the type of activity they perform

statement of cash flows a financial statement that shows a firm's cash receipts, cash payments, and investments for a period of time

stock dividend a distribution of new shares to existing stockholders in proportion to the percentage of shares that they own (pro rata); the value of the assets in a company does not change with a stock dividend

stock repurchase the purchase of stock by a company from its stockholders; an alternative way for the company to distribute value to the stockholders

stock split a pro-rata distribution of new shares to existing stockholders that is not associated with any change in the assets held by the firm; stock splits involve larger increases in the number of shares than stock dividends

strategic planning the process by which management establishes the firm's long-term goals, the strategies that will be used to achieve those goals, and the capabilities that are needed to sustain the firm's competitive position

strong-form of the efficient market hypothesis the theory that security prices reflect all information

sustainable growth rate (SGR) the rate of growth that a firm can sustain without selling additional equity while maintaining the same capital structure

systematic or nondiversifiable risk risk that cannot be eliminated through diversification

tangible assets physical assets such as property, plant, and equipment

targeted stock repurchase a stock repurchase that targets a specific stockholder

tender offer an open offer by a company to purchase shares

terminal value the value of the expected free cash flows beyond the period over which they are explicitly forecast

term loan a business loan with a maturity greater than one year

term structure of interest rates the relation between yield to maturity and term to maturity

time value of money the difference in value between a dollar in hand today and a dollar promised in the future; a dollar today is worth more than a dollar in the future

time zero the beginning of a transaction; often the current point in time

total contribution the total amount that a project contributes to help pay its fixed costs after covering all of its variable costs

total holding period return the total return on an asset over a specific period of time or holding period

trade-off theory the theory that managers trade off the benefits against the costs of using debt to identify the optimal capital structure for a firm

trade credit credit extended by one business to another

transactions analysis a valuation approach that uses transactions data from the sale of similar companies to estimate the value of another company's stock or its entire business

transnational corporation a multinational firm that has widely dispersed ownership and that is managed from a global perspective

treasury stock stock that the firm has repurchased from investors

trend analysis analysis of trends in financial data over time

true (intrinsic) value for a security, the present value of the cash flows an investor who owns that security can expect to receive in the future

Truth-in-Lending Act a federal law requiring lenders to fully inform borrowers of important information related to loans, including the annual percentage rate charged

Truth-in-Savings Act a federal law requiring institutions offering consumer savings vehicles, such as certificates of deposit (CDs), to fully inform consumers of important information about the savings vehicles, including the annual percentage rate paid

underinvestment problem the incentive that stockholders in a financially leveraged firm have to turn down positive NPV projects when the firm is in financial distress

underlying asset the asset from which the value of an option is derived

underpricing offering new securities for sale at a price below their true value

underwriting syndicate a group of underwriters that joins forces to reduce underwriting risk

unsystematic or diversifiable risk risk that can be eliminated through diversification

valuation date the date on which a value estimate applies

variable costs costs that vary directly with the number of units sold

variance (σ^2) a measure of the uncertainty associated with an outcome

venture capitalists individuals or firms that invest by purchasing equity in new businesses and often provide entrepreneurs with business advice

weak-form of the efficient market hypothesis the theory that security prices reflect all information in past prices but do not reflect all private or all public information

wealth the economic value of the assets someone possesses

weighted average cost of capital (WACC) the weighted average of the costs of the different types of capital (debt and equity) that have been used to finance a firm; the cost of each type of capital is weighted by the proportion of the total capital that it represents

yield curve a graph representing the term structure of interest rates, with the term to maturity on the horizontal axis and the yield on the vertical axis

yield to maturity for a bond, the discount rate that makes the present value of the coupon and principal payments equal to the price of the bond

Subject Index

E

Q

R

Company Index

Selected Abbreviations and Notation

β =	beta (a measure of systematic risk)
Δ =	change (e.g., ΔP = change in price level, ΔS = change in sales level)
ρ =	correlation
σ^2 (σ) =	variance (standard deviation)
x =	fractional weight of investment or component of capital
Add WC =	addition to working capital
APR =	annual percentage rate
ARR =	accounting rate of return
b =	dividend payout ratio
C =	coupon payment (bond), call option value
Cap Exp =	capital expenditures
CF =	cash flow
CF Opns =	cash flow from operations
CFI =	cash flow to investors
CFLTA =	cash flow invested in long-term assets
CFNWC =	cash flow invested in net working capital
CFOA =	cash flow from operating activity
CIP =	call interest premium
CO =	crossover level of unit sales
K_{cs} =	cost of common stock
COGS =	cost of goods sold
CV =	coefficient of variation
D =	dividend (stock)
D&A =	depreciation and amortization
DOL =	degree of operating leverage
DPO =	days' payables outstanding
DRP =	default risk premium
DSI =	days' sales in inventory
DSO =	days' sales outstanding
E(•) =	expected value (E(R) = expected return, etc.)
EAC =	equivalent annual cost
EAR = EAY =	effective annual rate (yield)
EBIT =	earnings before interest and taxes
EBITDA =	earnings before interest, taxes, depreciation, and amortization
EBT =	earnings before taxes
EFN =	external funding needed
EOQ =	economic order quantity
EROA =	EBIT return on assets
F =	face value (bond)
FC =	fixed costs
FCF =	free cash flows
FCFE =	free cash flow to equity

FCFF =	free cash flow from the firm
FV =	future value
FVA_n =	future value of an annuity
FXR =	foreign exchange or currency risk premium
g =	growth rate
i =	nominal rate of interest
IGR =	internal growth rate
IRR =	internal rate of return
k =	cost of capital (debt or equity)
m =	number of payments per year
MAT =	maturity adjustment to cost of a loan
MRP =	marketability risk premium
MV =	market value
n =	number of periods
NCF =	net cash flow
NCFOA =	net cash flow from operating activities
NOPAT =	net operating profits after tax
NPV =	net present value
NWC =	net working capital
OC =	operating cycle
Op Ex =	cash operating expenses
p =	probability
P =	price (P_0 = price at time zero, etc.), put option value
P/E ratio =	price/earnings ratio
PB =	payback period
PI =	profitability index
PR =	prime rate
PV =	present value
PV annuity factor =	present value of annuity factor
PVA_n =	present value of an annuity
PVP =	present value of a perpetuity
r =	real rate of interest
R =	return (R_{rf} = risk free, R_i, $R_{Portfolio}$, etc.)
$R_{Arithmetic\ average}$ =	arithmetic average growth rate
$R_{Geometric\ average}$ =	geometric average growth rate
ROA =	return on assets
ROE =	return on equity
S =	Sharpe Ratio
SGR =	sustainable growth rate
t =	tax rate
TV =	terminal value
V =	value (e.g., $V_{Firm} = V_{Assets} = V_{Debt} + V_{Equity}$)
VC =	variable costs
WACC =	weighted average cost of capital

BUILDING INTUITION

Throughout the book important finance principles and concepts are identified and emphasized in *Building Intuition* boxes. These boxes restate an important finance concept that has been discussed in the main text, such as the importance of cash flows, and provide an intuitive example or explanation of the concept. The *Building Intuition* boxes and the pages on which they appear are as follows:

PAGE